THE
OXFORD GERMAN
MINIDICTIONARY

German – English
English – German

Deutsch – Englisch
Englisch – Deutsch

GUNHILD PROWE
JILL SCHNEIDER

Oxford   New York
OXFORD UNIVERSITY PRESS

Oxford University Press, Walton Street, Oxford OX2 6DP

Oxford New York Toronto
Delhi Bombay Calcutta Madras Karachi
Kuala Lumpur Singapore Hong Kong Tokyo
Nairobi Dar es Salaam Cape Town
Melbourne Auckland Madrid

and associated companies in
Berlin Ibadan

Oxford is a trade mark of Oxford University Press

British Library Cataloguing in Publication Data

Data available

Library of Congress Cataloging in Publication Data

Data available

ISBN 0–19–864150–8

3 5 7 9 10 8 6 4

Printed in Great Britain by
Charles Letts (Scotland) Ltd.
Dalkeith, Scotland

Contents

Preface

This is a completely new work in the Oxford Mini-dictionary range and is designed for both English and German users.

It provides a handy and comprehensive reference work for tourists and business people, and covers the needs of the student for GCSE.

We should like to express our thanks to Dr Michael Clark of Oxford University Press for his advice and support, and to Roswitha and Neil Morris for reading the proofs.

G.P. & J.S.

March 1993

Introduction

A swung dash ~ represents the headword or that part of the headword preceding a vertical bar |. The initial letter of a German headword is given to show whether or not it is a capital.

The vertical bar | follows the part of the headword which is not to be repeated in compounds or derivatives.

Square brackets [ ] are used for optional material.

Angled brackets ⟨ ⟩ are used after a verb translation to indicate the object; before a verb translation to indicate the subject; before an adjective to indicate a typical noun which it qualifies.

Round brackets ( ) are used for field or style labels (see list on page vi) and for explanatory matter.

A box □ indicates a new part of speech within an entry.

od (oder) and *or* denote that words or portions of a phrase are synonymous. An oblique stroke / is used where there is a difference in usage or meaning.

≈ is used where no exact equivalent exists in the other language.

A dagger † indicates that a German verb is irregular and that the parts can be found in the verb table on page 705. Compound verbs are not listed there as they follow the pattern of the basic verb.

The stressed vowel is marked in a German headword by – (long) or · (short). A phonetic transcription is only given for words which do not follow the normal rules of pronunciation. These rules can be found on page 703.

Phonetics are given for all English headwords and for derivatives where there is a change of pronunciation or stress. In blocks of compounds, if no stress is shown, it falls on the first element.

A change in pronunciation or stress shown within a block of compounds applies only to that particular word (subsequent entries revert to the pronunciation and stress of the headword).

German headword nouns are followed by the gender and, with the exception of compound nouns, by the genitive and plural. These are only given at compound nouns if they present some difficulty. Otherwise the user should refer to the final element.

Nouns that decline like adjectives are entered as follows: **-e(r)** *m|f*, **-e(s)** *nt*.

Adjectives which have no undeclined form are entered in the feminine form with the masculine and neuter in brackets **-e(r,s)**.

The reflexive pronoun **sich** is accusative unless marked (*dat*).

Proprietary terms

This dictionary includes some words which are, or are asserted to be, proprietary names or trade marks. Their inclusion does not imply that they have acquired for legal purposes a non-proprietary or general significance, nor is any other judgement implied concerning their legal status. In cases where the editor has some evidence that a word is used as a proprietary name or trade mark this is indicated by the letter (P), but no judgement concerning the legal status of such words is made or implied thereby.

Abbreviations/Abkürzungen

adjective	a	Adjektiv
abbreviation	abbr	Abkürzung
accusative	acc	Akkusativ
Administration	Admin	Administration
adverb	adv	Adverb
American	Amer	amerikanisch
Anatomy	Anat	Anatomie
Archaeology	Archaeol	Archäologie
Architecture	Archit	Architektur
Astronomy	Astr	Astronomie
attributive	attrib	attributiv
Austrian	Aust	österreichisch
Motor vehicles	Auto	Automobil
Aviation	Aviat	Luftfahrt
Biology	Biol	Biologie
Botany	Bot	Botanik
Chemistry	Chem	Chemie
collective	coll	Kollektivum
Commerce	Comm	Handel
conjunction	conj	Konjunktion
Cookery	Culin	Kochkunst
dative	dat	Dativ
definite article	def art	bestimmter Artikel
demonstrative	dem	Demonstrativ-
dialect	dial	Dialekt
Electricity	Electr	Elektrizität
something	etw	etwas
feminine	f	Femininum
familiar	fam	familiär
figurative	fig	figurativ
genitive	gen	Genitiv
Geography	Geog	Geographie
Geology	Geol	Geologie
Geometry	Geom	Geometrie

Pronunciation of the alphabet
Aussprache des Alphabets

English/Englisch   *German/Deutsch*

English		German
eɪ	a	aː
biː	b	beː
siː	c	tseː
diː	d	deː
iː	e	eː
ef	f	ɛf
dʒiː	g	geː
eɪtʃ	h	haː
aɪ	i	iː
dʒeɪ	j	jɔt
keɪ	k	kaː
el	l	ɛl
em	m	ɛm
en	n	ɛn
əʊ	o	oː
piː	p	peː
kjuː	q	kuː
aː(r)	r	ɛr
es	s	ɛs
tiː	t	teː
juː	u	uː
viː	v	faʊ
ˈdʌbljuː	w	veː
eks	x	ɪks
waɪ	y	ˈʏpsilɔn
zed	z	tsɛt
eɪ umlaut	ä	ɛː
əʊ umlaut	ö	øː
juː umlaut	ü	yː
esˈzed	ß	ɛsˈtsɛt

predicative	pred	prädikativ
prefix	pref	Präfix
preposition	prep	Präposition
present	pres	Präsens
present participle	pres p	erstes Partizip
pronoun	pron	Pronomen
Psychology	Psych	Psychologie
past tense	pt	Präteritum
Railway	Rail	Eisenbahn
reflexive	refl	reflexiv
regular	reg	regelmäßig
relative	rel	Relativ-
Religion	Relig	Religion
see	s.	siehe
School	Sch	Schule
separable	sep	trennbar
singular	sg	Singular
South German	S Ger	Süddeutsch
slang	sl	Slang
someone	s.o.	jemand
something	sth	etwas
Technical	Techn	Technik
Telephone	Teleph	Telefon
Textiles	Tex	Textilien
Theatre	Theat	Theater
Television	TV	Fernsehen
Typography	Typ	Typographie
University	Univ	Universität
auxiliary verb	v aux	Hilfsverb
intransitive verb	vi	intransitives Verb
reflexive verb	vr	reflexives Verb
transitive verb	vt	transitives Verb
vulgar	vulg	vulgär
Zoology	Zool	Zoologie

Grammar	Gram	Grammatik
Horticulture	Hort	Gartenbau
impersonal	impers	unpersönlich
indefinite article	indef art	unbestimmter Artikel
inseparable	insep	untrennbar
interjection	int	Interjektion
invariable	inv	unveränderlich
irregular	irreg	unregelmäßig
someone	jd	jemand
someone	jdm	jemandem
someone	jdn	jemanden
someone's	jds	jemandes
Journalism	Journ	Journalismus
Law	Jur	Jura
Language	Lang	Sprache
literary	liter	dichterisch
masculine	m	Maskulinum
Mathematics	Math	Mathematik
Medicine	Med	Medizin
Meteorology	Meteorol	Meteorologie
Military	Mil	Militär
Mineralogy	Miner	Mineralogie
Music	Mus	Musik
noun	n	Substantiv
Nautical	Naut	nautisch
North German	N Ger	Norddeutsch
nominative	nom	Nominativ
neuter	nt	Neutrum
or	od	oder
Proprietary term	P	Warenzeichen
pejorative	pej	abwertend
Photography	Phot	Fotografie
Physics	Phys	Physik
plural	pl	Plural
Politics	Pol	Politik
possessive	poss	Possessiv-
past participle	pp	zweites Partizip

A

Aal *m* -[e]s,-e eel. **a~en (sich)** *vr* laze; *(ausgestreckt)* stretch out

Aas *nt* -es carrion; *(sl)* swine

ab *prep* (+ *dat*) from; **ab Montag** from Monday **a~** off; *(weg)* away; *(auf Fahrplan)* departs; **von jetzt ab** from now on; **ab und zu** now and then; **auf und ab** up and down

abändern *vt sep* alter; *(abwandeln)* modify

abarbeiten *vt sep* work off; **sich a~** slave away

Abart *f* variety. **a~ig** *a* abnormal

Abbau *m* dismantling; *(Kohlen-)* mining; *(fig)* reduction. **a~en** *vt sep* dismantle; mine *(Kohle)*; *(fig)* reduce, cut

abbeißen† *vt sep* bite off

abbeizen *vt sep* strip

abberufen† *vt sep* recall

abbestellen *vt sep* cancel; **jdn a~** put s.o. off

abbiegen† *vi sep* (sein) turn off; **[nach] links a~** turn left

Abbild *nt* image. **a~en** *vt sep* depict, portray. **A~ung** *f* -,-en illustration

Abbitte *f* **A~ leisten** apologize

abblättern *vi sep* (sein) flake off

abblend|en *vt/i sep* (haben) **[die Scheinwerfer] a~** dip one's headlights. **A~licht** *nt* dipped headlights *pl*

abbrechen† *v sep* □*vt* break off; *(abreißen)* demolish □ *vi* (sein/haben) break off

abbrennen *v sep* □*vt* burn off; *(niederbrennen)* burn down; let off *(Feuerwerkskörper)* □ *vi* (sein) burn down

abbringen† *vt sep* dissuade (**von** from)

Abbruch *m* demolition; *(Beenden)* breaking off; **etw** *(dat)* **keinen A~ tun** do no harm to sth

abbuchen *vt sep* debit

abbürsten *vt sep* brush down; *(entfernen)* brush off

abdank|en *vi sep* (haben) resign; *⟨Herrscher:⟩* abdicate. **A~ung** *f* -,-en resignation; abdication

abdecken *vt sep* uncover; *(wegnehmen)* take off; *(zudecken)* cover; **den Tisch a~** clear the table

abdichten *vt sep* seal

abdrehen *vt sep* turn off

Abdruck *m* (*pl* -̈e) impression; *(Finger-)* print; *(Nachdruck)* reprint. **a~en** *vt sep* print

abdrücken *vt/i sep* (haben) fire; **sich a~** leave an impression

Abend *m* -s,-e evening; **am A~** in the evening. **a~** *adv* heute **a~** this evening, tonight; **gestern a~** yesterday evening, last night. **A~brot** *nt* supper. **A~essen** *nt* dinner; *(einfacher)* supper. **A~kurs[us]** *m* evening class. **A~mahl** *nt* (Relig) [Holy] Communion. **a~s** *adv* in the evening

Abenteuer *nt* -s,- adventure; *(Liebes-)* affair. **a~lich** *a* fantastic; *(gefährlich)* hazardous

Abenteurer *m* -s,- adventurer

aber *conj* but; **oder a~** or else □ *adv* *(wirklich)* really; **a~ ja!** but of course! **Tausende und a~ Tausende** thousands upon thousands

Aberglaube *m* superstition. **a~gläubisch** *a* superstitious

abermals *adv* once again

abfahren|**en**† *v sep* □*vi* (sein) leave; ⟨*Auto:*⟩ drive off □*vt* take away; (*entlangfahren*) drive along; use (*Fahrkarte*); **abgefahrene Reifen** worn tyres. **A~t** *f* departure; (*Talfahrt*) descent; (*Piste*) run; (*Ausfahrt*) exit

Abfall *m* refuse, rubbish, (*Amer*) garbage; (*auf der Straße*) litter; (*Industrie-*) waste. **A~eimer** *m* rubbish-bin; litter-bin

abfallen† *vi sep* (sein) drop, fall; (*übrigbleiben*) be left (**für** for); (*sich neigen*) slope away; (*fig*) compare badly (**gegen** with); **vom Glauben a~** renounce one's faith. **a~d** *a* sloping

Abfallhaufen *m* rubbish-dump

abfällig *a* disparaging, *adv* -ly

abfangen† *vt sep* intercept; (*beherrschen*) bring under control

abfärben *vi sep* (haben) ⟨*Farbe:*⟩ run; ⟨*Stoff:*⟩ not be colour-fast; **a~ auf** (+ *acc*) (*fig*) rub off on

abfassen *vt sep* draft

abfertigen *vt sep* attend to; (*zollamtlich*) clear; **jdn kurz a~** (*fam*) give s.o. short shrift

abfeuern *vt sep* fire

abfind|**en**† *vt sep* pay off; (*entschädigen*) compensate; **sich a~en mit** come to terms with. **A~ung** *f* -,-en compensation

abflauen *vi sep* (sein) decrease

abfliegen† *vi sep* (sein) fly off; (*Aviat*) take off

abfließen† *vi sep* (sein) drain or run away

Abflug *m* (*Aviat*) departure

Abfluß *m* drainage; (*Öffnung*) drain. **A~rohr** *nt* drain-pipe

abfragen *vt sep* **jdn od jdm Vokabeln a~** test s.o. on vocabulary

Abfuhr *f* - removal; (*fig*) rebuff

abführ|**en** *vt sep* take *or* lead away. **a~end** *a* laxative. **A~mittel** *nt* laxative

abfüllen *vt sep* **auf od in Flaschen a~** bottle

Abgabe *f* handing in; (*Verkauf*) sale; (*Fußball*) pass; (*Steuer*) tax

Abgang *m* departure; (*Theat*) exit; (*Schul-*) leaving

Abgase *ntpl* exhaust fumes

abgeben† *vt sep* hand in; (*abliefern*) deliver; (*verkaufen*) sell; (*zur Aufbewahrung*) leave; (*Fußball*) pass; (*ausströmen*) give off; (*abfeuern*) fire; (*verlauten lassen*) give; ⟨*aus Stimme*⟩ cast; **jdm etw a~** give s.o. a share of sth; **sich a~ mit** occupy oneself with

abgedroschen *a* hackneyed

abgehen† *v sep* □*vi* (sein) leave; (*Theat*) exit; (*sich lösen*) come off; (*abgezogen werden*) be deducted; (*abbiegen*) turn off; (*verlaufen*) go off; **ihr geht jeglicher Humor ab** she totally lacks a sense of humour □*vt* walk along

abgehetzt *a* harassed. **abgelegen** *a* remote. **abgeneigt** *a* **etw** (*dat*) **nicht abgeneigt sein** not be averse to sth. **abgenutzt** *a* worn.

Abgeordnete(r) *m/f* deputy; (*Pol*) Member of Parliament. **abgepackt** *a* pre-packed. **abgerissen** *a* ragged

abgeschieden *a* secluded. **A~heit** *f* - seclusion

abgeschlossen *a* (*fig*) complete; ⟨*Wohnung*⟩ self-contained. **abgeschmackt** *a* (*fig*) tasteless. **abgesehen** *prep* apart (from **von**). **abgespannt** *a* exhausted. **abgestanden** *a* stale. **abgestorben** *a* dead; ⟨*Glied*⟩ numb. **abgetragen** *a* worn. **abgewetzt** *a* threadbare

abgewinnen† *vt sep* win (**jdm** from s.o.); **etw** (*dat*) **Geschmack a~** get a taste for sth

abgewöhnen *vt sep* **jdm/sich das Rauchen a~** cure s.o. of/ give up smoking

abgezehrt *a* emaciated

abgießen† _vt sep_ pour off; drain ⟨_Gemüse_⟩

abgleiten _vi sep_ (_sein_) slip

Abgott _m_ idol

abgöttisch _adv_ a ~ lieben idolize

abgrenz|en _vt sep_ divide off; ⟨_fig_⟩ define. **A~ung** _f_ - demarcation

Abgrund _m_ abyss; ⟨_fig_⟩ depths _pl_

abgucken _vt sep_ (_fam_) copy

Abguß _m_ cast

abhacken _vt sep_ chop off

abhaken _vt sep_ tick off

abhalten† _vt sep_ keep off; ⟨_hindern_⟩ keep, prevent (**von** from); ⟨_veranstalten_⟩ hold

abhanden _adv_ a~ **kommen** get lost

Abhandlung _f_ treatise

Abhang _m_ slope

abhängen¹ _vt sep_ (_reg_) take down; ⟨_abkuppeln_⟩ uncouple

abhäng|en²† _vi sep_ (_haben_) depend (**von** on). **a~ig** _a_ dependent (**von** on). **A~igkeit** _f_ - dependence

abhärten _vt sep_ toughen up

abhauen† _v sep_ □_vt_ chop off □_vi_ (_sein_) (_fam_) clear off

abheben† _v sep_ □_vt_ take off; ⟨_vom Konto_⟩ withdraw; **sich a~** stand out (**gegen** against) □_vi_ (_haben_) ⟨_Cards_⟩ cut [the cards]; ⟨_Aviat_⟩ take off; ⟨_Rakete:_⟩ lift off

abheften _vt sep_ file

abhelfen† _vt sep_ (+ _dat_) remedy

Abhilfe _f_ remedy; **A~ schaffen** take [remedial] action

abholen _vt sep_ collect; call for ⟨_Person_⟩; **jdn am Bahnhof a~** meet s.o. at the station

abhorchen _vt sep_ ⟨_Med_⟩ sound

abhör|en _vt sep_ listen to; ⟨_überwachen_⟩ tap; **jdn** _od_ **jdm Vokabeln a~** en test s.o. on vocabulary. **A~gerät** _nt_ bugging device

Abitur _nt_ -s ≈ A levels _pl._ **A~ient(in)** _m_ -en,-en _f_ (-,-nen) pupil taking the '_Abitur_'

abkanzeln _vt sep_ (_fam_) reprimand

abkaufen _vt sep_ buy (_dat_ from)

abkehren (sich) _vr sep_ turn away

abkette[l]n _vt/i sep_ (_haben_) cast off

abklingen† _vi sep_ (_sein_) die away; ⟨_nachlassen_⟩ subside

abkochen _vt sep_ boil

abkommen† _vi sep_ (_sein_) a~ **von** stray from; ⟨_aufgeben_⟩ give up; **vom Thema a~** digress. **A~** _nt_ -s,- agreement

abkömmlich _a_ available

Abkömmling _m_ -s,-e descendant

abkratzen _v sep_ □_vt_ scrape off □_vi_ (_sein_) (_sl_) die

abkühlen _vt/i sep_ (_haben_) cool; **sich a~** cool [down]; ⟨_Wetter:_⟩ turn cooler

Abkunft _f_ - origin

abkuppeln _vt sep_ uncouple

abkürz|en _vt sep_ shorten; abbreviate ⟨_Wort_⟩. **A~ung** _f_ short cut; ⟨_Wort_⟩ abbreviation

abladen† _vt sep_ unload

Ablage _f_ shelf; ⟨_für Akten_⟩ tray

ablager|n _vt sep_ deposit; **sich a~n** be deposited. **A~ung** _f_ -,-en deposit

ablassen† _v sep_ □_vt_ drain [off]; let off ⟨_Dampf_⟩; ⟨_vom Preis_⟩ knock off □_vi_ (_haben_) **a~ von** give up; **von jdm a~** leave s.o. alone

Ablauf _m_ drain; ⟨_Verlauf_⟩ course; ⟨_Ende_⟩ end; ⟨_einer Frist_⟩ expiry. **a~en†** _v sep_ □_vi_ (_sein_) run or drain off; ⟨_verlaufen_⟩ go off; ⟨_enden_⟩ expire; ⟨_Zeit:_⟩ run out; ⟨_Uhrwerk:_⟩ run down □_vt_ walk along; ⟨_absuchen_⟩ scour (**nach** for); **sich** _dat_ **die Schuhe a~en** wear down one's shoes

ablegen _v sep_ □_vt_ put down; discard ⟨_Karte_⟩; ⟨_abheften_⟩ file; ⟨_ausziehen_⟩ take off; ⟨_aufgeben_⟩ give up; sit, take ⟨_Prüfung_⟩; **abgelegte Kleidung** cast-offs _pl_ □_vi_ (_haben_) take off one's coat; ⟨_Naut_⟩ cast off. **A~er** _m_ -s,- ⟨_Bot_⟩ cutting; ⟨_Schößling_⟩ shoot

ablehn|en vt sep refuse; (mißbilli-
gen) reject. A~**ung** f -,-en refusal; rejection

ableit|en vt sep divert; sich a~ en
be derived (von/aus from).
A~**ung** f derivation; (Wort) derivative

ablenk|en vt sep deflect; divert
⟨Aufmerksamkeit⟩; (zerstreuen)
distract. A~**ung** f -,-en distraction

ablesen† vt sep read; (absuchen)
pick off

ableugnen vt sep deny

ablicht|en vt sep photocopy.
A~**ung** f photocopy

abliefern vt sep deliver

ablös|en vt sep detach; (abwech-
seln) relieve; sich a~en come
off; (sich abwechseln) take turns.
A~**ung** f relief

abmach|en vt sep remove; (aus-
machen) arrange; (vereinbaren)
agree; **abgemacht!** agreed!
A~**ung** f -,-en agreement

abmager|n vi sep (sein) lose
weight. A~**ungskur** f slimming
diet

abmarschieren vi sep (sein)
march off

abmelden vt sep cancel ⟨Zei-
tung⟩; sich a~ report that one is
leaving; (im Hotel) check out

abmess|en† vt sep measure.
A~**ungen** fpl measurements

abmühen (sich) vr sep struggle

abnäh|en vt sep take in. A~**er** m
-s,- dart

Abnahme f -removal; (Kauf) purchase; (Verminderung) decrease

abnehm|en† v sep ⟨vt take off,
remove; pick up ⟨Hörer⟩; jdm
etw a~en take/(kaufen) buy sth
from s.o. ⟨vi (haben) decrease;
(nachlassen) decline; ⟨Person:⟩
lose weight; ⟨Mond:⟩ wane.
A~**er** m -s,- buyer

Abneigung f dislike (gegen of)

abnorm a abnormal, adv -ly

abnutz|en vt sep wear out; sich
a~en wear out. A~**ung** f- wear
[and tear]

Abon|nement /abonə'mã:/ nt -s,-s
subscription. A~**nent** m -en,-en
subscriber. a~**nieren** vt take
out a subscription to

Abordnung f -,-en deputation

abpassen vt sep wait for; **gut a~**
time well

abprallen vi sep (sein) rebound;
⟨Geschoß:⟩ ricochet

abraten† vi sep (haben) jdm von
etw a~ advise s.o. against sth

abräumen vt/i (haben) clear
away; clear ⟨Tisch⟩

abrechn|en v sep ⟨vt deduct ⟨vi
(haben) settle up; (fig) get even.
A~**ung** f settlement [of ac-
counts]; (Rechnung) account

Abre¹se f departure. a~**n** vi sep
(sein) leave

abreißen† v sep ⟨vt tear off; (demolieren) pull down ⟨vi (sein)
come off; (fig) break off

abrichten vt sep train

abriegeln vt sep bolt; (absperren)
seal off

Abriß m demolition; (Übersicht)
summary

abrufen† vt sep call away; (Computer) retrieve

abrunden vt sep round off; **nach
unten/oben a~** round down/up

abrupt a abrupt, adv -ly

abrüst|en vi sep (haben) disarm.
A~**ung** f disarmament

abrutschen vi sep (sein) slip

Absage f -,-n cancellation; (Ablehnung) refusal. a~**n** v sep ⟨vt
cancel ⟨vi (haben) [jdm] a~n
cancel an appointment [with
s.o.]; (auf Einladung) refuse
[s.o.'s invitation]

absägen vt sep saw off; (fam) sack

Absatz m heel; (Abschnitt) paragraph; (Verkauf) sale

abschaff|en *vt sep* abolish; get rid of ⟨*Auto, Hund*⟩. A~ung *f* abolition

abschalten *vt/i sep* (haben) switch off

abschätzig *a* disparaging, *adv* -ly

Abschaum *m* (fig) scum

Abscheu *m* - revulsion

abscheulich *a* revolting; (fam) horrible, *adv* -bly

abschicken *vt sep* send off

Abschied *m* -[e]s,-e farewell; (*Trennung*) parting; A~ nehmen say goodbye (von to)

abschießen† *vt sep* shoot down; (*abtrennen*) shoot off; (*abfeuern*) fire; launch ⟨*Rakete*⟩

abschirmen *vt sep* shield

abschlagen† *vt sep* knock off; (*verweigern*) refuse; (*abwehren*) repel

abschlägig *a* negative; a~e Antwort refusal

Abschlepp|dienst *m* breakdown service. a~en *vt sep* tow away. A~seil *nt* tow-rope. A~wagen *m* breakdown vehicle

abschließen† *v sep* □*vt* lock; (*beenden, abmachen*) conclude; make ⟨*Wette*⟩; balance ⟨*Bücher*⟩; sich a~ ⟨*fig*⟩ cut oneself off □*vi* (*haben*) lock up; (*enden*) end. a~d *adv* in conclusion

Abschluß *m* conclusion. A~prüfung *f* final examination. A~zeugnis *nt* diploma

abschmecken *vt sep* season

abschmieren *vt sep* lubricate

abschneiden† *v sep* □*vt* cut off; den Weg a~ take a short cut □*vi* (*haben*) gut/schlecht a~ do well/badly

Abschnitt *m* section; (*Stadium*) stage; (*Absatz*) paragraph; (*Kontroll-*) counterfoil

abschöpfen *vt sep* skim off

abschrauben *vt sep* unscrew

abschreck|en† *vt sep* deter; (*Culin*) put in cold water ⟨*Ei*⟩.

a~end *a* repulsive, *adv* -ly; a~endes Beispiel warning. A~ungsmittel *nt* deterrent

abschreib|en† *v sep* □*vt* copy; (*Comm* & *fig*) write off □*vi* (*haben*) copy. A~ung *f* (*Comm*) depreciation

Abschrift *f* copy

Abschuß *m* shooting down; (*Abfeuern*) firing; (*Raketen-*) launch

abschüssig *a* sloping; (*steil*) steep

abschwächen *vt sep* lessen; sich a~ lessen; (*schwächer werden*) weaken

abschweifen *vi sep* (sein) digress

abschwellen† *vi sep* (sein) go down

abschwören† *vi sep* (haben) (+*dat*) renounce

abseh|bar *a* in a~barer Zeit in the foreseeable future. a~en† *vt/i sep* (haben) copy; (*voraussehen*) foresee; a~en von disregard; (*aufgeben*) refrain from; es abgesehen haben auf (+*acc*) have one's eye on; (*schikanieren*) have it in for

absein† *vi sep* (fam) have come off; (*erschöpft*) be worn out

abseits *adv* apart; (*Sport*) offside □*prep* (+*gen*) away from. A~ *nt* (*Sport*) offside

absend|en† *vt sep* send off. A~er *m* sender

absetzen *v sep* □*vt* put *or* set down; (*ablagern*) deposit; (*abnehmen*) take off; (*absagen*) cancel; (*abbrechen*) stop; (*entlassen*) dismiss; (*verkaufen*) sell; (*abziehen*) deduct; sich a~ be deposited; (*fliehen*) flee □*vi* (haben) pause

Absicht *f* -,-en intention; mit A~ intentionally, on purpose

absichtlich *a* intentional, *adv* -ly, deliberate, *adv* -ly

absitzen† *v sep* □*vi* (sein) dismount □*vt* (fam) serve ⟨*Strafe*⟩

absolut *a* absolute, *adv* -ly

Absolution/-'tsjo:n/ f- absolution

absolvieren vt complete; (*bestehen*) pass

absonderlich a odd

absonder|n vt sep separate; (*ausscheiden*) secrete; sich ~ keep apart (**von** from). **A~ung** f -,-en secretion

absor|bieren vt absorb. **A~ption** /-'tsjo:n/ f- absorption

abspeisen vt sep fob off (**mit** with)

abspenstig a a~ machen take (**jdm** from s.o.)

absperr|en vt sep cordon off; (*abstellen*) turn off; (*SGer*) lock. **A~ung** f-,-en barrier

abspielen vt sep play; (*Fußball*) pass; **sich a~** take place

Absprache f agreement

absprechen vt sep arrange; **sich a~** agree; **jdm etw a~** deny s.o. sth

abspring|en† vi sep (sein) jump off; (*mit Fallschirm*) parachute; (*abgehen*) come off; (*fam: zurücktreten*) back out

Absprung m jump

abspülen vt sep rinse; (*entfernen*) rinse off

abstamm|en vi sep (haben) be descended (**von** from). **A~ung** f- descent

Abstand m distance; (*zeitlich*) interval; **A~ halten** keep one's distance; **A~ nehmen von** (*fig*) refrain from

abstatten vt sep **jdm einen Besuch a~** pay s.o. a visit

abstauben vt sep dust

abstech|en† vi sep (haben) stand out. **A~er** m -s,- detour

abstehen† vi sep (haben) stick out; **a~** be away from

absteig|en† vi sep (sein) dismount; (*niedersteigen*) descend; (*Fußball*) be relegated

abstell|en vt sep put down; (*lagern*) store; (*parken*) park; (*abschalten*) turn off; (*fig: beheben*)

remedy. **A~gleis** nt siding. **A~raum** m box-room

absterben† vi sep (sein) die; (*gefühllos werden*) go numb

Abstieg m -[e]s,-e descent; (*Fußball*) relegation

abstimm|en v sep □vi (haben) vote (**über**+acc on) □vt coordinate (**auf**+acc with). **A~ung** f vote

Abstinenz /-st-/ f - abstinence. **A~ler** m -s,- teetotaller

abstoßen† vt sep knock off; (*abschieben*) push off; (*verkaufen*) sell; (*fig: ekeln*) repel. **a~d** a repulsive, adv -ly

abstrakt /-st-/ a abstract

abstreifen vt sep remove; slip off ⟨*Kleidungsstück, Schuhe*⟩

abstreiten† vt sep deny

Abstrich m (*Med*) smear; (*Kürzung*) cut

abstufen vt sep grade

Absturz m fall; (*Aviat*) crash

abstürzen vi sep (sein) fall; (*Aviat*) crash

absuchen vt sep search; (*ablesen*) pick off

absurd a absurd

Abszeß m -sses,-sse abscess

Abt m -[e]s, ̈-e abbot

abtasten vt sep feel; (*Techn*) scan

abtauen vt/i sep (sein) thaw; (*entfrosten*) defrost

Abtei f -,-en abbey

Abteil nt compartment

abteilen vt sep divide off

Abteilung f-,-en section; (*Admin, Comm*) department

abtragen† vt sep clear; (*einebnen*) level; (*abnutzen*) wear out; (*abzahlen*) pay off

abträglich a detrimental (**dat** to)

abtreib|en† v sep □vt (Naut) drive off course; **ein Kind a~en lassen** have an abortion □vi (sein) drift off course. **A~ung** f -,-en abortion

abtrennen vt sep detach; (abteilen) divide off

abtreten† v sep □vt cede (an + acc to); sich (dat) die Füße a~en wipe one's feet □vi (sein) (Theat) exit; (fig) resign. A~er m -s,- doormat

abtrocknen vt/i sep (haben) dry; sich a~ dry oneself

abtropfen vi sep (sein) drain

abtrünnig a renegade; a~ werden (+ dat) desert

abtun† vt sep (fig) dismiss

abverlangen vt sep demand (dat from)

abwägen† vt sep (fig) weigh

abwandeln vt sep modify

abwandern vi sep (sein) move away

abwarten v sep □vt wait for □vi (haben) wait [and see]

abwärts adv down[wards]

Abwasch m -s washing-up; (Geschirr) dirty dishes pl. **a~en†** v sep □vt wash; wash up (Geschirr); (entfernen) wash off □vi (haben) wash up. A~lappen m dishcloth

Abwasser nt -s,- sewage. A~kanal m sewer

abwechsel|n vi/r sep (haben) [sich] a~ alternate (Personen:) take turns. **a~d** a alternate, adv -ly

Abwechslung f-,-en change; zur A~ for a change. **a~sreich** a varied

Abweg m auf A~e geraten (fig) go astray. **a~ig** a absurd

Abwehr f- defence; (Widerstand) resistance; (Pol) counter-espionage. a~en vt sep ward off; (Mil) repel; (zurückweisen) dismiss. A~system nt immune system

abweich|en† vi sep (sein) deviate; (von Regel) depart (von from); (sich unterscheiden) differ (von from). a~end a divergent; (verschieden) different. A~ung f -,-en deviation; difference

abweis|en† vt sep turn down; turn away (Person); (abwehren) repel. a~end a unfriendly. A~ung f rejection; (Abfuhr) rebuff

abwenden† vt sep turn away; (verhindern) avert; sich a~ turn away; den Blick a~ look away

abwerfen† vt sep throw off; throw (Reiter); (Aviat) drop; (Kartenspiel) discard; shed (Haut, Blätter); yield (Gewinn)

abwerten vt sep devalue. **a~end** a pejorative, adv -ly. A~ung f -,-en devaluation

abwesen|d a absent; (zerstreut) absent-minded. A~heit f - absence; absent-mindedness

abwickeln vt sep unwind; (erledigen) settle

abwischen vt sep wipe; (entfernen) wipe off

abwürgen vt sep stall (Motor)

abzahlen vt sep pay off

abzählen vt sep count

Abzahlung f instalment

abzapfen vt sep draw

Abzeichen nt badge

abzeichnen vt sep copy; (unterzeichnen) initial; sich a~ stand out

Abzieh|bild nt transfer. a~en† v sep □vt pull off; take off (Laken); strip (Bett); (häuten) skin; (Phot) print; run off (Kopien); (zurückziehen) withdraw; (abrechnen) deduct □vi (sein) go away; (Rauch:) escape

abzielen vi sep (haben) a~ auf (+ acc) (fig) be aimed at

Abzug m withdrawal; (Abrechnung) deduction; (Phot) print; (Korrektur-) proof; (am Gewehr) trigger; (A~söffnung) vent; A~e pl deductions

abzüglich prep (+ gen) less

Abzugshaube f [cooker] hood

abzweig|en *v sep* □*vi* (*sein*) branch off □*vt* divert. **A~ung** *f* -,-en junction; (*Gabelung*) fork

ach *int* oh; **a~ je!** oh dear! **a~ so** I see; **mit A~ und Krach** (*fam*) by the skin of one's teeth

Achse *f* -,-n axis; (*Rad-*) axle

Achsel *f* -,-n shoulder; **die A~n zucken** shrug one's shoulders. **A~höhle** *f* armpit. **A~zucken** *nt* -s shrug

acht¹ *inv a,* **A~** *f* -,-en eight; **heute in a~ Tagen** a week today

acht² **außer a~ lassen** disregard; **sich in a~ nehmen** be careful

acht|e(r,s) *a* eighth. **a~eckig** *a* octagonal. **A~el** *nt* -s,- eighth. **A~elnote** *f* quaver, (*Amer*) eighth note

achten *vt* respect □*vi* (*haben*) **a~ auf** (+ *acc*) pay attention to; (*aufpassen*) look after; **darauf a~, daß** take care that

ächten *vt* ban; ostracize 〈*Person*〉

Achter|bahn *f* roller-coaster. **a~n** *adv* (*Naut*) aft

achtgeben† *vi sep* (*haben*) be careful; **a~ auf** (+ *acc*) look after

achtlos *a* careless, *adv* -ly

achtsam *a* careful, *adv* -ly

Achtung *f* - respect (**vor** + *dat* for); **A~!** I look out! (*Mil*) attention! **'A~ Stufe** 'mind the step'

acht|zehn *inv a* eighteen. **a~zehnte(r,s)** *a* eighteenth. **a~zig** *a inv* eighty. **a~zigste(r,s)** *a* eightieth

ächzen *vi* (*haben*) groan

Acker *m* -s,- field. **A~bau** *m* agriculture. **A~land** *nt* arable land

addieren *vt/i* (*haben*) add; (*zusammenzählen*) add up

Addition /-ˈtsjoːn/ *f* -,-en addition

ade *int* goodbye

Adel *m* -s nobility

Ader *f* -,-n vein; **künstlerische A~** artistic bent

Adjektiv *nt* -s,-e adjective

Adler *m* -s,- eagle

adlig *a* noble. **A~e(r)** *m* nobleman

Administration /-ˈtsjoːn/ *f* - administration

Admiral *m* -s,-e admiral

adop|tieren *vt* adopt. **A~tion** /-ˈtsjoːn/ *f* -,-en adoption. **A~tiveltern** *pl* adoptive parents. **A~tivkind** *nt* adopted child

Adrenalin *nt* -s adrenalin

Adress|e *f* -,-n address. **a~ieren** *vt* address

adrett *a* neat, *adv* -ly

Adria *f* - Adriatic

Advent *m* -s Advent. **A~skranz** *m* Advent wreath

Adverb *nt* -s,-ien /-jən/ adverb

Affäre *f* -,-n affair

Affe *m* -n,-n monkey; (*Menschen-*) ape

Affekt *m* -[e]s,-e **im A~** in the heat of the moment

affektiert *a* affected. **A~heit** *f* - affectation

affig *a* affected; (*eitel*) vain

Afrika *nt* -s Africa

Afrikan|er(in) *m* -s,- (*f* -,-nen) African. **a~isch** *a* African

After *m* -s,- anus

Agen|t(in) *m* -en,-en (*f* -,-nen) agent. **A~tur** *f* -,-en agency

Aggres|sion *f* -,-en aggression. **a~siv** *a* aggressive, *adv* -ly. **A~sivität** *f* - aggressiveness

Agitation /-ˈtsjoːn/ *f* - agitation

Agnostiker *m* -s,- agnostic

Ägypt|en /ɛˈɡʏptən/ *nt* -s Egypt. **Ä~er(in)** *m* -s,- (*f* -,-nen) Egyptian. **ä~isch** *a* Egyptian

ähneln *vi* (*haben*) (+ *dat*) resemble; **sich ä~** be alike

ahnen *vt* have a presentiment of; (*vermuten*) suspect

Ahnen *mpl* ancestors. **A~forschung** *f* genealogy. **A~tafel** *f* family tree

ähnlich *a* similar, *adv* -ly; **jdm ä~ sehen** resemble s.o.; *(typisch sein)* be just like s.o. **Ä~keit** *f* -,-en similarity; *resemblance*

Ahnung *f* -,-en premonition; *(Vermutung)* idea, hunch; **keine A~** *(fam)* no idea. **a~slos** *a* unsuspecting

Ahorn *m* -s,-e maple

Ähre *f* -,-n ear [of corn]

Aids /eːts/ *nt* - Aids

Akademie *f* -,-n academy

Akadem|iker(in) *m* -s,- *(f-,-nen)* university graduate. **a~isch** *a* academic, *adv* -ally

akklimatisieren (sich) *vr* become acclimatized

Akkord *m* -[e]s,-e *(Mus)* chord; **im A~ arbeiten** be on piece-work. **A~arbeit** *f* piece-work

Akkordeon *nt* -s,-s accordion

Akkumulator *m* -s,-en /ˈtoːrən/ *(Electr)* accumulator

Akkusativ *m* -s,-e accusative. **A~objekt** *nt* direct object

Akrobat|(in) *m* -en,-en *(f-,-nen)* acrobat. **a~isch** *a* acrobatic

Akt *m* -[e]s,-e act; *(Kunst)* nude

Akte *f* -,-n file; **A~n** documents. **A~ndeckel** *m* folder. **A~nkoffer** *m* attaché case. **A~nschrank** *m* filing cabinet. **A~ntasche** *f* briefcase

Aktie /ˈaktsjə/ *f* -,-n *(Comm)* share. **A~ngesellschaft** *f* joint-stock company

Aktion /akˈtsjoːn/ *f* -,-en action; *(Kampagne)* campaign. **A~är** *m* -s,-e shareholder

aktiv *a* active, *adv* -ly. **a~ieren** *vt* activate. **A~ität** *f* -,-en activity

Aktualität *f* -,-en topicality; **A~en** current events

aktuell *a* topical; *(gegenwärtig)* current; **nicht mehr a~** no longer relevant

Akupunktur *f* - acupuncture

Akust|ik *f* - acoustics *pl.* **a~isch** *a* acoustic, *adv* -ally

akut *a* acute

Akzent *m* -[e]s,-e accent

akzept|abel *a* acceptable. **a~ieren** *vt* accept

Alarm *m* -s alarm; *(Mil)* alert; **A~ schlagen** raise the alarm. **a~ieren** *vt* alert; *(beunruhigen)* alarm. **a~ierend** *a* alarming

albern *a* silly □*adv* in a silly way □*vi (haben)* play the fool

Album *nt* -s,-ben album

Algebra *f* - algebra

Algen *fpl* algae

Algerien /-iən/ *nt* -s Algeria

Alibi *nt* -s,-s alibi

Alkohol *m* -s alcohol. **a~frei** *a* non-alcoholic

Alkohol|iker(in) *m* -s,- *(f-,-nen)* alcoholic. **a~isch** *a* alcoholic. **A~ismus** *m* - alcoholism

all *inv pron* **all das/mein Geld** all the/my money; **all dies** all this

All *nt* -s universe

alle *pred a* finished, *(fam)* all gone; **a~ machen** finish up

all|e(r,s) *pron* all; *(jeder)* every; **a~es** everything, all; *(alle Leute)* everyone; **a~e** *pl* all; **a~es Geld** all the money; **a~e meine Freunde** all my friends; **wir a~e** we all; **a~e Tage** every day; **a~e drei Jahre** every three years; **in a~er Unschuld** in all innocence; **ohne a~en Grund** without any reason; **vor a~em** above all; **a~es in a~em** all in all; **a~es ausnützen!** all change! **a~edem** *pron* **bei/trotz a~edem** with/despite all that

Allee *f* -,-n avenue

Alleg|orie *f* -,-n allegory. **a~orisch** *a* allegorical

allein *adv* alone; *(nur)* only; **a~ der Gedanke** the mere thought; **von a~[e]** of its/⟨*Person*⟩ one's own accord; (*automatisch*) automatically; **einzig u a~** solely □*conj* but. **A~erziehende(r)** *m/f* single parent. **a~ig** *a* sole. **a~stehend** *a* single; **a~stehende** *pl* single people

allemal *adv* every time; (*gewiß*) certainly; **ein für a~** once and for all

allenfalls *adv* at most; (*eventuell*) possibly

aller|beste(r,s) *a* very best; **am a~besten** best of all. **a~dings** *adv* indeed; (*zwar*) admittedly. **a~erste(r,s)** *a* very first

Allergie *f* -,-n allergy

allergisch *a* allergic (**gegen** to)

aller|hand *inv a* all sorts of □*pron* all sorts of things; **das ist a~hand!** that's quite something! (*empört*) that's a bit much! **A~heiligen** *nt* -s All Saints Day. **a~höchstens** *adv* at the very most. **a~lei** *inv a* all sorts of □*pron* all sorts of things. **a~letzte(r,s)** *a* very last. **a~liebst** *a* enchanting. **a~liebste(r,s)** *a* favourite □*adv* **am a~liebsten** for preference; **am a~liebsten haben** like best of all. **a~meiste(r,s)** *a* most □*adv* **am a~meisten** most of all. **A~seelen** *nt* -s All Souls Day. **a~seits** *adv* generally; **guten Morgen a~seits!** good morning everyone! **a~wenigste(r,s)** *a* very least □*adv* **am a~wenigsten** least of all

alle|s u. alle(r,s). a~samt *adv* all. **A~swisser** *m* -s,- (*fam*) know-all

allgemein *a* general, *adv* -ly; **im a~en** in general. **A~heit** *f* - community; (*Öffentlichkeit*) general public

Allheilmittel *nt* panacea

Allianz *f* -,-en alliance

Alligator *m* -s,-en /-'to:rən/ alligator

alliiert *a* allied; **die A~en** *pl* the Allies

alljährlich *a* annual, *adv* -ly. **der A~mächtige** almighty; **der A~mächtige** the Almighty. **a~mählich** *a* gradual, *adv* -ly

Alltag *m* working day; **der A~** (*fig*) everyday life

alltäglich *a* daily; (*gewöhnlich*) everyday; (*Mensch*) ordinary □*adv* daily

alltags *adv* on weekdays

allzu *adv* [far] too; **a~ vorsichtig** over-cautious. **a~bald** *adv* all too soon. **a~oft** *adv* all too often. **a~sehr** *adv* far too much. **a~viel** *adv* far too much

a~weit *adv* far too much

Alm *f* -,-en alpine pasture

Almosen *ntpl* alms

Alpdruck *m* nightmare

Alpen *pl* Alps. **A~veilchen** *nt* cyclamen

Alphabet *nt* -[e]s,-e alphabet. **a~isch** *a* alphabetical, *adv* -ly

Alptraum *m* nightmare

als *conj* as; (*zeitlich*) when; (*mit Komparativ*) than; **nichts als** nothing but; **als ob** as if or though; **so tun als ob** (*fam*) pretend

also *adv* & *conj* so; **a~ gut** all right then; **na a~!** there you are!

alt *a* (*älter*, **ältest**) old; (*gebraucht*) second-hand; (*ehemalig*) former; **alt werden** grow old; **alles beim a~en lassen** leave things as they are

Alt *m* -s (*Mus*) contralto

Altar *m* -s,-ͤe altar

Alt|e(r) *m/f* old man/woman; **die A~en** old people. **A~eisen** *nt* scrap iron. **A~enheim** *nt* old people's home

Alter *nt* -s,- age; (*Bejahrtheit*) old age; **im A~ von** at the age of; **im A~** in old age

älter *a* older; **mein ä~er Bruder** my elder brother

altern *vi* (*sein*) age

Alternative *f* -,-n alternative

Alters|grenze f age limit.
A~heim nt old people's home.
A~rente f old-age pension.
a~schwach a old and infirm;
⟨Ding⟩ decrepit

Alter|tum nt -s,-̈er antiquity.
a~tümlich a old; (altmodisch)
old-fashioned

ältest|e(r,s) a oldest; **der ä~e Sohn** the eldest son

althergebracht a traditional

altklug a precocious, adv -ly

ältlich a elderly

alt|modisch old-fashioned □adv
in an old-fashioned way. **A~papier** nt waste paper. **A~stadt** f old [part of a] town. **A~warenhändler** m second-hand dealer.
A~weibermärchen nt old
wives' tale. **A~weibersommer**
m Indian summer; (Spinnfäden)
gossamer

Alufolie f [aluminium] foil

Aluminium nt -s aluminium,
(Amer) aluminum

am prep = an dem; **am Montag** on
Monday; **am Morgen** in the
morning; **am besten/meisten**
[the] best/most; **am teuersten
sein** be the most expensive

Amateur /-'tøːɐ̯/ m -s,-e amateur

Ambition /-'tsi̯oːn/ f -,-en ambition

Amboß m -sses,-sse anvil

ambulan|t a out-patient ... □adv
a~t behandeln treat as an out-patient. **A~z** f -,-en out-patients'
department; (Krankenwagen)
ambulance

Ameise f -,-n ant

amen int, **A~** nt -s amen

Amerika nt -s America

Amerikan|er(in) m -s,- (f-,-nen)
American. **a~isch** a American

Ami m -s,-s (fam) Yank

Ammoniak nt -s ammonia

Amnestie f -,-n amnesty

amoralisch a amoral

Ampel f -,-n traffic lights pl;
(Blumen-) hanging basket

Amphib|ie /-i̯ə/ f -,-n amphibian.
a~isch a amphibious

Amphitheater nt amphitheatre

Amput|ation /-'tsi̯oːn/ f -,-en amputation. **a~ieren** vt amputate

Amsel f -,-n blackbird

Amt nt -[e]s,-̈er office; (Aufgabe)
task; (Teleph) exchange. **a~ieren** (haben) hold office; **a~ierend** acting. **a~lich** a official,
adv -ly. **A~szeichen** nt dialling
tone

Amulett nt -[e]s,-e [lucky] charm

amüs|ant a amusing, adv -ly.
a~ieren vt amuse; **sich a~ieren** be amused (über + acc at);
(sich vergnügen) enjoy oneself

an prep (+ dat/acc) at; (haftend,
berührend) on; (gegen) against;
(+ acc) (schicken) to; **an der/die
Universität** at/to university; **an
dem Tag** on that day; **es ist an
mir** it is up to me; **an [und für]
sich** actually; **die Arbeit an sich**
the work as such □adv (angeschaltet) on; (auf Fahrplan) arriving; **an die zwanzig Mark/
Leute** about twenty marks/
people; **von heute an** from today

analog a analogous; (Computer)
analog. **A~ie** f -,-n analogy

Analphabet m -en,-en illiterate
person. **A~entum** nt -s illiteracy

Analy|se f -,-n analysis. **a~sieren** vt analyse. **A~tiker** m -s,-
analyst. **a~tisch** a analytical

Anämie f - anaemia

Ananas f -,-[se] pineapple

Anarch|ie f - anarchy. **A~ist** m
-en,-en anarchist

Anat|omie f - anatomy. **a~omisch** a anatomical, adv -ly

anbahnen (sich) vr sep develop

Anbau m cultivation; (Gebäude)
extension. **a~en** vt sep build on;
(anpflanzen) cultivate, grow

anbehalten† vt sep keep on

anbei adv enclosed

anbeißen† v sep □vt take a bite of □vi (haben) ⟨Fisch:⟩ bite; (fig) take the bait

anbelangen vt sep = **anbetreffen**

anbellen vt sep bark at

anbeten vt sep worship

Anbetracht m in A~ (+gen) in view of

anbetreffen† vt sep was mich/ das anbetrifft as far as I am/ that is concerned

Anbetung f- worship

anbiedern (sich) vr sep ingratiate oneself (bei with)

anbieten† vt sep offer; **sich a~** offer (zu to)

anbinden† vt sep tie up

Anblick m sight. **a~en** vt sep look at

anbrechen v sep □vt start on; break into ⟨Vorräte⟩ □vi (sein) begin; ⟨Tag:⟩ break; ⟨Nacht:⟩ fall

anbrennen v sep □vt light □vi (sein) burn; (Feuer fangen) catch fire

anbringen† vt sep bring [along]; (befestigen) fix

Anbruch m ⟨fig⟩ dawn; A~ des Tages/der Nacht daybreak/ nightfall

anbrüllen vt sep (fam) bellow at

Andacht f -,-en reverence; (Gottesdienst) prayers pl

andächtig a reverent, adv -ly; (fig) rapt, adv -ly

andauern vi sep (haben) last; (anhalten) continue. **a~d** a persistent, adv -ly; (ständig) constant, adv -ly

Andenken nt -s,- memory; (Souvenir) souvenir; **zum A~ an** (+acc) in memory of

ander|e(r,s) a other; (verschieden) different; (nächste) next; ein a~er, eine a~e another □pron der a~e/die a~en the other/ others; ein a~er another [one];

(Person) someone else; **kein a~er** no one else; **einer nach dem a~en** one after the other; **alles a~e/nichts a~e** everything/nothing else; **etwas ganz a~es** something quite different; **alles a~e als** anything but; **unter a~en** among other things. **a~enfalls** adv otherwise. **a~erseits** adv on the other hand. **a~mal** adv ein a~mal another time

ändern vt alter; (wechseln) change; **sich ä~** change

andernfalls adv otherwise

anders pred a different; **a~ werden** change □adv differently; ⟨riechen, schmecken⟩ different; (sonst) else; **jemand/niemand/ irgendwo a~** someone/no one/ somewhere else

anderseits adv on the other hand

anders|herum adv the other way round. **a~wo** adv (fam) somewhere else

anderthalb inv a one and a half; **a~ Stunden** an hour and a half

Änderung f -,-en alteration; (Wechsel) change

anderweitig a other □adv otherwise; (anderswo) elsewhere

andeuten vt sep indicate; (anspielen) hint at. **A~ung** f -,-en indication; hint

andicken vt sep (Culin) thicken

Andrang m rush (nach for); (Gedränge) crush

andre a & pron = **andere**

andrehen vt sep turn on; **jdm etw a~** (fam) palm sth off on s.o.

androhen vt sep jdm etw a~ threaten s.o. with sth

aneignen vt sep sich (dat) a~ appropriate; (lernen) learn

aneinander adv & pref together; ⟨denken⟩ of one another; **a~ vorbei** past one another. **a~geraten†** vi sep (sein) quarrel

Anekdote f -,-n anecdote

anekeln vt sep nauseate

anerkannt a acknowledged

anerkenn|en† vt sep acknowledge, recognize; ⟨würdigen⟩ appreciate. **A~end** a approving, adv -ly. **A~ung** f - acknowledgement, recognition; appreciation

anfahr|en† v sep ▸vt deliver; ⟨streifen⟩ hit; ⟨schimpfen⟩ snap at ▸vi (sein) start; **angefahren kommen** drive up

Anfall m fit, attack. **a~en†** v sep ▸vt attack ▸vi (sein) arise; ⟨Zinsen:⟩ accrue

anfällig a susceptible (**für** to); ⟨zart⟩ delicate. **A~keit** f - susceptibility (**für** to)

Anfang m -s,ⁿe beginning, start; **zu** od **am A~** at the beginning; ⟨anfangs⟩ at first. **a~en†** vt/i sep ⟨haben⟩ begin, start; ⟨tun⟩ do

Anfäng|er(in) m -s,- (f -,-nen) beginner. **a~lich** a initial, adv -ly

anfangs adv at first. **A~buchstabe** m initial letter. **A~gehalt** nt starting salary. **A~gründe** mpl rudiments

anfassen v sep ▸vt touch; ⟨behandeln⟩ treat; tackle ⟨Arbeit⟩; **jdn a~** take s.o.'s hand; **sich a~** hold hands; **sich weich a~** feel soft ▸vi ⟨haben⟩ **mit a~** lend a hand

anfechten† vt sep contest; ⟨fig: beunruhigen⟩ trouble

anfeinden vt sep be hostile to

anfertigen vt sep make

anfeuchten vt sep moisten

anfeuern vt sep spur on

anflehen vt sep implore, beg

Anflug m ⟨Aviat⟩ approach; ⟨fig: Spur⟩ trace

anforder|n vt sep demand; ⟨Comm⟩ order. **A~ung** f demand

Anfrage f enquiry. **a~n** vi sep ⟨haben⟩ enquire, ask

anfreunden (sich) vr sep make friends (**mit** with); ⟨miteinander⟩ become friends

anfügen vt sep add

anfühlen vt sep feel; **sich weich a~** feel soft

anführ|en vt sep lead; ⟨zitieren⟩ quote; ⟨angeben⟩ give; **jdn a~n** ⟨fam⟩ have s.o. on. **A~er** m leader. **A~ungszeichen** ntpl quotation marks

Angabe f statement; ⟨Anweisung⟩ instruction; ⟨Tennis⟩ service; ⟨fam: Angeberei⟩ showing-off; **nähere A~n** particulars

angeb|en† v sep ▸vt state; give ⟨Namen, Grund⟩; ⟨anzeigen⟩ indicate; set ⟨Tempo⟩ ▸vi ⟨haben⟩ ⟨Tennis⟩ serve; ⟨fam: protzen⟩ show off. **A~er(in)** m -s,- (f -,-nen) ⟨fam⟩ show-off. **A~erei** f -⟨fam⟩ showing-off

angeblich a alleged, adv -ly

angeboren a innate; ⟨Med⟩ congenital

Angebot nt offer; ⟨Auswahl⟩ range; **A~ und Nachfrage** supply and demand

angebracht a appropriate

angebunden a **kurz a~** curt

angegriffen a worn out; ⟨Gesundheit:⟩ poor

angeheiratet a ⟨Onkel, Tante⟩ by marriage

angeheitert a ⟨fam⟩ tipsy

angehen† v sep ▸vi ⟨sein⟩ begin, start; ⟨Licht, Radio:⟩ come on; ⟨anwachsen⟩ take root; **a~ gegen** fight ▸vt attack; tackle ⟨Arbeit⟩; ⟨bitten⟩ ask (**um** for); ⟨betreffen⟩ concern; **das geht dich nichts an** it's none of your business. **a~d** a future; ⟨Künstler⟩ budding

angehör|en vi sep ⟨haben⟩ (+ dat) belong to. **A~ige(r)** m/f relative; ⟨Mitglied⟩ member

Angeklagte(r) m/f accused

Angel f -,-n fishing rod; ⟨Tür-⟩ hinge

Angelegenheit f matter; **auswärtige A~en** in foreign affairs

Angel|haken m fish-hook. **a~n** vi ⟨haben⟩ fish ⟨nach for⟩; **a~n gehen** go fishing □vt ⟨fangen⟩ catch. **A~rute** f fishing-rod

angelsächsisch a Anglo-Saxon

angemessen a commensurate ⟨dat with⟩; ⟨passend⟩ appropriate, adv -ly

angenehm a pleasant, adv -ly; ⟨bei Vorstellung⟩ **a~!** delighted to meet you!

angenommen a ⟨Kind⟩ adopted; ⟨Name⟩ assumed

angeregt a animated, adv -ly

angesehen a respected; ⟨Firma⟩ reputable

angesichts prep (+ gen) in view of

angespannt a intent, adv -ly; ⟨Lage⟩ tense

Angestellte(r) m/f employee

angetan a **a~ sein von** be taken with

angetrunken a slightly drunk

angewandt a applied

angewiesen a dependent **(auf** + acc on); **auf sich selbst a~** on one's own

angewöhnen vt sep **jdm etw a~** get s.o. used to sth; **sich** ⟨dat⟩ **etw a~** get into the habit of doing sth

Angewohnheit f habit

Angina f - tonsillitis

angleichen† vt sep adjust ⟨dat to⟩

Angler m -s,- angler

anglikanisch a Anglican

Anglistik f - English [language and literature]

Angorakatze f Persian cat

angreifen† vt sep attack; tackle ⟨Arbeit⟩; ⟨schädigen⟩ damage; ⟨anbrechen⟩ break into; ⟨anfassen⟩ touch. **A~er** m -s,- attacker; ⟨Pol⟩ aggressor

angrenzen vi sep ⟨haben⟩ adjoin ⟨an etw acc sth⟩. **a~d** a adjoining

Angriff m attack; **in A~ nehmen** tackle. **a~slustig** a aggressive

Angst f -,-̈e fear; ⟨Psych⟩ anxiety; ⟨Sorge⟩ worry (um about); **A~ haben** be afraid (vor + dat of); ⟨sich sorgen⟩ be worried (um about); □**jdm a~ machen** frighten s.o.; **mir ist a~** I am frightened; I am worried (um about)

ängstigen vt frighten; ⟨Sorge machen⟩ worry; **sich ä~** be frightened; be worried (um about)

ängstlich a nervous, adv -ly; ⟨scheu⟩ timid, adv -ly; ⟨verängstigt⟩ frightened, scared; ⟨besorgt⟩ anxious, adv -ly. **Ä~keit** f -nervousness; timidity; anxiety

angstvoll a anxious, adv -ly; ⟨verängstigt⟩ frightened

angucken vt sep ⟨fam⟩ look at

angurten ⟨sich⟩ vr sep fasten one's seat-belt

anhaben† vt sep have on; **er/es kann mir nichts a~** ⟨fig⟩ he/it cannot hurt me

anhalt|en† v sep □vt stop; hold ⟨Atem⟩; **jdn zur Arbeit/Ordnung a~** en urge s.o. to work/be tidy □vi ⟨haben⟩ stop; ⟨andauern⟩ continue. **a~end** a persistent, adv -ly; ⟨Beifall⟩ prolonged. **A~er(in)** m -s,- ⟨f -,-nen⟩ hitch-hiker; **per A~er fahren** hitch-hike. **A~spunkt** m clue

anhand prep (+ gen) with the aid of

Anhang m appendix; ⟨fam: Angehörige⟩ family

anhängen† vt sep ⟨reg⟩ hang up; ⟨befestigen⟩ attach; ⟨hinzufügen⟩ add

anhäng|en²† vi ⟨haben⟩ be a follower of. **A~er** m -s,- follower; ⟨Auto⟩ trailer; ⟨Schild⟩ [tie-on] label; ⟨Schmuck⟩ pendant; ⟨Aufhänger⟩ loop. **A~erin** f -,-nen follower. **A~erschaft** f - following, followers pl. **a~lich** a affectionate. **A~sel** nt -s,- appendage

anhäufen vt sep pile up; **sich a~** pile up, accumulate

anheben† vt sep lift; (erhöhen) raise

Anhieb m **auf A~** straight away

Anhöhe f hill

anhören vt sep listen to; **mit a~** overhear; **sich gut a~** sound good

animieren vt encourage (zu to)

Anis m **-es** aniseed

Anker m **-s,-** anchor; **vor A~ gehen** drop anchor. **a~n** vi (haben) anchor; (liegen) be anchored

anketten vt sep chain up

Anklage f accusation; (Jur) charge; (Ankläger) prosecution. **A~bank** f dock. **a~n** vt sep accuse (gen of); (Jur) charge (gen with)

Ankläger m accuser; (Jur) prosecutor

anklammern vt sep clip on; peg on the line ⟨Wäsche⟩; **sich a~** cling (an+acc to)

Anklang m **bei jdm A~ finden** meet with s.o.'s approval

ankleben v sep ○vt stick on ○vi (sein) stick (an+dat to)

Ankleide|kabine f changing cubicle; (zur Anprobe) fitting-room. **a~n** vt sep dress; **sich a~n** dress

anklopfen vi sep (haben) knock

anknipsen vt sep (fam) switch on

anknüpfen v sep ○vt tie on; (fig) enter into ⟨Gespräch, Beziehung⟩ ○vi (haben) refer (an+acc to)

ankommen† vi sep (sein) arrive; (sich nähern) approach; **gut a~** arrive safely; (fig) go down well (bei with); **nicht a~ gegen** (fig) be no match for; **a~ auf** (+acc) depend on; **es a~ lassen auf** (+acc) risk; **das kommt darauf an** it [all] depends

ankreuzen vt sep mark with a cross

ankündig|en vt sep announce. **A~ung** f announcement

Ankunft f **-** arrival

ankurbeln vt sep (fig) boost

anlächeln vt sep smile at

anlachen vt sep smile at

Anlage f **-,-n** installation; (Industrie-) plant; (Komplex) complex; (Geld-) investment; (Plan) layout; (Beilage) enclosure; (Veranlagung) aptitude; (Neigung) predisposition; **öffentliche** A~n [public] gardens; **als A~** enclosed

Anlaß m **-sses,-̈sse** reason; (Gelegenheit) occasion; **A~ geben zu** give cause for

anlass|en† vt sep (Auto) start; (fam) leave on ⟨Licht⟩; keep on ⟨Mantel⟩; **sich gut/schlecht a~en** start off well/badly. **A~er** m **-s,-** starter

anläßlich prep (+gen) on the occasion of

Anlauf m (Sport) run-up; (fig) attempt. **a~en†** v sep ○vi (sein) start; (beschlagen) mist up; ⟨Metall-⟩ tarnish; **rot a~en** go red; (erröten) blush; **angelaufen kommen** come running up ○vt (Naut) call at

anlegen v sep ○vt put (an+acc against); put on ⟨Kleidung, Verband⟩; lay back ⟨Ohren⟩; aim ⟨Gewehr⟩; (investieren) invest; (ausgeben) spend (für on); (erstellen) build; (gestalten) lay out; draw up ⟨Liste⟩; **[mit] Hand a~** lend a hand; **es darauf a~** (fig) aim (zu to); **sich a~ mit** quarrel with ○vi (haben) ⟨Schiff:⟩ moor; **a~ auf** (+acc) aim at

anlehnen vt sep lean (an+acc against); **sich a~** lean (an+acc on); **eine Tür angelehnt lassen** leave a door ajar

Anleihe f **-,-n** loan

anleinen vt sep put on a lead

anleit|en vt sep instruct. **A~ung** f instructions pl

anlernen vt sep train

Anliegen *nt* -s,- request; (*Wunsch*) desire

anlieg|**en**† *vi sep* (*haben*) [**eng**] **a**~**en** fit closely; [**eng**] **a**~**end** close-fitting. **A**~**er** *mpl* residents; '**A**~**er frei**' 'access for residents only'

anlocken *vt sep* attract

anlügen† *vt sep* lie to

anmachen *vt sep* (*fam*) fix; (*anschalten*) turn on; (*anzünden*) light; (*Culin*) dress ⟨*Salat*⟩

anmalen *vt sep* paint

Anmarsch *m* (*Mil*) approach

anmaß|**en** *vt sep* **sich** (*dat*) **a**~**en** presume (**zu** to); **sich** (*dat*) **ein Recht a**~**en** claim a right. **a**~**end** *a* presumptuous, *adv* -ly; (*arrogant*) arrogant, *adv* -ly. **A**~**ung** *f* - presumption; arrogance

anmeld|**en** *vt sep* announce; (*Admin*) register; **sich a**~**en** say that one is coming; (*Admin*) register; (*Sch*) enrol; (*im Hotel*) check in; (*beim Arzt*) make an appointment. **A**~**ung** *f* announcement; (*Admin*) registration; (*Sch*) enrolment; (*Termin*) appointment

anmerk|**en** *vt sep* mark; **sich** (*dat*) **etw a**~**en lassen** show sth. **A**~**ung** *f* -,-**en** note

Anmut *f* - grace; (*Charme*) charm

anmuten *vt sep* **es mutet mich seltsam/vertraut an** it seems odd/familiar to me

anmutig *a* graceful, *adv* -ly; (*lieblich*) charming, *adv* -ly

annähen *vt sep* sew on

annäher|**nd** *a* approximate, *adv* -ly. **A**~**ungsversuche** *mpl* advances

Annahme *f* -,-**n** acceptance; (*Adoption*) adoption; (*Vermutung*) assumption

annehm|**bar** *a* acceptable. **a**~**en**† *vt sep* accept; (*verrechnen*) allow ⟨*Summe*⟩; (*sich zulegen, vermuten*) assume;

sich a~**en** (+ *gen*) take care of; **angenommen, daß** assuming that. **A**~**lichkeiten** *fpl* comforts

annektieren *vt* annex

Anno *adv* **A**~ **1920** in the year 1920

Annon|**ce** /a'nõ:sə/ *f* -,-**n** advertisement. **a**~**cieren** /-'si:-/ *vt*/*i* (*haben*) advertise

annullieren *vt* annul; cancel ⟨*Flug*⟩

anöden *vt sep* (*fam*) bore

Anomalie *f* -,-**n** anomaly

anonym *a* anonymous, *adv* -ly

Anorak *m* -s,-s anorak

anordn|**en** *vt sep* arrange; (*befehlen*) order. **A**~**ung** *f* arrangement; order

anorganisch *a* inorganic

anormal *a* abnormal

anpacken *v sep* ⊡*vt* grasp; tackle ⟨*Arbeit, Problem*⟩ ⊡*vi* (*haben*) **mit a**~ lend a hand

anpass|**en** *vt sep* try on; (*angleichen*) adapt (**dat** to); **sich a**~ adapt (**dat** to). **A**~**ung** *f* - adaptation. **a**~**ungsfähig** *a* adaptable. **A**~**ungsfähigkeit** *f* adaptability

Anpfiff *m* (*Sport*) kick-off; (*fam*: *Rüge*) reprimand

anpflanzen *vt sep* plant; (*anbauen*) grow

Anprall *m* -[e]s impact. **a**~**en** *vi sep* (*sein*) strike (**an** *acc* sth)

anprangern *vt sep* denounce

anpreisen† *vt sep* commend

Anprob|**e** *f* fitting. **a**~**ieren** *vt sep* try on

anrechnen *vt sep* count (**als** as); (*berechnen*) charge for; (*verrechnen*) allow ⟨*Summe*⟩; **ich rechne ihm seine Hilfe hoch an** I very much appreciate his help

Anrecht *nt* right (**auf** + *acc* to)

Anrede *f* [form of] address. **a**~**n** *vt sep* address; (*ansprechen*) speak to

anreg|en vt sep stimulate; (ermuntern) encourage (zu to); (vorschlagen) suggest. **a~end** a stimulating. **A~ung** f stimulation; (Vorschlag) suggestion

anreichern vt sep enrich

Anreise f journey; (Ankunft) arrival. **a~n** vi sep (sein) arrive

Anreiz m incentive

anrempeln vt sep jostle

Anrichte f -,-n sideboard. **a~n** vt sep (Culin) prepare; (garnieren) garnish (mit with); (verursachen) cause

anrüchig a disreputable

Anruf m call. **A~beantworter** m -s,- answering machine. **a~en†** v sep □vt call to; (bitten) call on (um for); (Teleph) ring □vi (haben) ring (bei jdm s.o.)

anrühren vt sep touch; (verrühren) mix

ans prep = **an das**

Ansage f announcement. **a~n** vt sep announce; **sich a~n** say that one is coming. **A~r(in)** m -s,- (f -,-nen) announcer

ansamm|eln vt sep collect; (anhäufen) accumulate; **sich a~eln** collect; (sich häufen) accumulate; (Leute:) gather. **A~lung** f collection; (Menschen-) crowd

ansässig a resident

Ansatz m beginning; (Haar-) hairline; (Versuch) attempt; (Techn) extension

anschaff|en vt sep [**sich** dat] etw **a~en** acquire; (kaufen) buy sth. **A~ung** f -,-en acquisition; (Kauf) purchase

anschalten vt sep switch on

anschau|en vt sep look at. **a~lich** a vivid, adv -ly. **A~ung** f -,-en (fig) view

Anschein m appearance; **den A~ haben** seem. **a~end** adv apparently

anschicken (sich) vr sep be about (zu to)

anschirren vt sep harness

Anschlag m notice; (Vor-) estimate; (Überfall) attack (**auf** + acc on); (Mus) touch; (Techn) stop; **240 A~e in der Minute** ≈ 50 words per minute. **A~brett** nt notice board. **a~en†** v sep □vt put up (Aushang); (Note, Taste) cast on (Masche); (beschädigen) chip □vi (haben) strike/(stoßen) knock (**an** + acc against); (Hund:) bark; (wirken) be effective □vi (sein) knock (**an** + acc against); **mit dem Kopf a~en** hit one's head. **A~zettel** m notice

anschließen† v sep □vt connect (**an** + acc to); (zufügen) add; **sich a~** an (+ acc) (anstoßen) adjoin; (folgen) follow; (sich anfreunden) become friendly with; **sich jdm a~** join s.o. □vi (haben) **a~ an** (+ acc) adjoin; (folgen) follow. **a~d** a adjoining; (zeitlich) following □adv afterwards; **a~d an** (+ acc) after

Anschluß m connection; (Kontakt) contact; **A~ finden** make friends; **im A~ an** (+ acc) after

anschmieg|en (sich) vr sep snuggle up/(Kleid:) cling (**an** + acc to). **a~sam** a affectionate

anschmieren vt sep smear; (fam: täuschen) cheat

anschnallen vt sep strap on; **sich a~** fasten one's seat-belt

anschneiden† vt sep cut into; broach (Thema)

anschreiben† vt sep write (**an** + acc on); (Comm) put on s.o.'s account; (sich wenden) write to; **bei jdm gut/schlecht angeschrieben sein** be in s.o.'s good/bad books

anschreien† vt sep shout at

Anschrift f address

anschuldig|en vt sep accuse. **A~ung** f -,-en accusation

anschwellen† vi sep (sein) swell

anschwemmen vt sep wash up

anschwindeln vt sep (fam) lie to

ansehen† vt sep look at; (einschätzen) regard (als as); [sich dat] etw a~ look at sth.; (TV) watch sth. A~ nt -s respect; (Ruf) reputation

ansehnlich a considerable

ansetzen v sep □vt join (an + acc to); (festsetzen) fix; (veranschlagen) estimate; Rost a~ get rusty; sich a~ form □vi (haben) (anbrennen) burn; zum Sprung a~ get ready to jump

Ansicht f view; meiner A~ nach in my view; zur A~ (Comm) on approval. A~s[post]karte f picture postcard. A~ssache f matter of opinion

ansiedeln (sich) vr sep settle

ansonsten adv apart from that

anspannen vt sep hitch up; (anstrengen) strain; tense (Muskel)

anspiel|en vi sep (haben) a~en auf (+ acc) allude to; (versteckt) hint at. A~ung f -,-en allusion; hint

Anspitzer m -s,- pencil-sharpener

Ansporn m (fig) incentive. a~en vt sep spur on

Ansprache f address

ansprechen v sep □vt speak to; (fig) appeal to □vi (haben) respond (auf + acc to). a~d a attractive

anspringen v sep □vt jump at □vi (sein) (Auto) start

Anspruch m claim/(Recht) right (auf + acc to); A~ haben be entitled (auf + acc to); in A~ nehmen make use of; (erfordern) demand; take up (Zeit); occupy (Person); hohe A~e stellen be very demanding. a~slos a undemanding; (bescheiden) unpretentious. a~svoll a demanding; (kritisch) discriminating; (vornehm) up-market

anspucken vt sep spit at

anstacheln vt sep (fig) spur on

Anstalt f -,-en institution; A~en/keine A~en machen prepare/make no move (zu to)

Anstand m decency; (Benehmen) [good] manners pl

anständig a decent, adv -ly; (ehrbar) respectable, adv -bly; (fam: beträchtlich) considerable, adv -bly; (richtig) proper, adv -ly

Anstands|dame f chaperon. a~los adv without any trouble; (bedenkenlos) without hesitation

anstarren vt sep stare at

anstatt conj & prep (+ gen) instead of; a~ zu arbeiten instead of working

anstecken vt sep tap (Faß)

anstecken v sep □vt pin (an + acc to/on); put on (Ring); (anzünden) light; (in Brand stecken) set fire to; (Med) infect; sich a~en catch an infection (bei from) □vi (haben) be infectious. a~end a infectious, (fam) catching. A~ung f -,-en infection

anstehen† vi sep (haben) queue, (Amer) stand in line

ansteigen† vi sep (sein) climb; (Gelände, Preise:) rise

anstelle prep (+ gen) instead of

anstell|en vt sep put, stand (an + acc against); (einstellen) employ; (anschalten) turn on; (tun) do; sich a~en queue [up], (Amer) stand in line; (sich haben) make a fuss. A~ung f employment; (Stelle) job

Anstieg m -[e]s,-e climb; (fig) rise

anstiften vt sep cause; (anzetteln) instigate; jdn a~n put s.o. up (zu to). A~r m instigator

Anstoß m (Anregung) impetus; (Stoß) knock; (Fußball) kick-off; A~ erregen/nehmen give/take offence (an + dat at). a~en† v sep □vt knock; (mit dem Ellbogen) nudge □vi (sein) knock (an + acc against) □ *vi* (*haben*) adjoin (**an etw** *acc* sth); [mit den Gläsern] **a~en** clink glasses; **a~en auf** (+ *acc*) drink to; **mit der Zunge a~en** lisp

anstößig *a* offensive, *adv* -ly

anstrahlen *vt sep* floodlight; (*anlachen*) beam at

anstreiche|n† *vt sep* paint; (*anmerken*) mark. **A~r** *m* -s, painter

anstreng|en *vt sep* strain; (*ermüden*) tire; **sich a~en** exert oneself; (*sich bemühen*) make an effort (**zu** to). **a~end** *a* strenuous; (*ermüdend*) tiring. **A~ung** *f* -,-en strain; (*Mühe*) effort

Anstrich *m* coat [of paint]

Ansturm *m* rush; (*Mil*) assault

Ansuchen *nt* -s,- request

Antagonismus *m* - antagonism

Antarktis *f* - Antarctic

Anteil *m* share; **A~ nehmen** take an interest (**an** + *dat* in); (*mitfühlen*) sympathize. **A~nahme** *f* - interest (**an** + *dat* in); (*Mitgefühl*) sympathy

Antenne *f* -,-n aerial

Anthologie *f* -,-n anthology

Anthropologie *f* - anthropology

Anti|alkoholiker *m* teetotaler. **A~biotikum** *nt* -s,-ka antibiotic

antik *a* antique. **A~e** *f* - [classical] antiquity

Antikörper *m* antibody

Antilope *f* -,-n antelope

Antipathie *f* - antipathy

Anti|quariat *nt* -[e]s,-e antiquarian bookshop. **a~quarisch** *a* & *adv* second-hand

Antiquitäten *fpl* antiques. **A~händler** *m* antique dealer

Antisemitismus *m* - anti-Semitism

Antisept|ikum *nt* -s,-ka antiseptic. **a~isch** *a* antiseptic

Antrag *m* -[e]s,-̈e proposal; (*Pol*) motion; (*Gesuch*) application. **A~steller** *m* -s,- applicant

antreffen† *vt sep* find

antreiben† *v sep* □ *vt* urge on; (*Techn*) drive; (*anschwemmen*) wash up □ *vi* (*sein*) be washed up

antreten† *v sep* □ *vt* start; take up

antreten† *v sep* □ *vt* start; take up ⟨*Amt*⟩ □ *vi* (*sein*) line up; (*Mil*) fall in

Antrieb *m* urge; (*Techn*) drive; **aus eigenem A~** of one's own accord

antrinken† *vt sep* **sich** (*dat*) **einen Rausch a~** get drunk; **sich** (*dat*) **Mut a~** give oneself Dutch courage

Antritt *m* start; **bei A~ eines Amtes** when taking office. **A~srede** *f* inaugural address

antun† *vt sep* **jdm etw a~** do sth to s.o.; **sich** (*dat*) **etwas a~** take one's own life; **es jdm angetan haben** appeal to s.o.

Antwort *f* -,-en answer, reply (**auf** + *acc* to). **a~en** *vt/i* (*haben*) answer (**jdm** s.o.)

anvertrauen *vt sep* entrust/(*mitteilen*) confide (**jdm** to s.o.); **sich jdm a~** confide in s.o.

anwachsen† *vi sep* (*sein*) take root; (*zunehmen*) grow

Anwalt *m* -[e]s,-̈e, **Anwältin** *f* -,-nen lawyer; (*vor Gericht*) counsel

Anwandlung *f* -,-en fit (**von** of)

Anwärter(in) *m*(*f*) candidate

anweis|en† *vt sep* assign (*dat* to); (*beauftragen*) instruct. **A~ung** *f* instruction; (*Geld-*) money order

anwend|en† *vt sep* apply (**auf** + *acc* to); (*gebrauchen*) use. **A~ung** *f* application; use

anwerben† *vt sep* recruit

Anwesen *nt* -s,- property

anwesend *a* present (**bei** at); **die A~den** those present. **A~heit** *f* - presence

anwidern *vt sep* disgust

Anwohner *mpl* residents

Anzahl *f* number

anzahl|en *vt sep* pay a deposit on; pay on account ⟨*Summe*⟩. **A∼ung** *f* deposit

anzapfen *vt sep* tap

Anzeichen *nt* sign

Anzeige *f* -,-n announcement; (*Inserat*) advertisement; **A∼ erstatten gegen jdn** report s.o. to the police. **a∼n** *vt sep* announce; (*inserieren*) advertise; (*melden*) report [to the police]; (*angeben*) indicate, show. **A∼r** *m* indicator

anzieh|en† *vt sep* ⟨*vt* attract; (*festziehen*) tighten; put on ⟨*Kleider, Bremse*⟩; draw up ⟨*Beine*⟩; (*ankleiden*) dress; **sich a∼en** get dressed; **was soll ich a∼en?** what shall I wear? **gut angezogen** well-dressed ⟨*vt* (*haben*) start pulling; ⟨*Preise*⟩ go up. **a∼end** *a* attractive. **A∼ung** *f* attraction. **A∼ungskraft** *f* attraction; (*Phys*) gravity

Anzug *m* suit; **im A∼ sein** (*fig*) be imminent

anzüglich *a* suggestive; ⟨*Bemerkung*⟩ personal

anzünden *vt sep* light; (*in Brand stecken*) set fire to

anzweifeln *vt sep* question

apart *a* striking, *adv* -ly

Apathie *f* - apathy

apathisch *a* apathetic, *adv* -ally

Aperitif *m* -s,-s aperitif

Apfel *m* -s,⸚ apple. **A∼mus** *nt* apple purée

Apfelsine *f* -,-n orange

Apostel *m* -s,- apostle

Apostroph *m* -s,-e apostrophe

Apotheke *f* -,-n pharmacy. **A∼er(in)** *m* -s,- (*f* -,-nen) pharmacist, [dispensing] chemist

Apparat *m* -[e]s,-e device; (*Phot*) camera; (*Radio, TV*) set; (*Teleph*) telephone; **am A∼!** speaking! **A∼ur** *f* -,-en apparatus

Appell *m* -s,-e appeal; (*Mil*) roll-call. **a∼ieren** *vi* (*haben*) appeal (**an** + *acc* to)

Appetit *m* -s appetite; **guten A∼!** enjoy your meal! **a∼lich** *a* appetizing, *adv* -ly

applaudieren *vi* (*haben*) applaud

Applaus *m* -es applause

Aprikose *f* -,-n apricot

April *m* -[s] April; **in den A∼ schicken** (*fam*) make an April fool of

Aquarell *nt* -s,-e water-colour

Aquarium *nt* -s,-ien aquarium

Äquator *m* -s equator

Ära *f* - era

Araber(in) *m* -s,- (*f* -,-nen) Arab

arabisch *a* Arab; (*Geog*) Arabian; ⟨*Ziffer*⟩ Arabic

Arbeit *f* -,-en work; (*Anstellung*) employment, job; (*Aufgabe*) task; (*Sch*) [written] test; (*Abhandlung*) treatise; (*Qualität*) workmanship; **bei der A∼** at work; **zur A∼ gehen** go to work; **an die A∼ gehen, sich an die A∼ machen** set to work; **sich** (*dat*) **viel A∼ machen** go to a lot of trouble. **a∼en** *v sep* ⟨*vi* (*haben*) work (**an** + *dat* on) ⟨*vt*: make; **einen Anzug a∼en lassen** have a suit made; **sich durch etw a∼en** work one's way through sth. **A∼er(in)** *m* -s,- (*f* -,-nen) worker; (*Land-, Hilfs-*) labourer. **A∼erklasse** *f* working class

Arbeitgeber *m* -s,- employer. **A∼nehmer** *m* -s,- employee. **a∼sam** *a* industrious

Arbeits|amt *nt* employment exchange. **A∼erlaubnis, A∼genehmigung** *f* work permit. **A∼kraft** *f* worker; **Mangel an A∼kräften** shortage of labour. **a∼los** *a* unemployed; **a∼los sein** be out of work. **A∼lose(r)** *m/f* unemployed person; **die A∼losen** the unemployed *pl.*

A~losenunterstützung *f* unemployment benefit. A~losigkeit *f* - unemployment
arbeitsparend *a* labour-saving
Arbeitsplatz *m* job. A~tag *m* working day. A~zimmer *nt* study
Archäologe *m* -n,-n archaeologist. A~logie *f* - archaeology. A~logisch *a* archaeological
Arche *f* - die A~ Noah Noah's Ark
Architekt(in) *m* -en,-en (*f* -,-nen) architect. a~tonisch *a* architectural. a~tur *f* - architecture
Archiv *nt* -s,-e archives *pl*
Arena *f* -,-nen arena
arg *a* (ärger, ärgst) bad; (groß) terrible; sein ärgster Feind his worst enemy □ *adv* badly; (sehr) terribly
Argentinien /-jən/ *nt* -s Argentina. a~isch *a* Argentinian
Ärger *m* -s annoyance; (Unannehmlichkeit) trouble. ä~lich *a* annoyed; (leidig) annoying; ä~lich sein be annoyed. ä~n *vt* annoy; (necken) tease; sich ä~n get annoyed (über jdn/etw with s.o./ about sth). Ä~nis *nt* -ses, -se annoyance; öffentliches Ä~nis public nuisance
Arglist *f* - malice. a~ig *a* malicious, *adv* -ly
arglos *a* unsuspecting; (unschuldig) innocent, *adv* -ly
Argument *nt* -[e]s,-e argument. a~ieren *vi* (haben) argue (daß that)
Argwohn *m* -s suspicion
argwöhnen *vt* suspect. a~isch *a* suspicious, *adv* -ly
Arie /'a:rjə/ *f* -,-n aria
Aristokrat *m* -en,-en aristocrat. A~kratie *f* - aristocracy. a~kratisch *a* aristocratic
Arithmetik *f* - arithmetic

Arktis *f* - Arctic. a~isch *a* Arctic
arm *a* (ärmer, ärmst) poor; arm und reich rich and poor
Arm *m* -[e]s,-e arm; jdn auf den Arm nehmen (fam) pull s.o.'s leg
Armaturenbrett *nt* instrument panel; (Auto) dashboard
Armband *nt* (*pl* -bänder) bracelet; (Uhr-) watch-strap. A~uhr *f* wrist-watch
Arme(r) *m*/*f* poor man/woman; die A~en the poor *pl*; du A~e *od* Ärmste! you poor thing!
Armee *f* -,-n army
Ärmel *m* -s,- sleeve. A~kanal *m* [English] Channel. a~los *a* sleeveless
Armlehne *f* arm. A~leuchter *m* candelabra
ärmlich *a* poor, *adv* -ly; (elend) miserable, *adv* -bly
armselig *a* miserable, *adv* -bly
Armut *f* - poverty
Aroma *nt* -s,-men & -mas aroma; (Culin) essence. a~tisch *a* aromatic
Arrangement /arãʒə'mã:/ *nt* -s,-s arrangement. a~gieren /-'ʒi:-/ *vt* arrange; sich a~gieren come to an arrangement
Arrest *m* -[e]s (Mil) detention
arrogant *a* arrogant, *adv* -ly. A~z *f* - arrogance
Arsch *m* -[e]s,¨e (vulg) arse
Arsen *nt* -s arsenic
Art *f* -,-en manner; (Weise) way; (Natur) nature; (Sorte) kind; (Biol) species; auf diese Art in this way. a~en *vi* (sein) a~en nach take after
Arterie /-jə/ *f* -,-n artery
Arthritis *f* - arthritis
artig *a* well-behaved; (höflich) polite, *adv* -ly; sei a~! be good!
Artikel *m* -s,- article
Artillerie *f* -,-n artillery
Artischocke *f* -,-n artichoke

Artist(in) *m* -en,-en (*f* -,-nen)
[circus] artiste

Arznei *f* -,-en medicine. **A~mit-**
tel *nt* drug

Arzt *m* -[e]s,⸚e doctor

Ärztin *f* -,-nen [woman] doctor.
ä~lich *a* medical

As *nt* -ses,-se ace

Asbest *m* -[e]s asbestos

Asche *f* - ash. **A~nbecher** *m*
ashtray. **A~rmittwoch** *m* Ash
Wednesday

Asiat(in) *m* -en,-en (*f* -,-nen)
Asian. **a~isch** *a* Asian

Asien /'a:zjən/ *nt* -s Asia

asozial *a* antisocial

Aspekt *m* -[e]s,-e aspect

Asphalt *m* -[e]s asphalt. **a~ie-**
ren *vt* asphalt

Assistent(in) *m* -en,-en (*f* -,-nen)
assistant

Ast *m* -[e]s,⸚e branch

ästhetisch *a* aesthetic

Asthma *nt* -s asthma. **a~ma-**
tisch *a* asthmatic

Astro|loge *m* -n,-n astrologer.
A~logie *f* - astrology. **A~naut**
m -en,-en astronaut. **A~nom** *m*
-en,-en astronomer. **A~nomie**
f - astronomy. **a~nomisch** *a*
astronomical

Asyl *nt* -s,-e home; (*Pol*) asylum.
A~ant *m* -en,-en asylum-seeker

Atelier /-'lje:/ *nt* -s,-s studio

Atem *m* -s breath; **tief A~** holen
take a deep breath. **a~berau-**
bend *a* breath-taking. **a~los** *a*
breathless, *adv* -ly. **A~pause** *f*
breather. **A~zug** *m* breath

Atheist *m* -en,-en atheist

Äther *m* -s ether

Äthiopien /-jən/ *nt* -s Ethiopia

Athlet(in) *m* -en,-en (*f* -,-nen)
athlete. **a~isch** *a* athletic

Atlantik *m* -s Atlantic. **a~isch** *a*
Atlantic; **der A~ische Ozean**
the Atlantic Ocean

Atlas *m* -lasses,-lanten atlas

atmen *vt/i* (*haben*) breathe

Atmosphär|e *f* -,-n atmosphere.
a~isch *a* atmospheric

Atmung *f* - breathing

Atom *nt* -s,-e atom. **a~ar** *a* atomic. **A~bombe** *f* atom bomb.
A~krieg *m* nuclear war

Attentat *nt* -[e]s,-e assassination
attempt. **A~täter** *m* [would-be]
assassin

Attest *nt* -[e]s,-e certificate

Attrak|tion /-'tsjo:n/ *f* -,-en at-
traction. **a~tiv** *a* attractive, *adv*
-ly

Attrappe *f* -,-n dummy

Attribut *nt* -[e]s,-e attribute.
a~iv *a* attributive, *adv* -ly

ätzen *vt* corrode; (*Med*) cauterize;
(*Kunst*) etch. **ä~d** *a* corrosive;
(*Spott*) caustic

au *int* ouch; **au fein!** oh good!

Aubergine /ober'ʒi:nə/ *f* -,-n aubergine

auch *adv* & *conj* also, too; (*außer-*
dem) what's more; (*selbst*) even;
a~ wenn even if; ich mag ihn—
ich a~ I like him—so do I; **ich**
bin nicht müde—ich a~ nicht
I'm not tired—nor or neither am
I; **sie weiß es a~** nicht she
doesn't know either; **wer/wie/**
was a~ immer whoever/how-
ever/whatever; **ist das a~**
wahr? is that really true?

Audienz *f* -,-en audience

audiovisuell *a* audio-visual

Auditorium *nt* -s,-ien (*Univ*) lecture hall

auf *prep* (+ *dat*) on; (+ *acc*) on [to];
(*bis*) until, till; (*Proportion*) to;
auf deutsch/englisch in Ger-
man/English; **auf einer/eine**
Party at/to a party; **auf der**
Straße in the street; **auf seinem**
Zimmer in one's room; **auf ei-**
nem Ohr taub deaf in one ear;
auf einen Stuhl steigen climb
on [to] a chair; **auf die Toilette**
gehen go to the toilet; **auf ein**
paar Tage verreisen go away

for a few days; **auf 10 Kilometer
zu sehen** visible for 10 kilometres □*adv* open; (*in die Höhe*)
up; **auf und ab** up and down; **sich
auf und davon machen** make
off; **Tür auf!** open the door!

aufarbeiten *vt sep* do up; **Rückstände a~** clear arrears [of
work]

aufatmen *vi sep* (*haben*) heave a
sigh of relief

aufbahren *vt sep* lay out

Aufbau *m* construction; (*Struktur*) structure. **a~en** *v sep* □*vt*
construct, build; (*errichten*)
erect; (*schaffen*) build up; (*arrangieren*) arrange; **sich a~en** (*fig*)
be based (**auf**+*dat* on) □*vi* (*haben*) be based (**auf**+*dat* on)

aufbäumen (**sich**) *vr sep* rear
[up]; (*fig*) rebel

aufbauschen *vt sep* puff out; (*fig*)
exaggerate

aufbehalten† *vt sep* keep on

aufbekommen† *vt sep* get open;
(*Sch*) be given [as homework]

aufbessern *vt sep* improve; (*erhöhen*) increase

aufbewahr|en *vt sep* keep; (*la-
gern*) store. **A~ung** *f* · safe keeping; storage; (*Gepäck-*) left-luggage office

aufbieten† *vt sep* mobilize; (*fig*)
summon up

aufblas|bar *a* inflatable. **a~en†**
vt sep inflate; **sich a~en** (*fig*)
give oneself airs

aufbleiben† *vi sep* (*sein*) stay
open; (*Person.*) stay up

aufblenden *vt/i sep* (*haben*)
(*Auto*) switch to full beam

aufblicken *vi sep* (*haben*) look up
(**zu** at/(*fig*) to)

aufblühen *vi sep* (*sein*) flower;
(*Knospe.*) open

aufbocken *vt sep* jack up

aufbraten *vt sep* fry up

aufbrauchen *vt sep* use up

aufbrausen *vi sep* (*sein*) (*fig*)
flare up. **a~d** *a* quick-tempered

aufbrechen† *v sep* □*vt* break
open □*vi* (*sein*) (*Knospe.·*) open;
(*sich aufmachen*) set out, start

aufbringen† *vt sep* raise (*Geld*)
find (*Kraft*); (*wütend machen*) infuriate

Aufbruch *m* start, departure

aufbrühen *vt sep* make (*Tee*)

aufbürden *vt sep* jdm etw **a~**
(*fig*) burden s.o. with sth

aufdecken *vt sep* (*auflegen*) put
on; (*abdecken*) uncover; (*fig*) expose

aufdrängen *vt sep* force (*dat* on);
sich jdm a~ force one's company on s.o.

aufdrehen *vt sep* turn on

aufdringlich *a* persistent

aufeinander *adv* one on top of
the other; (*schießen*) at each
other; (*warten*) for each other.
a~folgen *vi sep* (*sein*) follow one
another. **a~folgend** *a* successive; (*Tage*) consecutive

Aufenthalt *m* stay; **10 Minuten
A~ haben** (*Zug.·*) stop for 10
minutes. **A~serlaubnis, A~s-
genehmigung** *f* residence permit. **A~sraum** *m* recreation
room; (*im Hotel*) lounge

auferlegen *vt sep* impose (*dat* on)

auferstehen† *vi sep* (*sein*) rise
from the dead. **A~ung** *f* · resur-
rection

aufessen† *vt sep* eat up

auffahr|en† *vi sep* (*sein*) drive up;
(*aufprallen*) crash, run (**auf**+*acc*
into); (*aufschrecken*) start up;
(*aufbrausen*) flare up. **A~t** *f*
drive; (*Autobahn-*) access road,
slip road; (*Bergfahrt*) ascent

auffallen† *vi sep* (*sein*) be conspicuous; **unangenehm a~** make a
bad impression; **jdm a~** strike
s.o. **a~d** *a* striking, *adv* -ly

auffällig *a* conspicuous, *adv* -ly;
(*grell*) gaudy, *adv* -ily

auffangen† *vt sep* catch; pick up ⟨*Funkspruch*⟩

auffass|en *vt sep* understand; (*deuten*) take; **falsch a~en** misunderstand. **A~ung** *f* understanding; (*Ansicht*) view. **A~ungsgabe** *f* grasp

aufforder|n *vt sep* ask; (*einladen*) invite; **jdn zum Tanz a~n** ask s.o. to dance. **A~ung** *f* request; invitation

auffrischen *v sep* □*vt* freshen up; revive ⟨*Erinnerung*⟩; **seine Englischkenntnisse a~** brush up one's English

aufführ|en *vt sep* perform; (*angeben*) list; **sich a~en** behave. **A~ung** *f* performance

auffüllen *vt sep* fill up; **[wieder] a~** replenish

Aufgabe *f* task; (*Rechen-*) problem; (*Verzicht*) giving up; **A~n** (*Sch*) homework *sg*

Aufgang *m* way up; (*Treppe*) stairs *pl*; (*Astr*) rise

aufgeben† *v sep* □*vt* give up; post ⟨*Brief*⟩; send ⟨*Telegramm*⟩; place ⟨*Bestellung*⟩; register ⟨*Gepäck*⟩; put in the paper ⟨*Annonce*⟩; **jdm eine Aufgabe/ein Rätsel a~** set s.o. a task/a riddle; **jdm Suppe a~** serve s.o. with soup □*vi* (*haben*) give up

aufgeblasen *a* (*fig*) conceited

Aufgebot *nt* contingent (**an**+*dat* of); (*Relig*) banns *pl*; **unter A~ aller Kräfte** with all one's strength

aufgebracht *a* (*fam*) angry

aufgedunsen *a* bloated

aufgehen† *vi sep* (*sein*) open; (*sich lösen*) come undone; (*Teig, Sonne:*) rise; (*Saat:*) come up; (*Math*) come out exactly; **in Flammen a~** go up in flames; **in etw** (*dat*) **a~** (*fig*) be wrapped up in sth; **ihm ging auf** (*fam*) he realized (**daß** that)

aufgelegt *a* **a~ sein zu** be in the mood for; **gut/schlecht a~ sein** be in a good/bad mood

aufgelöst *a* (*fig*) distraught; **in Tränen a~** in floods of tears

aufgeregt *a* excited, *adv* -ly; (*erregt*) agitated, *adv* -ly

aufgeschlossen *a* (*fig*) open-minded

aufgesprungen *a* chapped

aufgeweckt *a* (*fig*) bright

aufgießen† *vt sep* pour on; (*aufbrühen*) make ⟨*Tee*⟩

aufgreifen† *vt sep* pick up; take up ⟨*Vorschlag, Thema*⟩

aufgrund *prep* (+*gen*) on the strength of

Aufguß *m* infusion

aufhaben† *vt sep* □*vt* have on; **den Mund a~** have one's mouth open; **viel a~** (*Sch*) have a lot of homework □*vi* (*haben*) be open

aufhalsen *vt sep* (*fam*) saddle with

aufhalten† *vt sep* hold up; (*anhalten*) stop; (*abhalten*) keep, detain; (*offenhalten*) hold open; hold out ⟨*Hand*⟩; **sich a~** stay; (*sich befassen*) spend one's time (**mit** on)

aufhäng|en *vt/i sep* (*haben*) hang up; (*henken*) hang; **sich a~en** hang oneself. **A~er** *m* -s,- loop. **A~ung** *f* (*Auto*) suspension

aufheben† *vt sep* pick up; (*hochheben*) raise; (*aufbewahren*) keep; (*beenden*) end; (*rückgängig machen*) lift; (*abschaffen*) abolish; (*Jur*) quash ⟨*Urteil*⟩; repeal ⟨*Gesetz*⟩; (*ausgleichen*) cancel out; **sich a~** cancel each other out; **gut aufgehoben sein** be well looked after. **A~** *nt* **-s viel A~s machen** make a great fuss (**von** about)

aufheitern *vt sep* cheer up; **sich a~** ⟨*Wetter:*⟩ brighten up

aufhellen *vt sep* lighten; **sich a~** ⟨*Himmel:*⟩ brighten

aufhetzen *vt sep* incite

aufholen v sep ⊳vt make up ⊳vi ⟨haben⟩ catch up; (zeitlich) make up time

aufhorchen vi sep ⟨haben⟩ prick up one's ears

aufhören vi sep ⟨haben⟩ stop; mit der Arbeit a~, a~ zu arbeiten stop working

aufklappen vt/i sep ⟨sein⟩ open

aufklär|en vt sep solve; jdn a~en enlighten s.o.; (sexuell) tell s.o. the facts of life; sich a~en be solved; ⟨Wetter:⟩ clear up. A~ung f solution; enlightenment; (Mil) reconnaissance; sexuelle A~ung sex education

aufkleb|en vt sep stick on. A~er m -s,- sticker

aufknöpfen vt sep unbutton

aufkochen v sep ⊳vt bring to the boil ⊳vi ⟨sein⟩ come to the boil

aufkommen† vi sep ⟨sein⟩ start; ⟨Wind:⟩ spring up; ⟨Mode:⟩ come in; a~ für pay for

aufkrempeln vt sep roll up

aufladen† vt sep load; (Electr) charge

Auflage f impression; (Ausgabe) edition; (Zeitungs-) circulation; (Bedingung) condition; (Überzug) coating

auflassen† vt sep leave open; leave on ⟨Hut⟩

auflauern vi sep ⟨haben⟩ jdm a~ lie in wait for s.o

Auflauf m crowd; (Culin) ≈ soufflé. a~en† vi sep ⟨sein⟩ ⟨Naut⟩ run aground

auflegen v sep ⊳vt apply (auf +acc to); put down ⟨Hörer⟩; neu a~ reprint ⊳vi ⟨haben⟩ ring off

auflehn|en (sich) vr sep ⟨fig⟩ rebel. A~ung f -rebellion

auflesen† vt sep pick up

aufleuchten vi sep ⟨haben⟩ light up

aufliegen† vi sep ⟨haben⟩ rest (auf +dat on)

auflisten vt sep list

auflockern vt sep break up; (entspannen) relax; ⟨fig⟩ liven up

auflös|en vt sep dissolve; close ⟨Konto⟩; sich a~en dissolve; ⟨Nebel:⟩ clear. A~ung f dissolution; (Lösung) solution

aufmach|en v sep ⊳vt open; (lösen) undo; sich a~en set out (nach for); (sich schminken) make oneself up ⊳vi ⟨haben⟩ open; jdm a~en open the door to s.o. A~ung f -,-en get-up; (Comm) presentation

aufmerksam a attentive, adv -ly; a~ werden auf (+acc) notice; jdn a~ machen auf (+acc) draw s.o.'s attention to. A~keit f -,-en attention; (Höflichkeit) courtesy

aufmucken vi sep ⟨haben⟩ rebel

aufmuntern vt sep cheer up

Aufnahme f -,-n acceptance; (Empfang) reception; (in Klub, Krankenhaus) admission; (Einbeziehung) inclusion; (Beginn) start; (Foto) photograph; (Film-) shot; (Mus) recording; (Band-) tape recording. a~fähig a receptive. A~prüfung f entrance examination

aufnehmen† vt sep pick up; (absorbieren) absorb; take ⟨Nahrung, Foto⟩; ⟨fassen⟩ hold; (annehmen) accept; (leihen) borrow; (empfangen) receive; (in Klub, Krankenhaus) admit; (beherbergen, geistig erfassen) take in; (einbeziehen) include; (beginnen) take up; (niederschreiben) take down; (filmen) film, shoot; (Mus) record; auf Band a~ tape[-record]; etw gelassen a~ take sth calmly; es a~ können mit ⟨fig⟩ be a match for

aufopfer|n vt sep sacrifice; sich a~n sacrifice oneself. a~nd a devoted, adv -ly. A~ung f self-sacrifice

aufpassen *vi sep* ⟨haben⟩ pay attention; (*sich vorsehen*) take care; a~ auf (+ *acc*) look after

aufpflanzen (sich) *vr sep* ⟨fam⟩ plant oneself

aufplatzen *vi sep* ⟨sein⟩ split open

aufplustern (sich) *vr sep* ⟨*Vogel:*⟩ ruffle up its feathers

Aufprall *m* -[e]s impact. a~en *vi sep* ⟨sein⟩ a~en auf (+ *acc*) hit

aufpumpen *vt sep* pump up, inflate

aufputsch|en *vt sep* incite; **sich a~en** take stimulants. **A~mittel** *nt* stimulant

aufquellen† *vi sep* ⟨sein⟩ swell

aufraffen *vt sep* pick up; **sich a~** pick oneself up; (*fig*) pull oneself together; (*sich aufschwingen*) find the energy (**zu** for)

aufragen *vi sep* ⟨sein⟩ rise [up]

aufräumen *vt/i sep* ⟨haben⟩ tidy up; (*wegräumen*) put away; **a~mit** (*fig*) get rid of

aufrecht *a & adv* upright. **a~erhalten†** *vt sep* ⟨fig⟩ maintain

aufreg|en *vt sep* excite; (*beunruhigen*) upset; (*ärgern*) annoy; **sich a~en** get excited; (*sich erregen*) get worked up. **a~end** *a* exciting. **A~ung** *f* excitement

aufreiben† *vt sep* chafe; (*fig*) wear down; **sich a~** wear oneself out. **a~d** *a* trying, wearing

aufreißen† *v sep* ⟨vt⟩ tear open; dig up ⟨*Straße*⟩; open wide ⟨*Augen, Mund*⟩ ⟨vi⟩ split open

aufreizend *a* provocative, *adv* -ly

aufrichten *vt sep* erect; (*fig: trösten*) comfort; **sich a~** straighten up; (*sich setzen*) sit up

aufrichtig *a* sincere, *adv* -ly. **A~keit** *f* - sincerity

aufriegeln *vt sep* unbolt

aufrollen *vt sep* roll up; (*entrollen*) unroll

aufrücken *vi sep* ⟨sein⟩ move up; (*fig*) be promoted

Aufruf *m* appeal (**an** + *dat* to). **a~en†** *vt sep* call out ⟨*Namen*⟩; **jdn a~en** call s.o.'s name; (*fig*) call on s.o. (**zu** to)

Aufruhr *m* -s,-e turmoil; (*Empörung*) revolt

aufrühr|en *vt sep* stir up. **A~er** *m* -s,- rebel. **a~erisch** *a* inflammatory; (*rebellisch*) rebellious

aufrunden *vt sep* round up

aufrüsten *vi sep* ⟨haben⟩ arm

aufs *prep* = **auf das**

aufsagen *vt sep* recite

aufsammeln *vt sep* gather up

aufsässig *a* rebellious

Aufsatz *m* top; (*Sch*) essay

aufsaugen† *vt sep* soak up

aufschauen *vi sep* ⟨haben⟩ look up (**zu** at)/(*fig*/to)

aufschichten *vt sep* stack up

aufschieben† *vt sep* slide open; (*verschieben*) put off, postpone

Aufschlag *m* impact; (*Tennis*) service; (*Hosen-*) turn-up; (*Ärmel-*) upturned cuff; (*Revers*) lapel; (*Comm*) surcharge. **a~en†** *v sep* ⟨vt⟩ open; crack ⟨*Ei*⟩; (*hochschlagen*) turn up; (*errichten*) put up; (*erhöhen*) increase; cast on ⟨*Masche*⟩; **sich** ⟨*dat*⟩ **das Knie a~en** cut [open] one's knee ⟨vi⟩ ⟨haben⟩ hit (**auf etw** *acc/dat* sth); (*Tennis*) serve; (*teurer werden*) go up

aufschließen† *v sep* ⟨vt⟩ unlock ⟨vi⟩ ⟨haben⟩ unlock the door

aufschlitzen *vt sep* slit open

Aufschluß *m* **A~ geben** give information (**über** + *acc* on). **a~reich** *a* revealing; (*lehrreich*) informative

aufschneid|en† *v sep* ⟨vt⟩ cut open; (*in Scheiben*) slice; carve ⟨*Braten*⟩ ⟨vi⟩ ⟨haben⟩ exaggerate. **A~er** *m* -s,- (*fam*) showoff

Aufschnitt *m* sliced sausage, cold meat [and cheese]

aufschrauben vt sep screw on; (abschrauben) unscrew

aufschrecken v sep □vt startle □vi (sein) start up; **aus dem Schlaf a~** wake up with a start

Aufschrei m [sudden] cry

aufschreiben† vt sep write down; (fam: verschreiben) prescribe; **jdn a~** ⟨Polizist:⟩ book s.o.

aufschreien† vi sep (haben) cry out

Aufschrift f inscription; (Etikett) label

Aufschub m delay; (Frist) grace

aufschürfen vt sep **sich** (dat) **das Knie a~** graze one's knee

aufschwatzen vt sep **jdm etw a~** talk s.o. into buying sth

aufschwingen† (sich) vr sep find the energy (zu for)

Aufschwung m (fig) upturn

aufsehen† vi sep (haben) look up (zu at/(fig) to). **A~** nt -s **A~erregen** cause a sensation.

a~erregend a sensational

Aufseher(in) m -s,- (f -,-nen) supervisor; (Gefängnis:) warder

aufsein† vi sep (sein) be open; ⟨Person:⟩ be up

aufsetzen vt sep put on; (verfassen) draw up; (entwerfen) draft; **sich a~** sit up

Aufsicht f supervision; (Person) supervisor. **A~srat** m board of directors

aufsitzen† vi sep (sein) mount

aufspannen vt sep put up

aufsparen vt sep save, keep

aufsperren vt sep open wide

aufspielen v sep □vi (haben) play □vr **sich a~** show off; **sich als Held a~** play the hero

aufspießen vt sep spear

aufspringen† vi sep (sein) jump up; (aufprallen) bounce; (sich öffnen) burst open; (Haut:) become chapped; **auf** (+ acc) jump on

aufspüren vt sep track down

aufstacheln vt sep incite

aufstampfen vi sep (haben) **mit dem Fuß a~** stamp one's foot

Aufstand m uprising, rebellion

aufständisch a rebellious. **A~e(r)** m rebel, insurgent

aufstapeln vt sep stack up

aufstauen vt sep dam [up]

aufstehen† vi sep (sein) get up; (offen sein) be open; (fig) rise up

aufsteigen† vi sep (sein) get on; ⟨Reiter:⟩ mount; ⟨Bergsteiger:⟩ climb up; (hochsteigen) rise [up]; (fig: befördert werden) rise (zu to); (Sport) be promoted

aufstell|en vt sep put up; (Culin) put on; (postieren) post; (in einer Reihe) line up; (nominieren) nominate; (Sport) select ⟨Mannschaft:⟩; make out ⟨Liste:⟩; lay down ⟨Regel:⟩; make ⟨Behauptung:⟩; set up ⟨Rekord:⟩; **sich a~en** rise [up]; (in einer Reihe) line up. **A~ung** f nomination; (Liste) list

Aufstieg m ascent; (fig) rise; (Sport) promotion

aufstöbern vt sep flush out; (fig) track down

aufstoßen† v sep □vt push open □vi burp; **a~ auf** (+acc) strike. **A~** nt -s burping

aufstrebend a (fig) ambitious

Aufstrich m (sandwich) spread

aufstützen vt sep rest (auf + acc on); **sich a~** lean (auf+ acc on)

aufsuchen vt sep look for; (besuchen) go to see

Auftakt m (fig) start

auftauchen vi sep (sein) emerge; ⟨U-Boot:⟩ surface; (fig) turn up; ⟨Frage:⟩ crop up

auftauen vt/i sep (sein) thaw

aufteil|en vt sep divide [up]. **A~ung** f division

auftischen vt sep serve [up]

Auftrag m -[e]s, -̈e task; (Kunst) commission; (Comm) order; **im A~** (+ gen) on behalf of. **a~en†** v sep □vt apply; (servieren) serve;

(abtragen) wear out; **jdm a~en** instruct s.o. (zu to) □*vi (haben)* **dick a~en** *(fam)* exaggerate. **A~geber** *m* -s,- client

auftreiben† *vt sep* distend; *(fam: beschaffen)* get hold of

auftrennen *vt sep* unpick, undo

auftreten† *v sep* □*vi (sein)* tread; *(sich benehmen)* behave, act; *(Theat)* appear; *(die Bühne betreten)* enter; *(vorkommen)* occur □*vt* kick open. **A~** *nt* -s occurrence; *(Benehmen)* manner

Auftrieb *m* buoyancy; *(fig)* boost

Auftritt *m (Theat)* appearance; *(auf die Bühne)* entrance; *(Szene)* scene

auftun† *vt sep* jdm Suppe a~ serve s.o. with soup; **sich** *(dat)* **etw a~** help oneself to sth; **sich a~** open

aufwachen *vi sep (sein)* wake up

aufwachsen† *vi sep (sein)* grow up

Aufwand *m* -[e]s expenditure; *(Luxus)* extravagance; *(Mühe)* trouble; **A~ treiben** be extravagant

aufwärmen *vt sep* heat up; *(fig)* rake up; **sich a~** warm oneself; *(Sport)* warm up

Aufwartefrau *f* cleaner

aufwärts *adv* upwards; *(bergauf)* uphill. **a~gehen** *vi sep (sein)* **es geht a~ mit jdm/etw** s.o./sth is improving

Aufwartung *f* - cleaner; **jdm seine A~ machen** call on s.o.

aufwaschen† *vt/i sep (haben)* wash up

aufwecken *vt sep* wake up

aufweichen *v sep* □*vt* soften *(fig)* □*vi (sein)* become soft

aufweisen† *vt sep* have, show

aufwend|en† *vt sep* spend; **Mühe a~en** take pains. **a~ig** *a* lavish, *adv* -ly; *(teuer)* expensive, *adv* -ly

aufwerfen† *vt sep (fig)* raise

aufwert|en *vt sep* revalue. **A~ung** *f* revaluation

aufwickeln *vt sep* roll up; *(auswickeln)* unwrap

aufwiegeln *vt sep* stir up

aufwiegen† *vt sep* compensate for

Aufwiegler *m* -s,- agitator

aufwirbeln *vt sep* **Staub a~** stir up dust; *(fig)* cause a stir

aufwisch|en *vt sep* wipe up; wash *(Fußboden)*. **A~lappen** *m* floorcloth

aufwühlen *vt sep* churn up; *(fig)* stir up

aufzähl|en *vt sep* enumerate, list. **A~ung** *f* list

aufzeichn|en *vt sep* record; *(zeichnen)* draw. **A~ung** *f* recording; **A~ungen** notes

aufzieh|en† *v sep* □*vt* pull up; hoist *(Segel)*; *(öffnen)* open; draw *(Vorhang)*; *(auftrennen)* undo; *(großziehen)* bring up; rear *(Tier)*; mount *(Bild)*; thread *(Perlen)*; wind up *(Uhr)*; *(arrangieren)* organize; *(fam: necken)* tease □*vi (sein)* approach

Aufzucht *f* rearing

Aufzug *m* hoist; *(Fahrstuhl)* lift, *(Amer)* elevator; *(Prozession)* procession; *(Theat)* act; *(fam: Aufmachung)* get-up

Augapfel *m* eyeball

Auge *nt* -s,-n eye; *(Punkt)* spot; **vier A~n werfen** throw a four; **gute A~n** good eyesight; **unter vier A~n** in private; **aus den A~n verlieren** lose sight of; **im A~ behalten** keep in sight; *(fig)* bear in mind

Augenblick *m* moment; **im/ jeden A~** at the/at any moment; **A~!** just a moment! **a~lich** *a* immediate; *(derzeitig)* present □*adv* immediately; *(derzeit)* at present

Augen|braue *f* eyebrow. **A~höhle** *f* eye socket. **A~licht** *nt*

sight. A~lid nt eyelid. A~
schein m in A~schein nehmen
inspect. A~zeuge m eyewitness

August m -[s] August

Auktion /-'tsi̯o:n/ f -,-en auction.
A~ator m -s,-en /-'to:rən/ auctioneer

Aula f -,-len (Sch) [assembly] hall

Au-pair-Mädchen /o'pɛ:r-/ nt au-pair

aus prep (+ dat) out of; (von) from;
(bestehend) [made] of; aus Angst
from or out of fear; aus Spaß for
fun □adv out; ⟨Licht, Radio⟩ off;
aus und ein in and out; nicht
mehr aus noch ein wissen be at
one's wits' end; von ... aus from
...; von sich aus of one's own
accord; von mir aus as far as I'm
concerned

ausarbeiten vt sep work out

ausarten vi sep (sein) degenerate
(in + acc into)

ausatmen vt/i sep (haben)
breathe out

ausbaggern vt sep excavate;
dredge ⟨Fluß⟩

ausbauen vt sep remove; (vergrößern)
extend; (fig) expand

ausbedingen vt sep sich (dat)
a~ insist on; (zur Bedingung
machen) stipulate

ausbesser|n vt sep mend, repair.
A~ung f repair

ausbeulen vt sep remove the
dents from; (dehnen) make baggy

Ausbeute f yield. a~en vt sep
exploit. A~ung f- exploitation

ausbild|en vt sep train; (formen)
form; (entwickeln) develop; sich
a~en train (als/zu as); (entstehen)
develop. A~er m -s,- instructor.
A~ung f training;
(Sch) education

ausbitten† vt sep sich (dat) a~
ask for; (verlangen) insist on

ausblasen† vt sep blow out

ausbleiben† vi sep (sein) fail to
appear/ ⟨Erfolg:⟩ materialize;

(nicht heimkommen) stay out; es
konnte nicht a~ it was inevitable. A~ nt -s absence

Ausblick m view

ausbrech|en vi sep (sein) break
out; ⟨Vulkan:⟩ erupt; (fliehen) escape;
in Tränen a~en burst into
tears. A~er m runaway

ausbreit|en vt sep spread [out];
sich a~en spread. A~ung f-
spread

ausbrennen vt sep □vt cauterize
□vi (sein) burn out; ⟨Haus:⟩ be
gutted [by fire]

Ausbruch m outbreak; ⟨Vulkan-⟩
eruption; (Wut-) outburst;
(Flucht) escape, break-out

ausbrüten vt sep hatch

Ausbund m A~ der Tugend paragon
of virtue

ausbürsten vt sep brush; (entfernen)
brush out

Ausdauer f perseverance; (körperlich)
stamina. a~nd a persevering;
(unermüdlich) untiring;
(Bot) perennial □adv with perseverance;
untiringly

ausdehn|en vt sep stretch; ⟨fig⟩
extend; sich a~en stretch; (Phys
& fig) expand; (dauern) last.
A~ung f expansion; (Umfang)
extent

ausdenken† vt sep sich (dat) a~
think up; (sich vorstellen)
imagine

ausdrehen vt sep turn off

Ausdruck m expression; (Fach-)
term; (Computer) printout. a~en
vt sep print

ausdrück|en vt sep squeeze out;
squeeze ⟨Zitrone⟩; stub out ⟨Zigarette⟩;
(äußern) express; sich
a~en express oneself. a~lich a
express, adv -ly

ausdrucks|los a expressionless.
a~voll a expressive

auseinander adv apart; (entzwei)
in pieces. a~falten vt sep unfold.
a~gehen† vi sep (sein)

part; ⟨Linien, Meinungen:⟩ diverge; ⟨Menge:⟩ disperse; ⟨Ehe:⟩ break up; ⟨entzweigehen⟩ come apart. **a~halten**† vt sep tell apart. **a~nehmen**† vt sep take apart or to pieces. **a~setzen** vt sep explain (jdm to s.o.); **sich a~setzen** have it out (mit jdm with s.o.); come to grips (mit einem Problem with a problem). **A~setzung** f -,-en discussion; ⟨Streit⟩ argument

auserlesen a select, choice

ausfahr|en| v sep □vt take for a drive; take out ⟨Baby⟩ (in the pram) □vi (sein) go for a drive. **A~t** f drive; ⟨Autobahn-, Garagen-⟩ exit

Ausfall m failure; ⟨Absage⟩ cancellation; ⟨Comm⟩ loss. **a~en**† vi sep fall out; ⟨versagen⟩ fail; ⟨abgesagt werden⟩ be cancelled; **gut/schlecht a~en** turn out to be good/poor

ausfallend, ausfällig a abusive

ausfertigen† vt sep make out. **A~ung** f -,-en in doppelter/dreifacher **A~ung** in duplicate/triplicate

ausfindig a **a~ machen** find

ausflippen vi (sein) freak out

Ausflucht f -,-e excuse

Ausflug m excursion, outing

Ausflügler m -s,- ⟨day-⟩tripper

Ausfluß m outlet; ⟨Abfluß⟩ drain; ⟨Med⟩ discharge

ausfragen vt sep question

ausfransen vi sep (sein) fray

Ausfuhr f -,-en ⟨Comm⟩ export

ausführen† vt sep take out; ⟨Comm⟩ export; ⟨durchführen⟩ carry out; ⟨erklären⟩ explain. **a~lich** a detailed □adv in detail. **A~ung** f execution; ⟨Comm⟩ version; ⟨äußere⟩ finish; ⟨Qualität⟩ workmanship; ⟨Erklärung⟩ explanation

Ausgabe f issue; ⟨Buch-⟩ edition; ⟨Comm⟩ version

Ausgang m way out, exit; ⟨Flugsteig⟩ gate; ⟨Ende⟩ end; ⟨Ergebnis⟩ outcome, result; **A~ haben** have time off. **A~spunkt** m starting-point. **A~ssperre** f curfew

ausgeben† vt sep hand out; issue ⟨Fahrkarten⟩; spend ⟨Geld⟩; buy ⟨Runde Bier⟩; **sich a~ als** pretend to be

ausgebeult a baggy

ausgebildet a trained

ausgebucht a fully booked; ⟨Vorstellung⟩ sold out

ausgedehnt a extensive; ⟨lang⟩ long

ausgedient a worn out; ⟨Person⟩ retired

ausgefallen a unusual

ausgefranst a frayed

ausgeglichen a [well-]balanced; ⟨gelassen⟩ even-tempered

ausgeh|en† vi sep (sein) go out; ⟨Haare:⟩ fall out; ⟨Vorräte, Geld:⟩ run out; ⟨verblassen⟩ fade; ⟨herrühren⟩ come (von from); ⟨abzielen⟩ aim (auf+acc at); **gut/schlecht a~en** end well/badly; **leer a~en** come away empty-handed; **davon a~en, daß** assume that. **A~verbot** nt curfew

ausgelassen a high-spirited; **a~ sein** be in high spirits

ausgelernt a [fully] trained

ausgemacht a agreed; ⟨fam: vollkommen⟩ utter

ausgenommen conj except; **a~ wenn** unless

ausgeprägt a marked

ausgerechnet adv **a~ heute** today of all days; **a~ er/Rom** he of all people/Rome of all places

ausgeschlossen pred a out of the question

ausgeschnitten a low-cut

ausgesprochen a marked □adv decidedly

ausgestorben a extinct; [wie] **a~** ⟨Straße:⟩ deserted

Ausgestoßene(r) m/f outcast

ausgewachsen a fully-grown

ausgewogen a [well-]balanced

ausgezeichnet a excellent, adv -ly

ausgiebig a extensive, adv -ly; (ausgedehnt) long; a~ Gebrauch machen von make full use of; a~ frühstücken have a really good breakfast

ausgießen† vt sep pour out; (leeren) empty

Ausgleich m -[e]s balance; (Entschädigung) compensation. a~en† v sep □vt balance; even out ⟨Höhe⟩; (ausgleichen) compensate for; sich a~en balance out ⟨□vi fishing⟩; (Sport) equalize. A~sgymnastik f keep-fit exercises pl. A~streffer m equalizer

ausgleiten† vi sep (sein) slip

ausgrab|en† vt sep dig up; (Archaeol) excavate. A~ung f -,-en excavation

Ausguck m -[e]s,-e look-out post; (Person) look-out

Ausguß m [kitchen] sink

aushaben† vt sep have finished ⟨Buch⟩; wann habt ihr Schule aus? when do you finish school?

aushalten† v sep □vt bear, stand; hold ⟨Note⟩; (Unterhalt zahlen für) keep; nicht auszuhalten, nicht zum A~ unbearable □vi (haben) hold out

aushandeln vt sep negotiate

aushändigen vt sep hand over

Aushang m [public] notice

aushängen¹ vt sep (reg) display; take off its hinges ⟨Tür⟩

aushäng|en²† vi sep (haben) be displayed. A~eschild nt sign

ausharren vi sep (haben) hold out

ausheben† vt sep excavate; take off its hinges ⟨Tür⟩

aushecken vt sep (fig) hatch

aushelfen† vi sep (haben) help out ⟨jdm s.o.⟩

Aushilf|e f [temporary] assistant; zur A~e to help out. A~skraft f temporary worker. a~sweise adv temporarily

aushöhlen vt sep hollow out

ausholen vi sep (haben) [zum Schlag] a~ raise one's arm [ready to strike]

aushorchen vt sep sound out

auskennen† (sich) vr sep know one's way around; sich mit/in etw ⟨dat⟩ a~ know all about sth

auskleiden vt sep undress; (Techn) line; sich a~ undress

ausknipsen vt sep switch off

auskommen† vi sep (sein) manage (mit/ohne with/without); (sich vertragen) get on ⟨gut well⟩. A~ nt -s sein A~/ein gutes A~ haben get by/be well off

auskosten vt sep enjoy [to the full]

auskugeln vt sep sich ⟨dat⟩ den Arm a~ dislocate one's shoulder

auskühlen vt/i sep (sein) cool

auskundschaften vt sep spy out; (erfahren) find out

Auskunft f -,-e information; (A~sstelle) information desk; (Büro) bureau; (Teleph) enquiries pl; eine A~ a piece of information. A~sbüro nt information bureau

auslachen vt sep laugh at

ausladen† vt sep unload; (fam: absagen) put off ⟨Gast⟩. a~d a projecting

Auslage f [window] display; A~n expenses

Ausland nt im/ins A~ abroad

Ausländ|er(in) m -s,- (f -,-nen) foreigner. a~isch a foreign

Auslandsgespräch nt international call

auslass|en† vt sep let out; let down ⟨Saum⟩; (weglassen) leave out; (versäumen) miss; (Culin) melt; (fig) vent ⟨Ärger⟩ (an + dat on); sich a~en über (+ acc) go on about. **A~ungszeichen** *nt* apostrophe

Auslauf *m* run. **a~en†** *vi sep* ⟨*sein*⟩ run out; ⟨*Farbe:*⟩ run; ⟨*Naut*⟩ put to sea; ⟨*leerlaufen*⟩ run dry; ⟨*enden*⟩ end; ⟨*Modell:*⟩ be discontinued

Ausläufer *m* ⟨*Geog*⟩ spur; ⟨*Bot*⟩ runner, sucker

ausleeren *vt sep* empty [out]

ausleg|en *vt sep* lay out; display ⟨*Waren*⟩; ⟨*bedecken*⟩ cover/ ⟨*auskleiden*⟩ line ⟨*mit* with⟩; ⟨*bezahlen*⟩ pay; ⟨*deuten*⟩ interpret. **A~ung** *f*, **-en** interpretation

ausleihen† *vt sep* lend; **sich** ⟨*dat*⟩ **a~** borrow

auslernen *vi sep* ⟨*haben*⟩ finish one's training

Auslese *f* - selection; ⟨*fig*⟩ pick; ⟨*Elite*⟩ elite. **a~n†** *vt sep* finish reading ⟨*Buch*⟩; ⟨*auswählen*⟩ pick out, select

ausliefer|n *vt sep* hand over; ⟨*Jur*⟩ extradite; **ausgeliefert sein** (+*dat*) be at the mercy of. **A~ung** *f* handing over; ⟨*Jur*⟩ extradition; ⟨*Comm*⟩ distribution

ausliegen† *vi sep* ⟨*haben*⟩ be on display

auslöschen *vt sep* extinguish; ⟨*abwischen*⟩ wipe off; ⟨*fig*⟩ erase

auslosen *vt sep* draw lots for

auslös|en *vt sep* set off, trigger; ⟨*fig*⟩ cause; arouse ⟨*Begeisterung*⟩; ⟨*einlösen*⟩ redeem; pay a ransom for ⟨*Gefangene*⟩. **A~er** *m* -s, - trigger; ⟨*Phot*⟩ shutter release

Auslosung *f* draw

auslüften *vt/i sep* ⟨*haben*⟩ air

ausmachen *vt sep* put out; ⟨*abschalten*⟩ turn off; ⟨*abmachen*⟩ arrange; ⟨*erkennen*⟩ make out; ⟨*betragen*⟩ amount to; ⟨*darstellen*⟩ represent; ⟨*wichtig sein*⟩ matter; **das macht mir nichts aus** I don't mind

ausmalen *vt sep* paint; ⟨*fig*⟩ describe; **sich** ⟨*dat*⟩ **a~** imagine

Ausmaß *nt* extent; **A~e** dimensions

ausmerzen *vt sep* eliminate

ausmessen† *vt sep* measure

Ausnahme *f* -,-n exception. **A~ezustand** *m* state of emergency. **a~slos** *adv* without exception. **a~sweise** *adv* as an exception

ausnehmen† *vt sep* take out; gut ⟨*Fisch*⟩; draw ⟨*Huhn*⟩; ⟨*ausschließen*⟩ exclude; ⟨*fam: schröpfen*⟩ fleece; **sich gut a~** look good. **a~d** *adv* exceptionally

ausnutz|en, ausnütz|en *vt sep* exploit; make the most of ⟨*Gelegenheit*⟩. **A~ung** *f* exploitation

auspacken *v sep* ⟨*vt* unpack; ⟨*auswickeln*⟩ unwrap ⟨*vi* ⟨*haben*⟩ ⟨*fam*⟩ talk

auspeitschen *vt sep* flog

auspfeifen *vt sep* whistle and boo

ausplaudern *vt sep* let out, blab

ausplündern *vt sep* loot; rob ⟨*Person*⟩

ausprobieren *vt sep* try out

Auspuff *m* -s exhaust [system]. **A~gase** *ntpl* exhaust fumes. **A~rohr** *nt* exhaust pipe

auspusten *vt sep* blow out

ausradieren *vt sep* rub out

ausrangieren *vt sep* ⟨*fam*⟩ discard

ausrauben *vt sep* rob

ausräuchern *vt sep* smoke out; fumigate ⟨*Zimmer*⟩

ausräumen *vt sep* clear out

ausrechnen *vt sep* work out, calculate

Ausrede *f* excuse. **a~n** *v sep* ⟨*vi* ⟨*haben*⟩ finish speaking; **laß mich a~n!** let me finish!⟨*vt* ⟨*jdm etw* **a~n** talk s.o. out of sth

ausreichen *vi sep* ⟨*haben*⟩ be enough; **a~ mit** have enough. **a~d** *a* adequate, *adv* -ly; ⟨*Sch*⟩ ≈ pass

Ausreise f departure [from a country]. **a~n** vi sep (sein) leave the country. **A~visum** nt exit visa

ausreiß|en† v sep □vt pull or tear out □vi (sein) (fam) run away. **A~er** m (fam) runaway

ausrenken vt sep dislocate; **sich** (dat) **den Arm a~** dislocate one's shoulder

ausrichten vt sep align; (bestellen) deliver; (erreichen) achieve; **jdm a~** tell s.o. (daß that); **kann ich etwas a~?** can I take a message? **ich soll Ihnen Grüße von X a~** X sends [you] his regards

ausrotten vt sep exterminate; (fig) eradicate

ausrücken vi sep (sein) (Mil) march off; (fam) run away

Ausruf m exclamation. **a~en†** vt sep exclaim; call out (Namen); (verkünden) proclaim; call (Streik); **jdn a~en lassen** have s.o. paged. **A~ezeichen** nt exclamation mark

ausruhen vt/i sep (haben) rest; **sich a~** have a rest

ausrüst|en vt sep equip. **A~ung** f equipment; (Mil) kit

ausrutschen vi sep (sein) slip

Aussage f -,-n statement; (Jur) testimony, evidence; (Gram) predicate. **a~n** vt/i sep (haben) state; (Jur) give evidence, testify

Aussatz m leprosy

Aussätzige(r) m/f leper

ausschachten vt sep excavate

ausschalten vt sep switch or turn off; (fig) eliminate

Ausschank m sale of alcoholic drinks; (Bar) bar

Ausschau f - **A~ halten nach** look out for. **a~en** vi sep (haben) (SGer) look; **a~en nach** look out for

ausscheiden† v sep □vi (sein) leave; (Sport) drop out; (nicht in Frage kommen) be excluded; **aus**

dem Dienst a~ retire □vt eliminate; (Med) excrete

ausschenken vt sep pour out; (verkaufen) sell

ausscheren vi sep (sein) (Auto) pull out

ausschildern vt sep signpost

ausschimpfen vt sep tell off

ausschlachten vt sep (fig) exploit

ausschlafen† v sep □vi/r (haben) [sich] **a~** get enough sleep; (morgens) sleep late; **nicht ausgeschlafen haben od sein** be still tired □vt sleep off (Rausch)

Ausschlag m (Med) rash; **den A~ geben** (fig) tip the balance. **a~en†** v sep □vi (haben) kick [out]; (Bot) sprout; (Baum:) come into leaf □vt knock out; (auskleiden) line; (ablehnen) refuse. **a~gebend** a decisive

ausschließen† vt sep lock out; (fig) exclude; (entfernen) expel. **a~lich** a exclusive, adv -ly

ausschlüpfen vi sep (sein) hatch

Ausschluß m exclusion; expulsion; **unter A~ der Öffentlichkeit** in camera

ausschmücken vt sep decorate; (fig) embellish

ausschneiden† vt sep cut out

Ausschnitt m excerpt, extract; (Zeitungs-) cutting; (Hals-) neckline

ausschöpfen vt sep ladle out; (Naut) bail out; exhaust (Möglichkeiten)

ausschreiben† vt sep write out; (ausstellen) make out; (bekanntgeben) announce; put out to tender (Auftrag)

Ausschreitungen fpl riots; (Exzesse) excesses

Ausschuß m committee; (Comm) rejects pl

ausschütten vt sep tip out; (verschütten) spill; (leeren) empty; **sich vor Lachen a~** (fam) be in stitches

ausschweif|end *a* dissolute.
Ä~**ung** *f* -,-en debauchery;
A~**ungen** excesses

ausschwenken *vt sep* rinse [out]

aussehen† *vi sep* (haben) look; es
sieht nach Regen aus it looks
like rain; **wie sieht er/es aus?**
what does he/it look like? A~ *nt*
-s appearance

aussein† *vi sep* (sein) be out;
⟨Licht, Radio:⟩ be off; (zu Ende
sein) be over; a~ **auf** (+acc) be
after; mit ihm ist es aus he's had
it

außen *adv* [on the] outside; nach
a~ outwards. A~**bordmotor** *m*
outboard motor. A~**handel** *m*
foreign trade. A~**minister** *m*
Foreign Minister. A~**politik** *f*
foreign policy. A~**seite** *f* outside. A~**seiter** *m* -s,- outsider;
(fig) misfit. A~**stände** *mpl* outstanding debts. A~**stehende(r)**
m/f outsider

außer *prep* (+dat) except [for],
apart from; (außerhalb) out of;
a~ **Atem/Sicht** out of breath/
sight; a~ **sich** (fig) beside oneself □conj except; a~ **wenn** unless. a~**dem** *adv* in addition, as
well □conj moreover

äußer|e(r,s) *a* external; ⟨Teil,
Schicht⟩ outer. Ä~**e(s)** *nt* exterior; (Aussehen) appearance

außer|ehelich *a* extramarital.
a~**gewöhnlich** *a* exceptional,
adv -ly. a~**halb** *prep* (+gen) outside □adv a~**halb wohnen** live
outside town

äußer|lich *a* external, adv -ly;
(fig) outward, adv -ly. ä~**n** *vt*
express; **sich** ä~**n** comment;
(sich zeigen) manifest itself

außerordentlich *a* extraordinary, adv -ily; (außergewöhnlich)
exceptional, adv -ly

äußerst *adv* extremely

außerstande *adv* unable (zu to)

äußerste|(r,s) *a* outermost; (wei-
teste) furthest; (höchste) utmost,
extreme; (letzte) last; (schlimmste) worst; am ä~**n Ende** at the
very end; aufs ä~ extremely.
Ä~**(s)** *nt* das Ä~ the limit;
(Schlimmste) the worst; **sein**
Ä~s **tun** do one's utmost

Äußerung *f* -,-en comment; (Bemerkung) remark

aussetzen *v sep* □vt expose (dat
to); abandon ⟨Kind, Hund⟩;
launch ⟨Boot⟩; offer ⟨Beloh-
nung⟩; etwas auszusetzen haben an (+dat) find fault with □vi
(haben) stop; ⟨Motor:⟩ cut out

Aussicht *f* -,-en view/(fig) prospect (auf+acc of); in A~ stellen promise; **weitere** A~**en**
(Meteorol) further outlook sg.
a~**slos** *a* hopeless, adv -ly. a~s-
reich *a* promising

aussöhnen *vt sep* reconcile; **sich**
a~ become reconciled

aussortieren *vt sep* pick out;
(ausscheiden) eliminate

ausspannen *v sep* □vt spread
out; unhitch ⟨Pferd⟩; (fam: wegnehmen) take (dat from) □vi (haben) rest. A~**ung** *f* rest

aussperren *vt sep* lock out.
A~**ung** *f* -,-en lock-out

ausspielen *v sep* □vt play
⟨Karte⟩; (fig) play off (**gegen**
against) □vi (haben) (Kartenspiel) lead

Aussprache *f* pronunciation;
(Sprechweise) diction; (Gespräch) talk

aussprechen† *v sep* □vt pronounce; (äußern) express; **sich**
a~ talk; come out (**für/gegen** in
favour of/against) □vi (haben)
finish [speaking]

Ausspruch *m* saying

ausspucken *v sep* □vt spit out □vi
(haben) spit

ausspülen *vt sep* rinse out

ausstaffieren *vt sep* (fam) kit out

Ausstand m strike; **in den A~ treten** go on strike

ausstatt|en† vt sep equip; **mit Möbeln a~en** furnish. **A~ung** f -,-en equipment; (Innen-) furnishings pl; (Theat) scenery and costumes pl; (Aufmachung) get-up

ausstehen† v sep □vt suffer; **Angst a~** be frightened; **ich kann sie nicht a~** I can't stand her □vi (haben) be outstanding

aussteig|en† vi sep (sein) get out; (aus Bus, Zug) get off; (fam: ausscheiden) opt out; (aus einem Geschäft) back out; **alles a~!** all change! **A~er(in)** m -s,- (f -,-nen) (fam) drop-out

ausstell|en vt sep exhibit; (Comm) display; (ausfertigen) make out; issue (Paß). **A~er** m -s,- exhibitor. **A~ung** f exhibition; (Comm) display. **A~ungsstück** nt exhibit

aussterben† vi sep (sein) die out; (Biol) become extinct. **A~** nt -s extinction

Aussteuer f trousseau

Ausstieg m -[e]s,-e exit

ausstopfen vt sep stuff

ausstoßen† vt sep emit; utter ⟨Fluch⟩; heave ⟨Seufzer⟩; (ausschließen) expel

ausstrahl|en vt/i sep (sein) radiate, emit; (Radio, TV) broadcast. **A~ung** f radiation; (fig) charisma

ausstrecken vt sep stretch out; put out ⟨Hand⟩; **sich a~** stretch out

ausstreichen† vt sep cross out

ausstreuen vt sep scatter; spread ⟨Gerüchte⟩

ausströmen v sep □vi (sein) pour out; (entweichen) escape □vt emit; (ausstrahlen) radiate

aussuchen vt sep pick, choose

Austausch m exchange. **a~bar** a interchangeable. **a~en** vt sep exchange; (auswechseln) replace

austeilen vt sep distribute; (ausgeben) hand out

Auster f -,-n oyster

austoben (sich) vr sep ⟨Sturm:⟩ rage; ⟨Person:⟩ let off steam; ⟨Kinder:⟩ romp about

austragen† vt sep deliver; hold ⟨Wettkampf⟩; play ⟨Spiel⟩

Australi|en /-jən/ nt -s Australia. **A~ier(in)** m -s,- (f -,-nen) Australian. **a~isch** a Australian

austreiben† v sep □vt drive out; (Relig) exorcize □vi (haben) (Bot) sprout

austreten† v sep □vt stamp out; (abnutzen) wear down □vi (sein) come out; (ausscheiden) leave (aus etw sth); [mal] a~ (fam) go to the loo; (Sch) be excused

austrinken† vt/i sep (haben) drink up; (leeren) drain

Austritt m resignation

austrocknen vt/i sep (sein) dry out

ausüben vt sep practise; carry on ⟨Handwerk⟩; exercise ⟨Recht⟩; exert ⟨Druck, Einfluß⟩; have ⟨Wirkung⟩

Ausverkauf m [clearance] sale. **a~t** a sold out; **a~tes Haus** full house

auswachsen† vt sep outgrow

Auswahl f choice, selection; (Comm) range; (Sport) team

auswählen vt sep choose, select

Auswander|er m emigrant. **a~n** vi sep (sein) emigrate. **A~ung** f emigration

auswärt|ig a non-local; (ausländisch) foreign. **a~s** adv outwards; (Sport) away; **a~s essen** eat out; **a~s arbeiten** not work locally. **A~sspiel** nt away game

auswaschen† vt sep wash out

auswechseln vt sep change; (ersetzen) replace; (Sport) substitute

Ausweg m (fig) way out. **a~los** a (fig) hopeless

ausweich|en† vi sep (sein) get out of the way; **jdm/etw a~en** avoid/ (sich entziehen) evade s.o./sth. **a~end** a evasive, adv -ly

ausweinen vt sep sich (dat) die Augen **a~** cry one's eyes out; **sich a~** have a good cry

Ausweis m -es,-e pass; (Mitglieds-, Studenten-) card. **a~en†** vt sep deport; **sich a~en** prove one's identity. **A~papiere** ntpl identification papers. **A~ung** f deportation

ausweiten vt sep stretch; (fig) expand

auswendig adv by heart

auswerten vt sep evaluate; (nutzen) utilize

auswickeln vt sep unwrap

auswirk|en (sich) vr sep have an effect (**auf**+acc on). **A~ung** f effect; (Folge) consequence

auswischen vt sep wipe out; **jdm eins a~** (fam) play a nasty trick on s.o.

auswringen† vt sep wring out

Auswuchs m excrescence; Auswüchse (fig) excesses

auszahlen vt sep pay out; (entlohnen) pay off; (abfinden) buy out; **sich a~** (fig) pay off

auszählen vt sep count; (Boxen) count out

Auszahlung f payment

auszeichn|en vt sep (Comm) price; (ehren) honour; (mit einem Preis) award a prize to; (Mil) decorate; **sich a~en** distinguish oneself. **A~ung** f honour; (Preis) award; (Mil) decoration; (Sch) distinction

ausziehen† v sep □vt pull out; (auskleiden) undress; take off ⟨Mantel, Schuhe⟩; **sich a~** take off one's coat; (sich entkleiden) undress □vi (sein) move out; (sich aufmachen) set out

Auszubildende(r) m/f trainee

Auszug m departure; (Umzug) move; (Ausschnitt) extract, excerpt; (Bank-) statement

authentisch a authentic

Auto nt -s,-s car; **A~ fahren** drive; (mitfahren) go in the car. **A~bahn** f motorway, (Amer) freeway

Autobiographie f autobiography

Auto|bus m bus. **A~fähre** f car ferry. **A~fahrer(in)** m(f) driver, motorist. **A~fahrt** f drive

Autogramm nt -s,-e autograph

autokratisch a autocratic

Automat m -en,-en automatic device; (Münz-) slot-machine; (Verkaufs-) vending-machine; (Fahrkarten-) machine; (Techn) robot. **A~ik** f - automatic mechanism; (Auto) automatic transmission

Auto|mation /-'tsio:n/ f - automation. **a~matisch** a automatic, adv -ally

autonom a autonomous. **A~ie** f - autonomy

Autonummer f registration number

Autopsie f -,-n autopsy

Autor m -s,-en /-'to:rən/ author

Auto|reisezug m Motorail. **A~rennen** nt motor race

Autorin f -,-nen author[ess]

Autori|sation /-'tsio:n/ f - authorization. **a~sieren** vt authorize. **a~tär** a authoritarian. **A~tät** f -,-en authority

Auto|schlosser m motor mechanic. **A~skooter** /-sku:tɐ/ m -s,- dodgem. **A~stopp** m -s per **A~stopp fahren** hitch-hike. **A~verleih** m car hire [firm]. **A~waschanlage** f car wash

autsch int ouch

Aversion f -,-en aversion (**gegen** to)

Axt f -,-̈e axe

B

B, b /be:/ *nt* - (*Mus*) B flat

Baby /'be:bi/ *nt* -s,-s baby.
B~ausstattung *f* layette. **B~-
sitter** /-sɪtɐ/ *m* -s,- babysitter

Bach *m* -[e]s,̈-e stream

Backbord *nt* -[e]s port [side]

Backe *f* -,-n cheek

backen *v* □ut/i † (*haben*) bake;
(*braten*) fry □*vi* (*reg*) (*haben*) (*kleben*) stick (**an** + *dat* to)

Backenzahn *m* molar

Bäcker *m* -s,- baker. **B~ei** *f* -,-en.
B~laden *m* baker's shop

Back|form *f* baking tin. **B~obst**
nt dried fruit. **B~ofen** *m* oven.
B~pfeife *f* (*fam*) slap in the face.
B~pflaume *f* prune. **B~-
pulver** *nt* baking-powder. **B~-
rohr** *nt* oven. **B~stein** *m* brick.
B~werk *nt* cakes and pastries *pl*

Bad *nt* -[e]s,̈-er bath; (*im Meer*)
bathe; (*Zimmer*) bathroom;
(*Schwimm-*) pool; (*Ort*) spa

Bade|anstalt *f* swimming baths
pl. **B~anzug** *m* swim-suit.
B~hose *f* swimming trunks *pl*.
B~kappe *f* bathing-cap. **B~-
mantel** *m* bathrobe. **B~-
matte** *f* bath-mat. **B~mütze** *f*
bathing-cap. **b~n** *vi* (*haben*)
have a bath; (*im Meer*) bathe □*vt*
bath; (*waschen*) bathe. **B~ort** *m*
seaside resort; (*Kurort*) spa.
B~tuch *nt* bath-towel. **B~-
wanne** *f* bath[-tub]. **B~zimmer**
nt bathroom

Bagatelle *f* -,-n trifle; (*Mus*) bagatelle

Bagger *m* -s,- excavator; (*Naß-*)
dredger. **b~n** *vt/i* (*haben*) excavate; dredge. **B~see** *m* flooded
gravel-pit

Bahn *f* -,-en path; (*Astr*) orbit;
(*Sport*) track; (*einzelne*) lane;
(*Rodel-*) run; (*Stoff-, Papier-*)

width; (*Rock-*) panel; (*Eisen-*) railway; (*Zug*) train; (*Straßen-*) tram;
auf die schiefe B~ kommen
(*fig*) get into bad ways. **b~bre-
chend** *a* (*fig*) pioneering. **b~en**
vt sich (*dat*) **einen Weg b~en**
clear a way (**durch** through).
B~hof *m* [railway] station.
B~steig *m* -[e]s,-e platform.
B~übergang *m* level crossing,
(*Amer*) grade crossing

Bahre *f* -,-n stretcher; (*Toten-*)
bier

Baiser /bɛˈzeː/ *nt* -s,-s meringue

Bajonett *nt* -[e]s,-e bayonet

Bake *f* -,-n (*Naut, Aviat*) beacon

Bakterien /-jən/ *fpl* bacteria

Balanc|e /baˈlãːsə/ *f* - balance; **die
B~e halten/verlieren** keep/lose
one's balance. **b~ieren** *vt/i* (*ha-
ben/sein*) balance

bald *adv* soon; (*fast*) almost; **b~
... b~ ... now ... now ...**

Baldachin /-xiːn/ *m* -s,-e canopy

bald|ig *a* early; (*Besserung*)
speedy. **b~möglichst** *adv* as
soon as possible

Balg *nt* & *m* -[e]s,̈-er (*fam*) brat.
b~en (**sich**) *vr* tussle. **B~erei**
f -,-en tussle

Balkan *m* -s Balkans *pl*

Balken *m* -s,- beam

Balkon /balˈkõː/ *m* -s,-s balcony;
(*Theat*) circle

Ball¹ *m* -[e]s,̈-e ball

Ball² *m* -[e]s,̈-e (*Tanz*) ball

Ballade *f* -,-n ballad

Ballast *m* -[e]s ballast. **B~stoffe**
mpl roughage *sg*

ballen *vt* **die** [**Hand zur**] **Faust
b~** clench one's fist; **sich b~**
gather, mass. **B~** *m* -s,- bale;
(*Anat*) ball of the hand/(*Fuß-*)
foot; (*Med*) bunion

Ballerina *f* -,-nen ballerina

Ballett *nt* -s,-e ballet

Ballettänzer(in) *m(f)* ballet
dancer

ballistisch *a* ballistic

Ballon /ba'lõ:/ *m* -s,-s balloon

Ball|saal *m* ballroom. **B~ungs-gebiet** *nt* conurbation. **B~-wechsel** *m* (*Tennis*) rally

Balsam *m* -s balm

Balt|ikum *nt* -s Baltic States *pl*. **b~isch** *a* Baltic

Balustrade *f* -,-n balustrade

Bambus *m* -ses,-se bamboo

banal *a* banal. **B~ität** *f* -,-en banality

Banane *f* -,-n banana

Banause *m* -n,-n philistine

Band¹ *nt* -[e]s,¨er ribbon; (*Naht-, Ton-, Ziel-*) tape; (*Anat*) ligament; **auf B~** aufnehmen tape; **lau-fendes B~** conveyor belt; **am laufenden B~** (*fam*) non-stop

Band² *m* -[e]s,¨e volume

Band³ *nt* -[e]s,-e (*fig*) bond; **B~e der Freundschaft** bonds of friendship

Band⁴ /bent/ *f* -,-s [jazz] band

Bandag|e /ban'da:ʒə/ *f* -,-n bandage. **b~ieren** *vt* bandage

Bande *f* -,-n gang

bändigen *vt* control, restrain; (*zähmen*) tame

Bandit *m* -en,-en bandit

Band|maß *nt* tape-measure. **B~nudeln** *fpl* noodles. **B~scheibe** *f* (*Anat*) disc. **B~scheibenvorfall** *m* slipped disc. **B~wurm** *m* tapeworm

bang|[e] *a* (**bänger, bängst**) anxious; **jdm b~e machen** frighten s.o. **B~e f/B~e haben** be afraid. **b~en** *vi* (*haben*) fear (**um** for); **mir b~t davor** I dread it

Banjo *nt* -s,-s banjo

Bank¹ *f* -,¨e bench

Bank² *f* -,-en (*Comm*) bank. **B~einzug** *m* direct debit

Bankett *nt* -s,-e banquet

Bankier /baŋ'kje:/ *m* -s,-s banker

Bank|konto *nt* bank account. **B~note** *f* banknote

Bankrott *m* -s,-s bankruptcy; **B~ machen** go bankrupt. **b~ a** bankrupt

Bankwesen *nt* banking

Bann *m* -[e]s,-e (*fig*) spell; **in jds B~** under s.o.'s spell. **b~en** *vt* exorcize; (*abwenden*) avert; (*wie*) **gebannt** spellbound

Banner *nt* -s,- banner

Baptist(in) *m* -en,-en (*f* -,-nen) Baptist

bar *a* (*rein*) sheer; (*Gold*) pure; **b~es Geld** cash; **[in] bar bezah-len** pay cash; **etw für b~e Münze nehmen** (*fig*) take sth as gospel

Bar *f* -,-s bar

Bär *m* -en,-en bear; **jdm einen B~en aufbinden** (*fam*) pull s.o.'s leg

Baracke *f* -,-n (*Mil*) hut

Barbar *m* -en,-en barbarian. **b~arisch** *a* barbaric

bar|fuß *adv* barefoot. **B~geld** *nt* cash

Bariton *m* -s,-e /-'to:nə/ baritone

Barkasse *f* -,-n launch

Barmann *m* (*pl* -männer) bar-man

barmherzig *a* merciful. **B~keit** *f* -mercy

barock *a* baroque. **B~ nt & m** -[s] baroque

Barometer *nt* -s,- barometer

Baron *m* -s,-e baron. **B~in** *f* -,-nen baroness

Barren *m* -s,- (*Gold-*) bar, ingot; (*Sport*) parallel bars *pl*. **B~gold** *nt* gold bullion

Barriere *f* -,-n barrier

Barrikade *f* -,-n barricade

barsch *a* gruff, *adv* -ly; (*kurz*) curt, *adv* -ly

Barsch *m* -[e]s,-e (*Zool*) perch

Barschaft *f* - **meine ganze B~** all I have/had on me

Bart *m* -[e]s,¨e beard; (*der Katze*) whiskers *pl*

bärtig *a* bearded

Barzahlung f cash payment

Basar m -s,-e bazaar

Base¹ f -,-n (female) cousin

Base² f -,-n (Chem) alkali, base

Basel nt -s Basle

basieren vi (haben) be based (**auf** + dat on)

Basilikum nt -s basil

Basis f -,**Basen** base; (fig) basis

basisch a (Chem) alkaline

Bask|enmütze f beret. **b~isch** a Basque

Baß m -sses,-̈sse bass; (Kontra-) double-bass

Bassin /ba'sɛ̃:/ nt -s,-s pond; (Brunnen-) basin; (Schwimm-) pool

Bassist m -en,-en bass player; (Sänger) bass

Baßstimme f bass voice

Bast m -[e]s raffia

basta int [und damit] **b~**! and that's that!

bast|eln vt make □vi (haben) do handicrafts; (herum-) tinker (**an** + dat with). **B~ler** m -s,- amateur craftsman; (Heim-) do-it-yourselfer

Bataillon /batal'jo:n/ nt -s,-e battalion

Batterie f -,-n battery

Bau¹ m -[e]s,-e burrow; (Fuchs-) earth

Bau² m -[e]s,-ten construction; (Gebäude) building; (Auf-) structure; (Körper-) build; (B~stelle) building site; **im Bau** under construction. **B~arbeiten** fpl building work sg; (Straßen-) roadworks. **B~art** f design; (Stil) style

Bauch m -[e]s, **Bäuche** abdomen, belly; (Magen) stomach; (Schmer-) paunch; (Bauchung) bulge. **b~ig** a bulbous. **B~nabel** m navel. **B~redner** m ventriloquist. **B~schmerzen** mpl stomachache sg. **B~speicheldrüse** f

pancreas. **B~weh** nt stomachache

bauen vt build; (konstruieren) construct; (an-) grow; **einen Unfall b~** (fam) have an accident (sth); **b~ auf** (+ acc) (fig) rely on

Bauer¹ m -s,-n farmer; (Schach) pawn

Bauer² m -s,- [bird]cage

Bäuer|in f -,-nen farmer's wife. **b~lich** a rustic

Bauern|haus nt farmhouse. **B~hof** m farm

bau|fällig a dilapidated. **B~genehmigung** f planning permission. **B~gerüst** nt scaffolding. **B~jahr** nt year of construction; **B~jahr 1985** (Auto) 1985 model. **B~kasten** m box of building bricks; (Modell-) construction kit. **B~klotz** m building brick. **B~kunst** f architecture. **b~lich** a structural, adv -ly. **B~lichkeiten** fpl buildings

Baum m -[e]s, **Bäume** tree

baumeln vi (haben) dangle; **die Beine b~ lassen** dangle one's legs

bäumen (sich) vr rear [up]

Baum|schule f [tree] nursery. **B~stamm** m tree-trunk. **B~wolle** f cotton. **b~wollen** a cotton

Bauplatz m building plot

bäurisch a rustic; (plump) uncouth

Bausch m -[e]s, **Bäusche** wad; **in B~ und Bogen** (fig) wholesale. **b~en** vt puff out; **sich b~en** billow [out]. **b~ig** a puffed [out]; ⟨Ärmel⟩ full

Bau|sparkasse f building society. **B~stein** m building brick; (fig) element. **B~stelle** f building site; (Straßen-) roadworks pl. **B~unternehmer** m building contractor. **B~werk** nt building. **B~zaun** m hoarding

Bayer|(in) m -s,-n (f -,-nen) Bavarian. **B~n** nt -s Bavaria
bay[e]risch a Bavarian
Bazillus m -,-len bacillus; (fam: Keim) germ

beabsichtig|en vt intend. **b~t** a intended; (absichtlich) intentional

beacht|en vt take notice of; (einhalten) observe; (folgen) follow; **nicht b~en** ignore. **b~lich** a considerable. **B~ung** f - observance; etw (dat) **keine B~ung schenken** take no notice of sth

Beamte(r) m, **Beamtin** f -,-nen official; (Staats-) civil servant; (Schalter-) clerk

beängstigend a alarming

beanspruchen vt claim; (erfordern) demand; (brauchen) take up; (Techn) stress; **die Arbeit beansprucht ihn sehr** his work is very demanding

beanstand|en vt find fault with; (Comm) make a complaint about. **B~ung** f -,-en complaint

beantragen vt apply for

beantworten vt answer

bearbeiten vt work; (weiter-) process; (behandeln) treat (mit with); (Admin) deal with; (redigieren) edit; (Theat) adapt; (Mus) arrange; (fam: bedrängen) pester; (fam: schlagen) pummel

Beatmung f künstliche **B~** artificial respiration. **B~sgerät** nt ventilator

beaufsichtig|en vt supervise. **B~ung** f - supervision

beauftragen vt instruct; (Kommission 〈Künstler〉); **jdn mit einer Arbeit b~en** assign a task to s.o. **B~te(r)** m/f representative

bebauen vt build on; (bestellen) cultivate

beben vi (haben) tremble

bebildert a illustrated

Becher m -s,- beaker; (Henkel-) mug; (Joghurt-, Sahne-) carton

Becken nt -s,- basin; (Schwimm-) pool; (Mus) cymbals pl; (Anat) pelvis

bedacht a careful; **b~ auf** (+ dat) concerned about; **darauf b~** anxious (zu to)

bedächtig a careful, adv -ly; (langsam) slow, adv -ly

bedanken (sich) vr thank (bei jdm s.o.)

Bedarf m -s need/(Comm) demand (an + dat for); bei **B~** if required. **B~sartikel** mpl requisites. **B~shaltestelle** f request stop

bedauer|lich a regrettable. **b~licherweise** adv unfortunately. **b~n** vt regret; (bemitleiden) feel sorry for; **bedaure!** sorry! **B~n** nt -s regret; (Mitgefühl) sympathy. **b~nswert** a pitiful; (bedauerlich) regrettable

bedeck|en vt cover; **sich b~en** 〈Himmel:〉 cloud over. **b~t** a covered; 〈Himmel〉 overcast

bedenk|en† vt consider; (überlegen) think over; **jdn b~** give s.o. a present; **sich b~** consider. **B~** pl misgivings; **ohne B~** without hesitation. **b~los** a unhesitating, adv -ly

bedenklich a doubtful; (verdächtig) dubious; (bedrohlich) worrying; (ernst) serious

bedeut|en vi (haben) mean; **jdm viel/nichts b~en** mean a lot/ nothing to s.o.; **es hat nichts zu b~en** it is of no significance. **b~end** a important; (beträchtlich) considerable. **b~sam** a = **b~ungsvoll**. **B~ung** f -,-en meaning; (Wichtigkeit) importance. **b~ungslos** a meaningless; (unwichtig) unimportant. **b~ungsvoll** a significant; (vielsagend) meaningful, adv -ly

bedien|en vt serve; (betätigen) operate; **sich [selbst] b~en** help

oneself. **B~ung** f -,-en service;
(Betätigung) operation; (Kellner)
waiter; (Kellnerin) f waitress.
B~ungsgeld nt, **B~ungs-
zuschlag** m service charge
bedingt a conditional; (einge-
schränkt) qualified
Bedingung f -,-en condition;
B~en conditions; (Comm)
terms. **b~slos** a unconditional,
adv -ly; (unbedingt) unquestion-
ing, adv -ly
bedrängen vt press; (belästigen)
pester
bedrohen vt threaten. **b~lich** a
threatening. **B~ung** f threat
bedrück|en vt depress. **b~end** a
depressing. **b~t** a depressed
bedruckt a printed
bedürf|en† vi (haben) (+gen)
need. **B~nis** nt -ses,-se need.
B~nisanstalt f public convenience. **b~tig** a needy
Beefsteak /'bi:fste:k/ nt -s,-s
steak; **deutsches B~** hamburger
beeilen (sich) vr hurry; hasten
(zu to); **beeilt euch!** hurry up!
beeindrucken vt impress
beeinflussen vt influence
beeinträchtigen vt mar; (schädigen) impair
beend|ig|en vt end
beengen vt restrict; **beengt wohnen** live in cramped conditions
beerben vt jdn **b~** inherit s.o.'s
property
beerdig|en vt bury. **B~ung** f
-,-en funeral
Beere f -,-n berry
Beet nt -[e]s,-e (Hort) bed
Beete f -,-n **rote B~** beetroot
befähig|en vt enable; (qualifizie-
ren) qualify. **B~ung** f- qualification; (Fähigkeit) ability
befahr|bar a passable. **b~en**† vt
drive along; **stark b~ene**
Straße busy road
befallen† vt attack; 〈Angst:〉 seize

befangen a shy; (gehemmt) self-
conscious; (Jur) biased. **B~heit**
f - shyness; self-consciousness;
bias
befassen (sich) vr concern one-
self/(behandeln) deal (mit with)
Befehl m -[e]s,-e order; (Leitung)
command (über + acc of). **b~en**†
vt jdm etw **b~en** order s.o. to do
sth □ vi (haben) give the orders.
b~igen vt (Mil) command.
B~sform f (Gram) imperative.
B~shaber m -s,- commander
befestig|en vt fasten (**an** + dat to);
(stärken) strengthen; (Mil) for-
tify. **B~ung** f -,-en fastening;
(Mil) fortification
befeuchten vt moisten
befind|en† (sich) vr be. **B~** nt -s
[state of] health
beflecken vt stain
befliss|en a assiduous, adv -ly
befolgen vt follow
beförder|n vt transport; (im
Rang) promote. **B~ung** f -,-en
transport; promotion
befragen vt question
befrei|en vt free; (räumen) clear
(**von** of); (freistellen) exempt
(**von** from); **sich b~en** free oneself. **B~er** m -s,- liberator. **b~t** a
(erleichtert) relieved. **B~ung** f -
liberation; exemption
befremd|en vt disconcert. **B~en**
nt -s surprise. **b~lich** a strange
befreunden (sich) vr make
friends; **befreundet sein** be
friends
befriedig|en vt satisfy. **b~end** a
satisfying; (zufriedenstellend) satisfactory. **B~ung** f- satisfaction
befrucht|en vt fertilize. **B~ung**
f - fertilization; **künstliche
B~ung** artificial insemination
Befugnis f -,-se authority. **b~t**
a authorized
Befund m result
befürcht|en vt fear. **B~ung** f
-,-en fear

befürworten vt support
begab|t a gifted. **B~ung** f -,-en gift, talent
begatten (sich) vr mate
begeben† (**sich**) vr go; (liter: geschehen) happen; **sich in Gefahr b~** expose oneself to danger. **B~heit** f -,-en incident
begegn|en vi (sein) **jdm/etw b~en** meet s.o./sth; **sich b~en** meet. **B~ung** f -,-en meeting; (Sport) encounter
begehen† vt walk along; (verüben) commit; (feiern) celebrate
begehr|en vt desire. **b~enswert** a desirable. **b~t** a sought-after
begeister|n vt **jdn b~n** arouse s.o.'s enthusiasm; **sich b~n** be enthusiastic (**für** about). **b~t** a enthusiastic, adv -ally; (eifrig) keen. **B~ung** f - enthusiasm
Begier|de f -,-n desire. **b~ig** a eager (**auf+**acc for)
begießen† vt water; (Culin) baste; (fam: feiern) celebrate
Beginn m -s beginning; **zu B~** at the beginning. **b~en†** vt/i (haben) start, begin; (anstellen) do
beglaubigen vt authenticate
begleichen† vt settle
begleit|en vt accompany. **B~er** m -s,-, **B~erin** f -,-nen companion; (Mus) accompanist. **B~ung** f -,-en company; (Gefolge) entourage; (Mus) accompaniment
beglück|en vt make happy. **b~t** a happy. **b~wünschen** vt congratulate (**zu** on)
begnadigen vt (Jur) pardon. **B~ung** f -,-en (Jur) pardon
begnügen (sich) vr content oneself (**mit** with)
Begonie /-iə/ f -,-n begonia
begraben† vt bury
Begräbnis n -ses,-se burial; (Feier) funeral
begreif|en† vt understand; **nicht zu b~en** incomprehensible.

b~lich a understandable; **jdm etw b~lich machen** make s.o. understand sth. **b~licherweise** adv understandably
begrenz|en vt form the boundary of; (beschränken) restrict. **b~t** a limited. **B~ung** f -,-en restriction; (Grenze) boundary
Begriff m -[e]s,-e concept; (Ausdruck) term; (Vorstellung) idea; **für meine B~** to my mind; **im B~ sein** od **stehen** be about (**zu** to); **schwer von B~** (fam) slow on the uptake. **b~sstutzig** a obtuse
begründ|en vt give one's reason for; (gründen) establish. **b~et** a justified. **B~ung** f -,-en reason
begrüßen vt greet; (billigen) welcome. **b~enswert** a welcome. **B~ung** f - greeting; welcome
begünstigen vt favour; (fördern) encourage
begutachten vt give an opinion on; (fam: ansehen) look at
begütert a wealthy
begütigen vt placate
behaart a hairy
behäbig a portly; (gemütlich) comfortable, adv -bly
behagen vi (haben) please (**jdm** s.o.). **B~en** nt -s contentment; (Genuß) enjoyment. **b~lich** a comfortable, adv -bly. **B~lichkeit** f -comfort
behalten† vt keep; (sich merken) remember; **etw für sich b~** (verschweigen) keep sth to oneself
Behälter m -s,- container
behand|eln vt treat; (sich befassen) deal with. **B~lung** f treatment
beharr|en vi (haben) persist (**auf +dat** in). **b~lich** a persistent, adv -ly; (hartnäckig) dogged, adv -ly. **B~lichkeit** f - persistence
behaupt|en† vt maintain; (vorgeben) claim; (sagen) say; (bewahren) retain; **sich b~en** hold one's

own. B~ung f -,-en assertion;
claim; (Äußerung) statement

beheben† vt remedy; (beseitigen)
remove

behelf|en† (sich) vr make do
(mit with). b~mäßig a make-
shift □adv provisionally

behelligen vt bother

behende a nimble, adv -bly

beherbergen vt put up

beherrsch|en vt rule over; (domi-
nieren) dominate; (meistern, zügeln) control; (können) know;
sich b~en control oneself. b~t
a self-controlled. B~ung f -con-
trol; (Selbst-) self-control; (Können) mastery

beherzigen vt heed. b~t a courageous, adv -ly

beherzt a courageous, adv -ly

behilflich a jdm b~ sein help
s.o.

behinder|n vt hinder; (blockie-
ren) obstruct. b~t a handicapped; (schwer) disabled. B~-
te(r) m/f handicapped/disabled
person. B~ung f -,-en obstruc-
tion; (Med) handicap; disability

Behörde f -,-n [public] authority

behüte|n vt protect; Gott behüte!
heaven forbid! b~t a sheltered

behutsam a careful, adv -ly;
(zart) gentle, adv -ly

bei prep (+ dat) near; (dicht) by; at
‹Firma, Veranstaltung›; bei der
Hand nehmen take by the hand;
bei sich haben have with one;
bei mir at my place; (in meinem
Fall) in my case; Herr X bei
Meyer Mr X c/o Meyer; bei Re-
gen when/(falls) if it rains; bei
Feuer in case of fire; bei Tag/
Nacht by day/night; bei der An-
kunft on arrival; bei Tisch/der
Arbeit at table/work; bei guter
Gesundheit in good health; bei
der hohen Miete [what] with the
high rent; bei all seiner Klug-
heit for all his cleverness

beibehalten† vt sep keep

beibringen† vt sep jdm etw b~
teach s.o. sth; (mitteilen) break
sth to s.o.; (zufügen) inflict sth on
s.o.

Beicht|e f -,-n confession. b~en
vt/i (haben) confess. B~stuhl m
confessional

beide a & pron both; die b~n
Brüder the two brothers; b~s
both; dreißig b~ (Tennis) thirty
all. b~rseitig a mutual.
b~rseits adv & prep (+ gen) on
both sides (of)

beidrehen vi sep (haben) heave to

beieinander adv together

Beifahrer|(in) m(f) [front-seat]
passenger; (Lkw) driver's mate;
(Motorrad) pillion passenger.
B~sitz m passenger seat

Beifall m -[e]s applause; (Billigung) approval; B~ klatschen
applaud

beifällig a approving, adv -ly

beifügen vt sep add; (beilegen)
enclose

beige /be:ʒ/ inv a beige

beigeben† v sep vt add □vi (haben) klein b~ give in

Beigeschmack m [slight] taste

Beihilfe f financial aid; (Studien-)
grant; (Jur) aiding and abetting

beikommen† vi sep (sein) jdm
b~ get the better of s.o.

Beil nt -[e]s,-e hatchet, axe

Beilage f supplement; (Gemüse)
vegetable; als B~ Reis (Culin)
served with rice

beiläufig a casual, adv -ly

beilegen vt sep enclose; (schlich-
ten) settle

beileibe adv b~ nicht by no
means

Beileid nt condolences pl.
B~sbrief m letter of condolence

beiliegend a enclosed

beim prep = bei dem; b~ Militär
in the army; b~ Frühstück at
breakfast; b~ Lesen when reading; b~ Lesen sein be reading

beimessen† *vt sep* ⟨*fig*⟩ attach ⟨*dat* to⟩

Bein *nt* -[e]s,-e leg; **jdm ein B~ stellen** trip s.o. up

beinah[e] *adv* nearly, almost

Beiname *m* epithet

beipflichten *vi sep* (*haben*) agree ⟨*dat* with⟩

Beirat *m* advisory committee

beirren *vt* **sich nicht b~ lassen** not let oneself be put off

beisammen *adv* together. **b~sein**† *vi sep* (*sein*) be together. **B~sein** *nt* -s get-together

Beisein *nt* presence

beiseite *adv* aside; (*abseits*) apart; **b~ legen** put aside; (*sparen*) put by; **Spaß** *od* **Scherz b~** joking apart

beisetz|**en** *vt sep* bury. **B~ung** *f* -,-en funeral

Beispiel *nt* example; **zum B~** for example. **b~haft** *a* exemplary. **b~los** *a* unprecedented. **b~sweise** *adv* for example

beispringen† *vi sep* (*sein*) **jdm b~** come to s.o.'s aid

beiß|**en**† *vt* & *i* (*haben*) bite; (*brennen*) sting; **sich b~en** ⟨*Farben*⟩ clash. **b~end** *a* ⟨*fig*⟩ biting; ⟨*Bemerkung*⟩ caustic. **B~zange** *f* pliers *pl*

Bei|**stand** *m* -[e]s help. **B~stand leisten** help s.o. **b~stehen**† *vi sep* (*haben*) **jdm b~stehen** help s.o.

beisteuern *vi sep* contribute

beistimmen *vi sep* (*haben*) agree

Beistrich *m* comma

Beitrag *m* -[e]s,-e contribution; (*Mitglieds-*) subscription; (*Versicherungs-*) premium; (*Zeitungs-*) article. **b~en**† *vt*/*i* (*haben*) contribute

bei|**treten**† *vi sep* (*sein*) (+*dat*) join. **B~tritt** *m* joining

beiwohnen *vi sep* (*haben*) (+*dat*) be present at

Beize *f* -,-n ⟨*Holz-*⟩ stain; (*Culin*) marinade

beizeiten *adv* in good time

beizen *vt* stain ⟨*Holz*⟩

bejahen *vt* answer in the affirmative; (*billigen*) approve of

bejahrt *a* aged, old

bejubeln *vt* cheer

bekämpfen *vt* fight. **B~ung** *f* -fight ⟨*gen* against⟩

bekannt *a* well-known; (*vertraut*) familiar; **jdm b~ sein** be known to s.o.; **jdn b~ machen** introduce s.o. **B~e(r)** *m*/*f* acquaintance; (*Freund*) friend. **B~gabe** *f* announcement. **b~geben**† *vt sep* announce. **b~lich** *adv* as is well known. **b~machen** *vt sep* announce. **B~machung** *f* -,-en announcement; (*Anschlag*) notice. **B~schaft** *f* - acquaintance; (*Leute*) acquaintances *pl*; (*Freunde*) friends *pl*. **b~werden**† *vi sep* (*sein*) become known

bekehr|**en** *vt* convert; **sich b~en** become converted. **B~ung** *f* -,-en conversion

bekenn|**en**† *vt* confess; profess ⟨*Glauben*⟩; **sich [für] schuldig b~en** admit one's guilt; **sich b~en zu** confess to ⟨*Tat*⟩; profess ⟨*Glauben*⟩; ⟨*jdm stehen*⟩ stand by. **B~tnis** *nt* -ses,-se confession; (*Konfession*) denomination

beklag|**en** *vt* lament; (*bedauern*) deplore; **sich b~en** complain. **b~enswert** *a* unfortunate. **B~te(r)** *m*/*f* ⟨*Jur*⟩ defendant

beklatschen *vt* applaud

bekleid|**en** *vt* hold ⟨*Amt*⟩. **b~et** *a* dressed ⟨mit in⟩. **B~ung** *f* clothing

Beklemmung *f* -,-en feeling of oppression

beklommen *a* uneasy; (*ängstlich*) anxious, *adv* -ly

bekommen† *vt* get; have ⟨*Baby*⟩; catch ⟨*Erkältung*⟩; **Angst/Hunger b~** get frightened/hungry;

etw geliehen b~ be lent sth □ *vi* (*sein*) **jdm gut b~** do s.o. good; ⟨*Essen:*⟩ agree with s.o.

bekömmlich *a* digestible

beköstigien *vt* feed; **sich selbst b~en** cater for oneself. **B~ung** *f* - board; ⟨*Essen*⟩ food

bekräftigen *vt* reaffirm; (*bestätigen*) confirm

bekreuzigen (sich) *vr* cross oneself

bekümmert *a* troubled; (*besorgt*) worried

bekunden *vt* show; (*bezeugen*) testify

belächeln *vt* laugh at

beladen† *vt* load □*a* laden

Belag *m* -[e]s,-̈e coating; (*Fußboden-*) covering; (*Brot-*) topping; (*Zahn-*) tartar; (*Brems-*) lining

belagerin *vt* besiege. **B~ung** *f* -,-en siege

Belang *m* von/ohne **b~** of/of no importance; **B~e** *pl* interests. **b~en** *vt* (*Jur*) sue. **b~los** *a* irrelevant; (*unwichtig*) trivial. **B~losigkeit** *f* -,-en triviality

belassen† *vt* leave; **es dabei b~** leave it at that

belasten *vt* load; (*fig*) burden; (*beanspruchen*) put a strain on; (*Comm*) debit; (*Jur*) incriminate

belästigen *vt* bother; (*bedrängen*) pester; (*unsittlich*) molest

Belastung *f* -,-en load; (*fig*) strain; (*Last*) burden; (*Comm*) debit. **B~smaterial** *nt* incriminating evidence. **B~szeuge** *m* prosecution witness

belaufen† (**sich**) *vr* amount (**auf** + *acc* to)

belauschen *vt* eavesdrop on

belebien *vt* (*fig*) revive; (*lebhaft machen*) enliven; **sich b~en** revive; ⟨*Stadt:*⟩ come to life. **b~t** *a* lively; ⟨*Straße*⟩ busy

Beleg *m* -[e]s,-e evidence; (*Beispiel*) instance (**für** of); (*Quittung*) receipt. **b~en** *vt* cover/

(*garnieren*) garnish (**mit** with); (*besetzen*) reserve; (*Univ*) enrol for; (*nachweisen*) provide evidence for; **den ersten Platz b~en** (*Sport*) take first place. **B~schaft** *f* -,-en work-force. **b~t** *a* occupied; ⟨*Zunge*⟩ coated; ⟨*Stimme*⟩ husky; **b~te Brote** open sandwiches; **der Platz ist b~t** this seat is taken

belehren *vt* instruct; (*aufklären*) inform

beleibt *a* corpulent

beleidigien *vt* offend; (*absichtlich*) insult. **B~ung** *f* -,-en insult

belesen *a* well-read

beleuchtien *vt* light; (*anleuchten*) illuminate. **B~ung** *f* -,-en illumination; (*elektrisch*) lighting; (*Licht*) light

belfern *vi* -[jə]n/ *nt* -s Belgium. **B~ier(in)** *m* -s,- (*f* -,-nen) Belgian. **b~isch** *a* Belgian

belichtien *vt* (*Phot*) expose. **B~ung** *f* - exposure

Beliebien *nt* -s **nach B~en** [just] as one likes; (*Culin*) if liked. **b~ig** *a* **eine b~ige Zahl/Farbe** any number/colour you like □ *adv* **b~ig lange/oft** as long/often as one likes. **b~t** *a* popular. **B~theit** *f* - popularity

beliefern *vt* supply (**mit** with)

bellien *vi* (*haben*) bark

belohnien *vt* reward. **B~ung** *f* -,-en reward

belüften *vt* ventilate

belügen† *vt* lie to; **sich [selbst] b~** deceive oneself

belustigien *vt* amuse. **B~ung** *f* -,-en amusement

bemächtigen (sich) *vr* (+ *gen*) seize

bemalen *vt* paint

bemängeln *vt* criticize

bemannt *a* manned

bemerkibar *a* **sich b~bar machen** attract attention; ⟨*Ding:*⟩ become noticeable. **b~en** *vt*

notice; (äußern) remark. b~ens-
wert a remarkable, adv ~bly.
B~ung f ~,-en remark
bemitleiden vt pity
bemittelt a well-to-do
bemüh|en vt trouble; sich b~en
try (zu to; um etw to get sth);
(sich kümmern) attend (um to);
b~t sein endeavour (zu to).
B~ung f ~,-en effort; (Mühe)
trouble
bemuttern vt mother
benachbart a neighbouring
benachrichtig|en vt inform;
(amtlich) notify. B~ung f ~,-en
notification
benachteilig|en vt discriminate
against; (ungerecht sein) treat un-
fairly. B~ung f ~,-en discrimination (gen against)
benehmen† (sich) vr behave.
B~ nt -s behaviour
beneiden vt envy (um etw sth).
b~swert a enviable
Bengel m -s,- boy; (Rüpel) lout
benommen a dazed
benötigen vt need
benutz|en, (SGer) benütz|en vt
use; take (Bahn). B~er m -s,-
user. b~erfreundlich a user-
friendly. B~ung f use
Benzin nt -s petrol, (Amer) gasoline. B~tank m petrol tank
beobacht|en vt observe. B~er m
-s,- observer. B~ung f ~,-en ob-
servation
bepacken vt load (mit with)
bepflanzen vt plant (mit with)
bequem a comfortable, adv ~bly;
(mühelos) easy, adv ~ily; (faul)
lazy. b~en (sich) vr deign (zu
to). B~lichkeit f ~,-en comfort;
(Faulheit) laziness
berat|en† vt advise; (überlegen)
discuss; sich b~en confer; sich
b~en lassen get advice Uvi (haben) discuss (über etw acc sth);
(beratschlagen) confer. B~er
m -s,-, B~erin f ~,-nen adviser.

b~schlagen vi (haben) confer.
B~ung f ~,-en guidance; (Rat)
advice; (Besprechung) discussion; (Med, Jur) consultation.
B~ungsstelle f advice centre
berauben vt rob (gen of)
berauschen vt intoxicate. b~d a
intoxicating, heady
berechn|en vt calculate; (anrech-
nen) charge for; (abfordern)
charge. b~end a (fig) calculat-
ing. B~ung f calculation
berechtig|en vt entitle; (befugen)
authorize; (fig) justify. b~t a
justified, justifiable. B~ung f
~,-en authorization; (Recht) right;
(Rechtmäßigkeit) justification
bered|en vt talk about; (klat-
schen) gossip about; (überreden)
talk round; sich b~en talk.
B~samkeit f ~ eloquence
beredt a eloquent, adv ~ly
Bereich m -[e]s,-e area; (fig)
realm; (Fach-) field
bereichern vt enrich; sich b~
grow rich (an + dat on)
Bereifung f ~ tyres pl
bereinigen vt (fig) settle
bereit a ready. b~en vt prepare;
(verursachen) cause; give (Überraschung). b~halten† vt sep
have/(ständig) keep ready.
b~legen vt sep put out [ready].
b~machen vt sep get ready;
sich b~machen get ready. b~s
adv already
Bereitschaft f ~,-en readiness;
(Einheit) squad. B~sdienst m
B~sdienst haben (Mil) be on
stand-by; ⟨Arzt:⟩ be on call;
⟨Apotheke:⟩ be open for out-of-
hours dispensing. B~spolizei f
riot police
bereit|stehen† vi sep (haben) be
ready. b~stellen vt sep put out
ready; (verfügbar machen) make
available. B~ung f ~ preparation. b~willig a willing, adv ~ly.
B~willigkeit f ~ willingness

bereuen vt regret

Berg m -[e]s,-e mountain; (Anhöhe) hill; **in den B~en** in the mountains. **b~ab** adv downhill. **b~an** adv uphill. **b~arbeiter** m miner. **b~auf** adv uphill; **es geht b~auf** (fig) things are looking up. **B~bau** m -[e]s mining

bergen† vt recover; (Naut) salvage; (retten) rescue

Berg|führer m mountain guide. **b~ig** a mountainous. **B~kette** f mountain range. **B~mann** m (pl -leute) miner. **B~steigen** nt -s mountaineering. **B~steiger(in)** m -s,- (f -,-nen) mountaineer, climber. **B~-und-Talbahn** f roller-coaster

Bergung f -recovery; (Naut) salvage; (Rettung) rescue

Berg|wacht f mountain rescue service. **B~werk** nt mine

Bericht m -[e]s,-e report; (Reise-) account; **B~ erstatten** report (über + acc on). **b~en** vt/i (haben) report; (erzählen) tell (von of). **B~erstatter(in)** m -s,- (f -,-nen) reporter; (Korrespondent) correspondent

berichtigen vt correct. **B~ung** f -,-en correction

berieseln vt irrigate. **B~ungsanlage** f sprinkler system

beritten a (Polizei) mounted

Berlin nt -s Berlin. **B~er** m -s,- Berliner; (Culin) doughnut □ a Berlin ...

Bernhardiner m -s,- St Bernard

Bernstein m amber

bersten† vi (sein) burst

berüchtigt a notorious

berückend a entrancing

berücksichtigen vt take into consideration. **B~ung** f -consideration

Beruf m profession; (Tätigkeit) occupation; (Handwerk) trade. **b~en†** vt appoint; **sich b~en** refer (auf + acc to); (vorgeben)

plead (auf etw acc sth) □ a competent; **b~en sein** be destined (zu to). **b~lich** a professional; (Ausbildung) vocational □ adv professionally; **b~lich tätig sein** work, have a job. **B~saussichten** fpl career prospects. **B~sberater(in)** m(f) careers officer. **B~sberatung** f vocational guidance. **b~smäßig** adv professionally. **B~sschule** f vocational school. **B~ssoldat** m regular soldier. **b~stätig** a working; **b~stätig sein** work, have a job. **B~stätige(r)** m/f working man/woman. **B~sverkehr** m rush-hour traffic. **B~ung** f -,-en appointment; (Bestimmung) vocation; (Jur) appeal; **B~ung einlegen** appeal. **B~ungsgericht** nt appeal court

beruhen vi (haben) be based (auf + dat on); **eine Sache auf sich b~ lassen** let a matter rest

beruhigen vt calm [down]; (zuversichtlich machen) reassure; **sich b~en** calm down. **b~end** a calming; (tröstend) reassuring; (Med) sedative. **B~ung** f -calming; reassurance; (Med) sedation. **B~ungsmittel** nt sedative; (bei Psychosen) tranquillizer

berühmt a famous. **B~heit** f -,-en fame; (Person) celebrity

berühr|en vt touch; (erwähnen) touch on; (beeindrucken) affect; **sich b~en** touch. **B~ung** f -,-en touch; (Kontakt) contact

besagen vt say; (bedeuten) mean. **b~t** a [afore]said

besänftigen vt soothe; **sich b~** calm down

Besatz m -es,-e trimming

Besatzung f -,-en crew; (Mil) occupying force

besaufen† (sich) vr (sl) get drunk

beschädigen vt damage. **B~ung** f -,-en damage

beschaffen vt obtain, get □a so
b~ sein, daß be such that; wie
ist es b~ mit? what about?
B~heit f - consistency; (Art) nature

beschäftig|en vt occupy; ⟨Arbeit-
geber:⟩ employ; **sich b~en**
occupy oneself. **b~t** a busy;
(angestellt) employed (bei at).
B~te(r) m/f employee. **B~ung**
f -,-en occupation; (Anstellung)
employment. **b~ungslos** a unemployed. **B~ungstherapie** f
occupational therapy

beschäm|en vt make ashamed.
b~end a shameful; (demüti-
gend) humiliating. **b~t** a
ashamed; (verlegen) embarrassed

beschatten vt shade; (überwachen) shadow

beschau|en [SGer] (sich (dat)]
etw b~en look at sth. **b~lich** a
tranquil; (Relig) contemplative

Bescheid m -[e]s information;
jdm B~ sagen od geben let s.o.
know; **B~ wissen** know

bescheiden a modest, adv -ly.
B~heit f - modesty

bescheinen† vt shine on; **von der
Sonne beschienen** sunlit

bescheinig|en vt certify. **B~ung**
f -,-en [written] confirmation;
(Schein) certificate

beschenken vt give a present/
presents to

bescher|en vt jdn b~en give s.o.
presents; jdm etw b~en give s.o.
sth. **B~ung** f -,-en distribution
of Christmas presents; (fam:
Schlamassel) mess

beschießen† vt fire at; (mit Artillerie) shell, bombard

beschildern vt signpost

beschimpf|en vt abuse, swear at.
B~ung f -,-en abuse

beschirmen vt protect

Beschlag m in B~ nehmen, mit
B~ belegen monopolize. **b~en†**
vt shoe □vi (sein) steam or mist

up □a steamed or misted up; (erfahren) knowledgeable (in + dat
about). **B~nahme** f -,-n confis-
cation; (Jur) seizure. **b~nah-
men** vt confiscate; (Jur) seize;
(fam) monopolize

beschleunig|en vt hasten;
(schneller machen) speed up;
quicken ⟨Schritt, Tempo⟩; sich
b~en speed up; quicken □vi (haben) accelerate. **B~ung** f -
acceleration

beschließen† vt decide; (beenden)
end □vi (haben) decide (über
+ acc about)

Beschluß m decision

beschmieren vt smear/(bestreichen) spread (mit with)

beschmutzen vt make dirty; sich
b~ get [oneself] dirty

beschneid|en† vt trim; (Hort)
prune; (fig: kürzen) cut back;
(Relig) circumcise. **B~ung** f -
circumcision

beschneit a snow-covered

beschnüffeln, beschnuppern
vt sniff at

beschönigen vt (fig) gloss over

beschränken vt limit, restrict;
sich b~ auf (+ acc) confine oneself to; ⟨Sache:⟩ be limited to

beschrankt a ⟨Bahnübergang⟩
with barrier[s]

beschränkt a limited; (geistig)
dull-witted; (borniert) narrow-
minded. **B~ung** f -,-en limitation, restriction

beschreib|en† vt describe;
(schreiben) write on. **B~ung** f
-,-en description

beschuldig|en vt accuse.
B~ung f -,-en accusation

beschummeln vt (fam) cheat

Beschuß m -sses (Mil) fire; (Artil-
lerie-) shelling

beschütz|en vt protect. **B~er** m
-s,- protector

Beschwer|de f -,-n complaint;
B~den (Med) trouble sg. **b~en**

vt weight down; **sich b~en** complain. **b~lich** *a* difficult

beschwichtigen *vt* placate

beschwindeln *vt* cheat (**um** out of); (*belügen*) lie to

beschwingt *a* elated; (*munter*) lively

beschwipst *a* (*fam*) tipsy

beschwören† *vt* swear to; (*anflehen*) implore; (*herauf-*) invoke

besehen† *vt* look at

beseitig|en *vt* remove. **B~ung** *f* -removal

Besen *m* -s,- broom. **B~ginster** *m* (*Bot*) broom. **B~stiel** *m* broomstick

besessen *a* obsessed (**von** by)

besetz|en *vt* occupy; fill ⟨*Posten*⟩; (*Theat*) cast ⟨*Rolle*⟩; (*verzieren*) trim (**mit** with). **b~t** *a* occupied; ⟨*Toilette, Leitung*⟩ engaged; ⟨*Zug, Bus*⟩ full up; **der Platz ist b~t** this seat is taken; **mit Perlen b~t** set with pearls. **B~tzeichen** *nt* engaged tone. **B~ung** *f* -,-en occupation; (*Theat*) cast

besichtig|en *vt* look round ⟨*Stadt, Museum*⟩; (*prüfen*) inspect; (*besuchen*) visit. **B~ung** *f* -,-en visit; (*Prüfung*) inspection; (*Stadt-*) sightseeing

besiedelt *a* **dünn/dicht b~** sparsely/densely populated

besiegeln *vt* (*fig*) seal

besieg|en† *vt* defeat; (*fig*) overcome. **B~te(r)** *m/f* loser

besinn|en† (**sich**) *vr* think, reflect; (*sich erinnern*) remember (**auf jdn/etw** s.o./sth); **sich anders b~en** change one's mind. **b~lich** *a* contemplative; (*nachdenklich*) thoughtful. **B~ung** *f* - reflection; (*Bewußtsein*) consciousness; **bei/ohne B~ung** conscious/unconscious; **zur B~ung kommen** regain consciousness; (*fig*) come to one's senses. **b~ungslos** *a* unconscious

Besitz *m* possession; (*Eigentum, Land-*) property; (*Gut*) estate. **b~anzeigend** *a* (*Gram*) possessive. **b~en†** *vt* own, possess; (*haben*) have. **B~er(in)** *m* -s,- (*f* -,-nen) owner; (*Comm*) proprietor. **B~ung** *f* -,-en [landed] property; (*Gut*) estate

besoffen *a* (*sl*) drunken; **b~ sein** be drunk

besohlen *vt* sole

besold|en *vt* pay. **B~ung** *f* - pay

besonder|e(r,s) *a* special; (*bestimmt*) particular; (*gesondert*) separate; **nichts B~es** nothing special. **B~heit** *f* -,-en peculiarity. **b~s** *adv* [e]specially, particularly; (*gesondert*) separately

besonnen *a* calm, *adv* -ly

besorg|en *vt* get; (*kaufen*) buy; (*erledigen*) attend to; (*versorgen*) look after. **B~nis** *f* -,-se anxiety; (*Sorge*) worry. **b~niserregend** *a* worrying. **b~t** *a* worried/(*bedacht*) concerned (**um** about). **B~ung** *f* -,-en errand; **B~ungen machen** do shopping

bespielt *a* recorded

bespitzeln *vt* spy on

besprech|en† *vt* discuss; (*rezensieren*) review; **sich b~en** confer; **ein Tonband b~en** make a tape recording. **B~ung** *f* -,-en discussion; review; (*Konferenz*) meeting

bespritzen *vt* splash

besser *a & adv* better. **b~n** *vt* improve; **sich b~n** get better, improve. **B~ung** *f* - improvement; **gute B~ung!** get well soon! **B~wisser** *m* -s,- know-all

Bestand *m* -[e]s,ˑe existence; (*Vorrat*) stock (**an** + *dat* of); **haben, von B~ sein** last

beständig *a* constant, *adv* -ly; ⟨*Wetter*⟩ settled; **b~ gegen** resistant to

Bestand|saufnahme *f* stocktaking. **B~teil** *m* part

bestärken vt (fig) strengthen

bestätig|en vt confirm;·· acknowledge ⟨Empfang⟩; **sich b∼en** prove to be true. **B∼ung** f -,-en confirmation

bestatt|en vt bury. **B∼ung** f -,-en funeral. **B∼ungsinstitut** nt [firm of] undertakers pl, (Amer) funeral home

bestäuben vt pollinate

bestaubt a dusty

Bestäubung f - pollination

bestaunen vt gaze at in amazement; (bewundern) admire

best|e(r,s) a best; **b∼en Dank!** many thanks! **am b∼en sein** be best; **zum b∼en geben** recite ⟨Gedicht⟩; tell ⟨Geschichte, Witz⟩; sing ⟨Lied⟩; **jdn zum b∼en halten** (fam) pull s.o.'s leg. **B∼e(r,s)** m/f/nt best; **sein B∼es tun** do one's best; **zum B∼en der Armen** for the benefit of the poor

bestech|en vt bribe; (bezaubern) captivate. **b∼end** a captivating. **b∼lich** a corruptible. **B∼ung** f bribery. **B∼ungsgeld** nt bribe

Besteck nt -[e]s,-e [set of] knife, fork and spoon; (coll) cutlery

bestehen vi (haben) exist; (fortdauern) last; (bei Prüfung) pass; **b∼ aus** consist/(gemacht sein) be made of; **b∼ auf** (+ dat) insist on □vt pass ⟨Prüfung⟩. **B∼** nt -s existence

bestehlen† vt rob

besteig|en† vt climb; (einsteigen) board; (aufsteigen) mount; ascend ⟨Thron⟩. **B∼ung** f ascent

bestell|en vt order; (vor-) book; (ernennen) appoint; (bebauen) cultivate; (ausrichten) tell; **zu sich b∼en** send for; **b∼t sein** have an appointment; **kann ich etwas b∼en?** can I take a message? **b∼en Sie Ihrer Frau Grüße von mir** give my regards to your wife. **B∼schein** m order

form. **B∼ung** f order; (Botschaft) message; (Bebauung) cultivation

besten|falls adv at best. **b∼s** adv very well

besteuer|n vt tax. **B∼ung** f -taxation

bestialisch /-st-/ a bestial

Bestie /'bɛstjə/ f -,-n beast

bestimm|en vt fix; (entscheiden) decide; (vorsehen) intend; (ernennen) appoint; (ermitteln) determine; (definieren) define; (Gram) qualify □vi (haben) be in charge ⟨über + acc of⟩. **b∼t** a definite, adv -ly; (gewiß) certain, adv -ly; (fest) firm, adv -ly. **B∼theit** f -firmness; **mit B∼theit** for certain. **B∼ung** f fixing; (Vorschrift) regulation; (Ermittlung) determination; (Definition) definition; (Zweck) purpose; (Schicksal) destiny. **B∼ungsort** m destination

Bestleistung f (Sport) record

bestraf|en vt punish. **B∼ung** f -,-en punishment

bestrahl|en vt shine on; (Med) treat with radiotherapy; irradiate ⟨Lebensmittel⟩. **B∼ung** f radiotherapy

Bestreb|en nt -s endeavour; (Absicht) aim. **b∼t a b∼t sein** endeavour (**zu** to). **B∼ung** f -,-en effort

bestreichen† vt spread (**mit** with)

bestreikt a strike-hit

bestreit|en† vt dispute; (leugnen) deny; (bezahlen) pay for

bestreuen vt sprinkle (**mit** with)

bestürmen vt (fig) besiege

bestürz|t a dismayed; (erschüttert) stunned. **B∼ung** f dismay, consternation

Bestzeit f (Sport) record [time]

Besuch m -[e]s,-e visit; (kurz) call; (Schul-) attendance; (Gast) visitor; (Gäste) visitors pl; **B∼ haben** have a visitor/visitors; **bei**

jdm zu *od* **auf B~** sein be staying with s.o. **b~en** *vt* visit; *(kurz)* call on; *(teilnehmen)* attend; go to ⟨*Schule, Ausstellung*⟩; **gut b~t** well attended. **B~er(in)** *m* -s,- *(f -,-nen)* visitor; caller; *(Theat)* patron. **B~szeit** *f* visiting hours *pl*

betagt *a* aged, old

betasten *vt* feel

betätig|en *vt* operate; **sich b~en** work **(als** as); **sich politisch b~en** engage in politics. **B~ung** *f* -,-en operation; *(Tätigkeit)* activity

betäub|en *vt* stun; *(Lärm:)* deafen; *(Med)* anaesthetize; *(lindern)* ease; deaden ⟨*Schmerz*⟩; **wie b~t** dazed. **B~ung** *f* - daze; *(Med)* anaesthesia; **unter örtlicher B~ung** under local anaesthetic. **B~ungsmittel** *nt* anaesthetic

Bete *f* -,-n **rote B~** beetroot

beteilig|en *vt* give a share to; **sich b~en** take part **(an +** *dat* in); *(beitragen)* contribute **(an +** *dat* to). **b~t a b~t sein** take part/*(an Unfall)* be involved/*(Comm)* have a share **(an +** *dat* in); **alle B~ten** all those involved. **B~ung** *f* -,-en participation; involvement; *(Anteil)* share

beten *vi* *(haben)* pray; *(bei Tisch)* say grace □ *vt* say

beteuer|n *vt* protest. **B~ung** *f* -,-en protestation

Beton /be'tɔŋ/ *m* -s concrete

betonen *vt* stress, emphasize

betonieren *vt* concrete

beton|t *a* stressed; *(fig)* pointed, *adv* -ly. **B~ung** *f* -,-en stress, emphasis

betören *vt* bewitch

betr., Betr. *abbr* **(betreffs)** re

Betracht *m* **in B~ ziehen** consider; **außer B~ lassen** disregard; **nicht in B~ kommen** be out of the question. **b~en** *vt* look at; *(fig)* regard **(als** as)

beträchtlich *a* considerable, *adv* -bly

Betrachtung *f* -,-en contemplation; *(Überlegung)* reflection

Betrag *m* -[e]s,⸚e amount. **b~en†** *vt* amount to; **sich b~en** behave. **B~en** *nt* -s behaviour; *(Sch)* conduct

betrauen *vt* entrust **(mit** with)

betrauern *vt* mourn

betreff|en† *vt* affect; *(angehen)* concern; **was mich betrifft** as far as I am concerned. **b~end** *a* relevant; **der b~ende Brief** the letter in question. **b~s** *prep* (+ *gen*) concerning

betreib|en† *vt* *(leiten)* run; *(ausüben)* carry on; *(vorantreiben)* pursue; *(antreiben)* run **(mit** on)

betret|en† *vt* step on; *(eintreten)* enter; **'B~ verboten** 'no entry'; **den Rasen** 'keep off [the grass]' □ *a* embarrassed □ *adv* in embarrassment

betreu|en *vt* look after. **B~er(in)** *m* -s,- *(f -,-nen)* helper; *(Kranken-)* nurse. **B~ung** *f* -care

Betrieb *m* business; *(Firma)* firm; *(Treiben)* activity; *(Verkehr)* traffic; **in B~** working; *(in Gebrauch)* in use; **außer B~** not in use; *(defekt)* out of order

Betriebsanleitung, B~anweisung *f* operating instructions *pl*. **B~ferien** *pl* firm's holiday; **'B~ferien** 'closed for the holidays'. **B~leitung** *f* management. **B~rat** *m* works committee. **B~ruhe** *f* 'montags B~ruhe** 'closed on Mondays'. **B~störung** *f* breakdown

betrinken (sich) *vr* get drunk

betroffen *a* disconcerted; **b~ sein** be affected (von by); **die B~en** those affected □ *adv* in consternation

betrüb|en *vt* sadden. **b~lich** *a* sad. **b~t** *a* sad, *adv* -ly

Betrug m -[e]s deception; (Jur) fraud

betrüg|en† vt cheat, swindle; (Jur) defraud; (in der Ehe) be unfaithful to; **sich b~en** deceive oneself. **B~er(in)** m -s, (f -,-nen) swindler. **B~erei** f -,-en fraud. **b~erisch** a fraudulent; (Person) deceitful

betrunken a drunken; **b~ sein** be drunk. **B~e(r)** m drunk

Bett nt -[e]s,-en bed; **im B~** in bed; **ins** od **zu B~ gehen** go to bed. **B~couch** f sofa-bed. **B~decke** f blanket; (Tages-) bedspread

bettel|arm a destitute. **B~ei** f -begging. **b~n** vi (haben) beg

bett|en vt lay, put; **sich b~en** lie down. **b~lägerig** a bedridden. **B~laken** nt sheet

Bettler(in) m -s,- (f -,-nen) beggar

Bett|pfanne f bedpan. **B~tuch** nt sheet

Bett|vorleger m bedside rug. **B~wäsche** f bed linen. **B~zeug** nt bedding

betupfen vt dab (mit with)

beug|en vt bend; (Gram) decline; conjugate ⟨Verb⟩; **sich b~en** bend; (lehnen) lean; (sich fügen) submit (dat to). **B~ung** f -,-en (Gram) declension; conjugation

Beule f -,-n bump; (Delle) dent

beunruhig|en vt worry; **sich b~en** worry. **B~ung** f - worry

beurlauben vt give leave to; (des Dienstes entheben) suspend

beurteil|en vt judge. **B~ung** f -,-en judgement; (Ansicht) opinion

Beute f - booty, haul; (Jagd-) bag; (B~tier) quarry; (eines Raubtiers) prey

Beutel m -s,- bag; (Geld-) purse; (Tabak- & Zool) pouch. **B~tier** nt marsupial

bevölker|n vt populate. **B~ung** f -,-en population

bevollmächtig|en vt authorize. **B~te(r)** m/f [authorized] agent

bevor conj before; **b~ nicht** until

bevormunden vt treat like a child

bevorstehen† vi sep (haben) approach; (unmittelbar) be imminent; **jdm b~** be in store for s.o. **b~d** a approaching, forthcoming; **unmittelbar b~d** imminent

bevorzug|en vt prefer; (begünstigen) favour. **b~t** a privileged; ⟨Behandlung⟩ preferential; (beliebt) favoured

bewachen vt guard; **bewachter Parkplatz** car park with an attendant

bewachsen a covered (mit with)

Bewachung f - guard; **unter B~** under guard

bewaffn|en vt arm. **b~et** a armed. **B~ung** f - armament; (Waffen) arms pl

bewahren vt protect (vor + dat from); (behalten) keep; **die Ruhe b~** keep calm; **Gott bewahre!** heaven forbid!

bewähren (sich) vr prove one's/⟨Ding:⟩ its worth; (erfolgreich sein) prove a success

bewahrheiten (sich) vr prove to be true

bewährt a reliable; (erprobt) proven. **B~ung** f - (Jur) probation. **B~ungsfrist** f [period of] probation. **B~ungsprobe** f (fig) test

bewaldet a wooded

bewältigen vt cope with; (überwinden) overcome; (schaffen) manage

bewandert a knowledgeable

bewässer|n vt irrigate. **B~ung** f - irrigation

bewegen¹ vt (reg) move; **sich b~** move; (körperlich) take exercise

bewegen²† vt jdn dazu b~, etw zu tun induce s.o. to do sth

Beweg|grund m motive. **b~lich** a movable, mobile; (wendig) agile. **B~lichkeit** f - mobility; agility. **b~t** a moved; (ereignisreich) eventful; ⟨See⟩ rough. **B~ung** f -,-en movement; (Phys) motion; (Rührung) emotion; (Gruppe) movement; **körperliche B~ung** physical exercise; **sich in B~ung setzen** [start to] move. **B~ungsfreiheit** f freedom of movement/⟨fig⟩ of action. **b~unglos** a motionless

beweinen vt mourn

Beweis m -es,-e proof; (Zeichen) token; **B~e** evidence sg. **b~en†** vt prove; (zeigen) show; **sich b~en** prove oneself ⟨Ding:⟩ itself. **B~material** nt evidence

bewenden vi es dabei **b~ lassen** leave it at that

bewerb|en† (sich) vr apply (**um** for; **bei** to). **B~er(in)** m -s,- (f -,-nen) applicant. **B~ung** f -,-en application

bewerkstelligen vt manage

bewerten vt value; (einschätzen) rate; (Sch) mark, grade

bewilligen vt grant

bewirken vt cause; (herbeiführen) bring about; (erreichen) achieve

bewirt|en vt entertain. **B~ung** f - hospitality

bewohn|bar a habitable. **b~en** vt inhabit, live in. **B~er(in)** m -s,- (f -,-nen) resident, occupant; (Einwohner) inhabitant

bewölk|en (sich) vr cloud over; **b~t** cloudy. **B~ung** f - clouds pl

bewundern vt admire. **B~nswert** a admirable. **B~ung** f - admiration

bewußt a conscious (gen of); (absichtlich) deliberate, adv -ly; (besagt) said; **sich** (dat) **etw** (gen) **b~ sein/werden** be/become

aware of sth. **b~los** a unconscious. **B~losigkeit** f - unconsciousness. **b~sein** n -s consciousness; (Gewißheit) awareness; **bei [vollem] B~sein** [fully] conscious; **mir kam zum B~sein** I realized (**daß** that)

bez. abbr (**bezahlt**) paid; (**bezüglich**) re

bezahl|en vt/i (haben) pay; pay for ⟨Ware, Essen⟩; **sich b~ machen** (fig) pay off. **B~ung** f - payment; (Lohn) pay

bezähmen vt control; (zügeln) restrain; **sich b~** restrain oneself

bezaubern vt enchant. **b~d** a enchanting

bezeichn|en vt mark; (bedeuten) denote; (beschreiben, nennen) describe (**als** as). **b~end** a typical. **B~ung** f marking; (Beschreibung) description (**als** as); (Ausdruck) term; (Name) name

bezeugen vt testify to

bezichtigen vt accuse (gen of)

bezieh|en† vt cover; (einziehen) move into; (beschaffen) obtain; (erhalten) get, receive; take ⟨Zeitung⟩; (in Verbindung bringen) relate (**auf**+acc to); **sich b~en** (bewölken) cloud over; **sich b~en auf** (+acc) refer to; **das Bett frisch b~en** put clean sheets on the bed. **B~ung** f -,-en relation; (Verhältnis) relationship; (Bezug) respect; **in dieser B~ung** in this respect; [**gute**] **B~ungen haben** have [good] connections. **b~ungsweise** adv respectively; (vielmehr) or rather

beziffern (sich) vr amount to (**auf**+acc)

Bezirk m -[e]s,-e district

Bezug m cover; (Kissen-) case; (Beschaffung) obtaining; (Kauf) purchase; (Zusammenhang) reference; **B~e** pl earnings; **B~nehmen** refer (**auf**+acc to);

b~ auf (+acc) regarding, concerning

bezüglich prep (+gen) regarding, concerning □a relating (**auf**+acc to); (Gram) relative

bezwecken vt (fig) aim at

bezweifeln vt doubt

bezwingen† vt conquer

BH /be:'ha:/ m -[s],-[s] bra

bibbern vi (haben) tremble; (vor Kälte) shiver

Bibel f -,-n Bible

Biber[1] m -s,- beaver

Biber[2] m & nt -s flannelette

Biblio|graphie f -,-n bibliography. **B~thek** f -,-en library. **B~thekar(in)** m -s,- (f -,-nen) librarian

biblisch a biblical

bieder a honest, upright; (ehrenwert) worthy; (einfach) simple

bieg|en† vt bend; **sich b~en** bend; **sich vor Lachen b~en** (fam) double up with laughter □vi (sein) curve (**nach** to); **um die Ecke b~en** turn the corner. **b~sam** a flexible, supple. **B~ung** f -,-en bend

Biene f -,-n bee. **B~nhonig** m natural honey. **B~nstock** m beehive. **B~nwabe** f honeycomb

Bier nt -s,-e beer. **B~deckel** m beer-mat. **B~krug** m beer-mug

Biest nt -[e]s,-er (fam) beast

bieten† vt offer; (bei Auktion) bid; (zeigen) present; **das lasse ich mir nicht b~** I won't stand for that

Bifokalbrille f bifocals pl

Biga|mie f -,-en bigamy. **B~mist** m -en,-en bigamist

bigott a over-pious

Bikini m -s,-s bikini

Bilanz f -,-en balance sheet; (fig) result; **die B~ ziehen** (fig) draw conclusions (**aus** from)

Bild nt -[e]s,-er picture; (Theat) scene; **jdn ins B~ setzen** put s.o. in the picture

bilden vt form; (sein) be; (erziehen) educate; **sich b~** form; (geistig) educate oneself

Bild|erbuch nt picture-book. **B~ergalerie** f picture gallery. **B~fläche** f screen; **von der B~fläche verschwinden** disappear from the scene. **B~hauer** m -s,- sculptor. **B~hauerei** f - sculpture. **b~hübsch** a very pretty. **b~lich** a pictorial; (figurativ) figurative, adv -ly. **B~nis** nt -ses,-se portrait. **B~schirm** m (TV) screen. **B~schirmgerät** nt visual display unit, VDU. **b~schön** a very beautiful

Bildung f - formation; (Erziehung) education; (Kultur) culture

Billard /'bɪljart/ nt -s billiards sg. **B~tisch** m billiard table

Billett /bɪl'jɛt/ nt -[e]s,-e & -s ticket

Billiarde f -,-n thousand million million

billig a cheap, adv -ly; (dürftig) poor; (gerecht) just; **recht und b~** right and proper. **b~en** vt approve. **B~ung** f - approval

Billion /bɪl'jo:n/ f -,-en million million, billion

bimmeln vi (haben) tinkle

Bimsstein m pumice stone

bin s. sein; **ich bin** I am

Binde f -,-n band; (Verband) bandage; (Damen-) sanitary towel. **B~hautentzündung** f conjunctivitis. **b~n**† vt tie (**an**+acc to); make ⟨Strauß⟩; bind ⟨Buch⟩; (fesseln) tie up; (Culin) thicken; **sich b~n** commit oneself. **b~nd** a (fig) binding. **B~strich** m hyphen. **B~wort** nt (pl -wörter) (Gram) conjunction

Bind|faden m string; **ein b~fa-
den** a piece of string. **B~ung** f
-,-en (fig) tie, bond; (Beziehung)
relationship; (Verpflichtung)
commitment; (Ski-) binding;
(Tex) weave

binnen prep (+dat) within; **b~
kurzem** shortly. **B~handel** m
home trade

Binse f -,-n (Bot) rush.
B~nwahrheit, B~nweisheit
f truism

Bio- pref organic

Bio|chemie f biochemistry.
b~dynamisch m organic.
B~graphie f -,-n biography

Bio|hof m organic farm. **B~
laden** m health-food store

Biolog|e m -n,-n biologist. **B~ie**
f biology. **b~isch** a biological,
adv -ly; **b~ischer Anbau** organic farming; **b~isch angebaut** organically grown

Birke f -,-n birch [tree]

Birm|a nt -s Burma. **b~anisch** a
Burmese

Birn|baum m pear-tree. **B~e** f
-,-n pear; (Electr) bulb

bis prep (+acc) as far as, [up] to;
(zeitlich) until, till; (spätestens)
by; **bis zu up** to; **bis jetzt** up to
now, so far; **bis dahin** until/(spätestens) by then; **bis auf** (+acc)
(einschließlich) [down] to; (ausgenommen) except [for]; **drei bis
vier Mark** three to four marks;
bis morgen! see you tomorrow!
□ conj until

Bischof m -s,ءe bishop

bisher adv so far, up to now.
b~ig attrib a (Präsident-) outgoing; **meine b~igen Erfahrun-
gen** my experiences so far

Biskuit|rolle /bis'kvi:t-/ f Swiss
roll. **B~teig** m sponge mixture

bislang adv so far, up to now

Biß m -sses,-sse bite

bißchen inv pron **ein b~** a bit, a
little; **ein b~ Brot** a bit of bread;
kein b~ not a bit

Biss|en m -s,- bite, mouthful.
b~ig a vicious; (fig) caustic

bist s. **sein**; **du b~** you are

Bistum nt -s,ءer diocese, see

bisweilen adv from time to time

bitt|e adv please; (nach Klopfen)
come in; (als Antwort auf 'danke')
don't mention it, you're welcome;
wie b~e? pardon? (empört) I beg
your pardon? (empört) **möchten Sie Kaffee?—ja b~e** would you like
some coffee?—yes please. **B~e** f
-,-n request/(dringend) plea (um
for). **b~en†** vt/i (haben) ask/
(dringend) beg (um for); (einladen) invite, ask; **ich b~e dich!** I
beg [of] you! (empört) I ask you!
b~end a pleading, adv -ly

bitter a bitter, adv -ly. **B~keit** f
-bitterness. **b~lich** adv bitterly

Bittschrift f petition

bizarr a bizarre, adv -ly

bläh|en vt swell; puff out ⟨Vor-
hang⟩; **sich b~en** swell; ⟨Vor-
hang, Segel;⟩ billow □vi (haben)
cause flatulence. **B~ungen** fpl
flatulence sg, (fam) wind sg

Blamage /bla'ma:ʒə/ f -,-n humi-
liation/(Schande) disgrace

blamier|en vt disgrace; **sich b~**
disgrace oneself; (sich lächerlich
machen) make a fool of oneself

blanchieren /blã'ʃi:rən/ vt (Culin)
blanch

blank a shiny; (nackt) bare; **b~
sein** (fam) be broke. **B~o-
scheck** m blank cheque

Blase f -,-n bubble; (Med) blister;
(Anat) bladder. **B~balg** m
-[e]s,ءe bellows pl. **b~n†** vt/i
(haben) blow; play ⟨Flöte⟩. **B~n-
entzündung** f cystitis

Bläser m -s,- (Mus) wind player;
die B~ the wind section sg

blasiert a blasé

Blas|instrument nt wind instrument. **B~kapelle** f brass band

Blasphemie f- blasphemy

blaß a (blasser, blassest) pale; (schwach) faint; **b~ werden** turn pale

Blässe f- pallor

Blatt nt -[e]s,̈-er (Bot) leaf; (Papier) sheet; (Zeitung) paper; **kein B~ vor den Mund nehmen** (fig) not mince one's words

blätter|n vi (haben) **b~n in** (+dat) leaf through. **B~teig** m puff pastry

Blattlaus f greenfly

blau a, **B~** nt -s,- blue; **b~er Fleck** bruise; **b~es Auge** black eye; **b~ sein** (fam) be tight; **Fahrt ins B~e** mystery tour. **B~beere** f bilberry. **B~licht** nt blue flashing light. **b~machen** vi sep (haben) (fam) skive off work

Blech nt -[e]s,-e sheet metal; (Weiß-) tin; (Platte) metal sheet; (Back-) baking sheet; (Mus) brass; (fam: Unsinn) rubbish. **b~en** vt/i (haben) (fam) pay. **B~(blas)instrument** nt brass instrument. **B~schaden** m (Auto) damage to the bodywork

Blei nt -[e]s lead

Bleibe f- place to stay. **b~n†** vi (sein) remain, stay; (übrig-) be left; **ruhig b~n** keep calm; **bei etw b~n** (fig) stick to sth; **b~n Sie am Apparat** hold the line. **b~nd** a permanent; (anhaltend) lasting. **b~nlassen†** vt sep **etw b~nlassen** not do sth; (aufhören) stop doing sth

bleich a pale. **b~en†** vi (sein) bleach; (ver-) fade □vt (reg) bleach. **B~mittel** nt bleach

blei|ern a leaden. **b~frei** a unleaded. **B~stift** m pencil. **B~stiftabsatz** m stiletto heel. **B~stiftspitzer** m -s,- pencil-sharpener

Blende f-,-n shade, shield; (Sonnen-) [sun] visor; (Phot) diaphragm; (Öffnung) aperture; (an Kleid) facing. **b~n** vt dazzle, blind. **b~nd** a (fig) dazzling; (prima) marvellous, adv -ly

Blick m -[e]s,-e look; (kurz) glance; (Aussicht) view; **auf den ersten B~** at first sight; **einen B~ für etw haben** (fig) have an eye for sth. **b~en** vi (haben) look/ (kurz) glance (**auf**+acc at). **B~punkt** m (fig) point of view

blind a blind; (trübe) dull; **b~er Alarm** false alarm; **b~er Passagier** stowaway. **B~darm** m appendix. **B~darmentzündung** f appendicitis. **B~e(r)** m/f blind man/woman; **die B~en** the blind pl. **B~enhund** m guidedog. **B~enschrift** f braille. **B~gänger** m -s,- (Mil) dud. **B~heit** f- blindness. **b~lings** adv (fig) blindly

blink|en vi (haben) flash; (funkeln) gleam; (Auto) indicate. **B~er** m -s,- (Auto) indicator. **B~licht** nt flashing light

blinzeln vi (haben) blink

Blitz m -[e]s,-e [flash of] lightning; (Phot) flash; **ein B~ aus heiterem Himmel** (fig) a bolt from the blue. **B~ableiter** m lightning-conductor. **b~artig** a lightning...□adv like lightning. **B~birne** f flashbulb. **b~en** vi (haben) flash; (funkeln) sparkle; **es hat geblitzt** there was a flash of lightning. **B~gerät** nt flash [unit]. **B~licht** nt (Phot) flash. **b~sauber** a spick and span. **b~schnell** a lightning...□adv like lightning. **B~strahl** m flash of lightning

Block m -[e]s,̈-e block □ -[e]s,-s & ̈-e (Schreib-) [note-]pad; (Häuser-) block; (Pol) bloc

Blockade f-,-n blockade

Blockflöte f recorder

blockieren vt block; (Mil) blockade

Blockschrift f block letters pl

blöd[e] a feeble-minded; (dumm) stupid, adv -ly

Blödsinn m -[e]s idiocy; (Unsinn) nonsense. **b~ig** a feeble-minded; (verrückt) idiotic

blöken vi (haben) bleat

blond a fair-haired; ⟨Haar⟩ fair. **B~ine** f -,-n blonde

bloß a bare; (alleinig) mere; **mit b~em Auge** with the naked eye □adv only, just; **was mache ich b~?** whatever shall I do?

Blöße f -,-n nakedness; **sich** (dat) **eine B~ geben** (fig) show a weakness

bloß|legen vt sep uncover; **b~-stellen** vt sep compromise; **sich b~stellen** show oneself up

Bluff m -s,-s bluff. **b~en** vt/i (haben) bluff

blühen vi (haben) flower; (fig) flourish. **b~d** a flowering; (fig) flourishing, thriving; ⟨Phantasie⟩ fertile

Blume f -,-n flower; (vom Wein) bouquet. **B~nbeet** n flower-bed. **B~ngeschäft** nt flower-shop, florist's [shop]. **B~nkohl** m cauliflower. **B~nmuster** nt floral design. **B~nstrauß** m bunch of flowers. **B~ntopf** m flowerpot; (Pflanze) [flowering] pot plant. **B~nzwiebel** f bulb

blumig a (fig) flowery

Bluse f -,-n blouse

Blut nt -[e]s blood. **b~arm** a anaemic. **b~bahn** f bloodstream. **b~befleckt** a bloodstained. **b~bild** nt blood count. **B~buche** f copper beech. **B~druck** m blood pressure. **b~dürstig** a bloodthirsty

Blüte f -,-n flower, bloom; (vom Baum) blossom; (B~zeit) flowering period; (Baum-) blossom

time; (fig) flowering; (Höhepunkt) peak, prime; (fam: Banknote) forged note, (fam) dud

Blut|egel m -s,- leech. **b~en** vi (haben) bleed

Blüten|blatt nt petal. **B~staub** m pollen

Blut|er m -s,- haemophiliac. **B~erguß** m bruise. **B~gefäß** nt blood-vessel. **B~gruppe** f blood group. **B~hund** m bloodhound. **b~ig** a bloody. **b~jung** a very young. **B~körperchen** nt -s,- [blood] corpuscle. **B~probe** f blood test. **b~rünstig** a (fig) bloody, gory; ⟨Person⟩ bloodthirsty. **B~schande** f incest. **B~spender** m blood donor. **B~sturz** m haemorrhage. **B~s-verwandte(r)** m/f blood relation. **B~transfusion**, **B~-übertragung** f blood transfusion. **B~ung** f -,-en bleeding; (Med) haemorrhage; (Regel-) period. **b~unterlaufen** a bruised; ⟨Auge⟩ bloodshot. **B~vergießen** nt -s bloodshed. **B~vergiftung** f blood-poisoning. **B~wurst** f black pudding

Bö f -,-en gust; (Regen-) squall

Bock m -[e]s,ˆe buck; (Ziege) billy goat; (Schaf) ram; (Gestell) support; **einen B~ schießen** (fam) make a blunder. **b~en** vi (haben) ⟨Pferd:⟩ buck; ⟨Kind:⟩ be stubborn. **b~ig** a (fam) stubborn. **B~springen** nt leap-frog

Boden m -s,ˆ ground; (Erde) soil; (Fuß-) floor; (Grundfläche) bottom; (Dach-) loft, attic. **B~kammer** f attic [room]. **b~los** a bottomless; (fam) incredible. **B~satz** m sediment. **B~schätze** mpl mineral deposits. **B~see (der)** Lake Constance

Bogen m -s,- & ˆ curve; (Geom) arc; (beim Skilauf) turn; (Archit)

arch; (*Waffe, Geigen-*) bow; (*Papier*) sheet; **einen großen B~ um jdn/etw machen** (*fam*) give s.o./sth a wide berth. **B~ gang** *m* arcade. **B~ schießen** *nt* archery

Bohle *f* -,-n [thick] plank

Böhm|en *nt* -s Bohemia. **b~isch** *a* Bohemian

Bohne *f* -,-n bean; **grüne B~n** French beans. **B~nkaffee** *m* real coffee

bohner|n *vt* polish. **B~wachs** *nt* floor-polish

bohr|en *vt/i* (*haben*) drill (**nach** for); drive (*Tunnel*); sink (*Brunnen*); (*Insekt:*) bore; **in der Nase b~en** pick one's nose. **B~er** *m* -s,- drill. **B~insel** *f* [offshore] drilling rig. **B~maschine** *f* electric drill. **B~turm** *m* derrick

Boje *f* -,-n buoy

Böllerschuß *m* gun salute

Bolzen *m* -s,- bolt; (*Stift*) pin

bombardieren *vt* bomb; (*fig*) bombard (**mit** with)

bombastisch *a* bombastic

Bombe *f* -,-n bomb. **B~nangriff** *m* bombing raid. **B~nerfolg** *m* huge success. **B~r** *m* -s,- (*Aviat*) bomber

Bon /bɔŋ/ *m* -s,-s voucher; (*Kassen-*) receipt

Bonbon /bɔŋˈbɔŋ/ *m* & *nt* -s,-s sweet

Bonus *m* -[sses],-[sse] bonus

Boot *nt* -[e]s,-e boat. **B~ssteg** *m* landing-stage

Bord¹ *nt* -[e]s,-e shelf

Bord² *m* (*Naut*) **an B~** aboard, on board; **über B~** overboard. **B~buch** *nt* log[-book]

Bordell *nt* -s,-e brothel

Bord|karte *f* boarding-pass. **B~stein** *m* kerb

borgen *vt* borrow; **jdm etw b~** lend s.o. sth

Borke *f* -,-n bark

borniert *a* narrow-minded

Börse *f* -,-n purse; (*Comm*) stock exchange. **B~nmakler** *m* stockbroker

Borste *f* -,-n bristle. **b~ig** *a* bristly

Borte *f* -,-n braid

bösartig *a* vicious; (*Med*) malignant

Böschung *f* -,-en embankment; (*Hang*) slope

böse *a* wicked, evil; (*unartig*) naughty; (*schlimm*) bad, *adv* -ly; (*zornig*) cross; **jdm** *od* **auf jdn b~ sein** be cross with s.o. **B~wicht** *m* -[e]s,-e villain; (*Schlingel*) rascal

bos|haft *a* malicious, *adv* -ly; (*gehässig*) spiteful, *adv* -ly. **B~heit** *f* -,-en malice; spite; (*Handlung*) spiteful act/(*Bemerkung*) remark

böswillig *a* malicious, *adv* -ly. **B~keit** *f* - malice

Botanik *f* - botany. **B~ker(in)** *m* -s,- (*f* -,-nen) botanist. **b~sch** *a* botanical

Bot|e *m* -n,-n messenger. **B~engang** *m* errand. **B~schaft** *f* -,-en message; (*Pol*) embassy. **B~schafter** *m* -s,- ambassador

Bottich *m* -[e]s,-e vat; (*Wasch-*) tub

Bouillon /bulˈjɔŋ/ *f* -,-s clear soup. **B~würfel** *m* stock cube

Bowle /ˈboːlə/ *f* -,-n punch

box|en *vi* (*haben*) box □ *vt* punch. **B~en** *nt* -s boxing. **B~er** *m* -s,- boxer. **B~kampf** *m* boxing match; (*Boxen*) boxing

Boykott *m* -[e]s,-s boycott. **b~ieren** *vt* boycott; (*Comm*) black

brachliegen† *vi sep* (*haben*) lie fallow

Branche /ˈbrãːʃə/ *f* -,-n [line of] business. **B~nverzeichnis** *nt* (*Teleph*) classified directory

Brand *m* -[e]s,¨e fire; (*Med*) gangrene; (*Bot*) blight; **in B~ geraten** catch fire; **in B~ setzen** *od*

stecken set on fire. **B~bombe** f incendiary bomb

branden vi (haben) surge; (sich brechen) break

Brand|geruch m smell of burning. **b~marken** vt (fig) brand. **B~stifter** m arsonist. **B~stiftung** f arson

Brandung f surf. **B~sreiten** nt surfing

Brand|wunde f burn. **B~zeichen** nt brand

Branntwein m spirit; (coll) spirits pl. **B~brennerei** f distillery

bras|ilianisch a Brazilian. **B~i-lien** /-jən/ nt -s Brazil

Brat|apfel m baked apple. **b~en†** vt/i (haben) roast; (in der Pfanne) fry. **B~en** m -s, roast; (B~stück) joint. **B~ensoße** f gravy. **B~fertig** a oven-ready. **B~hähnchen, B~huhn** nt roast/(zum Braten) roasting chicken. **B~kartoffeln** fpl fried potatoes. **B~klops** m rissole. **B~pfanne** f frying-pan

Bratsche f -,-n (Mus) viola

Brat|spieß m spit. **B~wurst** f sausage for frying; (gebraten) fried sausage

Brauch m -[e]s,¨e custom. **b~bar** a usable; (nützlich) useful. **b~en** vt need; (ge-, verbrauchen) use; take ⟨Zeit⟩; er b~t es nur zu sagen he has only to say; du b~st nicht zu gehen you needn't go

Braue f -,-n eyebrow

brau|en vt brew. **B~er** m -s, brewer. **B~erei** f -,-en brewery

braun a, **B~** nt -s, brown; b~ werden (Person:) get a tan

Bräune f - [sun-]tan. **b~n** vt/i (haben) brown; (in der Sonne) tan

braungebrannt a [sun-]tanned

Braunschweig nt -s Brunswick

Brause f -,-n (Dusche) shower; (an Gießkanne) rose; (B~limonade) fizzy drink. **b~n** vi (haben) roar;

(duschen) shower □vi (sein) rush [along] □vr sich b~n shower. **b~nd** a roaring; (sprudelnd) effervescent

Braut f -,¨e bride; (Verlobte) fiancée

Bräutigam m -s,-e bridegroom; (Verlobter) fiancé

Brautkleid nt wedding dress

bräutlich a bridal

Brautpaar nt bridal couple; (Verlobte) engaged couple

brav a good, well-behaved; (redlich) honest □adv dutifully; (redlich) honestly

bravo int bravo!

BRD abbr (Bundesrepublik Deutschland) FRG

Brech|eisen nt jemmy; (B~stange) crowbar. **b~en†** vt break; (Phys) refract ⟨Licht⟩; (erbrechen) vomit; **sich b~en** (Wellen:) break; ⟨Licht:⟩ be refracted; **sich** (dat) **den Arm b~en** break one's arm □vi (sein) break □vi (haben) vomit, be sick; **mit jdm b~en** (fig) break with s.o. **B~er** m -s,- breaker. **B~reiz** m nausea. **B~stange** f crowbar

Brei m -[e]s,-e paste; (Culin) purée; (Grieß-) pudding; (Hafer-) porridge. **b~ig** a mushy

breit a wide; (Schultern, Grinsen) broad □adv b~ grinsen grin broadly. **b~beinig** a & adv with legs apart. **B~e** f -,-n width; breadth; (Geog) latitude. **b~en** vt spread ⟨über+acc over⟩. **B~en-grad** m [degree of] latitude. **B~enkreis** m parallel. **B~seite** f long side; (Naut) broadside

Bremse¹ f -,-n horsefly

Bremse² f -,-n brake. **b~n** vt slow down; (fig) restrain □vi (haben) brake

Bremslicht nt brake-light

brenn|bar a combustible; **leicht b~bar** highly [in]flammable.

b~en† *vi* (*haben*) burn; ⟨*Licht:*⟩ be on; ⟨*Zigarette:*⟩ be alight; (*weh tun*) smart, sting; **es b~t in X** there's a fire in X; **darauf b~en, etw zu tun be dying to do sth** □ *vt* burn; (*rösten*) roast; (*im Brennofen*) fire; (*destillieren*) distil. **b~end** *a* burning; (*angezündet*) lighted; (*fig*) fervent □ *adv* ich würde b~end gern ... I'd love to ... **B~erei** *f* -,-en distillery

Brennnessel *f* -,-n stinging nettle **Brenn|holz** *nt* firewood. **B~ofen** *m* kiln. **B~punkt** *m* (*Phys*) focus; **im B~punkt des Interesses stehen be the focus of attention. B~spiritus** *m* methylated spirits. **B~stoff** *m* fuel

brenzlig *a* (*fam*) risky; **b~er Geruch** smell of burning

Bresche *f* -,-n breach

Bretagne /bre'tanjə/ (**die**) - Brittany

Brett *nt* -[e]s,-er board; (*im Regal*) shelf; **schwarzes B~** notice board. **B~chen** *nt* -s,- slat; (*Frühstücks-*) small board (*used as plate*). **B~spiel** *nt* board game

Brezel *f* -,-n pretzel

Bridge /brɪtʃ/ *nt* - (*Spiel*) bridge

Brief *m* -[e]s,-e letter. **B~beschwerer** *m* -s,- paperweight. **B~block** *m* writing pad. **B~freund(in)** *m(f)* pen-friend. **B~kasten** *m* letter-box, (*Amer*) mailbox. **B~kopf** *m* letter-head. **b~lich** *a & adv* by letter. **B~marke** *f* [postage] stamp. **B~öffner** *m* paper-knife. **B~papier** *nt* notepaper. **B~porto** *nt* letter rate. **B~tasche** *f* wallet. **B~träger** *m* postman, (*Amer*) mailman. **B~umschlag** *m* envelope. **B~wahl** *f* postal vote. **B~wechsel** *m* correspondence

Brigade *f* -,-n brigade

Brikett *nt* -s,-s briquette

brillan|t /brɪl'jant/ *a* brilliant, *adv* -ly. **B~t** *m* -en,-en [cut] diamond. **B~z** *f* - brilliance

Brille *f* -,-n glasses *pl*, spectacles *pl*; (*Schutz-*) goggles *pl*; (*Klosett-*) toilet seat

bringen† *vt* bring; (*fort-*) take; (*ein-*) yield; (*veröffentlichen*) publish; (*im Radio*) broadcast; show ⟨*Film*⟩; **ins Bett b~** put to bed; **jdn nach Hause b~** take/(*begleiten*) see s.o. home; **an sich** (*acc*) **b~** get possession of; **mit sich b~** entail; **um etw b~** deprive of; **etw hinter sich** (*acc*) **b~** get sth over [and done] with; **jdn dazu b~, etw zu tun** get s.o. to do sth; **es weit b~** (*fig*) go far

brisant *a* explosive

Brise *f* -,-n breeze

Brit|e *m* -n,-n, **B~in** *f* -,-nen Briton. **b~isch** *a* British

Bröck|chen *nt* -s,- (*Culin*) crouton. **b~elig** *a* crumbly; ⟨*Gestein*⟩ friable. **b~eln** *vt/i* (*haben/sein*) crumble

Brocken *m* -s,- chunk; (*Erde, Kohle*) lump; **ein paar B~ Englisch** (*fam*) a smattering of English

Brokat *m* -[e]s,-e brocade

Brokkoli *pl* broccoli *sg*

Brombeer|e *f* blackberry. **B~strauch** *m* bramble [bush]

Bronchitis *f* - bronchitis

Bronze /'brõːsə/ *f* -,-n bronze

Brosch|e *f* -,-n brooch. **b~iert** *a* paperback. **B~üre** *f* -,-n brochure; (*Heft*) booklet

Brösel *mpl* (*Culin*) breadcrumbs

Brot *nt* -[e]s,-e bread; **ein B~** a loaf [of bread]; (*Scheibe*) a slice of bread; **sein B~ verdienen** (*fig*) earn one's living (**mit** by)

Brötchen *n* -s,- [bread] roll

Brot|krümel *m* breadcrumb. **B~verdiener** *m* breadwinner

Bruch *m* -[e]s,¨-e break; (*Brechen*) breaking; (*Rohr-*) burst; (*Med*)

fracture; (*Eingeweide-*) rupture, hernia; (*Math*) fraction; (*fig*) breach; (*in Beziehung*) break-up

brüchig *a* brittle

Bruch|landung *f* crash-landing. **B~rechnung** *f* fractions *pl.* **B~stück** *nt* fragment. **b~stückhaft** *a* fragmentary. **B~teil** *m* fraction

Brücke *f* -,-n bridge; (*Teppich*) rug

Bruder *m* -s, ̈ brother

brüderlich *a* brotherly, fraternal

Brügge *nt* -s Bruges

Brühe *f* -,-n broth; (*Knochen-*) stock; **klare B~** clear soup. **b~en** *vt* scald; (*auf-*) make ⟨*Kaffee*⟩. **B~würfel** *m* stock cube

brüllen *vt/i* (*haben*) roar; ⟨*Kuh:*⟩ moo; (*fam: schreien*) bawl

brumm|eln *vt/i* (*haben*) mumble. **b~en** *vi* (*haben*) ⟨*Insekt:*⟩ buzz; ⟨*Bär:*⟩ growl; ⟨*Motor:*⟩ hum; (*murren*) grumble □*vt* mutter. **B~er** *m* -s,- (*fam*) bluebottle. **b~ig** *a* (*fam*) grumpy, *adv* -ily

brünett *a* dark-haired. **B~e** *f* -,-n brunette

Brunnen *m* -s,- well; (*Spring-*) fountain; (*Heil-*) spa water. **B~kresse** *f* watercress

brüsk *a* brusque, *adv* -ly. **b~ieren** *vt* snub

Brüssel *nt* -s Brussels

Brust *f* -,̈e chest; (*weibliche, Culin: B~stück*) breast. **B~bein** *nt* breastbone. **B~beutel** *m* purse worn round the neck

brüsten (sich) *vr* boast

Brust|fellentzündung *f* pleurisy. **B~schwimmen** *nt* breaststroke

Brüstung *f* -,-en parapet

Brustwarze *f* nipple

Brut *f* -,-en incubation; (*Junge*) brood; (*Fisch-*) fry

brutal *a* brutal, *adv* -ly. **B~ität** *f* -,-en brutality

brüten *vi* (*haben*) sit (*on* eggs); (*fig*) ponder (*über* + *dat* over); **b~de Hitze** oppressive heat

Brutkasten *m* (*Med*) incubator

brutto *adv*, **B~** - *pref* gross

brutzeln *vi* (*haben*) sizzle □*vt* fry

Bub *m* -en,-en (*SGer*) boy. **B~e** *m* -n,-n. (*Karte*) jack, knave

Bubikopf *m* bob

Buch *nt* -[e]s,̈er book; **B~ führen** keep a record (*über* + *acc* of); **die B~er führen** keep the accounts. **B~drucker** *m* printer

Buche *f* -,-n beech

buchen *vt* book; (*Comm*) enter

Bücher|bord, B~brett *nt* bookshelf. **B~ei** *f* -,-en library. **B~regal** *nt* bookcase, bookshelves *pl.* **B~schrank** *m* bookcase. **B~wurm** *m* bookworm

Buchfink *m* chaffinch

Buch|führung *f* bookkeeping. **B~halter(in)** *m* -s,- (*f* -,-nen) bookkeeper, accountant. **B~haltung** *f* bookkeeping, accountancy; (*Abteilung*) accounts department. **B~händler(in)** *m(f)* bookseller. **B~handlung** *f* bookshop. **B~macher** *m* -s,- bookmaker. **B~prüfer** *m* auditor

Büchse *f* -,-n box; (*Konserven-*) tin, can; (*Gewehr*) [sporting] gun. **B~nmilch** *f* evaporated milk. **B~nöffner** *m* tin *or* can opener

Buch|stabe *m* -n,-n letter. **b~stabieren** *vt* spell [out]. **b~stäblich** *adv* literally

Buchstützen *fpl* book-ends

Bucht *f* -,-en (*Geog*) bay

Buchung *f* -,-en booking, reservation; (*Comm*) entry

Buckel *m* -s,- hump; (*Beule*) bump; (*Hügel*) hillock; **einen B~ machen** ⟨*Katze:*⟩ arch its back

bücken (sich) *vr* bend down

bucklig *a* hunchbacked. **B~e(r)** *m/f* hunchback

Bückling *m* -s,-e smoked herring; (*fam: Verbeugung*) bow

buddeln vt/i (haben) (fam) dig

Buddhis|mus m - Buddhism. **B~t(in)** m -en,-en (f -,-nen) Buddhist. **b~tisch** a Buddhist

Bude f -,-n hut; (Kiosk) kiosk; (Markt-) stall; (fam: Zimmer) room; (Studenten-) digs pl

Budget /by'dʒe:/ nt -s,-s budget

Büfett nt -[e]s,-e sideboard; (Theke) bar; **kaltes B~** cold buffet

Büffel m -s, buffalo. **b~n** vt/i (haben) (fam) swot

Bug m -[e]s,-e (Naut) bow[s pl]

Bügel m -s,- frame; (Kleider-) coathanger; (Steig-) stirrup; (Brillen-) sidepiece. **B~brett** nt ironing-board. **B~eisen** nt iron. **B~falte** f crease. **b~frei** a non-iron. **b~n** vt/i (haben) iron

bugsieren vt (fam) manœuvre

buhen vi (haben) boo

Buhne f -,-n breakwater

Bühne f -,-n stage. **B~nbild** nt set. **B~neingang** m stage door

Buhrufe mpl boos

Bukett nt -[e]s,-e bouquet

Bulette f -,-n (meat) rissole

Bulgarien /-jən/ nt -s Bulgaria

Bull|auge nt (Naut) porthole. **B~dogge** f bulldog. **B~dozer** /-do:ze/ m -s,- bulldozer. **B~e** m -n,-n bull; (sl: Polizist) cop

Bummel|l m -s,- (fam) stroll. **B~lant** m -en,-en (fam) dawdler; (Faulenzer) loafer. **B~lei** f -,-en (fam) dawdling; (Nach-lässigkeit) carelessness

bummel|ig a (fam) slow; (nach-lässig) careless. **b~n** vi (sein) (fam) stroll □vi (haben) (fam) dawdle. **B~streik** m go-slow. **B~zug** m (fam) slow train

Bums m -es,-e (fam) bump, thump

Bund¹ nt -[e]s,-e bunch; (Stroh-) bundle

Bund² m -[e]s,-e association; (Bündnis) alliance; (Pol) federation; (Rock-, Hosen-) waistband; **im B~e sein** be in league (mit with); **der B~** the Federal Government; (fam: Bundeswehr) the [German] Army

Bündel nt -s,- bundle. **b~n** vt bundle [up]

Bundes|- pref Federal. **B~genosse** m ally. **B~kanzler** m Federal Chancellor. **B~land** nt [federal] state; (Aust) province. **B~liga** f German national league. **B~rat** m Upper House of Parliament. **B~regierung** f Federal Government. **B~republik** f **die B~republik Deutschland** the Federal Republic of Germany. **B~straße** f ≈ A road. **B~tag** m Lower House of Parliament. **B~wehr** f [Federal German] Army

bünd|ig a & adv **kurz und b~ig** short and to the point. **B~nis** nt -sses,-sse alliance

Bunker m -s,- bunker; (Luft-schutz-) shelter

bunt a coloured; (farbenfroh) colourful; (grell) gaudy; (gemischt) varied; (wirr) confused; **b~er Abend** social evening; **b~e Platte** assorted cold meats □ adv **b~ durcheinander** higgledy-piggledy; **es zu b~ treiben** (fam) go too far. **B~stift** m crayon

Bürde f -,-n (fig) burden

Burg f -,-en castle

Bürge m -n,-n guarantor. **b~n** vi (haben) **b~n für** vouch for; (fig) guarantee

Bürger|(in) m -s,- (f -,-nen) citizen. **B~krieg** m civil war. **b~lich** a civil; (Pflicht) civic; (mittelständisch) middle-class; **b~liche Küche** plain cooking. **B~liche(r)** m/f commoner. **B~meister** m mayor.

B~rechte *npl* civil rights.
B~steig *m* -[e]s,-e pavement,
(*Amer*) sidewalk
Burggraben *m* moat
Bürgschaft *f* -,-en surety; B~
leisten stand surety
Burgunder *m* -s,- (*Wein*) Bur-
gundy
Burleske *f* -,-n burlesque
Büro *nt* -s,-s office. B~ange-
stellte(r) *m/f* office-worker.
B~klammer *f* paper-clip.
B~krat *m* -en,-en bureaucrat.
B~kratie *f* -,-n bureaucracy.
b~kratisch *a* bureaucratic
Bursch|e *m* -n,-n lad, youth;
(*fam: Kerl*) fellow. b~ikos *a*
hearty; (*männlich*) mannish
Bürste *f* -,-n brush. b~n *vt* brush.
B~nschnitt *m* crew cut
Bus *m* -ses, -se bus; (*Reise-*) coach.
B~bahnhof *m* bus and coach
station
Busch *m* -[e]s,-e bush
Büschel *nt* -s,- tuft
buschig *a* bushy
Busen *m* -s,- bosom
Bussard *m* -s,-e buzzard
Buße *f* -,-n penance; (*Jur*) fine
büßen *vt/i* (*haben*) (*für*) etw a~
atone for sth; (*fig: bezahlen*) pay
for sth
bußfertig *a* penitent. B~geld *nt*
(*Jur*) fine
Büste *f* -,-n bust; (*Schneider-*)
dummy. B~nhalter *m* -s,- bra
Butter *f* - butter. B~blume *f*
buttercup. B~brot *nt* slice of
bread and butter. B~brotpa-
pier *nt* grease-proof paper.
B~faß *nt* churn. B~milch *f*
buttermilk. b~n *vi* (*haben*) make
butter □ *vt* butter
b.w. *abbr* (*bitte wenden*) P.T.O.
bzgl. *abbr* s. bezüglich
bzw. *abbr* s. beziehungsweise

C

ca. *abbr* (*circa*) about
Café /ka'fe:/ *nt* -s,-s café
Cafeteria /kafete'ri:a/ *f* -,-s cafe-
teria
campen /'kɛmpən/ *vi* (*haben*) go
camping. C~ing *nt* -s camping.
C~ingplatz *m* campsite
Cape /ke:p/ *nt* -s,-s cape
Caravan /'ka[:]ravan/ *m* -s,-s
(*Auto*) caravan; (*Kombi*) estate
car
Cassette /ka'sɛtə/ *f* -,-n cassette.
C~nrecorder /-rɛkɔrdɐ/ *m* -s,-
cassette recorder
CD /tse:'de:/ *f* -,-s compact disc, CD
Cell|ist(in) /tʃɛ'lɪst(ɪn)/ *m* -en,-en
(*f* -,-nen) cellist. C~o /'tʃɛlo/ *nt*
-,-los & -li cello
Celsius /'tsɛlzjus/ *inv* Celsius,
centigrade
Cembalo /'tʃɛmbalo/ *nt* -s,-los &
-li harpsichord
Champagner /ʃam'panjɐ/ *m* -s
champagne
Champignon /'ʃampɪnjɔŋ/ *m*
-s,-s [field] mushroom
Chance /'ʃã:s[ə]/ *f* -,-n chance
Chaos /'ka:ɔs/ *nt* - chaos
chaotisch /ka'o:tɪʃ/ *a* chaotic
Charakter /ka'rakte/ *m* -s,-e
/-'te:rə/ character. c~isieren *vt*
characterize. c~istisch *a* characteristic (*für* d), *adv* -ally
Charisma /ka'rɪsma/ *nt* -s charisma. c~atisch *a* charismatic
charm|ant /ʃar'mant/ *a* charm-
ing, *adv* -ly. C~e /ʃarm/ *m* -s
charm
Charter|flug /'tʃ-, 'ʃartə-/ *m*
charter flight. c~n *vt* charter
Chassis /ʃa'si:/ *nt* -,- /-'si:[s], -'si:s/
chassis
Chauffeur /ʃo'fø:ɐ/ *m* -s,-e chauffeur; (*Taxi-*) driver

Chauvinis|mus /ʃovi'nɪsmʊs/ m -
  chauvinism. **C~t** m -en,-en
  chauvinist

Chef /ʃɛf/ m -s,-s head; (fam) boss

Chem|ie /çe'mi:/ f - chemistry.
  C~ikalien /-jən/ fpl chemicals

Chem|iker(in) /'çe:-/ m -s,- (f
  -,-nen) chemist. **c~isch** a chemical, adv -ly; **c~ische Reinigung**
  dry-cleaning; (Geschäft) dry-
  cleaner's

Chicorée /'ʃikore:/ m -s chicory

Chiffr|e /'ʃifə, 'ʃifrə/ f -,-n cipher;
  (bei Annonce) box number.
  c~iert a coded

Chile /'çi:le/ nt -s Chile

China /'çi:na/ nt -s China. **C~ese**
  m -n,-n, **C~esin** f -,-nen Chinese. **c~esisch** a Chinese. **C~e-
  sisch** nt -[s] (Lang) Chinese

Chip /tʃɪp/ m -s,-s [micro]chip.
  C~s pl crisps, (Amer) chips

Chirurg /çi'rʊrk/ m -en,-en surgeon. **C~ie** /-'gi:/ f - surgery.
  c~isch /-g-/ a surgical, adv -ly

Chlor /klo:ɐ̯/ nt -s chlorine. **C~o-
  form** /kloro'form/ nt -s chloroform

Choke /tʃo:k/ m -s,-s (Auto) choke

Cholera /'ko:lera/ f - cholera

cholerisch /ko'le:rɪʃ/ a irascible

Cholesterin /ço-, koleste'ri:n/ nt
  -s cholesterol

Chor /ko:ɐ̯/ m -[e]s,Ꞌe choir;
  (Theat) chorus; **im C~** in chorus

Choral /ko'ra:l/ m -[e]s,Ꞌe chorale

Choreographie /koreogra'fi:/ f
  -,-n choreography

Chor|knabe /'ko:ɐ̯-/ m choirboy.
  C~musik f choral music

Christ /krɪst/ m -en,-en Christian.
  C~baum m Christmas tree.
  C~entum nt -s Christianity.
  C~in f -,-nen Christian.
  C~kind nt Christ-child; (als
  Geschenkbringer) ≈ Father
  Christmas. **c~lich** a Christian

Christus /'krɪstʊs/ m -ti Christ

Chrom /kro:m/ nt -s chromium

Chromosom /kromo'zo:m/ nt
  -s,-en chromosome

Chronik /'kro:nɪk/ f -,-en chronicle

chron|isch /'kro:nɪʃ/ a chronic,
  adv -ally. **c~ologisch** a chronological, adv -ly

Chrysantheme /kryzan'te:mə/ f
  -,-n chrysanthemum

circa /'tsɪrka/ adv about

Clique /'klɪkə/ f -,-n clique

Clou /klu:/ m -s,-s highlight, (fam)
  high spot

Clown /klaʊn/ m -s,-s clown.
  c~en vi (haben) clown

Club /klʊp/ m -s,-s club

Cocktail /'kɔkte:l/ m -s,-s cocktail

Code /ko:t/ m -s,-s code

Cola /'ko:la/ f -,- (fam) Coke (P)

Comic-Heft /'kɔmɪk-/ nt comic

Computer /kɔm'pju:tɐ/ m -s,-
  computer. **c~isieren** vt compu-
  terize

Conférencier /kõferã'sje:/ m -s,-s
  compère

Cord /kɔrt/ m -s, **C~samt** m corduroy. **C~[samt]hose** f cords pl

Couch /kaʊtʃ/ f -,-es settee.
  C~tisch m coffee-table

Coupon /ku'põ/ m -s,-s = **Kupon**

Cousin /ku'zɛ̃/ m -s,-s [male]
  cousin. **C~e** /-'zi:nə/ f -,-n [fe-
  male] cousin

Crem|e /kre:m/ f -s,-s cream;
  (Speise) cream dessert. **c~efar-
  ben** a cream. **c~ig** a creamy

Curry /'kari, 'kœri/ nt & m -s
  curry powder □nt -s,-s (Gericht)
  curry

D

da adv there; (hier) here; (zeitlich)
  then; (in dem Fall) in that case;
  von da an from then on □conj as,
  since

dabehalten† vt sep keep there

dabei (emphatic: **dabei**) adv
nearby; (daran) with it;
(eingeschlossen) included; (hinsichtlich) about it; (währenddem)
during this; (gleichzeitig) at the
same time; (doch) and yet; **d~**
close by; **d~ bleiben** vi (fig)
remain adamant; **was ist denn
d~?** (fam) so what? **d~sein†** vi
sep (sein) be present; (mitmachen) be involved; **d~sein, etw
zu tun** be just doing sth

dableiben† vi sep (sein) stay
there

Dach nt -[e]s,ˉer roof. **D~boden**
m loft. **D~gepäckträger** m
roof-rack. **D~kammer** f attic
room. **D~luke** f skylight.
D~rinne f gutter

Dachs m -es,-e badger

Dach|sparren m -s,- rafter.
D~ziegel m [roofing] tile

Dackel m -s,- dachshund

dadurch (emphatic: **dadurch**)
adv through it/them; (Ursache)
by it; (deshalb) because of that;
d~, daß because

dafür (emphatic: **dafür**) adv for
it/them; (anstatt) instead; (als
Ausgleich) but [on the other
hand]; **d~, daß** considering that.
d~können† vt sep (haben) **ich
kann nichts dafür** it's not my
fault

dagegen (emphatic: **dagegen**)
adv against it/them; (Mittel,
Tausch) for it; (verglichen damit)
by comparison; (jedoch) however; **hast du was d~?** do you
mind? **d~halten†** vt sep argue
(daß that)

daheim adv at home

daher (emphatic: **daher**) adv
from there; (deshalb) for that reason; **das kommt d~, weil** that's
because; **d~ meine Eile** hence
my hurry □conj that is why

dahin (emphatic: **dahin**) adv
there; **bis d~** up to there; (bis

dann) until/(Zukunft) by then;
jdn d~ bringen, daß er etw tut
get s.o. to do sth; **d~ sein** (fam)
be gone. **d~gehen†** vi sep (sein)
walk along; ⟨Zeit:⟩ pass. **d~ge-
stellt** a **d~gestellt lassen** (fig)
leave open; **das bleibt d~ge-
stellt** that remains to be seen

dahinten adv back there

dahinter (emphatic: **dahinter**)
adv behind it/them. **d~kom-
men†** vi sep (sein) (fig) get to the
bottom of it

Dahlie /-jə/ f -,-n dahlia

dalassen† vt sep leave there

daliegen† vi sep (haben) lie there

damalig a at that time; **der d~e
Minister** the then minister

damals adv at that time

Damast m -es,-e damask

Dame f -,-n lady; (Karte, Schach)
queen; (Spiel) draughts sg,
(Amer) checkers sg; (Doppel-
stein) king. **D~n-** pref ladies'/
lady's . . . **d~nhaft** a ladylike

damit (emphatic: **damit**) adv with
it/them; (dadurch) by it; **hör auf
d~!** stop it! □conj so that

dämlich a (fam) stupid, adv -ly

Damm m -[e]s,ˉe dam; (Insel-)
causeway; **nicht auf dem D~**
(fam) under the weather

dämmerig a dim; **es wird d~ig**
dusk is falling. **D~licht** nt twilight. **d~n** vi (haben) ⟨Morgen:⟩
dawn; **der Abend d~t** dusk is
falling; **es d~t** it is getting
light/(abends) dark. **D~ung** f -
dawn; (Abend-) dusk

Dämon m -s,-en /-'mo:nən/ demon

Dampf m -es,ˉe steam; (Chem)
vapour. **D~en** vi (haben) steam

dämpfen vt (Culin) steam; (fig)
muffle ⟨Ton⟩; lower ⟨Stimme⟩;
dampen ⟨Enthusiasmus⟩

Dampf|er m -s,- steamer.
D~kochtopf m pressure-
cooker. **D~maschine** f steam
engine. **D~walze** f steamroller

Damwild nt fallow deer pl

danach (emphatic: **danach**) adv after it/them; ⟨suchen⟩ for it/them; ⟨riechen⟩ of it; (später) afterwards; ⟨entsprechend⟩ accordingly; **es sieht d~ aus** it looks like it

Däne m -n,-n Dane

daneben (emphatic: **daneben**) adv beside it/them; (außerdem) in addition; ⟨verglichen damit⟩ by comparison. **d~gehen†** vi sep (sein) miss; (scheitern) fail

Dän|emark nt -s Denmark. **D~in** f -,-nen Dane. **d~isch** a Danish

Dank m -es thanks pl; **vielen D~!** thank you very much! **d~** prep (+ dat or gen) thanks to. **d~bar** a grateful, adv -ly; (erleichtert) thankful, adv -ly; (lohnend) rewarding. **D~barkeit** f - gratitude. **d~e** adv **d~e** [schön od sehr]! thank you [very much]! [nein] **d~e!** no thank you! **d~en** vi (haben) thank (jdm s.o.); (ablehnen) decline; **ich d~e!** no thank you! **nichts zu d~en!** don't mention it!

dann adv then; **d~ und wann** now and then; **nur/selbst d~, wenn** only/even if

daran (emphatic: **daran**) adv on it/them; at it/them; ⟨denken⟩ of it; **nahe d~** on the point (etw zu tun of doing sth); **denkt d~!** remember! **d~gehen†** vi sep (sein), **d~machen (sich)** vr sep set about (etw zu tun doing sth). **d~setzen** vt sep **alles d~setzen** do one's utmost (zu to)

darauf (emphatic: **darauf**) adv on it/them; ⟨warten⟩ for it; ⟨antworten⟩ to it; (danach) after that; (d~hin) as a result; **am Tag d~** the day after. **d~folgend** a following. **d~hin** adv as a result

daraus (emphatic: **daraus**) adv out of or from it/them; **er macht** sich nichts d~ he doesn't care for it; **was ist d~ geworden?** what has become of it?

Darbietung f -,-en performance; (Nummer) item

darin (emphatic: **darin**) adv in it/them

darlegen vt sep expound; (erklären) explain

Darlehen nt -s,- loan

Darm m -[e]s,⸚e intestine; (Wurst-) skin. **D~grippe** f gastric flu

darstell|en vt sep represent; (bildlich) portray; (Theat) interpret; (spielen) play; (schildern) describe. **D~er** m -s,- actor. **D~erin** f -,-nen actress. **D~ung** f representation; interpretation; description; (Bericht) account

darüber (emphatic: **darüber**) adv over it/them; (höher) above it/them; ⟨sprechen, lachen, sich freuen⟩ about it; (mehr) more; (inzwischen) in the meantime; **d~hinaus** beyond [it]; (dazu) on top of that

darum (emphatic: **darum**) adv round it/them; ⟨bitten, kämpfen⟩ for it; (deshalb) that is why; **d~, weil** because

darunter (emphatic: **darunter**) adv under it/them; (tiefer) below it/them; (weniger) less; (dazwischen) among them

das def art & pron s. **der**

dasein† vi sep (sein) be there/ (hier) here; (existieren) exist; **wieder d~** be back; **noch nie dagewesen** unprecedented. **D~** nt -s existence

dasitzen† vi sep (haben) sit there

dasjenige pron s. **derjenige**

daß conj that; **daß du nicht fällst!** mind you don't fall!

dasselbe pron s. **derselbe**

dastehen† vi sep (haben) stand there; **allein d~** (fig) be alone

Daten|sichtgerät *nt* visual display unit, VDU. **D~verarbeitung** *f* data processing

datieren *vt/i* (*haben*) date

Dativ *m* **-s,-e** dative. **D~objekt** *nt* indirect object

Dattel *f* **-,-n** date

Datum *nt* **-s,-ten** date; **Daten** (*Angaben*) data

Dauer *f* - duration, length; (*Jur*) term; **von D~** lasting; **auf die D~** in the long run. **D~auftrag** *m* standing order. **d~haft** *a* lasting, enduring; (*fest*) durable. **D~karte** *f* season ticket. **D~lauf** *m* im **D~lauf** at a jog. **D~milch** *f* long-life milk. **d~n** *vi* (*haben*) last; **lange d~n** take a long time. **d~nd** *a* lasting; (*ständig*) constant, *adv* **-ly**; **d~nd fragen** keep asking. **D~stellung** *f* permanent position. **D~welle** *f* perm. **D~wurst** *f* salami-type sausage

Daumen *m* **-s,-** thumb; **jdm den D~ drücken** *od* **halten** keep one's fingers crossed for s.o.

Daunen *fpl* down *sg*. **D~decke** *f* [down-filled] duvet

davon (*emphatic:* **davon**) *adv* from it/them; (*dadurch*) by it; (*damit*) with it/them; (*darüber*) about it; (*Menge*) of it/them; **die Hälfte d~** half of it/them; **das kommt d~!** it serves you right! **d~kommen†** *vi sep* (*sein*) escape (**mit dem Leben** with one's life). **d~laufen†** *vi sep* (*sein*) run away. **d~machen (sich)** *vr sep* (*fam*) make off. **d~tragen†** *vt sep* (*gewinnen*) carry off; (*erleiden*) suffer; (*gewinnen*) win

davor (*emphatic:* **davor**) *adv* in front of it/them; (*sich fürchten*) of it; (*zeitlich*) before it/them

dazu (*emphatic:* **dazu**) *adv* to it/them; (*damit*) with it/them; (*dafür*) for it; **noch d~** in addition to that; **jdn d~ bringen, etw zu**

tun get s.o. to do sth; **ich kam nicht d~** I didn't get round to [doing] it. **d~gehören** *vi sep* (*haben*) belong to it/them; **alles, was d~gehört** everything that goes with it. **D~kommen†** *vi sep* (*sein*) arrive [on the scene]; (*hinzukommen*) be added; **d~kommt, daß er krank ist** on top of that he is ill. **D~rechnen** *vt sep* add to it/them

dazwischen (*emphatic:* **dazwischen**) *adv* between them; in between; (*darunter*) among them. **d~fahren†** *vi sep* (*sein*) (*fig*) intervene. **d~kommen†** *vi sep* (*sein*) (*fig*) crop up; **wenn nichts d~kommt** if all goes well. **d~reden** *vi sep* (*haben*) interrupt. **d~treten†** *vi sep* (*sein*) (*fig*) intervene

DDR *f* - *abbr* (**Deutsche Demokratische Republik**) GDR

Debatte *f* **-,-n** debate; **zur D~te stehen** be at issue. **d~tieren** *vt/i* (*haben*) debate

Debüt /de'by:/ *nt* **-s,-s** début

dechiffrieren /deʃɪ'fri:rən/ *vt* decipher

Deck *nt* **-[e]s,-s** (*Naut*) deck; **an D~** on deck. **D~bett** *nt* duvet

Decke *f* **-,-n** cover; (*Tisch-*) tablecloth; (*Bett-*) blanket; (*Reise-*) rug; (*Zimmer-*) ceiling; **unter einer D~ stecken** (*fam*) be in league

Deckel *m* **-s,-** lid; (*Flaschen-*) top; (*Buch-*) cover

decken *vt* cover; tile (*Dach*); lay (*Tisch*); (*schützen*) shield; (*Sport*) mark; meet (*Bedarf*); **jdn d~** (*fig*) cover up for s.o.; **sich d~** (*fig*) cover oneself (**gegen** against); (*übereinstimmen*) coincide

Deck|mantel *m* (*fig*) pretence. **D~name** *m* pseudonym

Deckung f - (Mil) cover; (Sport) defence; (Mann-) marking; (Boxen) guard; (Sicherheit) security; **in D~ gehen** take cover

Defekt m - [e]s,-e defect. **d~** a defective

defensiv a defensive. **D~e** f - defensive

defilieren vi (sein/haben) file past

definieren vt define. **D~ition** /-ˈtsi̯oːn/ f -,-en definition. **d~itiv** a definite, adv -ly

Defizit nt -s,-e deficit

Deflation /-ˈtsi̯oːn/ f -,-en deflation

deformiert a deformed

deftig a (fam) ⟨Mahlzeit⟩ hearty; ⟨Witz⟩ coarse

Degen m -s,- sword; (Fecht-) epée

degenerieren vi (sein) degenerate. **d~t** a (fig) degenerate

degradieren vt (Mil) demote; (fig) degrade

dehnbar a elastic. **d~en** vt stretch; lengthen ⟨Vokal⟩; **sich d~en** stretch

Deich m - [e]s,-e dike

Deichsel f -,-n pole; (Gabel-) shafts pl

dein poss pron your. **d~e(r,s)** poss pron yours; **die D~en** pl your family sg. **d~erseits** adv for your part. **d~etwegen** adv for your sake; (wegen dir) because of you, on your account. **d~etwillen** adv um **d~etwillen** for your sake. **d~ige** poss pron der/die/das **d~ige** yours. **d~s** poss pron yours

Deka nt -[s],- (Aust) = **Dekagramm**

dekadent a decadent. **D~z** f - decadence

Dekagramm nt (Aust) 10 grams; **10 D~** 100 grams

Dekan m -s,-e dean

Deklination /-ˈtsi̯oːn/ f -,-en declension. **d~ieren** vt decline

Dekolleté /dekɔlˈteː/ nt -s,-s low neckline

Dekor m & nt -s decoration. **D~ateur** /-ˈtøːɐ̯/ m -s,-e interior decorator; (Schaufenster-) window-dresser. **D~ation** /-ˈtsi̯oːn/ f -,-en decoration; (Schaufenster-) window-dressing; (Auslage) display; **D~ationen** (Theat) scenery sg. **d~ativ** a decorative. **d~ieren** vt decorate; dress ⟨Schaufenster⟩

Delegation /-ˈtsi̯oːn/ f -,-en delegation. **d~ieren** vt delegate. **D~ierte(r)** m/f delegate

delikat a delicate; (lecker) delicious; (taktvoll) tactful, adv -ly. **D~esse** f -,-n delicacy. **D~essengeschäft** nt delicatessen

Delikt nt - [e]s,-e offence

Delinquent m -en,-en offender

Delirium nt -s delirium

Delle f -,-n dent

Delphin m -s,-e dolphin

Delta nt -s,-s delta

dem def art & pron s. der

Dementi nt -s,-s denial. **d~eren** vt deny

dementsprechend a corresponding; (passend) appropriate □adv accordingly; (passend) appropriately. **d~gemäß** adv accordingly. **d~nach** adv according to that; (folglich) consequently. **d~nächst** adv soon; (in Kürze) shortly

Demokrat m -en,-en democrat. **D~ie** f -,-n democracy. **d~isch** a democratic, adv -ally

demolieren vt wreck

Demonstrant m -en,-en demonstrator. **D~ation** /-ˈtsi̯oːn/ f -,-en demonstration. **d~ativ** a pointed, adv -ly; (Gram) demonstrative. **D~ativpronomen** nt demonstrative pronoun. **d~ieren** vt/i (haben) demonstrate

demontieren vt dismantle

demoralisieren vt demoralize

Demoskopie f - opinion research

Demut *f* - humility

demütig *a* humble, *adv* -bly.
d~en *vt* humiliate; **sich d~en**
humble oneself. **D~ung** *f* -,-en
humiliation

demzufolge *adv* = demnach

den *def art & pron s.* der. **d~en**
pron s. der

denk|bar *a* conceivable. **d~en†**
vt/i (haben) think (an + *acc* of);
(*sich erinnern*) remember (an
etw *acc* sth); **für jdn gedacht**
meant for s.o.; **das kann ich mir**
d~en I can imagine [that]; **ich**
d~e nicht daran I have no intention of doing it; **d~t daran!** don't
forget! **D~mal** *nt* monument.
d~-
würdig *a* memorable. **D~zettel**
m jdm einen **D~zettel geben**
(*fam*) teach s.o. a lesson

denn *conj* for; besser/mehr **d~**
je better/more than ever □*adv*
wie/wo **d~?** but how/where?
warum **d~ nicht?** why ever not?
es sei **d~ [, daß]** unless

dennoch *adv* nevertheless

Denunzi|ant *m* -en,-en informer.
d~ieren *vt* denounce

Deodorant *nt* -s,-s deodorant

deplaciert /-'tsi:ɐt/ *a* (*fig*) out of
place

Deponie *f* -,-n dump. **d~ren** *vt*
deposit

deportieren *vt* deport

Depot /de'po:/ *nt* -s,-s depot;
(*Lager*) warehouse; (*Bank-*) safe
deposit

Depression *f* -,-en depression

deprimieren *vt* depress. **d~d** *a*
depressing

Deputation /-'tsio:n/ *f* -,-en deputation

der, die, das, *pl* **die** *def art* (*acc*
den, die, das, *pl* die; *gen* des,
der, des, *pl* der; *dat* dem, der,
dem, *pl* den) the; **der Mensch**
man; **die Natur** nature; **das Le-**
ben life; **das Lesen/Tanzen**

reading/dancing; **sich** (*dat*) **das**
Gesicht/die Hände waschen
wash one's face/hands; **5 Mark**
das Pfund 5 marks a pound
□*pron* (*acc* den, die, das, *pl* die;
gen dessen, deren, dessen, *pl*
deren; *dat* dem, der, dem, *pl*
denen) □*dem pron* that; (*pl*)
those; (*substantivisch*) he, she, it;
(*Ding*) it; (*betont*) that; (*d~jenige*)
the one; (*pl*) they, those; (*Dinge*)
those; (*diejenigen*) the ones; **der**
und der such and such; **um die**
und die Zeit at such and such a
time; **das waren Zeiten!** those
were the days! □*rel pron* who;
(*Ding*) which, that

derart *adv* so; (*so sehr*) so much.
d~ig *a* such □*adv* = **derart**

derb *a* tough; (*kräftig*) strong;
(*grob*) coarse, *adv* -ly; (*unsanft*)
rough, *adv* -ly

deren *pron s.* der

dergleichen *inv a* such □*pron*
such a thing/such things; **nichts**
d~ nothing of the kind; **und die**
und die like

der-/die-/dasjenige, *pl* **diejeni-**
gen *pron* the one; (*Person*) he,
she; (*Ding*) it; (*pl*) those, the ones

dermaßen *adv* = **derart**

der-/die-/dasselbe, *pl* **diesel-**
ben *pron* the same; **ein- und**
dasselbe one and the same thing

derzeit *adv* at present

des *def art s.* der

Desert|eur /-'tø:ɐ/ *m* -s,-e de-
serter. **d~ieren** *vi* (*sein/haben*)
desert

desgleichen *adv* likewise □*pron*
the like

deshalb *adv* for this reason; (*also*)
therefore

Designer(in) /di'zaɪnɐ, -nərɪn/ *m*
-s,- (*f* -,-nen) designer

Desin|fektion /dɛs'ʔɪnfɛktsio:n/ *f* -
disinfecting. **D~fektionsmit-**
tel *nt* disinfectant. **d~fizieren**
vt disinfect

Desodorant nt -s,-s deodorant

Despot m -en,-en despot

dessen pron s. der

Dessert /dɛˈseːɐ̯/ nt -s,-s dessert, sweet. **D~löffel** m dessertspoon

Destill|ation /-ˈtsjoːn/ f - distillation. **d~ieren** vt distil

desto adv je mehr/eher, d~ besser the more/sooner the better

destruktiv a (fig) destructive

deswegen adv = deshalb

Detail /deˈtaj/ nt -s,-s detail

Detektiv m -s,-e detective. **D~roman** m detective story

Deton|ation /-ˈtsjoːn/ f -,-en explosion. **d~ieren** vi (sein) explode

deut|en vt interpret; predict (Zukunft) □vi (haben) point (auf + acc at/(fig) to). **d~lich** a clear, adv -ly; (eindeutig) plain, adv -ly. **D~lichkeit** f - clarity

deutsch a German; auf d~ in German. **D~** nt -[s] (Lang) German. **D~e(r)** m/f German. **D~land** nt -s Germany

Deutung f -,-en interpretation

Devise f -,-n motto. **D~n** pl foreign currency or exchange sg

Dezember m -s,- December

dezent a unobtrusive, adv -ly; (diskret) discreet, adv -ly

Dezernat nt -[e]s,-e department

Dezimal|system nt decimal system. **D~zahl** f decimal

dezimieren vt decimate

dgl. abbr s. dergleichen

d.h. abbr (das heißt) i.e.

Dia nt -s,-s (Phot) slide

Diabet|es m - diabetes. **D~iker** m -s,- diabetic

Diadem nt -s,-e tiara

Diagnos|e f -,-n diagnosis. **d~tizieren** vt diagnose

diagonal a diagonal, adv -ly. **D~e** f -,-n diagonal

Diagramm nt -s,-e diagram; (Kurven-) graph

Diakon m -s,-e deacon

Dialekt m -[e]s,-e dialect

Dialog m -[e]s,-e dialogue

Diamant m -en,-en diamond

Diameter m -s,- diameter

Diapositiv nt -s,-e (Phot) slide

Diaprojektor m slide projector

Diät f-,-en (Med) diet. **d~** adv d~ leben be on a diet. **D~assistent(in)** m(f) dietician

dich pron (acc of du) you; (refl) yourself

dicht a dense; (dick) thick; (undurchlässig) airtight; (wasser-) watertight □adv densely; thickly; (nahe) close (bei to). **D~e** f - density. **d~en¹** vt make watertight; (ab-) seal

dicht|en² vi (haben) write poetry. □vt write, compose. **D~er(in)** m -s,- (f -,-nen) poet. **d~erisch** a poetic. **D~ung¹** f -,-en poetry; (Gedicht) poem

Dichtung² f -,-en seal; (Ring) washer; (Auto) gasket

dick a thick, adv -ly; (beleibt) fat; (geschwollen) swollen; (fam: eng) close; **d~ werden** get fat; **d~ machen** be fattening; **ein d~es Fell haben** (fam) be thick-skinned. **D~e** f -,-n thickness; (D~leibigkeit) fatness. **d~fellig** a (fam) thick-skinned. **d~flüssig** a thick; (Phys) viscous. **D~kopf** m (fam) stubborn person; **einen D~kopf haben** be stubborn. **d~köpfig** a (fam) stubborn

didaktisch a didactic

die def art & pron s. der

Dieb|(in) m -[e]s,-e (f -,-nen) thief. **d~isch** a thieving; (Freude) malicious. **D~stahl** m -[e]s,-e theft; (geistig) plagiarism

diejenige pron s. derjenige

Diele f -,-n floorboard; (Flur) hall

dien|en vi (haben) serve. **D~er** m -s,- servant; (Verbeugung) bow.

D~erin f -,-nen maid, servant.
d~lich a helpful

Dienst m -[e]s,-e service; (*Arbeit*) work; (*Amtsausübung*) duty; **außer D~** off duty; (*pensioniert*) retired; **D~** haben work; (*Soldat, Arzt:*) be on duty; **jdm einen schlechten D~ erweisen** do s.o. a disservice

Dienstag m Tuesday. **d~s** adv on Tuesdays

Dienst|alter nt seniority. **d~bereit** a obliging; (*Apotheke*) open. **D~bote** m servant. **d~eifrig** a zealous, adv -ly. **d~frei** a **d~freier Tag** day off; **d~frei haben** have time off; (*Soldat, Arzt:*) be off duty. **D~grad** m rank. **d~habend** a duty ... **D~leistung** f service. **d~lich** a official □adv d~lich verreist away on business. **D~mädchen** nt maid. **D~reise** f business trip. **D~stelle** f office. **D~stunden** fpl office hours. **D~weg** m official channels pl

dies inv pron this. **d~bezüglich** a relevant □adv regarding this matter. **d~e(r,s)** pron this; (*pl*) these; (*substantivisch*) this [one]; (*pl*) these; **d~e Nacht** tonight; (*letzte*) last night

Diesel m -[s],- (*fam*) diesel

dieselbe pron s. derselbe

Diesel|kraftstoff m diesel [oil]. **D~motor** m diesel engine

diesig a hazy, misty

dies|mal adv this time. **d~seits** adv & prep (+ gen) this side (of)

Dietrich m -s,-e skeleton key

Diffam|ation /-'tsi̯o:n/ f defamation. **d~ierend** a defamatory

Differential /-'tsi̯a:l/ nt -s,-e differential

Differenz f -,-en difference. **d~ieren** vt/i (*haben*) differentiate (**zwischen** + dat between)

Digital- pref digital. **D~uhr** f digital clock/watch

Diktat nt -[e]s,-e dictation. **D~ator** m -s,-en /-'to:rən/ dictator. **d~atorisch** a dictatorial. **D~atur** f -,-en dictatorship. **d~ieren** vt/i (*haben*) dictate

Dilemma nt -s,-s dilemma

Dilettant(in) m -en,-en (f -,-nen) dilettante. **d~isch** a amateurish

Dill m -s dill

Dimension f -,-en dimension

Ding nt -[e]s,-e & (*fam*) -er thing; **guter D~e sein** be cheerful; **vor allen D~en** above all

Dinghi /'dɪŋgi/ nt -s,-s dinghy

Dinosaurier /-i̯ɐ/ m -s,- dinosaur

Diözese f -,-n diocese

Diphtherie f -,- diphtheria

Diplom nt -s,-e diploma; (*Univ*) degree

Diplomat m -en,-en diplomat. **D~ie** f -,- diplomacy. **d~isch** a diplomatic, adv -ally

dir pron (dat of du) [to] you; (*refl*) yourself; **ein Freund von dir** a friend of yours

direkt a direct □adv directly; (*wirklich*) really. **D~ion** /-'tsi̯o:n/ f - management; (*Vorstand*) board of directors. **D~or** m -s,-en /-'to:rən/, **D~orin** f -,-nen director; (*Bank-, Theater-*) manager; (*Sch*) head; (*Gefängnis*) governor. **D~übertragung** f live transmission

Dirig|ent m -en,-en (*Mus*) conductor. **d~ieren** vt direct; (*Mus*) conduct

Dirndl nt -s,- dirndl [dress]

Dirne f -,-n prostitute

Diskant m -s,-e (*Mus*) treble

Diskette f -,-n floppy disc

Disko f -,-s (*fam*) disco. **D~thek** f -,-en discothèque

Diskrepanz f -,-en discrepancy

diskret a discreet, adv -ly. **D~ion** /-'tsi̯o:n/ f - discretion

diskrimin|ier|en vt discriminate against. **D~ung** f · discrimination

Diskus m -, -se & **Disken** discus

Disku|ssion f · -en discussion. **d~tieren** vt/i (haben) discuss

disponieren vi (haben) make arrangements; **d~ [können] über** (+acc) have at one's disposal

Disput m -[e]s, -e dispute

Disqualifi|kation /-'tsio:n/ f disqualification. **d~zieren** vt disqualify

Dissertation /-tsio:n/ f · -en dissertation

Dissident m -en, -en dissident

Dissonanz f · -en dissonance

Distanz f · -en distance. **d~ieren (sich)** vr dissociate oneself (**von** from). **d~iert** a aloof

Distel f · -n thistle

distinguiert /dıstıŋ'gi:ɐt/ a distinguished

Disziplin f · -en discipline. **d~arisch** _,_ a disciplinary. **d~iert** a disciplined

dito adv ditto

diverse attrib a pl various

Divid|ende f · -n dividend. **d~ieren** vt divide (**durch** by)

Division f · -en division

DJH abbr (**Deutsche Jugendherberge**) [German] youth hostel

DM abbr (**Deutsche Mark**) DM

doch conj & adv but; (dennoch) yet; (trotzdem) after all; wenn **d~ ...!** if only ...! **nicht d~!** don't [do that]! **er kommt d~?** he is coming, isn't he? **kommst du nicht?**— **d~!** aren't you coming?—yes, I am!

Docht m -[e]s, -e wick

Dock nt -s, -s dock. **d~en** vt/i (haben) dock

Dogge f · -n Great Dane

Dogm|a nt -s, -men dogma. **d~atisch** a dogmatic, adv -ally

Dohle f · -n jackdaw

Doktor m -s, -en /-'to:rən/ doctor. **D~arbeit** f [doctoral] thesis. **D~würde** f doctorate

Doktrin f · -en doctrine

Dokument nt -[e]s, -e document. **D~arbericht** m documentary. **D~arfilm** m documentary film

Dolch m -[e]s, -e dagger

doll a (fam) fantastic; (schlimm) awful □ adv beautifully; (sehr) very; (schlimm) badly

Dollar m -s, - dollar

dolmetsch|en vt/i (haben) interpret. **D~er(in)** m -s, - (f · -nen) interpreter

Dom m -[e]s, -e cathedral

domin|ant a dominant. **d~ieren** vi (haben) dominate; (vorherrschen) predominate

Domino nt -s, -s dominoes sg. **D~stein** m domino

Dompfaff m -en, -en bullfinch

Donau f · Danube

Donner m -s · thunder. **d~n** vi (haben) thunder

Donnerstag m Thursday. **d~s** adv on Thursdays

Donnerwetter nt (fam) telling-off; (Krach) row □ int /'--'-/ wow! (Fluch) damn it!

doof a (fam) stupid, adv -ly

Doppel nt -s, - duplicate; (Tennis) doubles pl. **D~bett** nt double bed. **D~decker** m -s, - double-decker [bus]. **D~deutig** a ambiguous. **D~gänger** m -s, - double. **D~kinn** nt double chin. **D~name** m double-barrelled name. **D~punkt** m (Gram) colon. **D~schnitte** f sandwich. **d~sinnig** a ambiguous. **D~stecker** m two-way adaptor. **d~t** a double; ⟨Boden⟩ false; **in d~ter Ausfertigung** in duplicate; **die d~te Menge** twice the amount (**als** von); (zweimal) twice; **d~t so viel** twice as much. **D~zimmer** nt double room

Dorf nt -[e]s,⸚er village. **D~be-wohner** m villager

dörflich a rural

Dorn m -[e]s,-en thorn. **d~ig** a thorny

Dörrobst nt dried fruit

Dorsch m -[e]s,-e cod

dort adv there; **d~ drüben** over there. **d~her** adv [von] **d~her** from there. **d~hin** adv there. **d~ig** a local

Dose f -,-n tin, can; (Schmuck-) box

dösen vi (haben) doze

Dosen|milch f evaporated milk. **D~öffner** m tin or can opener

dosieren vt measure out

Dosis f -, **Dosen** dose

Dotter m & nt -s,- [egg] yolk

Dozent(in) m -en,-en (f -,-nen) (Univ) lecturer

Dr. abbr (**Doktor**) Dr

Drache m -n,-n dragon. **D~n** m -s,- kite; (fam: Frau) dragon. **D~nfliegen** nt hang-gliding. **D~nflieger** m hang-glider

Draht m -[e]s,⸚e wire; **auf D~** (fam) on the ball. **d~ig** a (fig) wiry. **D~seilbahn** f cable railway

drall a plump; (Frau) buxom

Dram|a nt -s,-men drama. **D~a-tik** f - drama. **D~atiker** m -s,- dramatist. **d~atisch** a dramatic, adv -ally. **d~atisieren** vt dramatize

dran adv (fam) = **daran**; **gut/schlecht d~ sein** be well off/in a bad way; **ich bin d~** it's my turn

Dränage f -'na:ʒə/ f - drainage

Drang m -[e]s urge; (Druck) pressure

dräng|eln vt/i (haben) push; (bedrängen) pester. **d~en** vt push; (bedrängen) urge; **sich d~en** crowd (um round) □vi (haben) push; (eilen) be urgent; ⟨Zeit:⟩ press; **d~en auf** (+acc) press for

dran|halten† (**sich**) vr sep hurry. **d~kommen†** vi sep

(sein) have one's turn; **wer kommt dran?** whose turn is it?

drapieren vt drape

drastisch a drastic, adv -ally

drauf adv (fam) = **darauf**; **d~ und dran sein** be on the point (etw zu tun of doing sth).

D~gänger m -s,- daredevil. **d~gängerisch** a reckless

draus adv (fam) = **daraus**

draußen adv outside; (im Freien) out of doors

drechseln vt (Techn) turn

Dreck m -s dirt; (Morast) mud; (fam: Kleinigkeit) trifle; **in den D~ ziehen** (fig) denigrate. **d~ig** a dirty; muddy

Dreh m -s (fam) knack; **den D~ heraushaben** have got the hang of it. **D~bank** f lathe. **D~blei-stift** m propelling pencil. **D~buch** nt screenplay, script. **d~en** vt/i turn; (im Kreis) rotate; (verschlingen) twist; roll ⟨Zigarette⟩; shoot ⟨Film⟩; **lauter/leiser d~en** turn up/down; **sich d~en** turn; (im Kreis) rotate; (schnell) spin; ⟨Wind:⟩ change; **sich d~en um** revolve around; (sich handeln) be about □vi (haben) turn; ⟨Wind:⟩ change; **an etw** (dat) **d~en** turn sth. **D~orgel** f barrel organ. **D~stuhl** m swivel chair. **D~tür** f revolving door. **D~ung** f -,-en turn; (im Kreis) rotation. **D~zahl** f number of revolutions

drei inv a, **D~** f -,-en three; (Sch) ≈ pass. **D~eck** nt -[e]s,-e triangle. **d~eckig** a triangular. **D~einigkeit** f - die [Heilige] **D~einigkeit** the [Holy] Trinity. **d~erlei** inv a three kinds of □pron three things. **d~fach** a triple; **in d~facher Ausfertigung** in triplicate. **D~faltigkeit** f - = **D~einigkeit**. **d~mal** adv three times. **D~rad** nt tricycle

dreißig inv a thirty. **d~ste(r,s)** a thirtieth

dreist a impudent, adv -ly; (verwegen) audacious, adv -ly. **D~igkeit** f - impudence; audacity

dreiviertel inv a three-quarter. **D~stunde** f three quarters of an hour

dreizehn inv a thirteen. **d~te(r,s)** a thirteenth

dreschen† vt thresh

dress|ieren vt train. **D~ur** f - training

dribbeln vi (haben) dribble

Drill m -[e]s (Mil) drill. **d~en** vt drill

Drillinge mpl triplets

drin adv (fam) = **darin**; (drinnen) inside

dring|en† vi (sein) penetrate (in +acc into); (durch etw sth); (heraus-) come (aus out of); (~en auf (+acc) insist on. **d~end** a urgent, adv -ly. **d~lich** a urgent. **D~lichkeit** f - urgency

Drink m -[s],-s [alcoholic] drink

drinnen adv inside; (im Haus) indoors

dritt adv zu **d~** in threes; **wir waren zu d~** there were three of us. **d~e(r,s)** a third; **ein D~er** a third person. **D~el** nt -s,- third. **d~ens** adv thirdly. **d~rangig** a third-rate

Droge f -,-n drug. **D~nabhängige(r)** m/f drug addict. **D~erie** f -,-n chemist's shop, (Amer) drugstore. **D~ist** m -en,-en chemist

drohen vi (haben) threaten (jdm s.o.). **d~d** a threatening; (Gefahr) imminent

dröhnen vi (haben) resound; (tönen) boom

Drohung f -,-en threat

drollig a funny; (seltsam) odd

Drops m -,- [fruit] drop

Droschke f -,-n cab

Drossel f -,-n thrush

drosseln vt (Techn) throttle; (fig) cut back

drüben adv over there. **d~er** adv (fam) = **darüber**

Druck[^1] m -[e]s,-e pressure; **unter D~** setzen (fig) pressurize

Druck[^2] m -[e]s,-e printing; (Schrift, Reproduktion) print. **D~buchstabe** m block letter

Drückeberger m -s,- shirker

drucken vt print

drücken vt/i (haben) press; (aus-) squeeze; ⟨Schuh:⟩ pinch; (umarmen) hug; (fig: belasten) weigh down; **Preise d~** force down prices; (an Tür) **d~** push; **sich d~** (fam) make oneself scarce; **sich d~ vor** (+dat) (fam) shirk. **d~d** a heavy; (schwül) oppressive

Drucker m -s,- printer

Drücker m -s,- push-button; (Tür-) door knob

Druckerei f -,-en printing works

Druck|knopf m press-stud; (Drücker) push-button. **D~luft** f compressed air. **D~sache** f printed matter. **D~schrift** f type; (Veröffentlichung) publication; **in D~schrift** in block letters pl

drucksen vi (haben) hum and haw

Druck|stelle f bruise. **D~taste** f push-button. **D~topf** m pressure-cooker

drum adv (fam) = **darum**

drunter adv (fam) = **darunter**; **alles geht d~ und drüber** (fam) everything is topsy-turvy

Drüse f -,-n (Anat) gland

Dschungel m -s,- jungle

du pron (familiar address) you; **auf du und du** on familiar terms

Dübel m -s,- plug

duck|en vt (fig: demütigen) humiliate; **sich d~en** duck; (fig) cringe. **D~mäuser** m -s,- moral coward

Dudelsack m bagpipes pl

Duell nt -s,-e duel

Duett nt -s,-e [vocal] duet

Duft m -[e]s,-e fragrance, scent; (Aroma) aroma. **d~en** vi (haben) smell (nach of). **d~ig** a fine; (zart) delicate

duld|en vt tolerate; (erleiden) suffer □vi (haben) suffer. **d~sam** a tolerant

dumm a (dümmer, dümmst) stupid, adv -ly; (unklug) foolish, adv -ly; (fam: lästig) awkward; **wie d~!** what a nuisance! **der D~e sein** (fig) be the loser. **d~erweise** adv stupidly; (leider) unfortunately. **D~heit** f -,-en stupidity; (Torheit) foolishness; (Handlung) folly. **D~kopf** m (fam) fool.

dumpf a dull, adv -y; (muffig) musty. **D~ig** a musty

Düne f -,-n dune

Dung m -s manure

Düng|emittel nt fertilizer. **d~en** vt fertilize. **D~er** m -s,- fertilizer

dunk|el a dark; (vage) vague, adv -ly; (fragwürdig) shady; **d~les Bier** brown ale; **im D~eln** in the dark

Dünkel m -s conceit

dunkel|blau a dark blue. **d~braun** a dark brown. **d~haft** a conceited

Dunkel|heit f - darkness. **D~kammer** f dark-room. **d~n** vi (haben) get dark. **d~rot** a dark red

dünn a thin, adv -ly; (Buch) slim; (spärlich) sparse; (schwach) weak

Dunst m -es,-e mist, haze; (Dampf) vapour

dünsten vt steam

dunstig a misty, hazy

Dünung f - swell

Duo nt -s,-s [instrumental] duet

Duplikat nt -[e]s,-e duplicate

Dur nt - (Mus) major [key]; **in A-Dur** in A major

durch prep (+ acc) through; (mittels) by; **[geteilt] d~** (Math) divided by □adv **die Nacht d~** throughout the night; **sechs Uhr d~** (fam) gone six o'clock; **d~ und d~** wet through

durcharbeiten vt sep work through; **sich d~** work one's way through

durchaus adv absolutely; **d~ nicht** by no means

durchbeißen† vt sep bite through

durchblättern vt sep leaf through

durchblicken vi sep (haben) look through; **d~ lassen** (fig) hint at

Durchblutung f circulation

durchbohren vt insep pierce

durchbrechen¹† vt/i sep (haben) break [in two]

durchbrechen²† vt insep break through; break (Schallmauer)

durchbrennen† vi sep (sein) burn through; ⟨Sicherung:⟩ blow; (fam: weglaufen) run away

durchbringen† vt sep get through; (verschwenden) squander; (versorgen) support; **sich d~** mit make a living by

Durchbruch m breakthrough

durchdacht a **gut d~** well thought out

durchdrehen v sep □vt mince □ vi (haben/sein) (fam) go crazy

durchdringen¹† vt insep penetrate

durchdringen²† vi sep (sein) penetrate; (sich durchsetzen) get one's way. **d~d** a penetrating; ⟨Schrei⟩ piercing

durcheinander adv in a muddle; (Person) confused. **D~** nt -s muddle. **D~bringen**† vt sep muddle [up]; confuse (Person). **d~geraten**† vi sep (sein) get mixed up. **d~reden** vi sep (haben) all talk at once

durchfahren¹† vi sep (sein) drive through; ⟨Zug:⟩ go through

durchfahren²† *vt insep* drive/go through; **jdn d~** ⟨*Gedanke:*⟩ flash through s.o.'s mind

Durchfahrt *f* journey/drive through; **auf der D~** passing through; **'D~ verboten'** 'no thoroughfare'

Durchfall *m* diarrhoea; ⟨*fam: Versagen*⟩ flop. **d~en†** *vi sep* (sein) fall through; ⟨*fam: versagen*⟩ flop; ⟨*bei Prüfung*⟩ fail

durchfliegen¹† *vi sep* (sein) fly through; ⟨*fam: durchfallen*⟩ fail

durchfliegen²† *vt insep* fly through; ⟨*lesen*⟩ skim through

durchfroren *a* frozen

Durchfuhr *f* ⟨*Comm*⟩ transit

durchführ|bar *a* feasible. **d~en** *vt sep* carry out

Durchgang *m* passage; ⟨*Sport*⟩ round; **'D~ verboten'** 'no entry'. **D~sverkehr** *m* through traffic

durchgeben† *vt sep* pass through; ⟨*übermitteln*⟩ transmit; ⟨*Radio, TV*⟩ broadcast

durchgebraten *a* **gut d~** well done

durchgehen† *v sep* ⟨*vi*⟩ (sein) go through; ⟨*davonlaufen*⟩ run away; ⟨*Pferd:*⟩ bolt; **jdm etw d~ lassen** let s.o. get away with sth ⟨*vt*⟩ go through. **d~d** *a* continuous, *adv* -ly; **d~ geöffnet** open all day; **d~der Wagen/Zug** through carriage/train

durchgreifen† *vi sep* (haben) reach through; ⟨*vorgehen*⟩ take drastic action. **d~d** *a* drastic

durchhalte|n† *v sep* ⟨*fig*⟩ ⟨*vi/haben*⟩ hold out ⟨*vt*⟩ keep up. **D~vermögen** *nt* stamina

durchhängen† *vi sep* (haben) sag

durchkommen† *vi sep* (sein) come through; ⟨*gelangen, am Telefon*⟩ get through; ⟨*bestehen*⟩ pass; ⟨*überleben*⟩ pull through; ⟨*finanziell*⟩ get by ⟨*mit an*⟩

durchkreuzen *vt insep* thwart

durchlassen† *vt sep* let through

durchlässig *a* permeable; ⟨*undicht*⟩ leaky

durchlaufen¹† *v sep* ⟨*vi*⟩ (sein) run through ⟨*vt*⟩ wear out

durchlaufen²† *vt insep* pass through

Durchlauferhitzer *m* -s,- geyser

durchleben *vt insep* live through

durchlesen† *vt sep* read through

durchleuchten *vt insep* X-ray

durchlöchert *a* riddled with holes

durchmachen *vt sep* go through; ⟨*erleiden*⟩ undergo; have ⟨*Krankheit*⟩

Durchmesser *m* -s,- diameter

durchnäßt *a* wet through

durchnehmen† *vt sep* ⟨*Sch*⟩ do

durchnumeriert *a* numbered consecutively

durchpausen *vt sep* trace

durchqueren *vt insep* cross

Durchreiche *f* -,-n ⟨*serving*⟩ hatch. **d~n** *vt sep* pass through

Durchreise *f* journey through; **auf der D~** passing through. **d~n** *vi sep* (sein) pass through

durchreißen† *vt/i sep* (sein) tear

durchs *adv* = **durch das**

Durchsage *f* -,-n announcement. **d~n** *vt sep* announce

durchschauen *vt insep* ⟨*fig*⟩ see through

durchscheinend *a* translucent

Durchschlag *m* carbon copy; ⟨*Culin*⟩ colander. **d~en¹†** *v sep* ⟨*vt*⟩ ⟨*Culin*⟩ rub through a sieve; **sich d~en** ⟨*in fig*⟩ struggle through ⟨*vi*⟩ (sein) ⟨*Sicherung:*⟩ blow

durchschlagen²† *vt insep* smash

durchschlagend *a* ⟨*fig*⟩ effective; ⟨*Erfolg*⟩ resounding

durchschneiden† *vt sep* cut

Durchschnitt *m* average; **im D~** on average. **d~lich** *a* average ⟨*adv*⟩ on average. **D~s-** *pref* average

Durchschrift *f* carbon copy

durchsehen† v sep □vi (haben)
see through □ vt look through

durchseihen vt sep strain

durchsetzen[1] vt sep force
through; **sich d ~** assert oneself;
‹Mode:› catch on

durchsetzen[2] vt insep inter-
sperse; (infiltrieren) infiltrate

Durchsicht f check

durchsichtig a transparent

durchsickern vi sep (sein) seep
through; ‹Neuigkeit:› leak out

durchsprechen† vt sep discuss

durchstehen† vt sep ‹fig› come
through

durchstreichen† vt sep cross out

durchsuchen vt insep search.
D ~ ung f -,-en search

durchtrieben a cunning

durchwachsen a ‹Speck›
streaky; (fam: gemischt) mixed

durchwacht a sleepless ‹Nacht›

durchwählen vi sep (haben)
‹Teleph› dial direct

durchweg adv without exception

durchweicht a soggy

durchwühlen vt insep rummage
through; ransack ‹Haus›

durchziehen† v sep □vt pull
through □vi (sein) pass through

durchzucken vt sep ‹fig› shoot
through; **jdn d ~** ‹Gedanke:›
flash through s.o.'s mind

Durchzug m through draught

dürfen† vt & v aux etw [tun] d ~
be allowed to do sth; **darf ich?**
may I? **sie darf es nicht sehen**
she must not see it; **ich hätte es
nicht tun/sagen d ~** I ought not
to have done/said it; **das dürfte
nicht allzu schwer sein** that
should not be too difficult

dürftig a poor; ‹Mahlzeit› scanty

dürr a dry; ‹Boden› arid; (mager)
skinny. **D ~ e** f -,-n drought

Durst m -[e]s thirst; **D ~ haben**
be thirsty. **d ~ en** vi (haben) be
thirsty. **d ~ ig** a thirsty

Dusche f -,-n shower. **d ~ n** vi/r
(haben) [**sich**] **d ~** have a shower

Düse f -,-n nozzle. **D ~ nflugzeug**
nt jet

düster a gloomy, adv -ily; (dunkel) dark

Dutzend nt -s,-e dozen. **d ~ weise**
adv by the dozen

duzen vt jdn d ~ call s.o. 'du'

Dynamik f - dynamics sg; ‹fig›
dynamism. **d ~ isch** a dynamic;
‹Rente› index-linked

Dynamit nt -s dynamite

Dynamo m -s,-s dynamo

Dynastie f -,-n dynasty

D-Zug /'de:-/ m express [train]

E

Ebbe f -,-n low tide

eben a level; (glatt) smooth; **zu
e ~ er Erde** on the ground floor
□adv just; (genau) exactly; **e ~
noch** only just; (gerade vorhin)
just now; **das ist es e ~!** that's
just it! [**na**] **e ~!** exactly! **E ~ bild**
nt image. **e ~ bürtig** a equal; **jdm
e ~ bürtig sein** be s.o.'s equal

Ebene f -,-n ‹Geog› plain; ‹Geom›
plane; ‹fig: Niveau› level

eben|falls adv also; **danke,
e ~ falls** thank you, [the] same to
you. **E ~ holz** nt ebony. **e ~ mäßig** a regular, adv -ly. **e ~ so** adv
just the same; (ebensosehr) just
as much; **e ~ so gut/teuer** just as
good/expensive. **e ~ sogut** adv
just as well. **e ~ sosehr** adv just
as much. **e ~ soviel** adv just as
much/many. **e ~ sowenig** adv
just as little/few; (noch) no more

Eber m -s,- boar. **E ~ esche** f
rowan

ebnen vt level; ‹fig› smooth

Echo nt -s,-s echo. **e ~ en** vt/i (haben) echo

echt a genuine, real; (authentisch)
authentic; ‹Farbe› fast; (typisch)

typical □*adv* (*fam*) really; typ-
ically. **E~heit** *f* - authenticity
Eck|ball *m* (*Sport*) corner. **E~ef**
-,-n corner. **e~en** vt (*fam*)
(*fam*) bump off. **e~ig** *a* angular;
⟨*Klammern*⟩ square; (*unbeholfen*) awkward. **E~stein** *m* cor-
ner-stone. **E~stoß** *m* = **E~ball**.
E~zahn *m* canine tooth
Ecu, ECU /e'ky:/ *m* -[s],-[s] ecu
edel *a* noble, *adv* -bly; (*wertvoll*)
precious; (*fein*) fine. **E~mann** *m*
(*pl* -leute) nobleman. **E~mut** *m*
magnanimity. **e~mütig** *a* magnanimous, *adv* -ly. **E~stahl** *m*
stainless steel. **E~stein** *m* precious stone
Efeu *m* -s ivy
Effekt *m* -[e]s,-e effect. **E~en** *pl*
securities. **e~iv** *a* actual, *adv* -ly;
(*wirksam*) effective, *adv* -ly.
e~voll *a* effective
EG *f* - *abbr* (**Europäische Gemeinschaft**) EC
egal *a* das ist mir **e~** (*fam*) it's all
the same to me □*adv* **e~** **wie/wo**
no matter how/where. **e~itär** *a*
egalitarian
Egge *f* -,-n harrow
Ego|ismus *m* - selfishness. **E~-
ist(in)** *m* -en,-en (*f* -,-nen) egoist. **e~istisch** *a* selfish, *adv* -ly.
e~zentrisch *a* egocentric
eh *adv* (*Aust fam*) anyway; seit eh
und je from time immemorial
ehe *conj* before; ehe nicht until
Ehe *f* -,-n marriage. **E~bett** *nt*
double bed. **E~bruch** *m* adultery. **E~frau** *f* wife. **E~leute** *pl*
married couple *sg*. **e~lich** *a*
marital; (*Recht*) conjugal; ⟨*Kind*⟩
legitimate
ehemalig *a* former. **e~s** *adv* formerly
Ehe|mann *m* (*pl* -männer) hus-
band. **E~paar** *nt* married couple
eher *adv* earlier, sooner; (*lieber,
vielmehr*) rather; (*mehr*) more
Ehering *m* wedding ring

ehr|bar *a* respectable. **E~ef-,-n**
honour; jdm **E~e** machen do
credit to s.o. **e~en** vt honour.
e~enamtlich *a* honorary □*adv*
in an honorary capacity. **E~en-
doktorat** *nt* honorary doctorate.
E~engast *m* guest of honour.
e~enhaft *a* honourable, *adv*
-bly. **E~enmann** *m* (*pl* -män-
ner) man of honour. **E~enmit-
glied** *nt* honorary member.
e~enrührig *a* defamatory.
E~enrunde *f* lap of honour.
E~ensache *f* point of honour.
e~enwert *a* honourable.
E~enwort *nt* word of honour.
e~erbietig *a* deferential, *adv*
-ly. **E~erbietung** *f* - deference.
E~furcht *f* reverence; (*Scheu*)
awe. **e~fürchtig** *a* reverent, *adv*
-ly. **E~gefühl** *nt* sense of
honour. **E~geiz** *m* ambition.
e~geizig *a* ambitious. **e~lich** *a*
honest, *adv* -ly; **e~lich gesagt** to
be honest. **E~lichkeit** *f* -
honesty. **e~los** *a* dishonourable.
e~sam *a* respectable. **e~wür-
dig** *a* venerable; (*als Anrede*)
Reverend
Ei *nt* -[e]s,-er egg
Eibe *f* -,-n yew
Eiche *f* -,-n oak. **E~lf-,-n** acorn.
E~lhäher *m* -s,- jay
eichen vt standardize
Eichhörnchen *nt* -s,- squirrel
Eid *m* -[e]s,-e oath
Eidechse *f* -,-n lizard
eidesstattlich *a* sworn □*adv* on oath
Eidotter *m* & *nt* egg yolk
Ei|erbecher *m* egg-cup. **E~ku-
chen** *m* pancake; (*Omelett*) om-
elette. **E~schale** *f* eggshell.
E~schnee *m* beaten egg-white.
E~stock *m* ovary. **E~uhr** *f*
egg-timer
Eifer *m* -s eagerness; (*Streben*)
zeal. **E~sucht** *f* jealousy.
e~süchtig *a* jealous, *adv* -ly

eiförmig a egg-shaped; (oval) oval

eifrig a eager, adv -ly; (begeistert) keen, adv -ly

Eigelb nt -[e]s,-e [egg] yolk

eigen a own; (typisch) characteristic (dat of); (seltsam) odd, adv -ly; (genau) particular. **E~art** f peculiarity. **e~artig** a peculiar, adv -ly; (seltsam) odd. **e~brötler** m -s,- crank. **e~händig** a personal, adv -ly; (Unterschrift) own. **E~heit** f -,-en peculiarity. **e~mächtig** a high-handed; (unbefugt) unauthorized □adv highhandedly; without authority. **E~name** m proper name. **E~nutz** m self-interest. **e~nützig** a selfish, adv -ly. **e~s** adv specially. **E~schaft** f -,-en quality; (Phys) property; (Merkmal) characteristic; (Funktion) capacity. **E~schaftswort** nt (pl -wörter) adjective. **E~sinn** m obstinacy. **e~sinnig** a obstinate, adv -ly

eigentlich a actual, real; (wahr) true □adv actually, really; (streng genommen) strictly speaking; **wie geht es ihm e~?** by the way, how is he?

Eigen|tum nt own goal. **E~tum** nt -s property. **E~tümer(in)** m -s,- (f -,-nen) owner. **e~tümlich** a odd, adv -ly; (typisch) characteristic. **E~tumswohnung** f freehold flat. **e~willig** a self-willed; (Stil) highly individual

eign|en (sich) vr be suitable. **E~ung** f suitability

Eil|brief m express letter. **E~e** f hurry; **E~e haben** be in a hurry; (Sache:) be urgent. **e~en** vi (sein) hurry □(haben) (drängen) be urgent. **e~ends** adv hurriedly. **e~ig** a hurried, adv -ly; (dringend) urgent, adv -ly; **es**

e~ig **haben** be in a hurry. **E~zug** m semi-fast train

Eimer m -s,- bucket; (Abfall-) bin

ein¹ adj one; **e~es Tages/Abends** one day/evening; **mit jdm in einem Zimmer schlafen** sleep in the same room as s.o. □indef art a, (vor Vokal) an; **so ein** such a; **was für ein** (Frage) what kind of a? (Ausruf) what a!

ein² adv **ein und aus** in and out; **nicht mehr ein noch aus wissen** (fam) be at one's wits' end

einander pron one another

einarbeiten vt sep train

einäscher|n vt sep reduce to ashes; cremate (Leiche). **E~ung** f -,-en cremation

einatmen vt/i sep (haben) inhale, breathe in

einäugig a one-eyed. **E~bahnstraße** f one-way street

einbalsamieren vt sep embalm

Einband m binding

Einbau m installation; (Montage) fitting. **e~en** vt sep install; (montieren) fit. **E~küche** f fitted kitchen

einbegriffen pred a included

einberuf|en vt sep convene; (Mil) call up, (Amer) draft. **E~ung** f call-up, (Amer) draft

Einbettzimmer nt single room

einbeulen vt sep dent

einbeziehen† vt sep [mit] e~ include; (berücksichtigen) take into account

einbiegen vi sep (sein) turn

einbild|en vt sep **sich** (dat) **etw** e~en imagine sth; **sich** (dat) **viel** e~en be conceited. **E~ung** f imagination; (Dünkel) conceit. **E~ungskraft** f imagination

einblenden vt sep fade in

einbleuen vt sep **jdm etw** e~ (fam) drum sth into s.o.

Einblick m insight

einbrech|en† vi sep (haben/sein) break in; **bei uns ist eingebrochen worden** we have been burgled □ ⟨Nacht:⟩ fall. **E~er** m burglar

einbring|en† vt sep get in; bring in ⟨Geld⟩; **das bringt nichts ein** it's not worth while. **e~lich** a profitable

Einbruch m burglary; **bei E~ der Nacht** at nightfall

einbürger|n vt sep naturalize; **sich e~n** become established. **E~ung** f - naturalization

Ein|buße f loss (**an**+dat of). **e~büßen** vt sep lose

einchecken /-tʃɛkən/ vt/i sep (haben) check in

eindecken (sich) vr sep stock up

eindeutig a unambiguous; (deutlich) clear, adv -ly

eindicken vt sep (Culin) thicken

eindring|en† vi sep (sein) **e~en in** (+acc) penetrate into; (mit Gewalt) force one's/⟨Wasser:⟩ its way into; (Mil) invade; **auf jdn e~en** (fig) press s.o.; (bittend) plead with s.o. **e~lich** a urgent, adv -ly. **E~ling** m -s,-e intruder

Eindruck m impression; **E~ machen** impress (**auf jdn** s.o.)

eindrücken vt sep crush

eindrucksvoll a impressive

ein|e(r,s) pron one; (jemand) someone; (man) one, you; **e~ lei** inv a ⟨attrib a von uns one of us; **es macht e~en müde** it makes you tired

einebnen vt sep level

eineiig a ⟨Zwillinge⟩ identical

eineinhalb inv a one and a half; **e~ Stunden** an hour and a half

Eineltern|familie f one-parent family

einengen vt sep restrict

Einer m -s,- (Math) unit. **e~** pron s. **eine(r,s)**. **e~lei** inv a ⟨attrib a one kind of; (eintönig, einheitlich) the same □ pred a (fam) immaterial; **es ist mir e~lei** it's all the

same to me. **E~lei** nt -s monotony. **e~seits** adv on the one hand

einfach a simple, adv -ly; ⟨Essen⟩ plain; ⟨Faden, Fahrt, Fahrkarte⟩ single; **e~er Soldat** private. **E~heit** f - simplicity

einfädeln vt sep thread; (fig: arrangieren) arrange; **sich e~** (Auto) filter in

einfahr|en† v sep ⟨vi (sein) arrive; ⟨Zug:⟩ pull in □ vt (Auto) run in; **die Ernte e~en** get in the harvest. **E~t** f arrival; (Eingang) entrance, way in; (Auffahrt) drive; (Autobahn-) access road; **keine E~t** no entry

Einfall m idea; (Mil) invasion. **e~en†** vi sep (sein) collapse; (eindringen) invade; (einstimmen) join in; **jdm e~en** occur to s.o.; **sein Name fällt mir nicht ein** I can't think of his name; **was fällt ihm ein!** what does he think he is doing! **e~sreich** a imaginative

Einfalt f - naïvety

einfältig a simple; (naiv) naïve

Einfaltspinsel m simpleton

einfangen† vt sep catch

einfarbig a of one colour; ⟨Stoff, Kleid⟩ plain

einfass|en vt sep border, edging; set ⟨Edelstein⟩. **E~ung** f border, edging

einfetten vt sep grease

einfinden† (sich) vr sep turn up

einfließen† vi sep (sein) flow in

einflößen† vt sep **jdm etw e~** give s.o. sips of sth; **jdm Angst e~** (fig) frighten s.o.

Einfluß m influence. **e~reich** a influential

einförmig a monotonous, adv -ly. **E~keit** f - monotony

einfried[ig]|en vt sep enclose. **E~ung** f -,-en enclosure

einfrieren vt/i sep (sein) freeze

einfügen vt sep insert; (einschieben) interpolate; **sich e~** fit in

einfühl|en (sich) *vr sep* empathize (**in**+*acc* with). **e~sam** *a* sensitive

Einfuhr *f* -,-en import

einführ|en *vt sep* introduce; (*einstecken*) insert; (*einweisen*) initiate; (*Comm*) import. **e~end** *a* introductory. **E~ung** *f* introduction; (*Einweisung*) initiation

Eingabe *f* petition; (*Computer*) input

Eingang *m* entrance, way in; (*Ankunft*) arrival

eingebaut *a* built-in; ⟨*Schrank*⟩ fitted

eingeben† *vt sep* hand in; (*einflößen*) give ⟨*jdm* s.o.⟩; (*Computer*) feed in

eingebildet *a* imaginary; (*überheblich*) conceited

Eingeborene(r) *m/f* native

Eingebung *f* -,-en inspiration

eingedenk *prep* (+*gen*) mindful of

eingefleischt *a* **e~er Junggeselle** confirmed bachelor

eingehakt *adv* arm in arm

eingehen† *v sep* □*vi* (*sein*) come in; (*ankommen*) arrive; (*einlaufen*) shrink; (*sterben*) die; ⟨*Zeitung, Firma*:⟩ fold; *auf etw* (*acc*) **e~** go into sth; (*annehmen*) agree to sth □*vt* enter into; contract ⟨*Ehe*⟩; make ⟨*Wette*⟩; take ⟨*Risiko*⟩. **e~d** *a* detailed; (*gründlich*) thorough, *adv* -ly

eingelegt *a* inlaid; (*Culin*) pickled; (*mariniert*) marinaded

eingemacht *a* (*Culin*) bottled

eingenommen *pred a* (*fig*) taken (**von** with); prejudiced (**gegen** against); **von sich e~** conceited

eingeschneit *a* snowbound

eingeschrieben *a* registered

Einge|ständnis *nt* admission. **e~stehen†** *vt sep* admit

eingetragen *a* registered

Eingeweide *pl* bowels, entrails

eingewöhnen (sich) *vr sep* settle in

eingießen† *vt sep* pour in; (*einschenken*) pour

eingleisig *a* single-track

eingliedern *vt sep* integrate. **E~ung** *f* integration

eingraben† *vt sep* bury

eingravieren *vt sep* engrave

eingreifen† *vi sep* (*haben*) intervene. **E~** *nt* -s intervention

Eingriff *m* intervention; (*Med*) operation

einhaken *vt/r sep* **jdn e~** *od sich bei jdm e~** take s.o.'s arm

einhalten† *v sep* □*vt* keep; (*befolgen*) observe □*vi* (*haben*) stop

einhändigen *vt sep* hand in

einhängen *v sep* □*vt* hang; put down ⟨*Hörer*⟩; **sich bei jdm e~** take s.o.'s arm □*vi* (*haben*) hang up

einheimisch *a* local; (*eines Landes*) native; (*Comm*) home-produced. **E~e(r)** *m/f* local; native

Einheit *f* -,-en unity; (*Maß*-, *Mil*) unit. **e~lich** *a* uniform, *adv* -ly; (*vereinheitlicht*) standard. **E~spreis** *m* standard price; (*Fahrpreis*) flat fare

einhellig *a* unanimous, *adv* -ly

einholen *vt sep* catch up with; (*aufholen*) make up for; (*erbitten*) seek; (*einkaufen*) buy; **e~ gehen** go shopping

einhüllen *vt sep* wrap

einhundert *inv a* one hundred

einig *a* united; [**sich** (*dat*)] **e~ werden/sein** come to an/be in agreement

einig|e(r,s) *pron* some; (*ziemlich viel*) quite a lot of; (*substantivisch*) some; **e~e** *pl* some; (*mehrere*) several; (*ziemlich viele*) quite a lot; **e~es** *sg* some things; **vor e~er Zeit** some time ago. **e~emal** *adv* a few times

einigen vt unite; unify ⟨Land⟩; **sich e~** come to an agreement; (ausmachen) agree (**auf**+acc **on**)

einigermaßen adv to some extent; (ziemlich) fairly; (ziemlich gut) fairly well

Einig|keit f unity; (Übereinstimmung) agreement. **E~ung** f unification; (Übereinkunft) agreement

einjährig a one-year-old; (ein Jahr dauernd) one year's ...; **e~e Pflanze** annual

einkalkulieren vt sep take into account

einkassieren vt sep collect

Einkauf m purchase; (Einkaufen) shopping; **Einkäufe machen** do some shopping. **e~en** vt sep buy; **e~en gehen** go shopping. **E~skorb** m shopping/(im Geschäft) wire basket. **E~stasche** f shopping bag. **E~swagen** m shopping trolley. **E~szentrum** nt shopping centre

einkehren vi sep (sein) [in einem Lokal] **e~** stop for a meal/drink [at an inn]

einklammern vt sep bracket

Einklang m harmony; **in E~ stehen** be in accord (**mit** with)

einkleben vt sep stick in

einkleiden vt sep fit out

einklemmen vt sep clamp; **sich (dat) den Finger in der Tür e~** catch one's finger in the door

einkochen v sep □vi (sein) boil down □vt preserve

Einkommen nt -s income. **E~[s]steuer** f income tax

einkreisen vt sep encircle; **rot e~** ring in red

Einkünfte pl income sg; (Einnahmen) revenue sg

einlad|en† vt sep load; (auffordern) invite; (bezahlen für) treat. **e~end** a inviting. **E~ung** f invitation

Einlage f enclosure; (Schuh-) arch support; (Zahn-) temporary filling; (Programm-) interlude; (Comm) investment; (Bank-) deposit; **Suppe mit E~** soup with noodles/dumplings

Einlaß m -sses admittance. **e~lassen†** vt sep let in; run ⟨Bad, Wasser⟩; **sich auf etw (acc)/mit jdm e~lassen** get involved in sth/with s.o.

einlaufen† vi sep (sein) come in; (ankommen) arrive; ⟨Wasser:⟩ run in; (schrumpfen) shrink; **[in den Hafen] e~** enter port

einleben (sich) vr sep settle in

Einlege|arbeit f inlaid work. **e~n** vt sep put in; lay in ⟨Vorrat⟩; lodge ⟨Protest, Berufung⟩; (einfügen) insert; (Auto) engage ⟨Gang⟩; (verzieren) inlay; (Culin) pickle; (marinieren) marinade; **eine Pause e~n** have a break. **E~sohle** f insole

einleit|en vt sep initiate; (eröffnen) begin. **e~end** a introductory. **E~ung** f introduction

einlenken vi sep (haben) (fig) relent

einleuchten vi sep (haben) be clear (dat to). **e~d** a convincing

einliefern vt sep take (**ins Krankenhaus** to hospital). **E~ung** f admission

einlösen vt sep cash ⟨Scheck⟩; redeem ⟨Pfand⟩; (fig) keep

einmachen vt sep preserve

einmal adv once; (eines Tages) one or some day; **noch/schon e~** again/before; **noch e~ so teuer** twice as expensive; **auf e~** at the same time; (plötzlich) suddenly; **nicht e~** not even; **es geht nun e~ nicht** it's just not possible. **E~eins** nt - [multiplication] tables pl. **e~ig** a single; (einzigartig) unique; (fam: großartig) fantastic, adv -ally

einmarschieren *vi sep* (sein) march in

einmisch|en (sich) *vr sep* interfere. **E~ung** *f* interference

einmütig *a* unanimous, *adv* -ly

Einnahme *f* -,-n taking; (*Mil*) capture; **E~n** *pl* income *sg*; (*Einkünfte*) revenue *sg*; (*Comm*) receipts; (*eines Ladens*) takings

einnehmen† *vt sep* take; have ⟨*Mahlzeit*⟩; (*Mil*) capture; take up ⟨*Platz*⟩; (*fig*) prejudice (**gegen** against); **jdn für sich e~** win s.o. over. **e~d** *a* engaging

einnicken *vi sep* (sein) nod off

Einöde *f* wilderness

einordnen *vt sep* put in its proper place; (*klassifizieren*) classify; **sich e~** fit in; (*Auto*) get in lane

einpacken *vt sep* pack; (*einhüllen*) wrap

einparken *vt sep* park

einpauken *vt sep* **jdm etw e~** (*fam*) drum sth into s.o.

einpflanzen *vt sep* plant; implant ⟨*Organ*⟩

einplanen *vt sep* allow for

einpräg|en *vt sep* impress (**jdm** [up]on s.o.); **sich** (*dat*) **etw e~** memorize sth. **e~sam** *a* easy to remember; ⟨*Melodie*⟩ catchy

einquartieren *vt sep* (*Mil*) billet (**bei** on); **sich in einem Hotel e~** put up at a hotel

einrahmen *vt sep* frame

einrasten *vi sep* (sein) engage

einräumen *vt sep* put away; (*zugeben*) admit; (*zugestehen*) grant

einrechnen *vt sep* include

einreden *v sep* □*vt* **jdm/sich** (*dat*) **etw e~** persuade s.o./oneself of sth □*vi* (haben) **auf jdn e~** talk insistently to s.o.

einreib|en† *vt sep* rub (**mit** with). **E~mittel** *nt* liniment

einreichen *vt sep* submit; **die Scheidung e~** file for divorce

Einreih|er *m* -s,- single-breasted suit. **e~ig** *a* single-breasted

Einreise *f* entry. **e~n** *vi sep* (sein) enter (**nach Irland** Ireland). **E~visum** *nt* entry visa

einreißen† *v sep* □*vt* tear; (*abreißen*) pull down □*vi* (sein) tear; ⟨*Sitte:*⟩ become a habit

einrenken *vt sep* (*Med*) set

einrichten *vt sep* fit out; (*möblieren*) furnish; (*anordnen*) arrange; (*Med*) set ⟨*Bruch*⟩; (*eröffnen*) set up; **sich e~en** furnish one's home; (*sich einschränken*) economize; (*sich vorbereiten*) prepare (**auf**+*acc* for). **E~ung** *f* furnishing; (*Möbel*) furnishings *pl*; (*Techn*) equipment; (*Vorrichtung*) device; (*Eröffnung*) setting up; (*Institution*) institution; (*Gewohnheit*) practice. **E~ungsgegenstand** *m* piece of equipment/(*Möbelstück*) furniture

einrollen *vt sep* roll up; put in rollers ⟨*Haare*⟩

einrosten *vi sep* (sein) rust; (*fig*) get rusty

einrücken *v sep* □*vi* (sein) (*Mil*) be called up; (*einmarschieren*) move in □*vt* indent

eins *inv a & pron* one; **noch e~** one other thing; **mir ist alles e~** (*fam*) it's all the same to me. **E~** *f* -,-en one; (*Sch*) ≈ A

einsam *a* lonely; (*allein*) solitary; (*abgelegen*) isolated. **E~keit** *f* loneliness; solitude; isolation

einsammeln *vt sep* collect

Einsatz *m* use; (*Mil*) mission; (*Wett-*) stake; (*E~teil*) insert; **im E~** in action. **e~bereit** *a* ready for action

einschalt|en *vt sep* switch on; (*einschieben*) interpolate; (*fig: beteiligen*) call in; **sich e~en** (*fig*) intervene. **E~quote** *f* (*TV*) viewing figures *pl*; ≈ ratings *pl*

einschärfen *vt sep* **jdm etw e~** impress sth [up]on s.o.

einschätz|en vt sep assess; (bewerten) rate. **E~ung** f assessment; estimation

einschenken vt sep pour

einscheren vi sep (sein) pull in

einschicken vt sep send in

einschieben† vt sep push in; (einfügen) insert; (fig) interpolate

einschiff|en (sich) vr sep embark. **E~ung** f embarkation

einschlafen† vi sep (sein) go to sleep; (aufhören) peter out

einschläfern vt sep lull to sleep; (betäuben) put out; (töten) put to sleep. **e~d** a soporific

Einschlag m impact; (fig: Beimischung) element. **e~en†** v sep □vt knock in; (zerschlagen) smash; (einwickeln) wrap; (falten) turn up; (drehen) turn (in etw acc sth); (einordnen) take up ⟨Laufbahn⟩ □vi (haben) hit/⟨Blitz:⟩ strike (in etw acc sth); (zustimmen) shake hands [on a deal]; (Erfolg haben) be a hit; **auf jdn e~** in beat s.o.

einschlägig a relevant

einschleusen vt sep infiltrate

einschließ|en† vt sep lock in; (umgeben) enclose; (einkreisen) surround; (einbeziehen) include; **sich e~en** lock oneself in; **Bedienung eingeschlossen** service included. **e~lich** adv inclusive □prep (+ gen) including

einschmeicheln (sich) vr sep ingratiate oneself (**bei** with)

einschnappen vi sep (sein) click shut; **eingeschnappt sein** (fam) be in a huff

einschneiden† vt/i sep (haben) **[in]** etw acc **e~** cut into sth. **e~d** a (fig) drastic, adv -ally

Einschnitt m cut; (Med) incision; (Lücke) gap; (fig) decisive event

einschränk|en vt sep restrict; (reduzieren) cut back; **sich e~en** economize. **E~ung** f -,-en restriction; (Reduzierung) reduction; (Vorbehalt) reservation

Einschreib[e]brief m registered letter. **e~en†** vt sep enter; register ⟨Brief⟩; **sich e~en** put one's name down; (sich anmelden) enrol. **E~en** nt registered letter/packet; **als** od **per E~en** by registered post

einschreiten† vi sep (sein) intervene

einschüchter|n vt sep intimidate. **E~ung** f - intimidation

einsegnen vt sep (Relig) confirm. **E~ung** f -,-en confirmation

einseh|en† vt sep inspect; (lesen) consult; (begreifen) see. **E~** nt -s **ein E~ haben** show some understanding; (vernünftig sein) see reason

einseitig a one-sided; (Pol) unilateral □adv on one side; (fig) one-sidedly; (Pol) unilaterally

einsenden† vt sep send in

einsetzen v sep □vt put in; (einfügen) insert; (verwenden) use; put on ⟨Zug⟩; call out ⟨Truppen⟩; (Mil) deploy; (ernennen) appoint; (wetten) stake; (riskieren) risk; **sich e~** für support □vi (haben) start; ⟨Winter, Regen:⟩ set in

Einsicht f insight; (Verständnis) understanding; (Vernunft) reason; **zur E~ kommen** see reason. **e~ig** a understanding; (vernünftig) sensible

Einsiedler m hermit

einsilbig a monosyllabic; (Person) taciturn

einsinken† vi sep (sein) sink in

einspannen vt sep harness; **jdn e~** (fam) rope s.o. in; **sehr eingespannt** (fam) very busy

einsparen vt sep save

einsperren vt sep shut/(im Gefängnis) lock up

einspielen vr sep warm up; **gut aufeinander eingespielt sein** work well together

einsprachig a monolingual

einspringen† vi sep (sein) step in (für for)

einspritzen vt sep inject

Einspruch m objection; **E~ erheben** object; (Jur) appeal

einspurig a single-track; (Auto) single-lane

einst adv once; (Zukunft) one day

Einstand m (Tennis) deuce

einstecken vt sep put in; post (Brief); (Electr) plug in; (fam: behalten) pocket; (fam: hinnehmen) take; suffer (Niederlage); etw e~ put sth in one's pocket

einstehen† vi sep (haben) **e~ für** vouch for; answer for (Folgen)

einsteigen† vi sep (sein) get in; (in Bus/Zug) get on

einstell|en vt sep put in; (anstellen) employ; (aufhören) stop; (regulieren) adjust, set; (Optik) focus; tune (Motor, Zündung); tune to (Sender); **sich e~** turn up; (ankommen) arrive; (eintreten) occur; (Schwierigkeiten:) arise; **sich e~ auf** (+ acc) adjust to; (sich vorbereiten) prepare for (für). **E~ung** f employment; (Aufhören) cessation; (Regulierung) adjustment; (Optik) focusing; (TV, Auto) tuning; (Haltung) attitude

Einstieg m -(e)s,-e entrance

einstig a former

einstimmen vi sep (haben) join in

einstimmig a unanimous, adv -ly. **E~keit** f - unanimity

einstöckig a single-storey

einstudieren vt sep rehearse

einstufen vt sep classify

Ein|sturz m collapse. **e~stürzen** vi sep (sein) collapse

einstweil|en adv for the time being; (inzwischen) meanwhile. **e~ig** a temporary

eintasten vt sep key in

eintauchen vt/i sep (sein) dip in; (heftiger) plunge in

eintauschen vt sep exchange

eintausend inv a one thousand

einteil|en vt sep divide (in + acc into); (Biol) classify; (Admin) (dat); **seine Zeit gut e~en** organize one's time well. **e~ig** a one-piece. **E~ung** f division; classification

eintönig a monotonous, adv -ly. **E~keit** f - monotony

Eintopf m, **E~gericht** nt stew

Ein|tracht f - harmony. **e~trächtig** a harmonious □ adv in harmony

Eintrag m -[e]s,-̈e entry. **e~en†** vt sep enter; (Admin) register; (einbringen) bring in; **sich e~en** put one's name down

einträglich a profitable

Eintragung f -,-en registration; (Eintrag) entry

eintreffen† vi sep (sein) arrive; (fig) come true; (geschehen) happen. **E~** nt -s arrival

eintreiben† vt sep drive in; (einziehen) collect

eintreten v sep □ vi (sein) enter; (geschehen) occur; **in einen Klub e~** join a club; **e~ für** (fig) stand up for □ vt kick in

Eintritt m entrance; (zu Veranstaltung) admission; (Beitritt) joining; (Beginn) beginning. **E~skarte** f (admission) ticket

eintrocknen vi sep (sein) dry up

einüben vt sep practise

einundachtzig inv a eighty-one

einverleiben vt sep incorporate (dat into); **sich** (dat) **etw e~** (fam) consume sth

Einvernehmen nt -s understanding; (Übereinstimmung) agreement; **in bestem E~** on the best of terms

einverstanden a **e~ sein** agree

Einverständnis nt agreement; (Zustimmung) consent

Einwand m -[e]s,-̈e objection

Einwander|er m immigrant. **e~n** vi sep (sein) immigrate. **E~ung** f immigration

einwandfrei *a* perfect, *adv* -ly;
  (*untadelig*) impeccable, *adv* -bly;
  (*eindeutig*) indisputable, *adv* -bly

einwärts *adv* inwards

einwechseln *vt sep* change

einwecken *vt sep* preserve, bottle

Einweg- *pref* non-returnable;
  ⟨*Feuerzeug*⟩ throw-away

einweichen *vt sep* soak

einweih|en *vt sep* inaugurate;
  (*Relig*) consecrate; (*einführen*)
  initiate; (*fam*) use for the first
  time; **in ein Geheimnis e~en** let
  into a secret. **E~ung** *f*-,-en inau-
  guration; consecration; initiation

einweisen† *vt sep* direct; (*einführen*) initiate; **ins Krankenhaus
e~** send to hospital

einwenden† *vt sep* **etwas e~** object (**gegen** to); **dagegen hätte
ich nichts einzuwenden** (*fam*) I
  wouldn't say no

einwerfen† *vt sep* insert; post
  ⟨*Brief*⟩; (*Sport*) throw in; (*vorbringen*) interject; (*zertrümmern*)
  smash

einwickeln *vt sep* wrap [up]

einwillig|en *vi sep* (*haben*) con-
  sent, agree (**in** + *acc* to). **E~ung**
  f- consent

einwirken *vi sep* (*haben*) **e~ auf**
  (+ *acc*) have an effect on; (*beeinflussen*) influence

Einwohner|(in) *m* -s,- (*f* -,-nen)
  inhabitant. **E~zahl** *f* population

Einwurf *m* interjection; (*Einwand*) objection; (*Sport*) throw-
  in; (*Münz-*) slot

Einzahl *f* (*Gram*) singular

einzahl|en *vt sep* pay in. **E~ung**
  f payment; (*Einlage*) deposit

einzäunen *vt sep* fence in

Einzel *nt* -s,- (*Tennis*) singles *pl*.
  E~bett *nt* single bed. **E~fall** *m*
  individual/(*Sonderfall*) isolated
  case. **E~gänger** *m* -s,- loner.
  E~haft *f* solitary confinement.
  E~handel *m* retail trade.
  E~händler *m* retailer. **E~-**

haus *nt* detached house. **E~-
heit** *f* -,-en detail. **E~karte** *f*
single ticket. **E~kind** *nt* only
child

einzeln *a* single, *adv* -gly; (*individuell*) individual, *adv* -ly; (*gesondert*) separate, *adv* -ly; odd
  ⟨*Handschuh, Socken*⟩; **e~e Fälle**
  some cases. **e~e(r,s)** *pron der/
die e~e** the individual; **ein e~er**
  a single one; **jeder e~e** every
single one; **im e~en** in detail;
  e~e *pl* some

Einzel|person *f* single person.
  E~teil *nt* [component] part.
  E~zimmer *nt* single room

einziehen† *v sep* □*vt* pull in; draw
  ⟨*Atem, Krallen*⟩; (*Zool, Techn*)
  retract; indent ⟨*Zeile*⟩; (*aus dem
Verkehr ziehen*) withdraw;
  (*beschlagnahmen*) confiscate;
  (*eintreiben*) collect; make ⟨*Er-
kundigungen*⟩; (*Mil*) call up; (*einfügen*) insert; (*einbauen*) put in;
  den Kopf e~ duck [one's head]
  □*vi* (*sein*) enter; (*umziehen*) move
  in; (*eindringen*) penetrate

einzig *a* only; (*einmalig*) unique;
  eine/keine e~e Frage a/not a
  single question; **ein e~es Mal**
  only once □*adv* only; **e~ und
allein** solely. **e~artig** *a* unique;
  (*unvergleichlich*) unparalleled.
  e~e(r,s) *pron der/die/das* **e~e** the
  only one; **ein/kein e~er**
  a/not a single one; **das war, was
mich stört** the only thing that
  bothers me

Einzug *m* entry; (*Umzug*) move
  (**in** + *acc* into). **E~sgebiet** *nt*
  catchment area

Eis *nt* -es ice; (*Speise-*) ice-cream.
  Eis am Stiel ice lolly. **E~bahn**
  f ice rink. **E~bär** *m* polar bear.
  E~becher *m* ice-cream sundae.
  E~bein *nt* (*Culin*) knuckle of
  pork. **E~berg** *m* iceberg.
  E~diele *f* ice-cream parlour

Eisen nt -s,- iron. E~**bahn** f railway. E~**bahner** m -s,- railwayman

eisern a iron; (fest) resolute, adv -ly; e~er Vorhang (Theat) safety curtain; (Pol) Iron Curtain

Eis|fach nt freezer compartment. e~**gekühlt** a chilled. e~**ig** a icy. E~**kaffee** m iced coffee. e~**kalt** a ice cold; (fig) icy, adv -ily. E~**kunstlauf** m figure skating. E~**lauf** m skating. e~**laufen**† vi sep (sein) skate. E~**läufer(in)** m(f) skater. E~**pickel** m ice-axe. E~**scholle** f ice-floe. E~**schrank** m refrigerator. E~**vogel** m kingfisher. E~**würfel** m icecube. E~**zapfen** m icicle. E~**zeit** f ice age

eitel a vain; (rein) pure. E~**keit** f -vanity

Eiter m -s pus. e~**n** vi (haben) discharge pus

Eiweiß nt -es,-e egg-white; (Chem) protein

Ekel[1] m -s disgust; (Widerwille) revulsion

Ekel[2] nt -s,- (fam) beast

ekel|erregend a nauseating. e~**haft** a nauseating; (widerlich) repulsive. e~**n** vt/i (haben) mich od mir e~t [es] davor it makes me feel sick □ vr sich e~**n** vor (+ dat) find repulsive

eklig a disgusting, repulsive

Ekstase f - ecstasy. e~**tisch** a ecstatic, adv -ally

Ekzem nt -s,-e eczema

elastisch a elastic; (federnd) springy; (fig) flexible. E~**zität** f - elasticity; flexibility

Elch m -[e]s,-e elk

Elefant m -en,-en elephant

elegant a elegant, adv -ly. E~**z** f - elegance

elektrifizieren vt electrify

Elektri|ker m -s,- electrician. e~**sch** a electric, adv -ally

elektrisieren vt electrify; **sich** e~ get an electric shock

Elektrizität f - electricity. E~**werk** nt power station

Elektro|artikel mpl electrical appliances. E~**ode** f -,-n electrode. E~**oherd** m electric cooker. E~**on** nt -s,-en /-'trɔːnən/ electron. E~**onik** f - electronics sg. e~**onisch** a electronic

Element nt -[e]s,-e element; (An-bau-) unit. e~**ar** a elementary

Elend nt -s misery; (Armut) poverty. e~ a miserable, adv -bly, wretched, adv -ly; (krank) poorly; (gemein) contemptible; (fam: schrecklich) dreadful, adv -ly. E~**sviertel** nt slum

elf inv a, E~ f -,-en eleven

Elfe f -,-n fairy

Elfenbein nt ivory

Elfmeter m (Fußball) penalty

elfte(r,s) a eleventh

eliminieren vt eliminate

Elite f -,-n élite

Elixier nt -s,-e elixir

Ell[en]bogen m elbow

Ellip|se f -,-n ellipse. e~**tisch** a elliptical

Elsaß nt - Alsace

elsässisch a Alsatian

Elster f -,-n magpie

elter|lich a parental. E~**n** pl parents. E~**nhaus** nt [parental] home. e~**nlos** a orphaned. E~**nteil** m parent

Email /e'maj/ nt -s,-s, E~**le** /e'maljə/ f -,-n enamel. e~**lieren** /ema[l]'jiːrən/ vt enamel

Emanzi|pation /-'tsjoːn/ f - emancipation. e~**piert** a emancipated

Embargo nt -s,-s embargo

Emblem nt -s,-e emblem

Embryo m -s,-s embryo

Emigr|ant(in) m -en,-en (f -,-nen) emigrant. E~**ation** /-'tsjoːn/ f - emigration. e~**ieren** vi (sein) emigrate

eminent a eminent, adv -ly

Emission f -,-en emission; (Comm) issue

Emotion /-'tsjo:n/ f -,-en emotion. **e~al** a emotional

Empfang m -[e]s,⁻e reception; (Erhalt) receipt; **in E~ nehmen** receive; (annehmen) accept. **e~en†** vt receive; (Biol) conceive

Empfänger m -s,- recipient; (Post-) addressee; (Zahlungs-) payee; (Radio, TV) receiver. **e~lich** a receptive/(Med) susceptible (für to). **E~nis** f- (Biol) conception

Empfängnisverhütung f contraception. **E~smittel** nt contraceptive

Empfangs|bestätigung f receipt. **E~chef** m reception manager. **E~dame** f receptionist. **E~halle** f [hotel] foyer

empfehl|en† vt recommend; sich **e~en** be advisable; (verabschieden) take one's leave. **e~enswert** a to be recommended; (ratsam) advisable. **E~ung** f -,-en recommendation; (Gruß) regards pl

empfind|en† vt feel. **e~lich** a sensitive (gegen to); (zart) delicate; (wund) tender; (reizbar) touchy; (hart) severe, adv -ly. **E~lichkeit** f - sensitivity; delicacy; tenderness; touchiness. **e~sam** a sensitive; (sentimental) sentimental. **E~ung** f -,-en sensation; (Regung) feeling

emphatisch a emphatic, adv -ally

empor adv (liter) up[wards]

Empor|kömmling m -s,-e upstart. **e~ragen** vi sep (haben) rise [up]

empör|t a indignant, adv -ly. **E~ung** f - indignation; (Auflehnung) rebellion

emsig a busy, adv -ily

Ende nt -s,-n end; (eines Films, Romans) ending; (am: Stück) bit; **E~ Mai** at the end of May; **zu E~ sein/gehen** be finished/come to an end; **etw zu E~ schreiben** finish writing sth; **am E~** at the end; (schließlich) in the end; (fam: vielleicht) perhaps; (fam: erschöpft) at the end of one's tether

end|en vi (haben) end. **e~gültig** a final, adv -ly; (bestimmt) definite, adv -ly

Endivie /-jə/ f -,-n endive

end|lich adv at last, finally; (schließlich) in the end. **e~los** a endless, adv -ly. **E~resultat** nt final result. **E~spiel** nt final. **E~spurt** m -[e]s final spurt. **E~station** f terminus. **E~ung** f -,-en (Gram) ending

Energie f - energy

energisch a resolute, adv -ly; (nachdrücklich) vigorous, adv -ly; **e~ werden** put one's foot down

eng a narrow; (beengt) cramped; (anliegend) tight; (nah) close, adv -ly

Enga|gement /āgaʒə'mã:/ nt -s,-s (Theat) engagement; (fig) commitment. **e~gieren** /-'ʒi:rən/ vt (Theat) engage; **sich e~gieren** become involved; **e~giert** committed

eng|anliegend a tight-fitting. **E~ef~** narrowness; **in die E~e treiben** (fig) drive into a corner

Engel m -s,- angel. **e~haft** a angelic

engherzig a petty

England nt -s England

Engländer m -s,- Englishman; (Techn) monkey-wrench; **die E~** the English pl. **E~in** f -,-nen Englishwoman

englisch a English; **auf e~** in English. **E~** nt -[s] (Lang) English

Engpaß m (fig) bottle-neck

en gros /ã'gro:/ *adv* wholesale

engstirnig *a* (*fig*) narrow-minded

Enkel *m* -s,-. grandson; **E~** *pl* grandchildren. **E~in** *f* -,-nen granddaughter. **E~kind** *nt* grandchild. **E~sohn** *m* grandson. **E~tochter** *f* granddaughter

enorm *a* enormous, *adv* -ly; (*fam*: *großartig*) fantastic

Ensemble /ã'sã:bəl/ *nt* -s,-s ensemble; (*Theat*) company

entart|en *vi* (*sein*) degenerate. **e~et** *a* degenerate

entbehr|en *vt* do without; (*vermissen*) miss. **e~lich** *a* dispensable; (*überflüssig*) superfluous. **E~ung** *f* -,-en privation

entbind|en† *vt* release (**von** from); (*Med*) deliver (**von** of) □ *vi* (*haben*) give birth. **E~ung** *f* delivery. **E~ungsstation** *f* maternity ward

entblöß|en *vt* bare. **e~t** *a* bare

entdeck|en *vt* discover. **E~er** *m* -s,- discoverer; (*Forscher*) explorer. **E~ung** *f* -,-en discovery

Ente *f* -,-n duck

entehren *vt* dishonour

enteign|en *vt* dispossess; expropriate (*Eigentum*)

enterben *vt* disinherit

Enterich *m* -s,-e drake

entfachen *vt* kindle

entfallen† *vi* (*sein*) not apply; **jdm e~** slip from s.o.'s hand; (*aus dem Gedächtnis*) slip s.o.'s mind; **auf jdn e~** be s.o.'s share

entfalt|en *vt* unfold; (*entwickeln*) develop; (*zeigen*) display; **sich e~en** unfold; develop. **E~ung** *f* development

entfern|en *vt* remove; **sich e~en** leave. **e~t** *a* distant; (*schwach*) vague, *adv* -ly; **2 Kilometer e~t** 2 kilometres away; **e~t verwandt** distantly related; **nicht im e~testen** not in the least.

E~ung *f* -,-en removal; (*Abstand*) distance; (*Reichweite*) range. **E~ungsmesser** *m* range-finder

entfesseln *vt* (*fig*) unleash

entfliehen† *vi* (*sein*) escape

entfremd|en *vt* alienate. **E~ung** *f* -alienation

entfrosten *vt* defrost

entführ|en *vt* abduct, kidnap; hijack (*Flugzeug*). **E~er** *m* abductor, kidnapper; hijacker. **E~ung** *f* abduction, kidnapping; hijacking

entgegen *adv* towards □ *prep* (+ *dat*) contrary to. **e~gehen†** *vi sep* (*sein*) (+ *dat*) go to meet; (*fig*) be heading for. **e~gesetzt** *a* opposite; (*gegensätzlich*) opposing. **e~halten†** *vt sep* (*fig*) object. **e~kommen†** *vi sep* (*sein*) (+ *dat*) come to meet; (*zukommen auf*) come towards; (*fig*) oblige. **E~kommen** *nt* -s helpfulness; (*Zugeständnis*) concession. **e~kommend** *a* approaching; (*Verkehr*) oncoming; (*fig*) obliging. **e~nehmen†** *vt sep* accept. **e~sehen** *vi sep* (*haben*) (+ *dat*) (*fig*) await; (*freudig*) look forward to. **e~setzen** *vt sep* **Widerstand e~setzen** (+ *dat*) resist. **e~treten†** *vi sep* (*sein*) (+ *dat*) (*fig*) confront; (*bekämpfen*) fight. **e~wirken** *vi sep* (*haben*) (+ *dat*) counteract; (*fig*) oppose

entgegn|en *vt* reply (**auf** (+ *acc* to). **E~ung** *f* -,-en reply

entgehen† *vi sep* (*sein*) (+ *dat*) escape; **jdm e~** (*unbemerkt bleiben*) escape s.o.'s notice; **sich** (*dat*) **etw e~ lassen** miss sth

entgeistert *a* flabbergasted

Entgelt *nt* -[e]s payment; **gegen E~** for money. **e~en** *vt* **jdn etw e~en lassen** (*fig*) make s.o. pay for sth

entgleis|en vi (sein) be derailed; (fig) make a gaffe. **E~ung** f -,-en derailment; (fig) gaffe

entgleiten† vi (sein) jdm e~ slip from s.o.'s grasp

entgräten vt fillet, bone

Enthaarungsmittel nt depilatory

enthalt|en† vt contain; **in etw** (dat) **e~en sein** be contained/ (eingeschlossen) included in sth; **sich der Stimme e~en** (Pol) abstain. **e~sam** a abstemious. **E~samkeit** f - abstinence. **E~ung** f (Pol) abstention

enthaupten vt behead

entheben† vt jdn seines Amtes **e~** relieve s.o. of his post

enthüll|en vt unveil; (fig) reveal. **E~ung** f -,-en revelation

Enthusias|mus m - enthusiasm. **E~t** m -en,-en enthusiast. **e~tisch** a enthusiastic, adv -ally

entkernen vt stone; core (Apfel)

entkleid|en vt undress; **sich e~en** undress. **E~ungsnummer** f strip-tease [act]

entkommen† vi (sein) escape

entkorken vt uncork

entkräft|en vt weaken; (fig) invalidate. **E~ung** f - debility

entkrampfen vt relax; **sich e~** relax

entlad|en† vt unload; (Electr) discharge; **sich e~** discharge; (Gewitter:) break; (Zorn:) erupt

entlang adv & prep (+ preceding acc or following dat) along; **die Straße e~**, **e~ der Straße** along the road; **an etw** (dat) **e~** along sth. **e~fahren†** vi sep (sein) drive along. **e~gehen†** vi sep (sein) walk along

entlarven vt unmask

entlass|en† vt dismiss; (aus Krankenhaus) discharge; (aus der Haft) release; **aus der Schule e~en werden** leave school.

E~ung f -,-en dismissal; discharge; release

entlast|en vt relieve the strain on; ease (Gewissen, Verkehr); relieve (von of); (Jur) exonerate. **E~ung** f - relief; exoneration. **E~ungszug** m relief train

entlaufen† vi (sein) run away

entledigen (sich) vr (+ dat) rid oneself of; (ausziehen) take off; (erfüllen) discharge

entleeren vt empty

entlegen a remote

entleihen† vt borrow (von from)

entlocken vt coax (dat from)

entlohnen vt pay

entlüft|en vt ventilate. **E~er** m -s,- extractor fan. **E~ung** f ventilation

entmündigen vt declare incapable of managing his own affairs

entmutigen vt discourage

entnehmen† vt take (dat from); (schließen) gather (dat from)

Entomologie f - entomology

entpuppen (sich) vr (fig) turn out (als etw to be sth)

entrahmen vt skimmed

entreißen† vt snatch (dat from)

entrichten vt pay

entrinnen† vi (sein) escape

entrollen vt unroll; unfurl (Fahne); **sich e~** unroll; unfurl

entrüst|en vt fill with indignation; **sich e~en** be indignant (über + acc at). **e~et** a indignant, adv -ly. **E~ung** f - indignation

entsaft|en vt extract the juice from. **E~er** m -s,- juice extractor

entsag|en vi (haben) (+ dat) renounce. **E~ung** f - renunciation

entschädig|en vt compensate. **E~ung** f -,-en compensation

entschärfen vt defuse

entscheid|en vt/i (haben) decide; **sich e~en** decide; (Sache:) be decided. **e~end** a decisive,

adv -ly; (kritisch) crucial.
E ~ ung f decision

entschieden a decided, adv -ly;
(fest) firm, adv -ly

entschlafen† vi (sein) (liter) pass
away

entschließen† (sich) vr decide,
make up one's mind; sich anders
e ~ change one's mind

entschlossen a determined;
(energisch) resolute, adv -ly;
kurz e ~ without hesitation;
(spontan) on the spur of the moment. E ~ heit f - determination

Entschluß m decision; einen E ~
fassen make a decision

entschlüsseln vt decode

entschuld|bar a excusable. e ~ i-
gen vt excuse; sich e ~ igen apologize (bei to); e ~ igen Sie
[bitte]! sorry! (bei Frage) excuse
me. E ~ igung f -,-en apology;
(Ausrede) excuse; [jdn] um E ~ i-
gung bitten apologize [to s.o.];
E ~ igung! sorry! (bei Frage) excuse me

entsetz|en vt horrify. E ~ en nt -s
horror. e ~ lich a horrible, adv
-bly; (schrecklich) terrible, adv
-bly. e ~ t a horrified

entsinnen† (sich) vr (+ gen) remember

Entsorgung f - waste disposal

entspann|en vt relax; sich e ~ en
relax; ⟨Lage:⟩ ease. E ~ ung f -
relaxation; easing; (Pol) détente

entsprech|en† vi (haben) (+ dat)
correspond to; (übereinstimmen)
agree with; (nachkommen) comply with. e ~ end a corresponding; (angemessen) appropriate;
(zuständig) relevant □adv cor-
respondingly; appropriately;
(demgemäß) accordingly □prep
(+ dat) in accordance with.
E ~ ung f -,-en equivalent

entspringen† vi (sein) ⟨Fluß:⟩
rise; (fig) arise, spring (dat from);
(entfliehen) escape

entstammen vi (sein) come/(abstammen) be descended (dat
from)

entsteh|en† vi (sein) come into
being; (sich bilden) form; (sich
entwickeln) develop; ⟨Brand:⟩
start; (stammen) originate/(sich
ergeben) result (aus from).
E ~ ung f - origin; formation;
development; (fig) birth

entsteinen vt stone

entstell|en vt disfigure; (verzer-
ren) distort. E ~ ung f disfigure-
ment; distortion

entstört a (Electr) suppressed

enttäusch|en vt disappoint.
E ~ ung f disappointment

entvölkern vt depopulate

entwaffnen vt disarm. e ~ d a
(fig) disarming

Entwarnung f all-clear [signal]

entwässer|n vt drain. E ~ ung
f - drainage

entweder conj & adv either

entweichen† vi (sein) escape

entweih|en vt desecrate. E ~ ung
f - desecration

entwenden vt steal (dat from)

entwerfen† vt design; (aufsetzen)
draft; (skizzieren) sketch

entwert|en vt devalue; (ungültig
machen) cancel. E ~ er m -s,-; tick-
et-cancelling machine. E ~ ung f
devaluation; cancelling

entwick|eln vt develop; sich
e ~ eln develop. E ~ lung f -,-en
development; (Biol) evolution.
E ~ lungsland nt developing
country

entwinden† vt wrench (dat from)

entwirren vt disentangle; (fig)
unravel

entwischen vi (sein) jdm e ~
(fam) give s.o. the slip

entwöhnen vt wean (gen from);
cure ⟨Süchtige⟩

entwürdigend a degrading

Entwurf m design; (Konzept)
draft; (Skizze) sketch

entwurzeln *vt* uproot

entzie|**hen**† *vt* take away (*dat* from); jdm den Führerschein e~hen disqualify s.o. from driving; **sich e~hen** (+*dat*) withdraw from; (*entgehen*) evade. **E~hungskur** *f* treatment for drug/alcohol addiction

entziffern *vt* decipher

entzücken *vt* delight. **E~** *nt* -s delight. **e~d** *a* delightful

Entzug *m* withdrawal; (*Vorenthaltung*) deprivation. **E~serscheinungen** *fpl* withdrawal symptoms

entzünd|**en** *vt* ignite; (*anstecken*) light; (*fig: erregen*) inflame; **sich e~en** ignite; (*Med*) become inflamed. **e~et** *a* (*Med*) inflamed. **e~lich** *a* inflammable. **E~ung** *f* (*Med*) inflammation

entzwei *a* broken. **e~en** (**sich**) *vr* quarrel. **e~gehen**† *vi sep* (*sein*) break

Enzian *m* -s,-e gentian

Enzyklo|**pädie** *f* -,-en encyclopaedia. **e~pädisch** *a* encyclopaedic

Enzym *nt* -s,-e enzyme

Epidemie *f* -,-n epidemic

Epi|**lepsie** *f* epilepsy. **E~leptiker(in)** *m* -s,- (*f* -,-nen) epileptic. **e~leptisch** *a* epileptic

Epilog *m* -s,-e epilogue

episch *a* epic

Episode *f* -,-n episode

Epitaph *nt* -s,-e epitaph

Epoche *f* -,-n epoch. **e~machend** *a* epoch-making

Epos *nt* -/Epen epic

er *pron* he; (*Ding, Tier*) it

erachten *vt* consider (**für nötig** necessary). **E~** *nt* -s **meines E~s** in my opinion

erbarmen (**sich**) *vr* have pity/ ⟨*Gott:*⟩ mercy (*gen* on). **E~** *nt* -s pity; mercy

erbärmlich *a* wretched, *adv* -ly; (*stark*) terrible, *adv* -bly

erbarmungslos *a* merciless, *adv* -ly

erbau|**en** *vt* build; (*fig*) edify; **sich e~en** be edified (**an**+*dat* by); **nicht e~t von** (*fam*) not pleased about. **e~lich** *a* edifying

Erbe¹ *m* -n,-n heir

Erbe² *nt* -s inheritance; (*fig*) heritage. **e~n** *vt* inherit

erbeuten *vt* get; (*Mil*) capture

Erbfolge *f* (*Jur*) succession

erbieten† (**sich**) *vr* offer (**zu** to)

Erbin *f* -,-nen heiress

erbitten† *vt* ask for

erbittert *a* bitter; (*heftig*) fierce, *adv* -ly

erblassen *vi* (*sein*) turn pale

erblich *a* hereditary

erblicken *vt* catch sight of

erblinden *vi* (*sein*) go blind

erbost *a* angry, *adv* -ily

erbrechen† *vt* vomit □ *vi/r* [**sich**] **e~** vomit. **E~** *nt* -s vomiting

Erbschaft *f* -,-en inheritance

Erbse *f* -,-n pea

Erb|**stück** *nt* heirloom. **E~teil** *nt* inheritance

Erd|**apfel** *m* (*Aust*) potato. **E~beben** *nt* -s,- earthquake. **E~beere** *f* strawberry. **E~boden** *m* ground

Erde *f* -,-n earth; (*Erdboden*) ground; (*Fußboden*) floor; **auf der E~** on earth; (*auf dem Boden*) on the ground/floor. **e~n** *vt* (*Electr*) earth

erdenklich *a* imaginable

Erd|**gas** *nt* natural gas. **E~geschoß** *nt* ground floor, (*Amer*) first floor. **e~ig** *a* earthy. **E~kugel** *f* globe. **E~kunde** *f* geography. **E~nuß** *f* peanut. **E~öl** *nt* (*mineral*) oil. **E~reich** *nt* soil

erdreisten (**sich**) *vr* have the audacity (**zu** to)

erdrosseln *vt* strangle

erdrücken *vt* crush to death. **e~d** *a* (*fig*) overwhelming

Erd|rutsch *m* landslide. **E~teil** *m* continent

erdulden *vt* endure

ereifern (sich) *vr* get worked up

ereignen (sich) *vr* happen

Ereignis *nt* -ses,-se event. **e~los** *a* uneventful. **e~reich** *a* eventful

Eremit *m* -en,-en hermit

ererbt *a* inherited

erfahr|en† *vt* learn, hear; *(erleben)* experience □ *a* experienced. **E~ung** *f* -,-en experience; **in E~ung bringen** find out

erfassen *vt* seize; *(begreifen)* grasp; *(einbeziehen)* include; *(aufzeichnen)* record; **von einem Auto erfaßt werden** be struck by a car

erfind|en† *vt* invent. **E~er** *m* -s,-, inventor. **e~erisch** *a* inventive. **E~ung** *f* -,-en invention

Erfolg *m* -[e]s,-e success; *(Folge)* result; **E~ haben** be successful. **e~en** *vi (sein)* take place; *(geschehen)* happen. **e~los** *a* unsuccessful, *adv* -ly. **e~reich** *a* successful, *adv* -ly. **e~versprechend** *a* promising

erforder|lich *a* required, necessary. **e~n** *vt* require, demand. **E~nis** *nt* -ses,-se requirement

erforsch|en *vt* explore; *(untersuchen)* investigate. **E~ung** *f* exploration; investigation

erfreu|en *vt* please; **sich guter Gesundheit e~en** enjoy good health. **e~lich** *a* pleasing, gratifying; *(willkommen)* welcome. **e~licherweise** *adv* happily. **e~t** *a* pleased

erfrier|en† *vi (sein)* freeze to death; *⟨Glied:⟩* become frostbitten; *⟨Pflanze:⟩* be killed by the frost. **E~ung** *f* -,-en frostbite

erfrisch|en *vt* refresh; **sich e~en** refresh onself. **e~end** *a* refreshing. **E~ung** *f* -,-en refreshment

erfüll|en *vt* fill; *(nachkommen)* fulfil; serve *⟨Zweck⟩*; discharge *⟨Pflicht⟩*; **sich e~en** come true. **E~ung** *f* fulfilment; **in E~ung gehen** come true

erfunden invented; *(fiktiv)* fictitious

ergänz|en *vt* complement; *(nachtragen)* supplement; *(auffüllen)* replenish; *(vervollständigen)* complete; *(hinzufügen)* add; **sich e~en** complement each other. **E~ung** *f* complement; supplement; *(Zusatz)* addition. **E~ungsband** *m* supplement

ergeb|en† *vt* produce; *(zeigen)* show, establish; **sich e~en** result; *⟨Schwierigkeit:⟩* arise; *(kapitulieren)* surrender; *(sich fügen)* submit; **es ergab sich** it turned out *(daß* that*)* □ *a* devoted, *adv* -ly; *(resigniert)* resigned, *adv* -ly. **E~enheit** *f* devotion

Ergebnis *nt* -ses,-se result. **e~los** *a* fruitless, *adv* -ly

ergehen† *vi (sein)* be issued; **etw über sich** *(acc)* **e~ lassen** submit to sth; **wie ist es dir ergangen?** how did you get on? □ *vr* **sich e~ in** (+ *dat*) indulge in

ergiebig *a* productive; *(fig)* rich

ergötzen *vt* amuse

ergreif|en† *vt* seize; take *⟨Maßnahme, Gelegenheit⟩*; take up *⟨Beruf⟩*; *(rühren)* move; **die Flucht e~** flee. **e~d** *a* moving

ergriffen *a* deeply moved. **E~heit** *f* emotion

ergründen *vt (fig)* get to the bottom of

erhaben *a* raised; *(fig)* sublime; **über etw** *(acc)* **e~ sein** *(fig)* be above sth

Erhalt *m* -[e]s receipt. **e~en†** *vt* receive, get; *(gewinnen)* obtain; *(bewahren)* preserve, keep; *(instandhalten)* maintain; *(unterhalten)* support; **am Leben e~en** keep alive □ *a* **gut/schlecht**

e~en in good/bad condition;
e~en bleiben survive
erhältlich *a* obtainable
Erhaltung *f* - (*s*. erhalten) preservation; maintenance
erhängen (sich) *vr* hang oneself
erhärten *vt* (*fig*) substantiate
erheb|en† *vt* raise; levy ⟨*Steuer*⟩; charge ⟨*Gebühr*⟩; **Anspruch** e~en lay claim (**auf**+*acc* to); **Protest** e~en protest; **sich** e~en rise; ⟨*Frage:*⟩ arise; (*sich empören*) rise up. e~lich *a* considerable, *adv* -bly. **E~ung** *f* -,-en elevation; (*Anhöhe*) rise; (*Aufstand*) uprising; (*Ermittlung*) survey
erheiter|n *vt* amuse. **E~ung** *f* - amusement
erhitzen *vt* heat; **sich** e~ get hot; (*fig*) get heated
erhoffen *vt* **sich** (*dat*) **etw** e~ hope for sth
erhöh|en *vt* raise; (*fig*) increase; **sich** e~en rise, increase. **E~ung** *f* -,-en increase. **E~ungszeichen** *nt* (*Mus*) sharp
erhol|en (sich) *vr* recover (**von** from); (*nach Krankheit*) convalesce, recuperate; (*sich ausruhen*) have a rest. e~sam *a* restful. **E~ung** *f* - recovery; convalescence; (*Ruhe*) rest. **E~ungsheim** *nt* convalescent home
erhören *vt* (*fig*) answer
erinner|n *vt* remind (**an**+*acc* of); **sich** e~n remember (**an jdn/etw** s.o./sth). **E~ung** *f* -,-en memory; (*Andenken*) souvenir
erkält|en (**sich**) *vr* catch a cold; e~et sein have a cold. **E~ung** *f* -,-en cold
erkenn|bar *a* recognizable; (*sichtbar*) visible. e~en† *vt* recognize; (*wahrnehmen*) distinguish; (*einsehen*) realize. e~t-lich *a* **sich** e~tlich zeigen show one's appreciation. **E~tnis** *f* -,-se recognition; realization;

⟨*Wissen*⟩ knowledge; **die neuesten** E~tnisse the latest findings
Erker *m* -s,- bay
erklär|en *vt* declare; (*erläutern*) explain; **sich bereit** e~en agree (**zu** to); **ich kann es mir nicht** e~en I can't explain it. e~end *a* explanatory. e~lich *a* explicable; (*verständlich*) understandable. e~licherweise *adv* understandably. e~t *attrib a* declared. **E~ung** *f* -,-en declaration; explanation; **öffentliche E~ung** public statement
erklingen† *vi* (*sein*) ring out
erkrank|en *vi* (*sein*) fall ill; be taken ill (**an**+*dat* with). **E~ung** *f* -,-en illness
erkunden *vt* explore; (*Mil*) reconnoitre
erkundig|en (sich) *vr* enquire (**nach jdm/etw** after s.o./about sth). **E~ung** *f* -,-en enquiry
erlahmen *vi* (*sein*) tire; ⟨*Kraft, Eifer:*⟩ flag
erlangen *vt* attain, get
Erlaß *m* -sses, ̈-sse (*Admin*) decree; (*Befreiung*) exemption; (*Straf-*) remission
erlassen† *vt* (*Admin*) issue; **jdm etw** e~ exempt s.o. from sth; let s.o. off ⟨*Strafe*⟩
erlauben *vt* allow, permit; **sich** e~, **etw zu tun** take the liberty of doing sth; **ich kann es mir nicht** e~ I can't afford it
Erlaubnis *f* - permission. **E~schein** *m* permit
erläuter|n *vt* explain. **E~ung** *f* -,-en explanation
Erle *f* -,-n alder
erleb|en *vt* experience; (*mit-*) see; have ⟨*Überraschung, Enttäuschung*⟩; **etw nicht mehr** e~en not live to see sth. **E~nis** *nt* -ses,-se experience
erledig|en *vt* do; (*sich befassen mit*) deal with; (*beenden*) finish;

(*entscheiden*) settle; (*töten*) kill; **e~t sein** be done/settled/ (*fam: müde*) worn out/(*fam: ruiniert*) finished

erleichter|n *vt* lighten; (*vereinfachen*) make easier; (*befreien*) relieve; (*lindern*) ease; **sich e~n** (*fig*) unburden oneself. **e~t a** relieved. **E~ung** *f* -relief

erleiden† *vt* suffer

erlernen *vt* learn

erlesen *a* exquisite; (*auserlesen*) choice, select

erleucht|en *vt* illuminate; **hell e~et** brightly lit. **E~ung** *f* -,-en (*fig*) inspiration

erliegen† *vi* (*sein*) succumb (*dat* to); **seinen Verletzungen e~** die of one's injuries

erlogen *a* untrue, false

Erlös *m* -es proceeds *pl*

erlöschen† *vi* (*sein*) go out; (*vergehen*) die; (*aussterben*) die out; (*ungültig werden*) expire; **erloschener Vulkan** extinct volcano

erlös|en *vt* save; (*befreien*) release (*von* from); (*Relig*) redeem. **e~t** *a* relieved. **E~ung** *f* release; (*Erleichterung*) relief; (*Relig*) redemption

ermächtig|en *vt* authorize. **E~ung** *f* -,-en authorization

ermahn|en *vt* exhort; (*zurechtweisen*) admonish. **E~ung** *f* exhortation; admonition

ermäßig|en *vt* reduce. **E~ung** *f* -,-en reduction

ermatt|en *vi* (*sein*) grow weary □*vt* weary. **e~et** *a* weary. **E~ung** *f* - weariness

ermessen† *vt* judge; (*begreifen*) appreciate. **E~** *nt* -s discretion; (*Urteil*) judgement; **nach eigenem E~** at one's own discretion

ermitt|eln *vt* establish; (*herausfinden*) find out □*vi* (*haben*) investigate (**gegen jdn** s.o.). **E~lungen** *fpl* investigations.

E~lungsverfahren *nt* (*Jur*) preliminary inquiry

ermöglichen *vt* make possible

ermord|en *vt* murder. **E~ung** *f* -,-en murder

ermüd|en *vt* tire □*vi* (*sein*) get tired. **E~ung** *f* - tiredness

ermunter|n *vt* encourage; **sich e~n** rouse oneself. **E~ung** *f* - encouragement

ermutigen *vt* encourage. **e~d** *a* encouraging

ernähr|en *vt* feed; (*unterhalten*) support, keep; **sich e~en von** live/⟨*Tier:*⟩ feed on. **E~er** *m* -s,- breadwinner. **E~ung** *f* - nourishment; nutrition; (*Kost*) diet

ernenn|en† *vt* appoint. **E~ung** *f* - an appointment

erneu|ern *vt* renew; (*auswechseln*) replace; change ⟨*Verband*⟩; (*renovieren*) renovate. **E~erung** *f* renewal; replacement; renovation. **e~t a** renewed; (*neu*) new □ *adv* again

erniedrig|en *vt* degrade; **sich e~en** lower oneself. **e~end** *a* degrading. **E~ungszeichen** *nt* (*Mus*) flat

ernst *a* serious, *adv* -ly; **e~ nehmen** take seriously. **E~** *m* -es seriousness; **im E~** seriously; **mit einer Drohung E~ machen** carry out a threat; **ist das dein E~?** are you serious? **im E~fall** when the real thing happens. **e~haft** *a* serious, *adv* -ly. **e~lich** *a* serious, *adv* -ly

Ernte *f* -,-n harvest; (*Ertrag*) crop. **E~dankfest** *nt* harvest festival. **e~n** *vt* harvest; (*fig*) reap, win

ernüchter|n *vt* sober up; (*fig*) bring down to earth; (*enttäuschen*) disillusion. **e~nd a** (*fig*) sobering. **E~ung** *f* - disillusionment

Erober|er *m* -s,- conqueror. **e~n** *vt* conquer. **E~ung** *f* -,-en conquest

eröffn|en *vt* open; **jdm etw e~en** announce sth to s.o.; **sich jdm e~en** 〈*Aussicht:*〉 present itself to s.o. **E~ung** *f* opening; (*Mitteilung*) announcement. **E~ungsansprache** *f* opening address

erörter|n *vt* discuss. **E~ung** *f* -,-en discussion

Erosion *f* -,-en erosion

Erot|ik *f* - eroticism. **e~isch** *a* erotic

Erpel *m* -s,- drake

erpicht *a* **e~ auf** (+ *acc*) keen on

erpress|en *vt* extort; blackmail 〈*Person*〉. **E~er** *m* -s,- blackmailer. **E~ung** *f* - extortion; blackmail

erprob|en *vt* test. **e~t** *a* proven

erquicken *vt* refresh

erraten† *vt* guess

erreg|bar *a* excitable. **e~en** *vt* excite; (*hervorrufen*) arouse; **sich e~en** get worked up. **e~end** *a* exciting. (*hitzig*) **e~t** *a* -s,- (*Med*) germ. **e~t** *a* agitated; (*hitzig*) heated. **E~ung** *f* - excitement; (*Erregtheit*) agitation

erreich|bar *a* within reach; 〈*Ziel:*〉 attainable; 〈*Person:*〉 available. **e~en** *vt* reach; catch 〈*Zug:*〉; live to 〈*Alter:*〉; (*durchsetzen*) achieve

erretten *vt* save

errichten *vt* erect

erringen† *vt* gain, win

erröten *vi* (*sein*) blush

Errungenschaft *f* -,-en achievement; (*fam: Anschaffung*) acquisition; **E~en der Technik** technical advances

Ersatz *m* -es replacement, substitute; (*Entschädigung*) compensation. **E~dienst** *m* = Zivildienst. **E~reifen** *m* spare tyre. **E~spieler(in)** *m(f)* substitute. **E~teil** *nt* spare part

ersäufen *vt* drown

erschaffen† *vt* create

erschallen† *vi* (*sein*) ring out

erschein|en† *vi* (*sein*) appear; 〈*Buch:*〉 be published; **jdm merkwürdig e~en** seem odd to s.o. **E~en** *nt* -s appearance; publication. **E~ung** *f* -,-en appearance; (*Person*) figure; (*Phänomen*) phenomenon; (*Symptom*) symptom; (*Geist*) apparition

erschieß|en† *vt* shoot [dead]. **E~ungskommando** *nt* firing squad

erschlaffen *vi* (*sein*) go limp; 〈*Haut, Muskeln:*〉 become flabby

erschlagen† *vt* beat to death; (*tödlich treffen*) strike dead; **vom Blitz e~ werden** be killed by lightning. □*a* (*fam*) (*erschöpft*) worn out; (*fassungslos*) stunned

erschließen† *vt* develop; (*zugänglich machen*) open up; (*nutzbar machen*) tap

erschöpf|en *vt* exhaust. **e~end** *a* exhausting; (*fig: vollständig*) exhaustive. **e~t** *a* exhausted. **E~ung** *f* - exhaustion

erschreck|en† *vt* (*sein*) get a fright □*vt* (*reg*) startle; (*beunruhigen*) alarm; **du hast mich e~t** you gave me a fright □*vr* (*reg & irreg*) **sich e~en** get a fright. **e~end** *a* alarming, *adv* -ly

erschrocken *a* frightened; (*erschreckt*) startled; (*bestürzt*) dismayed

erschütter|n *vt* shake; (*ergreifen*) upset deeply. **E~ung** *f* -,-en shock

erschweren *vt* make more difficult

erschwinglich *a* affordable

ersehen† *vt* (*fig*) see (aus from)

ersetzen *vt* replace; make good 〈*Schaden:*〉; refund 〈*Kosten:*〉; **jdm etw e~** compensate s.o. for sth

ersichtlich *a* obvious, apparent

erspar|en *vt* save; **jdm etw e~en** save/(*fernhalten*) spare s.o. sth. **E~nis** *f* -,-se saving; **E~nisse** savings

erst adv (zuerst) first; (noch nicht mehr als) only; (nicht vor) not until; e~ dann only then; eben od gerade e~ [only] just; das machte ihn e~ recht wütend it made him all the more angry

erstarren vi (sein) solidify; (gefrieren) freeze; (steif werden) go stiff; (vor Schreck) be paralysed

erstatten vt (zurück-) refund; Bericht e~ report (jdm to s.o.)

Erstaufführung f first performance, première

erstaun|en vt amaze, astonish. E~en nt amazement, astonishment. e~lich a amazing, adv -ly. e~licherweise adv amazingly

Erstausgabe f first edition. e~e(r,s) a first; (beste) best; E~e Hilfe first aid; er kam als e~er he arrived first; als e~es first of all; fürs e~e for the time being; der e~e beste the first one to come along; (fam) any Tom, Dick or Harry. E~e(r) m/f best; er ist der/sie ist die E~e in Latein he/she is top in Latin

erstechen† vt stab to death

erstehen† vt buy

ersteigern vt buy at an auction

erst|ens adv firstly, in the first place. e~ere(r,s) a the former; der/die/das e~ere the former

ersticken vt suffocate; smother ⟨Flammen⟩; (unterdrücken) suppress □ vi (sein) suffocate. E~ nt -s suffocation; zum E~ stifling

erst|klassig a first-class. e~mals adv for the first time

erstreben vt strive for. e~swert a desirable

erstrecken (sich) vr stretch; sich e~ auf (+ acc) (fig) apply to

ersuchen vt ask, request. E~ nt -s request

ertappen vt (fam) catch

erteilen vt give (jdm s.o.)

ertönen vi (sein) sound; (erschallen) ring out

Ertrag m -[e]s,-̈e yield. e~en† vt bear

erträglich a bearable; (leidlich) tolerable

ertränken vt drown

ertrinken† vi (sein) drown

erübrigen (sich) vr be unnecessary

erwachen vi (sein) awake

erwachsen a grown-up. E~e(r) m/f adult, grown-up

erwägen† vt consider. E~ung f -,-en consideration; in E~ung ziehen consider

erwähn|en vt mention. E~ung f -,-en mention

erwärmen vt warm; sich e~ warm up; (fig) warm (für to)

erwart|en vt expect; (warten auf) wait for. E~ung f -,-en expectation. e~ungsvoll a expectant, adv -ly

erwecken vt (fig) arouse; give ⟨Anschein⟩

erweichen vt soften; (fig) move; sich e~ lassen (fig) relent

erweisen† vt prove; (bezeigen) do ⟨Gefallen, Dienst, Ehre⟩; sich e~ als prove to be

erweitern vt widen; dilate ⟨Pupille⟩; (fig) extend, expand

Erwerb m -[e]s acquisition; (Kauf) purchase; (Brot-) livelihood; (Verdienst) earnings pl. e~en† vt acquire; (kaufen) purchase; (fig: erlangen) gain. e~slos a unemployed. e~stätig a [gainfully] employed. E~ung f -,-en acquisition

erwider|n vt reply; return (Besuch, Gruß). E~ung f -,-en reply

erwirken vt obtain

erwischen vt (fam) catch

erwünscht a desired

erwürgen vt strangle

Erz nt -es,-e ore

erzähl|en vt tell (jdm s.o.) □ vi (haben) talk (von about). E~er *m* -s,- narrator. **E~ung** *f* -,-en story, tale

Erzbischof *m* archbishop

erzeug|en *vt* produce; (*Electr*) generate; (*fig*) create. **E~er** *m* -s,- producer; (*Vater*) father. **E~nis** *nt* -ses,-se product; landwirtschaftliche **E~nisse** farm produce *sg*. **E~ung** *f* - production; generation

Erz|feind *m* arch-enemy. **E~herzog** *m* archduke

erzieh|en† *vt* bring up; (*Sch*) educate. **E~er** *m* -s,- (*private*) tutor. **E~erin** *f* -,-nen governess. **E~ung** *f* -,-nen upbringing; education

erzielen *vt* achieve; score ⟨*Tor*⟩

erzogen *a* gut/schlecht **e~** well/ badly brought up

erzürnt *a* angry

erzwingen† *vt* force

es *pron* it; (*Mädchen*) she; (*acc*) her; *impers* **es** regnet it is raining; **es** gibt there is/(*pl*) are; **ich hoffe es** I hope so

Esche *f* -,-n ash

Esel *m* -s,- donkey; (*fam: Person*) ass. **E~sohr** *nt* **E~sohren haben** ⟨*Buch:*⟩ be dog-eared

Eskal|ation /-'tsjo:n/ *f* - escalation. **e~ieren** *vt/i* (*haben*) escalate

Eskimo *m* -[s],-[s] eskimo

Eskort|e *f* -,-n (*Mil*) escort. **e~ieren** *vt* escort

eßbar *a* edible. **Eßecke** *f* dining area

essen† *vt/i* (*haben*) eat; **zu Mittag/Abend e~** have lunch/supper; [auswärts] **e~ gehen** eat out; **chinesisch e~** have a Chinese meal. **E~** *nt* -s,- food; (*Mahl*) meal; (*festlich*) dinner

Essenz *f* -,-en essence

Esser(in) *m* -s,- (*f* -,-nen) eater

Essig *m* -s vinegar. **E~gurke** *f* [pickled] gherkin

Eßkastanie *f* sweet chestnut. **Eßlöffel** *m* ≈ dessertspoon. **Eß-**

stäbchen *ntpl* chopsticks. **Eßtisch** *m* dining-table. **Eßwaren** *fpl* food *sg*; (*Vorräte*) provisions. **Eßzimmer** *nt* dining-room

Estland *nt* -s Estonia

Estragon *m* -s tarragon

etablieren (sich) *vr* establish oneself/⟨*Geschäft:*⟩ itself

Etage /e'ta:ʒə/ *f* -,-n storey. **E~nbett** *nt* bunk-beds *pl*. **E~nwohnung** *f* flat, (*Amer*) apartment

Etappe *f* -,-n stage

Etat /e'ta:/ *m* -s,-s budget

etepetete *a* (*fam*) fussy

Eth|ik *f* -ethic; (*Sittenlehre*) ethics *sg*. **e~isch** *a* ethical

Etikett *nt* -[e]s,-e[n] label; (*Preis-*) tag. **E~e** *f* -,-n etiquette; (*Aust*) = Etikett. **e~ieren** *vt* label

etlich|e(r,s) *pron* some; (*mehrere*) several; **e~es** a number of things; (*ziemlich viel*) quite a lot. **e~emal** *adv* several times

Etui /e'tvi:/ *nt* -s,-s case

etwa *adv* (*ungefähr*) about; (*zum Beispiel*) for instance; (*womöglich*) perhaps; nicht **e~**, daß ... not that ...; **denkt nicht e~** ... don't imagine ...; du hast doch nicht **e~** Angst? you're not afraid, are you? **e~ig** *a* possible

etwas *pron* something; (*fragend/ verneint*) anything; (*ein bißchen*) some, a little; ohne **e~** zu sagen without saying anything; sonst noch **e~**? anything else? noch **e~** Tee? some more tea? so **e~** Ärgerliches! what a nuisance!
□*adv* a bit

Etymologie *f* - etymology

euch *pron* (*acc of* ihr *pl*) you; (*dat*) [to] you; (*refl*) yourselves; (*einander*) each other; ein Freund von **e~** a friend of yours

euer *poss pron pl* your. **e~e**, **e~t-** s. eure, euret-

Eule *f* -,-n owl

Euphorie *f* - euphoria

eur|e *poss pron pl* your. e~e(r,s) *poss pron* yours. e~erseits *adv* for your part. e~etwegen *adv* for your sake; (*wegen euch*) because of you, on your account. e~etwillen *adv* um e~etwillen for your sake. e~ige *poss pron* der/die/das e~ige yours

Euro- *pref* Euro-

Europa *nt* -s Europe. E~- *pref* European

Europä|er(in) *m* -s,- (*f* -,-nen) European. e~isch *a* European; E~ische Gemeinschaft European Community

Euro|paß *m* Europasport. E~- scheck *m* Eurocheque

Euter *nt* -s,- udder

evakuier|en *vt* evacuate. E~ung *f* - evacuation

evan|gelisch *a* Protestant. E~gelist *m* -en,-en evangelist. E~gelium *nt* -s,-ien gospel

evaporieren *vt/i* (*sein*) evaporate

Eventu|alität *f* -,-en eventuality. e~ell *a* possible □ *adv* possibly; (*vielleicht*) perhaps

Evolution *f* -/tsjo:n/ *f* - evolution

evtl. *abbr s.* eventuell

ewig *a* eternal, *adv* -ly; (*fam: ständig*) constant, *adv* -ly; (*endlos*) never-ending; e~ dauern (*fam*) take ages. E~keit *f* - eternity; eine E~keit (*fam*) ages

exakt *a* exact, *adv* -ly. E~heit *f* - exactitude

Examen *nt* -s,- *and* -mina (*Sch*) examination

Exekutive *f* -(-*Pol*) executive

Exempel *nt* -s,- example; ein E~ an jdm statuieren make an example of s.o.

Exemplar *nt* -s,-e specimen; (*Buch*) copy. e~isch *a* exemplary

exerzieren *vt/i* (*haben*) (*Mil*) drill; (*üben*) practise

exhumieren *vt* exhume

Exil *nt* -s exile

Existenz *f* -,-en existence; (*Lebensgrundlage*) livelihood; (*pej: Person*) individual

existieren *vi* (*haben*) exist

exklusiv *a* exclusive. e~e *prep* (+ *gen*) excluding

exkommunizieren *vt* excommunicate

Exkremente *npl* excrement *sg*

exotisch *a* exotic

expan|dieren *vt/i* (*haben*) expand. E~sion *f* - expansion

Expedition /-'tsjo:n/ *f* -,-en expedition

Experiment *nt* -[e]s,-e experiment. e~ell *a* experimental. e~ieren *vi* (*haben*) experiment

Experte *m* -n,-n expert

explo|dieren *vi* (*sein*) explode. E~sion *f* -,-en explosion. e~siv *a* explosive

Expor|t *m* -[e]s,-e export. E~teur /-'tø:ɐ/ *m* -s,-e exporter. e~tieren *vt* export

Expreß *m* -sses,-sse express

extra *adv* separately; (*zusätzlich*) extra; (*eigens*) specially; (*fam: absichtlich*) on purpose

Extrakt *m* -[e]s,-e extract

Extras *npl* (*Auto*) extras

extravagan|t *a* flamboyant, *adv* -ly; (*übertrieben*) extravagant. E~z *f* -,-en flamboyance; extravagance; (*Überspanntheit*) folly

extravertiert *a* extrovert

extrem *a* extreme, *adv* -ly. E~ *nt* -s,-e extreme. E~ist *m* -en,-en extremist. E~itäten *fpl* extremities

Exzellenz *f* - (*title*) Excellency

Exzentriker *m* -s,- eccentric. e~isch *a* eccentric

Exzeß *m* -sses,-sse excess

F

Fabel *f* -,-n fable. f~haft *a* (*fam*) fantastic, *adv* -ally

Fabrik f -,-en factory. **F~ant** m -en,-en manufacturer. **F~at** nt -[e]s,-e product; (Marke) make. **F~ation** /-'tsioːn/ f - manufacture

Facette /fa'sɛtə/ f -,-n facet

Fach nt -[e]s,ˑer compartment; (Schub-) drawer; (Gebiet) field; (Sch) subject. **F~arbeiter** m skilled worker. **F~arzt** m, **F~ärztin** f specialist. **F~ausdruck** m technical term

fäch|eln (sich) vr fan oneself. **F~er** m -s,- fan

Fach|gebiet nt field. **f~gemäß**, **f~gerecht** a expert, adv -ly. **F~hochschule** f ≈ technical university. **f~kundig** a expert, adv -ly. **f~lich** a technical, adv -ly; (beruflich) professional. **F~mann** m (pl -leute) expert. **f~männisch** a expert, adv -ly. **F~schule** f technical college. **f~simpeln** vi (haben) (fam) talk shop. **F~werkhaus** nt half-timbered house. **F~wort** nt (pl -wörter) technical term

Fackel f -,-n torch. **F~zug** m torchlight procession

fade a insipid; (langweilig) dull

Faden m -s,ˑ thread; (Bohnen-) string; (Naut) fathom. **f~scheinig** a threadbare; (Grund) flimsy

Fagott nt -[e]s,-e bassoon

fähig a capable (zu/gen of); (tüchtig) able, competent. **F~keit** f -,-en ability; competence

fahl a pale

fahnd|en vi (haben) search (nach for). **F~ung** f -,-en search

Fahne f -,-n flag; (Druck-) galley [proof]; **eine F~ haben** (fam) reek of alcohol. **F~nflucht** f desertion. **f~nflüchtig** a · **f~flüchtig werden** desert

Fahr|ausweis m ticket. **F~bahn** f carriageway; (Straße) road. **f~bar** a mobile

Fähre f -,-n ferry

fahr|en† vi (sein) go, travel; ⟨Fahrer:⟩ drive; ⟨Radfahrer:⟩ ride; (verkehren) run; (ab-) leave; ⟨Schiff:⟩ sail; **mit dem Auto/Zug f~en** go by car/train; **in die Höhe f~en** start up; **in die Kleider f~en** throw on one's clothes; **mit der Hand über etw** (acc) **f~en** run one's hand over sth; **was ist in ihn gefahren?** (fam) what has got into him? □ vt drive; ride ⟨Fahrrad⟩; take ⟨Kurve⟩. **f~end** a moving; (f~bar) mobile; (nicht seßhaft) travelling, itinerant. **F~er** m -s,- driver. **F~erflucht** f failure to stop after an accident. **F~erhaus** nt driver's cab. **F~erin** f -,-nen woman driver. **F~gast** m passenger; (im Taxi) fare. **F~geld** nt fare. **F~gestell** nt chassis; (Aviat) undercarriage. **f~ig** a nervy; (zerstreut) distracted. **F~karte** f ticket. **F~kartenausgabe** f, **F~kartenschalter** m ticket office. **f~lässig** a negligent, adv -ly. **F~lässigkeit** f - negligence. **F~lehrer** m driving instructor. **F~plan** m timetable. **f~planmäßig** a scheduled □ adv according to/(pünktlich) on schedule. **F~preis** m fare. **F~prüfung** f driving test. **F~rad** nt bicycle. **F~schein** m ticket

Fährschiff nt ferry

Fahr|schule f driving school. **F~schüler(in)** m(f) learner driver. **F~spur** f [traffic] lane. **F~stuhl** m lift, (Amer) elevator. **F~stunde** f driving lesson

Fahrt f -,-en journey; (Auto) drive; (Ausflug) trip; (Tempo) speed; **in voller F~** at full speed. **F~ausweis** m ticket

Fährte f -,-n track; (Witterung) scent; **auf der falschen F~** (fig) on the wrong track

Fahr|tkosten pl travelling expenses. **F~werk** nt undercarriage. **F~zeug** nt -[e]s,-e vehicle; (Wasser-) craft, vessel

fair /fɛːɐ̯/ a fair, adv -ly. **F~neß** f-fairness

Fakten pl facts

Faktor m -s,-en /-'toːrən/ factor

Fakul|tät f-,-en faculty. **f~tativ** a optional

Falke m -n,-n falcon

Fall m -[e]s,-e fall; (Jur, Med, Gram) case; im **F~[e]** in case (gen of); **auf jeden F~** , **auf alle F~** e in any case; (bestimmt) definitely; **für alle F~** e just in case; **auf keinen F~** on no account

Falle f-,-n trap; **eine F~ stellen** set a trap (dat for)

fallen† vi (sein) fall; (sinken) go down; (im Krieg) **f~** be killed in the war; **f~ lassen** drop

fällen vt fell; (fig) pass (Urteil:); make (Entscheidung)

fallenlassen† vt sep (fig) drop; make (Bemerkung)

fällig a due; (Wechsel) mature; **längst f~** long overdue. **F~keit** f- (Comm) maturity

Fallobst nt windfalls pl

falls conj in case; (wenn) if

Fallschirm m parachute. **F~jäger** m paratrooper. **F~springer** m parachutist

Falltür f trapdoor

falsch a wrong (nicht echt, unaufrichtig) false; (gefälscht) forged (Geld) counterfeit; (Schmuck) fake □adv wrongly; falsely; (singen) out of tune; **f~ gehen** (Uhr:) be wrong

fälsch|en vt forge, fake. **F~er** m -s,- forger

Falsch|geld nt counterfeit money. **F~heit** f- falseness

fälschlich a wrong, adv -ly; (irrtümlich) mistaken, adv -ly. **f~erweise** adv by mistake

Falsch|meldung f false report; (absichtlich) hoax report. **F~münzer** m -s,- counterfeiter

Fälschung f-,-en forgery, fake; (Fälschen) forging

Falte f-,-n fold; (Rock-) pleat; (Knitter) crease; (im Gesicht) line; (Runzel) wrinkle

falten vt fold; sich **f~** (Haut:) wrinkle. **F~rock** m pleated skirt

Falter m -s,- butterfly; (Nacht-) moth

faltig a creased; (Gesicht) lined; (runzlig) wrinkled

familiär a family . . . ; (vertraut, zudringlich) familiar; (zwanglos) informal

Familie /-iə/ f -,-n family. **F~nanschluß** m **F~nanschluß haben** live as one of the family. **F~nforschung** f genealogy. **F~nleben** nt family life. **F~nname** m surname. **F~nplanung** f family planning. **F~nstand** m marital status

Fan /fɛn/ m -s,-s fan

Fana|tiker m -s,- fanatic. **f~tisch** a fanatical, adv -ly. **F~tismus** m - fanaticism

Fanfare f -,-n trumpet; (Signal) fanfare

Fang m -[e]s,-e capture; (Beute) catch; **F~** e (Krallen) talons; (Zähne) fangs. **F~arm** m tentacle. **f~en†** vt catch; (ein-) capture; **sich f~en** get caught (in + dat in); (fig) regain one's balance / (seelisch) composure. **F~en** nt -s **F~en spielen** play tag. **F~frage** f catch question. **F~zahn** m fang

fantastisch a = **phantastisch**

Farb|aufnahme f colour photograph. **F~band** nt (pl -bänder) typewriter ribbon. **F~e** f-,-n colour; (Maler-) paint; (zum Färben) dye; (Karten) suit. **f~echt** a colour-fast

färben vt colour; dye ⟨Textilien, Haare⟩; (fig)slant ⟨Bericht⟩; **sich [rot] f~** turn [red] □vi (haben) not be colour-fast

farb|enblind a colour-blind. **f~enfroh** a colourful. **F~fernsehen** nt colour television. **F~film** m colour film. **F~foto** nt colour photo. **f~ig** a coloured □adv in colour. **F~ige(r)** m/f coloured man/woman. **F~kasten** m box of paints. **f~los** a colourless. **F~stift** m crayon. **F~stoff** m dye; ⟨Lebensmittel-⟩ colouring. **F~ton** m shade

Färbung f -,-en colouring; (fig: Anstrich) bias

Farce /'farsə/ f -,-n farce; (Culin) stuffing

Farn m -[e]s, -e, **F~kraut** nt fern

Färse f -,-n heifer

Fasan m -[e]s,-e[n] pheasant

Faschierte(s) nt (Aust) mince

Fasching m -s (SGer) carnival

Faschis|mus m - fascism. **F~t** m -en,-en fascist. **f~tisch** a fascist

faseln vt/i (haben) (fam) (Unsinn) **f~** talk nonsense

Faser f -,-n fibre. **f~n** vi (haben) fray

Faß nt -sses,̈-sser barrel, cask; **Bier vom Faß** draught beer; **Faß ohne Boden** (fig) bottomless pit

Fassade f -,-n façade

faßbar a comprehensible; (greifbar) tangible

fassen vt take [hold of], grasp; (ergreifen) seize; (fangen) catch; (ein-) set; (enthalten) hold; (fig: begreifen) take in, grasp; conceive ⟨Plan⟩; make ⟨Entschluß⟩; **sich f~** compose oneself; **sich kurz/in Geduld f~** be brief/ patient; **in Worte f~** put into words; **nicht zu f~** (fig) unbelievable □vi (haben) **f~ an** (+ acc) touch; **f~ nach** reach for

faßlich a comprehensible

Fasson /fa'sõ:/ f - style; (Form) shape; (Weise) way

Fassung f -,-en mount; (Edelstein-) setting; (Electr) socket; (Version) version; (Beherrschung) composure; **aus der F~ bringen** disconcert. **f~slos** a shaken; (erstaunt) flabbergasted. **F~svermögen** nt capacity

fast adv almost, nearly; **f~ nie** hardly ever

fast|en vi (haben) fast. **F~enzeit** f Lent. **F~nacht** f Shrovetide; (Karneval) carnival. **F~nachtsdienstag** m Shrove Tuesday. **F~tag** m fast-day

Faszin|ation /-'tsjo:n/ f - fascination. **f~ieren** vt fascinate; **f~ierend** fascinating

fatal a fatal; (peinlich) embarrassing. **F~ismus** m - fatalism. **F~ist** m -en,-en fatalist

Fata Morgana f -/- -nen mirage

fauchen vi (haben) spit, hiss □vi snarl

faul a lazy; (verdorben) rotten, bad; ⟨Ausrede⟩ lame; (zweifelhaft) bad; (verdächtig) fishy

Fäule f - decay

faul|en vi (sein) rot; ⟨Zahn:⟩ decay; (verwesen) putrefy. **F~enzen** vi (haben) be lazy. **F~enzer** m -s,- lazy-bones sg. **F~heit** f - laziness. **f~ig** a rotting; ⟨Geruch⟩ putrid

Fäulnis f - decay

Faulpelz m (fam) lazy-bones sg

Fauna f - fauna

Faust f -,̈Fäuste fist; **auf eigene F~** (fig) off one's own bat. **F~handschuh** m mitten. **F~schlag** m punch

Fauxpas /fo'pa/ m -,- /-[s],-s/ gaffe

Favorit(in) /favo'ri:t(in)/ m -en,-en (f -,-nen) (Sport) favourite

Fax nt -,-[e] fax. **f~en** vt fax

Faxen *fpl* (*fam*) antics; **F~**
machen fool about; **F~ schnei-**
den pull faces

Faxgerät *nt* fax machine

Feber *m* -s, (*Aust*) February

Februar *m* -s,-e February

fecht|en† *vi* (*haben*) fence. **F~er**
m -s,- fencer

Feder *f* -,-n feather; (*Schreib-*)
pen; (*Spitze*) nib; (*Techn*) spring.
F~ball *m* shuttlecock; (*Spiel*)
badminton. **F~busch** *m* plume.
f~leicht *a* as light as a feather.
F~messer *nt* penknife. **f~n** *vi*
(*haben*) be springy; (*nachgeben*)
give; (*hoch-*) bounce; **f~nd**
springy; (*elastisch*) elastic.
F~ung *f* - (*Techn*) springs *pl*;
(*Auto*) suspension

Fee *f* -,-n fairy

Fegefeuer *nt* purgatory

fegen *vt* sweep □ *vi* (*sein*) (*rasen*)
tear

Fehde *f* -,-n feud

fehl *a* **f~ am Platze** out of place.
F~betrag *m* deficit. **f~en** *vi*
(*haben*) be missing/(*Sch*) absent;
(*mangeln*) be lacking; **es f~t an**
(+ *dat*) there is a shortage of; **mir**
f~t die Zeit I haven't got the
time; **sie/es f~t mir sehr** I miss
her/it very much; **was f~t ihm?**
what's the matter with him? **es**
f~te nicht viel und er ... he
very nearly ...; **das hat uns**
noch gefehlt! that's all we need!
f~end *a* missing; (*Sch*) absent

Fehler *m* -s,- mistake, error;
(*Sport & fig*) fault; (*Makel*) flaw.
f~frei *a* faultless, *adv* -ly.
f~haft *a* faulty. **f~los** *a* flawless, *adv* -ly

Fehl|geburt *f* miscarriage. **f~ge-**
hen† *vi sep* (*sein*) go wrong;
(*Schuß:*) miss; (*fig*) be mistaken.
F~griff *m* mistake. **F~kal-**
kulation *f* miscalculation.
F~schlag *m* failure. **f~schla-**
gen† *vi sep* (*sein*) fail. **F~start**

m (*Sport*) false start. **F~tritt** *m*
false step; (*fig*) [moral] lapse.
F~zündung *f* (*Auto*) misfire

Feier *f* -,-n celebration; (*Zeremo-*
nie) ceremony; (*Party*) party.
F~abend *m* end of the working
day; **F~abend machen** stop
work, (*fam*) knock off; **nach**
F~abend after work. **f~lich** *a*
solemn, *adv* -ly; (*förmlich*) formal, *adv* -ly. **F~lichkeit** *f* -,-en
solemnity; **F~lichkeiten** festivities. **f~n** *vt* celebrate; hold
⟨*Fest*⟩; (*ehren*) fête □ *vi* (*haben*)
celebrate; (*lustig sein*) make
merry. **F~tag** *m* [public] holiday; (*kirchlicher*) feast-day; **er-**
ster/zweiter F~tag Christmas
Day / Boxing Day. **f~tags** *adv* on
public holidays

feige *a* cowardly; **f~ sein** be a
coward □ *adv* in a cowardly way

Feige *f* -,-n fig. **F~nbaum** *m* fig
tree

Feig|heit *f* cowardice. **F~ling** *m*
-s,-e coward

Feile *f* -,-n file. **f~n** *vt/i* (*haben*)
file

feilschen *vi* (*haben*) haggle

Feilspäne *mpl* filings

fein *a* fine; (*zart*) delicate,
adv -ly; (*Strümpfe*) sheer; (*Un-*
terschied) subtle; (*scharf*) keen;
(*vornehm*) refined; (*elegant*) elegant; (*prima*) great; **sich f~ ma-**
chen dress up. **F~arbeit** *f* precision work

Feind|(in) *m* -es,-e (*f* -,-nen)
enemy. **f~lich** *a* enemy; (*f~se-*
lig) hostile. **F~schaft** *f* -,-en
enmity. **F~selig** *a* hostile. **F~-**
seligkeit *f* -,-en hostility

fein|fühlig *a* sensitive. **F~ge-**
fühl *nt* sensitivity; (*Takt*) delicacy. **F~heit** *f* -,-en (*s. fein*)
fineness; delicacy; subtlety;
keenness; refinement; **F~heiten**
subtleties. **F~kostgeschäft** *nt*

delicatessen [shop]. **F~schmecker** m -s,- gourmet

feist a fat

feixen vi (haben) smirk

Feld nt -[e]s,-er field; (Fläche) ground; (Sport) pitch; (Schach-) square; (auf Formular) box. **F~bau** m agriculture. **F~bett** nt camp-bed, (Amer) cot. **F~forschung** f fieldwork. **F~herr** m commander. **F~marschall** m Field Marshal. **F~stecher** m -s,- field-glasses pl. **F~webel** m (Mil) sergeant. **F~zug** m campaign

Felge f -,-n [wheel] rim

Fell nt -[e]s,-e (Zool) coat; (Pelz) fur; (abgezogen) skin, pelt; **ein dickes F~ haben** (fam) be thick-skinned

Fels m -en,-en rock. **F~block** m boulder. **F~en** m -s,- rock. **f~enfest** a (fig) firm, adv -ly. **f~ig** a rocky

feminin a feminine; (weibisch) effeminate

Femininum nt -s,-na (Gram) feminine

Feminist|(in) m -en,-en (f-,-nen) feminist. **f~isch** a feminist

Fenchel m -s fennel

Fenster nt -s,- window. **F~brett** nt window-sill. **F~laden** m [window] shutter. **F~leder** nt chamois[-leather]. **F~putzer** m -s,- window-cleaner. **F~scheibe** f [window-]pane

Ferien /'fe:rjən/ pl holidays; (Univ) vacation sg; **F~ haben** be on holiday. **F~ort** m holiday resort

Ferkel nt -s,- piglet

fern a distant; **der F~e Osten** the Far East □ adv far away; **von f~** from a distance □ prep (+ dat) far [away] from. **F~bedienung** f remote control. **f~bleiben†** vi sep (sein) stay away (dat from). **F~e** f - distance; **in/aus der F~e** in the/from a distance; **in weiter**

F~e far away; (zeitlich) in the distant future. **f~er** a further □ adv (außerdem) furthermore; (in Zukunft) in future. **f~gelenkt** a remote-controlled; ⟨Rakete⟩ guided. **F~gespräch** nt long-distance call. **f~gesteuert** a = f~gelenkt. **F~glas** nt binoculars pl. **f~halten†** vt sep keep away; **sich f~** halten keep away. **F~kopieren** m -s,- fax machine. **F~kurs[us]** m correspondence course. **F~lenkung** f remote control. **F~licht** nt (Auto) full beam. **F~meldewesen** nt telecommunications pl. **F~rohr** nt telescope. **F~schreiben** nt telex. **F~schreiber** m -s,- telex [machine]

Fernseh|apparat m television set. **f~en†** vi sep (haben) watch television. **F~en** nt -s television. **F~er** m -s,- [television] viewer; (Gerät) television set. **F~gerät** nt television set

Fernsprech|amt nt telephone exchange, (Amer) central. **F~er** m telephone. **F~nummer** f telephone number. **F~zelle** f telephone box

Fernsteuerung f remote control

Ferse f -,-n heel. **F~ngeld** nt **F~ngeld geben** (fam) take to one's heels

fertig a finished; (bereit) ready; (Comm) ready-made; (Gericht) ready-to-serve; **f~ werden mit** finish; (bewältigen) cope with; **f~ sein** have finished; (fig) be through (**mit jdm** with s.o.); (fam: erschöpft) be all in; (see-lisch) shattered □ adv **f~ essen/lesen** finish eating/reading. **F~bau** m (pl -bauten) prefabricated building. **f~bringen†** vt sep manage to do; (beenden) finish; **ich bringe es nicht f~** I can't bring myself to do it. **f~en** vt make. **F~gericht** nt ready-to-

serve meal. F~**haus** nt prefabricated house. F~**keit** f-,-en skill.
f~**kriegen** vt sep (fam) = f~**bringen**. f~**machen** vt sep finish; (bereitmachen) get ready; (fam: erschöpfen) wear out; (seelisch) shatter; (fam: abkanzeln) carpet; **sich** f~**machen** get ready. f~**stellen** vt sep complete. F~**stellung** f completion. F~**ung** f - manufacture
fesch a (fam) attractive; (flott) smart; (Aust: nett) kind
Fessel f -,-n ankle
fesseln vt tie up; tie (an + acc to); (fig) fascinate; **ans Bett gefesselt** confined to bed. F~ fpl bonds. f~**d** a (fig) fascinating; (packend) absorbing
fest a firm; (nicht flüssig) solid; (erstarrt) set; (haltbar) strong; (nicht locker) tight; (feststehend) fixed; (ständig) steady; (Anstellung) permanent; (Schlaf) sound; (Blick, Stimme) steady; f~ **werden** harden; (Gelee:) set; f~**e Nahrung** solids pl □adv firmly; tightly; steadily; soundly; (kräftig, tüchtig) hard; f~ **schlafen** be fast asleep
Fest nt -[e]s,-e celebration; (Party) party; (Relig) festival; **frohes F~!** happy Christmas!
fest|angestellt a permanent. f~**binden**† vt sep tie (an + dat to). f~**bleiben** vi sep (sein) (fig) remain firm. f~**e** vt sep (fam) hard. F~**essen** nt = F~**mahl**. f~**fahren** vi/r sep (sein) [sich] f~**fahren** get stuck; (Verhandlungen:) reach deadlock. f~**halten**† v sep □vt hold on to; (aufzeichnen) record; **sich** f~**halten** hold on □vi (haben) f~**halten an** (+ dat) (fig) stick to; cling to (Tradition). f~**igen** vt strengthen; **sich** f~**igen** grow stronger. F~**iger** m -s,- styling lotion/ (Schaum-) mousse. F~**igkeit** f -

(s. fest) firmness; solidity; strength; steadiness. f~**klammern** vt sep clip (an + dat to); **sich** f~**klammern** cling (an + dat to). F~**land** nt mainland; (Kontinent) continent. f~**legen** vt sep (fig) fix, settle; lay down (Regeln); tie up (Geld); **sich** f~**legen** commit oneself
festlich a festive, adv -ly. F~**keiten** fpl festivities
fest|liegen† vi sep (haben) be fixed, settled. f~**machen** v sep □vt fasten/(binden) tie (an + dat to); (f~legen) fix, settle □vi (haben) (Naut) moor. F~**mahl** nt feast; (Bankett) banquet. F~**nahme** f -,-n arrest. f~**nehmen**† vt sep arrest. F~**ordner** m steward. f~**setzen** vt sep fix, settle; (inhaftieren) gaol; **sich** f~**setzen** collect. f~**sitzen**† vi sep (haben) be firm/(Schraube:) tight; (haften) stick; (nicht weiterkommen) be stuck. F~**spiele** npl festival sg. f~**stehen**† vi sep (haben) be certain. f~**stellen** vt sep fix; (ermitteln) establish; (bemerken) notice; (sagen) state. F~**stellung** f establishment; (Aussage) statement; (Erkenntnis) realization. F~**tag** m special day

Festung f -,-en fortress
Fest|zelt nt marquee. f~**ziehen**† vt sep pull tight. F~**zug** m [grand] procession
Fete /'fe:tə, 'fɛ:tə/ f -,-n party
fett a fat; (f~reich) fatty; (fettig) greasy; (üppig) rich; (Druck) bold. F~ nt -[e]s,-e fat; (flüssig) grease. F~**arm** a low-fat. f~**en** vt grease □vi (haben) be greasy. F~**fleck** m grease mark. f~**ig** a greasy. f~**leibig** a obese. F~**näpfchen** nt ins F~**näpfchen treten** (fam) put one's foot in it

Fetzen m -s,- scrap; (Stoff) rag; **in F~** in shreds

feucht a damp, moist; ⟨Luft⟩ humid. **F~heiß** a humid. **F~igkeit** f - dampness; (Nässe) moisture; ⟨Luft⟩ humidity. **F~igkeits- creme** f moisturizer

feudal a (fam: vornehm) sumptuous, adv -ly. **F~ismus** m - feudalism

Feuer nt -s,- fire; (für Zigarette) light; (Begeisterung) passion; **F~ machen** light a fire; **F~ fangen** catch fire; (fam: sich verlieben) be smitten; **jdm F~ geben** give s.o. a light. **F~alarm** m fire alarm. **F~bestattung** f cremation. **f~gefährlich** a [in]flammable. **F~leiter** f fire-escape. **F~löscher** m -s,- fire extinguisher. **F~melder** m -s,- fire alarm. **f~n** vi (haben) fire (auf+acc on) □ vt (fam) (schleudern) fling; (entlassen) fire. **F~probe** f (fig) test. **f~rot** a crimson. **f~speiend** a **f~speiender Berg** volcano. **F~stein** m flint. **F~stelle** f hearth. **F~treppe** f fire-escape. **F~wache** f fire station. **F~waffe** f firearm. **F~wehr** f -,-en fire brigade. **F~wehrauto** nt fire-engine. **F~wehrmann** m (pl -männer & -leute) fireman. **F~werk** nt firework display, fireworks pl. **F~werkskörper** m firework. **F~zeug** nt lighter

feurig a fiery; (fig) passionate

Fiaker m -s,- (Aust) horse-drawn cab

Fichte f -,-n spruce

fidel a cheerful

Fieber nt -s [raised] temperature; **F~ haben** have a temperature. **f~haft** a (fig) feverish, adv -ly. **f~n** vi (haben) have a temperature. **F~thermometer** nt thermometer

fiebrig a feverish

fies a (fam) nasty, adv -ily

Figur f -,-en figure; (Roman-, Film-) character; (Schach-) piece

Fiktion /-'tsio:n/ f -,-en fiction. **f~tiv** a fictitious

Filet /fi'le:/ nt -s,-s fillet

Filiale f -,-n, **F~geschäft** nt (Comm) branch

Filigran nt -s filigree

Film m -[e]s,-e film; (Kino-) film, (Amer) movie; (Schicht) coating. **f~en** vt/i (haben) film. **F~kamera** f cine/(für Kinofilm) film camera

Filter m & (Techn) nt -s,- filter; (Zigaretten-) filter-tip. **f~ern** vt filter. **F~erzigarette** f filtertipped cigarette. **f~rieren** vt filter

Filz m -es felt. **f~en** vi (haben) become matted □ vt (fam) (durchsuchen) frisk; (stehlen) steal. **F~schreiber** m -s,-, **F~stift** m felt-tipped pen

Fimmel m -s,- (fam) obsession

Finale nt -s,- (Mus) finale; (Sport) final. **F~list(in)** m -en,-en (f -,-nen) finalist

Finanz f -,-en finance. **F~amt** nt tax office. **f~iell** a financial, adv -ly. **f~ieren** vt finance. **F~minister** m minister of finance

finden vt (meinen) think; **den Tod f~en** meet one's death; **wie f~est du das?** what do you think of that? **f~est du?** do you think so? **es wird sich f~en** it'll turn up; (fig) it'll be all right □ vi (haben) find one's way. **F~er** m -s,- finder. **F~erlohn** m reward. **f~ig** a resourceful. **F~ling** m -s,-e boulder

Finesse f -,-n (Kniff) trick; **F~n** (Techn) refinements

Finger m -s,- finger; **die F~ lassen von** (fam) leave alone; **etw im kleinen F~ haben** (fam) have sth at one's fingertips. **F~abdruck** m finger-mark;

(*Admin*) fingerprint. **F~hut** *m* thimble. **F~nagel** *m* finger-nail. **F~ring** *m* ring. **F~spitze** *f* finger-tip. **F~zeig** *m* -[e]s,-e hint

fingier|en *vt* fake. **f~t** *a* fictitious

Fink *m* -en,-en finch

Finn|e *m* -n,-n, **F~in** *f* -,-nen Finn. **f~isch** *a* Finnish. **F~land** *nt* -s Finland

finster *a* dark; (*düster*) gloomy; (*unheildrohend*) sinister; **im F~n** in the dark. **F~nis** *f* - darkness; (*Astr*) eclipse

Finte *f* -,-n trick; (*Boxen*) feint

Firma *f* -,-men firm, company

firmen *vt* (*Relig*) confirm

Firmen|wagen *m* company car. **F~zeichen** *nt* trade mark, logo

Firmung *f* -,-en (*Relig*) confirmation

Firnis *m* -ses,-se varnish. **f~sen** *vt* varnish

First *m* -[e]s,-e [roof] ridge

Fisch *m* -[e]s,-e fish; **F~e** (*Astr*) Pisces. **F~dampfer** *m* trawler. **f~en** *vt/i* (*haben*) fish; **aus dem Wasser f~en** (*fam*) fish out of the water. **F~er** *m* -s,- fisherman. **F~erei** *f* -, **F~fang** *m* fishing. **F~gräte** *f* fishbone. **F~händler** *m* fishmonger. **F~otter** *m* otter. **F~reiher** *m* heron. **F~stäbchen** *nt* -s,- fish finger. **F~teich** *m* fish-pond

Fiskus *m* - der **F~** the Treasury

Fisole *f* -,-n (*Aust*) French bean

fit *a* fit. **F~neß** *f* - fitness

fix *a* (*fam*) quick, adv -ly; (*geistig*) bright; **f~e Idee** obsession; **fix und fertig** all finished; (*bereit*) all ready; (*fam: erschöpft*) shattered. **F~er** *m* -s,- (*sl*) junkie

fixieren *vt* stare at; (*Phot*) fix

Fjord *m* -[e]s,-e fiord

FKK *abbr* (Freikörperkultur) naturism

flach *a* flat; (*eben*) level; (*niedrig*) low; (*nicht tief*) shallow; **f~er**

Teller dinner plate; **die f~e Hand** the flat of the hand

Fläche *f* -,-n area; (*Ober-*) surface; (*Seite*) face. **F~nmaß** *nt* square measure

Flachs *m* -es flax. **f~blond** *a* flaxen-haired; (*Haar*) flaxen

flackern *vi* (*haben*) flicker

Flagg|e *f* -,-n flag

flagrant *a* flagrant

Flair /flɛ:ɐ̯/ *nt* -s air, aura

Flak *f* -,-[s] anti-aircraft artillery/ (*Geschütz*) gun

flämisch *a* Flemish

Flamme *f* -,-n flame; (*Koch-*) burner; **in F~n** in flames

Flanell *m* -s (*Tex*) flannel

Flank|e *f* -,-n flank. **f~ieren** *vt* flank

Flasche *f* -,-n bottle. **F~nbier** *nt* bottled beer. **F~nöffner** *m* bottle-opener

flatter|haft *a* fickle. **f~n** *vi* (*sein/haben*) flutter; (*Segel:*) flap

flau *a* (*schwach*) faint; (*Comm*) slack; **mir ist f~** I feel faint

Flaum *m* -[e]s down. **f~ig** *a* downy; **f~ig rühren** (*Aust Culin*) cream

flauschig *a* fleecy; (*Spielzeug*) fluffy

Flausen *fpl* (*fam*) silly ideas; (*Ausflüchte*) silly excuses

Flaute *f* -,-n (*Naut*) calm; (*Comm*) slack period; (*Schwäche*) low

fläzen (sich) *vr* (*fam*) sprawl

Flechte *f* -,-n (*Med*) eczema; (*Bot*) lichen; (*Zopf*) plait. **f~n†** *vt* plait; weave (*Korb*)

Fleck *m* -[e]s,-e[n] spot; (*größer*) patch; (*Schmutz-*) stain, mark; **blauer F~** bruise; **nicht vom F~ kommen** (*fam*) make no progress. **f~en** *vi* (*haben*) stain. **F~en** *m* -s,- = **Fleck**; (*Ortschaft*) small town. **f~enlos** *a* spotless. **F~entferner** *m* -s,- stain remover. **f~ig** *a* stained; (*Haut*) blotchy

Fledermaus f bat

Flegel m -s,- lout. **f~haft** a loutish. **F~jahre** npl (fam) awkward age sg. **f~n (sich)** vr loll

flehen vi (haben) beg (**um** for).
f~tlich a pleading, adv -ly

Fleisch nt -[e]s flesh; (Culin) meat; (Frucht-) pulp. **F~er** m -s,- butcher. **F~erei** f -,-en, **F~erladen** m butcher's shop. **F~fressend** a carnivorous. **F~fresser** m -s,- carnivore. **F~hauer** m -s,- (Aust) butcher. **f~ig** a fleshy. **f~lich** a carnal. **F~wolf** m mincer. **F~wunde** f flesh-wound

Fleiß m -es diligence; (der Arbeit) diligently; (absichtlich) on purpose. **f~ig** a diligent, adv -ly; (arbeitsam) industrious, adv -ly

flektieren vt (Gram) inflect

fletschen vt **die Zähne f~** ⟨Tier:⟩ bare its teeth

flex|ibel a flexible; ⟨Einband⟩ limp. **F~ibilität** f - flexibility.
F~ion f -,-en (Gram) inflexion

flicken vt mend; (mit Flicken) patch. **F~** m -s,- patch

Flieder m -s lilac. **f~farben** a lilac

Fliege f -,-n fly; (Schleife) bow-tie; **zwei F~n mit einer Klappe schlagen** kill two birds with one stone. **f~n†** vi (sein) fly; (geworfen werden) be thrown; (fam: fallen) fall; (fam: entlassen werden) be fired; (von der Schule) be expelled; **in die Luft f~n** blow up ⟹vt fly. **f~nd** a flying; ⟨Händler⟩ itinerant; **in F~nder Eile** in great haste. **F~r** m -s,- airman; (Pilot) pilot; (fam: Flugzeug) plane. **F~rangriff** m air raid

flieh|en† vi (sein) flee (**vor** + dat from); (entweichen) escape ⟹vt shun. **f~end** a fleeing; ⟨Kinn, Stirn⟩ receding. **F~kraft** f centrifugal force

Fliese f -,-n tile

Fließ|band nt assembly line.
f~en† vi (sein) flow; (aus Wasserhahn) run. **f~end** a flowing; ⟨Wasser⟩ running; ⟨Verkehr⟩ moving; (geläufig) fluent, adv -ly.
F~heck nt fastback. **F~wasser** nt running water

flimmern vi (haben) shimmer; (TV) flicker; **es flimmert mir vor den Augen** everything is dancing in front of my eyes

flink a nimble, adv -bly; (schnell) quick, adv -ly

Flinte f -,-n shotgun

Flirt /flœɐt/ m -s,-s flirtation.
f~en vi (haben) flirt

Flitter m -s sequins pl; (F~schmuck) tinsel. **F~wochen** fpl honeymoon sg

flitzen vi (sein) (fam) dash; ⟨Auto:⟩ whizz

Flocke f -,-n flake; (Wolle) tuft.
f~ig a fluffy

Floh m -[e]s,ˆe flea. **F~markt** m flea market. **F~spiel** nt tiddlywinks sg

Flor m -s gauze; (Trauer-) crape; (Samt-, Teppich-) pile

Flora f - flora

Florett nt -[e]s,-e foil

florieren vi (haben) flourish

Floskel f -,-n (empty) phrase

Floß nt -es,ˆe raft

Flosse f -,-n fin; (Seehund-, Gummi-) flipper; (sl: Hand) paw

Flöt|e f -,-n flute; (Block-) recorder. **f~en** vi (haben) play the flute/recorder; (fam: pfeifen) whistle ⟹vt play on the flute/recorder. **F~ist(in)** m -en,-en (f -,-nen) flautist

flott a quick, adv -ly; (lebhaft) lively; (schick) smart, adv -ly; **f~leben** live it up

Flotte f -,-n fleet

flottmachen vt sep **wieder f~** (Naut) refloat; get going again ⟨Auto⟩; put back on its feet ⟨Unternehmen⟩

Flöz nt -es,-e [coal] seam

Fluch m -[e]s,-̈e curse. **f~en** vi (haben) curse, swear

Flucht[1] f -,-en (Reihe) line; (Zimmer-) suite

Flucht[2] f - flight; (Entweichen) escape; **die F~ ergreifen** take flight. **f~artig** a hasty, adv -ily

flücht|en vi (sein) flee (vor + dat from); (entweichen) escape □vr **sich f~en** take refuge. **f~ig** a fugitive; (kurz) brief, adv -ly; (Blick, Gedanke) fleeting; (Bekanntschaft) passing; (oberflächlich) cursory, adv -ily; (nicht sorgfältig) careless, adv -ly; (Chem) volatile; **f~ig sein** be on the run; **f~ig kennen** know slightly. **F~igkeitsfehler** m slip. **F~ling** m -s,-e fugitive; (Pol) refugee

Fluchwort nt (pl -wörter) swearword

Flug m -[e]s,-̈e flight. **F~abwehr** f anti-aircraft defence. **F~ball** m (Tennis) volley. **F~blatt** nt pamphlet

Flügel m -s,- wing; (Fenster-) casement; (Mus) grand piano

Fluggast m [air] passenger

flügge a fully-fledged

Flug|gesellschaft f airline. **F~hafen** m airport. **F~lotse** m air-traffic controller. **F~platz** m airport; (klein) airfield. **F~preis** m air fare. **F~schein** m air ticket. **F~schneise** f flight path. **F~schreiber** m -s,- flight recorder. **F~schrift** f pamphlet. **F~steig** m -[e]s,-e gate. **F~wesen** nt aviation. **F~zeug** nt -[e]s,-e aircraft, plane

Fluidum nt -s aura

Flunder f -,-n flounder

flunkern vi (haben) (fam) tell fibs; (aufschneiden) tell tall stories

Flunsch m -[e]s,-e pout

fluoreszierend a fluorescent

Flur m -[e]s,-e [entrance] hall; (Gang) corridor

Flusen fpl fluff sg

Fluß m -sses,-̈sse river; (Fließen) flow; **im F~** (fig) in a state of flux. **f~abwärts** adv downstream. **f~aufwärts** adv upstream. **F~bett** nt river-bed

flüssig a liquid; (Lava) molten; (fließend) fluent, adv -ly; (Verkehr) freely moving. **F~keit** f -,-en liquid; (Anat) fluid

Flußpferd nt hippopotamus

flüstern vt/i (haben) whisper

Flut f -,-en high tide; (fig) flood; **F~en** waters. **F~licht** nt floodlight. **F~welle** f tidal wave

Föderation /-'tsio:n/ f -,-en federation

Fohlen nt -s,- foal

Föhn m -s föhn [wind]

Folge f -,-n consequence; (Reihe) succession; (Fortsetzung) instalment; (Teil) part; **F~ leisten** (+ dat) accept (Einladung); obey (Befehl). **f~en** vi (sein) follow (jdm/etw s.o./sth); (zuhören) listen (dat to); **daraus f~t, daß it** follows that; **wie f~t** as follows □ (haben) (gehorchen) obey (jdm s.o.). **f~end** a following; **f~endes** the following. **f~endermaßen** adv as follows

folger|n vt conclude (aus from). **F~ung** f -,-en conclusion

folglich adv consequently. **f~sam** a obedient, adv -ly

Folie /'fo:liə/ f -,-n foil; (Plastik-) film

Folklore f - folklore

Folter f -,-n torture; **auf die F~ spannen** (fig) keep on tenterhooks. **f~n** vt torture

Fön (P) m -s,-e hair-drier

Fonds /fõ:/ m -,- /-[s],-s/ fund

fönen vt [blow-]dry

Fontäne f -,-n jet; (Brunnen) fountain

Förder|band nt (pl -bänder) conveyor belt. **f~lich** a beneficial

fordern vt demand; (beanspruchen) claim; (zum Kampf) challenge; **gefordert werden** (fig) be stretched

fördern vt promote; (unterstützen) encourage; (finanziell) sponsor; (gewinnen) extract

Forderung f -,-en demand; (Anspruch) claim

Förderung f - (s. fördern) promotion; encouragement; (Techn) production

Forelle f -,-n trout

Form f -,-en form; (Gestalt) shape; (Culin, Techn) mould; (Back-) tin; **[gut] in F~** in good form

Formalität f -,-en formality

Format nt -[e]s,-e format; (Größe) size; (fig: Bedeutung) stature

Formation /-'tsjo:n/ f -,-en formation

Formel f -,-n formula

formell a formal, adv -ly

formen vt shape, mould; (bilden) form; **sich f~** take shape

förmlich a formal, adv -ly; (regelrecht) virtual, adv -ly. **F~keit** f -,-en formality

form|los a shapeless; (zwanglos) informal, adv -ly. **F~sache** f formality

Formular nt -s,-e [printed] form

formulier|en vt formulate, word. **F~ung** f -,-en wording

forsch a brisk, adv -ly; (schneidig) dashing, adv -ly

forsch|en vi (haben) search (nach for). **f~end** a searching. **F~er** m -s,- research scientist; (Reisender) explorer. **F~ung** f -,-en research. **F~ungsreisende(r)** m explorer

Forst m -[e]s,-e forest

Förster m -s,- forester

Forstwirtschaft f forestry

Forsythie /-tsjə/ f -,-n forsythia

Fort nt -s,-s (Mil) fort

fort adv away; **f~ sein** be away; (gegangen/verschwunden) have gone; **und so f~** and so on; **in einem f~** continuously. **f~bewegen** vt sep move; **sich f~bewegen** move. **F~bewegung** f locomotion. **F~bildung** f further education/training. **f~bleiben†** vi sep (sein) stay away. **f~bringen†** vt sep take away. **f~fahren†** vi sep (sein) go away □ (haben/sein) continue (zu to). **f~fallen†** vi sep (sein) be dropped/(ausgelassen) omitted; (entfallen) no longer apply; (aufhören) cease. **f~führen** vt sep continue. **F~gang** m departure; (Verlauf) progress. **f~gehen** vi sep (sein) leave, go away; (ausgehen) go out; (andauern) go on. **f~geschritten** a advanced; (spät) late. **F~geschrittene(r)** m/f advanced student. **f~gesetzt** a constant, adv -ly. **f~jagen** vt sep chase away. **f~lassen†** vt sep let go; (auslassen) omit. **f~laufen** vi sep (sein) run away; (sich f~setzen) continue. **f~laufend** a consecutive, adv -ly. **f~nehmen†** vt sep take away. **f~pflanzen (sich)** vr sep reproduce; (Ton, Licht:) travel. **F~pflanzung** f - reproduction. **F~pflanzungsorgan** nt reproductive organ. **f~reißen†** vt sep carry away; (entreißen) tear away. **f~schaffen** vt sep take away. **f~schicken** vt sep send away; (abschicken) send off. **f~schreiten†** vi sep (sein) continue; (Fortschritte machen) progress, advance. **F~schreiten** nt progress, advance. **f~schreitend** a progressive; (Alter) advancing. **F~schritt** m progress; **F~schritte machen** make progress. **f~schrittlich** a progressive. **f~setzen** vt sep continue; **sich f~setzen** continue. **F~setzung**

f -,-en continuation; ⟨*Folge*⟩ instalment; **F~setzung folgt** to be continued. **F~setzungsroman** *m* serialized novel, serial.
f~während *a* constant, *adv* -ly.
f~werfen† *vt sep* throw away.
f~ziehen† *v sep* □*vt* pull away □*vi* (*sein*) move away

Fossil *nt* -,-ien /-i̯ən/ fossil
Foto *nt* -s,-s photo. **F~apparat** *m* camera. **f~gen** *a* photogenic
Fotograf(in) *m* -en,-/-in (*f*-,-nen) photographer. **F~ie** *f* -,-n photography; ⟨*Bild*⟩ photograph.
f~ieren *vt* take a photo[graph] of; **sich f~ieren lassen** have one's photo[graph] taken □*vi* (*haben*) take photographs. **f~isch** *a* photographic

Fotokopie *f* photocopy. **f~ren** *vt* photocopy. **F~rgerät** *nt* photocopier

Fötus *m* -,-ten foetus
Foul /faʊl/ *nt* -s,-s (*Sport*) foul.
f~en *vt* foul
Foyer /foa'je:/ *nt* -s,-s foyer
Fracht *f* -,-en freight. **F~er** *m* -s,-freighter. **F~gut** *nt* freight.
F~schiff *nt* cargo boat
Frack *m* -[e]s,-̈e & -s tailcoat; **im F~** in tails *pl*
Frage *f* -,-n question; **eine F~ stellen** ask a question; **etw in F~ stellen** question sth; ⟨*ungewiß machen*⟩ make sth doubtful; **ohne F~** undoubtedly; **nicht in F~ kommen** be out of the question. **F~bogen** *m* questionnaire.
f~n *vt/i* (*haben*) ask; **sich f~n** wonder (ob whether). **f~nd** *a* questioning, *adv* -ly; (*Gram*) interrogative. **F~zeichen** *nt* question mark

fraglich *a* doubtful; ⟨*Person, Sache*⟩ in question. **f~los** *adv* undoubtedly
Fragment *nt* -[e]s,-e fragment.
f~arisch *a* fragmentary

fragwürdig *a* questionable; ⟨*verdächtig*⟩ dubious
fraisefarben /'frɛ:s-/ *a* strawberry-pink
Fraktion /-'tsi̯o:n/ *f* -,-en parliamentary party
Franken¹ *m* -s,- (*Swiss*) franc
Franken² *nt* -s Franconia
Frankfurter *f* -,- frankfurter
frankieren *vt* stamp, frank
Frankreich *nt* -s France
Fransen *fpl* fringe *sg*
Franz|ose *m* -n,-n Frenchman; **die F~osen** the French *pl*. **F~ösin** *f* -,-nen Frenchwoman.
f~ösisch *a* French. **F~ösisch** *nt* -[s] (*Lang*) French
frapp|ant *a* striking. **f~ieren** *vt* (*fig*) strike; **f~ierend** striking
fräsen *vt* (*Techn*) mill
Fraß *m* -es feed; (*pej: Essen*) muck
Fratze *f* -,-n grotesque face; (*Grimasse*) grimace; (*pej: Gesicht*) face; **F~n schneiden** pull faces
Frau *f* -,-en woman; (*Ehe-*) wife; **F~ Thomas** Mrs/(*unverheiratet*) Miss/(*Admin*) Ms Thomas; **Unsere Liebe F~** (*Relig*) Our Lady. **F~chen** *nt* -s,- mistress
Frauen|arzt *m*, **F~ärztin** *f* gynaecologist. **F~rechtlerin** *f* -,-nen feminist. **F~zimmer** *nt* woman
Fräulein *nt* -s,- single woman; (*jung*) young lady; (*Anrede*) Miss
fraulich *a* womanly
frech *a* cheeky, *adv* -ily; (*unverschämt*) impudent, *adv* -ly.
F~dachs *m* (*fam*) cheeky monkey. **F~heit** *f* -,-en cheekiness; impudence; (*Äußerung, Handlung*) impertinence
frei *a* free; (*freischaffend*) freelance; ⟨*Künstler*⟩ independent; (*nicht besetzt*) vacant; (*offen*) open; (*bloß*) bare; **F~er Tag** day off; **sich** (*dat*) **f~ nehmen** take time off; **f~ machen** (*räumen*) clear; vacate ⟨*Platz*⟩; (*befreien*)

liberate; (*entkleiden*) bare; **f~
lassen** leave free; **jdm f~e Hand
lassen** give s.o. a free hand; **ist
dieser Platz f~?** is this seat tak-
en? '**Zimmer f~**' 'vacancies'
□*adv* freely; (*ohne Notizen*) without notes; (*umsonst*) free

Frei|bad *nt* open-air swimming
pool. **f~bekommen†** *vt sep* get
released; **einen Tag f~bekom-
men** get a day off. **f~beruflich**
a & adv freelance. **F~e** *nt* **im
F~en** in the open air, out of
doors. **F~frau** *f* baroness. **F~
gabe** *f* release. **f~geben†** *v sep*
□*vt* release; (*eröffnen*) open; **jdm
einen Tag f~geben** give s.o. a
day off□ *vi* (*haben*) **jdm f~geben**
give s.o. time off. **f~gebig** *a* generous, *adv* -ly. **F~gebigkeit** *f*-
generosity. **f~haben†** *v sep* □*vt*
eine Stunde f~haben have an
hour off; (*Sch*) have a free period
□*vi* (*haben*) be off work/(*Sch*)
school; (*beurlaubt sein*) have
time off. **f~halten†** *vt sep* keep
clear; (*belegen*) keep; **einen Tag/
sich f~halten** keep a day/one-
self free; **jdn f~halten** treat s.o.
[to a meal/drink]. **F~handels-
zone** *f* free-trade area. **f~hän-
dig** *adv* without holding on

Freiheit *f* -,-en freedom, liberty;
sich (*dat*) **F~en erlauben** take
liberties. **F~strafe** *f* prison
sentence

freiheraus *adv* frankly

Frei|herr *m* baron. **F~karte** *f*
free ticket. **F~körperkultur** *f*
naturism. **f~lassen†** *vt sep* release, set free. **F~lassung** *f* -
release. **F~lauf** *m* free-wheel.
f~legen *vt sep* expose. **f~lich**
adv admittedly; (*natürlich*) of
course. **F~lichttheater** *nt*
open-air theatre. **f~machen** *v
sep* □*vt* (*frankieren*) frank□ *vi/r*
(*haben*) [**sich**] **f~machen** take
time off. **F~marke** *f* [postage]

stamp. **F~maurer** *m* Freema-
son. **f~mütig** *a* candid, *adv* -ly.
F~platz *m* free seat; (*Sch*) free
place. **f~schaffend** *a* freelance.
f~schwimmen† (**sich**) *vr sep*
pass one's swimming test. **f~set-
zen** *vt sep* release; (*entlassen*)
make redundant. **f~sprechen†**
vt sep acquit. **F~spruch** *m* acquittal. **f~stehen†** *vi sep* (*haben*) stand empty; **es steht ihm
f~** (*fig*) he is free (**zu** to). **f~stel-
len** *vt sep* exempt (**von** from);
jdm etw f~stellen leave sth up
to s.o. **f~stempeln** *vt sep* frank.
F~stil *m* freestyle. **F~stoß** *m*
free kick. **F~stunde** *f* (*Sch*) free
period

Freitag *m* Friday. **f~s** *adv* on
Fridays

Frei|tod *m* suicide. **F~übungen**
fpl [physical] exercises. **F~
umschlag** *m* stamped envelope.
f~weg *adv* freely; (*offen*) openly.
f~willig *a* voluntary, *adv* -ily.
F~willige(r) *m/f* volunteer.
F~zeichen *nt* ringing tone;
(*Rufzeichen*) dialling tone.
F~zeit *f* free or spare time;
(*Muße*) leisure; (*Tagung*) [week-
end/holiday] course. **F~zeit-
pref** leisure ... **F~zeitbeklei-
dung** *f* casual wear. **f~zügig** *a*
unrestricted; (*großzügig*) liberal;
(*moralisch*) permissive

fremd *a* foreign; (*unbekannt, ungewohnt*) strange; (*nicht das
eigene*) other people's; **ein f~er
Mann** a stranger; **f~e Leute**
strangers; **unter f~em Namen**
under an assumed name; **jdm f~
sein** be unknown/(*wesens-*) alien
to s.o.; **ich bin hier f~** I'm a
stranger here. **f~artig** *a*
strange, *adv* -ly; (*exotisch*) exotic.
F~e *f* - in der **F~e** away from
home; (*im Ausland*) in a foreign
country. **F~e(r)** *m/f* stranger;
(*Ausländer*) foreigner; (*Tourist*)

tourist. **F~enführer** *m* [tourist] guide. **F~enverkehr** *m* tourism. **F~enzimmer** *nt* room [to let]; (*Gäste-*) guest room. **f~gehen†** *vi sep* (*sein*) (*fam*) be unfaithful. **F~körper** *m* foreign body. **f~ländisch** *a* foreign; (*exotisch*) exotic. **F~ling** *m* -s,-e stranger. **F~sprache** *f* foreign language. **F~wort** *nt* (*pl* -wörter) foreign word

frenetisch *a* frenzied

frequen|tieren *vt* frequent. **F~enz** *f* -,-en frequency

Freske *f* -,-n, **Fresko** *nt* -s,-ken fresco

Fresse *f* -,-n (*sl*) (*Mund*) gob; (*Gesicht*) mug; **halt die F~!** shut your trap! **f~n†** *vt/i* (*haben*) eat. **F~n** *nt* -s feed; (*sl: Essen*) grub

Freßnapf *m* feeding bowl

Freud|e *f* -,-n pleasure; (*innere*) joy; **mit F~en** with pleasure; **jdm eine F~e machen** please s.o. **f~ig** *a* joyful, adv -ly; **f~iges Ereignis** (*fig*) happy event. **f~los** *a* cheerless; (*traurig*) sad

freuen *vt* please; **sich f~** be pleased (*über* + *acc* about); **sich f~ auf** (+ *acc*) look forward to; **es freut mich, ich freue mich** I'm glad *or* pleased (**daß** that)

Freund *m* -es,-e friend; (*Verehrer*) boyfriend; (*Anhänger*) lover (*gen* of). **F~in** *f* -,-nen friend; (*Liebste*) girlfriend; (*Anhängerin*) lover (*gen* of). **f~lich** *a* kind, adv -ly; (*umgänglich*) friendly; (*angenehm*) pleasant; **wären Sie so f~lich?** would you be so kind? **f~licherweise** *adv* kindly. **F~lichkeit** *f* -,-en kindness; friendliness; pleasantness

Freundschaft *f* -,-en friendship; **F~ schließen** become friends. **f~lich** *a* friendly

Frevel /'fre:fəl/ *m* -s,- (*liter*) outrage. **f~haft** *a* (*liter*) wicked

Frieden *m* -s peace; **F~ schließen** make peace; **im F~** in peacetime; **laß mich in F~!** leave me alone! **F~srichter** *m* ≈ magistrate. **F~svertrag** *m* peace treaty

fried|fertig *a* peaceable. **F~hof** *m* cemetery. **f~lich** *a* peaceful, adv -ly; (*verträglich*) peaceable. **f~liebend** *a* peace-loving

frieren† *vi* (*haben*) (*Person:*) be cold; *impers* **es friert/hat gefroren** it is freezing/there has been a frost; **frierst du? friert [es] dich?** are you cold? □ (*sein*) (*gefrieren*) freeze

Fries *m* -es,-e frieze

Frikadelle *f* -,-n [meat] rissole

frisch *a* fresh; (*sauber*) clean; (*leuchtend*) bright; (*munter*) lively; (*rüstig*) fit; **sich f~ machen** freshen up □ *adv* freshly, newly; **f~ gelegte Eier** new-laid eggs; **ein Bett f~ beziehen** put clean sheets on a bed; **f~ gestrichen! wet paint!** **F~e** *f* - freshness; brightness; liveliness; fitness. **F~haltepackung** *f* vacuum pack. **F~käse** *m* ≈ cottage cheese. **f~weg** *adv* freely

Friseur /fri'zø:ɐ/ *m* -s,-e hairdresser; (*Herren-*) barber. **F~seursalon** *m* hairdressing salon. **F~seuse** /-'zø:zə/ *f* -,-n hairdresser

frisier|en *vt* **jdn/sich f~en** do s.o.'s/one's hair; **die Bilanz/einen Motor f~en** (*fam*) fiddle the accounts/soup up an engine. **F~kommode** *f* dressing-table. **F~salon** *m* = Friseursalon. **F~tisch** *m* dressing-table

Frisör *m* -s,-e = Friseur

Frist *f* -,-en period; (*Termin*) deadline; (*Aufschub*) time; **drei Tage F~** three days' grace. **f~en** *vt* **sein Leben f~en** eke out an existence. **f~los** *a* instant, adv -ly

Frisur f -,-en hairstyle
fritieren vt deep-fry
frivol /fri'vo:l/ a frivolous, adv -ly; (schlüpfrig) smutty
froh a happy; (freudig) joyful; (erleichtert) glad; **f~e Ostern!** happy Easter!
fröhlich a cheerful, adv -ly; (vergnügt) merry, adv -ily; **f~e Weihnachten!** merry Christmas! **F~keit** f - cheerfulness; merriment
frohlocken vi (haben) rejoice; (schadenfroh) gloat
Frohsinn m - cheerfulness
fromm a (frömmer, frömmst) devout, adv -ly; (gutartig) docile, adv -ly; **f~er Wunsch** idle wish
Frömm|igkeit f - devoutness, piety. **f~lerisch** a sanctimonious, adv -ly
frönen vi (haben) indulge (dat in)
Fronleichnam m Corpus Christi
Front f -,-en in front. **f~al** a frontal; (Zusammenstoß) head-on □adv from the front; (zusammenstoßen) head-on. **F~alzusammenstoß** m head-on collision
Frosch m -[e]s,-̈e frog. **F~laich** m frog-spawn. **F~mann** m (pl -männer) frogman
Frost m -[e]s,-̈e frost. **F~beule** f chilblain
fröst|eln vi (haben) shiver; **mich fröstelte [es]** I shivered/(fror) felt chilly
frost|ig a frosty, adv -ily. **F~schutzmittel** nt antifreeze
Frottee nt & m -s towelling
frottier|en vt rub down. **F~[hand]tuch** nt terry towel
frotzeln vt/i (haben) [über] jdn **f~** make fun of s.o.
Frucht f -,-̈e fruit; **F~ tragen** bear fruit. **F~bar** a fertile; (fig) fruitful. **F~barkeit** f - fertility. **f~en** vi (haben) **wenig/nichts f~en** have little/no effect. **f~ig** a

fruity. **f~los** a fruitless, adv -ly.
F~saft m fruit juice
frugal a frugal, adv -ly
früh a early □adv early; (morgens) in the morning; **heute/gestern/morgen f~** this/yesterday/tomorrow morning; **von f~ an** from an early age. **f~auf** adv **von f~auf** from an early age. **F~aufsteher** m -s,- early riser. **F~e** f - in aller **F~e** bright and early; **in der F~e** (SGer) in the morning. **f~er** adv earlier; (eher) sooner; (ehemals) formerly; (vor langer Zeit) in the old days; **f~er oder später** sooner or later; **ich wohnte f~er in X** I used to live in X. **f~ere(r,s)** a earlier; (ehemalig) former; (vorige) previous; **in f~eren Zeiten** in former times. **f~estens** adv at the earliest. **F~geburt** f premature birth/(Kind) baby. **F~jahr** nt spring. **F~jahrsputz** m spring-cleaning. **F~kartoffeln** fpl new potatoes. **F~ling** m -s,-e spring. **f~morgens** adv early in the morning. **f~reif** a precocious
Frühstück nt breakfast. **f~en** vi (haben) have breakfast
frühzeitig a & adv early; (vorzeitig) premature, adv -ly
Frustr|ation /-'tsio:n/ f -,-en frustration. **f~ieren** vt frustrate; **f~ierend** frustrating
Fuchs m -es,-̈e fox; (Pferd) chestnut. **f~en** vt (fam) annoy
Füchsin f -,-nen vixen
fuchteln vi (haben) **mit etw f~** (fam) wave sth about
Fuder nt -s,- cart-load
Fuge¹ f -,-n joint; **aus den F~n gehen** fall apart
Fuge² f -,-n (Mus) fugue
fügen vt fit (in + acc into); (an-) join (an + acc on to); (dazu-) add (zu to); (fig: bewirken) ordain; **sich f~** vt fit (in + acc into); adjoin/(folgen) follow (an etw acc

sth); (fig: gehorchen) submit (dat to); **sich in sein Schicksal f~en** resign oneself to one's fate; es f~te sich so zu haben (daß that). f~sam a obedient, adv -ly.

F~ung f -,-en **eine F~ung des Schicksals** a stroke of fate

fühl|bar a noticeable. f~en vt/i (haben) feel; **sich f~en** feel (krank/einsam ill/lonely); (fam: stolz sein) fancy oneself; **sich [nicht] wohl f~en** [not] feel well. **F~er** m -s,- feeler. F~ung f - contact; **F~ung aufnehmen** get in touch

Fuhre f -,-n load

führ|en vt lead; guide ⟨Tourist⟩; (geleiten) take; (leiten) run; (befehligen) command; (verkaufen) stock; bear ⟨Namen, Titel⟩; keep ⟨Liste, Bücher, Tagebuch⟩; **bei od mit sich f~en** carry; **sich gut/schlecht f~en** conduct oneself well/badly □vi (haben) lead; (verlaufen) go, run; **zu etw f~en** lead to sth. f~end a leading.
F~er m -s,- leader; (Fremden-) guide; (Buch) guide[book].
F~erhaus nt driver's cab.
F~erschein m driving licence; **den F~erschein machen** take one's driving test. **F~erscheinentzug** m disqualification from driving. **F~ung** f -,-en leadership; (Leitung) management; (Mil) command; (Betragen) conduct; (Besichtigung) guided tour; (Vorsprung) lead; **in F~ung gehen** go into the lead

Fuhr|unternehmer m haulage contractor. **F~werk** nt cart

Fülle f -,-n abundance, wealth (an+dat of); (Körper-) plumpness. f~n vt fill; (Culin) stuff; **sich f~n** fill [up]

Füllen nt -s,- foal

Füll|er m -s,- (fam) F~federhalter m fountain pen. f~ig a plump; ⟨Busen⟩ ample. F~ung f

-,-en filling; (Kissen-, Braten-) stuffing; (Pralinen-) centre

fummeln vi (haben) fumble (an+dat with)

Fund m -[e]s,-e find

Fundament nt -[e]s,-e foundations pl. f~al a fundamental

Fund|büro nt lost-property office. **F~grube** f (fig) treasure trove. **F~sachen** fpl lost property sg

fünf inv a, F~ f -,-en five; (Sch) ≈ fail mark. **F~linge** mpl quintuplets. **f~te(r,s)** a fifth. **f~zehn** inv a fifteen. **f~zehnte(r,s)** a fifteenth. f~zig inv a fifty. **F~ziger** m -s,- man in his fifties; (Münze) 50-pfennig piece. **f~zigste(r,s)** a fiftieth

fungieren vi (haben) act (als as)

Funk m -s radio; **über F~** over the radio. **F~e** m -n,-n spark.
f~eln vi (haben) sparkle; ⟨Stern:⟩ twinkle. **f~elnagelneu** a (fam) brand-new. **F~en** m -s,- spark. **F~en** vt radio. **F~er** m -s,- radio operator. **F~gerät** nt walkie-talkie. **F~spruch** m radio message. **F~streife** f [police] radio patrol

Funktion /-'tsjo:n/ f -,-en function; (Stellung) position; (Funktionieren) working; **außer F~** out of action. **F~är** m -s,-e official. **f~ieren** vi (haben) work

für prep (+acc) for; **Schritt für Schritt** step by step; **was für [ein]** what [a]? (fragend) what sort of [a]? **für sich** by oneself; ⟨Ding:⟩ itself. **Für** nt **das Für und Wider** the pros and cons pl.
F~bitte f intercession

Furche f -,-n furrow

Furcht f - fear (vor+dat of).
f~bar a terrible, adv -bly

fürchten vt/i (haben) fear; **sich f~en** be afraid (vor+dat of); **ich f~e, das geht nicht** I'm afraid that's impossible. **f~erlich** a dreadful, adv -ly

furcht|erregend a terrifying. **f~los** a fearless, adv -ly. **f~sam** a timid, adv -ly

füreinander adv for each other

Furnier nt -s,-e veneer. **f~t** a veneered

fürs prep = für das

Fürsorge f care; (Admin) welfare; (fam: Geld) ≈ social security. **F~er(in)** m -s, (f -,-nen) social worker. **f~lich** a solicitous

Fürsprache f intercession; **f~ einlegen** intercede

Fürsprecher m (fig) advocate

Fürst m -en,-en prince. **F~entum** nt -s,-er principality. **F~in** f -,-nen princess. **f~lich** a princely; (üppig) lavish, adv -ly

Furt f -,-en ford

Furunkel m -s,- (Med) boil

Fürwort nt (pl -wörter) pronoun

Furz m -es,-e (vulg) fart. **f~en** vi (haben) (vulg) fart

Fusion f -,-en fusion; (Comm) merger. **f~ieren** vi (haben) (Comm) merge

Fuß m -es,-e foot; (Lampen-) base; (von Weinglas) stem; **zu Fuß** on foot; **zu Fuß gehen** walk; **auf freiem Fuß** free; **auf freundschaftlichem/großem Fuß** on friendly terms/in grand style. **F~abdruck** m footprint. **F~abtreter** m -s,- doormat. **F~bad** nt footbath. **F~ball** m football. **F~ballspieler** m footballer. **F~balltoto** nt football pools pl. **F~bank** f footstool. **F~boden** m floor. **F~bremse** f footbrake

Fussel f -,-n & m -s,-[n] piece of fluff; **f~n** vi fluff sg. **f~n** vi (haben) shed fluff

fußen vi (haben) be based (auf + dat on). **F~ende** nt foot

Fußgänger|(in) m -s,- (f -,-nen) pedestrian. **F~brücke** f footbridge. **F~überweg** m pedestrian crossing. **F~zone** f pedestrian precinct

Fuß|geher m -s,- (Aust) = **F~gänger. F~gelenk** nt ankle. **F~hebel** m pedal. **F~nagel** m toenail. **F~note** f footnote. **F~pflege** f chiropody. **F~pfleger(in)** m(f) chiropodist. **F~rücken** m instep. **F~sohle** f sole of the foot. **F~stapfen** pl in jds **F~stapfen treten** (fig) follow in s.o.'s footsteps. **F~tritt** m kick. **F~weg** m footpath; **eine Stunde F~weg** an hour's walk

futsch pred a (fam) gone

Futter¹ nt -s feed; (Trocken-) fodder

Futter² nt -s,- (Kleider-) lining

Futteral nt -s,-e case

füttern¹ vt feed

füttern² vt line

Futur nt -s (Gram) future; **zweites F~** future perfect. **f~istisch** a futuristic

G

Gabe f -,-n gift; (Dosis) dose

Gabel f -,-n fork. **g~n (sich)** vr fork. **G~stapler** m -s,- fork-lift truck. **G~ung** f -,-en fork

gackern vi (haben) cackle

gaffen vi (haben) gape, stare

Gag /gεk/ m -s,-s (Theat) gag

Gage /'ga:ʒə/ f -,-n (Theat) fee

gähnen vi (haben) yawn. **G~** nt -s yawn; (wiederholt) yawning

Gala f ceremonial dress

galant a gallant, adv -ly

Galavorstellung f gala performance

Galerie f -,-n gallery

Galgen m -s,- gallows sg. **G~frist** f (fam) reprieve

Galionsfigur f figurehead

Galle f - bile; (G~nblase) gall-
bladder. **G~nblase** f gall-bladder. **G~nstein** m gallstone

Gallert nt g~s,-e, **Gallerte** f-,-n
[meat] jelly

Galopp m -s gallop; im G~ at a
gallop. **g~ieren** vi (sein) gallop

galvanisieren vt galvanize

gamm|eln vi (haben) (fam) loaf
around. **G~ler(in)** m -s,- (f
-,-nen) drop-out

Gams f-,-en (Aust) chamois

gang pred a g~ und gäbe quite
usual

Gang m -[e]s,-e walk; (G~art)
gait; (Boten-) errand; (Funktionieren) running; (Verlauf, Culin)
course; (Durch-) passage; (Korridor) corridor; (zwischen Sitz-
reihen) aisle, gangway; (Anat)
duct; (Auto) gear; in G~ brin-
gen/halten get/keep going; in
G~ kommen get going/(fig)
under way; im G~e/in vollem
G~e sein be in progress/in full
swing; Essen mit vier G~en
four-course meal. **G~art** f gait

gängig a common; (Comm) popular

Gangschaltung f gear change

Gangster /ˈgɛŋstə/ m -s,- gangster

Gangway /ˈgɛŋweː/ f-,-s gangway

Ganove m -n,-n (fam) crook

Gans f -,-e goose

Gänse|blümchen nt -s,- daisy.
G~füßchen ntpl inverted commas. **G~haut** f goose-pimples pl.
G~marsch m im G~marsch in
single file. **G~rich** m -s,-e
gander

ganz a whole, entire; (vollständig)
complete; (fam: heil) un-
damaged, intact; die g~e Zeit all
the time, the whole time; eine
g~e Weile/Menge quite a while/
lot; g~e zehn Mark all of ten
marks; meine g~en Bücher all
my books; inv g~ Deutschland
the whole of Germany; g~ bleiben (fam) remain intact; wieder
g~ machen (fam) mend; im
g~en in all, altogether; im großen und g~en on the whole
□adv quite; (völlig) completely,
entirely; (sehr) very; nicht g~
not quite; g~ allein all on one's
own; ein g~ alter Mann a very
old man; g~ wie du willst just as
you like; es war g~ nett it was
quite nice; g~ und gar completely, totally; g~ und gar
nicht not at all. **G~e(s)** nt whole;
es geht ums G~e it's all or
nothing. **g~jährig** adv all the
year round

gänzlich adv completely, entirely

ganz|tägig a & adv full-time;
(geöffnet) all day. **g~tags** adv all
day; (arbeiten) full-time

gar [1] a done, cooked

gar [2] adv gar nicht/nichts/nie-
mand not/nothing/no one at all;
oder gar even

Garage /ga'ra:ʒə/ f-,-n garage

Garantie f-,-n guarantee. **g~ren**
vt/i (haben) [für] etw g~ren
guarantee sth; er kommt g~rt
zu spät (fam) he's sure to be late.
G~schein m guarantee

Garbe f-,-n sheaf

Garderobe f-,-n (Kleider) wardrobe; (Ablage) cloakroom, (Amer)
checkroom; (Flur-) coat-rack;
(Künstler-) dressing-room. **G~n-
frau** f cloakroom attendant

Gardine f -,-n curtain. **G~n-
stange** f curtain rail

garen vt/i (haben) cook

gären† vi (haben) ferment; (fig)
seethe

Garn nt -[e]s,-e yarn; (Näh-) cotton

Garnele f -,-n shrimp; (rote)
prawn

garnieren vt decorate; (Culin)
garnish

Garnison f-,-en garrison

Garnitur f -,-en set; (*Wäsche*) set
of matching underwear; (*Möbel-*)
suite; **erste/zweite G~ sein**
(*fam*) be first-rate/second best

garstig a nasty

Garten m -s,¨ garden; **bota-
nischer G~** botanical gardens
pl. **G~arbeit** f gardening.
G~bau m horticulture. **G~
haus** nt, **G~laube** f summer-
house. **G~lokal** nt open-air café.
G~schere f secateurs pl

Gärtner|(in) m -s,- (f -,-nen) gar-
dener. **G~ei** f -,-en nursery;
(*fam: Gartenarbeit*) gardening

Gärung f - fermentation

Gas nt -es,-e gas; **Gas geben** (*Auto*)
accelerate. **G~herd** m gas
cooker. **G~maske** f gas mask.
G~pedal nt (*Auto*) accelerator

Gasse f -,-n alley; (*Aust*) street

Gast m -[e]s,¨e guest; (*Hotel-, Ur-
laubs-*) visitor; (*im Lokal*) patron;
zum Mittag G~e haben have
people to lunch; **bei jdm zu G~
sein** be staying with s.o. **G~ar-
beiter** m foreign worker.
G~bett nt spare bed

Gäste|bett nt spare bed.
G~buch nt visitors' book.
G~zimmer nt [hotel] room;
(*privat*) spare room; (*Aufenthaltsraum*) residents' lounge

gast|frei, g~freundlich a hos-
pitable, adv -bly. **G~freund-
schaft** f hospitality. **G~geber**
m -s,- host. **G~geberin** f -,-nen
hostess. **G~haus** nt, **G~hof** m
inn, hotel

gastieren vi (*haben*) make a guest
appearance; (*Truppe, Zirkus:*)
perform (in + dat in)

gastlich a hospitable, adv -bly.
G~keit f - hospitality

Gastro|nomie f - gastronomy.
g~nomisch a gastronomic

Gast|spiel nt guest performance.
G~spielreise f (*Theat*) tour.
G~stätte f restaurant. **G~-**

stube f bar; (*Restaurant*) restaurant. **G~wirt** m landlord.
G~wirtin f landlady. **G~-
wirtschaft** f restaurant

Gas|werk nt gasworks sg.
G~zähler m gas-meter

Gatte m -n,-n husband

Gatter nt -s,- gate; (*Gehege*) pen

Gattin f -,-nen wife

Gattung f -,-en kind; (*Biol*) genus;
(*Kunst*) genre. **G~sbegriff** m
generic term

Gaudi f - (*Aust, fam*) fun

Gaul m -[e]s, Gäule [old] nag

Gaumen m -s,- palate

Gauner m -s,- crook, swindler.
G~ei f -,-en swindle

Gaze /'ga:zə/ f - gauze

Gazelle f -,-n gazelle

geachtet a respected

geädert a veined

geartet a **gut g~** good-natured;
anders g~ different

Gebäck nt -s [cakes and] pastries
pl; (*Kekse*) biscuits pl

Gebälk nt -s timbers pl

geballt a ⟨*Faust*⟩ clenched

Gebärde f -,-n gesture. **g~n
(sich)** vr behave (**wie** like)

Gebaren nt -s behaviour

gebär|en† vt give birth to, bear;
geboren werden be born.
G~mutter f womb, uterus

Gebäude nt -s,- building

Gebeine ntpl [mortal] remains

Gebell nt -s barking

geben† vt give; (*tun, bringen*) put;
(*Karten*) deal; (*aufführen*) perform; (*unterrichten*) teach; **etw
verloren g~** give sth up as lost;
von sich g~ utter; (*fam: erbrechen*) bring up; **viel/wenig
g~ auf** (+ *acc*) set great/little
store by; **sich g~** (*nachlassen*)
wear off; (*besser werden*) get
better; (*sich verhalten*) behave;
sich geschlagen g~ admit defeat □ *impers* **es gibt** there is/are;
was gibt es Neues/zum Mittag/

im Kino? what's the news/for lunch/on at the cinema? **es wird Regen g~** it's going to rain; **das gibt es nicht** there's no such thing □*vi (haben) (Karten)* deal

Gebet *nt* -[e]s,-e prayer

Gebiet *nt* -[e]s,-e area; *(Hoheits-)* territory; *(Sach-)* field

gebiet|en† *vt* command; *(erfordern)* demand □*vi (haben) (haben)* rule. **G~er** *m* -s,- master; *(Herrscher)* ruler. **g~erisch** *a* imperious, *adv* -ly; *⟨Ton⟩* peremptory

Gebilde *nt* -s,- structure

gebildet *a* educated; *(kultiviert)* cultured

Gebirg|e *nt* -s,- mountains *pl*. **g~ig** *a* mountainous

Gebiß *nt* -sses, -sse teeth *pl*; *(künstliches)* false teeth *pl*, dentures *pl*; *(des Zaumes)* bit

geblümt *a* floral, flowered

gebogen *a* curved

geboren *a* born; **g~er Deutscher** German by birth; **Frau X, g~e Y Mrs X, née Y**

geborgen *a* safe, secure. **G~heit** *f* -security

Gebot *nt* -[e]s,-e rule; *(Relig)* commandment; *(bei Auktion)* bid

gebraten *a* fried

Gebrauch *m* use; *(Sprach-)* usage; **Gebräuche** customs; **in G~** in use; **G~ machen von** make use of. **g~en** *vt* use; **ich kann es nicht/gut g~en** I have no use for/can make good use of it; **zu nichts zu g~en** useless

gebräuchlich *a* common; *⟨Wort⟩* in common use

Gebrauch|sanleitung, G~sanweisung *f* directions *pl* for use. **g~t** *a* used; *(Comm)* secondhand. **G~twagen** *m* used car

gebrechlich *a* frail, infirm

gebrochen *a* broken □*adv* -g~ **Englisch sprechen** speak broken English

Gebrüll *nt* -s roaring; *(fam: Schreien)* bawling

Gebrumm *nt* -s buzzing; *(Motoren-)* humming

Gebühr *f* -,-en charge, fee; **über G~** excessively; **g~en** *vi (haben)* **ihm g~t** Respekt he deserves respect; **wie es sich g~t** as is right and proper. **g~end** *a* due, *adv* duly; *(geziemend)* proper, *adv* -ly. **g~enfrei** *a* free □*adv* free of charge. **g~enpflichtig** *a* & *adv* subject to a charge; **g~enpflichtige Straße** toll road

gebunden *a* bound; *⟨Suppe⟩* thickened

Geburt *f* -,-en birth; **von G~** by birth. **G~enkontrolle, G~enregelung** *f* birth-control. **G~enziffer** *f* birth-rate

gebürtig *a* native **(aus)**; **g~er Deutscher** German by birth

Geburts|datum *nt* date of birth. **G~helfer** *m* obstetrician. **G~hilfe** *f* obstetrics *sg.* **G~ort** *m* birthplace. **G~tag** *m* birthday. **G~urkunde** *f* birth certificate

Gebüsch *nt* -[e]s,-e bushes *pl*

Gedächtnis *nt* -ses memory; **aus dem G~** from memory

gedämpft *a* *⟨Ton⟩* muffled; *⟨Stimme⟩* hushed; *⟨Musik⟩* soft; *⟨Licht, Stimmung⟩* subdued

Gedanke *m* -ns,-n thought **(an + acc of)**; *(Idee)* idea; **sich** *(dat)* **G~n machen** worry **(über + acc** about). **G~nblitz** *m* brainwave. **g~nlos** *a* thoughtless, *adv* -ly; *(zerstreut)* absent-minded, *adv* -ly. **G~nstrich** *m* dash. **G~nübertragung** *f* telepathy. **g~nvoll** *a* pensive, *adv* -ly

Gedärme *ntpl* intestines; *(Tier-)* entrails

Gedeck *nt* -[e]s,-e place setting; *(auf Speisekarte)* set meal; **ein G~ auflegen** set a place. **g~t** *a* covered; *⟨Farbe⟩* muted

gedeihen† vi (sein) thrive, flourish

gedenken† vi (haben) propose (etw zu tun to do sth); jds/etw G~ remember s.o./sth. G~ nt -s memory; zum G~ an (+acc) in memory of

Gedenk|feier f commemoration. G~gottesdienst m memorial service. G~stätte f memorial. G~tafel f commemorative plaque. G~tag m day of remembrance; (Jahrestag) anniversary

Gedicht nt -[e]s,-e poem

gediegen a quality ...; (solide) well-made; (Charakter) upright; (Gold) pure □ adv g~ gebaut well built

Gedränge nt -s crush, crowd. g~t a (knapp) concise □ adv g~t voll packed

gedrückt a depressed

gedrungen a stocky

Geduld f- patience; G~ haben be patient. g~en (sich) vr be patient. g~ig a patient, adv -ly. G~[s]spiel nt puzzle

gedunsen a bloated

geehrt a honoured; sehr g~er Herr X dear Mr X

geeignet a suitable; im g~en Moment at the right moment

Gefahr f -,-en danger; auf eigene G~ in/out of danger; auf eigene G~ at one's own risk; G~ laufen run the risk (etw zu tun of doing sth)

gefähr|den vt endanger; (fig) jeopardize. g~lich a dangerous, adv -ly; (riskant) risky

gefahrlos a safe

Gefährt nt -[e]s,-e vehicle

Gefährte m -n,-n, **Gefährtin** f -,-nen companion

gefahrvoll a dangerous, perilous

Gefälle nt -s,- slope; (Straßen-) gradient

gefallen† vi (haben) jdm g~ please s.o.; er/es gefällt mir I

like him/it; sich (dat) etw g~ lassen put up with sth

Gefallen[1] m -s,- favour

Gefallen[2] nt -s pleasure (an + dat in); G~ finden an (+ dat) like; dir zu G~ to please you

Gefallene(r) m soldier killed in the war

gefällig a pleasing; (hübsch) attractive, adv -ly; (hilfsbereit) obliging; jdm g~ sein do s.o. a good turn; [sonst] noch etwas g~? will there be anything else? G~keit f -,-en favour; (Freundlichkeit) kindness. g~st adv (fam) kindly

Gefangen|e(r) m/f prisoner. g~halten† vt sep hold prisoner; keep in captivity (Tier). G~nahme f - capture. g~nehmen† vt sep take prisoner. G~schaft f - captivity; in G~schaft geraten be taken prisoner

Gefängnis nt -ses,-se prison; (Strafe) imprisonment. G~strafe f imprisonment; (Urteil) prison sentence. G~wärter m [prison] warder, (Amer) guard

Gefäß nt -es,-e container, receptacle; (Blut-) vessel

gefaßt a composed; (ruhig) calm, adv -ly; g~ sein auf (+acc) be prepared for

Gefecht nt -[e]s,-e fight; (Mil) engagement; außer G~ setzen put out of action

gefedert a sprung

gefeiert a celebrated

Gefieder nt -s plumage. g~t a feathered

Geflecht nt -[e]s,-e network; (Gewirr) tangle; (Korb-) wickerwork

gefleckt a spotted

geflissentlich adv studiously

Geflügel nt -s poultry. G~klein nt -s giblets pl. g~t a winged; g~tes Wort familiar quotation

Geflüster nt -s whispering

Gefolge nt -s retinue, entourage. **G~schaft** f- followers pl, following; (Treue) allegiance

gefragt a popular; **g~ sein** be in demand

gefräßig a voracious; ⟨Mensch⟩ greedy

Gefreite(r) m lance-corporal

gefrier|en† vi (sein) freeze. **G~fach** nt freezer compartment. **G~punkt** m freezing point. **G~schrank** m upright freezer. **G~truhe** f chest freezer

gefroren a frozen. **G~e(s)** nt (Aust) ice-cream

Gefüge nt -s,- structure; (fig) fabric

gefügig a compliant; (gehorsam) obedient

Gefühl nt -[e]s,-e feeling; (Empfindung) sensation; (Erregung) emotion; **im G~ haben** know instinctively. **g~los** a insensitive; (herzlos) unfeeling; (taub) numb. **g~sbetont** a emotional. **g~skalt** a (fig) cold. **g~smäßig** a emotional, adv -ly; (instinktiv) instinctive, adv -ly. **G~sregung** f emotion. **g~voll** a sensitive, adv -ly; (sentimental) sentimental, adv -ly

gefüllt a filled; (voll) full; (Bot) double; (Culin) stuffed; ⟨Schokolade⟩ with a filling

gefürchtet a feared, dreaded

gefüttert a lined

gegeben a given; (bestehend) present; (passend) appropriate; **zu g~er Zeit** at the proper time. **g~enfalls** adv if need be. **G~heiten** fpl realities, facts

gegen prep (+ acc) against; (Sport) versus; (g~über) to[wards]; (Vergleich) compared with; (Richtung, Zeit) towards; (ungefähr) around; **ein Mittel g~** a remedy for □adv g~ 100 Leute about 100

people. **G~angriff** m counterattack

Gegend f -,-en area, region; (Umgebung) neighbourhood

gegeneinander adv against/ (gegenüber) towards one another

Gegen|fahrbahn f opposite carriageway. **G~gift** nt antidote. **G~leistung** f **als G~leistung** in return. **G~maßnahme** f countermeasure. **G~satz** m contrast; (Widerspruch) contradiction; (G~teil) opposite; **im G~satz zu** unlike. **g~sätzlich** a contrasting; (widersprüchlich) opposing. **g~seitig** a mutual, adv -ly; **sich g~seitig hassen** hate one another. **G~spieler** m opponent. **G~sprechanlage** f intercom. **G~stand** m object; (Gram, Gesprächs-) subject. **g~standslos** a unfounded; (überflüssig) irrelevant; (abstrakt) abstract. **G~stück** nt counterpart; (G~teil) opposite. **G~teil** nt opposite, contrary; **im G~teil** on the contrary. **g~teilig** a opposite

gegenüber prep (+ dat) opposite; (Vergleich) compared with; **jdm g~ höflich sein** be polite to s.o. □adv opposite. **G~ nt -s** person opposite. **g~liegen†** vi sep (haben) be opposite (etw dat sth). **g~liegend** a opposite. **g~stehen†** vi sep (haben) (+ dat) face; **feindlich g~stehen** (+ dat) be hostile to. **g~stellen** vt sep confront; (vergleichen) compare. **g~treten†** vi sep (sein) (+ dat) face

Gegen|verkehr m oncoming traffic. **G~vorschlag** m counter-proposal. **G~wart** f - present; (Anwesenheit) presence. **g~wärtig** a present □adv at present. **G~wehr** f - resistance. **G~wert** m equivalent.

G~**wind** *m* head wind.
g~**zeichnen** *vt sep* countersign

geglückt *a* successful

Gegner|(in) *m* -s,- (*f* -,-nen) opponent. g~**isch** *a* opposing

Gehabe *nt* -s affected behaviour

Gehackte(s) *nt* mince, (*Amer*) ground meat

Gehalt¹ *m* -[e]s content

Gehalt² *nt* -[e]s,⸚er salary.
G~**serhöhung** *f* rise, (*Amer*) raise

gehaltvoll *a* nourishing

gehässig *a* spiteful, *adv* -ly

gehäuft *a* heaped

Gehäuse *nt* -s,- case; (*TV, Radio*) cabinet; (*Schnecken-*) shell; (*Kern-*) core

Gehege *nt* -s,- enclosure

geheim *a* secret; **im g~en** secretly. G~**dienst** *m* Secret Service. g~**halten†** *vt sep* keep secret. G~**nis** *nt* -ses,-se secret.
g~**nisvoll** *a* mysterious, *adv* -ly.
G~**polizei** *f* secret police

gehemmt *a* (*fig*) inhibited

gehen† *vi* (*sein*) go; (*zu Fuß*) walk; (*fort-*) leave; (*funktionieren*) work; (*Teig:*) rise; **tanzen/einkaufen g~** go dancing/shopping; **an die Arbeit g~** set to work; **in Schwarz [gekleidet] g~** dress in black; **nach Norden g~** (*Fenster:*) face north; **wenn es nach mir ginge** if I had my way; **über die Straße g~** cross the road; **was geht hier vor sich?** what is going on here? **das geht zu weit** (*fam*) that's going too far; *impers* **wie geht es [Ihnen]?** how are you? **es geht mir gut/ besser** I am well/better; **es geht nicht/nicht anders** it's impossible/there is no other way; **es ging ganz schnell** it was very quick; **es geht um Geld** she is only interested in the money; **es geht [so]** (*fam*) not too bad □ *vt*

walk. g~**lassen†** (**sich**) *vr sep* lose one's self-control; (*sich vernachlässigen*) let oneself go

geheuer *a* **nicht g~** eerie; (*verdächtig*) suspicious; **mir ist nicht g~** I feel uneasy

Geheul *nt* -s howling

Gehilfe *m* -n,-n, **Gehilfin** *f* -,-nen trainee; (*Helfer*) assistant

Gehirn *nt* -s brain; (*Verstand*) brains *pl*. G~**erschütterung** *f* concussion. G~**hautentzündung** *f* meningitis. G~**wäsche** *f* brainwashing

gehoben *a* (*fig*) superior; (*Sprache*) elevated

Gehöft *nt* -[e]s,-e farm

Gehölz *nt* -es,-e coppice, copse

Gehör *nt* -s hearing; G~ **schenken** (+ *dat*) listen to

gehorchen *vi* (*haben*) (+ *dat*) obey

gehören *vi* (*haben*) belong (*dat* to); **zu den Besten g~** be one of the best; **dazu gehört Mut** that takes courage; **sich g~** be [right and] proper; **es gehört sich nicht** it isn't done

gehörig *a* proper, *adv* -ly; **jdn g~ verprügeln** give s.o. a good hiding

gehörlos *a* deaf

Gehörn *nt* -s,-e horns *pl*; (*Geweih*) antlers *pl*

gehorsam *a* obedient, *adv* -ly.
G~ *m* -s obedience

Gehsteig *m* -[e]s,-e pavement, (*Amer*) sidewalk. G~**weg** *m* = **Gehsteig;** (*Fußweg*) footpath

Geier *m* -s,- vulture

Geige *f* -,-n violin. g~**n** *vi* (*haben*) play the violin □ *vt* play on the violin. G~**r(in)** *m* -s,- (*f* -,-nen) violinist

geil *a* lecherous; (*fam*) randy; (*fam: toll*) great

Geisel *f* -,-n hostage

Geiß *f* -,-en (*SGer*) [nanny-]goat.
G~**blatt** *nt* honeysuckle

Geißel f -,-n scourge

Geist m -[e]s,-er mind; (*Witz*) wit; (*Gesinnung*) spirit; (*Gespenst*) ghost; **der Heilige G~** the Holy Ghost or Spirit; **im G~** in one's mind. **g~erhaft** a ghostly **geistes|abwesend** a absent-minded, adv -ly. **G~blitz** m brainwave. **G~gegenwart** f presence of mind. **g~gegen-wärtig** adv with great presence of mind. **g~gestört** a [mentally] deranged. **g~krank** a mentally ill. **G~krankheit** f mental illness. **G~wissenschaften** fpl arts. **G~zustand** m mental state **geist|ig** a mental, adv -ly; (*intellektuell*) intellectual, adv -ly; **g~ige Getränke** spirits. **g~lich** a spiritual, adv -ly; (*religiös*) religious; (*Musik*) sacred; (*Tracht*) clerical. **G~liche(r)** m clergyman. **G~lichkeit** f - clergy. **g~los** a uninspired. **g~reich** a clever; (*witzig*) witty

Geiz m -es meanness. **g~en** vi (haben) be mean (**mit** with). **G~hals** m (fam) miser. **g~ig** a mean, miserly. **G~kragen** m (fam) miser

Gekicher nt -s giggling

geknickt a (fam) dejected, adv -ly

gekonnt a accomplished □adv expertly

Gekrakel nt -s scrawl

gekränkt a offended, hurt

Gekritzel nt -s scribble

gekünstelt a affected, adv -ly

Gelächter nt -s laughter

geladen a loaded; (fam: wütend) furious

Gelage nt -s,- feast

gelähmt a paralysed

Gelände nt -s,- terrain; (*Grundstück*) site. **G~lauf** m cross-country run

Geländer nt -s,- railings pl; (*Treppen-*) banisters pl; (*Brücken-*) parapet

gelangen vi (sein) reach/(fig) attain (**zu etw/an etw** acc sth); **in jds Besitz g~** come into s.o.'s possession

gelassen a composed; (*ruhig*) calm, adv -ly. **G~heit** f - equanimity; (*Fassung*) composure

Gelatine /ʒela-/ f - gelatine

geläufig a common, current; (*fließend*) fluent, adv -ly; **jdm g~ sein** be familiar to s.o.

gelaunt a **gut/schlecht g~ sein** be in a good/bad mood

gelb a yellow; (*bei Ampel*) amber; **g~e Rübe** (SGer) carrot; **das G~e vom Ei** the yolk of the egg. **G~** nt -s,- yellow; **bei G~** (*Auto*) on [the] amber. **g~lich** a yellowish. **G~sucht** f jaundice

Geld nt -es,-er money; **öffentliche G~er** public funds. **G~beutel** m, **G~börse** f purse. **G~geber** m -s,- backer. **g~lich** a financial, adv -ly. **G~mittel** ntpl funds. **G~schein** m banknote. **G~schrank** m safe. **G~strafe** f fine. **G~stück** nt coin

Gelee /ʒe'le:/ nt -s,-s jelly

gelegen a situated; (*passend*) convenient; **jdm sehr g~ sein od kommen** suit s.o. well; **mir ist viel/wenig daran g~** I'm very/not keen on it; (*es ist wichtig*) it matters a lot/little to me

Gelegenheit f -,-en opportunity, chance; (*Anlaß*) occasion; (*Comm*) bargain; **bei G~** some time. **G~sarbeit** f casual work. **G~sarbeiter** m casual worker. **G~skauf** m bargain

gelegentlich a occasional □adv occasionally; (*bei Gelegenheit*) some time □prep (+gen) on the occasion of

gelehrt a learned. **G~e(r)** m/f scholar

Geleise nt -s,- = Gleis

Geleit nt -[e]s escort; freies G~
safe conduct. **g~en** vt escort.
G~zug m (Naut) convoy

Gelenk nt -[e]s,-e joint. **g~ig** a
supple; (Techn) flexible

gelernt a skilled

Geliebte(r) m/f lover; (liter) beloved

gelieren /ʒe-/ vi (haben) set

gelinde a mild, adv -ly; **g~** gesagt
to put it mildly

gelingen† vi (sein) succeed, be
successful; **es gelang ihm, zu
entkommen** he succeeded in escaping. **G~** nt -s success

gell int (SGer) = gelt

gellend a shrill, adv -y

geloben vt promise [solemnly];
sich (dat) **g~** vow (zu to); **das
Gelobte Land** the Promised
Land

Gelöbnis nt -ses,-se vow

gelöst a (fig) relaxed

Gelse f -,-n (Aust) mosquito

gelt int (SGer) **das ist schön, g~?**
it's nice, isn't it? **ihr kommt
doch, g~?** you are coming,
aren't you?

gelten† vi (haben) be valid; (Regel:) apply; **g~ als** be regarded
as; **etw nicht g~ lassen** not
accept sth; **wenig/viel g~** be
worth/(fig) count for little/a lot;
jdm g~ be meant for s.o.; **das gilt
nicht** that doesn't count. **g~d** a
valid; (Preise) current; (Meinung) prevailing; **g~d machen**
assert (Recht, Forderung); bring
to bear (Einfluß)

Geltung f - validity; (Ansehen)
prestige; **G~ haben** be valid; **zur
G~ bringen/kommen** set off/
show to advantage

Gelübde nt -s,- vow

gelungen a successful

Gelüst nt -[e]s,-e desire/(stark)
craving (nach for)

gemächlich a leisurely □ adv in a
leisurely manner

Gemahl m -s,-e husband. **G~in** f
-,-nen wife

Gemälde nt -s,- painting. **G~ga-
lerie** f picture gallery

gemäß prep (+ dat) in accordance
with □ a etw (dat) **g~ sein** be in
keeping with sth

gemäßigt a moderate; (Klima)
temperate

gemein a common; (unanständig) vulgar; (niederträchtig)
mean; **g~er Soldat** private; **etw
g~ haben** have sth in common
□ adv shabbily; (fam: schrecklich) terribly

Gemeinde f -,-n [local] community; (Admin) borough; (Pfarr-)
parish; (bei Gottesdienst) congre-
gation. **G~rat** m local council/
(Person) councillor. **G~wahlen**
fpl local elections

gemein|gefährlich a dangerous.
G~heit f -,-en (s. gemein) com-
monness; vulgarity; meanness;
(Bemerkung, Handlung) mean
thing [to say/do]; **so eine
G~heit!** how mean! (wie ärgerlich) what a nuisance! **G~kos-
ten** pl overheads. **g~nützig** a
charitable. **G~platz** m platitude. **g~sam** a common; **etw
g~sam haben** have sth in common □ adv together

Gemeinschaft f -,-en community. **g~lich** a joint; (Besitz)
communal □ adv jointly; (zusammen) together. **G~sarbeit** f
team-work

Gemenge nt -s,- mixture

gemessen a measured; (würdevoll) dignified

Gemetzel nt -s,- carnage

Gemisch nt -[e]s,-e mixture. **g~t**
a mixed

Gemme f -,-n engraved gem

Gemse f -,-n chamois

Gemurmel nt -s murmuring

Gemüse nt -s,- vegetable; (coll) vegetables pl. **G~händler** m greengrocer

gemustert a patterned

Gemüt nt -[e]s,-er nature, disposition; (Gefühl) feelings pl; (Person) soul

gemütlich a cosy; (gemächlich) leisurely; (zwanglos) informal; ⟨Person⟩ genial; es sich (dat) g~ machen make oneself comfortable □adv cosily; in a leisurely manner; informally. **G~keit** f- cosiness; leisureliness

Gemüts|art f nature, disposition. **G~mensch** m (fam) placid person. **G~ruhe** f in aller **G~ruhe** (fam) calmly. **G~verfassung** f frame of mind

Gen nt -s,-e gene

genau a exact, adv -ly, precise, adv -ly; ⟨Waage, Messung⟩ accurate, adv -ly; (sorgfältig) meticulous, adv -ly; (ausführlich) detailed; **nichts G~es wissen** not know any details; **es ist nicht so g~ nehmen** not be too particular; **g~!** exactly! **g~genommen** adv strictly speaking. **G~igkeit** f- exactitude; precision; accuracy; meticulousness

genauso adv just the same; (g~sehr) just as much; **g~ gut/teuer** just as good/expensive. **g~gut** adv just as well. **g~sehr** adv just as much. **g~viel** adv just as much/many, **g~wenig** adv just as little/few; (noch) no more

Gendarm /ʒã'darm/ m -en,-en (Aust) policeman

Genealogie f- genealogy

genehmig|en vt grant; approve ⟨Plan⟩. **G~ung** f -,-en permission; (Schein) permit

geneigt a sloping, inclined; (fig) well-disposed (dat towards); **[nicht] g~ sein** (fig) [not] feel inclined (zu to)

General m -s,-̈e general. **G~direktor** m managing director. **g~isieren** vt (haben) generalize. **G~probe** f dress rehearsal. **G~streik** m general strike. **g~überholen** vt insep (inf & pp only) completely overhaul

Generation /-'tsio:n/ f -,-en generation

Generator m -s,-en /-'to:rən/ generator

generell a general, adv -ly

genes|en† vi (sein) recover. **G~ung** f- recovery; (Erholung) convalescence

Genet|ik f- genetics sg. **g~isch** a genetic, adv -ally

Genf nt -s Geneva. **G~er** a Geneva …; **G~er** See Lake Geneva

genial a brilliant, adv -ly; **ein g~er Mann** a man of genius. **G~ität** f- genius

Genick nt -s,-e [back of the] neck; **sich** (dat) **das G~ brechen** break one's neck

Genie /ʒe'ni:/ nt -s,-s genius

genieren /ʒe'ni:rən/ vt embarrass; **sich g~** feel or be embarrassed

genieß|bar a fit to eat/drink. **g~en†** vt enjoy; (verzehren) eat/drink. **G~er** m -s,- gourmet. **g~erisch** a appreciative □adv with relish

Genitiv m -s,-e genitive

Genosse m -n,-n (Pol) comrade. **G~nschaft** f -,-en cooperative

Genre /'ʒã:rə/ nt -s,-s genre

Gentechnologie f genetic engineering

genug inv a & adv enough

Genüge f zur **G~** sufficiently. **g~n** vi (haben) be enough; **jds Anforderungen g~n** meet s.o.'s requirements. **g~nd** inv a sufficient, enough; (Sch) fair □adv sufficiently, enough

genügsam a frugal, adv -ly; (bescheiden) modest, adv -ly

Genugtuung f - satisfaction

Genuß m -sses, ¨sse enjoyment; (Vergnügen) pleasure; (Verzehr) consumption. **genüßlich** a pleasurable □ adv with relish

geöffnet a open

Geo|graphie f - geography. **g~graphisch** a geographical, adv -ly. **G~loge** m -n,-n geologist. **G~logie** f - geology. **g~logisch** a geological, adv -ly. **G~meter** m -s,- surveyor. **G~metrie** f - geometry. **g~metrisch** a geometric[al]

geordnet a well-ordered; (stabil) stable; **alphabetisch g~** in alphabetical order

Gepäck nt -s luggage, baggage. **G~ablage** f luggage-rack. **G~aufbewahrung** f left-luggage office. **G~schalter** m luggage office. **G~schein** m left-luggage ticket; (Aviat) baggage check. **G~stück** nt piece of luggage. **G~träger** m porter; (Fahrrad-) luggage carrier; (Dach-) roof-rack. **G~wagen** m luggage-van

Gepard m -s,-e cheetah

gepflegt a well-kept; ⟨Person⟩ well-groomed; ⟨Hotel⟩ first-class

Gepflogenheit f -,-en practice; (Brauch) custom

Gepolter nt -s [loud] noise

gepunktet a spotted

gerade a straight; (direkt) direct; (aufrecht) upright; (aufrichtig) straightforward; ⟨Zahl⟩ even □ adv straight; directly; (eben) just; (genau) exactly; (besonders) especially; **nicht g~ billig** not exactly cheap; **g~ erst** only just; **g~ an dem Tag** on that very day. **G~ f -,-n** straight line. **g~aus** adv straight ahead/on

gerade|biegen† vt sep straighten; (fig) straighten out. **g~halten†** (sich) vr sep hold oneself straight. **g~heraus** adv (fig)

straight out. **g~sitzen†** vi sep (haben) sit [up] straight. **g~so** adv just the same; **g~so gut** just as good. **g~sogut** adv just as well. **g~stehen†** vi sep (haben) stand up straight; (fig) accept responsibility (für for). **g~wegs** adv directly, straight. **g~zu** adv virtually; (wirklich) absolutely

Geranie /-iə/ f -,-n geranium

Gerät nt -[e]s,-e tool; (Acker-) implement; (Küchen-) utensil; (Elektro-) appliance; (Radio-, Fernseh-) set; (Turn-) piece of apparatus; (coll) equipment

geraten† vi (sein) get; **in Brand g~** catch fire; **in Wut g~** get angry; **in Streit g~** start quarrelling; **gut/schlecht g~** turn out well/badly; **nach jdm g~** take after s.o.

Geratewohl nt aufs **G~** at random

geräuchert a smoked

geräumig a spacious, roomy

Geräusch nt -[e]s,-e noise. **g~los** a noiseless, adv -ly. **g~voll** a noisy, adv -ily

gerben vt tan

gerecht a just, adv -ly; (fair) fair, adv -ly; **g~ werden** (+ dat) do justice to. **g~fertigt** a justified. **G~igkeit** f - justice; fairness

Gerede nt -s talk; (Klatsch) gossip

geregelt a regular

gereift a mature

gereizt a irritable, adv -bly. **G~heit** f - irritability

gereuen vt es gereut mich nicht I don't regret it

Geriatrie f - geriatrics sg

Gericht¹ nt -[e]s,-e (Culin) dish

Gericht² nt -[e]s,-e court [of law]; **vor G~** in court; **das Jüngste G~** the Last Judgement; **mit jdm ins G~ gehen** take s.o. to task. **g~lich** a judicial; ⟨Verfahren⟩ legal □ adv **g~lich vorgehen** take legal action. **G~sbarkeit** f-

jurisdiction. **G~shof** *m* court of justice. **G~smedizin** *f* forensic medicine. **G~ssaal** *m* courtroom. **G~svollzieher** *m* -s,- bailiff

gerieben *a* grated; (*fam: schlau*) crafty

gering *a* small; (*niedrig*) low; (*g~fügig*) slight. **g~achten** *vt sep* have little regard for; (*verachten*) despise. **g~fügig** *a* slight, *adv* -ly. **g~schätzig** *a* contemptuous, *adv* -ly; (*Bemerkung*) disparaging. **g~ste(r,s)** *a* least; **nicht im g~sten** not in the least

gerinnen† *vi* (*sein*) curdle; ⟨*Blut:*⟩ clot

Gerippe *nt* -s,- skeleton; (*fig*) framework

gerissen *a* (*fam*) crafty

Germ *m* -[e]s (*Aust*) *f* - yeast

German|**e** *m* -n,-n [ancient] German. **g~isch** *a* Germanic. **G~ist(in)** *m* -en,-en (*f* -,-nen) Germanist. **G~istik** *f* - German [language and literature]

gern[e] *adv* gladly; **g~ haben** like; (*lieben*) be fond of; **ich tanze/schwimme g~** I like dancing/swimming; **das kannst du g~ tun** you're welcome to do that; **willst du mit?**—**g~!** do you want to come?—I'd love to!

gerötet *a* red

Gerste *f* - barley. **G~nkorn** *nt* (*Med*) stye

Geruch *m* -[e]s,-e smell (**von/ nach** of). **g~los** *a* odourless. **G~ssinn** *m* sense of smell

Gerücht *nt* -[e]s,-e rumour

geruhen *vi* (*haben*) deign (**zu** to)

gerührt *a* (*fig*) moved, touched

Gerümpel *nt* -s lumber, junk

Gerüst *nt* -[e]s,-e scaffolding; (*fig*) framework

gesalzen *a* salted; (*gefaßt*) steep

gesammelt *a* collected; (*gefaßt*) composed

gesamt *a* entire, whole. **G~aus-gabe** *f* complete edition. **G~be-trag** *m* total amount. **G~ein-druck** *m* overall impression. **G~heit** *f* - whole. **G~schule** *f* comprehensive school. **G~-summe** *f* total

Gesandte(r) *m*|*f* envoy

Gesang *m* -[e]s,-e singing; (*Lied*) song; (*Kirchen-*) hymn. **G~buch** *nt* hymn-book. **G~verein** *m* choral society

Gesäß *nt* -es buttocks *pl.* **G~-tasche** *f* hip pocket

Geschäft *nt* -[e]s,-e business; (*Laden*) shop, (*Amer*) store; (*Transaktion*) deal; (*fam: Büro*) office; **schmutzige G~e** shady dealings; **ein gutes G~ machen** do very well (mit out of); **sein G~ verstehen** know one's job. **g~e-halber** *adv* on business. **g~ig** *a* busy, *adv* -ily; (*Treiben*) bustling. **G~igkeit** *f* - activity. **g~lich** *a* business ... □ *adv* on business

Geschäfts|brief *m* business letter. **G~führer** *m* manager; (*Vereins-*) secretary. **G~mann** *m* (*pl* -leute) businessman. **G~reise** *f* business trip. **G~stelle** *f* office; (*Zweigstelle*) branch. **G~tüchtig** *a* **g~tüchtig sein** be a good businessman/-woman. **G~viertel** *nt* shopping area. **G~zeiten** *fpl* hours of business

geschehen† *vi* (*sein*) happen (*dat* to); **es ist ein Unglück g~** there has been an accident; **es ist um uns g~** we are done for; **das geschieht dir recht!** it serves you right! **gern g~!** you're welcome! **G~** *nt* -s events *pl*

gescheit *a* clever; **daraus werde ich nicht g~** I can't make head or tail of it

Geschenk *nt* -[e]s,-e present, gift. **G~korb** *m* gift hamper

Geschicht|e f -,-n history; (*Erzählung*) story; (*fam: Sache*) business. **g~lich** a historical, adv -ly

Geschick nt -[e]s fate; (*Talent*) skill; **G~ haben** be good (**zu** at). **G~lichkeit** f skilfulness, skill. **g~t** a skilful, adv -ly; (*klug*) clever, adv -ly

geschieden a divorced. **G~e(r)** m/f divorcee

Geschirr nt -s,-e (*coll*) crockery; (*Porzellan*) china; (*Service*) service; (*Pferde-*) harness; **schmutziges G~** dirty dishes pl. **G~spülmaschine** f dishwasher. **G~tuch** nt tea-towel

Geschlecht nt -[e]s,-er sex; (*Gram*) gender; (*Familie*) family; (*Generation*) generation. **g~lich** a sexual, adv -ly. **G~skrankheit** f venereal disease. **G~steile** ntpl genitals. **G~sverkehr** m sexual intercourse. **G~swort** nt (pl -wörter) article

geschliffen a (*fig*) polished

geschlossen a closed □adv unanimously; (*vereint*) in a body

Geschmack m -[e]s,-̈e taste; (*Aroma*) flavour; (*G~ssinn*) sense of taste; **einen guten G~ haben** (*fig*) have good taste; **G~ finden an** (+ dat) acquire a taste for. **g~los** a tasteless, adv -ly; **g~los sein** (*fig*) be in bad taste. **G~ssache** f matter of taste. **g~voll** a (*fig*) tasteful, adv -ly

geschmeidig a supple; (*weich*) soft

Geschöpf nt -[e]s,-e creature

Geschoß nt -sses,-sse missile; (*Stockwerk*) storey, floor

geschraubt a (*fig*) stilted

Geschrei nt -s screaming; (*fig*) fuss

Geschütz nt -es,-e gun, cannon

geschützt a protected; (*Stelle*) sheltered

Geschwader nt -s,- squadron

Geschwätz nt -es talk. **g~ig** a garrulous

geschweift a curved

geschweige conj **g~ denn** let alone

geschwind a quick, adv -ly

Geschwindigkeit f -,-en speed; (*Phys*) velocity. **G~sbegrenzung,** **G~sbeschränkung** f speed limit

Geschwister pl brother[s] and sister[s]; siblings

geschwollen a swollen; (*fig*) pompous, adv -ly

Geschworene(r) m/f juror; **die G~n** the jury sg

Geschwulst f -,-̈e swelling; (*Tumor*) tumour

geschwungen a curved

Geschwür nt -s,-e ulcer

Geselle m -n,-n fellow; (*Handwerks-*) journeyman

gesellig a sociable; (*Zool*) gregarious; (*unterhaltsam*) convivial; **g~er Abend** social evening. **G~keit** f -,-en entertaining; **die G~keit lieben** love company

Gesellschaft f -,-en company; (*Veranstaltung*) party; **die G~** society; **jdm G~ leisten** keep s.o. company. **g~lich** a social, adv -ly. **G~sreise** f group tour. **G~sspiel** nt party game

Gesetz nt -es,-e law. **G~entwurf** m bill. **g~gebend** a legislative. **G~gebung** f legislation. **g~lich** a legal, adv -ly. **g~los** a lawless. **g~mäßig** a lawful, adv -ly; (*gesetzlich*) legal, adv -ly

gesetzt a staid; (*Sport*) seeded □conj **g~ den Fall** supposing

gesetzwidrig a illegal, adv -ly

gesichert a secure

Gesicht nt -[e]s,-er face; (*Aussehen*) appearance; **zu G~ bekommen** set eyes on. **G~sausdruck** m [facial] expression. **G~sfarbe** f complexion.

G~spunkt *m* point of view. **G~szüge** *mpl* features

Gesindel *nt* -s riff-raff

gesinnt *a* **gut/übel g~** well/ill disposed (*dat* towards)

Gesinnung *f* -,-en mind; (*Einstellung*) attitude; **politische G~** political convictions *pl*

gesittet *a* well-mannered; (*zivilisiert*) civilized

gesondert *a* separate, *adv* -ly

Gespann *nt* -[e]s,-e team; (*Wagen*) horse and cart/carriage

gespannt *a* taut; (*fig*) tense, *adv* -ly; (*Beziehungen*) strained; (*neugierig*) eager, *adv* -ly; (*erwartungsvoll*) expectant, *adv* -ly; **g~ sein, ob** wonder whether; **auf etw/jdn g~ sein** look forward eagerly to sth/to seeing s.o.

Gespenst *nt* -[e]s,-er ghost. **g~isch** *a* ghostly; (*unheimlich*) eerie

Gespött *nt* -[e]s mockery; **zum G~ werden** become a laughingstock

Gespräch *nt* -[e]s,-e conversation; (*Telefon-*) call; **ins G~ kommen get** talking; **im G~ sein** be under discussion. **g~ig** *a* talkative. **G~sgegenstand** *m*, **G~sthema** *nt* topic of conversation

gesprenkelt *a* speckled

Gespür *nt* -s feeling; (*Instinkt*) instinct

Gestalt *f* -,-en figure; (*Form*) shape, form; **G~ annehmen** (*fig*) take shape. **g~en** *vt* shape; (*organisieren*) arrange; (*schaffen*) create; (*entwerfen*) design; **sich g~en** turn out

geständ|ig *a* confessed; **g~ig sein** have confessed. **G~nis** *nt* -ses,-se confession

Gestank *m* -s stench, [bad] smell

gestatten *vt* allow, permit; nicht **gestattet** prohibited; **g~ Sie?** may I?

Geste /'gɛ-, 'ge:stə/ *f* -,-n gesture

Gesteck *nt* -[e]s,-e flower arrangement

gestehen† *vt/i* (*haben*) confess; confess to (*Verbrechen*); **offen gestanden** to tell the truth

Gestein *nt* -[e]s,-e rock

Gestell *nt* -[e]s,-e stand; (*Flaschen-*) rack; (*Rahmen*) frame

gestellt *a* **gut/schlecht g~** well/ badly off; **auf sich** (*acc*) **selbst g~ sein** be thrown on one's own resources

gestelzt *a* (*fig*) stilted

gesteppt *a* quilted

gestern *adv* yesterday; **g~ nacht** last night

Gestik /'ɡɛstik/ *f* - gestures *pl*. **g~ulieren** *vi* (*haben*) gesticulate

gestrandet *a* stranded

gestreift *a* striped

gestrichelt *a* (*Linie*) dotted

gestrichen *a* **g~er Teelöffel** level teaspoon[ful]

gestrig /'ɡɛstrɪç/ *a* yesterday's; **am g~en Tag** yesterday

Gestrüpp *nt* -s,-e undergrowth

Gestüt *nt* -[e]s,-e stud [farm]

Gesuch *nt* -[e]s,-e request; (*Admin*) application. **g~t** *a* soughtafter; (*gekünstelt*) contrived

gesund *a* healthy, *adv* -ily; **g~ sein** be in good health; (*Sport, Getränk:*) be good for one; **wieder g~ werden** get well again

Gesundheit *f* - health; **G~!** (*bei Niesen*) bless you! **g~lich** *a* health ...; **in g~licher Zustand** state of health □*adv* **es geht ihm g~lich gut/schlecht** he is in good/poor health. **g~shalber** *adv* for health reasons. **g~sschädlich** *a* harmful. **G~szustand** *m* state of health

getäfelt *a* panelled

getigert *a* tabby

Getöse *nt* -s racket, din

getragen *a* solemn, *adv* -ly

Getränk nt -[e]s,-e drink. **G~karte** f wine-list

getrauen vt sich (dat) etw g~ dare [to] do sth; **sich g~** dare

Getreide nt -s (coll) grain

getrennt a separate, adv -ly; **g~ leben** live apart. **g~schreiben†** vt sep write as two words

getreu a faithful, adv -ly ⟨prep (+dat) true to; **der Wahrheit g~** truthfully. **g~lich** adv faithfully

Getriebe nt -s,- bustle; (Techn) gear; (Auto) transmission; (Gehäuse) gearbox

getrost adv with confidence

Getto nt -s,-s ghetto

Getue nt -s (fam) fuss

Getümmel nt -s tumult

getüpfelt a spotted

geübt a skilled; ⟨Auge, Hand⟩ practised

Gewächs nt -es,-e plant; (Med) growth

gewachsen a jdm/etw g~ sein be a match for s.o./be equal to sth

Gewächshaus nt greenhouse; (Treibhaus) hothouse

gewagt a daring

gewählt a refined

gewahr a g~ werden become aware (acc/gen of)

Gewähr f- guarantee

gewahren vt notice

gewähr|en vt grant; (geben) offer; **jdn g~en lassen** let s.o. have his way. **g~leisten** vt guarantee

Gewahrsam m -s safekeeping; (Haft) custody

Gewährsmann m (pl -männer & -leute) informant, source

Gewalt f -,-en power; (Kraft) force; (Brutalität) violence; **mit G~** by force; **G~ anwenden** use force; **sich in der G~ haben** be in control of oneself. **G~herrschaft** f tyranny. **g~ig** a powerful; (fam: groß) enormous, adv -ly; (stark) tremendous, adv -ly. **g~sam** a forcible, adv -bly;

⟨Tod⟩ violent. **g~tätig** a violent. **G~tätigkeit** f -,-en violence; (Handlung) act of violence

Gewand nt -[e]s,-er robe

gewandt a skilful, adv -ly; (flink) nimble, adv -bly. **G~heit** f- skill; nimbleness

Gewässer nt -s,- body of water; **G~ pl** waters

Gewebe nt -s,- fabric; (Anat) tissue

Gewehr nt -s,-e rifle, gun

Geweih nt -[e]s,-e antlers pl

Gewerb|e nt -s,- trade. **g~lich** a commercial, adv -ly. **g~smäßig** a professional, adv -ly

Gewerkschaft f -,-en trade union. **G~ler(in)** m -s,- (f -,-nen) trade unionist

Gewicht nt -[e]s,-e weight; (Bedeutung) importance. **G~heben** nt -s weight-lifting. **g~ig** a important

gewieft a (fam) crafty

gewillt a g~ sein be willing

Gewinde nt -s,- [screw] thread

Gewinn m -[e]s,-e profit; (fig) gain, benefit; (beim Spiel) winnings pl; (Preis) prize; (Los) winning ticket. **G~beteiligung** f profit-sharing. **g~bringend** a profitable, adv -bly. **g~en†** vt win; (erlangen) gain; (fördern) extract; **jdn für sich g~en** win s.o. over ⟨vi (haben) win; **g~en an** (+ dat) gain in. **g~end** a engaging. **G~er(in)** m -s,- (f -,-nen) winner

Gewirr nt -s,-e tangle; (Straßen-) maze; **G~ von Stimmen** hubbub of voices

gewiß a (gewisser, gewissest) certain, adv -ly

Gewissen nt -s,- conscience. **g~haft** a conscientious, adv -ly. **g~los** a unscrupulous. **G~sbisse** mpl pangs of conscience

gewissermaßen adv to a certain extent; (sozusagen) as it were

Gewißheit f - certainty

Gewitt|er nt -s,- thunderstorm. **g~ern** vi (haben) es g~ert it is thundering. **g~rig** a thundery

gewogen a (fig) well-disposed (dat towards)

gewöhnen vt jdn/sich g~ an (+ acc) get s.o. used to/get used to; **[an] jdn/etw gewöhnt sein** to be used to s.o./sth

Gewohnheit f -,-en habit. **g~smäßig** a habitual, adv -ly. **G~srecht** nt common law

gewöhnlich a ordinary, adv -ily; (üblich) usual, adv -ly; (ordinär) common

gewohnt a customary; (vertraut) familiar; (üblich) usual; etw (acc) **g~ sein** to be used to sth

Gewöhnung f - getting used (an + acc to); (Süchtigkeit) addiction

Gewölb|e nt -s,- vault. **g~t** a curved; (Archit) vaulted

gewollt a forced

Gewühl nt -[e]s crush

gewunden a winding

gewürfelt a check[ed]

Gewürz nt -es,-e spice. **G~nelke** f clove

gezackt a serrated

gezähnt a serrated; (Säge) toothed

Gezeiten fpl tides

gezielt a specific; (Frage) pointed

geziemend a proper, adv -ly

geziert a affected, adv -ly

gezwungen a forced □ adv **g~lachen** give a forced laugh. **g~ermaßen** adv of necessity; etw a **g~ermaßen tun** be forced to do sth

Gicht f - gout

Giebel m -s,- gable

Gier f - greed (nach for). **g~ig** a greedy, adv -ily

gieß|en† vt pour; water (Blumen, Garten); (Techn) cast □ v impers es **g~t** it is pouring [with rain].

G~erei f -,-en foundry. **G~kanne** f watering-can

Gift nt -[e]s,-e poison; (Schlangen-) venom; (Biol, Med) toxin. **g~ig** a poisonous; (Schlange) venomous; (Med, Chem) toxic; (fig) spiteful, adv -ly. **G~müll** m toxic waste. **G~pilz** m poisonous fungus, toadstool. **G~zahn** m [poison] fang

gigantisch a gigantic

Gilde f -,-n guild

Gimpel m -s,- bullfinch; (fam: Tölpel) simpleton

Gin /dʒɪn/ m -s gin

Ginster m -s (Bot) broom

Gipfel m -s,- summit, top; (fig) peak. **G~konferenz** f summit conference. **g~n** vi (haben) culminate (in + dat in)

Gips m -es plaster. **G~abguß** m plaster cast. **G~er** m -s,- plasterer. **G~verband** m (Med) plaster cast

Giraffe f -,-n giraffe

Girlande f -,-n garland

Girokonto /ˈʒiːro-/ nt current account

Gischt m -[e]s a f spray

Gitar|re f -,-n guitar. **G~rist(in)** m -en,-en (f -,-nen) guitarist

Gitter nt -s,- bars pl; (Rost) grating, grid; (Geländer, Zaun) railings pl; (Fenster-) grille; (Draht-) wire screen; **hinter G~n** (fam) behind bars. **G~netz** nt grid

Glanz m -es shine; (von Farbe, Papier) gloss; (Seiden-) sheen; (Politur) polish; (fig) brilliance; (Pracht) splendour

glänzen vi (haben) shine. **g~d** a shining, bright; (Papier, Haar) glossy; (fig) brilliant, adv -ly

glanz|los a dull. **G~stück** nt masterpiece; (einer Sammlung) show-piece. **g~voll** a (fig) brilliant, adv -ly; (prachtvoll) splendid, adv -ly. **G~zeit** f heyday

Glas nt -es,-̈er glass; (Brillen-)
lens; (Fern-) binoculars pl. (Mar-
meladen-) [glass] jar. **G~er** m -s,-
glazier

gläsern a glass . . .

Glashaus nt greenhouse

glasieren vt glaze; ice ⟨Kuchen⟩

glas|ig a glassy; (durchsichtig)
transparent. **G~scheibe** f pane

Glasur f -,-en glaze; (Culin) icing

glatt a smooth; (eben) even;
⟨Haar⟩ straight; (rutschig) slippery; (einfach) straightforward.
(eindeutig) downright; ⟨Absage⟩
flat □adv smoothly; evenly; (fam:
völlig) completely; (gerade)
straight; (leicht) easily; ⟨ableh-
nen⟩ flatly; **g~ verlaufen** go off
smoothly; **das ist g~ gelogen** it's
a downright lie

Glätte f - smoothness; (Rutschig-
keit) slipperiness

Glatteis nt [black] ice; **aufs G~
führen** (fam) take for a ride

glätten vt smooth; **sich g~** become smooth; ⟨Wellen:⟩ subside

glatt|gehen† vi sep (sein) (fig) go
off smoothly. **g~rasiert** a clean-
shaven. **g~streichen**† vt sep
smooth out. **g~weg** adv (fam)
outright

Glatz|e f -,-n bald patch; (Voll-)
bald head; **eine G~e bekommen**
go bald. **g~köpfig** a bald

Glaube m -ns belief (an + acc in);
(Relig) faith; **in gutem G~n** in
good faith; **G~n schenken** (+
dat) believe. **g~n** vt/i (haben)
believe (an + acc in); (vermuten)
think; **jdm g~n** believe s.o.;
nicht zu g~n unbelievable, incredible. **G~nsbekenntnis** nt
creed

glaubhaft a credible; (überzeugend) convincing, adv -ly

gläubig a religious; (vertrauend)
trusting, adv -ly. **G~e(r)** m/f⟨Re-
lig⟩ believer; **die G~en** the faithful. **G~er** m -s,- (Comm) creditor

glaub|lich a **kaum g~lich**
scarcely believable. **g~würdig**
a credible; ⟨Person⟩ reliable.
G~würdigkeit f - credibility;
reliability

gleich a same; (identisch) identical; (g~wertig) equal; **2 mal 5
[ist] g~ 10** two times 5 equals 10;
das ist mir g~ it's all the same to
me; **ganz g~, wo/wer** no matter
where/who □adv equally; (übereinstimmend) identically, the
same; (sofort) immediately; (in
Kürze) in a minute; (fast) nearly;
(direkt) right; **g~ alt/schwer**
sein be the same age/weight.
g~altrig a [of] the same age.
g~artig a similar. **g~bedeu-
tend** a synonymous. **g~berech-
tigt** a equal. **G~berechtigung** f
equality. **g~bleibend** a constant

gleichen† vi (haben) jdm/etw **g~**
be like or resemble s.o./sth; **sich
g~** be alike

gleich|ermaßen adv equally.
g~falls adv also, likewise;
danke g~falls thank you, the
same to you. **g~förmig** a uniform, adv -ly; (eintönig) monotonous, adv -ly. **G~förmigkeit** f
uniformity; monotony. **g~ge-
sinnt** a like-minded. **G~ge-
wicht** nt balance; (Phys & fig)
equilibrium. **g~gültig** a indifferent, adv -ly; (unwichtig) unimportant. **G~gültigkeit** f indif-
ference. **G~heit** f - equality;
(Ähnlichkeit) similarity. **g~ma-
chen** vt sep make equal; **dem
Erdboden g~machen** raze to
the ground. **g~mäßig** a even,
adv -ly, regular, adv -ly; (beständig) constant, adv -ly. **G~mä-
ßigkeit** f regularity. **G~mut** m
equanimity. **g~mütig** a calm,
adv -ly

Gleichnis nt -ses, -se parable

gleich|sam *adv* as it were. **G~schritt** *m* im **G~schritt** in step. **g~sehen** *vi sep (haben)* jdm **g~sehen** look like s.o.; *(fam: typisch sein)* be just like s.o. **g~setzen** *vt sep* equate/ *(g~stellen)* place on a par *(dat/ mit* with). **g~stellen** *vt sep* place on a par *(dat* with). **G~strom** *m* direct current. **g~tun†** *vi sep (haben)* es jdm **g~tun** emulate s.o.

Gleichung *f* -,-en equation

gleich|viel *adv* no matter *(ob/wer* whether/who). **g~wertig** *a* of equal value. **g~zeitig** *a* simultaneous, *adv* -ly

Gleis *nt* -es,-e track; *(Bahnsteig)* platform; **G~5** platform 5

gleiten† *vi (sein)* glide; *(rutschen)* slide. **g~d** *a* sliding; **g~de Arbeitszeit** flexitime

Gleitzeit *f* flexitime

Gletscher *m* -s,- glacier. **G~spalte** *f* crevasse

Glied *nt* -[e]s,-er limb; *(Teil)* part; *(Ketten-)* link; *(Mitglied)* member; *(Mil)* rank. **g~ern** *vt* arrange; *(einteilen)* divide; **sich g~ern** be divided *(in + acc* into). **G~maßen** *fpl* limbs

glimmen† *vi (haben)* glimmer

glimpflich *a* lenient, *adv* -ly; **g~ davonkommen** get off lightly

glitschig *a* slippery

glitzern *vi (haben)* glitter

global *a* global, *adv* -ly

Globus *m* -(busses), -ben *&* -busse globe

Glocke *f* -,-n bell. **G~nturm** *m* bell-tower, belfry

glorifizieren *vt* glorify

glorreich *a* glorious

Glossar *nt* -s,-e glossary

Glosse *f* -,-n comment

glotzen *vi (haben)* stare

Glück *nt* -[e]s [good] luck; *(Zufriedenheit)* happiness; **G~/kein G~ haben** be lucky/unlucky;

zum G~ luckily, fortunately; **auf gut G~** on the off chance; *(wahllos)* at random. **g~bringend** *a* lucky. **g~en** *vi (sein)* succeed; **es ist mir geglückt** I succeeded

gluckern *vi (haben)* gurgle

glücklich *a* lucky, fortunate; *(zufrieden)* happy; *(sicher)* safe □ *adv* happily; safely; *(fam: endlich)* finally. **g~erweise** *adv* luckily, fortunately

glückselig *a* blissfully happy. **G~keit** *f* bliss

glucksen *vi (haben)* gurgle

Glücks|spiel *nt* game of chance; *(Spielen)* gambling

G~wunsch *m* good wishes *pl*; *(Gratulation)* congratulations *pl*; **herzlichen G~!** congratulations! *(zum Geburtstag)* happy birthday! **G~karte** *f* greetings card

Glüh|birne *f* light-bulb. **g~en** *vi (haben)* glow. **g~end** *a* glowing; *(rot-)* red-hot; *(Hitze)* scorching; *(leidenschaftlich)* fervent, *adv* -ly. **G~faden** *m* filament. **G~wein** *m* mulled wine. **G~würmchen** *nt* -s,- glow-worm

Glukose *f* - glucose

Glut *f* - embers *pl*; *(Röte)* glow; *(Hitze)* heat; *(fig)* ardour

Glyzinie /-jə/ *f* -,-n wisteria

GmbH *abbr* **(Gesellschaft mit beschränkter Haftung)** ≈ plc

Gnade *f* - mercy; *(Gunst)* favour; *(Relig)* grace. **G~nfrist** *f* reprieve. **g~nlos** *a* merciless, *adv* -ly

gnädig *a* gracious, *adv* -ly; *(mild)* lenient, *adv* -ly; **g~e Frau** Madam

Gnom *m* -en,-en gnome

Gobelin /gobaˈlɛ̃/ *m* -s,-s tapestry

Gold *nt* -[e]s gold. **g~en** *a* gold ...; *(g~farben)* golden; **g~ene Hochzeit** golden wedding. **G~fisch** *m* goldfish. **G~grube** *f*

gold-mine. g~ig *a* sweet, lovely. **G~lack** *m* wallflower. **G~regen** *m* laburnum. **G~schmied** *m* goldsmith

Golf[1] *m* -[e]s,-e (Geog) gulf

Golf[2] *m* -s golf. **G~platz** *m* golf-course. **G~schläger** *m* golf-club. **G~spieler(in)** *m(f)* golfer

Gondel *f* -,-n gondola; (Kabine) cabin

Gong *m* -s,-s gong

gönnen *vt* jdm etw g~ not begrudge s.o. sth; **jdm etw nicht g~** begrudge s.o. sth; **sie gönnte sich** (dat) **keine Ruhe** she allowed herself no rest

Gönner *m* -s,- patron. **g~haft** *a* patronising, adv -ly

Gör *nt* -s,-en, **Göre** *f* -,-n (fam) kid

Gorilla *m* -s,-s gorilla

Gosse *f* -,-n gutter

Got|ik *f* -. **g~isch** *a* Gothic

Gott *m* -[e]s,ˌer God; (Myth) god

Götterspeise *f* jelly

Gottes|dienst *m* service. **g~lästerlich** *a* blasphemous, adv -ly. **G~lästerung** *f* blasphemy

Gottheit *f* -,-en deity

Göttin *f* -,-nen goddess

göttlich *a* divine, adv -ly

gott|los *a* ungodly; (atheistisch) godless. **g~verlassen** *a* God-forsaken

Götze *m* -n,-n, **G~nbild** *nt* idol

Gouver|nante /guvɐˈnantə/ *f* -,-n governess. **G~neur** /-ˈnøːɐ̯/ *m* -s,-e governor

Grab *nt* -[e]s,ˌer grave

graben† *vi* (haben) dig

Graben *m* -s,ˌ ditch; (Mil) trench

Grab|mal *nt* tomb. **G~stein** *m* gravestone, tombstone

Grad *m* -[e]s,-e degree

Graf *m* -en,-en count

Grafik *f* -,-en graphics *sg*; (Kunst) graphic arts *pl*; (Druck) print

Gräfin *f* -,-nen countess

grafisch *a* graphic; **g~e Darstellung** diagram

Grafschaft *f* -,-en county

Gram *m* -s grief

grämen (sich) *vr* grieve

grämlich *a* morose, adv -ly

Gramm *nt* -s,-e gram

Gram|matik *f* -,-en grammar. **g~matikalisch, g~matisch** *a* grammatical, adv -ly

Granat *m* -[e]s,-e (Miner) garnet. **G~apfel** *m* pomegranate. **G~e** *f* -,-n shell; (Hand-) grenade

Granit *m* -s,-e granite

Graph|ik *f*, **g~isch** *a* = **Grafik, grafisch**

Gras *nt* -es,ˌer grass. **g~en** *vi* (haben) graze. **G~hüpfer** *m* -s,- grasshopper

grassieren *vi* (haben) be rife

gräßlich *a* dreadful, adv -ly

Grat *m* -[e]s,-e (mountain) ridge

Gräte *f* -,-n fishbone

Gratifikation /-ˈtsi̯oːn/ *f* -,-en bonus

gratis *adv* free (of charge). **G~probe** *f* free sample

Gratu|lant(in) *m* -en,-en (f -,-nen) well-wisher. **G~lation** /-ˈtsi̯oːn/ *f* -,-en congratulations *pl*; (Glückwünsche) best wishes *pl*. **g~lieren** *vi* (haben) jdm **g~lieren** congratulate s.o. (zu on); (zum Geburtstag) wish s.o. happy birthday; **[ich] g~liere!** congratulations!

grau *a*, **G~** *nt* -s,- grey. **G~brot** *nt* mixed rye and wheat bread

grauen[1] *vi* (haben) **der Morgen** od **es graut** dawn is breaking

grauen[2] *v impers* **mir graut** [es] **davor** I dread it. **G~** *nt* -s dread. **g~haft, g~voll** *a* gruesome; (gräßlich) horrible, adv -bly

gräulich *a* greyish

Graupeln *fpl* soft hail *sg*

grausam *a* cruel, adv -ly. **G~keit** *f* -,-en cruelty

grausen *v impers* **mir graust davor** I dread it. **G~en** *nt* -s horror, dread. **g~ig** *a* gruesome

gravieren vt engrave. g~d a (fig) serious

Grazie /ˈgraːtsi̯ə/ f - grace

graziös a graceful, adv -ly

greifbar a tangible; in g~er Nähe within reach

greifen† vt take hold of; (fangen) catch ● vi (haben) reach (nach for); g~ zu (fig) turn to; um sich g~ (fig) spread. G~ nt G~ - spielen play tag

Greis m -es,-e old man. G~enalter nt extreme old age. g~enhaft a old. G~in f -,-nen old woman

grell a glaring; (Farbe) garish; (schrill) shrill, adv -y

Gremium nt -s,-ien committee

Grenze f -,-n border; (Staats-) frontier; (Grundstücks-) boundary; (fig) limit. g~en vi (haben) border (an + acc on); (fig) border on a boundless; (maßlos) infinite, adv -ly. G~fall m borderline case

Greuel m -s,- horror. G~tat f atrocity

greulich a horrible, adv -bly

Griech|e m -n,-n Greek. G~enland nt -s Greece. G~in f -,-nen Greek woman. g~isch a Greek. G~isch nt -[s] (Lang) Greek

griesgrämig a (fam) grumpy

Grieß m -es semolina

Griff m -[e]s,-e grasp, hold; (Hand-) movement of the hand; (Tür-, Messer-) handle; (Schwert-) hilt. g~bereit a handy

Grill m -s,-s grill; (Garten-) barbecue

Grille f -,-n (Zool) cricket; (fig: Laune) whim

grill|en vt/i (im Freien) barbecue ● vi (haben) have a barbecue. G~fest nt barbecue. G~gericht nt grill

Grimasse f -,-n grimace; G~n schneiden pull faces

grimmig a furious; (Kälte) bitter

grinsen vi (haben) grin. G~ nt -s grin

Grippe f -,-n influenza, (fam) flu

grob a (gröber, gröbst) coarse, adv -ly; (unsanft, ungefähr) rough, adv -ly; (unhöflich) rude, adv -ly; (schwer) gross, adv -ly; (Fehler) bad; g~e Arbeit rough work; g~ geschätzt roughly. G~ian m -s,-e brute

gröblich a gross, adv -ly

grölen vt/i (haben) bawl

Groll m -[e]s resentment; einen G~ gegen jdn hegen bear s.o. a grudge. g~en vi (haben) be angry (dat with); (Donner:) rumble

Grönland nt -s Greenland

Gros¹ nt -ses,- (Maß) gross

Gros² /groː/ nt - majority, bulk

Groschen m -s,- (Aust) groschen; (fam) ten-pfennig piece; der G~ ist gefallen (fam) the penny's dropped

groß a (größer, größt) big; (Anzahl, Summe) large; (bedeutend, stark) great; (g~artig) grand; (Buchstabe) capital; g~e Ferien summer holidays; g~e Angst haben be very frightened; der größte Teil the majority or bulk; g~ werden (Person:) grow up; g~ in etw (dat) sein be good at sth; g~ und klein young and old; im g~en und ganzen on the whole □adv (feiern) in style; (fam: viel) much; jdn g~ ansehen look at s.o. in amazement

großartig a magnificent, adv -ly. G~aufnahme f close-up. G~britannien nt -s Great Britain. G~buchstabe m capital letter. G~e(r) m/f unser G~er our eldest; die G~en the grown-ups; (fig) the great pl

Größe f -,-n size; (Ausmaß) extent; (Körper-) height; (Bedeutsamkeit) greatness; (Math) quantity; (Person) great figure

Groß|eltern pl grandparents. **g~enteils** adv largely

Größenwahnsinn m megalomania

Groß|handel m wholesale trade. **G~händler** m wholesaler. **g~herzig** a magnanimous, adv -ly. **G~macht** f superpower. **G~mut** f - magnanimity. **g~mütig** a magnanimous, adv -ly. **G~mutter** f grandmother. **G~onkel** m great-uncle. **G~reinemachen** nt -s springclean. **G~schreibung** f capitalization. **g~sprecherisch** a boastful. **g~spurig** a pompous, adv -ly; (überheblich) arrogant, adv -ly. **G~stadt** f [large] city. **g~städtisch** a city ... **G~tante** f great-aunt. **G~teil** m large proportion; (Hauptteil) bulk

größtenteils adv for the most part

groß|tun† (sich) vr sep brag. **G~vater** m grandfather. **g~ziehen†** vt sep bring up; rear ⟨Tier⟩. **g~zügig** a generous, adv -ly; (weiträumig) spacious. **G~zügigkeit** f - generosity

grotesk a grotesque, adv -ly

Grotte f -,-n grotto

Grübchen nt -s,- dimple

Grube f -,-n pit

grübeln vi (haben) brood

Gruft f -,-e [burial] vault

grün a green; im G~en out in the country; die G~en the Greens. **G~** nt -s,- green; (Laub, Zweige) greenery

Grund m -[e]s,-e ground; (Boden) bottom; (Hinter-) background; (Ursache) reason; auf G~ + (+gen) on the strength of; aus diesem G~e for this reason; von G~auf (fig) radically; im G~e [genommen] basically; auf G~ laufen (Naut) run aground. **G~begriffe** mpl basics. **G~besitz** m

landed property. **G~besitzer** m landowner

gründ|en vt found, set up; start ⟨Familie⟩; (fig) base (auf + acc on); sich g~en be based (auf + acc on). **G~er(in)** m -s,- (f -,-nen) founder

Grund|farbe f primary colour. **G~form** f (Gram) infinitive. **G~gesetz** nt (Pol) constitution. **G~lage** f basis, foundation. **g~legend** a fundamental, adv -ly

gründlich a thorough, adv -ly. **G~keit** f - thoroughness

grund|los a bottomless; (fig) groundless ⬜ adv without reason. **G~mauern** fpl foundations

Gründonnerstag m Maundy Thursday

Grund|regel f basic rule. **G~riß** m ground-plan; (fig) outline. **G~satz** m principle. **g~sätzlich** a fundamental, adv -ly; (im allgemeinen) in principle; (prinzipiell) on principle. **G~schule** f primary school. **G~stein** m foundation-stone. **G~stück** nt plot [of land]

Gründung f -,-en foundation

grün|en vi (haben) become green. **G~gürtel** m green belt. **G~span** m verdigris. **G~streifen** m grass verge; (Mittel-) central reservation; (Amer) median strip

grunzen vi (haben) grunt

Gruppe f -,-n group; (Reise-) party

gruppieren vt group; sich g~ form a group/groups

Grusel|geschichte f horror story. **g~ig** a creepy

Gruß m -es,-e greeting; (Mil) salute; einen schönen G~ an X give my regards to X; viele/herzliche G~e regards; Mit freundlichen G~en Yours sincerely; (Comm) faithfully

grüßen vt/i (haben) say hallo (jdn to s.o.); (Mil) salute; g~ Sie X von mir give my regards to X;

jdn g~ lassen send one's regards to s.o.; grüß Gott! (SGer,
Aust) good morning/afternoon/
evening!

guck|en vi (haben) (fam) look.
G~loch nt peep-hole

Guerilla /ge'rılja/ f guerilla warfare. G~kämpfer m guerilla

Gulasch nt & m -s goulash

gültig a valid, adv -ly. G~keit f
validity

Gummi m & nt -s,-[s] rubber;
(Harz) gum. G~band nt (pl
-bänder) elastic or rubber band;
(G~zug) elastic

gummiert a gummed

Gummi|knüppel m truncheon.
G~stiefel m gumboot, well-
ington. G~zug m elastic

Gunst f favour; zu jds G~en in
s.o.'s favour

günstig a favourable, adv -bly;
(passend) convenient, adv -ly

Günstling m -s,-e favourite

Gurgel f -,-n throat. g~n vi (haben) gargle. G~wasser nt gargle

Gurke f -,-n cucumber; (Essig-)
gherkin

gurren vi (haben) coo

Gurt m -[e]s,-e strap; (Gürtel)
belt; (Auto) safety-belt. G~band
nt (pl -bänder) waistband

Gürtel m -s,- belt. G~linie f
waistline. G~rose f shingles sg

GUS abbr (Gemeinschaft Unab-
hängiger Staaten) CIS

Guß m -sses,-̈sse (Techn) casting;
(Strom) stream; (Regen-) down-
pour; (Torten-) icing. G~eisen
nt cast iron. g~eisern a cast-
iron

gut a (besser, best) good; (Gewis-
sen-) clear; (gütig) kind (zu to);
jdm gut sein be fond of s.o.; im
g~en amicably; zu g~er Letzt
in the end; schon gut that's all
right □ adv well; (schmecken, riechen) good; (leicht) easily; es gut
haben be well off; (Glück haben)

be lucky; gut zu sehen clearly
visible; gut drei Stunden a good
three hours; du hast gut reden
it's easy for you to talk

Gut nt -[e]s,-̈er possession, prop-
erty; (Land-) estate; Gut und
Böse good and evil; Güter
(Comm) goods

Gutacht|en nt -s,- expert's report.
G~er m -s,- expert

gut|artig a good-natured; (Med)
benign. g~aussehend a good-
looking. g~bezahlt a well-paid.
G~dünken nt -s nach eigenem
G~dünken at one's own discretion

Gute(s) nt etwas/nichts G~s
something/nothing good; G~s
tun do good; das G~ daran the
good thing about it all; alles G~!
all the best!

Güte f -,-n goodness, kindness;
(Qualität) quality; du meine
G~! my goodness!

Güterzug m goods/(Amer) freight
train

gut|gehen† vi sep (sein) go well;
es geht mir gut I am well;(geschäftlich) doing well. g~ge-
hend a flourishing, thriving.
g~gemeint a well-meant.
g~gläubig a trusting. g~ha-
ben† vt sep fünfzig Mark g~ha-
ben have fifty marks credit (bei
with). G~haben nt -s,- [credit]
balance; (Kredit) credit. g~hei-
ßen† vt sep approve of

gütig a kind, adv -ly

gütlich a amicable, adv -bly

gut|machen vt sep make up for;
make good (Schaden). g~mütig
a good-natured, adv -ly. G~mü-
tigkeit f - good nature.
G~schein m credit note; (Bon)
voucher; (Geschenk-) gift token.
g~schreiben† vt sep credit.
G~schrift f credit

Guts|haus nt manor house.
G~hof m manor

gut|situiert *a* well-to-do. **g~-**
tun† *vi sep (haben)* jdm/etw
g~tun do s.o./sth good. **g~wil-**
lig *a* willing, *adv* -ly

Gymnasium *nt* -s,-ien ≈ grammar school

Gymnast|ik *f* - [keep-fit] exer-
cises *pl*; *(Turnen)* gymnastics *sg*.
g~isch *a* g~ische Übung exercise

Gynäko|loge *m* -n,-n gynaecolo-
gist. **G~logie** *f* - gynaecology.
g~logisch *a* gynaecological

H

H, h /ha:/ *nt* -,- *(Mus)* B, b

Haar *nt* -[e]s,-e hair; **sich** *(dat)*
die Haare *od* **das H~ waschen**
wash one's hair; **um ein H~**
(fam) very nearly. **H~bürste**
f hairbrush. **h~en** *vi (haben)* shed
hairs; *⟨Tier:⟩* moult □ *vr* **sich**
h~en moult. **h~ig** *a* hairy;
(fam) tricky. **H~klammer,**
H~klemme *f* hair-grip. **H~na-**
del *f* hairpin. **H~nadelkurve** *f*
hairpin bend. **H~schleife** *f*
bow. **H~schnitt** *m* haircut.
H~spange *f* slide. **h~sträu-**
bend *a* hair-raising; *(empörend)*
shocking. **H~trockner** *m* -s,-
hair-drier. **H~waschmittel** *nt*
shampoo

Habe *f* - possessions *pl*

haben† *vt* have; **Angst/Hunger/**
Durst h~ be frightened/hun-
gry/thirsty; **ich hätte gern** I'd
like; **sich h~** *(fam)* make a fuss;
es gut/schlecht h~ be well/
badly off; **etw gegen jdn h~**
have sth against s.o.; **was hat er?**
what's the matter with him? □ *v*
aux have; **ich habe/hatte ge-**
schrieben I have/had written; **er**
hätte ihr geholfen he would
have helped her

Habgier *f* greed. **h~ig** *a* greedy

Habicht *m* -[e]s,-e hawk

Hab|seligkeiten *fpl* belongings.
H~sucht *f* = Habgier

Hack|beil *nt* chopper. **H~bra-**
ten *m* meat loaf

Hacke¹ *f* -,-n hoe; *(Spitz-)* pick

Hacke² *f* -,-n, **Hacken** *m* -s,- heel

hacken *vt/i (haben)* hoe; *(schlagen, zerklei-*
nern) chop; *⟨Vogel:⟩* peck; **ge-**
hacktes Rindfleisch minced/
(Amer) ground beef. **H~fleisch**
nt mince, *(Amer)* ground meat

Hafen *m* -s,- harbour; *(See-)* port.
H~arbeiter *m* docker. **H~-**
damm *m* mole. **H~stadt** *f* port

Hafer *m* -s oats *pl*. **H~flocken**
fpl [rolled] oats. **H~mehl** *nt* oatmeal

Haft *f* - *(Jur)* custody; *(Haft-)*
imprisonment. **h~bar** *a* *(Jur)*
liable. **H~befehl** *m* warrant [of
arrest]

haften *vi (haben)* cling; *(kleben)*
stick; *(bürgen)* vouch/*(Jur)* be
liable (**für** for)

Häftling *m* -s,-e detainee

Haftpflicht *f* *(Jur)* liability.
H~versicherung *f* *(Auto)*
third-party insurance

Haftstrafe *f* imprisonment

Haftung *f* - *(Jur)* liability

Hagebutte *f* -,-n rose-hip

Hagel *m* -s hail. **H~korn** *nt* hail-
stone. **h~n** *vi (haben)* hail

hager *a* gaunt

Hahn *m* -[e]s,-e cock; *(Techn)* tap,
(Amer) faucet

Hähnchen *nt* -s,- *(Culin)* chicken

Hai|[fisch] *m* -[e]s,-e shark

Häkchen *nt* -s,- tick

häkel|n *vt/i (haben)* crochet.
H~nadel *f* crochet-hook

Haken *m* -s,- hook; *(Häkchen)*
tick; *(fam: Schwierigkeit)* snag.
h~ *vt* hook (**an** + *acc* to). **H~-**
kreuz *nt* swastika. **H~nase** *f*
hooked nose

halb *a* half; **eine h~e Stunde** half an hour; **zum h~en Preis** at half price; **auf h~em Weg** half-way □ *adv* half; **h~ drei** half past two; **fünf [Minuten] vor/nach h~** vier twenty-five [minutes] past three/to four; **h~ und h~** half and half; (*fast ganz*) more or less. **H~blut** *nt* half-breed. **H~dunkel** *nt* semi-darkness. **H~e(r)** *f*|*m*|*nt* half [a litre]

halber *prep* (+ *gen*) for the sake of; **Geschäfte h~** on business

Halb|finale *nt* semifinal. **H~heit** *f* -,-**en** (*fig*) half-measure

halbieren *vt* halve, divide in half; (*Geom*) bisect

Halb|insel *f* peninsula. **H~kreis** *m* semicircle. **H~kugel** *f* hemisphere. **h~laut** *a* low □ *adv* in an undertone. **h~mast** *adv* at half-mast. **H~messer** *m* -**s**,- radius. **H~mond** *m* half moon. **H~pension** *f* half-board. **h~rund** *a* semicircular. **H~schuh** *m* [flat] shoe. **h~stündlich** *a & adv* half-hourly. **h~tags** *adv* [for] half a day; **h~tags arbeiten** ≈ work part-time. **H~ton** *m* semitone. **h~wegs** *adv* half-way; (*ziemlich*) more or less. **h~wüchsig** *a* adolescent. **H~zeit** *f* (*Sport*) half-time; (*Spielzeit*) half

Halde *f* -,-**n** dump, tip

Hälfte *f* -,-**n** half; **zur H~** half

Halfter[1] *m & nt* -**s**,- halter

Halfter[2] *f* -,-**n** & *nt* -**s**,- holster

Hall *m* -[e]**s**,-**e** sound

Halle *f* -,-**n** hall; (*Hotel-*) lobby; (*Bahnhofs-*) station concourse

hallen *vi* (*haben*) resound; (*wider-*) echo

Hallen- *pref* indoor

hallo *int* hallo

Halluzination /-'tsi̯o:n/ *f* -,-**en** hallucination

Halm *m* -[e]**s**,-**e** stalk; (*Gras-*) blade

Hals *m* -**es**,-**e** neck; (*Kehle*) throat; **aus vollem H~e** at the top of one's voice; (*lachen*) out loud. **H~ausschnitt** *m* neckline. **H~band** *nt* (*pl* -**bänder**) collar. **H~kette** *f* necklace. **H~schmerzen** *mpl* sore throat *sg*. **h~starrig** *a* stubborn. **H~tuch** *nt* scarf

halt[1] *adv* (*SGer*) just; **es geht h~ nicht** it's just not possible

halt[2] *int* stop! (*Mil*) halt! (*fam*) wait a moment!

Halt *m* -[e]**s**,-**e** hold; (*Stütze*) support; (*innerer*) stability; (*Anhalten*) stop. **h~bar** *a* durable; (*Tex*) hard-wearing; (*fig*) tenable; **h~bar bis ...** (*Comm*) use by ...

halten† *vt* hold; make 〈*Rede*〉; give 〈*Vortrag*〉; (*einhalten, bewahren*) keep; [**sich** (*dat*)] **etw h~** keep 〈*Hund*〉; take 〈*Zeitung*〉; run 〈*Hund*〉; **warm h~** keep warm; **h~ für** regard as; **viel/nicht viel h~ von** think highly/little of; **sich h~** hold on (**an**+ *dat* to); (*fig*) hold out; (*Geschäft:*) keep going; (*haltbar sein*) keep; (*Wetter:*) hold; (*Blumen:*) last; **sich links h~** keep left; **sich gerade h~** hold oneself upright; **sich h~ an** (+ *acc*) (*fig*) keep to □ *vi* (*haben*) hold; (*haltbar sein, bestehen bleiben*) keep; (*Freundschaft, Blumen:*) last; (*haltmachen*) stop; **h~ auf** (+ *acc*) (*fig*) set great store by; **auf sich** (*acc*) **h~** take pride in oneself; **an sich** (*acc*) **h~** contain oneself; **zu jdm h~** be loyal to s.o.

Halter *m* -**s**,- holder

Halte|stelle *f* stop. **H~verbot** *nt* waiting restriction; 'H~verbot' 'no waiting'

halt|los *a* (*fig*) unstable; (*unbegründet*) unfounded. **h~machen** *vi sep* (*haben*) stop

Haltung f -,-en (Körper-) posture; (Verhalten) manner; (Einstellung) attitude; (Fassung) composure; (Halten) keeping; h~ annehmen (Mil) stand to attention

Halunke m -n,-n scoundrel

Hamburger m -s,- hamburger

hämisch a malicious, adv -ly

Hammel m -s,- ram; (Culin) mutton. H~fleisch nt mutton

Hammer m -s,: hammer

hämmern vt/i (haben) hammer; ⟨Herz:⟩ pound

Hämorrhoiden /hɛmɔrɔˈiːdən/ fpl haemorrhoids

Hamster m -s,- hamster. h~n vt/i (fam) hoard

Hand f -,:e hand; jdm die H~ geben shake hands with s.o.; rechter/linker H~ on the right/left; [aus] zweiter H~ secondhand; unter der H~ unofficially; (geheim) secretly; an H~ von with the aid of; H~ und Fuß haben (fig) be sound. H~arbeit f manual work; (handwerklich) handicraft; (Nadelarbeit) needlework; (Gegenstand) hand-made article. H~ball m [German] handball. H~besen m brush. H~bewegung f gesture. H~bremse f handbrake. H~buch nt handbook, manual

Händedruck m handshake

Handel m -s trade, commerce; (Unternehmen) business; (Geschäft) deal; H~ treiben trade. h~n vi (haben) act; (Handel treiben) trade (mit in); von etw od über etw (acc) h~n deal with sth; sich h~n um be about, concern. H~smarine f merchant navy. H~sschiff nt merchant vessel. H~sschule f commercial college. h~süblich a customary. H~sware f merchandise

Hand|feger m -s,- brush. H~fertigkeit f dexterity. h~fest a sturdy; (fig) solid. H~fläche f

palm. h~gearbeitet a handmade. H~gelenk nt wrist. h~gemacht a handmade. H~gemenge nt -s,- scuffle. H~gepäck nt hand-luggage. h~geschrieben a hand-written. H~granate f hand-grenade. h~greiflich a tangible; h~greiflich werden become violent. H~griff m handle; mit einem H~griff with a flick of the wrist

handhaben vt insep (reg) handle

Handikap /'hɛndɪkæp/ nt -s,-s handicap

Hand|kuß m kiss on the hand. H~lauf m handrail

Händler m -s,- dealer, trader

handlich a handy

Handlung f -,-en act; (Handeln) action; (Roman-) plot; (Geschäft) shop. H~sweise f conduct

Hand|schellen fpl handcuffs. H~schlag m handshake. H~schrift f handwriting; (Text) manuscript. H~schuh m glove. H~schuhfach nt glove compartment. H~stand m handstand. H~tasche f handbag. H~tuch nt towel. H~voll f -,- handful

Handwerk nt craft, trade; sein H~ verstehen know one's job. H~er m -s,- craftsman; (Arbeiter) workman

Hanf m -[e]s hemp

Hang m -[e]s,:e slope; (fig) inclination, tendency

Hänge|brücke f suspension bridge. H~lampe f [light] pendant. H~matte f hammock

hängen¹ vt (reg) hang

hängen²†vi (haben) hang; h~ an (+dat) (fig) be attached to. h~bleiben† vi sep (sein) stick (an+dat on); ⟨Kleid:⟩ catch (an +dat on). h~lassen† vt sep leave; den Kopf h~lassen be downcast

Hannover nt -s Hanover

hänseln vt tease

hantieren vi (haben) busy oneself

hapern vi (haben) **es hapert** there's a lack (an + dat of)

Happen m -s, mouthful; **eine H~ essen** have a bite to eat

Harfe f -,-n harp

Harke f -,-n rake. **h~n** vt/i (haben) rake

harmlos a harmless; (arglos) innocent, adv -ly. **H~igkeit** f - harmlessness; innocence

Harmonie f -,-n harmony. **h~ren** vi (haben) harmonize; (gut auskommen) get on well

Harmonika f -,-s accordion; (Mund-) mouth-organ

harmonisch a harmonious, adv -ly

Harn m -[e]s urine. **H~blase** f bladder

Harpune f -,-n harpoon

hart (härter, härtest) a hard; (heftig) violent; (streng) harsh □ adv hard; (streng) harshly

Härte f -,-n hardness; (Strenge) harshness; (Not) hardship. **h~n** vt harden

Hart|faserplatte f hardboard. **h~gekocht** a hard-boiled. **h~herzig** a hard-hearted. **h~näckig** a stubborn, adv -ly; (ausdauernd) persistent, adv -ly. **H~näckigkeit** f - stubbornness; persistence

Harz nt -es,-e resin

Haschee nt -s,-s (Culin) hash

haschen vi (haben) **h~ nach** try to catch

Haschisch nt & m -[s] hashish

Hase m -n,-n hare; **falscher H~** meat loaf

Hasel f -,-n hazel. **H~maus** f dormouse. **H~nuß** f hazel-nut

Hasenfuß m (fam) coward

Haß m -sses hatred

hassen vt hate

häßlich a ugly; (unfreundlich) nasty, adv -ily. **H~keit** f - ugliness; nastiness

Hast f - haste. **h~en** vi (sein) hasten, hurry. **h~ig** a hasty, adv -ily, hurried, adv -ly

hast, hat, hatte, hätte s. haben

Haube f -,-n cap; (Trocken-) drier; (Kühler-) bonnet, (Amer) hood

Hauch m -[e]s breath; (Luft-) breeze; (Duft) whiff; (Spur) tinge. **h~dünn** a very thin; (Strümpfe) sheer. **h~en** vt/i (haben) breathe

Haue f - pick; (fam: Prügel) beating. **h~n†** vt beat; (hämmern) knock; (meißeln) hew; **sich h~n** fight; **übers Ohr h~n** (fam) cheat □ vi (haben) **bang** (auf + acc on); **jdm ins Gesicht h~n** hit s.o. in the face

Haufen m -s, heap, pile; (Leute) crowd

häufen vt heap or pile [up]; **sich h~** pile up; (zunehmen) increase

haufenweise adv in large numbers; **h~ Geld** pots of money

häufig a frequent, adv -ly. **H~keit** f - frequency

Haupt nt -[e]s, Häupter head. **H~bahnhof** m main station. **H~darsteller** m, **H~darstellerin** f male/female lead. **H~fach** nt main subject. **H~gericht** nt main course. **H~hahn** m mains tap; (Wasser-) stopcock

Häuptling m -s,-e chief

Haupt|mahlzeit f main meal. **H~mann** m (pl -leute) captain. **H~person** f most important person; (Theat) principal character. **H~post** f main post office. **H~quartier** nt headquarters pl. **H~rolle** f lead; (fig) leading role. **H~sache** f main thing; **in der H~sache** in the main. **h~sächlich** a main, adv -ly,

H~satz m main clause. H~-
schlüssel m master key. H~-
stadt f capital. H~straße f main
street. H~verkehrsstraße f
main road. H~verkehrszeit f
rush-hour. H~wort nt (pl
-wörter) noun

Haus nt -es, Häuser house; (Gebäude) building; (Schnecken-)
shell; zu H~e at home; nach
H~e home. H~angestellte(r)
m/f domestic servant. H~arbeit
f housework; (Sch) homework.
H~arzt m family doctor. H~-
aufgaben fpl homework sg.
H~besetzer m -s, squatter.
H~besuch m house-call

hausen vi (haben) live; (wüten)
wreak havoc

Haus|frau f housewife. H~ge-
hilfin f domestic help. h~ge-
macht a home-made. H~halt m
-[e]s,-e household; (Pol) budget.
h~halten† vi sep (haben) h~-
halten mit manage carefully;
conserve ⟨Kraft⟩. H~hälterin f
-,-nen housekeeper. H~halts-
geld nt housekeeping [money].
H~haltsplan m budget. H~-
herr m head of the household;
(Gastgeber) host. H~hoch a
huge; (fam) big □ adv (fam) vast-
ly; (verlieren) by a wide margin

hausier|en vi (haben) h~en mit
hawk. H~er m -s,- hawker

Hauslehrer m [private] tutor.
H~in f governess

häuslich a domestic; ⟨Person⟩
domesticated

Haus|meister m caretaker.
H~nummer f house number.
H~ordnung f house rules pl.
H~putz m cleaning. H~rat m
-[e]s household effects pl.
H~schlüssel m front-door key.
H~schuh m slipper. H~stand
m household. H~suchung f
[police] search. H~suchungs-
befehl m search-warrant.

H~tier nt domestic animal;
(Hund, Katze) pet. H~tür f front
door. H~wart m -[e]s,-e caretaker. H~wirt m landlord.
H~wirtin f landlady

Haut f-,Häute skin; (Tier-) hide;
aus der H~ fahren (fam) fly off
the handle. H~arzt m dermatologist

häuten vt skin; sich h~ moult

haut|eng a skin-tight. H~farbe f
colour; (Teint) complexion

Haxe f-,-n = Hachse

Hbf. abbr s. Hauptbahnhof

Hebamme f-,-n midwife

Hebel m -s,- lever. H~kraft f,
H~wirkung f leverage

heben† vt lift; (hoch-, steigern)
raise; sich h~ rise; ⟨Nebel:⟩ lift;
(sich verbessern) improve

hebräisch a Hebrew

hecheln vi (haben) pant

Hecht m -[e]s,-e pike

Heck nt -s,-s (Naut) stern; (Aviat)
tail; (Auto) rear

Hecke f-,-n hedge. H~nschütze
m sniper

Heck|fenster nt rear window.
H~motor m rear engine.
H~tür f hatchback

Heer nt -[e]s,-e army

Hefe f- yeast. H~teig m yeast
dough. H~teilchen nt Danish
pastry

Heft¹ nt -[e]s,-e haft, handle

Heft² nt -[e]s,-e booklet; (Sch)
exercise book; (Zeitschrift) issue.
h~en vt (nähen) tack; (stecken)
pin/(klammern) clip/(mit Heftmaschine) staple (an+acc to).
H~er m -s,- file

heftig a fierce, adv -ly, violent,
adv -ly; ⟨Schlag, Regen⟩ heavy,
adv -ily; ⟨Schmerz, Gefühl⟩ intense, adv -ly; ⟨Person⟩ quick-
tempered. H~keit f- fierceness,
violence; intensity

Heft|klammer f staple; (Büro-)
paper-clip. H~maschine f

stapler. H~**pflaster** nt sticking plaster. H~**zwecke** f -,-n drawing-pin

hegen vt care for; (fig) cherish ⟨Hoffnung⟩; harbour ⟨Verdacht⟩

Hehl nt & m **kein[en]** H~ **machen aus** make no secret of. H~**er** m -s,- receiver, fence

Heide[1] m -n,-n heathen

Heide[2] f -,-n heath; (Bot) heather. H~**kraut** nt heather

Heidelbeere f bilberry, (Amer) blueberry

Heid|in f -,-nen heathen. h~**nisch** a heathen

heikel a difficult, tricky; (delikat) delicate; (dial) (Person) fussy

heil a undamaged, intact; (Person) unhurt; (gesund) well; mit h~**er Haut** (fam) unscathed

Heil nt -s salvation; sein H~ **versuchen** try one's luck

Heiland m -s (Relig) Saviour

Heil|anstalt f sanatorium; (Nerven-) mental hospital. H~**bad** nt spa. h~**bar** a curable

Heilbutt m -[e]s,-e halibut

heilen vt cure; heal ⟨Wunde⟩ □ vi (sein) heal

heilfroh a (fam) very relieved

Heilgymnastik f physiotherapy

heilig a holy; (geweiht) sacred; der H~**e Abend** Christmas Eve; die h~**e Anna** Saint Anne. H~**abend** m Christmas Eve. H~**e(r)** m/f saint. h~**en** vt keep, observe. H~**enschein** m halo. h~**halten**† vt sep hold sacred; keep ⟨Feiertag⟩. H~**keit** f sanctity, holiness. H~**sprechen**† vt sep canonize. H~**tum** nt -s,-er shrine

heil|kräftig a medicinal. H~**kräuter** ntpl medicinal herbs. h~**los** a unholy. H~**mittel** nt remedy. H~**praktiker** m -s,- practitioner of alternative medicine. h~**sam** a

(fig) salutary. H~**sarmee** f Salvation Army. H~**ung** f - cure

Heim nt -[e]s,-e home; (Studenten-) hostel. h~ adv home

Heimat f -,-en home; (Land) native land. H~**abend** m folk evening. h~**los** a homeless. H~**stadt** f home town

heim|begleiten vt sep see home. h~**bringen**† vt sep bring home; (begleiten) see home. H~**computer** m home computer. h~**fahren**† v sep □ vi (sein) go/drive home □ vt take/drive home. H~**fahrt** f way home. h~**gehen**† vi sep (sein) go home; (sterben) die

heimisch a native, indigenous; (Pol) domestic; h~ **sein/sich h~ fühlen** be/feel at home

Heim|kehr f - return [home]. h~**kehren** vi sep (sein) return home. h~**kommen**† vi sep (sein) come home

heimlich a secret, adv -ly. H~**keit** f -,-en secrecy. H~**keiten** secrets. H~**tuerei** f - secretiveness

Heim|reise f journey home. h~**reisen** vi sep (sein) go home. H~**spiel** nt home game. h~**suchen** vt sep afflict. h~**tückisch** a treacherous; (Krankheit) insidious. h~**wärts** adv home. h~**weg** m way home. H~**weh** nt -s homesickness; H~**weh haben** be homesick. H~**werker** m -s,- [home] handyman. h~**zahlen** vt sep jdm etw h~**zahlen** (fig) pay s.o. back for sth

Heirat f -,-en marriage. h~**en** vt/i (haben) marry. H~**santrag** m proposal; **jdm einen H~santrag machen** propose to s.o. H~**sfähig** a marriageable

heiser a hoarse, adv -ly. H~**keit** f - hoarseness

heiß a hot, adv -ly; (hitzig) heated; (leidenschaftlich) fervent, adv -ly; **mir ist h~** I am hot

heißen† vi (haben) be called; (bedeuten) mean; **ich heiße ...** my name is ...; **wie heißt du?** what is your name? **wie heißt ... auf englisch?** what's the English for ...? **es heißt** it says; (man sagt) it is said; **das heißt** that is [to say]; **was soll das h~?** what does it mean? (empört) what's the meaning of this? □ vt call; **jdn etw tun h~** tell s.o. to do sth

heiß|geliebt a beloved. **h~hungrig** a ravenous. **H~wasserbereiter** m -s, water heater

heiter a cheerful, adv -ly; (Wetter) bright; (amüsant) amusing; **aus h~em Himmel** (fig) out of the blue. **H~keit** f - cheerfulness; (Gelächter) mirth

Heiz|anlage f heating; (Auto) heater. **H~decke** f electric blanket. **h~en** vt heat; legit (Ofen) □ vi (haben) put the heating on; ⟨Ofen:⟩ give out heat. **H~gerät** nt heater. **H~kessel** m boiler. **H~körper** m radiator. **H~lüfter** m -s, fan heater. **H~material** nt fuel. **H~ofen** m heater. **H~ung** f -,-en heating; (Heizkörper) radiator

Hektar nt & m -s, hectare

hektisch a hectic

Held m -en,-en hero. **h~enhaft** a heroic, adv -ally. **H~enmut** m heroism. **h~enmütig** a heroic, adv -ally. **H~entum** nt s heroism. **H~in** f -,-nen heroine

helf|en† vi (haben) help (jdm s.o.); (nützen) be effective; **sich** (dat) **nicht zu h~ en wissen** not know what to do; **es hilft nichts** it's no use. **H~er(in)** m -s, (f -,-nen) helper, assistant. **H~ershelfer** m accomplice

hell a light; (Licht ausstrahlend, klug) bright; ⟨Stimme⟩ clear;

(fam: völlig) utter; **h~es Bier** ≈ lager □ adv brightly; **h~ begeistert** absolutely delighted. **h~hörig** a poorly sound-proofed; **h~hörig werden** (fig) sit up and take notice

hellicht a **h~er Tag** broad daylight

Hell|igkeit f - brightness. **H~seher(in)** m -s, (f -,-nen) clairvoyant. **h~wach** a wide awake

Helm m -[e]s,-e helmet

Hemd nt -[e]s,-en vest, (Amer) undershirt; (Ober-) shirt. **H~bluse** f shirt

Hemisphäre f -,-n hemisphere

hemm|en vt check; (verzögern) impede; (fig) inhibit. **H~ung** f -,-en (fig) inhibition; (Skrupel) scruple; **H~ungen haben** be inhibited. **h~ungslos** a unrestrained, adv -ly

Hendl nt -s,-[n] (Aust) chicken

Hengst m -[e]s,-e stallion. **H~fohlen** nt colt

Henkel m -s,- handle

henken vt hang

Henne f -,-n hen

her adv here; (zeitlich) ago; **her mit ...!** give me ...! **von oben/unten/Norden/weit her** from above/below/the north/far away; **vor/hinter jdm/etw her** in front of/behind s.o./sth; **von der Farbe/vom Thema her** as far as the colour/subject is concerned

herab adv down [here]; **von oben h~** from above; (fig) condescending, adv -ly. **h~blicken** vi sep (haben) = **h~sehen**

herablass|en† vt sep let down; **sich h~en** condescend (zu to). **h~end** a condescending, adv -ly. **H~ung** f - condescension

herab|sehen† vi sep (haben) look down (auf+acc on). **h~setzen** vt sep reduce, cut; (fig) belittle. **h~setzend** a disparaging, adv

-ly. **h~würdigen** vt sep belittle, disparage

Heraldik f -heraldry

heran adv near; [bis] **h~** an (+acc) up to. **h~bilden** vt sep train. **h~gehen**† vi sep (sein) **h~gehen an** (+acc) go up to; get down to ⟨Arbeit⟩. **h~kommen**† vi sep (sein) approach; **h~kommen an** (+acc) come up to; (erreichen) get at; (fig) measure up to. **h~machen (sich)** vr sep **sich h~machen an** (+acc) approach; get down to ⟨Arbeit⟩. **h~reichen** vi sep (haben) **h~reichen an** (+acc) reach; (fig) measure up to. **h~wachsen**† vi sep (sein) grow up. **h~ziehen**† v sep □vt pull up (an +acc to); (züchten) raise; (h~bilden) train; (hinzuziehen) call in □vi (sein) approach

herauf adv up [here]; die Treppe **h~** up the stairs. **h~beschwören**† vt sep evoke; (verursachen) cause. **h~kommen**† vi sep (sein) come up. **h~setzen** vt sep raise, increase

heraus adv out (aus of); **h~ damit** od mit der Sprache! out with it! **h~bekommen**† vt sep get out; (ausfindig machen) find out; (lösen) solve; Geld **h~bekommen** get change. **h~bringen**† vt sep bring out; (fam) get out. **h~finden**† v sep □vt find out □vi (haben) find one's way out. **H~forderer** m -s,- challenger. **h~fordern** vt sep provoke; challenge ⟨Person⟩. **H~forderung** f provocation; challenge. **h~gabe** f handing over; (Admin) issue; (Veröffentlichung) publication. **h~geben**† vt sep hand over; (Admin) issue; (veröffentlichen) publish; edit ⟨Zeitschrift⟩; **jdm Geld h~geben** give s.o. change □vi (haben) give change (auf +acc for).

H~geber m -s,- publisher; editor. **h~gehen**† vi sep (sein) ⟨Fleck:⟩ come out; **aus sich h~gehen** (fig) come out of one's shell. **h~halten (sich)** vr sep (fig) keep out (aus of). **h~holen** vt sep get out. **h~kommen**† vi sep (sein) come out; (aus Schwierigkeit, Takt) get out; **auf eins od dasselbe h~kommen** (fam) come to the same thing. **h~lassen**† vt sep let out. **h~machen** vt sep get out; **sich gut h~machen** (fig) do well. **h~nehmen**† vt sep take out; **sich zuviel h~nehmen** (fig) take liberties. **h~platzen** vi sep (haben) (fam) burst out laughing. **h~putzen (sich)** vr sep doll oneself up. **h~ragen** vi sep (haben) jut out; (fig) stand out. **h~reden** (sich) vr sep make excuses. **h~rücken** v sep □vt move out; (hergeben) hand over □vi (sein) **h~rücken mit** hand over; (fig: sagen) come out with. **h~rutschen** vi sep (sein) slip out. **h~schlagen**† vt sep knock out; (fig) gain. **h~stellen** vt sep put out; **sich h~stellen** turn out (als to be; daß that). **h~suchen** vt sep pick out. **h~ziehen**† vt sep pull out

herb a sharp; ⟨Wein⟩ dry; ⟨Landschaft⟩ austere; (fig) harsh

herbei adv here. **h~führen** vt sep (fig) bring about. **h~lassen**† (sich) vr sep condescend (zu to). **h~schaffen** vt sep get. **h~sehnen** vt sep long for

Herberg|e f -,-n [youth] hostel; (Unterkunft) lodging. **H~svater** m warden

herbestellen vt sep summon

herbitten† vt sep ask to come

herbringen† vt sep bring [here]

Herbst m -[e]s,-e autumn. **h~lich** a autumnal

Herd m -[e]s,-e stove, cooker; (fig) focus

Herde f -,-n herd; (Schaf-) flock
herein adv in [here]; h~! come in!
h~bitten† vt sep ask in. **h~bre-
chen**† vi sep (sein) burst in; (fig)
set in; ⟨Nacht:⟩ fall; **h~brechen
über** (+acc) (fig) overtake.
h~fallen† vi sep (sein) (fam) be
taken in (**auf**+acc by). **h~kom-
men**† vi sep (sein) come in.
h~lassen† vt sep let in. **h~le-
gen** vt sep (fam) take for a ride.
h~rufen† vt sep call in
Herfahrt f journey/drive here
herfallen† vi sep (sein) **h~über**
(+acc) attack; fall upon ⟨Essen⟩
hergeben† vt sep hand over; (fig)
give up; **sich h~zu** (fig) be a
party to
hergebracht a traditional
hergehen† vi sep (sein) **h~vor/
neben/hinter** (+dat) walk along
in front of/beside/behind; **es ging
lustig her** (fam) there was a lot
of merriment
herhalten† vt sep (haben) hold
out; **h~müssen** be the one to
suffer
herholen vt sep fetch; **weit hergeholt** (fig) far-fetched
Hering m -s,-e herring; (Zelt-
pflock) tent-peg
her|kommen† vi sep (sein) come
here; **wo kommt das her?** where
does it come from? **h~kömm-
lich** a traditional. **H~kunft** f -
origin
herlaufen† vi sep (sein) **h~vor/
neben/hinter** (+dat) run/
⟨gehen⟩ walk along in front of/
beside/behind
herleiten vt sep derive
hermachen vt sep **viel/wenig
h~** be impressive/unimpressive;
(wichtig nehmen) make a lot of/
little fuss (**von** of); **sich h~über**
(+acc) fall upon; tackle ⟨Arbeit⟩
Hermelin[1] nt -s,-e (Zool) stoat
Hermelin[2] m -s,-e (Pelz) ermine
hermetisch a hermetic, adv -ally

Hernie /ˈhɛrnjə/ f -,-n hernia
Heroin nt -s heroin
Herr m -en,-en gentleman; (Ge-
bieter) master (**über**+acc of);
[**Gott,**] **der H~** the Lord [God];
H~ Meier Mr Meier; **Sehr
geehrte H~en** Dear Sirs.
H~chen nt -s,- master. **H~en-
haus** nt manor [house]. **h~en-
los** a ownerless; ⟨Tier⟩ stray.
H~ensitz m manor
Herrgott m **der H~** the Lord; **H~
[noch mal]!** damn it!
herrichten vt sep prepare;
wieder h~ renovate
Herrin f -,-nen mistress
herrisch a imperious, adv -ly;
⟨Ton⟩ peremptory; (herrschsüchtig) overbearing
herrlich a marvellous, adv -ly;
(großartig) magnificent, adv -ly.
H~keit f -,-en splendour
Herrschaft f -,-en rule; (Macht)
power; (Kontrolle) control; **meine H~en!** ladies and gentlemen!
herrsch|en vi (haben) rule; (ver-
breitet sein) prevail; **es h~te
Stille/große Aufregung** there
was silence/great excitement.
H~er(in) m -s,- (f -,-nen) ruler.
h~süchtig a domineering
herrühren vi sep (haben) stem
(**von** from)
hersein† vi sep (sein) come (**von**
from); **h~hinter** (+dat) be after;
**es ist schon lange/drei Tage
her** it was a long time/three days
ago
herstammen vi sep (haben) come
(**aus/von** from)
herstell|en vt sep establish;
(Comm) manufacture, make.
H~er m -s,- manufacturer,
maker. **H~ung** f - establishment; manufacture
herüber adv over [here].
h~kommen† vi sep (sein) come
over [here]

herum *adv* im Kreis h~ [round] in a circle; falsch h~ the wrong way round; um ... h~ round ...; (*ungefähr*) [round] about ... h~**albern** *vi sep* (*haben*) fool around. h~**drehen** *vt sep* turn round/(*wenden*) over; turn ⟨*Schlüssel*⟩; **sich** h~**drehen** turn round/over. h~**gehen**† *vi sep* (*sein*) walk around; ⟨*Zeit:*⟩ pass; h~**gehen um** go round. h~**kommen**† *vi sep* (*sein*) get about; h~**kommen um** get round; come round ⟨*Ecke*⟩; **um etw** [**nicht**] h~**kommen** [not] get out of sth. h~**kriegen** *vt sep* h~**kriegen** (*fam*) talk s.o. round. h~**liegen**† *vi sep* (*sein*) lie around. h~**lungern** *vi sep* (*haben*) loiter. h~**schnüffeln** *vi sep* (*haben*) (*fam*) nose about. h~**sitzen**† *vi sep* (*haben*) sit around; h~**sitzen um** sit round. h~**sprechen** (**sich**) *vr sep* ⟨*Gerücht:*⟩ get about. h~**stehen**† *vi sep* (*haben*) stand around; h~**stehen um** stand round. h~**treiben**† (**sich**) *vr sep* hang around. h~**ziehen**† *vi sep* (*sein*) move around; (*ziellos*) wander about

herunter *adv* down [here]; **die Treppe** h~ down the stairs. h~**fallen**† *vi* fall off. h~**gehen**† *vi sep* come down; (*sinken*) go/come down. h~**gekommen** *a* (*fig*) run-down; ⟨*Gebäude*⟩ dilapidated; ⟨*Person*⟩ down-at-heel. h~**kommen**† *vi sep* (*sein*) come down; (*fig*) go to rack and ruin; ⟨*Firma, Person:*⟩ go downhill; (*gesundheitlich*) get run down. h~**lassen**† *vt sep* let down, lower. h~**machen** *vt sep* (*fam*) reprimand; (*herabsetzen*) run down. h~**spielen** *vt sep* (*fig*) play down. h~**ziehen**† *vt sep* pull down

hervor *adv* out (**aus** of). h~**bringen**† *vt sep* produce; utter ⟨*Wort*⟩. h~**gehen**† *vi sep* (*sein*) come/(*sich ergeben*) emerge/(*folgen*) follow (**aus** from). h~**heben**† *vt sep* (*fig*) stress, emphasize. h~**quellen**† *vi sep* (*sein*) stream out; (*h~treten*) bulge. h~**ragen** *vi sep* (*haben*) jut out; (*fig*) stand out. h~**ragend** *a* (*fig*) outstanding. h~**rufen**† *vt sep* (*fig*) cause. h~**stehen**† *vi sep* (*haben*) protrude. h~**treten**† *vi sep* (*sein*) protrude, bulge; (*fig*) stand out. h~**tun**† (**sich**) *vr sep* (*fig*) distinguish oneself; (*angeben*) show off

Herweg *m* way here

Herz *nt* -ens,-en heart; (*Kartenspiel*) hearts *pl*; **sich** (*dat*) **ein** H~ **fassen** pluck up courage. H~**anfall** *m* heart attack

herzeigen *vt sep* show

herz|**en** *vt* hug. H~**enslust** *f* **nach** H~**enslust** to one's heart's content. h~**haft** *a* hearty, *adv* -ily; (*würzig*) savoury

herziehen† *vi sep* ⟨*hinter sich* (*dat*) h~⟩ pull along [behind one] ⟨*vii* hinter jdm h~ follow along behind s.o.; **über jdn** h~ (*fam*) run s.o. down

herz|**ig** *a* sweet, adorable. H~**infarkt** *m* heart attack. H~**klopfen** *nt* -s palpitations *pl*; **ich hatte** H~**klopfen** my heart was pounding

herzlich *a* cordial, *adv* -ly; (*warm*) warm, *adv* -ly; (*aufrichtig*) sincere, *adv* -ly; h~**en Dank!** many thanks! h~**e Grüße** kind regards; h~ **wenig** precious little. H~**keit** *f* - cordiality; warmth; sincerity

herzlos *a* heartless

Herzog *m* -s,-̈e duke. H~**in** *f* -,-nen duchess. H~**tum** *nt* -s,-̈er duchy

Herz|schlag *m* heartbeat; *(Med)* heart failure. **h~zerreißend** *a* heart-breaking

Hessen *nt* -s Hesse

heterosexuell *a* heterosexual

Hetze *f* - rush; *(Kampagne)* virulent campaign **(gegen** against). **h~n** *vt* chase; **sich h~n** hurry □*vi (haben)* agitate; *(sich beeilen)* hurry □*vi (sein)* rush

Heu *nt* -s hay; **Geld wie Heu haben** *(fam)* have pots of money

Heuchelei *f* - hypocrisy

heuch|eln *vt* feign □*vi (haben)* pretend. **H~ler(in)** *m* -s,- *(f* -,-nen)* hypocrite. **h~lerisch** *a* hypocritical, *adv* -ly

heuer *adv (Aust)* this year

Heuer *f* -,-n *(Naut)* pay. **h~n** *vt* hire; sign on *(Matrosen)*

heulen *vi (haben)* howl; *(fam: weinen)* cry; *(Sirene)* wail

Heurige(r) *m (Aust)* new wine

Heu|schnupfen *m* hay fever. **H~schober** *m* -s,- haystack. **H~schrecke** *f* -,-n grasshopper; *(Wander-)* locust

heut|e *adv* today; *(heutzutage)* nowadays; **h~e früh** *od* **morgen** this morning; **von h~e auf morgen** from one day to the next. **h~ig** *a* today's ...; *(gegenwärtig)* present; **der h~ige Tag** today. **h~zutage** *adv* nowadays

Hexe *f* -,-n witch. **h~n** *vi (haben)* work magic; **ich kann nicht h~n** *(fam)* I can't perform miracles. **H~njagd** *f* witch-hunt. **H~nschuß** *m* lumbago. **H~rei** *f* - witchcraft

Hieb *m* -[e]s,-e blow; *(Peitschen-)* lash; **H~e** hiding *sg*

hier *adv* here; **h~ und da** here and there; *(zeitlich)* now and again

Hierarchie /hierar'çi:/ *f* -,-n hierarchy

hier|auf *adv* on this/these; *(antworten)* to this; *(zeitlich)* after

this. **h~aus** *adv* out of or from this/these. **h~behalten†** *vt sep* keep here. **h~bleiben†** *vi sep (sein)* stay here. **h~durch** *adv* through this/these; *(Ursache)* as a result of this. **h~für** *adv* for this/these. **h~her** *adv* here. **h~hin** *adv* here. **h~in** *adv* in this/these. **h~lassen†** *vt sep* leave here. **h~mit** *adv* with this/these; *(Comm)* herewith; *(Admin)* hereby. **h~nach** *adv* after this/these; *(demgemäß)* according to this/these. **h~sein†** *vi sep (sein)* be here. **h~über** *adv* over/*(höher)* above this/these; *(sprechen, streiten)* about this/these. **h~unter** *adv* under/*(tiefer)* below this/these; *(dazwischen)* among these. **h~von** *adv* from this/these; *(h~über)* about this/these; *(Menge)* of this/these. **h~zu** *adv* to this/these; *(h~für)* for this/these. **h~zulande** *adv* here

hiesig *a* local. **H~e(r)** *m/f* local

Hilfe *f* -,-n help, aid; **um H~e rufen** call for help; **jdm zu H~e kommen** come to s.o.'s aid. **h~los** *a* helpless, *adv* -ly. **H~losigkeit** *f* - helplessness. **h~reich** *a* helpful

Hilfs|arbeiter *m* unskilled labourer. **h~bedürftig** *a* needy; **h~bedürftig sein** be in need of help. **h~bereit** *a* helpful, *adv* -ly. **H~kraft** *f* helper. **H~mittel** *nt* aid. **H~verb, H~zeitwort** *nt* auxiliary verb

Himbeere *f* raspberry

Himmel *m* -s,- sky; *(Relig & fig)* heaven; *(Bett-)* canopy; **am H~** in the sky; **unter freiem H~** in the open air. **H~bett** *nt* four-poster [bed]. **H~fahrt** *f* Ascension; **Mariä H~fahrt** Assumption. **h~schreiend** *a* scandalous. **H~srichtung** *f* compass point;

in alle H~richtungen in all directions. h~weit a (fam) vast

himmlisch a heavenly

hin adv there; hin und her to and fro; hin und zurück there and back; (Rail) return; hin und wieder now and again; an (+ dat) ... hin along; auf (+ acc) ... hin in reply to ⟨Brief, Anzeige⟩; on ⟨jds Rat⟩; zu od nach ... hin towards; vor sich hin reden talk to oneself

hinab adv down [there]

hinauf adv up [there]; die Treppe/Straße h~ up the stairs/road. h~gehen† vi sep (sein) go up. h~setzen vt sep raise

hinaus adv out [there]; (nach draußen) outside; zur Tür h~ out of the door; auf Jahre h~ for years to come; über etw (acc) h~ beyond sth; ⟨Menge⟩ [over and] above sth. h~fliegen† v sep □ vi (sein) fly out; (fam) get the sack □ vt fly out. h~gehen† vi sep (sein) go out; ⟨Zimmer:⟩ face (nach Norden north); h~gehen über (+ acc) go beyond, exceed. h~kommen† vi sep (sein) get out; h~kommen über (+ acc) get beyond. h~laufen† vi sep (sein) run out; h~laufen auf (+ acc) (fig) amount to. h~lehnen (sich) vr sep lean out. h~ragen vi sep (haben) h~ragen über (+ acc) rise above; (fig) stand out above. h~schicken vt sep send out. h~schieben† vt sep (fig) put off. h~sehen† vi sep (haben) look out. h~sein† vi sep (sein) über etw (acc) h~sein (fig) be past sth. h~werfen† vt sep throw out; (fam: entlassen) fire. h~wollen† vi sep (haben) want to go out; h~wollen auf (+ acc) (fig) aim at; hoch h~wollen (fig) be ambitious. h~ziehen† v sep □ vt

pull out; (in die Länge ziehen) drag out; (verzögern) delay; sich h~ziehen drag on; be delayed □ vi (sein) move out. h~zögern vt delay; sich h~zögern be delayed

Hinblick m im H~ auf (+ acc) in view of; (hinsichtlich) regarding

hinbringen† vt sep take there; (verbringen) spend

hinderlich a awkward; jdm h~lich sein hamper s.o. h~n vt hamper; (verhindern) prevent. H~nis nt -ses,-se obstacle. H~nisrennen nt steeplechase

hindeuten vi sep (haben) point (auf + acc to)

Hindu m -s,-s Hindu. H~ismus m - Hinduism

hindurch adv through it/them; den Sommer h~ throughout the summer

hinein adv in [there]; (nach innen) inside; h~ in (+ acc) into. h~fallen† vi sep (sein) fall in. h~gehen† vi sep (sein) go in; h~gehen in (+ acc) go into. h~laufen† vi sep (sein) run in; h~laufen in (+ acc) run into. h~reden vi sep (haben) jdm h~reden interrupt s.o.; (sich einmischen) interfere in s.o.'s affairs. h~versetzen (sich) vr sep sich in jds Lage h~versetzen put oneself in s.o.'s position. h~ziehen† vt sep pull in; in etw (acc) h~gezogen werden (fig) become involved in sth

hinfahren† v sep □ vi (sein) go/drive there □ vt take/drive there. H~fahrt f journey/drive there; (Rail) outward journey. h~fallen† vi sep (sein) fall. h~fällig a (gebrechlich) frail; (ungültig) invalid. h~fliegen† v sep □ vi (sein) fly there; (fam) fall □ vt fly there. H~flug m flight there; (Admin) outward flight.

H~gabe f - devotion; (*Eifer*) dedication

hingeb|en† vt sep give up; **sich h~en** (*fig*) devote oneself (**einer Aufgabe** to a task); abandon oneself (**dem Vergnügen** to pleasure). **H~ung** f - devotion. **h~ungsvoll** a devoted, adv -ly

hingegen adv on the other hand

hingehen† vi sep (sein) go/(*zu Fuß*) walk there; (*vergehen*) pass; **h~ zu** go up to; **wo gehst du hin?** where are you going? **etw h~ lassen** (*fig*) let sth pass

hingerissen a rapt, adv -ly; **h~ sein** be carried away (**von** by)

hin|halten† vt sep hold out; (*warten lassen*) keep waiting. **h~hocken (sich)** vr sep squat down. **h~kauern (sich)** vr sep crouch down

hinken vi (haben/sein) limp

hin|knien (sich) vr sep kneel down. **h~kommen**† vi sep (sein) get there; (*h~gehören*) belong, go; (*fam: auskommen*) manage (**mit** with); (*fam: stimmen*) be right. **h~länglich** a adequate, adv -ly. **h~laufen**† vi sep (sein) run/(*gehen*) walk there. **h~legen** vt sep lay or put down; **sich h~legen** lie down. **h~nehmen**† vt sep (*fig*) accept

hinreichen v sep □vt hand (**dat** to) □vi (haben) extend (**bis** to); (*ausreichen*) be adequate. **h~d** a adequate, adv -ly

Hinreise f journey there; (*Rail*) outward journey

hinreißen† vt sep (*fig*) carry away; **sich h~ lassen** get carried away. **h~d** a ravishing, adv -ly

hinricht|en vt sep execute. **H~ung** f execution

hinschicken vt sep send there

hinschleppen vt sep drag there; (*fig*) drag out; **sich h~** drag oneself along; (*fig*) drag on

hinschreiben† vt sep write there; (*aufschreiben*) write down

hinsehen† vi sep (haben) look

hinsein† vi sep (sein) (*fam*) be gone; (*kaputt, tot*) have had it; [**ganz**] **h~ von** be overwhelmed by; **es ist noch/nicht mehr lange hin** it's a long time yet/not long to go

hinsetzen vt sep put down; **sich h~** sit down

Hinsicht f - in dieser/gewisser **H~** in this respect/in a certain sense; **in finanzieller H~** financially. **h~lich** prep (+ gen) regarding

hinstellen vt sep put or set down; park ⟨*Auto*⟩; (*fig*) make out (**als** to be); **sich h~** stand

hinstrecken vt sep hold out; **sich h~** extend

hintan|setzen, h~stellen vt sep ignore; (*vernachlässigen*) neglect

hinten adv at the back; **dort h~** back there; **nach/von h~** to the back/from behind. **h~herum** adv round the back; (*fam*) by devious means; (*erfahren*) in a roundabout way

hinter prep (+ dat/acc) behind; (*nach*) after; **h~ jdm/etw herlaufen** run after s.o./sth; **h~ etw** (dat) **stecken** (*fig*) be behind sth; **h~ etw** (acc) **kommen** (*fig*) get to the bottom of sth; **etw h~ sich** (acc) **bringen** get sth over [and done] with. **H~bein** nt hind leg

Hinterbliebene pl (Admin) surviving dependants; **die H~n** the bereaved family sg

hinterbringen† vt tell (**jdm** s.o.)

hintere(r,s) a back, rear; **h~s Ende** far end

hintereinander adv one behind/ (*zeitlich*) after the other; **dreimal h~** three times in succession/ (*fam*) in a row

Hintergedanke m ulterior motive

hintergehen† *vt* deceive

Hinter|grund *m* background.
H~halt *m* -[e]s,-e ambush; aus
dem H~halt überfallen am-
bush. h~hältig *a* underhand

hinterher *adv* behind, after; *(zeitlich)* afterwards. h~gehen† *vi
sep* *(sein)* follow [jdm behind].
h~kommen† *vi sep* *(sein)* follow [behind]. h~laufen† *vi sep*
(sein) run after (jdm s.o.)

Hinter|hof *m* back yard. H~~
kopf *m* back of the head

hinterlassen† *vt* leave [behind];
(Jur) leave, bequeath (dat to).
H~schaft *f* -,-en *(Jur)* estate

hinterlegen† *vt* deposit

Hinter|leib *m* *(Zool)* abdomen.
H~list *f* deceit. h~listig *a* de-
ceitful, *adv* -ly. h~m *prep*
= hinter dem. H~mann *m* (pl
-männer) person behind.
h~n *prep* = hinter den. H~n
m -s,- *(fam)* bottom, backside.
h~rad *nt* rear or back wheel.
h~rücks *adv* from behind. h~s
prep = hinter das. h~ste(r,s) *a*
last; h~ste Reihe back row.
H~teil *nt* *(fam)* behind

hintertreiben† *vt* *(fig)* block

Hinter|treppe *f* back stairs *pl*.
H~tür *f* back door; *(fig)* loop-
hole

hinterziehen† *vt* *(Admin)* evade

Hinterzimmer *nt* back room

hinüber *adv* over or across
[there]. h~gehen† *vi sep* *(sein)*
go over or across; h~gehen über
(+ acc) cross

hinunter *adv* down [there]; die
Treppe/Straße h~ down the
stairs/road. h~gehen† *vi sep*
(sein) go down. h~schlucken *vt
sep* swallow

Hinweg *m* way there

hinweg *adv* away, off; h~ über
(+ acc) over; über eine Zeit h~
over a period. h~gehen† *vi sep*
(sein) h~gehen über (+ acc)

(fig) pass over. h~kommen† *vi
sep* *(sein)* h~kommen über
(+ acc) *(fig)* get over. h~sehen†
vi sep *(haben)* h~sehen über
(+ acc) see over; *(fig)* overlook.
h~setzen (sich) *vr sep* sich
h~setzen über (+ acc) ignore

Hinweis *m* -es,-e reference; *(Andeutung)* hint; *(Anzeichen)* indication; unter H~ auf (+ acc)
with reference to. h~en† *v sep*
□*vi (haben)* point (auf + acc to)
□*vt* jdn auf etw (acc) h~en
point sth out to s.o. h~end *a (Gram)*
demonstrative

hin|wenden† *vt sep* turn; sich
h~wenden turn (zu to).
h~werfen† *vt sep* throw down;
drop *(Bemerkung)*; *(schreiben)*
jot down; *(zeichnen)* sketch; *(fam:
aufgeben)* pack in

hinwieder *adv* on the other hand

hin|zeigen *vi sep* *(haben)* point
(auf + acc to). h~ziehen† *vt sep*
pull; *(fig: in die Länge ziehen)*
drag out; *(verzögern)* delay; sich
h~ziehen drag on; be delayed;
sich h~gezogen fühlen zu *(fig)*
feel drawn to

hinzu *adv* in addition. h~fügen
vt sep add. h~kommen† *vi sep*
(sein) be added; *(ankommen)*
arrive [on the scene]; join (zu
jdm s.o.). h~rechnen *vt sep*
add. h~ziehen† *vt sep* call in

Hiobsbotschaft *f* bad news *sg*

Hirn *nt* -s brain; *(Culin)* brains *pl*.
H~gespinst *nt* -[e]s,-e figment
of the imagination. H~haut~~
zündung *f* meningitis. h~ver-
brannt *a (fam)* crazy

Hirsch *m* -[e]s,-e deer; *(männlich)*
stag; *(Culin)* venison

Hirse *f* - millet

Hirt *m* -en,-en, **Hirte** *m* -n,-n
shepherd

hissen *vt* hoist

Histor|iker *m* -s,- historian.
h~isch *a* historical; (*bedeutend*)
historic

Hit *m* -s,-s (*Mus*) hit

Hitz|e *f* - heat. **H~ewelle** *f* heat
wave. **h~ig** *a* (*fig*) heated, *adv*
-ly; (*Person*) hot-headed; (*jähzornig*) hot-tempered. **H~kopf**
m hothead. **H~schlag** *m* heat-
stroke

H-Milch /'ha:-/ *f* long-life milk

Hobby *nt* -s,-s hobby

Hobel *m* -s,- (*Techn*) plane; (*Culin*) slicer. **h~n** *vt/i* (*haben*)
plane. **H~späne** *mpl* shavings

hoch *a* (höher, höchst; *attrib*
hohe(r,s)) high; (*Baum, Mast*)
tall; (*Offizier*) high-ranking; (*Alter*) great; (*Summe*) large;
(*Strafe*) heavy; **hohe Schuhe**
ankle boots □ *adv* high; (*sehr*)
highly; **die Treppe/den Berg
h~** up the stairs/hill; **sechs
Mann h~** six of us/them. **H~** *nt*
-s,-s cheer; (*Meteorol*) high

Hoch|achtung *f* high esteem.
H~achtungsvoll *adv* Yours
faithfully. **H~amt** *nt* High Mass.
h~arbeiten (sich) *vr sep* work
one's way up. **h~begabt** *attrib a*
highly gifted. **H~betrieb** *m*
great activity; **in den Geschäf-
ten herrscht H~betrieb** the
shops are terribly busy.
H~burg *f* (*fig*) stronghold.
H~deutsch *nt* High German.
H~druck *m* high pressure.
H~ebene/plateau. **h~fahren†**
vi sep (*sein*) go up; (*auffahren*)
start up; (*aufbrausen*) flare up.
h~fliegend *a* (*fig*) ambitious.
h~gehen† *vi sep* (*sein*) go up;
(*explodieren*) blow up; (*aufbrausen*) flare up. **h~gestellt** *attrib a*
high-ranking; (*Zahl*) superior.
h~gewachsen *a* tall. **H~glanz**
m high gloss. **h~gradig** *a* extreme, *adv* -ly. **h~hackig** *a* high-
heeled. **h~halten†** *vt sep* hold

up; (*fig*) uphold. **H~haus** *nt*
high-rise building. **h~heben†** *vt
sep* lift up; raise (*Kopf, Hand*).
h~herzig *a* magnanimous, *adv*
-ly. **h~kant** *adv* on end.
h~kommen† *vi sep* (*sein*) come
up; (*aufstehen*) get up; (*fig*) get on
[in the world]. **H~konjunktur** *f*
boom. **h~krempeln** *vt sep* roll
up. **h~leben** *vi sep* (*haben*)
h~leben lassen give three
cheers for; **... lebe hoch!** three
cheers for ...! **H~mut** *m* pride,
arrogance. **h~mütig** *a* arrogant, *adv* -ly. **h~näsig** *a* (*fam*)
snooty. **h~nehmen†** *vt sep* pick
up; (*fam*) tease. **H~ofen** *m* blast-
furnace. **h~ragen** *vi sep* rise
[up]; (*Turm*:) soar. **H~ruf** *m*
cheer. **H~saison** *f* high season.
H~schätzung *f* high esteem.
h~schlagen† *vt sep* turn up
(*Kragen*). **h~schrecken†** *vi sep*
(*sein*) start up. **H~schule** *f*
university; (*Musik-, Kunst-*)
academy. **h~sehen†** *vi sep* (*haben*) look up. **H~sommer** *m*
midsummer. **H~spannung** *f*
high/(*fig*) great tension. **h~
spielen** *vt sep* (*fig*) magnify.
H~sprache *f* standard language. **H~sprung** *m* high jump

höchst *adv* extremely, most

Hochstapler *m* -s,- confidence
trickster

höchst|e(r,s) *a* highest; (*Baum,
Turm*) tallest; (*oberste, größte*)
top; **es ist h~e Zeit** it is high
time. **h~ens** *adv* at most; (*es sei
denn*) except perhaps. **H~fall** *m
im H~fall* at most. **H~ge-
schwindigkeit** *f* top or maximum speed. **H~maß** *nt* maximum. **h~persönlich** *adv* in person. **H~preis** *m* top price.
H~temperatur *f* maximum
temperature. **h~wahrschein-
lich** *adv* most probably

hoch|trabend a pompous, adv
-ly. **h~treiben†** vt sep push up
⟨Preis⟩. **H~verrat** m high treason. **H~wasser** nt high tide;
(Überschwemmung) floods pl.
H~würden m -s Reverend; (Anrede) Father

Hochzeit f -,-en wedding; **h~**
feiern get married. **H~skleid** nt
wedding dress. **H~sreise** f
honeymoon [trip]. **H~stag** m
wedding day/(Jahrestag) anniversary

hochziehen† vt sep pull up; (hissen) hoist; raise ⟨Augenbrauen⟩

Hocke f -in der H~ sitzen squat;
in die H~ gehen squat down.
h~n vi (haben) squat □vr sich
h~n squat down

Hocker m -s,- stool

Höcker m -s,- bump; (Kamel-)
hump

Hockey /'hɔki/ nt -s hockey

Hode f -,-n, **Hoden** m -s,- testicle

Hof m -[e]s,-̈e [court]yard;
(Bauern-) farm; (Königs-) court;
(Schul-) playground; (Astr) halo

hoffen vt/i (haben) hope (**auf**+acc
for). **h~tlich** adv I hope, let us
hope; (als Antwort) **h~tlich/**
h~tlich nicht let's hope so/not

Hoffnung f -,-en hope. **h~slos** a
hopeless, adv -ly. **h~svoll** a
hopeful, adv -ly

höflich a polite, adv -ly, courteous, adv -ly. **H~keit** f -,-en politeness, courtesy; (Äußerung)
civility

hohe(r,s) a s. hoch

Höhe f -,-n height; (Aviat, Geog)
altitude; (Niveau) level; (einer
Summe) size; (An-) hill; **in die**
H~ gehen rise, go up; **nicht auf**
der H~ (fam) under the
weather; **das ist die H~!** (fam)
that's the limit!

Hoheit f -,-en (Staats-) sovereignty; (Titel) Highness. **H~sge-**
biet nt [sovereign] territory.

H~szeichen nt national emblem

Höhe|nlinie f contour line.
H~nsonne f sun-lamp. **H~n-**
zug m mountain range. **H~-**
punkt m (fig) climax, peak;
(einer Vorstellung) highlight.
h~r a & adv higher; **h~re**
Schule secondary school

hohl a hollow; (leer) empty

Höhle f -,-n cave; (Tier-) den;
(Hohlraum) cavity; (Augen-)
socket

Hohl|maß nt measure of capacity. **H~raum** m cavity

Hohn m -s scorn, derision

höhn|en vi deride □vi (haben)
jeer. **h~isch** a scornful, adv -ly

holen vt fetch, get; (kaufen) buy;
(nehmen) take (**aus** from); **h~**
lassen send for; [tief] **Atem** od
Luft h~ take a [deep] breath;
sich (dat) etw h~ get sth; catch
⟨Erkältung⟩

Holland nt -s Holland

Holländ|er m -s,- Dutchman; **die**
H~er the Dutch pl. **H~erin** f
-,-nen Dutchwoman. **h~isch**
a Dutch

Höll|e f - hell. **h~isch** a infernal;
(schrecklich) terrible, adv -bly

holpern vi (sein) jolt or bump
along □vi (haben) be bumpy

holp[e]rig a bumpy

Holunder m -s (Bot) elder

Holz nt -es,-̈er wood; (Nutz-) timber. **H~blasinstrument** nt
woodwind instrument

hölzern a wooden

Holz|hammer m mallet. **h~ig** a
woody. **H~kohle** f charcoal.
H~schnitt m woodcut.
H~schuh m [wooden] clog.
H~wolle f wood shavings pl.
H~wurm m woodworm

homogen a homogeneous

Homöopathie f- homoeopathy

homosexuell a homosexual.
H~e(r) m/f homosexual

Honig *m* -s honey. **H~wabe** *f* honeycomb

Hono|rar *nt* -s,-e fee. **H~rieren** *vt* remunerate; (*fig*) reward

Hopfen *m* -s hops *pl*; (*Bot*) hop

hopsen *vi* (*sein*) jump

Hör|apparat *m* hearing-aid. **h~bar** *a* audible, *adv* -bly

horchen *vi* (*haben*) listen (**auf** + *acc* to); (*heimlich*) eavesdrop

Horde *f* -,-n horde; (*Gestell*) rack

hören *vt* hear; (*an-*) listen to □ *vi* (*haben*) hear; (*horchen*) listen; (*gehorchen*) obey; **h~ auf** (+ *acc*) listen to. **H~sagen** *nt* vom **H~sagen** from hearsay

Hör|er *m* -s,- listener; (*Teleph*) receiver. **H~funk** *m* radio. **H~gerät** *nt* hearing-aid

Horizon|t *m* -[e]s horizon. **h~tal** *a* horizontal, *adv* -ly

Hormon *nt* -s,-e hormone

Horn *nt* -s,¨er horn. **H~haut** *f* hard skin; (*Augen-*) cornea

Hornisse *f* -,-n hornet

Horoskop *nt* -[e]s,-e horoscope

Hörrohr *nt* stethoscope

Horrorfilm *m* horror film

Hör|saal *m* (*Univ*) lecture hall. **H~spiel** *nt* radio play

Hort *m* -[e]s,-e (*Schatz*) hoard; (*fig*) refuge. **h~en** *vt* hoard

Hortensie /-iə/ *f* -,-n hydrangea

Hörweite *f* in/außer **H~** within/out of earshot

Hose *f* -,-n, **Hosen** *pl* trousers *pl*. **H~nrock** *m* culottes *pl*. **H~nschlitz** *m* fly, flies *pl*. **H~nträger** *mpl* braces, (*Amer*) suspenders

Hostess, Hosteß *f* -,-tessen hostess; (*Aviat*) air hostess

Hostie /'hɔstiə/ *f* -,-n (*Relig*) host

Hotel *nt* -s,-s hotel; **H~ garni** /gar'ni:/ bed-and-breakfast hotel. **H~ier** /-'lie:/ *m* -s,-s hotelier

hübsch *a* pretty, *adv* -ily; (*nett*) nice, *adv* -ly; (*Summe*) tidy

Hubschrauber *m* -s,- helicopter

---

huckepack *adv* jdn **h~ tragen** give s.o. a piggyback

Huf *m* -[e]s,-e hoof. **H~eisen** *nt* horseshoe

Hüft|e *f* -,-n hip. **H~gürtel**, **H~halter** *m* -s,- girdle

Hügel *m* -s,- hill. **H~ig** *a* hilly

Huhn *nt* -s,¨er chicken; (*Henne*) hen

Hühn|chen *nt* -s,- chicken. **H~erauge** *nt* corn. **H~erbrühe** *f* chicken broth. **H~erstall** *m* henhouse, chicken-coop

huldig|en *vi* (*haben*) pay homage (*dat* to). **H~ung** *f* - homage

Hülle *f* -,-n cover; (*Verpackung*) wrapping; (*Platten-*) sleeve; **in H~ und Fülle** in abundance. **h~n** *vt* wrap

Hülse *f* -,-n (*Bot*) pod; (*Etui*) case. **H~nfrüchte** *fpl* pulses

human *a* humane, *adv* -ly. **h~itär** *a* humanitarian. **H~ität** *f* - humanity

Hummel *f* -,-n bumble-bee

Hummer *m* -s,- lobster

Hum|or *m* -s humour; **H~or haben** have a sense of humour. **h~oristisch** *a* humorous. **h~orvoll** *a* humorous, *adv* -ly

humpeln *vi* (*sein/haben*) hobble

Humpen *m* -s,- tankard

Hund *m* -[e]s,-e dog; (*Jagd-*) hound. **H~ehalsband** *nt* dog-collar. **H~ehütte** *f* kennel. **H~eleine** *f* dog lead

hundert *inv a* one/a hundred. **H~ nt** -s,-e hundred; **H~e von** hundreds of. **H~jahrfeier** *f* centenary, (*Amer*) centennial. **h~prozentig** *a* adv one hundred per cent. **h~ste(r,s)** *a* hundredth. **H~stel** *nt* -s,- hundredth

Hündin *f* -,-nen bitch

Hüne *m* -n,-n giant

Hunger *m* -s hunger; **H~ haben** be hungry. **h~n** *vi* (*haben*)

starve; h~n nach (fig) hunger for. H~snot f famine

hungrig a hungry, adv -ily

Hupe f -,-n (Auto) horn. h~n vi (haben) sound one's horn

hüpf|en vi (sein) skip; ⟨Vogel, Frosch:⟩ hop; ⟨Grashüpfer:⟩ jump. H~er m -s,- skip, hop

Hürde f -,-n (Sport & fig) hurdle; ⟨Schaf:⟩ pen, fold

Hure f -,-n whore

hurra int hurray. H~ nt -s,-s hurray; (Beifallsruf) cheer

Husche f -,-n [short] shower. h~n vi (sein) slip; ⟨Eidechse:⟩ dart; ⟨Maus:⟩ scurry; ⟨Lächeln:⟩ flit

hüsteln vi (haben) give a slight cough

husten vi (haben) cough. H~ m -s cough. H~ m -s cough mixture

Hut¹ m -[e]s,̈ e hat; (Pilz-) cap

Hut² f - auf der H~ sein to be on one's guard (vor + dat against)

hüten vt watch over; tend ⟨Tiere⟩; (aufpassen) look after; das Bett h~ müssen be confined to bed; sich h~ be on one's guard (vor + dat against); sich h~, etw zu tun take care not to do sth

Hütte f -,-n hut; (Hunde-) kennel; (Techn) iron and steel works. H~nkäse m cottage cheese. H~nkunde f metallurgy

Hyäne f -,-n hyena

Hybride f -,-n hybrid

Hydrant m -en,-en hydrant

hydraulisch a hydraulic, adv -ally

hydroelektrisch /hydro'e'lek-trɪʃ/ a hydroelectric

Hygien|e /hy'gie:nə/ f - hygiene. h~isch a hygienic, adv -ally

hypermodern a ultra-modern

Hypno|se f - hypnosis. h~tisch a hypnotic. H~tiseur /-'zø:ɐ/ m -s,-e hypnotist. h~tisieren vt hypnotize

Hypochonder /hypo'xɔndɐ/ m -s,- hypochondriac

Hypothek f -,-en mortgage

Hypothe|se f -,-n hypothesis. h~tisch a hypothetical, adv -ly

Hys|terie f - hysteria. h~terisch a hysterical, adv -ly

I

ich pron I; ich bin's it's me. Ich nt -[s],-[s] self; (Psych) ego

IC-Zug /i'tse:-/ m inter-city train

ideal a ideal. I~ nt -s,-e ideal. i~isieren vt idealize. I~ismus m -idealism. I~ist(in) m -en,-en (f -,-nen) idealist. i~istisch a idealistic

Idee f -,-n idea; fixe I~ obsession; eine I~ ⟨fam: wenig⟩ a tiny bit

identifizieren vt identify

iden|tisch a identical. I~tät f -,-en identity

Ideo|logie f -,-n ideology. i~lo-gisch a ideological

idiomatisch a idiomatic

Idiot m -en,-en idiot. i~isch a idiotic, adv -ally

Idol nt -s,-e idol

idyllisch /i'dʏlɪʃ/ a idyllic

Igel m -s,- hedgehog

ignorieren vt ignore

ihm pron (dat of er, es) [to] him; (Ding, Tier) [to] it; Freunde von ihm friends of his

ihn pron (acc of er) him; (Ding, Tier) it. i~en pron (dat of sie pl) [to] them; Freunde von i~en friends of theirs. I~en pron (dat of Sie) [to] you; Freunde von I~en friends of yours

ihr pron (2nd pers pl) you □ (dat of sie sg) [to] her; (Ding, Tier) [to] it; Freunde von ihr friends of hers □poss pron her; (Ding, Tier) its; (pl) their. Ihr poss pron your. i~e(r,s) poss pron hers; (pl) theirs. I~e(r,s) poss pron yours.

i~**erseits** adv for her/(pl) their part. I~**erseits** adv on your part. i~**etwegen** adv for her/(Ding, Tier) its/(pl) their sake; (wegen) because of her/it/them, on her/its/their account. I~**etwegen** adv for your sake; (wegen) because of you, on your account. i~**etwillen** adv um i~**etwillen** for her/(Ding, Tier) its/(pl) their sake. I~**etwillen** adv um I~**etwillen** for your sake. i~**ige** poss pron der/die/ das i~**ige** hers; (pl) theirs. I~**ige** poss pron der/die/das I~**ige** yours. i~s poss pron hers; (pl) theirs. I~s poss pron yours

Ikone f -,-n icon

illegal a illegal, adv -ly

Illusion f -,-en illusion; sich (dat) I~**ionen machen** delude oneself. i~**orisch** a illusory

Illustration /-'tsjo:n/ f -,-en illustration. i~**ieren** vt illustrate. I~**ierte** f -n,-[n] [illustrated] magazine

Iltis m -ses,-se polecat

im prep = in dem; im Mai in May; im Kino at the cinema

Image /'ımıdʒ/ nt -[s],-s /-ıs/ [public] image

Imbiß m snack. I~**halle**, I~**stube** f snack-bar

Imitation /-'tsjo:n/ f -,-en imitation. i~**ieren** vt imitate

Imker m -s,- bee-keeper

Immatrikulation /-'tsjo:n/ f - (Univ) enrolment. i~**ieren** vt (Univ) enrol; sich i~**ieren** enrol

immer adv always; für i~ for ever; (endgültig) for good; i~ noch still; i~ mehr/weniger/ wieder more and more/less and less/again and again; wer/was [auch] i~ whoever/whatever. i~**fort** adv = i~zu. i~**grün** a evergreen. i~**hin** adv (wenigstens) at least; (trotzdem) all the

same; (schließlich) after all. i~**zu** adv all the time

Immobilien /-jən/ pl real estate sg. I~**händler**, I~**makler** m estate agent, (Amer) realtor

immun a immune (**gegen** to). i~**isieren** vt immunize. I~**ität** f immunity

Imperativ m -s,-e imperative

Imperfekt nt -s,-e imperfect

Imperialismus m - imperialism

impfen vt vaccinate, inoculate. I~**stoff** m vaccine. I~**ung** f -,-en vaccination, inoculation

Implantat nt -[e]s,-e implant

imponieren vi (haben) impress (jdm s.o.)

Import m -[e]s,-e import. I~**teur** /-'tø:ɐ/ m -s,-e importer. i~**tieren** vt import

imposant a imposing

impotent a (Med) impotent. I~**z** f - (Med) impotence

imprägnieren vt waterproof

Impressionismus m - impressionism

improvisieren vt/i (haben) improvise

Impuls m -es,-e impulse. i~**iv** a impulsive, adv -ly

imstande pred a able (zu zu); capable (etw zu tun of doing sth)

in prep (+ dat) in; (+ acc) into, in; (bei Bus, Zug) on; in der Schule/Oper at school/the opera; in die Schule to school □ a in prof a indeed

Inbegriff m embodiment. i~**en** prof a included

Inbrunst f - fervour

inbrünstig a fervent, adv -ly

indem conj (während) while; (da-durch) by (+ -ing)

Inder(in) m -s,- (f -,-nen) Indian

indessen conj while □ adv (unter-dessen) meanwhile; (jedoch) however

Indian m -s,-e (Aust) turkey

Indian|er(in) m -s,- (f -,-nen) (American) Indian. **i~isch** a Indian

Indien /'ɪndjən/ nt -s India

indigniert a indignant, adv -ly

Indikativ m -s,-e indicative

indirekt a indirect, adv -ly

indisch a Indian

indiskre|t a indiscreet. **I~tion** /-'tsjo:n/ f -,-en indiscretion

indiskutabel a out of the question

indisponiert a indisposed

Individu|alist m -en,-en individualist. **I~alität** f - individuality. **i~ell** a individual, adv -ly. **I~um** /-'vi:duʊm/ nt -s,-duen individual

Indizienbeweis /ɪn'di:tsjən-/ m circumstantial evidence

indoktrinieren vt indoctrinate

industr|ialisiert a industrialized. **I~ie** f -,-n industry. **i~iell** a industrial. **I~ielle(r)** m industrialist

ineinander adv in/into one another

Infanterie f - infantry

Infektion /-'tsjo:n/ f -,-en infection. **I~skrankheit** f infectious disease

Infinitiv m -s,-e infinitive

infizieren vt infect; **sich i~** become/ ⟨Person:⟩ be infected

Inflation /-'tsjo:n/ f - inflation. **i~är** a inflationary

infolge prep (+ gen) as a result of. **i~dessen** adv consequently

Inform|atik f - information science. **I~ation** /-'tsjo:n/ f -,-en information; **I~ationen** Information sg. **i~ieren** vt inform; **sich i~ieren** find out (**über** + acc about)

infrarot a infra-red

Ingenieur /ɪnʒe'njø:ɐ̯/ m -s,-e engineer

Ingwer m -s ginger

Inhaber(in) m -s,- (f -,-nen) holder; (Besitzer) proprietor; (Scheck-) bearer

inhaftieren vt take into custody

inhalieren vt/i (haben) inhale

Inhalt m -[e]s,-e contents pl; (Bedeutung, Gehalt) content; (Geschichte) story. **I~sangabe** f summary. **I~sverzeichnis** nt list/(in Buch) table of contents

Initiale /initsi'a:lə/ f -,-n initial

Initiative /initsia'ti:və/ f -,-n initiative

Injektion /-'tsjo:n/ f -,-en injection. **injizieren** vt inject

inklusive prep (+ gen) including □ adv inclusive

inkognito adv incognito

inkonsequen|t a inconsistent, adv -ly. **I~z** f -,-en inconsistency

inkorrekt a incorrect, adv -ly

Inkubationszeit /-'tsjo:ns-/ f (Med) incubation period

Inland nt -[e]s home country; (Binnenland) interior. **I~sgespräch** nt inland call

inmitten prep (+ gen) in the middle of; (unter) amongst □ adv **i~ von** amongst, amidst

inne|haben vt sep hold, have. **i~halten†** vi sep (haben) pause

innen adv inside; **nach i~** inwards. **I~architekt(in)** m(f) interior designer. **I~minister** m Minister of the Interior; (in UK) Home Secretary. **I~politik** f domestic policy. **I~stadt** f town centre

inner|e(r,s) a inner; (Med, Pol) internal. **I~e(s)** nt interior; (Mitte) centre; (fig: Seele) inner being. **I~eien** fpl (Culin) offal sg. **i~halb** prep (+ gen) inside; (zeitlich & fig) within; (während) during □ adv **i~halb von** within. **i~lich** a internal; (seelisch) inner; (besinnlich) introspective

□*adv* internally; (*im Inneren*) inwardly. **i∼ste(r,s)** innermost; **im I∼sten** (*fig*) deep down

innig *a* sincere, *adv* -ly; (*tief*) deep, *adv* -ly; (*eng*) intimate, *adv* -ly

Innung *f* -,-en guild

inoffiziell *a* unofficial, *adv* -ly

ins *prep* = **in das; ins Kino/Büro** to the cinema/office

Insasse *m* -n,-n inmate; (*im Auto*) occupant; (*Passagier*) passenger

insbesondere *adv* especially

Inschrift *f* inscription

Insekt *nt* -[e]s,-en insect. **I∼envertilgungsmittel** *nt* insecticide

Insel *f* -,-n island

Inserat *nt* -[e]s,-e [newspaper] advertisement. **I∼ent** *m* -en,-en advertiser. **i∼ieren** *vt/i* (*haben*) advertise

insge|heim *adv* secretly. **i∼samt** *adv* [all] in all

Insignien /-iən/ *pl* insignia

insofern, insoweit *adv* /-'zo:-/ in this respect; **i∼ als** in as much as □*conj* /-zo'fɛrn, -'vaɪt/ **i∼ als** in so far as

Inspektion /ɪnspɛk'tsjo:n/ *f* -,-en inspection. **I∼ektor** *m* -en,-en /-'to:rən/ inspector

Inspiration /ɪnspira'tsjo:n/ *f* -,-en inspiration. **i∼ieren** *vt* inspire

inspizieren /-sp-/ *vt* inspect

Install|ateur /ɪnstala'tø:ɐ̯/ *m* -s,-e fitter; (*Klempner*) plumber. **i∼ieren** *vt* install

instand *adv* **i∼ halten** maintain; (*pflegen*) look after; **i∼ setzen** restore; (*reparieren*) repair. **I∼haltung** *f* - maintenance, upkeep

inständig *a* urgent, *adv* -ly

Instandsetzung *f* - repair

Instant- /ˈɪnstant-/ *pref* instant

Instanz /-st-/ *f* -,-en authority

Instinkt /-st-/ *m* -[e]s,-e instinct. **i∼iv** *a* instinctive, *adv* -ly

Institut /-st-/ *nt* -[e]s,-e institute. **I∼tion** /-'tsjo:n/ *f* -,-en institution

Instrument /-st-/ *nt* -[e]s,-e instrument. **I∼almusik** *f* instrumental music

Insulin *nt* -s insulin

inszenier|en *vt* (*Theat*) produce. **I∼ung** *f* -,-en production

Integr|ation /-'tsjo:n/ *f* - integration. **i∼ieren** *vt* integrate; **sich i∼ieren** integrate. **I∼ität** *f* - integrity

Intellekt *m* -[e]s intellect. **i∼uell** *a* intellectual

intelligen|t *a* intelligent, *adv* -ly. **I∼z** *f* - intelligence; (*Leute*) intelligentsia

Intendant *m* -en,-en director

Intens|ität *f* - intensity. **i∼iv** *a* intensive, *adv* -ly. **i∼ivieren** *vt* intensify. **I∼ivstation** *f* intensive-care unit

inter|essant *a* interesting. **I∼esse** *nt* -s,-n interest; **I∼esse haben** be interested (**an** + *dat* in). **I∼essengruppe** *f* pressure group. **I∼essent** *m* -en,-en interested party; (*Käufer*) prospective buyer. **i∼essieren** *vt* interest; **sich i∼essieren** be interested (**für** in)

intern *a* (*fig*) internal, *adv* -ly

Inter|nat *nt* -[e]s,-e boarding school. **i∼national** *a* international, *adv* -ly. **i∼nieren** *vt* intern. **I∼nierung** *f* -,-en internment. **I∼nist** *m* -en, -en specialist in internal diseases. **I∼pretation** /-'tsjo:n/ *f* -,-en interpretation. **i∼pretieren** *vt* interpret. **I∼punktion** /-'tsjo:n/ *f* -,-en punctuation. **I∼rogativpronomen** *nt* interrogative pronoun. **I∼vall** *nt* -s,-e interval. **I∼vention** /-'tsjo:n/ *f* -,-en intervention

Interview /'ɪntɐvju:/ *nt* -s,-s interview. **i~en** /-'vju:ən/ *vt* interview

intim *a* intimate, *adv* -ly. **I~ität** *f* -,-en intimacy

intolerant|**t** *a* intolerant. **I~z** *f* -intolerance

intransitiv *a* intransitive, *adv* -ly

intravenös *a* intravenous, *adv* -ly

Intrig|**e** *f* -,-n intrigue. **i~ieren** *vi* (*haben*) plot

introvertiert *a* introverted

Intui|**tion** /-'tsjo:n/ *f* -,-en intuition. **i~tiv** *a* intuitive, *adv* -ly

Invalidenrente *f* disability pension

Invasion *f* -,-en invasion

Inven|**tar** *nt* -s,-e furnishings and fittings *pl*; (*Techn*) equipment; (*Bestand*) stock; (*Liste*) inventory. **I~tur** *f* -,-en stock-taking

investieren *vt* invest

inwendig *a & adv* inside

inwie|**fern** *adv* in what way. **i~weit** *adv* how far, to what extent

Inzest *m* -[e]s incest

inzwischen *adv* in the meantime

Irak (der) -[s] Iraq. **i~isch** *a* Iraqi

Iran (der) -[s] Iran. **i~isch** *a* Iranian

irdisch *a* earthly

Ire *m* -n,-n Irishman; **die I~n** the Irish *pl*

irgend *adv* **i~ jemand/etwas** someone/something; (*fragend, verneint*) anyone/anything; **wer/was/wann i~** whoever/what-ever/whenever; **wenn i~ möglich** if at all possible. **i~ein** *indef art* some/any; (*j~*) **ein anderer** someone/anyone else. **i~eine(r,s)** *pron* any one; (*jemand*) someone/anyone. **i~wann** *pron* at some time [or other]/at any time. **i~was** *pron* (*fam*) something [or other]/any-thing. **i~welche(r,s)** *pron* any.

i~wer *pron* someone/anyone. **i~wie** *adv* somehow [or other]. **i~wo** *adv* somewhere/any-where; **i~wo anders** somewhere else

Irin *f* -,-nen Irishwoman

Iris *f* -,- (*Anat, Bot*) iris

irisch *a* Irish

Irland *nt* -s Ireland

Ironie *f* -irony

ironisch *a* ironic, *adv* -ally

irr *a* = **irre**

irrational *a* irrational

irre *a* mad, crazy; (*fam: gewaltig*) incredible, *adv* -bly; **i~ werden** get confused. **I~(r)** *m/f* lunatic. **i~führen** *vt sep* (*fig*) mislead. **i~gehen†** *vi sep* (*sein*) lose one's way; (*sich täuschen*) be wrong

irrelevant *a* irrelevant

irre|**machen** *vt sep* confuse. **i~n** *vi/r* (*haben*) [sich] **i~n** be mistaken; **wenn ich mich nicht i~** if I am not mistaken □ *vi* (*sein*) wander. **I~nanstalt** *f,* **I~n-haus** *nt* lunatic asylum. **i~re-den** *vi sep* (*haben*) ramble

Irr|**garten** *m* maze. **i~ig** *a* erroneous

irritieren *vt* irritate

Irr|**sinn** *m* madness, lunacy. **i~sinnig** *a* mad; (*fam: gewaltig*) incredible, *adv* -bly. **I~tum** *m* -s,-̈er mistake. **i~tümlich** *a* mistaken, *adv* -ly

Ischias *m & nt* - sciatica

Islam (der) -[s] Islam. **islamisch** *a* Islamic

Island *nt* -s Iceland

Isolier|**band** *nt* insulating tape. **i~en** *vt* isolate; (*Phys, Electr*) insulate; (*gegen Schall*) sound-proof. **I~ung** *f* - isolation; insulation; soundproofing

Israel /'izrae:l/ *nt* -s Israel. **I~eli** *m* -[s],-s & *f* -,-[s] Israeli. **i~elisch** *a* Israeli

ist *s.* **sein**; **er ist** he is

Ital|ien /-jən/ nt -s Italy. **I~ie-ner(in)** m -s,- (f -,-nen) Italian. **i~ienisch** a Italian. **I~ienisch** nt -[s] (Lang) Italian

J

ja adv yes; **ich glaube ja** I think so; **ja nicht!** not on any account! **seid 'ja vorsichtig!** whatever you do, be careful! **da seid ihr ja!** there you are! **das ist es ja** that's just it; **das mag ja wahr sein** that may well be true

Jacht f -,-en yacht

Jacke f -,-n jacket; (Strick-) cardigan

Jackett /ʒa'kɛt/ nt -s,-s jacket

Jade m -[s] & f- jade

Jagd f -,-en hunt; (Schießen) shoot; (Jagen) hunting; shooting; (fig) pursuit (**nach** of); **auf die J~ gehen** go hunting/shooting. **J~flugzeug** nt fighter aircraft. **J~gewehr** nt sporting gun. **J~hund** m gun-dog; (Hetzhund) hound

jagen vt hunt; (schießen) shoot; (verfolgen, wegjagen) chase; (treiben) drive; **sich j~** chase each other; **in die Luft j~** blow up □vi (haben) hunt; (rasen) rush; (fig) chase (**nach** after) □vi (sein) race, dash

Jäger m -s,- hunter

jäh a sudden, adv -ly; (steil) steep, adv -ly

Jahr nt -[e]s,-e year. **J~buch** nt year-book. **j~elang** adv for years. **J~estag** m anniversary. **J~eszahl** f year. **J~eszeit** f season. **J~gang** m year; (Wein) vintage. **J~hundert** nt century. **J~hundertfeier** f centenary. (Amer) centennial

jährlich a annual, yearly □adv annually, yearly

Jahr|markt m fair. **J~tausend** nt millenium. **J~zehnt** nt -[e]s,-e decade

Jähzorn m violent temper. **j~ig** a hot-tempered

Jalousie /ʒalu'zi:/ f -,-n venetian blind

Jammer m -s misery; (Klagen) lamenting; **es ist ein J~** it is a shame

jämmerlich a miserable, adv -bly; (mitleiderregend) pitiful, adv -ly

jammer|n vi (haben) lament □vt **jdn j~n** arouse s.o.'s pity. **j~schade** a **j~schade sein** (fam) be a terrible shame

Jänner m -s,- (Aust) January

Januar m -s,-e January

Jap|an nt -s Japan. **J~aner(in)** m -s,- (f -,-nen) Japanese. **j~anisch** a Japanese. **J~anisch** nt -[s] (Lang) Japanese

Jargon /ʒar'gõ:/ m -s jargon

jäten vt/i (haben) weed

jauchzen vi (haben) (liter) exult

jaulen vi (haben) yelp

Jause f -,-n (Aust) snack

jawohl adv yes

Jawort nt **jdm sein J~ geben** accept s.o.'s proposal [of marriage]

Jazz /jats, dʒɛs/ m - jazz

je adv (jemals) ever; (jeweils) each; (pro) per; **je nach** according to; **seit eh und je** always; **besser denn je** better than ever □conj **je mehr, desto** od **um so besser** the more the better □prep (+ acc) per

Jeans /dʒi:ns/ pl jeans

jed|e(r,s) pron every; (j~ einzelne) each; (j~ beliebige) any; (substantivisch) everyone; each one; anyone; **ohne j~n Grund** without any reason. **j~enfalls** adv in any case; (wenigstens) at least. **j~ermann** pron everyone.

j~erzeit adv at any time. **j~es-mal** adv every time; **j~esmal wenn** whenever

jedoch adv & conj however

jeher adv von od seit j~ always

jemals adv ever

jemand pron someone, somebody; ⟨fragend, verneint⟩ anyone, anybody

jen|e(r,s) pron that; ⟨pl⟩ those; ⟨substantivisch⟩ that one; ⟨pl⟩ those. **j~seits** prep (+gen) [on] the other side of

jetzig a present; ⟨Preis⟩ current

jetzt adv now. **J~zeit** f present

jeweil|ig a respective. **J~s** adv at a time

jiddisch a, **J~** nt [-s] Yiddish

Job /dʒɔp/ m -s,-s job. **j~ben** vi (haben) (fam) work

Joch nt [-e]s,-e yoke

Jockei, Jockey /'dʒɔki/ m -s,-s jockey

Jod nt -[e]s iodine

jodeln vi (haben) yodel

Joga m & nt -[s] yoga

joggen /'dʒɔgən/ vi (haben/sein) jog. **J~ing** nt -[s] jogging

Joghurt m & nt -[s] yoghurt

Johannisbeere f redcurrant; **schwarze J~** blackcurrant

johlen vi (haben) yell; (empört) jeer

Joker m -s,- ⟨Karte⟩ joker

Jolle f -,-n dinghy

Jongl|eur /ʒõ'glø:ɐ/ m -s,-e juggler. **j~ieren** vi (haben) juggle

Joppe f -,-n [thick] jacket

Jordanien /-jən/ nt -s Jordan

Journal|ismus /ʒʊrna'lɪsmʊs/ m - journalism. **J~t(in)** m -en,-en (f -,-nen) journalist

Jubel m -s rejoicing, jubilation. **j~n** vi (haben) rejoice

Jubil|ar(in) m -s,-e (f -,-nen) person celebrating an anniversary. **J~äum** nt -s,-äen jubilee; ⟨Jahrestag⟩ anniversary

juck|en vi (haben) itch; **sich j~en** scratch; **es j~t mich** I have an itch; (fam: möchte) I'm itching (zu tu). **J~reiz** m itch[ing]

Jude m -n,-n Jew. **J~ntum** nt -s Judaism; (Juden) Jewry

Jüd|in f -,-nen Jewess. **j~isch** a Jewish

Judo nt -[s] judo

Jugend f - youth; (junge Leute) young people pl. **J~herberge** f youth hostel. **J~klub** m youth club. **J~kriminalität** f juvenile delinquency. **j~lich** a youthful. **J~liche(r)** m/f young man/woman; (Admin) juvenile. **J~liche** pl young people. **J~stil** m art nouveau. **J~zeit** f youth

Jugoslaw|ien /-jən/ nt -s Yugoslavia. **j~isch** a Yugoslav

Juli m -[s],-s July

jung a (jünger, jüngst) young; ⟨Wein⟩ new. **j~** pron j~ und alt young and old. **J~e** m -n,-n boy. **J~e(s)** nt young animal/bird; (Katzen-) kitten; (Bären-, Löwen-) cub; (Hunde-, Seehund-) pup; die **J~en** the young pl. **j~enhaft** a boyish

Jünger m -s,- disciple

Jungfer f -,-n alte **J~** old maid. **J~nfahrt** f maiden voyage

Jung|frau f virgin; (Astr) Virgo. **j~fräulich** a virginal. **J~geselle** m bachelor

Jüngling m -s,-e youth

jüngst|e(r,s) a youngest; (neueste) latest; in **j~er Zeit** recently

Juni m -[s],-s June

junior a, **J~** m -s,-en /-'o:rən/ junior

Jura pl law sg

Jurist|(in) m -en,-en (f -,-nen) lawyer. **j~isch** a legal, adv -ly

Jury /ʒy'ri:/ f -,-s jury; (Sport) judges pl

justieren vt adjust

Justiz f - die **J~** justice. **J~irr-tum** m miscarriage of justice.

J~minister *m* Minister of Justice
Juwel *nt* -s,-en & (*fig*) -e jewel.
J~ier *m* -s,-e jeweller
Jux *m* -es,-e (*fam*) joke; aus Jux for fun

K

Kabarett *nt* -s,-s & -e cabaret
kabbelig *a* choppy
Kabel *nt* -s,- cable. K~fernsehen *nt* cable television
Kabeljau *m* -s,-e & -s cod
Kabine *f* -,-n cabin; (*Umkleide-*) cubicle; (*Telefon-*) booth; (*einer K~nbahn*) car. K~nbahn *f* cable-car
Kabinett *nt* -s,-e (*Pol*) Cabinet
Kabriolett *nt* -s,-s convertible
Kachel *f* -,-n tile. k~n *vt* tile
Kadaver *m* -s,- carcass
Kadenz *f* -,-en (*Mus*) cadence; (*für Solisten*) cadenza
Kadett *m* -en,-en cadet
Käfer *m* -s,- beetle
Kaff *nt* -s,-s (*fam*) dump
Kaffee /'kafe:, ka'fe:/ *m* -s,-s coffee; (*Mahlzeit*) afternoon coffee. K~grund *m* = K~satz. K~kanne *f* coffee-pot. K~maschine *f* coffee-maker. K~mühle *f* coffee-grinder. K~satz *m* coffee-grounds *pl*
Käfig *m* -s,-e cage
kahl *a* bare; (*haarlos*) bald. k~geschoren *a* shaven. k~köpfig *a* bald-headed
Kahn *m* -s,-e boat; (*Last-*) barge
Kai *m* -s,-s quay
Kaiser *m* -s,- emperor. K~in *f* -,-nen empress. k~lich *a* imperial. K~reich *nt* empire. K~schnitt *m* Caesarean [section]
Kajüte *f* -,-n (*Naut*) cabin
Kakao /ka'kau/ *m* -s cocoa
Kakerlak *m* -s & -en,-en cockroach

Kaktee /kak'te:ə/ *f* -,-n, Kaktus *m* -,-teen /-'te:ən/ cactus
Kalb *nt* -[e]s,-er calf. K~fleisch *nt* veal
Kalender *m* -s,- calendar; (*Taschen-, Termin-*) diary
Kaliber *nt* -s,- calibre; (*Gewehr-*) bore
Kalium *nt* -s potassium
Kalk *m* -[e]s,-e lime; (*Kalzium*) calcium. k~en *vt* whitewash. K~stein *m* limestone
Kalkulation /-'tsio:n/ *f* -,-en calculation. k~ieren *vt/i* (*haben*) calculate
Kalorie *f* -,-n calorie
kalt *a* (kälter, kältest) cold; es ist k~ it is cold; mir ist k~ I am cold. k~blütig *a* cold-blooded, *adv* -ly; (*ruhig*) cool, *adv* -ly
Kälte *f* - cold; (*Gefühls-*) coldness; 10 Grad K~ 10 degrees below zero. K~welle *f* cold spell
kaltherzig *a* cold-hearted. k~schnäuzig *a* (*fam*) cold, *adv* -ly
Kalzium *nt* -s calcium
Kamel *nt* -s,-e camel; (*fam: Idiot*) fool
Kamera *f* -,-s camera
Kamerad(in) *m* -en,-en (*f* -,-nen) companion; (*Freund*) mate; (*Mil, Pol*) comrade. K~schaft *f* - comradeship
Kameramann *m* (*pl* -männer & -leute) cameraman
Kamille *f* - camomile
Kamin *m* -s,-e fireplace; (*SGer: Schornstein*) chimney. K~feger *m* -s,- (*SGer*) chimney-sweep
Kamm *m* -[e]s,-e comb; (*Berg-*) ridge; (*Zool, Wellen-*) crest
kämmen *vt* comb; jdn/sich k~ comb s.o.'s/one's hair
Kammer *f* -,-n small room; (*Techn, Biol, Pol*) chamber. K~diener *m* valet. K~musik *f* chamber music
Kammgarn *nt* (*Tex*) worsted

Kampagne /kam'panjə/ *f* -,-n
(*Pol, Comm*) campaign
Kampf *m* -es,-̈e fight; (*Schlacht*)
battle; (*Wett-*) contest; (*fig*)
struggle; **schwere K~e** heavy
fighting *sg*; **den K~ ansagen**
(+ *dat*) (*fig*) declare war on
kämpf|en *vi* (*haben*) fight; **sich
k~en durch** fight one's way
through. **K~er(in)** *m* -s,- (*f*
-,-nen) fighter
kampf|los *adv* without a fight.
K~richter *m* (*Sport*) judge
kampieren *vi* (*haben*) camp
Kanada *nt* -s Canada
Kanad|ier(in) /-iɐ, -iərɪn/ *m* -s,-
(*f* -,-nen) Canadian. **k~isch**
a Canadian
Kanal *m* -s,-̈e canal; (*Abfluß-*)
drain, sewer; (*Radio, TV*) channel; **der K~ the** [English] Channel
Kanalisation /-'tsjo:n/ *f* - sewer-
age system, drains *pl.* **k~ieren**
vt canalize; (*fig: lenken*) channel
Kanarienvogel /-iən-/ *m* canary
Kanarisch *a* **K~e Inseln**
Canaries
Kandi|dat(in) *m* -en,-en (*f*
-,-nen) candidate. **k~dieren** *vi*
(*haben*) stand (für for)
kandiert *a* candied
Känguruh *nt* -s,-s kangaroo
Kaninchen *nt* -s,- rabbit
Kanister *m* -s,- canister;
(*Benzin-*) can
Kännchen *nt* -s,- [small] jug;
(*Kaffee-*) pot
Kanne *f* -,-n jug; (*Kaffee-, Tee-*) pot;
(*Öl-*) can; (*große Milch-*) churn;
(*Gieß-*) watering-can
Kannibal|e *m* -n,-n cannibal.
K~ismus *m* - cannibalism
Kanon *m* -s,-s canon; (*Lied*)
round
Kanone *f* -,-n cannon, gun; (*fig:
Könner*) ace
kanonisieren *vt* canonize
Kantate *f* -,-n cantata

Kante *f* -,-n edge; **auf die hohe
K~ legen** (*fam*) put by
Kanten *m* -s,- crust [of bread]
Kanter *m* -s,- canter
kantig *a* angular
Kantine *f* -,-n canteen
Kanton *m* -s,-e (*Swiss*) canton
Kantor *m* -s,-en /-'to:rən/ choir-
master and organist
Kanu *nt* -s,-s canoe
Kanzel *f* -,-n pulpit; (*Aviat*) cock-
pit
Kanzleistil *m* officialese
Kanzler *m* -s,- chancellor
Kap *nt* -s,-s (*Geog*) cape
Kapazität *f* -,-en capacity; (*Ex-
perte*) authority
Kapelle *f* -,-n chapel; (*Mus*) band
Kaper *f* -,-n (*Culin*) caper
kapern *vt* (*Naut*) seize
kapieren *vt* (*fam*) understand,
(*fam*) get
Kapital *nt* -s capital; **K~ schla-
gen aus** (*fig*) capitalize on.
K~ismus *m* - capitalism. **K~ist**
m -en,-en capitalist. **k~istisch** *a*
capitalist
Kapitän *m* -s,-e captain
Kapitel *nt* -s,- chapter
Kapitulation /-'tsjo:n/ *f* - capit-
ulation. **k~ieren** *vi* (*haben*) ca-
pitulate
Kaplan *m* -s,-e curate
Kappe *f* -,-n cap. **k~n** *vt* cut
Kapsel *f* -,-n capsule; (*Flaschen-*)
top
kaputt *a* (*fam*) broken; (*zerrissen*) torn; (*defekt*) out of order;
(*ruiniert*) ruined; (*erschöpft*)
worn out. **k~gehen** *vi sep*
(*sein*) (*fam*) break; (*zerreißen*)
tear; (*defekt werden*) pack up;
(*Ehe, Freundschaft*) break up.
k~lachen (sich) *vr sep* (*fam*)
be in stitches. **k~machen** *vt sep*
(*fam*) break; (*zerreißen*) tear; (*defekt machen*) put out of order;
(*erschöpfen*) wear out; **sich
k~machen** wear oneself out

Kapuze f -,-n hood

Kapuzinerkresse f nasturtium

Karaffe f -,-n carafe; (mit Stöpsel) decanter

Karambolage /karambo'la:ʒə/ f -,-n collision

Karamel m -s caramel. **K~bonbon** m & nt ≈ toffee

Karat nt -[e]s,-e carat

Karawane f -,-n caravan

Kardinal m -s,-e cardinal. **K~zahl** f cardinal number

Karfiol m -s (Aust) cauliflower

Karfreitag m Good Friday

karg a (kärger, kärgst) meagre; (frugal) frugal; (spärlich) sparse; (unfruchtbar) barren; (gering) scant. **k~en** vi (haben) be sparing (mit with)

kärglich a poor, meagre; (gering) scant

Karibik f - Caribbean

kariert a check[ed]; ⟨Papier⟩ squared; schottisch k~ tartan

Karik|atur f -,-en caricature; (Journ) cartoon. **k~ieren** vt caricature

karitativ a charitable

Karneval m -s,-e & -s carnival

Karnickel nt -s,- (dial) rabbit

Kärnten nt -s Carinthia

Karo nt -s,- (Raute) diamond; (Viereck) square; (Muster) check; (Kartenspiel) diamonds pl. **K~muster** nt check

Karosserie f -,-n bodywork

Karotte f -,-n carrot

Karpfen m -s,- carp

Karre f -,-n = **Karren**

Karree nt -s,-s square; ums K~ round the block

Karren m -s,- cart; (Hand-) barrow. **k~** vt cart

Karriere /ka'rje:rə/ f -,-n career; **K~ machen** get to the top

Karte f -,-n card; (Eintritts-, Fahr-) ticket; (Speise-) menu; (Land-) map

Kartei f -,-en card index. **K~karte** f index card

Karten|spiel nt card-game; (Spielkarten) pack/(Amer) deck of cards. **K~vorverkauf** m advance booking

Kartoffel f -,-n potato. **K~brei** m, **K~püree** nt mashed potatoes pl. **K~salat** m potato salad

Karton /kar'tɔŋ/ m -s,-s cardboard; (Schachtel) carton, cardboard box

Karussell nt -s,-e & -s roundabout

Karwoche f Holy Week

Käse m -s,- cheese. **K~kuchen** m cheesecake

Kaserne f -,-n barracks pl

Kasino nt -s,-s casino

Kasperle nt & m -s,- Punch. **K~theater** nt Punch and Judy show

Kasse f -,-n till; (Registrier-) cash register; (Zahlstelle) cash desk; (im Supermarkt) check-out; (Theater-) box-office; (Geld) pool [of money], (fam) kitty; (Kranken-) health insurance scheme; (Spar-) savings bank; **knapp/gut bei K~ sein** (fam) be short of cash/be flush. **K~npatient** m ≈ NHS patient. **K~nschlager** m box-office hit. **K~nwart** m -[e]s,-e treasurer. **K~nzettel** m receipt

Kasserolle f -,-n saucepan [with one handle]

Kassette f -,-n cassette; (Film-, Farbband-) cartridge; (Schmuck-) case; (Geld-) money-box. **K~nrecorder** /-rəkɔrdə/ m -s,- cassette recorder

kassier|en vi (haben) collect the money (im Bus) than collect the fares □ vt collect. **K~er(in)** m -s,- (f -,-nen) cashier

Kastagnetten /kastan'jɛtən/ pl castanets

Kastanie /kas'ta:nịə/ f -,-n [horse] chestnut, (fam) conker. **k~n-braun** a chestnut

Kaste f -,-n caste

Kasten m -s,⁼ box; (Brot-) bin; (Flaschen-) crate; (Brief-) letter-box; (Aust: Schrank) cupboard; (Kleider-) wardrobe

kastrieren vt castrate; neuter (Tier)

Kasus m -,- /-u:s/ (Gram) case.

Katalog m -[e]s,-e catalogue. **k~isieren** vt catalogue

Katalysator m -s,-en /-'to:rən/ catalyst; (Auto) catalytic converter

Katapult nt -[e]s,-e catapult. **k~ieren** vt catapult

Katarrh m -s,-e catarrh

katastrophal a catastrophic. **K~ophe** f -,-n catastrophe

Katechismus m - catechism

Kategorie f -,-n category. **k~o-risch** a categorical, adv -ly

Kater m -s,- tom-cat; (fam: Katzenjammer) hangover

Kathedrale f -,-n cathedral

Kathedrale f -,-n cathedral

Kath|olik(in) m -en,-en (f -,-nen) Catholic. **k~olisch** a Catholic. **K~olizismus** m - Catholicism

Kätzchen nt -s,- kitten; (Bot) cat-kin

Katze f -,-n cat. **K~njammer** m (fam) hangover. **K~nsprung** m ein K~nsprung (fam) a stone's throw

Kauderwelsch nt -[s] gibberish

kauen vt/i (haben) chew; bite (Nägel)

kauern vi (haben) crouch; sich **k~** crouch down

Kauf m -[e]s, Käufe purchase; guter K~ bargain; in K~ nehmen (fig) put up with. **k~en** vt/i (haben) buy; **k~en bei** shop at

Käufer(in) m -s,- (f -,-nen) buyer; (im Geschäft) shopper

Kauf|haus nt department store. **K~kraft** f purchasing power. **k~laden** m shop

käuflich a saleable; (bestechlich) corruptible; **k~ sein** be for sale; **k~ erwerben** buy

Kauf|mann m (pl -leute) businessman; (Händler) dealer; (dial) grocer. **k~männisch** a commercial. **K~preis** m purchase price

Kaugummi m chewing-gum

Kaulquappe f -,-n tadpole

kaum adv hardly; **k~ glaublich** od zu glauben hard to believe

kauterisieren vt cauterize

Kaution /-'tsịo:n/ f -,-en surety; (Jur) bail; (Miet-) deposit

Kautschuk m -s rubber

Kauz m -es, Käuze owl; **komischer K~** (fam) odd fellow

Kavalier -s,-e gentleman

Kavallerie f - cavalry

Kaviar m -s caviare

keck a bold; (frech) cheeky

Kegel m -s,- skittle; (Geom) cone; **mit Kind und K~** (fam) with all the family. **K~bahn** f skittle-alley. **k~förmig** a conical. **k~n** vi (haben) play skittles

Kehle f -,-n throat; **aus voller K~e** at the top of one's voice; **etw in die falsche K~e bekommen** (fam) take sth the wrong way. **K~kopf** m larynx. **K~kopf-entzündung** f laryngitis

Kehre f -,-n (hairpin) bend. **k~en** vi (haben) (fegen) sweep □vt sweep; (wenden) turn; **den Rücken k~en** turn one's back (dat on); sich k~en an (+ acc) not care about. **K~icht** m -[e]s sweepings pl. **K~reim** m refrain. **K~seite** f (fig) drawback; **die K~seite der Medaille** the other side of the coin. **k~tmachen** vi *sep (haben)* turn back; *(sich um-drehen)* turn round. **K~twen-dung** *f* about-turn; *(fig)* U-turn

keifen *vi (haben)* scold

Keil *m* -[e]s,-e wedge

Keile *f* - *(fam)* hiding. **k~n (sich)** *vr (fam)* fight. **K~rei** *f* -,-en *(fam)* punch-up

Keil|kissen *nt* [wedge-shaped] bolster. **K~riemen** *m* fan belt

Keim *m* -[e]s,-e *(Bot)* sprout; *(Med)* germ; **im K~ ersticken** *(fig)* nip in the bud. **k~en** *vi (haben)* germinate; *(austreiben)* sprout. **k~frei** *a* sterile

kein *pron* no; not a; **auf k~en Fall** on no account; **k~e fünf Minuten** less than five minutes. **k~e(r,s)** *pron* no one, nobody; *(Ding)* none, not one. **k~esfalls** *adv* on no account. **k~eswegs** *adv* by no means. **k~mal** *adv* not once. **k~s** *pron* none, not one

Keks *m* -[es],-[e] biscuit, *(Amer)* cookie

Kelch *m* -[e]s,-e goblet, cup; *(Relig)* chalice; *(Bot)* calyx

Kelle *f* -,-n ladle; *(Maurer-, Pflanz-)* trowel

Keller *m* -s,- cellar. **K~ei** *f* -,-en winery. **K~geschoß** *nt* cellar; *(bewohnbar)* basement. **K~wohnung** *f* basement flat

Kellner *m* -s,- waiter. **K~in** *f* -,-nen waitress

keltern *vt* press

keltisch *a* Celtic

Kenia *nt* -s Kenya

kennen| *vt* know. **k~enlernen** *vt sep* get to know; *(treffen)* meet; **sich k~enlernen** meet; *(näher)* get to know one another. **K~er** *m* -s,-, **K~erin** *f* -,-nen connois-seur; *(Experte)* expert. **k~melo-die** *f* signature tune. **k~tlich** *a* recognizable; **k~tlich machen** mark. **K~tnis** *f* -,-se knowledge; **zur K~tnis nehmen** take note of; **in K~tnis setzen** inform

(von of). **K~wort** *nt* (*pl* -wörter) reference; *(geheimes)* password. **K~zeichen** *nt* dis-tinguishing mark or feature; *(Merkmal)* characteristic; *(Mar-kierung)* mark, marking; *(Abzei-chen)* badge; *(Auto)* registration. **k~zeichnen** *vt* distinguish; *(markieren)* mark. **k~zeich-nend** *a* typical *(für* of). **K~ziffer** *f* reference number

kentern *vi (sein)* capsize

Keramik *f* -,-en pottery, ceramics *sg*; *(Gegenstand)* piece of pottery

Kerbe *f* -,-n notch

Kerbholz *nt* **etwas auf dem K~ haben** *(fam)* have a record

Kerker *m* -s,- dungeon; *(Gefäng-nis)* prison

Kerl *m* -s,-e *(fam)* fellow, bloke

Kern *m* -s,-e pip; *(Kirsch-)* stone; *(Nuß-)* kernel; *(Techn)* core; *(Atom-, Zell- & fig)* nucleus; *(Stadt-)* centre; *(einer Sache)* heart. **K~energie** *f* nuclear energy. **K~gehäuse** *nt* core. **k~gesund** *a* perfectly healthy. **k~ig** *a* robust; *⟨Ausspruch⟩* pithy. **k~los** *a* seedless. **K~physik** *f* nuclear physics *sg*

Kerze *f* -,-n candle. **K~ngerade** *a & adv* straight. **K~nhalter** *m* -s,- candlestick

keß *a* (kesser, kessest) pert

Kessel *m* -s,- kettle; *(Heiz-)* boiler. **K~stein** *m* fur

Kette *f* -,-n chain; *(Hals-)* neck-lace. **k~n** *vt* chain (an + *acc* to). **K~nladen** *m* chain store. **K~nraucher** *m* chain-smoker. **K~nreaktion** *f* chain reaction

Ketze|r(in) *m* -s,- (*f* -,-nen) heretic. **K~rei** *f* - heresy

keuchen *vi (haben)* pant. **K~husten** *m* whooping cough

Keule *f* -,-n club; *(Culin)* leg; *(Hühner-)* drumstick

keusch *a* chaste. **K~heit** *f* - chastity

Kfz *abbr s.* Kraftfahrzeug

Khaki *nt* - khaki. **k~farben** *a* khaki

kichern *vi* (haben) giggle

Kiefer[1] *f* -,-n pine[-tree]

Kiefer[2] *m* -s,- jaw

Kiel *m* -s,-e (Naut) keel. **K~wasser** *nt* wake

Kiemen *fpl* gills

Kies *m* -es gravel. **K~el** *m* -s,-, **K~elstein** *m* pebble. **K~grube** *f* gravel pit

Kilo *nt* -s,-[s] kilo. **K~gramm** *nt* kilogram. **K~hertz** *nt* kilohertz. **K~meter** *m* kilometre. **K~meterstand** *m* ≈ mileage. **K~watt** *nt* kilowatt

Kind *nt* -es,-er child; **von K~ auf** from childhood

Kinder|arzt *m,* **K~ärztin** *f* paediatrician. **K~bett** *nt* child's cot. **K~ei** *f* -,-en childish prank. **K~garten** *m* nursery school. **K~gärtnerin** *f* nursery school teacher. **K~geld** *nt* child benefit. **K~gottesdienst** *m* Sunday school. **K~lähmung** *f* polio. **k~leicht** *a* very easy. **K~los** *a* childless. **K~mädchen** *nt* nanny. **k~reich** *a* **k~reiche Familie** large family. **K~reim** *m* nursery rhyme. **K~spiel** *nt* children's game; **das ist ein/kein K~spiel** that is dead easy/ not easy. **K~tagesstätte** *f* day nursery. **K~teller** *m* children's menu. **K~wagen** *m* pram, (Amer) baby carriage. **K~zimmer** *nt* child's/children's room; (für Baby) nursery

Kind|heit *f* - childhood. **k~isch** *a* childish, puerile. **k~lich** *a* childlike

kinetisch *a* kinetic

Kinn *nt* -[e]s,-e chin. **K~lade** *f* jaw

Kino *nt* -s,-s cinema

Kiosk *m* -[e]s,-e kiosk

Kippe *f* -,-n (Müll-) dump; (fam: Zigaretten-) fag-end; **auf der K~ stehen** (fam) be in a precarious position; (unsicher sein) hang in the balance. **k~lig** *a* wobbly. **k~ln** *vi* (haben) wobble. **k~n** *vt* tilt; (schütten) tip (in + acc into) □ *vi* (sein) topple

Kirche *f* -,-n church. **K~enbank** *f* pew. **K~endiener** *m* verger. **K~enlied** *nt* hymn. **K~enschiff** *nt* nave. **K~hof** *m* churchyard. **k~lich** *a* church ... □ *adv* **k~lich getraut werden** be married in church. **K~turm** *m* church tower, steeple. **K~weih** *f* -,-en [village] fair

Kirmes *f* -,-sen = Kirchweih

Kirsche *f* -,-n cherry. **K~wasser** *nt* kirsch

Kissen *nt* -s,- cushion; (Kopf-) pillow

Kiste *f* -,-n crate; (Zigarren-) box

Kitsch *m* -es sentimental rubbish; (Kunst) kitsch. **k~ig** *a* slushy; (Kunst) kitschy

Kitt *m* -s [adhesive] cement; (Fenster-) putty

Kittel *m* -s,- overall, smock; (Arzt-, Labor-) white coat

kitten *vt* stick; (fig) cement

Kitz *nt* -es,-e (Zool) kid

Kitz|el *m* -s,- tickle; (Nerven-) thrill. **k~eln** *vt/i* (haben) tickle. **k~lig** *a* ticklish

Kladde *f* -,-n notebook

klaffen *vi* (haben) gape

kläffen *vi* (haben) yap

Klage *f* -,-n lament; (Beschwerde) complaint; (Jur) action. **k~n** *vi* (haben) lament; (sich beklagen) complain; (Jur) sue

Kläger(in) *m* -s,- (f -,-nen) (Jur) plaintiff

kläglich *a* pitiful, adv -ly; (erbärmlich) miserable, adv -bly

klamm *a* cold and damp; (steif) stiff. **K~** *f* -,-en (Geog) gorge

Klammer f -,-n (*Wäsche-*) peg; (*Büro-*) paper-clip; (*Heft-*) staple; (*Haar-*) grip; (*für Zähne*) brace; (*Techn*) clamp; (*Typ*) bracket. **k~n (sich)** vr cling (**an**+*acc* to)

Klang m -[e]s,⁻e sound; (*K~farbe*) tone. **k~voll** a resonant; ⟨*Stimme*⟩ sonorous

Klapp|bett nt folding bed. **K~e** f -,-n flap; (*fam: Mund*) trap. **k~en** vt fold; (*hoch-*) tip up □vi (*haben*) (*fam*) work out. **K~entext** m blurb

Klapper f -,-n rattle. **k~n** vi (*haben*) rattle. **K~schlange** rattlesnake

klapp|rig a rickety; (*schwach*) decrepit. **K~stuhl** m folding chair. **K~tisch** m folding table

Klaps m -es,-e pat; (*strafend*) smack. **k~en** vt smack

klar a clear; **sich** (*dat*) **k~ od im k~en sein** realize □*adv* clearly; (*fam: natürlich*) of course. **K~e(r)** m (*fam*) schnapps

klären vt clarify; **sich k~** clear; (*fig: sich lösen*) resolve itself

Klarheit f - clarity

Klarinette f -,-n clarinet

klar|machen vt sep make clear (*dat* to); **sich** (*dat*) **etw k~machen** understand sth. **K~sichtfolie** f transparent(*haftend*) cling film. **k~stellen** vt sep clarify

Klärung f - clarification

klarwerden† vi sep (*sein*) (*fig*) become clear (*dat* to); **sich** (*dat*) **k~** make up one's mind; (*erkennen*) realize

Klasse f -,-n class; (*Sch*) class, form, (*Amer*) grade; (*Zimmer*) classroom; **erster/zweiter K~** first/second class. **k~** inv a (*fam*) super. **K~narbeit** f [written] test. **K~nbuch** nt ≈ register. **K~nkamerad(in)** m(*f*) class-mate. **K~nkampf** m class

struggle. **K~nzimmer** nt classroom

klassifizier|en vt classify. **K~ung** f -,-en classification

Klass|ik f - classicism; (*Epoche*) classical period. **K~iker** m -s,-, classical author(*Mus*) composer. **k~isch** a classical; (*mustergültig, typisch*) classic

Klatsch m -[e]s gossip. **K~base** f (*fam*) gossip. **k~en** vt slap; Beifall **k~en** applaud □vi (*haben*) make a slapping sound; (*im Wasser*) splash; (*tratschen*) gossip; (*applaudieren*) clap; [**in die Hände**] **k~en** clap one's hands □vi (*haben/sein*) slap (*gegen* against). **K~maul** nt gossip. **k~naß** a (*fam*) soaking wet

klauben vt pick

Klaue f -,-n claw; (*fam: Schrift*) scrawl. **k~n** vt/i (*haben*) (*fam*) steal

Klausel f -,-n clause

Klaustrophobie f - claustrophobia

Klausur f -,-en (*Univ*) [examination] paper; (*Sch*) written test

Klaviatur f -,-en keyboard

Klavier nt -s,-e piano. **K~spieler(in)** m(*f*) pianist

kleb|en vt stick/(*mit Klebstoff*) glue (**an**+*acc* to) □vi (*haben*) stick (**an**+*dat* to). **k~rig** a sticky. **K~stoff** m adhesive, glue. **K~streifen** m adhesive tape

kleckern vi (*haben*) (*fam*) = **klecksen**

Klecks m -es,-e stain; (*Tinten-*) blot; (*kleine Menge*) dab. **k~en** vi (*haben*) make a mess

Klee m -s clover. **K~blatt** nt clover leaf

Kleid nt -[e]s,-er dress; **K~er** dresses; (*Kleidung*) clothes. **k~en** vt dress; (*gut stehen*) suit; **sich k~en** dress. **K~erbügel** m coat-hanger. **K~erbürste** f clothes-brush. **K~erhaken** *m* coat-hook. **K~errock** *m* pinafore dress. **K~erschrank** *m* wardrobe, (*Amer*) clothes closet. **k~sam** *a* becoming. **K~ung** *f* clothes *pl*, clothing. **K~ungsstück** *nt* garment

Kleie *f* - bran

klein *a* small, little; (*von kleinem Wuchs*) short; **von k~ auf** from childhood. **K~arbeit** *f* painstaking work. **K~bus** *m* minibus. **K~e(r,s)** *m/f/nt* little one. **K~geld** *nt* [small] change. **k~hacken** *vt sep* chop up small. **K~handel** *m* retail trade. **K~heit** *f* - smallness; (*Wuchs*) short stature. **K~holz** *nt* firewood. **K~igkeit** *f* -,-en trifle; (*Mahl*) snack. **K~kind** *nt* infant. **K~kram** *m* (*fam*) odds and ends *pl*; (*Angelegenheiten*) trivia *pl*. **k~laut** *a* subdued. **k~lich** *a* petty. **K~lichkeit** *f* - pettiness. **k~mütig** *a* faint-hearted

Kleinod *nt* -[e]s,-e jewel

klein|schneiden† *vt sep* cut into small pieces. **K~stadt** *f* small town. **k~städtisch** *a* provincial. **K~wagen** *m* small car

Kleister *m* -s paste. **k~n** *vt* paste

Klemme *f* -,-n [hair~]grip; **in der K~ sitzen** (*fam*) be in a fix. **k~n** *vt* jam; **sich** (*dat*) **den Finger k~n** get one's finger caught □ *vi* (*haben*) jam, stick

Klempner *m* -s, - plumber

Klerus (*der*) - the clergy

Klette *f* -,-n burr; **wie eine K~** (*fig*) like a limpet

klettern *vi* (*sein*) climb. **K~pflanze** *f* climber. **K~rose** *f* climbing rose

Klettverschluß *m* Velcro (P) fastening

klicken *vi* (*haben*) click

Klient(in) /kli'ɛnt(ɪn)/ *m* -en,-en (*f* -,-nen) (*Jur*) client

Kliff *nt* -[e]s,-e cliff

Klima *nt* -s climate. **K~anlage** *f* air-conditioning

klimatisch *a* climatic. **k~isiert** *a* air-conditioned

klimpern *vi* (*haben*) jingle; **k~ auf** (+*dat*) tinkle on ⟨*Klavier*⟩; strum ⟨*Gitarre*⟩

Klinge *f* -,-n blade

Klingel *f* -,-n bell. **k~n** *vi* (*haben*) ring; **es k~t** there's a ring at the door

klingen† *vi* (*haben*) sound

Klinik *f* -,-en clinic. **k~sch** *a* clinical, *adv* -ly

Klinke *f* -,-n [door] handle

klipp *pred a* **k~ und klar** quite plain, *adv* -ly

Klipp *m* -s,-s = **Klips**

Klippe *f* -,-n [submerged] rock

Klips *m* -es,-e clip; (*Ohr~*) clip-on ear-ring

klirren *vi* (*haben*) rattle; ⟨*Geschirr, Glas:*⟩ chink

Klischee *nt* -s,-s cliché

Klo *nt* -s,-s (*fam*) loo, (*Amer*) john

klobig *a* clumsy

klönen *vi* (*haben*) (*NGer fam*) chat

klopf|en *vi* (*haben*) knock; (*leicht*) tap; ⟨*Herz:*⟩ pound; **es k~te** there was a knock at the door □ *vt* beat; (*ein-*) knock

Klops *m* -es,-e meatball; (*Brat~*) rissole

Klosett *nt* -s,-s lavatory

Kloß *m* -es,ꞏe dumpling; **ein K~ im Hals** (*fam*) a lump in one's throat

Kloster *nt* -s,ꞏ monastery; (*Nonnen-*) convent

klösterlich *a* monastic

Klotz *m* -es,ꞏe block

Klub *m* -s,-s club

Kluft[1] *f* -,ꞏe cleft; (*fig: Gegensatz*) gulf

Kluft[2] *f* -,-en outfit; (*Uniform*) uniform

klug *a* (klüger, klügst) intelligent, *adv* -ly; (*schlau*) clever, *adv*

-ly; **nicht k~ werden aus** not understand. **K~heit** f - cleverness

Klump|en m -s,- lump. **k~en** vi (haben) go lumpy. **k~ig** a lumpy

knabbern vt/i (haben) nibble

Knabe m -n,-n boy. **k~nhaft** a boyish

Knäckebrot nt crispbread

knack|en vt/i (haben) crack. **K~s** m -es,-e crack; **einen K~s haben** be cracked/(fam: verrückt sein) crackers

Knall m -[e]s,-e bang. **K~bonbon** m cracker. **k~en** vi (haben) go bang; ⟨Peitsche:⟩ crack □vt (fam: werfen) chuck; **jdm eine k~en** (fam) clout s.o. **k~ig** a (fam) gaudy. **k~rot** a bright red

knapp a ⟨gering⟩ scant; ⟨mangelnd⟩ scarce; ⟨gerade ausreichend⟩ bare; ⟨eng⟩ tight; **ein k~es Pfund** just under a pound. **k~halten†** vt sep (fam) keep short (mit of). **K~heit** f - scarcity

Knarre f -,-n rattle. **k~n** vi (haben) creak

Knast m -[e]s (fam) prison

knattern vi (haben) crackle; ⟨Gewehr:⟩ stutter

Knäuel m & nt -s,- ball

Knauf m -[e]s,Knäufe knob

knauser|ig a (fam) stingy. **k~n** vi (haben) (fam) be stingy

knautschen vt (fam) crumple □ vi (haben) crease

Knebel m -s,- gag. **k~n** vt gag

Knecht m -[e]s,-e farm-hand; (fig) slave. **k~en** vt (fig) enslave. **K~schaft** f - (fig) slavery

kneif|en† vt (vi (haben) pinch; (fam: sich drücken) chicken out. **K~zange** f pincers pl

Kneipe f -,-n (fam) pub, (Amer) bar

knet|en vt knead; ⟨formen⟩ mould. **K~masse** f Plasticine (P)

Knick m -[e]s,-e bend; (im Draht) kink; (Kniff) crease. **k~en** vt bend; ⟨kniffen⟩ fold; **geknickt sein** (fam) be dejected. **k~[e]rig** a (fam) stingy

Knicks m -es,-e curtsy. **k~en** vi (haben) curtsy

Knie nt -s,- /'kni:ə/ knee. **K~bundhose** f knee-breeches pl. **K~kehle** f hollow of the knee

knien /'kni:ən/ vi (haben) kneel □vr **sich k~** kneel [down]

Knie|scheibe f kneecap. **K~strumpf** m knee-length sock

Kniff m -[e]s,-e pinch; (Falte) crease; (fam: Trick) trick. **k~en** vt fold. **k~[e]lig** a (fam) tricky

knipsen vt (lochen) punch; (Phot) photograph □vi (haben) take a photograph/photographs

Knirps m -es,-e (fam) little chap; (P) (Schirm) telescopic umbrella

knirschen vi (haben) grate; ⟨Schnee, Kies:⟩ crunch; **mit den Zähnen k~** grind one's teeth

knistern vi (haben) crackle; ⟨Papier:⟩ rustle

Knitter|falte f crease. **k~frei** a crease-resistant. **k~n** vi (haben) crease

knobeln vi (haben) toss (**um** for); (fam: überlegen) puzzle

Knoblauch m -s garlic

Knöchel m -s,- ankle; (Finger-) knuckle

Knochen m -s,- bone. **K~mark** nt bone marrow. **k~trocken** a bone-dry

knochig a bony

Knödel m -s,- (SGer) dumpling

Knolle f -,-n tuber. **k~ig** a bulbous

Knopf m -[e]s,-e button; (Kragen-) stud; (Griff) knob

knöpfen vt button

Knopfloch nt buttonhole

Knorpel m -s gristle; (Anat) cartilage

knorrig a gnarled

Knospe f bud

Knötchen nt -s,- nodule

Knoten m -s,- knot; ⟨Med⟩ lump; ⟨Haar-⟩ bun, chignon. **k~** vt knot. **K~punkt** m junction

knotig a knotty; ⟨Hände⟩ gnarled

knuffen vt poke

knüll|en vt crumple □vi (haben) crease. **K~er** m -s,- (fam) sensation

knüpfen vt knot; ⟨verbinden⟩ attach (**an**+acc to)

Knüppel m -s,- club; ⟨Gummi-⟩ truncheon

knurr|en vi (haben) growl; ⟨Magen:⟩ rumble; ⟨fam: schimpfen⟩ grumble. **k~ig** a grumpy

knusprig a crunchy, crisp

knutschen vi (haben) ⟨fam⟩ smooch

k.o. /ka⁰o:/ a **k.o. schlagen** knock out; **k.o. sein** ⟨fam⟩ be worn out. **K.o.** m -s,-s knock-out

Koalition /koali'tsio:n/ f -,-en coalition

Kobold m -[e]s,-e goblin, imp

Koch m -[e]s,¨e cook; ⟨im Restaurant⟩ chef. **K~buch** nt cookery book, ⟨Amer⟩ cookbook. **k~en** vt cook; ⟨sieden⟩ boil; make ⟨Kaffee, Tee⟩ □vi (haben) cook; ⟨sieden⟩ boil; ⟨fam⟩ seethe (**vor**+dat with). **K~en** nt -s cooking; ⟨Sieden⟩ boiling; **zum K~en bringen/kommen** bring/come to the boil. **k~end** a boiling □adv **k~end heiß** boiling hot. **K~er** m -s,- cooker. **K~gelegenheit** f cooking facilities pl. **K~herd** m cooker, stove

Köchin f -,-nen [woman] cook

Kochkunst f cookery. **K~löffel** m wooden spoon. **K~nische** f kitchenette. **K~platte** f hot-plate. **K~topf** m saucepan

Kode /ko:t/ m -s,-s code

Köder m -s,- bait

Koexist|enz /'ko:ʔeksɪstɛnts/ f co-existence. **k~ieren** vi (haben) coexist

Koffein /kɔfe'i:n/ nt -s caffeine. **k~frei** a decaffeinated

Koffer m -s,- suitcase. **K~kuli** m luggage trolley. **K~radio** nt portable radio. **K~raum** m ⟨Auto⟩ boot, ⟨Amer⟩ trunk

Kognak /'kɔnjak/ m -s,-s brandy

Kohl m -[e]s cabbage

Kohle f -,-n coal. **K~[n]hydrat** nt -[e]s,-e carbohydrate. **K~n-bergwerk** nt coal-mine, colliery. **K~ndioxyd** nt carbon dioxide. **K~ngrube** f = **K~nbergwerk**. **K~nherd** m [kitchen] range. **K~nsäure** f carbon dioxide. **K~nstoff** m carbon. **K~papier** nt carbon paper

Kohl|kopf m cabbage. **K~rabi** m -[s],-[s] kohlrabi. **K~rübe** f swede

Koje f -,-n ⟨Naut⟩ bunk

Kokain /koka'i:n/ nt -s cocaine

kokett a flirtatious. **k~ieren** vi (haben) flirt

Kokon /ko'kõ:/ m -s,-s cocoon

Kokosnuß f coconut

Koks m -es coke

Kolben m -s,- ⟨Gewehr-⟩ butt; ⟨Mais-⟩ cob; ⟨Techn⟩ piston; ⟨Chem⟩ flask

Kolibri m -s,-s humming-bird

Kolik f -,-en colic

Kollabora|teur /-'tø:ɐ̯/ m -s,-e collaborator. **K~tion** /-'tsio:n/ f collaboration

Kolleg nt -s,-s & -ien /-jən/ ⟨Univ⟩ course of lectures

Kolleg|e m -n,-n, **K~in** f -,-nen colleague. **K~ium** nt -s,-ien staff

Kollek|te f -,-n ⟨Relig⟩ collection. **K~tion** /-'tsio:n/ f -,-en collection. **K~tiv** a collective. **K~ti-vum** nt -s,-va collective noun

kolli|dieren vi (sein) collide. **K~sion** f -,-en collision

Köln nt -s Cologne. **K~isch-wasser**, **K~isch Wasser** nt eau-de-Cologne

Kolonialwaren fpl groceries

Kolonie f -,-n colony. **k~isieren** vt colonize

Kolonne f -,-n column; (Mil) convoy

Koloß m -sses,-sse giant

kolossal a enormous, adv -ly

Kolumne f -,-n (Journ) column

Koma nt -s,-s coma

Kombi m -s,-s = **K~wagen**. **K~nation** /-'tsjo:n/ f -,-en combination; (Folgerung) deduction; (Kleidung) co-ordinating outfit. **k~nieren** vt combine; (fig) reason; (folgern) deduce. **K~wagen** m estate car, (Amer) station-wagon

Kombüse f -,-n (Naut) galley

Komet m -en,-en comet. **k~enhaft** a (fig) meteoric

Komfort /kɔm'fo:g/ m -s comfort; (Luxus) luxury. **k~abel** /-'ta:bl/ a comfortable, adv -bly; (luxuriös) luxurious, adv -ly

Komik f - humour. **K~er** m -s, comic, comedian

komisch a funny; (Oper) comic; (sonderbar) odd, funny □ adv funnily; oddly. **k~erweise** adv funnily enough

Komitee nt -s,-s committee

Komma nt -s,-s & -ta comma; (Dezimal-) decimal point; **drei K~fünf** three point five

Kommandant m -en,-en commanding officer. **K~deur** /-'dø:g/ m -s commander. **k~dieren** vt command; (befehlen) order; (fam: herum-) order about □ vi (haben) give the orders

Kommando nt -s,-s order; (Befehlsgewalt) command; (Einheit) detachment. **K~brücke** f bridge

kommen vi (sein) come; (eintreffen) arrive; (gelangen) get (nach to); **k~lassen** send for; **auf/**

hinter etw (acc) **k~** think of/find out about sth; **um/zu etw k~** lose/acquire sth; **wieder zu sich k~** come round; **wie kommt das?** why is that? **K~** nt -s coming; **K~und Gehen** coming and going. **k~d** a coming; **k~den Montag** next Monday

Kommentar m -s,-e commentary; (Bemerkung) comment. **K~tator** m -s,-en /-'to:rən/ commentator. **k~tieren** vt comment on

kommerzialisieren vt commercialize. **k~ziell** a commercial, adv -ly

Kommilitone m -n,-n, **K~tonin** f -,-nen fellow student

Kommiß m -sses (fam) army

Kommissar m -s,-e commissioner; (Polizei-) superintendent

Kommission f -,-en commission; (Gremium) committee

Kommode f -,-n chest of drawers

Kommunalwahlen fpl local elections

Kommunikation /-'tsjo:n/ f -,-en communication

Kommunion f -,-en [Holy] Communion

Kommuniqué /kɔmyni'ke:/ nt -s,-s communiqué

Kommunismus m -s Communism. **K~ist(in)** m -en,-en (f -,-nen) Communist. **k~istisch** a Communist

kommunizieren vi (haben) receive [Holy] Communion

Komödie /ko'mø:dja/ f -,-n comedy

Kompagnon /'kɔmpanjõ/ m -s,-s (Comm) partner

kompakt a compact. **K~schallplatte** f compact disc

Kompanie f -,-n (Mil) company

Komparativ m -s,-e comparative

Komparse m -n,-n (Theat) extra

Kompaß m -sses,-sse compass

kompatibel a compatible

kompeten|t a competent. **K~z** f -,-en competence

komplett a complete, adv -ly

Komplex m -es,-e complex. **k~** a complex

Komplikation /-'tsio:n/ f -,-en complication

Kompliment nt -[es]s,-e compliment

Komplize m -n,-n accomplice

komplizier|en vt complicate. **k~t** a complicated

Komplott nt -[e]s,-e plot

kompo|nieren vt/i (haben) compose. **K~nist** m -en,-en composer. **K~sition** /-'tsio:n/ f -,-en composition

Kompositum nt -s,-ta compound

Kompost m -[e]s compost

Kompott nt -[e]s,-e stewed fruit

Kompresse f -,-n compress

komprimieren vt compress

Kompromiß m -sses,-sse compromise; **einen K~ schließen** compromise. **k~los** a uncompromising

kompromittieren vt compromise

Kondensation /-'tsio:n/ f - condensation. **k~sieren** vt condense

Kondensmilch f evaporated/(gesüßt) condensed milk

Kondition /-'tsio:n/ f - (Sport) fitness; **in K~** in form. **K~al** m -s,-e (Gram) conditional

Konditor m -s,-en /-'to:rən/ confectioner. **K~ei** f -,-en patisserie

Kondo|lenzbrief m letter of condolence. **k~lieren** vi (haben) express one's condolences

Kondom nt & m -s,-e condom

Konfekt nt -[e]s confectionery; (Pralinen) chocolates pl

Konfektion /-'tsio:n/ f - ready-to-wear clothes pl

Konferenz f -,-en conference; (Besprechung) meeting

Konfession f -,-en [religious] denomination. **k~ell** a denominational. **k~slos** a non-denominational

Konfetti nt -s confetti

Konfirm|and(in) m -en,-en (f -,-nen) candidate for confirmation. **K~ation** /-'tsio:n/ f -,-en (Relig) confirmation. **k~ieren** vt (Relig) confirm

Konfitüre f -,-n jam

Konflikt m -[e]s,-e conflict

Konföderation /-'tsio:n/ f confederation

Konfront|ation /-'tsio:n/ f -,-en confrontation. **k~ieren** vt confront

konfus a confused

Kongreß m -sses,-sse congress

König m -s,-e king. **K~in** f -,-nen queen. **k~lich** a royal, adv -ly; (hoheitsvoll) regal, adv -ly; (großzügig) handsome, adv -ly; (fam: groß) tremendous, adv -ly. **K~reich** nt kingdom

konisch a conical

Konjugation /-'tsio:n/ f -,-en conjugation. **k~ieren** vt conjugate

Konjunktion /-'tsio:n/ f -,-en (Gram) conjunction

Konjunktiv m -s,-e subjunctive

Konjunktur f - economic situation; (Hoch-) boom

konkav a concave

konkret a concrete

Konkurren|t(in) m -en,-en (f -,-nen) competitor, rival. **K~z** f - competition; **jdm K~z machen** compete with s.o. **k~zfähig** a (Comm) competitive. **K~zkampf** m competition, rivalry

konkurrieren vi (haben) compete

Konkurs m -es,-e bankruptcy; **K~ machen** go bankrupt

können† vt/i (mod) be able to do sth; (beherrschen) know sth; **k~ Sie Deutsch?** do you know any German? **das**

kann ich nicht I can't do that; **er kann nicht mehr** he can't go on; **für etw nichts k~** not be to blame for sth □*v aux lesen/schwimmen* k~ be able to read/swim; **er kann/konnte es tun** he can/could do it; **das kann** *od* **könnte [gut] sein** that may [well] be. **K~** *nt* **-s** ability; (*Wissen*) knowledge

Könner(in) *m* -s,- (*f* -,-nen) expert

konsequen|t *a* consistent, *adv* -ly; (*logisch*) logical, *adv* -ly. **K~z** *f* -,-en consequence

konservativ *a* conservative

Konserv|en *fpl* tinned *or* canned food *sg.* **K~enbüchse, K~endose** *f* tin, can. **k~ieren** *vt* preserve; (*in Dosen*) tin, can. **K~ierungsmittel** *nt* preservative

Konsistenz *f* - consistency

konsolidieren *vt* consolidate

Konsonant *m* -en,-en consonant

konsterniert *a* dismayed

Konstitution /-'tsjo:n/ *f* -,-en constitution. **k~ell** *a* constitutional

konstruieren *vt* construct; (*entwerfen*) design

Konstruk|tion /-'tsjo:n/ *f* -,-en construction; (*Entwurf*) design. **k~tiv** *a* constructive

Konsul *m* -s,-n consul. **K~at** *nt* -[e]s,-e consulate

Konsult|ation /-'tsjo:n/ *f* -,-en consultation. **k~ieren** *vt* consult

Konsum *m* -s consumption. **K~ent** *m* -en,-en consumer. **K~güter** *npl* consumer goods

Kontakt *m* -[e]s,-e contact. **K~linsen** *fpl* contact lenses. **K~person** *f* contact

kontern *vt/i* (*haben*) counter

Kontinent /'kɔn-, kɔnti'nɛnt/ *m* -s,-e continent

Kontingent *nt* -[e]s,-e (*Comm*) quota; (*Mil*) contingent

Kontinuität *f* - continuity

Konto *nt* -s,-s account. **K~auszug** *m* [bank] statement. **K~nummer** *f* account number. **K~stand** *m* [bank] balance

Kontrabaß *m* double-bass

Kontrast *m* -[e]s,-e contrast

Kontroll|abschnitt *m* counterfoil. **K~e** *f*-,-n control; (*Prüfung*) check. **K~eur** /-'lø:ɐ/ *m* -s,-e [ticket] inspector. **k~ieren** *vt* check; inspect (*Fahrkarten*); (*beherrschen*) control

Kontroverse *f* -,-n controversy

Kontur *f* -,-en contour

Konvention /-'tsjo:n/ *f* -,-en convention. **k~ell** *a* conventional, *adv* -ly

Konversation /-'tsjo:n/ *f* -,-en conversation. **K~slexikon** *nt* encyclopaedia

konvert|ieren *vi* (*haben*) (*Relig*) convert. **K~it** *m* -en,-en convert

konvex *a* convex

Konvoi /kɔn'vɔy/ *m* -s,-s convoy

Konzentr|ation /-'tsjo:n/ *f* -,-en concentration. **K~slager** *nt* concentration camp

konzentrieren *vt* concentrate; **sich k~** concentrate (**auf**+ *acc* on)

Konzept *nt* -[e]s,-e [rough] draft; **jdn aus dem K~ bringen** put s.o. off his stroke. **K~papier** *nt* rough paper

Konzern *m* -s,-e (*Comm*) group [of companies]

Konzert *nt* -[e]s,-e concert; (*Klavier-, Geigen-*) concerto. **K~meister** *m* leader, (*Amer*) concertmaster

Konzession *f* -,-en licence; (*Zugeständnis*) concession

Konzil *nt* -s,-e (*Relig*) council

Kooperation /ko'ɔpera'tsjo:n/ *f* co-operation

Koordin|ation /koʊˈɔːdɪnaˈtsjoːn/
f · co-ordination. **k~ieren** *vt* co-
ordinate

Kopf *m* -[e]s,ⁿe head; **ein K~**
Kohl/Salat a cabbage/lettuce;
aus dem K~ from memory; (*aus-*
wendig) by heart; **auf dem K~**
(*verkehrt*) upside down; **K~ an**
K~ neck and neck; (*stehen*)
shoulder to shoulder; **sich** (*dat*)
den K~ waschen wash one's
hair; **sich** (*dat*) **den K~ zerbre-**
chen rack one's brains. **K~ball**
m header. **K~bedeckung** *f*
head-covering

Köpf|chen *nt* -s,- little head;
K~chen haben (*fam*) be clever.
k~en *vt* behead; (*Fußball*) head

Kopf|ende *nt* head. **K~haut** *f*
scalp. **K~hörer** *m* headphones
pl. **K~kissen** *nt* pillow. **K~kis-**
senbezug *m* pillow-case. **k~los**
a panic-stricken. **k~nicken** *nt*
-s nod. **K~rechnen** *nt* mental
arithmetic. **K~salat** *m* lettuce.
K~schmerzen *mpl* headache
sg. **K~schütteln** *nt* -s shake of
the head. **K~sprung** *m* header,
dive. **K~stand** *m* headstand.
K~steinpflaster *nt* cobblestones *pl*. **K~stütze** *f* head-rest.
K~tuch *nt* headscarf. **k~über**
adv head first; (*fig*) headlong.
K~wäsche *f* shampoo. **K~weh**
nt headache. **K~zerbrechen** *nt*
-s **sich** (*dat*) **K~zerbrechen ma-**
chen rack one's brains; (*sich sor-*
gen) worry

Kopie *f* -,-n copy. **k~ren** *vt* copy

Koppel¹ *f* -,-n enclosure; (*Pferde-*)
paddock

Koppel² *nt* -s,- (*Mil*) belt. **k~n** *vt*
couple

Koralle *f* -,-n coral

Korb *m* -[e]s,ⁿe basket; **jdm einen**
K~ geben (*fig*) turn s.o. down.
K~ball *m* [kind of] netball.
K~stuhl *m* wicker chair

Kord *m* -s (*Tex*) corduroy

Kordel *f* -,-n cord

Korinthe *f* -,-n currant

Kork *m* -s cork. **K~en** *m* -s,- cork.
K~enzieher *m* -s,- corkscrew

Korn¹ *nt* -[e]s,ⁿer grain; (*Samen-*)
seed; (*coll: Getreide*) grain, corn;
(*am Visier*) front sight

Korn² *m* -[e]s,- (*fam*) grain
schnapps

Körn|chen *nt* -s,- granule. **k~ig**
a granular

Körper *m* -s,- body; (*Geom*) solid.
K~bau *m* build, physique.
k~behindert *a* physically disabled. **k~lich** *a* physical, *adv* -ly;
(*Strafe*) corporal. **K~pflege** *f*
personal hygiene. **K~puder** *m*
talcum powder. **K~schaft** *f* -,-en
corporation, body. **K~strafe** *f*
corporal punishment. **K~teil** *m*
part of the body

Korps /koːɐ̯/ *nt* -,- /-[s],-s/ corps

korpulent *a* corpulent

korrekt *a* correct, *adv* -ly. **K~or**
m -s,-en /-ˈtoːrən/ proof-reader.
K~ur *f* -,-en correction. **K~ur-**
abzug, K~urbogen *m* proof

Korrespon|dent(in) *m* -en,-en (*f*
-,-nen) correspondent. **K~denz**
f -,-en correspondence. **k~-**
dieren *vi* (*haben*) correspond

Korridor *m* -s,-e corridor

korrigieren *vt* correct

Korrosion *f* - corrosion

korrumpieren *vt* corrupt

korrupt *a* corrupt. **K~tion**
/-ˈtsjoːn/ *f* - corruption

Korsett *nt* -[e]s,-e corset

koscher *a* kosher

Kose|name *m* pet name.
K~wort *nt* (*pl -wörter*) term of
endearment

Kosmet|ik *f* - beauty culture.
K~ika *ntpl* cosmetics. **K~ike-**
rin *f* -,-nen beautician. **k~isch**
a cosmetic; (*Chirurgie*) plastic

kosm|isch a cosmic. **K~o-naut(in)** m -en, -en (f -, -nen) cosmonaut. **k~opolitisch** a cosmopolitan

Kosmos m - cosmos

Kost f - food; (Ernährung) diet; (Verpflegung) board

kostbar a precious. **K~keit** f -, -en treasure

kosten¹ vt/i (haben) [von] etw **k~** taste sth

kosten² vt cost; (brauchen) take; wieviel kostet es? how much is it? **K~** pl expense sg, cost sg; (Jur) costs; **auf meine K~** at my expense. **K~[vor]anschlag** m estimate. **k~los** a free □ adv free [of charge]

Kosthappen m taste

köstlich a delicious; (entzückend) delightful. **K~keit** f -, -en (fig) gem; (Culin) delicacy

Kost|probe f taste; (fig) sample. **k~spielig** a expensive, costly

Kostüm nt -s, -e (Theat) costume; (Verkleidung) fancy dress; (Schneider-) suit. **K~fest** nt fancy-dress party. **k~iert** a **k~iert sein** be in fancy dress

Kot m -[e]s excrement; (Schmutz) dirt

Kotelett /kɔtˈlɛt/ nt -s, -e chop, cutlet. **K~en** pl sideburns

Köter m -s, - (pej) dog

Kotflügel m (Auto) wing, (Amer) fender

kotzen vi (haben) (sl) throw up; **es ist zum K~** it makes you sick

Krabbe f -, -n crab; (Garnele) shrimp; (rote) prawn

krabbeln vi (haben) (sl) crawl

Krach m -[e]s, -̈e (Techn) din, racket; (Knall) crash; (fam: Streit) row; (fam: Ruin) crash. **k~en** vi (haben) crash; **es hat gekracht** there was a bang/(fam: Unfall) a crash □ (sein) break, crack; (auf-treffen) crash (gegen into)

krächzen vi (haben) croak

Kraft f -, -̈e strength; (Gewalt) force; (Arbeits-) worker; **in/außer K~** in/no longer in force; **in K~ treten** come into force. **k~** prep (+ gen) by virtue of. **K~ausdruck** m swear-word. **K~fahrer** m driver. **K~fahrzeug** nt motor vehicle. **K~fahrzeugbrief** m [vehicle] registration document

kräftig a strong; (gut entwickelt) sturdy; (nahrhaft) nutritious; (heftig) hard □ adv strongly; (heftig) hard. **k~en** vt strengthen

kraft|los a weak. **K~post** f post bus service. **K~probe** f trial of strength. **K~rad** nt motorcycle. **K~stoff** m (Auto) fuel. **k~voll** a strong, powerful. **K~wagen** m motor car. **K~werk** nt power station

Kragen m -s, - collar

Krähe f -, -n crow

krähen vi (haben) crow

krakeln vt/i (haben) scrawl

Kralle f -, -n claw. **k~n (sich)** vr clutch (**an jdn/etw** s.o./sth); (Katze:) dig its claws (**in** + acc into)

Kram m -s (fam) things pl, (fam) stuff; (Angelegenheiten) business; **wertloser K~** junk. **k~en** vi (haben) rummage about (**in** + dat in; **nach** for). **K~laden** m [small] general store

Krampf m -[e]s, -̈e cramp. **K~-adern** fpl varicose veins. **k~haft** a convulsive, adv -ly; (verbissen) desperate, adv -ly

Kran m -[e]s, -̈e (Techn) crane

Kranich m -s, -e (Zool) crane

krank a (kränker, kränkst) sick; (Knie, Herz) bad; **k~ sein/werden/machen** be/fall/make ill; **sich k~ melden** report sick. **K~e(r)** m/f sick man/woman, invalid; **die K~en** the sick pl

kränkeln vi (haben) be in poor health. **k~d** a ailing

kranken vi (haben) (fig) suffer
(an + dat from)

kränken vt offend, hurt

Kranken|bett nt sick-bed.
K~geld nt sickness benefit.
K~gymnast(in) m -en,-en (f
-,-nen) physiotherapist. **K~-
gymnastik** f physiotherapy.
K~haus nt hospital. **K~kasse** f
health insurance scheme/(Amt)
office. **K~pflege** f nursing.
K~pfleger(in) m(f) nurse.
K~saal m [hospital] ward.
K~schein m certificate of en-
titlement to medical treatment.
K~schwester f nurse. **K~ur-
laub** m sick-leave. **K~ver-
sicherung** f health insurance.
K~wagen m ambulance.
K~zimmer nt sick-room

krank|haft a morbid; (patholo-
gisch) pathological. **K~heit** f
-,-en illness, disease

kränk|lich a sickly. **K~ung** f
-,-en slight

Kranz m -es,-̈e wreath; (Ring)
ring

Krapfen m -s,- doughnut

kraß a (krasser, krassest) glaring; (offensichtlich) blatant;
(stark) gross; rank (Außenseiter)

Krater m -s,- crater

krätz|bürstig a (fam) prickly.
k~en vt/i (haben) scratch; sich
k~en scratch oneself/(Tier:) itself. **K~er** m -s,- scratch; (Werkzeug) scraper

Kraul nt -s (Sport) crawl. **k~en**[1]
vi (haben/sein) (Sport) do the
crawl

kraulen[2] vt tickle; **sich am Kopf
k~** scratch one's head

kraus a wrinkled; (Haar) frizzy;
(verworren) muddled; **k~ ziehen**
wrinkle. **K~e** f -,-n frill, ruffle;
(Haar) frizziness

kräuseln vt wrinkle; frizz
(Haar); gather (Stoff); ripple
(Wasser); **sich k~** wrinkle; (sich

kringeln curl; (Haar:) go frizzy;
(Wasser:) ripple

krausen vt wrinkle; frizz (Haar);
gather (Stoff); **sich k~** wrinkle;
(Haar:) go frizzy

Kraut nt -[e]s, Kräuter herb;
(SGer) cabbage; (Sauer-) sauerkraut; **wie K~ und Rüben** (fam)
higgledy-piggledy

Krawall m -s,-e riot; (Lärm) row

Krawatte f -,-n [neck]tie

kraxeln vi (sein) (fam) clamber

krea|tiv /krea'ti:f/ a creative.
K~tur f -,-en creature

Krebs m -es,-e crayfish; (Med)
cancer; (Astr) Cancer. **k~ig** a
cancerous

Kredit m -s,-e credit; (Darlehen)
loan; **auf K~** on credit.
K~karte f credit card

Kreide f -,-n chalk. **k~ebleich** a
deathly pale. **k~ig** a chalky

kreieren /kre'i:rən/ vt create

Kreis m -es,-e circle; (Admin)
district

kreischen vt/i (haben) screech;
(schreien) shriek

Kreisel m -s,- [spinning] top;
(fam: Kreisverkehr) roundabout

kreis|en vi (haben) circle; revolve
(um around). **k~förmig** a circular. **K~lauf** m cycle; (Med) circulation. **k~rund** a circular.
K~säge f circular saw. **K~ver-
kehr** m [traffic] roundabout,
(Amer) traffic circle

Krem f -,-s & m -s,-e cream

Krematorium nt -s,-ien crematorium

Krempe f -,-n [hat] brim

Krempel m -s (fam) junk

krempeln vt turn (nach oben up)

Kren m -[e]s (Aust) horseradish

krepieren vi (sein) explode; (sl:
sterben) die

Krepp m -s,-e & -s crêpe

Kreppapier nt crêpe paper

Kresse f -,-n cress; (Kapuziner-)
nasturtium

Kreta nt -s Crete

Kreuz nt -es,-e cross; (Kreuzung) intersection; (Mus) sharp; (Kartenspiel) clubs pl; (Anat) small of the back; über K~ crosswise; das K~ schlagen cross oneself. k~ adv k~ und quer in all directions. k~en vt cross; sich k~en cross; ⟨Straßen:⟩ intersect; ⟨Meinungen:⟩ clash □vi (haben/sein) cruise; ⟨Segelschiff:⟩ tack. K~er m -s,- cruiser. K~fahrt f (Naut) cruise; (K~zug) crusade. K~feuer nt crossfire. K~gang m cloister

kreuzig|en vt crucify. K~ung f -,-en crucifixion

Kreuz|otter f adder, common viper. K~ung f -,-en intersection; (Straßen-) crossroads sg; (Hybride-) cross. K~verhör nt cross-examination; ins K~verhör nehmen cross-examine. K~weg m crossroads pl; (Relig) Way of the Cross. k~weise adv crosswise. K~worträtsel nt crossword [puzzle]. K~zug m crusade

kribbel|ig a (fam) edgy. k~n vi (haben) tingle; (kitzeln) tickle

kriech|en† vi (sein) crawl; (fig) grovel (vor + dat to). k~erisch a grovelling. K~spur f (Auto) crawler lane. K~tier nt reptile

Krieg m -[e]s,-e war

kriegen vt (fam) get; ein Kind k~ have a baby

Krieger|denkmal nt war memorial. k~isch a warlike; (militärisch) military

kriegs|beschädigt a war-disabled. K~dienstverweigerer m -s,- conscientious objector. K~gefangene(r) m prisoner of war. K~gefangenschaft f captivity. K~gericht nt court martial. K~list f stratagem. K~rat m council of war. K~recht nt

martial law. K~schiff nt warship. K~verbrechen nt war crime

Krimi m -s,-s (fam) crime story/film. K~nalität f - crime; (Vorkommen) crime rate. K~nalpolizei f criminal investigation department. K~nalroman m crime novel. K~nell a criminal. K~nelle(r) m criminal

kringeln (sich) vr curl [up]; (vor Lachen) fall about

Kripo f - = Kriminalpolizei

Krippe f -,-n manger; (Weihnachts-) crib; (Kinder-) crèche

Krise f -,-n crisis

Kristall¹ nt -s (Glas) crystal; (geschliffen) cut glass

Kristall² m -s,-e crystal. k~isieren vi/r (haben) [sich] k~isieren crystallize

Kriterium nt -s,-ien criterion

Kriti|k f -,-en criticism; (Rezension) review; unter aller K~ (fam) abysmal

Kriti|ker m -s,- critic; (Rezensent) reviewer. k~sch a critical, adv -ly. k~sieren vt criticize; review

kritteln vi (haben) find fault (an + acc with)

kritzeln vt/i (haben) scribble

Krokette f -,-n (Culin) croquette

Krokodil nt -s,-e crocodile

Krokus m -,-[se] crocus

Krone f -,-n crown; (Baum-) top

krönen vt crown

Kron|leuchter m chandelier. K~prinz m crown prince

Krönung f -,-en coronation; (fig: Höhepunkt) crowning event/(Leistung) achievement

Kropf m -[e]s,-e (Zool) crop; (Med) goitre

Kröte f -,-n toad

Krücke f -,-n crutch; (Stock-) handle; an K~n on crutches

Krug m -[e]s,-e jug; (Bier-) tankard

Krume f -,-n soft part [of loaf]; (Krümel) crumb; (Acker-) topsoil

Krümel m -s,- crumb. **k~ig** a crumbly. **k~n** vt crumble □vi (haben) be crumbly; ⟨Person:⟩ drop crumbs

krumm a crooked; (gebogen) curved; (verbogen) bent. **k~bei-nig** a bow-legged

krümmen vt bend; crook ⟨Finger⟩; **sich k~** bend; (sich winden) writhe; (vor Schmerzen/ Lachen) double up

krummnehmen† vt sep (fam) take amiss

Krümmung f -,-en bend; (Kurve) curve

Krüppel m -s,- cripple

Kruste f -,-n crust; (Schorf) scab

Kruzifix nt -es,-e crucifix

Krypta /ˈkrypta/ f -,-ten crypt

Kuba nt -s Cuba. **k~anisch** a Cuban

Kübel m -s,- tub; (Eimer) bucket; (Techn) skip

Kubik- pref cubic. **K~meter** m & nt cubic metre

Küche f -,-n kitchen; (Kochkunst) cooking; **kalte/warme K~** cold/ hot food; **französische K~** French cuisine

Kuchen m -s,- cake

Küchen|herd m cooker, stove. **K~maschine** f food processor, mixer. **K~schabe** f -,-n cock-roach. **K~zettel** m menu

Kuckuck m -s,-e cuckoo; **zum K~!** (fam) hang it! **K~suhr** f cuckoo clock

Kufe f -,-n [sledge] runner

Kugel f -,-n ball; (Geom) sphere; (Gewehr-) bullet; (Sport) shot. **k~förmig** a spherical. **K~-lager** nt ball-bearing. **k~n** vt/i (haben) roll; **sich k~n** roll/ (vor Lachen) fall about. **k~rund** a spherical; (fam: dick) tubby. **K~schreiber** m ballpoint

[pen]. **k~sicher** a bullet-proof.

K~stoßen nt -s shot-putting

Kuh f -,̈e cow

kühl a cool, adv -ly; (kalt) chilly. **K~box** f -,-en cool-box. **K~e** f - coolness; chilliness. **k~en** vt cool; refrigerate ⟨Lebensmittel⟩; chill ⟨Wein⟩. **K~er** m -s,- ice-bucket; (Auto) radiator. **K~er-haube** f bonnet, (Amer) hood. **K~fach** nt frozen-food compart-ment. **K~raum** m cold store. **K~schrank** m refrigerator. **K~truhe** f freezer. **K~ung** f - cooling; (Frische) coolness. **K~wasser** nt [radiator] water

Kuhmilch f cow's milk

kühn a bold, adv -ly; (wagemutig) daring. **K~heit** f - boldness

Kuhstall m cowshed

Küken nt -s,- chick; (Enten-) duckling

Kukuruz m -[es] (Aust) maize

kulant a obliging

Kuli m -s,-s (fam: Kugelschreiber) ballpoint [pen], Biro (P)

kulinarisch a culinary

Kulissen fpl (Theat) scenery sg; (seitlich) wings; **hinter den K~** (fig) behind the scenes

kullern vt/i (sein) (fam) roll

Kult m -[e]s,-e cult

kultivier|en vt cultivate. **k~t** a cultured

Kultur f -,-en culture; **K~en** plantations. **K~beutel** m toilet-bag. **k~ell** a cultural. **K~film** m documentary film

Kultusminister m Minister of Education and Arts

Kümmel m -s caraway; (Getränk) kümmel

Kummer m -s sorrow, grief; (Sorge) worry; (Ärger) trouble

kümmer|lich a puny; (dürftig) meagre; (armselig) wretched. **k~n** vt concern; **sich k~n um** look after; (sich befassen) con-cern oneself with; (beachten) take notice of; **ich werde mich darum k~n** I shall see to it; **k~e dich um deine eigenen Angelegenheiten!** mind your own business!

kummervoll *a* sorrowful **Kumpel** *m* -s,- (*fam*) mate **Kunde** *m* -n,-n customer. **K~ndienst** *m* [after-sales] service **Kund|gebung** *f* -,-en (*Pol*) rally. **k~ig** *a* knowledgeable; (*sach*-) expert

kündig|en *vt* cancel ⟨*Vertrag*⟩; give notice of withdrawal for ⟨*Geld*⟩; give notice to quit ⟨*Wohnung*⟩; **seine Stellung k~en** give [in one's] notice □*vi* (*haben*) give [in one's] notice; **jdm k~en** give s.o. notice [of dismissal/⟨*Vermieter:*⟩ to quit]. **K~ung** *f* -,-en cancellation; notice [of withdrawal/dismissal/to quit]; (*Entlassung*) dismissal. **K~ungsfrist** *f* period of notice

Kund|in *f* -,-nen [woman] customer. **K~machung** *f* -,-en (*Aust*) [public] notice. **K~schaft** *f* - clientele, customers *pl*

künftig *a* future □*adv* in future

Kunst *f* -,ˍe art; (*Können*) skill. **K~dünger** *m* artificial fertilizer. **K~faser** *f* synthetic fibre. **k~fertig** *a* skilful. **K~fertigkeit** *f* skill. **K~galerie** *f* art gallery. **K~gerecht** *a* expert, *adv* -ly. **K~geschichte** *f* history of art. **K~gewerbe** *nt* arts and crafts *pl*. **K~griff** *m* trick. **K~händler** *m* art dealer

Künstler *m* -s,- artist; (*Könner*) master. **K~in** *f* -,-nen [woman] artist. **k~isch** *a* artistic, *adv* -ally. **K~name** *m* pseudonym; (*Theat*) stage name

künstlich *a* artificial, *adv* -ly

kunst|los *a* simple. **K~maler** *m* painter. **K~stoff** *m* plastic. **K~stopfen** *nt* invisible mending. **K~stück** *nt* trick; (*große*

Leistung) feat. **k~voll** *a* artistic; (*geschickt*) skilful, *adv* -ly; (*kompliziert*) elaborate, *adv* -ly. **K~werk** *nt* work of art

kunterbunt *a* multicoloured; (*gemischt*) mixed □*adv* **k~ durcheinander** higgledy-piggledy

Kupfer *nt* -s copper. **k~n** *a* copper

kupieren *vt* crop

Kupon /ku'põ:/ *m* -s,-s voucher; (*Zins*-) coupon; (*Stoff*-) length

Kuppe *f* -,-n [rounded] top; (*Finger*-) end, tip

Kuppel *f* -,-n dome

kupp|eln *vt* couple (**an** + *acc* to) □*vi* (*haben*) (*Auto*) operate the clutch. **K~lung** *f* -,-en coupling; (*Auto*) clutch

Kur *f* -,-en course of treatment; (*im Kurort*) cure

Kür *f* -,-en (*Sport*) free exercise; (*Eislauf*) free programme

Kurbel *f* -,-n crank. **k~n** *vt* wind (**nach oben/unten** up/down). **K~welle** *f* crankshaft

Kürbis *m* -ses,-se pumpkin; (*Flaschen*-) marrow

Kurgast *m* health-resort visitor

Kurier *m* -s,-e courier

kurieren *vt* cure

kurios *a* curious, odd. **K~ität** *f* -,-en oddness; (*Objekt*) curiosity; (*Kunst*) curio

Kur|ort *m* health resort; (*Badeort*) spa. **K~pfuscher** *m* quack

Kurs *m* -es,-e course; (*Aktien*-) price. **K~buch** *nt* timetable

kursieren *vi* (*haben*) circulate

kursiv *a* cursive □*adv* in italics. **K~schrift** *f* italics *pl*

Kursus *m* -,Kurse course

Kurswagen *m* through carriage

Kurtaxe *f* visitors' tax

Kurve *f* -,-n curve; (*Straßen*-) bend

kurz a (kürzer, kürzest) short;
(knapp) brief; (rasch) quick;
(schroff) curt; **k~e Hosen**
shorts; **vor k~em** a short time
ago; **seit k~em** lately; **binnen
k~em** shortly; **den kürzeren
ziehen** get the worst of it □adv
briefly; quickly; curtly; **k~ vor/
nach** a little way/(zeitlich)
shortly before/after; **sich k~ fassen** be brief; **k~ und gut** in
short; **über k~ oder lang** sooner
or later; **zu k~ kommen** get less
than one's fair share. **K~arbeit**
f short-time working. **k~ärme-
lig** a short-sleeved. **k~atmig** a
k~atmig sein be short of breath
Kürze f - shortness; (Knappheit)
brevity; **in K~** shortly. **k~n** vt
shorten; (verringern) cut
kurz|erhand adv without further
ado. **k~fristig** a short-term
□adv at short notice. **k~ge-
schichte** f short story. **k~lebig**
a short-lived
kürzlich adv recently
Kurz|meldung f newsflash.
K~nachrichten fpl news head-
lines. **K~schluß** m short circuit;
(fig) brainstorm. **K~schrift** f
shorthand. **k~sichtig** a short-
sighted. **K~sichtigkeit** f- short-
sightedness. **K~streckenra-
kete** f short-range missile.
k~um adv in short
Kürzung f -,-en shortening;
(Verringerung) cut (gen in)
Kurz|waren fpl haberdashery
sg, (Amer) notions. **k~weilig** a
amusing. **K~welle** f short wave
kuscheln (sich) vr snuggle
(an + acc up to)
Kusine f -,-n [female] cousin
Kuß m -sses,-sse kiss
küssen vt/i (haben) kiss; **sich k~**
kiss
Küste f -,-n coast. **K~nwache**,
K~nwacht f coastguard
Küster m -s,- verger

Kustos m -,-oden /-'to:-/ curator
Kutsch|e f -,-n [horse-drawn] car-
riage/(geschlossen) coach. **K~er**
m -s,- coachman, driver. **k~ie-
ren** vt/i (haben) drive
Kutte f -,-n (Relig) habit
Kutter m -s,- (Naut) cutter
Kuvert /ku've:ɐ/ nt -s,-s envelope
KZ /ka:'tset/ nt -[s],-[s] concentra-
tion camp

L

labil a unstable
Labor nt -s,-s & -e laboratory.
L~ant(in) m -en,-en (f -,-nen)
laboratory assistant. **L~ato-
rium** nt -s,-ien laboratory
Labyrinth nt -[e]s,-e maze, labyrinth
Lache f -,-n puddle; (Blut-) pool
lächeln vi (haben) smile. **L~** nt -s
smile. **l~d** a smiling
lachen vi (haben) laugh. **L~** nt -s
laugh; (Gelächter) laughter
lächerlich a ridiculous, adv -ly;
sich l~ machen make a fool of
oneself. **L~keit** f -,-en ridicu-
lousness; (Kleinigkeit) triviality
lachhaft a laughable
Lachs m -es,-e salmon. **l~far-
ben**, **l~rosa** a salmon-pink
Lack m -[e]s,-e varnish; (Japan-)
lacquer; (Auto) paint. **l~en** vt
varnish. **l~ieren** vt varnish;
(spritzen) spray. **L~schuhe** mpl
patent-leather shoes
Lade f -,-n drawer
laden† vt load; (Electr) charge;
(Jur: vor-) summons
Laden m -s,- shop, (Amer) store;
(Fenster-) shutter. **L~dieb** m
shop-lifter. **L~diebstahl** m
shop-lifting. **L~schluß** m [shop]
closing-time. **L~tisch** m counter
Laderaum m (Naut) hold
lädieren vt damage

Ladung f -,-en load; (Naut, Aviat) cargo; (elektrische, Spreng-) charge; (Jur: Vor-) summons

Lage f -,-n position; (Situation) situation; (Schicht) layer; (fam: Runde) round; **nicht in der L~ sein** not be in a position (**zu** to)

Lager nt -s,- camp; (L~haus) warehouse; (Vorrat) stock; (Techn) bearing; (Erz-, Ruhe-) bed; (eines Tieres) lair; **[nicht] auf L~** [not] in stock. **L~haus** nt warehouse. l~n vt store; (legen) lay; **sich l~n** settle; (sich legen) lie down □vi (haben) camp; (liegen) lie; ⟨Waren:⟩ be stored. **L~raum** m store-room. **L~stätte** f (Geol) deposit. **L~ung** f -storage

Lagune f -,-n lagoon

lahm a lame. **l~en** vi (haben) be lame

lähmen vt paralyse

lahmlegen vt sep (fig) paralyse

Lähmung f -,-en paralysis

Laib m -[e]s,-e loaf

Laich m -(e)s (Zool) spawn. **l~en** vi (haben) spawn

Laie m -n,-n layman; (Theat) amateur. **l~nhaft** a amateurish. **L~nprediger** m lay preacher

Lake f -,-n brine

Laken nt -s,- sheet

lakonisch a laconic, adv -ally

Lakritze f - liquorice

lallen vt/i (haben) mumble; ⟨Baby:⟩ babble

Lametta nt -s tinsel

Lamm nt -[e]s,-̈er lamb

Lampe f -,-n lamp; (Decken-, Wand-) light; (Glüh-) bulb. **L~nfieber** nt stage fright. **L~nschirm** m lampshade

Lampion /lam'pjɔŋ/ m -s,-s Chinese lantern

lancieren /lã'siːrən/ vt (Comm) launch

Land nt -[e]s,-̈er country; (Fest-) land; (Bundes-) state, Land; (Aust) province; **Stück L~** piece of land; **auf dem L~e** in the country; **an L~ gehen** (Naut) go ashore. **L~arbeiter** m agricultural worker. **L~ebahn** f runway. **l~einwärts** adv inland. **l~en** vt/i (sein) land; (fam: gelangen) end up

Ländereien pl estates

Länderspiel nt international

Landesteg m landing-stage

Landesverrat m treason

Land|karte f map. **l~läufig** a popular

ländlich a rural

Land|maschinen fpl agricultural machinery sg. **L~schaft** f -,-en scenery; (Geog, Kunst) landscape; (Gegend) country[side]. **l~schaftlich** a scenic; (regional) regional. **L~smann** m (pl -leute) fellow countryman, compatriot. **L~smännin** f -,-nen fellow countrywoman. **L~straße** f country road; (Admin) ≈ B road. **L~streicher** m -s,- tramp. **L~tag** m state/(Aust) provincial parliament

Landung f -,-en landing. **L~sbrücke** f landing-stage

Land|vermesser m -s,- surveyor. **L~weg** m country lane; **auf dem L~weg** overland. **L~wirt** m farmer. **L~wirtschaft** f agriculture; (Hof) farm. **l~wirtschaftlich** a agricultural

lang[1] adv & prep (+ preceding acc or preceding an + dat) along; **den od am Fluß l~** along the river

lang[2] a (länger, längst) long; (groß) tall; **seit l~em** for a long time □adv **eine Stunde/Woche l~** for an hour/a week; **mein Leben l~** all my life. **l~ärmelig** a long-sleeved. **l~atmig** a long-winded. **l~e** adv a long time; ⟨schlafen⟩ late; **wie/zu l~e** how/too long; **schon l~e** [for] a long time; (zurückliegend) a long time ago; l~e nicht not for a long time; (bei weitem nicht) nowhere near

Länge f -,-n length; (Geog) longitude; der L~ nach lengthways; ⟨liegen, fallen⟩ full length

langen vt hand (dat to) □vi (haben) reach (an etw acc sth; nach for); (genügen) be enough

Läng|engrad m degree of longitude. L~enmaß nt linear measure. l~er a & adv longer; (längere Zeit) [for] some time

Langeweile f - boredom; L~ haben be bored

lang|fristig a long-term; ⟨Vorhersage⟩ long-range. l~jährig a long-standing; ⟨Erfahrung⟩ long. l~lebig a long-lived

länglich a oblong. l~rund a oval

langmütig a long-suffering

längs adv & prep (+gen/dat) along; (der Länge nach) lengthways

lang|sam a slow, adv -ly. L~samkeit f - slowness. L~schläfer(in) m(f) (fam) late riser. L~schrift f longhand

längst adv [schon] l~ for a long time; (zurückliegend) a long time ago; l~ nicht nowhere near

Lang|strecken- pref long-distance; (Mil, Aviat) long-range. l~weilen vt bore; sich l~weilen be bored. l~weilig a boring, adv -ly. L~welle f long wave. l~wierig a lengthy

Lanze f -,-n lance

Lappalie /la'pa:lja/ f -,-n trifle

Lappen m -s,- cloth; (Anat) lobe

läppisch a silly

Lapsus m -,- slip

Lärche f -,-n larch

Lärm m -s noise. l~en vi (haben) make a noise. l~end a noisy

Larve /'larfə/ f -,-n larva; (Maske) mask

lasch a listless; (schlaff) limp; (fade) insipid

Lasche f -,-n tab; (Verschluß-) flap; (Zunge) tongue

Laser /'le:-, 'la:zɐ/ m -s,- laser

lassen† vt leave; (zulassen) let; jdm etw l~ let s.o. keep sth; sein Leben l~ lose one's life; etw [sein od bleiben] l~ not do sth; (aufhören) stop [doing] sth; laß das! stop it! jdn schlafen/gewinnen l~ let s.o. sleep/win; jdn warten l~ keep s.o. waiting; etw machen/reparieren l~ have sth done/repaired; etw verschwinden l~ make sth disappear; sich [leicht] biegen/öffnen l~ bend/open [easily]; sich gut waschen l~ wash well; es läßt sich nicht leugnen it is undeniable; laßt uns gehen! let's go!

lässig a casual, adv -ly. L~keit f - casualness

Lasso nt -s,-s lasso

Last f -,-en load; (Gewicht) weight; (fig) burden; L~en charges; (Steuern) taxes; jdm zur L~ fallen be a burden on s.o. L~auto nt lorry. l~en vi (haben) weigh heavily⟨(liegen⟩ rest (auf+dat on). L~enaufzug m goods lift

Laster¹ m -s,- (fam) lorry, (Amer) truck

Laster² nt -s,- vice. l~haft a depraved; (zügellos) dissolute

läster|lich a blasphemous. l~n vt blaspheme □vi (haben) make disparaging remarks (über+acc about). L~ung f -,-en blasphemy

lästig a troublesome; l~ sein/werden be/become a nuisance

Last|kahn m barge. L~[kraft]wagen m lorry, (Amer) truck. L~zug m lorry with trailer[s]

Latein nt -[s] Latin. L~amerika nt Latin America. l~isch a Latin

latent a latent

Laterne f -,-n lantern; (Straßen-) street lamp. L~npfahl m lamppost

latschen vi (sein) (fam) traipse; (schlurfen) shuffle

Latte f -,-n slat; (Tor-, Hochsprung-) bar

Latz m -es,⸚e bib

Lätzchen nt -s,- [baby's] bib

Latzhose f dungarees pl

lau a lukewarm; (mild) mild

Laub nt -[e]s leaves pl; (L~werk) foliage. **L~baum** m deciduous tree

Laube f -,-n summer-house; (gewachsen) arbour. **L~ngang** m pergola; (Archit) arcades pl

Laub|säge f fretsaw. **L~wald** m deciduous forest

Lauch m -[e]s leeks pl

Lauer f auf der L~ liegen lie in wait. **l~n** vi (haben) lurk; **l~n auf** (+ acc) lie in wait for

Lauf m -[e]s, Läufe run; (Laufen) running; (Verlauf) course; (Wett-) race; (Sport: Durchgang) heat; (Gewehr-) barrel; **im L~[e]** (+ gen) in the course of. **L~bahn** f career. **l~en†** vi (sein) run; (zu Fuß gehen) walk; (gelten) be valid; Ski/Schlittschuh l~en ski/skate. **l~end** a running; (gegenwärtig) current; (regelmäßig) regular; **l~ende Nummer** serial number; **auf dem l~enden sein/jdn auf dem l~enden halten** be/keep s.o. up to date □ adv continually. **l~enlassen†** vt sep (fam) let go

Läufer m -s,- (Person, Teppich) runner; (Schach) bishop

Lauf|gitter nt play-pen. **L~masche** f ladder. **L~rolle** f castor. **L~schritt** m im L~schritt at a run; (Mil) at the double. **L~stall** m play-pen. **L~zettel** m circular

Lauge f -,-n soapy water

Laun|e f -,-n mood; (Einfall) whim; **guter L~e sein**, **gute L~e haben** be in a good mood.

l~enhaft a capricious. **l~isch** a moody

Laus f -,Läuse louse; (Blatt-) greenfly. **L~bub** m (fam) rascal

lauschen vi (haben) listen; (heimlich) eavesdrop

lausig a (fam) lousy □ adv terribly

laut a loud, adv -ly; (geräuschvoll) noisy, adv -ily; **l~ lesen** read aloud; **l~er stellen** turn up □ prep (+ gen/dat) according to. **L~** m -es,-e sound

Laute f -,-n (Mus) lute

lauten vi (haben) (Text-) run, read; **auf jds Namen l~** be in s.o.'s name

läuten vt/i (haben) ring

lauter a pure; (ehrlich) honest; (Wahrheit) plain □ a inv sheer; (nichts als) nothing but. **L~keit** f -integrity

läutern vt purify

laut|hals adv at the top of one's voice; (lachen) out loud. **l~los** a silent, adv -ly; (Stille) hushed. **L~schrift** f phonetics pl. **L~sprecher** m loudspeaker. **l~stark** a vociferous, adv -ly. **L~stärke** f volume

lauwarm a lukewarm

Lava f -,-ven lava

Lavendel m -s lavender

lavieren vi (haben) manœuvre

Lawine f -,-n avalanche

lax a lax. **L~heit** f -laxity

Lazarett nt -[e]s,-e military hospital

leasen /'li:sən/ vt rent

Lebehoch nt cheer

leben vt/i (haben) live (von on); **leb wohl!** farewell! **L~** nt -s,- life; (Treiben) bustle; **am L~** alive. **l~d** a living

lebendig a live; (lebhaft) lively; (anschaulich) vivid, adv -ly; **l~ sein** be alive. **L~keit** f - liveliness; vividness

Lebens|abend m old age. **L~alter** nt age. **L~art** f manners pl. **l~fähig** a viable. **Lebensgefahr** f mortal danger; **in L~gefahr** in mortal danger; ⟨Patient⟩ critically ill. **l~gefährlich** a extremely dangerous; ⟨Verletzung⟩ critical □adv critically. **L~größe** f **in L~größe** life-sized. **L~haltungskosten** pl cost of living sg. **l~lang** a lifelong. **l~länglich** a life ... □adv for life. **L~lauf** m curriculum vitae. **L~mittel** ntpl food sg. **L~mittelgeschäft** nt food shop. **L~mittelhändler** m grocer. **l~notwendig** a vital. **L~retter** m rescuer; ⟨beim Schwimmen⟩ life-guard. **L~standard** m standard of living. **L~unterhalt** m livelihood; **seinen L~unterhalt verdienen** earn one's living. **L~versicherung** f life assurance. **L~wandel** m conduct. **l~wichtig** a vital. **L~zeichen** nt sign of life. **L~zeit** f **auf L~zeit** for life.

Leber f -,-n liver. **L~fleck** m mole. **L~wurst** f liver sausage **Lebe|wesen** nt living being. **L~wohl** nt -s,-s & -e farewell **leb|haft** a lively; ⟨Farbe⟩ vivid. **L~haftigkeit** f - liveliness. **L~kuchen** m gingerbread. **l~los** a lifeless. **L~tag** m **mein/dein L~tag** all my/your life. **L~zeiten** fpl **zu jds L~zeiten** in s.o.'s lifetime

leck a leaking. **L~** nt -s,-s leak. **l~en¹** vi (haben) leak. **lecken²** vt/i (haben) lick. **lecker** a tasty. **L~bissen** m delicacy. **L~ei** f -,-en sweet. **Leder** nt -s,- leather. **l~n** a leather; ⟨wie Leder⟩ leathery. **ledig** a single. **l~lich** adv merely **Lee** f & nt - **nach Lee** ⟨Naut⟩ to leeward

leer a empty; ⟨unbesetzt⟩ vacant; **l~ laufen** ⟨Auto⟩ idle. **L~e** f - emptiness; ⟨leerer Raum⟩ void. **l~en** vt empty; **sich l~en** empty. **L~lauf** m ⟨Auto⟩ neutral. **L~ung** f -,-en ⟨Post⟩ collection **legal** a legal, adv -ly. **l~isieren** vt legalize. **L~ität** f - legality **Legasthenie** f - dyslexia. **L~theniker** m -s,- dyslexic **L~thenisch** a dyslexic **legen** vt put; ⟨hin-, ver-⟩ lay; set ⟨Haare⟩; **Eier l~** lay eggs; **sich l~** lie down; ⟨Staub:⟩ settle; ⟨nachlassen⟩ subside **legendär** a legendary **Legende** f -,-n legend **leger** /le'ʒeːɐ̯/ a casual, adv -ly **legieren** vt alloy; ⟨Culin⟩ thicken. **L~ung** f -,-en alloy **Legion** f -,-en legion **Legislative** f - legislature **legitim** a legitimate, adv -ly. **l~ieren** (sich) vr prove one's identity. **L~ität** f - legitimacy **Lehm** m -s clay. **l~ig** a clayey **Lehne** f -,-n ⟨Rücken-⟩ back; ⟨Arm-⟩ arm. **l~en** vt lean (an + acc against); **sich l~en** lean (an + acc against) □vi (haben) be leaning (an + dat against). **L~sessel**, **L~stuhl** m armchair **Lehr|buch** nt textbook. **L~e** f -,-n apprenticeship; ⟨Anschauung⟩ doctrine; ⟨Theorie⟩ theory; ⟨Wissenschaft⟩ science; ⟨Ratschlag⟩ advice; ⟨Erfahrung⟩ lesson; **jdm eine L~e erteilen** ⟨fig⟩ teach s.o. a lesson. **l~en** vt/i ⟨haben⟩ teach. **L~er** m -s,- teacher; ⟨Fahr-, Ski-⟩ instructor. **L~erin** f -,-nen teacher. **L~erzimmer** nt staff-room. **L~fach** nt ⟨Sch⟩ subject. **L~gang** m course. **L~kraft** f teacher. **L~ling** m -s,-e apprentice; ⟨Auszubildender⟩ trainee. **L~plan** m syllabus. **l~reich** a instructive. **L~stelle** f apprenticeship.

L~stuhl m (Univ) chair. L~zeit f apprenticeship

Leib m -es,-er body; (Bauch) belly.
L~eserziehung f (Sch) physical education. L~eskraft f aus L~eskräften as hard/⟨schreien⟩ loud as one can. L~gericht nt favourite dish. l~haftig a der l~haftige Satan the devil incarnate □ adv in the flesh. l~lich a physical; (blutsverwandt) real, natural. L~speise f = L~gericht. L~wache f (coll) bodyguard. L~wächter m bodyguard. L~wäsche f underwear

Leiche f -,-n [dead] body; corpse. L~nbegängnis nt -ses,-se funeral. L~nbestatter m -s,- undertaker. l~nblaß a deathly pale. L~nhalle f mortuary. L~nwagen m hearse. L~nzug m funeral procession, cortège

Leichnam m -s,-e [dead] body

leicht a light, adv -ly; (Stoff, Anzug) lightweight; (gering) slight, adv -ly; (mühelos) easy, adv -ily. L~athletik f [track and field] athletics sg. l~fallen† vi sep (sein) be easy (dat for). l~fertig a thoughtless, adv -ly; (vorschnell) rash, adv -ly; (frivol) frivolous, adv -ly. L~gewicht nt (Boxen) lightweight. l~gläubig a gullible. l~hin adv casually. L~igkeit f -lightness; (Mühelosigkeit) ease; (L~sein) easiness; mit L~igkeit with ease. l~lebig a happy-go-lucky. l~machen† vt make easy (dat for); es sich (dat) l~machen take the easy way out. l~nehmen† vt sep (fig) take lightly. L~sinn m carelessness; recklessness; (Frivolität) frivolity. l~sinnig a careless, adv -ly; (unvorsichtig) reckless, adv -ly; (frivol) frivolous, adv -ly

Leid nt -[e]s sorrow, grief; (Böses) harm. l~ a jdn/etw l~ sein/

werden be/get tired of s.o./sth; es tut mir l~ I am sorry; er tut mir l~ I feel sorry for him

Leide|form f passive. l~n† vt/i (haben) suffer (an+dat from); jdn [gut] l~n können like s.o.; jdn/etw nicht l~n können dislike s.o./sth. L~n nt -s,- suffering; (Med) complaint; (Krankheit) disease. l~nd a suffering; l~nd sein be in poor health. L~nschaft f -,-en passion. l~nschaftlich a passionate, adv -ly

leid|er adv unfortunately. l~er ja/nicht I'm afraid so/not. l~ig a wretched. l~lich a tolerable, adv -bly. l~tragende(r) m/f person who suffers; (Trauernde) mourner. L~wesen nt zu meinem L~wesen to my regret

Leier f -,-n die alte L~ (fam) the same old story. L~kasten m barrel-organ. l~n vt/i (haben) wind; (herunter-) drone out

Leih|bibliothek, L~bücherei f lending library. L~e f -,-n loan. l~en† vt lend; sich (dat) etw l~en borrow sth. L~gabe f loan. L~gebühr f rental; (für Bücher) lending charge. L~haus nt pawnshop. L~wagen m hire-car. l~weise adv on loan

Leim m -s glue. l~en vt glue

Leine f -,-n rope; (Wäsche-) line; (Hunde-) lead, leash

Lein|en nt -s linen. l~en a linen. L~tuch nt sheet. L~wand f linen; (Kunst) canvas; (Film-) screen

leise a quiet, adv -ly; ⟨Stimme, Musik, Berührung⟩ soft, adv -ly; (schwach) faint, adv -ly; (leicht) light, adv -ly; l~r stellen turn down

Leiste f -,-n strip; (Holz-) batten; (Zier-) moulding; (Anat) groin

Leisten m -s,- [shoemaker's] last

leist|en vt achieve, accomplish; **sich** (dat) **etw l~en** treat oneself to sth; (fam: anstellen) get up to sth; **ich kann es mir nicht l~en** I can't afford it. **L~ung** f -,-en achievement; (Sport, Techn) performance; (Produktion) output; (Zahlung) payment. **l~ungs-fähig** a efficient; **L~ungsfähig-keit** f efficiency

Leit|artikel m leader, editorial. **L~bild** nt (fig) model. **l~en** vt run, manage; (an-/hinführen) lead; (Mus, Techn, Phys) conduct; (lenken, schicken) direct. **l~end** a leading; (Posten) executive

Leiter[1] f -,-n ladder

Leit|er[2] m -s,- director; (Comm) manager; (Führer) leader; (Sch) head; (Mus, Phys) conductor. **L~erin** f -,-nen director; manageress; leader; head. **L~faden** m manual. **L~kegel** m [traffic] cone. **L~planke** f crash barrier. **L~spruch** m motto. **L~ung** f -,-en (Führung) direction; (Comm) management; (Aufsicht) control; (Electr: Schnur) lead, flex; (Kabel) cable; (Telefon-) line; (Rohr-) pipe; (Haupt-) main. **L~ungswasser** nt tap water

Lektion /-'tsjo:n/ f -,-en lesson

Lekt|or m -s,-en /-'to:rən/, **L~o-rin** f -,-nen (Univ) assistant lecturer; (Verlags-) editor. **L~üre** f -,-n reading matter; (Lesen) reading

Lende f -,-n loin

lenk|bar a steerable; (fügsam) tractable. **l~en** vt guide (steuern) steer; (Aust) drive; (regeln) control; **jds Aufmerksam-keit auf sich** (acc) **l~en** attract s.o.'s attention. **L~er** m -s,- driver; (L~stange) handlebars pl. **L~rad** nt steering-wheel. **L~stange** f handlebars pl. **L~ung** f- steering

Leopard m -en,-en leopard

Lepra f- leprosy

Lerche f -,-n lark

lernen vt/i (haben) learn; (für die Schule) study; **schwimmen l~** learn to swim

lesbar a readable; (leserlich) legible

Lesb|ierin /'lɛsbjərɪn/ f -,-nen lesbian. **l~isch** a lesbian

Lese f -,-n harvest. **L~buch** nt reader. **l~n†** vt/i (haben) read; (Univ) lecture □ut pick, gather. **L~n** nt -s reading. **L~r(in)** m -s,- (f -,-nen) reader. **L~ratte** f (fam) bookworm. **l~rlich** a legible, adv -bly. **L~zeichen** nt bookmark

Lesung f -,-en reading

lethargisch a lethargic, adv -ally

Lettland nt -s Latvia

letzt|e(r,s) a last; (neueste) latest; **in l~er Zeit** recently; **l~en Endes** in the end. **l~emal** adv **das l~emal** the last time; **zum l~enmal** for the last time. **l~ens** adv recently; (zuletzt) lastly. **l~ere(r,s)** a the latter; **der/die/das l~ere** the latter

Leucht|e f -,-n light. **l~en** vi (haben) shine. **l~end** a shining. **L~er** m -s,- candlestick. **L~feuer** nt beacon. **L~kugel** f flare. **L~reklame** f neon sign. **L~[stoff]röhre** f fluorescent tube. **L~turm** m lighthouse. **L~zifferblatt** nt luminous dial

leugnen vt deny

Leukämie f- leukaemia

Leumund m -s reputation

Leute pl people; (Mil) men; (Arbeiter) workers

Leutnant m -s,-s second lieutenant

leutselig a affable, adv -bly

Levkoje /lɛf'ko:jə/ f -,-n stock

Lexikon nt -s,-ka encyclopaedia; (Wörterbuch) dictionary

Libanon (der) -s Lebanon

Libelle f -,-n dragonfly; (Techn) spirit-level; (Haarspange) slide

liberal a (Pol) Liberal

Libyen nt -s Libya

Licht nt -[e]s,-er light; (Kerze) candle; L~ **machen** turn on the light; **hinter** L~ **führen** (fam) dupe. l~ a bright; (Med) lucid; (spärlich) sparse. L~**bild** nt [passport] photograph; (Dia) slide. L~**bildervortrag** m slide lecture. L~**blick** m (fig) ray of hope. l~**en** vt thin out; **den Anker** l~**en** (Naut) weigh anchor; **sich** l~**en** become less dense; ⟨Haare:⟩ thin. L~**hupe** f headlight flasher; **die** L~**hupe betätigen** flash one's headlights. L~**maschine** f dynamo. L~**schalter** m light-switch. L~**ung** f -,-en clearing

Lid nt -[e]s,-er [eye]lid. L~**schatten** m eye-shadow

lieb a dear; (nett) nice; (artig) good; **es ist mir** l~ I'm glad (**daß** that); **es wäre mir** l~er I should prefer it (**wenn** if). l~**äugeln** vi (haben) l~**äugeln mit** fancy; toy with ⟨Gedanken⟩

Liebe f -,-n love. l~**lei** f -,-en flirtation. l~**n** vt love; (mögen) like; **sich** l~**n** love each other; (körperlich) make love. l~**nd** a loving ▭adv **etw** l~**nd gern tun** love to do sth. l~**nswert** a lovable. l~**nswürdig** a kind. l~**nswürdigerweise** adv very kindly. L~**nswürdigkeit** f -,-en kindness

lieber adv rather; (besser) better; l~ **mögen** like better; **ich trinke** l~ **Tee** I prefer tea

Liebes|brief m love letter. L~**dienst** m favour. L~**geschichte** f love story. L~**kummer** m heartache; L~**kummer haben** be depressed over an

unhappy love-affair. L~**paar** nt [pair of] lovers pl

lieb|evoll a loving, adv -ly; (zärtlich) affectionate, adv -ly. l~**gewinnen**† vt sep grow fond of. l~**haben**† vt sep be fond of; (lieben) love. L~**haber** m -s,-lover; (Sammler) collector. L~**haberei** f -,-en hobby. l~**kosen** vt caress. L~**kosung** f -,-en caress. l~**lich** a lovely; (sanft) gentle; (süß) sweet. L~**ling** m -s,-e darling; (Bevorzugte) favourite. L~**lings-** pref favourite. l~**los** a loveless; (Eltern) uncaring; (unfreundlich) unkind ▭adv unkindly; (ohne Sorgfalt) without care. L~**schaft** f -,-en [love] affair. l~**ste(r,s)** a dearest; (bevorzugt) favourite ▭adv **am** l~**sten** best [of all]; **jdn/etw am** l~**sten mögen** like s.o./sth best [of all]; **ich hätte am** l~**sten geweint** I felt like crying. L~**ste(r)** m/f beloved; (Schatz) sweetheart

Lied nt -[e]s,-er song

liederlich a slovenly; (unordentlich) untidy; (ausschweifend) dissolute. L~**keit** f - slovenliness; untidiness; dissoluteness

Lieferant m -en,-en supplier

liefer|bar a (Comm) available. l~**n** vt supply; (zustellen) deliver; (hervorbringen) yield. L~**ung** f -,-en delivery; (Sendung) consignment; (per Schiff) shipment. L~**wagen** m delivery van

Liege f -,-n couch. l~**n**† vi (haben) lie; (gelegen sein) be situated; l~**n an** (+dat) (fig) be due to; (abhängen) depend on; **jdm** [**nicht**] l~**n** [not] suit s.o.; (ansprechen) [not] appeal to s.o.; **mir liegt viel/nicht daran** it is very/ not important to me. l~**nbleiben**† vi sep (sein) remain lying [there]; (im Bett) stay in bed;

⟨*Ding:*⟩ be left; ⟨*Schnee:*⟩ settle; ⟨*Arbeit:*⟩ remain undone; (*zurückgelassen werden*) be left behind; (*Panne haben*) break down. l~**nlassen**† *vt sep* leave lying [there]; (*zurücklassen*) leave behind; (*nicht fortführen*) leave undone. L~**sitz** *m* reclining seat. L~**stuhl** *m* deck-chair. L~**stütz** *m* -es,-e press-up, (*Amer*) push-up. L~**wagen** *m* couchette car. L~**wiese** *f* lawn for sunbathing

Lift *m* -[e]s,-e & -s lift, (*Amer*) elevator

Liga *f* -,-gen league

Likör *m* -s,-e liqueur

lila *inv a* mauve; (*dunkel*) purple

Lilie /ˈliːliə/ *f* -,-n lily

Liliputaner(in) *m* -s,- (*f* -,-nen) dwarf

Limo *f* -,-[s] (*fam*), L~**nade** *f* -,-n fizzy drink, (*Amer*) soda; (*Zitronen-*) lemonade

Limousine /limuˈziːnə/ *f* -,-n saloon, (*Amer*) sedan; (*mit Trennscheibe*) limousine

lind *a* mild; (*sanft*) gentle

Linde *f* -,-n lime tree

linder|n *vt* relieve, ease. L~**ung** *f* - relief

Line|al *nt* -s,-e ruler. l~**ar** *a* linear

Linguistik *f* - linguistics *sg*

Linie /-iə/ *f* -,-n line; (*Zweig*) branch; (*Bus-*) route; L~ 4 number 4 [bus/tram]; in erster L~ primarily. L~**nflug** *m* scheduled flight. L~**nrichter** *m* linesman

lin[i]iert *a* lined, ruled

Link|e *f* -n,-n left side; (*Hand*) left hand; (*Boxen*) left; **die L~e** (*Pol*) the left; **zu meiner L~en** on my left. l~**e(r,s)** *a* left; (*Pol*) leftwing; l~**e Seite** left[-hand] side; (*von Stoff*) wrong side; l~**e Masche** purl. l~**isch** *a* awkward, *adv* -ly

links *adv* on the left; (*bei Stoff*) on the wrong side; (*verkehrt*) inside out; **von/nach** l~ from/to the left; l~ **stricken** purl. L~**händer(in)** *m* -s,- (*f* -,-nen) lefthander. l~**händig** *a & adv* left-handed. L~**verkehr** *m* driving on the left

Linoleum/-leum/ *nt* -s lino[leum]

Linse *f* -,-n lens; (*Bot*) lentil

Lippe *f* -,-n lip. L~**nstift** *m* lipstick

Liquid|ation /-ˈtsjoːn/ *f* -,-en liquidation. l~**ieren** *vt* liquidate

lispeln *vt/i* (*haben*) lisp

List *f* -,-en trick, ruse; (*Listigkeit*) cunning

Liste *f* -,-n list

listig *a* cunning, crafty

Litanei *f* -,-en litany

Litauen *nt* -s Lithuania

Liter *m & nt* -s,- litre

liter|arisch *a* literary. L~**atur** *f* - literature

Litfaßsäule *f* advertising pillar

Liturgie *f* -,-n liturgy

Litze *f* -,-n braid; (*Electr*) flex

live /laif/ *adv* (*Radio, TV*) live

Lizenz *f* -,-en licence

Lkw /ɛlkaˈveː/ *m* -[s],-s = Lastkraftwagen

Lob *nt* -[e]s praise

Lobby /ˈlɔbi/ *f* - (*Pol*) lobby

loben *vt* praise. l~**swert** *a* praiseworthy, laudable

löblich *a* praiseworthy

Lobrede *f* eulogy

Loch *nt* -[e]s,-er hole. l~**en** *vt* punch a hole/holes in; punch (*Fahrkarte*). L~**er** *m* -s,- punch

löcher|ig *a* full of holes. l~**n** *vt* (*fam*) pester

Locke *f* -,-n curl. l~**n**¹ *vt* curl; **sich** l~**n** curl

locken² *vt* lure, entice; (*reizen*) tempt. l~**d** *a* tempting

Lockenwickler *m* -s,- curler; (*Rolle*) roller

locker a loose, adv -ly; ⟨Seil⟩ slack; ⟨Erde, Kuchen⟩ light; ⟨zwanglos⟩ casual; ⟨zu frei⟩ lax; ⟨unmoralisch⟩ loose. l~n vt loosen; slacken ⟨Seil, Zügel⟩; break up ⟨Boden⟩; relax ⟨Griff⟩; sich l~n become loose; ⟨Seil:⟩ slacken; ⟨sich entspannen⟩ relax. L~ungsübungen fpl limbering-up exercises

lockig a curly

Lock|mittel nt bait. L~ung f -,-en lure; ⟨Versuchung⟩ temptation. L~vogel m decoy

Loden m -s ⟨Tex⟩ loden

lodern vi ⟨haben⟩ blaze

Löffel m -s,- spoon; ⟨L~voll⟩ spoonful. l~n vt spoon up

Logarithmus m -,-men logarithm

Logbuch nt ⟨Naut⟩ log-book

Loge /'lo:ʒə/ f -,-n lodge; ⟨Theat⟩ box

Logierbesuch /lo'ʒi:ɐ̯-/ m house guest/guests pl

Logik f - logic. l~isch a logical, adv -ly

Logo nt -s,-s logo

Lohn m -[e]s,:-e wages pl, pay; ⟨fig⟩ reward. L~empfänger m wage-earner. l~en vi/r ⟨haben⟩ [sich] l~en be worth it or worth while □vt be worth; jdm etw l~en reward s.o. for sth. l~end a worthwhile; ⟨befriedigend⟩ rewarding. L~erhöhung f [pay] rise; ⟨Amer⟩ raise. L~steuer f income tax

Lok f -,-s ⟨fam⟩ = **Lokomotive**

Lokal nt -s,-e restaurant; ⟨Trink-⟩ bar. l~ a local. l~isieren vt locate; ⟨begrenzen⟩ localize

Lokomotiv|e f -,-n engine, locomotive. L~führer m engine driver

London nt -s London. L~er a London ... □m -s,- Londoner

Lorbeer m -s,-en laurel; **Echter L~bay**. L~blatt nt ⟨Culin⟩ bay-leaf

Lore f -,-n ⟨Rail⟩ truck

Los nt -es,-e lot; ⟨Lotterie-⟩ ticket; ⟨Schicksal⟩ fate; **das Große Los ziehen** hit the jackpot

los pred a **los sein** be loose; **jdn/etw los sein** be rid of s.o./sth; **was ist [mit ihm] los?** what's the matter [with him]? □adv **los!** go on! **Achtung, fertig, los!** ready, steady, go!

lösbar a soluble

losbinden† vt sep untie

Lösch|blatt nt sheet of blotting-paper. l~en¹ vt put out, extinguish; quench ⟨Durst⟩; blot ⟨Tinte⟩; ⟨tilgen⟩ cancel; ⟨streichen⟩ delete; erase ⟨Aufnahme⟩

löschen² vt ⟨Naut⟩ unload

Lösch|fahrzeug nt fire-engine. L~gerät nt fire extinguisher. L~papier nt blotting-paper

lose a loose, adv -ly

Lösegeld nt ransom

losen vi ⟨haben⟩ draw lots ⟨um for⟩

lösen vt undo; ⟨lockern⟩ loosen; ⟨entfernen⟩ detach; ⟨klären⟩ solve; ⟨auflösen⟩ dissolve; cancel ⟨Vertrag⟩; break off ⟨Beziehung, Verlobung⟩; ⟨kaufen⟩ buy; **sich l~** come off; ⟨sich trennen⟩ detach oneself/itself; ⟨lose werden⟩ come undone; ⟨sich entspannen⟩ relax; ⟨sich klären⟩ resolve itself; ⟨sich auflösen⟩ dissolve

los|fahren† vi sep ⟨sein⟩ start; ⟨Auto:⟩ drive off; l~fahren auf (+ acc) head for ⟨fig: angreifen⟩ go for. l~gehen† vi sep ⟨sein⟩ set off; ⟨fam: anfangen⟩ start; ⟨fam: abgehen⟩ come off; ⟨Bombe, Gewehr:⟩ go off; l~gehen auf (+ acc) head for ⟨fig: angreifen⟩ go for. l~kommen† vi sep ⟨sein⟩ get away ⟨von from⟩; l~kommen auf (+ acc) come towards.

l~**lachen** *vi sep* (*haben*) burst out laughing. l~**lassen**† *vt sep* let go of; (*freilassen*) release

löslich *a* soluble

los|**lösen** *vt sep* detach; **sich l~lösen** become detached; (*fig*) break away (**von** from). l~**machen** *vt sep* detach; (*losbinden*) untie; **sich l~machen** free oneself/itself. l~**platzen** *vi sep* (*sein*) (*fam*) burst out laughing. l~**reißen**† *vt sep* tear off; **sich l~reißen** break free; (*fig*) tear oneself away. l~**sagen** (**sich**) *vr sep* renounce (**von etw** sth). l~**schicken** *vt sep* send off. l~**sprechen**† *vt sep* absolve (**von** from). l~**steuern** *vi sep* (*sein*) head (**auf** + *acc* for)

Losung *f* -,-**en** (*Pol*) slogan; (*Mil*) password

Lösung *f* -,-**en** solution. **L~smittel** *nt* solvent

los|**werden**† *vt sep* get rid of. l~**ziehen**† *vi sep* (*sein*) set off; l~**ziehen gegen** *od* **über** (+ *acc*) (*beschimpfen*) run down

Lot *nt* -[e]s,-**e** perpendicular; (*Blei-*) plumb[-bob]; **im Lot sein** (*fig*) be all right. l~**en** *vt* plumb

löt|**en** *vt* solder. **L~lampe** *f* blowlamp, (*Amer*) blowtorch. **L~metall** *nt* solder

lotrecht *a* perpendicular, *adv* -ly

Lotse *m* -n,-n (*Naut*) pilot. l~**n** *vt* (*Naut*) pilot; (*fig*) guide

Lotterie *f* -,-n lottery

Lotto *nt* -s,-s lotto; (*Lotterie*) lottery

Löwe *m* -n,-n lion; (*Astr*) Leo. **L~enanteil** *m* (*fig*) lion's share. **L~enzahn** *m* (*Bot*) dandelion. **L~in** *f* -,-nen lioness

loyal /lɔaˈjaːl/ *a* loyal. **L~ität** *f* - loyalty

Luchs *m* -es,-e lynx

Lücke *f* -,-n gap. **L~nbüßer** *m* -s,- stopgap. **l~nhaft** *a* incomplete;

〈*Wissen*〉 patchy. l~**nlos** *a* complete; (*Folge*) unbroken

Luder *nt* -s,- (*sl*) (*Frau*) bitch; **armes L~** poor wretch

Luft *f* -,⸚e air; **tief L~ holen** take a deep breath; **in die L~ gehen** explode. **L~angriff** *m* air raid. **L~aufnahme** *f* aerial photograph. **L~ballon** *m* balloon. **L~bild** *nt* aerial photograph. **L~blase** *f* air bubble

lüften *vt* air; raise 〈*Hut*〉; reveal 〈*Geheimnis*〉

Luft|**fahrt** *f* aviation. **L~fahrtgesellschaft** *f* airline. **L~gewehr** *nt* airgun. **L~hauch** *m* breath of air. **L~ig** *a* airy; 〈*Kleid*〉 light. **L~kissenfahrzeug** *nt* hovercraft. **L~krieg** *m* aerial warfare. **L~kurort** *m* climatic health resort. l~**leer** *a* l~**leerer Raum** vacuum. **L~linie** *f* 100 **km L~linie** 100 km as the crow flies. **L~loch** *nt* air-hole; (*Aviat*) air pocket. **L~matratze** *f* air-bed, inflatable mattress. **L~pirat** *m* [aircraft] hijacker. **L~post** *f* airmail. **L~pumpe** *f* air pump; (*Fahrrad-*) bicycle-pump. **L~röhre** *f* windpipe. **L~schiff** *nt* airship. **L~schlange** *f* [paper] streamer. **L~schlösser** *ntpl* castles in the air. **L~schutzbunker** *m* air-raid shelter

Lüftung *f* - ventilation

Luft|**veränderung** *f* change of air. **L~waffe** *f* air force. **L~weg** *m* **auf dem L~weg** by air. **L~zug** *m* draught

Lüge *f* -,-n lie. l~**n**† *vt/i* (*haben*) lie. **L~ner(in)** *m* -s,- (*f* -,-nen) liar. l~**nerisch** *a* untrue; 〈*Person*〉 untruthful

Luke *f* -,-n hatch; (*Dach-*) skylight

Lümmel *m* -s,- lout; (*fam: Schelm*) rascal. **l~n (sich)** *vr* loll

Lump *m* -en,-en scoundrel. **L~en** *m* -s,- rag; in **L~en** in rags. **l~en** *vt* sich nicht **l~en lassen** be generous. **L~engesindel, L~enpack** *nt* riff-raff. **L~ensammler** *m* rag-and-bone man. **l~ig** *a* mean, shabby; (*gering*) measly

Lunchpaket /'lan[t]ʃ-/ *nt* packed lunch

Lunge *f -,-n* lungs *pl*; (*L~nflügel*) lung. **L~nentzündung** *f* pneumonia

lungern *vi* (*haben*) loiter

Lunte *f* **L~ riechen** (*fam*) smell a rat

Lupe *f -,-n* magnifying glass

Lurch *m* -[e]s,-e amphibian

Lust *f -,̈-e* pleasure; (*Verlangen*) desire; (*sinnliche Begierde*) lust; **L~ haben** feel like (**auf** *etw acc* sth); **ich habe keine L~** I don't feel like it; (*will nicht*) I don't want to

Lüster *m* -s,- lustre; (*Kronleuchter*) chandelier

lüstern *a* greedy (**auf** + *acc* for); (*sinnlich*) lascivious; (*geil*) lecherous

lustig *a* jolly; (*komisch*) funny; **sich l~ machen über** (+ *acc*) make fun of

Lüstling *m* -s,-e lecher

lust|los *a* listless, *adv* -ly. **L~mörder** *m* sex killer. **L~spiel** *nt* comedy

lutherisch *a* Lutheran

lutsch|en *vt/i* (*haben*) suck. **L~er** *m* -s,- lollipop; (*Schnuller*) dummy, (*Amer*) pacifier

lütt *a* (*NGer*) little

Lüttich *nt* -s Liège

Luv *f* & *nt* - **nach Luv** (*Naut*) to windward

luxuriös *a* luxurious, *adv* -ly

Luxus *m* - luxury. **L~artikel** *m* luxury article. **L~ausgabe** *f* de luxe edition. **L~hotel** *nt* luxury hotel

Lymph|drüse /'lymf-/ *f*, **L~knoten** *m* lymph gland

lynchen /'lynçən/ *vt* lynch

Lyrik *f* - lyric poetry. **L~iker** *m* -s,- lyric poet. **l~isch** *a* lyrical; (*Dichtung*) lyric

M

Mach|art *f* style. **m~bar** *a* feasible. **m~en** *vt* make; get (*Mahlzeit*); take (*Foto*); (*ausführen, tun, in Ordnung bringen*) do; (*Math: ergeben*) be; (*kosten*) come to; **sich** (*dat*) **etw m~en lassen** have sth made; **was m~st du da?** what are you doing? **was m~t die Arbeit?** how is work? **das m~t 6 Mark [zusammen]** that's 6 marks [altogether]; **das m~t nichts** it doesn't matter; **sich** (*dat*) **wenig/nichts m~en aus** care little/ nothing for □ *vr* **sich m~en** do well; **sich an die Arbeit m~en** get down to work □ *vi* (*haben*) **ins Bett m~en** (*fam*) wet the bed; **schnell m~en** hurry. **M~enschaften** *fpl* machinations

Macht *f -,̈-e* power; **mit aller M~** with all one's might. **M~haber** *m* -s,- ruler

mächtig *a* powerful; (*groß*) enormous □ *adv* (*fam*) terribly

macht|los *a* powerless. **M~wort** *nt* **ein M~wort sprechen** put one's foot down

Mädchen *nt* -s,- girl; (*Dienst-*) maid. **m~haft** *a* girlish. **M~name** *m* girl's name; (*vor der Ehe*) maiden name

Made *f -,-n* maggot

Mädel *nt* -s,- girl

madig *a* maggoty; **jdn m~ machen** (*fam*) run s.o. down

Madonna *f -,-nen* madonna

Magazin nt -s,-e magazine; (Lager) warehouse; (Raum) store-room

Magd f -,-̈e maid

Magen m -s,-̈ stomach. **M~schmerzen** mpl stomach-ache sg. **M~verstimmung** f stomach upset

mager a thin; ⟨Fleisch⟩ lean; ⟨Boden⟩ poor; ⟨dürftig⟩ meagre. **M~keit** f - thinness; leanness. **M~sucht** f anorexia

Magie f - magic

Magier /'ma:giɐ/ m -s,- magician. **m~isch** a magic; (geheimnisvoll) magical

Magistrat m -s,-e city council

Magnesia f - magnesia

Magnet m -en & -[e]s,-e magnet. **m~isch** a magnetic. **m~isieren** vt magnetize. **M~ismus** m - magnetism

Mahagoni nt -s mahogany

Mähdrescher m -s,- combine harvester. **m~en** vt/i (haben) mow

Mahl nt -[es]s,-̈er meal

mahlen† vt grind

Mahlzeit f meal; **M~!** enjoy your meal!

Mähne f -,-n mane

mahnen vt/i (haben) remind (wegen about); (ermahnen) admonish; (auffordern) urge (zu to); **zur Vorsicht/Eile m~** urge caution/haste. **M~ung** f -,-en reminder; admonition; (Aufforderung) exhortation

Mai m -[e]s,-e May; **der Erste Mai** May Day. **M~glöckchen** nt -s,- lily of the valley. **M~käfer** m cockchafer

Mailand nt -s Milan

Mais m -es maize, (Amer) corn; (Culin) sweet corn. **M~kolben** m corn-cob

Majestät f -,-en majesty. **m~isch** a majestic, adv -ally

Major m -s,-e major

Majoran m -s marjoram

Majorität f -,-en majority

makaber a macabre

Makel m -s,- blemish; (Defekt) flaw; (fig) stain. **m~los** a flawless; (fig) unblemished

mäkeln vi (haben) grumble

Makkaroni pl macaroni sg

Makler m -s,- (Comm) broker

Makrele f -,-n mackerel

Makrone f -,-n macaroon

mal adv (Math) times; (bei Maßen) by; (fam: einmal) once; (eines Tages) one day; **schon mal** once before; (jemals) ever; **nicht mal** not even; **hört/seht mal!** listen!/ look!

Mal¹ nt -[es]s,-e time; **zum ersten Mal** for the first time; **mit einem Mal** all at once; **ein für alle Mal** once and for all

Mal² nt -[e]s,-e mark; (auf der Haut) mole; (Mutter-) birthmark

Malbuch nt colouring book. **m~en** vt/i (haben) paint. **M~er** m -s,- painter. **M~erei** f -,-en painting. **M~erin** f -,-nen painter. **m~erisch** a picturesque

Malheur /ma'løːɐ/ nt -s,-e & -s (fam) mishap; (Ärger) trouble

Mallorca /ma'lɔrka, -'jɔrka/ nt -s Majorca

malnehmen† vt sep multiply (mit by)

Malz nt -es malt. **M~bier** nt malt beer

Mama /'mama, ma'ma:/ f -s,-s mummy

Mammut nt -s,-e & -s mammoth

mampfen vt (fam) munch

man pron one, you; (die Leute) people, they; **man sagt** they say, it is said

Manager /'mɛnɪdʒɐ/ m -s,- manager

manch inv pron m~ ein(e) many a; m~ einer/eine many a man/woman. **m~e(r,s)** pron many a

[so] m~es Mal many a time;
m~e **Leute** some people □ (*substantivisch*) m~er/m~e many a
man/woman; m~e *pl* some;
(*Leute*) some people; (*viele*) many
[people]; m~es some things;
(*vieles*) many things. m~**erlei**
inv a various □*pron* various
things

manchmal *adv* sometimes
Mandant(in) *m* -en,-en (*f-,-nen*)
(*Jur*) client

Mandarine *f* -,-n mandarin
Mandat *nt* -[e]s,-e mandate; (*Jur*)
brief; (*Pol*) seat

Mandel *f* -,-n almond; (*Anat*) ton-
sil. M~**entzündung** *f* tonsillitis
Manege /ma'neːʒə/ *f* -,-n ring;
(*Reit-*) arena

Mangel[1] *m* -s,⸚ (*Knappheit*)
shortage; (*Med*) deficiency;
(*Fehler*) defect; M~ **leiden** go
short

Mangel[2] *f* -,-n mangle
mangel|haft a faulty, defective;
(*Sch*) unsatisfactory. m~n[1] *vi*
(*haben*) es m~t an (+ *dat*) there
is a lack/(*Knappheit*) shortage of.
mangeln[2] *vt* put through the
mangle

mangels *prep* (+ *gen*) for lack of
Mango *f* -,-s mango
Manie *f* -,-n mania; (*Sucht*) obses-
sion

Manier *f* -,-en manner; M~**en**
manners. m~**lich** a well-mannered □*adv* properly

Manifest *nt* -[e]s,-e manifesto.
m~**ieren (sich)** *vr* manifest itself

Maniküre *f* -,-n manicure; (*Person*) manicurist. m~**n** *vt* manicure

Manipul|ation /-'tsi̯oːn/ *f* -,-en
manipulation. m~**ieren** *vt* ma-
nipulate

Manko *nt* -s,-s disadvantage;
(*Fehlbetrag*) deficit

Mann *m* -[e]s,⸚er man; (*Ehe-*) husband

Männchen *nt* -s,- little man;
(*Zool*) male; M~ **machen**
(*Hund:*) sit up

Mannequin /'manəkɛ̃/ *nt* -s,-s
model

Männerchor *m* male voice choir
Mannes|alter *nt* manhood.
M~**kraft** *f* virility

mannhaft a manful, *adv* -ly
mannigfaltig a manifold; (*verschieden*) diverse

männlich a male; (*Gram & fig*)
masculine; (*mannhaft*) manly;
⟨*Frau*⟩ mannish. M~**keit** *f* -
masculinity; (*fig*) manhood

Mannschaft *f* -,-en team; (*Naut*)
crew. M~**sgeist** *m* team spirit

Manöver *nt* -s,- manœuvre;
(*Winkelzug*) trick. m~**rieren**
vt/i (*haben*) manœuvre

Mansarde *f* -,-n attic room; (*Wohnung*) attic flat

Manschette *f* -,-n cuff; (*Blumen-
topf-*) paper frill. M~**nknopf** *m*
cuff-link

Mantel *m* -s,⸚ coat; (*Jacke*) overcoat; (*Reifen-*) outer tyre

Manuskript *nt* -[e]s,-e manuscript

Mappe *f* -,-n folder; (*Akten-*) briefcase; (*Schul-*) bag

Marathon *m* -s,-s marathon
Märchen *nt* -s,- fairy-tale.
m~**haft** a fairy-tale . . . ; (*phantastisch*) fabulous

Margarine *f* - margarine
Marienkäfer /ma'riːən-/ *m* lady-
bird, (*Amer*) ladybug

Marihuana *nt* -s marijuana
Marille *f* -,-n (*Aust*) apricot
Marinade *f* -,-n marinade
Marine *f* marine; (*Kriegs-*) navy.
m~**blau** a navy [blue]. M~**-
infanterist** *m* marine

marinieren *vt* marinade
Marionette *f* -,-n puppet, marionette

Mark¹ f -,- mark; **drei M~** three marks

Mark² nt -[e]s (Knochen-) marrow; (Bot) pith; (Frucht-) pulp; **bis ins M~ getroffen** (fig) cut to the quick

markant a striking

Marke f -,-n token; (rund) disc; (Erkennungs-) tag; (Brief-) stamp; (Lebensmittel-) coupon; (Spiel-) counter; (Markierung) mark; (Fabrikat) make; (Tabak-) brand. **M~nartikel** m branded article

markier|en vt mark; (fam: vortäuschen) fake. **M~ung** f -,-en marking

Markise f -,-n awning

Markstück nt one-mark piece

Markt m -[e]s, ⸚e market; (M~platz) market-place. **M~forschung** f market research. **M~platz** m market-place

Marmelade f -,-n jam; (Orangen-) marmalade

Marmor m -s marble

Marokko nt -s Morocco

Marone f -,-n [sweet] chestnut

Marotte f -,-n whim

Marsch¹ f -,-en marsh

Marsch² m -[e]s, ⸚e march. **m~ int** (Mil) march! **m~ ins Bett!** off to bed!

Marschall m -s, ⸚e marshal

marschieren vi (sein) march

Marter f -,-n torture. **m~n** vt torture

Martinshorn nt [police] siren

Märtyrer(in) m -s,- (f -,-nen) martyr

Martyrium nt -s martyrdom

Mar|xismus m - Marxism. **m~xistisch** a Marxist

März m -,-e March

Marzipan nt -s marzipan

Masche f -,-n stitch; (im Netz) mesh; (fam: Trick) dodge. **M~ndraht** m wire netting

Maschin|e f -,-n machine; (Flugzeug) plane; (Schreib-) typewriter. **m~egeschrieben** a typewritten, typed. **m~ell** a machine ... □ adv by machine. **M~enbau** m mechanical engineering. **M~engewehr** nt machine-gun. **M~enpistole** f sub-machine-gun. **M~erie** f machinery. **M~eschreiben** nt typing. **M~ist** m -en,-en machinist; (Naut) engineer

Masern pl measles sg

Maserung f -,-en [wood] grain

Maske f -,-n mask; (Theat) makeup. **M~rade** f -,-n disguise; (fig: Heuchelei) masquerade

maskieren vt mask; **sich m~** dress up (als as)

Maskottchen nt -s,- mascot

maskulin a masculine

Maskulinum nt -s,-na (Gram) masculine

Masochis|mus /mazoˈxɪsmʊs/ m - masochism. **M~t** m -en,-en masochist

Maß¹ nt -es,-e measure; (Abmessung) measurement; (Grad) degree; (Mäßigung) moderation; **in od mit Maß[en]** in moderation; **in hohem Maße** to a high degree

Maß² f -,- (SGer) litre [of beer]

Massage /maˈsaːʒə/ f -,-n massage

Massaker nt -s,- massacre

Maßanzug m made-to-measure suit. **M~band** nt (pl -bänder) tape-measure

Masse f -,-n mass; (Culin) mixture; (Menschen-) crowd; **eine M~ Arbeit** (fam) masses of work. **M~nartikel** m mass-produced article. **m~nhaft** adv in huge quantities. **M~nmedien** pl mass media. **M~nproduktion** f mass production. **m~nweise** adv in huge numbers

Masseu|r /maˈsøːʁ/ m -s,-e masseur. **M~rin** f -,-nen, **M~se** /-ˈsøːzə/ f -,-n masseuse

maß|gebend a authoritative; *(einflußreich)* influential. **m~geblich** a decisive, adv -ly. **m~geschneidert** a made-to-measure. **m~halten†** vi sep *(haben)* exercise moderation

massieren[1] vt massage

massieren[2] (sich) vr mass

massig a massive

mäßig a moderate, adv -ly; *(mittelmäßig)* indifferent. **m~en** vt moderate; **sich m~en** moderate; *(sich beherrschen)* restrain oneself. **M~keit** f - moderation. **M~ung** f - moderation

massiv a solid; *(stark)* heavy

Maß|krug m beer mug. **m~los** a excessive; *(grenzenlos)* boundless; *(äußerst)* extreme, adv -ly. **M~nahme** f -,-n measure. **m~regeln** vt reprimand

Maßstab m scale; *(Norm & fig)* standard. **m~gerecht**, **m~sgetreu** a scale... □adv to scale

maßvoll a moderate

Mast[1] m -[e]s,-en pole; *(Überland-)* pylon; *(Naut)* mast

Mast[2] f - fattening. **M~darm** m rectum

mästen vt fatten

Masturb|ation /-'tsjo:n/ f - masturbation. **m~ieren** vi *(haben)* masturbate

Material nt -s,-ien /-jən/ material; *(coll)* materials pl. **M~ismus** m - materialism. **m~istisch** a materialistic

Mater|ie /ma'te:rjə/ f -,-n matter; *(Thema)* subject. **m~iell** a material

Mathe f - *(fam)* maths sg

Mathe|matik f - mathematics sg. **M~matiker** m -s,- mathematician. **m~matisch** a mathematical

Matinee f -,-n *(Theat)* morning performance

Matratze f -,-n mattress

Mätresse f -,-n mistress

Matrose m -n,-n sailor

Matsch m -[e]s mud; *(Schnee-)* slush. **m~ig** a muddy; slushy; *(weich)* mushy

matt a weak; *(gedämpft)* dim; *(glanzlos)* dull; *(Politur, Farbe)* matt; **jdn m~ setzen** checkmate s.o. **M~ ~ nt -s** *(Schach)* mate

Matte f -,-n mat

Mattglas nt frosted glass

Matt|igkeit f - weakness; *(Müdigkeit)* weariness. **M~scheibe** f *(fam)* television screen

Matura f *(Aust)* ≈ A levels pl

Mauer f -,-n wall. **m~n** vt build □vi *(haben)* lay bricks. **M~werk** nt masonry

Maul nt -[e]s,Mäuler *(Zool)* mouth; **halt's M~!** *(fam)* shut up! **m~en** vi *(haben)* grumble. **M~korb** m muzzle. **M~tier** nt mule. **M~wurf** m mole. **M~wurfshaufen, M~wurfshügel** m molehill

Maurer m -s,- bricklayer

Maus f -,Mäuse mouse. **M~efalle** f mousetrap

mausern (sich) vr moult; *(fam)* turn (zu into)

Maut f -,-en *(Aust)* toll. **M~straße** f toll road

maximal a maximum

Maximum nt -s,-ma maximum

Mayonnaise /majo'nɛ:zə/ f -,-n mayonnaise

Mäzen m -s,-e patron

Mechan|ik /me'ça:nɪk/ f - mechanics sg; *(Mechanismus)* mechanism. **M~iker** m -s,- mechanic. **m~isch** a mechanical, adv -ly. **m~isieren** vt mechanize. **M~ismus** m -,-men mechanism

meckern vi *(haben)* bleat; *(fam: nörgeln)* grumble

Medaille /me'daljə/ f -,-n medal. **M~on** /-'jő:/ nt -s,-s medallion; *(Schmuck)* locket

Medikament nt -[e]s,-e medicine

Medit|ation /-'tsio:n/ f -,-en meditation. **m~ieren** vi (haben) meditate

Medium nt -s,-ien medium; **die Medien** the media

Medizin f -,-en medicine. **M~er** m -s,- doctor; (Student) medical student. **m~isch** a medical; (heilkräftig) medicinal

Meer nt -[e]s,-e sea. **M~busen** m gulf. **M~enge** f strait. **M~esspiegel** m sea-level. **M~jungfrau** f mermaid. **M~rettich** m horseradish. **M~schweinchen** nt -s,- guinea-pig

Megaphon nt -s,-e megaphone

Mehl nt -[e]s flour. **m~ig** a floury. **M~schwitze** f (Culin) roux. **M~speise** f (Aust) dessert; (Kuchen) pastry. **M~tau** m (Bot) mildew

mehr pron & adv more; **nicht m~** no more; (zeitlich) no longer; **nichts m~** no more; (nichts weiter) nothing else; **nie m~** never again. **m~deutig** a ambiguous. **m~en** vt increase; **sich m~en** increase. **m~ere** pron several. **m~eres** pron several things pl. **m~fach** a multiple; (mehrmalig) repeated □ adv several times. **M~fahrtenkarte** f book of tickets. **m~farbig** a [multi]coloured. **M~heit** f -,-en majority. **m~malig** a repeated. **m~mals** adv several times. **m~sprachig** a multilingual. **m~stimmig** a (Mus) for several voices □ adv m~stimmig singen sing in harmony. **M~wertsteuer** f value-added tax, VAT. **M~zahl** f majority; (Gram) plural. **M~zweck-** pref multi-purpose

melden† vt avoid, shun

Meierei f -,-en (dial) dairy

Meile f -,-n mile. **M~nstein** m milestone. **m~nweit** adv [for] miles

mein poss pron my. **m~e(r,s)** poss pron mine; **die M~en** pl my family sg

Meineid m perjury; **einen M~ leisten** perjure oneself

meinen vt mean; (glauben) think; (sagen) say; **es gut m~** mean well

mein|erseits adv for my part. **m~etwegen** adv for me/ my sake; (wegen mir) because of me, on my account; (fam: von mir aus) as far as I'm concerned. **m~etwillen** adv um m~etwillen for my sake. **m~ige** poss pron **der/die/das m~ige** mine. **m~s** poss pron mine

Meinung f -,-en opinion; **jdm die M~ sagen** give s.o. a piece of one's mind. **M~sumfrage** f opinion poll

Meise f -,-n (Zool) tit

Meißel m -s,- chisel. **m~n** vt/i (haben) chisel

meist adv mostly; (gewöhnlich) usually. **m~e** a der/die/das m~e most; **die m~en Leute** most people; **die m~e Zeit** most of the time; **am m~en** [the] most □ pron das **m~e** most [of it]; **die m~en** most. **m~ens** adv mostly; (gewöhnlich) usually

Meister m -s,- master craftsman; (Könner) master; (Sport) champion. **m~haft** a masterly □ adv in masterly fashion. **m~n** vt master. **M~schaft** f -,-en mastery; (Sport) championship. **M~stück** n, **M~werk** nt masterpiece

Melanch|olie /melaŋko'li:/ f - melancholy. **m~olisch** a melancholy

meld|en vt report; (anmelden) register; (ankündigen) announce; **sich m~en** report (bei to); (zum Militär) enlist; (freiwillig) volunteer; (Teleph) answer; (Sch) put up one's hand; (von sich hören lassen) get in touch (bei with);

sich krank m~en report sick.
M~ung ƒ -,-en report; (*Anmeldung*) registration

meliert *a* mottled; **grau m~es Haar** hair flecked with grey

melken† *vt* milk

Melod|ie ƒ -,-n tune, melody.
m~iös *a* melodious

melodisch *a* melodic; (*melodiös*) melodious, tuneful

melodramatisch *a* melodramatic, *adv* -ally

Melone ƒ -,-n melon; [schwarze]
M~ (*fam*) bowler [hat]

Membran ƒ -,-en membrane

Memoiren |me'mǫa:rən| *pl* memoirs

Menge ƒ -,-n amount, quantity; (*Menschen-*) crowd; (*Math*) set; **eine M~ Geld** a lot of money.
m~n *vt* mix

Mensa ƒ -,-sen (*Univ*) refectory

Mensch *m* -en,-en human being;
der M~ man; die M~en people;
jeder/kein M~ everybody/nobody. M~enaffe *m* ape. M~enfeind *m* misanthropist. m~enfeindlich *a* antisocial. M~enfresser *m* -s,- cannibal; (*Zool*)
man-eater; (*fam*) ogre. M~enfreundlich *a* philanthropic.
M~enleben *nt* human life; (*Lebenszeit*) lifetime. m~enleer *a* deserted. M~enmenge ƒ crowd.
M~enraub *m* kidnapping.
M~enrechte *ntpl* human rights. m~enscheu *a* unsociable. M~enskind *int* (*fam*)
good heavens! M~enverstand *m* gesunder M~enverstand
common sense. m~enwürdig *a* humane, *adv* -ly. M~heit ƒ - die
M~heit mankind, humanity.
m~lich *a* human; (*human*)
humane, *adv* -ly. M~lichkeit ƒ - humanity

Menstru|ation /-'tsjo:n/ ƒ - menstruation. m~ieren *vi* (*haben*)
menstruate

Mentalität ƒ -,-en mentality

Menü *nt* -s,-s menu; (*festes M~*)
set meal

Menuett *nt* -[e]s,-e minuet

Meridian *m* -s,-e meridian

merk|bar *a* noticeable. M~blatt
nt [explanatory] leaflet. m~en *vt*
notice; sich (*dat*) etw m~en remember sth. m~lich *a* noticeable, *adv*-bly. M~mal *nt* feature

merkwürdig *a* odd, *adv* -ly,
strange, *adv* -ly. m~erweise
adv oddly enough

meß|bar *a* measurable. M~becher *m* (*Culin*) measure

Messe¹ ƒ -,-n (*Relig*) mass; (*Comm*)
[trade] fair

Messe² ƒ -,-n (*Mil*) mess

messen† *vt/i* (*haben*) measure;
(*ansehen*) look at; [bei jdm]
Fieber m~ take s.o.'s temperature; sich m~ compete (mit
jdm with); sich mit jdm m~/nicht
m~ können be a/no match for
s.o.

Messer *nt* -s,- knife

Messias *m* - Messiah

Messing *nt* -s brass

Messung ƒ -,-en measurement

Metabolismus *m* - metabolism

Metall *nt* -s,-e metal. m~en *a*
metal; (*metallisch*) metallic.
m~isch *a* metallic

Metallurgie ƒ - metallurgy

Metamorphose ƒ -,-n metamorphosis

Metaph|er ƒ -,-n metaphor.
m~orisch *a* metaphorical, *adv*
-ly

Meteor *m* -s,-e meteor. M~ologe
m -n,-n meteorologist. M~ologie ƒ - meteorology. m~ologisch *a* meteorological

Meter *m* & *nt* -s,- metre, (*Amer*)
meter. M~maß *nt* tape-measure

Method|e ƒ -,-n method. m~isch
a methodical

metrisch *a* metric

Metropole ƒ -,-n metropolis

metzeln vt (fig) massacre

Metzger m -s,- butcher. **M~ei** f -,-en butcher's shop

Meute f -,-n pack [of hounds]; (fig: Menge) mob

Meuterei f -,-en mutiny

meutern vi (haben) mutiny; (fam: schimpfen) grumble

Mexikan|er(in) m -s, (f -,-nen) Mexican. **m~isch** a Mexican

Mexiko nt -s Mexico

miauen vi (haben) mew, miaow

mich pron (acc of ich) me; (refl) myself

Mieder nt -s,- bodice (Korsett) corset

Miene f -,-n expression; **M~ machen** make as if (zu to)

mies a (fam) lousy; **mir ist m~** I feel rotten

Miet|e f -,-n rent; (Mietgebühr) hire charge; **zur M~e wohnen** live in rented accommodation. **m~en** vt rent ⟨Haus, Zimmer⟩; hire ⟨Auto, Boot, Fernseher⟩. **M~er(in)** m -s,- (f -,-nen) tenant. **m~frei** a & adv rent-free. **M~shaus** nt block of rented flats. **M~vertrag** m lease. **M~wagen** m hire-car. **M~wohnung** f rented flat; (zu vermieten) flat to let

Mieze f -,-n (fam) puss[y]

Migräne f -,-n migraine

Mikrobe f -,-n microbe

Mikro|chip m microchip. **M~computer** m microcomputer. **M~film** m microfilm

Mikro|fon, M~phon nt -s,-e microphone. **M~prozessor** m -s,-en /-'so:rən/ microprocessor. **M~skop** nt -s,-e microscope. **m~skopisch** a microscopic

Mikrowelle f microwave. **M~ngerät** nt, **M~nherd** m microwave oven

Milbe f -,-n mite

Milch f - milk. **M~bar** f milk bar. **M~geschäft** nt dairy. **M~glas**

nt opal glass. **m~ig** a milky. **M~kuh** f dairy cow. **M~mann** m (pl -männer) milkman. **M~mixgetränk** nt milk shake. **M~straße** f Milky Way

mild a mild; (nachsichtig) lenient; **m~e Gaben** alms. **M~e** f -mildness; leniency. **m~ern** vt make milder; (mäßigen) moderate; (lindern) alleviate, ease; **sich m~ern** become milder; (sich mäßigen) moderate; (nachlassen) abate; ⟨Schmerz:⟩ ease; **m~ernde Umstände** mitigating circumstances. **m~tätig** a charitable

Milieu /mi'ljø:/ nt -s,-s [social] environment

militant a militant

Militär nt -s army; (Soldaten) troops pl; **beim M~** in the army. **m~isch** a military

Miliz f -,-en militia

Milliarde /mɪr'ljardə/ f -,-n thousand million, billion

Milli|gramm nt milligram. **M~meter** m & nt millimetre. **M~meterpapier** nt graph paper

Million /mɪr'ljo:n/ f -,-en million. **M~är** m -s,-e millionaire. **M~ärin** f -,-nen millionairess

Milz f - (Anat) spleen

mimen vt (fam: vortäuschen) act. **M~ik** f - [expressive] gestures and facial expressions pl

Mimose f -,-n mimosa

minder a lesser □ adv less; **mehr oder m~** more or less. **M~heit** f -,-en minority

minderjährig a under-age; **m~ sein** be under age. **M~e(r)** m/f (Jur) minor. **M~keit** f - (Jur) minority

mindern vt diminish; decrease ⟨Tempo⟩. **M~ung** f -decrease

minderwertig a inferior. **M~keit** f - inferiority. **M~keitskomplex** m inferiority complex

Mindest- *pref* minimum. **m~e** *a & pron* der/die/das ~ the least; **zum m~en** at least; **nicht im m~en** not in the least. **m~ens** *adv* at least. **M~lohn** *m* minimum wage. **M~maß** *nt* minimum

Mine *f* -,-n mine; (*Bleistift*-) lead; (*Kugelschreiber*-) refill. **M~nfeld** *nt* minefield. **M~nräumboot** *nt* minesweeper

Mineral *nt* -s,-e & -ien /-iən/ mineral. **m~isch** *a* mineral. **M~ogie** *f* - mineralogy. **M~wasser** *nt* mineral water

Miniatur *f* -,-en miniature

Minigolf *nt* miniature golf

minimal *a* minimal

Minimum *nt* -s,-ma minimum

Minirock *m* miniskirt

Min|ster *m* -s,- minister. **m~steriell** *a* ministerial. **M~sterium** *nt* -s,-ien ministry

Minorität *f* -,-en minority

minus *conj, adv & prep* (+ *gen*) minus. **M~** *nt*- deficit; (*Nachteil*) disadvantage. **M~zeichen** *nt* minus [sign]

Minute *f* -,-n minute

mir *pron* (*dat of* ich) [to] me; (*refl*) myself; **mir nichts, dir nichts** without so much as a 'by your leave'

Misch|ehe *f* mixed marriage. **m~en** *vt* mix; blend ⟨*Tee, Kaffee*⟩; toss ⟨*Salat*⟩; shuffle ⟨*Karten*⟩; **sich m~en** mix; ⟨*Person:*⟩ mingle (unter + *acc* with); **sich m~en in** (+ *acc*) join in ⟨*Gespräch*⟩; meddle in ⟨*Angelegenheit*⟩ □*vi* (*haben*) shuffle the cards. **M~ling** *m* -s,-e half-caste; (*Hund*) cross. **M~masch** *m* -[e]s,-e (*fam*) hotchpotch. **M~ung** *f* -,-en mixture; blend

miserabel *a* abominable; (*erbärmlich*) wretched

mißachten *vt* disregard

Miß|achtung *f* disregard. **M~behagen** *nt* [feeling of] unease. **M~bildung** *f* deformity

mißbilligen *vt* disapprove of

Miß|billigung *f* disapproval. **M~brauch** *m* abuse; **M~brauch treiben mit** abuse

miß|brauchen *vt* abuse; (*vergewaltigen*) rape. **m~deuten** *vt* misinterpret

missen *vt* do without; **ich möchte es nicht m~** I should not like to be without it

Miß|erfolg *m* failure. **M~ernte** *f* crop failure

Misse|tat *f* misdeed. **M~täter** *m* (*fam*) culprit

mißfallen† *vi* (*haben*) displease (jdm s.o.)

Miß|fallen *nt* -s displeasure; (*Mißbilligung*) disapproval. **m~gebildet** *a* deformed. **M~geburt** *f* freak; (*fig*) monstrosity. **M~geschick** *nt* mishap; (*Unglück*) misfortune. **m~gestimmt** *a* **m~gestimmt sein** be in a bad mood

miß|glücken *vi* (*sein*) fail. **m~gönnen** *vt* begrudge

Miß|griff *m* mistake. **M~gunst** *f* resentment. **m~günstig** *a* resentful

mißhandeln *vt* ill-treat

Miß|handlung *f* ill-treatment. **M~helligkeit** *f* -,-en disagreement

Mission *f* -,-en mission

Missionar(in) *m* -s,-e (*f* -,-nen) missionary

Miß|klang *m* discord. **M~kredit** *m* discredit; **in M~kredit bringen** discredit. **m~lich** *a* awkward. **m~liebig** *a* unpopular

mißlingen† *vi* (*sein*) fail; **es mißlang ihr** she failed. **M~** *nt* -s failure

Mißmut *m* ill humour. **m~ig** *a* morose, *adv* -ly

mißraten† *vi (sein)* turn out badly

Miß|stand *m* abuse; *(Zustand)* undesirable state of affairs. **M~stimmung** *f* discord; *(Laune)* bad mood. **M~ton** *m* discordant note

mißtrauen *vi (haben)* jdm/etw m~ mistrust s.o./sth; *(Argwohn hegen)* distrust s.o./sth

Mißtrau|en *nt* -s mistrust; *(Argwohn)* distrust. **M~ensvotum** *nt* vote of no confidence. **m~isch** *a* distrustful; *(argwöhnisch)* suspicious

Miß|verhältnis *nt* disproportion. **M~verständnis** *nt* misunderstanding. **m~verstehen**† *vt* misunderstand. **M~wirtschaft** *f* mismanagement

Mist *m* -[e]s manure; *(fam)* rubbish

Mistel *f* -,-n mistletoe

Misthaufen *m* dungheap

mit *prep* (+ *dat*) with; *(sprechen)* to; *(mittels)* by; *(inklusive)* including; *(bei)* at; **mit Bleistift** in pencil; **mit lauter Stimme** in a loud voice; **mit drei Jahren** at the age of three □*adv (auch)* as well; **mit anfassen** *(fig)* lend a hand; **es ist mit das ärmste Land der Welt** it is among the poorest countries in the world

Mitarbeit *f* collaboration. **m~en** *vi sep* collaborate (**an** + *dat* on). **M~er(in)** *m(f)* collaborator; *(Kollege)* colleague; *(Betriebsangehörige)* employee

Mitbestimmung *f* co-determination

mitbringen|en† *vt sep* bring [along]; **jdm Blumen m~en** bring/(*hinbringen*) take s.o. flowers. **M~sel** *nt* -s,- present *(brought back from holiday etc)*

Mitbürger *m* fellow citizen

miteinander *adv* with each other

miterleben *vt sep* witness

Mitesser *m (Med)* blackhead

mitfahren† *vi sep (sein)* go/come along; **mit jdm m~** go with s.o.; *(mitgenommen werden)* be given a lift by s.o.

mitfühlen *vi sep (haben)* sympathize. **m~d** *a* sympathetic; *(mitleidig)* compassionate

mitgeben† *vt sep* **jdm etw m~** give s.o. sth to take with him

Mitgefühl *nt* sympathy

mitgehen† *vi sep (sein)* **mit jdm m~** go with s.o.; **etw m~ lassen** *(fam)* pinch sth

mitgenommen *a* worn; **m~ sein** be in a sorry state; *(erschöpft)* be exhausted

Mitgift *f* -,-en dowry

Mitglied *nt* member. **M~schaft** *f* - membership

mithalten† *vi sep (haben)* join in; **mit jdm nicht m~ können** not be able to keep up with s.o.

Mithilfe *f* assistance

mitkommen† *vi sep (sein)* come [along] too; *(fig: folgen können)* keep up; *(verstehen)* follow

Mitlaut *m* consonant

Mitleid *nt* pity, compassion. **M~enschaft** *f* **in M~enschaft ziehen** affect. **m~erregend** *a* pitiful. **m~ig** *a* pitying; *(mitfühlend)* compassionate. **m~slos** *a* pitiless

mitmachen *v sep* □*vt* take part in; *(erleben)* go through □*vi (haben)* join in

Mitmensch *m* fellow man

mitnehmen† *vt sep* take along; *(mitfahren lassen)* give a lift to; *(fig: schädigen)* affect badly; *(erschöpfen)* exhaust; **'zum M~n'** 'to take away', *(Amer)* 'to go'

mitnichten *adv* not at all

mitreden *vi sep (haben)* join in [the conversation]; *(mit entscheiden)* have a say (**bei** in)

mitreißen† *vt sep* sweep along; *(fig: begeistern)* carry away; **m~d** rousing

mitsamt prep (+dat) together with

mitschneiden† vt sep record

mitschreiben† vt sep (haben) take down

Mitschuld f partial blame. **m~ig** a m~ig sein be partly to blame

Mitschüler(in) m(f) fellow pupil

mitspielen vi sep (haben) join in; (Theat) be in the cast; (beitragen) play a part; **jdm übel m~en** treat s.o. badly. **M~er** m fellow player; (Mitwirkender) participant

Mittag m midday, noon; (Mahlzeit) lunch; (Pause) lunch-break; [zu] **M~ essen** have lunch. **m~** adv heute **m~** at lunch-time today. **M~essen** nt lunch. **m~s** adv at noon; (als Mahlzeit) for lunch; **um 12 Uhr m~s** at noon. **M~spause** f lunch-hour; (Pause) lunch-break. **M~sschlaf** m after-lunch nap. **M~tisch** m lunch table; (Essen) lunch. **M~szeit** f lunch-time

Mittäter(in) m(f) accomplice. **M~schaft** f complicity

Mitte f -,-n middle; (Zentrum) centre; **die goldene M~** the golden mean; **M~ Mai** in mid-May; **in unserer M~** in our midst

mitteilen vt sep jdm etw **m~en** tell s.o. sth; (amtlich) inform s.o. of sth. **m~sam** a communicative. **M~ung** f-,-en communication; (Nachricht) piece of news

Mittel nt -s, means sg; (Heilremedy; (Medikament) medicine; (M~wert) mean; (Durchschnitt) average; **m~** pl (Geld-) funds, resources. **m~** pred a medium; (m~mäßig) middling. **M~alter** nt Middle Ages pl. **m~alterlich** a medieval. **m~bar** a indirect, adv -ly. **M~ding** nt (fig) cross. **m~europäisch** a Central European. **M~finger** m middle finger. **m~groß** a medium-

sized; (Person) of medium height. **m~klasse** f middle range. **m~los** a destitute. **m~mäßig** a middling; [nur] **m~mäßig** mediocre. **M~meer** nt Mediterranean. **M~punkt** m centre; (fig) centre of attention

mittels prep (+gen) by means of

Mittelschule f = Realschule. **M~smann** m (pl -männer), **M~sperson** f intermediary, go-between. **M~stand** m middle class. **m~ste(r,s)** a middle. **M~streifen** m (Auto) central reservation, (Amer) median strip. **M~stürmer** m centre-forward. **M~weg** m (fig) middle course; **goldener M~weg** happy medium. **M~welle** f medium wave. **M~wort** nt (pl -wörter) participle

mitten adv **m~ in/auf** (dat/acc) in the middle of; **m~ unter** (dat/acc) amidst. **m~durch** adv [right] through the middle

Mitternacht f midnight

mittler e(r,s) a middle; (Größe, Qualität) medium; (durchschnittlich) mean, average. **m~weile** adv meanwhile; (seitdem) by now

Mittwoch m -s,-e Wednesday. **m~s** adv on Wednesdays

mitunter adv now and again

mitwirken vi sep (haben) take part; (helfen) contribute. **M~ung** f participation

mixen vt mix. **M~er** m -s,- (Culin) liquidizer, blender. **M~tur** f -,-en (Med) mixture

Möbel pl furniture sg. **M~stück** nt piece of furniture. **M~tischler** m cabinet-maker. **M~wagen** m removal van

mobil a mobile; (fam: munter) lively; (nach Krankheit) fit (and well]; **m~ machen** mobilize

Mobile nt -s,-s mobile

Mobiliar nt -s furniture

mobilisier|en vt mobilize.
 M~ung f - mobilization
Mobilmachung f - mobilization
möblier|en vt furnish; **m~tes
 Zimmer** furnished room
mochte, möchte s. **mögen**
Modalverb nt modal auxiliary
Mode f -,-n fashion; **M~ sein** be
 fashionable
Modell nt -s,-e model; **M~ stehen** pose (**jdm** for s.o.). **m~ie-
 ren** vt model
Modenschau f fashion show
Modera|tor m -s,-en /-ˈtoːrən/,
 M~torin f -,-nen (TV) presenter
modern[1] vi (haben) decay
modern[2] a modern; (modisch)
 fashionable. **m~isieren** vt modernize
Mode|schmuck m costume jew-
 ellery. **M~schöpfer** m fashion
 designer
Modifi|kation /-ˈtsjoːn/ f -,-en
 modification. **m~zieren** vt modify
modisch a fashionable
Modistin f -,-nen milliner
modrig a musty
modulieren vt modulate
Mofa nt -s,-s moped
mogeln vi (haben) (fam) cheat
mögen† vt like; **lieber m~** prefer
 □ v aux **ich möchte** I'd like;
 möchtest du nach Hause? do
 you want to go home? **ich mag
 nicht mehr** I've had enough; **ich
 hätte weinen m~** I could have
 cried; **ich mag mich irren** I may
 be wrong; **wer/was mag das
 sein?** whoever/whatever can it
 be? **wie mag es ihm ergangen
 sein?** I wonder how he got on;
 [das] mag sein that may well be;
 mag kommen, was da will
 come what may
möglich a possible; **alle m~en** in
 all sorts of. **m~erweise** adv possibly. **M~keit** f -,-en possibility.
 M~keitsform f subjunctive

m~st adv if possible; **m~st
 viel/früh** as much/early as possible
Mohammedan|er(in) m -s,- (f
 -,-nen) Muslim. **m~isch** a Muslim
Mohn m -s poppy; (Culin) poppy-
 seed. **M~blume** f poppy
Möhre, Mohrrübe f -,-n carrot
mokieren (sich) vr make fun
 (**über** + acc of)
Mokka m -s mocha; (Geschmack)
 coffee
Molch m -[e]s,-e newt
Mole f -,-n (Naut) mole
Molekül nt -s,-e molecule
Molkerei f -,-en dairy
Moll nt - (Mus) minor
mollig a cosy; (warm) warm;
 (rundlich) plump
Moment m -[e]s,-e moment; **im/je-
 den M~** at the/any moment; **M~
 [mal]!** just a moment! **m~an** a
 momentary, adv -ily; (gegenwärtig) at the moment
Momentaufnahme f snapshot
Monarch m -en,-en monarch.
 M~ie f -,-n monarchy
Monat m -s,-e month. **m~elang**
 adv for months. **m~lich** a & adv
 monthly. **M~skarte** f monthly
 season ticket
Mönch m -[e]s,-e monk
Mond m -[e]s,-e moon
mondän a fashionable, adv -bly
Mond|finsternis f lunar eclipse.
 m~hell a moonlit. **M~sichel** f
 crescent moon. **M~schein** m
 moonlight
monieren vt criticize
Monitor m -s,-en /-ˈtoːrən/ (Techn)
 monitor
Monogramm nt -s,-e monogram
Mono|log m -s,-e monologue.
 M~pol nt -s,-e monopoly.
 m~polisieren vt monopolize.
 m~ton a monotonous, adv -ly.
 m~tonie f - monotony
Monster nt -s,- monster

monstr|ös *a* monstrous. **M~osität** *f* -,-en monstrosity

Monstrum *nt* -s,-stren monster

Monsun *m* -s,-e monsoon

Montag *m* Monday

Montage /mɔn'taːʒə/ *f*,-/-,-n fitting; (*Zusammenbau*) assembly; (*Film-*) editing; (*Kunst*) montage

montags *adv* on Mondays

Montanindustrie *f* coal and steel industry

Monteur /mɔn'tøːɐ/ *m* -s,-e fitter. **M~anzug** *m* overalls *pl*

montieren *vt* fit; (*zusammenbauen*) assemble

Monument *nt* -[e]s,-e monument. **m~al** *a* monumental

Moor *nt* -[e]s,-e bog; (*Heide-*) moor

Moos *nt* -es,-e moss. **m~ig** *a* mossy

Mop *m* -s,-s mop

Moped *nt* -s,-s moped

Mops *m* -es,⸚e pug [dog]

Moral *f* - morals *pl*; (*Selbstvertrauen*) morale; (*Lehre*) moral. **m~isch** *a* moral, *adv* -ly. **m~isieren** *vi* (*haben*) moralize

Morast *m* -[e]s,-e morass; (*Schlamm*) mud

Mord *m* -[e]s,-e murder; (*Pol*) assassination. **M~anschlag** *m* murder/assassination attempt. **m~en** *vt/i* (*haben*) murder, kill

Mörder *m* -s,- murderer; (*Pol*) assassin. **M~in** *f*,-,-nen murderess. **m~isch** *a* murderous; (*fam: schlimm*) dreadful

Mords- *pref* (*fam*) terrific. **m~mäßig** *a* (*fam*) frightful, *adv* -ly

morgen *adv* tomorrow; **m~ früh/nachmittag** tomorrow morning/afternoon; **heute/gestern/Montag m~** this/yesterday/Monday morning

Morgen *m* -s,- morning; (*Maß*) ≈ acre; **am M~** in the morning. **M~dämmerung** *f* dawn. **m~dlich** *a* morning ...

M~grauen *nt* -s dawn; **im**

M~grauen at dawn. **M~mantel**, **M~rock** *m* dressing-gown. **M~rot** *nt* red sky in the morning. **m~s** *a* in the morning

morgig *a* tomorrow's; **der m~e Tag** tomorrow

Morphium *nt* -s morphine

morsch *a* rotten

Morsealphabet *nt* Morse code

Mörtel *m* -s mortar

Mosaik /moza'iːk/ *nt* -s,-e[n] mosaic

Moschee *f*,-,-n mosque

Mosel *f* - Moselle. **M~wein** *m* Moselle [wine]

Moskau *nt* -s Moscow

Moskito *m* -s,-s mosquito

Mos|lem *m* -s,-s Muslim. **m~lemisch** *a* Muslim

Most *m* -[e]s must; (*Apfel-*) ≈ cider

Mostrich *m* -s (*NGer*) mustard

Motel *nt* -s,-s motel

Motiv *nt* -s,-e motive; (*Kunst*) motif. **M~ation** /-'tsjoːn/ *f* - motivation. **m~ieren** *vt* motivate

Motor /'moːtɔr, moː'toːr/ *m* -s,-en /-'toːrən/ engine; (*Elektro-*) motor. **M~boot** *nt* motor boat

motorisieren *vt* motorize

Motor|rad *nt* motor cycle. **M~radfahrer** *m* motor-cyclist. **M~roller** *m* motor scooter

Motte *f*,-,-n moth. **M~nkugel** *f* mothball

Motto *nt* -s,-s motto

Möwe *f*,-,-n gull

Mücke *f*,-,-n gnat; (*kleine*) midge; (*Stech-*) mosquito

mucksen (sich) *vr* sich nicht **m~** (*fam*) keep quiet

müd|e *a* tired; nicht **m~e werden/es m~e sein** not tire/be tired (etw zu tun of doing sth). **M~igkeit** *f* - tiredness

Muff *m* -s,-e muff

muffig *a* musty; (*fam: mürrisch*) grumpy

Mühe *f* -,-n effort; (*Aufwand*) trouble; **sich** (*dat*) **M~ geben**

make an effort; (*sich bemühen*) try; **nicht der M~** wert not worth while; **mit M~ und Not** with great difficulty; (*gerade noch*) only just. **m~los** *a* effortless, *adv* -ly

muhen *vi* (*haben*) moo

mühe|n (**sich**) *vr* struggle. **m~voll** *a* laborious; (*anstrengend*) arduous

Mühl|e *f* -,-n mill; (*Kaffee-*) grinder. **M~stein** *m* millstone

Müh|sal *f* -,-e (*liter*) toil; (*Mühe*) trouble. **m~sam** *a* laborious, *adv* -ly; (*beschwerlich*) difficult, *adv* with difficulty. **m~selig** *a* laborious, *adv* -ly

Mulde *f* -,-n hollow

Müll *m* -s refuse, (*Amer*) garbage. **M~abfuhr** *f* refuse collection

Mullbinde *f* gauze bandage

Mülleimer *m* waste bin; (*Mülltonne*) dustbin, (*Amer*) garbage can

Müller *m* -s,- miller

Müll|halde *f* [rubbish] dump. **M~schlucker** *m* refuse chute. **M~tonne** *f* dustbin, (*Amer*) garbage can. **M~wagen** *m* dustcart, (*Amer*) garbage truck

mulmig *a* (*fam*) dodgy; (*Gefühl*) uneasy; **ihm war m~** he felt uneasy/(*übel*) queasy

multi|national *a* multinational. **M~plikation** /-'tsjo:n/ *f* -,-en multiplication. **m~plizieren** *vt* multiply

Mumie /'mu:mjə/ *f* -,-n mummy

mumifiziert *a* mummified

Mumm *m* -s (*fam*) energy

Mumps *m* - mumps

Mund *m* -[e]s,̈er mouth; **halt den M~!** be quiet! (*sl*) shut up! **M~art** *f* dialect. **m~artlich** *a* dialect

Mündel *nt* & *m* -s,- (*Jur*) ward. **m~sicher** *a* gilt-edged

münden *vi* (*sein*) flow/(*Straße*) lead (**in** + *acc* into)

mund|faul *a* taciturn. **M~geruch** *m* bad breath. **M~harmonika** *f* mouth-organ

mündig *a* **m~ sein/werden** (*Jur*) be /come of age. **M~keit** *f* - (*Jur*) majority

mündlich *a* verbal, *adv* -ly; **m~e Prüfung** oral

Mund|stück *nt* mouthpiece; (*Zigaretten-*) tip. **m~tot** *a* **m~tot machen** (*fig*) gag

Mündung *f* -,-en (*Fluß-*) mouth; (*Gewehr-*) muzzle

Mund|voll *m* -,- mouthful. **M~wasser** *nt* mouthwash. **M~werk** *nt* **ein gutes M~werk haben** (*fam*) be very talkative. **M~winkel** *m* corner of the mouth

Munition /-'tsjo:n/ *f* - ammunition

munkeln *vt/i* (*haben*) talk (**von** of); **es wird gemunkelt** rumour has it (**daß** that)

Münster *nt* -s,- cathedral

munter *a* lively; (*heiter*) merry; **m~ sein** (*wach*) be wide awake/ (*aufgestanden, gesund*) up and about; **gesund und m~** fit and well □ *adv* [*immer*] **m~** merrily

Münz|e *f* -,-n coin; (*M~stätte*) mint. **m~en** *vt* mint; **das war auf dich gemünzt** (*fam*) that was aimed at you. **M~fernsprecher** *m* coin-box telephone, payphone. **M~wäscherei** *f* launderette

mürbe *a* crumbly; (*Obst*) mellow; (*Fleisch*) tender; **jdn m~ machen** (*fig*) wear s.o. down. **M~teig** *m* short pastry

Murmel *f* -,-n marble

murmeln *vt/i* (*haben*) murmur; (*undeutlich*) mumble, mutter. **M~** *nt* -s murmur

Murmeltier *nt* marmot

murren *vt/i* (haben) grumble

mürrisch *a* surly

Mus *nt* -es purée

Muschel *f* -,-n mussel; (Schale) [sea] shell

Museum /mu'ze:ʊm/ *nt* -s,-seen /-'ze:ən/ museum

Musik *f* -music. **M~alien** /-jən/ *pl* [printed] music *sg.* **m~alisch** *a* musical

Musikbox *f* juke-box

Musiker(in) *m* -s,- (*f* -,-nen) musician

Musik|instrument *nt* musical instrument. **M~kapelle** *f* band. **M~lös** *m* bandstand **pavillon** *m* bandstand

musisch *a* artistic

musizieren *vi* (haben) make music

Muskat *m* -[e]s nutmeg

Muskel *m* -s,-n muscle. **M~kater** *m* stiff and aching muscles *pl*

Musku|latur *f* - muscles *pl*. **m~lös** *a* muscular

Müsli *nt* -s muesli

muß *s.* müssen. **Muß** *nt* - ein Muß a must

Muße *f* - leisure; mit M~ at leisure

müssen† *v aux* etw tun m~ have to/(fam) have got to do sth; ich muß jetzt gehen I have to or must go now; ich mußte lachen I had to laugh; ich muß es wissen I need to know; du müßtest es mal versuchen you might or should try it; muß das sein? is that necessary?

müßig *a* idle; (unnütz) futile. **M~gang** *m* -idleness

mußte, müßte *s.* müssen

Muster *nt* -s,- pattern; (Probe) sample; (Vorbild) model. **M~beispiel** *nt* typical example; (Vorbild) perfect example. **M~betrieb** *m* model factory.

m~gültig, m~haft *a* exemplary. **m~n** *vt* eye; (inspizieren) inspect. **M~schüler(in)** *m(f)* model pupil. **M~ung** *f* -,-en inspection; (Mil) medical; (Muster) pattern

Mut *m* -[e]s courage; jdm Mut machen encourage s.o.

Mutation /-'tsjo:n/ *f* -,-en (Biol) mutation

mut|ig *a* courageous, *adv* -ly. **m~los** *a* despondent; (entmutigt) disheartened

mutmaß|en *vt* presume; (Vermutungen anstellen) speculate. **m~lich** *a* probable, *adv*-bly; der **m~liche Täter** the suspect. **M~ung** *f* -,-en speculation, conjecture

Mutprobe *f* test of courage

Mutter¹ *f* -,¨ mother; werdende **M~** mother-to-be

Mutter² *f* -,-n (Techn) nut

Muttergottes *f* -,- madonna

Mutter|land *nt* motherland. **M~leib** *m* womb

mütterlich *a* maternal; (fürsorglich) motherly. **m~erseits** *adv* on one's/the mother's side

Mutter|mal *nt* birthmark; (dunkel) mole. **M~schaft** *f* - motherhood. **m~seelenallein** *a & adv* all alone. **M~sprache** *f* mother tongue. **M~tag** *m* Mother's Day

Mutti *f* -,-s (fam) mummy

Mutwill|e *m* wantonness. **m~ig** *a* wanton, *adv* -ly

Mütze *f* -,-n cap; wollene **M~** woolly hat

MwSt. *abbr* (Mehrwertsteuer) VAT

mysteriös *a* mysterious, *adv* -ly

Myst|ik /'mystɪk/ *f* - mysticism. **m~isch** *a* mystical

myth|isch *a* mythical. **M~ologie** *f* - mythology. **M~os** *m* -,-then myth

N

na *int* well; **na gut** all right then; **na ja** oh well; **na und?** so what?

Nabe *f* -,-n hub

Nabel *m* -s,-. navel. **N~schnur** *f* umbilical cord

nach *prep* (+ *dat*) after; (*Uhrzeit*) past; (*Richtung*) to; (*greifen, rufen, sich sehnen*) for; (*gemäß*) according to; **meiner Meinung n~** in my opinion; **n~ oben** upwards □*adv* **n~ und n~** gradually, bit by bit; **n~ wie vor** still

nachäffen *vt sep* mimic

nachahm|en *vt sep* imitate. **N~ung** *f* -,-en imitation

nacharbeiten *vt sep* make up for

nacharten *vi sep* (sein) **jdm n~** take after s.o.

Nachbar|(in) *m* -n,-n (*f* -,-nen) neighbour. **N~haus** *nt* house next door. **N~land** *nt* neighbouring country. **n~lich** *a* neighbourly; (*Nachbar-*) neighbouring. **N~schaft** *f* - neighbourhood; **gute N~schaft** neighbourliness

nachbestell|en *vt sep* reorder. **N~ung** *f* repeat order

nachbild|en *vt sep* copy, reproduce. **N~ung** *f* copy, reproduction

nachdatieren *vt sep* backdate

nachdem *conj* after; **je n~** it depends

nachdenk|en† *vi sep* (haben) think (**über** + *acc* about). **n~lich** *a* thoughtful, *adv* -ly

Nachdruck *m* (pl -e) reproduction; (*unveränderter*) reprint; (*Betonung*) emphasis

nachdrücklich *a* emphatic, *adv* -ally

nacheifern *vi sep* (haben) **jdm n~** emulate s.o.

nacheilen *vi sep* (sein) (+ *dat*) hurry after

nacheinander *adv* one after the other

Nachfahre *m* -n,-n descendant

Nachfolge *f* succession. **n~en** *vi sep* (sein) (+ *dat*) follow; (*im Amt*) succeed. **N~er(in)** *m* -s,- (*f* -,-nen) successor

nachforsch|en *vi sep* (haben) make enquiries. **N~ung** *f* enquiry; **N~ungen anstellen** make enquiries

Nachfrage *f* (Comm) demand. **n~n** *vi sep* (haben) enquire

nachfüllen *vt sep* refill ⟨Behälter⟩; **Wasser n~** fill up with water

nachgeben† *vi sep* □ *vi* (haben) give way; (sich fügen) give in, yield □*vt* **jdm Suppe n~** give s.o. more soup

Nachgebühr *f* surcharge

nachgehen† *vi sep* (sein) ⟨Uhr:⟩ be slow; **jdm/etw n~** follow s.o./sth; follow up ⟨Spur, Angelegenheit⟩; pursue ⟨Angelegenheit, Tätigkeit⟩; go about ⟨Arbeit⟩

nachgeraten† *vi sep* (sein) **jdm n~** take after s.o.

Nachgeschmack *m* after-taste

nachgiebig *a* indulgent; (gefällig) compliant. **N~keit** *f* - indulgence; compliance

nachgrübeln *vi sep* (haben) ponder (**über** + *acc* on)

nachhallen *vi sep* (haben) reverberate

nachhaltig *a* lasting

nachhelfen† *vi sep* (haben) help

nachher *adv* later; (danach) afterwards; **bis n~!** see you later!

Nachhilfeunterricht *m* coaching

nachhinein *adv* **im n~** afterwards

nachhinken *vi sep* (sein) (fig) lag behind

nachholen vt sep (später holen) fetch later; (mehr holen) get more; (später machen) do later; (aufholen) catch up on; make up for ⟨Zeit⟩

nachjagen vi sep (haben) (+ dat) chase after

Nachkomme m -n,-n descendant. **n~n†** vi sep (sein) follow [later], come later; (Schritt halten) keep up; etw (dat) n~n (fig) comply with ⟨Bitte, Wunsch⟩; carry out ⟨Versprechen, Pflicht⟩. **N~nschaft** f - descendants pl, progeny

Nachkriegszeit f post-war period

Nachlaß m -lasses,-lässe discount; (Jur) [deceased's] estate

nachlassen† v sep □vi (haben) decrease; ⟨Regen, Hitze:⟩ let up; ⟨Schmerz:⟩ ease; ⟨Sturm:⟩ abate; ⟨Augen, Kräfte, Leistungen:⟩ deteriorate; **er ließ nicht nach [mit Fragen]** he persisted [with his questions] □vt **etw vom Preis n~** take sth off the price

nachlässig a careless, adv -ly; (leger) casual, adv -ly; (unordentlich) sloppy, adv -ily. **N~keit** f - carelessness; sloppiness

nachlaufen† vi sep (sein) (+ dat) run after

nachlegen vt sep Holz/Kohlen n~ put more wood/coal on the fire

nachlesen† vt sep look up

nachlöse|n vi sep (haben) pay one's fare on the train/on arrival. **N~schalter** m excess-fare office

nachmachen vt sep (später machen) do later; (imitieren) imitate, copy; (fälschen) forge; **jdm etw n~** copy sth from s.o.; repeat ⟨Übung⟩ after s.o.

Nachmittag m afternoon. **n~** adv gestern/heute n~ yesterday/this afternoon. **n~s** adv in the afternoon

Nachnahme f etw per N~ schicken send sth cash on delivery or COD

Nachname m surname

Nachporto nt excess postage

nachprüfen vt sep check, verify

nachrechnen vt sep work out; (prüfen) check

Nachrede f üble N~ defamation

Nachricht f -,-en [piece of] news sg; (N~en) news sg; **eine N~ hinterlassen** leave a message; **jdm N~ geben** inform, notify s.o. **N~endienst** m (Mil) intelligence service. **N~ensendung** f news bulletin. **N~enwesen** nt communications pl

nachrücken vi sep (sein) move up

Nachruf m obituary

nachsagen vt sep repeat ⟨jdm after s.o.⟩; **jdm Schlechtes/ Gutes n~** speak ill/well of s.o.; **man sagt ihm nach, daß er geizig ist** he is said to be stingy

Nachsaison f late season

Nachsatz m postscript

nachschicken vt sep (später schicken) send later; (hinterher-) send after ⟨jdm s.o.⟩; send on ⟨Post⟩ ⟨jdm to s.o.⟩

nachschlag|en v sep □vt look up □vi (haben) **in einem Wörterbuch n~en** consult a dictionary; **jdm n~en** take after s.o. **N~ewerk** nt reference book

Nachschlüssel m duplicate key

Nachschrift f transcript; (Nachsatz) postscript

Nachschub m (Mil) supplies pl

nachsehen† v sep □vt (prüfen) check; (nachschlagen) look up; (hinwegsehen über) overlook □vi (prüfen) check; **im Wörterbuch n~** consult a dictionary; **jdm/etw n~** gaze after s.o./sth. **N~** nt **das N~ haben** (fam) go empty-handed

nachsenden *vt sep* forward ⟨*Post*⟩ ⟨jdm to s.o.⟩; '**bitte n~**' 'please forward'

Nachsicht *f* forbearance; (*Milde*) leniency; (*Nachgiebigkeit*) indulgence. **n~ig** *a* forbearing; lenient; indulgent

Nachsilbe *f* suffix

nachsitzen *vi sep* (haben) **n~ müssen** be kept in [after school]; **jdn n~ lassen** give s.o. detention. **N~** *nt* -s (*Sch*) detention

Nachspeise *f* dessert, sweet

Nachspiel *nt* (*fig*) sequel

nachspionieren *vi sep* (haben) **jdm n~** spy on s.o.

nachsprechen† *vt sep* repeat ⟨jdm after s.o.⟩

nachspülen *vt sep* rinse

nächst /-çst/ *prep* (+ *dat*) next to. **n~beste(r,s)** *a* (*zweitbeste*) next best. **n~e(r,s)** *a* next; (*nächstgelegene*) nearest; ⟨*Verwandte*⟩ closest; **n~e Woche** next week; **in er Nähe** close by; **am n~en sein** be nearest or closest □*pron* **der/die/das n~e** the next; **der n~e bitte** next please; **als n~es** next; **fürs n~e** for the time being. **N~e(r)** *m* fellow man

nachstehend *a* following □*adv* below

nachstellen *v sep* □*vt* readjust; put back ⟨*Uhr*⟩ □*vi* (haben) (+ *dat*) pursue

nächst|emal *adv* **das n~emal** [the] next time. **N~enliebe** *f* charity. **n~ens** *adv* shortly. **n~gelegen** *a* nearest. **n~liegend** *a* most obvious

nachstreben *vi sep* (haben) **jdm n~** emulate s.o.

nachsuchen *vi sep* (haben) search; **n~ um** request

Nacht *f* -,-̈e night; **über/bei N~** overnight/at night. **n~** *vor* Montag/morgen *n~* Monday/tomorrow night; **heute n~** tonight;

(*letzte Nacht*) last night; **gestern n~** last night; (*vorletzte Nacht*) the night before last. **N~dienst** *m* night duty

Nachteil *m* disadvantage; **zum N~s** to the detriment (*gen* of). **n~ig** *a* adverse, *adv* -ly

Nacht|essen *nt* (*SGer*) supper. **N~falter** *m* moth. **N~hemd** *nt* night-dress; (*Männer-*) night-shirt

Nachtigall *f* -,-en nightingale

Nachtisch *m* dessert

Nacht|klub *m* night-club. **N~leben** *nt* night-life

nächtlich *a* nocturnal, night...

Nacht|lokal *nt* night-club. **N~mahl** *nt* (*Aust*) supper

Nachtrag *m* postscript; (*Ergänzung*) supplement. **n~en†** *vt sep* add; **jdm etw n~en** walk behind s.o. carrying sth; (*fig*) bear a grudge against s.o. for sth. **n~end** *a* vindictive; **sein bear grudges**

nachträglich *a* subsequent, later; (*verspätet*) belated □*adv* later; (*nachher*) afterwards; (*verspätet*) belatedly

nachtrauern *vi sep* (haben) (+ *dat*) mourn the loss of

Nacht|ruhe *f* night's rest; **angenehme N~ruhe!** sleep well! **n~s** *adv* at night; **2 Uhr n~s** 2 o'clock in the morning. **N~schicht** *f* night-shift. **N~tisch** *m* bedside table. **N~tischlampe** *f* bedside lamp. **N~topf** *m* chamber-pot. **N~wächter** *m* night-watchman. **N~zeit** *f* night-time

Nachuntersuchung *f* check-up

nachwachsen† *vi sep* (sein) grow again

Nachwahl *f* by-election

Nachweis *m* -es,-e proof. **n~bar** *a* demonstrable. **n~en†** *vt sep* prove; (*aufzeigen*) show; (*vermitteln*) give details of; **jdm nichts**

n~en können have no proof against s.o. n~lich *a* demonstrable, *adv* -bly

Nachwelt *f* posterity

Nachwirkung *f* after-effect

Nachwort *nt* (*pl* -e) epilogue

Nachwuchs *m* new generation; (*fam: Kinder*) offspring. N~spieler *m* young player

nachzahlen *vt/i sep* (haben) pay extra; (*später zahlen*) pay later; **Steuern** n~ pay tax arrears

nachzählen *vt/i sep* (haben) count again; (*prüfen*) check

Nachzahlung *f* extra/later payment; (*Gehalts-*) back-payment

nachzeichnen *vt sep* copy

Nachzügler *m* -s,- late-comer; (*Zurückgebliebener*) straggler

Nacken *m* -s,- nape *or* back of the neck

nackt *a* naked; (*bloß, kahl*) bare; (*Schmuck-, Hut-*) pin. N~baden *nt* nude bathing. N~heit *f* -nakedness, nudity. N~kultur *f* nudism. N~schnecke *f* slug

Nadel *f* -,-n needle; (*Häkel-*) hook; (*Schmuck-, Hut-*) pin. N~arbeit *f* needlework. N~baum *m* conifer. N~kissen *nt* pincushion. N~stich *m* stitch; (*fig*) pinprick. N~wald *m* coniferous forest

Nagel *m* -s,- nail. N~bürste *f* nail-brush. N~feile *f* nail-file. N~haut *f* cuticle. N~lack *m* nail varnish. n~n *vt* nail. n~neu *a* brand-new. N~schere *f* nail scissors *pl*

nagen *vt/i* (haben) gnaw (an + *dat* at); n~d (*fig*) nagging

Nagetier *nt* rodent

nah *a*, *adv* & *prep* = nahe; **von nah und fern** from far and wide

Näharbeit *f* sewing; **eine N~** a piece of sewing

Nahaufnahme *f* close-up

nahe *a* (näher, nächst) nearby; (*zeitlich*) imminent; (*eng*) close;

der N~ Osten the Middle East; in n~r Zukunft in the near future; von n~m [from] close to; n~ sein be close (*dat* to); dem Tränen n~ close to tears □*adv* near, close; (*verwandt*) closely; n~ an (+ *acc/dat*) near [to], close to; n~ daran sein, etw zu tun nearly do sth; jdm zu n~ treten (*fig*) offend s.o. □*prep* (+ *dat*) near [to], close to

Nähe *f* - nearness, proximity; aus der N~ [from] close to; in der N~ near *or* close by; in der N~ der Kirche near the church

nahebei *adv* near *or* close by

nahe|gehen *vi sep* (sein) jdm n~gehen (*fig*) affect s.o. deeply. n~kommen *vi sep* (sein) (*fig*) come close (*dat* to); (*vertraut werden*) get close (*dat* to). n~legen *vt sep* recommend (*dat* to); jdm n~legen, etw zu tun urge s.o. to do sth. n~liegen† *vi sep* (haben) (*fig*) be highly likely. n~liegend *a* obvious

nahen *vi* (sein) (*liter*) approach

nähen *vt/i* (haben) sew; (*anfertigen*) make; (*Med*) stitch [up]

näher *a* closer; (*Weg*) shorter; (*Einzelheiten*) further □*adv* closer; (*genauer*) more closely; sich n~ erkundigen make further enquiries; n~ an (+ *acc/dat*) nearer [to], closer to □*prep* (+ *dat*) nearer [to], closer to. N~e[s] *nt* [further] details *pl*. n~kommen† *vi sep* (sein) come closer, approach; (*fig*) get closer (*dat* to). n~n (sich) *vr* approach

nahestehen† *vi sep* (haben) (*fig*) be close (*dat* to)

nahezu *adv* almost

Nähgarn *nt* [sewing] cotton

Nahkampf *m* close combat

Näh|maschine *f* sewing machine. N~nadel *f* sewing-needle

nähren vt feed; (fig) nurture; **sich n~ von** live on □vi (haben) be nutritious

nahrhaft a nutritious

Nährstoff m nutrient

Nahrung f - food, nourishment. **N~smittel** nt food

Nährwert m nutritional value

Naht f -,=e seam; (Med) suture. **n~los** a seamless

Nahverkehr m local service. **N~szug** m local train

Nähzeug nt sewing; (Zubehör) sewing kit

naiv /na'i:f/ a naïve, adv -ly. **N~ität** /-vi'tε:t/ f - naïvety

Name m -ns,-n name; **im N~n** (+ gen) in the name of; ⟨handeln⟩ on behalf of; **das Kind beim rechten N~n nennen** (fam) call a spade a spade. **n~nlos** a nameless; (unbekannt) unknown, anonymous. **n~ns** adv by the name of □prep (+ gen) on behalf of. **N~nstag** m name-day. **N~nsvetter** m namesake. **N~nszug** m signature. **n~ntlich** adv by name; (besonders) especially

namhaft a noted; (ansehnlich) considerable; **n~ machen** name

nämlich adv (und zwar) namely; (denn) because

nanu int hallo

Napf m -[e]s,=e bowl

Narbe f -,-n scar

Narkose f -,-n general anaesthetic. **N~arzt** m anaesthetist. **N~mittel** nt anaesthetic

Narkotikum nt -s,-ka narcotic; (Narkosemittel) anaesthetic. **n~isieren** vt anaesthetize

Narr m -en,-en fool; **zum N~en halten** od **halten** make a fool of. **n~en** vt fool. **n~ensicher** a foolproof. **N~heit** f -,-en folly

Närr|in f -,-nen fool. **n~isch** a foolish; (fam: verrückt) crazy (**auf** + acc about)

Narzisse f -,-n narcissus; **gelbe N~** daffodil

nasal a nasal

nasch|en vt/i (haben) nibble (**an** + dat at); **wer hat von Kuchen genascht?** who's been at the cake? **N~haft** a sweet-toothed

Nase f -,-n nose; **an der N~ herumführen** (fam) dupe

näseln vi (haben) speak through one's nose; **n~d** nasal

Nasen|bluten nt -s nosebleed. **N~loch** nt nostril. **N~rücken** m bridge of the nose

Naseweis m -es,-e (fam) know-all

Nashorn nt rhinoceros

naß a (nasser, nassest) wet

Nässe f - wet; (Naßsein) wetness. **n~n** vt wet

naßkalt a cold and wet

Nation /na'tsio:n/ f -,-en nation. **n~al** a national. **N~alhymne** f national anthem. **N~alismus** m - nationalism. **N~alität** f -,-en nationality. **N~alsozialismus** m National Socialism. **N~alspieler** m international

Natrium nt -s sodium

Natron nt -s doppeltkohlensaures **N~** bicarbonate of soda

Natter f -,-n snake; (Gift-) viper

Natur f -,-en nature; **von N~ aus** by nature. **N~alien** /-jən/ pl natural produce sg. **n~alisieren** vt naturalize. **N~alisierung** f -,-en naturalization

Naturell nt -s,-e disposition

Natur|erscheinung f natural phenomenon. **n~farben** a natural[-coloured]. **N~forscher** m naturalist. **N~kunde** f natural history. **N~lehrpfad** m nature trail

natürlich a natural □adv naturally; (selbstverständlich) of course. **N~keit** f - naturalness

natur|rein a pure. **N~schutz** m nature conservation; **unter**

N~schutz stehen be protected. N~schutzgebiet nt nature reserve. N~wissenschaft f [natural] science. N~wissenschaftler m scientist. n~wissenschaftlich a scientific; (Sch) science ...

nautisch a nautical

Navigation /-'tsjo:n/ f - navigation

Nazi m -s,-s Nazi

n.Chr. abbr (nach Christus) AD

Nebel m -s,- fog; (leicht) mist. n~haft a hazy. N~horn nt foghorn. n~ig a = neblig

neben prep (+ dat/acc) next to, beside; (+dat) (außer) apart from; n~ mir next to me. n~an adv next door

Neben|anschluß m (Teleph) extension. N~ausgaben fpl incidental expenses

nebenbei adv in addition; (beiläufig) casually; n~ bemerkt incidentally

Neben|bemerkung f passing remark. N~beruf m second job. N~beschäftigung f spare-time occupation. N~buhler(in) m -s,- (f -,-nen) rival

nebeneinander adv next to each other, side by side

Neben|eingang m side entrance. N~fach nt (Univ) subsidiary subject. N~fluß m tributary. N~gleis nt siding. N~haus nt house next door

nebenher adv in addition. n~gehen† vi sep (sein) walk alongside

nebenhin adv casually

Neben|höhle f sinus. N~kosten pl additional costs. N~mann m (pl -männer) person next to one. N~produkt nt by-product. N~rolle f supporting role; (kleine) minor role; eine

N~rolle spielen (fig) be unimportant. N~sache f unimportant matter. n~sächlich a unimportant. N~satz m subordinate clause. N~straße f minor road; (Seiten-) side street. N~verdienst m additional earnings pl. N~wirkung f side-effect. N~zimmer nt room next door

neblig a foggy; (leicht) misty

nebst prep (+ dat) [together] with

Necessaire /nesɛ'sɛːɐ/ nt -s,-s toilet bag; (Näh-, Nagel-) set

neck|en vt tease. N~erei f - teasing. n~isch a teasing; (keß) saucy

nee adv (fam) no

Neffe m -n,-n nephew

negativ a negative. N~ nt -s,-e (Phot) negative

Neger m -s,- Negro

nehmen† vt take (dat from); sich (dat) etw n~ take sth; help oneself to ⟨Essen⟩; jdn zu sich n~ have s.o. to live with one

Neid m -[e]s envy, jealousy. n~en vt jdm den Erfolg n~en be jealous of s.o.'s success. n~isch a envious, jealous (auf+acc of); auf jdn n~isch sein envy s.o.

neig|en vt incline; (zur Seite) tilt; (beugen) bend; sich n~en incline; ⟨Boden:⟩ slope; ⟨Person:⟩ bend (über+acc over) □vi (haben) n~en zu (fig) have a tendency towards; be prone to ⟨Krankheit⟩; incline towards ⟨Ansicht⟩; dazu n~en, etw zu tun tend to do sth. N~ung f -,-en inclination; (Gefälle) slope; (fig) tendency; (Hang) leaning; (Herzens-) affection

nein adv, N~ nt -s no

Nektar m -s nectar

Nelke f -,-n carnation; (Feder-) pink; (Culin) clove

nennen|en† vt call; (taufen) name; (angeben) give; (erwähnen) mention; **sich n~en** call oneself. **n~enswert** a significant. **N~ung f -,-en** mention; (Sport) entry. **N~wert m** face value
Neofaschismus m neofascism
Neon nt -s neon. **N~beleuchtung f** fluorescent lighting
neppen vt (fam) rip off
Nerv m -s,-en /-fən/ nerve; **die N~en verlieren** lose control of oneself. **n~en** vt jdn **n~en** (sl) get on s.o.'s nerves. **N~enarzt m** neurologist. **N~enaufreibend** a nerve-racking. **N~enbündel** nt (fam) bundle of nerves. **N~enkitzel m** (fam) thrill. **N~ensystem** nt nervous system. **N~enzusammenbruch m** nervous breakdown
nervös a nervy, edgy; (Med) nervous; **n~ sein** be on edge
Nervosität f -nerviness, edginess
Nerz m -es,-e mink
Nessel f -,-n nettle
Nest nt -[e]s,-er nest; (fam: Ort) small place
nesteln vi (haben) fumble (**an** + dat with)
Nesthäkchen nt -s,- (fam) baby of the family
nett a nice, adv -ly; (freundlich) kind, adv -ly
netto adv net. **N~gewicht** nt net weight
Netz nt -es,-e net; (Einkaufs-) string bag; (Spinnen-) web; (auf Landkarte) grid; (System) network; (Electr) mains pl. **N~haut f** retina. **N~karte f** area season-ticket. **N~werk** nt network
neu a new; (modern) modern; **wie neu** as good as new; **das ist mir neu** it's news to me; **aufs n~e** [once] again; **von n~em** all over again □adv newly; (gerade erst) only just; (erneut) again; **etw neu schreiben/streichen** rewrite/

repaint sth. **N~ankömmling m -s,-e** newcomer. **N~anschaffung f** recent acquisition. **n~artig** a new [kind of]. **N~auflage f** new edition; (unverändert) reprint. **N~bau m** (pl -ten) new house/building
Neu|e(r) m/f new person, newcomer; (Schüler) new boy/girl. **N~e(s)** nt das **N~e** the new; etwas **N~es** something new; (Neuigkeit) a piece of news; **was gibt's N~es?** what's the news?
neuer|dings adv [just] recently. **n~lich** a renewed, new □adv new. **N~ung f-,-en** innovation
neuest|e(r,s) a newest; (letzte) latest; **seit n~em** just recently. **N~e** nt das **N~e** the latest thing; (Neuigkeit) the latest news sg
neugeboren a newborn
Neugier, Neugierde f -curiosity. (Wißbegierde) inquisitiveness
neugierig a curious (**auf**+acc about), adv -ly; (wißbegierig) inquisitive, adv -ly
Neuheit f -,-en novelty; (Neusein) newness; **die letzte N~** the latest thing
Neuigkeit f -,-en piece of news; **N~en** news sg
Neujahr nt New Year's Day; **über N~** over the New Year
neulich adv the other day
Neu|ling m -s,-e novice. **N~modisch** a newfangled. **N~mond m** new moon
neun inv a, & **N~ f -,-en** nine. **N~malkluge(r) m** (fam) clever Dick. **n~te(r,s)** a ninth. **n~zehn** inv a nineteen. **n~zehnte(r,s)** a nineteenth. **n~zig** inv a ninety. **n~zigste(r,s)** a ninetieth
Neuralgie f -,-n neuralgia
neureich a nouveau riche
Neurolog|e m -n,-n neurologist. **N~ie f -,-n** neurology
Neuro|se f -,-n neurosis. **n~tisch** a neurotic

Neuschnee *m* fresh snow
Neuseeland *nt* -s New Zealand
neuste(r,s) *a* = **neueste(r,s)**

neutral *a* neutral. **N∼isieren** *vt* neutralize. **N∼ität** *f* - neutrality
Neutrum *nt* -s,-tra neuter noun
neu|vermählt *a* **n∼vermähltes Paar** newly-weds *pl*. **N∼zeit** *f* modern times *pl*

nicht *adv* not; **ich kann∼** I cannot *or* can't; **er ist n∼ ge-kommen** he hasn't come; **n∼ mehr/besser als no more/better than; bitte n∼!** please don't! **n∼ berühren!** do not touch! **du kommst doch auch, ∼ [wahr]?** you are coming too, aren't you? **du kennst ihn doch, n∼?** you know him, don't you?
Nichtachtung *f* disregard; (*Ge-ringschätzung*) disdain
Nichte *f* -,-n niece
nichtig *a* trivial; (*Jur*) [null and] void
Nichtraucher *m* non-smoker. **N∼abteil** *nt* non-smoking com-partment
nichts *pron & a* nothing; **n∼ an-deres/Besseres** nothing else/better; **n∼ mehr** no more; **ich weiß n∼** I know nothing *or* don't know anything. **N∼** *nt* - nothing-ness; (*fig: Leere*) void; (*Person*) nonentity. **n∼ahnend** *a* unsus-pecting
Nichtschwimmer *m* non-swim-mer
nichtsdesto|trotz *adv* all the same. **n∼weniger** *adv* never-theless
nichts|nutzig *a* good-for-no-thing; (*fam: unartig*) naughty. **n∼sagend** *a* meaningless; (*un-interessant*) nondescript. **N∼-tun** *nt* -s idleness
Nickel *nt* -s nickel
nicken *vi* (*haben*) nod. **N∼** *nt* -s nod

Nickerchen *nt* -s,- (*fam*) nap; **ein N∼ machen** have forty winks
nie *adv* never

nieder *a* low □*adv* down. **n∼brennen†** *vt/i sep* (*sein*) burn down. **N∼deutsch** *nt* Low Ger-man. **N∼gang** *m* (*fig*) decline. **n∼gedrückt** *a* (*fig*) depressed. **n∼gehen†** *vi sep* (*sein*) come down. **n∼geschlagen** *a* de-jected, despondent. **N∼ge-schlagenheit** *f* - dejection, des-pondency. **N∼kunft** *f* -,-e con-finement. **N∼lage** *f* defeat
Niederlande (die) *pl* the Nether-lands
Niederländ|er *m* -s,- Dutchman; **die N∼er** the Dutch *pl*. **N∼e-rin** *f* -,-nen Dutchwoman. **n∼isch** *a* Dutch
nieder|lassen† *vt sep* let down; **sich n∼lassen** settle; (*sich set-zen*) sit down. **N∼lassung** *f* -,-en settlement; (*Zweigstelle*) branch. **n∼legen** *vt sep* put *or* lay down; resign (*Amt*); **die Arbeit n∼le-gen** go on strike; **sich n∼legen** lie down. **n∼machen, n∼met-zeln** *vt sep* massacre. **n∼rei-ßen†** *vt sep* tear down. **N∼sach-sen** *nt* Lower Saxony. **N∼schlag** *m* precipitation; (*Re-gen*) rainfall; (*radioaktiver*) fall-out; (*Boxen*) knock-down. **n∼schlagen†** *vt sep* knock down; lower (*Augen*); (*unter-drücken*) crush. **n∼schmettern** *vt sep* (*fig*) shatter. **n∼schrei-ben†** *vt sep* write down. **n∼schreien** *vt sep* shout down. **n∼setzen** *vt sep* put *or* set down; **sich n∼setzen** sit down. **n∼strecken** *vt sep* fell; (*durch Schuß*) gun down
niederträchtig *a* base, vile
Niederung *f* -,-en low ground
nieder|walzen *vt sep* flatten. **n∼werfen†** *vt sep* throw down;

(*unterdrücken*) crush; **sich n~werfen** prostrate oneself

niedlich *a* pretty; (*goldig*) sweet; (*Amer*) cute

niedrig *a* low; (*fig: gemein*) base □ *adv* low

niemals *adv* never

niemand *pron* nobody, no one

Niere *f* -,-n kidney; **künstliche N~** kidney machine

niesel|n *vi* (*haben*) drizzle; **es n~t** it is drizzling. **N~regen** *m* drizzle

niesen *vi* (*haben*) sneeze. **N~** *nt* -s sneezing; (*Nieser*) sneeze

Niet *m* & *nt* -[e]s,-e, **Niete¹** *f* -,-n rivet; (*an Jeans*) stud

Niete² *f* -,-n blank; (*fam*) failure

nieten *vt* rivet

Nikotin *nt* -s nicotine

Nil *m* -[s] Nile. **N~pferd** *nt* hippopotamus

nimmer *adv* (*SGer*) not any more; **nie und n~** never. **n~müde** *a* tireless. **n~satt** *a* insatiable. **N~wiedersehen** *nt* **auf N~wiedersehen** (*fam*) for good

nippen *vi* (*haben*) take a sip (**an** + *dat of*)

nirgend|s, n~wo *adv* nowhere

Nische *f* -,-n recess, niche

nisten *vi* (*haben*) nest

Nitrat *nt* -[e]s,-e nitrate

Niveau /niˈvoː/ *nt* -s,-s level; (*geistig, künstlerisch*) standard

nix *adv* (*fam*) nothing

Nixe *f* -,-n mermaid

nobel *a* noble; (*fam: luxuriös*) luxurious; (*fam: großzügig*) generous

noch *adv* still; (*zusätzlich*) as well; (*mit Komparativ*) even; **n~ nicht** not yet; **gerade n~** only just; **n~ immer** od **immer n~** still; **n~ letzte Woche** only last week; **es ist n~ viel Zeit** there's plenty of time yet; **wer/was/wo n~?** who/what/where else? **n~**

jemand/etwas someone/something else; (*Frage*) anyone/anything else? **n~ einmal** again; **n~ ein Bier** another beer; **n~ größer** even bigger; **n~ so sehr/schön** however much/beautiful □ *conj* **weder ... n~** neither ... nor

nochmal|ig *a* further. **n~s** *adv* again

Nomad|e *m* -n,-n nomad. **n~isch** *a* nomadic

Nominativ *m* -s,-e nominative

nominell *a* nominal, *adv* -ly

nominier|en *vt* nominate. **N~ung** *f* -,-en nomination

nonchalant /nõʃaˈlãː/ *a* nonchalant, *adv* -ly

Nonne *f* -,-n nun. **N~nkloster** *nt* convent

Nonstopflug *m* direct flight

Nord *m* -[e]s north. **N~amerika** *nt* North America. **n~deutsch** *a* North German

Norden *m* -s north; **nach N~** north

nordisch *a* Nordic

nördlich *a* northern; (*Richtung*) northerly □ *adv* & *prep* (+ *gen*) **n~ [von] der Stadt** [to the] north of the town

Nordosten *m* north-east

Nordpol *m* North Pole. **N~see** *f* - North Sea. **n~wärts** *adv* northwards. **N~westen** *m* north-west

Nörgelei *f* -,-en grumbling

nörgeln *vi* (*haben*) grumble

Norm *f* -,-en norm; (*Techn*) standard; (*Soll*) quota

normal *a* normal, *adv* -ly. **n~erweise** *adv* normally. **n~isieren** *vt* normalize; **sich n~isieren** return to normal

normen, normieren *vt* standardize

Norwe|gen *nt* -s Norway. **N~ger(in)** *m* -s,- (*f* -,-nen) Norwegian. **n~gisch** *a* Norwegian

Nost|algie *f* - nostalgia. n~algisch *a* nostalgic

Not *f* -,⁻e need; (*Notwendigkeit*) necessity; (*Entbehrung*) hardship; (*seelisch*) trouble; Not leiden be in need, suffer hardship; mit knapper Not only just; zur Not if need be; (*äußerstenfalls*) at a pinch

Notar *m* -s,-e notary public

Not|arzt *m* emergency doctor. N~ausgang *m* emergency exit. N~behelf *m* -[e]s,-e makeshift. N~bremse *f* emergency brake. N~dienst *m* N~dienst haben be on call. n~dürftig *a* scant; (*behelfsmäßig*) makeshift

Note *f* -,-n note; (*Zensur*) mark; ganze/halbe N~ (*Mus*) semibreve/minim, (*Amer*) whole/half note; N~n lesen read music; persönliche N~ personal touch. N~nblatt *nt* sheet of music. N~nschlüssel *m* clef. N~nständer *m* music-stand

Notfall *m* emergency; im N~ in an emergency; (*notfalls*) if need be; für den N~ just in case. n~s *adv* if need be

not|gedrungen *adv* of necessity. N~groschen *m* nest-egg

notieren *vt* note down; (*Comm*) quote; sich (*dat*) etw n~ make a note of sth

nötig *a* necessary; n~ haben need; das N~ste the essentials *pl* □*adv* urgently. n~en *vt* force; (*auffordern*) press; laßt euch nicht n~en help yourselves. n~enfalls *adv* if need be. N~ung *f* - coercion

Notiz *f* -,-en note; (*Zeitungs-*) item; [keine] N~ nehmen von take [no] notice of. N~buch *nt* notebook. N~kalender *m* diary

Not|lage *f* plight. n~landen *vi* (*sein*) make a forced landing. N~landung *f* forced landing.

n~leidend *a* needy. N~lösung *f* stopgap. N~lüge *f* white lie

notorisch *a* notorious

Not|ruf *m* emergency call; (*Naut, Aviat*) distress call; (*Nummer*) emergency services number. N~signal *nt* distress signal. N~stand *m* state of emergency. N~unterkunft *f* emergency accommodation. N~wehr *f* - (*Jur*) self-defence

notwendig *a* necessary; (*unerläßlich*) essential □*adv* urgently. N~keit *f* -,-en necessity

Notzucht *f* - (*Jur*) rape

Nougat /'nu:gat/ *m* & *nt* -s nougat

Novelle *f* -,-n novella; (*Pol*) amendment

November *m* -s,- November

Novität *f* -,-en novelty

Novize *m* -n,-n, Novizin *f* -,-nen (*Relig*) novice

Nu *m* im Nu (*fam*) in a flash

Nuance /'nÿã:sə/ *f* -,-n nuance; (*Spur*) shade

nüchtern *a* sober; (*sachlich*) matter-of-fact; (*schmucklos*) bare; (*ohne Würze*) bland; auf n~en Magen on an empty stomach □*adv* soberly

Nudel *f* -,-n piece of pasta; N~n pasta *sg*; (*Band-*) noodles. N~holz *nt* rolling-pin

Nudist *m* -en,-en nudist

nuklear *a* nuclear

null *inv a* zero, nought; (*Teleph*) 0; (*Sport*) nil; (*Tennis*) love; n~ Fehler no mistakes; n~ und nichtig (*Jur*) null and void. N~ *f* -,-en nought, zero; (*fig: Person*) nonentity; drei Grad unter N~ three degrees below zero. N~punkt *m* zero

numerieren *vt* number

numerisch *a* numerical

Nummer *f* -,-n number; (*Ausgabe*) issue; (*Darbietung*) item; (*Zirkus-*) act; (*Größe*) size.

N~nschild *nt* number-/(*Amer*) license-plate

nun *adv* now; (*na*) well; (*halt*) just; **von nun an** from now on; **nun gut!** very well then! **das Leben ist nun mal so** so life's like that

nur *adv* only, just; **wo kann ich sie nur sein?** wherever can she be? **alles, was ich nur will** everything I could possibly want; **er soll es nur versuchen!** (*drohend*) just let him try! **könnte/hätte ich nur . . . !** if only I could/had . . . ! **nur Geduld!** just be patient!

Nürnberg *nt* -s Nuremberg

nuscheln *vt/i* (*haben*) mumble

Nuß *f* -,**Nüsse** nut. **N~baum** *m* walnut tree. **N~knacker** *m* -s,-, nutcrackers *pl.* **N~schale** *f* nutshell

Nüstern *fpl* nostrils

Nut *f* -,-en, **Nute** *f* -,-n groove

Nutte *f* -,-n (*sl*) tart (*sl*)

nutz|bar *a* usable; **n~bar machen** utilize; **n~bringend** a profitable, *adv* -bly

nütze *a* **zu etwas/nichts n~ sein** be useful/useless

nutzen *vt* use, utilize; (*aus-*) take advantage of □ *vi* (*haben*) = **nützen**. **N~** -s benefit; (*Comm*) profit; **N~ ziehen aus** benefit from; **von N~ sein** be useful

nützen *vi* (*haben*) be useful or of use (*dat* to); (*Mittel:*) be effective; **nichts n~** be useless *or* no use; **was nützt mir das?** what good is that to me? □ *vt* = **nutzen**

Nutzholz *nt* timber

nützlich *a* useful; **sich n~ machen** make oneself useful. **N~keit** *f* - usefulness

nutz|los *a* useless; (*vergeblich*) vain. **N~losigkeit** *f* - uselessness. **N~nießer** *m* -s,- beneficiary. **N~ung** *f* - use, utilization

Nylon /'nailɔn/ *nt* -s nylon

Nymphe /'nʏmfə/ *f* -,-n nymph

O

o *int* o ja/nein! oh yes/no! **o weh!** oh dear!

Oase *f* -,-n oasis

ob *conj* whether; **ob reich, ob arm** rich or poor; **ob sie wohl krank ist?** I wonder whether she is ill; **und ob!** (*fam*) you bet!

Obacht *f* **O~ geben** pay attention; **O~ geben auf** (+*acc*) look after; **O~!** look out!

Obdach *nt* -[e]s shelter. **o~los** *a* homeless. **O~lose(r)** *m/f* homeless person; **die O~losen** the homeless *pl*

Obduktion /-'tsio:n/ *f* -,-en postmortem

O-Beine *ntpl* (*fam*) bow-legs, bandy legs. **O-beinig** *a* bandylegged

oben *adv* at the top; (*auf der Oberseite*) on top; (*eine Treppe hoch*) upstairs; **da o~** up there; **o~ im Norden** up in the north; **siehe o~** see above; **o~ auf** (+*acc/dat*) on top of; **nach o~** up[wards]; (*die Treppe hinauf*) upstairs; **von o~** from above/upstairs; **von o~ bis unten** from top to bottom; (*Person:*) to toe; **jdn von o~ bis unten mustern** look s.o. up and down. **o~an** *adv* at the top. **o~auf** *adv* on top; **o~auf sein** (*fig*) be cheerful. **o~drein** *adv* on top of that. **o~erwähnt**, **o~genannt** *a* above-mentioned. **o~hin** *adv* casually

Ober *m* -s,- waiter

Ober|arm *m* upper arm. **O~arzt** *m* = senior registrar. **O~befehlshaber** *m* commander-in-chief. **O~begriff** *m* generic term. **O~deck** *nt* upper deck. **o~e(r,s)** *a* upper; (*höhere*)

higher. **O~fläche** f surface.
o~flächlich a superficial, adv
-ly. **O~geschoß** nt upper storey.
o~halb adv & prep (+gen)
above; o~halb vom Dorf/des
Dorfes above the village.
O~hand f die **O~hand gewin-**
nen gain the upper hand.
O~haupt nt (fig) head.
O~haus nt (Pol) upper house;
(in UK) House of Lords.
O~hemd nt [man's] shirt

Oberin f -,-nen matron; (Relig)
mother superior
ober|irdisch a surface ... □adv
above ground. **O~kellner** m
head waiter. **O~kiefer** m upper
jaw. **O~körper** m upper part of
the body. **O~leutnant** m lieutenant. **O~licht** nt overhead
light; (Fenster) skylight; (über
Tür) fanlight. **O~lippe** f upper
lip
Obers nt - (Aust) cream
Ober|schenkel m thigh. **O~-**
schicht f upper class. **O~-**
schule f grammar school.
O~schwester f (Med) sister.
O~seite f upper/(rechte Seite)
right side
Oberst m -en & -s,-en colonel
oberste(r,s) a top; (höchste) highest; (Befehlshaber, Gerichtshof)
supreme; (wichtigste) first
Ober|stimme f treble. **O~stufe** f
upper school. **O~teil** nt top.
O~weite f chest/(der Frau) bust
size
obgleich conj although
Obhut f - care; in guter **O~** sein
be well looked after
obig a above
Objekt nt -[e]s,-e object; (Haus,
Grundstück) property; **O~** der
Forschung subject of research
Objektiv nt -s,-e lens. **o~** a objec-
tive, adv -ly. **O~ität** f - objectivity
Oblate f -,-n (Relig) wafer

obliga|t a (fam) inevitable.
O~tion /-'tsjo:n/ f -,-en obligation; (Comm) bond. **o~torisch** a
obligatory
Obmann m (pl -männer) [jury]
foreman; (Sport) referee
Oboe /o'bo:ə/ f -,-n oboe
Obrigkeit f - authorities pl
obschon conj although
Observatorium nt -s,-ien observatory
obskur a obscure; (zweifelhaft)
dubious
Obst nt -es (coll) fruit. **O~baum**
m fruit-tree. **O~garten** m orchard. **O~händler** m fruiterer.
O~kuchen m fruit flan. **O~sa-**
lat m fruit salad
obszön a obscene. **O~ität** f -,-en
obscenity
O-Bus m trolley bus
obwohl conj although
Ochse m -n,-n ox. **o~** vi (haben)
(fam) swot. **O~nschwanz-**
suppe f oxtail soup
öde a desolate; (unfruchtbar) barren; (langweilig) dull. **Öde** f -
desolation; barrenness; dullness;
(Gegend) waste
oder conj or; du kennst ihn doch,
o~? you know him, don't you?
Ofen m -,̈ stove; (Heiz-) heater;
(Back-) oven; (Techn) furnace
offen a open, adv -ly; (Haar)
loose; (Flamme) naked; (o~her-
zig) frank, adv -ly; (o~ gezeigt)
overt, adv -ly; (unentschieden)
unsettled; o~e Stelle vacancy;
Tag der o~en Tür open day;
Wein o~ verkaufen sell wine by
the glass; adv o~ gesagt od gestanden to be honest. **o~bar** a
obvious □adv apparently.
o~baren vt reveal. **O~barung**
f-,-en revelation. **o~bleiben**† vi
sep (sein) remain open. **o~hal-**
ten† vt sep hold open (Tür); keep
open (Mund, Augen). **o~heit** f -
frankness, openness. **o~herzig**

a frank, adv -ly. **O~herzigkeit** *f* - frankness. **o~kundig** *a* manifest, adv -ly. **o~lassen†** *vt sep* leave open; leave vacant ⟨Stelle⟩. **o~sichtlich** *a* obvious, adv -ly. **offensiv** *a* offensive. **O~e** *f* -,-n offensive

offenstehen† *vi sep* (haben) be open; ⟨Rechnung:⟩ be outstanding; **jdm o~** (fig) be open to s.o.

öffentlich *a* public, adv -ly. **Ö~keit** *f* - public; **an die Ö~keit gelangen** become public; **in aller Ö~keit** in public, publicly

Offerte *f* -,-n (Comm) offer

offiziell *a* official, adv -ly

Offizier *m* -s,-e (Mil) officer

öffn|en *vt/i* (haben) open; **sich ö~en** open. **Ö~er** *m* -s,- opener. **Ö~ung** *f* -,-en opening. **Ö~ungszeiten** *fpl* opening hours

oft adv often

öfter adv quite often. **o~e(r,s)** *a* frequent; **des ö~en** frequently. **ö~s** adv (fam) quite often

oftmals adv often

oh int oh!

ohne prep (+ acc) without; **o~mich!** count me out! **oben o~** topless; **nicht o~ sein** (fam) be not bad; **(nicht harmlos)** be quite nasty •conj **o~ zu** überlegen without thinking; **o~ daß ich es merkte** without my noticing it. **o~dies** adv anyway. **o~gleichen** *pred a* unparalleled; **eine Frechheit o~gleichen** a piece of unprecedented insolence. **o~hin** adv anyway

Ohn|macht *f* -,-en faint; (fig) powerlessness; **in O~macht fallen** faint. **o~mächtig** *a* unconscious; (fig) powerless; **o~mächtig werden** faint

Ohr nt -[e]s,-en ear; **übers Ohr hauen** (fam) cheat

Öhr nt -[e]s,-e eye

ohren|betäubend *a* deafening. **O~schmalz** *nt* ear-wax.

O~schmerzen *mpl* earache sg. **O~sessel** *m* wing-chair. **O~tropfen** *mpl* ear drops

Ohrfeige *f* slap in the face; **jdm eine O~n geben** slap s.o.'s face. **o~n** *vt* **jdn o~n** slap s.o.'s face

Ohr|läppchen nt -s,- ear-lobe. **O~ring** *m* ear-ring. **O~wurm** *m* earwig

oje int oh dear!

okay /o'ke:/ *a & adv* (fam) OK

okkult *a* occult

Öko|logie *f* - ecology. **ö~logisch** *a* ecological. **Ö~nomie** *f* - economy; (Wissenschaft) economics sg. **ö~nomisch** *a* economic; (sparsam) economical

Oktave *f* -,-n octave

Oktober *m* -s,- October

Okular nt -s,-e eyepiece

okulieren *vt* graft

ökumenisch *a* ecumenical

Öl nt -[e]s,-e oil; **in Öl malen** paint in oils. **Ölbaum** *m* olive-tree. **ölen** *vt* oil; **wie ein geölter Blitz** (fam) like greased lightning. **Ölfarbe** *f* oil-paint. **Ölfeld** nt oilfield. **Ölgemälde** nt oil-painting. **ölig** *a* oily

Oliv|e *f* -,-n olive. **O~enöl** nt olive oil. **o~grün** *a* olive[-green]

öll *a* (fam) old; (fam: häßlich) nasty

Ölmeßstab *m* dip-stick. **Ölsardinen** *fpl* sardines in oil. **Ölstand** *m* oil-level. **Öltanker** *m* oil-tanker. **Öltoppich** *m* oil slick

Olympiade *f* -,-n Olympic Games pl, Olympics pl

Olymp|iasieger(in) /o'lympia-/ *m(f)* Olympic champion. **o~isch** *a* Olympic; **O~ische Spiele** Olympic Games

Ölzeug nt oilskins pl

Oma *f* -,-s (fam) granny

Omelett nt -[e]s,-e & -s omelette

Omen nt -s,- omen

ominös *a* ominous

Omnibus *m* bus; (Reise-) coach

onanieren vi (haben) masturbate

Onkel m -s,- uncle

Opa m -s,-s (fam) grandad

Opal m -s,-e opal

Oper f -,-n opera

Operation /-'tsjo:n/ f -,-en operation. **O~ssaal** m operating-theatre

Operette f -,-n operetta

operieren vt operate on ⟨Patient, Herz⟩; **sich o~ lassen** have an operation □ vi (haben) operate

Opern|glas nt opera-glasses pl. **O~haus** nt opera-house. **O~sänger(in)** m(f) opera-singer

Opfer nt -s,- sacrifice; ⟨eines Unglücks⟩ victim; **ein O~ bringen** make a sacrifice; **jdm/etw zum O~ fallen** fall victim to s.o./sth. **o~n** vt sacrifice. **O~ung** f -,-en sacrifice

Opium nt -s opium

opponieren vi (haben) **o~ gegen** oppose

Opportun|ist m -en,-en opportunist. **o~isch** a opportunist

Opposition /-'tsjo:n/ f -,- opposition. **O~spartei** f opposition party

Optik f -optics sg; ⟨fam: Objektiv⟩ lens. **O~er** m -s,- optician

optimal a optimum

Optim|ismus m -optimism. **O~t** m -en,-en optimist. **o~tisch** a optimistic, adv -ally

Optimum nt -s,-ma optimum

Option /ɔp'tsjo:n/ f -,-en option

optisch a optical; ⟨Eindruck⟩ visual

Orakel nt -s,- oracle

Orange /o'rã:ʒə/ f -,-n orange. **o~** inv a orange. **O~ade** /orã'ʒa:də/ f -,-n orangeade. **O~nmarmelade** f [orange] marmalade. **O~nsaft** m orange juice

Oratorium nt -s,-ien oratorio

Orchest|er /ɔr'kɛstɐ/ nt -s,- orchestra. **o~rieren** vt orchestrate

Orchidee /ɔrçi'de:ə/ f -,-n orchid

Orden m -s,- ⟨Ritter-, Kloster-⟩ order; ⟨Auszeichnung⟩ medal, decoration; **jdm einen O~ verleihen** decorate s.o. **O~stracht** f ⟨Relig⟩ habit

ordentlich a neat, tidy; ⟨anständig⟩ respectable; ⟨ordnungsgemäß, fam: richtig⟩ proper; ⟨Mitglied, Versammlung⟩ ordinary; ⟨fam: gut⟩ decent; ⟨fam: gehörig⟩ good □ adv neatly, tidily; respectably; properly; ⟨fam: gut, gehörig⟩ well; ⟨sehr⟩ very; ⟨regelrecht⟩ really

Order f -,-s & -n order

ordinär a common

Ordin|ation /-'tsjo:n/ f -,-en ⟨Relig⟩ ordination; ⟨Aust⟩ surgery. **o~ieren** vt ⟨Relig⟩ ordain

ordn|en vt put in order; ⟨aufräumen⟩ tidy; ⟨an-⟩ arrange; **sich zum Zug o~** form a procession. **O~er** m -s,- steward; ⟨Akten-⟩ file

Ordnung f -order; **O~ halten** keep order; **O~ machen** tidy up; **in O~ bringen** put in order; ⟨aufräumen⟩ tidy; ⟨reparieren⟩ mend; ⟨fig⟩ put right; **in O~ sein** be in order; ⟨ordentlich sein⟩ be tidy; ⟨fig⟩ be all right; **ich bin mit dem Magen** od **mein Magen ist nicht ganz in O~** I have a slight stomach upset; **[geht] in O~!** OK! **o~sgemäß** a proper, adv -ly. **O~sstrafe** f ⟨Jur⟩ fine. **o~swidrig** a improper, adv -ly

Ordonnanz f -,-en ⟨Mil⟩ orderly

Organ nt -s,-e organ; ⟨fam: Stimme⟩ voice

Organi|sation /-'tsjo:n/ f -,-en organization. **O~sator** m -s,-en /-'to:rən/ organizer

organisch a organic, adv -ally

organisieren vt organize; (fam: beschaffen) get [hold of]

Organis|mus m -,-men organism; (System) system. **O~t** m -en,-en organist

Organspenderkarte f donor card

Orgasmus m -,-men orgasm

Orgel f -,-n (Mus) organ. **O~ pfeife** f organ-pipe

Orgie /ˈɔrgjə/ f -,-n orgy

Orient|t /ˈoːriɛnt/ m -s Orient. **o~ talisch** a Oriental

orientier|en /oriɛnˈtiːrən/ vt inform (über + acc about); **sich o~en** get one's bearings, orientate oneself; (unterrichten) inform oneself (über + acc about). **O~ung** f - orientation; **die O~ung verlieren** lose one's bearings

original a original. **O~** nt -s,-e original; (Person) character. **O~ität** f - originality. **O~ übertragung** f live transmission

originell a original; (eigenartig) unusual

Orkan m -s,-e hurricane

Ornament nt -[e]s,-e ornament

Ornat m -[e]s,-e robes pl

Ornithologie f - ornithology

Ort m -[e]s,-e place; (Ortschaft) [small] town; **am Ort** locally; **am Ort des Verbrechens** at the scene of the crime; **an Ort und Stelle** in the right place; (sofort) on the spot. **o~en** vt locate

ortho|dox a orthodox. **O~ gra phie** f -spelling. **o~graphisch** a spelling. **O~päde** m -n,-n orthopaedic specialist. **o~pädisch** a orthopaedic

örtlich a local, adv -ly. **Ö~keit** f -,-en locality

Ortschaft f -,-en [small] town; (Dorf) village; **geschlossene O~** (Auto) built-up area

orts|fremd a o~ fremd sein to a stranger. **O~gespräch** nt (Teleph) local call. **O~name** m place-name. **O~sinn** m sense of direction. **O~verkehr** m local traffic. **O~zeit** f local time

Öse f -,-n eyelet; (Schlinge) loop; **Haken und Öse** hook and eye

Ost m -[e]s east. **O~deutsch** a Eastern/(Pol) East German

Osten m -s east; **nach O~** east

ostentativ a pointed, adv -ly

Osteopath m -en,-en osteopath

Oster|ei /ˈoːstɐˌʔai/ nt Easter egg. **O~fest** nt Easter. **O~glocke** f daffodil. **O~montag** m Easter Monday. **o~n** nt -; Easter; **frohe o~n!** happy Easter!

Österreich nt -s Austria. **Ö~er** m -s,-, **Ö~erin** f -,-nen Austrian. **ö~isch** a Austrian

östlich a eastern; (Richtung) easterly □ adv & prep (+ gen) ö~ [von] der Stadt [to the] east of the town

Ost|see f Baltic [Sea]. **o~wärts** adv eastwards

oszillieren vi (haben) oscillate

Otter¹ m -s,- otter

Otter² f -,-n adder

Ouverture /uverˈtyːrə/ f -,-n overture

oval a oval. **O~** nt -s,-e oval

Ovation /-ˈtsi̯oːn/ f -,-en ovation

Ovulation /-ˈtsi̯oːn/ f -,-en ovulation

Oxid, Oxyd nt -[e]s,-e oxide

Ozean m -s,-e ocean

Ozon nt -s ozone. **O~loch** nt hole in the ozone layer. **O~schicht** f ozone layer

P

paar pron inv **ein p~** a few; **alle p~ Tage** every few days. **P~** nt -[e]s,-e pair; (Ehe, Liebes-, Tanzcouple. **p~en** vt mate; (verbinden) combine; **sich p~en** mate. **P~ung** f-,-en mating. **p~weise** adv in pairs, in twos

Pacht f-,-en lease; (P~summe) rent. **p~en** vt lease

Pächter m-s,- lessee; (eines Hofes) tenant

Pachtvertrag m lease

Pack¹ m-[e]s,-e bundle

Pack² nt-[e]s (sl) rabble

Päckchen nt-s,- package, small packet

pack|en vt/i (haben) pack; (ergreifen) seize; (fig: fesseln) grip; **p~ dich!** (sl) beat it! **P~en** m-s,- bundle. **p~end** a (fig) gripping. **P~papier** nt [strong] wrapping paper. **P~ung** f-,-en packet; (Med) pack

Pädagog|e m-n,-n educationalist; (Lehrer) teacher. **P~ik** f-educational science. **p~isch** a educational

Paddel nt-s,- paddle. **P~boot** nt canoe. **p~n** vi (haben/sein) paddle. **P~sport** m canoeing

Page /'pa:ʒə/ m-n,-n page

Paillette /paj'jɛtə/ f-,-n sequin

Paket nt-[e]s,-e packet; (Post-) parcel

Pakistan nt-s Pakistan. **P~aner(in)** m-s,- (f-,-nen) Pakistani. **p~anisch** a Pakistani

Pakt m-[e]s,-e pact

Palast m-[e]s,-e palace

Paläst|ina nt-s Palestine. **P~inenser(in)** m-s,- (f-,-nen) Palestinian. **p~inensisch** a Palestinian

Palette f-,-n palette

Palm|e f-,-n palm[-tree]; **jdn auf die P~e bringen** (fam) drive s.o. up the wall. **P~sonntag** m Palm Sunday

Pampelmuse f-,-n grapefruit

Panier|mehl nt (Culin) breadcrumbs pl. **p~t** a (Culin) breaded

Panik f- panic; **in P~ geraten** panic

panisch a **p~e Angst** panic

Panne f-,-n breakdown; (Reifen-) flat tyre; (Mißgeschick) mishap. **P~ndienst** m breakdown service

Panorama nt-s panorama

panschen vt adulterate □vi (haben) splash about

Pantine f-,-n [wooden] clog

Pantoffel m-s,-n slipper; (ohne Ferse) mule. **P~held** m (fam) henpecked husband

Pantomime¹ f-,-n mime

Pantomime² m-n,-n mime artist

pantschen vt/i = **panschen**

Panzer m-s,- armour; (Mil) tank; (Zool) shell. **p~n** vt armour-plate. **P~schrank** m safe

Papa /'papa, pa'pa:/ m-s,-s daddy

Papagei m-s & -en,-en parrot

Papier nt-s,-e paper. **P~korb** m waste-paper basket. **P~schlange** f streamer. **P~waren** fpl stationery sg

Pappe f- cardboard; (dial: Kleister) glue

Pappel f-,-n poplar

pappen vt/i (haben) (fam) stick

pappig a (fam) sticky

Papp|karton m, **P~schachtel** f cardboard box

Paprika m-s,-[s] [sweet] pepper; (Gewürz) paprika

Papst m-[e]s,-e pope

päpstlich a papal

Parade f-,-n parade

Paradeiser m-s,- (Aust) tomato

Paradies nt-es,-e paradise. **p~isch** a heavenly

Paradox nt-es,-e paradox. **p~** a paradoxical

Paraffin nt-s paraffin

Paragraph m-en,-en section

parallel a & adv parallel. **P~e** f-,-n parallel

Paranuß f Brazil nut

Parasit m-en,-en parasite

parat a ready

Pärchen nt -s,- pair; (Liebes-) couple

Parcours /par'ku:ɐ̯/ m -, -/-[s],-s (Sport) course

Pardon /par'dõ:/ int sorry!

Parfüm nt -s,-e & -s perfume, scent. **p~iert** a perfumed, scented

parieren[1] vt parry

parieren[2] vi (haben) (fam) obey

Parität f - parity; (in Ausschuß) equal representation

Park m -s,-s park. **p~en** vt/i (haben) park. **P~en** nt -s parking; 'P~en verboten' 'no parking'

Parkett nt -[e]s,-e parquet floor; (Theat) stalls pl

Park|haus nt multi-storey car park. **P~lücke** f parking space. **P~platz** m car park, (Amer) parking-lot; (für ein Auto) parking space; (Autobahn-) lay-by. **P~scheibe** f parking-disc. **P~schein** m car-park ticket. **P~uhr** f parking-meter. **P~verbot** nt parking ban; 'P~verbot' 'no parking'

Parlament nt -[e]s,-e parliament. **p~arisch** a parliamentary

Parodie f -,-n parody. **p~ren** vt parody

Parole f -,-n slogan; (Mil) password

Part m -s,-s (Theat, Mus) part

Partei f -,-en (Pol, Jur) party; (Miet-) tenant; **für jdn P~ ergreifen** take s.o.'s part. **p~isch** a biased. **p~los** a independent

Parterre /par'tɛr/ nt -s,-s ground floor; (Amer) first floor; (Theat) rear stalls pl. **p~** adv on the ground floor

Partie f -,-n part; (Tennis, Schach) game; (Golf) round; (Comm) batch; **eine gute P~ machen** marry well

Partikel[1] nt -s,- particle

Partikel[2] f -,-n (Gram) particle

Partitur f -,-en (Mus) full score

Partizip nt -s,-ien /-jən/ participle; **erstes/zweites P~** present/past participle

Partner(in) m -s,- (f -,-nen) partner. **P~schaft** f -,-en partnership. **P~stadt** f twin town

Party /'pa:ɐ̯ti/ f -,-s party

Parzelle f -,-n plot [of ground]

Paß m -sses,ˈsse passport; (Geog, Sport) pass

passabel a passable

Passage /pa'sa:ʒə/ f -,-n passage; (Einkaufs-) shopping arcade

Passagier /pasa'ʒi:ɐ̯/ m -s,-e passenger

Paßamt nt passport office

Passant(in) m -en,-en (f -,-nen) passer-by

Paßbild nt passport photograph

Passe f -,-n yoke

passen vi (haben) fit; (geeignet sein) be right (für for); (Sport) pass the ball; (aufgeben) pass; **p~ zu** go [well] with; (übereinstimmen) match; **jdm p~** fit s.o.; (gelegen sein) suit s.o.; **seine Art paßt mir nicht** I don't like his manner; [ich] **passe** pass. **p~d** a suitable; (angemessen) appropriate; (günstig) convenient; (übereinstimmend) matching

passier|bar a passable. **p~en** vt pass; cross (Grenze); (Culin) rub through a sieve ☐ vi (sein) happen (jdm to s.o.); **es ist ein Unglück p~t** there has been an accident. **P~schein** m pass

Passion f -,-en passion. **p~iert** a very keen ⟨Jäger, Angler⟩

passiv a passive. **P~** nt -s,-e (Gram) passive

Paßkontrolle f passport control. **P~straße** f pass

Paste f -,-n paste

Pastell nt -[e]s,-e pastel. **P~farbe** f pastel colour

Pastet|chen nt -s,- [individual] pie; (Königin-) vol-au-vent. **P~e** f -,-n pie; (Gänseleber-) paté

pasteurisieren /pastøri'ziːrən/ vt pasteurize

Pastille f -,-n pastille

Pastinake f -,-n parsnip

Pastor m -s,-en /-'toːrən/ pastor

Pate m -n,-n godfather; (fig) sponsor; **P~n** godparents. **P~nkind** nt godchild.**P~nschaft** f - sponsorship. **P~nsohn** m godson

Patent nt -[e]s,-e patent; (Offiziers-) commission. **p~** a (fam) clever, adv -ly; ⟨Person⟩ resourceful. **p~ieren** vt patent

Patentochter f god-daughter

Pater m -s,- (Relig) Father

pathetisch a emotional □adv with emotion

Patholog|e m -n,-n pathologist. **p~isch** a pathological, adv -ly

Pathos nt - emotion, feeling

Patience /pa'siɑ̃ːs/ f -,-n patience

Patient(in) /pa'tsjɛnt(m)/ m -en,-en (f -,-nen) patient

Patin f -,-nen godmother

Patriot|(in) m -en,-en (f -,-nen) patriot. **p~isch** a patriotic. **P~ismus** m - patriotism

Patrone f -,-n cartridge

Patrouille /pa'trʊljə/ f -,-n patrol. **p~ieren** /-'jiːrən/ vi (haben/sein) patrol

Patsch|e f in der **P~e** sitzen (fam) be in a jam. **p~en** vi (haben/sein) splash □vt slap. **p~naß** a (fam) soaking wet

Patt nt -s stalemate

Patz|er m -s,- (fam) slip. **p~ig** a (fam) insolent

Pauk|e f -,-n kettledrum; **auf die P~e hauen** (fam) have a good time; (prahlen) boast. **P~en** vt/i (haben) (fam) swot. **P~er** m -s,- (fam: Lehrer) teacher

pausbäckig a a chubby-cheeked

pauschal a all-inclusive; (einheitlich) flat-rate; (fig) sweeping ⟨Urteil⟩; **p~e Summe** lump sum □adv in a lump sum; (fig) wholesale. **P~e** f -,-n lump sum. **P~summe** f lump sum

P~reise f package tour.

P~summe f lump sum

Pause¹ f -,-n break; (beim Sprechen) pause; (Theat) interval; (im Kino) intermission; (Mus) rest; **p~ machen** have a break

Pause² f -,-n tracing. **p~n** vt trace

pausenlos a incessant, adv -ly

pausieren vi (haben) have a break; (ausruhen) rest

Pauspapier nt tracing-paper

Pavian m -s,-e baboon

Pavillon /'paviljõ/ m -s,-s pavilion

Pazifi|k m -s Pacific [Ocean]. **p~sch** a Pacific

Pazifist m -en,-en pacifist

Pech nt -s pitch; (Unglück) bad luck; **P~ haben** be unlucky. **p~schwarz** a pitch-black; ⟨Haare, Augen⟩ jet-black. **P~strähne** f run of bad luck. **P~vogel** m (fam) unlucky devil

Pedal nt -s,-e pedal

Pedant m -en,-en pedant. **p~isch** a pedantic, adv -ally

Pediküre f -,-n pedicure

Pegel m -s,- level; (Gerät) water-level indicator. **P~stand** m [water] level

peilen vt take a bearing on; **über den Daumen gepeilt** (fam) at a rough guess

Pein f - (liter) torment. **p~igen** vt torment

peinlich a embarrassing, awkward; (genau) scrupulous, adv -ly; **es war mir sehr p~** I was very embarrassed

Peitsche f -,-n whip. **p~n** vt whip; (fig) lash □vi (sein) lash **(an+** acc against). **P~nhieb** m lash

pekuniär a financial, adv -ly

Pelikan m -s,-e pelican

Pell|e f -,-n skin. **p∼en** vt peel; shell ⟨Ei⟩; **sich g∼en** peel. **P∼kartoffeln** fpl potatoes boiled in their skins

Pelz m -es,-e fur. **P∼mantel** m fur coat

Pendel nt -s,- pendulum. **p∼n** vi (haben) swing □vi (sein) commute. **P∼verkehr** m shuttle-service; (für Pendler) commuter traffic

Pendler m -s,- commuter

penetrant a penetrating; (fig) obtrusive, adv -ly

penibel a fastidious, fussy; (pedantisch) pedantic

Penis m -,-se penis

Penn|e f -,-n (fam) school. **p∼n** vi (haben) sleep. **P∼er** m -s,- (sl) tramp

Pension /pã'zio:n/ f -,-en pension; (Hotel) guest-house; **bei voller/ halber P∼** with full/half board. **P∼är(in)** m -s,-e (f -,-nen) pensioner. **P∼at** nt -[e]s,-e boarding-school. **p∼ieren** vt retire. **p∼iert** a retired. **P∼ierung** f -,-en retirement

Pensum nt -s [allotted] work

Peperoni f -,- chilli

per prep (+ acc) by; **per Luftpost** by airmail

perfekt a perfect, adv -ly; **p∼ sein** ⟨Vertrag:⟩ be settled

Perfekt nt -s (Gram) perfect

Perfektion /-'tsio:n/ f - perfection

perforiert a perforated

Pergament nt -[e]s,-e parchment. **P∼papier** nt grease-proof paper

Period|e f -,-n period. **p∼isch** a periodic, adv -ally

Perl|e f -,-n pearl; (Glas-, Holz-) bead; (Sekt-) bubble; (fam: Hilfe) treasure. **p∼en** vi (haben) bubble. **P∼mutt** nt -s, **P∼mutter** f - & nt -s mother-of-pearl

perplex a (fam) perplexed

Perserkatze f Persian cat

Pers|ien /-jǝn/ nt -s Persia. **p∼isch** a Persian

Person f -,-en person; (Theat) character; **ich für meine P∼** [I] for my part; **für vier P∼en** for four people

Personal nt -s personnel, staff. **P∼ausweis** m identity card. **P∼chef** m personnel manager. **P∼ien** /-jǝn/ pl personal particulars. **P∼mangel** m staff shortage. **P∼pronomen** nt personal pronoun

Personen|kraftwagen m private car. **P∼zug** m stopping train

personifizieren vt personify

persönlich a personal □adv personally, in person. **P∼keit** f -,-en personality

Perspektive f -,-n perspective; (Zukunfts-) prospect

Perücke f -,-n wig

pervers a [sexually] perverted. **P∼ion** f -,-en perversion

Pessimis|mus m - pessimism. **P∼t** m -en,-en pessimist. **p∼tisch** a pessimistic, adv -ally

Pest f - plague

Petersilie /-jǝ/ f - parsley

Petroleum /-leum/ nt -s paraffin, (Amer) kerosene

Petze f -,-n (fam) sneak. **p∼n** vi (haben) (fam) sneak

Pfad m -[e]s,-e path. **P∼finder** m -s,- [Boy] Scout. **P∼finderin** f -,-nen [Girl] Guide

Pfahl m -[e]s,-e stake, post

Pfalz (die) - the Palatinate

Pfand nt -[e]s,-er pledge; (beim Spiel) forfeit; (Flaschen-) deposit

pfänd|en vt (Jur) seize. **P∼erspiel** nt game of forfeits

Pfand|haus nt pawnshop. **P∼leiher** m -s,- pawnbroker

Pfändung f -,-en (Jur) seizure

Pfann|e f -,-n [frying-]pan. **P∼kuchen** m pancake; Berliner **P∼kuchen** doughnut

Pfarr|er m -s,- vicar, parson; (katholischer) priest. **P~haus** nt vicarage

Pfau m -s,-en peacock

Pfeffer m -s pepper. **P~kuchen** m gingerbread. **P~minzbonbon** m & nt [pepper]mint. **P~minze** f (Bot) peppermint. **P~minztee** m [pepper]mint tea. p~n vt pepper; (fam: schmeißen) chuck. **P~streuer** m -s,- pepperpot

Pfeife|e f -,-en whistle; (Tabak-, Orgel-) pipe. p~en† vt/i (haben) whistle; (als Signal) blow the whistle; ich p~e darauf (fam) I couldn't care less [about it]!

Pfeil m -[e]s,-e arrow

Pfeiler m -s,- pillar; (Brücken-) pier

Pfennig m -s,-e pfennig; 10 **P** > 10 pfennigs

Pferch m -s,-e [sheep] pen. p~en vt (fam) cram (in + acc into)

Pferd nt -es,-e horse; zu **P~e** on horseback; **das P~ beim Schwanz aufzäumen** put the cart before the horse. **P~erennen** nt horse-race; (als Sport) horse-|racing. **P~eschwanz** m horse's tail; (Frisur) pony-tail. **P~estall** m stable. **P~estärke** f horsepower. **P~ewagen** m horse-drawn cart

Pfiff m -[e]s,-e whistle; **P~ haben** (fam) have style

Pfifferling m -s,-e chanterelle

pfiffig a smart

Pfingst|en nt -s Whitsun. **P~montag** m Whit Monday. **P~rose** f peony

Pfirsich m -s,-e peach. p~farben a peach[-coloured]

Pflanz|e f -,-n plant. p~en vt plant. **P~enfett** nt vegetable fat. p~lich a vegetable; (Mittel) herbal. **P~ung** f -,-en plantation

Pflaster nt -s,- pavement; (Heft-) plaster. p~n vt pave. **P~stein** m paving-stone

Pflaume f -,-n plum

Pflege f - care; (Kranken-) nursing; in **P~ nehmen** look after; (Admin) foster (Kind). p~bedürftig a in need of care. **P~eltern** pl foster-parents. **P~kind** nt foster-child. p~leicht a easy-care. **P~mutter** f foster-mother. p~n vt look after, care for; nurse (Kranke); cultivate (Künste, Freundschaft). **P~r(in)** m -s,- (f -,-nen) nurse; (Tier-) keeper

Pflicht f -,-en duty; (Sport) compulsory exercise/routine. p~bewußt a conscientious, adv -ly. p~eifrig a zealous, adv -ly. **P~fach** nt (Sch) compulsory subject. **P~gefühl** nt sense of duty. p~gemäß a due□adv duly

Pflock m -[e]s,-e peg

pflücken vt pick

Pflug m -[e]s,-e plough

pflügen vt/i (haben) plough

Pforte f -,-n gate

Pförtner m -s,- porter

Pfosten m -s,- post

Pfote f -,-n paw

Pfropfen m -s,- stopper; (Korken-) cork. p~ vt graft (auf + acc on [to]); (fam: pressen) cram (in + acc into)

pfui int ugh! p~ schäm dich! you should be ashamed of yourself!

Pfund nt -[e]s,-e & - pound

Pfusch|arbeit f (fam) shoddy work. p~en vi (haben) (fam) botch one's work. **P~er** m -s,- (fam) shoddy worker. **P~erei** f -,-en (fam) botch-up

Pfütze f -,-n puddle

Phänomen nt -s,-e phenomenon. p~al a phenomenal

Phantasie f -,-n imagination. **P~n** fantasies; (Fieber-) hallucinations. p~los a unimaginative. p~ren vi (haben) fantasize; (im

Fieber) be delirious. **p~voll** *a*
imaginative, *adv* -ly

phant|astisch *a* fantastic, *adv*
-ally. **P~om** *nt* -s,-e phantom

pharma|zeutisch *a* pharmaceut-
ical. **P~zie** *f* - pharmacy

Phase *f* -,-n phase

Philanthrop *m* -en,-en philan-
thropist. **p~isch** *a* philanthropic

Philolo|ge *m* -n,-n teacher/stu-
dent of language and literature.
P~gie *f* - [study of] language and
literature

Philosoph *m* -en,-en philosopher. **P~ie** *f* -,-n philosophy.
p~ieren *vi* (*haben*) philosophize

philosophisch *a* philosophical,
adv -ly

phlegmatisch *a* phlegmatic

Phobie *f* -,-n phobia

Phonet|ik *f* - phonetics *sg*.
p~isch *a* phonetic, *adv* -ally

Phonotypistin *f* -,-nen audio
typist

Phosphor *m* -s phosphorus

Photo *nt*, **Photo-** *s.* Foto, Foto-

Phrase *f* -,-n empty phrase

Physik *f* - physics *sg*. **p~alisch** *a*
physical

Physiker(in) *m* -s,- (*f* -,-nen)
physicist

Physio|logie *f* - physiology.
P~therapie *f* physiotherapy

physisch *a* physical, *adv* -ly

Pianist(in) *m* -en,-en (*f* -,-nen)
pianist

Pickel *m* -s,- pimple, spot; (*Spitzhacke*) pick. **p~ig** *a* spotty

picken *vt/i* (*haben*) peck (nach
at); (*fam: nehmen*) pick (aus out
of); (*Aust fam: kleben*) stick

Picknick *nt* -s,-s picnic. **p~en** *vi*
(*haben*) picnic

piep[s]en *vi* (*haben*) ⟨*Vogel:*⟩
cheep; ⟨*Maus:*⟩ squeak; (*Techn*)
bleep. **P~er** *m* -s,- bleeper

Pier *m* -s,-e (*harbour*) pier

Pietät /pie'tɛːt/ *f* - reverence.
p~los *a* irreverent, *adv* -ly

Pigment *nt* -[e]s,-e pigment.
P~ierung *f* - pigmentation

Pik *nt* -s,-s (*Karten*) spades *pl*

pikant *a* piquant; (*gewagt*) racy

piken *vt* (*fam*) prick

pikiert *a* offended, hurt

piksen *vt* (*fam*) prick

Pilger|(in) *m* -s,- (*f* -,-nen) pil-
grim. **P~fahrt** *f* pilgrimage.
p~n *vi* (*sein*) make a pilgrimage

Pille *f* -,-n pill

Pilot *m* -en,-en pilot

Pilz *m* -es,-e fungus; (*eßbarer*)
mushroom; **wie P~e aus dem
Boden schießen** (*fig*) mushroom

pingelig *a* (*fam*) fussy

Pinguin *m* -s,-e penguin

Pinie /-jə/ *f* -,-n stone-pine

pink *pred a* shocking pink

pinkeln *vi* (*haben*) (*fam*) pee

Pinsel *m* -s,- [paint]brush

Pinzette *f* -,-n tweezers *pl*

Pionier *m* -s,-e (*Mil*) sapper; (*fig*)
pioneer. **P~arbeit** *f* pioneering
work

Pirat *m* -en,-en pirate

pirschen *vi* (*haben*) **p~ auf** (+
acc) stalk □ *vr* **sich p~** creep
(**an** + *acc* up to)

pissen *vi* (*haben*) (*sl*) piss

Piste *f* -,-n (*Ski-*) run, piste;
(*Renn-*) track; (*Aviat*) runway

Pistole *f* -,-n pistol

pitschnaß *a* (*fam*) soaking wet

pittoresk *a* picturesque

Pizza *f* -,-s pizza

Pkw /'pe:kave:/ *m* -s,-s (= *Perso-
nenkraftwagen*) [private] car

placieren /-'tsi:rən/*nt* = **plazieren**

Plackerei *f* - (*fam*) drudgery

plädieren *vi* (*haben*) plead (**für**
for); **auf Freispruch p~** (*Jur*)
ask for an acquittal

Plädoyer /plɛdoa'je:/ *nt* -s,-s (*Jur*)
closing speech; (*fig*) plea

Plage *f* -,-n [hard] labour; (*Mühe*)
trouble; (*Belästigung*) nuisance.

p~n vt torment, plague; (bedrängen) pester; sich p~n struggle; (arbeiten) work hard

Plagi|at nt -[e]s,-e plagiarism. p~ieren vt plagiarize

Plakat nt -[e]s,-e poster

Plakette f -,-n badge

Plan m -[e]s,⁼e plan

Plane f -,-n tarpaulin; (Boden-) groundsheet

planen vt/i (haben) plan

Planet m -en,-en planet

planier|en vt level. P~raupe f bulldozer

Planke f -,-n plank

plan|los a unsystematic, adv -ally. p~mäßig a systematic; ⟨Ankunft⟩ scheduled □adv systematically; (nach Plan) according to plan; ⟨ankommen⟩ on schedule

Plansch|becken nt paddling pool. p~en vi (haben) splash about

Plantage /plan'ta:ʒə/ f -,-n plantation

Planung f - planning

Plapper|maul nt (fam) chatterbox. p~n vi (haben) chatter □vt talk ⟨Unsinn⟩

plärren vi (haben) bawl; ⟨Radio:⟩ blare

Plasma nt -s plasma

Plastik¹ f -,-en sculpture

Plast|ik² nt -s plastic. p~isch a three-dimensional; (formbar) plastic; (anschaulich) graphic, adv -ally; p~ische Chirurgie plastic surgery

Platane f -,-n plane [tree]

Plateau /pla'to:/ nt -s,-s plateau

Platin nt -s platinum

Platitüde f -,-n platitude

platonisch a platonic

plätschern vi (haben) splash

plätschern vi (haben) splash; ⟨Bach:⟩ babble □ vi (sein) ⟨Bach:⟩ babble along

platt a & adv flat; p~ sein (fam) be flabbergasted. P~ nt -[s] ⟨Lang⟩ Low German

Plättbrett nt ironing-board

Platte f -,-n slab; (Druck-) plate; (Metall-, Glas-) sheet; (Fliese) tile; (Koch-) hotplate; (Tisch-) top; (Auszieh-) leaf; (Schall-) record, disc; (zum Servieren) [flat] dish, platter; kalte P~ assorted cold meats and cheeses pl

Plätt|eisen nt iron. p~en vt/i (haben) iron

Platten|spieler m record-player

Platt|form f -,-en platform. P~füße mpl flat feet. P~heit f -,-en platitude

Platz m -es,⁼e place; (von Häusern umgeben) square; (Sitz-) seat; (Sport-) ground; (Fußball-) pitch; (Tennis-) court; (Golf-) course; (freier Raum) room, space; P~ nehmen take a seat; P~ machen/lassen make/leave room; vom P~ stellen (Sport) send off. P~angst f agoraphobia; (Klaustrophobie) claustrophobia. P~anweiserin f -,-nen usherette

Plätzchen nt -s,- spot; (Culin) biscuit

platzen vi (sein) burst; (auf-) split; (fam: scheitern) fall through; ⟨Verlobung:⟩ be off; vor Neugier p~ be bursting with curiosity

Platz|karte f seat reservation ticket. P~konzert nt open-air concert. P~mangel m lack of space. P~patrone f blank. P~regen m downpour. P~verweis m (Sport) sending off. P~wunde f laceration

Plauderei f -,-en chat

plaudern vi (haben) chat

Plausch m -[e]s,-e (SGer) chat. p~en vi (haben) (SGer) chat

plausibel a plausible

plazieren vt place, put; sich p~ (Sport) be placed

pleite *a* (*fam*) **p~ sein** be broke; ⟨*Firma:*⟩ be bankrupt; **p~ gehen** go bankrupt. **P~** *f* -,-n (*fam*) bankruptcy; (*Mißerfolg*) flop; **P~ machen** go bankrupt

plissiert *a* (finely) pleated

Plombe *f* -,-n seal; (*Zahn-*) filling. **p~ieren** *vt* seal; fill ⟨*Zahn*⟩

plötzlich *a* sudden, *adv* -ly

plump *a* plump; (*ungeschickt*) clumsy, *adv* -ily

plumpsen *vi* (*sein*) (*fam*) fall

Plunder *m* -s (*fam*) junk, rubbish

plündern *vt/i* (*haben*) loot

Plunderstück *nt* Danish pastry

Plural *m* -s,-e plural

plus *adv, conj & prep* (+ *dat*) plus. **P~** *nt* - surplus; (*Gewinn*) profit; (*Vorteil*) advantage, plus. **P~punkt** *m* (*Sport*) point; (*fig*) plus. **P~quamperfekt** *nt* pluperfect. **P~zeichen** *nt* plus sign

Po *m* -s,-s (*fam*) bottom

Pöbel *m* -s mob, rabble. **p~haft** *a* loutish

pochen *vi* (*haben*) knock; ⟨*Herz:*⟩ pound; **p~ auf** (+ *acc*) (*fig*) insist on

pochieren /pɔ'ʃiːrən/ *vt* poach

Pocken *pl* smallpox *sg*

Podest *nt* -[e]s,-e rostrum

Podium *nt* -s,-ien /-jən/ platform; (*Podest*) rostrum

Poesie /poe'ziː/ *f* - poetry

poetisch *a* poetic

Pointe /'pŏɛ̃tə/ *f* -,-n point (*of a joke*)

Pokal *m* -s,-e goblet; (*Sport*) cup

pökeln *vt* (*Culin*) salt

Poker *nt* -s poker

Pol *m* -s,-e pole. **p~ar** *a* polar

polarisieren *vt* polarize

Polarstern *m* pole-star

Pole *m* -n,-n Pole. **P~n** *nt* -s Poland

Police /po'liːsə/ *f* -,-n policy

Polier *m* -s,-e foreman

polieren *vt* polish

Polin *f* -,-nen Pole

Politesse *f* -,-n [woman] traffic warden

Politik *f* - politics *sg*; (*Vorgehen, Maßnahme*) policy

Polit|iker(in) *m* -s, (*f* -,-nen) politician. **p~isch** *a* political, *adv* -ly

Politur *f* -,-en polish

Polizei *f* - police *pl*. **P~beamte(r)** *m* police officer. **p~lich** *a* police … *adv* by the police; ⟨*sich anmelden*⟩ with the police. **P~streife** *f* police patrol. **P~stunde** *f* closing time. **P~wache** *f* police station

Polizist *m* -en,-en policeman. **P~in** *f* -,-nen policewoman

Pollen *m* -s pollen

polnisch *a* Polish

Polohemd *nt* polo shirt

Polster *nt* -s,- pad; (*Kissen*) cushion; (*Möbel-*) upholstery; (*fig: Rücklage*) reserves *pl*. **P~er** *m* -s,- upholsterer. **P~möbel** *pl* upholstered furniture *sg*. **p~n** *vt* pad; upholster ⟨*Möbel*⟩. **P~ung** *f* - padding; upholstery

Polter|abend *m* wedding-eve party. **p~n** *vi* (*haben*) thump, bang; (*schelten*) bawl □ *vi* (*sein*) crash down; (*gehen*) clump [along]; (*fahren*) rumble [along]

Polyäthylen *nt* -s polythene

Polyester *m* -s polyester

Polyp *m* -en,-en polyp; (*sl: Polizist*) copper; **P~en** adenoids *pl*

Pomeranze *f* -,-n Seville orange

Pommes *pl* (*fam*) French fries

Pommes frites /pom'friːt/ *pl* chips; (*dünner*) French fries

Pomp *m* -s pomp

Pompon /pɔ̃'pŏ:/ *m* -s,-s pompon

pompös *a* ostentatious, *adv* -ly

Pony¹ *nt* -s,-s pony

Pony² *m* -s,-s fringe

Pop *m* -[s] pop. **P~musik** *f* pop music

Popo *m* -s,-s (*fam*) bottom

popul|är *a* popular. **P~arität** *f* - popularity

Pore *f* -,-n pore

Porno|graphie *f* - pornography. **p~graphisch** *a* pornographic

porös *a* porous

Porree *m* -s leeks *pl*; **eine Stange P~** a leek

Portal *nt* -s,-e portal

Portemonnaie /pɔrtmɔ'ne:/ *nt* -s,-s purse

Portier /pɔr'tje:/ *m* -s,-s doorman, porter

Portion /-'tsjo:n/ *f* -,-en helping, portion

Porto *nt* -s postage. **p~frei** *adv* post free, post paid

Porträt /pɔr'trɛ:/ *nt* -s,-s portrait. **p~tieren** *vt* paint a portrait of

Portugal *nt* -s Portugal

Portugies|e *m* -n,-n, **P~in** *f* -,-nen Portuguese. **p~isch** *a* Portuguese

Portwein *m* port

Porzellan *nt* -s china, porcelain

Posaune *f* -,-n trombone

Pose *f* -,-n pose

posieren *vi* (*haben*) pose

Position /-'tsjo:n/ *f* -,-en position

positiv *a* positive, *adv* -ly. **P~** *nt* -s,-e (*Phot*) positive

Posse *f* -,-n (*Theat*) farce. **P~n** *m* -s,- prank; **P~n** *pl* tomfoolery *sg*

Possessiv|pronomen *nt* possessive pronoun

possierlich *a* cute

Post *f* - post office; (*Briefe*) mail, post; **mit der P~** by post

postalisch *a* postal

Post|amt *nt* post office. **P~anweisung** *f* postal money order. **P~bote** *m* postman

Posten *m* -s,- post; (*Wache*) sentry; (*Waren-*) batch; (*Rechnungs-*) item, entry; **P~ stehen** stand guard; **nicht auf dem P~** (*fam*) under the weather

Poster *nt* & *m* -s,- poster

Postfach *nt* post-office *or* PO box

postieren *vt* post, station; **sich p~** station oneself

Post|karte *f* postcard. **p~lagernd** *adv* poste restante. **P~leitzahl** *f* postcode, (*Amer*) Zip code. **P~scheckkonto** *nt* ≈ National Girobank account. **P~stempel** *m* postmark

postum *a* posthumous, *adv* -ly

post|wendend *adv* by return of post. **P~wertzeichen** *nt* [postage] stamp

Poten|tial /-'tsja:l/ *nt* -s,-e potential. **p~tiell** /-'tsjɛl/ *a* potential, *adv* -ly

Potenz *f* -,-en potency; (*Math & fig*) power

Pracht *f* - magnificence, splendour. **P~exemplar** *nt* magnificent specimen

prächtig *a* magnificent, *adv* -ly; (*prima*) splendid, *adv* -ly

prachtvoll *a* magnificent, *adv* -ly

Prädikat *nt* -[e]s,-e rating; (*Comm*) grade; (*Gram*) predicate. **p~iv** *a* (*Gram*) predicative, *adv* -ly. **P~swein** *m* high-quality wine

präge|n *vt* stamp (**auf**+*acc* on); emboss 〈*Leder, Papier*〉; mint 〈*Münze*〉; coin 〈*Wort, Ausdruck*〉; (*fig*) shape. **P~stempel** *m* die

pragmatisch *a* pragmatic, *adv* -ally

prägnant *a* succinct, *adv* -ly

prähistorisch *a* prehistoric

prahl|en *vi* (*haben*) boast, brag (**mit** about). **p~erisch** *a* boastful, *adv* -ly

Prakti|k *f* -,-en practice. **P~kant(in)** *m* -en,-en (*f* -,-nen) trainee

Prakti|kum *nt* -s,-ka practical training. **p~sch** *a* practical; (*nützlich*) handy; (*tatsächlich*) virtual; **p~scher Arzt** general practitioner □*adv* practically;

virtually; (*in der Praxis*) in practice; **p~sch arbeiten** do practical work. **p~zieren** *vt/i* (*haben*) practise; (*anwenden*) put into practice; (*fam:* **bekommen**) get

Praline *f* -,-n chocolate; **Schachtel P~n** box of chocolates

prall *a* bulging; (*dick*) plump; ⟨*Sonne*⟩ blazing □ *adv* **p~gefüllt** full to bursting. **p~en** *vi* (*sein*) **p~auf** (+ *acc*)/**gegen** collide with, hit; ⟨*Sonne:*⟩ blaze down on

Prämie /-iə/ *f* -,-n premium; (*Preis*) award

präm[i]ieren *vt* award a prize to

Pranger *m* -s,- pillory

Pranke *f* -,-n paw

Präparat *nt* -[e]s,-e preparation. **p~ieren** *vt* prepare; (*zerlegen*) dissect; (*ausstopfen*) stuff

Präposition /-'tsio:n/ *f* -,-en preposition

Präsens *nt* - (*Gram*) present

präsentieren *vt* present; **sich p~** present itself/⟨*Person:*⟩ oneself

Präsenz *f* - presence

Präservativ *nt* -s,-e condom

Präsident(in) *m* -en,-en *f* -,-nen president. **P~schaft** *f* - presidency

Präsidium *nt* -s presidency; (*Gremium*) executive committee; (*Polizei-*) headquarters *pl*

prasseln *vi* (*haben*) ⟨*Regen:*⟩ beat down; (*Feuer:*) crackle □ *vi* (*sein*) **p~auf** (+ *acc*)/**gegen** beat down on/beat against

prassen *vi* (*haben*) live extravagantly; (*schmausen*) feast

Präteritum *nt* -s imperfect

präventiv *a* preventive

Praxis *f* -,-xen practice; (*Erfahrung*) practical experience; (*Arzt-*) surgery; **in der P~** in practice

Präzedenzfall *m* precedent

präzis[e] *a* precise, *adv* -ly

Präzision *f* - precision

predigen *vt/i* (*haben*) preach. **P~er** *m* -s,- preacher. **P~t** *f* -,-en sermon

Preis *m* -es,-e price; (*Belohnung*) prize; **um jeden/keinen P~** at any/not at any price. **P~ausschreiben** *nt* competition

Preiselbeere *f* (*Bot*) cowberry; (*Culin*) ≈ cranberry

preisen† *vt* praise; **sich glücklich p~** count oneself lucky

preisgeben† *vt sep* abandon (*dat* to); reveal ⟨*Geheimnis*⟩

preis|gekrönt *a* award-winning. **P~gericht** *nt* jury. **p~günstig** *a* reasonably priced □ *adv* at a reasonable price. **P~lage** *f* price range. **p~lich** *a* price . . . □ *adv* in price. **P~richter** *m* judge. **P~schild** *nt* price-tag. **P~träger(in)** *m(f)* prize-winner. **p~wert** *a* reasonable, *adv* -bly; (*billig*) inexpensive, *adv* -ly

prekär *a* difficult; (*heikel*) delicate

Prell|bock *m* buffers *pl*. **p~en** *vt* bounce; (*verletzen*) bruise; (*fam: betrügen*) cheat. **P~ung** *f* -,-en bruise

Premiere /prə'mie:rə/ *f* -,-n première

Premierminister(in) /prə'mie:-/ *m(f)* Prime Minister

Presse *f* -,-n press. **P~n** *vt* press; **sich p~** press (**an** + *acc* against)

pressieren *vi* (*haben*) (*SGer*) be urgent

Preßluft *f* compressed air. **P~bohrer** *m* pneumatic drill

Prestige /prɛs'ti:ʒə/ *nt* -s prestige

Preuß|en *nt* -s Prussia. **p~isch** *a* Prussian

prickeln *vi* (*haben*) tingle

Priester *m* -s,- priest

prima *a inv* first-class, first-rate; (*fam: toll*) fantastic, *adv* fantastically well

primär *a* primary, *adv* -ily

Primel f -,-n primula; (Garten-) polyanthus

primitiv a primitive

Prinz m -en,-en prince. **P~essin** f -,-nen princess

Prinzip nt -s,-ien /-jən/ principle; **im/aus P~** in/on principle. **p~iell** a ⟨Frage⟩ of principle □adv on principle; (im Prinzip) in principle

Priorität f -,-en priority

Prise f -,-n **P~ Salz** pinch of salt

Prisma nt -s,-men prism

privat a private, adv -ly; (persönlich) personal. **P~adresse** f home address. **p~isieren** vt privatize

Privatleben nt private life. **P~lehrer** m private tutor. **P~lehrerin** f governess. **P~patient(in)** m(f) private patient

Privileg nt -[e]s,-ien /-jən/ privilege. **p~iert** a privileged

pro prep (+ dat) per. **Pro** nt -s, **Pro und Kontra** the pros and cons pl

Probe f -,-n test, trial; (Menge, Muster) sample; (Theat) rehearsal; **auf die P~** stellen put to the test. **P~fahrt** f test drive. **p~n** vt/i (haben) (Theat) rehearse. **p~weise** adv on a trial basis. **P~zeit** f probationary period

probieren vt/i (haben) try; (kosten) taste; (proben) rehearse

Problem nt -s,-e problem. **p~atisch** a problematic

problemlos a problem-free □adv without any problems

Produkt nt -[e]s,-e product

Produktion /-'tsjo:n/ f -,-en production. **p~tiv** a productive. **P~tivität** f - productivity

Produzent m -en,-en producer. **p~zieren** vt produce; **sich p~zieren** (fam) show off

professionell a professional, adv -ly

Professor m -s,-en /-'so:rən/ professor

Profi m -s,-s (Sport) professional

Profil nt -s,-e profile; (Reifen-) tread; (fig) image. **p~iert** a (fig) distinguished

Profit m -[e]s,-e profit. **p~ieren** vi (haben) profit (von from)

Prognose f -,-n forecast; (Med) prognosis

Programm nt -s,-e programme; (Computer-) program; (TV) channel; (Comm: Sortiment) range. **p~ieren** vt/i (haben) (Computer) program. **P~ierer(in)** m -s, (f -,-nen) [computer] programmer

progressiv a progressive

Projekt nt -[e]s,-e project

Projektor m -s,-en /-'to:rən/ projector

projizieren vt project

Proklamation /-'tsjo:n/ f -,-en proclamation. **p~ieren** vt proclaim

Prolet m -en,-en boor. **P~ariat** nt -[e]s proletariat. **P~arier** /-jɐ/ m -s,- proletarian

Prolog m -s,-e prologue

Promenade f -,-n promenade. **P~nmischung** f (fam) mongrel

Promille pl (fam) alcohol level sg in the blood; **zuviel P~ haben** (fam) be over the limit

prominent a prominent. **P~z** f - prominent figures pl

Promiskuität f - promiscuity

promovieren vi (haben) obtain one's doctorate

prompt a prompt, adv -ly; (fam: natürlich) of course

Pronomen nt -s,- pronoun

Propaganda f - propaganda; (Reklame) publicity. **p~ieren** vt propagate

Propeller m -s,- propeller

Prophet m -en,-en prophet. **p~isch** a prophetic

prophezeien vt prophesy. **P~ung** f -,-en prophecy

Proportion /-'tsĭo:n/ f -,-en proportion. **p~al** a proportional. **p~iert** a gut **p~iert** well proportioned

Prosa f - prose

prosaisch a prosaic, adv -ally

prosit int cheers!

Prospekt m -[e]s,-e brochure; (Comm) prospectus

prost int cheers!

Prostitu|ierte f -n,-n prostitute. **P~tion** /-'tsĭo:n/ f - prostitution

Protest m -[e]s,-e protest

Protestant|(in) m -en,-en (f -,-nen) (Relig) Protestant. **p~isch** a (Relig) Protestant.

protestieren vi (haben) protest

Prothese f -,-e artificial limb; (Zahn-) denture

Protokoll nt -s,-e record; (Sitzungs-) minutes pl; (diplomatisches) protocol; (Strafzettel) ticket

Prototyp m -s,-en prototype

protz|en vi (haben) show off (mit etw sth). **p~ig** a ostentatious

Proviant m -s provisions pl

Provinz f -,-en province. **p~iell** a provincial

Provision f -,-en (Comm) commission

provisorisch a provisional, adv -ly, temporary, adv -ly

Provokation /-'tsĭo:n/ f -,-en provocation

provozieren vt provoke. **p~d** a provocative, adv -ly

Prozedur f -,-en [lengthy] business

Prozent nt -[e]s,-e & - per cent; 5 **P~** 5 per cent. **P~satz** m percentage. **p~ual** a percentage ...

Prozeß m -sses,-sse process; (Jur) lawsuit; (Kriminal-) trial

Prozession f -,-en procession

prüde a prudish

prüf|en vt test/(über-) check (auf + acc for); audit (Bücher); (Sch) examine; **p~ender Blick**

searching look. **P~er** m -s,-, inspector; (Buch-) auditor; (Sch) examiner. **P~ling** m -s,-e examination candidate. **P~ung** f -,-en examination; (Test) test; (Bücher-) audit; (fig) trial

Prügel m -s,-; cudgel; **P~** pl hiding sg, beating sg. **P~ei** f -,-en brawl, fight. **p~n** vt beat, thrash; **sich p~n** fight, brawl

Prunk m -[e]s magnificence, splendour. **p~en** vi (haben) show off (mit etw sth). **p~voll** a magnificent, adv -ly

prusten vi (haben) splutter; (schnauben) snort

Psalm m -s,-en psalm

Pseudonym nt -s,-e pseudonym

pst int shush!

Psychiater m -s,- psychiatrist. **P~atrie** f - psychiatry. **p~atrisch** a psychiatric

psychisch a psychological, adv -ly; (Med) mental, adv -ly

Psycho|analyse f psychoanalysis. **P~loge** m -n,-n psychologist. **P~logie** f - psychology. **p~logisch** a psychological, adv -ly

Pubertät f - puberty

publik a **p~ werden/machen** become/make public

Publikum nt -s public; (Zuhörer) audience; (Zuschauer) spectators pl. **p~zieren** vt publish

Pudding m -s,-e blancmange; (im Wasserbad gekocht) pudding

Pudel m -s,- poodle

Puder m & (fam) nt -s,- powder; (Körper-) talcum [powder]. **P~dose** f [powder] compact. **p~n** vt powder. **P~zucker** m icing sugar

Puff¹ m -[e]s,-e push, poke

Puff² m & nt -s,-s (sl) brothel

puffen vt (fam) poke □ vi (sein) puff along

Puffer m -s,- (Rail) buffer; (Culin) pancake. **P~zone** f buffer zone

Pull|i *m* -s,-s jumper. **P~over** *m* -s,- jumper; (*Herren-*)

Puls *m* -es pulse. **P~ader** *f* artery. **p~ieren** *vi* (*haben*) pulsate

Pult *nt* -[e]s,-e desk; (*Lese-*) lectern

Pulver *nt* -s,- powder. **p~ig** *a* powdery. **p~isieren** *vt* pulverize

Pulver|kaffee *m* instant coffee. **P~schnee** *m* powder snow

pummelig *a* (*fam*) chubby

Pump *m* auf **P~** (*fam*) on tick

Pumpe *f* -,-n pump. **p~n** *vt/i* (*haben*) pump; (*fam: leihen*) lend; [sich (*dat*)] etw **p~n** (*fam: borgen*) borrow sth

Pumps /pœmps/ *pl* court shoes

Punkt *m* -[e]s,-e dot; (*Tex*) spot; (*Geom, Sport & flg*) point; (*Gram*) full stop, period; **P~** sechs Uhr at six o'clock sharp; **nach P~en siegen** win on points. **p~iert** *a* ⟨*Linie, Note*⟩ dotted

pünktlich *a* punctual, *adv* -ly. **P~keit** *f* punctuality

Punsch *m* -[e]s,-e [hot] punch

Pupille *f* -,-n (*Anat*) pupil

Puppe *f* -,-n doll; (*Marionette*) puppet; (*Schaufenster-, Schneider-*) dummy; (*Zool*) chrysalis

pur *a* pure; (*fam: bloß*) sheer; **Whisky pur** neat whisky

Püree *nt* -s,-s purée; (*Kartoffel-*) mashed potatoes *pl*

puritanisch *a* puritanical

purpurrot *a* crimson

Purzel|baum *m* (*fam*) somersault. **p~n** *vi* (*sein*) (*fam*) tumble

pusseln *vi* (*haben*) (*fam*) potter

Puste *f* -. (*fam*) breath; **aus der P~** out of breath. **p~n** *vt/i* (*haben*) (*fam*) blow

Pute *f* -,-n turkey; (*Henne*) turkey hen. **P~r** *m* -s,- turkey cock

Putsch *m* -[e]s,-e coup

Putz *m* -es plaster; (*Staat*) finery. **p~en** *vt* clean; (*Aust*) dry-clean; (*zieren*) adorn; **sich p~en** dress

up; **sich** (*dat*) **die Zähne/Nase p~en** clean one's teeth/blow one's nose. **P~frau** *f* cleaner, charwoman. **p~ig** *a* (*fam*) amusing, cute; (*seltsam*) odd. **P~macherin** *f* -,-nen milliner

Puzzlespiel /'pazl-/ *nt* jigsaw

Pyramide *f* -,-n pyramid

Q

Quacksalber *m* -s,- quack

Quadrat *nt* -[e]s,-e square. **q~isch** *a* square. **Q~meter** *m* & *nt* square metre

quaken *vi* (*haben*) quack; ⟨*Frosch:*⟩ croak

quäken *vi* (*haben*) screech; ⟨*Baby:*⟩ whine

Quäker(in) *m* -s, (*f* -,-nen) Quaker

Qual *f* -,-en torment; (*Schmerz*) agony

quälen *vt* torment; (*foltern*) torture; (*bedrängen*) pester; **sich q~** torment oneself; (*leiden*) suffer; (*sich mühen*) struggle. **q~d** *a* agonizing

Quälerei *f* -,-en torture; (*Qual*) agony

Quälgeist *m* (*fam*) pest

Qualifi|kation /-'tsio:n/ *f* -,-en qualification. **q~zieren** *vt* qualify; **sich q~zieren** qualify. **q~ziert** *a* qualified; (*fähig*) competent; (*Arbeit*) skilled

Qualität *f* -,-en quality

Qualle *f* -,-n jellyfish

Qualm *m* -s [thick] smoke. **q~en** *vi* (*haben*) smoke

qualvoll *a* agonizing

Quantität *f* -,-en quantity

Quantum *nt* -s,-ten quantity; (*Anteil*) share, quota

Quarantäne *f* - quarantine

Quark *m* -s quark, ≈ curd cheese; (*fam: Unsinn*) rubbish

Quartal nt -s,-e quarter
Quartett nt -[e]s,-e quartet
Quartier nt -s,-e accommodation; (Mil) quarters pl; ein Q~ suchen look for accommodation
Quarz m -es quartz
quasseln vi (haben) (fam) jabber
Quaste f -,-n tassel
Quatsch m -[e]s (fam) nonsense, rubbish; Q~ machen (Unfug machen) fool around; (etw falsch machen) do a silly thing. **q~en** (fam) vi (haben) talk; (schwatzen) natter; (Wasser, Schlamm:) squelch □ vt talk. **q~naß** a (fam) soaking wet
Quecksilber nt mercury
Quelle f -,-n spring; (Fluß- & fig) source. **q~n†** vi (sein) well [up]/ (fließen) pour (aus from); (aufquellen) swell; (hervortreten) bulge
quengeln vi (fam) whine; (Baby:) grizzle
quer adv across, crosswise; (schräg) diagonally
Quere f - der Q~ nach across, crosswise; jdm in die Q~ kommen get in s.o.'s way
querfeldein adv across country
quer|gestreift a horizontally striped. **q~köpfig** a (fam) awkward. **Q~latte** f crossbar. **Q~schiff** nt transept. **Q~schnitt** m cross-section. **Q~schnittsgelähmt** a paraplegic. **Q~straße** f side-street; die erste Q~straße links the first turning on the left. **Q~verweis** m cross-reference
quetsch|en vt squash; (drücken) squeeze; (zerdrücken) crush; (Culin) mash; sich **q~en** in (+ acc) squeeze into; sich (dat) den Arm **q~en** bruise one's arm. **Q~ung** f -,-en, **Q~wunde** f bruise
Queue /kø:/ nt -s,-s cue
quicklebendig a very lively

quieken vi (haben) squeal; (Maus:) squeak
quietschen vi (haben) squeal; (Tür, Dielen:) creak
Quintett nt -[e]s,-e quintet
Quirl m -[e]s,-e blender with a star-shaped head. **q~en** vt mix
quitt a q~ sein (fam) be quits
Quitte f -,-n quince
quittieren vt receipt (Rechnung); sign for (Geldsumme, Sendung); (reagieren auf) greet (mit with); den Dienst q~ resign
Quittung f -,-en receipt
Quiz /kvɪs/ nt -,- quiz
Quote f -,-n proportion

R

Rabatt m -[e]s,-e discount
Rabatte f (Hort) border
Rabattmarke f trading stamp
Rabbiner m -s,- rabbi
Rabe m -n,-n raven. **r~nschwarz** a pitch-black
rabiat a violent, adv -ly; (wütend) furious, adv -ly
Rache f - revenge, vengeance
Rachen m -s,- pharynx; (Maul) jaws pl
rächen vt avenge; sich r~ take revenge (an + dat on); (Fehler, Leichtsinn:) cost s.o. dear
Racker m -s,- (fam) rascal
Rad nt -[e]s,-er wheel; (Fahr-) bicycle, (fam) bike
Radar m & nt -s radar
Radau m -s (fam) din, racket
radebrechen vt/i (haben) [Deutsch/Englisch] r~ speak broken German/English
radeln vi (sein) (fam) cycle
Rädelsführer m ringleader
radfahr|en† vi sep (sein) cycle; ich fahre gern Rad I like cycling. **R~er(in)** m(f) -s,- (f -,-nen) cyclist

radier|en vt/i (haben) rub out; (Kunst) etch. **R~ung** f -,-en etching

Radieschen /-'di:sçən/ nt -s,- radish

radikal a radical, adv -ly; (drastisch) drastic, adv -ally. **R~e(r)** m/f (Pol) radical

Radio nt -s,-s radio

radioaktiv a radioactive. **R~ität** f - radioactivity

Radioapparat m radio [set]

Radius m -,-ien /-jən/ radius

Rad|kappe f hub-cap. **R~ler** m -s,- cyclist; (Getränk) shandy. **R~weg** m cycle track

raff|en vt grab; (kräuseln) gather; (kürzen) condense. **r~gierig** a avaricious

Raffin|ade f - refined sugar. **R~erie** f -,-n refinery. **R~esse** f -,-n refinement; (Schlauheit) cunning. **r~ieren** vt refine. **r~iert** a ingenious, adv -ly; (durchtrieben) crafty, adv -ily

Rage /'ra:ʒə/ f - (fam) fury

ragen vi (haben) rise [up]

Rahm m -s (SGer) cream

rahmen vt frame. **R~** m -s,- frame; (fig) framework; (Grenze) limits pl; (einer Feier) setting

Rain m -[e]s,-e grass verge

räkeln v = rekeln

Rakete f -,-n rocket; (Mil) missile

Rallye /'rali/ nt -s,-s rally

rammen vt ram

Rampe f -,-n ramp; (Theat) front of the stage. **R~nlicht** nt im **R~nlicht stehen** (fig) be in the limelight

ramponier|en vt (fam) damage; (ruinieren) ruin; **r~t** battered

Ramsch m -es junk. **R~laden** m junk-shop

ran adv = heran

Rand m -[e]s,-̈er edge; (Teller-, Gläser-, Brillen-) rim; (Zier-) border, edging; (Buch-, Brief-) margin; (Stadt-) outskirts pl; (Ring) ring; **am R~e des Ruins** on the brink of ruin; **am R~e erwähnen** mention in passing; **zu R~e kommen mit** (fam) cope with; **außer R~ und Band** (fam: ausgelassen) very boisterous

randalieren vi (haben) rampage

Rand|bemerkung f marginal note. **R~streifen** m (Auto) hard shoulder

Rang m -[e]s,-̈e rank; (Theat) tier; **erster/zweiter R~** (Theat) dress/upper circle; **ersten R~es** first-class

rangieren /raŋ'ʒi:rən/ vt shunt □vi (haben) rank (vor + dat before); **an erster Stelle r~** come first

Rangordnung f order of importance; (Hierarchie) hierarchy

Ranke f -,-n tendril; (Trieb) shoot

ranken (sich) vr (haben) trail; (in die Höhe) climb; **sich r~ um** twine around

Ranzen m -s,- (Sch) satchel

ranzig a rancid

Rappe m -n,-n black horse

rappeln v (fam) □vi (haben) rattle □vr sich **r~** pick oneself up; (fig) rally

Raps m -es (Bot) rape

rar a rare; **er macht sich rar** (fam) we don't see much of him. **R~ität** f -,-en rarity

rasant a fast; (schnittig, schick) stylish □adv fast; stylishly

rasch a quick, adv -ly

rascheln vi (haben) rustle

Rasen m -s,- lawn

rasen vi (sein) tear [along]; (Puls:) race; (Zeit:) fly; **gegen eine Mauer r~** career into a wall □vi (haben) rave; (Sturm:) rage; **vor Begeisterung r~** go wild with enthusiasm. **r~d** a furious; (*tobend*) raving; ⟨*Sturm, Durst*⟩ raging; (*Schmerz*) excruciating; ⟨*Beifall*⟩ tumultuous □*adv* terribly

Rasenmäher *m* lawn-mower

Raserei *f* - speeding; (*Toben*) frenzy

Rasier|apparat *m* razor. **r~en** *vt* shave; **sich r~en** shave. **R~klinge** *f* razor blade. **R~pinsel** *m* shaving-brush. **R~wasser** *nt* aftershave [lotion]

Raspel *f*-,-n rasp; (*Culin*) grater. **r~n** *vt* grate

Rasse *f* -,-n race. **R~hund** *m* pedigree dog

Rassel *f*-,-n rattle. **r~n** *vi* (*haben*) rattle; ⟨*Schlüssel:*⟩ jangle; ⟨*Kette:*⟩ clank □*vi* (*sein*) rattle [along]

Rassen|diskriminierung *f* racial discrimination. **R~trennung** *f* racial segregation

Rassepferd *nt* thoroughbred

rassisch *a* racial

Rassis|mus *m* - racism. **r~tisch** *a* racist

Rast *f*-,-en rest. **r~en** *vi* (*haben*) rest. **R~haus** *nt* motorway restaurant. **r~los** *a* restless, *adv* -ly; (*ununterbrochen*) ceaseless, *adv* -ly. **R~platz** *m* picnic area. **R~stätte** *f* motorway restaurant [and services]

Rasur *f*-,-en shave

Rat[1] *m* -[e]s [piece of] advice; **guter Rat** good advice; **zu Rat[e] ziehen** consult; **sich** (*dat*) **keinen Rat wissen** not know what to do

Rat[2] *m* -[e]s,-̈e (*Admin*) council; (*Person*) councillor

Rate *f*-,-n instalment

raten† *vt* guess; (*empfehlen*) advise □*vi* (*haben*) guess; **jdm r~** advise s.o.

Ratenzahlung *f* payment by instalments

Rat|geber *m* -s,- adviser; (*Buch*) guide. **R~haus** *nt* town hall

ratifizier|en *vt* ratify. **R~ung** *f* -,-en ratification

Ration /ra'tsjo:n/ *f* -,-en ration; **eiserne R~** iron rations *pl*. **r~al** *a* rational, *adv* -ly. **r~alisieren** *vt*/*i* (*haben*) rationalize. **r~ell** *a* efficient, *adv* -ly. **r~ieren** *vt* ration

rat|los *a* helpless, *adv* -ly; **r~los sein** not know what to do. **r~sam** *pred a* advisable; (*klug*) prudent. **R~schlag** *m* piece of advice; **R~schläge** advice *sg*

Rätsel *nt* -s,- riddle; (*Kreuzwort-*) puzzle; (*Geheimnis*) mystery. **r~haft** *a* puzzling, mysterious. **r~n** *vi* (*haben*) puzzle

Ratte *f*-,-n rat

rattern *vi* (*haben*) rattle □*vi* (*sein*) rattle [along]

Raub *m* -[e]s robbery; (*Menschen-*) abduction; (*Beute*) loot, booty. **r~en** *vt* steal; abduct ⟨*Menschen*⟩; **jdm etw r~en** rob s.o. of sth

Räuber *m* -s,- robber

Raub|mord *m* robbery with murder. **R~tier** *nt* predator. **R~überfall** *m* robbery. **R~vogel** *m* bird of prey

Rauch *m* -[e]s smoke. **r~en** *vt*/*i* (*haben*) smoke. **R~en** *nt*-s smoking; 'R~en verboten' 'no smoking'. **R~er** *m*-s,- smoker. **R~erabteil** *nt* smoking compartment

Räucher|lachs *m* smoked salmon. **r~n** *vt* (*Culin*) smoke

Rauch|fang *m* (*Aust*) chimney. **r~ig** *a* smoky. **R~verbot** *nt* smoking ban

räudig *a* mangy

rauf *adv* = **herauf, hinauf**

raufen *vt* pull; **sich** (*dat*) **die Haare r~en** (*fig*) tear one's hair □*vr*/*i* (*haben*) [sich] **r~en** fight. **R~erei** *f*-,-en fight

rauh a rough, adv -ly; (unfreundlich) gruff, adv -ly; ⟨Klima, Wind⟩ harsh, raw; ⟨Landschaft⟩ rugged; (heiser) husky; ⟨Hals⟩ sore

Rauheit f - (s. rauh) roughness; gruffness; harshness; ruggedness

rauh|haarig a wire-haired. **R~reif** m hoar-frost

Raum m -[e]s, Räume room; (Gebiet) area; ⟨Welt-⟩ space

räumen vt clear; vacate ⟨Wohnung⟩; evacuate ⟨Gebäude, Gebiet, (Mil) Stellung⟩; ⟨bringen⟩ put (in/auf+acc into/on); (holen) get (aus out of); **beiseite r~** move/put to one side; **aus dem Weg r~** (fam) get rid of

Raum|fahrer m astronaut. **R~fahrt** f space travel. **R~fahrzeug** nt spacecraft. **R~flug** m space flight. **R~inhalt** m volume

räumlich a spatial. **R~keiten** fpl rooms

Raum|pflegerin f cleaner. **R~schiff** nt spaceship

Räumung f - (s. räumen) clearing; vacating; evacuation. **R~sverkauf** m clearance/closing-down sale

raunen vt/i (haben) whisper

Raupe f -,-n caterpillar

raus adv = heraus, hinaus

Rausch m -[e]s, Räusche intoxication; (fig) exhilaration; **einen R~ haben** be drunk

rauschen vi (haben) ⟨Wasser, Wind:⟩ rush; ⟨Bäume, Blätter:⟩ rustle □ vi (sein) rush [along]; **aus dem Zimmer r~** sweep out of the room. **r~d** a rushing; rustling; ⟨Applaus⟩ tumultuous

Rauschgift nt [narcotic] drug; (coll) drugs pl. **R~süchtige(r)** m/f drug addict

räuspern (sich) vr clear one's throat

rausschmeiß|en† vt sep (fam) throw out; (entlassen) sack. **R~er** m -s,- (fam) bouncer

Raute f -,-n diamond

Razzia f -,-ien /-jən/ [police] raid

Reagenzglas nt test-tube

reagieren vi (haben) react (auf+acc to)

Reaktion /-'tsjo:n/ f -,-en reaction. **r~är** a reactionary

Reaktor m -s,-en /-'to:rən/reactor

real a real; (gegenständlich) tangible; (realistisch) realistic, adv -ally. **r~isieren** vt realize

Realis|mus m - realism. **R~t** m -en, -en realist. **r~tisch** a realistic, adv -ally

Realität f -,-en reality

Realschule f ≈ secondary modern school

Rebe f -,-n vine

Rebell m -en, -en rebel. **r~ieren** vi (haben) rebel. **R~ion** f -,-en rebellion

rebellisch a rebellious

Rebhuhn nt partridge

Rebstock m vine

Rechen m -s,- rake. **r~** vt/i (haben) rake

Rechen|aufgabe f arithmetical problem; (Sch) sum. **R~fehler** m arithmetical error. **R~maschine** f calculator

Rechenschaft f - **R~ ablegen** give account (über+acc of); **jdn zur R~ ziehen** call s.o. to account

recherchieren /reʃɛr'ʃi:rən/ vt/i (haben) investigate; (Journ) research

rechnen vi (haben) do arithmetic; (schätzen) reckon; (zählen) count (zu among; auf+acc on); **r~ mit** reckon with; (erwarten) expect; **gut r~ können** be good at figures □ vt calculate, work out; do ⟨Aufgabe⟩; (dazu-) add (zu to); (fig) count (zu among). **R~** nt -s arithmetic

Rechner *m* -s,- calculator; (*Computer*) computer; **ein guter R~ sein** be good at figures

Rechnung *f* -,-en bill, (*Amer*) check; (*Comm*) invoice; (*Berechnung*) calculation; **R~ führen über** (+*acc*) keep account of; **etw** (*dat*) **R~ tragen** (*fig*) take sth into account. **R~sjahr** *nt* financial year. **R~sprüfer** *m* auditor

Recht *nt* -[e]s,-e law; (*Berechtigung*) right (**auf**+*acc* to); **im R~ sein** be in the right; **mit od zu R~** rightly; **von S~s wegen** by right; (*eigentlich*) by rights

recht *a* right; (*wirklich*) real; **ich habe keine r~e Lust** I don't really feel like it; **es jdm r~ machen** please s.o.; **jdm r~ sein** be all right with s.o. □ **r~ haben/behalten** be right; **r~ bekommen** be proved right; **jdm r~ geben** agree with s.o. □ *adv* correctly; (*ziemlich*) quite; (*sehr*) very; **r~ vielen Dank** many thanks

Recht|**e** *f* -n,-[n] right side; (*Hand*) right hand; (*Boxen*) right; **die R~e** (*Pol*) the right; **zu meiner R~en** on my right. **r~e(r,s)** *a* right; (*Pol*) right-wing; **r~e Masche** plain stitch. **R~e(r)** *m/f* **der/die R~e** the right man/woman; **du bist mir der/die R~e!** you're a fine one! **R~e(s)** *nt* **das R~e** the right thing; **etwas R~es lernen** learn something useful; **nach dem R~en sehen** see that everything is all right

Rechteck *nt* -[e]s,-e rectangle. **r~ig** *a* rectangular

rechtfertig|**en** *vt* justify; **sich r~en** justify oneself. **R~ung** *f* -justification

recht|**haberisch** *a* opinionated. **r~lich** *a* legal, *adv* -ly. **r~mäßig** *a* legitimate, *adv* -ly

rechts *adv* on the right; (*bei Stoff*) on the right side; **von/nach r~**

from/to the right; **zwei r~, zwei links stricken** knit two, purl two. **R~anwalt** *m*, **R~anwältin** *f* lawyer

rechtschaffen *a* upright; (*ehrlich*) honest, *adv* -ly; **r~ müde** thoroughly tired

rechtschreib|**en** *vi* (*inf only*) spell correctly. **R~fehler** *m* spelling mistake. **R~ung** *f* -spelling

Rechts|**händer(in)** *m* -s,- (*f* -,-nen) right-hander. **r~händig** *a* & *adv* right-handed. **r~kräftig** *a* legal, *adv* -ly. **R~streit** *m* law suit. **R~verkehr** *m* driving on the right. **r~widrig** *a* illegal, *adv* -ly. **R~wissenschaft** *f* jurisprudence

recht|**winklig** *a* right-angled. **r~zeitig** *a* & *adv* in time

Reck *nt* -[e]s,-e horizontal bar

recken *vt* stretch; **sich r~** stretch; **den Hals r~** crane one's neck

Redakteur /redak'tøːɐ/ *m* -s,-e editor; (*Radio, TV*) producer

Redaktion /-'tsjoːn/ *f* -,-en editing; (*Radio, TV*) production; (*Abteilung*) editorial/production department. **r~ell** *a* editorial

Rede *f* -,-n speech; **zur R~ stellen** demand an explanation from; **davon ist keine R~** there's no question of it; **nicht der R~ wert** not worth mentioning. **r~gewandt** *a* eloquent, *adv* -ly

reden *vi* (*haben*) talk (**von** about; **mit** to); (*eine Rede halten*) speak □ *vt* talk; speak (*Wahrheit*); **kein Wort r~** not say a word. **R~sart** *f* saying; (*Phrase*) phrase

Redewendung *f* idiom

redigieren *vt* edit

redlich *a* honest, *adv* -ly

Red|**ner** *m* -s,- speaker. **r~selig** *a* talkative

reduzieren *vt* reduce

Reeder *m* -s,- shipowner. **R~ei** *f*
-,-en shipping company

reell *a* real; (*ehrlich*) honest, *adv*
-ly; (*Preis, Angebot*) fair

Refer|**at** *nt* -[e]s,-e report; (*Ab-
handlung*) paper; (*Abteilung*) section. **R~ent(in)** *m* -en,-en (*f*
-,-nen) speaker; (*Sachbearbeiter*)
expert. **R~enz** *f* -,-en reference.
r~ieren *vi* (*haben*) deliver a
paper; (*berichten*) report (**über**
+ *acc* **on**)

reflektieren *vt/i* (*haben*) reflect
(**über** + *acc* **on**)

Reflex *m* -es,-e reflex; (*Wider-
schein*) reflection. **R~ion** *f* -,-en
reflection. **r~iv** *a* reflexive.
R~ivpronomen *nt* reflexive
pronoun

Reform *f* -,-en reform. **R~ation**
/-'tsio:n/ *f* (*Relig*) Reformation
Reform|**haus** *nt* health-food
shop. **r~ieren** *vt* reform

Refrain /ra'frɛ̃:/ *m* -s,-s refrain

Regal *nt* -s,-e [set of] shelves *pl*

Regatta *f* -,-ten regatta

rege *a* active; (*lebhaft*) lively;
(*geistig*) alert; (*Handel*) brisk
□ *adv* actively

Regel *f* -,-n rule; (*Monats-*) period;
in der R~ as a rule. **r~mäßig** *a*
regular, *adv* -ly. **r~n** *vt* regulate;
direct (*Verkehr*); (*erledigen*) settle. **r~recht** *a* real, proper □ *adv*
really. **R~ung** *f* -,-en regulation;
settlement. **r~widrig** *a* irregular, *adv* -ly

regen *vt* move; **sich r~** move;
(*wach werden*) stir

Regen *m* -s,- rain. **R~bogen** *m*
rainbow. **R~bogenhaut** *f* iris

Regener|**ation** /-'tsio:n/ *f* regen-
eration. **r~ieren** *vt* regenerate;
sich r~ieren regenerate

Regen|**mantel** *m* raincoat.
R~schirm *m* umbrella. **R~tag**
m rainy day. **R~tropfen** *m* rain-
drop. **R~wetter** *nt* wet weather.
R~wurm *m* earthworm

Regie /re'ʒi:/ *f* - direction; **R~**
führen direct

regier|**en** *vt/i* (*haben*) govern,
rule; (*Monarch:*) reign [over];
(*Gram*) take. **r~end** *a* ruling;
reigning. **R~ung** *f* -,-en government; (*Herrschaft*) rule; (*eines
Monarchen*) reign

Regime /re'ʒi:m/ *nt* -s,- /-mə/ regime

Regiment[1] *nt* -[e]s,-er regiment

Regiment[2] *nt* -[e]s,-e rule

Region *f* -,-en region. **r~al** *a*
regional, *adv* -ly

Regisseur /reʒɪ'sø:ɐ̯/ *m* -s,-e director

Register *nt* -s,- register; (*Inhalts-
verzeichnis*) index; (*Orgel-*) stop

registrier|**en** *vt* register; (*Techn*)
record. **R~kasse** *f* cash register

Regler *m* -s,- regulator

reglos *a* & *adv* motionless

regn|**en** *vi* (*haben*) rain; **es r~et** it
is raining. **r~erisch** *a* rainy

regul|**är** *a* normal, *adv* -ly; (*recht-
mäßig*) legitimate, *adv* -ly.
r~ieren *vt* regulate

Regung *f* -,-en movement; (*Ge-
fühls-*) emotion. **r~slos** *a* & *adv*
motionless

Reh *nt* -[e]s,-e roe-deer; (*Culin*)
venison

Rehabilit|**ation** /-'tsio:n/ *f* - re-
habilitation. **r~ieren** *vt* re-
habilitate

Rehbock *m* roebuck

Reib|**e** *f* -,-n grater. **r~en†** *vt* rub;
(*Culin*) grate; **blank r~en** polish
□ *vi* (*haben*) rub. **R~ereien** *fpl*
(*fam*) friction *sg*. **R~ung** *f* -
friction. **r~ungslos** *a* (*fig*)
smooth, *adv* -ly

reich *a* rich (**an** + *dat* **in**), *adv* -ly;
(*r~haltig*) abundant, *adv* -ly

Reich *nt* -[e]s,-e empire; (*König-*)
kingdom; (*Bereich*) realm

Reich|**e(r)** *m/f* rich man/woman;
die R~en the rich *pl*

reichen vt hand; ⟨anbieten⟩ offer □ vi ⟨haben⟩ be enough; ⟨in der Länge⟩ be long enough; r~ bis zu reach [up to]; ⟨sich erstrecken⟩ extend to; mit dem Geld r~ have enough money; mir reicht's! I've had enough!

reich|haltig a extensive, large ⟨Mahlzeit⟩ substantial. r~lich a ample; ⟨Vorrat⟩ abundant, plentiful; eine r~liche Stunde a good hour □ adv amply; abundantly; ⟨fam: sehr⟩ very. R~tum m -s,-tümer wealth (an + dat of); R~tümer riches. R~weite f reach; ⟨Techn, Mil⟩ range

Reif m -[e]s [hoar-]frost

reif a ripe; ⟨fig⟩ mature; r~ für ready for. R~e f - ripeness; ⟨fig⟩ maturity. r~en vi ⟨sein⟩ ripen; ⟨Wein, Käse & fig⟩ mature

Reifen m -s,- hoop; ⟨Arm-⟩ bangle; ⟨Auto-⟩ tyre. R~druck m tyre pressure. R~panne f puncture, flat tyre

Reifeprüfung f ≈ A levels pl

reiflich a careful, adv -ly

Reihe f -,-n row; ⟨Anzahl & Math⟩ series; der R~ nach in turn; außer der R~ out of turn; wer ist an der od kommt an die R~? whose turn is it? r~n (sich) vr sich r~n an etw (+ acc) follow. R~nfolge f order. R~nhaus nt terraced house. r~nweise adv in rows; ⟨fam⟩ in large numbers

Reiher m -s,- heron

Reim m -[e]s,-e rhyme. r~en vt rhyme; sich r~en rhyme

rein[1] a pure; ⟨sauber⟩ clean; ⟨Unsinn, Dummheit⟩ sheer; ins r~e schreiben make a fair copy of; ins r~e bringen ⟨fig⟩ sort out □ adv purely; ⟨fam⟩ absolutely

rein[2] adv =herein, hinein

Reineclaude /rɛːnə'kloːdə/ f -,-n greengage

Reinfall m ⟨fam⟩ let-down; ⟨Mißerfolg⟩ flop. r~en† vi sep

⟨sein⟩ fall in; ⟨fam⟩ be taken in (auf + acc by)

Rein|gewinn m net profit. R~heit f - purity

reinigen vt clean; ⟨chemisch⟩ dry-clean. R~ung f -,-en cleaning; ⟨chemische⟩ dry-cleaning; ⟨Geschäft⟩ dry cleaner's

Reinkarnation /-'reːnkarnaˈtsɪoːn/ f -,-en reincarnation

reinlegen vt sep put in; ⟨fam⟩ dupe; ⟨betrügen⟩ take for a ride

reinlich a clean. R~keit f - cleanliness

Rein|machefrau f cleaner. R~schrift f fair copy. r~seiden a pure silk

Reis m -es rice

Reise f -,-n journey; ⟨See-⟩ voyage; ⟨Urlaubs-, Geschäfts-⟩ trip. R~andenken nt souvenir. R~büro nt travel agency. R~bus m coach. R~führer m tourist guide; ⟨Buch⟩ guide. R~gesellschaft f tourist group. R~leiter(in) m(f) courier. r~n vi ⟨sein⟩ travel. R~nde(r) m/f traveller. R~paß m passport. R~scheck m traveller's cheque. R~unternehmer, R~veranstalter m -s,- tour operator. R~ziel nt destination

Reisig nt -s brushwood

Reißaus m R~ nehmen ⟨fam⟩ run away

Reißbrett nt drawing-board

reißen† vt tear; ⟨weg-⟩ snatch; ⟨töten⟩ kill; Witze r~ crack jokes; aus dem Schlaf r~ awaken rudely; an sich (acc) r~ snatch; seize ⟨Macht⟩; mit sich r~ sweep away; sich r~ um ⟨fam⟩ fight for; ⟨gern mögen⟩ be keen on; hin und her gerissen sein ⟨fig⟩ be torn □ vi ⟨sein⟩ tear; ⟨Seil, Faden;⟩ break □ vi ⟨haben⟩ r~ an (+ dat) pull at. r~d a raging; ⟨Tier⟩ ferocious; ⟨Schmerz⟩ violent

Reißer *m* -s,- (*fam*) thriller; (*Erfolg*) big hit. **r~isch** *a* (*fam*) sensational

Reiß|nagel *m* = **R~zwecke**. **R~verschluß** *m* zip [fastener]. **R~wolf** *m* shredder. **R~zwecke** *f* -,-n drawing-pin, (*Amer*) thumbtack

reit|en† *vt/i* (*sein*) ride. **R~er(in)** *m* -s,- (*f* -,-nen) rider. **R~hose** *f* riding breeches *pl*. **R~pferd** *nt* saddle-horse. **R~schule** *f* riding-school. **R~weg** *m* bridle-path

Reiz *m* -es,-e stimulus; (*Anziehungskraft*) attraction, appeal; (*Charme*) charm. **r~bar** *a* irritable. **R~barkeit** *f* - irritability. **r~en** *vt* provoke; (*Med*) irritate; (*interessieren, locken*) appeal to, attract; arouse (*Neugier*); (*beim Kartenspiel*) bid. **r~end** *a* charming, *adv* -ly; (*entzückend*) delightful. **R~ung** *f* -,-en (*Med*) irritation. **r~voll** *a* attractive

rekapitulieren *vt/i* (*haben*) recapitulate

rekeln (sich) *vr* stretch; (*lümmeln*) sprawl

Reklamation /-'tsjo:n/ *f* -,-en (*Comm*) complaint

Reklam|e /-,-n advertising, publicity; (*Anzeige*) advertisement; (*TV, Radio*) commercial; **R~e machen** advertise (**für** etw sth). **r~ieren** *vt* complain about; (*fordern*) claim □ *vi* (*haben*) complain

rekonstruieren *vt* reconstruct. **R~ktion** /-'tsjo:n/ *f* -,-en reconstruction

Rekonvaleszenz *f* - convalescence

Rekord *m* -[e]s,-e record

Rekrut *m* -en,-en recruit. **r~ieren** *vt* recruit

Rek|tor *m* -s,-en /-'to:rən/ (*Sch*) head[master]; (*Univ*) vice-chancellor. **R~torin** *f* -,-nen head[mistress]; vice-chancellor

Relais /rəˈlɛː/ *nt* -,- /-s,-s/ (*Electr*) relay

relativ *a* relative, *adv* -ly. **R~pronomen** *nt* relative pronoun

relevant *a* relevant (**für** to). **R~z** *f* - relevance

Relief /rəˈljɛf/ *nt* -s,-s relief

Religi|on *f* -,-en religion; (*Sch*) religious education. **r~ös** *a* religious

Reling *f* -,-s (*Naut*) rail

Reliquie /reˈliːkvjə/ *f* -,-n relic

Remouladensoße /remuˈlaːdən-/ *f* ≈ tartar sauce

rempeln *vt* jostle; (*stoßen*) push

Ren *nt* -s,-s reindeer

Reneklode *f* -,-n greengage

Renn|auto *nt* racing car. **R~bahn** *f* race-track; (*Pferde*) racecourse. **R~boot** *nt* speedboat. **r~en†** *vi/t* (*sein*) run; **um die Wette r~en** have a race. **R~en** *nt* -s,- race. **R~pferd** *nt* racehorse. **R~sport** *m* racing. **R~wagen** *m* racing car

renommiert *a* renowned; (*Hotel, Firma*) of repute

renovier|en *vt* renovate; redecorate (*Zimmer*). **R~ung** *f* - renovation; redecoration

rentabel *a* profitable, *adv* -bly

Rente *f* -,-n pension; **in R~ gehen** (*fam*) retire. **R~nversicherung** *f* pension scheme

Rentier *nt* reindeer

rentieren (sich) *vr* be profitable; (*sich lohnen*) be worth while

Rentner(in) *m* -s,- (*f* -,-nen) [old-age] pensioner

Reparatur *f* -,-en repair. **R~werkstatt** *f* repair workshop; (*Auto*) garage

reparieren *vt* repair, mend

repatriieren *vt* repatriate

Repertoire /reperˈtoaːʀ/ *nt* -s,-s repertoire

Reportage /-ˈtaːʒə/ *f* -,-n report

Reporter(in) *m* -s,- (*f* -,-nen) reporter

repräsent|ativ *a* representative (für of); (*eindrucksvoll*) imposing; (*Prestige verleihend*) prestigious. **r~ieren** *vt* represent (*v*) (haben) perform official/social duties

Repress|alie /-lịə/ *f* -,-n reprisal. **r~iv** *a* repressive

Reprodu|ktion /-'tsio:n/ *f* -,-en reproduction. **r~zieren** *vt* reproduce

Reptil *nt* -s,-ien /-jən/ reptile

Republik *f* -,-en republic. **r~a-nisch** *a* republican

requirieren *vt* (Mil) requisition

Requisiten *pl* (Theat) properties, (fam) props

Reservat *nt* -[e]s,-e reservation

Reserve *f* -,-n reserve; (Mil, Sport) reserves *pl*. **R~rad** *nt* spare wheel. **R~spieler** *m* reserve. **R~tank** *m* reserve tank

reservier|en *vt* reserve; **r~en lassen** book. **r~t** *a* reserved. **R~ung** *f* -,-en reservation

Reservoir /rezɛr'vŏa:ɐ̯/ *nt* -s,-s reservoir

Resid|enz *f* -,-en residence. **r~ieren** *vi* (haben) reside

Resignation /-'tsịo:n/ *f* -,- resignation. **r~ieren** *vi* (haben) (fig) give up. **r~iert** *a* resigned, *adv* -ly

resolut *a* resolute, *adv* -ly

Resolution /-'tsịo:n/ *f* -,-en resolution

Resonanz *f* -,-en resonance; (*fig: Widerhall*) response

Respekt /-sp-, /-'p- *m* -[e]s respect (vor + *dat* for). **r~abel** *a* respectable. **r~ieren** *vt* respect

respekt|los *a* disrespectful, *adv* -ly. **r~voll** *a* respectful, *adv* -ly

Ressort /rɛ'so:ɐ̯/ *nt* -s,-s department

Rest *m* -[e]s,-e remainder, rest; **R~e remains**; (*Essens-*) leftovers

Restaurant /rɛsto'rã:/ *nt* -s,-s restaurant

Restaur|ation /rɛstaura'tsịo:n/ *f* -restoration. **r~ieren** *vt* restore

Rest|betrag *m* balance. **r~lich** *a* remaining. **r~los** *a* utter, *adv* -ly

Resultat *nt* -[e]s,-e result

Retorte *f* -,-n (Chem) retort. **R~nbaby** *nt* (fam) test-tube baby

rett|en *vt* save (vor + *dat* from); (*aus Gefahr befreien*) rescue; **sich r~en** save oneself; (*flüchten*) escape. **R~er** *m* -s,- rescuer; (fig) saviour

Rettich *m* -s,-e white radish

Rettung *f* -,-en rescue; (fig) salvation; **jds letzte R~** s.o.'s last hope. **R~sboot** *nt* lifeboat. **R~sdienst** *m* rescue service. **R~sgürtel** *m* lifebelt. **r~slos** *adv* hopelessly. **R~sring** *m* lifebelt. **R~swagen** *m* ambulance

retuschieren *vt* (Phot) retouch

Reu|e *f* - remorse; (Relig) repentance. **r~en** *vt* fill with remorse; **es reut mich nicht** I don't regret it. **r~ig** *a* penitent. **r~mütig** *a* contrite, *adv* -ly

Revanche /re'vã:ʃə/ *f* -,-n revenge. **R~e fordern** (Sport) ask for a return match. **r~ieren** (sich) *vr* take revenge; (*sich erkenntlich zeigen*) reciprocate (mit with); **sich für eine Einladung r~ieren** return an invitation

Revers /re've:ɐ̯/ *nt* -,- /-[s],-s/ lapel

revidieren *vt* revise; (*prüfen*) check

Revier *nt* -s,-e district; (*Zool & fig*) territory; (*Polizei-*) [police] station

Revision *f* -,-en revision; (*Prüfung*) check; (*Bücher-*) audit; (Jur) appeal

Revolte *f* -,-n revolt

Revolution /-'tsịo:n/ *f* -,-en revolution. **r~är** *a* revolutionary. **r~ieren** *vt* revolutionize

Revolver *m* -s,- revolver

Revue /rə'vy:/ *f* -,-n revue

Rezen|sent *m* -en,-en reviewer. **r~sieren** *vt* review. **R~sion** *f* -,-en review

Rezept *nt* -[e]s,-e prescription; *(Culin)* recipe

Rezeption /-'tsɪo̯n/ *f* -,-en reception

Rezession *f* -,-en recession

rezitieren *vt* recite

R-Gespräch *nt* reverse-charge call, *(Amer)* collect call

Rhabarber *m* -s rhubarb

Rhapsodie *f* -,-n rhapsody

Rhein *m* -s Rhine. **R~land** *nt* -s Rhineland. **R~wein** *m* hock

Rhetori|k *f* - rhetoric. **r~sch** *a* rhetorical

Rheuma *nt* -s rheumatism. **r~tisch** *a* rheumatic. **R~atismus** *m* - rheumatism

Rhinozeros *nt* -[ses],-se rhinoceros

rhyth|misch /'ryt-/ *a* rhythmic[al], *adv* -ally. **R~mus** *m* -,-men rhythm

Ribisel *f* -,-n redcurrant

richten *vt* direct *(auf+ acc* at); address *(Frage, Briefe) (an+ acc* to); aim, train *(Waffe) (auf+ acc* at); *(einstellen)* set; *(vorbereiten)* prepare; *(reparieren)* mend; *(hinrichten)* execute; *(SGer: ordentlich machen)* tidy; **in die Höhe r~** raise [up]; **das Wort an jdn r~** address s.o.; **gegen** against; *(Blick:)* turn *(auf+ acc* on); **sich r~ nach** comply with *(Vorschrift, jds Wünschen)*; fit in with *(jds Plänen)*; *(befolgen)* go by; *(abhängen)* depend □*vi (haben)* **r~ über** *(+ acc)* judge

Richter *m* -s,- judge

Richtfest *nt* topping-out ceremony

richtig *a* right, correct; *(wirklich, echt)* real; **das R~e** the right

thing □*adv* correctly; really; **die Uhr geht r~** the clock is right. **R~keit** *f* - correctness. **r~stellen** *vt sep (fig)* correct

Richtlinien *fpl* guidelines

Richtung *f* -,-en direction; *(fig)* trend

riechen *vt/i (haben)* smell **(nach** of; **an etw** *dat* sth)

Riegel *m* -s,- bolt; *(Seife)* bar

Riemen *m* -s,- strap; *(Ruder)* oar

Riese *m* -n,-n giant

rieseln *vi (sein)* trickle; *(Schnee:)* fall lightly

Riesen|erfolg *m* huge success. **r~groß** *a* huge, enormous

riesig *a* huge; *(gewaltig)* enormous □*adv (fam)* terribly

Riff *nt* -[e]s,-e reef

rigoros *a* rigorous, *adv* -ly

Rille *f* -,-n groove

Rind *nt* -es,-er ox; *(Kuh)* cow; *(Stier)* bull; *(R~fleisch)* beef; **R~er** cattle *pl*

Rinde *f* -,-n bark; *(Käse-)* rind; *(Brot-)* crust

Rinderbraten *m* roast beef

Rind|fleisch *nt* beef. **R~vieh** *nt* cattle *pl; (fam: Idiot)* idiot

Ring *m* -[e]s,-e ring

ringeln (sich) *vr* curl; *(Schlange:)* coil itself **(um** round)

ring|en *vi (haben)* wrestle; *(fig)* struggle **(um/nach** for) □*vt* wring *(Hände)*. **R~en** *nt* -s wrestling. **R~er** *m* -s,- wrestler. **R~kampf** *m* wrestling match; *(als Sport)* wrestling. **R~richter** *m* referee

rings *adv* **r~ im Kreis** in a circle; **r~ um jdn/etw** all around s.o./sth. **r~herum, r~um** *adv* all around

Rinn|e *f* -,-n channel; *(Dach-)* gutter. **r~en** *vi (sein)* run; *(Sand:)* trickle. **R~stein** *m* gutter

Rippe *f* -,-n rib. **R~nfellentzündung** *f* pleurisy. **R~nstoß** *m* dig in the ribs

Risiko nt -s,-s & -ken risk; ein R~ eingehen take a risk

riskant a risky. **r~ieren** vt risk

Riß m -sses,-sse tear; (Mauer-) crack; (fig) rift

rissig a cracked; (Haut) chapped

Rist m -[e]s,-e instep

Ritt m -[e]s,-e ride

Ritter m -s,- knight. **r~lich** a chivalrous, adv -ly. **R~lichkeit** f -chivalry

rittlings adv astride

Ritual nt -s,-e ritual. **r~ell** a ritual

Ritz m -es,-e scratch. **R~e** f -,-n crack; (Fels-) cleft; (zwischen Betten, Vorhängen) gap. **r~en** vt scratch

Rival|**e** m -n,-n, R~in f -,-nen rival. **r~isieren** vi (haben) compete (mit with). **r~isierend** a rival ... **R~ität** f -,-en rivalry

Robbe f -,-n seal. **R~n** vi (sein) crawl

Robe f -,-n gown; (Talar) robe

Roboter m -s,- robot

robust a robust

röcheln vi (haben) breathe stertorously

Rochen m -s,- (Zool) ray

Rock[1] m -[e]s,-e skirt; (Jacke) jacket

Rock[2] m -[s] (Mus) rock

Rodel|**bahn** f toboggan run. **r~n** vi (sein/haben) toboggan. **R~schlitten** m toboggan

roden vt clear ⟨Land⟩; grub up ⟨Stumpf⟩

Rogen m -s,- [hard] roe

Roggen m -s rye

roh a rough; (ungekocht) raw; ⟨Holz⟩ bare; (brutal) brutal; **r~e Gewalt** brute force □ adv roughly; brutally. **R~bau** m -[e]s,-ten shell. **R~kost** f raw [vegetarian] food. **R~ling** m -s,-e brute. **R~material** nt raw material. **R~öl** nt crude oil

Rohr nt -[e]s,-e pipe; (Geschütz-) barrel; (Bot) reed; (Zucker-, Bambus-) cane

Röhr|**chen** nt -s,- [drinking] straw; (Auto, fam) breathalyser (P). **R~e** f -,-n tube; (Radio-) valve; (Back-) oven

Rohstoff m raw material

Rokoko nt -s rococo

Rolladen m roller shutter

Rollbahn f taxiway; (Start-/Landebahn) runway

Rolle f -,-n roll; (Garn-) reel; (Draht-) coil; (Techn) roller; (Seil-) pulley; (Wäsche-) mangle; (Lauf-) castor; (Schrift-) scroll; (Theat) part, role; **das spielt keine R~** (fig) that doesn't matter. **r~n** vt/i (haben); (auf-) roll up; roll out ⟨Teig⟩; put through the mangle ⟨Wäsche⟩; sich **r~n** roll; (sich ein-) curl up □ vi (sein) roll; (Flugzeug:) taxi □ vi (haben) ⟨Donner:⟩ rumble. **R~r** m -s,- scooter

Roll|**feld** nt airfield. **R~kragen** m polo-neck. **R~mops** m rollmop[s] sg

Rollo nt -s,-s [roller] blind

Roll|**schuh** m roller-skate. **R~schuh laufen** roller-skate. **R~splitt** m -s loose chippings pl. **R~stuhl** m wheelchair. **R~treppe** f escalator

Rom nt -s Rome

Roman m -s,-e novel. **r~isch** a Romanesque; ⟨Sprache⟩ Romance. **R~schriftsteller(in)** m(f) novelist

Romant|**ik** f - romanticism. **r~isch** a romantic, adv -ally

Romanze f -,-n romance

Röm|**er(in)** m -s,- (f -,-nen) Roman. **r~isch** a Roman

Rommé /'rome:/ nt -s rummy

röntgen vt X-ray. **R~aufnahme** f, **R~bild** nt X-ray. **R~strahlen** mpl X-rays

rosa inv a, R~ nt -[s],- pink

Rose f -,-n rose. **R~nkohl** m [Brussels] sprouts pl. **R~n- kranz** m (Relig) rosary. **R~nmontag** m Monday before Shrove Tuesday

Rosette f -,-n rosette

rosig a rosy

Rosine f -,-n raisin

Rosmarin m -s rosemary

Roß nt Rosses, Rösser horse. **R~kastanie** f horse-chestnut

Rost[1] m -[e]s,-e grating; (Kamin-) grate; (Brat-) grill

Rost[2] m -[e]s rust. **r~en** vi (haben) rust

röst|en vt roast; toast ⟨Brot⟩. **R~er** m -s,- toaster

rostfrei a stainless

rostig a rusty

rot a (röter, rötest), **Rot** nt -s,- red; **rot werden** turn red; (erröten) go red, blush

Rotation /-'tsjo:n/ f -,-en rotation

Röte f - redness; (Scham-) blush

Röteln pl German measles sg

röten vt redden; **sich r~** turn red

rothaarig a red-haired

rotieren vi (haben) rotate

Rot|kehlchen nt -s,- robin. **R~kohl** m red cabbage

rötlich a reddish

Rot|licht nt red light. **R~wein** m red wine

Roulade /ru'la:də/ f -,-n beef olive. **R~leau** /-'lo:/ nt -s,-s [roller] blind

Route /'ru:tə/ f -,-n route

Routin|e /ru'ti:nə/ f -,-n routine; (Erfahrung) experience. **r~e- mäßig** a routine , □adv rou- tinely. **r~iert** a experienced

Rowdy /'raʊdi/ m -s,-s hooligan

Rübe f -,-n beet; **rote R~** beetroot; **gelbe R~** (SGer) carrot

rüber adv = herüber, hinüber

Rubin m -s,-e ruby

Rubrik f -,-en column; (Katego- rie) category

Ruck m -[e]s,-e jerk

Rückantwort f reply

ruckartig a jerky, adv -ily

rück|bezüglich a (Gram) reflex- ive. **R~blende** f flashback. **R~blick** m (fig) review (auf + acc of). **r~blickend** adv in retrospect. **r~datieren** vt (inf & pp only) backdate

Rücken m -s,- back; (Buch-) spine; (Berg-) ridge. **R~lehne** f back. **R~mark** nt spinal cord. **R~schwimmen** nt backstroke. **R~wind** m following wind; (Aviat) tail wind

rückerstatten vt (inf & pp only) refund

Rückfahr|karte f return ticket. **R~t** f return journey

Rück|fall m relapse. **r~fällig** a **r~fällig werden** (Jur) re-offend. **R~flug** m return flight. **R~frage** f [further] query. **r~fragen** vi (haben) (inf & pp only) check (bei with). **R~gabe** f return. **R~gang** m decline; (Preis-) drop, fall. **r~gängig** a **r~gängig machen** cancel; break off ⟨Verlobung⟩. **R~grat** nt -[e]s,-e spine, backbone. **R~halt** m support. **R~hand** f backhand. **R~kehr** f return. **R~lagen** fpl reserves. **R~licht** nt rear-light. **r~lings** adv backwards; (von hinten) from behind. **R~reise** f return jour- ney

Rucksack m rucksack

Rück|schau f review. **R~schlag** m (Sport) return; (fig) set-back. **R~schluß** f conclusion. **R~schritt** m (fig) retrograde step. **r~schrittlich** a retro- grade. **R~seite** f back; (einer Münze) reverse

Rücksicht f -,-en consideration. **R~ nehmen auf** (+ acc) show consideration for; (*berücksichti-gen*) take into consideration. **R~nahme** *f* - consideration. **r~slos** *a* inconsiderate, *adv* -ly; (*schonungslos*) ruthless, *adv* -ly. **r~svoll** *a* considerate, *adv* -ly

Rück|sitz *m* back seat; (*Sozius*) pillion. **R~spiegel** *m* rear-view mirror. **R~spiel** *nt* return match. **R~sprache** *f* consultation; **R~sprache nehmen mit** consult. **R~stand** *m* (*Chem*) residue; (*Arbeits-*) backlog; **R~stände** arrears; **im R~stand sein** be behind. **r~ständig** *a* (*fig*) backward. **R~stau** *m* (*Auto*) tailback. **R~strahler** *m* -s-, reflector. **R~tritt** *m* resignation; (*Fahrrad*) back pedalling. **r~vergüten** *vt* (*inf & pp only*) refund. **R~wanderer** *m* repatriate

rückwärt|ig *a* back ..., rear ... **r~s** *adv* backwards. **R~sgang** *m* reverse [gear]

Rückweg *m* way back

ruckweise *adv* jerkily

rück|wirkend *a* retrospective, *adv* -ly. **R~wirkung** *f* retrospective effect; **mit R~wirkung vom** backdated to. **R~zahlung** *f* repayment. **R~zug** *m* retreat

Rüde *m* -n,-n [male] dog

Rudel *nt* -s,- herd; (*Wolfs-*) pack; (*Löwen-*) pride

Ruder *nt* -s,- oar; (*Steuer-*) rudder; **am R~** (*Naut & fig*) at the helm. **R~boot** *nt* rowing boat. **R~er** *m* -s,- oarsman. **r~n** *vt/i* (*haben/sein*) row

Ruf *m* -[e]s,-e call; (*laut*) shout; (*Telefon*) telephone number; (*Ansehen*) reputation; **Künstler von Ruf** artist of repute. **r~en†** *vt/i* (*haben*) call (**nach** for); **r~en lassen** send for

Rüffel *m* -s,- (*fam*) telling-off. **r~n** *vt* (*fam*) tell off

Ruf|name *m* forename by which one is known. **R~nummer** *f* telephone number. **R~zeichen** *nt* dialling tone

Rüge *f* -,-n reprimand. **r~n** *vt* reprimand; (*kritisieren*) criticize

Ruhe *f* - rest; (*Stille*) quiet; (*Frieden*) peace; (*innere*) calm; (*Gelassenheit*) composure; **die R~ bewahren** keep calm; **in R~ lassen** leave in peace; **sich zur R~ setzen** retire; **R~ [da]!** quiet! **R~gehalt** *nt* [retirement] pension. **r~los** *a* restless, *adv* -ly. **r~n** *vi* (*haben*) rest (**auf**+*dat* on); (*Arbeit, Verkehr:*) have stopped; **hier ruht** ... here lies ... **R~pause** *f* rest, break. **R~stand** *m* retirement; **in den R~stand treten** retire; **im R~stand** retired. **R~störung** *f* disturbance of the peace. **R~tag** *m* day of rest; 'Montag **R~tag**' 'closed on Mondays'

ruhig *a* quiet, *adv* -ly; (*erholsam*) restful; (*friedlich*) peaceful, *adv* -ly; (*unbewegt, gelassen*) calm, *adv* -ly; **r~ bleiben** remain calm; **sehen Sie sich r~ um** you're welcome to look round; **man kann r~ darüber sprechen** there's no harm in talking about it

Ruhm *m* -[e]s fame; (*Ehre*) glory

rühmen *vt* praise; **sich r~** boast (*gen* about)

ruhmreich *a* glorious

Ruhr *f* - (*Med*) dysentery

Rühr|ei *nt* scrambled eggs *pl.* **r~en** *vt* move; (*Culin*) stir; **sich r~en** move; **zu Tränen r~en** move to tears; **r~ euch!** (*Mil*) at ease! □*vi* (*haben*) stir; **r~en an** (+*acc*) touch; (*fig*) touch on; **r~en von** (*fig*) come from. **r~end** *a* touching, *adv* -ly. **rühr|ig** *a* active. **r~selig** *a* sentimental. **R~ung** *f* - emotion

Ruin m -s ruin. **R~e** f -,-n ruin; ruins pl (gen of). **r~ieren** vt ruin

rülpsen vi (haben) (fam) belch

Rum m -s rum

rum adv = herum

Rumänien /-jən/ nt -s Romania. **r~isch** a Romanian

Rummel m -s (fam) hustle and bustle; (Jahrmarkt) funfair. **R~platz** m fairground

rumoren vi (haben) make a noise; ⟨Magen:⟩ rumble

Rumpel|kammer f junk-room. **r~n** vi (haben/sein) rumble

Rumpf m -[e]s,-̈e body, trunk; (Schiffs-) hull; (Aviat) fuselage

rümpfen vt die Nase ~ turn up one's nose ⟨über + acc at⟩

rund a round □adv approximately; **r~ um** [a]round. **R~blick** m panoramic view. **R~brief** m circular [letter]

Runde f -,-n round; (Kreis) circle; (eines Polizisten) beat; (beim Rennen) lap; **eine R~ Bier** a round of beer. **r~n** vt round; **sich r~n** become round; ⟨Backen:⟩ fill out

Rund|fahrt f tour. **R~frage** f poll

Rundfunk m radio; **im R~** on the radio. **R~gerät** nt radio [set]

Rund|gang m round; (Spaziergang) walk (durch round). **r~heraus** adv straight out. **r~herum** adv all around. **r~lich** a rounded; (mollig) plump. **R~reise** f [circular] tour. **R~schreiben** nt circular. **r~um** adv all round. **R~ung** f -,-en curve. **r~weg** adv ⟨ablehnen⟩ flatly

runter adv = herunter, hinunter

Runzel f -,-n wrinkle. **r~n** vt die Stirn **r~n** frown

runzlig a wrinkled

Rüpel m -s,-. (fam) lout. **r~haft** a (fam) loutish

rupfen vt pull out; pluck ⟨Geflügel⟩; (fam: schröpfen) fleece

ruppig a rude, adv -ly

Rüsche f -,-n frill

Ruß m -es soot

Russe m -n,-n Russian

Rüssel m -s,- (Zool) trunk

rußen vi (haben) smoke. **r~ig** a sooty

Russ|in f -,-nen Russian. **r~isch** a Russian. **R~isch** nt -[s] (Lang) Russian

Rußland nt -s Russia

rüsten vi (haben) prepare (**zu/für** for); □vr **sich r~** get ready; **gerüstet sein** be ready

rüstig a sprightly

rustikal a rustic

Rüstung f -,-en armament; (Harnisch) armour. **R~skontrolle** f arms control

Rute f -,-n twig; (Angel-, Wünschel-) rod; (zur Züchtigung) birch; (Schwanz) tail

Rutsch m -[e]s,-e slide. **R~bahn** f slide. **R~e** f -,-n chute. **r~en** vt slide; (rücken) move □ vi (sein) slide; (aus-, ab-) slip; (Auto) skid; (rücken) move [along]. **r~ig** a slippery

rütteln vt shake □vi (haben) **r~ an** (+ dat) rattle

S

Saal m -[e]s,Säle hall; (Theat) auditorium; (Kranken-) ward

Saat f -,-en seed; (Säen) sowing; (Gesätes) crop. **S~gut** nt seed

sabbern vi (haben) (fam) slobber; ⟨Baby:⟩ dribble; (reden) jabber

Säbel m -s,- sabre

Sabo|tage /zabo'ta:ʒə/ f -sabotage. **S~teur** /'to:ɐ̯/ m -s,-e saboteur. **s~tieren** vt sabotage

Sach|bearbeiter m expert. **S~buch** nt non-fiction book. **s~dienlich** a relevant

Sache f -,-n matter, business; (*Ding*) thing; (*fig*) cause; **zur S~ kommen** come to the point

Sach|gebiet nt (*fig*) area, field. **s~gemäß** a proper, adv -ly. **S~kenntnis** f expertise. **s~kundig** a expert, adv -ly. **s~lich** a factual, adv -ly; (*nüchtern*) matter-of-fact, adv -ly; (*objektiv*) objective, adv -ly; (*schmucklos*) functional

sächlich a (*Gram*) neuter

Sachse m -n,-n Saxon. **S~n** nt -s Saxony

sächsisch a Saxon

sacht a gentle, adv -ly

Sach|verhalt m -[e]s facts pl. **s~verständig** a expert, adv -ly. **S~verständige(r)** m/f expert

Sack m -[e]s,⸚e sack; **mit S~ und Pack** with all one's belongings

sacken vi (*sein*) sink; (*zusammen~*) go down; (*Person:*) slump

Sack|gasse f cul-de-sac; (*fig*) impasse. **S~leinen** nt sacking

Sadis|mus m - sadism. **S~t** m -en,-en sadist. **s~tisch** a sadistic, adv -ally

säen vt/i (*haben*) sow

Safe /ze:f/ m -s,-s safe

Saft m -[e]s,⸚e juice; (*Bot*) sap. **s~ig** a juicy; (*Wiese*) lush; (*Preis, Rechnung*) hefty; (*Witz*) coarse. **s~los** a dry

Sage f -,-n legend

Säge f -,-n saw. **S~mehl** nt sawdust

sagen vt say; (*mitteilen*) tell; (*bedeuten*) mean; **das hat nichts zu s~** it doesn't mean anything

sägen vt/i (*haben*) saw

sagenhaft a legendary; (*fam: unglaublich*) fantastic, adv -ally

Säge|späne mpl wood shavings. **S~werk** nt sawmill

Sahne f - cream. **S~ebonbon** m & nt -s toffee. **s~ig** a creamy

Saison /zɛ'zõ:/ f -,-s season

Saite f -,-n (*Mus, Sport*) string. **S~ninstrument** nt stringed instrument

Sakko m & nt -s,-s sports jacket

Sakrament nt -[e]s,-e sacrament. **Sakrileg** nt -s,-e sacrilege

Sakrist|an m -s,-e verger. **S~ei** f -,-en vestry

Salat m -[e]s,-e salad; **ein Kopf S~** a lettuce. **S~soße** f salad-dressing

Salbe f -,-n ointment

Salbei m -s & f - sage

salben vt anoint

Saldo m -s,-dos & -den balance

Salon /za'lõ:/ m -s,-s salon; (*Naut*) saloon

salopp a casual, adv -ly; (*Benehmen*) informal, adv -ly; (*Ausdruck*) slangy

Salto m -s somersault

Salut m -[e]s,-e salute. **s~ieren** vi (*haben*) salute

Salve f -,-n volley; (*Geschütz:*) salvo; (*von Gelächter*) burst

Salz nt -es,-e salt. **s~en†** vt salt. **S~faß** nt salt-cellar. **s~ig** a salty. **S~kartoffeln** fpl boiled potatoes. **S~säure** f hydrochloric acid

Samen m -s,- seed; (*Anat*) semen, sperm

sämig a (*Culin*) thick

Sämling m -s,-e seedling

Sammel|becken nt reservoir. **S~begriff** m collective term. **s~n** vt/i (*haben*) collect; (*suchen, versammeln*) gather; **sich s~n** collect; (*sich versammeln*) gather; (*sich fassen*) collect oneself. **S~name** m collective noun

Sammler(in) m -s,- (f -,-nen) collector. **S~ung** f -,-en collection; (*innere*) composure

Samstag m -s,-e Saturday. **s~s** adv on Saturdays

samt prep (+ *dat*) together with □ adv **s~ und sonders** without exception

Samt m -[e]s velvet. **s~ig** a velvety

sämtlich indef pron inv all. **s~e(r,s)** indef pron all the; **s~e Werke** complete works; **meine s~en Bücher** all my books

Sanatorium nt -s,-ien sanatorium

Sand m -[e]s sand

Sandale f -,-n sandal. **S~ette** f -,-n high-heeled sandal

Sand|bank f sandbank. **S~burg** f sand-castle. **s~ig** a sandy. **S~kasten** m sand-pit. **S~kuchen** m Madeira cake. **S~papier** nt sandpaper. **S~stein** m sandstone

sanft a gentle, adv -ly. **s~mütig** a meek

Sänger(in) m -s,- (f -,-nen) singer

sanieren vt clean up; redevelop ⟨Gebiet⟩; ⟨modernisieren⟩ modernize; make profitable ⟨Industrie, Firma⟩; **sich s~** become profitable

sanitär a sanitary

Sanität|er m -s,- first-aid man; ⟨Fahrer⟩ ambulance man; ⟨Mil⟩ medical orderly. **S~swagen** m ambulance

Sanktion /zaŋkˈtsɪo:n/ f -,-en sanction. **s~ieren** vt sanction

Saphir m -s,-e sapphire

Sardelle f -,-n anchovy

Sardine f -,-n sardine

Sarg m -[e]s,⸚e coffin

Sarkas|mus m - sarcasm. **s~tisch** a sarcastic, adv -ally

Sat|an m -s Satan; ⟨fam: Teufel⟩ devil. **s~anisch** a satanic

Satellit m -en,-en satellite. **S~enfernsehen** nt satellite television

Satin /zaˈtɛŋ/ m -s satin

Satir|e f -,-n satire. **s~isch** a satirical, adv -ly

satt a full; ⟨Farbe⟩ rich; **s~ sein** have had enough [to eat]; **sich s~ essen** eat as much as one wants;

s~ machen feed; ⟨Speise:⟩ be filling; **etw s~ haben** ⟨fam⟩ be fed up with sth

Sattel m -s,⸚ saddle. **s~n** vt saddle. **S~schlepper** m tractor unit. **S~zug** m articulated lorry

sättigen vt satisfy; ⟨Chem & fig⟩ saturate □vi (haben) be filling. **s~d** a filling

Satz m -es,⸚e sentence; ⟨Teil-⟩ clause; ⟨These⟩ proposition; ⟨Math⟩ theorem; ⟨Mus⟩ movement; ⟨Tennis, Zusammengehöriges⟩ set; ⟨Boden-⟩ sediment; ⟨Kaffee-⟩ grounds pl; ⟨Steuer-, Zins-⟩ rate; ⟨Druck-⟩ setting; ⟨Schrift-⟩ type; ⟨Sprung⟩ leap, bound. **S~aussage** f predicate. **S~gegenstand** m subject. **S~zeichen** nt punctuation mark

Sau f -,⸚Säue sow; ⟨sl: schmutziger Mensch⟩ dirty pig

sauber a clean; ⟨ordentlich⟩ neat, adv -ly; ⟨anständig⟩ decent, adv -ly; ⟨fam: nicht anständig⟩ fine. **s~halten**† vt sep keep clean. **S~keit** f - cleanliness; neatness; decency

säuberlich a neat, adv -ly

saubermachen vt/i sep (haben) clean

säuber|n vt clean; ⟨befreien⟩ rid/ ⟨Pol⟩ purge (von of). **S~ungsaktion** f ⟨Pol⟩ purge

Sauce /ˈzo:sə/ f -,-n sauce; ⟨Braten-⟩ gravy

Saudi-Arabien /-jən/ nt -s Saudi Arabia

sauer a sour; ⟨Chem⟩ acid; ⟨eingelegt⟩ pickled; ⟨schwer⟩ hard; **saurer Regen** acid rain; **s~ sein** ⟨fam⟩ be annoyed

Sauerei f -,-en = Schweinerei

Sauerkraut nt sauerkraut

säuerlich a slightly sour

Sauer|stoff m oxygen

saufen† vt/i (haben) drink; ⟨sl⟩ booze

Säufer *m* -s,- (*sl*) boozer

saugen† *vt/i* (*haben*) suck; (*staub-*) vacuum, hoover; **sich voll Wasser s~** soak up water

säugen *vt* suckle

Sauger *m* -s,- [baby's] dummy, (*Amer-*) pacifier; (*Flaschen-*) teat

Säugetier *nt* mammal

saugfähig *a* absorbent

Säugling *m* -s,-e infant

Säule *f* -,-n column

Saum *m* -[e]s,Säume hem; (*Rand*) edge

säumen¹ *vt* hem; (*fig*) line

säum|en² *vi* (*haben*) delay. **s~ig** *a* dilatory

Sauna *f* -,-nas & -nen sauna

Säure *f* -,-n acidity; (*Chem*) acid

säuseln *vi* (*haben*) rustle [softly]

sausen *vi* (*haben*) rush; ⟨*Ohren:*⟩ buzz □*vi* (*sein*) rush [along]

Sauwetter *nt* (*sl*) lousy weather

Saxophon *nt* -s,-e saxophone

SB- /ɛs'be:-/ *pref* (= **Selbstbedienung**) self-service ...

S-Bahn *f* city and suburban railway

sch *int* shush! (*fort*) shoo!

Schabe *f* -,-n cockroach

schaben *vt/i* (*haben*) scrape

schäbig *a* shabby, *adv* -ily

Schablone *f* -,-n stencil; (*Muster*) pattern; (*fig*) stereotype

Schach *nt* -s chess; **S~!** check! **in S~ halten** (*fig*) keep in check. **S~brett** *nt* chessboard

schachern *vi* (*haben*) haggle

Schachfigur *f* chess-man

schachmatt *a* **s~ setzen** checkmate; **s~!** checkmate!

Schachspiel *nt* game of chess

Schacht *m* -[e]s,⸗e shaft

Schachtel *f* -,-n box; (*Zigaretten-*) packet

Schachzug *m* move

schade *a* **s~ sein** be a pity or shame; **zu s~ für** too good for; **[wie] s~!** [what a] pity or shame!

Schädel *m* -s,- skull. **S~bruch** *m* fractured skull

schaden *vi* (*haben*) (+ *dat*) damage; (*nachteilig sein*) hurt; **das schadet nichts** that doesn't matter. **S~** *m* -s,⸗ damage; (*Defekt*) defect; (*Nachteil*) disadvantage; **zu S~ kommen** be hurt. **S~ersatz** *m* damages *pl*. **S~freude** *f* malicious glee. **s~froh** *a* gloating

schadhaft *a* defective

schädig|en *vt* damage, harm. **S~ung** *f* -,-en damage

schädlich *a* harmful

Schädling *m* -s,-e pest. **S~sbekämpfungsmittel** *nt* pesticide

Schaf *nt* -[e]s,-e sheep; (*fam: Idiot*) idiot. **S~bock** *m* ram

Schäfchen *nt* -s,- lamb

Schäfer *m* -s,- shepherd. **S~hund** *m* sheepdog; **Deutscher S~hund** German shepherd, alsatian

Schaffell *nt* sheepskin

schaffen¹† *vt* create; (*herstellen*) establish; make ⟨*Platz*⟩; **wie geschaffen für** made for

schaffen² *v* (*reg*) □*vt* manage [to do]; pass ⟨*Prüfung*⟩; catch ⟨*Zug*⟩; (*bringen*) take; **jdm zu s~ machen** trouble s.o.; **sich** (*dat*) **zu s~ machen** busy oneself (**an** + *dat* with) □*vi* (*haben*) (*SGer: arbeiten*) work. **S~** *nt* -s work

Schaffner *m* -s,- conductor; (*Zug-*) ticket-inspector

Schaffung *f* - creation

Schaft *m* -[e]s,⸗e shaft; (*Gewehr-*) stock; (*Stiefel-*) leg. **S~stiefel** *m* high boot

Schal *m* -s,-e scarf

schal *a* insipid; (*abgestanden*) flat; (*fig*) stale

Schale *f* -,-n skin; (*abgeschält*) peel; (*Ei-, Nuß-, Muschel-*) shell; (*Schüssel*) dish

schälen *vt* peel; **sich s~** peel

schalkhaft *a* mischievous, *adv* -ly

Schall *m* -[e]s sound. **S~dämpfer** *m* silencer. **s~dicht** *a* soundproof. **s~en** *vi* (*haben*) ring out; (*nachhallen*) resound; **s~end lachen** roar with laughter. **S~mauer** *f* sound barrier. **S~platte** *f* record, disc

schalt|en *vt* switch (*vi* (*haben*) switch/⟨Ampel:⟩ turn (**auf**+*acc* to); (*Auto*) change gear; (*fam:* *begreifen*) catch on. **S~er** *m* -s,-switch; (*Post-, Bank-*) counter; (*Fahrkarten-*) ticket window. **S~hebel** *m* switch; (*Auto*) gearlever. **S~jahr** *nt* leap year. **S~kreis** *m* circuit. **S~ung** *f* -,-en circuit; (*Auto*) gear change

Scham *f* -shame; (*Anat*) private parts *pl*; **falsche S~** false modesty

schämen (sich) *vr* be ashamed; **schämt euch!** you should be ashamed of yourselves!

scham|haft *a* modest, *adv* -ly; (*schüchtern*) bashful, *adv* -ly. **s~los** *a* shameless, *adv* -ly

Schampon *nt* -s shampoo. **s~ieren** *vt* shampoo

Schande *f* - disgrace, shame; **S~machen** (+*dat*) bring shame on

schänd|en *vt* dishonour; (*fig*) defile; (*Relig*) desecrate; (*sexuell*) violate. **s~lich** *a* disgraceful, *adv* -ly. **S~ung** *f* -,-en defilement; desecration; violation

Schanktisch *m* bar

Schanze *f* -,-n [ski-]jump

Scharf *f* -,-en crowd; ⟨Vogel-⟩ flock; **in [hellen] S~en** in droves

Scharade *f* -,-n charade

scharen *vt* um **sich s~** gather round one; **sich s~ um** flock round. **s~weise** *adv* in droves

scharf *a* (**schärfer, schärfst**) sharp; (*stark*) strong; (*stark gewürzt*) hot; (*Geruch*) pungent; ⟨Frost, Wind, Augen, Verstand⟩ keen; (*streng*) harsh; ⟨Galopp, Ritt⟩ hard; (*Munition*) live; ⟨Hund⟩ fierce; **s~ einstellen** (*Phot*) focus; **s~ sein** (*Phot*) be in focus; **s~ sein auf** (+*acc*) (*fam*) be keen on ⟨adv sharply; ⟨hinsehen, nachdenken, bremsen, reiten⟩ hard; (*streng*) harshly; **s~ schießen** fire live ammunition

Scharfblick *m* perspicacity

Schärfe *f* - (*s. scharf*) sharpness; strength; hotness; pungency; keenness; harshness. **s~n** *vt* sharpen

scharf|machen *vt sep* (*fam*) incite. **S~richter** *m* executioner. **S~schütze** *m* marksman. **s~sichtig** *a* perspicacious. **S~sinn** *m* astuteness. **s~sinnig** *a* astute, *adv* -ly

Scharlach *m* -s scarlet fever

Scharlatan *m* -s,-e charlatan

Scharnier *nt* -s,-e hinge

Schärpe *f* -,-n sash

scharren *vi* (*haben*) scrape; ⟨Huhn:⟩ scratch; ⟨Pferd:⟩ paw the ground ⟨vt scrape

Schart|e *f* -,-n nick. **s~ig** *a* jagged

Schaschlik *m* & *nt* -s,-s kebab

Schatten *m* -s,- shadow; (*schattige Stelle*) shade; **im S~** in the shade. **s~haft** *a* shadowy. **S~riß** *m* silhouette. **S~seite** *f* shady side; (*fig*) disadvantage

schattier|en *vt* shade. **S~ung** *f* -,-en shading; (*fig:* *Variante*) shade

schattig *a* shady

Schatz *m* -es,-̈e treasure; (*Freund, Freundin*) sweetheart; (*Anrede*) darling

Schätzchen *nt* -s,- darling

schätzen *vt* estimate; (*taxieren*) value; (*achten*) esteem; (*würdigen*) appreciate; (*fam: vermuten*) reckon; **sich glücklich s~** consider oneself lucky

Schätzung f -,-en estimate; (*Taxierung*) valuation. **s~sweise** adv approximately

Schau f -,-en show; zur S~ stellen display. **S~bild** nt diagram

Schauder m -s shiver; (*vor Abscheu*) shudder. **s~haft** a dreadful, adv -ly. **s~n** vi (*haben*) shiver; (*vor Abscheu*) shudder; **mich s~te** I shivered/shuddered

schauen vi (*haben*) (*SGer, Aust*) look; **s~, daß** make sure that

Schauer m -s,- shower; (*Schauder*) shiver. **S~geschichte** f horror story. **s~lich** a ghastly. **s~n** vi (*haben*) shiver; **mich s~te** I shivered

Schaufel f -,-n shovel; (*Kehr-*) dustpan. **s~n** vt shovel; (*graben*) dig

Schaufenster nt shop-window. **S~bummel** m window-shopping. **S~puppe** f dummy

Schaukasten m display case

Schaukel f -,-n swing. **s~n** vt rock □ vi (*haben*) rock; (*auf einer Schaukel*) swing; (*schwanken*) sway. **S~pferd** nt rocking-horse. **S~stuhl** m rocking-chair

schaulustig a curious

Schaum m -[e]s foam; (*Seifen-*) lather; (*auf Bier*) froth; (*als Frisier-, Rasiermittel*) mousse

schäumen vi (*haben*) foam, froth; (*Seife:*) lather

Schaum|gummi m foam rubber. **s~ig** a, **s~ig rühren** (*Culin*) cream. **S~krone** f white crest; (*auf Bier*) head. **S~speise** f mousse. **S~stoff** m [synthetic] foam. **S~wein** m sparkling wine

Schauplatz m scene

schaurig a dreadful, adv -ly; (*unheimlich*) eerie, adv eerily

Schauspiel nt play; (*Anblick*) spectacle. **S~er** m actor. **S~erin** f actress. **s~ern** vi (*haben*) act; (*sich verstellen*) play-act

Scheck m -s,-s cheque, (*Amer*) check. **S~buch, S~heft** nt cheque-book. **S~karte** f cheque card

Scheibe f -,-n disc; (*Schieß-*) target; (*Glas-*) pane; (*Brot-, Wurst-*) slice. **S~nwaschanlage** f windscreen washer. **S~nwischer** m -s,- windscreen-wiper

Scheich m -s,-e & -s sheikh

Scheide f -,-n sheath; (*Anat*) vagina

scheid|en† vt separate; (*unterscheiden*) distinguish; dissolve (*Ehe*); **sich s~en lassen** get divorced; **sich s~en** diverge; (*Meinungen:*) differ □ vi (*sein*) leave; (*voneinander*) part. **S~ung** f -,-en divorce

Schein m -[e]s,-e light; (*Anschein*) appearance; (*Bescheinigung*) certificate; (*Geld-*) note; **etw nur zum S~** tun only pretend to do sth. **s~bar** a apparent, adv -ly. **s~en†** vi (*haben*) shine; (*den Anschein haben*) seem, appear; **mir s~t** it seems to me

scheinheilig a hypocritical, adv -ly. **S~keit** f hypocrisy

Scheinwerfer m -s,- floodlight; (*Such-*) searchlight; (*Auto*) headlight; (*Theat*) spotlight

Scheiß e, scheiß pref (*vulg*) bloody. **S~e** f - (*vulg*) shit. **s~en†** vi (*haben*) (*vulg*) shit

Scheit nt -[e]s,-e log

Scheitel m -s,- parting. **s~n** vt part (*Haar*)

scheitern vi (*sein*) fail

Schelle f -,-n bell. **s~n** vi (*haben*) ring

Schellfisch m haddock

Schelm m -s,-e rogue. **s~isch** a mischievous, adv -ly

Schelte f - scolding. **s~n†** vi (*haben*) grumble (*über + acc* about); **mit jdm s~n** scold s.o. □ vt scold; (*bezeichnen*) call

Schema *nt* -s,-mata model, pattern; (*Skizze*) diagram

Schemel *m* -s,- stool

Schenke *f* -,-n tavern

Schenkel *m* -s,- thigh; (*Geom*) side

schenken *vt* give [as a present]; **jdm Vertrauen/Glauben s~** trust/believe s.o.; **sich** (*dat*) **etw s~** give sth a miss

scheppern *vi* (*haben*) clank

Scherbe *f* -,-n [broken] piece

Schere *f* -,-n scissors *pl*; (*Techn*) shears *pl*; (*Hummer-*) claw. **s~n¹†** *vt* shear; crop ⟨*Haar*⟩; clip ⟨*Hund*⟩

scheren² *vt* (*reg*) (*fam*) bother; **sich nicht s~ um** not care about; **scher dich zum Teufel!** go to hell!

Scherenschnitt *m* silhouette

Scherereien *fpl* (*fam*) trouble *sg*

Scherz *m* -es,-e joke; **im/zum S~** as a joke. **s~en** *vi* (*haben*) joke. **S~frage** *f* riddle. **s~haft** *a* humorous

scheu *a* shy, *adv* -ly; ⟨*Tier*⟩ timid; **s~ werden** ⟨*Pferd*⟩: shy; **s~ machen** startle. **S~** *f* - shyness; (*bei Pferd*) timidity; (*Ehrfurcht*) awe

scheuchen *vt* shoo

scheuen *vt* be afraid of; (*meiden*) shun; **keine Mühe/Kosten s~** spare no effort/expense; **sich s~** be afraid (**vor** + *dat* of); shrink (**etw zu tun** from doing sth) □ *vi* (*haben*) ⟨*Pferd*⟩: shy

Scheuer|lappen *m* floor-cloth. **s~n** *vt* scrub; (*mit Scheuerpulver*) scour; (*wund*) rub; [**wund**] **s~n** chafe □ *vi* (*haben*) rub, chafe. **S~tuch** *nt* floor-cloth

Scheuklappen *fpl* blinkers

Scheune *f* -,-n barn

Scheusal *nt* -s,-e monster

scheußlich *a* horrible, *adv* -bly

Schi *m* -s,-er ski; **S~ fahren** *od* **laufen** ski

Schicht *f* -,-en layer; (*Geol*) stratum; (*Gesellschafts-*) class; (*Arbeits-*) shift. **S~arbeit** *f* shift work. **s~en** *vt* stack [up]

schick *a* stylish, *adv* -ly; ⟨*Frau*⟩ chic; (*fam: prima*) great. **S~** *m* -[e]s style

schicken *vt/i* (*haben*) send; **s~ nach** send for; **sich s~ in** (+ *acc*) resign oneself to

schicklich *a* fitting, proper

Schicksal *nt* -s,-e fate. **s~haft** *a* fateful. **S~sschlag** *m* misfortune

Schiebe|dach *nt* (*Auto*) sun-roof. **s~en†** *vt* push; (*gleitend*) slide; (*fam: handeln mit*) traffic in; **etw s~en auf** (+ *acc*) (*fig*) put sth down to; ⟨*Schuld, Verantwortung*⟩ on □ *vi* (*haben*) push. **S~er** *m* -s,- slide; (*Person*) black marketeer. **S~etür** *f* sliding door. **S~ung** *f* -,-en (*fam*) illicit deal; (*Betrug*) rigging, fixing

Schieds|gericht *nt* panel of judges; (*Jur*) arbitration tribunal. **S~richter** *m* referee; (*Tennis*) umpire; (*Jur*) arbitrator

schief *a* crooked; (*unsymmetrisch*) lopsided; (*geneigt*) slanting, sloping; (*nicht senkrecht*) leaning; ⟨*Winkel*⟩ oblique; (*fig*) false; (*mißtrauisch*) suspicious □ *adv* not straight; **jdn s~ ansehen** look at s.o. askance

Schiefer *m* -s slate

schief|gehen† *vi sep* (*sein*) (*fam*) go wrong. **s~lachen** (**sich**) *vr sep* double up with laughter

schielen *vi* (*haben*) squint

Schienbein *nt* shin; (*Knochen*) shinbone

Schiene *f* -,-n rail; (*Gleit-*) runner; (*Med*) splint. **s~n†** *vt* (*Med*) put in a splint

schier¹ *adv* almost

schier² *a* ⟨*Fleisch*⟩: lean

Schieß|bude *f* shooting-gallery. **s~en†** *vt* shoot; fire ⟨*Kugel*⟩:

score 〈Tor〉 □vi (haben) shoot, fire (auf+acc at) □ vi (sein) shoot [along]; (strömen) gush; **in die Höhe s~en** shoot up. **S~erei** f -,-en shooting. **S~scheibe** f target. **S~stand** m shooting-range

Schifahr|en nt skiing. **S~er(in)** m(f) skier

Schiff nt -[e]s,-e ship; (Kirchen-) nave; (Seiten-) aisle

Schiffahrt f shipping

schiff|bar a navigable. **S~bau** m shipbuilding. **S~bruch** m shipwreck. **s~brüchig** a shipwrecked. **S~chen** nt -s,- small boat; (Tex) shuttle. **S~er** m -s,- skipper

Schikan|e f -,-n harassment; **mit allen S~en** (fam) with every refinement. **s~ieren** vt harass; (tyrannisieren) bully

Schi|laufen nt -s skiing. **S~läufer(in)** m(f) skier

Schild[1] m -[e]s,-e shield; **etw im S~e führen** (fam) be up to sth

Schild[2] nt -[e]s,-er sign; (Namens-, Nummern-) plate; (Mützen-) badge; (Etikett) label

Schilddrüse f thyroid [gland]

schilder|n vt describe. **S~ung** f -,-en description

Schildkröte f tortoise; (See-) turtle. **S~patt** nt -[e]s tortoiseshell

Schilf nt -[e]s reeds pl

schillern vi (haben) shimmer

Schimmel m -s,- mould; (Pferd) white horse. **s~ig** a mouldy. **s~n** vi (haben/sein) go mouldy

Schimmer m -s gleam; (Spur) glimmer. **s~n** vi (haben) gleam

Schimpanse m -n,-n chimpanzee

schimpfen vi (haben) grumble (mit at; über+acc about); scold (mit jdm s.o.) □ vt call. **S~name** m term of abuse. **S~wort** nt (pl -wörter) swear-word; (Beleidigung) insult

schind|en† vt work or drive hard; (quälen) ill-treat; **sich s~en** slave [away]; **Eindruck s~en** (fam) try to impress. **S~er** m -s,- slave-driver. **S~erei** f - slave-driving; (Plackerei) hard slog

Schinken m -s,- ham. **S~speck** m bacon

Schippe f -,-n shovel. **s~n** vt shovel

Schirm m -[e]s,-e umbrella; (Sonnen-) sunshade; (Lampen-) shade; (Augen-) visor; (Mützen-) peak; (Ofen-, Bild-) screen; (fig: Schutz) shield. **S~herr** m patron. **S~herrschaft** f patronage. **S~mütze** f peaked cap

schizophren a schizophrenic. **S~ie** f - schizophrenia

Schlacht f -,-en battle

schlachten vt slaughter, kill

Schlachter, Schlächter m -s,- (NGer) butcher

Schlacht|feld nt battlefield. **S~haus** nt, **S~hof** m abattoir. **S~platte** f plate of assorted cooked meats and sausages. **S~schiff** nt battleship

Schlacke f -,-n slag

Schlaf m -[e]s sleep; **im S~** in one's sleep. **S~anzug** m pyjamas pl, (Amer) pajamas pl. **S~couch** f sofa bed

Schläfe f -,-n (Anat) temple

schlafen† vi (haben) sleep; (fam: nicht aufpassen) be asleep; **s~ gehen** go to bed; **er schläft noch** he is still asleep. **S~szeit** f bedtime

Schläfer(in) m -s,- (f -,-nen) sleeper

schlaff a limp, adv -ly; 〈Seil〉 slack; (Muskel) flabby

Schlaf|lied nt lullaby. **s~los** a sleepless. **S~losigkeit** f - insomnia. **S~mittel** nt sleeping drug

schläfrig a sleepy, adv -ily

Schlaf|saal m dormitory. **S~sack** m sleeping-bag. **S~tablette** f sleeping-pill. **s~trunken** a [still] half asleep. **S~wagen** m sleeping-car, sleeper. **s~wandeln** vi (haben/sein) sleep-walk. **S~zimmer** nt bedroom

Schlag m -[e]s,ˆe blow; (Faust-) punch; (Herz-, Puls-, Trommel-) beat; (einer Uhr) chime; (Glocken-, Gong- & Med) stroke; (elektrischer) shock; (Portion) helping; (Art) type; (Aust) whipped cream; **S~e bekommen** get a beating; **S~ auf S~** in rapid succession. **S~ader** f artery. **S~anfall** m stroke. **s~artig** a sudden, adv -ly. **S~baum** m barrier

schlagen† vt hit, strike; (fällen) fell; knock (Loch, Nagel) (in + acc into); (prügeln, besiegen) beat; (Culin) whisk (Eiweiß); whip (Sahne); (legen) throw; (wickeln) wrap; (hinzufügen) add (zu to); **sich s~** fight; **sich geschlagen geben** admit defeat □ vi (haben) beat; ⟨Tür:⟩ bang; ⟨Uhr:⟩ strike; (melodisch) chime; **mit den Flügeln s~** flap its wings; **um sich s~** lash out; **es schlug sechs** the clock struck six □ vi (sein) in etw (acc) s~ ⟨Blitz, Kugel:⟩ strike sth; **s~ an** (+ acc) knock against; **nach jdm s~** ⟨fig⟩ take after s.o. **s~d** a ⟨fig⟩ conclusive, adv -ly

Schlager m -s,- popular song; (Erfolg) hit

Schläger m -s,- racket; (Tischtennis-) bat; (Golf-) club; (Hockey-) stick; (fam: Raufbold) thug. **S~ei** f -,-en fight, brawl

schlag|fertig a quick-witted. **S~instrument** nt percussion instrument. **S~loch** nt pot-hole. **S~sahne** f whipped cream; (ungeschlagen) whipping cream. **S~seite** f (Naut) list. **S~stock** m truncheon. **S~wort** nt (pl -worte) slogan. **S~zeile** f headline. **S~zeug** nt (Mus) percussion. **S~zeuger** m -s,- percussionist; (in Band) drummer

schlaksig a gangling

Schlamassel m & nt -s (fam) mess

Schlamm m -[e]s mud. **s~ig** a muddy

Schlampe f -,-n (fam) slut. **s~en** vi (haben) (fam) be sloppy (bei in). **S~erei** f -,-en sloppiness; (Unordnung) mess. **s~ig** a slovenly; (Arbeit) sloppy □ adv in a slovenly way; sloppily

Schlange f -,-n snake; (Menschen-, Auto-) queue; **S~ stehen** queue; (Amer) stand in line

schlängeln (sich) vr wind; ⟨Person:⟩ weave (durch through)

Schlangen|biß m snakebite. **S~linie** f wavy line

schlank a slim. **S~heit** f slimness. **S~heitskur** f slimming diet

schlapp a tired; (schlaff) limp, adv -ly. **S~e** f -,-n (fam) setback

schlau a clever, adv -ly; (gerissen) crafty, adv -ily; **ich werde nicht s~ daraus** I can't make head or tail of it

Schlauch m -[e]s,Schläuche tube; (Wasser-) hose[pipe]. **S~boot** nt rubber dinghy. **s~en** vt (fam) exhaust

Schlaufe f -,-n loop

schlecht a bad; (böse) wicked; (unzulänglich) poor; **s~ werden** go bad; ⟨Wetter:⟩ turn bad; **s~er werden** get worse; **s~ aussehen** look bad; ⟨Person:⟩ unwell; **mir ist s~** I feel sick □ adv badly; poorly; (kaum) not really. **s~gehen**† vi sep ⟨jdm:⟩ go badly (+ dat) **es geht ihm s~** he's doing badly; (gesundheitlich) he's not well. **s~gelaunt** attrib a bad-tempered. **s~hin** adv quite simply.

S~**igkeit** f- wickedness. s~**machen** vt sep (fam) run down

schlecken vt/i (haben) lick (an etw dat sth); (auf-) lap up

Schlegel m -s,- mallet; (Trommel-) stick; (SGer: Keule) leg; (Hühner-) drumstick

schleichen† vi (sein) creep; (langsam gehen/fahren) crawl □vr sich s~ creep. s~**d** a creeping; ⟨Krankheit⟩ insidious

Schleier m -s,- veil; (fig) haze. s~**haft** a es ist mir s~haft (fam) it's a mystery to me

Schleife f -,-n bow; (Fliege) bowtie; (Biegung) loop

schleifen¹ v (reg) □vt drag; (zerstören) raze to the ground □vi (haben) trail, drag

schleifen²† vt grind; (schärfen) sharpen; cut ⟨Edelstein, Glas⟩; (drillen) drill

Schleim m -[e]s slime; (Anat) mucus; (Med) phlegm. s~**ig** a slimy

schlemmen vi (haben) feast □vt feast on. S~**er** m -s,- gourmet

schlendern vi (sein) stroll

schlenkern vt/i (haben) swing; s~ **mit** swing; dangle ⟨Beine⟩

Schlepp|dampfer m tug. S~**e** f -,-n train. s~**en** vt drag; (tragen) carry; (ziehen) tow; **sich s~en** drag oneself; (sich hinziehen) drag on; **sich s~en mit** carry. s~**end** a slow, adv -ly. S~**er** m -s,- tug; (Traktor) tractor.

S~kahn m barge. S~**lift** m T-bar lift. S~**tau** nt tow-rope; **ins S~tau nehmen** take in tow

Schleuder f -,-n catapult; (Wäsche-) spin-drier. s~**n** vt hurl; spin ⟨Wäsche⟩; extract ⟨Honig⟩ □vi (sein) skid; **ins S~n geraten** skid. S~**preise** mpl knock-down prices. S~**sitz** m ejector seat

schleunigst adv hurriedly; (sofort) at once

Schleuse f -,-n lock; (Sperre) sluice[-gate]. s~**n** vt steer

Schliche pl tricks; **jdm auf die S~ kommen** get on to s.o.

schlicht a plain, adv -ly; (einfach) simple, adv -ly

schlicht|en vt settle □vi (haben) arbitrate. S~**ung** f- settlement; (Jur) arbitration

Schlick m -[e]s silt

Schließe f -,-n clasp; (Schnalle) buckle

schließen† vt close; (ab-) lock; fasten ⟨Kleid, Verschluß⟩; (stillegen) close down; (beenden, folgern) conclude; enter into ⟨Vertrag⟩; **sich s~** close; **in die Arme s~** embrace; **etw s~ an** (+acc) connect sth to; **sich s~ an** (+acc) follow □vi (haben) close; (den Betrieb einstellen) close down; (den Schlüssel drehen) turn the key; (enden, folgern) conclude; **s~ lassen auf** (+acc) suggest

Schließ|fach nt locker. s~**lich** adv finally, in the end; (immerhin) after all. S~**ung** f -,-en closure

Schliff m -[e]s cut; (Schleifen) cutting; (fig) polish; **der letzte S~** the finishing touches pl

schlimm a bad, adv -ly; s~**er werden** get worse; **nicht so s~!** it doesn't matter! s~**stenfalls** adv if the worst comes to the worst

Schlinge f -,-n loop; (Henkers-) noose; (Med) sling; (Falle) snare

Schlingel m -s,- (fam) rascal

schling|en† vt wind, wrap; tie ⟨Knoten⟩; **sich s~en um** coil around (um + acc); **s~en** bolt one's food. S~**pflanze** f climber

Schlips m -es,-e tie

Schlitten m -s,- sledge; (Rodel-) toboggan; (Pferde-) sleigh; S~ **fahren** toboggan

schlittern vi (haben/ sein) slide

Schlittschuh m skate; S~ laufen skate. S~läufer(in) m(f)
skater

Schlitz m -es,-e slit; (für Münze)
slot; (Jacken-) vent; (Hosen-) flies
pl. s~en vt slit

Schloß nt -sses,-sser lock; (Vor-
hänge-) padlock; (Verschluß)
clasp; (Gebäude) castle; (Palast)
palace

Schlosser m -s,- locksmith;
(Auto-) mechanic; (Maschinen-)
fitter

Schlot m -[e]s,-e chimney

schlottern vi (haben) shake,
tremble; (Kleider:) hang loose

Schlucht f -,-en ravine, gorge

schluchz|en vi (haben) sob.
S~er m -s,- sob

Schluck m -[e]s,-e mouthful;
(klein) sip

Schluckauf m -s hiccups pl

schlucken vt/i (haben) swallow.
S~ m -s hiccups pl

schlud|ern vi (haben) be sloppy
(bei in). s~rig a sloppy, adv -ily;
(Arbeit) slipshod

Schlummer m -s slumber. s~n
vi (haben) slumber

Schlund m -[e]s [back of the]
throat; (fig) mouth

schlüpf|en vi (sein) slip; [aus
dem Ei] s~en hatch. S~er m -s,-
knickers pl. s~rig a slippery;
(anstößig) smutty

schlurfen vi (sein) shuffle

schlürfen vt/i (haben) slurp

Schluß m -sses,-sse end; (S~fol-
gerung) conclusion; **zum S~** finally; S~ machen stop (mit etw
sth); finish (mit jdm with s.o.)

Schlüssel m -s,- key; (Schrauben-)
spanner; (Geheim-) code; (Mus)
clef. S~bein nt collar-bone.
S~bund m & nt bunch of keys.
S~loch nt keyhole. S~ring m
key-ring

Schlußfolgerung f conclusion

schlüssig a conclusive, adv -ly;
sich (dat) s~ werden make up
one's mind

Schluß|licht nt rear-light. S~-
verkauf m [end of season] sale

Schmach f- disgrace

schmachten vi (haben) languish

schmächtig a slight

schmackhaft a tasty

schmal a narrow; (dünn) thin;
(schlank) slender; (karg) meagre

schmälern vt diminish; (herabsetzen) belittle

Schmalz[^1] nt -es lard; (Ohren-)
wax

Schmalz[^2] m -es (fam) schmaltz.
s~ig a (fam) schmaltzy, slushy

schmarotz|en vi (haben) be para-
sitic (auf+dat on); (Person:)
sponge (bei on). S~er m -s,-
parasite; (Person) sponger

Schmarren m -s,- (Aust) pancake
[torn into strips]; (fam: Unsinn)
rubbish

schmatzen vi (haben) eat noisily

schmausen vi (haben) feast

schmecken vi (haben) taste
(nach of); [gut] s~ taste good;
hat es dir geschmeckt? did you
enjoy it? □ vt taste

Schmeichelei f -,-en flattery;
(Kompliment) compliment

schmeichel|haft a complimen-
tary, flattering. s~n vi (haben)
(+ dat) flatter

schmeißen† vt/i (haben) s~ [mit]
(fam) chuck

Schmeißfliege f bluebottle

schmelz|en† vt/i (sein) melt;
smelt (Erze). S~wasser nt
melted snow

Schmerbauch m (fam) paunch

Schmerz m -es,-en pain; (Kummer) grief; S~en haben be in
pain. s~en vt hurt; (fig) grieve
□ vi (haben) hurt; be painful.
S~ensgeld nt compensation for
pain and suffering. s~haft a
painful. s~lich a (fig) painful;

(traurig) sad, *adv* -ly. **s~los** *a* painless, *adv* -ly. **s~stillend** *a* pain-killing; **s~stillendes Mittel** analgesic, pain-killer. **S~tablette** *f* pain-killer

Schmetterball *m (Tennis)* smash

Schmetterling *m* -s,-e butterfly

schmettern *vt* hurl; *(Tennis)* smash; *(singen)* sing; *(spielen)* blare out □*vi (haben)* sound; ⟨*Trompeten:*⟩ blare

Schmied *m* -[e]s,-e blacksmith

Schmiede *f* -,-n forge. **S~eisen** *nt* wrought iron. **s~n** *vt* forge; *(fig)* hatch; **Pläne s~n** make plans

schmieg|en *vt* press; **sich s~en an** (+ *acc*) nestle or snuggle up to; ⟨*Kleid:*⟩ cling to. **s~sam** *a* supple

Schmier|e *f* -,-n grease; *(Schmutz)* mess. **s~en** *vt* lubricate; *(streichen)* spread; *(schlecht schreiben)* scrawl; *(sl: bestechen)* bribe □*vi (haben)* smudge; *(schmieren)* scrawl. **S~fett** *nt* grease. **S~geld** *nt (fam)* bribe. **s~ig** *a* greasy; *(schmutzig)* grubby; *(anstößig)* smutty; ⟨*Person*⟩ slimy. **S~mittel** *nt* lubricant

Schminke *f* -,-n make-up. **s~n** *vt* make up; **sich s~n** put on make-up; **sich** *(dat)* **die Lippen s~n** put on lipstick

schmirgel|n *vt* sand down. **S~papier** *nt* emery-paper

schmökern *vt/i (haben) (fam)* read

schmollen *vi (haben)* sulk; *(s~d den Mund verziehen)* pout

schmor|en *vt/i (haben)* braise; *(fam: schwitzen)* roast. **S~topf** *m* casserole

Schmuck *m* -[e]s jewellery; *(Verzierung)* ornament, decoration

schmücken *vt* decorate, adorn; **sich s~** adorn oneself

schmuck|los *a* plain. **S~stück** *nt* piece of jewellery; *(fig)* jewel

schmuddelig *a* grubby

Schmuggel *m* -s smuggling. **s~n** *vt* smuggle. **S~ware** *f* contraband

Schmuggler *m* -s,- smuggler

schmunzeln *vi (haben)* smile

schmusen *vi (haben)* cuddle

Schmutz *m* -es dirt; **in den S~ ziehen** *(fig)* denigrate. **s~en** *vi (haben)* get dirty. **S~fleck** *m* dirty mark. **s~ig** *a* dirty

Schnabel *m* -s,¨ beak, bill; *(eines Kruges)* lip; *(Tülle)* spout

Schnake *f* -,-n mosquito; *(Kohl-)* daddy-long-legs

Schnalle *f* -,-n buckle. **s~n** *vt* strap; *(zu-)* buckle; **den Gürtel enger s~n** tighten one's belt

schnalzen *vi (haben)* **mit der Zunge/den Fingern s~** click one's tongue/snap one's fingers

schnapp|en *vi (haben)* **s~en nach** snap at; gasp for *(Luft)* □*vt* snatch, grab; *(fam: festnehmen)* nab. **S~schloß** *nt* spring lock. **S~schuß** *m* snapshot

Schnaps *m* -es,¨e schnapps

schnarchen *vi (haben)* snore

schnarren *vi (haben)* rattle; ⟨*Klingel:*⟩ buzz

schnattern *vi (haben)* cackle

schnauben *vi (haben)* snort □*vt* **sich** *(dat)* **die Nase s~** blow one's nose

schnaufen *vi (haben)* puff, pant

Schnauze *f* -,-n muzzle; *(eines Kruges)* lip; *(Tülle)* spout

Schnecke *f* -,-n snail; *(Nackt-)* slug; *(Spirale)* scroll; *(Gebäck)* ≈ Chelsea bun. **S~nhaus** *nt* snail-shell

Schnee *m* -s snow; *(Eier-)* beaten egg-white. **S~ball** *m* snowball. **S~besen** *m* whisk. **S~brille** *f* snow-goggles *pl*. **S~fall** *m* snow-fall. **S~flocke** *f* snowflake. **S~glöckchen** *nt* -s,- snowdrop. **S~kette** *f* snow chain.

S~**mann** m (pl -**männer**) snowman. S~**pflug** m snow-plough.
S~**schläger** m whisk. S~**sturm** m snowstorm, blizzard.
S~**wehe** f -,-n snow-drift

Schneid m -[e]s (SGer) courage

Schneide f -.-n (cutting) edge; (Klinge) blade

schneiden† vt cut; (in Scheiben) slice; (kreuzen) cross; (nicht beachten) cut dead; **Gesichter** s~ pull faces; **sich** s~ cut oneself; (über-) intersect; **sich** (dat/acc) **in den Finger** s~ cut one's finger. s~**d** a cutting; (kalt) biting

Schneider m -s,- tailor. S~**in** f -,-nen dressmaker. s~**n** vt make (Anzug, Kostüm)

Schneidezahn m incisor

schneidig a dashing, adv -ly

schneien vi (haben) snow; **es schneit** it is snowing

Schneise f -,-n path; (Feuer-) firebreak

schnell a quick; ⟨Auto, Tempo⟩ fast□ adv quickly; (in s~em Tempo) fast; (bald) soon; **mach** s~! hurry up! s~**en** vi (sein) **in die Höhe** s~en shoot up. S~**igkeit** f -,-rapidity; (Tempo) speed. S~**imbiß** m snack-bar. S~**kochtopf** m pressure-cooker. S~**reinigung** f express cleaners. s~**stens** adv as quickly as possible. S~**zug** m express [train]

schnetzeln vt cut into thin strips

schneuzen (sich) vr blow one's nose

schnippen vt flick

schnippisch a pert, adv -ly

Schnipsel m & nt -s,- scrap

Schnitt m -[e]s,-e cut; (Film-) cutting; (S~muster) [paper] pattern; **im** S~ (durchschnittlich) on average

Schnitte f -,-n slice [of bread]; (belegt) open sandwich

schnittig a stylish; (stromlinienförmig) streamlined

Schnitt|**käse** m hard cheese. S~**lauch** m chives pl. S~**muster** nt [paper] pattern. S~**punkt** m [point of] intersection. S~**wunde** f cut

Schnitzel nt -s,- scrap; (Culin) escalope. s~**n** vt shred

schnitzen vt/i (haben) carve. S~**er** m -s,- carver; (fam: Fehler) blunder. S~**erei** f -,-en carving

schnodderig a (fam) brash

schnöde a despicable, adv -bly; (verächtlich) contemptuous, adv -ly

Schnorchel m -s,- snorkel

Schnörkel m -s,- flourish; (Kunst) scroll. s~**ig** a ornate

schnorren vt/i (haben) (fam) scrounge

schnüffeln vi (haben) sniff (**an etw** dat sth); (fam: spionieren) snoop [around]

Schnuller m -s,- [baby's] dummy, (Amer) pacifier

schnupfen vt sniff; **Tabak** s~**en** take snuff. S~**en** m -s,- [head] cold. S~**tabak** m snuff

schnuppern vt/i (haben) sniff (**an etw** dat sth)

Schnur f -,¨e string; (Kordel) cord; (Besatz-) braid; (Electr) flex; **eine** S~ a piece of string

Schnür|**chen** nt -s,- **wie am** S~**chen** (fam) like clockwork. s~**en** vt tie; lace [up] ⟨Schuhe⟩

schnurgerade a & adv dead straight

Schnurr|**bart** m moustache. s~**en** vi (haben) hum; ⟨Katze:⟩ purr

Schnür|**schuh** m lace-up shoe. S~**senkel** m [shoe-]lace

schnurstracks adv straight

Schock m -[e]s,-e shock. s~**en** vt (fam) shock; **geschockt sein** be shocked. s~**ieren** vt shock; s~**ierend** shocking

Schöffe m -n,-n lay judge

Schokolade f - chocolate

Scholle f -,-n clod [of earth]; (Eis-) [ice-]floe; (Fisch) plaice

schon adv already; (allein) just; (sogar) even; (ohnehin) anyway; s~ **einmal** before; (jemals) ever; s~ **immer/oft/wieder** always/often/again; **hast du ihn s~ gesehen?** have you seen him yet? **s~ der Gedanke daran** the mere thought of it; **s~ deshalb** for that reason alone; **das ist s~ möglich** that's quite possible; **ja s~, aber** well yes, but; **nun geh/komm s~!** go/come on then!

schön a beautiful; (Wetter) fine; (angenehm, nett) nice; (gut) good; (fam: beträchtlich) pretty; s~en **Dank!** thank you very much! na **s~** all right then □adv beautifully; nicely; (gut) well; s~ **langsam** nice and slowly

schonen vt spare; (gut behandeln) look after; **sich s~** take things easy. **s~d** a gentle, adv -tly

Schönheit f -,-en beauty. S~**sfehler** m blemish. S~**skonkurrenz** f, S~**swettbewerb** m beauty contest

schönmachen vt sep smarten up; **sich s~** make oneself look nice

Schonung f -,-en gentle care; (nach Krankheit) rest; (Baum-) plantation. **s~slos** a ruthless, adv -ly

Schonzeit f close season

schöpf|en vt scoop [up]; ladle (Suppe); **Mut s~en** take heart; **frische Luft s~en** get some fresh air. S~**er** m -s,- creator; (Kelle) ladle. S~**erisch** a creative. S~**kelle** f, S~**löffel** m ladle. S~**ung** f -,-en creation

Schoppen m -s,- (SGer) ≈ pint

Schorf m -[e]s scab

Schornstein m chimney. S~**feger** m -s,- chimney-sweep

Schoß m -es,⸗e lap; (Frack-) tail

Schote f -,-n pod; (Erbse) pea

Schotte m -n,-n Scot, Scotsman

Schotter m -s gravel; (für Gleise) ballast

schott|isch a Scottish, Scots. S~**land** nt -s Scotland

schraffieren vt hatch

schräg a diagonal, adv -ly; (geneigt) sloping; s~ **halten** tilt. S~**e** f -,-n slope. S~**strich** m oblique stroke

Schramme f -,-n scratch. s~**n** vt scrape, scratch

Schrank m -[e]s,⸗e cupboard; (Kleider-) wardrobe; (Akten-, Glas-) cabinet

Schranke f -,-n barrier

Schraube f -,-n screw; (Schiffs-) propeller. **s~n** vt screw; (ab-) unscrew; (drehen) turn; **sich in die Höhe s~n** spiral upwards. S~**nmutter** f nut. S~**nschlüssel** m spanner. S~**nzieher** m -s,- screwdriver

Schraubstock m vice

Schrebergarten m ≈ allotment

Schreck m -[e]s,-e fright; jdm **einen s~ einjagen** give s.o. a fright. S~**en** m -s,- fright; (Entsetzen) horror. s~**en** vt (reg) frighten; (auf-) startle □ vi (sein) **in die Höhe s~en** start up

Schreck|gespenst nt spectre. s~**haft** a easily frightened; (nervös) jumpy. s~**lich** a terrible, adv -bly. S~**schuß** m warning shot

Schrei m -[e]s,-e cry, shout; (gellend) scream; **der letzte S~** (fam) the latest thing

Schreib|block m writing-pad. s~**en** vt/i (haben) write; (auf der Maschine) type; **richtig/falsch s~en** spell right/wrong; **sich s~en** (Wort:) be spelt; (korrespondieren) correspond; **sich krank s~en lassen** get a doctor's certificate. S~**en** nt -s,- writing; (Brief) letter. S~**fehler**

m spelling mistake. S~**heft** *nt* exercise book. S~**kraft** *f* clerical assistant; *(für Maschineschreiben)* typist. S~**maschine** *f* typewriter. S~**papier** *nt* writing-paper. S~**schrift** *f* script. S~**tisch** *m* desk. S~**ung** *f*,-**en** spelling. S~**waren** *fpl* stationery *sg.* S~**weise** *f* spelling

schreien† *vt/i (haben)* cry; *(gellend)* scream; *(rufen, laut sprechen)* shout; **zum S~** sein *(fam)* be a scream. **s~d** *a (fig)* glaring; *(grell)* garish

Schreiner *m* -s,- joiner

schreiten *vi (sein)* walk

Schrift *f* -,-**en** writing; *(Druck-)* type; *(Abhandlung)* paper; **die Heilige S~** the Scriptures *pl.* S~**führer** *m* secretary. **s~lich** *a* written □ *adv* in writing. S~**sprache** *f* written language. S~**steller(in)** *m* -s,- *(f* -,-**nen)** writer. S~**stück** *nt* document. S~**zeichen** *nt* character

schrill *a* shrill, *adv* -y

Schritt *m* -[e]s,-e step; *(Entfernung)* pace; *(Gangart)* walk; *(der Hose)* crotch; **im S~** in step; *(langsam)* at walking pace; S~ **halten mit** *(fig)* keep pace with. S~**weise** *adv* step by step

schroff *a* precipitous, *adv* -ly; *(abweisend)* brusque, *adv* -ly; *(unvermittelt)* abrupt, *adv* -ly; *(Gegensatz)* stark

schröpfen *vt (fam)* fleece

Schrot *m* & *nt* -[e]s coarse meal; *(Blei-)* small shot. **s~en** *vt* grind coarsely. S~**flinte** *f* shotgun

Schrott *m* -[e]s scrap[-metal]; **zu S~ fahren** *(fam)* write off. S~**platz** *m* scrap-yard. **s~reif** *a* ready for the scrap-heap

schrubb|**en** *vt/i (haben)* scrub. S~**er** *m* -s,- [long-handled] scrubbing-brush

Schrull|**e** *f* -,-**n** whim; **alte S~** *(fam)* old crone. **s~ig** *a* cranky

schrumpfen *vi (sein)* shrink; *⟨Obst:⟩* shrivel

schrump[**e**]**lig** *a* wrinkled

Schrunde *f* -,-**n** crack; *(Spalte)* crevasse

Schub *m* -[e]s,-̈e *(Phys)* thrust; *(S~fach)* drawer; *(Menge)* batch. S~**fach** *nt* drawer. S~**karre** *f*, S~**karren** *m* wheelbarrow. S~**lade** *f* drawer

Schubs *m* -es,-e push, shove. **s~en** *vt* push, shove

schüchtern *a* shy, *adv* -ly; *(zaghaft)* tentative, *adv* -ly. S~**heit** *f*- shyness

Schuft *m* -[e]s,-e *(pej)* swine. **s~en** *vi (haben)* *(fam)* slave away

Schuh *m* -[e]s,-e shoe. S~**anzieher** *m* -s,- shoehorn. S~**band** *nt (pl* -bänder) shoe-lace. S~**creme** *f* shoe-polish. S~**löffel** *m* shoehorn. S~**macher** *m* -s,- shoemaker; *(zum Flicken)* [shoe]mender. S~**werk** *nt* shoes *pl*

Schul|**abgänger** *m* -s,- school-leaver. S~**arbeiten**, S~**aufgaben** *fpl* homework *sg.* S~**buch** *nt* school-book

Schuld *f* -,-**en** guilt; *(Verantwortung)* blame; *(Geld-)* debt; S~**en machen** get into debt; S~ **haben an** (+ *dat*) to be to blame for □ **s~ haben** *od* **sein** to be to blame (**an** + *dat* for); **jdm s~ geben** blame s.o. **s~en** *vt* owe

schuldig *a* guilty *(gen* of); *(gebührend)* due; **jdm etw s~ sein** owe s.o. sth. S~**keit** *f* - duty

schuld|**los** *a* innocent. S~**ner** *m* -s,- debtor. S~**spruch** *m* guilty verdict

Schule *f* -,-**n** school; **in der/die S~** at/to school. **s~n** *vt* train

Schüler|**(in)** *m* -s,- *(f* -,-**nen)** pupil. S~**lotse** *m* pupil acting as crossing warden

schul|frei a s~freier Tag day without school; **wir haben morgen s~frei** there's no school tomorrow. **S~hof** m [school] playground. **S~jahr** nt school year; ⟨Klasse⟩ form. **S~junge** m schoolboy. **S~kind** nt schoolchild. **S~leiter(in)** m(f) head [teacher]. **S~mädchen** nt schoolgirl. **S~stunde** f lesson

Schulter f -,-n shoulder. **S~blatt** nt shoulder-blade. **s~n** vt shoulder. **S~tuch** nt shawl

Schulung f - training

schummeln vi (haben) (fam) cheat

Schund m -[e]s trash. **S~roman** m trashy novel

Schuppe f -,-n scale; **S~n** pl dandruff sg. **s~n (sich)** vr flake [off]

Schuppen m -s,- shed

Schur f - shearing

Schür|eisen nt poker. **s~en** vt poke; ⟨fig⟩ stir up

schürf|en vt mine; **sich** ⟨dat⟩ **das Knie s~en** graze one's knee □ vi (haben) **s~en nach** prospect for. **S~wunde** f abrasion, graze

Schürhaken m poker

Schurke m -n,-n villain

Schürze f -,-n apron. **s~n** vt ⟨raffen⟩ gather [up]; tie ⟨Knoten⟩; purse ⟨Lippen⟩. **S~njäger** m (fam) womanizer

Schuß m -sses, ·̈sse shot; ⟨kleine Menge⟩ dash

Schüssel f -,-n bowl; ⟨TV⟩ dish

schusselig a (fam) scatterbrained

Schuß|fahrt f ⟨Ski⟩ schuss. **S~waffe** f firearm

Schuster m -s,- = **Schuhmacher**

Schutt m -[e]s rubble. **S~ablade|platz** m rubbish dump

Schüttel|frost m shivering fit. **s~n** vt shake; **sich s~n** shake oneself/itself; ⟨vor Ekel⟩ shudder

jdm die Hand s~n shake s.o.'s hand

schütten vt pour; ⟨kippen⟩ tip; ⟨ver-⟩ spill □ vi (haben) **es schüttet** it is pouring [with rain]

Schutthaufen m pile of rubble

Schutz m -es protection; ⟨Zuflucht⟩ shelter; ⟨Techn⟩ guard; **S~ suchen** take refuge; **unter dem S~ der Dunkelheit** under cover of darkness. **S~anzug** m protective suit. **S~blech** nt mudguard. **S~brille** goggles pl

Schütze m -n,-n marksman; ⟨Tor-⟩ scorer; ⟨Astr⟩ Sagittarius; **guter S~** good shot

schützen vt protect ⟨Zuflucht gewähren⟩ shelter (**vor** + dat from) □ vi (haben) give protection/shelter (**vor** + dat from). **s~d** a protective, adv -ly

Schützenfest nt fair with shooting competition

Schutz|engel m guardian angel. **S~heilige(r)** m/f patron saint

Schützling m -s,-e charge; ⟨Protégé⟩ protégé

schutz|los a defenceless, helpless. **S~mann** m ⟨pl -männer & -leute⟩ policeman. **S~umschlag** m dust-jacket

Schwaben nt -s Swabia

schwäbisch a Swabian

schwach a ⟨schwächer, schwächst⟩ weak, adv -ly; ⟨nicht gut; gering⟩ poor, adv -ly; ⟨leicht⟩ faint, adv -ly

Schwäche f -,-n weakness. **s~n** vt weaken

Schwach|heit f - weakness. **S~kopf** m (fam) idiot

schwäch|lich a delicate. **S~ling** m -s,-e weakling

Schwachsinn m mental deficiency. **s~ig** a mentally deficient; ⟨fam⟩ idiotic

Schwächung f - weakening

schwafeln ⟨fam⟩ vi (haben) waffle □ vt talk

Schwager m -s,- brother-in-law

Schwägerin f -,-nen sister-in-law

Schwalbe f -,-n swallow

Schwall m -[e]s torrent

Schwamm m -[e]s,⁻e sponge; ⟨SGer: Pilz⟩ fungus; (eßbar) mushroom. **s~ig** a spongy; (aufgedunsen) bloated

Schwan m -[e]s,⁻e swan

schwanen vi (haben) (fam) mir **schwante, daß** I had a nasty feeling that

schwanger a pregnant

schwängern vt make pregnant

Schwangerschaft f -,-en pregnancy

Schwank m -[e]s,⁻e (Theat) farce

schwank|en vi (haben) sway; ⟨Boot:⟩ rock; (sich ändern) fluctuate; (unentschieden sein) be undecided □(sein) stagger. **S~ung** f -,-en fluctuation

Schwanz m -es,⁻e tail

schwänzen vt (fam) skip; **die Schule s~** play truant

Schwarm m -[e]s,⁻e swarm; (Fisch-) shoal; (fam: Liebe) idol

schwärmen vi (haben) swarm; **s~ für** (fam) adore; (verliebt sein) have a crush on; **s~ von** (fam) rave about

Schwarte f -,-n (Speck-) rind; (fam: Buch) tome

schwarz a (schwärzer, schwärzest) black; (fam: illegal) illegal, adv -ly; **s~er Markt** black market; **s~ gekleidet** dressed in black; **s~ auf weiß** in black and white; **ins S~e treffen** score a bull's-eye. **S~** nt -[e]s,- black. **S~arbeit** f moonlighting. **s~arbeiten** vi sep (haben) moonlight. **S~brot** nt black bread. **S~e(r)** m f black

Schwärze f - blackness. **s~n** vt blacken

Schwarz|fahrer m fare-dodger. **S~handel** m black market (mit

in). **S~händler** m black marketeer. **S~markt** m black market. **s~sehen** vi sep (haben) watch television without a licence; (fig) be pessimistic. **S~wald** m Black Forest. **s~weiß** a black and white

Schwatz m -es (fam) chat

schwatzen, (SGer) **schwätzen** vi (haben) chat; (klatschen) gossip; (Sch) talk [in class] □vt talk

schwatzhaft a garrulous

Schwebe f -in der S~ (fig) undecided. **S~bahn** f cable railway. **s~n** vi (haben) float; (fig) be undecided; ⟨Verfahren:⟩ be pending; **in Gefahr s~n** be in danger □⟨sein⟩ float

Schwede m -n,-n Swede. **S~n** nt -s Sweden. **S~in** f -,-nen Swede. **s~isch** a Swedish

Schwefel m -s sulphur. **S~säure** f sulphuric acid

schweigen† vi (haben) be silent; **ganz zu s~ von** to say nothing of, let alone. **S~** nt -s silence; **zum S~ bringen** silence. **s~d** a silent, adv -ly

schweigsam a silent; (wortkarg) taciturn

Schwein nt -[e]s,-e pig; (Culin) pork; (sl) (schmutziger Mensch) dirty pig; (Schuft) swine; **S~ haben** (fam) be lucky. **S~ebraten** m roast pork. **S~efleisch** nt pork. **S~ehund** m (sl) swine. **S~erei** f -,-en (sl) [dirty] mess; (Gemeinheit) dirty trick. **S~estall** m pigsty. **s~isch** a lewd. **S~sleder** nt pigskin

Schweiß m -es sweat

schweiß|en vt weld. **S~er** m -s,- welder

Schweiz (die) - Switzerland. **S~er** a & m -s,-, **S~erin** f -,-nen Swiss. **s~erisch** a Swiss

schwelen vi (haben) smoulder

schwelgen vi (haben) feast; **s~ in** (+ dat) wallow in

Schwelle f -,-n threshold; (*Eisenbahn-*) sleeper

schwellen† vi (*sein*) swell. **S~ung** f -,-en swelling

Schwemme f -,-n watering-place; (*fig: Überangebot*) glut. **s~n** vt wash; **an Land s~n** wash up

Schwenk m -[e]s swing. **s~en** vt swing; (*schwingen*) wave; (*spülen*) rinse; **in Butter s~en** toss in butter □ vi (*sein*) turn

schwer a heavy; (*schwierig*) difficult; (*mühsam, streng*) hard; (*ernst*) serious; (*schlimm*) bad; **3 Pfund s~** sein weigh 3 pounds □ adv heavily; with difficulty; (*mühsam, streng*) hard; (*schlimm, sehr*) badly, seriously; **s~ hören** be hard of hearing; **s~ arbeiten** work hard; **s~ zu sagen** difficult or hard to say

Schwere f -,- heaviness; (*Gewicht*) weight; (*Schwierigkeit*) difficulty; (*Ernst*) gravity. **S~losigkeit** f -- weightlessness

schwer|fallen† vi sep (*sein*) be hard (*dat* for). **s~fällig** a ponderous, adv -ly; (*unbeholfen*) clumsy, adv -ily. **S~gewicht** nt heavyweight. **s~hörig** a **s~hörig sein** be hard of hearing. **S~kraft** f (*Phys*) gravity. **s~krank** a seriously ill. **s~lich** adv hardly. **s~machen** vt sep make difficult (*dat* for). **s~mütig** a melancholic. **s~nehmen†** vt sep take seriously. **S~punkt** m centre of gravity; (*fig*) emphasis

Schwert nt -[e]s,-er sword. **S~lilie** f iris

schwer|tun (sich) vr sep have difficulty (*mit* with). **S~verbrecher** m serious offender. **s~verdaulich** a indigestible. **s~verletzt** a seriously injured. **s~wiegend** a weighty

Schwester f -,-n sister; (*Kranken-*) nurse. **s~lich** a sisterly

Schwieger|eltern pl parents-in-law. **S~mutter** f mother-in-law. **S~sohn** m son-in-law. **S~tochter** f daughter-in-law. **S~vater** m father-in-law

Schwiele f -,-n callus

schwierig a difficult. **S~keit** f -,-en difficulty

Schwimm|bad nt swimming-baths pl. **S~becken** nt swimming-pool. **s~en†** vt/i (*sein/haben*) swim; (*auf dem Wasser treiben*) float. **S~er** m -s,-, swimmer; (*Techn*) float. **S~weste** f life-jacket

Schwindel m -s dizziness, vertigo; (*Betrug*) fraud; (*Lüge*) lie. **S~anfall** m dizzy spell. **s~frei** a **s~frei sein** have a good head for heights. **s~n** vi (*haben*) (*lügen*) lie; **mir od mich s~t** I feel dizzy

schwinden† vi (*sein*) dwindle; (*vergehen*) fade; (*nachlassen*) fail

Schwindl|er m -s,- liar; (*Betrüger*) fraud, con-man. **s~ig** a dizzy; **mir ist od wird s~ig** I feel dizzy

schwing|en† vt/i (*haben*) swing; (*Phys*) oscillate; (*vibrieren*) vibrate □ vt swing; wave (*Fahne*); (*drohend*) brandish. **S~tür** f swing-door. **S~ung** f -,-en oscillation; vibration

Schwips m -es,-e einen **S~ haben** (*fam*) be tipsy

schwirren vi (*haben/sein*) buzz; (*surren*) whirr

Schwitz|e f -,-n (*Culin*) roux. **s~en** vi (*haben*) sweat; **ich s~e** od mich s~t I am hot □ vt (*Culin*) sweat

schwören† vt/i (*haben*) swear (*auf* + acc by); **Rache s~** swear revenge

schwul a (*fam: homosexuell*) gay

schwül a close. **S~e** f - closeness

schwülstig a bombastic, adv -ally

Schwung *m* -[e]s,⸚e swing; (*Bogen*) sweep; (*Schnelligkeit*) momentum; (*Kraft*) vigour; (*Feuer*) verve; (*fam: Anzahl*) batch; in S~ **kommen** gather momentum; (*fig*) get going. **s~haft** *a* brisk, adv -ly. **s~los** *a* dull. **s~voll** *a* vigorous, adv -ly; (*Bogen, Linie*) sweeping; (*mitreißend*) spirited, lively

Schwur *m* -[e]s,⸚e vow; (*Eid*) oath. **S~gericht** *nt* jury [court]

sechs *inv a*, **S~** *f* -,-en six; (*Sch*) ≈ fail mark. **s~eckig** *a* hexagonal. **s~te(r,s)** *a* sixth

sech|zehn *inv a* sixteen. **s~zehnte(r,s)** *a* sixteenth. **s~zig** *inv a* sixty. **s~zigste(r,s)** *a* sixtieth

sedieren *vt* sedate

See[1] *m* -s,-n /'ze:ən/ lake

See[2] *f* - sea; **an die/der See** to/at the seaside; **auf See** at sea. **S~bad** *nt* seaside resort. **S~fahrt** *f* [sea] voyage; (*Schiffahrt*) navigation. **S~gang** *m* schwerer S~gang rough sea. **S~hund** *m* seal. **s~krank** *a* seasick

Seele *f* -,-n soul. **s~nruhig** *a* calm, adv -ly

seelisch *a* psychological, adv -ly; (*geistig*) mental, adv -ly

Seelsorger *m* -s,- pastor

See|luft *f* sea air. **S~macht** *f* maritime power. **S~mann** *m* (*pl* -leute) seaman, sailor. **S~not** *f* in S~not in distress. **S~räuber** *m* pirate. **S~reise** *f* [sea] voyage. **S~rose** *f* water-lily. **S~sack** *m* kitbag. **S~stern** *m* starfish. **S~tang** *m* seaweed. **s~tüchtig** *a* seaworthy. **S~weg** *m* sea-route; **auf dem S~weg** by sea. **S~zunge** *f* sole

Segel *nt* -s,- sail. **S~boot** *nt* sailing-boat. **S~fliegen** *nt* gliding. **S~flieger** *m* glider pilot. **S~flugzeug** *nt* glider. **s~n** *vt/i*

(*sein/haben*) sail. **S~schiff** *nt* sailing-ship. **S~sport** *m* sailing. **S~tuch** *nt* canvas

Segen *m* -s blessing. **s~sreich** *a* beneficial; (*gesegnet*) blessed

Segler *m* -s,- yachtsman

Segment *nt* -[e]s,-e segment

segnen *vt* bless; **gesegnet mit** blessed with

sehen† *vt* see; watch (*Fernsehsendung*); **sich s~ lassen** show oneself ◇ *vi* (*haben*) see; (*blicken*) look (**auf**+*acc* at); (*ragen*) show (**aus** above); **gut/schlecht s~** have good/bad eyesight; **vom S~ kennen** know by sight; **s~ nach** keep an eye on; (*betreuen*) look after; (*suchen*) look for; **darauf s~, daß** see [to it] that. **s~swert, s~swürdig** *a* worth seeing. **S~swürdigkeit** *f* -,-en sight

Sehkraft *f* sight, vision

Sehne *f* -,-n tendon; (*eines Bogens*) string

sehnen (sich) *vr* long (**nach** for)

sehnig *a* sinewy; (*Fleisch*) stringy

sehn|lich[st] *a* ⟨*Wunsch*⟩ dearest □ *adv* longingly. **S~sucht** *f* longing (**nach** for). **s~süchtig** *a* longing, adv -ly; ⟨*Wunsch*⟩ dearest

sehr *adv* very; (*mit Verb*) very much

seicht *a* shallow

seid *s.* **sein**[1]; **ihr s~** you are

Seide *f* -,-n silk

Seidel *nt* -s,- beer-mug

seiden *a* silk ... **S~papier** *nt* tissue paper. **S~raupe** *f* silkworm. **s~weich** *a* silky-soft

seidig *a* silky

Seife *f* -,-n soap. **S~npulver** *nt* soap powder. **S~nschaum** *m* lather

seifig *a* soapy

seihen *vt* strain

Seil *nt* -[e]s,-e rope; (*Draht-*) cable. **S~bahn** *f* cable railway. **s~springen**† *vi* (*sein*) (*inf & pp* *only*) skip. S~**tänzer(in)** *m(f)* tightrope walker

sein[1]† *vi (sein)* be; **er ist Lehrer** he is a teacher; **sei still!** be quiet! **mir ist kalt/schlecht** I am cold/ feel sick; **wie dem auch sei** be that as it may □*v aux* have; **an- gekommen/gestorben s**~ have arrived/died; **er war/wäre ge- fallen** he had/would have fallen; **es ist/war viel zu tun/nichts zu sehen** there is/was a lot to be done/nothing to be seen

sein[2] *poss pron* his; *(Ding, Tier)* its; *(nach man)* one's; **sein Glück versuchen** try one's luck. **s~e(r,s)** *poss pron* his; *(nach man)* one's own; **das S~e** to do one's share. **s~erseits** *adv* for his part. **s~erzeit** *adv* in those days. **s~etwegen** *adv* for his sake; *(wegen ihm)* because of him, on his account. **s~etwillen** *adv* **um s~etwillen** for his sake. **s~ige** *poss pron* **der/die/das s~ige** his

seinlassen† *vt sep* leave; *(aufhö- ren mit)* stop

seins *poss pron* his; *(nach man)* one's own

seit *conj & prep (+ dat)* since; **s~ wann?** since when? **s~ einiger Zeit** for some time [past]; **ich wohne s~ zehn Jahren hier** I've lived here for ten years. **s~dem** *conj* & *adv* since □*adv* since then

Seite *f -,-n* side; *(Buch-)* page; **S~ an S~** side by side; **zur S~ le- gen/treten** put/step aside; **jds starke S~** s.o.'s strong point; **von S~n** (+ *gen)* on the part of; **auf der einen/anderen S~** *(fig)* on the one/other hand

seitens *prep (+ gen)* on the part of

Seiten|schiff *nt* [side] aisle. **S~sprung** *m* infidelity; **einen S~sprung machen** be unfaith- ful. **S~stechen** *nt -s (Med)*

stitch. **S~straße** *f* side-street. **S~streifen** *m* verge; *(Autobahn-)* hard shoulder

seither *adv* since then

seit|lich *a* side . . . □*adv* at/on the side; **s~lich von** to one side of □*prep (+ gen)* to one side of. **s~wärts** *adv* on/to one side; *(zur Seite)* sideways

Sekret *nt -[e]s,-e* secretion

Sekret|är *m -s,-e* secretary; *(Schrank)* bureau. **S~ariat** *nt -[e]s,-e* secretary's office. **S~ä- rin** *f -,-nen* secretary

Sekt *m -[e]s* [German] sparkling wine

Sekte *f -,-n* sect

Sektion *f -'ts̸jo:n/ f -,-en* section; *(Sezierung)* autopsy

Sektor *m -s,-en /-'to:rən/* sector

Sekundant *m -en,-en (Sport)* se- cond

sekundär *a* secondary

Sekunde *f -,-n* second

selber *pron (fam)* = **selbst**

selbst *pron* oneself; **ich/du/er/sie s**~ I myself /you yourself/ he himself/she herself; **wir/ihr/ sie s**~ we ourselves/you yourselves/ they themselves; **ich schneide mein Haar s**~ I cut my own hair; **von s**~ of one's own accord; *(au- tomatisch)* automatically □*adv* even. **S~achtung** *f* self-esteem, self-respect

selbständig *a* independent, *adv -ly*; self-employed ⟨*Handwerker*⟩; **sich s**~ **machen** set up on one's own. **S~keit** *f -* independence

Selbstaufopferung *f* self-sacri- fice

Selbstbedienung *f* self-service. **S~srestaurant** *nt* self-service restaurant, cafeteria

Selbst|befriedigung *f* masturba- tion. **S~beherrschung** *f* self- control. **S~bestimmung** *f* self- determination. **s~bewußt** *a* self-confident. **S~bewußtsein**

nt self-confidence. S~ bildnis *nt* self-portrait. S~ erhaltung *f* self-preservation. s~ gefällig *a* self-satisfied, smug, *adv* -ly. s~ gemacht *a* home-made. s~ gerecht *a* self-righteous. S~ gespräch *nt* soliloquy; S~ gespräche führen talk to oneself. s~ haftend *a* self-adhesive. s~ herrlich *a* autocratic, *adv* -ally. S~ hilfe *f* self-help. s~ klebend *a* self-adhesive. S~ kostenpreis *m* cost price. s~ laut *m* vowel. s~ los *a* selfless, *adv* -ly. S~ mitleid *nt* self-pity. S~ mord *m* suicide. S~ mörder(in) *m(f)* suicide. s~ mörderisch *a* suicidal. s~ porträt *nt* self-portrait. s~ sicher *a* self-assured. S~ sicherheit *f* self-assurance. s~ süchtig *a* selfish, *adv* -ly. S~ tanken *nt* self-service (for petrol). s~ tätig *a* automatic, *adv* -ally. S~ versorgung *f* self-catering. **selbstverständlich** *a* natural, *adv* -ly; etw für s~ halten take sth for granted; das ist s~ that goes without saying; s~! of course! S~ keit *f* - matter of course; das ist eine S~ keit that goes without saying. **Selbst|verteidigung** *f* self-defence. S~ vertrauen *nt* self-confidence. S~ verwaltung *f* self-government. s~ zufrieden *a* complacent, *adv* -ly

selig *a* blissfully happy; (Relig) blessed; (verstorben) late. S~ keit *f* - bliss

Sellerie *m* -s,-s & *f* -,- celeriac; (Stangen-) celery

selten *a* rare □ *adv* rarely, seldom; (besonders) exceptionally. S~ heit *f* -,-en rarity

Selterswasser *nt* seltzer [water]

seltsam *a* odd, *adv* -ly, strange, *adv* -ly. s~ erweise *adv* oddly/ strangely enough

Semester *nt* -s,- (Univ) semester

Semikolon *nt* -s,-s semicolon

Seminar *nt* -s,-e seminar; (Institut) department; (Priester-) seminary

Semmel *f* -,-n [bread] roll. S~ brösel *pl* breadcrumbs

Senat *m* -[e]s,-e senate. S~ or *m* -s,-en /-'to:rən/ senator

senden¹ *vt* send

sende|n² *vt* (reg) broadcast; (über Funk) transmit, send. S~ r *m* -s,- [broadcasting] station; (Anlage) transmitter. S~ reihe *f* series

Sendung *f* -,-en consignment, shipment; (Auftrag) mission; (Radio, TV) programme

Senf *m* -s mustard

sengend *a* scorching

senil *a* senile. S~ ität *f* - senility

Senior *m* -s,-en /-'o:rən/ senior; S~ en senior citizens. S~ enheim *nt* old people's home. S~ enteller *m* senior citizen's menu

Senke *f* -,-n dip, hollow

Senkel *m* -s,- [shoe-]lace

senken *vt* lower; bring down (Fieber, Preise); bow (Kopf); sich s~ come down, fall; (absinken) subside; (abfallen) slope down

senkrecht *a* vertical, *adv* -ly. S~ e *f* -n,-n perpendicular

Sensation /-'tsjo:n/ *f* -,-en sensation. S~ ell *a* sensational, *adv* -ly

Sense *f* -,-n scythe

sensib|el *a* sensitive, *adv* -ly. S~ ilität *f* - sensitivity

sentimental *a* sentimental. S~ ität *f* - sentimentality

separat *a* separate, *adv* -ly

September *m* -s,- September

Serenade *f* -,-n serenade

Serie /ˈzeːrɪə/ f -,-n series; (*Briefmarken*) set; (*Comm*) range.
S~nummer f serial number

seriös a respectable, adv -bly; (*zuverlässig*) reliable, adv -bly; (*ernstgemeint*) serious

Serpentine f -,-n winding road; (*Kehre*) hairpin bend

Serum nt -s,-Sera serum

Service[1] /ˈzœrviːs/ nt -[s],-/-ˈviːsəs/, -ˈviːsə/ service, set

Service[2] /ˈzøːɡvɪs/ m & nt -s /-vɪs/(*Comm, Tennis*) service

servier|en vt/i (*haben*) serve.
S~erin f -,-nen waitress.
S~wagen m trolley

Serviette f -,-n napkin, serviette

Servus m (*Aust*) cheerio; (*Begrüßung*) hallo

Sessel m -s,- armchair. **S~bahn** f, **S~lift** m chair-lift

seßhaft a settled; **s~ werden** settle down

Set /zɛt/ nt & m -[s],-s set; (*Deckchen*) place-mat

setz|en vt put; (*abstellen*) set down; (*hin-*) sit down ⟨*Kind*⟩; move ⟨*Spielstein*⟩; (*pflanzen*) plant; (*schreiben, wetten*) put; **sich s~en** sit down; (*sinken*) settle □vi (*sein*) leap □vi (*haben*) **s~en auf** (*+ acc*) back. **S~ling** m -s,-e seedling

Seuche f -,-n epidemic

seufz|en vi (*haben*) sigh. **S~er** m -s,- sigh

Sex /zɛks/ m -[es] sex. **s~istisch** a sexist

Sexu|alität f -sexuality. **s~ell** a sexual, adv -ly

sexy /ˈzɛksi/ inv a sexy

sezieren vt dissect

Shampoo /ˈʃampuː/, **Shampoon** /ˈʃampoːn/ nt -s shampoo

siamesisch a Siamese

sich refl pron oneself; (*mit er/sie/es*) himself/herself/itself; (*mit sie pl*) themselves; (*mit Sie*) yourself; (*pl*) yourselves; (*einander*) each other; **s~ kennen** know oneself/(*einander*) each other; **s~ waschen** have a wash; **s~** (*dat*) **die Zähne putzen/die Haare kämmen** clean one's teeth/comb one's hair; **s~** (*dat*) **das Bein brechen** break a leg; **s~ wundern/schämen** be surprised/ashamed; **s~ gut lesen/verkaufen** read/sell well; **von s~ aus** of one's own accord

Sichel f -,-n sickle

sicher a safe; (*gesichert*) secure; (*gewiß*) certain; (*zuverlässig*) reliable; sure ⟨*Urteil, Geschmack*⟩; steady ⟨*Hand*⟩; (*selbstbewußt*) self-confident; **sich** (*dat*) **etw** (*gen*) **s~ sein** be sure of sth; **bist du s~?** are you sure? □adv safely; securely; certainly; reliably; self-confidently; (*wahrscheinlich*) most probably; **er kommt s~** he is sure to come; **s~!** certainly! **s~gehen**† vi sep (*sein*) be sure

Sicherheit f - safety; (*Pol, Psych, Comm*) security; (*Gewißheit*) certainty; (*Zuverlässigkeit*) reliability; (*des Urteils, Geschmacks*) surety; (*Selbstbewußtsein*) self-confidence. **S~sgurt** m safety-belt; (*Auto*) seat-belt. **s~shalber** adv to be on the safe side. **S~snadel** f safety-pin

sicherlich adv certainly; (*wahrscheinlich*) most probably

sicher|n vt secure; (*garantieren*) safeguard; (*schützen*) protect; put the safety-catch on ⟨*Pistole*⟩; **sich** (*dat*) **etw s~n** secure sth. **s~stellen** vt sep safeguard; (*beschlagnahmen*) seize. **S~ung** f -,-en safeguard, protection; (*Gewehr-*) safety-catch; (*Electr*) fuse

Sicht f -,-n view; (*S~weite*) visibility; **in S~ kommen** come into view; **auf lange S~** in the long term. **s~bar** a visible, adv -bly. **s~en**

vt sight; *(durchsehen)* sift through. **s~lich** *a* obvious, *adv* -ly. **S~vermerk** *m* visa. **S~weite** *f* visibility; **in/ außer S~weite** within/out of sight

sickern *vi (sein)* seep

sie *pron (nom) (sg)* she; *(Ding, Tier)* it; *(pl)* they; *(acc) (sg)* her; *(Ding, Tier)* it; *(pl)* them

Sie *pron* you; **gehen/warten Sie!** go/wait!

Sieb *nt* -[e]s,-e sieve; *(Tee-)* strainer. **s~en¹** *vt* sieve, sift

sieben² *inv a,* **S~** *f* -,-en seven. **S~sachen** *fpl (fam)* belongings. **s~te(r,s)** *a* seventh

sieb|te(r,s) *a* seventh. **s~zehn** *inv a* seventeen. **s~zehnte(r,s)** *a* seventeenth. **s~zig** *inv a* seventy. **s~zigste(r,s)** *a* seventieth

siede|n† *vt/i (haben)* boil. **S~punkt** *m* boiling point

Siedl|er *m* -s,- settler. **S~ung** *f* -,-en [housing] estate; *(Niederlassung)* settlement

Sieg *m* -[e]s,-e victory

Siegel *nt* -s,- seal. **S~ring** *m* signet-ring

sieg|en *vi (haben)* win. **S~er(in)** *m* -s,- *(f* -,-nen) winner. **s~reich** *a* victorious

siezen *vt* jdn s~ call s.o. 'Sie'

Signal *nt* -s,-e signal. **s~isieren** *vt* signal

signieren *vt* sign

Silbe *f* -,-n syllable. **S~ntrennung** *f* word-division

Silber *nt* -s silver. **S~hochzeit** *f* silver wedding. **s~n** *a* silver. **S~papier** *nt* silver paper

Silhouette /zil'lυεtə/ *f* -,-n silhouette

Silizium *nt* -s silicon

Silo *m & nt* -s,-s silo

Silvester *nt* -s New Year's Eve

simpel *a* simple, *adv* -ply; *(einfältig)* simple-minded

Simplex *nt* -,-e simplex

Sims *m & nt* -es,-e ledge; *(Kamin-)* mantelpiece

Simul|ant *m* -en,-en malingerer. **s~ieren** *vt* feign; *(Techn)* simulate □ *vi (haben)* pretend; *(sich krank stellen)* malinger

simultan *a* simultaneous, *adv* -ly

sind s. **sein¹; wir/sie s~** we/they are

Sinfonie *f* -,-n symphony

singen† *vt/i (haben)* sing

Singular *m* -s,-e singular

Singvogel *m* songbird

sinken† *vi (sein)* sink; *(nieder-)* drop; *(niedriger werden)* go down, fall; **den Mut s~ lassen** lose courage

Sinn *m* -[e]s,-e sense; *(Denken)* mind; *(Zweck)* point; **im S~ haben** have in mind; **in gewissem S~e** in a sense; **es hat keinen S~** it is pointless; **nicht bei S~en sein** be out of one's mind. **S~bild** *nt* symbol. **s~en†** *vi (haben)* think; **auf Rache s~en** plot one's revenge

sinnlich *a* sensory; *(sexuell)* sensual; *(Genüsse)* sensuous. **S~keit** *f* - sensuality; **s~keit** *f* - sensuality; sensuousness

sinn|los *a* senseless, *adv* -ly; *(zwecklos)* pointless, *adv* -ly. **s~voll** *a* meaningful; *(vernünftig)* sensible, *adv* -bly

Sintflut *f* flood

Siphon /'zi:fõ/ *m* -s,-s siphon

Sippe *f* -,-n clan. **S~schaft** *f* - clan; *(Pack)* crowd

Sirene *f* -,-n siren

Sirup *m* -s,-e syrup; *(schwarzer)* treacle

Sitte *f* -,-n custom; **S~n** manners. **s~nlos** *a* immoral

sittlich *a* moral, *adv* -ly. **S~keit** *f* - morality. **S~keitsverbrecher** *m* sex offender

sittsam *a* well-behaved; *(züchtig)* demure, *adv* -ly

Situa|ation /-'tsɪoːn/ f -,-en situation. **s~iert** a gut/schlecht **s~iert** well/badly off

Sitz m -es,-e seat; (Paßform) fit **sitzen†** vi (haben) sit; (sich befinden) be; (passen) fit; (fam: treffen) hit home; **s~ bleiben** remain seated; [**im Gefängnis**] **s~** (fam) be in jail. **s~bleiben†** vi sep (sein) (fam) (Sch) stay or be kept down; (nicht heiraten) be left on the shelf; **s~ bleiben auf** (+ dat) be left with. **s~ d** a seated; (Tätigkeit) sedentary. **s~lassen†** vt sep (fam) (nicht heiraten) jilt; (im Stich lassen) leave in the lurch; (Sch) keep down

Sitz|gelegenheit f seat. **S~platz** m seat. **S~ung** f -,-en session

Sizilien /-jən/ nt -s Sicily

Skala f -,-len scale; (Reihe) range

Skalpell nt -s,-e scalpel

skalpieren vt scalp

Skandal m -s,-e scandal. **s~ös** a scandalous

skandieren vt scan ⟨Verse⟩; chant ⟨Parolen⟩

Skandinav|ien /-jən/ nt -s Scandinavia. **s~isch** a Scandinavian

Skat m -s skat

Skelett nt -[e]s,-e skeleton

Skep|sis f - scepticism. **s~tisch** a sceptical, adv -ly; (mißtrauisch) doubtful, adv -ly

Ski /ʃiː/ m -s,-er ski; **Ski fahren** od **laufen** ski. **S~fahrer(in)** od **S~läufer(in)** m(f) skier. **S~sport** m skiing

Skizze f -,-n sketch. **s~nhaft** a sketchy, adv -ily. **s~ieren** vt sketch

Sklav|e m -n,-n slave. **S~erei** f - slavery. **S~in** f -,-nen slave. **s~isch** a slavish, adv -ly

Skorpion m -s,-e scorpion; (Astr) Scorpio

Skrupel m -s,- scruple. **s~los** a unscrupulous

Skulptur f -,-en sculpture

skurril a absurd, adv -ly

Slalom m -s,-s slalom

Slang /slɛŋ/ m -s slang

Slaw|e m -n,-n, **S~in** f -,-nen Slav. **s~isch** a Slav; (Lang) Slavonic

Slip m -s,-s briefs pl

Smaragd m -[e]s,-e emerald

Smoking m -s,-s dinner jacket, (Amer) tuxedo

Snob m -s,-s snob. **S~ismus** m - snobbery. **s~istisch** a snobbish

so adv so; (so sehr) so much; (auf diese Weise) like this/that; (solch) such; (fam: sowieso) anyway; (fam: umsonst) free; (fam: ungefähr) about; **nicht so schnell** not so fast; **so gut/bald wie** as good/ soon as; **so ein Mann** a man like that; **so ein Zufall!** what a coincidence! **so nicht** not like that; **mir ist so, als ob** I feel as if; **so oder so** in any case; **eine Stunde oder so** an hour or so; **so um zehn Mark** (fam) about ten marks; [es ist] **gut** so that's fine; **so, das ist geschafft** there, that's done; **so?** really? **so kommt doch!** come on then! ⟨conj (also) so; (dann) then; **so daß** so that; **so gern ich auch käme** as much as I would like to come

sobald conj as soon as

Söckchen nt -s,- [ankle] sock

Socke f -,-n sock

Sockel m -s,- plinth, pedestal

Socken m -s,- sock

Soda nt & f - oda. **S~wasser** nt soda water

Sodbrennen nt -s heartburn

soeben adv just [now]

Sofa nt -s,-s settee, sofa

sofern adv provided [that]

sofort adv at once, immediately; (auf der Stelle) instantly. **s~ig** a immediate

Software /'zɔftvɛːɐ̯/ f - software

sogar adv even

sogenannt a so-called

sogleich adv at once

Sohle f -,-n sole; (Tal-) bottom

Sohn m -[e]s,-̈e son

Sojabohne f soya bean

solange conj as long as

solch inv pron such; s~ ein(e) such a; s~ einer/eine/eins one/ (Person) someone like that. s~e(r,s) pron such; ein s~er Mann/eine s~e Frau a man/woman like that; ich habe s~e Angst I am so afraid □ (substantivisch) ein s~er/eine s~e/ein s~es one/(Person) someone like that; s~e (pl) those; (Leute) people like that

Sold m -[e]s (Mil) pay

Soldat m -en,-en soldier

Söldner m -s,- mercenary

solidarisch a s~e Handlung act of solidarity; sich s~ erklären declare one's solidarity

Solidarität f - solidarity

solide a solid, adv -ly; (haltbar) sturdy, adv -ily; (sicher) sound, adv -ly; (anständig) respectable, adv -bly

Solist(in) m -en,-en (f -,-nen) soloist

Soll nt -s (Comm) debit; (Produktions-) quota

sollen† v aux er soll warten he is to wait; (möge) let him wait; was soll ich machen? what shall I do? du sollst nicht lügen you shouldn't lie; du sollst nicht töten (liter) thou shalt not kill; ihr sollt jetzt still sein! will you be quiet now! du solltest dich schämen you ought to or should be ashamed of yourself; es hat nicht sein s~ it was not to be; ich hätte es nicht tun s~ I ought not to or should not have done it; er soll sehr nett/reich sein he is supposed to be very nice/rich; sollte es regnen, so ... if it should rain then ...; das soll man nicht [tun] you're not

supposed to [do that]; **soll ich [mal versuchen]?** shall I [try]? **soll er doch!** let him! **was soll's!** so what!

Solo nt -s,-los & -li solo. **s~** adv solo

somit adv therefore, so

Sommer m -s,- summer. **S~ferien** pl summer holidays. **s~lich** a summery; (Sommer-) summer ... □ adv s~lich warm as warm as summer. **S~schlußverkauf** m summer sale. **S~sprossen** fpl freckles. **s~sprossig** a freckled

Sonate f -,-n sonata

Sonde f -,-n probe

Sonder|angebot nt special offer. **s~bar** a odd, adv -ly. **S~fahrt** f special excursion. **S~fall** m special case. **s~gleichen** a eine Gemeinheit/Grausamkeit s~gleichen unparalleled meanness/cruelty. **s~lich** a particular, adv -ly; (sonderbar) odd, adv -ly. **S~ling** m -s,-e crank. **S~marke** f special stamp

sondern conj but; nicht nur ... s~ auch not only ... but also

Sonder|preis m special price. **S~schule** f special school. **S~zug** m special train

sondieren vt sound out

Sonett nt -[e]s,-e sonnet

Sonnabend m -s,-e Saturday. **s~s** adv on Saturdays

Sonne f -,-n sun. **s~n (sich)** vr sun oneself; (fig) bask (in + dat in)

Sonnen|aufgang m sunrise. **s~baden** vi (haben) sunbathe. **S~bank** f sun-bed. **S~blume** f sunflower. **S~brand** m sunburn. **S~brille** f sun-glasses pl. **S~energie** f solar energy. **S~finsternis** f solar eclipse. **S~öl** nt sun-tan oil. **S~schein** m sunshine. **S~schirm** m sunshade.

S~**stich** m sunstroke. S~**uhr** f sundial. S~**untergang** m sunset. S~**wende** f solstice

sonnig a sunny

Sonntag m -s,-e Sunday. s~s adv on Sundays

sonst adv (gewöhnlich) usually; (im übrigen) apart from that; (andernfalls) otherwise, (or [else]; **wer/was/wie/wo** s~? who/what/how/where else? s~ **niemand/nichts** no one/nothing else; s~ **noch jemand/etwas?** anyone/anything else? s~ **noch Fragen?** any more questions? s~**ig** a other. s~**jemand** pron (fam) someone/(fragend, verneint) anyone else. s~**wer** pron = s~**jemand.** s~**wie** adv (fam) some/any other way. s~**wo** adv (fam) somewhere/anywhere else

sooft conj whenever

Sopran m -s,-e soprano

Sorge f -,-n worry (um about); (Fürsorge) care; in S~ sein be worried; **sich** (dat) S~**n machen** worry; **keine** S~! don't worry! s~**n** vi (haben) s~**n für** look after, care for; (versorgen) provide for; (sich kümmern) see to; **dafür** s~**n, daß** see [to it] or make sure that □or **sich** s~**n** worry. s~**nfrei** a carefree. s~**nvoll** a worried, adv -ly. S~**recht** nt (Jur) custody

Sorgfalt f -care. s~**fältig** a careful, adv -ly. s~**los** a careless, adv -ly; (unbekümmert) carefree. s~**sam** a careful, adv -ly

Sorte f -,-n kind, sort; (Comm) brand

sortieren vt sort [out]; (Comm) grade. S~**iment** nt-[e]s,-e range

sosehr conj however much

Soße f -,-n sauce; (Braten-) gravy; (Salat-) dressing

Souffl|eur /zu'lø:ɐ/ m -s,-e, S~**euse** /-ø:zə/ f -,-n prompter. s~**ieren** vi (haben) prompt

Souvenir /zuvə'ni:ɐ/ nt -s,-s souvenir

souverän /zuvə'rɛ:n/ a sovereign; (fig: überlegen) expert, adv -ly. S~**ität** f - sovereignty

soviel conj however much; s~ **ich weiß** as far as I know □adv as much (wie as); s~ **wie möglich** as much as possible

soweit conj as far as; (insoweit) [in] so far as □adv on the whole; s~ **wie möglich** as far as possible; s~ **sein** be ready; **es ist** s~ the time has come

sowenig conj however little □adv no more (wie than); s~ **wie möglich** as little as possible

sowie conj as well as; (sobald) as soon as

sowieso adv anyway, in any case

sowjet|isch a Soviet. S~**union** f - Soviet Union

sowohl adv ... **als** od **wie auch** ...... as well as ...; s~ **er als auch seine Frau** both he and his wife

sozial a social, adv -ly; (Einstellung, Beruf) caring. S~**arbeit** f social work. S~**arbeiter(in)** m(f) social worker. S~**demokrat** m social democrat. S~**hilfe** f social security

Sozial|ismus m - socialism. S~**t** m -en,-en socialist. s~**tisch** a socialist

Sozial|versicherung f National Insurance. S~**wohnung** f ≈ council flat

Soziologe m -n,-n sociologist. S~**ogie** f - sociology

Sozius m -,-se (Comm) partner; (Beifahrersitz) pillion

sozusagen adv so to speak

Spachtel m -s, & f -,-n spatula

Spagat m -[e]s,-e (Aust) string; S~ **machen** do the splits pl

Spaghetti pl spaghetti sg

spähen vi (haben) peer

Spalier nt -s,-e trellis; S~ **stehen** line the route

Spalt m -[e]s,-e crack; ⟨im Vorhang⟩ chink

Spalt|e f -,-n crack, crevice; ⟨Gletscher-⟩ crevasse; ⟨Druck-⟩ column; ⟨Orangen-⟩ segment. **s~en**† vt split; **sich s~en** split. **S~ung** f -,-en splitting; ⟨Kluft⟩ split; ⟨Phys⟩ fission

Span m -[e]s,¨e [wood] chip; ⟨Hobel-⟩ shaving

Spange f -,-n clasp; ⟨Haar-⟩ slide; ⟨Zahn-⟩ brace; ⟨Arm-⟩ bangle

Span|ien /-jən/ nt -s Spain. **S~ier** m -s,-, **S~ierin** f -,-nen Spaniard. **s~isch** a Spanish. **S~isch** nt -[s] ⟨Lang⟩ Spanish

Spann m -[e]s instep

Spanne f -,-n span; ⟨Zeit-⟩ space; ⟨Comm⟩ margin

spann|en vt stretch; put up ⟨Leine⟩; ⟨straffen⟩ tighten; ⟨an-⟩ harness (**an**+acc to); **den Hahn s~en** cock the gun; **sich s~en** tighten □vi ⟨haben⟩ be too tight. **s~end** a exciting. **S~er** m -s,- ⟨fam⟩ Peeping Tom. **S~ung** f -,-en tension; ⟨Erwartung⟩ suspense; ⟨Electr⟩ voltage

Spar|buch nt savings book. **S~büchse** f money-box. **s~en** vt/i ⟨haben⟩ save; ⟨sparsam sein⟩ economize (**mit/an** + dat on); **sich** (dat) **die Mühe s~en** save oneself the trouble. **S~er** m -s,- saver

Spargel m -s,- asparagus

Spar|kasse f savings bank. **S~konto** nt deposit account

spärlich a sparse, adv -ly; ⟨dürftig⟩ meagre; ⟨knapp⟩ scanty, adv -ily

Sparren m -s,- rafter

sparsam a economical, adv -ly; ⟨Person⟩ thrifty. **S~keit** f - economy; thrift

Sparschwein nt piggy bank

spartanisch a Spartan

Sparte f -,-n branch; ⟨Zeitungs-⟩ section; ⟨Rubrik⟩ column

Spaß m -es,¨e fun; ⟨Scherz⟩ joke; **im/aus/zum S~** for fun; **S~ machen** be fun; ⟨Person:⟩ be joking; **es macht mir keinen S~** I don't enjoy it; **viel S~!** I have a good time! **s~en** vi ⟨haben⟩ joke. **s~ig** a amusing, funny. **S~vogel** m joker

Spast|iker m -s,- spastic. **s~isch** a spastic

spät a & adv late; **wie s~ ist es?** what time is it? **zu s~** too late; **zu s~ kommen** be late. **s~abends** adv late at night

Spatel m -s,- & f -,-n spatula

Spaten m -s,- spade

später a later; ⟨zukünftig⟩ future □adv later

spätestens adv at the latest

Spatz m -en,-en sparrow

Spätzle pl ⟨Culin⟩ noodles

spazieren vi ⟨sein⟩ stroll. **s~gehen**† vi sep ⟨sein⟩ go for a walk

Spazier|gang m walk; **einen S~gang machen** go for a walk. **S~gänger(in)** m -s,- (f -,-nen) walker. **S~stock** m walking-stick

Specht m -[e]s,-e woodpecker

Speck m -s bacon; ⟨fam: Fettpolster⟩ fat. **S~ig** a greasy

Spedi|teur /ʃpedi'tøːɐ/ m -s,-e haulage/⟨für Umzüge⟩ removals contractor. **S~tion** /-'tsjoːn/ f -,-en carriage, haulage; ⟨Firma⟩ haulage/⟨für Umzüge⟩ removals firm

Speer m -[e]s,-e spear; ⟨Sport⟩ javelin

Speiche f -,-n spoke

Speichel m -s saliva

Speicher m -s,- warehouse; ⟨dial: Dachboden⟩ attic; ⟨Computer⟩ memory. **s~n** vt store

speien† vt spit; ⟨erbrechen⟩ vomit

Speise f -,-n food; ⟨Gericht⟩ dish; ⟨Pudding⟩ blancmange. **S~eis** nt ice-cream. S~**kammer** f larder. S~**karte** f menu. s~n vi (haben) eat; **zu Abend** s~n have dinner □vt feed. S~**röhre** f oesophagus. S~**saal** m dining-room. S~**wagen** m dining-car

Spektakel m -s (fam) noise

spektakulär a spectacular

Spektrum nt -s,-tra spectrum

Spekul|ant m -en,-en speculator. S~**ation** /-'tsio:n/ f -,-en speculation. s~**ieren** vi (haben) speculate; s~**ieren auf** (+acc) (fam) hope to get

Spelze f -,-n husk

spendabel a generous

Spende f -,-n donation. s~n vt donate; give ⟨Blut, Schatten⟩; Beifall s~n applaud. S~**r** m -s,-, donor; ⟨Behälter⟩ dispenser

spendieren vt pay for; **jdm etw/ein Bier** s~ treat s.o. to sth/stand s.o. a beer

Spengler m -s,- (SGer) plumber

Sperling m -s,-e sparrow

Sperr|e f -,-n barrier; ⟨Verbot⟩ ban; (Comm) embargo. s~n vt close; (ver-) block; (verbieten) ban; cut off ⟨Strom, Telefon⟩; stop ⟨Scheck, Kredit⟩; s~n in (+acc) put in ⟨Gefängnis, Käfig⟩; **sich** s~n balk (**gegen** at); **gesperrt gedruckt** (Typ) spaced

Sperr|holz nt plywood. s~**ig** a bulky. S~**müll** m bulky refuse. S~**stunde** f closing time

Spesen pl expenses

spezial|isieren (sich) vr specialize (**auf**+acc in). S~**ist** m -en,-en specialist. S~**ität** f -,-en speciality

speziell a special, adv -ly

spezifisch a specific, adv -ally

Sphäre /'sfɛ:rə/ f -,-n sphere

spicken vt (Culin) lard; **gespickt mit** (fig) full of □vi (haben) (fam) crib (**bei** from)

Spiegel m -s,- mirror; ⟨Wasser-, Alkohol-⟩ level. S~**bild** nt reflection. S~**ei** nt fried egg. s~n vt reflect; **sich** s~n be reflected □vi (haben) reflect [the light]; ⟨glänzen⟩ gleam. S~**ung** f -,-en reflection

Spiel nt -[e]s,-e game; ⟨Spielen⟩ playing; ⟨Glücks-⟩ gambling; ⟨Schau-⟩ play; ⟨Satz⟩ set; **ein** S~ **Karten** a pack/(Amer) deck of cards; **auf dem** S~ **stehen** be at stake; **aufs** S~ **setzen** risk. S~**art** f variety. S~**automat** m fruit machine. S~**bank** f casino. S~**dose** f musical box. s~**en** vt/i (haben) play; (im Glücksspiel) gamble; (vortäuschen) act; ⟨Roman:⟩ be set (**in**+dat in); s~**en mit** (fig) toy with. s~**end** a (mühelos) effortless, adv -ly

Spieler|(in) m -s,- (f -,-nen) player; ⟨Glücks-⟩ gambler. S~**ei** f -,-en amusement; (Kleinigkeit) trifle

Spiel|feld nt field, pitch. S~**gefährte** m, S~**gefährtin** f playmate. S~**karte** f playing-card. S~**marke** f chip. S~**plan** m programme. S~**platz** m playground. S~**raum** m (fig) scope; (Techn) clearance. S~**regeln** fpl rules [of the game]. S~**sachen** fpl toys. S~**verderber** m -s,- spoilsport. S~**waren** fpl toys. S~**warengeschäft** nt toyshop. S~**zeug** nt toy; (S~sachen) toys pl

Spieß m -es,-e spear; (Brat-) spit; (für Schaschlik) skewer; (Fleisch-) kebab; **den** S~ **umkehren** turn the tables on s.o. S~**bürger** m [petit] bourgeois. s~**bürgerlich** a bourgeois. s~**en** vt etw **auf etw** (acc) s~**en** spear sth with sth. S~**er** m -s,- [petit] bourgeois. S~**ig** a bourgeois. S~**ruten** fpl S~**ruten laufen** run the gauntlet

Spike[s]reifen /ˈʃpaɪk[s]-/ *m* studded tyre

Spinat *m* -s spinach

Spind *m & nt* -[e]s,-e locker

Spindel *f* -,-n spindle

Spinne *f* -,-n spider

spinn|en† *vt/i* (haben) spin; **er spinnt** (fam) he's crazy. **S~ennetz** *nt* spider's web. **S~[en]gewebe** *nt*, **S~webe** *f* -,-n cobweb

Spion *m* -s,-e spy

Spionage /ʃpi̯oˈnaːʒə/ *f* - espionage, spying; **S~** trailing (in comp) **S~abwehr** *f* counter-espionage

spionieren *vi* (haben) spy

Spionin *f* -,-nen [woman] spy

Spiral|e *f* -,-n spiral. **s~ig** *a* spiral

Spiritismus *m* - spiritualism. **s~tisch** *a* spiritualist

Spirituosen *pl* spirits

Spiritus *m* - alcohol; (Brenn) methylated spirits *pl.* **S~kocher** *m* spirit stove

Spital *nt* -s,-̈er (Aust) hospital

spitz *a* pointed; (scharf) sharp; (schrill) shrill; ⟨Winkel⟩ acute; **s~e Bemerkung** dig. **S~bube** *m* scoundrel; (Schlingel) rascal. **s~bübisch** *a* mischievous, *adv* -ly

Spitze *f* -,-n point; (oberer Teil) top; (vorderer Teil) front; (Pfeil-, Finger-, Nasen-) tip; (Schuh-, Strumpf-) toe; (Zigarren-, Zigaretten-) holder; (Höchstleistung) maximum; (Tex) lace; (fam: Anspielung) dig; **an der S~ liegen** be in the lead

Spitzel *m* -s,- informer

spitzen *vt* sharpen; purse ⟨Lippen⟩; prick up ⟨Ohren⟩; **sich s~ auf** (+ acc) (fam) look forward to. **S~geschwindigkeit** *f* top speed

spitz|findig *a* over-subtle. **S~hacke** *f* pickaxe. **S~name** *m* nickname

Spleen /ʃpliːn/ *m* -s,-e obsession; **einen S~ haben** be crazy. **s~ig** *a* eccentric

Splitter *m* -s,- splinter. **s~n** *vi* (sein) shatter. **s~[faser]nackt** *a* (fam) stark naked

sponsern *vt* sponsor

Sponsor *m* -s,- sponsor

spontan *a* spontaneous, *adv* -ly

sporadisch *a* sporadic, *adv* -ally

Spore *f* -,-n (Biol) spore

Sporn *m* -[e]s,**Sporen** spur; **einem Pferd die Sporen geben** spur a horse

Sport *m* -[e]s sport; (Hobby) hobby. **S~art** *f* sport. **S~fest** *nt* sports day. **S~ler** *m* -s,- sportsman. **S~lerin** *f* -,-nen sportswoman. **S~lich** *a* sports ...; (fair) sporting, *adv* -ly; (flott, schlank) sporty. **S~platz** *m* sports ground. **S~verein** *m* sports club. **S~wagen** *m* sports car; (Kinder-) push-chair, (Amer) stroller

Spott *m* -[e]s mockery. **s~billig** *a & adv* dirt cheap

spött|eln *vi* (haben) mock; **s~ über** (+ acc) poke fun at

spotten *vi* (haben) mock; **s~ über** (+ acc) make fun of; (höhnen) ridicule

spöttisch *a* mocking, *adv* -ly

Sprach|e *f* -,-n language; (Sprechfähigkeit) speech; **zur S~e bringen** bring up. **S~fehler** *m* speech defect. **S~labor** *nt* language laboratory. **s~lich** *a* linguistic, *adv* -ally. **s~los** *a* speechless

Spray /ʃpreː/ *nt & m* -s,-s spray. **S~dose** *f* aerosol [can]

Sprech|anlage *f* intercom. **S~chor** *m* chorus; **im S~chor** rufen chant

sprechen† *vi* (haben) speak/(sich unterhalten) talk **über** (+ acc) **von** about/(of); **deutsch/englisch s~** speak German/English □ *vt* speak; (sagen, aufsagen) say;

pronounce ⟨Urteil⟩; **schuldig s~** find guilty; **jdn s~** speak to s.o.; **Herr X ist nicht zu s~** Mr X is not available

Sprecher(in) m -s, (f -,-nen) speaker; (Radio, TV) announcer; (Wortführer) spokesman, f spokeswoman

Sprechstunde f consulting hours pl; (Med) surgery. **S~hilfe** f (Med) receptionist

Sprechzimmer nt consulting room

spreizen vt spread

Sprengel m -s, parish

sprengen vt blow up; blast ⟨Felsen⟩; (fig) burst; (begießen) water; (mit Sprenger) sprinkle; dampen ⟨Wäsche⟩. **S~er** m -s, sprinkler. **S~kopf** m warhead. **S~körper** m explosive device. **S~stoff** m explosive

Spreu f -chaff

Sprich|wort nt (pl -wörter) proverb. **s~wörtlich** a proverbial

sprießen† vi (sein) sprout

Springbrunnen m fountain

spring|en† vi (sein) jump; (Schwimmsport) dive; ⟨Ball⟩ bounce; (spritzen) spurt; (zer-) break; (rissig werden) crack; ⟨SGer: laufen⟩ run. **S~er** m -s, jumper; (Kunst-) diver; (Schach) knight. **S~reiten** nt show-jumping. **S~seil** nt skipping-rope

Sprint m -s, -s sprint

Sprit m -s (fam) petrol

Spritze f -,-n syringe; (Injektion) injection; (Feuer-) hose. **s~n** vt spray; (be-, ver-) splash; (Culin) pipe; (Med) inject □vi (haben) splash; ⟨Fett:⟩ spit □vi (sein) splash; (hervor-) spurt; (fam: laufen) dash. **S~er** m -s, splash; (Schuß) dash. **s~ig** a lively; ⟨Wein, Komödie⟩ sparkling. **S~tour** f (fam) spin

spröde a brittle; (trocken) dry; (rissig) chapped; ⟨Stimme⟩ harsh; (abweisend) aloof

Sproß m -sses,-sse shoot

Sprosse f -,-n rung. **S~nkohl** m (Aust) Brussels sprouts pl

Sprotte f -,-n sprat

Spruch m -[e]s,⁓e saying; (Denk-) motto; (Zitat) quotation. **S~band** nt (pl -bänder) banner

Sprudel m -s, sparkling mineral water. **s~n** vi (haben/sein) bubble

Sprüh|dose f aerosol [can]. **s~en** vt spray □vi (sein) ⟨Funken:⟩ fly; (fig) sparkle. **s~regen** m fine drizzle

Sprung m -[e]s,⁓e jump, leap; (Schwimmsport) dive; (fam: Katzen-) stone's throw; (Riß) crack; **auf einem S~** (fam) for a moment. **S~brett** nt springboard. **s~haft** a erratic; (plötzlich) sudden, adv -ly. **S~schanze** f ski-jump. **S~seil** nt skipping-rope

Spucke f - spit. **S~n** vt/i (haben) spit; (sich übergeben) be sick

Spuk m -[e]s,-e (ghostly) apparition. **s~en** vi (haben) ⟨Geist:⟩ walk; **in diesem Haus s~t es** this house is haunted

Spülbecken nt sink

Spule f -,-n spool

Spüle f -,-n sink unit; (Becken) sink

spulen vt spool

spül|en vt rinse; (schwemmen) wash; **Geschirr s~** wash up □vi (haben) flush [the toilet]. **S~kasten** m cistern. **S~mittel** nt washing-up liquid. **S~tuch** nt dishcloth

Spur f -,-en track; (Fahr-) lane; (Fährte) trail; (Anzeichen) trace; (Hinweis) lead; **keine od nicht die S~** (fam) not in the least

spürbar a noticeable, adv -bly

spuren vi (haben) (fam) toe the line

spür|en *vt* feel; *(seelisch)* sense. **S~hund** *m* tracker dog

spurlos *adv* without trace

spurten *vi (sein)* put on a spurt; *(fam: laufen)* sprint

sputen (sich) *vr* hurry

Staat *m* -[e]s,-en state; *(Land)* country; *(Putz)* finery. **s~lich** *a* state ... □ *adv* by the state

Staatsangehörige(r) *m/f* national. **S~keit** *f* - nationality

Staats|anwalt *m* state prosecutor. **S~beamte(r)** *m* civil servant. **S~besuch** *m* state visit. **S~bürger(in)** *m(f)* national. **S~mann** *m (pl -männer)* statesman. **S~streich** *m* coup

Stab *m* -[e]s,-e rod; *(Gitter-)* bar; *(Sport)* baton; *(Mitarbeiter-)* team; *(Mil)* staff

Stäbchen *ntpl* chopsticks

Stabhochsprung *m* pole-vault

stabil *a* stable; *(gesund)* robust; *(solide)* sturdy, *adv* -ily. **s~isieren** *vt* stabilize; *sich* **s~isieren** stabilize. **S~ität** *f* - stability

Stachel *m* -s,- spine; *(Gift-)* sting; *(Spitze)* spike. **S~beere** *f* gooseberry. **S~draht** *m* barbed wire. **s~ig** *a* prickly. **S~schwein** *nt* porcupine

Stadion *nt* -s,-ien stadium

Stadium *nt* -s,-ien stage

Stadt *f* -,-e town; *(Groß-)* city

Städt|chen *nt* -s,- small town. **s~isch** *a* urban; *(kommunal)* municipal

Stadt|mauer *f* city wall. **S~mitte** *f* town centre. **S~plan** *m* street map. **S~teil** *m* district. **S~zentrum** *nt* town centre

Staffel *f* -,-n team; *(S~lauf)* relay; *(Mil)* squadron

Staffelei *f* -,-en easel

Staffel|lauf *m* relay race. **s~n** *vt* stagger; *(abstufen)* grade

Stagn|ation *f* -'tsio:n/ *f* - stagnation. **s~ieren** *vi (haben)* stagnate

Stahl *m* -s steel. **S~beton** *m* reinforced concrete

Stall *m* -[e]s,-e stable; *(Kuh-)* shed; *(Schweine-)* sty; *(Hühner-)* coop; *(Kaninchen-)* hutch

Stamm *m* -[e]s,-e trunk; *(Sippe)* tribe; *(Kern)* core; *(Wort-)* stem. **S~baum** *m* family tree; *(eines Tieres)* pedigree

stammeln *vt/i (haben)* stammer

stammen *vi (haben)* come/*(zeitlich)* date *(von/aus* from); *das Zitat stammt von Goethe* the quotation is from Goethe

Stamm|gast *m* regular. **S~halter** *m* son and heir

Stammkundschaft *f* regulars *pl*. **S~lokal** *nt* favourite pub. **S~tisch** *m* table reserved for the regulars; *(Treffen)* meeting of the regulars

stämmig *a* sturdy

stampf|en *vi (haben)* stamp; *(Maschine:)* pound; *mit den Füßen* **s~en** stamp one's feet □ *vi (sein)* tramp □ *vt* pound; mash *(Kartoffeln)*. **S~kartoffeln** *fpl* mashed potatoes

Stand *m* -[e]s,-e standing position; *(Zustand)* state; *(Spiel-)* score; *(Höhe)* level; *(gesellschaftlich)* class; *(Verkaufs-)* stall; *(Messe-)* stand; *(Taxi-)* rank; *auf den neuesten S~ bringen* update

Standard *m* -s,-s standard. **s~isieren** *vt* standardize

Standarte *f* -,-n standard

Standbild *nt* statue

Ständchen *nt* -s,- serenade; *jdm ein S~ bringen* serenade s.o.

Ständer *m* -s,- stand; *(Geschirr-, Platten-)* rack; *(Kerzen-)* holder

Standesamt *nt* registry office. **S~beamte(r)** *m* registrar. **S~unterschied** *m* class distinction

stand|haft *a* steadfast, *adv* -ly. **s~halten†** *vi sep (haben)* stand firm; etw (dat) s~halten stand up to sth

ständig a constant, adv -ly; (fest) permanent, adv -ly

Stand|licht nt sidelights pl. S~ort m position; (Firmen-) location; (Mil) garrison. S~pauke f (fam) dressing-down. S~punkt m point of view. S~spur f hard shoulder. S~uhr f grandfather clock

Stange f -,-n bar; (Holz-) pole; (Gardinen-) rail; (Hühner-) perch; (Zimt-) stick; von der S~ (fam) off the peg. S~nbohne f runner bean. S~nbrot nt French bread

Stanniol nt -s tin foil. S~papier nt silver paper

stanzen vt stamp; (aus-) punch out; punch (Loch)

Stapel m -s,- stack, pile; vom S~ laufen be launched. S~lauf m launch[ing]. s~n vt stack or pile up; sich s~n pile up

stapfen vi (sein) tramp, trudge

Star[1] m -[e]s,-e starling

Star[2] m -[e]s (Med) [grauer] S~ cataract; grüner S~ glaucoma

Star[3] m -s,-s (Theat, Sport) star

stark a (stärker, stärkst) strong; (Motor) powerful; (Verkehr, Regen) heavy; (Hitze, Kälte) severe; (groß) big; (schlimm) bad; (dick) thick; (korpulent) stout □ adv strongly; heavily; badly; (sehr) very much

Stärk|e f -,-n (s. stark) strength; power; thickness; stoutness; (Größe) size; (Mais-, Wäsche-) starch. S~emehl nt cornflour. s~en vt strengthen; starch (Wäsche); sich s~en fortify oneself. S~ung f -,-en strengthening; (Erfrischung) refreshment

starr a rigid, adv -ly; (steif) stiff, adv -ly; (Blick) fixed; (unbeugsam) inflexible, adv -bly

starren vi (haben) stare; vor Schmutz s~ be filthy

starr|köpfig a stubborn. S~sinn m obstinacy. s~sinnig a obstinate, adv -ly

Start m -s,-s start; (Aviat) take-off. S~bahn f runway. s~en vi (sein) start; (Aviat) take off; (aufbrechen) set off; (teilnehmen) compete □ vt start; (fig) launch

Station /-'tsio:n/ f -,-en station; (Haltestelle) stop; (Abschnitt) stage; (Med) ward; S~ machen break one's journey; bei freier S~ all found. s~är a as an inpatient. s~ieren vt station

statisch a static

Statist(in) m -en,-en (f -,-nen) (Theat) extra

Statistik f -,-en statistics sg; (Aufstellung) statistics pl. s~sch a statistical, adv -ly

Stativ nt -s,-e (Phot) tripod

statt prep (+ gen) instead of; s~dessen instead □ conj s~ etw zu tun instead of doing sth

Stätte f -,-n place

statt|finden vi sep (haben) take place. s~haft a permitted

stattlich a imposing; (beträchtlich) considerable

Statue /'ʃta:tuə/ f -,-n statue

Statur f - build, stature

Status m - status. S~symbol nt status symbol

Statut nt -[e]s,-en statute

Stau m -[e]s,-s congestion; (Auto) [traffic] jam; (Rück-) tailback

Staub m -[e]s dust; S~ wischen dust; S~ saugen vacuum, hoover

Staubecken nt reservoir

staub|en vi (haben) raise dust; es s~t it's dusty. S~ig a dusty. s~saugen vt/i (haben) vacuum, hoover. S~sauger m vacuum cleaner, Hoover (P). S~tuch nt duster

Staudamm m dam

Staude f -,-n shrub

stauen *vt* dam up; **sich s~** accumulate; ⟨*Autos:*⟩ form a tailback

staunen *vi (haben)* be amazed or astonished. **S~** *nt* -s amazement, astonishment

Stau|see *m* reservoir. **S~ung** *f* -,-en congestion; ⟨*Auto*⟩ [traffic] jam

Steak /ʃteːk, steːk/ *nt* -s,-s steak

stechen† *vt* stick (**in** + *acc* in); ⟨*verletzen*⟩ prick; ⟨*mit Messer*⟩ stab; ⟨*Insekt:*⟩ sting; ⟨*Mücke:*⟩ bite; ⟨*gravieren*⟩ engrave □ *vi (haben)* prick; ⟨*Insekt:*⟩ sting; ⟨*Mücke:*⟩ bite; ⟨*mit Stechuhr*⟩ clock in/out; **in See s~** put to sea. **s~d** *a* stabbing; ⟨*Geruch*⟩ pungent

Stech|ginster *m* gorse. **S~kahn** *m* punt. **S~mücke** *f* mosquito. **S~palme** *f* holly. **S~uhr** *f* time clock

Steck|brief *m* 'wanted' poster. **S~dose** *f* socket. **s~en** *vt* put; ⟨*mit Nadel, Reißzwecke*⟩ pin; ⟨*pflanzen*⟩ plant □ *vi (haben)* be (*fest-*) be stuck; **hinter etw** (*dat*) **s~en** ⟨*fig*⟩ be behind sth

Stecken *m* -s,- ⟨*SGer*⟩ stick

stecken|bleiben† *vi sep (sein)* get stuck. **s~lassen†** *vt sep* leave. **S~pferd** *nt* hobby-horse

Steck|er *m* -s,- ⟨*Electr*⟩ plug. **S~ling** *m* -s,-e cutting. **S~nadel** *f* pin. **S~rübe** *f* swede

Steg *m* -[e]s,-e foot-bridge; ⟨*Boots-*⟩ landing-stage; ⟨*Brillen-*⟩ bridge. **S~reif** *m* **aus dem S~reif** extempore

stehen† *vi (haben)* stand; ⟨*sich befinden*⟩ be; (*still-*) be stationary; ⟨*Maschine, Uhr:*⟩ have stopped; **vor dem Ruin s~** face ruin; **jdm/etw s~** ⟨*fig*⟩ stand by s.o./sth; **gut s~** ⟨*Chancen, Aktien:*⟩ be doing well; ⟨*Chancen:*⟩ be good; **jdm [gut] s~** suit s.o.; **sich gut s~** be on good terms; **es**

steht 3 zu 1 the score is 3 – 1; **es steht schlecht um ihn** he is in a bad way. **S~** *nt* -s standing; **zum S~ bringen/kommen** bring/come to a standstill. **s~bleiben†** *vi sep (sein)* stop; ⟨*Motor:*⟩ stall; ⟨*Zeit:*⟩ stand still; ⟨*Gebäude:*⟩ be left standing. **s~d** *a* standing; ⟨*sich nicht bewegend*⟩ stationary; ⟨*Gewässer*⟩ stagnant. **s~lassen†** *vt sep* leave; **sich** (*dat*) **einen Bart s~lassen** grow a beard

Steh|lampe *f* standard lamp. **S~leiter** *f* step-ladder

stehlen† *vt/i (haben)* steal; **sich s~** steal, creep

Steh|platz *m* standing place. **S~vermögen** *nt* stamina, staying-power

steif *a* stiff, *adv* -ly. **S~heit** *f* - stiffness

Steig|bügel *m* stirrup. **S~eisen** *nt* crampon

steigen† *vi (sein)* climb; ⟨*hochgehen*⟩ rise, go up; ⟨*Schulden, Spannung:*⟩ mount; **s~ auf** (+*acc*) climb on [to] ⟨*Stuhl*⟩; climb ⟨*Berg, Leiter*⟩; get on ⟨*Pferd, Fahrrad*⟩; **s~ in** (+ *acc*) climb into; get in ⟨*Auto*⟩; get on ⟨*Bus, Zug*⟩; **s~ aus** climb out of; get out of ⟨*Bett, Auto*⟩; get off ⟨*Bus, Zug*⟩; **einen Drachen s~lassen** fly a kite; **s~de Preise** rising prices

steiger|n *vt* increase; **sich s~n** increase; ⟨*sich verbessern*⟩ improve. **S~ung** *f* -,-en increase; improvement; ⟨*Gram*⟩ comparison

Steigung *f* -,-en gradient; ⟨*Hang*⟩ slope

steil *a* steep, *adv* -ly. **S~küste** *f* cliffs *pl*

Stein *m* -[e]s,-e stone; ⟨*Ziegel-*⟩ brick; ⟨*Spiel-*⟩ piece. **s~alt** *a* ancient. **S~bock** *m* ibex; ⟨*Astr*⟩ Capricorn. **S~bruch** *m* quarry. **S~garten** *m* rockery. **S~gut** *nt*

earthenware. **s~hart** a rock-
hard. **s~ig** a stony. **s~igen** vt
stone. **S~kohle** f [hard] coal.
s~reich a (fam) very rich.
S~schlag m rock fall

Stelle f -,-n place; (Fleck) spot;
(Abschnitt) passage; (Stellung)
job, post; (Büro) office; (Behörde)
authority; **kahle S~** bare patch;
auf der S~ immediately; **an
deiner S~** in your place

stellen vt put; (aufrecht) stand; set
(Wecker, Aufgabe); ask (Frage);
make (Antrag, Forderung, Diagnose); **zur Verfügung s~** provide; **lauter/leiser s~** turn up/
down; **kalt/warm s~** chill/keep
hot; **sich s~** [go and] stand; give
oneself up (**der Polizei** to the
police); **sich tot/schlafend s~**
pretend to be dead/asleep; **gut
gestellt sein** to be well off

Stellen|anzeige f job advertise-
ment. **S~vermittlung** f employment agency. **s~weise** adv in
places

Stellung f -,-en position; (Arbeit)
job; **S~ nehmen** make a statement (**zu** on). **s~slos** a jobless.
S~suche f job-hunting

stellvertret|end a deputy ...
□adv as a deputy; **s~end für jdn**
on s.o.'s behalf. **S~er** m deputy

Stellwerk nt signal-box

Stelzen fpl stilts. **s~** vi (sein)
stalk

stemmen vt press; lift (Gewicht);
sich s~ gegen brace oneself
against

Stempel m -s,- stamp; (Post-) post-
mark; (Präge-) die; (Feingehalts-)
hallmark. **s~n** vt stamp; hallmark (Silber); cancel (Marke)

Stengel m -s,- stalk, stem

Steno f - (fam) shorthand

Steno|gramm nt -[e]s,-e short-
hand text. **S~graphie** f - shorthand. **s~graphieren** vt take
down in shorthand □vi (haben)

do shorthand. **S~typistin** f
-,-nen shorthand typist

Steppdecke f quilt

Steppe f -,-n steppe

Steptanz m tap-dance

sterben† vi (sein) die (**an**+dat
of); **im S~ liegen** be dying

sterblich a mortal. **S~e(r)** m/f
mortal. **S~keit** f - mortality

stereo adv in stereo. **S~anlage** f
stereo [system]

stereotyp a stereotyped

steril a sterile. **s~isieren** vt ster-
ilize. **S~ität** f - sterility

Stern m -[e]s,-e star. **S~bild** nt
constellation. **S~chen** nt -s,- asterisk. **S~kunde** f astronomy.
S~schnuppe f -,-n shooting
star. **S~warte** f -,-n observatory

stetig a steady, adv -ily

stets adv always

Steuer[1] nt -s,- steering-wheel;
(Naut) helm; **am S~** at the wheel

Steuer[2] f -,-n tax

Steuer|bord nt -[e]s starboard
[side]. **S~erklärung** f tax return. **s~frei** a & adv tax-free.
S~mann m (pl -leute) helms-
man; (beim Rudern) cox. **s~n** vt
steer; (Aviat) pilot; (Techn) control □vi (haben) be at the wheel/
(Naut) helm □(sein) head (**nach**
for). **s~pflichtig** a taxable.
S~rad nt steering-wheel.
S~ruder nt helm. **S~ung** f -
steering; (Techn) controls pl.
S~zahler m -s,- taxpayer

Stewardeß /ˈstjuːədɛs/ f -,-dessen
air hostess, stewardess

Stich m -[e]s,-e prick; (Messer-)
stab; (S~wunde) stab wound;
(Bienen-) sting; (Mücken-) bite;
(Schmerz) stabbing pain; (Näh-)
stitch; (Kupfer-) engraving; (Kartenspiel) trick; **S~ ins Rötliche**
tinge of red; **jdn im S~ lassen**
leave s.o. in the lurch; (Gedächtnis:) fail s.o. **s~eln** vi (haben)
make snide remarks

Stich|flamme f jet of flame.
s~haltig a valid. **S~probe** f
spot check. **S~wort** nt (pl
-wörter) headword; (pl -worte)
(Theat) cue; **S~worte** notes

stick|en vt/i (haben) embroider.
S~erei f embroidery

stickig a stuffy

Stickstoff m nitrogen

Stiefbruder m stepbrother

Stiefel m -s,- boot

Stief|kind nt stepchild. **S~mut-**
ter f stepmother. **S~mütter-**
chen nt -s,- pansy. **S~schwe-**
ster f stepsister. **S~sohn** m step-
son. **S~tochter** f stepdaughter.
S~vater m stepfather

Stiege f -,-n stairs pl

Stiel m -[e]s,-e handle; (Blumen-
Gläser-) stem; (Blatt-) stalk

Stier m -[e]s,-e bull; (Astr)
Taurus

stieren vi (haben) stare

Stier|kampf m bullfight

Stift¹ m -[e]s,-e pin; (Nagel) tack;
(Blei-) pencil; (Farb-) crayon

Stift² nt -[e]s,-e [endowed] foundation. **s~en** vt endow; (spenden) donate; create (Unheil, Verwirrung); bring about (Frieden).
S~er m -s,- founder; (Spender)
donor. **S~ung** f -,-en foundation;
(Spende) donation

Stigma nt -s (fig) stigma

Stil m -[e]s,-e style; in großem
S~ in style. **s~isiert** a stylized.
s~istisch a stylistic, adv -ally

still a quiet, adv -ly; (reglos, ohne
Kohlensäure) still; (heimlich)
secret, adv -ly; der **S~e** Ozean
the Pacific; im **s~en** secretly;
(bei sich) inwardly. **S~e** f -
quiet; (Schweigen) silence

Stilleben nt still life

stilleg|en vt sep close down.
S~ung f -,-en closure

stillen vt satisfy; quench (Durst);
stop (Schmerzen, Blutung);
breast-feed (Kind)

stillhalten† vi sep (haben) keep
still

Stillschweigen nt silence. **s~d** a
silent, adv -ly; (fig) tacit, adv -ly

still|sitzen† vi sep (haben) sit
still. **S~stand** m standstill; zum
S~stand bringen stop. **s~ste-**
hen† vi sep (haben) stand still;
(anhalten) stop; (Verkehr:) be at a
standstill

Stil|möbel pl reproduction furni-
ture sg. **s~voll** a stylish, adv -ly

Stimm|bänder ntpl vocal cords.
s~berechtigt a entitled to vote.
S~bruch m er ist im **S~bruch**
his voice is breaking

Stimme f -,-n voice; (Wahl-) vote

stimmen vi (haben) be right;
(wählen) vote; **stimmt das?** is
that right/(wahr) true? □ vt tune;
jdn traurig/fröhlich s~ make
s.o. feel sad/happy

Stimm|enthaltung f abstention.
S~recht nt right to vote

Stimmung f -,-en mood; (Atmosphäre) atmosphere. **s~svoll** a
full of atmosphere

Stimmzettel m ballot-paper

stimulieren vt stimulate

stink|en† vi (haben) smell/(stark)
stink (nach of). **S~tier** nt skunk

Stipendium nt -s,-ien scholarship; (Beihilfe) grant

Stirn f -,-en forehead; die **S~**
bieten (+ dat) (fig) defy. **S~-**
runzeln nt -s frown

stöbern vi (haben) rummage

stochern vi (haben) **s~ in** (+ dat)
poke (Feuer); pick at (Essen);
pick (Zähne)

Stock¹ m -[e]s,-e stick; (Ski-) pole;
(Bienen-) hive; (Rosen-) bush;
(Reb-) vine

Stock² m -[e]s,- storey, floor.
S~bett nt bunk-beds pl. **s~dun-**
kel a (fam) pitch-dark

stock|en vi (haben) stop; (Verk-
kehr:) come to a standstill; (Person:) falter. **s~end** a hesitant,

adv -ly. s~**taub** a (fam) stone-deaf. S~**ung** f -,-en hold-up

Stockwerk nt storey, floor

Stoff m -[e]s,-e substance; (Tex) fabric, material; (Thema) subject [matter]; (Gesprächs-) topic. S~**tier** nt soft toy. S~**wechsel** m metabolism

stöhnen vi (haben) groan, moan. S~ nt -s groan, moan

stoisch a stoic, adv -ally

Stola f -,-len stole

Stollen m -s,- gallery; (Kuchen) stollen

stolpern vi (sein) stumble; s~ **über** (+ acc) trip over

stolz a proud (auf + acc of), adv -ly. S~ m -es pride

stolzieren vi (sein) strut

stopfen vt stuff; (stecken) put; (ausbessern) darn □ vi (haben) be constipating; (fam: essen) guzzle

Stopp m -s,-s stop. s~ int stop!

stoppel|ig a stubbly. S~n fpl stubble sg

stopp|en vt stop; (Sport) time □ vi (haben) stop. S~**schild** nt stop sign. S~**uhr** f stop-watch

Stöpsel m -s,- plug; (Flaschen-) stopper

Storch m -[e]s,-̈e stork

Store f /ʃtoːɐ̯/ m -s,-s net curtain

stören vt disturb; disrupt (Rede, Sitzung); jam (Sender); (mißfallen) bother; **stört es Sie, wenn ich rauche?** do you mind if I smoke? □ vi (haben) be a nuisance; **entschuldigen Sie, daß ich störe** I'm sorry to bother you

stornieren vt cancel

störrisch a stubborn, adv -ly

Störung f -,-en (s. stören) disturbance; disruption; (Med) trouble; (Radio) interference; **technische S~** technical fault

Stoß m -es,-̈e push, knock; (mit Ellbogen) dig; (Hörner-) butt; (mit Waffe) thrust; (Schwimm-) stroke; (Ruck) jolt; (Erd-) shock;

(Stapel) stack, pile. S~**dämpfer** m -s,- shock absorber

stoßen† vt push, knock; (mit Füßen) kick; (mit Kopf, Hörnern) butt; (an-) poke, nudge; (treiben) thrust; **sich s~** knock oneself; **sich (dat) den Kopf s~** hit one's head □ vi (haben) push; s~ **an** (+ acc) knock against; (angrenzen) adjoin □ vi (sein) s~ **gegen** knock against; bump into (Tür); s~ **auf** (+ acc) bump into; (entdecken) come across; strike (Öl); (fig) meet with (Ablehnung)

Stoß|stange f bumper. S~**verkehr** m rush-hour traffic. S~**zahn** m tusk. S~**zeit** f rush-hour

stottern vt/i (haben) stutter, stammer

Str. abbr (Straße) St

Straf|anstalt f prison. S~**arbeit** f (Sch) imposition. s~**bar** a punishable; **sich s~bar machen** commit an offence

Strafe f -,-n punishment; (Jur & fig) penalty; (Geld-) fine; (Freiheits-) sentence. s~n vt punish

straff a tight, taut. s~en vt tighten; **sich s~en** tighten

Strafgesetz nt criminal law

sträf|lich a criminal, adv -ly. S~**ling** m -s,-e prisoner

Straf|mandat nt (Auto) [parking/speeding] ticket. S~**porto** nt excess postage. S~**predigt** f (fam) lecture. S~**raum** m penalty area. S~**stoß** m penalty. S~**tat** f crime. S~**zettel** m (fam) = S~**mandat**

Strahl m -[e]s,-en ray; (einer Taschenlampe) beam; (Wasser-) jet. s~**en** vi (haben) shine; (funkeln) sparkle; (lächeln) beam. S~**enbehandlung** f radiotherapy. s~**end** a shining; sparkling; beaming; radiant (Schönheit)

S~**entherapie** f radiotherapy. S~**ung** f - radiation

Strähn|e f -,-n strand. s~**ig** a straggly

stramm a tight, adv -ly; (kräftig) sturdy; (gerade) upright

Strampel|**höschen** nt -s,- rompers pl. s~**n** vi (haben) ⟨Baby:⟩ kick

Strand m -[e]s,-̈e beach. s~**en** vi (sein) run aground; (fig) fail. S~**korb** m wicker beach-chair. S~**promenade** f promenade

Strang m -[e]s,-̈e rope

Strapaz|e f -,-n strain. s~**ieren** vt be hard on; tax ⟨Nerven, Geduld⟩. s~**ierfähig** a hard-wearing. s~**iös** a exhausting

Straß m - &-sses paste

Straße f -,-n road; (in der Stadt auch) street; (Meeres-) strait; **auf der S~** in the road/street. S~**nbahn** f tram, (Amer) streetcar. S~**nkarte** f road-map. S~**nlaterne** f street lamp. S~**nsperre** f road-block

Strat|**egie** f -,-n strategy. s~**egisch** a strategic, adv -ally

sträuben vt ruffle up ⟨Federn⟩; **sich s~** ⟨Fell, Haar:⟩ stand on end; (fig) resist

Strauch m -[e]s,Sträucher bush

straucheln vi (sein) stumble

Strauß[1] m -es, Sträuße bunch [of flowers]; (Bukett) bouquet

Strauß[2] m -es,-e ostrich

Strebe f -,-n brace, strut

streben vi (haben) strive (**nach** for) □ vi (sein) head (**nach/zu** for)

Streb|**er** m -s,- pushy person; (Sch) swot. s~**sam** a industrious

Strecke f -,-n stretch, section; (Entfernung) distance; (Rail) line; (Route) route

strecken vt stretch; (aus-) stretch out; (gerade machen) straighten; (Culin) thin down; **sich s~**

stretch; (sich aus-) stretch out; **den Kopf aus dem Fenster s~** put one's head out of the window

Streich m -[e]s,-e prank, trick; **jdm einen S~ spielen** play a trick on s.o.

streicheln vt stroke

streichen† vt spread; (weg-) smooth; (an-) paint; (aus-) delete; (kürzen) cut □ vi (haben) s~ **über** (+ acc) stroke

Streicher m -s,- string-player; **die S~** the strings

Streichholz nt match. S~**schachtel** f matchbox

Streich|**instrument** nt stringed instrument. S~**käse** m cheese spread. S~**orchester** nt string orchestra. S~**ung** f -,-en deletion; (Kürzung) cut

Streife f -,-n patrol

streifen vt brush against; (berühren) touch; (verletzen) graze; (fig) touch on ⟨Thema⟩; (ziehen) slip (**über** + acc over); **mit dem Blick s~** glance at □ vi (sein) roam

Streifen m -s,- stripe; (Licht-) streak; (auf der Fahrbahn) line; (schmales Stück) strip

Streifenwagen m patrol car. s~**ig** a streaky. S~**schuß** m glancing shot; (Wunde) graze

Streik m -s,-s strike; **in den S~ treten** go on strike. S~**brecher** m strike-breaker, (pej) scab. s~**en** vi (haben) strike; (fam) refuse; (versagen) pack up. S~**ende(r)** m striker. S~**posten** m picket

Streit m -[e]s,-e quarrel; (Auseinandersetzung) dispute. s~**en**† vr/i (haben) [**sich**] s~**en** quarrel. s~**ig** a **jdm etw s~ig machen** dispute s.o.'s right to sth. S~**igkeiten** fpl quarrels. S~**kräfte** fpl armed forces. S~**süchtig** a quarrelsome

streng a strict, adv -ly; ⟨Blick, Ton⟩ stern, adv -ly; ⟨rauh, nüchtern⟩ severe, adv -ly; ⟨Geschmack⟩ sharp. **S~e** f - strictness; sternness; severity. **s~genommen** adv strictly speaking. **s~gläubig** a strict; ⟨orthodox⟩ orthodox. **s~stens** adv strictly

Streß m -sses,-sse stress

stressig a (fam) stressful

streuen vt spread; (ver-) scatter; sprinkle ⟨Zucker, Salz⟩; **die Straßen s~** grit the roads

streunen vi (sein) roam; **s~der Hund** stray dog

Strich m -[e]s,-e line; ⟨Feder-, Pinsel-⟩ stroke; ⟨Morse-, Gedanken-⟩ dash; **gegen den S~** the wrong way; (fig) against the grain. **S~kode** m bar code. **S~punkt** m semicolon

Strick m -[e]s,-e cord; ⟨Seil⟩ rope; (fam: Schlingel) rascal

strick|en vt/i (haben) knit. **S~jacke** f cardigan. **S~leiter** f rope-ladder. **S~nadel** f knitting-needle. **S~waren** fpl knitwear sg. **S~zeug** nt knitting

striegeln vt groom

strikt a strict, adv -ly

strittig a contentious

Stroh nt -[e]s straw. **S~blumen** fpl everlasting flowers. **S~dach** nt thatched roof. **S~gedeckt** a thatched. **S~halm** m straw

Strolch m -[e]s,-e (dated) rascal

Strom m -[e]s,-e river; ⟨Menschen-, Auto-, Blut-⟩ stream; ⟨Tränen-⟩ flood; ⟨Schwall⟩ torrent; ⟨Electr⟩ current, power; **gegen den S~** (fig) against the tide; **es regnet in Strömen** it is pouring with rain. **s~abwärts** adv downstream. **s~aufwärts** adv upstream

strömen vi (sein) flow; ⟨Menschen, Blut:⟩ stream; pour; **s~der Regen** pouring rain

Strom|kreis m circuit. **s~linienförmig** a streamlined. **S~sperre** f power cut

Strömung f -,-en current

Strophe f -,-n verse

strotzen vi (haben) be full (**vor** + dat of); **vor Gesundheit s~** bursting with health

Strudel m -s,- whirlpool; ⟨SGer Culin⟩ strudel

Struktur f -,-en structure; ⟨Tex⟩ texture

Strumpf m -[e]s,-e stocking; ⟨Knie-⟩ sock. **S~band** nt (pl -bänder) suspender, (Amer) garter. **S~bandgürtel** m suspender/(Amer) garter belt. **S~halter** m = **S~band. S~hose** f tights pl, (Amer) pantyhose

Strunk m -[e]s,-e stalk; ⟨Baum-⟩ stump

struppig a shaggy

Stube f -,-n room. **s~nrein** a house-trained

Stuck m -s stucco

Stück nt -[e]s,-e piece; ⟨Zucker-⟩ lump; ⟨Seife⟩ tablet; ⟨Theater-⟩ play; ⟨Gegenstand⟩ item; ⟨Exemplar⟩ specimen; **20 S~ Vieh** 20 head of cattle; **ein S~** (Entfernung) some way; **aus freien S~en** voluntarily. **S~chen** nt -s,- [little] bit. **s~weise** adv bit by bit; (einzeln) singly

Student|(in) m -en,-en (f -,-nen) student. **s~isch** a student . . .

Studie f -ja/ f -,-n study

studier|en vt/i (haben) study. **S~zimmer** nt study

Studio nt -s,-s studio

Studium nt -s,-ien studies pl

Stufe f -,-n step; ⟨Treppen-⟩ stair; ⟨Raketen-⟩ stage; ⟨Niveau⟩ level. **s~n** vt terrace; ⟨staffeln⟩ grade

Stuhl m -[e]s,-e chair; ⟨Med⟩ stools pl. **S~gang** m bowel movement

stülpen vt put (**über** + acc over)

stumm a dumb; (*schweigsam*) silent, adv -ly

Stummel m -s,- stump; (*Zigaretten-*) butt; (*Bleistift-*) stub

Stümper m -s,- bungler. s~**haft** a incompetent, adv -ly

stumpf a blunt; (*Winkel*) obtuse; (*glanzlos*) dull; (*fig*) apathetic, adv -ally. S~ m -[e]s,-e stump

Stumpfsinn m apathy; (*Langweiligkeit*) tedium. s~**ig** a apathetic, adv -ally; (*langweilig*) tedious

Stunde f -,-n hour; (*Sch*) lesson

stunden vt jdm eine Schuld s~ give s.o. time to pay a debt

Stunden|kilometer mpl kilometres per hour. s~**lang** adv for hours. S~**lohn** m hourly rate. S~**plan** m timetable. s~**weise** adv by the hour

stündlich a & adv hourly

Stups m -es,-e nudge; (*Schubs*) push. s~**en** vt nudge; (*schubsen*) push. S~**nase** f snub nose

stur a pigheaded; (*phlegmatisch*) stolid, adv -ly; (*unbeirrbar*) dogged, adv -ly

Sturm m -[e]s,-̈e gale; (*schwer*) storm; (*Mil*) assault

stürm|en vi (*haben*) (*Wind:*) blow hard; **es s~t** it's blowing a gale □vi (*sein*) rush □vt storm; (*bedrängen*) besiege. S~**er** m -s,- forward. s~**isch** a stormy; (*Überfahrt*) rough; (*fig*) tumultuous, adv -ly; (*ungestüm*) tempestuous, adv -ly

Sturz m -es,-̈e [heavy] fall; (*Preis-, Kurs-*) sharp drop; (*Pol*) overthrow

stürzen vi (*sein*) fall [heavily]; (*in die Tiefe*) plunge; (*Preise, Kurse:*) drop sharply; (*Regierung:*) fall; (*eilen*) rush □vt throw; (*umkippen*) turn upside down; turn out (*Speise, Kuchen*); (*Pol*) overthrow, topple; **sich s~** throw oneself (**aus/in** + acc out of/into); **sich s~ auf** (+ acc) pounce on

Sturz|flug m (*Aviat*) dive. S~**helm** m crash-helmet

Stute f -,-n mare

Stütze f -,-n support; (*Kopf-, Arm-*) rest

stutzen vi (*haben*) stop short □vt trim; (*Hort*) cut back; (*kupieren*) crop

stützen vt support; (*auf-*) rest; **sich s~ auf** (+ acc) lean on; (*beruhen*) be based on

Stutzer m -s,- dandy

stutzig a puzzled; (*mißtrauisch*) suspicious

Stützpunkt m (*Mil*) base

Subjekt nt -[e]s,-e subject. s~**iv** a subjective, adv -ly

Subskription /-'tsjoːn/ f -,-en subscription

Substantiv nt -s,-e noun

Substanz f -,-en substance

subtil a subtle, adv -tly

subtrahieren vt subtract. S~**k-tion** /-'tsjoːn/ f -,-en subtraction

Subvention /-'tsjoːn/ f -,-en subsidy. s~**ieren** vt subsidize

subversiv a subversive

Suche f - search; **auf der S~e nach** looking for. s~**en** vt look for; (*intensiv*) search for; seek (*Hilfe, Rat*); '**Zimmer gesucht**' 'room wanted' □vi (*haben*) look, search (**nach** for). S~**er** m -s,- (*Phot*) viewfinder

Sucht f -,-̈e addiction; (*fig*) mania

süchtig a addicted. S~**e(r)** m/f addict

Süd m -[e]s south. S~**afrika** nt South Africa. S~**amerika** nt South America. s~**deutsch** a South German

Süden m -s south; **nach S~** south

Süd|frucht f tropical fruit. s~**lich** a southern; (*Richtung*) southerly □adv & prep (+ gen) s~**lich** [**von**] **der Stadt** [to the] south of the town. s~**osten** m south-east. S~**pol** m South Pole.

s~wärts *adv* southwards.
S~westen *m* south-west

süffisant *a* smug, *adv* -ly

suggerieren *vt* suggest (*dat to*)

Suggest|ion /-'tjo:n/ *f* ~,-en suggestion. s~iv *a* suggestive

Sühne *f* ~,-n atonement; (*Strafe*) penalty. s~n *vt* atone for

Sultanine *f* ~,-n sultana

Sülze *f* ~,-n [meat] jelly; (*Schweinskopf-*) brawn

Summe *f* ~,-n sum

summ|en *vi* (*haben*) hum; (*Biene:*) buzz □*vt* hum. S~er *m* ~-s,- buzzer

summieren (sich) *vr* add up; (*sich häufen*) increase

Sumpf *m* ~[e]s,ˑe marsh, swamp. s~ig *a* marshy

Sünd|e *f* ~,-n sin. S~enbock *m* scapegoat. S~er(in) *m* ~-s,- (*f* ~,-nen) sinner. s~haft *a* sinful. s~igen *vi* (*haben*) sin

super *inv a* (*fam*) great. S~lativ *m* ~-s,-e superlative. S~markt *m* supermarket

Suppe *f* ~,-n soup. S~nlöffel *m* soup-spoon. S~nteller *m* soup-plate. S~nwürfel *m* stock cube

Surf|brett /'sœ:ɐf-/ *nt* surfboard. S~en *nt* ~-s surfing

surren *vi* (*haben*) whirr

süß *a* sweet, *adv* -ly. S~e *f* ~ sweetness. s~en *vt* sweeten. S~igkeit *f* ~,-en sweet. s~lich *a* sweetish; (*fig*) sugary. S~speise *f* sweet. S~stoff *m* sweetener. S~waren *fpl* confectionery *sg*, sweets *pl*. S~wasser- *pref* freshwater

Sylvester *nt* ~-s = Silvester

Symbol *nt* ~-s,-e symbol. S~ik *f* ~ symbolism. s~isch *a* symbolic, *adv* -ally. s~isieren *vt* symbolize

Sym|metrie *f* ~ symmetry. s~metrisch *a* symmetrical, *adv* -ly

Sympathie *f* ~,-n sympathy

sympath|isch *a* agreeable; (*Person*) likeable. s~isieren *vi* (*haben*) be sympathetic (mit to)

Symphonie *f* ~,-n = Sinfonie

Symptom *nt* ~-s,-e symptom. s~atisch *a* symptomatic

Synagoge *f* ~,-n synagogue

synchronisieren /zynkroni'zi:ran/ *vt* synchronize; dub (*Film*)

Syndikat *nt* ~-[e]s,-e syndicate

Syndrom *nt* ~-s,-e syndrome

synonym *a* synonymous, *adv* -ly. S~ *nt* ~-s,-e synonym

Syntax /'zyntaks/ *f* ~ syntax

Synthe|se *f* ~,-n synthesis. S~tik *nt* ~-s synthetic material. s~tisch *a* synthetic, *adv* -ally

Syrien /-jən/ *nt* ~-s Syria

System *nt* ~-s,-e system. s~atisch *a* systematic, *adv* -ally

Szene *f* ~,-n scene. S~rie *f* ~ scenery

T

Tabak *m* ~-s,-e tobacco

Tabelle *f* ~,-n table; (*Sport*) league table

Tablett *nt* ~-[e]s,-s tray

Tablette *f* ~,-n tablet

tabu *a* taboo. T~ *nt* ~-s,-s taboo

Tacho *m* ~-s, Tachometer *m* & *nt* speedometer

Tadel *m* ~-s,- reprimand; (*Kritik*) censure; (*Sch*) black mark. t~los *a* impeccable, *adv* -bly. t~n *vt* reprimand; censure. t~nswert *a* reprehensible

Tafel *f* ~,-n (*Tisch, Tabelle*) table; (*Platte*) slab; (*Anschlag-, Hinweis-*) board; (*Gedenk-*) plaque; (*Schiefer-*) slate; (*Wand-*) blackboard; (*Bild-*) plate; (*Schokolade*) bar. t~n *vi* (*haben*) feast

Täfelung *f* ~ panelling

Tag *m* ~-[e]s,-e day; Tag für Tag day by day; am T~e in the daytime; eines T~es one day; unter

T~e underground; es wird Tag it is getting light; guten Tag! good morning/afternoon! t~aus adv t~aus, t~ein day in, day out

Tage|buch nt diary. t~lang adv for days

tagen vi (haben) meet; ⟨Gericht:⟩ sit; es tagt day is breaking

Tages|anbruch m daybreak. T~ausflug m day trip. T~decke f bedspread. T~karte f day ticket; ⟨Speise⟩ menu of the day. T~licht nt daylight. T~mutter f child-minder. T~ordnung f agenda. T~rückfahrkarte f day return [ticket]. T~zeit f time of the day. T~zeitung f daily [news]paper

täglich a & adv daily; zweimal t~ twice a day

tags adv by day; t~ zuvor/darauf the day before/after

tagsüber adv during the day

tag|täglich a daily □adv every single day. T~traum m daydream. T~undnachtgleiche f ·,-n equinox. T~ung f ·,-en meeting; ⟨Konferenz⟩ conference

Taill|e /'taljə/ f ·,-n waist. t~iert /ta'ji:ɐt/ a fitted

Takt m ·[e]s,-e tact; ⟨Mus⟩ bar; ⟨Tempo⟩ time; ⟨Rhythmus⟩ rhythm; im T~ in time [to the music]. T~gefühl nt tact

Takt|ik f ·tactics pl. t~isch a tactical, adv ·ly

takt|los a tactless, adv ·ly. T~losigkeit f ·tactlessness. T~stock m baton. t~voll a tactful, adv ·ly

Tal nt ·[e]s,-er valley

Talar m ·s,-e robe; ⟨Univ⟩ gown

Talent nt ·[e]s,-e talent. t~iert a talented

Talg m ·s tallow; ⟨Culin⟩ suet

Talsperre f dam

Tampon /tam'põ:/ m ·s,-s tampon

Tang m ·s seaweed

Tangente f ·,-n tangent; ⟨Straße⟩ bypass

Tank m ·s,-s tank. t~en vt fill up with ⟨Benzin⟩. □vi (haben) fill up with petrol; ⟨Aviat⟩ refuel; ich muß t~en I need petrol. T~er m ·s,- tanker. T~stelle f petrol/⟨Amer⟩ gas station. T~wart m ·[e]s,-e petrol-pump attendant

Tanne f ·,-n fir [tree]. T~nbaum m fir tree; ⟨Weihnachtsbaum⟩ Christmas tree. T~nzapfen m fir cone

Tante f ·,-n aunt

Tantiemen /tan'tje:mən/ pl royalties

Tanz m ·es,-e dance. t~en vt/i (haben) dance

Tänzer(in) m ·s,- (f ·,-nen) dancer

Tanz|lokal nt dance-hall. T~musik f dance music

Tapete f ·,-n wallpaper. T~nwechsel m ⟨fam⟩ change of scene

tapezier|en vt paper. T~er m ·s,- paperhanger, decorator

tapfer a brave, adv ·ly. T~keit f · bravery

tappen vi (sein) walk hesitantly; ⟨greifen⟩ grope (nach for)

Tarif m ·s,-e rate; ⟨Verzeichnis⟩ tariff

tarn|en vt disguise; ⟨Mil⟩ camouflage; sich t~en disguise/camouflage oneself. T~ung f ·disguise; camouflage

Tasche f ·,-n pocket; ⟨Hosen-, Hand-tel-⟩ pocket. T~nbuch nt paperback. T~ndieb m pickpocket. T~ngeld nt pocket-money. T~nlampe f torch, ⟨Amer⟩ flashlight. T~nmesser nt penknife. T~ntuch nt handkerchief

Tasse f ·,-n cup

Tastatur f ·,-en keyboard

tast|bar a palpable. T~e f ·,-n key; ⟨Druck-⟩ push-button. t~en vi (haben) feel, grope (nach for)

□ *vt* key in ⟨*Daten*⟩; **sich t~en** feel one's way (**zu** to). **t~end** *a* tentative, *adv* -ly

Tat *f* -,-en action; ⟨*Helden*-⟩ deed; ⟨*Straf*-⟩ crime; **in der Tat** indeed; **auf frischer Tat ertappt** caught in the act. **t~enlos** *adv* passively

Täter(in) *m* -s,- (*f* -,-nen) culprit; ⟨*Jur*⟩ offender

tätig *a* active, *adv* -ly; **t~ sein** work. **T~keit** *f* -,-en activity; ⟨*Funktionieren*⟩ action; ⟨*Arbeit*⟩ work, job

Tatkraft *f* energy

tätlich *a* physical, *adv* -ly; **t~ werden** become violent. **T~keiten** *fpl* violence *sg*

Tatort *m* scene of the crime

tätowier|en *vt* tattoo. **T~ung** *f* -,-en tattooing; ⟨*Bild*⟩ tattoo

Tatsache *f* fact. **T~nbericht** *m* documentary

tatsächlich *a* actual, *adv* -ly

tätscheln *vt* pat

Tatze *f* -,-n paw

Tau¹ *m* -[e]s dew

Tau² *nt* -[e]s,-e rope

taub *a* deaf; ⟨*gefühllos*⟩ numb; ⟨*Nuß*⟩ empty; ⟨*Gestein*⟩ worthless

Taube *f* -,-n pigeon; ⟨*Turtel- & fig*⟩ dove. **T~nschlag** *m* pigeon-loft

Taub|heit *f* - deafness; ⟨*Gefühllosigkeit*⟩ numbness. **t~stumm** *a* deaf and dumb

tauch|en *vt* dip, plunge; ⟨*unter*-⟩ duck □ *vi* (*haben/sein*) dive/⟨*ein*-⟩ plunge (**in** + *acc* into); ⟨*auf*-⟩ appear (**aus** out of). **T~er** *m* -s,- diver. **T~eranzug** *m* diving-suit. **T~sieder** *m* -s,- [small, portable] immersion heater

tauen *vi* (*sein*) melt, thaw □ *impers* **es taut** it is thawing

Tauf|becken *nt* font. **T~e** *f* -,-n christening, baptism. **t~en** *vt* christen, baptize. **T~pate** *m* godfather. **T~stein** *m* font

tauge|n *vi* (*haben*) **etwas/nichts t~n** be good/no good; **zu etw t~n/nicht t~n** be good/no good for sth. **T~nichts** *m* -es,-e good-for-nothing

tauglich *a* suitable; ⟨*Mil*⟩ fit. **T~keit** *f* - suitability; fitness

Taumel *m* -s daze; **wie im T~** in a daze. **t~n** *vi* (*sein*) stagger

Tausch *m* -[e]s,-e exchange, ⟨*fam*⟩ swap. **t~en** *vt* exchange/⟨*handeln*⟩ barter (**gegen** for); **die Plätze t~en** change places □ *vi* (*haben*) swap (**mit etw** sth; **mit jdm** with s.o.)

täuschen *vt* deceive, fool; betray ⟨*Vertrauen*⟩; **sich t~** delude oneself; ⟨*sich irren*⟩ be mistaken □ *vi* (*haben*) be deceptive. **t~d** *a* deceptive; ⟨*Ähnlichkeit*⟩ striking

Tausch|geschäft *nt* exchange. **T~handel** *m* barter; ⟨*T~geschäft*⟩ exchange

Täuschung *f* -,-en deception; ⟨*Irrtum*⟩ mistake; ⟨*Illusion*⟩ delusion

tausend *inv a* one/a thousand. **T~** *nt* -s,-e thousand. **T~füßler** *m* -s,- centipede. **t~ste(r,s)** *a* thousandth. **T~stel** *nt* -s,- thousandth

Tau|tropfen *m* dewdrop. **T~wetter** *nt* thaw. **T~ziehen** *nt* -s tug of war

Taxe *f* -,-n charge; ⟨*Kur*-⟩ tax; ⟨*Taxi*⟩ taxi

Taxi *nt* -s,-s taxi, cab

taxieren *vt* estimate/⟨*im Wert*⟩ value (**auf** + *acc* at); ⟨*fam*: *mustern*⟩ size up

Taxi|fahrer *m* taxi driver. **T~stand** *m* taxi rank

Teakholz /'tiːk-/ *nt* teak

Team /tiːm/ *nt* -s,-s team

Technik *f* -,-en technology; ⟨*Methode*⟩ technique. **T~ker** *m* -s,- technician. **t~sch** *a* technical, *adv* -ly; ⟨*technologisch*⟩ technological, *adv* -ly; **T~sche**

Hochschule Technical University

Techno|logie f -,-n technology.
t~**logisch** a technological
Teckel m -s,- dachshund
Teddybär m teddy bear
Tee m -s,-s tea. T~**beutel** m tea-bag. T~**kanne** f teapot. T~**kessel** m kettle. T~**löffel** m teaspoon
Teer m -s tar. t~**en** vt tar
Tee|sieb nt tea-strainer. t~**tasse** f teacup. T~**wagen** m [tea] trolley
Teich m -[e]s,-e pond
Teig m -[e]s,-e pastry; (Knet-) dough; (Rühr-) mixture; (Pfannkuchen-) batter. T~**rolle** f, T~**roller** m rolling-pin. T~**waren** fpl pasta sg
Teil m -[e]s,-e part; (Bestand-) component; (Jur) party; der vordere T~ the front part; zum T~ partly; zum großen/größten T~ for the most part □m & nt -[e]s (Anteil) share; sein[en] T~ beitragen do one's share; ich für mein[en] T~ for my part □nt -[e]s,-e part; (Ersatz-) spare part; (Anbau-) unit
teil|bar a divisible. T~**en** vt divide; (auf-) share out; (gemeinsam haben) share; (Pol) partition ⟨Land⟩; sich (dat) etw [mit jdm] t~**en** share sth [with s.o.]; sich t~**en** divide; (sich gabeln) fork; ⟨Vorhang:⟩ open; ⟨Meinungen:⟩ differ □vi (haben) share
teilhab|en† vi sep (haben) share (an etw dat sth). T~**er** m -s,- (Comm) partner
Teilnahm|e f - participation; (innere) interest; (Mitgefühl) sympathy. t~**slos** a apathetic, adv -ally
teilnehm|en† vi sep (haben) t~**en an** (+dat) take part in; (mitfühlen) share [in]. T~**er(in)**

m -s,- (f -,-nen) participant; (an Wettbewerb) competitor
teil|s adv partly. T~**ung** f -,-en division; (Pol) partition. t~**weise** a partial □adv partially, partly; (manchmal) in some cases. T~**zahlung** f part-payment; (Rate) instalment. T~**zeitbeschäftigung** f part-time job
Teint /tɛ̃/ m -s,-s complexion
Telefax nt fax
Telefon nt -s,-e [tele]phone. T~**anruf** m, T~**at** nt -[e]s,-e [tele]phone call. T~**buch** nt [tele]phone book. t~**ieren** vi (haben) [tele]phone
telefon|isch a [telephone ... □adv by [tele]phone. T~**ist(in)** m -en,-en (f -,-nen) telephonist. T~**karte** f phone card. T~**nummer** f [tele]phone number. T~**zelle** f [tele]phone box
Telegraf m -en,-en telegraph. T~**enmast** m telegraph pole. t~**ieren** vi (haben) send a telegram. t~**isch** a telegraphic □adv by telegram
Telegramm nt -s,-e telegram
Telegraph m -en,-en = Telegraf
Teleobjektiv nt telephoto lens
Telepathie f - telepathy
Telephon nt -s,-e = Telefon
Teleskop nt -s,-e telescope. t~**isch** a telescopic
Telex nt -,-[e] telex. t~**en** vt telex
Teller m -s,- plate
Tempel m -s,- temple
Temperament nt -s,-e temperament; (Lebhaftigkeit) vivacity. t~**los** a dull. t~**voll** a vivacious; ⟨Pferd:⟩ spirited
Temperatur f -,-en temperature
Tempo nt -s,-s speed; (Mus: pl -pi) tempo; T~ [T~]! hurry up!
Tenden|z f -,-en trend; (Neigung) tendency. t~**ieren** vi (haben) tend (zu towards)

Tennis nt - tennis. T~platz m tennis-court. T~schläger m tennis-racket

Tenor m -s,-̈e (Mus) tenor

Teppich m -s,-e carpet. T~boden m fitted carpet

Termin m -s,-e date; (Arzt-) appointment; [letzter] T~ deadline. T~kalender m [appointments] diary

Terminologie f -,-n terminology

Terpentin nt -s turpentine

Terrain /tɛˈrɛ̃ː/ nt -s,-s terrain

Terrasse f -,-n terrace

Terrier /ˈtɛriɐ/ m -s,- terrier

Terrine f -,-n tureen

Territorium nt -s,-ien territory

Terror m -s terror. t~isieren vt terrorize. T~ismus m - terrorism. T~ist m -en,-en terrorist

Terzett nt -[e]s,-e [vocal] trio

Tesafilm (P) m ≈ Sellotape (P)

Test m -[e]s,-s & -e test

Testament nt -[e]s,-e will; Altes/ Neues T~ Old/New Testament. T~svollstrecker m -s,- executor

testen vt test

Tetanus m - tetanus

teuer a expensive, adv -ly; (lieb) dear; wie t~? how much? T~ung f -,-en rise in prices

Teufel m -s,- devil; zum T~! (sl) damn [it]! T~skreis m vicious circle

teuflisch a fiendish

Text m -[e]s,-e text; (Passage) passage; (Bild-) caption; (Lied-) lyrics pl, words pl; (Opern-) libretto. T~er m -s,- copy-writer; (Schlager-) lyricist

Textil|ien /-jən/ pl textiles; (Textilwaren) textile goods. T~industrie f textile industry

Textverarbeitungssystem nt word processor

TH abbr = Technische Hochschule

Theater nt -s,- theatre; (fam: Getue) fuss, to-do; T~ spielen act; (fam) put on an act. T~kasse f box-office. T~stück nt play

theatralisch a theatrical, adv -ly

Theke f -,-n bar; (Ladentisch) counter

Thema nt -s,-men subject; (Mus) theme

Themse f - Thames

Theolo|ge m -n,-n theologian. T~gie f - theology

theor|etisch a theoretical, adv -ly. T~ie f -,-n theory

Therapeut(in) m -en,-en (f -,-nen) therapist. t~isch a therapeutic

Therapie f -,-n therapy

Thermal|bad nt thermal bath; (Ort) thermal spa. T~quelle f thermal spring

Thermometer nt -s,- thermometer

Thermosflasche (P) f Thermos flask (P)

Thermostat m -[e]s,-e thermostat

These f -,-n thesis

Thrombose f -,-n thrombosis

Thron m -[e]s,-e throne. t~en vi (haben) sit [in state]. T~folge f succession. T~folger m -s,- heir to the throne

Thunfisch m tuna

Thymian m -s thyme

Tick m -s,-s (fam) quirk; einen T~ haben be crazy

ticken vi (haben) tick

tief a deep; (t~liegend, niedrig) low; (t~gründig) profound; t~er Teller soup-plate; im t~sten Winter in the depths of winter ◻ adv deep; low; (sehr) deeply, profoundly; ⟨schlafen⟩ soundly. T~ nt -s,-s (Meteorol) depression. T~bau m civil engineering. T~e f -,-n depth

Tief|ebene f [lowland] plain. T~garage f underground car

park. t~gekühlt a [deep-]fro-
zen. t~greifend a radical, adv
-ly. t~gründig a (fig) profound
Tiefkühl|fach nt freezer com-
partment. **T~kost** f frozen food.
T~truhe f deep-freeze
Tief|land nt lowlands pl.
T~punkt m (fig) low.
t~schürfend a (fig) profound.
t~sinnig a (fig) profound; (trüb-
sinnig) melancholy. **T~stand** m
(fig) low
Tiefsttemperatur f minimum
temperature
Tier nt [e]s,-e animal. **T~arzt**
m, **T~ärztin** f vet, veterinary
surgeon. **T~garten** m zoo.
t~isch a animal ...; (fig: roh)
bestial. **T~kreis** m zodiac.
T~kreiszeichen nt sign of the
zodiac. **T~kunde** f zoology.
T~quälerei f cruelty to animals
Tiger m -s,- tiger
tilgen vt pay off (Schuld); (streichen) delete; (fig: auslöschen)
wipe out
Tinte f -,-n ink. **T~nfisch** m
squid
Tip m -s,-s (fam) tip
tipp|en vt (fam) type □vi (haben)
(berühren) touch (auf/an etw acc
sth); (fam: maschineschreiben)
type; t~en auf (+ acc) (fam: wetten) bet on. **T~fehler** m (fam)
typing error. **T~schein** m pools/
lottery coupon
tipptopp a (fam) immaculate,
adv -ly
Tirol nt -s [the] Tyrol
Tisch m -[e]s,-e table; (Schreib-)
desk; nach T~ after the meal.
T~decke f table-cloth. **T~ge-
bet** nt grace. **T~ler** m -s,- joiner;
(Möbel-) cabinet-maker. **T~rede**
f after-dinner speech. **T~tennis**
nt table tennis. **T~tuch** nt table-
cloth
Titel m -s,- title. **T~rolle** f title-
role

Toast /to:st/ m -[e]s,-e toast;
(Scheibe) piece of toast; einen T~
ausbringen propose a toast (auf
+ acc to). **T~er** m -s,- toaster
tob|en vi (haben) rave; (Sturm:)
rage; (Kinder:) play boisterously
□vi (sein) rush. t~süchtig a
raving mad
Tochter f -,: daughter. **T~ge-
sellschaft** f subsidiary
Tod m -es death. t~ernst a
deadly serious, adv -ly
Todes|angst f mortal fear.
T~anzeige f death announcement; (Zeitungs-) obituary.
T~fall m death. **T~opfer** nt
fatality, casualty. **T~strafe** f
death penalty. **T~urteil** nt
death sentence
Tod|feind m mortal enemy.
t~krank a dangerously ill
tödlich a fatal, adv -ly; (Gefahr)
mortal, adv -ly; (groß) deadly;
t~ gelangweilt bored to death
tod|müde a dead tired. t~sicher
a (fam) dead certain □adv for
sure. **T~sünde** f deadly sin.
t~unglücklich a desperately
unhappy
Toilette /tɔa'lɛta/ f -,-n toilet.
T~npapier nt toilet paper
toler|ant a tolerant. **T~anz** f -
tolerance. t~ieren vt tolerate
toll a crazy, mad; (fam: prima)
fantastic; (schlimm) awful □adv
beautifully; (sehr) very;
(schlimm) badly. t~en vi
(haben/sein) romp. t~kühn a
foolhardy. **T~wut** f rabies.
t~wütig a rabid
Tölpel m -s,- fool
Tomate f -,-n tomato. **T~nmark**
nt tomato purée
Tombola f -,-s raffle
Ton[1] m -[e]s clay
Ton[2] m -[e]s,-e tone; (Klang)
sound; (Note) note; (Betonung)
stress; (Farb-) shade; der gute

Ton (*fig*) good form. **T~ab-
nehmer** *m* -s,- pick-up. **t~an-
gebend** *a* (*fig*) leading. **T~art**
f tone [of voice]; (*Mus*) key. **T~-
band** *nt* (*pl* -bänder) tape. **T~-
bandgerät** *nt* tape recorder

tönen *vi* (*haben*) sound □*vt* tint

Ton|fall *m* tone [of voice]; (*Ak-
zent*) intonation. **T~leiter** *f*
scale. **t~los** *a* toneless, *adv* -ly

Tonne *f* -,-n barrel, cask; (*Müll-*)
bin; (*Maß*) tonne, metric ton

Topf *m* -[e]s,¨e pot; (*Koch-*) pan

Topfen *m* -s (*Aust*) ≈ curd cheese

Töpfer|(in) *m* -s,- (*f* -,-nen) pot-
ter. **T~ei** *f* -,-en pottery

Töpferwaren *fpl* pottery *sg*

Topf|lappen *m* oven-cloth.
T~pflanze *f* potted plant

Tor¹ *m* -en,-en fool

Tor² *nt* -[e]s,-e gate; (*Einfahrt*)
gateway; (*Sport*) goal. **T~bogen**
m archway

Torf *m* -s peat

Torheit *f* -,-en folly

Torhüter *m* -s,- goalkeeper

töricht *a* foolish, *adv* -ly

torkeln *vi* (*sein/haben*) stagger

Tornister *m* -s,- knapsack; (*Sch*)
satchel

torp|edieren *vt* torpedo. **T~edo**
m -s,-s torpedo

Torpfosten *m* goal-post

Torte *f* -,-n gâteau; (*Obst-*) flan

Tortur *f* -,-en torture

Torwart *m* -s,-e goalkeeper

tosen *vi* (*haben*) roar; (*Sturm:*)
rage

tot *a* dead; **einen t~en Punkt
haben** (*fig*) be at a low ebb

total *a* total, *adv* -ly. **t~itär** *a*
totalitarian. **T~schaden** *m*
≈ write-off

Tote(r) *m/f* dead man/woman;
(*Todesopfer*) fatality; **die T~n**
the dead *pl*

töten *vt* kill

toten|blaß *a* deathly pale.
T~gräber *m* -s,- grave-digger.
T~kopf *m* skull. **T~schein** *m*
death certificate. **T~stille** *f*
deathly silence

tot|fahren† *vt sep* run over and
kill. **t~geboren** *a* stillborn. **t~-
lachen (sich)** *vr sep* (*fam*) be in
stitches

Toto *nt & m* -s football pools *pl.*
T~schein *m* pools coupon

tot|schießen† *vt sep* shoot dead.
T~schlag *m* (*Jur*) manslaughter. **t~schlagen†** *vt sep*
kill. **t~schweigen†** *vt sep* (*fig*)
hush up. **t~stellen (sich)** *vr sep*
pretend to be dead

Tötung *f* -,-en killing; **fahrläs-
sige T~** (*Jur*) manslaughter

Toup|et /tu'pe:/ *nt* -s,-s toupee.
t~ieren *vt* back-comb

Tour /tu:ɐ̯/ *f* -,-en tour; (*Ausflug*)
trip; (*Auto-*) drive; (*Rad-*) ride;
(*Strecke*) distance; (*Techn*) revolution; (*fam: Weise*) way; **auf
vollen T~en** at full speed; (*fam*)
flat out

Touris|mus /tu'rɪsmus/ *m* - tour-
ism. **T~t** *m* -en,-en tourist

Tournee /tʊr'ne:/ *f* -,-n tour

Trab *m* -[e]s trot

Trabant *m* -en,-en satellite

traben *vi* (*haben/sein*) trot

Tracht *f* -,-en [national] costume;
eine T~ Prügel a good hiding

trachten *vi* (*haben*) strive (**nach**
for); **jdm nach dem Leben t~** be
out to kill s.o.

trächtig *a* pregnant

Tradition /-'tsio:n/ *f* -,-en tradition. **t~ell** *a* traditional, *adv* -ly

Trafik *f* -,-en (*Aust*) tobacconist's

Trag|bahre *f* stretcher. **t~bar** *a*
portable; (*Kleidung*) wearable;
(*erträglich*) bearable

träge *a* sluggish, *adv* -ly; (*faul*)
lazy, *adv* -ily; (*Phys*) inert

tragen† *vt* carry; *(an-/ aufhaben)* wear; *(fig)* bear □*vi (haben)* carry; **gut t~** *(Baum:)* produce a good crop; **schwer t~** carry a heavy load; *(fig)* be deeply affected **(an +** *dat* by). **t~d** *a (Techn)* load-bearing; *(trächtig)* pregnant

Träger *m* -s,- porter; *(Inhaber)* bearer; *(eines Ordens)* holder; *(Bau-)* beam; *(Stahl-)* girder; *(Achsel-)* [shoulder] strap. **T~kleid** *nt* pinafore dress

Trag|etasche *f* carrier bag. **T~fläche** *f (Aviat)* wing; *(Naut)* hydrofoil. **T~flächenboot, T~flügelboot** *nt* hydrofoil

Trägheit *f* - sluggishness; *(Faulheit)* laziness; *(Phys)* inertia

Trag|ik *f* - tragedy. **t~isch** *a* tragic, *adv* -ally

Tragödie /-jə/ *f* -,-n tragedy

Tragweite *f* range; *(fig)* consequence

Train|er /ˈtrɛːnɐ/ *m* -s,- trainer; *(Tennis-)* coach. **t~ieren** *vt/i (haben)* train

Training /ˈtrɛːnɪŋ/ *nt* -s training. **T~sanzug** *m* tracksuit. **T~schuhe** *mpl* trainers

Trakt *m* -[e]s,-e section; *(Flügel)* wing

traktieren *vt (haben)* mit Schlägen/Tritten **t~** beat/kick

Traktor *m* -s,-en /-ˈtoːrən/ tractor

trampeln *vi (haben)* stamp one's feet □*vi (sein)* trample **(auf +** *acc* on) □*vt* trample

trampen /ˈtrɛmpən/ *vi (sein) (fam)* hitch-hike

Trance /ˈtrãːsə/ *f* -,-n trance

Tranchier|messer /trãˈʃiːɐ̯-/ *nt* carving-knife. **t~en** *vt* carve

Träne *f* -,-n tear. **t~n** *vi (haben)* water. **T~ngas** *nt* tear-gas

Tränke *f* -,- watering-place; *(Trog)* drinking-trough. **t~n** *vt* water ⟨*Pferd*⟩; *(nässen)* soak **(mit** with)

Trans|aktion *f* transaction.

T~fer *m* -s,-s transfer. **T~formator** *m* -s,-en /-ˈtoːrən/ transformer. **T~fusion** *f* -,-en [blood] transfusion

Transistor *m* -,-en /-ˈtoːrən/ transistor

Transit /tranˈziːt/ *m* -s transit

transitiv *a* transitive, *adv* -ly

Transparent *nt* -[e]s,-e banner; *(Bild)* transparency

transpirieren *vi (haben)* perspire

Transplantation /-ˈtsjoːn/ *f* -,-en transplant

Transport *m* -[e]s,-e transport; *(Güter-)* consignment. **t~ieren** *vt* transport. **T~mittel** *nt* means of transport

Trapez *nt* -es,-e trapeze; *(Geom)* trapezium

Tratsch *m* -[e]s *(fam)* gossip. **t~en** *vi (haben) (fam)* gossip

Tratte *f* -,-n *(Comm)* draft

Traube *f* -,-n bunch of grapes; *(Beere)* grape; *(fig)* cluster. **T~nzucker** *m* glucose

trauen *vi (haben)* (+*dat*) trust; **ich traute kaum meinen Augen** I could hardly believe my eyes □*vt* marry; **sich t~** dare **(etw zu tun** [to] do sth); venture **(in +** *acc*/**aus** into/out of)

Trauer *f* - mourning; *(Schmerz)* grief **(um** for); **T~ tragen** be [dressed] in mourning. **T~fall** *m* bereavement. **T~feier** *f* funeral service. **T~marsch** *m* funeral march. **t~n** *vi (haben)* grieve; **t~n um** mourn [for]. **T~spiel** *nt* tragedy. **T~weide** *f* weeping willow

traulich *a* cosy, *adv* -ily

Traum *m* -[e]s,Träume dream

Trau|ma *nt* -s,-men trauma. **t~matisch** *a* traumatic

träumen *vt/i (haben)* dream

traumhaft *a* dreamlike; *(schön)* fabulous, *adv* -ly

traurig *a* sad, *adv* -ly; (*erbärm-lich*) sorry. T~**keit** *f* - sadness

Trau|ring *m* wedding-ring. T~**schein** *m* marriage certifi-cate. T~**ung** *f* -,-en wedding [ce-remony]

Treck *m* -s,-s trek

Trecker *m* -s,- tractor

Treff *nt* -s,-s (*Karten*) spades *pl*

treffen† *vt* hit; (*Blitz*:) strike; (*fig: verletzen*) hurt; (*zusammen-kommen mit*) meet; take (*Maß-nahme*); **sich t~en** meet (**mit jdm** s.o.); **sich gut t~en** be con-venient; **es traf sich, daß** it so happened that; **es gut/schlecht t~en** be lucky/unlucky *vi* (*ha-ben*) hit the target; **t~en auf** (+ *acc*) meet; (*fig*) meet with. T~**en** *nt* -s,- meeting. t~**end** *a* apt, *adv* -ly; (*Ähnlichkeit*) strik-ing. T~**er** *m* -s,- hit; (*Los*) win-ner. T~**punkt** *m* meeting-place

treiben† *vt* drive; (*sich befassen mit*) do; carry on (*Gewerbe*); in-dulge in (*Luxus*); get up to (*Un-fug*); **Handel t~** trade; **Blü-ten/Blätter t~** come into flower/leaf; **zur Eile t~** hurry [up]; **was treibt ihr da?** (*fam*) what are you up to? *vi* (*sein*) drift; (*schwimmen*) float *vi* (*haben*) (*Bot*) sprout. T~ *nt* -s activity; (*Getriebe*) bustle

Treib|haus *nt* hothouse. T~**hauseffekt** *m* greenhouse effect. T~**holz** *nt* driftwood. T~**riemen** *m* transmission belt. T~**sand** *m* quicksand. T~**stoff** *m* fuel

Trend *m* -s,-s trend

trenn|bar *a* separable. t~**en** *vt* separate/(*abmachen*) detach (**von** from); divide, split (*Wort*); **sich t~en** separate; (*auseinan-dergehen*) part; **sich t~en von** leave; (*fortgeben*) part with.

T~**ung** *f* -,-en separation; (*Sil-ben-*) division. T~**ungsstrich** *m* hyphen. T~**wand** *f* partition

trepp|ab *adv* downstairs. t~**auf** *adv* upstairs

Treppe *f* -,-n stairs *pl*; (*Außen-*) steps *pl*; **eine T~** a flight of stairs/steps. T~**nflur** *m* landing. T~**ngeländer** *nt* banisters *pl*. T~**nhaus** *nt* stairwell. T~**nstufe** *f* stair, step

Tresor *m* -s,-e safe

Tresse *f* -,-n braid

Treteimer *m* pedal bin

treten† *vi* (*sein/haben*) step; (*ver-sehentlich*) tread; (*ausschlagen*) kick (**nach** at); **in Verbindung t~** get in touch *vt* tread; (*mit Füßen*) kick

treu *a* faithful, *adv* -ly; (*fest*) loyal, *adv* -ly. T~**e** *f* - faithfulness; loyalty; (*eheliche*) fidelity. T~**händer** *m* -s,- trustee. t~**herzig** *a* trusting, *adv* -ly; (*arglos*) innocent, *adv* -ly. t~**los** *a* disloyal, *adv* -ly; (*untreu*) un-faithful

Tribüne *f* -,-n platform; (*Zu-schauer-*) stand

Tribut *m* -[e]s,-e tribute; (*Opfer*) toll

Trichter *m* -s,- funnel; (*Bomben-*) crater

Trick *m* -s,-s trick. T~**film** *m* cartoon. t~**reich** *a* clever

Trieb *m* -[e]s,-e drive, urge; (*In-stinkt*) instinct; (*Bot*) shoot. T~**täter,** T~**verbrecher** *m* sex offender. T~**werk** *nt* (*Aviat*) en-gine; (*Uhr-*) mechanism

triefen† *vi* (*haben*) drip; (*naß sein*) be dripping (**von/vor** + *dat* with). t~**naß** *a* dripping wet

triftig *a* valid

Trigonometrie *f* - trigonometry

Trikot[1] /tri'ko:/ *m* -s (*Tex*) jersey

Trikot[2] *nt* -s,-s (*Sport*) jersey; (*Fußball-*) shirt

Trimester *nt* -s,- term

Trimm-dich nt -s keep-fit

trimmen vt trim; (fam) train; tune ⟨Motor⟩; **sich t~** keep fit

trink|bar a drinkable. **t~en†** vt/i (haben) drink. **T~er(in)** m -s,- (f -,-nen) alcoholic. **T~geld** nt tip. **T~halm** m [drinking-]straw. **T~spruch** m toast. **T~wasser** nt drinking-water

Trio nt -s,-s trio

trippeln vi (sein) trip along

trist a dreary

Tritt m -[e]s,-e step; ⟨Fuß-⟩ kick. **T~brett** nt step. **T~leiter** f step-ladder

Triumph m -s,-e triumph. **t~ie-ren** vi (haben) rejoice; **t~ieren über** (+ acc) triumph over. **t~ierend** a triumphant, adv -ly

trocken a dry, adv drily. **T~haube** f drier. **T~heit** f -,-en dryness; ⟨Dürre⟩ drought. **t~le-gen** vt sep change ⟨Baby⟩; drain ⟨Sumpf⟩. **T~milch** f powdered milk

trockn|en vt/i (sein) dry. **T~er** m -s,- drier

Troddel f -,-n tassel

Trödel m -s (fam) junk. **T~laden** m (fam) junk-shop. **T~markt** m (fam) flea market. **t~n** vi (haben) dawdle

Trödler m -s,- (fam) slowcoach; ⟨Händler⟩ junk-dealer

Trog m -[e]s,-e trough

Trommel f -,-n drum. **T~fell** nt ear-drum. **t~n** vi (haben) drum

Trommler m -s,- drummer

Trompete f -,-n trumpet. **T~r** m -s,- trumpeter

Tropen pl tropics

Tropf m -[e]s,-e (Med) drip

tröpfeln vt/i (sein/haben) drip; es tröpfelt it's spitting with rain

tropfen vt/i (sein/haben) drip. **T~** m -s,- drop; ⟨fallend⟩ drip. **t~weise** adv drop by drop

tropf|naß a dripping wet. **T~stein** m stalagmite; ⟨hängend⟩ stalactite

Trophäe /tro'fɛ:ə/ f -,-n trophy

tropisch a tropical

Trost m -[e]s consolation, comfort

tröst|en vt console, comfort; **sich t~en** console oneself. **t~lich** a comforting

trost|los a desolate; ⟨elend⟩ wretched; ⟨reizlos⟩ dreary. **T~preis** m consolation prize. **t~reich** a comforting

Trott m -s amble; (fig) routine

Trottel m -s,- (fam) idiot

trotten vi (sein) traipse; ⟨Tier:⟩ amble

Trottoir /tro'toa:ɐ/ nt -s,-s pavement, (Amer) sidewalk

trotz prep (+ gen) despite, in spite of. **T~** m -es defiance. **t~dem** adv nevertheless. **t~en** vi (haben) (+ dat) defy. **t~ig** a defiant, adv -ly; ⟨Kind⟩ stubborn

trübe a dull; ⟨Licht⟩ dim; ⟨Flüssigkeit⟩ cloudy; (fig) gloomy

Trubel m -s bustle

trüben vt dull; make cloudy ⟨Flüssigkeit⟩; (fig) spoil; strain ⟨Verhältnis⟩; **sich t~** ⟨Flüssigkeit:⟩ become cloudy; ⟨Himmel:⟩ cloud over; ⟨Augen:⟩ dim; ⟨Verhältnis, Erinnerung:⟩ deteriorate

Trüb|sal f - misery; (fam) mope. **t~selig** a miserable; ⟨trübe⟩ gloomy, adv -ily. **T~sinn** m melancholy. **t~sin-nig** a melancholy

Trugbild nt illusion

trüg|en† vt deceive □ vi (haben) be deceptive. **t~erisch** a false; ⟨täuschend⟩ deceptive

Trugschluß m fallacy

Truhe f -,-n chest

Trümmer pl rubble sg; ⟨T~teile⟩ wreckage sg; (fig) ruins. **T~haufen** m pile of rubble

Trumpf m -[e]s,·̈e trump [card];
T~ **sein** be trumps. **t~en** vi
(haben) play trumps

Trunk m -[e]s drink. **T~enbold**
m -[e]s,-e drunkard. **T~enheit** f
- drunkenness; **T~enheit am
Steuer** drunken driving.
T~sucht f alcoholism

Trupp m -s,-s group; (Mil) squad.
T~e f -,-n (Mil) unit; (Theat)
troupe; **T~en** troops

Truthahn m turkey

Tschech|e m -n,-n, **T~in** f -,-nen
Czech. **t~isch** a Czech. **T~o-
slowakei** (die) - Czechoslovakia

tschüs int bye, cheerio

Tuba f -,-ben (Mus) tuba

Tube f -,-n tube

Tuberkulose f - tuberculosis

Tuch¹ nt -[e]s,·̈er cloth; (Hals-,
Kopf-) scarf; (Schulter-) shawl

Tuch² nt -[e]s,-e (Stoff) cloth

tüchtig a competent; (reichlich,
beträchtlich) good; (groß) big
□adv competently; (ausreichend)
well; ⟨regnen, schneien⟩ hard.
T~keit f - competence

Tück|e f -,-n malice; **T~en haben**
be temperamental; (gefährlich
sein) be treacherous. **t~isch** a
malicious, adv -ly; (gefährlich)
treacherous

tüfteln vi (haben) (fam) fiddle
(an + dat with); (geistig) puzzle
(an + dat over)

Tugend f -,-en virtue. **t~haft** a
virtuous

Tülle f -,-n spout

Tulpe f -,-n tulip

tummeln (sich) vr romp [about];
(sich beeilen) hurry [up]

Tümmler m -s,- porpoise

Tumor m -s,-en /-'mo:rən/ tumour

Tümpel m -s,- pond

Tumult m -[e]s,-e commotion;
(Aufruhr) riot

tun† vt do; take ⟨Schritt, Blick⟩;
work ⟨Wunder⟩; (bringen) put
(in + acc into); **sich tun** happen;

jdm etwas tun hurt s.o.; **viel zu
tun haben** have a lot to do; **das
tut man nicht** it isn't done; **das
tut nichts** it doesn't matter □vi
(haben) act (als ob as if); **über-
rascht tun** pretend to be surprised; **er tut nur so** he's just
pretending; **zu tun haben** have
things/work to do; **[es] zu tun
haben mit** have to deal with; **[es]
mit dem Herzen zu tun haben**
have heart trouble. **Tun** nt -s
actions pl

Tünche f -,-n whitewash; (fig)
veneer. **t~n** vt whitewash

Tunesien /-jən/ nt -s Tunisia

Tunke f -,-n sauce. **t~n** vt/i
(haben) dip (in + acc into)

Tunnel m -s,- tunnel

tupfen vt dab □vi (haben) t~ an
an/auf (+acc) touch. **T~en** m
-s,- spot. **T~er** m -s,- spot; (Med)
swab

Tür f -,-en door

Turban m -s,-e turban

Turbine f -,-n turbine

turbulent a turbulent. **T~z** f
-,-en turbulence

Türk|e m -n,-n Turk. **T~ei** (die) -
Turkey. **T~in** f -,-nen Turk

türkis inv a turquoise. **T~** m
-es,-e turquoise

türkisch a Turkish

Turm m -[e]s,·̈e tower; (Schach)
rook, castle

Türm|chen nt -s,- turret. **t~en** vt
pile [up]; **sich t~en** pile up □vi
(sein) (fam) escape

Turmspitze f spire

turn|en vi (haben) do gymnastics.
T~en nt -s gymnastics sg; (Sch)
physical education, (fam) gym.
T~er(in) m -s,- (f -,-nen) gymnast. **T~halle** f gymnasium

Turnier nt -s,-e tournament;
(Reit-) show

Turnschuhe mpl gym shoes

Türschwelle f doorstep, threshold

Tusch m -[e]s,-e fanfare

Tusche f-,-n (drawing) ink; (*Wasserfarbe*) watercolour

tuscheln vt/i (haben) whisper

Tüte f -,-n bag; (*Comm*) packet; (*Eis-*) cornet; **in die T~ blasen** (*fam*) be breathalysed

tuten vi (haben) hoot; ⟨*Schiff:*⟩ sound its hooter; ⟨*Sirene:*⟩ sound

TÜV m - ≈ MOT [test]

Typ m -s,-e en type; (*fam: Kerl*) bloke. **T~e** f -,-n type; (*fam: Person*) character

Typhus m - typhoid

typisch a typical, adv -ly (**für** of)

Typographie f - typography

Typus m -,**Typen** type

Tyrann m -en,-en tyrant. **T~ei** f - tyranny. **t~isch** a tyrannical. **t~isieren** vt tyrannize

U

u.a. abbr (**unter anderem**) amongst other things

U-Bahn f underground, (*Amer*) subway

übel a bad; (*häßlich*) nasty, adv -ily; **mir ist/wird ü~** I feel sick. **Ü~** nt -s,- evil. **Ü~keit** f - nausea. **ü~nehmen†** vt sep take amiss; **jdm etw ü~nehmen** hold sth against s.o. **Ü~täter** m culprit

üben vt/i (haben) practise; **sich in etw** (dat) **ü~** practise sth

über prep (+ dat/acc) over; (*höher als*) above; (*betreffend*) about; ⟨*Buch, Vortrag*⟩ on; ⟨*Scheck, Rechnung*⟩ for; (*quer ü~*) across; **ü~ Köln fahren** go via Cologne; **ü~ Ostern** over Easter; **die Woche ü~** during the week; **heute ü~ eine Woche** a week today; **Fehler ü~ Fehler** mistake after mistake □adv **ü~ und ü~** all over; **jdm ü~ sein** be better/(*stärker*) stronger than s.o. □a (*fam*) **ü~ sein** be left

over; **etw ü~ sein** be fed up with sth

überall adv everywhere

überanstrengen vt insep overtax; strain ⟨*Augen*⟩; **sich ü~** overexert oneself

überarbeiten vt insep revise; **sich ü~en** overwork. **Ü~ung** f - revision; overwork

überaus adv extremely

überbewerten vt insep overrate

überbieten† vt insep outbid; (*fig*) outdo; (*übertreffen*) surpass

Überblick m overall view; (*Abriß*) summary

überblicken vt insep overlook; (*abschätzen*) assess

überbringen† vt insep deliver

überbrücken vt insep (*fig*) bridge

überdauern vt insep survive

überdenken† vt insep think over

überdies adv moreover

überdimensional a oversized

Überdosis f overdose

Überdruß m -sses surfeit; **bis zum Ü~** ad nauseam

überdrüssig a **ü~ sein/werden** be/grow tired (gen of)

übereignen vt insep transfer

übereilt a over-hasty, adv -ily

übereinander adv one on top of/above the other; ⟨*sprechen*⟩ about each other. **ü~schlagen†** vt sep cross ⟨*Beine*⟩; fold ⟨*Arme*⟩

überein|kommen† vi sep (sein) agree. **Ü~kunft** f - agreement. **ü~stimmen** vi sep (haben) agree; ⟨*Zahlen:*⟩ tally; ⟨*Ansichten:*⟩ coincide; ⟨*Farben:*⟩ match. **Ü~stimmung** f agreement

überempfindlich a over-sensitive; (*Med*) hypersensitive

überfahren† vt insep run over

Überfahrt f crossing

Überfall m attack; (*Bank-*) raid

überfallen† vt insep attack; raid ⟨*Bank*⟩; (*bestürmen*) bombard

(mit with); (*überkommen*) come over; (*fam: besuchen*) surprise
überfällig *a* overdue
überfliegen† *vt insep* fly over; (*lesen*) skim over
überflügeln *vt insep* outstrip
Überfluß *m* abundance; (*Wohlstand*) affluence
überflüssig *a* superfluous
überfluten† *vt insep* flood
überfordern *vt insep* overtax
überführ|en *vt insep* transfer; (*Jur*) convict (*gen* of). **Ü~ung** *f* transfer; (*Straße*) flyover; (*Fußgänger-*) foot-bridge
überfüllt *a* overcrowded
Übergabe *f* (s. **übergeben**) handing over; transfer
Übergang *m* crossing; (*Wechsel*) transition. **Ü~sstadium** *nt* transitional stage
übergeben† *vt insep* hand over; (*übereignen*) transfer; **sich ü~** be sick
übergehen¹ *vi sep* (*sein*) pass (**an**+*acc* to); (*überwechseln*) go over (**zu** to); (*werden zu*) turn (**in**+*acc* into); **zum Angriff ü~** start the attack
übergehen²† *vt insep* (*fig*) pass over; (*nicht beachten*) ignore; (*auslassen*) leave out
Übergewicht *nt* excess weight; (*fig*) predominance; **Ü~ haben** be overweight
übergießen† *vt insep* **mit Wasser ü~** pour water over
überglücklich *a* overjoyed
übergreifen† *vi sep* (*haben*) spread (**auf**+*acc* to). **Ü~griff** *m* infringement
über|groß *a* outsize; (*übertrieben*) exaggerated. **Ü~größe** *f* outsize
überhaben† *vt sep* have on; (*fam: satthaben*) be fed up with
überhandnehmen† *vi sep* (*haben*) increase alarmingly
überhängen *v sep* □*vi*† (*haben*) overhang □*vt* (*reg*) **sich** (*dat*) **etw**

ü~ sling over one's shoulder (*Gewehr*); put round one's shoulders (*Jacke*)
überhäufen† *vt insep* inundate (**mit** with)
überhaupt *adv* (*im allgemeinen*) altogether; (*eigentlich*) anyway; (*überdies*) besides; **ü~ nicht**/**nichts** not/nothing at all
überheblich *a* arrogant, *adv* -ly. **Ü~keit** *f* arrogance
überhol|en *vt insep* overtake; (*reparieren*) overhaul. **ü~t** *a* outdated. **Ü~ung** *f* -,-en overhaul. **Ü~verbot** *nt* 'Ü~verbot' 'no overtaking'
überhören *vt insep* fail to hear; (*nicht beachten*) ignore
überirdisch *a* supernatural
überkochen *vi sep* (*sein*) boil over
überladen† *vt insep* overload □*a* over-ornate
überlassen† *vt insep* **jdm etw ü~** leave sth to s.o.; (*geben*) let s.o. have sth; **sich seinem Schmerz ü~** abandon oneself to one's grief; **sich** (*dat*) **selbst ü~ sein** be left to one's own devices
überlasten *vt insep* overload; overtax (*Person*)
Überlauf *m* overflow
überlaufen¹ *vi sep* (*sein*) overflow; (*Mil, Pol*) defect
überlaufen²† *vt insep* **jdn ü~** ⟨*Gefühl:*⟩ come over s.o. □*a* over-run; (*Kursus*) over-subscribed
Überläufer *m* defector
überleben *vt*/*i insep* (*haben*) survive. **Ü~de(r)** *m*/*f* survivor
überlegen¹ *vt sep* put over
überlegen² *v insep* □*vt* (**sich** *dat*) **ü~** think over, consider; **sich** (*dat*) **anders ü~** change one's mind □*vi* (*haben*) think, reflect; **ohne zu ü~** without thinking
überlegen³ *a* superior; (*herablassend*) supercilious, *adv* -ly. **Ü~heit** *f* superiority

Überlegung *f* -,-en reflection

überliefer|n *vt insep* hand down. **Ü~ung** *f* tradition

überlisten *vt insep* outwit

überm *prep* = **über dem**

Über|macht *f* superiority. **ü~mächtig** *a* superior; ⟨*Gefühl*⟩ overpowering

übermannen *vt insep* overcome

Über|maß *nt* excess. **ü~mäßig** *a* excessive, *adv* -ly

Übermensch *m* superman. **ü~lich** *a* superhuman

übermitteln *vt insep* convey; ⟨*senden*⟩ transmit

übermorgen *adv* the day after tomorrow

übermüdet *a* overtired

Über|mut *m* high spirits *pl.* **ü~mütig** *a* high-spirited □ *adv* in high spirits

übern *prep* = **über den**

übernächst|e(r,s) *a* next ... but one; **ü~es Jahr** the year after next

übernacht|en *vi insep* ⟨*haben*⟩ stay overnight. **Ü~ung** *f* -,-en overnight stay; **Ü~ung und Frühstück** bed and breakfast

Übernahme *f* - taking over; ⟨*Comm*⟩ take-over

übernatürlich *a* supernatural

übernehmen† *vt insep* take over; ⟨*annehmen*⟩ take on; **sich ü~** overdo things; ⟨*finanziell*⟩ overreach oneself

überprüf|en *vt insep* check. **Ü~ung** *f* check

überqueren *vt insep* cross

überragen *vt insep* tower above; ⟨*fig*⟩ surpass. **Ü~d** *a* outstanding

überrasch|en *vt insep* surprise. **ü~end** *a* surprising, *adv* -ly; ⟨*unerwartet*⟩ unexpected, *adv* -ly. **Ü~ung** *f* -,-en surprise

überreden *vt insep* persuade

überreichen *vt insep* present

überreizt *a* overwrought

überrennen† *vt insep* overrun

Überreste *mpl* remains

überrumpeln *vt insep* take by surprise

übers *prep* = **über das**

Überschall- *pref* supersonic

überschatten *vt insep* overshadow

überschätzen *vt insep* overestimate

Überschlag *m* rough estimate; ⟨*Sport*⟩ somersault

überschlagen¹† *vt sep* cross ⟨*Beine*⟩

überschlagen²† *vt insep* estimate roughly; ⟨*auslassen*⟩ skip; **sich ü~** somersault; ⟨*Ereignisse:*⟩ happen fast □ *a* tepid

überschnappen *vi sep* ⟨*sein*⟩ ⟨*fam*⟩ go crazy

überschneiden† **(sich)** *vr insep* intersect, cross; ⟨*zusammenfallen*⟩ overlap

überschreiben† *vt insep* entitle; ⟨*übertragen*⟩ transfer

überschreiten† *vt insep* cross; ⟨*fig*⟩ exceed

Überschrift *f* heading; ⟨*Zeitungs-*⟩ headline

Über|schuß *m* surplus. **ü~schüssig** *a* surplus

überschütten *vt insep* **ü~ mit** cover with; ⟨*fig*⟩ shower with

überschwemm|en *vt insep* flood; ⟨*fig*⟩ inundate. **Ü~ung** *f* -,-en flood

überschwenglich *a* effusive, *adv* -ly

Übersee *in/nach* **Ü~** overseas; *aus/von* **Ü~** from overseas. **Ü~dampfer** *m* ocean liner. **ü~isch** *a* overseas

übersehen† *vt insep* look out over; ⟨*abschätzen*⟩ assess; ⟨*nicht sehen*⟩ overlook, miss; ⟨*ignorieren*⟩ ignore

übersenden† *vt insep* send

übersetzen¹ *vi sep* ⟨*haben/sein*⟩ cross [over]

übersetz|en² *vt insep* translate. Ü~**er(in)** *m* -s, *(f* -,-nen) translator. Ü~**ung** *f* -,-en translation

Übersicht *f* overall view; *(Abriß)* summary; *(Tabelle)* table. ü~**lich** *a* clear, *adv* -ly

übersied|eln *vi insep (sein)*, **übersied|eln** *vi insep (sein)* move *(nach* to). Ü~**ung** *f* move

übersinnlich *a* supernatural

überspannt *a* exaggerated; *(verschroben)* eccentric

überspielen *vt insep (fig)* cover up; **auf Band** ü~ tape

überspitzt *a* exaggerated

überspringen† *vt insep* jump [over]; *(auslassen)* skip

überstehen¹† *vi sep (haben)* project, jut out

überstehen²† *vt insep* come through; get over *(Krankheit)*; *(überleben)* survive

übersteigen† *vt insep* climb [over]; *(fig)* exceed

überstimmen *vt insep* outvote

überstreifen *vt sep* slip on

Überstunden *fpl* overtime *sg*; Ü~ **machen** work overtime

überstürz|en *vt insep* rush; **sich** ü~**en** *(Ereignisse:)* happen fast; *(Worte:)* tumble out. ü~**t** *a* hasty, *adv* -ily

übertölpeln *vt insep* dupe

übertönen *vt insep* drown [out]

übertrag|bar *a* transferable; *(Med)* infectious. ü~**en†** *vt insep* transfer; *(übergeben)* assign *(dat* to); *(Techn, Med)* transmit; *(Radio, TV)* broadcast; *(übersetzen)* translate; *(anwenden)* apply *(auf+acc* to) ü~**en** transferred, figurative. Ü~**ung** *f* -,-en transfer; transmission; broadcast; translation; application

übertreffen† *vt insep* surpass; *(übersteigen)* exceed; **sich selbst** ü~ excel oneself

übertreib|en† *vt insep* exaggerate; *(zu weit treiben)* overdo. Ü~**ung** *f* -,-en exaggeration

übertreten¹† *vi sep (sein)* step over the line; *(Pol)* go over/*(Relig)* convert *(zu* to)

übertret|en²† *vt insep* infringe; break *(Gesetz)*. Ü~**ung** *f* -,-en infringement; breach

übertrieben *a* exaggerated; *(übermäßig)* excessive, *adv* -ly

übervölkert *a* overpopulated

übervorteilen *vt insep* cheat

überwach|en *vt insep* supervise; *(kontrollieren)* monitor; *(bespitzeln)* keep under surveillance

überwachsen *a* overgrown

überwältigen *vt insep* overpower; *(fig)* overwhelm. ü~**d** *a* overwhelming

überweis|en† *vt insep* transfer; refer *(Patienten)*. Ü~**ung** *f* transfer; *(ärztliche)* referral

überwerfen¹† *vt sep* throw on *(Mantel)*

überwerfen²† *(sich)* *vr insep* fall out *(mit* with)

überwiegen† *v insep □vi (haben)* predominate □*vt* outweigh. ü~**d** *a* predominant, *adv* -ly

überwind|en *vt insep* overcome; **sich** ü~**en** force oneself. Ü~**ung** *f* effort

Überwurf *m* wrap; *(Bett-)* bedspread

Über|zahl *f* majority. ü~**zählig** *a* spare

überzeug|en *vt insep* convince; **sich [selbst]** ü~**en** satisfy oneself. ü~**end** *a* convincing, -ly. Ü~**ung** *f* -,-en conviction

überziehen¹† *vt sep* put on

überziehen²† *vt insep* cover; overdraw *(Konto)*

Überzug *m* cover; *(Schicht)* coating

üblich *a* usual; *(gebräuchlich)* customary

U-Boot *nt* submarine

übrig *a* remaining; (*andere*) other; **alles ü~e** [all] the rest; **im ü~en** besides; (*ansonsten*) apart from that; **ü~ sein** be left [over]; **etw ü~ haben** have sth left [over]. **ü~behalten**† *vt sep* have left [over]. **ü~bleiben**† *vi sep* (*sein*) be left [over]; **uns blieb nichts anderes ü~** we had no choice. **ü~ens** *adv* by the way. **ü~lassen**† *vt sep* leave [over]

Übung *f* -,-en exercise; (*Üben*) practice; **außer** *od* **aus der Ü~** out of practice

UdSSR *f* - USSR

Ufer *nt* -s,- shore; (*Fluß*) bank

Uhr *f* -,-en clock; (*Armband-*) watch; (*Zähler*) meter; **um ein U~** at one o'clock; **wieviel U~ ist es?** what's the time? **U~armband** *nt* watch-strap. **U~macher** *m* -s,- watch and clockmaker. **U~werk** *nt* clock/ watch mechanism. **U~zeiger** *m* [clock-/watch-]hand. **U~zeigersinn** *m* im/entgegen dem **U~zeigersinn** clockwise/ anti-clockwise. **U~zeit** *f* time

Uhu *m* -s,-s eagle owl

UKW *abbr* (Ultrakurzwelle) VHF

Ulk *m* -s fun; (*Streich*) trick. **u~en** *vi* (*haben*) joke. **u~ig** *a* funny; (*seltsam*) odd, *adv* -ly

Ulme *f* -,-n elm

Ultimatum *nt* -s,-ten ultimatum

Ultrakurzwelle *f* very high frequency

Ultraschall *m* ultrasound

ultraviolett *a* ultraviolet

um *prep* (+ *acc*) [a]round; (*Uhrzeit*) at; (*bitten, kämpfen*) for; (*streiten*) over; (*sich sorgen*) about; (*betrügen*) out of; (*bei Angabe einer Differenz*) by; **um** [...herum] around, [round] about; **Tag um Tag** day after day; **um den andern** every other day; **um seinetwillen** for his

sake □*adv* (*ungefähr*) around, about □*conj* um zu to; (*Absicht*) [in order] to; **zu müde, um zu ...** too tired to ...; **um so besser** all the better

umändern *vt sep* alter

umarbeiten *vt sep* alter; (*bearbeiten*) revise

umarm|en *vt insep* embrace, hug. **U~ung** *f* -,-en embrace, hug

Umbau *m* rebuilding; conversion (zu into). **u~en** *vt sep* rebuild; convert (**zu** into)

umbild|en *vt sep* change; (*umgestalten*) reorganize; reshuffle (*Kabinett*). **U~ung** *f* reorganisation; (*Pol*) reshuffle

umbinden† *vt sep* put on

umblättern *v sep* □*vt* turn [over] □*vi* (*haben*) turn the page

umblicken (sich) *vr sep* look round; (*zurück-*) look back

umbringen† *vt sep* kill; **sich u~** kill oneself

Umbruch *m* (*fig*) radical change

umbuchen *v sep* □*vt* change; (*Comm*) transfer □*vi* (*haben*) change one's booking

umdrehen *v sep* □*vt* turn round/ (*wenden*) over; turn (*Schlüssel*); (*umkrempeln*) turn inside out; **sich u~** turn round; (*im Liegen*) turn over □*vi* (*haben/sein*) turn back

Umdrehung *f* turn; (*Motor-*) revolution

umeinander *adv* around each other; **sich u~ sorgen** worry about each other

umfahren¹† *vt sep* run over

umfahren²† *vt insep* go round; bypass (*Ort*)

umfallen† *vi sep* (*sein*) fall over; (*Person:*) fall down

Umfang *m* girth; (*Geom*) circumference; (*Größe*) size; (*Ausmaß*) extent; (*Mus*) range

umfangen† *vt insep* embrace; (*fig*) envelop

umfangreich a extensive; (*dick*) big

umfassen vt insep consist of, comprise; (*umgeben*) surround. **u~d** a comprehensive

Umfrage f survey, poll

umfüllen vt sep transfer

umfunktionieren vt sep convert

Umgang m [social] contact; (*Umgehen*) dealing (mit with); **U~ haben mit** associate with

umgänglich a sociable

Umgangs|formen fpl manners. **U~sprache** f colloquial language. **u~sprachlich** a colloquial, adv -ly

umgeben† vt/i insep (haben) surround □a u~en von surrounded by. **U~ung** f,-,-en surroundings pl

umgehen¹ vi sep (sein) go round; **u~ mit** treat, handle; (*verkehren*) associate with; **in dem Schloß geht ein Gespenst um** the castle is haunted

umgehen² vt insep avoid; (*nicht beachten*) evade; (*Straße:*) bypass

umgehend a immediate, adv -ly

Umgehungsstraße f bypass

umgekehrt a inverse; (*Reihen-folge*) reverse; **es war u~** it was the other way round □adv conversely; **und u~** and vice versa

umgraben† vt sep dig [over]

umhaben† vt sep have on

Umhang m cloak

umhauen† vt sep knock down; (*fällen*) chop down

umher adv weit u~ all around. **u~gehen†** vi sep (sein) walk about

umhören (sich) vr sep ask around

Umkehr f - turning back. **u~en** v sep □vi sep (sein) turn back or round; turn inside out (*Tasche*); (*fig*) reverse □vt turn round; turn inside out

umkippen v sep □vt tip over; (*versehentlich*) knock over □vi

(sein) fall over; (*Boot:*) capsize; (*fam: ohnmächtig werden*) faint

Umkleide|kabine f changing-cubicle. **u~n (sich)** vr sep change. **U~raum** m changing-room

umknicken v sep □vt bend; (*falten*) fold □vi (sein) bend; (*mit dem Fuß*) go over on one's ankle

umkommen vi sep (sein) perish; **u~ lassen** waste (*Lebensmittel*)

Umkreis m surroundings pl; **im U~ von** within a radius of

umkreisen vt insep circle; (*Astr*) revolve around; (*Satellit:*) orbit

umkrempeln vt sep turn up; (*von innen nach außen*) turn inside out; (*ändern*) change radically

Umlauf m circulation; (*Astr*) revolution. **U~bahn** f orbit

Umlaut m umlaut

umlegen vt sep lay or put down; flatten (*Getreide*); turn down (*Kragen*); put on (*Schal*); throw (*Hebel*); (*verlegen*) transfer; (*fam: niederschlagen*) knock down; (*töten*) kill

umleiten vt sep divert. **U~ung** f diversion

umliegend a surrounding

umpflanzen vt sep transplant

umrahmen vt insep frame

umranden vt insep edge

umräumen vt sep rearrange

umrechnen vt sep convert. **U~ung** f conversion

umreißen¹ vt sep tear down; knock down (*Person*)

umreißen² vt insep outline

umringen vt insep surround

Umriß m outline

umrühren vt/i sep (haben) stir

ums pron = um das; **u~ Leben kommen** lose one's life

Umsatz m (*Comm*) turnover

umschalten vt/i sep (haben) switch over; **auf Rot u~** (*Ampel:*) change to red

Umschau f U~ halten nach look
out for. **u~en (sich)** vr sep look
round/⟨zurück⟩ back
Umschlag m cover; ⟨Schutz-⟩
jacket; ⟨Brief-⟩ envelope; ⟨Med⟩
compress; ⟨Hosen-⟩ turn-up;
⟨Wechsel⟩ change. **u~en†** v sep
□vt turn up; turn over ⟨Seite⟩;
⟨fällen⟩ chop down □vi ⟨sein⟩ topple over; ⟨Boot:⟩ capsize; ⟨Wet-
ter:⟩ change; ⟨Wind:⟩ veer
umschließen† vt insep enclose
umschnallen vt sep buckle on
umschreiben¹† vt sep rewrite
umschreib|en²† vt insep define;
⟨anders ausdrücken⟩ paraphrase.
U~ung f definition; paraphrase
umschulen vt sep retrain; ⟨Sch⟩
transfer to another school
Umschweife pl keine U~ machen come straight out with it;
ohne U~ straight out
Umschwung m ⟨fig⟩ change;
⟨Pol⟩ U-turn
umsehen† (sich) vr sep look
round; ⟨zurück⟩ look back; sich
u~ nach look for
umsein† vi sep ⟨sein⟩ ⟨fam⟩ be
over; ⟨Zeit:⟩ be up
umseitig a & adv overleaf
umsetzen vt sep move; ⟨umpflan-
zen⟩ transplant; ⟨Comm⟩ sell
Umsicht f circumspection. **u~ig**
a circumspect, adv -ly
umsied|eln v sep □vt resettle □vi
⟨sein⟩ move. **U~lung** f resettle-
ment
umsonst adv in vain; ⟨grundlos⟩
without reason; ⟨gratis⟩ free
umspringen† vi sep ⟨sein⟩
change; ⟨Wind:⟩ veer; **übel u~
mit** treat badly
Umstand m circumstance; ⟨Tat-
sache⟩ fact; ⟨Aufwand⟩ fuss;
⟨Mühe⟩ trouble; **unter U~̃en** possibly; **U~̃e machen** make a fuss;
jdm U~̃e machen put s.o. to
trouble; **in andern U~̃en** be pregnant

umständlich a laborious, adv -ly;
⟨kompliziert⟩ involved; ⟨Person⟩
fussy
Umstands|kleid nt maternity
dress. **U~wort** nt (pl -wörter)
adverb
umstehen† vi insep surround
Umstehende pl bystanders
umsteigen† vi sep ⟨sein⟩ change
umstellen¹ vt insep surround
umstell|en² vt sep rearrange;
transpose ⟨Wörter⟩; ⟨anders ein-
stellen⟩ reset; ⟨Techn⟩ convert;
⟨ändern⟩ change; sich u~en adjust. **U~ung** f rearrangement;
transposition; resetting; conversion; change; adjustment
umstimmen vt sep **jdn u~**
change s.o's mind
umstoßen† vt sep knock over;
⟨fig⟩ overturn; upset ⟨Plan⟩
umstritten a controversial; ⟨un-
geklärt⟩ disputed
umstülpen vt sep turn upside
down; ⟨von innen nach außen⟩
turn inside out
Um|sturz m coup. **u~stürzen** v
sep □vt overturn; ⟨Pol⟩ overthrow □vi ⟨sein⟩ fall over
umtaufen vt sep rename
Umtausch m exchange. **u~en** vt
sep change; exchange ⟨gegen for⟩
umwälzend a revolutionary
umwandeln vt sep convert; ⟨fig⟩
transform
umwechseln vt sep change
Umweg m detour; **auf U~en** in a
roundabout way
Umwelt f environment.
u~freundlich a environment-
ally friendly. **U~schutz** m protection of the environment. **U~-
schützer** m environmentalist
umwenden† vt sep turn over;
sich u~ turn round
umwerfen† vt sep knock over;
⟨fig⟩ upset ⟨Plan⟩; ⟨fam⟩ bowl
over ⟨Person⟩

umziehen† v sep □ vi (sein) move
□ vt change; **sich u~** change

umzingeln vt insep surround

Umzug m move; (Prozession) procession

unabänderlich a irrevocable; ⟨Tatsache⟩ unalterable

unabhängig a independent, adv -ly; **u~ davon, ob** irrespective of whether. **U~keit** f - independence

unabkömmlich pred a busy

unablässig a incessant, adv -ly

unabsehbar a incalculable

unabsichtlich a unintentional, adv -ly

unachtsam a careless, adv -ly. **U~keit** f - carelessness

unangebracht a inappropriate

unangemeldet a unexpected, adv -ly

unangemessen a inappropriate, adv -ly

unangenehm a unpleasant, adv -ly; (peinlich) embarrassing

Unannehmlichkeiten fpl trouble sg

unansehnlich a shabby; ⟨Person⟩ plain

unanständig a indecent, adv -ly

unantastbar a inviolable

unappetitlich a unappetizing

Unart f -,-en bad habit. **u~ig** a naughty

unauffällig a inconspicuous, adv -ly, unobtrusive, adv -ly

unauffindbar a u~ sein be nowhere to be found

unaufgefordert adv without being asked

unaufhaltsam a inexorable, adv -bly. **u~hörlich** a incessant, adv -ly

unaufmerksam a inattentive

unaufrichtig a insincere

unausbleiblich a inevitable

unausgeglichen a unbalanced; ⟨Person⟩ unstable

unauslöschlich a (fig) indelible, adv -bly. **u~sprechlich** a indescribable, adv -bly. **u~stehlich** a insufferable

unbarmherzig a merciless, adv -ly

unbeabsichtigt a unintentional, adv -ly

unbedacht a rash, adv -ly

unbedenklich a harmless □ adv without hesitation

unbedeutend a insignificant; (geringfügig) slight, adv -ly

unbedingt a absolute, adv -ly; **nicht u~** not necessarily

unbefangen a natural, adv -ly; (unparteiisch) impartial

unbefriedigend a unsatisfactory. **u~t** a dissatisfied

unbefugt a unauthorized □ adv without authorization

unbegreiflich a incomprehensible

unbegrenzt a unlimited □ adv indefinitely

unbegründet a unfounded

Unbehag|en nt unease; (körperlich) discomfort. **u~lich** a uncomfortable, adv -bly

unbeholfen a awkward, adv -ly

unbekannt a unknown; (nicht vertraut) unfamiliar. **U~e(r)** m/f stranger

unbekümmert a unconcerned; (unbeschwert) carefree

unbeliebt a unpopular. **U~heit** f unpopularity

unbemannt a unmanned

unbemerkt a & adv unnoticed

unbenutzt a unused

unbequem a uncomfortable, adv -bly; (lästig) awkward

unberechenbar a unpredictable

unberechtigt a unjustified; (unbefugt) unauthorized

unberufen int touch wood!

unberührt a untouched; (fig) virgin; ⟨Landschaft⟩ unspoilt

unbescheiden a presumptuous

unbeschrankt a unguarded
unbeschränkt a unlimited □adv without limit
unbeschreiblich a indescribable, adv -bly
unbeschwert a carefree
unbesiegbar a invincible
unbesiegt a undefeated
unbesonnen a rash, adv -ly
unbespielt a blank
unbeständig a inconsistent; ⟨Wetter⟩ unsettled
unbestechlich a incorruptible
unbestimmt a indefinite; ⟨Alter⟩ indeterminate; ⟨ungewiß⟩ uncertain; ⟨unklar⟩ vague □adv vaguely
unbestreitbar a indisputable, adv -bly
unbestritten a undisputed □adv indisputably
unbeteiligt a indifferent; u~ an (+ dat) not involved in
unbetont a unstressed
unbewacht a unguarded
unbewaffnet a unarmed
unbeweglich a & adv motionless, still
unbewohnt a uninhabited
unbewußt a unconscious, adv -ly
unbezahlbar a priceless
unbezahlt a unpaid
unbrauchbar a useless
und conj and; **und so weiter** and so on; **nach und nach** bit by bit
Undank m ingratitude. **u~bar** a ungrateful; (nicht lohnend) thankless. **U~barkeit** f ingratitude
undefinierbar a indefinable
undenk|bar a unthinkable. **u~lich** a seit u~lichen Zeiten from time immemorial
undeutlich a indistinct, adv -ly; (vage) vague, adv -ly
undicht a leaking; **u~e Stelle** leak
Unding nt absurdity

undiplomatisch a undiplomatic, adv -ally
unduldsam a intolerant
undurch|dringlich a impenetrable; ⟨Miene⟩ inscrutable. **u~-führbar** a impracticable
undurch|lässig a impermeable. **u~sichtig** a opaque; (fig) doubtful
uneben a uneven, adv -ly. **U~heit** f -,-en unevenness; (Buckel) bump
unecht a false; **u~er Schmuck/ Pelz** imitation jewellery/fur
unehelich a illegitimate
unehr|enhaft a dishonourable, adv -bly. **u~lich** a dishonest, adv -ly. **U~lichkeit** f dishonesty
uneinig a (fig) divided; [sich (dat)] u~ sein disagree. **U~keit** f disagreement; (Streit) discord
uneins a u~ sein be at odds
unempfindlich a insensitive (gegen to); (widerstandsfähig) tough; (Med) immune
unendlich a infinite, adv -ly; (endlos) endless, adv -ly. **U~keit** f - infinity
unentbehrlich a indispensable
unentgeltlich a free; ⟨Arbeit⟩ unpaid □adv free of charge; ⟨arbeiten⟩ without pay
unentschieden a undecided; (Sport) drawn; **u~ spielen** draw. **U~** nt -s,- draw
unentschlossen a indecisive; (unentschieden) undecided. **U~heit** f indecision
unentwegt a persistent, adv -ly; (unaufhörlich) incessant, adv -ly
unerbittlich a implacable, adv -bly; ⟨Schicksal⟩ inexorable
unerfahren a inexperienced. **U~heit** f - inexperience
unerfreulich a unpleasant, adv -ly
unergründlich a unfathomable
unerhört a enormous, adv -ly; (empörend) outrageous, adv -ly

unerklärlich *a* inexplicable

unerläßlich *a* essential

unerlaubt *a* unauthorized □*adv* without permission

unermeßlich *a* immense, *adv* -ly

unermüdlich *a* tireless, *adv* -ly

unersättlich *a* insatiable

unerschöpflich *a* inexhaustible

unerschütterlich *a* unshakeable

unerschwinglich *a* prohibitive

unersetzlich *a* irreplaceable; ⟨*Verlust*⟩ irreparable

unerträglich *a* unbearable, *adv* ·bly

unerwartet *a* unexpected, *adv* -ly

unerwünscht *a* unwanted; ⟨*Besuch*⟩ unwelcome

unfähig *a* incompetent; u~, etw zu tun incapable of doing sth; (*nicht in der Lage*) unable to do sth. U~keit *f* incompetence; inability (zu to)

unfair *a* unfair, *adv* -ly

Unfall *m* accident. U~flucht *f* failure to stop after an accident. U~station *f* casualty department

unfaßbar *a* incomprehensible; (*unglaublich*) unimaginable

unfehlbar *a* infallible. U~keit *f* infallibility

unfolgsam *a* disobedient

unförmig *a* shapeless

unfreiwillig *a* involuntary, *adv* -ily; (*unbeabsichtigt*) unintentional, *adv* -ly

unfreundlich *a* unfriendly; (*unangenehm*) unpleasant, *adv* -ly. U~keit *f* unfriendliness; unpleasantness

Unfriede[n] *m* discord

unfruchtbar *a* infertile; (*fig*) unproductive. U~keit *f* infertility

Unfug *m* -s mischief; (*Unsinn*) nonsense

Ungar|(in) *m* -n,-n (*f* -,-nen) Hungarian. u~isch *a* Hungarian. U~n *nt* -s Hungary

ungastlich *a* inhospitable

ungeachtet *prep* (+ *gen*) in spite of. ungebärdig *a* unruly. ungebeugt *a* (*Gram*) uninflected. ungebraucht *a* unused. ungebührlich *a* improper, *adv* -ly. ungedeckt *a* uncovered; (*Sport*) unmarked; ⟨*Tisch*⟩ unlaid

Ungeduld *f* impatience. u~ig *a* impatient, *adv* -ly

ungeeignet *a* unsuitable

ungefähr *a* approximate, *adv* -ly, rough, *adv* -ly

ungefährlich *a* harmless

ungehalten *a* angry, *adv* -ily

ungeheuer *a* enormous, *adv* -ly. U~ *nt* -s,- monster

ungeheuerlich *a* outrageous

ungehobelt *a* uncouth

ungehörig *a* improper, *adv* -ly; (*frech*) impertinent, *adv* -ly

ungehorsam *a* disobedient. U~ *m* disobedience

ungeklärt *a* unsolved; ⟨*Frage*⟩ unsettled; ⟨*Ursache*⟩ unknown

ungeladen *a* unloaded; ⟨*Gast*⟩ uninvited

ungelegen *a* inconvenient. U~heiten *fpl* trouble *sg*

ungelernt *a* unskilled. ungemein *a* tremendous, *adv* -ly

ungemütlich *a* uncomfortable, *adv* -bly; (*unangenehm*) unpleasant, *adv* -ly

ungenau *a* inaccurate, *adv* -ly; (*vage*) vague, *adv* -ly. U~igkeit *f* -,-en inaccuracy

ungeniert /'unʒeni:ɐt/ *a* uninhibited □*adv* openly

ungenießbar *a* inedible; ⟨*Getränk*⟩ undrinkable. ungenügend *a* inadequate, *adv* -ly; (*Sch*) unsatisfactory. ungepflegt *a* neglected; ⟨*Person*⟩ unkempt. ungerade *a* ⟨*Zahl*⟩ odd

ungerecht *a* unjust, *adv* -ly. U~igkeit *f* -,-en injustice

ungern *adv* reluctantly

ungesalzen *a* unsalted

ungeschehen *a* u~ machen undo

Ungeschick|lichkeit *f* clumsiness. **u~t** *a* clumsy, *adv* -ily

ungeschminkt *a* without makeup; ⟨*Wahrheit*⟩ unvarnished. **ungeschrieben** *a* unwritten. **ungesehen** *a* & *adv* unseen. **ungesellig** *a* unsociable. **ungesetzlich** *a* illegal, *adv* -ly. **ungestört** *a* undisturbed. **ungestraft** *a* with impunity. **ungestüm** *a* impetuous, *adv* -ly. **ungesund** *a* unhealthy. **ungesüßt** *a* unsweetened. **ungetrübt** *a* perfect

Ungetüm *nt* -s,-e monster

ungewiß *a* uncertain; **im ungewissen lassen** leave in the dark. **U~heit** *f* uncertainty

ungewöhnlich *a* unusual, *adv* -ly. **ungewohnt** *a* unaccustomed; (*nicht vertraut*) unfamiliar. **ungewollt** *a* unintentional, *adv* -ly; ⟨*Schwangerschaft*⟩ unwanted

Ungeziefer *nt* -s vermin

ungezogen *a* naughty, *adv* -ily

ungezwungen *a* informal, *adv* -ly; (*natürlich*) natural, *adv* -ly

ungläubig *a* incredulous

unglaublich *a* incredible, *adv* -bly, unbelievable, *adv* -bly

ungleich *a* unequal, *adv* -ly; (*verschieden*) different. **U~heit** *f* - inequality. **u~mäßig** *a* uneven, *adv* -ly

Unglück *nt* -s,-e misfortune; (*Pech*) bad luck; (*Mißgeschick*) mishap; (*Unfall*) accident; **U~bringen** be unlucky. **u~lich** *a* unhappy, *adv* -ily; (*ungünstig*) unfortunate, *adv* -ly. **u~licherweise** *adv* unfortunately. **u~selig** *a* unfortunate. **U~sfall** *m* accident

ungültig *a* invalid; (*Jur*) void

ungünstig *a* unfavourable, *adv* -bly; (*unpassend*) inconvenient, *adv* -ly

ungut *a* ⟨*Gefühl*⟩ uneasy; **nichts für u~!** no offence!

unhandlich *a* unwieldy

Unheil *nt* -s disaster; **U~ anrichten** cause havoc

unheilbar *a* incurable, *adv* -bly

unheimlich *a* eerie; (*gruselig*) creepy; (*fam: groß*) terrific □ *adv* eerily; (*fam: sehr*) terribly

unhöflich *a* rude, *adv* -ly. **U~keit** *f* rudeness

unhörbar *a* inaudible, *adv* -bly

unhygienisch *a* unhygienic

Uni *f* -,-s (*fam*) university

uni /y'ni:/ *inv* *a* plain

Uniform *f* -,-en uniform

uninteress|ant *a* uninteresting. **u~iert** *a* uninterested; (*unbeteiligt*) disinterested

Union *f* -,-en union

universal *a* universal

universell *a* universal, *adv* -ly

Universität *f* -,-en university

Universum *nt* -s universe

unkenntlich *a* unrecognizable. **U~nis** *f* ignorance

unklar *a* unclear; (*ungewiß*) uncertain; (*vage*) vague, *adv* -ly; **im u~en sein** be in the dark. **U~heit** *f* -,-en uncertainty

unklug *a* unwise, *adv* -ly

unkompliziert *a* uncomplicated

Unkosten *pl* expenses

Unkraut *nt* weed; (*coll*) weeds *pl*; **U~ jäten** weed. **U~vertilgungsmittel** *nt* weed-killer

unkultiviert *a* uncultured

unlängst *adv* recently

unlauter *a* dishonest; (*unfair*) unfair

unleserlich *a* illegible, *adv* -bly

unleugbar *a* undeniable, *adv* -bly

unlogisch *a* illogical, *adv* -ly

unlös|bar *a* (*fig*) insoluble. **u~lich** *a* (*Chem*) insoluble

unlustig *a* listless, *adv* -ly

unmäßig *a* excessive, *adv* -ly; (*äußerst*) extreme, *adv* -ly

Unmenge f enormous amount/ (Anzahl) number

Unmensch m (fam) brute. **u~lich** a inhuman; (entsetzlich) appalling, adv -ly

unmerklich a imperceptible, adv -bly

unmißverständlich a unambiguous, adv -ly; (offen) unequivocal, adv -ly

unmittelbar a immediate, adv -ly; (direkt) direct, adv -ly

unmöbliert a unfurnished

unmodern a old-fashioned

unmöglich a impossible, adv -bly. **U~keit** f - impossibility

Unmoral f immorality. **u~isch** a immoral, adv -ly

unmündig a under-age

Unmut m displeasure

unnachahmlich a inimitable

unnachgiebig a intransigent

unnatürlich a unnatural, adv -ly

unnormal a abnormal, adv -ly

unnötig a unnecessary, adv -ly

unnütz a useless □adv needlessly

unordentlich a untidy, adv -ly; (nachlässig) sloppy, adv -ily. **U~nung** f disorder; (Durcheinander) muddle

unorganisiert a disorganized

unorthodox a unorthodox □adv in an unorthodox manner

unparteiisch a impartial, adv -ly

unpassend a inappropriate, adv -ly; (Moment) inopportune

unpäßlich a indisposed

unpersönlich a impersonal

unpraktisch a impractical

unpünktlich a unpunctual □adv late

unrasiert a unshaven

Unrast f restlessness

unrealistisch a unrealistic, adv -ally

unrecht a wrong, adv -ly □n u~ haben be wrong; jdm u~ tun do s.o. an injustice; jdm u~ geben disagree with s.o. **U~nt** wrong;

zu U~ wrongly. **u~mäßig** a unlawful, adv -ly

unregelmäßig a irregular, adv -ly. **U~keit** f irregularity

unreif a unripe; (fig) immature

unrein a impure; (Luft) polluted; (Haut) bad; **ins u~e schreiben** make a rough draft of

unrentabel a unprofitable, adv -bly

unrichtig a incorrect

Unruhe f -,-n restlessness; (Erregung) agitation; (Besorgnis) anxiety; **U~en** (Pol) unrest sg. **u~ig** a restless, adv -ly; (Meer) agitated; (laut) noisy, adv -ily; (besorgt) anxious, adv -ly

uns pron (acc/dat of wir) us; (refl) ourselves; (einander) each other; **ein Freund von uns** a friend of ours

unsagbar, unsäglich a indescribable, adv -bly

unsanft a rough, adv -ly

unsauber a dirty; (nachlässig) sloppy, adv -ily; (unlauter) dishonest, adv -ly

unschädlich a harmless

unscharf a blurred

unschätzbar a inestimable

unscheinbar a inconspicuous

unschicklich a improper, adv -ly

unschlagbar a unbeatable

unschlüssig a undecided

Unschuld f - innocence; (Jungfräulichkeit) virginity. **u~ig** a innocent, adv -ly

unselbständig a dependent □adv **u~ denken** not think for oneself

unser poss pron our. **u~e(r,s)** poss pron ours. **u~erseits** adv for our part. **u~twegen** adv for our sake; (wegen uns) because of us, on our account. **u~twillen** adv um u~twillen for our sake

unsicher a unsafe; (ungewiß) uncertain; (nicht zuverlässig) unreliable; (Schritte, Hand) unsteady; (Person) insecure □adv unsteadily. **U~heit** *f* uncertainty; unreliability; insecurity

unsichtbar *a* invisible

Unsinn *m* nonsense. **u~ig** *a* nonsensical, absurd

Unsitte *f* bad habit. **u~lich** *a* indecent, *adv* -ly

unsportlich *a* not sporty; (*unfair*) unsporting, *adv* -ly

uns|re(r,s) *poss pron* = **unsere(r,s)**. **u~rige** *poss pron* **der/die/das u~rige** ours

unsterblich *a* immortal. **U~keit** *f* immortality

unstet *a* restless, *adv* -ly; (*unbeständig*) unstable

Unstimmigkeit *f* -,-en inconsistency; (*Streit*) difference

Unsumme *f* vast sum

unsymmetrisch *a* not symmetrical

unsympathisch *a* unpleasant; **er ist mir u~** I don't like him

untätig *a* idle, *adv* idly. **U~keit** *f* - idleness

untauglich *a* unsuitable; (*Mil*) unfit

unteilbar *a* indivisible

unten *adv* at the bottom; (*auf der Unterseite*) underneath; (*eine Treppe tiefer*) downstairs; **hier/da u~** down here/there; **nach u~** down[wards]; (*die Treppe hinunter*) downstairs

unter *prep* (+*dat/acc*) under; (*niedriger als*) below; (*inmitten, zwischen*) among; **u~ anderem** among other things; **u~ der Woche** during the week; **u~ sich** by themselves; **u~ uns gesagt** between ourselves

Unter|arm *m* forearm. **U~bewußtsein** *nt* subconscious

unterbieten† *vt insep* undercut; beat ⟨*Rekord*⟩

unterbinden† *vt insep* stop

unterbleiben† *vi insep* (sein) cease; **es hat zu u~** it must stop

unterbrech|en† *vt insep* interrupt; break ⟨*Reise*⟩. **U~ung** *f* -,-en interruption; break

unterbreiten *vt insep* present

unterbringen† *vt sep* put; (*beherbergen*) put up

unterdessen *adv* in the meantime

unterdrück|en *vt insep* suppress; oppress ⟨*Volk*⟩. **U~ung** *f* suppression; oppression

untere(r,s) *a* lower

untereinander *adv* one below the other; (*miteinander*) among ourselves/yourselves/themselves

unterernährt *a* undernourished. **U~ung** *f* malnutrition

Unterfangen *nt* -s,- venture

Unterführung *f* underpass; (*Fußgänger-*) subway

Untergang *m* (*Astr*) setting; (*Naut*) sinking; (*Zugrundegehen*) disappearance; (*der Welt*) end

Untergebene(r) *m/f* subordinate

untergehen† *vi sep* (sein) (*Astr*) set; (*versinken*) go under; ⟨*Schiff:*⟩ go down, sink; (*zugrunde gehen*) disappear; ⟨*Welt:*⟩ come to an end

untergeordnet *a* subordinate

Untergeschoß *nt* basement

untergraben† *vt insep* (*fig*) undermine

Untergrund *m* foundation; (*Hintergrund*) background; (*Pol*) underground. **U~bahn** *f* underground [railway]; (*Amer*) subway

unterhaken *vt sep* jdn **u~** take s.o.'s arm; **untergehakt** arm in arm

unterhalb *adv* & *prep* (+ *gen*) below

Unterhalt *m* maintenance

unterhalt|en† *vt insep* maintain; (*ernähren*) support; (*betreiben*) run; (*erheitern*) entertain; **sich u~en** talk; (*sich vergnügen*) enjoy oneself. **u~sam** *a* entertaining. **U~ung** *f* -,-en maintenance;

(*Gespräch*) conversation; (*Zeitvertrieb*) entertainment

unterhandeln *vi insep* (*haben*) negotiate

Unter|haus *nt* (*Pol*) lower house; (*in UK*) House of Commons. U~**hemd** *nt* vest. U~**holz** *nt* undergrowth. U~**hose** *f* underpants *pl.* u~**irdisch** *a & adv* underground

unterjochen *vt insep* subjugate

Unterkiefer *m* lower jaw

unter|kommen† *vi insep* (*sein*) find accommodation; (*eine Stellung finden*) get a job. u~**kriegen** *vt sep* (*fam*) get down

Unterkunft *f* -,-künfte accommodation

Unterlage *f* pad; U~**n** papers

Unterlaß *m* ohne U~ incessantly

unterlass|en† *vt insep* etw u~en refrain from [doing] sth; (*es u~en, etw zu tun* fail or omit to do sth. U~**ung** *f* -,-en omission

unterlaufen† *vi insep* (*sein*) occur; **mir ist ein Fehler u~** I made a mistake

unterlegen¹ *vt sep* put underneath

unterlegen² *a* inferior; (*Sport*) losing; **zahlenmäßig u~** outnumbered (*dat* by). U~**e(r)** *m/f* loser

Unterleib *m* abdomen

unterliegen† *vi insep* (*sein*) lose (*dat* to); (*unterworfen sein*) be subject (*dat* to)

Unterlippe *f* lower lip

unterm *prep* = unter dem

Untermiete *f* zur U~ wohnen be a lodger. U~**r(in)** *m(f)* lodger

unterminieren *vt insep* undermine

untern *prep* = unter den

unternehm|en† *vt insep* undertake; take ⟨Schritte⟩; **etw/nichts u~en** do sth/nothing. U~**en** *nt*

-s,- undertaking, enterprise; (*Betrieb*) concern. U~**end** *a* enterprising. U~**er** *m* -s,- employer; (*Bau*-) contractor; (*Industrieller*) industrialist. U~**ung** *f* -,-en undertaking, (*Comm*) venture. u~**ungslustig** *a* enterprising; (*abenteuerlustig*) adventurous

Unteroffizier *m* non-commissioned officer

unterordnen *vt sep* subordinate; **sich u~** accept a subordinate role

Unterredung *f* -,-en talk

Unterricht *m* -[e]s teaching; (*Privat*-) tuition; (U~**sstunden**) lessons *pl*; U~ **geben/nehmen** give/have lessons

unterrichten *vt/i insep* (*haben*) teach; (*informieren*) inform; **sich u~** inform oneself

Unterrock *m* slip

unters *prep* = unter das

untersagen *vt insep* forbid

Untersatz *m* mat; (*mit Füßen*) stand; (*Gläser*-) coaster

unterschätzen *vt insep* underestimate

unterscheid|en† *vt/i insep* (*haben*) distinguish; (*auseinanderhalten*) tell apart; **sich u~en** differ. U~**ung** *f* -,-en distinction

Unterschied *m* -[e]s,-e difference; (*Unterscheidung*) distinction; **im U~ zu ihm** unlike him. u~**lich** *a* different; (*wechselnd*) varying; **das ist u~lich** it varies. u~**slos** *a* equal, *adv* -ly

unterschlag|en† *vt insep* embezzle; (*verheimlichen*) suppress. U~**ung** *f* -,-en embezzlement; suppression

Unterschlupf *m* -[e]s shelter; (*Versteck*) hiding-place

unterschreiben† *vt/i insep* (*haben*) sign

Unter|schrift *f* signature; *(Bild-)* caption. **U~seeboot** *nt* submarine. **U~setzer** *m* -s,- = **Untersatz**

untersetzt *a* stocky

Unterstand *m* shelter

unterste(r,s) *a* lowest, bottom

unterstehen¹† *vi sep (haben)* shelter

unterstehen² *v insep □vi (haben)* be answerable *(dat* to); *(unterliegen)* be subject *(dat* to) *□vr* **sich u~** dare; **untersteh dich!** don't you dare!

unterstellen¹ *vt sep* put underneath; *(abstellen)* store; **sich u~** shelter

unterstellen² *vt insep* place under the control *(dat* of); *(annehmen)* assume; *(fälschlich zuschreiben)* impute *(dat* to)

unterstreichen† *vt insep* underline

unterstütz|en *vt insep* support; *(helfen)* aid. **U~ung** *f* -,-en support; *(finanziell)* aid; *(regelmäßiger Betrag)* allowance; *(Arbeitslosen-)* benefit

untersuch|en *vt insep* examine; *(Jur)* investigate; *(prüfen)* test; *(überprüfen)* check; *(durchsuchen)* search. **U~ung** *f* -,-en examination; investigation; test; check; search. **U~ungshaft** *f* detention on remand; **in U~ungshaft** on remand. **U~ungsrichter** *m* examining magistrate

Untertan *m* -s & -en,-en subject

Untertasse *f* saucer

untertauchen *v sep □vt* duck □*vi (sein)* go under; *(fig)* disappear

Unterteil *nt* bottom (part)

unterteilen *vt insep* subdivide; *(aufteilen)* divide

Untertitel *m* subtitle

Unterton *m* undertone

untervermieten *vt/i insep (haben)* sublet

unterwandern *vt insep* infiltrate

Unterwäsche *f* underwear

Unterwasser- *pref* underwater

unterwegs *adv* on the way; *(außer Haus)* out; *(verreist)* away

unterweisen† *vt insep* instruct

Unterwelt *f* underworld

unterwerfen† *vt insep* subjugate; **sich u~en** submit *(dat* to); **etw** *(dat)* **unterworfen sein** be subject to sth

unterwürfig *a* obsequious, *adv* -ly

unterzeichnen *vt insep* sign

unterziehen¹† *vt sep* put on underneath; *(Culin)* fold in

unterziehen²† *vt insep* **etw einer Untersuchung/Überprüfung u~** examine/ check sth; **sich einer Operation/Prüfung u~** have an operation/take a test

Untier *nt* monster

untragbar *a* intolerable

untrennbar *a* inseparable

untreu *a* disloyal; *(in der Ehe)* unfaithful. **U~e** *f* disloyalty; infidelity

untröstlich *a* inconsolable

untrüglich *a* infallible

Untugend *f* bad habit

überlegt *a* rash, *adv* -ly

unüber|sehbar *a* obvious; *(groß)* immense. **u~troffen** *a* unsurpassed

unum|gänglich *a* absolutely necessary. **u~schränkt** *a* absolute. **u~wunden** *adv* frankly

ununterbrochen *a* incessant, *adv* -ly

unveränderlich *a* invariable; *(gleichbleibend)* unchanging

unverändert *a* unchanged

unverantwortlich *a* irresponsible, *adv* -bly

unverbesserlich *a* incorrigible

unverbindlich *a* non-committal; *(Comm)* not binding □*adv* without obligation

unverblümt *a* blunt □*adv* -ly

unverdaulich *a* indigestible

unver|einbar *a* incompatible.
u~geßlich *a* unforgettable.
u~gleichlich *a* incomparable
unver|hältnismäßig *a*
disproportionate. **u~heiratet**
a unmarried. **u~hofft** *a* unexpected, *adv* -ly. **u~hohlen** *a* un-
disguised □*adv* openly. **u~käuf-
lich** *a* not for sale; ⟨*Muster*⟩ free
unverkennbar *a* unmistakable,
adv -bly
unverletzt *a* unhurt
unvermeidlich *a* inevitable
unver|mindert *a & adv* undi-
minished. **u~mittelt** *a* abrupt,
adv -ly. **u~mutet** *a* unexpected,
adv -ly
Unver|nunft *f* folly. **u~nünftig**
a foolish, *adv* -ly
unverschämt *a* insolent, *adv* -ly;
(*fam: ungeheuer*) outrageous,
adv -ly. **u~heit** *f* -,-en insolence
unver|sehens *adv* suddenly.
u~sehrt *a* unhurt; (*unbeschädigt*) intact. **u~söhnlich** *a* irreconcilable; ⟨*Gegner*⟩ implacable
unverständ|lich *a* incompre-
hensible; (*undeutlich*) indistinct.
U~nis *f* lack of understanding
unverträglich *a* incompatible;
⟨*Person*⟩ quarrelsome; (*unbe-
kömmlich*) indigestible
unverwandt *a* fixed, *adv* -ly
unver|wundbar *a* invulnerable.
u~wüstlich *a* indestructible;
⟨*Person, Humor*⟩ irrepressible;
⟨*Gesundheit*⟩ robust. **u~zeih-
lich** *a* unforgivable
unverzüglich *a* immediate, *adv*
-ly
unvollendet *a* unfinished
unvollkommen *a* imperfect; (*unvollständig*) incomplete. **U~heit**
f -,-en imperfection
unvollständig *a* incomplete
unvor|bereitet *a* unprepared.
u~eingenommen *a* unbiased.
u~hergesehen *a* unforeseen

unvorsichtig *a* careless, *adv* -ly.
U~keit *f* - carelessness
unvorstellbar *a* unimaginable,
adv -bly
unvorteilhaft *a* unfavourable;
(*nicht hübsch*) unattractive;
⟨*Kleid, Frisur*⟩ unflattering
unwahr *a* untrue. **U~heit** *f* -,-en
untruth. **u~scheinlich** *a* unlikely; (*unglaublich*) improbable;
(*fam: groß*) incredible, *adv* -bly
unweigerlich *a* inevitable, *adv*
-bly
unweit *adv & prep* (+ *gen*) not far;
u~ vom Fluß/des Flusses not
far from the river
unwesentlich *a* unimportant
□*adv* slightly
Unwetter *nt* -s,- storm
unwichtig *a* unimportant
unwider|legbar *a* irrefutable.
u~ruflich *a* irrevocable, *adv*
-bly. **u~stehlich** *a* irresistible
Unwille|e *m* displeasure. **u~ig** *a*
angry, *adv* -ily; (*widerwillig*) reluctant, *adv* -ly. **u~kürlich** *a*
involuntary, *adv* -ily; (*instinktiv*)
instinctive, *adv* -ly
unwirklich *a* unreal
unwirksam *a* ineffective
unwirsch *a* irritable, *adv* -bly
unwirtlich *a* inhospitable
unwirtschaftlich *a* uneconomic,
adv -ally
unwissen|d *a* ignorant. **U~heit**
f - ignorance
unwohl *a* unwell; (*unbehaglich*)
uneasy. **U~sein** *nt* -s indisposi-
tion
unwürdig *a* unworthy (*gen* of);
(*würdelos*) undignified
Unzahl *f* vast number. **unzählig**
a innumerable, countless
unzerbrechlich *a* unbreakable
unzerstörbar *a* indestructible
unzertrennlich *a* inseparable
Unzucht *f* sexual offence; **ge-
werbsmäßige U~** prostitution

unzüchtig a indecent, adv -ly; ⟨Schriften⟩ obscene

unzufrieden a dissatisfied; (innerlich) discontented. **U~heit** f dissatisfaction; (Pol) discontent

unzulänglich a inadequate, adv -ly

unzulässig a inadmissible

unzumutbar a unreasonable

unzurechnungsfähig a insane. **U~keit** f insanity

unzusammenhängend a incoherent

unzutreffend a inapplicable; (falsch) incorrect

unzuverlässig a unreliable

unzweckmäßig a unsuitable, adv -bly

unzweideutig a unambiguous

unzweifelhaft a undoubted, adv -ly

üppig a luxuriant, adv -ly; (überreichlich) lavish, adv -ly; ⟨Busen, Figur⟩ voluptuous

uralt a ancient

Uran nt -s uranium

Uraufführung f first performance

urbar a u~ machen cultivate

Ureinwohner mpl native inhabitants

Urenkel m great-grandson; (pl) great-grandchildren

Urgroß|mutter f great-grandmother. **U~vater** m great-grandfather

Urheber m -s,- originator; (Verfasser) author. **U~recht** nt copyright

Urin m -s,-e urine

Urkunde f -,-n certificate; (Dokument) document

Urlaub m -s holiday; (Mil, Admin) leave; **auf U~** on holiday/ leave; **U~ haben** be on holiday/ leave. **U~er(in)** m (f -,-nen) holiday-maker. **U~sort** m holiday resort

Urne f -,-n urn; (Wahl-) ballot-box

Ursache f cause; (Grund) reason; **keine U~!** don't mention it!

Ursprung m origin

ursprünglich a original, adv -ly; (anfänglich) initial, adv -ly; (natürlich) natural

Urteil nt -s,-e judgement; (Meinung) opinion; (U~sspruch) verdict; (Strafe) sentence. **u~en** vi (haben) judge. **U~svermögen** nt [power of] judgement

Urwald m primeval forest; (tropischer) jungle

urwüchsig a natural; (derb) earthy

Urzeit f primeval times pl; **seit U~en** from time immemorial

USA pl USA sg

usw. abbr (und so weiter) etc.

Utensilien /-jən/ ntpl utensils

utopisch a Utopian

V

vage /'va:gə/ a vague, adv -ly

Vakuum /'va:kuʊm/ nt -s vacuum. **v~verpackt** a vacuum-packed

Vanille /va'nɪljə/ f - vanilla

vari|abel /va'rja:bəl/ a variable. **V~ante** f -,-n variant. **V~ation** /-'tsjo:n/ f -,-en variation. **v~ieren** vt/i (haben) vary

Vase /'va:zə/ f -,-n vase

Vater m -s,- father. **V~land** nt fatherland

väterlich a paternal; (fürsorglich) fatherly. **v~erseits** adv on one's/the father's side

Vater|schaft f -fatherhood; (Jur) paternity. **V~unser** nt -s,- Lord's Prayer

Vati m -s,-s (fam) daddy

v. Chr. abbr (vor Christus) BC

Vegetar|ier(in) /vege'ta:rjɐ, -jərɪn/ m(f) -s,- (f -,-nen) vegetarian. **v~isch** a vegetarian

Vegetation /vegeta'tsjo:n/ *f* -,-en vegetation

Veilchen *nt* -s,- violet

Vene /'ve:nə/ *f* -,-n vein

Venedig /ve'ne:dɪç/ *nt* -s Venice

Ventil /vɛn'ti:l/ *nt* -s,-e valve.
V~**ator** *m* -s,-en /-'to:rən/ fan

verabreden *vt* arrange; **sich [mit jdm]** v~-en arrange to meet [s.o.]. V~**ung** *f* -,-en arrangement; *(Treffen)* appointment

verabreichen *vt* administer

verabscheuen *vt* detest, loathe

verabschieden *vt* say goodbye to; *(aus dem Dienst)* retire; pass *(Gesetz)*; **sich** v~ say goodbye

verachten *vt* despise. v~**swert** *a* contemptible

verächtlich *a* contemptuous, *adv* -ly; *(unwürdig)* contemptible

Verachtung *f* - contempt

verallgemeiner|n *vt/i (haben)* generalize. V~**ung** *f* -,-en generalization

veralte|n *vi (sein)* become obsolete. v~**t** *a* obsolete

Veranda /ve'randa/ *f* -,-den veranda

veränder|lich *a* changeable; *(Math)* variable. v~**n** *vt* change; **sich** v~**n** change; *(beruflich)* change one's job. V~**ung** *f* change

verängstigt *a* frightened, scared

verankern *vt* anchor

veranlagt *a* künstlerisch/musikalisch v~**t** sein have an artistic/a musical bent; **praktisch** v~**t** practically minded. V~**ung** *f* -,-en disposition; *(Neigung)* tendency; *(künstlerisch)* bent

veranlass|en *vt (reg)* arrange for; *(einleiten)* institute; **jdn** v~**en** prompt s.o. *(zu* to). V~**ung** *f* -,-en reason; **auf meine** V~**ung** at my suggestion; *(Befehl)* on my orders

veranschaulichen *vt* illustrate

veranschlagen *vt (reg)* estimate

veranstalt|en *vt* organize; hold, give *(Party)*; make *(Lärm)*. V~**er** *m* -s,- organizer. V~**ung** *f* -,-en event

verantwort|en *vt* take responsibility for; **sich** v~**en** answer (für for). v~**lich** *a* responsible; v~**lich machen** hold responsible. V~**ung** *f* -,-en responsibility. v~**ungsbewußt** *a* responsible, *adv* -bly. v~**ungslos** *a* irresponsible, *adv* -bly. v~**ungsvoll** *a* responsible

verarbeiten *vt* use; *(Techn)* process; *(verdauen & fig)* digest; v~ **zu** make into

verärgern *vt* annoy

verarmt *a* impoverished

verästeln (sich) *vr* branch out

verausgaben (sich) *vr* spend all one's money; *(körperlich)* wear oneself out

veräußern *vt* sell

Verb /vɛrp/ *nt* -s,-en verb. v~**al** /vɛr'ba:l/ *a* verbal, *adv* -ly

Verband *m* -[e]s,⁻e association; *(Mil)* unit; *(Med)* bandage; *(Wund-)* dressing. V~**szeug** *nt* first-aid kit

verbann|en *vt* exile; *(fig)* banish. V~**ung** *f* - exile

verbarrikadieren *vt* barricade

verbeißen† *vt* suppress; **ich konnte mir kaum das Lachen** v~ I could hardly keep a straight face

verbergen† *vt* hide; **sich** v~ hide

verbesser|n *vt* improve; *(berichtigen)* correct. V~**ung** *f* -,-en improvement; correction

verbeug|en *vr* bow. V~**ung** *f* bow

verbeulen *vt* dent

verbiegen† *vt* bend; **sich** v~ bend

verbieten† *vt* forbid; *(Admin)* prohibit, ban

verbillig|en *vt* reduce [in price]. v~**t** *a* reduced

verbinden† vt connect (**mit** to); (zusammenfügen) join; (verknüpfen) combine; (in Verbindung bringen) associate; (Med) bandage; dress ⟨Wunde⟩; **sich v~** combine; (sich zusammentun) join together; **jdm die Augen v~** blindfold s.o.; **jdm verbunden sein** (fig) be obliged to s.o.

verbindlich a friendly; (bindend) binding. **V~keit** f-,-en friendliness; **V~keiten** obligations; (Comm) liabilities

Verbindung f connection; (Verknüpfung) combination; (Kontakt) contact; (Vereinigung) association; **chemische V~** chemical compound; **in V~ stehen/sich in V~ setzen** be/get in touch

verbissen a grim, adv -ly; (zäh) dogged, adv -ly

verbitten† vt **sich** ⟨dat⟩ **etw v~** not stand for sth

verbittern vt make bitter. **v~t** a bitter. **V~ung** f - bitterness

verblassen vi (sein) fade

Verbleib m -s whereabouts pl. **v~en†** vi (sein) remain

verbleichen† vi (sein) fade

verbleit a ⟨Benzin⟩ leaded

verblüffen vt amaze, astound. **V~ung** f - amazement

verblühen vi (sein) wither, fade

verbluten vi (sein) bleed to death

verborgen¹ a hidden

verborgen² vt lend

Verbot nt -[e]s,-e ban. **v~en** a forbidden; (Admin) prohibited; **'Rauchen v~en'** 'no smoking'

Verbrauch m -[e]s consumption. **v~en** vt use; consume ⟨Lebensmittel⟩; (erschöpfen) use up, exhaust. **V~er** m -s,- consumer. **v~t** a worn; ⟨Luft⟩ stale

verbrechen† vt (fam) perpetrate. **V~** nt -s,- crime

Verbrecher m -s,- criminal. **v~isch** a criminal

verbreiten vt spread; **sich v~en** spread. **v~ern** vt widen. **v~ern** widen. **v~et** a widespread. **V~ung** f - spread; (Verbreiten) spreading

verbrennen† vt/i (sein) burn; cremate ⟨Leiche⟩. **V~ung** f -,-en burning; cremation; (Wunde) burn

verbringen† vt spend

verbrühen vt scald

verbuchen vt enter; (fig) notch up ⟨Erfolg⟩

verbünden (sich) vr form an alliance. **V~ete(r)** m/f ally

verbürgen vt guarantee; **sich v~ für** vouch for

verbüßen vt serve ⟨Strafe⟩

Verdacht m -[e]s suspicion; **in** or **im V~ haben** suspect

verdächtig a suspicious, adv -ly. **v~en** vt suspect (gen of). **V~te(r)** m/f suspect

verdammen vt condemn; (Relig) damn. **V~nis** f - damnation. **v~t** a & adv (sl) damned; **v~t!** damn!

verdampfen vt/i (sein) evaporate

verdanken vt owe (dat to)

verdauen vt digest. **v~lich** a digestible. **V~ung** f - digestion

Verdeck nt -[e]s,-e hood; (Oberdeck) top deck. **v~en** vt cover; (verbergen) hide, conceal

verdenken† vt **das kann man ihm nicht v~** you can't blame him for it

verderben† vt/i (sein) spoil; ⟨Lebensmittel:⟩ go bad ⟨vt spoil; (zerstören) ruin; (moralisch) corrupt; **ich habe mir den Magen verdorben** I have an upset stomach. **V~en** nt -s ruin. **v~lich** a perishable; (schädlich) pernicious

verdeutlichen vt make clear

verdichten vt compress; **sich v~** ⟨Nebel:⟩ thicken

verdienen vt/i (haben) earn; (fig) deserve. **V~er** m -s,- wage-earner

Verdienst[1] *m* -[e]s earnings *pl*

Verdienst[2] *nt* -[e]s,-e merit

verdient *a* well-deserved; ⟨*Person*⟩ of outstanding merit. **v~er-maßen** *adv* deservedly

verdoppeln *vt* double; ⟨*fig*⟩ re-double; **sich v~** double

verdorben *a* spoilt, ruined; ⟨*Magen*⟩ upset; ⟨*moralisch*⟩ corrupt; ⟨*verkommen*⟩ depraved

verdorren *vi* (*sein*) wither

verdrängen *vt* force out; ⟨*fig*⟩ displace; ⟨*psychisch*⟩ repress

verdreh|en *vt* twist; roll ⟨*Augen*⟩; ⟨*fig*⟩ distort. **v~t** *a* ⟨*fam*⟩ crazy

verdreifachen *vt* treble, triple

verdreschen† *vt* ⟨*fam*⟩ thrash

verdrießlich *a* morose, *adv* -ly

verdrücken *vt* crumple; ⟨*fam: essen*⟩ polish off; **sich v~** ⟨*fam*⟩ slip away

Verdruß *m* -sses annoyance

verdunk|eln *vt* darken; black out ⟨*Zimmer*⟩; **sich v~** darken. **V~[e]lung** *f* black-out

verdünnen *vt* dilute; **sich v~** taper off

verdunst|en *vi* (*sein*) evaporate. **V~ung** *f* evaporation

verdursten *vi* (*sein*) die of thirst

verdutzt *a* baffled

veredeln *vt* refine; ⟨*Hort*⟩ graft

verehr|en *vt* revere; ⟨*Relig*⟩ worship; ⟨*bewundern*⟩ admire; ⟨*schenken*⟩ give. **V~er(in)** *m* -s, (*f* -,-nen) admirer. **V~ung** *f* veneration; worship; admiration

vereidigen *vt* swear in

Verein *m* -s,-e society; ⟨*Sport*⟩ club

vereinbar *a* compatible. **v~en** *vt* arrange; **nicht zu v~en** incompatible. **V~ung** *f* -,-en agreement

vereinen *vt* unite; **sich v~** unite

vereinfachen *vt* simplify

vereinheitlichen *vt* standardize

vereinig|en *vt* unite; merge ⟨*Firmen*⟩; **sich v~en** unite; **V~te**

Staaten [von Amerika] United States *sg* [of America]. **V~ung** *f* -,-en union; ⟨*Organisation*⟩ organization

vereinsamt *a* lonely

vereinzelt *a* isolated □ *adv* occasionally

vereist *a* frozen; ⟨*Straße*⟩ icy

vereiteln *vt* foil, thwart

vereitert *a* septic

verenden *vi* (*sein*) die

verengen *vt* restrict; **sich v~** narrow; ⟨*Pupille:*⟩ contract

vererb|en *vt* leave ⟨*dat* to); ⟨*Biol & fig*⟩ pass on ⟨*dat* to). **V~ung** *f* heredity

verewigen *vt* immortalize; **sich v~** ⟨*fam*⟩ leave one's mark

verfahren† *vi* (*sein*) proceed; **v~ mit deal with** □ *vr* **sich v~** lose one's way □ *a* muddled. **V~** *nt* -s, procedure; ⟨*Techn*⟩ process; ⟨*Jur*⟩ proceedings *pl*

Verfall *m* decay; ⟨*eines Gebäudes*⟩ dilapidation; ⟨*körperlich & fig*⟩ decline; ⟨*Ablauf*⟩ expiry. **v~en†** *vi* (*sein*) decay; ⟨*Person, Sitten:*⟩ decline; ⟨*ablaufen*⟩ expire; **v~en in** (+ *acc*) lapse into; **v~en auf** (+ *acc*) hit on ⟨*Idee*⟩; **jdm/etw v~en** be under the spell of s.o./sth; be addicted to ⟨*Alkohol*⟩

verfälschen *vt* falsify; adulterate ⟨*Wein, Lebensmittel*⟩

verfänglich *a* awkward

verfärben (sich) *vr* change colour; ⟨*Stoff:*⟩ discolour

verfass|en *vt* write; ⟨*Jur*⟩ draw up; ⟨*entwerfen*⟩ draft. **V~er** *m* -s, author. **V~ung** *f* ⟨*Pol*⟩ constitution; ⟨*Zustand*⟩ state

verfaulen *vi* (*sein*) rot, decay

verfechten† *vt* advocate

verfehlen *vt* miss

verfeind|en (sich) *vr* become enemies; **v~t sein** be enemies

verfeinern *vt* refine; ⟨*verbessern*⟩ improve

verfilmen *vt* film

verfilzt a matted
verflieg|en† vi (sein) evaporate; ⟨Zeit:⟩ fly
verflixt a (fam) awkward; (verdammt) blessed; **v~!** damn!
verfluch|en vt curse. **v~t** a & adv (fam) damned; **v~t!** damn!
verflüchtigen (sich) vr evaporate
verflüssigen vt liquefy
verfolg|en† vt pursue; (fig) follow; (bedrängen) pester; (Pol) persecute; **strafrechtlich v~en** prosecute. **V~er** m -s,- pursuer. **V~ung** f - pursuit; persecution
verfrachten vt ship
verfrüht a premature
verfügbar a available
verfüg|en vt order; (Jur) decree □ vi (haben) **v~en über** (+ acc) have at one's disposal. **V~ung** f -,-en order; (Jur) decree; **jdm zur V~ung stehen/stellen** be/place at s.o.'s disposal
verführ|en vt seduce; (verlocken) tempt. **V~er** m seducer. **V~erisch** a seductive; tempting. **V~ung** f seduction; temptation
vergammelt a rotten; (Gebäude) decayed; ⟨Person⟩ scruffy
vergangen a past; (letzte) last. **V~heit** f - past; (Gram) past tense
vergänglich a transitory
vergas|en vt gas. **V~er** m -s,- carburettor
vergeb|en† vt award (an + dat to); (weggeben) give away; (verzeihen) forgive. **v~ens** adv in vain. **v~lich** a futile, vain □ adv in vain. **V~ung** f - forgiveness
vergehen† vi (sein) pass; **v~ vor** (+ dat) nearly die of; **sich v~** violate (gegen etw sth); (sexuell) sexually assault (an jdm s.o.). **V~** nt -s,- offence
vergelt|en† vt repay. **V~ung** f - retaliation; (Rache) revenge. **V~ungsmaßnahme** f reprisal

vergessen† vt forget; (liegenlassen) leave behind. **V~heit** f - oblivion; **in V~heit geraten** be forgotten
vergeßlich a forgetful. **V~keit** f - forgetfulness
vergeuden vt waste, squander
vergewaltig|en vt rape. **V~ung** f -,-en rape
vergewissern (sich) vr make sure (gen of)
vergieß|en† vt spill; shed ⟨Tränen, Blut⟩
vergift|en vt poison. **V~ung** f -,-en poisoning
Vergißmeinnicht nt -[e]s,-[e] forget-me-not
vergittert a barred
verglasen vt glaze
Vergleich m -[e]s,-e comparison; (Jur) settlement. **v~bar** a comparable. **v~en**† vt compare (mit with/to). **v~sweise** adv comparatively
vergnüg|en (sich) vr enjoy oneself. **V~en** nt -s,- pleasure; (Spaß) fun; **viel V~en!** have a good time! **v~lich** a enjoyable. **v~t** a cheerful, adv -ly; (zufrieden) happy, adv -ily; (vergnüglich) enjoyable. **V~ungen** fpl entertainments
vergolden vt gild; (plattieren) gold-plate
vergönnen vt grant
vergöttern vt idolize
vergraben† vt bury
vergreifen† (sich) vr **sich v~ an** (+ dat) assault; (stehlen) steal
vergriffen a out of print
vergrößer|n vt enlarge; ⟨Linse:⟩ magnify; (vermehren) increase; (erweitern) extend; expand ⟨Geschäft⟩; **sich v~n** grow bigger; ⟨Firma:⟩ expand; (zunehmen) increase. **V~ung** f -,-en magnification; increase; expansion; (Phot) enlargement. **V~ungsglas** nt magnifying glass

Vergünstigung f -,-en privilege

vergüt|en vt pay for; **jdm etw v~en** reimburse s.o. for sth. **V~ung** f -,-en remuneration; (*Erstattung*) reimbursement

verhaft|en vt arrest. **V~ung** f -,-en arrest

verhalten† (*sich*) vr behave; (*handeln†*) act; (*beschaffen sein*) be; **sich still v~** keep quiet. **V~** nt -s behaviour, conduct

Verhältnis nt -ses,-se relationship; (*Liebes-*) affair; (*Math*) ratio; **V~se** circumstances; (*Bedingungen*) conditions; **über seine V~se leben** live beyond one's means. **v~mäßig** adv comparatively, relatively

verhand|eln vt discuss; (*Jur*) try □vi (*haben*) negotiate; **v~eln gegen** (*Jur*) try. **V~lung** f (*Jur*) trial; **V~lungen** negotiations

verhängen vt cover; (*fig*) impose

Verhängnis nt -ses fate, doom. **v~voll** a fatal, disastrous

verharmlosen vt play down

verharren vi (*haben*) remain

verhärten vt/i (*sein*) harden; **sich v~** harden

verhaßt a hated

verhätscheln vt spoil, pamper

verhauen† vt (*fam*) beat; **make a mess of** ⟨*Prüfung*⟩

verheerend a devastating; (*fam*) terrible

verhehlen vt conceal

verheilen vi (*sein*) heal

verheimlichen vt keep secret

verheirat|en vt get married (**mit** to). **v~et** a married

verhelfen† vi (*haben*) **jdm zu etw v~** help s.o. get sth

verherrlichen vt glorify

verhexen vt bewitch; **es ist wie verhext** (*fam*) there is a jinx on it

verhinder|n vt prevent; **v~t sein** be unable to come. **V~ung** f -prevention

verhöhnen vt deride

Verhör nt -s,-e interrogation; **ins V~ nehmen** interrogate. **v~en** vt interrogate; **sich v~en** mishear

verhüllen vt cover; (*fig*) disguise

v~d a euphemistic, adv -ally

verhungern vi (*sein*) starve

verhüt|en vt prevent. **V~ung** f -prevention. **V~ungsmittel** nt contraceptive

verhutzelt a wizened

verirren (sich) vr get lost

verjagen vt chase away

verjüngen vt rejuvenate; **sich v~** taper

verkalkt a (*fam*) senile

verkalkulieren (sich) vr miscalculate

Verkauf m sale; **zum V~** for sale. **v~en** vt sell; **zu v~en** for sale

Verkäufer|in m seller; (*im Geschäft*) shop assistant

Verkehr m -s traffic; (*Kontakt*) contact; (*Geschlechts-*) intercourse; **aus dem V~ ziehen** take out of circulation. **v~en** vi (*haben*) operate; ⟨*Bus, Zug:*⟩ run; (*Umgang haben*) associate, mix (**mit** with); (*Gast sein*) visit (**bei jdm** s.o.); frequent (**in einem Lokal** a restaurant); **brieflich v~en** correspond □vt **ins Gegenteil v~en** turn round

Verkehrs|ampel f traffic lights pl. **V~büro** nt = **V~verein**. **V~funk** m [radio] traffic information. **V~unfall** m road accident. **V~verein** m tourist office. **V~zeichen** nt traffic sign

verkehrt a wrong, adv -ly. **v~herum** adv the wrong way round; (*links*) inside out

verkennen† vt misjudge

verklagen vt sue (**auf+** acc for)

verkleid|en vt disguise; (*Techn*) line; **sich v~en** disguise oneself; (*für Kostümfest*) dress up. **V~ung** f -,-en disguise; (*Kostüm*) fancy dress; (*Techn*) lining

verkleiner|n vt reduce [in size].
V~**ung** f - reduction. V~**ungs-
form** f diminutive
verklemmt a jammed; (psychisch) inhibited
verkneifen† vr **sich** (dat) etw v~
do without sth; (verbeißen) suppress sth
verknittern vt/i (sein) crumple
verknüpfen vt knot together;
(verbinden) connect, link; (zugleich tun) combine
verkommen† vi (sein) be neglected; (sittlich) go to the bad;
(verfallen) decay; (Haus:) fall
into disrepair; (Gegend:) become
run-down; (Lebensmittel:) go bad
□a neglected; (sittlich) depraved;
(Haus) dilapidated; (Gegend)
run-down
verkörper|n vt embody, per-
sonify. V~**ung** f -,-en embodiment, personification
verkraften vt cope with
verkrampft a (fig) tense
verkriechen† (sich) vr hide
verkrümmt a crooked, bent
verkrüppelt a crippled; (Glied)
deformed
verkühl|en (sich) vr catch a
chill. V~**ung** f -,-en chill
verkümmer|n vi (sein) waste/
(Pflanze:) wither away. v~t a
stunted
verkünd|en vt announce; pro-
nounce (Urteil). v~**igen** vt announce; (predigen) preach
verkürzen vt shorten; (verringern) reduce; (abbrechen) cut
short; while away (Zeit)
verladen† vt load
Verlag m -[e]s,-e publishing firm
verlangen vt ask for; (fordern)
demand; (berechnen) charge; am
Telefon verlangt werden be
wanted on the telephone. V~ nt
-s desire; (Bitte) request; auf V~
on demand

verlänger|n vt extend; lengthen
(Kleid); (zeitlich) prolong; renew
(Paß, Vertrag); (Culin) thin
down. V~**ung** f -,-en extension;
renewal. V~**ungsschnur** f extension cable
verlangsamen vt slow down
Verlaß m -sses auf ihn ist kein
V~ you cannot rely on him
verlassen† vt leave; (im Stich lassen) desert; **sich** v~ **auf** (+acc)
rely or depend on □a deserted.
V~**heit** f - desolation
verläßlich a reliable
Verlauf m course; im V~ (+gen)
in the course of. v~**en†** vi (sein)
run; (ablaufen) go; (zerlaufen)
melt; gut v~en go [off] well □vr
sich v~**en** lose one's way;
(Menge:) disperse; (Wasser:)
drain away
verleben vt spend
verlegen vt move; (verschieben)
postpone; (vor-) bring forward;
(verlieren) mislay; (versperren)
block; (legen) lay (Teppich,
Rohre); (veröffentlichen) publish;
sich v~ **auf** (+acc) take up
(Beruf, Fach); resort to (Taktik,
Bitten) □a embarrassed; **nie** v~
um never at a loss for. V~**heit** f -
embarrassment
Verleger m -s,- publisher
verleihen† vt lend; (gegen Gebühr) hire out; (überreichen)
award, confer; (fig) give
verleiten vt induce/(verlocken)
tempt (zu to)
verlernen vt forget
verlesen†[1] vt read out; **ich habe
mich** v~ I misread it
verlesen†[2] vt sort out
verletz|en vt injure; (kränken)
hurt; (verstoßen gegen) infringe;
violate (Grenze). v~**end** a hurt-
ful, wounding. v~**lich** a vulnerable. V~**te(r)** m/f injured person; (bei Unfall) casualty.

V~ung f -,-en injury; (Verstoß) infringement; violation

verleugnen vt deny; disown ⟨Freund⟩

verleumd|en vt slander; (schriftlich) libel. v~erisch a slanderous; libellous. V~ung f -,-en slander; (schriftlich) libel

verlieben (sich) vr fall in love (in+acc with); verliebt sein be in love (in+acc with)

verlier|en† vt lose; shed ⟨Laub⟩; sich v~en disappear; ⟨Weg:⟩ peter out □vi (haben) lose (an etw dat sth). V~er m -s,- loser

verlob|en (sich) vr get engaged (mit to); v~t sein be engaged. V~te f fiancée. V~te(r) m fiancé. V~ung f -,-en engagement

verlock|en vt tempt; v~end tempting. V~ung f -,-en temptation

verlogen a lying

verloren a lost; v~e Eier poached eggs. v~gehen† vi sep (sein) get lost

verlos|en vt raffle. V~ung f -,-en raffle; (Ziehung) draw

verlottert a run-down; ⟨Person⟩ scruffy; (sittlich) dissolute

Verlust m -[e]s,-e loss

vermachen vt leave, bequeath

Vermächtnis nt -ses,-se legacy

vermähl|en (sich) vr marry. V~ung f -,-en marriage

vermehren vt increase; propagate ⟨Pflanzen⟩; sich v~ increase; (sich fortpflanzen) breed, multiply

vermeiden† vt avoid

vermeintlich a supposed, adv -ly

Vermerk m -[e]s,-e note. v~en vt note [down]; übel v~en take amiss

vermess|en† vt measure; survey ⟨Gelände⟩ □a presumptuous. V~enheit f - presumption

V~ung f measurement; (Land-) survey

vermiet|en vt let, rent [out]; hire out ⟨Boot, Auto⟩; zu v~en to let ⟨Boot:⟩ for hire. V~er m landlord. V~erin f landlady

vermind|ern vt reduce, lessen. V~ung f - reduction, decrease

vermischen vt mix; sich v~ mix

vermissen vt miss

vermißt a missing. V~e(r) m missing person/(Mil) soldier

vermitt|eln vi (haben) mediate □vt arrange; (beschaffen) find; place ⟨Arbeitskräfte⟩; impart ⟨Wissen⟩; convey ⟨Eindruck⟩. V~s prep (+gen) by means of

Vermittl|er m -s,- agent; (Schlichter) mediator. V~ung f -,-en arrangement; (Agentur) agency; (Teleph) exchange; (Schlichtung) mediation

vermögen† vt be able (zu to). V~ nt -s,- fortune. v~d a wealthy

vermut|en vt suspect; (glauben) presume. v~lich a probable □ adv presumably. V~ung f -,-en supposition; (Verdacht) suspicion; (Mutmaßung) conjecture

vernachlässig|en vt neglect. V~ung f - neglect

vernehm|en† vt hear; (verhören) question; (Jur) examine. V~ung f -,-en questioning

verneig|en (sich) vr bow. V~ung f -,-en bow

vernein|en vt answer in the negative; (ablehnen) reject. v~end a negative. V~ung f -,-en negative answer; (Gram) negative

vernicht|en vt destroy; (ausrotten) exterminate. v~end a devastating; ⟨Niederlage⟩ crushing. V~ung f - destruction; extermination

Vernunft f - reason. V~ annehmen see reason

vernünftig *a* reasonable, sensible; (*fam: ordentlich*) decent □*adv* sensibly; (*fam*) properly

veröffentlich|en *vt* publish. **V~ung** *f -,-en* publication.

verordn|en *vt* prescribe (*dat* for). **V~ung** *f -,-en* prescription; (*Verfügung*) decree

verpachten *vt* lease [out]

verpack|en *vt* pack; (*einwickeln*) wrap. **V~ung** *f* packaging, wrapping

verpassen *vt* miss; (*fam: geben*) give

verpfänden *vt* pawn

verpflanzen *vt* transplant

verpfleg|en *vt* feed; **sich selbst v~en** cater for oneself. **V~ung** *f -* board; (*Essen*) food; Unterkunft und **V~ung** board and lodging

verpflicht|en *vt* oblige; (*einstellen*) engage; (*Sport*) sign; **sich v~en** undertake/(*vertraglich*) promise (**zu** to); (*vertraglich*) sign a contract; **jdm v~et sein** be indebted to s.o. **V~ung** *f -,-en* obligation, commitment

verpfuschen *vt* make a mess of

verpönt *a* **v~ sein** be frowned upon

verprügeln *vt* beat up, thrash

Verputz *m* **-es** plaster. **v~en** *vt* plaster; (*fam: essen*) polish off

Verrat *m* **-[e]s** betrayal, treachery. **v~en†** *vt* betray; give away (*Geheimnis*); (*fam: sagen*) tell; **sich v~en** give oneself away

Verräter *m* **-s,-** traitor. **v~isch** *a* treacherous; (*fig*) revealing

verräuchert *a* smoky

verrechn|en *vt* settle; clear (*Scheck*); **sich v~nen** make a mistake; (*fig*) miscalculate. **V~nungsscheck** *m* crossed cheque

verregnet *a* spoilt by rain; (*Tag*) rainy, wet

verreisen *vi* (*sein*) go away; **verreist sein** be away

verreißen† *vt* (*fam*) pan, slate

verrenk|en *vt* dislocate; **sich v~** contort oneself

verricht|en *vt* perform, do; say (*Gebet*). **V~ung** *f -,-en* task

verriegeln *vt* bolt

verringer|n *vt* reduce; **sich v~n** decrease. **V~ung** *f -* reduction; decrease

verrost|en *vi* (*sein*) rust. **v~et** *a* rusty

verrücken *vt* move

verrückt *a* crazy, mad; **v~ werden/machen** go/drive crazy. **V~e(r)** *m/f* lunatic. **V~heit** *f -,-en* madness; (*Torheit*) folly

Verruf *m* disrepute. **v~en** *a* disreputable

verrühren *vt* mix

verrunzelt *a* wrinkled

verrutschen *vi* (*sein*) slip

Vers /fɛrs/ *m* **-es,-e** verse

versag|en *vi* (*haben*) fail □*vt* **jdm/sich etw v~en** deny s.o./oneself sth. **V~en** *nt* **-s,-** failure. **V~er** *m* **-s,-** failure

versalzen† *vt* put too much salt in/on; (*fig*) spoil

versamm|eln *vt* assemble; **sich v~eln** assemble, meet. **V~lung** *f* assembly, meeting

Versand *m* **-[e]s** dispatch. **V~haus** *nt* mail-order firm

versäum|en *vt* miss; lose (*Zeit*); (*unterlassen*) neglect; [**es**] **v~en, etw zu tun** fail/neglect to do sth. **V~nis** *nt* **-ses,-se** omission

verschaffen *vt* get; **sich** (*dat*) **v~** obtain; gain (*Respekt*)

verschämt *a* bashful, *adv* -ly

verschandeln *vt* spoil

verschärfen *vt* intensify; tighten (*Kontrolle*); increase (*Tempo*); aggravate (*Lage*); **sich v~** intensify; increase; (*Lage:*) worsen

verschätzen (**sich**) *vr* **sich v~ in** (+ *dat*) misjudge

verschenken *vt* give away
verscheuchen *vt* shoo/(*jagen*)
chase away
verschicken *vt* send; (*Comm*) dispatch
verschieb|**en**† *vt* move; (*aufschieben*) put off, postpone; (*sl: handeln mit*) traffic in; **sich v~en** move, shift; (*verrutschen*) slip; (*zeitlich*) be postponed. **V~ung** *f* shift; postponement
verschieden *a* different; **v~e** (*pl*) different; (*mehrere*) various; **v~es** some things; (*dieses und jenes*) various things; **die v~sten Farben** a whole variety of colours; **das ist v~** it varies □*adv* differently; **v~ groß/lang** of different sizes/lengths. **v~artig** *a* diverse. **V~heit** *f* difference; (*Vielfalt*) diversity. **v~tlich** *adv* several times
verschimmel|**n** *vi* (*sein*) go mouldy. **v~t** *a* mouldy
verschlafen† *vi* (*haben*) oversleep □*vt* sleep through ⟨*Tag*⟩; (*versäumen*) miss ⟨*Zug, Termin*⟩; **sich v~** oversleep □*a* sleepy; **noch v~** still half asleep
Verschlag *m* -[e]s,⸚e shed
verschlagen† *vt* lose ⟨*Seite*⟩; **jdm die Sprache/den Atem v~** leave s.o. speechless/take s.o.'s breath away; **nach X v~ werden** end up in X □*a* sly, *adv* -ly
verschlechter|**n** *vt* make worse; **sich v~n** get worse, deteriorate. **V~ung** *f* -,-en deterioration
verschleiern *vt* veil; (*fig*) hide
Verschleiß *m* -es wear and tear; (*Verbrauch*) consumption. **v~en**† *vt/i* (*sein*) wear out
verschleppen *vt* carry off; (*entführen*) abduct; spread ⟨*Seuche*⟩; neglect ⟨*Krankheit*⟩; (*hinauszuhen*) delay
verschleudern *vt* sell at a loss; (*verschwenden*) squander

verschließen† *vt* close; (*abschließen*) lock; (*einschließen*) lock up
verschlimmer|**n** *vt* make worse; aggravate ⟨*Lage*⟩; **sich v~n** get worse, deteriorate. **V~ung** *f* -,-en deterioration
verschlingen† *vt* intertwine; (*fressen*) devour; (*fig*) swallow
verschlissen *a* worn
verschlossen *a* reserved. **V~heit** *f* - reserve
verschlucken *vt* swallow; **sich v~** choke (**an** + *dat* on)
Verschluß *m* -sses,⸚sse fastener, clasp; (*Fenster-, Koffer-*) catch; (*Flaschen-*) top; (*luftdicht*) seal; (*Phot*) shutter; **unter V~** under lock and key
verschlüsselt *a* coded
verschmähen *vt* spurn
verschmelzen† *vt/i* (*sein*) fuse
verschmerzen *vt* get over
verschmutz|**en** *vt* soil; pollute ⟨*Luft*⟩ □*vi* (*sein*) get dirty. **V~ung** *f* - pollution
verschnaufen *vi/r* (*haben*) [**sich**] **v~** get one's breath
verschneit *a* snow-covered
verschnörkelt *a* ornate
verschnüren *vt* tie up
verschollen *a* missing
verschonen *vt* spare
verschönern *vt* brighten up; (*verbessern*) improve
verschossen *a* faded
verschrammt *a* scratched
verschränken *vt* cross
verschreiben† *vt* prescribe; **sich v~** make a slip of the pen
verschrie[e]n *a* notorious
verschroben *a* eccentric
verschrotten *vt* scrap
verschulden *vt* be to blame for. **V~** *nt* -s fault
verschuldet *a* v ~ **sein** be in debt
verschütten *vt* spill; (*begraben*) bury
verschweigen† *vt* conceal, hide

verschwend|en vt waste. **v~e-risch** a extravagant, adv -ly; (üppig) lavish, adv -ly. **V~ung** f - extravagance; (Vergeudung) waste

verschwiegen a discreet; (Ort) secluded. **V~heit** f - discretion

verschwimmen† vi (sein) become blurred

verschwinden† vi (sein) disappear; [mal] ~ (fam) spend a penny. **V~** nt -s disappearance

verschwommen a blurred

verschwör|en† (sich) vr conspire. **V~ung** f -,-en conspiracy

versehen† vt perform; hold (Posten); keep (Haushalt); ~ mit provide with; **sich v~** make a mistake; **ehe man sich's versieht** before you know where you are. **V~** nt -s,-oversight; (Fehler) slip; **aus V~** by mistake. **v~tlich** adv by mistake

Versehrte(r) m disabled person

versenden† vt send [out]

versengen vt singe; (stärker) scorch

versenken vt sink; **sich v~ in** (+acc) immerse oneself in

versessen a keen (auf+acc on)

versetzen vt move; transfer (Person); (Sch) move up; (verpfänden) pawn; (verkaufen) sell; (vermischen) blend; (antworten) reply; **jdn v~en** (fam: warten lassen) stand s.o. up; **jdm einen Stoß/Schreck v~en** give s.o. a push/fright; **jdn in Angst/Erstaunen v~en** frighten/astonish s.o.; **sich in jds Lage v~en** put oneself in s.o.'s place. **V~ung** f -,-en move; transfer; (Sch) move to a higher class

verseuch|en vt contaminate. **V~ung** f - contamination

versicher|n vt insure; (bekräftigen) affirm; **jdm v~n** assure s.o. (daß that). **V~ung** f -,-en insurance; assurance

versiegeln vt seal

versiegen vi (sein) dry up

versiert /ver'zi:ɐt/ a experienced

versilbert a silver-plated

versinken vi (sein) sink; **in Gedanken versunken** lost in thought

Version /ver'zjo:n/ f -,-en version

Versmaß /'fɛrs-/ nt metre

versöhn|en vt reconcile; **sich v~en** become reconciled. **v~lich** a conciliatory. **V~ung** f -,-en reconciliation

versorg|en vt provide, supply (mit with); provide for (Familie); (betreuen) look after; keep (Haushalt). **V~ung** f - provision, supply; (Betreuung) care

verspät|en (sich) vr be late. **v~et** a (Zug) delayed; (Dank, Glückwunsch) belated □adv late; belatedly. **V~ung** f - lateness; **V~ung haben** be late

versperren vt block; bar (Weg)

verspiel|en vt gamble away; **sich v~en** play a wrong note. **v~t** a playful, adv -ly

verspotten vt mock, ridicule

versprech|en† vt promise; **sich v~en** make a slip of the tongue; **sich** (dat) **viel v~en von** have high hopes of. **V~en** nt -s,- promise. **V~ungen** fpl promises

verspüren vt feel

verstaatlich|en vt nationalize. **V~ung** f - nationalization

Verstand m -[e]s mind; (Vernunft) reason; **den V~ verlieren** go out of one's mind. **v~esmäßig** a rational, adv -ly

verständig a sensible, adv -bly; (klug) intelligent, adv -ly. **v~en** vt notify, inform; **sich v~en** communicate; (sich verständlich machen) make oneself understood; (sich einigen) reach agreement. **V~ung** f - notification; communication; (Einigung) agreement

verständlich a comprehensible, adv -bly; (deutlich) clear, adv -ly; (begreiflich) understandable; **sich v~ machen** make oneself understood. **v~erweise** adv understandably

Verständnis nt -ses understanding. **v~los** a uncomprehending, adv -ly. **v~voll** a understanding, adv -ly

verstärk|en vt strengthen, reinforce; (steigern) intensify, increase; amplify ⟨Ton⟩; **sich v~en** intensify. **v~er** m -s,- amplifier. **V~ung** f reinforcement; increase; amplification; (Truppen) reinforcements pl

verstaubt a dusty

verstauchen vt sprain

verstauen vt stow

Versteck nt -[e]s,-e hiding-place; **V~ spielen** play hide-and-seek. **v~en** vt hide; **sich v~en** hide. **v~t** a hidden; (heimlich) secret; (verstohlen) furtive, adv -ly

verstehen† vt understand; (können) know; **falsch v~** misunderstand; **sich v~** understand one another; (auskommen) get on; **das versteht sich von selbst** that goes without saying

versteifen vt stiffen; **sich v~** stiffen; **(fig) insist (auf+acc on)**

versteiger|n vt auction. **V~ung** f auction

versteinert a fossilized

verstell|bar a adjustable. **v~en** vt adjust; (versperren) block; (verändern) disguise; **sich v~en** pretend. **V~ung** f disguise

versteuern vt pay tax on

verstiegen a (fig) extravagant

verstimm|t a disgruntled; ⟨Magen⟩ upset; (Mus) out of tune. **V~ung** f ill humour; (Magen-) upset

verstockt a stubborn, adv -ly

verstohlen a furtive, adv -ly

verstopf|en vt plug; (versperren) block; **v~t** blocked; (Med) constipated. **V~ung** f -,-en blockage; (Med) constipation

verstorben a late, deceased. **V~e(r)** m/f deceased

verstört a bewildered

Verstoß m infringement. **v~en†** vt disown □vi (haben) **v~en gegen** contravene, infringe; offend ⟨Anstand⟩

verstreichen† vt spread □vi (sein) pass

verstreuen vt scatter

verstümmeln vt mutilate; garble ⟨Text⟩

verstummen vi (sein) fall silent; ⟨Gespräch, Lärm:⟩ cease

Versuch m -[e]s,-e attempt; (Experiment) experiment. **v~en** vt/i (haben) try; **sich v~en in** (+dat) try one's hand at; **v~t sein** be tempted (zu to). **V~skaninchen** nt (fig) guinea-pig. **v~sweise** adv as an experiment. **V~ung** f -,-en temptation

versündigen (sich) vr sin (an +dat against)

vertagen vt adjourn; (aufschieben) postpone; **sich v~** adjourn

vertauschen vt exchange; (verwechseln) mix up

verteidig|en vt defend. **V~er** m -s,- defender; (Jur) defence counsel. **V~ung** f -,-en defence

verteil|en vt distribute; (zuteilen) allocate; (ausgeben) hand out; (verstreichen) spread; **sich v~en** spread out. **V~ung** f - distribution; allocation

vertief|en vt deepen; **v~t sein in** (+acc) be engrossed in. **V~ung** f -,-en hollow, depression

vertikal /verti'ka:l/ a vertical, adv -ly

vertilgen vt exterminate; kill [off] ⟨Unkraut⟩; (fam: essen) demolish

vertippen (sich) vr make a typing mistake

vertonen vt set to music

Vertrag m -[e]s,-̈e contract; (Pol) treaty

vertragen† vt tolerate, stand; take ⟨Kritik, Spaß⟩; **sich v~** get on; (passen) go (mit with); **sich wieder v~** make it up □ a worn

verträglich a contractual

verträglich a good-natured; (bekömmlich) digestible

vertrauen vi (haben) trust (jdm/etw s.o./sth; auf+acc in). **V~** nt -s trust, confidence (zu in); **im V~** in confidence. **V~smann** m (pl -leute) representative; (Sprecher) spokesman. **v~svoll** a trusting, adv -ly. **v~swürdig** a trustworthy

vertraulich a confidential, adv -ly; (intim) familiar, adv -ly

vertraut a intimate; (bekannt) familiar; **sich v~ machen mit** familiarize oneself with. **V~heit** f -intimacy; familiarity

vertreiben† vt drive away; drive out ⟨Feind⟩; (Comm) sell; ⟨dat⟩ **die Zeit v~en** pass the time. **V~ung** f -,-en expulsion

vertret|en† vt represent; (einspringen für) stand in or deputize for; (verfechten) support; hold ⟨Meinung⟩; **sich** ⟨dat⟩ **den Fuß v~en** twist one's ankle; **sich** ⟨dat⟩ **die Beine v~en** stretch one's legs. **V~er** m -s,- representative; deputy; (Arzt-) locum; (Verfechter) supporter, advocate. **V~ung** f -,-en representation; (Person) deputy; (eines Arztes) locum; (Handels-) agency

Vertrieb m -[e]s (Comm) sale. **V~ene(r)** m/f displaced person

vertrocknen vi (sein) dry up

vertrösten† vt auf später **v~** put s.o. off until later

vertun† vt waste; **sich v~** (fam) make a mistake

vertuschen vt hush up

verübeln vt **jdm etw v~** hold sth against s.o.

verüben vt commit

verunglimpfen vt denigrate

verunglücken vi (sein) be involved in an accident; (fam: mißglücken) go wrong; **tödlich v~** be killed in an accident

verunreinigen vt pollute; (verseuchen) contaminate; (verschmutzen) soil

verunstalten vt disfigure

veruntreu|en vt embezzle. **V~ung** f - embezzlement

verursachen vt cause

verurteil|en vt condemn; (Jur) convict (wegen of); sentence (zum Tode to death). **V~ung** f - condemnation; (Jur) conviction

vervielfachen vt multiply

vervielfältigen vt duplicate

vervollkommnen vt perfect

vervollständigen vt complete

verwachsen a deformed

verwählen (sich) vr misdial

verwahren vt keep; (verstauen) put away; **sich v~** (fig) protest

verwahrlost a neglected; ⟨Haus⟩ dilapidated; (sittlich) depraved

Verwahrung f - keeping; **in V~ nehmen** take into safe keeping

verwaist a orphaned

verwalt|en vt administer; (leiten) manage; govern ⟨Land⟩. **V~er** m -s,- administrator; manager. **V~ung** f -,-en administration; management; government

verwand|eln vt transform, change (in+acc into); **sich v~eln** change, turn (in+acc into). **V~lung** f transformation

verwandt a related (mit to). **V~e(r)** m/f relative. **V~schaft** f - relationship; (Menschen) relatives pl

verwarn|en vt warn, caution. **V~ung** f warning, caution

verwaschen a washed out, faded

verwechs|eln *vt* mix up, confuse; *(halten für)* mistake (mit for). **V~lung** *f* -,-en mix-up

verwegen *a* audacious, *adv* -ly

Verwehung *f* -,-en [snow-]drift

verweichlich|t *a (fig)* soft

verweiger|n *vt/i (haben)* refuse *(jdm etw* to sth); **den Gehorsam v~n** refuse to obey. **V~ung** *f* refusal

verweilen *vi (haben)* stay

Verweis *m* -es,-e reference *(auf+acc* to); *(Tadel)* reprimand. **v~en†** *vt* refer *(auf/an+acc* to); *(tadeln)* reprimand; **von der Schule v~en** expel

verwelken *vi (sein)* wilt

verwend|en† *vt* use; spend *⟨Zeit, Mühe⟩*. **V~ung** *f* use

verwerf|en† *vt* reject; **sich v~en** warp. **v~lich** *a* reprehensible

verwert|en *vt* utilize, use; *(Comm)* exploit. **V~ung** *f* - utilization; exploitation

verwesen *vi (sein)* decompose

verwick|eln *vt* involve (in+acc in); **sich v~eln** get tangled up; **in etw (acc) v~elt sein** *(fig)* be involved or mixed up in sth. **v~elt** *a* complicated

verwilder|t *a* wild; *⟨Garten⟩* overgrown; *⟨Aussehen⟩* unkempt

verwinden† *vt (fig)* get over

verwirken *vt* forfeit

verwirklichen *vt* realize; **sich v~** be realized

verwirr|en *vt* tangle up; *(fig)* confuse; **sich v~en** get tangled; *(fig)* become confused. **v~t** *a* confused. **V~ung** *f* - confusion

verwischen *vt* smudge

verwittert *a* weathered; *⟨Gesicht⟩* weather-beaten

verwitwet *a* widowed

verwöhn|en *vt* spoil. **v~t** *a* spoilt; *(anspruchsvoll)* discriminating

verworren *a* confused

verwund|bar *a* vulnerable. **v~en** *vt* wound

verwunder|lich *a* surprising. **v~n** *vt* surprise; **sich v~n** be surprised. **V~ung** *f* - surprise

Verwund|ete(r) *m* wounded soldier; **die V~eten** the wounded *pl.* **V~ung** *f* -,-en wound

verwünsch|en *vt* curse. **v~t** *a* confounded

verwüst|en *vt* devastate, ravage. **V~ung** *f* -,-en devastation

verzagen *vi (haben)* lose heart

verzählen (sich) *vr* miscount

verzärteln *vt* mollycoddle

verzauber|n *vt* bewitch; *(fig)* enchant; **v~n in** (+*acc*) turn into

Verzehr *m* -s consumption. **v~en** *vt* eat; *(aufbrauchen)* use up; **sich v~en** *(fig)* pine away

verzeich|nen *vt* list; *(registrieren)* register. **V~nis** *nt* -ses,-se list; *⟨Inhalts⟩* index

verzeih|en† *vt* forgive; **v~en Sie!** excuse me! **V~ung** *f* - forgiveness; **um V~ung bitten** apologize; **V~ung!** sorry! *(bei Frage)* excuse me!

verzerren *vt* distort; contort *⟨Gesicht⟩*; pull *⟨Muskel⟩*

Verzicht *m* -[e]s renunciation *(auf+acc* of). **v~en** *vi (haben)* do without; **v~en auf** (+*acc*) give up; renounce *⟨Recht, Erbe⟩*

verziehen† *vt* pull out of shape; *(verwöhnen)* spoil; **sich v~** lose shape; *⟨Holz⟩* warp; *⟨Gesicht⟩* twist; *(verschwinden)* disappear; *⟨Nebel⟩* disperse; *⟨Gewitter⟩* pass; **das Gesicht v~** pull a face □ *vi (sein)* move [away]

verzier|en *vt* decorate. **V~ung** *f* -,-en decoration

verzinsen *vt* pay interest on

verzöger|n *vt* delay; *(verlangsamen)* slow down; **sich v~n** be delayed. **V~ung** *f* -,-en delay

verzollen vt pay duty on; **haben Sie etwas zu v~?** have you anything to declare?

verzück|t a ecstatic, adv -ally. **V~ung** f rapture, ecstasy

Verzug m delay; **in V~** in arrears

verzweif|eln vi (sein) despair. **v~elt** a desperate, adv -ly; **v~elt sein** be in despair; (ratlos) be desperate. **V~lung** f despair; (Ratlosigkeit) desperation

verzweigen (sich) vr branch [out]

verzwickt a (fam) tricky

Veto /'ve:to/ nt -s,-s veto

Vetter m -s,-n cousin. **V~nwirtschaft** f nepotism

vgl. abbr (vergleiche) cf

Viadukt /vja'dʊkt/ nt -[e]s,-e viaduct

vibrieren /vi'bri:rən/ vi (haben) vibrate

Video /'vi:deo/ nt -s,-s video. **V~kassette** f video cassette. **V~recorder** /-rəkɔrdɐ/ m -s,- video recorder

Vieh nt -[e]s livestock; (Rinder) cattle pl; (fam: Tier) creature. **v~isch** a brutal, adv -ly

viel pron a great deal/(fam) a lot of; (pl) many, (fam) a lot of; (substantivisch) **v~[es]** much, (fam) a lot; **nicht/zu v~** not/too much; **v~e** pl many; **das v~e Geld/Lesen** all that money/reading □adv much, (fam) a lot; **v~ mehr/weniger** much more/less; **v~ zu groß/klein** much or far too big/small

viel|deutig a ambiguous. **v~erlei** inv a many kinds of □pron many things. **v~fach** a multiple □adv many times; (fam: oft) frequently. **V~falt** f -diversity, [great] variety. **v~fältig** a diverse, varied

vielleicht adv perhaps, maybe; (fam: wirklich) really

vielmals adv very much; **danke v~!** I thank you very much!

viel mehr adv rather; (im Gegenteil) on the contrary. **v~sagend** a meaningful, adv -ly

vielseitig a varied; (Person) versatile □adv **v~ begabt** versatile. **V~keit** f -versatility

vielversprechend a promising

vier inv a, V~ f -,-en four; (Sch) ≈ fair. **V~eck** nt -[e]s,-e oblong, rectangle; (Quadrat) square. **v~eckig** a oblong, rectangular; square. **v~fach** a quadruple. **V~linge** mpl quadruplets

Viertel /'fɪrtl/ nt -s,- quarter; (Wein) quarter litre; **V~ vor/nach sechs** [a] quarter to/past six; **V~ neun** [a] quarter past eight; **drei V~ neun** [a] quarter to nine. **V~finale** nt quarterfinal. **V~jahr** nt three months pl; (Comm) quarter. **v~jährlich** a & adv quarterly. **v~n** vt quarter. **V~note** f crotchet, (Amer) quarter note. **V~stunde** f quarter of an hour

vier|zehn /'fɪr-/ inv a fourteen. **v~zehnte(r,s)** a fourteenth. **v~zig** inv a forty. **v~zigste(r,s)** a fortieth

Villa /'vɪla/ f -,-len villa

violett /vio'let/ a violet

Vio|line /vio'li:nə/ f -,-n violin. **V~linschlüssel** m treble clef. **V~loncello** /-lɔn'tʃelo/ nt cello

Virtuose /vɪr'tuo:zə/ m -n,-n virtuoso

Virus /'vi:rʊs/ nt -,-ren virus

Visier /vi'zi:ɐ/ nt -s,-e visor

Vision /vi'zio:n/ f -,-en vision

Visite /vi'zi:tə/ f -,-n round; **V~ machen** do one's round

visuell /vi'zuɛl/ a visual, adv -ly

Visum /'vi:zʊm/ nt -s,-sa visa

vital /vi'ta:l/ a vital; (Person) energetic. **V~ität** f -vitality

Vitamin /vita'mi:n/ nt -s,-e vitamin

Vitrine /vi'triːnə/ *f* -,-n display cabinet/(*im Museum*) case

Vizepräsident /'fiːtsə-/ *m* vice president

Vogel *m* -s,ˉ bird; **einen V~ haben** (*fam*) have a screw loose. **V~scheuche** *f* -,-n scarecrow

Vokab|eln /vo'kaːbəln/ *fpl* vocabulary *sg*. **V~ular** *nt* -s,-e vocabulary

Vokal /vo'kaːl/ *m* -s,-e vowel

Volant /vo'lãː/ *m* -s,-s flounce; (*Auto*) steering-wheel

Volk *nt* -[e]s,ˉer people *sg*; (*Bevölkerung*) people *pl*; (*Bienen-*) colony

Völker|kunde *f* ethnology. **V~mord** *m* genocide. **V~recht** *nt* international law

Volks|abstimmung *f* plebiscite. **V~fest** *nt* public festival. **V~hochschule** *f* adult education classes *pl*/(*Gebäude*) centre. **V~lied** *nt* folk-song. **V~tanz** *m* folk-dance. **v~tümlich** *a* popular. **V~wirt** *m* economist. **V~wirtschaft** *f* economics *sg*. **V~zählung** *f* [national] census

voll *a* full (**von** *od* **mit** *d*); (*Haar*) thick; (*Erfolg, Ernst*) complete; (*Wahrheit*) whole; **v~ machen** fill up; **die Uhr schlug v~** (*fam*) the clock struck the hour □ *adv* (*ganz*) completely; (*arbeiten*) full-time; (*auszahlen*) in full; **v~ und ganz** fully, completely

vollauf *adv* fully, completely

Voll|beschäftigung *f* full employment. **V~blut** *nt* thoroughbred

vollbringen† *vt insep* accomplish; work (*Wunder*)

vollende|n *vt insep* complete. **v~t** *a* perfect, *adv* -ly; **v~te Gegenwart/Vergangenheit** perfect/pluperfect

vollends *adv* completely

Vollendung *f* completion; (*Vollkommenheit*) perfection

voller *inv a* full of; **v~ Angst/Freude** filled with fear/joy; **v~ Flecken** covered with stains

Völlerei *f* - gluttony

Volleyball /'vɔli-/ *m* volleyball

vollführen *vt insep* perform

vollfüllen *vt sep* fill up

Vollgas *nt* **V~ geben** put one's foot down; **mit V~** flat out

völlig *a* complete, *adv* -ly

volljährig *a* **v~ sein** (*Jur*) be of age. **V~keit** *f* - (*Jur*) majority

Vollkaskoversicherung *f* fully comprehensive insurance

vollkommen *a* perfect, *adv* -ly; (*völlig*) complete, *adv* -ly. **V~heit** *f* - perfection

Voll|kornbrot *nt* wholemeal bread. **V~macht** *f* -,-en authority; (*Jur*) power of attorney. **V~mond** *m* full moon. **V~pension** *f* full board. **v~schlank** *a* with a fuller figure

vollständig *a* complete, *adv* -ly

vollstrecken *vt insep* execute; carry out (*Urteil*)

volltanken *vi sep* (*haben*) (*Auto*) fill up [with petrol]

Volltreffer *m* direct hit

vollzählig *a* complete; **sind wir v~?** are we all here?

vollzieh|en† *vt insep* carry out; perform (*Handlung*); consummate (*Ehe*); **sich v~** take place

Volt /vɔlt/ *nt* -[s],- volt

Volumen /vo'luːmən/ *nt* -s,- volume

vom *prep* = **von dem**; **vom Rauchen** from smoking

von *prep* (+ *dat*) of; (*über*) about; (*Ausgangspunkt, Ursache*) from; (*beim Passiv*) by; **Musik von Mozart** music by Mozart; **einer von euch** one of you; **von hier/heute an** from here/today; **von mir aus** I don't mind

voneinander *adv* from each other; (*abhängig*) on each other

vonstatten *adv* **v~ gehen** take
place; **gut v~ gehen** go [off] well

vor *prep* (+ *dat/acc*) in front of;
(*zeitlich, Reihenfolge*) before;
(+ *dat*) (*bei Uhrzeit*) to; ⟨*warnen,
sich fürchten/schämen*⟩ of;
⟨*schützen, davonlaufen*⟩ from;
⟨*Respekt haben*⟩ for; **vor Angst/
Kälte zittern** tremble with fear/
cold; **vor drei Tagen/Jahren**
three days/years ago; **vor sich**
(*acc*) **hin murmeln** mumble to
oneself; **vor allen Dingen** above
all □*adv* forward; **vor und zurück** backwards and forwards

Vor|abend *m* eve. **V~ahnung** *f*
premonition

voran *adv* at the front; (*voraus*)
ahead; (*vorwärts*) forward.
v~gehen *vi sep* (*sein*) lead the
way; (*Fortschritte machen*) make
progress; **jdm/etw v~gehen**
precede s.o./sth. **v~kommen†**
vi sep (*sein*) make progress; (*fig*)
get on

Vor|anschlag *m* estimate.
V~anzeige *f* advance notice.
V~arbeit *f* preliminary work.
V~arbeiter *m* foreman

voraus *adv* ahead (*dat* of); (*vorn*)
at the front; (*vorwärts*) forward
□**im voraus** in advance. **v~be-
zahlen** *vt sep* pay in advance.
v~gehen† *vi sep* (*sein*) go on
ahead; **jdm/etw v~gehen** precede s.o./sth. **V~sage** *f-,-n* predic-
tion. **v~sagen** *vt sep* predict.
v~sehen† *vt sep* foresee

voraussetz|en *vt sep* take for
granted; (*erfordern*) require; **vorausgesetzt, daß** provided that.
V~ung *f-,-en* assumption; (*Erfordernis*) prerequisite; **unter
der V~ung, daß** on condition
that

Voraussicht *f* foresight; **aller
V~ nach** in all probability.
v~lich *a* anticipated, expected
□*adv* probably

Vorbehalt *m* -[e]s,-e reservation.
v~en† *vt sep* **sich** (*dat*) **v~en**
reserve ⟨*Recht*⟩; **jdm v~en
sein/bleiben** be left to s.o. **v~los**
a unreserved, *adv* -ly

vorbei *adv* past (**an jdm/etw** s.o./
sth); (*zu Ende*) over. **v~fahren†**
vi sep (*sein*) drive/go past. **v~ge-
hen†** *vi sep* (*sein*) go past; (*verfehlen*) miss; (*vergehen*) pass; (*fam:
besuchen*) drop in (**bei** on).
v~kommen† *vi sep* (*sein*)
pass/(*v~können*) get past (**an
jdm/etw** s.o./sth); (*fam: besuchen*) drop in (**bei** on)

vorbereit|en *vt sep* prepare; pre-
pare for ⟨*Reise*⟩; **sich v~en** prepare [oneself] (**auf**+*acc* for).
V~ung *f-,-en* preparation

vorbestellen *vt sep* order/(*im
Theater, Hotel*) book in advance

vorbestraft *a* **v~ sein** have a
[criminal] record

vorbeug|en *v sep* □*vt* bend for-
ward; **sich v~en** bend or lean
forward □*vi* (*haben*) prevent (**etw**
dat sth); **v~end** preventive.
V~ung *f* preventive

Vorbild *nt* model. **v~lich** *a* exemplary, model □*adv* in an exemplary manner

vorbringen† *vt sep* put forward;
offer ⟨*Entschuldigung*⟩

vordatieren *vt sep* post-date

Vorder|bein *nt* foreleg. **v~e(r,s)**
a front. **V~grund** *m* fore-
ground. **V~mann** *m* (*pl* -män-
ner) person in front; **auf
V~mann bringen** (*fam*) lick
into shape; (*aufräumen*) tidy up.
V~rad *nt* front wheel. **V~seite**
f front; (*einer Münze*) obverse.
v~ste(r,s) *a* front, first. **V~teil**
nt front

vor|drängeln (sich) *vr sep* (*fam*)
jump the queue. **v~drängen
(sich)** *vr sep* push forward.
v~dringen† *vi sep* (*sein*) advance

vor|ehelich *a* pre-marital. **v~ei-lig** *a* rash, adv -ly

voreingenommen *a* biased, prejudiced. **V~heit** *f* - bias

vorenthalten† *vt sep* withhold

vorerst *adv* for the time being

Vorfahr *m* -en,-en ancestor

vorfahren† *vi sep (sein)* drive up; *(vorwärts-)* move forward; *(voraus-)* drive on ahead

Vorfahrt *f* right of way; 'V~ beachten' 'give way'. **V~straße** *f* ≈ major road

Vorfall *m* incident. **v~en†** *vi sep (sein)* happen

vorfinden† *vt sep* find

Vorfreude *f* [happy] anticipation

vorführ|en *vt sep* present, show; *(demonstrieren)* demonstrate; *(aufführen)* perform. **V~ung** *f* presentation; demonstration; performance

Vor|gabe *f (Sport)* handicap. **V~gang** *m* occurrence; *(Techn)* process. **V~gänger(in)** *m* -s,- *(f -,-nen)* predecessor. **V~garten** *m* front garden

vorgeben† *vt sep* pretend

vorge|faßt *a* preconceived. **v~fertigt** *a* prefabricated

vorgehen† *vi sep (sein)* go forward; *(voraus-)* go on ahead; *(Uhr:)* be fast; *(wichtig sein)* take precedence; *(verfahren)* act, proceed; *(geschehen)* happen, go on. **V~** *nt -s* action

vorgeschichtlich *a* prehistoric. **V~geschmack** *m* foretaste. **V~gesetzte(r)** *m/f* superior. **v~gestern** *adv* the day before yesterday

vorhaben† *vt sep* propose, intend *(zu* to*)*; **etw v~** have sth planned; **nichts v~** have no plans. **V~** *nt -s,-* plan; *(Projekt)* project

vorhalt|en *v sep* ⊓*vt* hold up; **jdm etw v~** en reproach s.o. for sth ⊓*vi (haben)* last. **V~ungen**

fpl **jdm V~ungen machen** reproach s.o. **(wegen** for*)*

Vorhand *f (Sport)* forehand

vorhanden *a* existing; **v~ sein** exist; *(verfügbar sein)* be available. **V~sein** *nt -s* existence

Vorhang *m* curtain

Vorhängeschloß *nt* padlock

vorher *adv* before[hand]

vorhergehend *a* previous

vorherig *a* prior; *(vorhergehend)* previous

Vorherrschaft *f* supremacy. **v~en** *vi sep (haben)* predominate. **v~end** *a* predominant

Vorher|sage *f -,-n* prediction; *(Wetter-)* forecast. **v~sagen** *vt sep* predict; forecast ⟨*Wetter*⟩. **v~sehen†** *vt sep* foresee

vorhin *adv* just now

vorige(r,s) *a* last, previous

Vor|kämpfer *m (fig)* champion. **V~kehrungen** *fpl* precautions. **V~kenntnisse** *fpl* previous knowledge *sg*

vorkommen† *vi sep (sein)* happen; *(vorhanden sein)* occur; *(nach vorn kommen)* come forward; *(hervorkommen)* come out; *(zu sehen sein)* show; **jdm bekannt/verdächtig v~** seem familiar/suspicious to s.o.; **sich** *(dat)* **dumm/alt v~** feel stupid/old. **V~** *nt -s,-* occurrence; *(Geol)* deposit

Vorkriegszeit *f* pre-war period

vorlad|en† *vt sep (Jur)* summons. **V~ung** *f* summons

Vorlage *f* model; *(Muster)* pattern; *(Gesetzes-)* bill

vorlassen† *vt sep* admit; **jdn v~** *(fam)* let s.o. pass; *(den Vortritt lassen)* let s.o. go first

Vor|lauf *m (Sport)* heat. **V~läufer** *m* forerunner. **V~läufig** *a* provisional, adv -ly; *(zunächst)* for the time being.

v~**laut** a forward. **V**~**leben** nt past

vorleg|en vt sep put on ⟨Kette⟩; (unterbreiten) present; (vorzeigen) show; **jdm Fleisch v~en** serve s.o. with meat. **V**~**er** m -s,- mat; (Bett-) rug

vorles|en† vt sep read [out]; **jdm v~en** read to s.o. **V**~**ung** f lecture

vorletzt|e(r,s) a last ... but one; ⟨Silbe⟩ penultimate; **v~es Jahr** the year before last

Vorliebe f preference

vorliebnehmen† vt sep make do (mit with)

vorlieg|en† vi sep (haben) be present/(verfügbar) available; (bestehen) exist, be; **es muß ein Irrtum v~** there must be some mistake. **v~d** a present, ⟨Frage⟩ at issue

vorlügen† vt sep lie (dat to)

vorm prep = **vor dem**

vormachen vt sep put up; put on ⟨Kette⟩; push ⟨Riegel⟩; (zeigen) demonstrate; **jdm etwas v~** (fam: täuschen) kid s.o.

Vormacht f supremacy

vormals adv formerly

Vormarsch m (Mil & fig) advance

vormerken vt sep make a note of; (reservieren) reserve

Vormittag m morning. **v**~ adv **gestern/heute v~** yesterday/ this morning. **v~s** adv in the morning

Vormund m -[e]s,-munde & -münder guardian

vorn adv at the front; **nach v~** to the front; **von v~** from the front; (vom Anfang) beginning; **von v~ anfangen** start afresh

Vorname m first name

vorne adv = **vorn**

vornehm a distinguished; (elegant) smart, adv -ly

vornehmen† vt sep carry out; **sich** (dat) **v~, etw zu tun** plan/(beschließen) resolve to do sth

vorn|herein adv **von v~herein** from the start. **v~über** adv forward

Vor|ort m suburb. **V**~**rang** m priority, precedence (**vor** + dat over). **V**~**rat** m -[e]s,-e supply, stock (**an** + dat of). **v~rätig** a available; **v~rätig haben** have in stock. **V**~**ratskammer** f larder. **V**~**raum** m ante-room. **V**~**recht** nt privilege. **V**~**richtung** f device

vorrücken vt sep (haben) move forward; (Mil) advance

Vorrunde f qualifying round

vors prep = **vor das**

vorsagen vt/i sep (haben) recite; **jdm** [**die Antwort**] **v~** tell s.o. the answer

Vor|satz m resolution. **v~sätzlich** a deliberate, adv -ly; (Jur) premeditated

Vorschau f preview; (Film-) trailer

Vorschein m **zum V~ kommen** appear

vorschießen† vt sep advance ⟨Geld⟩

Vorschlag m suggestion, proposal. **v~en†** vt sep suggest, propose

vorschnell a rash, adv -ly

vorschreiben† vt sep lay down; dictate (dat to); **vorgeschriebene Dosis** prescribed dose

Vorschrift f regulation; (Anweisung) instruction; **jdm v~en machen** tell s.o. what to do; **Dienst nach V~** work to rule. **v~smäßig** a correct, adv -ly

Vorschule f nursery school

Vorschuß m advance

vorschützen vt sep plead [as an excuse]; feign ⟨Krankheit⟩

vorseh|en† v sep □vt intend (für/ als for/as); (planen) plan; sich v~en be careful (vor + dat of) □vi (haben) peep out. V~ung f - providence

vorsetzen vt sep move forward; jdm etw v~ serve s.o. sth

Vorsicht f - care; (bei Gefahr) caution; V~! careful! (auf Schild) 'caution'. v~ig a careful, adv -ly; cautious, adv -ly. v~shalber adv to be on the safe side. V~smaßnahme f pre- caution

Vorsilbe f prefix

Vorsitz m chairmanship; den V~ führen be in the chair. V~en† vi sep (haben) preside (dat over). V~ende(r) m/f chairman

Vorsorge f V~ treffen take pre- cautions; make provisions (für for). v~n vi sep (haben) provide (für for). V~untersuchung f check-up

vorsorglich adv as a precaution

Vorspeise f starter

Vorspiel nt prelude. v~en v sep □vt perform; (Mus) play (dat for) □vi (haben) audition

vorsprechen† v sep □vt recite; (zum Nachsagen) say (dat to) □vi (haben) (Theat) audition; bei jdm v~ call on s.o.

vorspringen† vi sep (sein) jut out; v~des Kinn prominent chin

Vor|sprung m projection; (Fels-) ledge; (Vorteil) lead (vor + dat over). V~stadt f suburb. v~städtisch a suburban. V~stand m board [of directors]; (Vereins-) committee; (Partei-) executive

vorsteh|en† vi sep (haben) pro- ject, protrude; einer Abteilung v~en be in charge of a depart- ment; v~end protruding; (Augen) bulging. V~er m -s,- head; (Gemeinde-) chairman

vorstell|bar a imaginable, con- ceivable. v~en vt sep put for- ward (Bein, Uhr); (darstellen) re- present; (bekanntmachen) intro- duce; sich v~en introduce one- self; (als Bewerber) go for an in- terview; sich (dat) etw v~en imagine sth. V~ung f introduc- tion; (bei Bewerbung) interview; (Aufführung) performance; (Idee) idea; (Phantasie) imagina- tion. V~ungsgespräch nt inter- view. V~ungskraft f imagina- tion

Vorstoß m advance

Vorstrafe f previous conviction

Vortag m day before

vortäuschen vt sep feign, fake

Vorteil m advantage. v~haft a advantageous, adv -ly; (Kleidung, Farbe) flattering

Vortrag m -[e]s,-̈e talk; (wissen- schaftlich) lecture; (Klavier-, Ge- dicht-) recital. v~en† vt sep per- form; (aufsagen) recite; (singen) sing; (darlegen) present (dat to); express (Wunsch)

vortrefflich a excellent, adv -ly

vortreten† vi sep (sein) step for- ward; (hervor-) protrude

Vortritt m precedence; jdm den V~ lassen let s.o. go first

vorüber adv v~ sein be over; an etw (dat) v~ past sth. v~ge- hen† vi sep (sein) walk past; (ver- gehen) pass. v~gehend a tem- porary, adv -ily

Vor|urteil nt prejudice. V~ver- kauf m advance booking

vorverlegen vt sep bring forward

Vor|wahl[nummer] f dialling code. V~wand m -[e]s,-̈e pre- text; (Ausrede) excuse

vorwärts adv forward[s]. v~kommen† vi sep (sein) make progress; (fig) get on

vorweg adv beforehand; (vorn) in front; (voraus) ahead. v~neh- men† vt sep anticipate

vorweisen† *vt sep* show

vorwerfen† *vt sep* throw (*dat* to); **jdm etw v~** reproach s.o. with sth; (*beschuldigen*) accuse s.o. of sth

vorwiegend *adv* predominantly

Vorwort *nt* (*pl -worte*) preface

Vorwurf *m* reproach; **jdm Vorwürfe machen** reproach s.o. **v~svoll** *a* reproachful, *adv* -ly

Vorzeichen *nt* sign; (*fig*) omen

vorzeigen *vt sep* show

vorzeitig *a* premature, *adv* -ly

vorziehen† *vt sep* pull forward; draw ⟨*Vorhang*⟩; (*vorverlegen*) bring forward; (*lieber mögen*) prefer; (*bevorzugen*) favour

Vor|zimmer *nt* ante-room; (*Büro*) outer office. **V~zug** *m* preference; (*gute Eigenschaft*) merit, virtue; (*Vorteil*) advantage

vorzüglich *a* excellent, *adv* -ly

vorzugsweise *adv* preferably

vulgär /vul'gε:g/ *a* vulgar ▫ *adv* in a vulgar way

Vulkan /vul'ka:n/ *m* -s,-e volcano

W

Waage *f* -,-n scales *pl*; (*Astr*) Libra. **W~recht** *a* horizontal, *adv* -ly

Wabe *f* -,-n honeycomb

wach *a* awake; (*aufgeweckt*) alert; **w~ werden** wake up

Wach|e *f* -,-n guard; (*Posten*) sentry; (*Dienst*) guard duty; (*Naut*) watch; (*Polizei-*) station; **W~e halten** keep watch; **W~e stehen** stand guard. **w~en** *vi* (*haben*) be awake; **w~en über** (+ *acc*) watch over. **W~hund** *m* guard-dog

Wacholder *m* -s juniper

Wachposten *m* sentry

Wachs *nt* -es wax

wachsam *a* vigilant, *adv* -ly. **W~keit** *f* -vigilance

wachsen†[1] *vi* (*sein*) grow

wachs|en[2] *vt* (*reg*) wax. **W~figur** *f* waxwork. **W~tuch** *nt* oil-cloth

Wachstum *nt* -s growth

Wächter *m* -s,- guard; (*Park-*) keeper; (*Parkplatz-*) attendant

Wacht|meister *m* (*police*) constable. **W~posten** *m* sentry

Wachturm *m* watch-tower

wackelig *a* wobbly; ⟨*Stuhl*⟩ rickety; ⟨*Person*⟩ shaky. **W~kontakt** *m* loose connection. **w~n** *vi* (*haben*) wobble; (*zittern*) shake ▫ *vi* (*sein*) totter

wacklig *a* = **wackelig**

Wade *f* -,-n (*Anat*) calf

Waffe *f* -,-n weapon; **W~n** arms

Waffel *f* -,-n waffle; (*Eis-*) wafer

Waffen|ruhe *f* cease-fire. **W~schein** *m* firearms licence. **W~stillstand** *m* armistice

Wagemut *m* daring. **w~ig** *a* daring, *adv* -ly

wagen *vt* risk; **es w~**, etw **zu tun** dare [to] do sth; **sich w~** (*gehen*) venture

Wagen *m* -s,- cart; (*Eisenbahn-*) carriage, coach; (*Güter-*) wagon; (*Kinder-*) pram; (*Auto*) car. **W~heber** *m* -s,- jack

Waggon /va'gõ:/ *m* -s,-s wagon

waghalsig *a* daring, *adv* -ly

Wagnis *nt* -ses,-se risk

Wahl *f* -,-en choice; (*Pol, Admin*) election; (*geheime*) ballot; **zweite W~** (*Comm*) seconds *pl*

wähl|en *vt/i* (*haben*) choose; (*Pol, Admin*) elect; (*stimmen*) vote; (*Teleph*) dial. **W~er(in)** *m* -s,- (*f* -,-nen) voter. **w~erisch** *a* choosy, fussy

Wahl|fach *nt* optional subject. **w~frei** *a* optional. **W~kampf** *m* election campaign. **W~kreis** *m* constituency. **W~lokal** *nt* polling-station. **w~los** *a* indiscriminate, *adv* -ly. **W~recht** *nt* [right to] vote

Wählscheibe *f* (*Teleph*) dial

Wahl|spruch m motto. **W~urne**
f ballot-box

Wahn m -[e]s delusion; (Manie)
mania

wähnen vt believe

Wahnsinn m madness. **w~ig** a
mad, insane; (fam: unsinnig)
crazy; (fam: groß) terrible; **w~ig**
werden go mad □ adv (fam) terribly. **W~ige(r)** m/f maniac

wahr a true; (echt) real; **w~ werden** come true; **du kommst**
doch, nicht w~? you are coming, aren't you?

wahren vt keep; (verteidigen)
safeguard; **den Schein w~** keep
up appearances

währen vi (haben) last

während prep (+ gen) during
□ conj while; (wohingegen) whereas. **w~dessen** adv in the meantime

wahrhaben vt etw nicht **w~**
wollen refuse to admit sth

wahrhaftig adv really, truly

Wahrheit f -,-en truth. **w~sge-**
mäß a truthful, adv -ly

wahrnehm|bar a perceptible.
w~en† vt sep notice; (nutzen)
take advantage of; exploit (Vorteil); look after (Interessen).
W~ung f -,-en perception

wahrsag|en v sep □ vt predict □ vi
(haben) jdm **w~en** tell s.o.'s fortune. **W~erin** f -,-nen fortuneteller

wahrscheinlich a probable, adv
-bly. **W~keit** f -probability

Währung f -,-en currency

Wahrzeichen nt symbol

Waise f -,-n orphan. **W~nhaus**
nt orphanage. **W~nkind** nt
orphan

Wal m -[e]s,-e whale

Wald m -[e]s,¨er wood; (groß) forest. **w~ig** a wooded

Walis|er m -s,- Welshman.
w~isch a Welsh

Wall m -[e]s,¨e mound; (Mil) rampart

Wallfahr|er(in) m(f) pilgrim.
W~t f pilgrimage

Walnuß f walnut

Walze f -,-n roller. **w~n** vt roll

wälzen vt roll; pore over
⟨Bücher⟩; mull over (Probleme);
sich w~ roll [about]; (schlaflos)
toss and turn

Walzer m -s,- waltz

Wand f -,¨e wall; (Trenn-) partition; (Seite) side; (Fels-) face

Wandel m -s change. **w~bar** a
changeable. **w~n** vi (sein) stroll
□ vr sich **w~n** change

Wander|er m -s,-, **W~in** f -,-nen
hiker, rambler. **w~n** vi (sein)
hike, ramble; (ziehen) travel; (gemächlich gehen) wander; (ziellos)
roam. **W~schaft** f - travels pl.
W~ung f -,-en hike, ramble;
(länger) walking tour. **W~weg**
m footpath

Wandgemälde nt mural

Wandlung f -,-en change, transformation

Wand|malerei f mural. **W~ta-**
fel f blackboard. **W~teppich** m
tapestry

Wange f -,-n cheek

wank|elmütig a fickle. **w~en** vi
(haben) sway; ⟨Person:⟩ stagger;
(fig) waver □ vi (sein) stagger

wann adv when

Wanne f -,-n tub

Wanze f -,-n bug

Wappen nt -s,- coat of arms.
W~kunde f heraldry

war, wäre s. **sein¹**

Ware f -,-n article; (Comm) commodity; (coll) merchandise;
W~n goods. **W~nhaus nt department store. **W~nprobe** f
sample. **W~nzeichen** nt trademark

warm a (wärmer, wärmst)
warm; ⟨Mahlzeit⟩ hot; **w~**

machen heat □ *adv* warmly; **w ~ essen** have a hot meal

Wärm|e *f* - warmth; *(Phys)* heat; **10 Grad W ~ e** 10 degrees above zero. **w ~ en** *vt* warm; heat ⟨*Essen, Wasser*⟩. **W ~ flasche** *f* hot-water bottle

warmherzig *a* warm-hearted

Warn|blinkanlage *f* hazard [warning] lights *pl.* **w ~ en** *vt/i (haben)* warn **(vor + *dat* of). W ~ ung** *f* **-,-en** warning

Warteliste *f* waiting list

warten *vi (haben)* wait **(auf + *acc* for); auf sich (*acc*) w ~ lassen** take one's/its time □ *vt* service

Wärter(in) *m* -s,- *(f* -,-nen) keeper; *(Museums-)* attendant; *(Gefängnis-)* warder, *(Amer)* guard; *(Kranken-)* orderly

Warte|raum *m* waiting-room. **W ~ saal** *m* exit waiting-room. **W ~ zimmer** *nt (Med)* waiting-room

Wartung *f* - *(Techn)* service

warum *adv* why

Warze *f* -,-n wart

was *pron* what; **was für [ein]?** what kind of [a]? **was für ein Pech!** what bad luck! **das gefällt dir, was?** you like that, don't you? □ *rel pron* that; **alles, was ich brauche** all [that] I need □ *indef pron (fam: etwas)* something; *(fragend, verneint)* anything; **was zu essen** something to eat; **so was Ärgerliches!** what a nuisance! □ *adv (fam) (warum)* why; *(wie)* how

wasch|bar *a* washable. **W ~ becken** *nt* wash-basin. **W ~ beutel** *m* sponge-bag

Wäsche *f* - washing; *(Unter-)* underwear; **in der W ~** in the wash

waschecht *a* colour-fast; *(fam)* genuine

Wäsche|klammer *f* clothes-peg. **W ~ leine** *f* clothes-line

waschen† *vt* wash; **sich w ~** have a wash; **sich (*dat*) die Hände w ~** wash one's hands; **W ~ und Legen** shampoo and set □ *vi (haben)* do the washing

Wäscherei *f* -,-en laundry

Wäsche|schleuder *f* spin-drier. **W ~ trockner** *m* tumble-drier

Wasch|küche *f* laundry-room. **W ~ lappen** *m* washcloth; *(fam: Feigling)* sissy. **W ~ maschine** *f* washing machine. **W ~ mittel** *nt* detergent. **W ~ pulver** *nt* washing-powder. **W ~ raum** *m* washroom. **W ~ salon** *m* launderette. **W ~ zettel** *m* blurb

Wasser *nt* -s water; *(Haar-)* lotion; **ins W ~ fallen** *(fam)* fall through; **mir lief das W ~ im Mund zusammen** my mouth was watering. **W ~ ball** *m* beachball; *(Spiel)* water polo. **w ~ dicht** *a* watertight; ⟨*Kleidung*⟩ waterproof. **W ~ fall** *m* waterfall. **W ~ farbe** *f* watercolour. **W ~ hahn** *m* tap, *(Amer)* faucet. **W ~ kasten** *m* cistern. **W ~ kraft** *f* water-power. **W ~ kraftwerk** *nt* hydroelectric power-station. **W ~ leitung** *f* water-main; **aus der W ~ leitung** from the tap. **W ~ mann** *m (Astr)* Aquarius

wässern *vt* soak; *(begießen)* water □ *vi (haben)* water

Wasser|scheide *f* watershed. **W ~ ski** *nt* -s water-skiing. **W ~ stoff** *m* hydrogen. **W ~ straße** *f* waterway. **W ~ waage** *f* spirit-level. **W ~ werfer** *m* -s,- water-cannon. **W ~ zeichen** *nt* watermark

wäßrig *a* watery

waten *vi (sein)* wade

watscheln *vi (sein)* waddle

Watt¹ *nt* -[e]s mud-flats *pl*

Watt² *nt* -s,- *(Phys)* watt

Watt|e f - cotton wool. **w~iert** a padded; (gesteppt) quilted

WC /ve:'tse:/ nt -s,-s WC

web|en vt/i (haben) weave. **W~er** m -s,- weaver. **W~stuhl** m loom

Wechsel m -s,- change; (Tausch) exchange; (Comm) bill of exchange. **W~geld** nt change. **w~haft** a changeable. **W~jahre** npl menopause sg. **W~kurs** m exchange rate. **w~n** vt change; (tauschen) exchange; (ab-) alternate; (verschieden sein) vary. **w~nd** a changing; (verschieden) varying. **w~seitig** a mutual, adv -ly. **W~strom** m alternating current. **W~stube** f bureau de change. **w~weise** adv alternately. **W~wirkung** f interaction

weck|en vt wake [up]; (fig) awaken □vi (haben) ⟨Wecker:⟩ go off. **W~er** m -s,- alarm [clock]

wedeln vi (haben) wave; mit dem Schwanz **w~** wag its tail

weder conj **w~ ... noch** neither ... nor

Weg m -[e]s,-e way; (Fuß-) path; (Fahr-) track; (Gang) errand; **auf dem Weg** on the way (nach to); **sich auf den Weg machen** set off; **im Weg sein** be in the way

weg adv away, off; (verschwunden) gone; **weg sein** be away; (gegangen/verschwunden) have gone; (fam: schlafen) be asleep; **Hände weg!** hands off! **w~bleiben†** vi sep (sein) stay away. **w~bringen†** vt sep take away

wegen prep (+dat) because of; (um ... willen) for the sake of; (bezüglich) about

weg|fahren† vi sep (sein) go away; (abfahren) leave. **w~fallen†** vi sep (sein) be dropped/(ausgelassen) omitted; (entfallen) no longer apply; (aufhören) cease. **w~geben†** vt sep

give away; send to the laundry ⟨Wäsche⟩. **w~gehen†** vi sep (sein) leave, go away; (ausgehen) go out; ⟨Fleck:⟩ come out. **w~jagen** vt sep chase away. **w~kommen†** vi sep (sein) get away; (verlorengehen) disappear. **w~lassen†** vt sep let go; (auslassen) omit. **w~laufen†** vi sep (sein) run away. **w~machen** vt sep remove. **w~nehmen†** vt sep take away. **w~räumen** vt sep put away; (entfernen) clear away. **w~schicken** vt sep send away; (abschicken) send off. **w~tun†** vt sep put away; (wegwerfen) throw away

Wegweiser m -s,- signpost

weg|werfen† vt sep throw away. **w~ziehen†** v sep □vt pull away □vi (sein) move away

weh a sore; weh tun hurt; ⟨Kopf, Rücken:⟩ ache; **jdm weh tun** hurt s.o. □int **oh weh!** oh dear!

wehe int alas; **w~ [dir/euch]!** (drohend) don't you dare!

wehen vi (haben) blow; (flattern) flutter □vt blow

Wehen fpl contractions; **in den W~ liegen** be in labour

weh|leidig a soft; (weinerlich) whining. **W~mut** f- wistfulness. **w~mütig** a wistful, adv -ly

Wehr¹ nt -[e]s,-e weir

Wehr² f **sich zur W~ setzen** resist. **W~dienst** m military service. **W~dienstverweigerer** m -s,- conscientious objector

wehren vt (sich) vr resist; (gegen Anschuldigung) protest; (sich sträuben) refuse

wehr|los a defenceless. **W~macht** f armed forces pl. **W~pflicht** f conscription

Weib nt -[e]s,-er woman; (Ehe-) wife. **W~chen** nt -s,- (Zool) female. **W~erheld** m womanizer. **w~isch** a effeminate. **w~lich** a

feminine; (*Biol*) female. W~-
lichkeit *f* - femininity

weich *a* soft, *adv* -ly; (*gar*) done;
⟨*Ei*⟩ soft-boiled; ⟨*Mensch*⟩ soft-
hearted; **w~ werden** (*fig*) relent

Weiche *f* -,-n (*Rail*) points *pl*

weichen¹ *vi* (sein) (*reg*) soak

weichen² † *vi* (sein) give way (*dat*
to); **nicht von jds Seite w~** not
leave s.o.'s side

Weich|heit *f* - softness. **w~her-
zig** *a* soft-hearted. **w~lich** *a* soft;
⟨*Charakter*⟩ weak. **W~spüler** *m*
-s,- (*Tex*) conditioner. **W~tier** *nt*
mollusc

Weide¹ *f* -,-n (*Bot*) willow

Weide² *f* -,-n pasture. **w~n** *vt/i*
(haben) graze; **sich w~n an** (+
dat) enjoy; ⟨*schadenfroh*⟩ gloat
over

weiger|n (sich) *vr* refuse.
W~ung *f* -,-en refusal

Weihe *f* -,-n consecration; (*Priester*) ordination. **w~n** *vt* consecrate; (*zum Priester*) ordain; dedi-
cate ⟨*Kirche*⟩ (*dat* to)

Weiher *m* -s,- pond

Weihnacht|en *nt* -s & *pl* Christ-
mas. **w~lich** *a* Christmassy.
W~sbaum *m* Christmas tree.
W~sfest *nt* Christmas.
W~slied *nt* Christmas carol.
W~smann *m* (*pl* -männer)
Father Christmas. **W~stag** *m*
erster/zweiter W~stag Christ-
mas Day/Boxing Day

Weih|rauch *m* incense. **W~-
wasser** *nt* holy water

weil *conj* because; (*da*) since

Weile *f* - while

Wein *m* -[e]s,-e wine; (*Bot*) vines
pl; (*Trauben*) grapes *pl*. **W~bau**
m wine-growing. **W~beere** *f*
grape. **W~berg** *m* vineyard.
W~brand *m* -[e]s brandy

wein|en *vt/i* (haben) cry, weep.
w~erlich *a* tearful, *adv* -ly

Wein|glas *nt* wineglass. **W~-
karte** *f* wine-list. **W~keller** *m*

wine-cellar. **W~lese** *f* grape harvest. **W~liste** *f* wine-list.
W~probe *f* wine-tasting.
W~rebe *f* vine. **W~stock** *m* vine.
W~stube *f* wine-bar. **W~trau-
be** *f* bunch of grapes; (*W~beere*)
grape

weise *a* wise, *adv* -ly

Weise *f* -,-n way; (*Melodie*) tune;
auf diese W~ in this way

weisen† *vt* show; **von sich w~**
(*fig*) reject ⋄ *vi* (haben) point (**auf**
+ *acc* at)

Weisheit *f* -,-en wisdom.
W~szahn *m* wisdom tooth

weiß *a*, **W~** *nt* -,- white

weissag|en *vt/i insep* (haben)
prophesy. **W~ung** *f* -,-en prophecy

Weiß|brot *nt* white bread.
W~e(r) *m/f* white man/woman.
w~en *vt* whitewash. **W~wein**
m white wine

Weisung *f* -,-en instruction; (*Befehl*) order

weit *a* wide; (*ausgedehnt*) extensive; (*lang*) long □*adv* widely;
⟨*offen, öffnen*⟩ wide; (*lang*) far;
von w~em from a distance; **bei
w~em** by far; **w~ und breit** far
and wide; **ist es noch w~?** is it
much further? **ich bin so w~** I'm
ready; **zu w~ gehen** (*fig*) go too
far. **w~aus** *adv* far. **W~blick**
m (*fig*) far-sightedness. **w~-
blickend** *a* (*fig*) far-sighted

Weite *f* -,-n expanse; (*Entfernung*)
distance; (*Größe*) width. **w~n** *vt*
widen; stretch ⟨*Schuhe*⟩; **sich
w~n** widen; stretch; ⟨*Pupille*⟩
dilate

weiter *a* further □*adv* further;
(*außerdem*) in addition; (*an-
schließend*) then; **etw w~ tun** go
on doing sth; **w~ nichts/nie-
mand** nothing/no one else; **und
so w~** and so on. **w~arbeiten**
vi sep (haben) go on working

weiter|**e(r,s)** *a* further; **im w~en Sinne** in a wider sense; **ohne w~es** just like that; *(leicht)* easily; **bis auf w~es** until further notice; *(vorläufig)* for the time being

weiter|**erzählen** *vt sep* go on with; *(w~sagen)* repeat. **w~fahren†** *vi sep (sein)* go on. **w~geben†** *vt sep* pass on. **w~gehen†** *vi sep (sein)* go on. **w~hin** *adv (immer noch)* still; *(in Zukunft)* in future; *(außerdem)* furthermore; **etw w~hin tun** go on doing sth. **w~kommen†** *vi sep (sein)* get on. **w~machen** *vi sep (haben)* carry on. **w~sagen** *vt sep* pass on; *(verraten)* repeat

weit|**gehend** *adv* extensive □ *adv* to a large extent. **w~hin** *adv* a long way; *(fig)* widely. **w~läufig** *a* spacious; *(entfernt) adv* -ly; *(ausführlich)* lengthy, *adv* at length. **w~reichend** *a* far-reaching. **w~schweifig** *a* long-winded. **w~sichtig** *a* long-sighted; *(fig)* far-sighted. **W~sprung** *m* long jump. **w~verbreitet** *a* widespread

Weizen *m* -s wheat

welch *inv pron* what; **w~ ein(e)** what a. **w~e(r,s)** *pron* which; **um w~e Zeit?** at what time? □ *rel pron* which; *(Person)* who □ *indef pron* some; *(fragend)* any; **was für w~e?** what sort of?

welk *a* wilted; *⟨Laub⟩* dead. **w~en** *vi (sein)* wilt; *(fig)* fade

Wellblech *nt* corrugated iron

Welle *f* -,-n wave; *⟨Techn⟩* shaft. **W~enlänge** *f* wavelength. **W~enlinie** *f* wavy line. **W~enreiten** *nt* surfing. **W~ensittich** *m* -s,-e budgerigar. **w~ig** *a* wavy

Welt *f* -,-en world; **auf der W~** in the world; **auf die od zur W~ kommen** be born. **W~all** *nt* universe. **w~berühmt** *a* world-famous. **w~fremd** *a* unworldly.

w~gewandt *a* sophisticated. **W~kugel** *f* globe. **w~lich** *a* worldly; *(nicht geistlich)* secular. **Weltmeister**|**(in)** *m(f)* world champion. **W~schaft** *f* world championship

Weltraum *m* space. **W~fahrer** *m* astronaut

Welt|**rekord** *m* world record. **w~weit** *a & adv* world-wide

wem *pron (dat of wer)* to whom. **wen** *pron (acc of wer)* whom

Wende *f* -,-n change. **W~kreis** *m* *(Geog)* tropic

Wendeltreppe *f* spiral staircase

wenden[1] *vt (reg)* turn; **sich zum Guten w~** take a turn for the better □ *vi (haben)* turn [round]

wenden[2]† *(& reg)* *vt* turn; **sich w~** turn; **sich an jdn w~** turn/*(schriftlich)* write to s.o.

Wend|**epunkt** *m* *(fig)* turning-point. **w~ig** *a* nimble; *⟨Auto⟩* manœuvrable. **W~ung** *f* -,-en turn; *(Biegung)* bend; *(Veränderung)* change

wenig *pron* little; *(pl)* few; **w~e** *pl* few □ *adv* little; *(kaum)* not much. **w~er** *pron* less; *(pl)* fewer; **immer w~er** less and less □ *adv & conj* less. **w~ste(r,s)** *a* least; **am w~sten** least [of all]. **w~stens** *adv* at least

wenn *conj* if; *(sobald)* when; **immer w~** whenever; **w~ nicht** unless; **w~ auch** even though

wer *pron* who; *(fam: jemand)* someone; *(fragend)* anyone; **ist da wer?** is anyone there?

Werbe|**agentur** *f* advertising agency. **w~n†** *vt* recruit; attract *⟨Kunden, Besucher⟩* □ *vi (haben)* **w~n für** advertise; canvass for *⟨Partei⟩*; **w~n um** try to attract *⟨Besucher⟩*; court *⟨Frau, Gunst⟩*. **W~spot** */sp-/* *m* -s,-s commercial

Werbung *f* - advertising

werden† *vi* ⟨*sein*⟩ become; ⟨*müde, alt, länger*⟩ get, grow; ⟨*blind, wahnsinnig*⟩ go; **blaß w~** turn pale; **krank w~** fall ill; **es wird warm/dunkel** it is getting warm/dark; **mir wurde schlecht/schwindlig** I felt sick/dizzy; **er will Lehrer w~** he wants to be a teacher; **was ist aus ihm geworden?** what has become of him? □*v aux* ⟨*Zukunft*⟩ shall; **wir w~ sehen** we shall see; **es wird bald regnen** it's going to rain soon; **würden Sie so nett sein?** would you be so kind? □ ⟨*Passiv; pp* **worden**⟩ be; **geliebt/geboren w~** be loved/born; **es wurde gemunkelt** it was rumoured

werfen† *vt* throw; cast ⟨*Blick, Schatten*⟩; **sich w~** ⟨*Holz:*⟩ warp □*vi* ⟨*haben*⟩ **~ mit** throw

Werft *f* -,-en shipyard

Werk *nt* -[e]s,-e work; ⟨*Fabrik*⟩ works *sg*, factory; ⟨*Trieb-*⟩ mechanism. **W~en** *nt* -s ⟨*Sch*⟩ handicraft. **W~statt** *f* -,-ᵉen workshop; ⟨*Auto-*⟩ garage; ⟨*Künstler-*⟩ studio. **W~tag** *m* weekday. **w~tags** *adv* on weekdays. **w~tätig** *a* working. **W~unterricht** *m* ⟨*Sch*⟩ handicraft

Werkzeug *nt* tool; ⟨*coll*⟩ tools *pl*. **W~maschine** *f* machine tool

Wermut *m* -s vermouth

wert *a* **viel/50 Mark w~** worth a lot/50 marks; **nichts w~ sein** be worthless; **jds/etw** ⟨*gen*⟩ **w~ sein** be worthy of s.o./sth. **W~** *m* -[e]s,-e value; ⟨*Nenn-*⟩ denomination; **im W~ von** worth; **W~legen auf** (+*acc*) set great store by. **w~en** *vt* rate

Wert|gegenstand *m* object of value; **W~gegenstände** valuables. **w~los** *a* worthless. **W~minderung** *f* depreciation. **W~papier** *nt* ⟨*Comm*⟩ security.

W~sachen *fpl* valuables. **w~voll** *a* valuable

Wesen *nt* -s,- nature; ⟨*Lebe-*⟩ being; ⟨*Mensch*⟩ creature

wesentlich *a* essential; ⟨*grundlegend*⟩ fundamental; ⟨*erheblich*⟩ considerable; **im w~en** essentially □*adv* considerably, much

weshalb *adv* why

Wespe *f* -,-n wasp

wessen *pron* ⟨*gen of* **wer**⟩ whose

westdeutsch *a* West German

Weste *f* -,-n waistcoat; ⟨*Amer*⟩ vest

Westen *m* -s west; **nach W~** west

Western *m* -[s],- western

Westfalen *nt* -s Westphalia

Westindien *nt* West Indies *pl*

west|lich *a* western; ⟨*Richtung*⟩ westerly □*adv* & *prep* (+*gen*) **w~lich [von] der Stadt** [to the] west of the town. **w~wärts** *adv* westwards

weswegen *adv* why

wett *a* **w~ sein** be quits

Wett|bewerb *m* -s,-e competition. **W~büro** *nt* betting shop

Wette *f* -,-n bet; **um die W~ laufen** race ⟨*mit jdm* s.o.⟩

wetteifern *vi* ⟨*haben*⟩ compete

wetten *vt/i* ⟨*haben*⟩ bet ⟨*auf*+*acc* on⟩; **mit jdm w~** have a bet with s.o.

Wetter *nt* -s,- weather; ⟨*Un-*⟩ storm. **W~bericht** *m* weather report. **W~hahn** *m* weathercock. **W~lage** *f* weather conditions *pl*. **W~vorhersage** *f* weather forecast. **W~warte** *f* -,-n meteorological station

Wett|kampf *m* contest. **W~kämpfer(in)** *m(f)* competitor. **W~lauf** *m* race. **w~machen** *vt sep* make up for. **W~rennen** *nt* race. **W~streit** *m* contest

wetzen *vt* sharpen □*vi* ⟨*sein*⟩ ⟨*fam*⟩ dash

Whisky *m* -s whisky

wichsen *vt* polish

wichtig *a* important; **w~ neh-men** take seriously. **W~keit** *f* - importance. **w~tuerisch** *a* self-important

Wicke *f* -,-n sweet pea

Wickel *m* -s,- compress

wick|eln *vt* wind; (*ein-*) wrap; (*bandagieren*) bandage; **ein Kind frisch w~** change a baby. **W~ler** *m* -s,- curler

Widder *m* -s,- ram; (*Astr*) Aries

wider *prep* (+ *acc*) against; (*entgegen*) contrary to; **w~ Willen** against one's will

widerfahren† *vi insep* (*sein*) **jdm w~** happen to s.o.

widerhallen *vi sep* (*haben*) echo

widerlegen *vt insep* refute

wider|lich *a* repulsive; (*unangenehm*) nasty, *adv* -ily. **w~recht-lich** *a* unlawful, *adv* -ly. **W~rede** *f* contradiction; **keine W~rede!** don't argue!

widerrufen† *vt/i insep* (*haben*) retract; revoke ⟨*Befehl*⟩

Widersacher *m* -s,- adversary

widersetzen (**sich**) *vr insep* resist ⟨jdm/etw s.o./sth⟩

wider|sinnig *a* absurd. **w~spenstig** *a* unruly; (*störrisch*) stubborn

widerspiegeln *vt sep* reflect; **sich w~** be reflected

widersprechen† *vi insep* (*haben*) contradict ⟨jdm/etw s.o./sth⟩

Wider|spruch *m* contradiction; (*Protest*) protest. **w~sprüch-lich** *a* contradictory. **w~spruchslos** *adv* without protest

Widerstand *m* resistance; **W~leisten** resist. **w~sfähig** *a* resistant; (*Bot*) hardy

widerstehen† *vi insep* (*haben*) resist ⟨jdm/etw s.o./sth⟩; (*anwidern*) be repugnant ⟨jdm to s.o.⟩

widerstreben *vi insep* (*haben*) **es widerstrebt mir** I am reluctant (zu to). **W~ nt -s** reluctance. **w~d** *a* reluctant, *adv* -ly

widerwärtig *a* disagreeable, unpleasant; (*ungünstig*) adverse

Widerwille *m* aversion, repugnance. **w~ig** *a* reluctant, *adv* -ly

widm|en *vt* dedicate ⟨dat to⟩; (*verwenden*) devote ⟨dat to⟩; **sich w~en** (+ *dat*) devote oneself to. **W~ung** *f* -,-en dedication

widrig *a* adverse, unfavourable

wie *adv* how; **wie viele?** how many? **wie ist Ihr Name?** what is your name? **wie ist das Wetter?** what is the weather like? □ *conj* as; (*gleich wie*) like; (*sowie*) as well as; (*als*) when, as; **genau wie du** just like you; **so gut/reich wie** as good/rich as; **nichts wie** nothing but; **größer wie ich** (*fam*) bigger than me

wieder *adv* again; **er ist w~ da** he is back

Wiederaufbau *m* reconstruction. **w~en** *vt sep* reconstruct

wiederaufnehmen† *vt sep* resume. **W~aufrüstung** *f* rearmament

wieder|bekommen† *vt sep* get back. **w~beleben** *vt sep* revive. **W~belebung** *f* - resuscitation. **w~bringen†** *vt sep* bring back. **w~erkennen†** *vt sep* recognize. **W~gabe** *f* (s. **w~geben**) return; portrayal; rendering; reproduction. **w~geben†** *vt sep* give back, return; (*darstellen*) portray; (*ausdrücken, übersetzen*) render; (*zitieren*) quote; (*Techn*) reproduce. **W~geburt** *f* reincarnation

wiedergutmach|en *vt sep* (*fig*) make up for; redress ⟨*Unrecht*⟩; (*bezahlen*) pay for. **W~ung** *f* - reparation; (*Entschädigung*) compensation

wiederher|stellen vt sep re-es-
tablish; restore ⟨Gebäude⟩; restore to health ⟨Kranke⟩; **w~ge-
stellt sein** be fully recovered.
W~stellung f re-establishment;
restoration; ⟨Genesung⟩ recovery
wiederholen[1] vt sep get back
wiederhol|en[2] vt insep repeat;
⟨Sch⟩ revise; **sich w~en** recur;
⟨Person:⟩ repeat oneself. **w~t** a
repeated, adv -ly. **W~ung** f
-,-en repetition; ⟨Sch⟩ revision
Wieder|hören nt auf **W~hören!**
goodbye! **W~käuer** m -s,- ruminant. **W~kehr** f - return;
⟨W~holung⟩ recurrence. **w~-
kehren** vi sep (sein) return; ⟨sich
wiederholen⟩ recur. **w~-
kommen**† vi sep (sein) come
back
wiedersehen† vt sep see again.
W~ nt -s,- reunion; **auf W~!**
goodbye!
wiederum adv again; ⟨anderer-
seits⟩ on the other hand
wiedervereinig|en vt sep re-
unify ⟨Land⟩. **W~ung** f reuni-
fication
wieder|verheiraten (sich) vr
sep remarry. **W~verwenden**†
vt sep reuse. **w~verwerten** vt
sep recycle. **w~wählen** vt sep
re-elect
Wiege f -,-n cradle
wiegen[1]† vt/i (haben) weigh
wiegen[2] vt (reg) rock; **sich w~**
sway; ⟨schaukeln⟩ rock. **W~lied**
nt lullaby
wiehern vi (haben) neigh
Wien nt -s Vienna. **W~er** a Viennese; **W~er Schnitzel** Wiener
schnitzel □m -s,- Viennese □f
-,- ≈ frankfurter. **w~erisch** a
Viennese
Wiese f -,-n meadow
Wiesel nt -s,- weasel
wieso adv why
wieviel pron how much/⟨pl⟩
many; **um w~ Uhr?** at what

time? **w~te(r,s)** a which; **der
W~te ist heute?** what is the date
today?
wieweit adv how far
wild a wild, adv -ly; ⟨Stamm⟩
savage; **w~er Streik** wildcat
strike; **w~ wachsen** grow wild.
W~ nt -[e]s game; ⟨Rot-⟩ deer;
⟨Culin⟩ venison. **W~dieb** m
poacher. **W~e(r)** m/f savage
Wilderer m -s,- poacher. **w~n**
vt/i (haben) poach
wildfremd a totally strange;
w~e Leute total strangers
Wild|heger, W~hüter m -s,-
gamekeeper. **W~leder** nt suede.
w~ledern a suede. **W~nis** f -
wilderness. **W~schwein** nt wild
boar. **W~westfilm** m western
Wille m -ns will; **Letzter W~**
will; **seinen W~n durchsetzen**
get one's [own] way; **mit W~n**
intentionally
willen prep (+ gen) **um ... w~**
for the sake of . . .
Willens|kraft f will-power.
w~stark a strong-willed
willig a willing, adv -ly
willkommen a welcome; **w~
heißen** welcome. **W~** nt -s welcome
willkürlich a arbitrary, adv -ily
wimmeln vi (haben) swarm
wimmern vi (haben) whimper
Wimpel m -s,- pennant
Wimper f -,-n [eye]lash; **nicht
mit der W~ zucken** ⟨fam⟩ not
bat an eyelid. **W~ntusche** f
mascara
Wind m -[e]s,-e wind
Winde f -,-n ⟨Techn⟩ winch
Windel f -,-n nappy, ⟨Amer⟩ diaper

winden† vt wind; make ⟨Kranz⟩;
in die Höhe w~ winch up; **sich
w~** wind ⟨um round⟩; ⟨sich
krümmen⟩ writhe

Wind|hund m greyhound. **w~ig**
a windy. **W~mühle** f windmill.
W~pocken fpl chickenpox sg.
W~schutzscheibe f windscreen, (Amer) windshield.
w~still a calm. **W~stille** f
calm. **W~stoß** m gust of wind.
W~surfen nt windsurfing

Windung f -,-en bend; (Spirale)
spiral

Wink m -[e]s,-e sign; (Hinweis)
hint

Winkel m -s,- angle; (Ecke) corner. **W~messer** m -s,- protrac-
tor

winken vi (haben) wave; **jdm w~**
wave/(herbei~) beckon to s.o.

winseln vi (haben) whine

Winter m -s,- winter. **w~lich** a
wintry; (Winter-) winter ...
W~schlaf m hibernation.
W~schlaf halten hibernate.
W~sport m winter sports pl

Winzer m -s,- winegrower

winzig a tiny, minute

Wipfel m -s,- [tree]top

Wippe f -,-n see-saw. **w~n** vi
(haben) bounce; (auf Wippe) play
on the see-saw

wir pron we; **wir sind es** it's us

Wirbel m -s,- eddy; (Drehung)
whirl; (Trommel-) roll; (Anat)
vertebra; (Haar-) crown; (Aufsehen) fuss. **w~n** vt/i (sein/haben)
whirl. **W~säule** f spine.
W~sturm m cyclone. **W~tier**
nt vertebrate. **W~wind** m whirl-
wind

wird s. **werden**

wirken vi (haben) have an effect
(**auf**+ acc on); (zur Geltung kommen) be effective; (tätig sein)
work; (scheinen) seem □vt (Tex)
knit; **Wunder w~** work miracles

wirklich a real, adv -ly. **W~keit**
f -,-en reality

wirksam a effective, adv -ly.
W~keit f - effectiveness

Wirkung f -,-en effect. **w~slos** a
ineffective, adv -ly. **w~svoll** a
effective, adv -ly

wirr a tangled; (Haar) tousled;
(verwirrt, verworren) confused.
W~warr m -s tangle; (fig) confusion; (von Stimmen) hubbub

Wirt m -[e]s,-e landlord. **W~in** f
-,-nen landlady

Wirtschaft f -,-en economy;
(Gast-) restaurant; (Kneipe) pub.
w~en vi (haben) manage one's
finances; (sich betätigen) busy
oneself; **sie kann nicht w~en** she's a bad manager. **W~erin** f
-,-nen housekeeper. **w~lich** a
economic, adv -ally; (sparsam)
economical, adv -ly. **W~sgeld** nt
housekeeping [money]. **W~s-
prüfer** m auditor

Wirtshaus nt inn; (Kneipe) pub

Wisch m -[e]s,-e (fam) piece of
paper

wisch|en vt/i (haben) wipe; wash
(Fußboden) □vi (sein) slip;
(Maus-) scurry. **W~lappen** m
cloth; (Aufwisch-) floor-cloth

wispern vt/i (haben) whisper

wissen† vt/i (haben) know; **weißt
du noch?** do you remember?
nichts w~ wollen von not want
anything to do with. **W~** nt -s
knowledge; **meines W~s** to my
knowledge

Wissenschaft f -,-en science.
W~ler m -s,- academic; (Natur-)
scientist. **w~lich** a academic,
adv -ally; scientific, adv -ally

wissen|swert a worth knowing.
w~tlich a deliberate □adv
knowingly

witter|n vt scent; (ahnen) sense.
W~ung f - scent; (Wetter)
weather

Witwe f -,-n widow. **W~r** m -s,-
widower

Witz m -es,-e joke; (Geist) wit.
W~bold m -[e]s,-e joker. **w~ig**
a funny; (geistreich) witty

wo *adv* where; (*als*) when; (*irgend-wo*) somewhere; **wo immer** wherever □*conj* seeing that; (*ob-wohl*) although; (*wenn*) if

woanders *adv* somewhere else

wobei *adv* how; (*relativ*) during the course of which

Woche *f* -,-n week. **W~nende** *nt* weekend. **W~nkarte** *f* weekly ticket. **w~nlang** *adv* for weeks. **W~ntag** *m* day of the week; (*Werktag*) weekday. **w~tags** *adv* on weekdays

wöchentlich *a* & *adv* weekly

Wodka *m* -s vodka

wodurch *adv* how; (*relativ*) through/(*Ursache*) by which; (*Folge*) as a result of which

wofür *adv* what ... for; (*relativ*) for which

Woge *f* -,-n wave

wogegen *adv* what ... against; (*relativ*) against which □*conj* whereas

woher *adv* where from; **woher weißt du das?** how do you know that? **wohin** *adv* where [to]; **wohin gehst du?** where are you going? **wohin-gegen** *conj* whereas

wohl *adv* well; (*vermutlich*) probably; (*etwa*) about; (*zwar*) perhaps; **w~ kaum** hardly; **w~ oder übel** willy-nilly; **sich w~ fühlen** feel well/(*behaglich*) comfortable; **der ist w~ verrückt!** he must be mad! **W~** *nt* -[e]s welfare, well-being; **auf jds W~ trinken** drink s.o.'s health; **zum W~** (+ *gen*) for the good of; **zum W~!** cheers!

wohlauf *a* **w~ sein** to be well

Wohl|befinden *nt* well-being. **W~behagen** *nt* feeling of well-being. **w~behalten** *a* safe, *adv* -ly. **W~ergehen** *nt* -s welfare. **w~erzogen** *a* well brought-up

Wohlfahrt *f* - welfare. **W~sstaat** *m* Welfare State

Wohl|gefallen *nt* -s pleasure. **W~geruch** *m* fragrance. **w~-gesinnt** *a* well disposed (*dat* towards). **w~habend** *a* prosperous, well-to-do. **w~ig** *a* comfortable, *adv* -bly. **w~klingend** *a* melodious. **w~riechend** *a* fragrant. **w~schmeckend** *a* tasty

Wohlstand *m* prosperity. **W~sgesellschaft** *f* affluent society

Wohltat *f* [act of] kindness; (*Annehmlichkeit*) treat; (*Genuß*) bliss. **Wohltät|er** *m* benefactor. **w~ig** *a* charitable

wohl|tuend *a* agreeable, *adv* -bly. **w~tun†** *vi sep* (*haben*) **jdm w~-tun** do s.o. good. **w~verdient** *a* well-deserved. **w~weislich** *adv* deliberately

Wohlwollen *nt* -s goodwill; (*Gunst*) favour. **w~d** *a* benevolent, *adv* -ly

Wohn|anhänger *m* = **Wohnwagen**. **W~block** *m* block of flats. **w~en** *vi* (*haben*) live; (*vorübergehend*) stay. **W~gegend** *f* residential area. **w~haft** *a* resident. **W~haus** *nt* [dwelling-]house. **W~heim** *nt* hostel; (*Alten-*) home. **w~lich** *a* comfortable, *adv* -bly. **W~mobil** *nt* -s,-e camper. **W~ort** *m* place of residence. **W~raum** *m* living space; (*Zimmer*) living-room. **W~sitz** *m* place of residence

Wohnung *f* -,-en flat, (*Amer*) apartment; (*Unterkunft*) accommodation. **W~snot** *f* housing shortage

Wohn|wagen *m* caravan, (*Amer*) trailer. **W~zimmer** *nt* living-room

wölben *vt* curve; arch (*Rücken*). **W~ung** *f* -,-en curve; (*Archit*) vault

Wolf *m* -[e]s,¨e wolf; (*Fleisch-*) mincer; (*Reiß-*) shredder

Wolke *f* -,-n cloud. **W~enbruch** *m* cloudburst. **W~enkratzer** *m* skyscraper. **w~enlos** *a* cloudless. **w~ig** *a* cloudy

Wolldecke *f* blanket. **W~e** *f* -,-n wool

wollen[1]† *vt/i* (haben) & *v aux* want; **etw tun w~** want to do sth; *(beabsichtigen)* be going to do sth; **ich will nach Hause** I want to go home; **wir wollten gerade gehen** we were just going; **ich wollte, ich könnte dir helfen** I wish I could help you; **der Motor will nicht anspringen** the engine won't start

wollen[2] *a* woollen. **w~ig** *a* woolly. **W~sachen** *fpl* woollens

wollüstig *a* sensual, carnal

womit *adv* what ... with; *(relativ)* with which. **womöglich** *adv* possibly. **wonach** *adv* what ... after/ ⟨*suchen*⟩ for/⟨*riechen*⟩ of; *(relativ)* after/for/of which

Wonne *f* -,-n bliss; *(Freude)* joy. **w~ig** *a* sweet

woran *adv* what ... on/⟨*denken, sterben*⟩ of; *(relativ)* on/of which; **woran hast du ihn erkannt?** how did you recognize him? **worauf** *adv* what ... on/⟨*warten*⟩ for; *(relativ)* on/for which; *(woraufhin)* whereupon. **woraufhin** *adv* whereupon. **woraus** *adv* what ... from; *(relativ)* from which. **worin** *adv* what ... in; *(relativ)* in which

Wort *nt* -[e]s,¨er & -e word; **jdm ins W~ fallen** interrupt s.o.; **ein paar W~e sagen** say a few words. **w~brüchig** *a* **w~brüchig werden** break one's word

Wörterbuch *nt* dictionary

Wortführer *m* spokesman. **w~getreu** *a* & *adv* word-forword. **w~gewandt** *a* eloquent, *adv* -ly. **w~karg** *a* taciturn. **W~laut** *m* wording

wörtlich *a* literal, *adv* -ly; *(wortgetreu)* word-for-word

wortlos *a* silent □*adv* without a word. **W~schatz** *m* vocabulary. **W~spiel** *nt* pun, play on words. **W~wechsel** *m* exchange of words; *(Streit)* argument. **w~wörtlich** *a* & *adv* = **wörtlich**

worüber *adv* what ... over/⟨*lachen, sprechen*⟩ about; *(relativ)* over/about which. **worum** *adv* what ... round/⟨*bitten, kämpfen*⟩ for; *(relativ)* round/for which; **worum geht es?** what is it about?. **worunter** *adv* what ... under/ *(wozwischen)* among; *(relativ)* under/among which. **wovon** *adv* what ... from/⟨*sprechen*⟩ about; *(relativ)* from/about which. **wovor** *adv* what ... in front of; ⟨*sich fürchten*⟩ what ... of; *(relativ)* in front of which; of which. **wozu** *adv* what ... to/ ⟨*brauchen, benutzen*⟩ for; *(relativ)* to/for which; **wozu?** what for?

Wrack *nt* -s,-s wreck

wringen† *vt* wring

wuchern *vi* (haben/sein) grow profusely. **W~preis** *m* extortionate price. **W~ung** *f* -,-en growth

Wuchs *m* -es growth; *(Gestalt)* stature

Wucht *f* - force. **w~en** *vt* heave. **w~ig** *a* massive

wühlen *vi* (haben) rummage; *(in der Erde)* burrow □*vt* dig

Wulst *m* -[e]s,¨e bulge; *(Fett-)* roll. **w~ig** *a* bulging; ⟨*Lippen*⟩ thick

wund *a* sore; **w~ reiben** chafe. **W~brand** *m* gangrene

Wunde *f* -,-n wound

Wunder *nt* -s,- wonder, marvel; *(übernatürliches)* miracle; **kein W~!** no wonder! **w~bar** *a* miraculous; *(herrlich)* wonderful, *adv* -ly, marvellous, *adv* -ly. **W~kind** *nt* infant prodigy w ~ **lich** a odd, adv -ly. w ~ n vt surprise; **sich** w ~ n be surprised (**über** + acc at). w ~ **schön** a beautiful, adv -ly. w ~ **voll** a wonderful, adv -ly

Wundstarrkrampf m tetanus

Wunsch m -[e]s,-e wish; (*Verlangen*) desire; (*Bitte*) request

wünschen vt want; **sich** (*dat*) etw w ~ want sth; (*bitten um*) ask for sth; **jdm Glück/gute Nacht** w ~ wish s.o. luck/good night; **ich wünschte, ich könnte . . .** I wish I could . . .; **Sie** w ~ ? can I help you? w ~ **swert** a desirable

Wunsch|konzert nt musical request programme. W ~ **traum** m (*fig*) dream

wurde, würde s. werden

Würde f -,-n dignity; (*Ehrenrang*) honour. w ~ **los** a undignified. W ~ **nträger** m dignitary. w ~ **voll** a dignified □adv with dignity

würdig a dignified; (*wert*) worthy. w ~ **en** vt recognize; (*schätzen*) appreciate; **keines Blickes** w ~ **en** not deign to look at

Wurf m -[e]s,-e throw; (*Junge*) litter

Würfel m -s,- cube; (*Spiel-*) dice; (*Zucker-*) lump. w ~ **n** vi (*haben*) throw the dice; w ~ **n um** play dice for □vt throw; (*in Würfel schneiden*) dice. W ~ **zucker** m cube sugar

würgen vt choke □vi (*haben*) retch; choke (**an** + *dat* on)

Wurm m -[e]s,-er worm; (*Made*) maggot. w ~ **en** vi (*haben*) **jdn** w ~ **en** (*fam*) rankle [with s.o.]. w ~ **stichig** a worm-eaten

Wurst f -,-e sausage; **das ist mir** W ~ (*fam*) I couldn't care less

Würstchen nt -s,- small sausage; **Frankfurter** W ~ frankfurter

Würze f -,-n spice; (*Aroma*) aroma

Wurzel f -,-n root; W ~ **n schlagen** take root. w ~ **n** vi (*haben*) root

würz|en vt season. w ~ **ig** a tasty; (*aromatisch*) aromatic; (*pikant*) spicy

wüst a chaotic; (*wirr*) tangled; (*öde*) desolate; (*wild*) wild, adv -ly; (*schlimm*) terrible, adv -ly. **Wüste** f -,-n desert

Wut f - rage, fury. W ~ **anfall** m fit of rage

wüten vi (*haben*) rage. w ~ **d** a furious, adv -ly; w ~ **d machen** infuriate

X

x /1ks/ inv a (*Math*) x; (*fam*) umpteen. **X-Beine** ntpl knock-knees. **x-beinig** a knock-kneed. **x-beliebig** a (*fam*) any; **eine x-beliebige Zahl** any number [you like]; **x-mal** adv (*fam*) umpteen times

Y

Yoga /'jo:ga/ m & nt -[s] yoga

Z

Zack|e f -,-n point; (*Berg-*) peak; (*Gabel-*) prong. z ~ **ig** a jagged; (*gezackt*) serrated; (*fam: schneidig*) smart, adv -ly

zaghaft a timid, adv -ly; (*zögernd*) tentative, adv -ly

zäh a tough; (*hartnäckig*) tenacious, adv -ly; (*zähflüssig*) viscous; (*schleppend*) sluggish, adv -ly. z ~ **flüssig** a viscous; (*Verkehr*) slow-moving. Z ~ **igkeit** f - toughness; tenacity

Zahl f -,-en number; (*Ziffer, Betrag*) figure

zahl|bar a payable. **z~en** vt/i (haben) pay; (bezahlen) pay for; **bitte z~en!** the bill please!

zählen vi (haben) count; **z~ zu** (fig) be one/(pl) some of; **z~ auf** (+acc) count on□vt count; **z~ zu** add to; (fig) count among; **die Stadt zählt 5000 Einwohner** the town has 5000 inhabitants

zahlenmäßig a numerical, adv -ly

Zähler m -s,- meter

Zahl|grenze f fare-stage. **Z~karte** f paying-in slip. **z~los** a countless. **z~reich** a numerous; ⟨Anzahl, Gruppe⟩ large □ adv in large numbers. **Z~ung** f -,-en payment; **in Z~ung nehmen** take in part-exchange

Zählung f -,-en count

zahlungsunfähig a insolvent

Zahlwort nt (pl -wörter) numeral

zahm a tame

zähmen vt tame; (fig) restrain

Zahn m -[e]s,-̈e tooth; (am Zahnrad) cog. **Z~arzt** m, **Z~ärztin** f dentist. **Z~belag** m plaque. **Z~bürste** f toothbrush. **z~en** vi (haben) be teething. **Z~fleisch** nt gums pl. **z~los** a toothless. **Z~pasta** f -,-en toothpaste. **Z~rad** nt cog-wheel. **Z~schmelz** m enamel. **Z~schmerzen** mpl toothache sg. **Z~spange** f brace. **Z~stein** m tartar. **Z~stocher** m -s,- toothpick

Zange f -,-n pliers pl; (Kneif-) pincers pl; (Kohlen-, Zucker-) tongs pl; (Geburts-) forceps pl

Zank m -[e]s squabble. **z~en** vr **sich z~en** squabble □vi (haben) scold (mit jdm s.o.)

zänkisch a quarrelsome

Zäpfchen nt -s,- (Anat) uvula; (Med) suppository

Zapfen m -s,- (Bot) cone; (Stöpsel) bung; (Eis-) icicle. **z~** vt tap, draw. **Z~streich** m (Mil) tattoo

Zapf|hahn m tap. **Z~säule** f petrol-pump

zappelig a fidgety; (nervös) jittery. **z~n** vi (haben) wriggle; ⟨Kind:⟩ fidget

zart a delicate, adv -ly; (weich, zärtlich) tender, adv -ly; (sanft) gentle, adv -ly. **Z~gefühl** nt tact. **Z~heit** f - delicacy; tenderness; gentleness

zärtlich a tender, adv -ly; (liebevoll) loving, adv -ly. **Z~keit** f -,-en tenderness; (Liebkosung) caress

Zauber m -s magic; (Bann) spell. **Z~er** m -s,- magician. **z~haft** a enchanting. **Z~künstler** m conjurer. **Z~kunststück** nt = **Z~trick**. **z~n** vi (haben) do magic; (Zaubertricks ausführen) do conjuring tricks□vt produce as if by magic. **Z~stab** m magic wand. **Z~trick** m conjuring trick

zaudern vi (haben) delay; (zögern) hesitate

Zaum m -[e]s,Zäume bridle; **im Z~ halten** (fig) restrain

Zaun m -[e]s,Zäune fence. **Z~könig** m wren

z.B. abbr (zum Beispiel) e.g.

Zebra nt -s,-s zebra. **Z~streifen** m zebra-crossing

Zeche f -,-n bill; (Bergwerk) pit

zechen vi (haben) (fam) drink

Zeder f -,-n cedar

Zeh m -[e]s,-en toe. **Z~e** f -,-n toe; (Knoblauch-) clove. **Z~ennagel** m toenail

zehn inv a, **Z~** f -,-en ten. **z~te(r,s)** a tenth. **Z~tel** nt -s,- tenth

Zeichen nt -s,- sign; (Signal) signal. **Z~setzung** f - punctuation. **Z~trickfilm** m cartoon [film]

zeichn|en vt/i (haben) draw; (kenn-) mark; (unter-) sign. **Z~er** m -s,- draughtsman. **Z~ung** f

-,-en drawing; (*auf Fell*) markings *pl*

Zeige|finger *m* index finger. z~n *vt* show; **sich z~n** appear; (*sich herausstellen*) become clear; **das wird sich z~n** we shall see □*vi* (*haben*) point (**auf**+*acc* to). Z~r *m* -s,- pointer; (*Uhr-*) hand

Zeile *f* -,-n line; (*Reihe*) row

zeit *prep* (+*gen*) during. **Z~** (*dat*) **meines/seines Lebens** all my/his life

Zeit *f* -,-en time; (*Gram*) tense. **z~lebens** take one's time; **es hat Z~** there's no hurry; **mit der Z~** in time; **in nächster Z~** in the near future; **die erste Z~** at first; **von Z~ zu Z~** from time to time; **zur Z~** at present; (*rechtzeitig*) in time; **[ach] du liebe Z~!** (*fam*) good heavens!

Zeit|alter *nt* age, era. **Z~arbeit** *f* temporary work. **Z~bombe** *f* time bomb. **z~gemäß** *a* modern, up-to-date. **Z~genosse** *m*, **Z~genossin** *f* contemporary. **z~genössisch** *a* contemporary. **z~ig** *a* & *adv* early. **Z~lang** *f* **eine Z~lang** for a time or while. **z~lebens** *adv* all one's life

zeitlich *a* (*Dauer*) in time; (*Folge*) chronological □*adv* **z~begrenzt** for a limited time

zeit|los *a* timeless. **Z~lupe** *f* slow motion. **Z~punkt** *m* time. **z~raubend** *a* time-consuming. **Z~raum** *m* period. **Z~schrift** *f* magazine, periodical

Zeitung *f* -,-en newspaper. **Z~spapier** *nt* newspaper

Zeit|verschwendung *f* waste of time. **Z~vertreib** *m* pastime; **zum Z~vertreib** to pass the time. **z~weilig** *a* temporary □*adv* temporarily; (*hin und wieder*) at times. **z~weise** *adv* at times. **Z~wort** *nt* (*pl* **-wörter**) verb. **Z~zünder** *m* time fuse

Zelle *f* -,-n cell; (*Telefon-*) box

Zelt *nt* -[e]s,-e tent; (*Fest-*) marquee. **z~en** *vi* (*haben*) camp. **Z~en** *nt* -s camping. **Z~plane** *f* tarpaulin. **Z~platz** *m* campsite

Zement *m* -[e]s cement. **z~ieren** *vt* cement

zen|sieren *vt* (*Sch*) mark; censor (*Presse, Film*). **Z~sur** *f* -,-en (*Sch*) mark, (*Amer*) grade; (*Presse-*) censorship

Zentimeter *m* & *nt* centimetre. **Z~maß** *nt* tape-measure

Zentner *m* -s,- [metric] hundred-weight (*50 kg*)

zentral *a* central, *adv* -ly. **Z~e** *f* -,-n central office; (*Partei-*) headquarters *pl*; (*Teleph*) exchange. **Z~heizung** *f* central heating. **z~isieren** *vt* centralize

Zentrum *nt* -s,-tren centre

zerbrech|en† *vt/i* (*sein*) break; **sich** (*dat*) **den Kopf z~en** rack one's brains. **z~lich** *a* fragile

zerdrücken *vt* crush; mash (*Kartoffeln*)

Zeremonie *f* -,-n ceremony

Zeremoniell *nt* -s,-e ceremonial. **z~** *a* ceremonial, *adv* -ly

Zerfall *m* disintegration; (*Verfall*) decay. **z~en†** *vi* (*sein*) disintegrate; (*verfallen*) decay; **in drei Teile z~en** be divided into three parts

zerfetzen *vt* tear to pieces

zerfließen† *vi* (*sein*) melt; (*Tinte:*) run

zergehen† *vi* (*sein*) melt; (*sich auflösen*) dissolve

zergliedern *vt* dissect

zerkleinern *vt* chop/(*schneiden*) cut up; (*mahlen*) grind

zerknirscht *a* contrite

zerknüllen *vt* crumple [up]

zerkratzen *vt* scratch

zerlassen† *vt* melt

zerlegen *vt* take to pieces, dismantle; (*zerschneiden*) cut up; (*tranchieren*) carve

zerlumpt *a* ragged

zermalmen vt crush

zermürb|en vt ⟨fig⟩ wear down. Z~**ungskrieg** m war of attrition

zerplatzen vi (sein) burst

zerquetschen vt squash, crush; mash ⟨Kartoffeln⟩

Zerrbild nt caricature

zerreißen† vt tear; ⟨in Stücke⟩ tear up; break ⟨Faden, Seil⟩ □ vi (sein) tear; break

zerren vt drag; pull ⟨Muskel⟩ □ vi (haben) pull (an + dat at)

zerrinnen† vi (sein) melt

zerrissen a torn

zerrütten vt ruin, wreck; shatter ⟨Nerven⟩; zerrüttete Ehe broken marriage

zerschlagen† vt smash; smash up ⟨Möbel⟩; **sich z~** ⟨Hoffnung:⟩ be dashed □ a ⟨erschöpft⟩ worn out

zerschmettern vt/i (sein) smash

zerschneiden† vt cut; ⟨in Stücke⟩ cut up

zersetzen vt corrode; undermine ⟨Moral⟩; **sich z~** decompose

zersplittern vi (sein) splinter; ⟨Glas:⟩ shatter □ vt shatter

zerspringen† vi (sein) shatter; ⟨bersten⟩ burst

Zerstäuber m -s,- atomizer

zerstör|en vt destroy; ⟨zunichte machen⟩ wreck. Z~**er** m -s,- destroyer. Z~**ung** f destruction

zerstreu|en vt scatter; disperse ⟨Menge⟩; dispel ⟨Zweifel⟩; **sich z~en** disperse; ⟨sich unterhalten⟩ amuse oneself. z~t a absentminded, adv -ly. Z~**ung** f -,-en ⟨Unterhaltung⟩ entertainment

zerstückeln vt cut up into pieces

zerteilen vt divide up

Zertifikat nt -[e]s,-e certificate

zertreten† vt stamp on; ⟨zerdrücken⟩ crush

zertrümmern vt smash [up]; wreck ⟨Gebäude, Stadt⟩

zerzausen vt tousle; **z~t** a dishevelled; ⟨Haar⟩ tousled

Zettel m -s,- piece of paper; ⟨Notiz⟩ note; ⟨Bekanntmachung⟩ notice; ⟨Reklame-⟩ leaflet

Zeug nt -s ⟨fam⟩ stuff; ⟨Sachen⟩ things pl; ⟨Ausrüstung⟩ gear; **dummes Z~** nonsense; **das Z~ haben zu** have the makings of

Zeuge m -n,-n witness. **z~n** vi (haben) testify; **z~n von** ⟨fig⟩ show □ vt father. Z~**naussage** f testimony. Z~**nstand** m witness box/⟨Amer⟩ stand

Zeugin f -,-nen witness

Zeugnis nt -ses,-se certificate; ⟨Sch⟩ report; ⟨Referenz⟩ reference; ⟨fig: Beweis⟩ evidence

Zickzack m -[e]s,-e zigzag

Ziege f -,-n goat

Ziegel m -s,- brick; ⟨Dach-⟩ tile. Z~**stein** m brick

ziehen† vt pull; ⟨sanfter: zücken; zeichnen⟩ draw; ⟨heraus-⟩ pull out; extract ⟨Zahn⟩; raise ⟨Hut⟩; put on ⟨Bremse⟩; move ⟨Schachfigur⟩; put up ⟨Leine, Zaun⟩; ⟨dehnen⟩ stretch; make ⟨Grimasse, Scheitel⟩; ⟨züchten⟩ breed; grow ⟨Rosen, Gemüse⟩; **nach sich z~** ⟨fig⟩ entail □ vr **sich z~** ⟨sich erstrecken⟩ run; ⟨sich verziehen⟩ warp □ vi (haben) pull (an + dat on/at); ⟨Tee, Ofen:⟩ draw; ⟨Culin⟩ simmer; **es zieht** there is a draught; **solche Filme z~ nicht mehr** films like that are no longer popular □ vi (sein) ⟨um-⟩ move (nach to); ⟨Menge:⟩ march; ⟨Vögel:⟩ migrate; ⟨Wolken, Nebel:⟩ drift. Z~ nt -s ache

Ziehharmonika f accordion

Ziehung f -,-en draw

Ziel nt -[e]s,-e destination; ⟨Sport⟩ finish; ⟨Z~scheibe & Mil⟩ target; ⟨Zweck⟩ aim, goal. **z~bewußt** a purposeful, adv -ly. **z~en** vi (haben) aim (**auf** + acc at). **z~los** a aimless, adv -ly. Z~**scheibe** f target;

(fig) butt. **z~strebig** *a* single-minded, *adv* -ly

ziemen (sich) *vr* be seemly

ziemlich *a* *(fam)* fair □*adv* rather, fairly; *(fast)* pretty well

Zier|de *f* -,-n ornament. **z~en** *vt* adorn; **sich z~en** make a fuss; *(sich bitten lassen)* need coaxing

zierlich *a* dainty, *adv* -ily; *(fein)* delicate, *adv* -ly; *(Frau)* petite

Ziffer *f* -,-n figure, digit; *(Zahlzeichen)* numeral. **Z~blatt** *nt* dial

zig *inv a (fam)* umpteen

Zigarette *f* -,-n cigarette

Zigarre *f* -,-n cigar

Zigeuner(in) *m* -s,- *(f* -,-nen*)* gypsy

Zimmer *nt* -s,- room. **Z~mädchen** *nt* chambermaid. **Z~mann** *m (pl* -leute*)* carpenter. **z~n** *vt* make □*vi (haben)* do carpentry. **Z~nachweis** *m* accommodation bureau. **Z~pflanze** *f* house plant

zimperlich *a* squeamish; *(wehleidig)* soft; *(prüde)* prudish

Zimt *m* -[e]s cinnamon

Zink *nt* -s zinc

Zinke *f* -,-n prong; *(Kamm-)* tooth

Zinn *m* -s tin; *(Gefäße)* pewter

Zins|en *mpl* interest *sg;* **Z~en tragen** earn interest. **Z~eszins** *m* -es,-en compound interest. **Z~fuß**, **Z~satz** *m* interest rate

Zipfel *m* -s,- corner; *(Spitze)* point; *(Wurst-)* [tail-]end

zirka *adv* about

Zirkel *m* -s,- [pair of] compasses *pl; (Gruppe)* circle

Zirkul|ation /-'tsjo:n/ *f* circulation. **z~ieren** *vi (sein)* circulate

Zirkus *m* -,-se circus

zirpen *vi (haben)* chirp

zischen *vi (haben)* hiss; *(Fett:)* sizzle □*vt* hiss

Zitat *nt* -[e]s,-e quotation. **z~ieren** *vt/i (haben)* quote; *(rufen)* summon

Zitr|onat *nt* -[e]s candied lemon-peel. **Z~one** *f* -,-n lemon. **Z~onenlimonade** *f* lemonade

zittern *vi (haben)* tremble; *(vor Kälte)* shiver; *(beben)* shake

zittrig *a* shaky, *adv* -ily

Zitze *f* -,-n teat

zivil *a* civilian; *(Ehe, Recht, Luftfahrt)* civil; *(mäßig)* reasonable. **Z~** *nt* -s civilian clothes *pl.* **Z~courage** /-kura:ʒə/ *f* - courage of one's convictions. **Z~dienst** *m* community service

Zivili|sation /-'tsjo:n/ *f* -,-en civilization. **z~sieren** *vt* civilize. **z~siert** *a* civilized □*adv* in a civilized manner

Zivilist *m* -en,-en civilian

zögern *vi (haben)* hesitate. **Z~** *nt* -s hesitation. **z~d** *a* hesitant, *adv* -ly

Zoll¹ *m* -[e]s,- inch

Zoll² *m* -[e]s,-̈e [customs] duty; *(Behörde)* customs *pl.* **Z~abfertigung** *f* customs clearance. **Z~beamte(r)** *m* customs officer. **z~frei** *a & adv* duty-free. **Z~kontrolle** *f* customs check

Zone *f* -,-n zone

Zoo *m* -s,-s zoo

Zoo|loge /tsoo'lo:gə/ *m* -n,-n zoologist. **Z~logie** *f* - zoology. **z~logisch** *a* zoological

Zopf *m* -[e]s,-̈e plait

Zorn *m* -[e]s anger. **z~ig** *a* angry, *adv* -ily

zotig *a* smutty, dirty

zottig *a* shaggy

z.T. *abbr (zum Teil)* partly

zu *prep (+ dat)* to; *(dazu)* with; *(zeitlich, preislich)* at; *(Zweck)* for; *(über)* about; **zu ...** *hin* towards; **zu Hause** at home; **zu Fuß/Pferde** on foot/horseback; **zu beiden Seiten** on both sides; **zu Ostern** at Easter; **zu diesem Zweck** for this purpose; **zu meinem Erstaunen/Entsetzen** to my surprise/horror; **zu Dutzenden** by the dozen; **eine Marke zu 60 Pfennig** a 60-pfennig stamp; **das Stück zu zwei Mark** at two marks each; **wir waren zu dritt/viert** there were three/four of us; **es steht 5 zu 3** the score is 5–3; **zu etw werden** turn into sth □*adv* (*allzu*) too; (*Richtung*) towards; (*geschlossen*) closed; (*an Schalter, Hahn*) off; **zu groß/weit** too big/far; **nach dem Fluß zu** towards the river; **Augen zu!** close your eyes! **Tür zu!** shut the door! **nur zu!** go on! **mach zu!** (*fam*) hurry up! □*conj* to; **etwas zu essen** something to eat; **nicht zu glauben** unbelievable; **zu erörternde Probleme** problems to be discussed

zuallererst *adv* first of all. **z~letzt** *adv* last of all

Zubehör *nt* -s accessories *pl*

zubereit|en *vt sep* prepare. **Z~ung** *f* - preparation; (*in Rezept*) method

zubilligen *vt sep* grant

zubinden† *vt sep* tie [up]

zubring|en† *vt sep* spend. **Z~er** *m* -s,- access road; (*Bus*) shuttle

Zucchini /tsu'ki:ni/ *pl* courgettes

Zucht *f* -,-en breeding; (*Pflanzen-*) cultivation; (*Art, Rasse*) breed; (*von Pflanzen*) strain; (*Z~farm*) farm; (*Pferde-*) stud; (*Disziplin*) discipline

zücht|en *vt* breed; cultivate, grow (*Rosen, Gemüse*). **Z~er** *m* -s,- breeder; grower

Zuchthaus *nt* prison

züchtigen *vt* chastise

Züchtung *f* -,-en breeding; (*Pflanzen-*) cultivation; (*Art, Rasse*) breed; (*von Pflanzen*) strain

zucken *vi* (*haben*) twitch; (*sich z~d bewegen*) jerk; (*Blitz:*) flash; (*Flamme:*) flicker □*vt* **die Achseln z~** shrug one's shoulders

zücken *vt* draw (*Messer*)

Zucker *m* -s sugar. **Z~dose** *f* sugar basin. **Z~guß** *m* icing. **z~krank** *a* diabetic. **Z~krankheit** *f* diabetes. **z~n** *vt* sugar. **Z~rohr** *nt* sugar cane. **Z~rübe** *f* sugar beet. **z~süß** *a* sweet; (*fig*) sugary. **Z~watte** *f* candyfloss. **Z~zange** *f* sugar tongs *pl*

zuckrig *a* sugary

zudecken *vt sep* cover up; (*im Bett*) tuck up; cover (*Topf*)

zudem *adv* moreover

zudrehen *vt sep* turn off; **jdm den Rücken z~** turn one's back on s.o.

zudringlich *a* pushing, (*fam*) pushy

zudrücken *vt sep* press *or* push shut; close (*Augen*)

zueinander *adv* to one another; **z~ passen** go together. **z~halten†** *vi sep* (*haben*) (*fig*) stick together

zuerkennen† *vt sep* award (*dat* to)

zuerst *adv* first; (*anfangs*) at first; **mit dem Kopf z~** head first

zufahr|en† *vi sep* (*sein*) **z~en auf** (+ *acc*) drive towards. **Z~t** *f* access; (*Einfahrt*) drive

Zufall *m* chance; (*Zusammentreffen*) coincidence; **durch Z~** by chance/coincidence. **z~en†** *vi sep* (*sein*) close, shut; **jdm z~en** (*Aufgabe:*) fall/(*Erbe:*) go to s.o.

zufällig *a* chance, accidental □*adv* by chance; **ich war z~ da** I happened to be there

Zuflucht *f* refuge; (*Schutz*) shelter. **Z~sort** *m* refuge

zufolge *prep* (+ *dat*) according to

zufrieden *a* contented, *adv* -ly; (*befriedigt*) satisfied. **z~geben†** (**sich**) *vr sep* be satisfied. **Z~heit** *f* - contentment; satisfaction. **z~lassen†** *vt sep* leave in peace. **z~stellen** *vt sep* satisfy. **z~stellend** *a* satisfactory, *adv* -ly

zufrieren† *vi sep (sein)* freeze over

zufügen *vt sep* inflict *(dat* on); do *⟨Unrecht⟩ (dat* to)

Zufuhr *f -* supply

zuführen *vt sep □vt* supply □ *vi (haben)* z~ **auf** (+*acc*) lead to

Zug *m -[e]s,-̈e* train; *(Kolonne)* column; *(Um-)* procession; *(Mil)* platoon; *(Vogelschar)* flock; *(Ziehen, Zugkraft)* pull; *(Wandern, Ziehen)* migration; *(Schluck, Luft-)* draught; *(Atem-)* breath; *(beim Rauchen)* puff; *(Schach-)* move; *(beim Schwimmen, Rudern)* stroke; *(Gesichts-)* feature; *(Wesens-)* trait; **etw in vollen Zügen genießen** enjoy sth to the full; **in einem Zug[e]** at one go

Zugabe *f (Geschenk)* [free] gift; *(Mus)* encore

Zugang *m* access

zugänglich *a* accessible; *⟨Mensch:⟩* approachable; *(fig)* amenable *(dat/für* to)

Zugbrücke *f* drawbridge

zugeben† *vt sep* add; *(gestehen)* admit; *(erlauben)* allow. **zuge-gebenermaßen** *adv* admittedly

zugegen *a* z~ **sein** be present

zugehen† *vi sep (sein)* close; **jdm** z~ be sent to s.o.; **z~ auf** (+*acc*) go towards; **dem Ende z~** draw to a close; *⟨Vorräte:⟩* run low; **auf der Party ging es lebhaft zu** the party was pretty lively

Zugehörigkeit *f -* membership

Zügel *m -s,-* rein

zugelassen *a* registered

zügel|los *a* unrestrained, *adv -ly*; *(sittenlos)* licentious. **z~n** *vt* rein in; *(fig)* curb

Zuge|ständnis *nt* concession. **z~stehen†** *vt sep* grant

zugetan *a* fond *(dat* of)

zugig *a* draughty

zügig *a* quick, *adv -ly*

Zug|kraft *f* pull; *(fig)* attraction. **z~kräftig** *a* effective; *(anreizend)* popular; *⟨Titel⟩* catchy

zugleich *adv* at the same time

Zug|luft *f* draught. **Z~pferd** *nt* draught-horse; *(fam)* drudge

zugreifen *vi sep (haben)* grab it/them; *(bei Tisch)* help o.s.; *(bei Angebot)* jump at it; *(helfen)* lend a hand

zugrunde *adv* z~ **richten** destroy; z~ **gehen** be destroyed; *⟨Ehe:⟩* founder; *(sterben)* die; z~ **liegen** form the basis *(dat* of)

zugucken *vi sep (haben)* = zuse-hen

zugunsten *prep* (+*gen*) in favour of; *⟨Sammlung⟩* in aid of

zugute *adv* **jdm/etw** z~ **kommen** benefit s.o./sth; **jdm seine Jugend** z~ **halten** make allowances for s.o.'s youth

Zugvogel *m* migratory bird

zuhalten† *v sep □vt* keep closed; *(bedecken)* cover; **sich** *(dat)* **die Nase** z~ hold one's nose □*vi (haben)* z~ **auf** (+*acc*) head for

Zuhälter *m -s,-* pimp

Zuhause *nt -s,-* home

zuhören *vi sep (haben)* listen *(dat* to). **Z~er(in)** *m(f)* listener

zujubeln *vi sep (haben)* **jdm** z~ cheer s.o.

zukehren *vt sep* turn *(dat* to)

zukleben *vt sep* seal

zuknallen *vt/i sep (sein)* slam

zuknöpfen *vt sep* button up

zukommen† *vi sep (sein)* z~ **auf** (+*acc*) come towards; *(sich nähern)* approach; z~ **lassen** send *(jdm* s.o.); *⟨devote* *⟨Pflege⟩* jdm; z~ **lassen** devote *⟨Pflege⟩*; **jdm** z~ be s.o.'s right

Zukunft *f -* future. **zukünftig** *a* future □*adv* in future

zulächeln *vi sep (haben)* smile *(dat* at)

Zulage *f -,-n* extra allowance

zulangen *vi sep (haben)* help oneself; **tüchtig** z~ tuck in

zulassen† *vt sep* allow, permit; *(teilnehmen lassen)* admit; *(Admin)* license, register; *(geschlossen lassen)* leave closed; leave unopened ⟨*Brief*⟩

zulässig *a* permissible

Zulassung *f -,-en* admission; registration; *(Lizenz)* licence

zulaufen† *vi sep (sein)* z~ **auf** (+ *acc*) run towards; **spitz** z~ **in** taper to a point

zulegen *vt sep* add; **sich** (*dat*) etw z~ get sth; grow ⟨*Bart*⟩

zuleide *adv* jdm etwas z~ **tun** hurt s.o.

zuletzt *adv* last; *(schließlich)* in the end; **nicht** z~ not least

zuliebe *adv* jdm/etw z~ for the sake of s.o./sth

zum *prep* = **zu dem; zum Spaß** for fun; **etw zum Lesen** sth to read

zumachen *v sep* □*vt* close, shut; do up ⟨*Jacke*⟩; seal ⟨*Umschlag*⟩; turn off ⟨*Hahn*⟩; *(stillegen)* close down □*vi (haben)* close, shut; *(stillgelegt werden)* close down

zumal *adv* especially □*conj* especially since

zumeist *adv* for the most part

zumindest *adv* at least

zumutbar *a* reasonable

zumute *adv* mir ist traurig/elend z~ I feel sad/wretched; mir ist nicht danach z~ I don't feel like it

zumut|en *vt sep* jdm etw z~ **en** ask *or* expect sth of s.o.; **sich** (*dat*) **zuviel** z~**en** overdo things. **Z~ung** *f* - imposition; **eine** Z~**ung sein** be unreasonable

zunächst *adv* first [of all]; *(anfangs)* at first; *(vorläufig)* for the moment □*prep* (+ *dat*) nearest to

Zunahme *f -,-n* increase

Zuname *m* surname

zünd|en *vt/i (haben)* ignite; z~**ende Rede** rousing speech. **Z~er** *m -s,-* detonator, fuse. **Z~holz** *nt* match. **Z~kerze** *f*

sparking-plug. **Z~schlüssel** *m* ignition key. **Z~schnur** *f* fuse. **Z~ung** *f -,-en* ignition

zunehmen† *vt/i sep (haben)* increase **(an** + *dat* in); ⟨*Mond:*⟩ wax; *(an Gewicht)* put on weight. z~**d** *a* increasing, *adv* -ly

Zuneigung *f* - affection

Zunft *f -,¨e* guild

zünftig *a* proper, *adv* -ly

Zunge *f -,-n* tongue. **Z~n-brecher** *m* tongue-twister

zunichte *a* z~ **machen** wreck; z~ **werden** come to nothing

zunicken *vi sep (haben)* nod (*dat* to)

zunutze *a* **sich** (*dat*) **etw** z~ **machen** make use of sth; *(ausnutzen)* take advantage of sth

zuoberst *adv* right at the top

zuordnen *vt sep* assign (*dat* to)

zupfen *vt/i (haben)* pluck **(an** + *dat* in); pull out ⟨*Unkraut*⟩

zur *prep* = **zu der; zur Schule/Arbeit** to school/work; **zur Zeit** at present

zurechnungsfähig *a* of sound mind

zurecht|finden† *(sich)* *vr sep* find one's way. **z~kommen**† *vi sep (sein)* cope (**mit** with); *(rechtzeitig kommen)* be in time. **z~legen** *vt sep* put out ready; **sich** (*dat*) **eine Ausrede** z~**legen** have an excuse all ready. **z~machen** *vt sep* get ready; **sich** z~**machen** get ready. **z~weisen**† *vt sep* reprimand. **Z~weisung** *f* reprimand

zureden *vi sep (haben)* jdm z~ try to persuade s.o.

zurichten *vt sep* prepare; *(beschädigen)* damage; *(verletzen)* injure

zuriegeln *vt sep* bolt

zurück *adv* back; **Berlin, hin und** z~ return to Berlin. **z~behalten**† *vt sep* keep back; be left with ⟨*Narbe*⟩. **z~bekommen**† *vt sep* get back; **20 Pfennig z~bekommen** get 20 pfennigs change. **z~bleiben**† *vi sep (sein)* stay behind; *(nicht mithalten)* lag behind. **z~blicken** *vi sep (haben)* look back. **z~bringen**† *vt sep* bring back; *(wieder hinbringen)* take back. **z~erobern** *vt sep* recapture; *(fig)* regain. **z~erstatten** *vt sep* refund. **z~fahren**† *vi sep* □*vt* drive back □*vi (sein)* return, go back; *(im Auto)* drive back; *(z~weichen)* recoil. **z~finden**† *vi sep (haben)* find one's way back. **z~führen** *vt sep* □*vt* take back; *(fig)* attribute **(auf**+*acc* to) □*vi (haben)* lead back. **z~geben**† *vt sep* give back, return. **z~geblieben** *a* retarded. **z~gehen**† *vi sep (sein)* go back, return; *(abnehmen)* go down; **z~gehen auf** (+*acc*) *(fig)* go back to

zurückgezogen *a* secluded. **Z~heit** *f* - seclusion

zurückhalt|en† *vt sep* hold back; *(abhalten)* stop; **sich z~en** restrain oneself. **Z~ung** *f* - reserve

zurück|kehren *vi sep (sein)* return. **z~kommen**† *vi sep (sein)* come back, return; *(ankommen)* get back; **z~kommen auf** (+*acc*) *(fig)* come back to. **z~lassen**† *vt sep* leave behind; *(z~kehren lassen)* allow back. **z~legen** *vt sep* put back; *(reservieren)* keep; *(sparen)* put by; *(Strecke)* cover. **z~lehnen (sich)** *vr sep* lean back. **z~liegen**† *vi sep (haben)* be in the past; *(Sport)* be behind; **das liegt lange zurück** that was long ago. **z~melden (sich)** *vr sep* report back. **z~nehmen**† *vt sep* take back. **z~rufen**† *vt/i sep (haben)* call back. **z~scheuen** *vi sep (sein)* shrink **(vor**+*dat* from). **z~schicken** *vt sep* send

back. **z~schlagen**† *v sep* □*vi (haben)* hit back □*vt* hit back; *(abwehren)* beat back; *(umschlagen)* turn back. **z~schneiden**† *vt sep* cut back. **z~schrecken**† *vi sep (sein)* shrink back, recoil; *(fig)* shrink **(vor**+*dat* from). **z~setzen** *v sep* □*vt* put back; *(Auto)* reverse, back; *(herabsetzen)* reduce; *(fig)* neglect □*vi (haben)* reverse, back. **z~stellen** *vt sep* put back; *(reservieren)* keep; *(fig)* put aside; *(aufschieben)* postpone. **z~stoßen**† *v sep* □*vt* push back □*vi (sein)* reverse, back. **z~treten**† *vi sep (sein)* step back; *(vom Amt)* resign; *(verzichten)* withdraw. **z~weichen**† *vi sep (sein)* draw back; *(z~schrecken)* shrink back. **z~weisen**† *vt sep* turn away; *(fig)* reject. **z~werfen**† *vt* throw back; *(reflektieren)* reflect. **z~zahlen** *vt sep* pay back. **z~ziehen**† *vt sep* draw back; *(fig)* withdraw; **sich z~ziehen** withdraw; *(vom Beruf)* retire; *(Mil)* retreat

Zuruf *m* shout. **r~en**† *vt sep* shout *(dat* to)

Zusage *f* -,-n acceptance; *(Versprechen)* promise. **z~n** *v sep* □ *vt* promise □*vi (haben)* accept; **jdm z~n** appeal to s.o.

zusammen *adv* together; *(insgesamt)* altogether. **Z~arbeit** *f* co-operation. **z~arbeiten** *vi sep (haben)* co-operate. **z~bauen** *vt sep* assemble. **z~beißen**† *vt sep* **die Zähne z~beißen** clench/ *(fig)* grit one's teeth. **z~bleiben**† *vi sep (sein)* stay together. **z~brechen**† *vi sep (sein)* collapse. **z~bringen**† *vt sep* bring together; *(beschaffen)* raise. **Z~bruch** *m* collapse; *(Nerven-* & *fig)* breakdown. **z~fahren**† *vi sep (sein)* collide; *(z~zucken)* start. z~**fallen**† *vi sep* (*sein*) collapse; (*zeitlich*) coincide. z~**falten** *vt sep* fold up. z~**fassen** *vt sep* summarize, sum up. Z~**fassung** *f* summary. z~**fügen** *vt sep* fit together. z~**führen** *vt sep* bring together. z~**gehören** *vi sep* (*haben*) belong together; (*z~passen*) go together. z~**gesetzt** *a* (*Gram*) compound. z~**halten**† *v sep* □*vt* hold together; (*beisammenhalten*) keep together □*vi* (*haben*) (*fig*) stick together. Z~**hang** *m* connection; (*Kontext*) context. z~**hängen**† *vi sep* (*haben*) be connected. z~**hanglos** *a* incoherent, adv -ly. z~**klappen** *v sep* □*vt* fold up □ *vi* (*sein*) collapse. z~**kommen**† *vi sep* (*sein*) meet; (*sich sammeln*) accumulate. Z~**kunft** *f* -,̈e meeting. z~**laufen**† *vi sep* (*sein*) gather; (*Flüssigkeit:*) collect; (*Linien:*) converge. z~**leben** *vi sep* (*haben*) live together. z~**legen** *v sep* □*vt* put together; (*z~falten*) fold up; (*vereinigen*) amalgamate; pool (*Geld*) □ *vi* (*haben*) club together. z~**nehmen**† *vt sep* gather up; summon up (*Mut*); collect (*Gedanken*). **sich** z~**nehmen** pull oneself together. z~**passen** *vi sep* (*haben*) go together, match; (*Personen:*) be well matched. z~**prall** *m* collision. z~**prallen** *vi sep* (*sein*) collide. z~**rechnen** *vt sep* add up. z~**reißen**† (**sich**) *vr sep* (*fam*) pull oneself together. z~**rollen** *vt sep* roll up; **sich** z~**rollen** curl up. z~**schlagen**† *vt sep* smash up; (*prügeln*) beat up. z~**schließen**† (**sich**) *vr sep* join together; (*Firmen:*) merge. Z~**schluß** *m* union; (*Comm*) merger. z~**schreiben**† *vt sep* write as one word **zusammensein**† *vi sep* (*sein*) be together. Z~ *nt* -s get-together.

zusammensetz|**en** *vt sep* put together; (*Techn*) assemble; **sich** z~**en** sit [down] together; (*bestehen*) be made up (*aus* from). Z~**ung** *f* -,-en composition; (*Techn*) assembly; (*Wort*) compound

zusammen|**stellen** *vt sep* put together; (*gestalten*) compile. Z~**stoß** *m* collision; (*fig*) clash. z~**stoßen**† *vi sep* (*sein*) collide. z~**treffen**† *vi sep* (*sein*) meet; (*zeitlich*) coincide. Z~**treffen** *nt* meeting; coincidence. z~**zählen** *vt sep* add up. z~**ziehen**† *v sep* □*vt* draw together; (*addieren*) add up; (*konzentrieren*) mass; **sich** z~**ziehen** contract; (*Gewitter:*) gather □*vi* (*sein*) move in together; move in (**mit** with). z~**zucken** *vi sep* (*sein*) start; (*vor Schmerz*) wince

Zusatz *m* addition; (*Jur*) rider; (*Lebensmittel-*) additive. Z~**gerät** *nt* attachment. **zusätzlich** *a* additional □*adv* in addition

zuschanden *adv* z~ **machen** ruin, wreck; z~ **fahren** wreck

zuschau|en *vi sep* (*haben*) watch. Z~**er(in)** *m* -s,- (*f* -,-nen) spectator; (*TV*) viewer. Z~**erraum** *m* auditorium

zuschicken *vt sep* send (*dat* to)

Zuschlag *m* surcharge; (*D-Zug-*) supplement. z~**en**† *v sep* □*vt* shut; (*heftig*) slam; (*bei Auktion*) knock down (**jdm** to s.o.) □ *vi* (*haben*) hit out; (*Feind:*) strike □*vi* (*sein*) slam shut. z~**pflichtig** *a* for which a supplement is payable

zuschließen† *v sep* □*vt* lock □*vi* (*haben*) lock up

zuschneiden† *vt sep* cut out; cut to size (*Holz*)

zuschreiben† *vt sep* attribute (*dat* to); **jdm die Schuld** z~ blame s.o.

Zuschrift f letter; (auf Annonce) reply

zuschulden adv sich (dat) etwas z~ kommen lassen do wrong

Zuschuß m contribution; (staatlich) subsidy

zusehen† vi sep (haben) watch; z~, daß see [to it] that

zusehends adv visibly

zusein† vi sep (sein) be closed

zusenden vt sep send (dat to)

zusetzen v sep □vt add; (einbüßen) lose □vi (haben) jdm z~ pester s.o.; ⟨Hitze:⟩ take it out of s.o.

zusichern vt sep promise. Z~ung f promise

Zuspätkommende(r) m/f latecomer

zuspielen vt sep (Sport) pass

zuspitzen (sich) vr sep (fig) become critical

zusprechen† v sep □vt award (jdm s.o.); jdm Trost/Mut z~ comfort/encourage s.o. □vi (haben) dem Essen z~ eat heartily

Zustand m condition, state

zustande adv z~ bringen/kommen bring/come about

zuständig a competent; (verantwortlich) responsible. Z~keit f competence; responsibility

zustehen† vi sep (haben) jdm z~ be s.o.'s right; ⟨Urlaub:⟩ be due to s.o.; es steht ihm nicht zu he is not entitled to it; (gebührt) it is not for him (zu to)

zusteigen† vi sep (sein) get on; noch jemand zugestiegen? tickets please; (im Bus) any more fares please?

zustellen vt sep block; (bringen) deliver. Z~ung f delivery

zusteuern v sep □vi (sein) head (auf + acc for) □vt contribute

zustimmen vi sep (haben) agree. (billigen) approve (dat of). Z~ung f consent; approval

zustoßen† vi sep (sein) happen (dat to)

Zustrom m influx

zutage adv z~ treten od kommen/bringen come/bring to light

Zutat f (Culin) ingredient

zuteilen vt sep allocate; assign ⟨Aufgabe⟩. Z~ung f allocation

zutiefst adv deeply

zutragen† vt sep carry/(fig) report (dat to); sich z~ happen

zutrauen vt sep jdm etw z~ believe s.o. capable of sth. Z~en nt -s confidence. z~lich a trusting, adv -ly; ⟨Tier⟩ friendly

zutreffen† vi sep (haben) be correct; z~ auf (+acc) apply to. z~d a applicable (auf + acc to); (richtig) correct, adv -ly

zutrinken† vi sep (haben) jdm z~ drink to s.o.

Zutritt m admittance

zuunterst adv right at the bottom

zuverlässig a reliable, adv -bly. Z~keit f - reliability

Zuversicht f - confidence. z~lich a confident, adv -ly

zuviel pron & adv too much; (pl) too many

zuvor adv before; (erst) first

zuvorkommen† vi sep (sein) (+dat) anticipate; jdm z~ beat s.o. to it. z~d a obliging, adv -ly

Zuwachs m -es increase

zuwege adv z~ bringen achieve

zuweilen adv now and then

zuweisen† vt sep assign; (zuteilen) allocate

zuwenden† vt sep turn (dat to); sich z~en (+dat) turn to; (fig) devote oneself to. Z~ung f donation; ⟨Fürsorge⟩ care

zuwenig pron & adv too little; (pl) too few

zuwerfen† vt sep slam ⟨Tür⟩; jdm etw z~ throw s.o. sth; give s.o. ⟨Blick, Lächeln⟩

zuwider adv jdm z~ sein be repugnant to s.o. □prep (+dat) contrary to. z~**handeln** vi sep (haben) contravene (etw dat sth)

zuzahlen vt sep pay extra

zuziehen† v sep □vt pull tight; draw ⟨Vorhänge⟩; (hinzu-) call in; sich (dat) etw z~ contract ⟨Krankheit⟩; sustain ⟨Verletzung⟩; incur ⟨Zorn⟩ □vi (sein) move into the area

zuzüglich prep (+gen) plus

Zwang m -[e]s,ːe compulsion; (Gewalt) force; (Verpflichtung) obligation

zwängen vt squeeze

zwanglos a informal, adv -ly; ⟨Benehmen⟩ free and easy. Z~**igkeit** f - informality

Zwangs|jacke f straitjacket. Z~**lage** f predicament. z~**läufig** a inevitable, adv -ly

zwanzig inv a twenty. z~**ste(r,s)** a twentieth

zwar adv admittedly; **und z~** to be precise

Zweck m -[e]s,-e purpose; (Sinn) point; **es hat keinen Z~** there is no point. z~**dienlich** a appropriate; ⟨Information⟩ relevant. z~**los** a pointless. z~**mäßig** a suitable, adv -bly; (praktisch) functional, adv -ly. z~**s** prep (+gen) for the purpose of

zwei inv a, Z~ f -,-en two; (Sch) ≈ B. Z~**bettzimmer** nt twin-bedded room

zweideutig a ambiguous, adv -ly; (schlüpfrig) suggestive, adv -ly. Z~**keit** f -,-en ambiguity

zweierlei inv a two kinds of □pron two things. z~**fach** a double

Zweifel m -s,- doubt. z~**haft** a doubtful; (fragwürdig) dubious. z~**los** adv undoubtedly. z~**n** vi (haben) doubt (**an etw** dat sth)

Zweig m -[e]s,-e branch. Z~**geschäft** nt branch. Z~**stelle** f branch [office]

Zwei|kampf m duel. z~**mal** adv twice. z~**reihig** a double-breasted. z~**sprachig** a bilingual

zweit adv zu z~ in twos; **wir waren zu z~** there were two of us. z~**beste(r,s)** a second-best. z~**e(r,s)** a second

zwei|teilig a two-piece; ⟨Film, Programm⟩ two-part. z~**tens** adv secondly

zweitklassig a second-class

Zwerchfell nt diaphragm

Zwerg m -[e]s,-e dwarf

Zwetschge f -,-n quetsche

Zwickel m -s,- gusset

zwicken vt/i (haben) pinch

Zwieback m -[e]s,-e rusk

Zwiebel f -,-n onion; (Blumen-) bulb

Zwielicht nt half-light; (Dämmerlicht) twilight. Z~**ig** a shady

Zwie|spalt m conflict. z~**spältig** a conflicting. Z~**tracht** f - discord

Zwilling m -s,-e twin; Z~**e** (Astr) Gemini

zwingen† vt force; **sich z~** force oneself. z~**d** a compelling

Zwinger m -s,- run; (Zucht-) kennels pl

zwinkern vi (haben) blink; (als Zeichen) wink

Zwirn m -[e]s button thread

zwischen prep (+dat/acc) between; (unter) among[st]. Z~**bemerkung** f interjection. Z~**ding** nt (fam) cross. z~**durch** adv in between; (in der Z~zeit) in the meantime; (ab und zu) now and again. Z~**fall** m incident. Z~**händler** m middleman. Z~**landung** f stop-over. Z~**raum** m gap, space. Z~**ruf** m interjection. Z~**stecker** *m* adaptor. Z~**wand,** *f* partition. Z~**zeit** *f* **in der Z~zeit** in the meantime

Zwist *m* -[e]s,-e discord; (*Streit*) feud. Z~**igkeiten** *fpl* quarrels

zwitschern *vi* (*haben*) chirp

zwo *inv a* two

zwölf *inv a* twelve. z~**te(r,s)** *a* twelfth

zwote(r,s) *a* second

Zyklus *m* -,-**klen** cycle

Zylind|er *m* -s,- cylinder; (*Hut*) top hat. z~**risch** *a* cylindrical

Zyn|iker *m* -s,- cynic. z~**isch** *a* cynical, *adv* -ly. Z~**ismus** *m* - cynicism

Zypern *nt* -s Cyprus

Zypresse *f* -,-n cypress

Zyste /'tsysta/ *f* -,-n cyst

A

a /ə, *betont* eɪ/ *(vor einem Vokal* **an**) *indef art* ein(e); *(each)* pro; **not a** kein(e)

aback /əˈbæk/ *adv* **be taken ~** verblüfft sein

abandon /əˈbændən/ *vt* verlassen; *(give up)* aufgeben □*n* Hingabe *f*. **~ed** *a* verlassen; *⟨behaviour⟩* hemmungslos

abase /əˈbeɪs/ *vt* demütigen

abashed /əˈbæʃt/ *a* beschämt, verlegen

abate /əˈbeɪt/ *vi* nachlassen

abattoir /ˈæbətwɑː(r)/ *n* Schlachthof *m*

abbey /ˈæbɪ/ *n* Abtei *f*. **~ot** *n* Abt *m*

abbreviat|e /əˈbriːvɪeɪt/ *vt* abkürzen. **~ion** /-ˈeɪʃn/ *n* Abkürzung *f*

abdicat|e /ˈæbdɪkeɪt/ *vi* abdanken. **~ion** /-ˈkeɪʃn/ *n* Abdankung *f*

abdom|en /ˈæbdəmən/ *n* Unterleib *m*. **~inal** /-ˈdɒmɪnl/ *a* Unterleibs-

abduct /əbˈdʌct/ *vt* entführen. **~ion** /-ˈʌkʃn/ *n* Entführung *f*. **~or** *n* Entführer *m*

aberration /æbəˈreɪʃn/ *n* Abweichung *f*; *(mental)* Verwirrung *f*

abet /əˈbet/ *vt* (pt/pp **abetted**) **aid and ~** *(Jur)* Beihilfe leisten (+ *dat*)

abeyance /əˈbeɪəns/ *n* **in ~** [zeitweilig] außer Kraft; **fall into ~** außer Kraft kommen

abhor /əbˈhɔː(r)/ *vt* (pt/pp abhorred) verabscheuen. **~rence** /-ˈhɒrəns/ *n* Abscheu *f*. **~rent** /-ˈhɒrənt/ *a* abscheulich

abid|e /əˈbaɪd/ *vt* (pt/pp **abided**) *(tolerate)* aushalten; ausstehen ⟨*person*⟩ □*vi* **~e by** sich halten an (+ *acc*). **~ing** *a* bleibend

ability /əˈbɪlətɪ/ *n* Fähigkeit *f*; *(talent)* Begabung *f*

abject /ˈæbdʒekt/ *a* erbärmlich; *(humble)* demütig

ablaze /əˈbleɪz/ *a* in Flammen; **be ~** in Flammen stehen

able /ˈeɪbl/ *a* (-r, -st) fähig; **be ~ to do sth** etw tun können. **~-'bodied** *a* körperlich gesund; *(Mil)* tauglich

ably /ˈeɪblɪ/ *adv* gekonnt

abnormal /æbˈnɔːml/ *a* anormal; *(Med)* abnorm. **~ity** /-ˈmælətɪ/ *n* Abnormität *f*. **~ly** *adv* ungewöhnlich

aboard /əˈbɔːd/ *adv & prep* an Bord (+ *gen*)

abode /əˈbəʊd/ *n* Wohnsitz *m*

abol|ish /əˈbɒlɪʃ/ *vt* abschaffen. **~ition** /æbəˈlɪʃn/ *n* Abschaffung *f*

abominable /əˈbɒmɪnəbl/ *a*, **-bly** *adv* abscheulich

abominate /əˈbɒmɪneɪt/ *vt* verabscheuen

aborigines /æbəˈrɪdʒəniːz/ *npl* Ureinwohner *pl*

abort /əˈbɔːt/ *vt* abtreiben. **~ion** /-ˈɔːʃn/ *n* Abtreibung *f*; **have an ~ion** eine Abtreibung vornehmen lassen. **~ive** /-tɪv/ *a* ⟨*attempt*⟩ vergeblich

abound /əˈbaʊnd/ *vi* reichlich vorhanden sein; **~ in** reich sein an (+ *dat*)

about /əˈbaʊt/ *adv* umher, herum; *(approximately)* ungefähr; **be ~** *(in circulation)* umgehen; *(in existence)* vorhanden sein; **be up and ~** auf den Beinen sein; **be ~ to do sth** im Begriff sein, etw zu tun; **there are a lot ~** es gibt viele; **there was no one ~** es war

kein Mensch da; **run/play** ~ her-
umlaufen/-spielen □ *prep* um (+
acc) [... herum]; (*concerning*)
über (+ *dat*); **what is it** ~?
worum geht es? ⟨*book:*⟩ wovon
handelt es? **I know nothing** ~ **it**
ich weiß nichts davon; **talk/**
know ~ reden/wissen von
about: ~-'**face** n, ~-'**turn** n Kehrtwendung *f*
above /ə'bʌv/ *adv* oben □ *prep*
über (+ *dat/acc*); ~ **all** vor allem
above: ~-'**board** a legal.
~-'**mentioned** a obenerwähnt
abrasion /ə'breɪʒn/ n Schürfwunde *f*
abrasive /ə'breɪsɪv/ a Scheuer-;
⟨*remark*⟩ verletzend □ n Scheuer-
mittel *nt*; (*Techn*) Schleifmittel *nt*
abreast /ə'brest/ *adv* nebeneinander; **keep** ~ of Schritt halten mit
abridge /ə'brɪdʒ/ *vt* kürzen
abroad /ə'brɔːd/ *adv* im Ausland;
go ~ ins Ausland fahren
abrupt /ə'brʌpt/ a, -**ly** *adv* abrupt;
(*sudden*) plötzlich; (*curt*) schroff
abscess /'æbsɪs/ n Abszeß *m*
abscond /əb'skɒnd/ *vi* entfliehen
absence /'æbsəns/ n Abwesenheit *f*
absent[1] /'æbsənt/ a, -**ly** *adv* abwesend; **be** ~ fehlen
absent[2] /æb'sent/ *vt* ~ **oneself**
fernbleiben
absentee /æbsən'tiː/ n Abwe-
sende(r) *m/f*
absent-minded /æbsənt'maɪn-
dɪd/ a, -**ly** *adv* geistesabwesend;
(*forgetful*) zerstreut
absolute /'æbsəluːt/ a, -**ly** *adv* absolut
absolution /æbsə'luːʃn/ n Absolution *f*
absolve /əb'zɒlv/ *vt* lossprechen
absorb /əb'sɔːb/ *vt* absorbieren,
aufsaugen; ~ **ed in** vertieft in (+
acc). ~ **ent** /-ənt/ a saugfähig
absorption /əb'sɔːpʃn/ n Absorption *f*
abstain /əb'steɪn/ *vi* sich enthalten
(**from** *gen*); ~ **from voting** sich
der Stimme enthalten

abstemious /əb'stiːmɪəs/ a ent-
haltsam
abstention /əb'stenʃn/ n (*Pol*)
[Stimm]enthaltung *f*
abstinence /'æbstɪnəns/ n Ent-
haltsamkeit *f*
abstract /'æbstrækt/ a abstrakt
□ n (*summary*) Abriß *m*
absurd /əb'sɜːd/ a, -**ly** *adv* absurd.
~ **ity** n Absurdität *f*
abundan|ce /ə'bʌndəns/ n Fülle *f*
(**of** an + *dat*). ~ **t** a reichlich
abuse[1] /ə'bjuːz/ *vt* mißbrauchen;
(*insult*) beschimpfen
abuse[2] /ə'bjuːs/ n Mißbrauch *m*;
(*insults*) Beschimpfungen *pl*.
~ **ive** /-ɪv/ ausfallend
abut /ə'bʌt/ *vi* (*pt/pp* **abutted**) angrenzen (**on to** an + *acc*)
abysmal /ə'bɪzml/ a (*fam*) katastrophal
abyss /ə'bɪs/ n Abgrund *m*
academic /ækə'demɪk/ a, -**ally** *adv*
akademisch □ n Akademiker(in)
m(f)
academy /ə'kædəmɪ/ n Akademie *f*
accede /ək'siːd/ *vi* ~ **to** zustimmen
(+ *dat*); besteigen ⟨*throne*⟩
accelerat|e /ək'seləreɪt/ *vt* be-
schleunigen □ *vi* die Geschwindigkeit erhöhen. ~ **ion** /-'reɪʃn/ n
Beschleunigung *f*. ~ **or** n (*Auto*)
Gaspedal *nt*
accent[1] /'æksənt/ n Akzent *m*
accent[2] /ək'sent/ *vt* betonen
accentuate /ək'sentjʊeɪt/ *vt* betonen
accept /ək'sept/ *vt* annehmen; (*fig*)
akzeptieren □ *vi* zusagen. ~ **able**
/-əbl/ a annehmbar. ~ **ance** n Annahme *f*; (*of invitation*) Zusage *f*
access /'ækses/ n Zugang *m*;
(*road*) Zufahrt *f*. ~ **ible** /ək'sesəbl/
a zugänglich
accession /ək'seʃn/ n (**to** *throne*)
Thronbesteigung *f*
accessor|y /ək'sesərɪ/ n (*Jur*) Mit-
schuldige(r) *m/f*; ~ **ies** *pl*
(*fashion*) Accessoires *pl*; (*Techn*)
Zubehör *nt*

accident /'æksɪdənt/ *n* Unfall *m*; *(chance)* Zufall *m*; **by ~** zufällig; *(unintentionally)* versehentlich. **~al** /-'dentl/ *a*, **-ly** *adv* zufällig; *(unintentional)* versehentlich

acclaim /ə'kleɪm/ *n* Beifall *m* □ *vt* feiern **(as als)**

acclimate /ə'klaɪmətaɪz/ *vt* (*Amer*) = **acclimatize**

acclimatize /ə'klaɪmətaɪz/ *vt* **become ~d** sich akklimatisieren

accolade /'ækəleɪd/ *n* Auszeichnung *f*

accommodat|e /ə'kɒmədeɪt/ *vt* unterbringen; *(oblige)* entgegenkommen (+ *dat*). **~ing** *a* entgegenkommend. **~ion** /-'deɪʃn/ *n* (*rooms*) Unterkunft *f*

accompan|iment /ə'kʌmpənɪmənt/ *n* Begleitung *f*. **~ist** *n* (*Mus*) Begleiter(in) *m(f)*

accompany /ə'kʌmpənɪ/ *vt* (*pt/pp* **-ied**) begleiten

accomplice /ə'kʌmplɪs/ *n* Komplize/-zin *m/f*

accomplish /ə'kʌmplɪʃ/ *vt* erfüllen ⟨*task*⟩; *(achieve)* erreichen. **~ed** *a* fähig. **~ment** *n* Fertigkeit *f*; *(achievement)* Leistung *f*

accord /ə'kɔ:d/ *n* (*treaty*) Abkommen *nt*; **of one ~** einmütig; **of one's own ~** aus eigenem Antrieb □ *vt* gewähren. **~ance** *n* **in ~ance with** entsprechend (+ *dat*)

according /ə'kɔ:dɪŋ/ *adv* **~ to** nach (+ *dat*). **~ly** *adv* entsprechend

accordion /ə'kɔ:dɪən/ *n* Akkordeon *nt*

accost /ə'kɒst/ *vt* ansprechen

account /ə'kaʊnt/ *n* Konto *nt*; (*bill*) Rechnung *f*; *(description)* Darstellung *f*; (*report*) Bericht *m*; **~s** *pl* (*Comm*) Bücher *pl*; **on ~ of** wegen (+ *gen*); **on no ~** auf keinen Fall; **on this ~** deshalb; **on my ~** meinetwegen; **of no ~** ohne Bedeutung; **take into ~** in Betracht ziehen, berücksichtigen

□ *vi* **~ for** Rechenschaft ablegen für; *(explain)* erklären

accountant /ə'kaʊntənt/ *n* Buchhalter(in) *m(f)*; *(chartered)* Wirtschaftsprüfer *m*; (*for tax*) Steuerberater *m*

accoutrements /ə'ku:trəmənts/ *npl* Ausrüstung *f*

accredited /ə'kredɪtɪd/ *a* akkreditiert

accrue /ə'kru:/ *vi* sich ansammeln

accumulat|e /ə'kju:mjʊleɪt/ *vt* ansammeln, anhäufen □ *vi* sich ansammeln, sich anhäufen. **~ion** /-'leɪʃn/ *n* Ansammlung *f*, Anhäufung *f*. **~or** *n* (*Electr*) Akkumulator *m*

accura|cy /'ækjʊrəsɪ/ *n* Genauigkeit *f*. **~te** /-rət/ *a*, **-ly** *adv* genau

accusation /ækju:'zeɪʃn/ *n* Anklage *f*

accusative /ə'kju:zətɪv/ *a* & *n* **~ [case]** (*Gram*) Akkusativ *m*

accuse /ə'kju:z/ *vt* (*Jur*) anklagen (**of** *gen*); **~ s.o. of doing sth** jdn beschuldigen, etw getan zu haben. **~d** *n* **the ~d** der/die Angeklagte

accustom /ə'kʌstəm/ *vt* gewöhnen (**to an** + *dat*); **grow** *or* **get ~ed to** sich gewöhnen an (+ *acc*). **~ed** *a* gewohnt

ace /eɪs/ *n* (*Cards, Sport*) As *nt*

ache /eɪk/ *n* Schmerzen *pl* □ *vi* weh tun, schmerzen

achieve /ə'tʃi:v/ *vt* leisten; (*gain*) erzielen; *(reach)* erreichen. **~ment** *n* (*feat*) Leistung *f*

acid /'æsɪd/ *a* sauer; (*fig*) beißend □ *n* Säure *f*. **~ity** /ə'sɪdətɪ/ *n* Säure *f*. **~ 'rain** *n* saurer Regen *m*

acknowledge /ək'nɒlɪdʒ/ *vt* anerkennen; *(admit)* zugeben; erwidern ⟨*greeting*⟩; **~ receipt of** den Empfang bestätigen (+ *gen*). **~ment** *n* Anerkennung *f*; (*of letter*) Empfangsbestätigung *f*

acne /'æknɪ/ *n* Akne *f*

acorn /'eɪkɔ:n/ *n* Eichel *f*

acoustic /ə'ku:stɪk/ *a*, **-ally** *adv* akustisch. **~s** *npl* Akustik *f*

acquaint /ə'kweɪnt/ vt ~ s.o. with jdn bekannt machen mit; be ~ed with kennen; vertraut sein mit ⟨fact⟩. ~ance n Bekanntschaft f; ⟨person⟩ Bekannte(r) m/f; make s.o.'s ~ance jdn kennenlernen

acquiesce /ækwɪ'es/ vi einwilligen (to in + acc). ~nce n Einwilligung f

acquire /ə'kwaɪə(r)/ vt erwerben

acquisition /ækwɪ'zɪʃn/ n Erwerb m; ⟨thing⟩ Erwerbung f. ~ive /ə'kwɪzətɪv/ a habgierig

acquit /ə'kwɪt/ vt (pt/pp acquitted) freisprechen; ~ oneself well seiner Aufgabe gerecht werden. ~tal n Freispruch m

acre /'eɪkə(r)/ n ≈ Morgen m

acrid /'ækrɪd/ a scharf

acrimon|ious /ækrɪ'məʊnɪəs/ a bitter. ~y /'ækrɪmənɪ/ n Bitterkeit f

acrobat /'ækrəbæt/ n Akrobat(in) m(f). ~ic /-'bætɪk/ a akrobatisch

across /ə'krɒs/ adv hinüber/herüber; ⟨wide⟩ breit; ⟨not lengthwise⟩ quer; ⟨in crossword⟩ waagerecht; come ~ sth auf etw ⟨acc⟩ stoßen; go ~ hinübergehen; bring ~ herüberbringen • prep über (+ acc); ⟨crosswise⟩ quer über (+ acc/dat); ⟨on the other side of⟩ auf der anderen Seite (+ gen)

act /ækt/ n Tat f; ⟨action⟩ Handlung f; ⟨law⟩ Gesetz nt; ⟨Theat⟩ Akt m; ⟨item⟩ Nummer f; put on an ~ ⟨fam⟩ sich verstellen • vi handeln; ⟨behave⟩ sich verhalten; ⟨Theat⟩ spielen; ⟨pretend⟩ sich verstellen; ~ as fungieren als • vt spielen ⟨role⟩. ~ing a ⟨deputy⟩ stellvertretend □ n ⟨Theat⟩ Schauspielerei f. ~ing profession n Schauspielerberuf m

action /'ækʃn/ n Handlung f; ⟨deed⟩ Tat f; ⟨Mil⟩ Einsatz m; ⟨Jur⟩ Klage f; ⟨effect⟩ Wirkung f; ⟨Techn⟩ Mechanismus m; out of ~ ⟨machine⟩: außer Betrieb; take ~ handeln; killed in ~

gefallen. ~ 'replay n ⟨TV⟩ Wiederholung f

activate /'æktɪveɪt/ vt betätigen; ⟨Chem, Phys⟩ aktivieren

active /'æktɪv/ a, -ly adv aktiv; on ~ e service im Einsatz. ~ity /-'tɪvətɪ/ n Aktivität f

act|or /'æktə(r)/ n Schauspieler m. ~ress n Schauspielerin f

actual /'æktjʊəl/ a, -ly adv eigentlich; ⟨real⟩ tatsächlich. ~ity /-'ælətɪ/ n Wirklichkeit f

acumen /'ækjʊmən/ n Scharfsinn m

acupuncture /'ækjʊ-/ n Akupunktur f

acute /ə'kju:t/ a scharf; ⟨angle⟩ spitz; ⟨illness⟩ akut. ~ly adv sehr

ad /æd/ n ⟨fam⟩ = **advertisement**

AD abbr ⟨Anno Domini⟩ n.Chr.

adamant /'ædəmənt/ a be ~ that darauf bestehen, daß

adapt /ə'dæpt/ vt anpassen; bearbeiten ⟨play⟩ • vi sich anpassen. ~ability /-ə'bɪlətɪ/ n Anpassungsfähigkeit f. ~able /-əbl/ a anpassungsfähig

adaptation /ædæp'teɪʃn/ n ⟨Theat⟩ Bearbeitung f

adapter, adaptor /ə'dæptə(r)/ n ⟨Techn⟩ Adapter m; ⟨Electr⟩ ⟨twoway⟩ Doppelstecker m

add /æd/ vt hinzufügen; ⟨Math⟩ addieren • vi zusammenzählen, addieren; ~ to hinzufügen zu; ⟨fig: increase⟩ steigern; ⟨compound⟩ verschlimmern. ~ up vt zusammenzählen ⟨figures⟩ • vi zusammenzählen, addieren; ~ up to machen; it doesn't ~ up ⟨fig⟩ da stimmt etwas nicht

adder /'ædə(r)/ n Kreuzotter f

addict /'ædɪkt/ n Süchtige(r) m/f

addict|ed /ə'dɪktɪd/ a süchtig; ~ed to drugs drogensüchtig. ~ion /-ɪkʃn/ n Sucht f. ~ive /-ɪv/ a be ~ive zur Süchtigkeit führen

addition /ə'dɪʃn/ n Hinzufügung f; ⟨Math⟩ Addition f; ⟨thing added⟩

Ergänzung f; **in** ~ zusätzlich. ~ **al** a, **-ly** adv zusätzlich.

additive /'ædɪtɪv/ n Zusatz m

address /ə'dres/ n Adresse f, Anschrift f; (speech) Ansprache f; **form of** ~ Anrede f □ vt adressieren (**to an** + acc); (speak to) anreden ⟨person⟩; sprechen von (+ dat) ⟨meeting⟩. ~ **ee** /ædre'si:/ n Empfänger m

adenoids /'ædənɔɪdz/ npl [Rachen]polypen pl

adept /'ædept/ a geschickt (**at in** + dat)

adequate /'ædɪkwət/ a, **-ly** adv ausreichend

adhere /əd'hɪə(r)/ vi kleben/(fig) festhalten (**to an** + dat). ~ **nce** n Festhalten nt

adhesive /əd'hi:sɪv/ a klebend □ n Klebstoff m

adjacent /ə'dʒeɪsnt/ a angrenzend

adjective /'ædʒɪktɪv/ n Adjektiv nt

adjoin /ə'dʒɔɪn/ vt angrenzen an (+ acc). ~ **ing** a angrenzend

adjourn /ə'dʒɜ:n/ vt vertagen (**until auf** + acc) □ vi sich vertagen. ~ **ment** n Vertagung f

adjudicate /ə'dʒu:dɪkeɪt/ vi entscheiden; (in competition) Preisrichter sein

adjust /ə'dʒʌst/ vt einstellen; (alter) verstellen □ vi sich anpassen (**to** dat). ~ **able** /-əbl/ a verstellbar. ~ **ment** n Einstellung f; Anpassung f

ad lib /æd'lɪb/ adv aus dem Stegreif □ vi (pt/pp **ad libbed**) (fam) improvisieren

administer /əd'mɪnɪstə(r)/ vt verwalten; verabreichen ⟨medicine⟩

administration /ədmɪnɪ'streɪʃn/ n Verwaltung f; (Pol) Regierung f. ~ **or** /əd'mɪnɪstreɪtə(r)/ n Verwaltungsbeamte(r) m /-beamtin f

admirable /'ædmərəbl/ a bewundernswert

admiral /'ædmərəl/ n Admiral m

admiration /ædmə'reɪʃn/ n Bewunderung f

admire /əd'maɪə(r)/ vt bewundern. ~ **r** n Verehrer(in) m(f)

admissable /əd'mɪsəbl/ a zulässig

admission /əd'mɪʃn/ n Eingeständnis nt; (entry) Eintritt m

admit /əd'mɪt/ vt (pt/pp **admitted**) (let in) hereinlassen; (acknowledge) zugeben; ~ **to sth** etw zugeben. ~ **tance** n Eintritt m. ~ **tedly** adv zugegebenermaßen

admonish /əd'mɒnɪʃ/ vt ermahnen. ~ **tion** /ædmə'nɪʃn/ n Ermahnung f

ado /ə'du:/ n **without more** ~ ohne weiteres

adolescen|ce /ædə'lesns/ n Jugend f, Pubertät f. ~ **t** a Jugend-; ⟨boy, girl⟩ halbwüchsig □ n Jugendliche(r) m/f

adopt /ə'dɒpt/ vt adoptieren; ergreifen ⟨measure⟩; (Pol) annehmen ⟨candidate⟩. ~ **ion** /-ɒpʃn/ n Adoption f. ~ **ive** /-ɪv/ a Adoptiv-

ador|able /ə'dɔ:rəbl/ a bezaubernd. ~ **ation** /ædə'reɪʃn/ n Anbetung f

adore /ə'dɔ:(r)/ vt (worship) anbeten; (fam: like) lieben

adorn /ə'dɔ:n/ vt schmücken. ~ **ment** n Schmuck m

adrenalin /ə'drenəlɪn/ n Adrenalin nt

Adriatic /eɪdrɪ'ætɪk/ a & n ~ **[Sea]** Adria f

adrift /ə'drɪft/ a **be** ~ treiben; **come** ~ sich loslösen

adroit /ə'drɔɪt/ a, **-ly** adv gewandt, geschickt

adulation /ædju'leɪʃn/ n Schwärmerei f

adult /'ædʌlt/ n Erwachsene(r) m/f

adulterate /ə'dʌltəreɪt/ vt verfälschen; panschen ⟨wine⟩

adultery /ə'dʌltərɪ/ n Ehebruch m

advance /əd'va:ns/ n Fortschritt m; (Mil) Vorrücken nt; (payment) Vorschuß m; **in** ~ im voraus □ vi vorankommen; (Mil) vorrücken;

(make progress) Fortschritte machen □ *vt* fördern ⟨cause⟩; vorbringen ⟨idea⟩; vorschießen ⟨money⟩. ~ **booking** *n* Kartenvorverkauf *m*. ~**d** *a* fortgeschritten; (progressive) fortschrittlich. ~**ment** *n* Förderung *f*; (promotion) Beförderung *f*

advantage /əd'vɑ:ntɪdʒ/ *n* Vorteil *m*; **take** ~ **of** ausnutzen. ~**ous** /ædvən'teɪdʒəs/ *a* vorteilhaft

advent /'ædvent/ *n* Ankunft *f*; **A~** (season) Advent *m*

adventur|e /əd'ventʃə(r)/ *n* Abenteuer *nt*. ~**er** *n* Abenteurer *m*. ~**ous** /-rəs/ *a* abenteuerlich; ⟨person⟩ abenteuerlustig

adverb /'ædvɜ:b/ *n* Adverb *nt*

adversary /'ædvəsərɪ/ *n* Widersacher *m*

advers|e /'ædvɜ:s/ *a* ungünstig. ~**ity** /əd'vɜ:sətɪ/ *n* Not *f*

advert /'ædvɜ:t/ *n* (fam) = **advertisement**

advertise /'ædvətaɪz/ *vt* Reklame machen für; (by small ad) inserieren □ *vi* Reklame machen; inserieren; ~ **for** per Anzeige suchen

advertisement /əd'vɜ:tɪsmənt/ *n* Anzeige *f*; (publicity) Reklame *f*; (small ad) Inserat *nt*

advertis|er /'ædvətaɪzə(r)/ *n* Inserent *m*. ~**ing** *n* Werbung *f* □ attrib Werbe-

advice /əd'vaɪs/ *n* Rat *m*. ~ **note** *n* Benachrichtigung *f*

advisable /əd'vaɪzəbl/ *a* ratsam

advis|e /əd'vaɪz/ *vt* raten (s.o. jdm); (counsel) beraten; (inform) benachrichtigen; ~ **e s.o. against** sth jdm von etw abraten □ *vi* raten. ~**er** *n* Berater(in) *m(f)*. ~**ory** *a* beratend

advocate[1] /'ædvəkət/ *n* [Rechts]anwalt *m*/-anwältin *f*; (supporter) Befürworter *m*

advocate[2] /'ædvəkeɪt/ *vt* befürworten

aerial /'eərɪəl/ *a* Luft- □ *n* Antenne *f*

aerobics /eə'rəʊbɪks/ *n* Aerobic *nt*

aero|drome /'eərədrəʊm/ *n* Flugplatz *m*. ~**plane** *n* Flugzeug *nt*

aerosol /'eərəsɒl/ *n* Spraydose *f*

aesthetic /i:s'θetɪk/ *a* ästhetisch

afar /ə'fɑ:(r)/ *adv* **from** ~ aus der Ferne

affable /'æfəbl/ *a*, **-bly** *adv* freundlich

affair /ə'feə(r)/ *n* Angelegenheit *f*, Sache *f*; (scandal) Affäre *f*; [love-]~ [Liebes]verhältnis *nt*

affect /ə'fekt/ *vt* sich auswirken auf (+ *acc*); (concern) betreffen; (move) rühren; (pretend) vortäuschen. ~**ation** /æfek'teɪʃn/ *n* Affektiertheit *f*. ~**ed** *a* affektiert

affection /ə'fekʃn/ *n* Liebe *f*. ~**ate** /-ət/ *a*, **-ly** *adv* liebevoll

affiliated /ə'fɪlɪeɪtɪd/ *a* angeschlossen (to *dat*)

affinity /ə'fɪnətɪ/ *n* Ähnlichkeit *f*; (attraction) gegenseitige Anziehung *f*

affirm /ə'fɜ:m/ *vt* behaupten; (Jur) eidesstattlich erklären

affirmative /ə'fɜ:mətɪv/ *a* bejahend □ *n* Bejahung *f*

affix /ə'fɪks/ *vt* anbringen (to *dat*); (stick) aufkleben (to auf + *acc*); setzen ⟨signature⟩ (to unter + *acc*)

afflict /ə'flɪkt/ *vt* **be** ~**ed** with behaftet sein mit. ~**ion** /-ɪkʃn/ *n* Leiden *nt*

affluen|ce /'æflʊəns/ *n* Reichtum *m*. ~**t** *a* wohlhabend. ~**t society** *n* Wohlstandsgesellschaft *f*

afford /ə'fɔ:d/ *vt* (provide) gewähren; **be able to** ~ sth sich (*dat*) etw leisten können. ~**able** /-əbl/ *a* erschwinglich

affray /ə'freɪ/ *n* Schlägerei *f*

affront /ə'frʌnt/ *n* Beleidigung *f* □ *vt* beleidigen

afield /ə'fi:ld/ *adv* **further** ~ weiter weg

afloat /ə'fləʊt/ *a* **be** ~ ⟨ship:⟩ flott sein; **keep** ~ ⟨person:⟩ sich über Wasser halten

afoot /ə'fʊt/ *a* im Gange

aforesaid /ə'fɔ:sed/ a (Jur) obenerwähnt

afraid /ə'freɪd/ a be ~ Angst haben
(of vor + dat); I'm ~ not leider
nicht; I'm ~ so [ja] leider; I'm ~
I can't help you ich kann Ihnen
leider nicht helfen

afresh /ə'freʃ/ adv von vorne

Africa /'æfrɪkə/ n Afrika nt. ~n a
afrikanisch □n Afrikaner(in)
m(f)

after /'ɑ:ftə(r)/ adv danach □prep
nach (+ dat); ~ that danach; ~
all schließlich; the day ~ tomorrow übermorgen; be ~ aus-
sein auf (+ acc) □conj nachdem

after-: ~effect n Nachwirkung f.
~math /-mɑ:θ/ n Auswirkungen
pl. ~'noon n Nachmittag m;
good ~noon! guten Tag! ~-
sales service n Kundendienst
m. ~shave n Rasierwasser nt.
~thought n nachträglicher Einfall m. ~wards adv nachher

again /ə'geɪn/ adv wieder; (once
more) noch einmal; (besides)
außerdem; ~ and ~ immer
wieder

against /ə'geɪnst/ prep gegen (+
acc)

age /eɪdʒ/ n Alter nt; (era) Zeitalter
nt; ~s (fam) ewig; under ~ minderjährig; of ~ volljährig; two
years of ~ zwei Jahre alt □v
(pres p ageing) □vt älter machen
□vi altern; (mature) reifen

aged¹ /eɪdʒd/ a ~ two zwei Jahre
alt

aged² /'eɪdʒɪd/ a betagt □n the
~ pl die Alten

ageless /'eɪdʒlɪs/ a ewig jung

agency /'eɪdʒənsɪ/ n Agentur f; (office) Büro nt; have the ~ for die
Vertretung haben für

agenda /ə'dʒendə/ n Tagesord-
nung f; on the ~ auf dem Programm

agent /'eɪdʒənt/ n Agent(in) m(f);
(Comm) Vertreter(in) m(f); (substance) Mittel nt

aggravat|e /'ægrəveɪt/ vt ver-
schlimmern; (fam: annoy) ärgern. ~ion /-'veɪʃn/ n (fam)
Ärger m

aggregate /'ægrɪgət/ a gesamt □n
Gesamtzahl f; (sum) Gesamtsumme f

aggress|ion /ə'greʃn/ n Aggres-
sion f. ~ive /-sɪv/ a, -ly adv aggressiv. ~iveness n Aggressivi-
tät f. ~or n Angreifer(in) m(f)

aggrieved /ə'gri:vd/ a verletzt

aggro /'ægrəʊ/ n (fam) Ärger m

aghast /ə'gɑ:st/ a entsetzt

agil|e /'ædʒaɪl/ a flink, behende;
⟨mind⟩ wendig. ~ity /ə'dʒɪlətɪ/ n
Flinkheit f, Behendigkeit f

agitat|e /'ædʒɪteɪt/ vt bewegen;
(shake) schütteln □vi (fig) ~ for
agitieren für. ~ed a, -ly adv erregt. ~ion /-'teɪʃn/ n Erregung f;
(Pol) Agitation f. ~or n Agitator
m

agnostic /æg'nɒstɪk/ n Agnostiker m

ago /ə'gəʊ/ adv vor (+ dat); a
month ~ vor einem Monat; a
long time ~ vor langer Zeit; how
long ~ is it? wie lange ist es her?

agog /ə'gɒg/ a gespannt

agoniz|e /'ægənaɪz/ vi [innerlich]
ringen. ~ing a qualvoll

agony /'ægənɪ/ n Qual f; be in ~
furchtbare Schmerzen haben

agree /ə'gri:/ vt vereinbaren; (admit) zugeben; ~ to do sth sich
bereit erklären, etw zu tun □vi
⟨people, figures:⟩ übereinstimmen; (reach agreement) sich einigen; (get on) gut miteinander auskommen; (consent) einwilligen
(to in + acc); I ~ der Meinung bin
ich auch; ~ with s.o. jdm zustimmen; ⟨food:⟩ jdm bekommen;
~ with sth (approve of) mit etw
einverstanden sein

agreeable /ə'gri:əbl/ a angenehm;
be ~ einverstanden sein (to mit)

agreed /ə'gri:d/ a vereinbart

agreement /ə'griːmənt/n Übereinstimmung f; (consent) Einwilligung f; (contract) Abkommen nt; **reach** ~ sich einigen

agricultural /ˌægrɪ'kʌltʃərəl/ a landwirtschaftlich. ~**e** /'ægrɪkʌltʃə(r)/ n Landwirtschaft f

aground /ə'graʊnd/ a gestrandet; **run** ~ ⟨ship:⟩ stranden

ahead /ə'hed/ adv straight ~ geradeaus; **be** ~ **of** s.o./sth vor jdm/etw sein; (fig) voraus sein; **draw** ~ nach vorne ziehen; **go on** ~ vorgehen; **get** ~ vorankommen; **go** ~! (fam) bitte! **look/plan** ~ vorausblicken/-planen

aid /eɪd/ n Hilfe f; (financial) Unterstützung f; **in** ~ **of** zugunsten (+ gen) □vt helfen (+ dat)

aide /eɪd/ n Berater m

Aids /eɪdz/ n Aids nt

ailing /'eɪlɪŋ/ a kränkelnd. ~**ment** n Leiden nt

aim /eɪm/ n Ziel nt; **take** ~ zielen □vt richten (**at** auf + acc) □vi zielen (**at** auf + acc); ~ **to do** sth beabsichtigen, etw zu tun. ~**less** a, -**ly** adv ziellos

air /eə(r)/ n Luft f; (tune) Melodie f; (expression) Miene f; (appearance) Anschein m; **be on the** ~ ⟨programme:⟩ gesendet werden; ⟨person:⟩ senden, auf Sendung sein; **put on** ~s vornehm tun; **by** ~ auf dem Luftweg; (airmail) mit Luftpost □vt lüften; vorbringen ⟨views⟩

air: ~-**bed** n Luftmatratze f. ~-**conditioned** a klimatisiert. ~-**conditioning** n Klimaanlage f. ~**craft** n Flugzeug nt. ~**fare** n Flugpreis m. ~**field** n Flugplatz m. ~ **force** n Luftwaffe f. ~ **freshener** n Raumspray nt. ~**gun** n Luftgewehr nt. ~ **hostess** n Stewardeß f. ~ **letter** n Aerogramm nt. ~**line** n Fluggesellschaft f. ~**lock** n Luftblase f. ~**mail** n Luftpost f. ~**man** n Flieger m. ~**plane** n (Amer)

Flugzeug nt. ~ **pocket** n Luftloch nt. ~**port** n Flughafen m. ~**raid** n Luftangriff m. ~-**raid shelter** n Luftschutzbunker m. ~**ship** n Luftschiff nt. ~ **ticket** n Flugschein m. ~**tight** a luftdicht. ~ **traffic** n Luftverkehr m. ~-**traffic controller** n Fluglotse m. ~**worthy** a flugtüchtig

airy /'eərɪ/ a (-ier, -iest) luftig; ⟨manner⟩ nonchalant

aisle /aɪl/ n Gang m

ajar /ə'dʒɑː(r)/ a angelehnt

akin /ə'kɪn/ a ~ **to** verwandt mit; (similar) ähnlich (**to** dat)

alabaster /'æləbɑːstə(r)/ n Alabaster m

alacrity /ə'lækrətɪ/ n Bereitschaft f

alarm /ə'lɑːm/ n Alarm m; (device) Alarmanlage f; (clock) Wecker m; (fear) Unruhe f □vt erschrecken; alarmieren. ~ **clock** n Wecker m

alas /ə'læs/ int ach!

album /'ælbəm/ n Album nt

alcohol /'ælkəhɒl/ n Alkohol m. ~**ic** /-'hɒlɪk/ a alkoholisch □n Alkoholiker(in) m(f). ~**ism** n Alkoholismus m

alcove /'ælkəʊv/ n Nische f

alert /ə'lɜːt/ a aufmerksam □n Alarm m; **on the** ~ auf der Hut □vt alarmieren

algae /'ældʒiː/ npl Algen pl

algebra /'ældʒɪbrə/ n Algebra f

Algeria /æl'dʒɪərɪə/ n Algerien nt

alias /'eɪlɪəs/ n Deckname m □adv alias

alibi /'ælɪbaɪ/ n Alibi nt

alien /'eɪlɪən/ a fremd □n Ausländer(in) m(f)

alienat|e /'eɪlɪəneɪt/ vt entfremden. ~**ion** /-'neɪʃn/ n Entfremdung f

alight[1] /ə'laɪt/ vi aussteigen (**from** aus); ⟨bird:⟩ sich niederlassen

alight[2] a **be** ~ brennen; **set** ~ anzünden

align /ə'laɪn/ vt ausrichten. ~**ment** n Ausrichtung f; **out of** ~ nicht richtig ausgerichtet

alike /ə'laɪk/ a & adv ähnlich; (same) gleich; **look ~** sich (dat) ähnlich sehen

alimony /'ælɪmənɪ/ n Unterhalt m

alive /ə'laɪv/ a lebendig; **be ~** leben; **be ~ with** wimmeln von

alkali /'ælkəlaɪ/ n Base f, Alkali nt

all /ɔːl/ a alle pl; (whole) ganz; **~ [the] children** alle Kinder; **our children** alle unsere Kinder; **~ the others** alle anderen; **~ day** den ganzen Tag; **~ the wine** der ganze Wein; **for ~ that** (nevertheless) trotzdem; **in ~ innocence** in aller Unschuld □pron alle pl; (everything) alles; **~ of you/them** Sie/sie alle; **~ of the town** die ganze Stadt; **not at ~** gar nicht; **in ~** insgesamt; **~ in ~** alles in allem; **most of ~** am meisten; **once and for ~** ein für allemal □adv ganz; **~ but** fast; **at once** auf einmal; **~ too soon** viel zu früh; **~ the same** (nevertheless) trotzdem; **~ the better** um so besser; **be ~ in** (fam) völlig erledigt sein; **four ~** (Sport) vier zu vier

allay /ə'leɪ/ vt zerstreuen

allegation /ælɪ'ɡeɪʃn/ n Behauptung f

allege /ə'ledʒ/ vt behaupten. **~d a, -ly** /-ɪdlɪ/ adv angeblich

allegiance /ə'liːdʒəns/ n Treue f

allegor|ical /ælɪ'ɡɒrɪkl/ a allegorisch. **~y** /'ælɪɡərɪ/ n Allegorie f

allerg|ic /ə'lɜːdʒɪk/ a allergisch (to gegen). **~y** /'ælədʒɪ/ n Allergie f

alleviate /ə'liːvɪeɪt/ vt lindern

alley /'ælɪ/ n Gasse f; (for bowling) Bahn f

alliance /ə'laɪəns/ n Verbindung f; (Pol) Bündnis nt

allied /'ælaɪd/ a alliiert; (fig: related) verwandt (to mit)

alligator /'ælɪɡeɪtə(r)/ n Alligator m

allocat|e /'æləkeɪt/ vt zuteilen; (share out) verteilen. **~ion** /-'keɪʃn/ n Zuteilung f

allot /ə'lɒt/ vt (pt/pp allotted) zuteilen (s.o. jdm). **~ment** n ≈ Schrebergarten m

allow /ə'laʊ/ vt erlauben; (give) geben; (grant) gewähren; (reckon) rechnen; (agree, admit) zugeben; **~ for** berücksichtigen; **s.o. to do sth** jdm erlauben, etw zu tun; **be ~ed to do sth** etw tun dürfen

allowance /ə'laʊəns/ n [finanzielle] Unterstützung f; **~ for petrol** Benzingeld nt; **make ~s for** berücksichtigen

alloy /'ælɔɪ/ n Legierung f

allude /ə'luːd/ vi anspielen (to auf + acc)

allure /ə'lʊə(r)/ n Reiz m

allusion /ə'luːʒn/ n Anspielung f

ally¹ /'ælaɪ/ n Verbündete(r) m/f; **the Allies** pl die Alliierten

ally² /ə'laɪ/ vt (pt/pp -ied) verbinden; **~ oneself with** sich verbünden mit

almighty /ɔːl'maɪtɪ/ a allmächtig; (fam: big) Riesen- □ n **the A~** der Allmächtige

almond /'ɑːmənd/ n (Bot) Mandel f

almost /'ɔːlməʊst/ adv fast, beinahe

alms /ɑːmz/ npl (liter) Almosen pl

alone /ə'ləʊn/ a & adv allein; **leave me ~** laß mich in Ruhe; **leave that ~!** laß die Finger davon! **let ~** ganz zu schweigen von

along /ə'lɒŋ/ prep entlang (+ acc); **~ the river** den Fluß entlang □adv **~ with** zusammen mit; **all ~** die ganze Zeit; **come ~** komm doch; **I'll bring it ~** ich bringe es mit; **move ~** weitergehen

along|side adv daneben □prep neben (+ dat)

aloof /ə'luːf/ a distanziert

aloud /ə'laʊd/ adv laut

alphabet /'ælfəbet/ n Alphabet nt. **~ical** /-'betɪkl/ a, **-ly** adv alphabetisch

alpine /'ælpaɪn/ a alpin; **A~** Alpen-

Alps /ælps/ npl Alpen pl

already /ɔːlˈredɪ/ adv schon

Alsace /ælˈsæs/ n Elsaß nt

Alsatian /ælˈseɪʃn/ n (dog) [deutscher] Schäferhund m

also /ˈɔːlsəʊ/ adv auch

altar /ˈɔːltə(r)/ n Altar m

alter /ˈɔːltə(r)/ vt ändern □ vi sich verändern. ~**ation** /-ˈreɪʃn/ n Änderung f

alternate[1] /ˈɔːltəneɪt/ vi [sich] abwechseln □ vt abwechseln

alternate[2] /ɔːlˈtɜːnət/ a, -ly adv abwechselnd; (Amer: alternative) andere(r,s); on ~ days jeden zweiten Tag

'alternating current n Wechselstrom m

alternative /ɔːlˈtɜːnətɪv/ a andere(r,s) □n Alternative f. ~**ly** adv oder aber

although /ɔːlˈðəʊ/ conj obgleich, obwohl

altitude /ˈæltɪtjuːd/ n Höhe f

altogether /ɔːltəˈgeðə(r)/ adv insgesamt; (on the whole) alles in allem

altruistic /æltruˈɪstɪk/ altruistisch

aluminium /æljʊˈmɪnɪəm/ n, (Amer) **aluminum** /əˈluːmɪnəm/ n Aluminium nt

always /ˈɔːlweɪz/ adv immer

am /æm/ see be

a.m. abbr (ante meridiem) vormittags

amalgamate /əˈmælgəmeɪt/ vt vereinigen; (Chem) amalgamieren □ vi sich vereinigen; (Chem) sich amalgamieren

amass /əˈmæs/ vt anhäufen

amateur /ˈæmətə(r)/ n Amateur m □attrib Amateur-; (Theat) Laien-. ~**ish** a laienhaft

amaze /əˈmeɪz/ vt erstaunen. ~**d** a erstaunt. ~**ment** n Erstaunen nt

amazing /əˈmeɪzɪŋ/ a, -ly adv erstaunlich

ambassador /æmˈbæsədə(r)/ n Botschafter m

amber /ˈæmbə(r)/ n Bernstein m □a (colour) gelb

ambidextrous /æmbɪˈdekstrəs/ a be ~ mit beiden Händen gleich geschickt sein

ambience /ˈæmbɪəns/ n Atmosphäre f

ambiguity /æmbɪˈgjuːətɪ/ n Zweideutigkeit f. ~**ous** /-ˈbɪgjʊəs/ a, -ly adv zweideutig

ambition /æmˈbɪʃn/ n Ehrgeiz m; (aim) Ambition f. ~**ous** /-ʃəs/ a ehrgeizig

ambivalent /æmˈbɪvələnt/ a zwiespältig; be/feel ~ im Zwiespalt sein

amble /ˈæmbl/ vi schlendern

ambulance /ˈæmbjʊləns/ n Krankenwagen m. ~ **man** n Sanitäter m

ambush /ˈæmbʊʃ/ n Hinterhalt m □ vt aus dem Hinterhalt überfallen

amen /ɑːˈmen/ int amen

amenable /əˈmiːnəbl/ a ~ to zugänglich (to dat)

amend /əˈmend/ vt ändern. ~**ment** n Änderung f. ~**s** npl make ~s for sth etw wiedergutmachen

amenities /əˈmiːnətɪz/ npl Einrichtungen pl

America /əˈmerɪkə/ n Amerika nt. ~**n** a amerikanisch □n Amerikaner(in) m(f). ~**nism** n Amerikanismus m

amiable /ˈeɪmɪəbl/ a nett

amicable /ˈæmɪkəbl/ a, -bly adv freundschaftlich; ⟨agreement⟩ gütlich

amid[st] /əˈmɪd[st]/ prep inmitten (+ gen)

amiss /əˈmɪs/ a be ~ nicht stimmen □adv not come ~ nicht unangebracht sein; take sth ~ etw übelnehmen

ammonia /əˈməʊnɪə/ n Ammoniak nt

ammunition /æmjʊˈnɪʃn/ n Munition f

amnesia /æmˈniːzɪə/ n Amnesie f

amnesty /'æmnəstɪ/ n Amnestie f

among[st] /ə'mʌŋ[st]/ prep unter (+ dat/acc); ~ **yourselves** untereinander

amoral /eɪ'mɒrəl/ a amoralisch

amorous /'æmərəs/ a zärtlich

amount /ə'maʊnt/ n Menge f; (sum of money) Betrag m; (total) Gesamtsumme f □vi – to sich belaufen auf (+ acc); (fig) hinauslaufen auf (+ acc)

amp /æmp/ n Ampere nt

amphibi|an /æm'fɪbɪən/ n Amphibie f. ~**ous** /-ɪəs/ a amphibisch

amphitheatre /'æmfɪ/ n Amphitheater nt

ample /'æmpl/ a (-r, -st), -ly adv reichlich; (large) füllig

amplif|ier /'æmplɪfaɪə(r)/ n Verstärker m. ~**y** /-faɪ/ vt (pt/pp -ied) weiter ausführen; verstärken ⟨sound⟩

amputat|e /'æmpjʊteɪt/ vt amputieren. ~**ion** /-'teɪʃn/ n Amputation f

amuse /ə'mju:z/ vt amüsieren, belustigen; (entertain) unterhalten. ~**ment** n Belustigung f; Unterhaltung f. ~**ment arcade** n Spielhalle f

amusing /ə'mju:zɪŋ/ a amüsant

an /ən, betont ən/ see **a**

anaem|ia /ə'ni:mɪə/ n Blutarmut f, Anämie f. ~**ic** a blutarm

anaesthesia /ænəs'θi:zɪə/ n Betäubung f

anaesthetic /ænəs'θetɪk/ n Narkosemittel nt, Betäubungsmittel nt; **under [an]** ~ in Narkose; **give s.o. an** ~ jdm eine Narkose geben

anaesthet|ist /ə'ni:sθətɪst/ n Narkosearzt m. ~**ize** /-taɪz/ vt betäuben

analog[ue] /'ænəlɒg/ a Analog-

analogy /ə'nælədʒɪ/ n Analogie f

analyse /'ænəlaɪz/ vt analysieren

analysis /ə'næləsɪs/ n Analyse f

analyst /'ænəlɪst/ n Chemiker(in) m(f); (Psych) Analytiker m

analytical /ænə'lɪtɪkl/ a analytisch

anarch|ist /'ænəkɪst/ n Anarchist m. ~**y** n Anarchie f

anathema /ə'næθəmə/ n Greuel m

anatom|ical /ænə'tɒmɪkl/ a, -**ly** adv anatomisch. ~**y** /ə'nætəmɪ/ n Anatomie f

ancest|or /'ænsestə(r)/ n Vorfahr m. ~**ry** n Abstammung f

anchor /'æŋkə(r)/ n Anker m □vi ankern □vt verankern

anchovy /'æntʃəvɪ/ n Sardelle f

ancient /'eɪnʃənt/ a alt

ancillary /æn'sɪlərɪ/ n Hilfs- **and**, betont ænd/ conj und; ~ **so on** und so weiter; **six hundred** ~ **two** sechshundertzwei; **more** ~ **more** immer mehr; **nice** ~ **warm** schön warm; **try** ~ **come** versuche zu kommen

anecdote /'ænɪkdəʊt/ n Anekdote f

anew /ə'nju:/ adv von neuem

angel /'eɪndʒl/ n Engel m. ~**ic** /æn'dʒelɪk/ a engelhaft

anger /'æŋgə(r)/ n Zorn m □vt zornig machen

angle¹ /'æŋgl/ n Winkel m; (fig) Standpunkt m; **at an** ~ schräg

angle² vi angeln; ~ **for** (fig) fischen nach. ~**r** n Angler m

Anglican /'æŋglɪkən/ a anglikanisch □n Anglikaner(in) m(f)

Anglo-Saxon /æŋgləʊ'sæksn/ a angelsächsisch □n Angelsächsisch nt

angry /'æŋgrɪ/ a (-ier, -iest), -**ily** adv zornig; **be** ~ **with** böse sein auf (+ acc)

anguish /'æŋgwɪʃ/ n Qual f

angular /'æŋgjʊlə(r)/ a eckig; ⟨features⟩ kantig

animal /'ænɪml/ n Tier nt □a tierisch

animate¹ /'ænɪmət/ a lebendig

animate² /'ænɪmeɪt/ vt beleben. ~**ed** a lebhaft. ~**ion** /-'meɪʃn/ n Lebhaftigkeit f

animosity /ænɪ'mɒsətɪ/ n Feindseligkeit f

aniseed /'ænɪsi:d/ n Anis m

ankle /'æŋkl/ n [Fuß]knöchel m
annex /ə'neks/ vt annektieren
annex[e] /'æneks/ n Nebengebäude nt; (extension) Anbau m
annihilat|e /ə'naɪəleɪt/ vt vernichten. **~ion** /-'leɪʃn/ n Vernichtung f
anniversary /ænɪ'vɜːsərɪ/ n Jahrestag m
annotate /'ænəteɪt/ vt kommentieren
announce /ə'naʊns/ vt bekanntgeben; (over loudspeaker) durchsagen; (at reception) ankündigen; (Radio, TV) ansagen; (in newspaper) anzeigen. **~ment** n Bekanntgabe f, Bekanntmachung f; Durchsage f; Ansage f; Anzeige f. **~r** n Ansager(in) m(f)
annoy /ə'nɔɪ/ vt ärgern; (pester) belästigen; **get ~ed** sich ärgern. **~ance** n Ärger m. **~ing** a ärgerlich
annual /'ænjʊəl/ a, **-ly** adv jährlich □ n (Bot) einjährige Pflanze f; (book) Jahresalbum nt
annuity /ə'njuːɪtɪ/ n [Leib]rente f
annul /ə'nʌl/ vt (pt/pp annulled) annullieren
anoint /ə'nɔɪnt/ vt salben
anomaly /ə'nɒmǝlɪ/ n Anomalie f
anonymous /ə'nɒnɪməs/ a, **-ly** adv anonym
anorak /'ænəræk/ n Anorak m
anorexia /ænə'reksɪə/ n Magersucht f
another /ə'nʌðə(r)/ a & pron ein anderer/eine andere/ein anderes; (additional) noch ein(e); **~ [one]** noch einer/eine/eins; **~ day** an einem anderen Tag; **in ~ way** auf andere Weise; **~ time** ein andermal; **one ~** einander
answer /'ɑːnsə(r)/ n Antwort f; (solution) Lösung f □ vt antworten (s.o. jdm); beantworten (question, letter); **~ the door/telephone** an die Tür/ans Telefon gehen □ vi antworten; (Teleph) sich melden; **~ back** eine freche

Antwort geben; **~ for** verantwortlich sein für. **~able** /-əbl/ a verantwortlich. **~ing machine** n (Teleph) Anrufbeantworter m
ant /ænt/ n Ameise f
antagonis|m /æn'tægənɪzm/ n Antagonismus m. **~tic** /-'nɪstɪk/ a feindselig
antagonize /æn'tægənaɪz/ vt gegen sich aufbringen
Antarctic /ænt'ɑːktɪk/ n Antarktis f
antelope /'æntɪləʊp/ n Antilope f
antenatal /æntɪ'neɪtl/ a **~ care** Schwangerschaftsfürsorge f
antenna /æn'tenə/ n Fühler m; (Amer: aerial) Antenne f
ante-room /'æntɪ-/ n Vorraum m
anthem /'ænθəm/ n Hymne f
anthology /æn'θɒlədʒɪ/ n Anthologie f
anthropology /ænθrə'pɒlədʒɪ/ n Anthropologie f
anti-aircraft /æntɪ-/ a Flugabwehr-
antibiotic /æntɪbaɪ'ɒtɪk/ n Antibiotikum nt
'antibody n Antikörper m
anticipat|e /æn'tɪsɪpeɪt/ vt vorhersehen; (forestall) zuvorkommen (+ dat); (expect) erwarten. **~ion** /-'peɪʃn/ n Erwartung f
anti'climax n Enttäuschung f
anti'clockwise a & adv gegen den Uhrzeigersinn
antics /'æntɪks/ npl Mätzchen pl
anti'cyclone n Hochdruckgebiet nt
antidote /'æntɪdəʊt/ n Gegengift nt
'antifreeze n Frostschutzmittel nt
antipathy /æn'tɪpəθɪ/ n Abneigung f, Antipathie f
antiquarian /æntɪ'kweərɪən/ a antiquarisch. **~ bookshop** n Antiquariat nt
antiquated /'æntɪkweɪtɪd/ a veraltet

antique /æn'ti:k/ *a* antik □*n* Antiquität *f.* ~ **dealer** *n* Antiquitätenhändler *m*

antiquity /æn'tɪkwətɪ/ *n* Altertum *nt*

anti-Semitic /ˌæntɪsɪ'mɪtɪk/ *a* antisemitisch

anti'septic *a* antiseptisch □*n* Antiseptikum *nt*

anti'social *a* asozial; (*fam*) ungesellig

antithesis /æn'tɪθəsɪs/ *n* Gegensatz *m*

antlers /'æntləz/ *npl* Geweih *nt*

anus /'eɪnəs/ *n* After *m*

anvil /'ænvɪl/ *n* Amboß *m*

anxiety /æŋ'zaɪətɪ/ *n* Sorge *f*

anxious /'æŋkʃəs/ *a*, **-ly** *adv* ängstlich; (*worried*) besorgt; **be ~ to do sth** etw gerne machen wollen

any /'enɪ/ *a* irgendein(e); *pl* irgendwelche; (*every*) jede(r,s); *pl* alle; (*after negative*) kein(e); *pl* keine; **~ colour/number you like** eine beliebige Farbe/Zahl; **have you ~ wine/apples?** haben Sie Wein/Äpfel? **for ~ reason** aus irgendeinem Grund □*pron* [irgend]einer/eine/eins; *pl* [irgend]welche; (*some*) welche(r,s); *pl* welche; (*all*) alle *pl*; (*negative*) keiner/keine/keins; *pl* keine; **I don't want ~ of it** ich will nichts davon; **there aren't ~** es gibt keine; **I need wine/apples/money—have we ~?** ich brauche Wein/Äpfel/Geld—haben wir welchen/welche/welches? □*adv* noch; **~ quicker/slower** noch schneller/langsamer; **is it ~ better?** geht es etwas besser? **would you like ~ more?** möchten Sie noch [etwas]? **I can't eat ~ more** ich kann nichts mehr essen; **I can't go ~ further** ich kann nicht mehr weiter

'anybody *pron* [irgend] jemand; (*after negative*) niemand; **~ can do that** das kann jeder

'anyhow *adv* jedenfalls; (*nevertheless*) trotzdem; (*badly*) irgendwie

'anyone *pron* = **anybody**

'anything *pron* [irgend] etwas; (*after negative*) nichts; (*everything*) alles

'anyway *adv* jedenfalls; (*in any case*) sowieso

'anywhere *adv* irgendwo; (*after negative*) nirgendwo; ⟨*be, live*⟩ überall; **I'd go ~** ich würde überallhin gehen

apart /ə'pɑ:t/ *adv* auseinander; **live ~** getrennt leben; **~ from** abgesehen von

apartment /ə'pɑ:tmənt/ *n* Zimmer *nt*; (*Amer: flat*) Wohnung *f*

apathy /'æpəθɪ/ *n* Apathie *f*

ape /eɪp/ *n* [Menschen]affe *m* □*vt* nachäffen

aperitif /ə'perɪtɪf/ *n* Aperitif *m*

aperture /'æpətʃə(r)/ *n* Öffnung *f*; (*Phot*) Blende *f*

apex /'eɪpeks/ *n* Spitze *f*; (*fig*) Gipfel *m*

apiece /ə'pi:s/ *adv* pro Person; (*thing*) pro Stück

apologetic /əpɒlə'dʒetɪk/ *a*, **-ally** *adv* entschuldigend; **be ~** sich entschuldigen

apologize /ə'pɒlədʒaɪz/ *vi* sich entschuldigen (**to** bei)

apology /ə'pɒlədʒɪ/ *n* Entschuldigung *f*

apostle /ə'pɒsl/ *n* Apostel *m*

apostrophe /ə'pɒstrəfɪ/ *n* Apostroph *m*

appal /ə'pɔ:l/ *vt* (*pt/pp* **appalled**) entsetzen. **~ling** *a* entsetzlich

apparatus /æpə'reɪtəs/ *n* Apparatur *f*; (*Sport*) Geräte *pl*; (*single piece*) Gerät *nt*

apparel /ə'pærəl/ *n* Kleidung *f*

apparent /ə'pærənt/ *a* offenbar; (*seeming*) scheinbar. **~ly** *adv* offenbar, anscheinend

apparition /æpə'rɪʃn/ *n* Erscheinung *f*

appeal /ə'pi:l/ *n* Appell *m*, Aufruf *m*; (*request*) Bitte *f*; (*attraction*)

Reiz m; (Jur) Berufung f □ vi appellieren (to an + acc); (ask) bitten (for um); (be attractive) zusagen (to dat); (Jur) Berufung einlegen. ~ing a ansprechend

appear /ə'pɪə(r)/ vi erscheinen; (seem) scheinen; (Theat) auftreten. ~ance n Erscheinen nt; (look) Aussehen nt; to all ~ances allem Anschein nach

appease /ə'pi:z/ vt beschwichtigen

append /ə'pend/ vt nachtragen; setzen ⟨signature⟩ (to unter + acc). ~age /-ɪdʒ/ n Anhängsel nt

appendicitis /əpendɪ'saɪtɪs/ n Blinddarmentzündung f

appendix /ə'pendɪks/ n (pl -ices /-ɪsi:z/) (of book) Anhang m □ (pl -es) (Anat) Blinddarm m

appertain /æpə'teɪn/ vi ~ to betreffen

appetite /'æpɪtaɪt/ n Appetit m

appetizing /'æpɪtaɪzɪŋ/ a appetitlich

applaud /ə'plɔ:d/ vt/i Beifall klatschen (+ dat). ~se n Beifall m

apple /'æpl/ n Apfel m

appliance /ə'plaɪəns/ n Gerät nt

applicable /'æplɪkəbl/ a anwendbar (to auf + acc); (on form) nicht ~ nicht zutreffend

applicant /'æplɪkənt/ n Bewerber(in) m(f)

application /æplɪ'keɪʃn/ n Anwendung f; (request) Antrag m; (for job) Bewerbung f; (diligence) Fleiß m

applied /ə'plaɪd/ a angewandt

apply /ə'plaɪ/ vt (pt/pp -ied) auftragen ⟨paint⟩; anwenden ⟨force, rule⟩ □ vi zutreffen (to auf + acc); ~ for beantragen; sich bewerben um ⟨job⟩

appoint /ə'pɔɪnt/ vt ernennen; (fix) festlegen; well ~ed gut ausgestattet. ~ment n Ernennung f; (meeting) Verabredung f; (at doctor's, hairdresser's) Termin m; (job) Posten m; make an ~ment sich anmelden

apposite /'æpəzɪt/ a treffend

appraise /ə'preɪz/ vt abschätzen

appreciable /ə'pri:ʃəbl/ a merklich; (considerable) beträchtlich

appreciat|e /ə'pri:ʃɪeɪt/ vt zu schätzen wissen; (be grateful for) dankbar sein für; (enjoy) schätzen; (understand) verstehen □ vi (increase in value) im Wert steigen. ~ion /-'eɪʃn/ n (gratitude) Dankbarkeit f; in ~ion als Dank (of für). ~ive /-ətɪv/ a dankbar

apprehend /æprɪ'hend/ vt festnehmen

apprehens|ion /æprɪ'henʃn/ n Festnahme f; (fear) Angst f. ~ive /-sɪv/ a ängstlich

apprentice /ə'prentɪs/ n Lehrling m. ~ship n Lehre f

approach /ə'prəʊtʃ/ n Näherkommen nt; (of time) Nahen nt; (access) Zugang m; (road) Zufahrt f □ vi sich nähern; ⟨time:⟩ nahen □ vt sich nähern (+ dat); (with request) herantreten an (+ acc); (set about) sich heranmachen an (+ acc). ~able /-əbl/ a zugänglich

approbation /æprə'beɪʃn/ n Billigung f

appropriate¹ /ə'prəʊprɪət/ a angebracht, angemessen

appropriate² /ə'prəʊprɪeɪt/ vt sich (dat) aneignen

approval /ə'pru:vl/ n Billigung f; on ~ zur Ansicht

approv|e /ə'pru:v/ vt billigen □ vi ~e of sth/s.o. mit etw/jdm einverstanden sein. ~ing a, -ly adv anerkennend

approximate¹ /ə'prɒksɪmeɪt/ vi ~ to nahekommen (+ dat)

approximate² /ə'prɒksɪmət/ a ungefähr. ~ly adv ungefähr, etwa

approximation /əprɒksɪ'meɪʃn/ n Schätzung f

apricot /'eɪprɪkɒt/ n Aprikose f

April /'eɪprəl/ n April m; make an ~ fool of s.o. im April schicken

apron /'eɪprən/ n Schürze f

apropos /'æprəpəʊ/ adv ~ [of] betreffs (+ gen)

apt /æpt/ *a*, **-ly** *adv* passend; ⟨*pupil*⟩ begabt; **be ~ to do sth** dazu neigen, etw zu tun

aptitude /'æptɪtjuːd/ *n* Begabung *f*

aqualung /'ækwəlʌŋ/ *n* Tauchgerät *nt*

aquarium /ə'kweərɪəm/ *n* Aquarium *nt*

Aquarius /ə'kweərɪəs/ *n* (*Astr*) Wassermann *m*

aquatic /ə'kwætɪk/ *a* Wasser-

Arab /'ærəb/ *a* arabisch ☐ *n* Araber(in) *m(f)*. **~ian** /ə'reɪbɪən/ *a* arabisch

Arabic /'ærəbɪk/ *a* arabisch

arable /'ærəbl/ *a* **~ land** Ackerland *nt*

arbitrary /'ɑːbɪtrərɪ/ *a*, **-ily** *adv* willkürlich

arbitrat|e /'ɑːbɪtreɪt/ *vi* schlichten. **~ion** /-'treɪʃn/ *n* Schlichtung *f*

arc /ɑːk/ *n* Bogen *m*

arcade /ɑː'keɪd/ *n* Laubengang *m*; (*shops*) Einkaufspassage *f*

arch /ɑːtʃ/ *n* Bogen *m*; (*of foot*) Gewölbe *nt* ☐ *vt* **~ its back** ⟨*cat:*⟩ einen Buckel machen

archaeological /ɑːkɪə'lɒdʒɪkl/ *a* archäologisch

archaeolog|ist /ɑːkɪ'ɒlədʒɪst/ *n* Archäologe *m*/-login *f*. **~y** *n* Archäologie *f*

archaic /ɑː'keɪɪk/ *a* veraltet

arch'bishop /ɑːtʃ-/ *n* Erzbischof *m*

arch-'enemy *n* Erzfeind *m*

archer /'ɑːtʃə(r)/ *n* Bogenschütze *m*. **~y** *n* Bogenschießen *nt*

architect /'ɑːkɪtekt/ *n* Architekt(in) *m(f)*. **~ural** /ɑːkɪ'tektʃərəl/ *a*, **-ly** *adv* architektonisch

architecture /'ɑːkɪtektʃə(r)/ *n* Architektur *f*

archives /'ɑːkaɪvz/ *npl* Archiv *nt*

archway /'ɑːtʃweɪ/ *n* Torbogen *m*

Arctic /'ɑːktɪk/ *a* arktisch ☐ *n* **the ~** die Arktis

ardent /'ɑːdənt/ *a*, **-ly** *adv* leidenschaftlich

ardour /'ɑːdə(r)/ *n* Leidenschaft *f*

arduous /'ɑːdjʊəs/ *a* mühsam

are /ɑː(r)/ *see* **be**

area /'eərɪə/ *n* (*surface*) Fläche *f*; (*Geom*) Flächeninhalt *m*; (*region*) Gegend *f*; (*fig*) Gebiet *nt*. **~ code** *n* (*Amer*) Vorwahlnummer *f*

arena /ə'riːnə/ *n* Arena *f*

aren't /ɑːnt/ = **are not**. *See* **be**

Argentina /ɑːdʒən'tiːnə/ *n* Argentinien *nt*

Argentin|e /'ɑːdʒəntaɪn/, **~ian** /-'tɪnɪən/ *a* argentinisch

argue /'ɑːgjuː/ *vi* streiten (**about** über + *acc*); (*two people:*) sich streiten; (*debate*) diskutieren; **don't ~!** keine Widerrede! ☐ *vt* (*debate*) diskutieren; (*reason*) **~ that** argumentieren, daß

argument /'ɑːgjʊmənt/ *n* Streit *m*, Auseinandersetzung *f*; (*reasoning*) Argument *nt*; **have an ~** sich streiten. **~ative** /-'mentətɪv/ *a* streitlustig

aria /'ɑːrɪə/ *n* Arie *f*

arid /'ærɪd/ *a* dürr

Aries /'eəriːz/ *n* (*Astr*) Widder *m*

arise /ə'raɪz/ *vi* (*pt* **arose**, *pp* **arisen**) sich ergeben (**from** aus)

aristocracy /ærɪ'stɒkrəsɪ/ *n* Aristokratie *f*

aristocrat /'ærɪstəkræt/ *n* Aristokrat(in) *m(f)*. **~ic** /-'krætɪk/ *a* aristokratisch

arithmetic /ə'rɪθmətɪk/ *n* Rechnen *nt*

ark /ɑːk/ *n* **Noah's A~** die Arche Noah

arm /ɑːm/ *n* Arm *m*; (*of chair*) Armlehne *f*; **~s** *pl* (*weapons*) Waffen *pl*; (*Heraldry*) Wappen *nt*; **up in ~s** (*fam*) empört ☐ *vt* bewaffnen

armament /'ɑːməmənt/ *n* Bewaffnung *f*; **~s** *pl* Waffen *pl*

'armchair *n* Sessel *m*

armed /ɑːmd/ *a* bewaffnet; **~ forces** Streitkräfte *pl*

armistice /'ɑːmɪstɪs/ *n* Waffenstillstand *m*

armour /'ɑːmə(r)/ *n* Rüstung *f*. **~ed** *a* Panzer-

'armpit *n* Achselhöhle *f*

army /ˈɑːmɪ/ n Heer nt; (specific) Armee f; **join the** ~ zum Militär gehen

aroma /əˈrəʊmə/ n Aroma nt, Duft m. ~**tic** /ærəˈmætɪk/ a aromatisch

arose /əˈrəʊz/ see **arise**

around /əˈraʊnd/ adv [all] ~ rings herum; **he's not** ~ er ist nicht da; **look/turn** ~ sich umsehen/umdrehen; **travel** ~ herumreisen □prep um (+ acc) ... herum; (approximately) gegen

arouse /əˈraʊz/ vt aufwecken; (excite) erregen

arrange /əˈreɪndʒ/ vt arrangieren; (furniture, books); (settle) abmachen; **I have** ~**d to go there** ich habe abgemacht, daß ich dahingehe. ~**ment** n Anordnung f; (agreement) Vereinbarung f; (of flowers) Gesteck nt; **make** ~**ments** Vorkehrungen treffen

arrears /əˈrɪəz/ npl Rückstände pl; **in** ~ im Rückstand

arrest /əˈrest/ n Verhaftung f; **under** ~ verhaftet □vt verhaften

arrival /əˈraɪvl/ n Ankunft f; **new** ~**s** pl Neuankömmlinge pl

arrive /əˈraɪv/ vi ankommen; ~ **at** (fig) gelangen zu

arrogan|ce /ˈærəgəns/ n Arroganz f. ~**t** a, **-ly** adv arrogant

arrow /ˈærəʊ/ n Pfeil m

arse /ɑːs/ n (vulg) Arsch m

arsenic /ˈɑːsənɪk/ n Arsen nt

arson /ˈɑːsn/ n Brandstiftung f. ~**ist** /-sənɪst/ n Brandstifter m

art /ɑːt/ n Kunst f; **work of** ~ Kunstwerk nt; ~**s and crafts** pl Kunstgewerbe nt; **A** ~**s** pl (Univ) Geisteswissenschaften pl

artery /ˈɑːtərɪ/ n Schlagader f, Arterie f

artful /ˈɑːtfl/ a gerissen

'art gallery n Kunstgalerie f

arthritis /ɑːˈθraɪtɪs/ n Arthritis f

artichoke /ˈɑːtɪtʃəʊk/ n Artischocke f

article /ˈɑːtɪkl/ n Artikel m; (object) Gegenstand m; ~ **of clothing** Kleidungsstück nt

articulate¹ /ɑːˈtɪkjʊlət/ a deutlich; **be** ~ sich gut ausdrücken können

articulate² /ɑːˈtɪkjʊleɪt/ vt aussprechen. ~**d lorry** n Sattelzug m

artifice /ˈɑːtɪfɪs/ n Arglist f

artificial /ɑːtɪˈfɪʃl/ a, **-ly** adv künstlich

artillery /ɑːˈtɪlərɪ/ n Artillerie f

artist /ˈɑːtɪst/ n Künstler(in) m(f)

artiste /ɑːˈtiːst/ n (Theat) Artist(in) m(f)

artistic /ɑːˈtɪstɪk/ a, **-ally** adv künstlerisch

artless /ˈɑːtlɪs/ a unschuldig

as /æz/ conj (because) da; (when) als; (while) während □prep als; **as a child/foreigner** als Kind/Ausländer □adv as well auch; **as soon as** sobald; **as much as** soviel wie; **as quick as** so schnell wie du; **as you know** wie Sie wissen; **as far as I'm concerned** was mich betrifft

asbestos /æzˈbestəs/ n Asbest m

ascend /əˈsend/ vi [auf]steigen □vt besteigen ⟨throne⟩

Ascension /əˈsenʃn/ n (Relig) [Christi] Himmelfahrt f

ascent /əˈsent/ n Aufstieg m

ascertain /æsəˈteɪn/ vt ermitteln

ascribe /əˈskraɪb/ vt zuschreiben (to dat)

ash¹ /æʃ/ n (tree) Esche f

ash² n Asche f

ashamed /əˈʃeɪmd/ a beschämt; **be** ~ sich schämen (of über + acc)

ashore /əˈʃɔː(r)/ adv an Land

ash: ~**tray** n Aschenbecher m. **A** ~ **'Wednesday** n Aschermittwoch m

Asia /ˈeɪʃə/ n Asien nt. ~**n** a asiatisch □n Asiat(in) m(f). ~**tic** /eɪʃɪˈætɪk/ a asiatisch

aside /əˈsaɪd/ adv beiseite; ~ **from** (Amer) außer (+ dat)

ask /ɑːsk/ vt/i fragen; stellen ⟨question⟩; (invite) einladen; ~ **for** bitten um; verlangen ⟨s.o.⟩; ~ **after** sich erkundigen nach; ~ **s.o. in** jdn hereinbitten; ~ **s.o. to do sth** jdn bitten, etw zu tun

askance /əˈskɑːns/ adv look ~ **at** schief ansehen

askew /əˈskjuː/ a & adv schief

asleep /əˈsliːp/ a **be** ~ schlafen; **fall** ~ einschlafen

asparagus /əˈspærəgəs/ n Spargel m

aspect /ˈæspekt/ n Aspekt m

aspersions /əˈspɜːʃnz/ npl **cast** ~ **on** schlechtmachen

asphalt /ˈæsfælt/ n Asphalt m

asphyxia /æsˈfɪksɪə/ n Erstickung f. ~ **te** /æˈsfɪksɪeɪt/ vt/i ersticken. ~**tion** /-ˈeɪʃn/ n Erstickung f

aspirations /æspəˈreɪʃnz/ npl Streben nt

aspire /əˈspaɪə(r)/ vi ~ **to** streben nach

ass /æs/ n Esel m

assail /əˈseɪl/ vt bestürmen. ~**ant** n Angreifer(in) m(f)

assassin /əˈsæsɪn/ n Mörder(in) m(f). ~**ate** vt ermorden. ~**ation** /-ˈeɪʃn/ n [politischer] Mord m

assault /əˈsɔːlt/ n (Mil) Angriff m; (Jur) Körperverletzung f □vt [tätlich] angreifen

assemble /əˈsembl/ vi sich versammeln □vt versammeln; (Techn) montieren

assembly /əˈsemblɪ/ n Versammlung f; (Sch) Andacht f; ~ **line** n Fließband nt

assent /əˈsent/ n Zustimmung f □vi zustimmen (**to** dat)

assert /əˈsɜːt/ vt behaupten; ~ **oneself** sich durchsetzen. ~**ion** /-ˈɜːʃn/ n Behauptung f. ~**ive** /-tɪv/ a **be** ~**ive** sich durchsetzen können

assess /əˈses/ vt bewerten; (fig & for tax purposes) einschätzen;

schätzen ⟨value⟩. ~**ment** n Einschätzung f; (of tax) Steuerbescheid m

asset /ˈæset/ n Vorteil m; ~**s** pl (money) Vermögen nt; (Comm) Aktiva pl

assiduous /əˈsɪdjʊəs/ a, **-ly** adv fleißig

assign /əˈsaɪn/ vt zuweisen (**to** dat). ~**ment** n (task) Aufgabe f

assimilate /əˈsɪmɪleɪt/ vt aufnehmen; (integrate) assimilieren

assist /əˈsɪst/ vt/i helfen (+ dat). ~**ance** n Hilfe f. ~**ant** a Hilfs- □n Assistent(in) m(f); (in shop) Verkäufer(in) m(f)

associate[1] /əˈsəʊʃɪeɪt/ vt verbinden; (Psych) assoziieren □vi ~ **with** verkehren mit. ~**ion** /-ˈeɪʃn/ n Verband m. **A~ion football** n Fußball m

associate[2] /əˈsəʊʃɪət/ a assoziiert □n Kollege m/-gin f

assort|**ed** /əˈsɔːtɪd/ a gemischt. ~**ment** n Mischung f

assum|**e** /əˈsjuːm/ vt annehmen; übernehmen ⟨office⟩; ~**ing that** angenommen, daß

assumption /əˈsʌmpʃn/ n Annahme f; **on the** ~ in der Annahme (**that** daß)

assurance /əˈʃʊərəns/ n Versicherung f; (confidence) Selbstsicherheit f

assure /əˈʃʊə(r)/ vt versichern (s.o. jdm); **I** ~ **you** [**of that**] das versichere ich Ihnen. ~**d** a sicher

asterisk /ˈæstərɪsk/ n Sternchen nt

astern /əˈstɜːn/ adv achtern

asthma /ˈæsmə/ n Asthma nt. ~**tic** /-ˈmætɪk/ a asthmatisch

astonish /əˈstɒnɪʃ/ vt erstaunen. ~**ing** a erstaunlich. ~**ment** n Erstaunen nt

astound /əˈstaʊnd/ vt in Erstaunen setzen

astray /əˈstreɪ/ adv **go** ~ verlorengehen; ⟨person:⟩ sich verlaufen; (fig) vom rechten Weg abkommen; **lead** ~ verleiten

astride /ə'straɪd/ *adv* rittlings □*prep* rittlings auf (+ *dat*/*acc*)

astringent /ə'strɪndʒənt/ *a* adstringierend; (*fig*) beißend

astrolog|er /ə'strɒlədʒə(r)/ *n* Astrologe *m*/-gin *f*. ~ **y** *n* Astrologie *f*

astronaut /'æstrənɔ:t/ *n* Astronaut(in) *m(f)*

astronom|er /ə'strɒnəmə(r)/ *n* Astronom *m*. ~**ical** /æstrə'nɒmɪkl/ *a* astronomisch. ~**y** *n* Astronomie *f*

astute /ə'stju:t/ *a* scharfsinnig. ~**ness** *n* Scharfsinn *m*

asylum /ə'saɪləm/ *n* Asyl *nt*; [**lunatic**] ~ Irrenanstalt *f*

at /ət, *betont* æt/ *prep* an (+ *dat*/ *acc*); (*with house*) in; (*price*) zu; (*speed*) mit; **at the station** am Bahnhof; **at the beginning**/**end** am Anfang/Ende; **at home** zu Hause; **at John's** bei John; **at work**/**the hairdresser's** bei der Arbeit/beim Friseur; **at school**/ **the office** in der Schule/im Büro; **at a party**/**wedding** auf einer Party/Hochzeit; **at one o'clock** um ein Uhr; **at Christmas**/**Easter** zu Weihnachten/ Ostern; **at the age of** im Alter von; **not at all** gar nicht; **at times** manchmal; **two at a time** zwei auf einmal; **good**/**bad at languages** gut/schlecht in Sprachen
ate /et/ *see* **eat**

atheist /'eɪθɪɪst/ *n* Atheist(in) *m(f)*

athlet|e /'æθli:t/ *n* Athlet(in) *m(f)*. ~**ic** /-'letɪk/ *a* sportlich. ~**ics** /-'letɪks/ *n* Leichtathletik *f*

Atlantic /ət'læntɪk/ *a* & *n* the ~ **[Ocean]** der Atlantik

atlas /'ætləs/ *n* Atlas *m*

atmospher|e /'ætməsfɪə(r)/ *n* Atmosphäre *f*. ~**ic** /-'ferɪk/ *a* atmosphärisch

atom /'ætəm/ *n* Atom *nt*. ~ **bomb** *n* Atombombe *f*

atomic /ə'tɒmɪk/ *a* Atom-

atone /ə'təʊn/ *vi* büßen (**for** für). ~**ment** *n* Buße *f*

atrocious /ə'trəʊʃəs/ *a* abscheulich

atrocity /ə'trɒsɪtɪ/ *n* Greueltat *f*

attach /ə'tætʃ/ *vt* befestigen (**to** an + *dat*); beimessen ⟨*importance*⟩ (**to** *dat*); **be** ~ **ed to** (*fig*) hängen an (+ *dat*)

attaché /ə'tæʃeɪ/ *n* Attaché *m*. ~ **case** *n* Aktenkoffer *m*

attachment /ə'tætʃmənt/ *n* Bindung *f*; (*tool*) Zubehörteil *nt*; (*additional*) Zusatzgerät *nt*

attack /ə'tæk/ *n* Angriff *m*; (*Med*) Anfall *m* □*vt*/*i* angreifen. ~**er** *n* Angreifer *m*

attain /ə'teɪn/ *vt* erreichen; (*get*) erlangen. ~**able** /-əbl/ *a* erreichbar

attempt /ə'tempt/ *n* Versuch *m*. □*vt* versuchen

attend /ə'tend/ *vt* anwesend sein bei; (*go regularly to*) besuchen; (*take part in*) teilnehmen an (+ *dat*); (*accompany*) begleiten; ⟨*doctor:*⟩ behandeln □*vi* anwesend sein; (*pay attention*) aufpassen; ~ **to** sich kümmern um; (*in shop*) bedienen. ~**ance** *n* Anwesenheit *f*; (*number*) Besucherzahl *f*. ~**ant** *n* Wärter(in) *m(f)*; (*in car park*) Wächter *m*

attention /ə'tenʃn/ *n* Aufmerksamkeit *f*; ~! (*Mil*) stillgestanden! **pay** ~ aufpassen; **pay** ~ **to** beachten, achten auf (+ *acc*); **need** ~ reparaturbedürftig sein; **for the** ~ **of** zu Händen von

attentive /ə'tentɪv/ *a*, -**ly** *adv* aufmerksam

attest /ə'test/ *vt*/*i* ~ [**to**] bezeugen

attic /'ætɪk/ *n* Dachboden *m*

attire /ə'taɪə(r)/ *n* Kleidung *f* □*vt* kleiden

attitude /'ætɪtju:d/ *n* Haltung *f*

attorney /ə'tɜ:nɪ/ *n* (*Amer: lawyer*) Rechtsanwalt *m*; **power of** ~ Vollmacht *f*

attract /ə'trækt/ *vt* anziehen; erregen ⟨*attention*⟩; ~ **s.o.'s attention** jds Aufmerksamkeit auf sich ⟨*acc*⟩ lenken. ~**ion** /-ækʃn/ *n* Anziehungskraft *f*; ⟨*charm*⟩ Reiz *m*; ⟨*thing*⟩ Attraktion *f*. ~**ive** /-tɪv/ *a*, **-ly** *adv* attraktiv

attribute[1] /'ætrɪbju:t/ *n* Attribut *nt*

attribute[2] /ə'trɪbju:t/ *vt* zuschreiben (**to** *dat*). ~**ive** /-tɪv/ *a*, **-ly** *adv* attributiv

attrition /ə'trɪʃn/ *n* **war of** ~ Zermürbungskrieg *m*

aubergine /'əʊbəʒiːn/ *n* Aubergine *f*

auburn /'ɔːbən/ *a* kastanienbraun

auction /'ɔːkʃn/ *n* Auktion *f*, Versteigerung *f* □ *vt* versteigern. ~**eer** /-ʃə'nɪə(r)/ *n* Auktionator *m*

audaci|ous /ɔː'deɪʃəs/ *a*, **-ly** *adv* verwegen. ~**ty** /-'dæsətɪ/ *n* Verwegenheit *f*; ⟨*impudence*⟩ Dreistigkeit *f*

audible /'ɔːdəbl/ *a*, **-bly** *adv* hörbar

audience /'ɔːdɪəns/ *n* Publikum *nt*; ⟨*Theat, TV*⟩ Zuschauer *pl*; ⟨*Radio*⟩ Zuhörer *pl*; ⟨*meeting*⟩ Audienz *f*

audio /'ɔːdɪəʊ/: ~ **typist** *n* Phonotypistin *f*. ~'**visual** *a* audiovisuell

audit /'ɔːdɪt/ *n* Bücherrevision *f* □ *vt* ⟨*Comm*⟩ prüfen

audition /ɔː'dɪʃn/ *n* ⟨*Theat*⟩ Vorsprechen *nt*; ⟨*Mus*⟩ Vorspielen *nt*; ⟨*for singer*⟩ Vorsingen *nt* □ *vi* vorsprechen; vorspielen; vorsingen

auditor /'ɔːdɪtə(r)/ *n* Buchprüfer *m*

auditorium /ɔːdɪ'tɔːrɪəm/ *n* Zuschauerraum *m*

augment /ɔːg'ment/ *vt* vergrößern

augur /'ɔːgə(r)/ *vi* ~ **well/ill** etwas/nichts Gutes verheißen

august /ɔː'gʌst/ *a* hoheitsvoll

August /'ɔːgəst/ *n* August *m*

aunt /ɑːnt/ *n* Tante *f*

au pair /əʊ'peə(r)/ *n* ~ [**girl**] Au-pair-Mädchen *nt*

aura /'ɔːrə/ *n* Fluidum *nt*

auspices /'ɔːspɪsɪz/ *npl* ⟨*protection*⟩ Schirmherrschaft *f*

auspicious /ɔː'spɪʃəs/ *a* günstig; ⟨*occasion*⟩ freudig

auster|e /ɒ'stɪə(r)/ *a* streng; ⟨*simple*⟩ nüchtern. ~**ity** /-terɪtɪ/ *n* Strenge *f*; ⟨*hardship*⟩ Entbehrung *f*

Australia /ɒ'streɪlɪə/ *n* Australien *nt*. ~**n** *a* australisch □*n* Australier(in) *m(f)*

Austria /'ɒstrɪə/ *n* Österreich *nt*. ~**n** *a* österreichisch □*n* Österreicher(in) *m(f)*

authentic /ɔː'θentɪk/ *a* echt, authentisch. ~**ate** *vt* beglaubigen. ~**ity** /-'tɪsətɪ/ *n* Echtheit *f*

author /'ɔːθə(r)/ *n* Schriftsteller *m*, Autor *m*; ⟨*of document*⟩ Verfasser *m*

authoritarian /ɔːθɒrɪ'teərɪən/ *a* autoritär

authoritative /ɔː'θɒrɪtətɪv/ *a* maßgebend; **be** ~ Autorität haben

authority /ɔː'θɒrətɪ/ *n* Autorität *f*; ⟨*public*⟩ Behörde *f*; **in** ~ verantwortlich

authorization /ɔːθərar'zeɪʃn/ *n* Ermächtigung *f*

authorize /'ɔːθəraɪz/ *vt* ermächtigen ⟨*s.o.*⟩; genehmigen ⟨*sth*⟩

autobi'ography /ɔːtə-/ *n* Autobiographie *f*

autocratic /ɔːtə'krætɪk/ *a* autokratisch

autograph /'ɔːtə-/ *n* Autogramm *nt*

automatic /ɔːtə'mætɪk/ *a*, **-ally** *adv* automatisch □*n* ⟨*car*⟩ Fahrzeug *nt* mit Automatikgetriebe; ⟨*washing machine*⟩ Waschautomat *m*

automation /ɔːtə'meɪʃn/ *n* Automation *f*

automobile /'ɔːtəməbiːl/ *n* Auto *nt*

autonom|ous /ɔː'tɒnəməs/ *a* autonom. ~**y** *n* Autonomie *f*

autopsy /'ɔːtɒpsɪ/ *n* Autopsie *f*

autumn /'ɔːtəm/ *n* Herbst *m*. ~**al** /-'tʌmnl/ *a* herbstlich

auxiliary /ɔːgˈzɪlɪərɪ/ a Hilfs- □ n Helfer(in) m(f), Hilfskraft f

avail /əˈveɪl/ n to no ~ vergeblich □ vi ~ oneself of Gebrauch machen von

available /əˈveɪləbl/ a verfügbar; (obtainable) erhältlich

avalanche /ˈævəlɑːnʃ/ n Lawine f

avari|ce /ˈævərɪs/ n Habsucht f. ~ious /-ˈrɪʃəs/ a habgierig, habsüchtig

avenge /əˈvendʒ/ vt rächen

avenue /ˈævənjuː/ n Allee f

average /ˈævərɪdʒ/ a Durchschnitts-, durchschnittlich □ n Durchschnitt m; on ~ im Durchschnitt, durchschnittlich □ vt durchschnittlich schaffen □ vi ~ out at im Durchschnitt ergeben

avers|e /əˈvɜːs/ a not be ~e to etw (dat) nicht abgeneigt sein. ~ion /-ɜːʃn/ n Abneigung f (to gegen)

avert /əˈvɜːt/ vt abwenden

aviary /ˈeɪvɪərɪ/ n Vogelhaus nt

aviation /eɪvɪˈeɪʃn/ n Luftfahrt f

avid /ˈævɪd/ a gierig (for nach); (keen) eifrig

avocado /ævəˈkɑːdəʊ/ n Avocado f

avoid /əˈvɔɪd/ vt vermeiden; ~ s.o. jdm aus dem Weg gehen. ~able /-əbl/ a vermeidbar. ~ance n Vermeidung f

await /əˈweɪt/ vt warten auf (+ acc)

awake /əˈweɪk/ a wach; wide ~ hellwach □ vi (pt awoke, pp awoken) erwachen

awaken /əˈweɪkn/ vt wecken □ vi erwachen. ~ing n Erwachen nt

award /əˈwɔːd/ n Auszeichnung f; (prize) Preis m □ vt zuerkennen (to s.o. dat); verleihen ⟨prize⟩

aware /əˈweə(r)/ a become ~ gewahr werden (of gen); be ~ that wissen, daß. ~ness n Bewußtsein nt

awash /əˈwɒʃ/ a be ~ unter Wasser stehen

away /əˈweɪ/ adv weg, fort; (absent) abwesend; be ~ nicht da

sein; far ~ weit weg; four kilometres ~ vier Kilometer entfernt; play ~ (Sport) auswärts spielen; go/stay ~ weggehen/ -bleiben. ~ game n Auswärtsspiel nt

awe /ɔː/ n Ehrfurcht f

awful /ˈɔːfl/ a, -ly adv furchtbar

awhile /əˈwaɪl/ adv eine Weile

awkward /ˈɔːkwəd/ a schwierig; (clumsy) ungeschickt; (embarrassing) peinlich; (inconvenient) ungünstig. ~ly adv ungeschickt; (embarrassedly) verlegen

awning /ˈɔːnɪŋ/ n Markise f

awoke(n) /əˈwəʊk(ən)/ see awake

awry /əˈraɪ/ adv schief

axe /æks/ n Axt f □ vt (pres p axing) streichen; (dismiss) entlassen

axis /ˈæksɪs/ n (pl axes /-siːz/) Achse f

axle /ˈæksl/ n (Techn) Achse f

ay[e] /aɪ/ adv ja □ n Jastimme f

B

B /biː/ n (Mus) H nt

BA abbr of Bachelor of Arts

babble /ˈbæbl/ vi plappern; ⟨stream⟩ plätschern

baboon /bəˈbuːn/ n Pavian m

baby /ˈbeɪbɪ/ n Baby nt; (Amer, fam) Schätzchen nt

baby: ~ carriage n (Amer) Kinderwagen m. ~ish a kindisch. ~-minder n Tagesmutter f. ~-sit vi babysitten. ~-sitter n Babysitter m

bachelor /ˈbætʃələ(r)/ n Junggeselle m; B~ of Arts/Science Bakkalaureus Artium/Scientium

bacillus /bəˈsɪləs/ n (pl -lli) Bazillus m

back /bæk/ n Rücken m; (reverse) Rückseite f; (of chair) Rückenlehne f; (Sport) Verteidiger m; at/ (Auto) in the ~ hinten; on the ~ auf der Rückseite; ~ to front verkehrt; at the ~ of beyond am Ende der Welt □a Hinter- zurück; ~ here/there hier/da hinten; ~ at home zu Hause; go/ pay ~ zurückgehen/-zahlen □vt (support) unterstützen; (with money) finanzieren; (Auto) zurücksetzen; (Betting) [Geld] setzen auf(+ acc); (cover the back of) mit einer Verstärkung versehen □vi (Auto) zurücksetzen. ~ down vi klein beigeben. ~ in vi rückwärts hineinfahren. ~ out vi rückwärts hinaus-/herausfahren; (fig) aussteigen (of aus). ~ up vt unterstützen; (confirm) bestätigen □vi (Auto) zurücksetzen

back: ~ache n Rückenschmerzen pl. ~biting n gehässiges Gerede nt. ~bone n Rückgrat nt. ~chat n Widerrede f. ~comb vt toupieren. ~date vt rückdatieren; ~dated to rückwirkend von. ~door n Hintertür f

backer /'bækə(r)/ n Geldgeber m

back: ~fire n (Auto) fehlzünden; (fig) fehlschlagen. ~ground n Hintergrund m; family ~ground Familienverhältnisse pl. ~hand n (Sport) Rückhand f. ~handed a (compliment) zweifelhaft. ~hander n (Sport) Rückhandschlag m; (fam: bribe) Schmiergeld nt

backing /'bækɪŋ/ n (support) Unterstützung f; (material) Verstärkung f

back: ~lash n (fig) Gegenschlag m. ~log n Rückstand m (of an + dat). ~ 'seat n Rücksitz m. ~side n (fam) Hintern m. ~stage adv hinter die Bühne. ~stroke n Rückenschwimmen nt. ~-up n Unterstützung f; (Amer: traffic jam) Stau m

backward /'bækwəd/ a zurückgeblieben; (country) rückständig □adv rückwärts. ~s rückwärts; ~s and forwards hin und her

back: ~water n (fig) unberührtes Fleckchen n. ~ 'yard n Hinterhof m; not in my ~ yard (fam) nicht vor meiner Haustür

bacon /'beɪkn/ n [Schinken]speck m

bacteria /bæk'tɪərɪə/ npl Bakterien pl

bad /bæd/ a (worse, worst) schlecht; (serious) schwer, schlimm; (naughty) unartig. ~ language gemeine Ausdrucksweise f; feel ~ sich schlecht fühlen; (feel guilty) ein schlechtes Gewissen haben; go ~ schlecht werden

bade /bæd/ see bid²

badge /bædʒ/ n Abzeichen nt

badger /'bædʒə(r)/ n Dachs m □vt plagen

badly /'bædlɪ/ adv schlecht; (seriously) schwer; ~ off schlecht gestellt; ~ behaved unerzogen; want ~ sich (dat) sehnsüchtig wünschen; need ~ dringend brauchen

bad-mannered a mit schlechten Manieren

badminton /'bædmɪntən/ n Federball m

bad-tempered a schlecht gelaunt

baffle /'bæfl/ vt verblüffen

bag /bæg/ n Tasche f; (of paper) Tüte f; (pouch) Beutel m; ~s of (fam) jede Menge □vt (fam: reserve) in Beschlag nehmen

baggage /'bægɪdʒ/ n [Reise]gepäck nt

baggy /'bægɪ/ a (clothes) ausgebeult

bagpipes npl Dudelsack m

bail /beɪl/ n Kaution f; on ~ gegen Kaution □vt □ s.o. out jdn gegen Kaution freibekommen; (fig) jdm aus der Patsche helfen. ~ out vt (Naut) ausschöpfen □vi (Aviat) abspringen

bailiff /'beɪlɪf/ n Gerichtsvollzieher m; (of estate) Gutsverwalter m

bait /beɪt/ n Köder m □vt mit einem Köder versehen; (fig: torment) reizen

bake /beɪk/ vt/i backen

baker /'beɪkə(r)/ n Bäcker m; ~'s [shop] Bäckerei f. ~y n Bäckerei f

baking /'beɪkɪŋ/ n Backen m. ~-powder n Backpulver nt. ~-tin n Backform f

balance /'bæləns/ n (equilibrium) Gleichgewicht nt, Balance f; (scales) Waage f; (Comm) Saldo m; (outstanding sum) Restbetrag m; [bank] ~ Kontostand m; **in the ~** (fig) in der Schwebe □vt balancieren; (equalize) ausgleichen; (Comm) abschließen ⟨books⟩ □vi balancieren; (fig & Comm) sich ausgleichen. ~d a ausgewogen. ~-sheet n Bilanz f

balcony /'bælkənɪ/ n Balkon m

bald /bɔːld/ a (-er, -est) kahl; ⟨person⟩ kahlköpfig; **go ~** eine Glatze bekommen

balderdash /'bɔːldədæʃ/ n Unsinn m

bald|ing /'bɔːldɪŋ/ a **be ~ing** eine Glatze bekommen. ~ly adv unverblümt. ~ness n Kahlköpfigkeit f

bale /beɪl/ n Ballen m

baleful /'beɪlfl/ a, **-ly** adv böse

balk /bɔːlk/ vt vereiteln □vi ~ **at** zurückschrecken vor (+ dat)

Balkans /'bɔːlkənz/ npl Balkan m

ball[1] /bɔːl/ n Ball m; (Billiards, Croquet) Kugel f; (of yarn) Knäuel m & nt; **on the ~** (fam) auf Draht

ball[2] n (dance) Ball m

ballad /'bæləd/ n Ballade f

ballast /'bæləst/ n Ballast m

ball-'bearing n Kugellager nt

ballerina /bælə'riːnə/ n Ballerina f

ballet /'bæleɪ/ n Ballett nt. ~-dancer n Balletttänzer(in) m(f)

ballistic /bə'lɪstɪk/ a ballistisch. ~s n Ballistik f

balloon /bə'luːn/ n Luftballon m; (Aviat) Ballon m

ballot /'bælət/ n [geheime] Wahl f; (on issue) [geheime] Abstimmung f. ~-box n Wahlurne f. ~-paper n Stimmzettel m

ball: ~-point ['pen] n Kugelschreiber m. ~-room n Ballsaal m

balm /bɑːm/ n Balsam m

balmy /'bɑːmɪ/ a (-ier, -iest) a sanft; (fam: crazy) verrückt

Baltic /'bɔːltɪk/ a & n **the ~ [Sea]** die Ostsee

balustrade /bælə'streɪd/ n Balustrade f

bamboo /bæm'buː/ n Bambus m

bamboozle /bæm'buːzl/ vt (fam) übers Ohr hauen

ban /bæn/ n Verbot nt □vt (pt/pp banned) verbieten

banal /bə'nɑːl/ a banal. ~ity /-'ælətɪ/ n Banalität f

banana /bə'nɑːnə/ n Banane f

band /bænd/ n Band nt; (stripe) Streifen m; (group) Schar f; (Mus) Kapelle f □vi ~ **together** sich zusammenschließen

bandage /'bændɪdʒ/ n Verband m; (for support) Bandage f □vt verbinden; bandagieren ⟨limb⟩

b. & b. abbr of **bed and breakfast**

bandit /'bændɪt/ n Bandit m

band: ~-stand n Musikpavillon m. ~-wagon n **jump on the ~-wagon** (fig) sich einer erfolgreichen Sache anschließen

bandy[1] /'bændɪ/ vt (pt/pp -ied) wechseln ⟨words⟩

bandy[2] a (-ier, -iest) **be ~** O-Beine haben. ~-**legge**d a O-beinig

bang /bæŋ/ n (noise) Knall m; (blow) Schlag m □adv **go ~** knallen □int bums! peng! □vt knallen; (shut noisily) zuknallen; (strike) schlagen auf (+ acc); ~ **one's head** sich (dat) den Kopf stoßen (on an + acc) □vi schlagen; ⟨door:⟩ zuknallen

banger /'bæŋə(r)/ n (firework) Knallfrosch m; (fam: sausage) Wurst f; **old ~** (fam: car) Klapperkiste f

bangle /'bæŋgl/ n Armreifen m

banish /'bænɪʃ/ vt verbannen

banisters /'bænɪstəz/ npl [Treppen]geländer nt

banjo /'bændʒəʊ/ n Banjo nt

bank¹ /bæŋk/ n (of river) Ufer nt; (slope) Hang m □ vi (Aviat) in die Kurve gehen

bank² n Bank f □ vt einzahlen; ~ with ein Konto haben bei. ~ on vt sich verlassen auf (+ acc)

'bank account n Bankkonto nt

'banker /'bæŋkə(r)/ n Bankier m

bank: ~ **'holiday** n gesetzlicher Feiertag m. ~**ing** n Bankwesen nt. ~**note** n Banknote f

bankrupt /'bæŋkrʌpt/ a bankrott; go ~ bankrott machen □ n Bankrotteur m □ vt bankrott machen. ~**cy** n Bankrott m

banner /'bænə(r)/ n Banner nt; (carried by demonstrators) Transparent nt, Spruchband nt

banns /bænz/ npl (Relig) Aufgebot nt

banquet /'bæŋkwɪt/ n Bankett nt

banter /'bæntə(r)/ n Spöttelei f

bap /bæp/ n weiches Brötchen nt

baptism /'bæptɪzm/ n Taufe f

Baptist /'bæptɪst/ n Baptist(in) m(f)

baptize /bæp'taɪz/ vt taufen

bar /bɑ:(r)/ n Stange f, (of cage) [Gitter]stab m; (of gold) Barren m; (of chocolate) Tafel f; (of soap) Stück m; (long) Riegel m; (café) Bar f; (counter) Theke f; (Mus) Takt m; (fig: obstacle) Hindernis nt; parallel ~s (Sport) Barren m; be called to the ~ (Jur) als plädierender Anwalt zugelassen werden; behind ~s (fam) hinter Gittern □ vt (pt/pp barred) versperren ⟨way, door⟩; ausschließen ⟨person⟩ □ prep außer; none ohne Ausnahme

barbarian /bɑ:'beərɪən/ n Barbar m

barbar|ic /bɑ:'bærɪk/ a barbarisch. ~**ity** n Barbarei f. ~**ous** /'bɑ:bərəs/ a barbarisch

barbecue /'bɑ:bɪkju:/ n Grill m; (party) Grillfest nt □ vt [im Freien] grillen

barbed /bɑ:bd/ a ~ **wire** Stacheldraht m

barber /'bɑ:bə(r)/ n [Herren]friseur m

barbiturate /bɑ:'bɪtjʊrət/ n Barbiturat nt

'bar code n Strichcode m

bare /beə(r)/ a (-r, -st) nackt, bloß; ⟨tree⟩ kahl; ⟨empty⟩ leer; (mere) bloß □ vt entblößen; fletschen ⟨teeth⟩

bare: ~**back** adv ohne Sattel. ~**faced** a schamlos. ~**foot** adv barfuß. ~**'headed** a mit unbedecktem Kopf

barely /'beəlɪ/ adv kaum

bargain /'bɑ:gɪn/ n (agreement) Geschäft nt; (good buy) Gelegenheitskauf m; **into the** ~ noch dazu; **make a** ~ sich einigen □ vi handeln; (haggle) feilschen; ~ **for** (expect) rechnen mit

barge /bɑ:dʒ/ n Lastkahn m; (towed) Schleppkahn m □ vi ~ **in** (fam) hereinplatzen

baritone /'bærɪtəʊn/ n Bariton m

bark¹ /bɑ:k/ n (of tree) Rinde f

bark² n Bellen nt □ vi bellen

barley /'bɑ:lɪ/ n Gerste f

bar: ~**maid** n Schankmädchen nt. ~**man** n Barmann m

barmy /'bɑ:mɪ/ a (fam) verrückt

barn /bɑ:n/ n Scheune f

barometer /bə'rɒmɪtə(r)/ n Barometer nt

baron /'bærn/ n Baron m. ~**ess** n Baronin f

baroque /bə'rɒk/ a barock □ n Barock nt

barracks /'bærəks/ npl Kaserne f

barrage /'bærɑ:ʒ/ n (in river) Wehr nt; (Mil) Sperrfeuer nt; (fig) Hagel m

barrel /'bærl/ n Faß nt; (of gun) Lauf m; (of cannon) Rohr nt. ~**organ** n Drehorgel f

barren /'bærn/ a unfruchtbar; ⟨landscape⟩ öde

barricade /ˈbærɪˈkeɪd/ n Barrikade f □ vt verbarrikadieren

barrier /ˈbærɪə(r)/ n Barriere f; (across road) Schranke f; (Rail) Sperre f; (fig) Hindernis nt

barring /ˈbɑːrɪŋ/ prep ~ accidents wenn alles gutgeht

barrister /ˈbærɪstə(r)/ n [plädierender] Rechtsanwalt m

barrow /ˈbærəʊ/ n Karre f, Karren m. ~ boy n Straßenhändler m

barter /ˈbɑːtə(r)/ vt tauschen (for gegen)

base /beɪs/ n Fuß m; (fig) Basis f; (Mil) Stützpunkt m □ a gemein; ⟨metal⟩ unedel □ vt stützen (on auf + acc); be ~d on basieren auf (+ dat)

base: ~ball n Baseball m. ~less a unbegründet. ~ment n Kellergeschoß nt. ~ment flat n Kellerwohnung f

bash /bæʃ/ n Schlag m; have a ~! (fam) probier es mal! □ vt hauen; (dent) einbeulen; ~ed in verbeult

bashful /ˈbæʃfl/ a, -ly adv schüchtern

basic /ˈbeɪsɪk/ a Grund-; (fundamental) grundlegend; (essential) wesentlich; ⟨unadorned⟩ einfach; the ~s das Wesentliche. ~ally adv grundsätzlich

basil /ˈbæzl/ n Basilikum nt

basilica /bəˈzɪlɪkə/ n Basilika f

basin /ˈbeɪsn/ n Becken nt; (for washing) Waschbecken nt; (for food) Schüssel f

basis /ˈbeɪsɪs/ n (pl -ses /-siːz/) Basis f

bask /bɑːsk/ vi sich sonnen

basket /ˈbɑːskɪt/ n Korb m. ~ball n Basketball m

Basle /bɑːl/ n Basel nt

bass /beɪs/ a Baß-; ~ voice Baßstimme f □ n Baß m; (person) Bassist m

bassoon /bəˈsuːn/ n Fagott nt

bastard /ˈbɑːstəd/ n (sl) Schuft m

baste¹ /beɪst/ vt (sew) heften

baste² vt (Culin) begießen

bastion /ˈbæstɪən/ n Bastion f

bat¹ /bæt/ n Schläger m; off one's own ~ (fam) auf eigene Faust □ vt (pt/pp batted) schlagen; not ~ an eyelid (fig) nicht mit der Wimper zucken

bat² n (Zool) Fledermaus f

batch /bætʃ/ n (of people) Gruppe f; (of papers) Stoß m; (of goods) Sendung f; (of bread) Schub m

bated /ˈbeɪtɪd/ a with ~ breath mit angehaltenem Atem

bath /bɑːθ/ n (pl ~s /bɑːðz/) Bad nt; (tub) Badewanne f; ~s pl Badeanstalt f; have a ~ baden □ vt/i baden

bathe /beɪð/ n Bad nt □ vt/i baden. ~r n Badende(r) m/f

bathing /ˈbeɪðɪŋ/ n Baden nt. ~-cap n Bademütze f. ~-costume n Badeanzug m

bath: ~-mat n Badematte f. ~robe n (Amer) Bademantel m. ~room n Badezimmer nt. ~-towel n Badetuch nt

baton /ˈbætn/ n (Mus) Taktstock m; (Mil) Stab m

battalion /bəˈtælɪən/ n Bataillon nt

batten /ˈbætn/ n Latte f

batter /ˈbætə(r)/ n (Culin) flüssiger Teig m □ vt schlagen. ~ed a ⟨car⟩ verbeult; ⟨wife⟩ mißhandelt

battery /ˈbætərɪ/ n Batterie f

battle /ˈbætl/ n Schlacht f; (fig) Kampf m □ vi (fig) kämpfen (for um)

battle: ~axe n (fam) Drachen m. ~field n Schlachtfeld nt. ~ship n Schlachtschiff nt

batty /ˈbætɪ/ a (fam) verrückt

Bavaria /bəˈveərɪə/ n Bayern f. ~n a bayrisch □ n Bayer(in) m(f)

bawdy /ˈbɔːdɪ/ a (-ier, -iest) derb

bawl /bɔːl/ vt/i brüllen

bay¹ /beɪ/ n (Geog) Bucht f; (Archit) Erker m

bay² n keep at ~ fernhalten

bay³ n (horse) Braune(r) m

bay⁴ n (Bot) [echter] Lorbeer m. ~-leaf n Lorbeerblatt nt

bayonet /ˈbeɪənet/ n Bajonett nt

bay 'window n Erkerfenster nt

bazaar /bə'zɑː(r)/ n Basar m

BC abbr (before Christ) v. Chr.

be /biː/ vi (pres am, are, is, pl are; pt was, pl were; pp been) sein; (lie) liegen; (stand) stehen; (cost) kosten; **he is a teacher** er ist Lehrer; **be quiet!** sei still! **I am cold/hot** mir ist kalt/heiß; **how are you?** wie geht es Ihnen? **I am well** mir geht es gut; **there is/are** es gibt; **what do you want to be?** was willst du werden? **I have been to Vienna** ich bin in Wien gewesen; **has the postman been?** war der Briefträger schon da? **it's hot, isn't it?** es ist heiß, nicht [wahr]? **you are coming too, aren't you?** du kommst mit, nicht [wahr]? **it's yours, is it?** das gehört also Ihnen? yes he is/I am ja; (negating previous statement) doch; **three and three are six** drei und drei macht sechs □ v aux ~ reading/going lesen/ gehen; **I am coming/staying** ich komme/bleibe; **what is he doing?** was macht er? **I am being lazy** ich faulenze; **I was thinking of you** ich dachte an dich; **you were going to ...** du wolltest ...; **I am to stay** ich soll bleiben; **you are not to ...** du darfst nicht ...; **you are to do that immediately** das mußt du sofort machen □ passive werden; **be attacked/deceived** überfallen/betrogen werden

beach /biːtʃ/ n Strand m. ~wear n Strandkleidung f

beacon /'biːkn/ n Leuchtfeuer nt; (Naut, Aviat) Bake f

bead /biːd/ n Perle f

beak /biːk/ n Schnabel m

beaker /'biːkə(r)/ n Becher m

beam /biːm/ n Balken m; (of light) Strahl m □ vi strahlen. ~ing a [freude]strahlend

bean /biːn/ n Bohne f; **spill the ~s** (fam) alles ausplaudern

bear[1] /beə(r)/ n Bär m

bear[2] vt/i (pt bore, pp borne) tragen; (endure) ertragen; gebären ⟨child⟩; ~ right rechts halten. ~able /-əbl/ a erträglich

beard /bɪəd/ n Bart m. ~ed a bärtig

bearer /'beərə(r)/ n Träger m; (of news, cheque) Überbringer m; (of passport) Inhaber(in) m(f)

bearing /'beərɪŋ/ n Haltung f; (Techn) Lager nt; **have a** ~ on von Belang sein für; **get one's ~s** sich orientieren; **lose one's ~s** die Orientierung verlieren

beast /biːst/ n Tier nt; (fam: person) Biest nt

beastly /'biːstlɪ/ a (-ier, -iest) (fam) scheußlich; ⟨person⟩ gemein

beat /biːt/ n Schlag m; (of policeman) Runde f; (rhythm) Takt m □ vt/i (pt beat, pp beaten) schlagen; (thrash) verprügeln; klopfen ⟨carpet⟩; (hammer) hämmern (on an + acc); ~ a retreat (Mil) sich zurückziehen; ~ it! (fam) hau ab! it ~s me (fam) das begreife ich nicht. ~ up vt zusammenschlagen

beaten /'biːtn/ a off the ~en track abseits. ~ing n Prügel pl

beautician /bjuː'tɪʃn/ n Kosmetikerin f

beauti|ful /'bjuːtɪfl/ a, -ly adv schön. ~fy /-faɪ/ vt (pt/pp -ied) verschönern

beauty /'bjuːtɪ/ n Schönheit f. ~ parlour n Kosmetiksalon m. ~ spot n Schönheitsfleck m; (place) landschaftlich besonders reizvolle Stelle f

beaver /'biːvə(r)/ n Biber m

became /bɪ'keɪm/ see become

because /bɪ'kɒz/ conj weil □ adv ~ of wegen (+ gen)

beckon /'bekn/ vt/i ~ [to] herbeiwinken

become /bɪ'kʌm/ vt/i (pt became, pp become) werden. ~ing n sich ⟨clothes⟩ kleidsam

bed /bed/ n Bett nt; (layer) Schicht f; (of flowers) Beet nt; **in** ~ im Bett; **go to** ~ ins od zu Bett gehen; ~ **and breakfast** Zimmer mit Frühstück. ~ **clothes** npl, ~ **ding** n Bettzeug nt

bedlam /'bedləm/ n Chaos nt

bedpan n Bettpfanne f

bedraggled /bɪ'drægld/ a naß und verschmutzt

bed: ~ **ridden** a bettlägerig. ~ **room** n Schlafzimmer nt

bedside n **at his** ~ an seinem Bett. ~ **lamp** n Nachttischlampe f. ~ '**rug** n Bettvorleger m. ~ '**table** n Nachttisch m

bed: ~ '**sitter** n, ~ -'**sitting-room** n Wohnschlafzimmer nt. ~ **spread** n Tagesdecke f. ~ **time** n **at** ~ **time** vor dem Schlafengehen

bee /biː/ n Biene f

beech /biːtʃ/ n Buche f

beef /biːf/ n Rindfleisch nt. ~ **burger** n Hamburger m

bee: ~ **hive** n Bienenstock m. ~ **keeper** n Imker(in) m(f). ~ **keeping** n Bienenzucht f. ~ **line** n **make a** ~ **line for** (fam) zusteuern auf (+ acc)

been /biːn/ see **be**

beer /bɪə(r)/ n Bier nt

beet /biːt/ n (Amer: beetroot) rote Bete f; [**sugar**] ~ Zuckerrübe f

beetle /'biːtl/ n Käfer m

beetroot n rote Bete f

before /bɪ'fɔː(r)/ prep vor (+ dat/acc); **the day** ~ **yesterday** vorgestern; ~ **long** bald □adv vorher; (already) schon; **never** ~ noch nie; ~ **that** davor □conj (time) ehe, bevor. ~ **hand** adv vorher, im voraus

befriend /bɪ'frend/ vt sich anfreunden mit

beg /beg/ v (pt/pp begged) □vi betteln; ~ **(entreat)** anflehen; (ask) bitten (**for** um)

began /bɪ'gæn/ see **begin**

beggar /'begə(r)/ n Bettler(in) m(f); (fam) Kerl m

begin /bɪ'gɪn/ vt/i (pt began, pp begun, pres p beginning) anfangen, beginnen; **to** ~ **with** anfangs. ~ **ner** n Anfänger(in) m(f). ~ **ning** n Anfang m, Beginn m

begonia /bɪ'gəʊnɪə/ n Begonie f

begrudge /bɪ'grʌdʒ/ vt mißgönnen

beguile /bɪ'gaɪl/ vt betören

begun /bɪ'gʌn/ see **begin**

behalf /bɪ'hɑːf/ n **on** ~ **of** im Namen von; **on my** ~ meinetwegen

behave /bɪ'heɪv/ vi sich verhalten; ~ **oneself** sich benehmen

behaviour /bɪ'heɪvjə(r)/ n Verhalten nt; **good/bad** ~ gutes/schlechtes Benehmen nt; ~ **pattern** Verhaltensweise f

behead /bɪ'hed/ vt enthaupten

beheld /bɪ'held/ see **behold**

behind /bɪ'haɪnd/ prep hinter (+ dat/acc); **be** ~ **sth** hinter etw (dat) stecken □adv hinten; (late) im Rückstand; **a long way** ~ weit zurück; **in the car** ~ im Wagen dahinter □n (fam) Hintern m. ~ **hand** adv im Rückstand

behold /bɪ'həʊld/ vt (pt/pp beheld) (liter) sehen

beholden /bɪ'həʊldn/ a verbunden (**to** dat)

beige /beɪʒ/ a beige

being /'biːɪŋ/ n Dasein nt; **living** ~ Lebewesen nt; **come into** ~ entstehen

belated /bɪ'leɪtɪd/ a, **-ly** adv verspätet

belch /beltʃ/ vi rülpsen □vt ~ **out** ausstoßen (smoke)

belfry /'belfrɪ/ n Glockenstube f; (tower) Glockenturm m

Belgian /'beldʒən/ a belgisch □n Belgier(in) m(f)

Belgium /'beldʒəm/ n Belgien nt

belief /bɪ'liːf/ n Glaube m

believable /bɪ'liːvəbl/ a glaubhaft

believe /bɪ'liːv/ vt/i glauben (s.o. jdm; **in** an + acc). ~ **r** n (Relig) Gläubige(r) m/f

belittle /bɪ'lɪtl/ vt herabsetzen

bell /bel/ n Glocke f; (on door) Klingel f

belligerent /bɪ'lɪdʒərənt/ a kriegführend; (aggressive) streitlustig

bellow /'beləʊ/ vt/i brüllen

bellows /'beləʊz/ npl Blasebalg m

belly /'belɪ/ n Bauch m

belong /bɪ'lɒŋ/ vi gehören (to dat); (be member) angehören (to dat). ~ings npl Sachen pl

beloved /bɪ'lʌvɪd/ a geliebt □ n Geliebte(r) m/f

below /bɪ'ləʊ/ prep unter (+ dat/ acc) □ adv unten; (Naut) unter Deck

belt /belt/ n Gürtel m; (area) Zone f; (Techn) [Treib]riemen m □ vi (fam: rush) rasen □ vt (fam: hit) hauen

bemused /bɪ'mju:zd/ a verwirrt

bench /bentʃ/ n Bank f; (work-) Werkbank f; the B~ (Jur) die Richter pl

bend /bend/ n Biegung f; (in road) Kurve f; round the ~ (fam) verrückt □ v (pt/pp bent) □ vt biegen; beugen (arm, leg) □ vi sich bücken; (thing:) sich biegen; (road:) eine Biegung machen. ~ **down** vi sich bücken. ~ **over** vi sich vornüberbeugen

beneath /bɪ'ni:θ/ prep unter (+ dat/acc); ~ **him** (fig) unter seiner Würde; ~ **contempt** unter aller Würde □ adv darunter

benediction /benɪ'dɪkʃn/ n (Relig) Segen m

benefactor /'benɪfæktə(r)/ n Wohltäter(in) m(f)

beneficial /benɪ'fɪʃl/ a nützlich

beneficiary /benɪ'fɪʃərɪ/ n Begünstigte(r) m/f

benefit /'benɪfɪt/ n Vorteil m; (allowance) Unterstützung f; (insurance) Leistung f; **sickness** ~ Krankengeld nt □ v (pt/pp -fited, pres p -fiting) □ vt nützen (+ dat) □ vi profitieren (from von)

benevolen|ce /bɪ'nevələns/ n Wohlwollen nt. ~t a, -ly adv wohlwollend

benign /bɪ'naɪn/ a, -ly adv gütig; (Med) gutartig

bent /bent/ see **bend** □ a (person) gebeugt; (distorted) verbogen; (fam: dishonest) korrupt; be ~ **on doing sth** darauf erpicht sein, etw zu tun □ n Hang m, Neigung f (for zu); **artistic** ~ künstlerische Ader f

bequeath /bɪ'kwi:ð/ vt vermachen (to dat). ~**quest** /-'kwest/ n Vermächtnis nt

bereave|d /bɪ'ri:vd/ n the ~d pl die Hinterbliebenen. ~**ment** n Trauerfall m; (state) Trauer f

bereft /bɪ'reft/ a ~ **of** beraubt (+ gen)

beret /'bereɪ/ n Baskenmütze f

Berne /bɜ:n/ n Bern nt

berry /'berɪ/ n Beere f

berserk /bə'sɜ:k/ a **go** ~ wild werden

berth /bɜ:θ/ n (on ship) [Schlaf]koje f; (ship's anchorage) Liegeplatz m; **give a wide** ~ **to** (fam) einen großen Bogen machen um □ vi anlegen

beseech /bɪ'si:tʃ/ vt (pt/pp beseeched or besought) anflehen

beside /bɪ'saɪd/ prep neben (+ dat/ acc); ~ **oneself** außer sich (dat)

besides /bɪ'saɪdz/ prep außer (+ dat) □ adv außerdem

besiege /bɪ'si:dʒ/ vt belagern

besought /bɪ'sɔ:t/ see **beseech**

bespoke /bɪ'spəʊk/ a (suit) maßgeschneidert

best /best/ a & adv der/die/das Beste; **at** ~ bestenfalls; **all the** ~! alles Gute! **do one's** ~ sein Bestes tun; **the** ~ **part of a year** fast ein Jahr; **to the** ~ **of my knowledge** soviel ich weiß; **make the** ~ **of it** das Beste daraus machen □ adv am besten; **as** ~ **I could** so gut ich konnte. ~ '**man** n ≈ Trauzeuge m

bestow /bɪ'stəʊ/ vt schenken (**on** dat)

best'seller n Bestseller m

bet /bet/ n Wette f □ v (pt/pp **bet** or **betted**) □ vt ~ **s.o. £5** mit jdm um £5 wetten □ vi wetten; ~ **on** [Geld] setzen auf (+ acc)

betray /bɪ'treɪ/ vt verraten. ~**al** n Verrat m

better /'betə(r)/ a besser; **get** ~ sich bessern; (after illness) sich erholen □ adv besser; ~ **off** besser dran; ~ **not** lieber nicht; **all the** ~ um so besser; **the sooner the** ~ je eher, desto besser; **think** ~ **of sth** sich eines Besseren besinnen; **you'd** ~ **stay** du bleibst am besten hier □ vt ~ **oneself** sich verbessern; (do better than) übertreffen; ~ **oneself** sich verbessern

'betting shop n Wettbüro nt

between /bɪ'twiːn/ prep zwischen (+ dat/acc); ~ **you and me** unter uns; ~ **us** (together) zusammen □ adv **[in]** ~ dazwischen

beverage /'bevərɪdʒ/ n Getränk nt

bevy /'bevɪ/ n Schar f

beware /bɪ'weə(r)/ vi sich in acht nehmen (**of** vor + dat); ~ **of the dog!** Vorsicht, bissiger Hund!

bewilder /bɪ'wɪldə(r)/ vt verwirren. ~**ment** n Verwirrung f

bewitch /bɪ'wɪtʃ/ vt verzaubern; (fig) bezaubern

beyond /bɪ'jɒnd/ prep/adv (+ acc) ... hinaus; (further) weiter als; ~ **reach** außer Reichweite; ~ **doubt** ohne jeden Zweifel; **it's** ~ **me** (fam) das geht über meinen Horizont □ adv darüber hinaus

bias /'baɪəs/ n Voreingenommenheit f; (preference) Vorliebe f; (Jur) Befangenheit f; **cut on the** ~ schräg geschnitten □ vt (pt/pp **biased**) (influence) beeinflussen. ~**ed** a voreingenommen; (Jur) befangen

bib /bɪb/ n Lätzchen nt

Bible /'baɪbl/ n Bibel f

biblical /'bɪblɪkl/ a biblisch

bibliography /bɪblɪ'ɒgrəfɪ/ n Bibliographie f

bicarbonate /baɪ'kɑːbəneɪt/ n ~ **of soda** doppeltkohlensaures Natron nt

bicker /'bɪkə(r)/ vi sich zanken

bicycle /'baɪsɪkl/ n Fahrrad nt □ vi mit dem Rad fahren

bid[1] /bɪd/ n Gebot nt; (attempt) Versuch m □ vt/i (pt/pp **bid**, pres p **bidding**) bieten (**for** auf + acc); (Cards) reizen

bid[2] vt (pt **bade** or **bid**, pp **bidden** or **bid**, pres p **bidding**) (liter) heißen; ~ **s.o. welcome** jdn willkommen heißen

bidder /'bɪdə(r)/ n Bieter(in) m(f)

bide /baɪd/ vt ~ **one's time** den richtigen Moment abwarten

biennial /baɪ'enɪəl/ a zweijährlich; (lasting two years) zweijährig

bier /bɪə(r)/ n [Toten]bahre f

bifocals /baɪ'fəʊklz/ npl [**pair of**] ~ Bifokalbrille f

big /bɪg/ a (**bigger, biggest**) groß □ adv **talk** ~ (fam) angeben

bigam|ist /'bɪgəmɪst/ n Bigamist m. ~**y** n Bigamie f

big-'headed a (fam) eingebildet

bigot /'bɪgət/ n Eiferer m. ~**ed** a engstirnig

'bigwig n (fam) hohes Tier nt

bike /baɪk/ n (fam) [Fahr]rad nt

bikini /bɪ'kiːnɪ/ n Bikini m

bilberry /'bɪlbərɪ/ n Heidelbeere f

bile /baɪl/ n Galle f

bilingual /baɪ'lɪŋgwəl/ a zweisprachig

bilious /'bɪljəs/ a (Med) ~ **attack** verdorbener Magen m

bill[1] /bɪl/ n Rechnung f; (poster) Plakat nt; (Pol) Gesetzentwurf m; (Amer: note) Banknote f. ~ **of exchange** Wechsel m □ vt eine Rechnung schicken (+ dat)

bill[2] n (beak) Schnabel m

billet /'bɪlɪt/ n (Mil) Quartier nt □ vt (pt/pp **billeted**) einquartieren (**on** bei)

'billfold n (Amer) Brieftasche f

billiards /'bɪljədz/ n Billard nt

billion /'bɪljən/ n (thousand million) Milliarde f; (million million) Billion f

billy-goat /'bɪlɪ-/ n Ziegenbock m

bin /bɪn/ n Mülleimer m; (for bread) Kasten m

bind /baɪnd/ vt (pt/pp bound) binden (to an + acc); (bandage) verbinden; (Jur) verpflichten; (cover the edge of) einfassen. ~ing n verbindlich □ n Einband m; (braid) Borte f; (on ski) Bindung f

binge /bɪndʒ/ n □'bɪndʒ/ go on the ~ eine Sauftour machen

binoculars /bɪ'nɒkjʊləz/ npl (pair of) ~ Fernglas nt

bio|**chemistry** /baɪəʊ-/ n Biochemie f. ~**degradable** /-dɪ'greɪdəbl/ a biologisch abbaubar

biograph|**er** /baɪ'ɒgrəfə(r)/ n Biograph(in) m(f). ~**y** n Biographie f

biological /baɪə'lɒdʒɪkl/ a biologisch

biolog|**ist** /baɪ'ɒlədʒɪst/ n Biologe m. ~**y** n Biologie f

birch /bɜːtʃ/ n Birke f; (whip) Rute f

bird /bɜːd/ n Vogel m; (fam: girl) Mädchen nt; kill two ~s with one stone zwei Fliegen mit einer Klappe schlagen

Biro(P) /'baɪrəʊ/ n Kugelschreiber m

birth /bɜːθ/ n Geburt f

birth: ~ **certificate** n Geburtsurkunde f. ~**control** n Geburtenregelung f. ~**day** n Geburtstag m. ~**mark** n Muttermal nt. ~**rate** n Geburtenziffer f. ~**right** n Geburtsrecht nt

biscuit /'bɪskɪt/ n Keks m

bisect /baɪ'sekt/ vt halbieren

bishop /'bɪʃəp/ n Bischof m; (Chess) Läufer m

bit[1] /bɪt/ n Stückchen nt; (for horse) Gebiß nt; (Techn) Bohreinsatz m; a ~ ein bißchen m; ~ by ~ nach und nach; a ~ of bread ein bißchen Brot; do one's ~ sein Teil tun

bit[2] see **bite**

bitch /bɪtʃ/ n Hündin f; (sl) Luder nt. ~**y** a gehässig

bit|**e** /baɪt/ n Biß m; [insect] ~ Stich m; (mouthful) Bissen m □ vt/i (pt bit, pp bitten) beißen; (insect:) stechen; kauen (one's nails). ~**ing** a beißend

bitter /'bɪtə(r)/ a, -**ly** adv bitter; **cry** ~**ly** bitterlich weinen; ~**ly cold** bitterkalt □ n bitteres Bier nt. ~**ness** n Bitterkeit f

bitty /'bɪtɪ/ a zusammengestoppelt

bizarre /bɪ'zɑː(r)/ a bizarr

blab /blæb/ vi (pt/pp **blabbed**) alles ausplaudern

black /blæk/ a (-**er**, -**est**) schwarz; **be** ~ **and blue** grün und blau sein □ n Schwarz nt; (person) Schwarze(r) m/f □ vt schwärzen; boykottieren (goods). ~ **out** vt verdunkeln □ vi (lose consciousness) das Bewußtsein verlieren

black: ~**berry** n Brombeere f. ~**bird** n Amsel f. ~**board** n (Sch) [Wand]tafel f. ~'**currant** n schwarze Johannisbeere f

blacken /blækn/ vt/i schwärzen

black: ~'**eye** n blaues Auge nt. B~ **Forest** n Schwarzwald m. ~'**ice** n Glatteis nt. ~ **leg** n Streikbrecher m. ~**list** vt auf die schwarze Liste setzen. ~**mail** n Erpressung f □ vt erpressen. ~**mailer** n Erpresser(in) m(f). ~'**market** n schwarzer Markt m. ~**out** n Verdunkelung f; **have a** ~**out** (Med) das Bewußtsein verlieren. ~'**pudding** n Blutwurst f. ~**smith** n [Huf]schmied m

bladder /'blædə(r)/ n (Anat) Blase f

blade /bleɪd/ n Klinge f; (of grass) Halm m

blame /bleɪm/ n Schuld f □ vt die Schuld geben (+ dat); **no one is to** ~ keiner ist schuld daran. ~**less** a schuldlos

blanch /blɑːntʃ/ vi blaß werden □vt (Culin) blanchieren

blancmange /bləˈmɒnʒ/ n Pudding m

bland /blænd/ a (-er, -est) mild

blank /blæŋk/ a leer; ⟨look⟩ ausdruckslos □n Lücke f; ⟨cartridge⟩ Platzpatrone f. ~ 'cheque n Blankoscheck m

blanket /ˈblæŋkɪt/ n Decke f; wet ~ (fam) Spielverderber(in) m(f)

blank 'verse n Blankvers m

blare /bleə(r)/ vt/i schmettern

blasé /ˈblɑːzeɪ/ a blasiert

blaspheme /blæsˈfiːm/ vi lästern

blasphem|ous /ˈblæsfəməs/ a[gottes]lästerlich. ~y n [Gottes]lästerung f

blast /blɑːst/ n ⟨gust⟩ Luftstoß m; ⟨sound⟩ Stoß m □vt sprengen □int ⟨sl⟩ verdammt. ~ed a ⟨sl⟩ verdammt

blast: ~-furnace n Hochofen m. ~-off n ⟨of missile⟩ Start m

blatant /ˈbleɪtənt/ a offensichtlich

blaze /bleɪz/ n Feuer nt □vi brennen

blazer /ˈbleɪzə(r)/ n Blazer m

bleach /bliːtʃ/ n Bleichmittel nt □vt/i bleichen

bleak /bliːk/ a (-er, -est) öde; ⟨fig⟩ trostlos

bleary-eyed /ˈblɪərɪ-/ a mit trüben/ ⟨on waking up⟩ verschlafenen Augen

bleat /bliːt/ vi blöken; ⟨goat:⟩ meckern

bleed /bliːd/ v (pt/pp bled) □vi bluten □vt entlüften ⟨radiator⟩

bleep /bliːp/ n Piepton m □vi piepsen □vt mit dem Piepser rufen. ~er n Piepser m

blemish /ˈblemɪʃ/ n Makel m

blend /blend/ n Mischung f □vt mischen □vi sich vermischen. ~er n (Culin) Mixer m

bless /bles/ vt segnen. ~ed /ˈblesɪd/ a heilig; ⟨sl⟩ verflixt. ~ing n Segen m

blew /bluː/ see **blow²**

blight /blaɪt/ n (Bot) Brand m □vt ⟨spoil⟩ vereiteln

blind /blaɪnd/ a blind; ⟨corner⟩ unübersichtlich; ~ man/woman Blinde(r) m/f □n [roller] ~ Rouleau nt □vt blenden

blind: ~ 'alley n Sackgasse f. ~fold a & adv mit verbundenen Augen □n Augenbinde f □vt die Augen verbinden (+ dat). ~ly adv blindlings. ~ness n Blindheit f

blink /blɪŋk/ vi blinzeln; ⟨light:⟩ blinken

blinkers /ˈblɪŋkəz/ npl Scheuklappen pl

bliss /blɪs/ n Glückseligkeit f. ~ful a glückselig

blister /ˈblɪstə(r)/ n (Med) Blase f □vi ⟨paint:⟩ Blasen werfen

blitz /blɪts/ n Luftangriff m; (fam) Großaktion f

blizzard /ˈblɪzəd/ n Schneesturm m

bloated /ˈbləʊtɪd/ a aufgedunsen

blob /blɒb/ n Klecks m

bloc /blɒk/ n (Pol) Block m

block /blɒk/ n Block m; (of wood) Klotz m; (of flats) [Wohn]block m □vt blockieren. ~ up vt zustopfen

blockade /blɒˈkeɪd/ n Blockade f □vt blockieren

blockage /ˈblɒkɪdʒ/ n Verstopfung f

block: ~head n (fam) Dummkopf m. ~ 'letters npl Blockschrift f

bloke /bləʊk/ n (fam) Kerl m

blonde /blɒnd/ a blond □n Blondine f

blood /blʌd/ n Blut nt

blood: ~ count n Blutbild nt. ~-curdling a markerschütternd. ~ donor n Blutspender m. ~ group n Blutgruppe f. ~hound n Bluthund m. ~-poisoning n Blutvergiftung f. ~ pressure n Blutdruck m. ~ relative n Blutsverwandte(r) m/f. ~shed n Blutvergießen nt.

~**shot** a blutunterlaufen. ~
sports npl Jagdsport m.
~**-stained** a blutbefleckt.
~**stream** n Blutbahn f. ~ **test** n
Blutprobe f. ~**thirsty** a blutdür-
stig. ~ **transfusion** n Blutüber-
tragung f. ~**-vessel** n Blutgefäß
nt

bloody /'blʌdɪ/ a (-ier, -iest) blutig; (sl) verdammt. ~'**minded** a
(sl) stur

bloom /blu:m/ n Blüte f □vi
blühen

bloom|er /'blu:mə(r)/ n (fam)
Schnitzer m. ~**ing** a (fam) verdammt

blossom /'blɒsəm/ n Blüte f □vi
blühen. ~ **out** vi (fig) aufblühen

blot /blɒt/ n [Tinten]klecks m;
(fig) Fleck m □vt (pt/pp blotted)
löschen. ~ **out** vt (fig) auslöschen

blotch /blɒtʃ/ n Fleck m. ~**y** a
fleckig

'**blotting-paper** n Löschpapier nt

blouse /blaʊz/ n Bluse f

blow[1] /bləʊ/ n Schlag m

blow[2] v (pt blew, pp blown) □vt
blasen; (fam: squander) verpul-
vern; ~ **one's nose** sich (dat) die
Nase putzen □vi blasen; (fuse:)
durchbrennen. ~ **away** vt weg-
blasen □vi wegfliegen. ~ **down**
vt umwehen □vi umfallen. ~ **out**
vt (extinguish) ausblasen. ~
over vi umfallen; (fig) vorübergehen. ~ **up** vt (inflate)
aufblasen; (enlarge) vergrößern;
(shatter by explosion) sprengen
□vi explodieren

blow: ~**-dry** vt fönen. ~**fly** n
Schmeißfliege f. ~**lamp** n Lötlampe f

blown /bləʊn/ see **blow**[2]

'**blowtorch** n (Amer) Lötlampe f

blowy /'bləʊɪ/ a windig

bludgeon /'blʌdʒn/ vt (fig) zwingen

blue /blu:/ a (-r, -st) blau; feel ~
deprimiert sein □n Blau nt; have

the ~**s** deprimiert sein; **out of**
the ~ aus heiterem Himmel.

blue: ~**bell** n Sternhyazinthe f.
~**berry** n Heidelbeere f.
~**bottle** n Schmeißfliege f. ~
film n Pornofilm m. ~**print** n
(fig) Entwurf m

bluff /blʌf/ n Bluff m □vi bluffen

blunder /'blʌndə(r)/ n Schnitzer m
□vi einen Schnitzer machen

blunt /blʌnt/ a stumpf; (person)
geradeheraus. ~**ly** adv unverblümt, geradeheraus

blur /blɜ:(r)/ n it's all a ~ alles ist
verschwommen □vt (pt/pp
blurred) verschwommen ma-
chen; ~**red** verschwommen

blurb /blɜ:b/ n Klappentext m

blurt /blɜ:t/ vt ~ **out** heraus-
platzen mit

blush /blʌʃ/ n Erröten nt □vi
erröten

bluster /'blʌstə(r)/ n Großtuerei f.
~**y** a windig

boar /bɔ:(r)/ n Eber m

board /bɔ:d/ n Brett nt; (for noti-
ces) schwarzes Brett nt; (committee) Ausschuß m; (of directors)
Vorstand m; on ~ an Bord; full
~ Vollpension f; ~ **and lodging**
Unterkunft und Verpflegung pl;
go by the ~ (fam) unter den
Tisch fallen □vt einsteigen in (+
acc); (Naut, Aviat) besteigen □vi
an Bord gehen; ~ **with** in Pension wohnen bei. ~ **up** vt mit
Brettern verschlagen

boarder /'bɔ:də(r)/ n Pensionsgast
m; (Sch) Internatsschüler(in)
m(f)

board: ~**-game** n Brettspiel nt.
~**ing-house** n Pension f. ~**ing-**
school n Internat nt

boast /bəʊst/ vt sich rühmen (+
gen) □vi prahlen (about mit).
~**ful** a, ~**ly** adv prahlerisch

boat /bəʊt/ n Boot nt; (ship) Schiff
nt. ~**er** n (hat) flacher Strohhut
m

bob /bɒb/ n Bubikopf m □vi (pt/pp
bobbed) (curtsy) knicksen; ~ **up**

and down sich auf und ab bewegen

bobbin /'bɒbɪn/ n Spule f

'bob-sleigh n Bob m

bode /bəʊd/ vi ~ **well/ill** etwas/ nichts Gutes verheißen

bodice /'bɒdɪs/ n Mieder nt

bodily /'bɒdɪlɪ/ a körperlich □adv (forcibly) mit Gewalt

body /'bɒdɪ/ n Körper m; (corpse) Leiche f; (corporation) Körperschaft f; **the main** ~ der Hauptanteil. ~**guard** n Leibwächter m. ~**work** n (Auto) Karosserie f

bog /bɒg/ n Sumpf m □vt **get** ~**ged down** steckenbleiben

boggle /'bɒgl/ vi **the mind** ~**s** es ist kaum vorstellbar

bogus /'bəʊgəs/ a falsch

boil[1] /bɔɪl/ n Furunkel m

boil[2] n bring/come to the ~ zum Kochen bringen/kommen □vt/i kochen; ~**ed potatoes** Salzkartoffeln pl. ~ **down** vi (fig) hinauslaufen (**to** auf + acc). ~ **over** vi überkochen. ~ **up** vt aufkochen

boiler /'bɔɪlə(r)/ n Heizkessel m. ~**suit** n Overall m

'boiling point n Siedepunkt m

boisterous /'bɔɪstərəs/ a übermütig

bold /bəʊld/ a (-er, -est), -**ly** adv kühn; (Typ) fett. ~**ness** n Kühnheit f

bollard /'bɒlɑːd/ n Poller m

bolster /'bəʊlstə(r)/ n Nackenrolle f □vt ~ **up** Mut machen (+ dat)

bolt /bəʊlt/ n Riegel m; (Techn) Bolzen m; **nuts and** ~**s** Schrauben und Muttern pl □vt verschrauben (**to** an + acc); verriegeln ⟨door⟩; hinunterschlingen ⟨food⟩ □vi abhauen; ⟨horse:⟩ durchgehen □adv ~ **upright** adv kerzengerade

bomb /bɒm/ n Bombe f □vt bombardieren

bombard /bɒm'bɑːd/ vt beschießen; (fig) bombardieren

bombastic /bɒm'bæstɪk/ a bombastisch

bomb|er /'bɒmə(r)/ n (Aviat) Bomber m; (person) Bombenleger(in) m(f). ~**shell** n **be a** ~**shell** (fig) wie eine Bombe einschlagen

bond /bɒnd/ n (fig) Band nt; (Comm) Obligation f; **be in** ~ unter Zollverschluß stehen

bondage /'bɒndɪdʒ/ n (fig) Sklaverei f

bone /bəʊn/ n Knochen m; (of fish) Gräte f □vt von den Knochen lösen ⟨meat⟩; entgräten ⟨fish⟩. ~'**dry** a knochentrocken

bonfire /'bɒn-/ n Gartenfeuer nt; (celebratory) Freudenfeuer nt

bonnet /'bɒnɪt/ n Haube f

bonus /'bəʊnəs/ n Prämie f; (gratuity) Gratifikation f; (fig) Plus nt

bony /'bəʊnɪ/ a (-ier, -iest) knochig; ⟨fish⟩ grätig

boo /buː/ int buh! □vt ausbuhen □vi buhen

boob /buːb/ n (fam: mistake) Schnitzer m □vi (fam) einen Schnitzer machen

book /bʊk/ n Buch nt; (of tickets) Heft nt; **keep the** ~**s** (Comm) die Bücher führen □vt/i buchen; (reserve) [vor]bestellen; **for offence** aufschreiben. ~**able** /-əbl/ a im Vorverkauf erhältlich

book: ~**case** n Bücherregal nt. ~**ends** npl Bücherstützen pl. ~**ing-office** n Fahrkartenschalter m. ~**keeping** n Buchführung f. ~**let** n Broschüre f. ~**maker** n Buchmacher m. ~**mark** n Lesezeichen nt. ~**seller** n Buchhändler(in) m(f). ~**shop** n Buchhandlung f. ~**stall** n Bücherstand m. ~**worm** n Bücherwurm m

boom /buːm/ n (Comm) Hochkonjunktur f; (upturn) Aufschwung m □vi dröhnen; (fig) blühen

boon /buːn/ n Segen m

boor /bʊə(r)/ n Flegel m. ~**ish** a flegelhaft

boost /bu:st/ n Auftrieb m □vt Auftrieb geben (+ dat). ~**er** n (Med) Nachimpfung f

boot /bu:t/ n Stiefel m; (Auto) Kofferraum m

booth /bu:ð/ n Bude f; (cubicle) Kabine f

booty /'bu:tɪ/ n Beute f

booze /bu:z/ n (fam) Alkohol m □vi (fam) saufen

border /'bɔ:də(r)/ n Rand m; (frontier) Grenze f; (in garden) Rabatte f □vi ~ **on** grenzen an (+ acc). ~**line** n Grenzlinie f. ~**line case** n Grenzfall m

bore¹ /bɔ:(r)/ see **bear**²

bore² vt/i (Techn) bohren

bore³ n (of gun) Kaliber nt; (person) langweiliger Mensch m; (thing) langweilige Sache f □vt langweilen; **be** ~ **ed** sich langweilen. ~**edom** n Langeweile f. ~**ing** a langweilig

born /bɔ:n/ pp **be** ~ geboren werden □a geboren

borne /bɔ:n/ see **bear**²

borough /'bʌrə/ n Stadtgemeinde f

borrow /'bɒrəʊ/ vt [sich (dat)] borgen od leihen (**from** von)

bosom /'bʊzm/ n Busen m

boss /bɒs/ n (fam) Chef m □vt herumkommandieren. ~**y** a herrschsüchtig

botanical /bə'tænɪkl/ a botanisch

botan|ist /'bɒtənɪst/ n Botaniker(in) m(f). ~**y** n Botanik f

botch /bɒtʃ/ vt verpfuschen

both /bəʊθ/ a & pron beide; ~ [**the**] **children** beide Kinder; ~ **of them** beide [von ihnen] □adv ~ **men and women** sowohl Männer als auch Frauen

bother /'bɒðə(r)/ n Mühe f; (minor trouble) Ärger m □int (fam) verflixt!□vt belästigen; (disturb) stören □vi sich kümmern (**about** um); **don't** ~ nicht nötig

bottle /'bɒtl/ n Flasche f □vt auf Flaschen abfüllen; (preserve) einmachen. ~ **up** vt (fig) in sich (dat) aufstauen

bottle: ~**neck** n (fig) Engpaß m. ~-**opener** n Flaschenöffner m

bottom /'bɒtəm/ a unterste(r,s)□n (of container) Boden m; (of river) Grund m; (of page, hill) Fuß m; (buttocks) Hintern m; **at the** ~ **unten**; **get to the** ~ **of sth** (fig) hinter etw (acc) kommen. ~**less** a bodenlos

bough /baʊ/ n Ast m

bought /bɔ:t/ see **buy**

boulder /'bəʊldə(r)/ n Felsblock m

bounce /baʊns/ vi (aufspringen; ⟨cheque⟩ (fam) nicht gedeckt sein □vt aufspringen lassen ⟨ball⟩

bouncer /'baʊnsə(r)/ n (fam) Rausschmeißer m

bouncing /'baʊnsɪŋ/ a ~ **baby** strammer Säugling m

bound¹ /baʊnd/ n Sprung m □vi springen

bound² see **bind** □a ~ **for** ⟨ship⟩ mit Kurs auf (+ acc); **be** ~ **to do sth** etw bestimmt machen; (obliged) verpflichtet sein, etw zu machen

boundary /'baʊndərɪ/ n Grenze f

boundless a grenzenlos

bounds /baʊndz/ npl (fig) Grenzen pl; **out of** ~ verboten

bouquet /bʊ'keɪ/ n [Blumen]strauß m; (of wine) Bukett nt

bourgeois /'bʊəʒwɑ:/ a (pej) spießbürgerlich

bout /baʊt/ n (Med) Anfall m; (Sport) Kampf m

bow¹ /bəʊ/ n (weapon & Mus) Bogen m; (knot) Schleife f

bow² /baʊ/ n Verbeugung f □vi sich verbeugen □vt neigen ⟨head⟩

bow³ /baʊ/ n (Naut) Bug m

bowel /'baʊəl/ n Darm m; ~ **movement** Stuhlgang m. ~**s** pl Eingeweide pl; (digestion) Verdauung f

bowl¹ /bəʊl/ n Schüssel f; (shallow) Schale f; (of pipe) Kopf m; (of spoon) Schöpfteil m

bowl² n (ball) Kugel f □ vt/i werfen. **~ over** vt umwerfen

bow-legged /bəʊˈlegd/ a O-beinig

bowler¹ /ˈbəʊlə(r)/ n (Sport) Werfer m

bowler² n **~** [hat] Melone f

bowling /ˈbəʊlɪŋ/ n Kegeln nt. **~-alley** n Kegelbahn f

bowls /bəʊlz/ n Boulespiel nt

bow-tie /bəʊ-/ n Fliege f

box¹ /bɒks/ n Schachtel f; (wooden) Kiste f; (cardboard) Karton m; (Theat) Loge f

box² vt/i (Sport) boxen; **~ s.o.'s ears** jdn ohrfeigen

box|er /ˈbɒksə(r)/ n Boxer m. **~ing** n Boxen nt. **B~ing Day** n zweiter Weihnachtstag m

box: ~office n (Theat) Kasse f. **~room** n Abstellraum m

boy /bɔɪ/ n Junge m

boycott /ˈbɔɪkɒt/ n Boykott m □ vt boykottieren

boy: ~friend n Freund m. **~ish** a jungenhaft

bra /brɑː/ n BH m

brace /breɪs/ n Strebe f, Stütze f; (dental) Zahnspange f; **~s** npl Hosenträger mpl □ vt **~ oneself** sich stemmen (**against** gegen); (fig) sich gefaßt machen (**for** auf + acc)

bracelet /ˈbreɪslɪt/ n Armband nt

bracing /ˈbreɪsɪŋ/ a stärkend

bracken /ˈbrækn/ n Farnkraut nt

bracket /ˈbrækɪt/ n Konsole f; (group) Gruppe f; (Typ) round/square **~s** runde/eckige Klammern □ vt einklammern

brag /bræg/ vi (pt/pp bragged) prahlen (**about** mit)

braid /breɪd/ n Borte f

braille /breɪl/ n Blindenschrift f

brain /breɪn/ n Gehirn nt; **~s** (fig) Intelligenz f

brain: ~child n geistiges Produkt m. **~less** a dumm. **~wash**

vt einer Gehirnwäsche unterziehen. **~wave** n Geistesblitz m

brainy /ˈbreɪnɪ/ a (-ier, -iest) klug

braise /breɪz/ vt schmoren

brake /breɪk/ n Bremse f □ vt/i bremsen. **~-light** n Bremslicht nt

bramble /ˈbræmbl/ n Brombeerstrauch m

bran /bræn/ n Kleie f

branch /brɑːntʃ/ n Ast m; (fig) Zweig m; (Comm) Zweigstelle f, (shop) Filiale f □ vi sich gabeln. **~off** vi abzweigen. **~ out** vi **~ out into** sich verlegen auf (+ acc)

brand /brænd/ n Marke f; (on animal) Brandzeichen nt □ vt mit dem Brandeisen zeichnen (animal); (fig) brandmarken als

brandish /ˈbrændɪʃ/ vt schwingen

brand-new a nagelneu

brandy /ˈbrændɪ/ n Weinbrand m

brash /bræʃ/ a naßforsch

brass /brɑːs/ n Messing nt; (Mus) Blech nt; **get down to ~ tacks** (fam) zur Sache kommen; **top ~** (fam) hohe Tiere pl. **~ band** n Blaskapelle f

brassiere /ˈbræzɪə(r)/ n Büstenhalter m

brassy /ˈbrɑːsɪ/ a (-ier, -iest) (fam) ordinär

brat /bræt/ n (pej) Balg nt

bravado /brəˈvɑːdəʊ/ n Forschheit f

brave /breɪv/ a (-r, -st), **-ly** adv tapfer □ vt die Stirn bieten (+ dat). **~ry** /-ərɪ/ n Tapferkeit f

bravo /brɑːˈvəʊ/ int bravo!

brawl /brɔːl/ n Schlägerei f □ vi sich schlagen

brawn /brɔːn/ n (Culin) Sülze f

brawny /ˈbrɔːnɪ/ a muskulös

bray /breɪ/ vi iahen

brazen /ˈbreɪzn/ a unverschämt

brazier /ˈbreɪzɪə(r)/ n Kohlenbecken nt

Brazil /brəˈzɪl/ n Brasilien nt. **~ian** a brasilianisch. **~ nut** n Paranuß f

breach /briːtʃ/ n Bruch m; (Mil & fig) Bresche f; ~ **of contract** Vertragsbruch m □ vt durchbrechen; brechen (contract)

bread /bred/ n Brot nt; **slice of ~ and butter** Butterbrot nt

bread: ~**crumbs** npl Brotkrümel pl; (Culin) Paniermehl nt. ~**line** n be on the ~ **line** gerade genug zum Leben haben

breadth /bredθ/ n Breite f

'bread-winner n Brotverdiener m

break /breik/ n Bruch m; (interval) Pause f; (interruption) Unterbrechung f; (fam: chance) Chance f □ vt (pt **broke**, pp **broken**) □ vt brechen; (smash) zerbrechen; (damage) kaputtmachen (fam); (interrupt) unterbrechen; ~ **one's arm** sich (dat) den Arm brechen □ vi brechen; (day:) anbrechen; (storm:) losbrechen; (thing:) kaputtgehen (fam); (rope, thread:) reißen; (news:) bekanntwerden; **his voice is** ~**ing** er ist im Stimmbruch. ~ **away** vi sich losreißen √ (fig) sich absetzen (from von). ~ **down** vi zusammenbrechen; (Techn) eine Panne haben; (negotiations:) scheitern □ vt aufbrechen (door); aufgliedern (figures). ~ **in** vi einbrechen. ~ **off** vt/i abbrechen; lösen (engagement). ~ **out** vi ausbrechen. ~ **up** vt zerbrechen □ vi (crowd:) sich zerstreuen; (marriage, couple:) auseinandergehen; (Sch) Ferien bekommen

'break|able /'breikəbl/ a zerbrechlich. ~**age** /-ɪdʒ/ n Bruch m. ~**down** n (Techn) Panne f; (Med) Zusammenbruch m; (of figures) Aufgliederung f. ~**er** n (wave) Brecher m

breakfast /'brekfəst/ n Frühstück nt

break: ~**through** n Durchbruch m. ~**water** n Buhne f

breast /brest/ n Brust f. ~**bone** n Brustbein nt. ~**feed** vt stillen. ~**stroke** n Brustschwimmen nt

breath /breθ/ n Atem m; **out of** ~ außer Atem; **under one's** ~ vor sich (acc) hin

breathalyse /'breθəlaɪz/ vt ins Röhrchen blasen lassen. ~**r (P)** n Röhrchen nt. ~**r test** n Alcotest (P) m

breathe /briːð/ vt/i atmen. ~ **in** vt/i einatmen. ~ **out** vt/i ausatmen

breath|er /'briːðə(r)/ n Atempause f. ~**ing** n Atmen nt

breath /breθ/-/: ~**less** a atemlos. ~**taking** a atemberaubend. ~ **test** n Alcotest (P) m

bred /bred/ see **breed**

breeches /'britʃɪz/ npl Kniehose f; (for riding) Reithose f

breed /briːd/ n Rasse f □ v (pt/pp **bred**) □ vt züchten; (give rise to) erzeugen □ vi sich vermehren. ~**er** n Züchter m. ~**ing** n Zucht f; (fig) [gute] Lebensart f

breez|e /briːz/ n Lüftchen nt; (Naut) Brise f. ~**y** a [leicht] windig

brevity /'brevətɪ/ n Kürze f

brew /bruː/ n Gebräu nt □ vt brauen; kochen (tea) □ vi (fig) sich zusammenbrauen. ~**er** n Brauer m. ~**ery** n Brauerei f

bribe /braɪb/ n (money) Bestechungsgeld n □ vt bestechen. ~**ry** /-ərɪ/ n Bestechung f

brick /brɪk/ n Ziegelstein m, Backstein m □ vt ~ **up** zumauern

'bricklayer n Maurer m

bridal /'braɪdl/ a Braut-

bride /braɪd/ n Braut f. ~**groom** n Bräutigam m. ~**smaid** n Brautjungfer f

bridge¹ /brɪdʒ/ n Brücke f; (of nose) Nasenrücken m; (of spectacles) Steg m □ vt (fig) überbrücken

bridge² (Cards) Bridge nt

bridle /'braɪdl/ n Zaum m. ~**-path** n Reitweg m

brief¹ /briːf/ a (-er, -est) kurz; **be ~** ⟨person:⟩ sich kurz fassen

brief² n Instruktionen pl; ⟨Jur: case⟩ Mandat nt □vt Instruktionen geben (+ dat); ⟨Jur⟩ beauftragen. **~case** n Aktentasche f

briefing /ˈbriːfɪŋ/ n Informationsgespräch nt. **~ly** adv kurz. **~ness** n Kürze f

briefs /briːfs/ npl Slip m

brigad|e /brɪˈgeɪd/ n Brigade f. **~ier** /-əˈdɪə(r)/ n Brigadegeneral m

bright /braɪt/ a (-er, -est), **-ly** adv hell; ⟨day⟩ heiter; **~ red** hellrot

bright|en /ˈbraɪtn/ v **~en [up]** □vt aufheitern □vi sich aufheitern. **~ness** n Helligkeit f

brilliance /ˈbrɪljəns/ n Glanz m; ⟨of person⟩ Genialität f

brilliant /ˈbrɪljənt/ a, **-ly** adv glänzend; ⟨person⟩ genial

brim /brɪm/ n Rand m; ⟨of hat⟩ Krempe f □vi (pt/pp **brimmed**) **~ over** überfließen

brine /braɪn/ n Salzwasser nt; ⟨Culin⟩ [Salz]lake f

bring /brɪŋ/ vt (pt/pp **brought**) bringen; **~ them with you** bring sie mit. **~ about** vt verursachen. **~ along** vt mitbringen. **~ back** vt zurückbringen. **~ down** vt herunterbringen; senken ⟨price⟩. **~ off** vt vollbringen. **~ on** vt ⟨cause⟩ verursachen. **~ out** vt herausbringen. **~ round** vt vorbeibringen; ⟨persuade⟩ überreden; wieder zum Bewußtsein bringen ⟨unconscious person⟩. **~ up** vt heraufbringen; ⟨vomit⟩ erbrechen; aufziehen ⟨children⟩; erwähnen ⟨question⟩

brink /brɪŋk/ n Rand m

brisk /brɪsk/ a (-er, -est), **-ly** adv lebhaft; ⟨quick⟩ schnell

bristl|e /ˈbrɪsl/ n Borste f. **~ly** a borstig

Brit|ain /ˈbrɪtn/ n Großbritannien nt. **~ish** a britisch; **the ~ish** die Briten pl. **~on** n Brite m/Britin f

Brittany /ˈbrɪtənɪ/ n die Bretagne

brittle /ˈbrɪtl/ a brüchig, spröde

broach /brəʊtʃ/ vt anzapfen; anschneiden ⟨subject⟩

broad /brɔːd/ a (-er, -est) breit; ⟨hint⟩ deutlich; **in ~ daylight** am hellichten Tag. **~ beans** npl dicke Bohnen pl

'broadcast n Sendung f □vt/i (pt/pp **-cast**) senden. **~er** n Rundfunk- und Fernsehpersönlichkeit f. **~ing** n Funk und Fernsehen pl

broaden /ˈbrɔːdn/ vt verbreitern; ⟨fig⟩ erweitern □vi sich verbreitern

broadly /ˈbrɔːdlɪ/ adv breit; **~ speaking** allgemein gesagt

broad'minded a tolerant

brocade /brəˈkeɪd/ n Brokat m

broccoli /ˈbrɒkəlɪ/ n inv Brokkoli pl

brochure /ˈbrəʊʃə(r)/ n Broschüre f

brogue /brəʊg/ n ⟨shoe⟩ Wanderschuh m; **Irish ~** irischer Akzent m

broke /brəʊk/ see **break** □ a (fam) pleite

broken /ˈbrəʊkn/ see **break** □ a zerbrochen, ⟨fam⟩ kaputt; **~ English** gebrochenes Englisch nt. **~-hearted** a untröstlich

broker /ˈbrəʊkə(r)/ n Makler m

brolly /ˈbrɒlɪ/ n ⟨fam⟩ Schirm m

bronchitis /brɒŋˈkaɪtɪs/ n Bronchitis f

bronze /brɒnz/ n Bronze f

brooch /brəʊtʃ/ n Brosche f

brood /bruːd/ n Brut f □vi brüten; ⟨fig⟩ grübeln

brook¹ /brʊk/ n Bach m

brook² vt dulden

broom /bruːm/ n Besen m; ⟨Bot⟩ Ginster m. **~stick** n Besenstiel m

broth /brɒθ/ n Brühe f

brothel /ˈbrɒθl/ n Bordell m

brother /ˈbrʌðə(r)/ n Bruder m

brother: ~**-in-law** n (pl **-s-in-law**) Schwager m. ~**ly** a brüderlich

brought /brɔːt/ see **bring**

brow /brau/ n Augenbraue f; ⟨forehead⟩ Stirn f; ⟨of hill⟩ [Berg]kuppe f

'browbeat vt (pt **-beat**, pp **-beaten**) einschüchtern

brown /braun/ a (-er, -est) braun; ~ '**paper** Packpapier m. ~ Braun nt □vt bräunen □vi braun werden

Brownie /'brauni/ n Wichtel m

browse /brauz/ vi ⟨read⟩ schmökern; (in shop) sich umsehen

bruise /bruːz/ n blauer Fleck m □vt beschädigen ⟨fruit⟩; ~ one's **arm** sich (dat) den Arm quetschen

brunch /brʌntʃ/ n Brunch m

brunette /bruː'net/ n Brünette f

Brunswick /'brʌnzwik/ n Braunschweig nt

brunt /brʌnt/ n the ~ of die volle Wucht (+ gen)

brush /brʌʃ/ n Bürste f; (with handle) Handfeger m; ⟨for paint, pastry⟩ Pinsel m; (bushes) Unterholz nt; ⟨fig: conflict⟩ Zusammenstoß m □vt bürsten; putzen ⟨teeth⟩; ~ **against** streifen {gegen}, ~ **aside** ⟨fig⟩ abtun. ~ **off** vt abbürsten; ⟨reject⟩ zurückweisen. ~ **up** vt/i ⟨fig⟩ ~up [on] auffrischen

brusque /brusk/ a, **-ly** adv brüsk

Brussels /'brʌslz/ n Brüssel nt. ~ **sprouts** npl Rosenkohl m

brutal /'bruːtl/ a, **-ly** adv brutal. ~**ity** /-'tælətɪ/ n Brutalität f

brute /bruːt/ n Unmensch m. ~ **force** n rohe Gewalt f

B.Sc. abbr = **Bachelor of Science**

bubble /'bʌbl/ n [Luft]blase f □vi sprudeln

buck¹ /bʌk/ n ⟨deer & Gym⟩ Bock m; ⟨rabbit⟩ Rammler m □vi ⟨horse:⟩ bocken. ~ **up** vi (fam)

sich aufheitern; (hurry) sich beeilen

buck² n (Amer, fam) Dollar m

buck³ n **pass the** ~ die Verantwortung abschieben

bucket /'bʌkɪt/ n Eimer m

buckle /'bʌkl/ n Schnalle f □vt zuschnallen □vi sich verbiegen

bud /bʌd/ n Knospe f □vi (pt/pp **budded**) knospen

Buddhism /'budizm/ n Buddhismus m. ~**t a** buddhistisch □n Buddhist(in) m(f)

buddy /'bʌdɪ/ n (fam) Freund m

budge /bʌdʒ/ vt bewegen □vi sich [von der Stelle] rühren

budgerigar /'bʌdʒərɪgaː(r)/ n Wellensittich m

budget /'bʌdʒɪt/ n Budget nt; (Pol) Haushaltsplan m; (money available) Etat m □vi (pt/pp **budgeted**) ~ **for sth** etw einkalkulieren

buff /bʌf/ a ⟨colour⟩ sandfarben □n Sandfarbe f; (Amer, fam) Fan m □vt polieren

buffalo /'bʌfələʊ/ n (inv or pl **-es**) Büffel m

buffer /'bʌfə(r)/ n (Rail) Puffer m; **old** ~ (fam) alter Knacker m; ~ **zone** Pufferzone f

buffet¹ /'bʊfeɪ/ n Büfett nt; (on station) Imbissstube f

buffet² /'bʌfɪt/ vt (pt/pp **buffeted**) hin und her werfen

buffoon /bə'fuːn/ n Narr m

bug /bʌg/ n Wanze f; (fam: virus) Bazillus m; (fam: device) Abhörgerät nt, (fam) Wanze f □vt (pt/pp **bugged**) (fam) verwanzen ⟨room⟩; abhören ⟨telephone⟩; (Amer: annoy) ärgern

buggy /'bʌgɪ/ n [Kinder]sportwagen m

bugle /'bjuːgl/ n Signalhorn n

build /bɪld/ n (of person) Körperbau m □vt/i (pt/pp **built**) bauen. ~ **on** vt anbauen (**to** an + acc). ~ **up** vt aufbauen □vi zunehmen; ⟨traffic:⟩ sich stauen

builder /'bɪldə(r)/ n Bauunternehmer m

building /'bɪldɪŋ/ n Gebäude nt. ~
site n Baustelle f. ~ society n
Bausparkasse f

built /bɪlt/ see **build**. ~-in a eingebaut. ~-in 'cupboard n Ein-
bauschrank m. ~-up area n be-
bautes Gebiet nt; (Auto) geschlossene Ortschaft f

bulb /bʌlb/ n [Blumen]zwiebel f;
(Electr) [Glüh]birne f

bulbous /'bʌlbəs/ a bauchig

Bulgaria /bʌl'geərɪə/ n Bulgarien nt

bulge /bʌldʒ/ n Ausbauchung f
□vi sich ausbauchen. ~ing a
prall; ⟨eyes⟩ hervorquellend;
~ing with prall gefüllt mit

bulk /bʌlk/ n Masse f; (greater
part) Hauptteil m; in ~ en gros;
(loose) lose. ~y a sperrig; (large)
massig

bull /bʊl/ n Bulle m, Stier m

'bulldog n Bulldogge f

bulldozer /'bʊldəʊzə(r)/ n Planier-
raupe f

bullet /'bʊlɪt/ n Kugel f

bulletin /'bʊlɪtɪn/ n Bulletin nt

'bullet-proof a kugelsicher

'bullfight n Stierkampf m. ~er n
Stierkämpfer m

'bullfinch n Dompfaff m

bullion /'bʊlɪən/ n gold ~ Barren-
gold nt

bullock /'bʊlək/ n Ochse m

bull: ~ring n Stierkampfarena f.
~'s-eye n score a ~'s-eye ins
Schwarze treffen

bully /'bʊlɪ/ n Tyrann m □vt tyrannisieren

bum[1] /bʌm/ n (sl) Hintern m

bum[2] n (Amer, fam) Landstreicher m

bumble-bee /'bʌmbl-/ n Hummel f

bump /bʌmp/ n Bums m; (swelling) Beule f; (in road) holperige
Stelle f □vt stoßen. ~ into stoßen
gegen; (meet) zufällig treffen. ~
off (fam) um die Ecke bringen

bumper /'bʌmpə(r)/ a Rekord- □n
(Auto) Stoßstange f

bumpkin /'bʌmpkɪn/ n country
~ Tölpel m

bumptious /'bʌmpʃəs/ a aufgeblasen

bumpy /'bʌmpɪ/ a holperig

bun /bʌn/ n Milchbrötchen nt;
(hair) [Haar]knoten m

bunch /bʌntʃ/ n (of flowers)
Strauß m; (of radishes, keys)
Bund m; (of people) Gruppe f; ~
of grapes [ganze] Weintraube f

bundle /'bʌndl/ n Bündel nt □vt
~ [up] bündeln

bung /bʌŋ/ vt (fam) (throw)
schmeißen. ~ up vt (fam) verstopfen

bungalow /'bʌŋgələʊ/ n Bungalow m

bungle /'bʌŋgl/ vt verpfuschen

bunion /'bʌnjən/ n (Med) Ballen m

bunk /bʌŋk/ n [Schlaf]koje f.
~-beds npl Etagenbett nt

bunker /'bʌŋkə(r)/ n Bunker m

bunkum /'bʌŋkəm/ n Quatsch m

bunny /'bʌnɪ/ n (fam) Kaninchen
nt

buoy /bɔɪ/ n Boje f. ~ up vt (fig)
stärken

buoyan|cy /'bɔɪənsɪ/ n Auftrieb m.
~t a be ~t schwimmen; ⟨water:⟩
gut tragen

burden /'bɜːdn/ n Last f □vt belasten. ~some /-səm/ a lästig

bureau /'bjʊərəʊ/ n (pl -x /-əʊz/ or
~s) (desk) Sekretär m; (office)
Büro nt

bureaucracy /bjʊə'rɒkrəsɪ/ n
Bürokratie f

bureaucrat /'bjʊərəkræt/ n Büro-
krat m. ~ic /-'krætɪk/ a bürokra-
tisch

burger /'bɜːgə(r)/ n Hamburger m

burglar /'bɜːglə(r)/ n Einbrecher
m. ~ alarm n Alarmanlage f

burglar|ize /'bɜːgləraɪz/ vt (Amer)
einbrechen in (+ acc). ~y n Einbruch m

burgle /'bɜːgl/ vt einbrechen in (+
acc); they have been ~d bei
ihnen ist eingebrochen worden

Burgundy /'bɜːgəndɪ/ n Burgund nt; **b~** (wine) Burgunder m

burial /'berɪəl/ n Begräbnis nt

burlesque /bɜːˈlesk/ n Burleske f

burly /'bɜːlɪ/ a (-ier, -iest) stämmig

Burma /'bɜːmə/ n Birma nt. **~ese** /-'miːz/ a birmanisch

burn /bɜːn/ n Verbrennung f; (on skin) Brandwunde f; (on material) Brandstelle f □v (pt/pp **burnt** or **burned**) □vt verbrennen □vi brennen; ⟨food:⟩ anbrennen. **~ down** vt/i niederbrennen

burnish /'bɜːnɪʃ/ vt polieren

burnt /bɜːnt/ see **burn**

burp /bɜːp/ vi (fam) aufstoßen

burrow /'bʌrəʊ/ n Bau m □vi wühlen

bursar /'bɜːsə(r)/ n Rechnungsführer m. **~y** n Stipendium nt

burst /bɜːst/ n Bruch m; (surge) Ausbruch m □v (pt/pp **burst**) □vt platzen machen □vi platzen; ⟨bud:⟩ aufgehen; **~ into tears** in Tränen ausbrechen

bury /'berɪ/ vt (pt/pp **-ied**) begraben; (hide) vergraben

bus /bʌs/ n [Auto]bus m □vt/i (pt/pp **bussed**) mit dem Bus fahren

bush /bʊʃ/ n Strauch m; (land) Busch m. **~y** a (-ier, -iest) buschig

busily /'bɪzɪlɪ/ adv eifrig

business /'bɪznɪs/ n Angelegenheit f; (Comm) Geschäft nt; **on ~** geschäftlich; **he has no ~ to** er hat kein Recht, zu; **mind one's own ~** sich um seine eigenen Angelegenheiten kümmern; **that's none of your ~** das geht Sie nichts an. **~-like** a geschäftsmäßig. **~man** n Geschäftsmann m

busker /'bʌskə(r)/ n Straßenmusikant m

bus-stop n Bushaltestelle f

bust¹ /bʌst/ n Büste f. **~ size** n Oberweite f

bust² a (fam) kaputt; **go ~** pleite machen □v (pt/pp **busted** or

bust) (fam) □vt kaputtmachen □vi kaputtgehen

bustle /'bʌsl/ n Betrieb m, Getriebe nt □vi **~ about** geschäftig hin und her laufen. **~ing** a belebt

bust-up n (fam) Streit m, Krach m

busy /'bɪzɪ/ a (-ier, -iest) beschäftigt; ⟨day⟩ voll; ⟨street⟩ belebt; (with traffic) stark befahren; (Amer Teleph) besetzt; **be ~** zu tun haben □vt **~ oneself** sich beschäftigen (with mit)

busybody n Wichtigtuer(in) m(f)

but /bʌt/, unbetont bət/ conj aber; (after negative) sondern ●prep außer (+ dat); **~ for** (without) ohne (+ acc); **the last ~ one** der/die/das vorletzte; **the next ~ one** der/die/das übernächste □adv nur

butcher /'bʊtʃə(r)/ n Fleischer m, Metzger m; **~'s [shop]** Fleischerei f, Metzgerei f □vt [ab]schlachten

butler /'bʌtlə(r)/ n Butler m

butt /bʌt/ n (of gun) [Gewehr]kolben m; (fig: target) Zielscheibe f; ⟨of cigarette⟩ Stummel m; (for water) Regentonne f □vt mit dem Kopf stoßen □vi **~ in** unterbrechen

butter /'bʌtə(r)/ n Butter f □vt mit Butter bestreichen. **~ up** vt (fam) schmeicheln (+ dat)

butter: ~cup n Butterblume f, Hahnenfuß m. **~fly** n Schmetterling m

buttocks /'bʌtəks/ npl Gesäß nt

button /'bʌtn/ n Knopf m □vt **~ [up]** zuknöpfen □vi geknöpft werden. **~hole** n Knopfloch nt

buttress /'bʌtrɪs/ n Strebepfeiler m; **flying ~** Strebebogen m

buxom /'bʌksəm/ a drall

buy /baɪ/ n Kauf m □vt (pt/pp **bought**) kaufen. **~er** n Käufer(in) m(f)

buzz /bʌz/ n Summen nt □vi summen. **~ off** vi (fam) abhauen

buzzard /ˈbʌzəd/ n Bussard m

buzzer /ˈbʌzə(r)/ n Summer m

by /baɪ/ prep (close to) bei (+ dat); (next to) neben (+ dat/acc); (past) an (+ dat) ... vorbei; (to the extent of) um (+ acc); (at the latest) bis; (by means of) durch; **by Mozart/Dickens** von Mozart/Dickens; **~ oneself** allein; **~ the sea** am Meer; **~ car/bus** mit dem Auto/Bus; **~ sea** mit dem Schiff; **~ day/night** bei Tag/Nacht; **~ the hour** pro Stunde; **~ the metre** meterweise; **six metres ~ four** sechs mal vier Meter; **win ~ a length** mit einer Länge Vorsprung gewinnen; **miss the train ~ a minute** den Zug um eine Minute verpassen □ adv **~ and ~** mit der Zeit; **~ and large** im großen und ganzen; **put ~** beiseite legen; **go/pass ~** vorbeigehen

bye /baɪ/ int (fam) tschüs

by: **~-election** n Nachwahl f. **~gone** a vergangen. **~-law** n Verordnung f. **~pass** n Umgehungsstraße f; (Med) Bypass m □ vt umfahren. **~-product** n Nebenprodukt m. **~-road** n Nebenstraße f. **~stander** n Zuschauer(in) m(f)

Byzantine /bɪˈzæntaɪn/ a byzantinisch

C

cab /kæb/ n Taxi nt; (of lorry, train) Führerhaus nt

cabaret /ˈkæbəreɪ/ n Kabarett nt

cabbage /ˈkæbɪdʒ/ n Kohl m

cabin /ˈkæbɪn/ n Kabine f; (hut) Hütte f

cabinet /ˈkæbɪnɪt/ n Schrank m; [display] ~ Vitrine f; (TV, Radio) Gehäuse nt; C~ (Pol) Kabinett nt. **~-maker** n Möbeltischler m

cable /ˈkeɪbl/ n Kabel nt; (rope) Tau nt. **~ railway** n Seilbahn f.

~ television n Kabelfernsehen nt

cache /kæʃ/ n Versteck nt; **~ of arms** Waffenlager nt

cackle /ˈkækl/ vi gackern

cactus /ˈkæktəs/ n (pl -ti /-taɪ/ or -tuses) Kaktus m

caddie /ˈkædɪ/ n Caddie m

caddy /ˈkædɪ/ n [tea-] ~ Teedose f

cadet /kəˈdet/ n Kadett m

cadge /kædʒ/ vt/i (fam) schnorren

Caesarean /sɪˈzeərɪən/ a & n ~ [section] Kaiserschnitt m

café /ˈkæfeɪ/ n Café nt

cafeteria /kæfəˈtɪərɪə/ n Selbstbedienungsrestaurant nt

caffeine /ˈkæfiːn/ n Koffein nt

cage /keɪdʒ/ n Käfig m

cagey /ˈkeɪdʒɪ/ a (fam) **be ~** mit der Sprache nicht herauswollen

cajole /kəˈdʒəʊl/ vt gut zureden (+ dat)

cake /keɪk/ n Kuchen m; (of soap) Stück m. **~d** a verkrustet (with mit)

calamity /kəˈlæmətɪ/ n Katastrophe f

calcium /ˈkælsɪəm/ n Kalzium nt

calculat|e /ˈkælkjʊleɪt/ vt berechnen; (estimate) kalkulieren. **~ing** a (fig) berechnend. **~ion** /-ˈleɪʃn/ n Rechnung f, Kalkulation f. **~or** n Rechner m

calendar /ˈkælɪndə(r)/ n Kalender m

calf¹ /kɑːf/ n (pl calves) Kalb nt

calf² /kɑːf/ n (pl calves) (Anat) Wade f

calibre /ˈkælɪbə(r)/ n Kaliber nt

calico /ˈkælɪkəʊ/ n Kattun m

call /kɔːl/ n Ruf m; (Teleph) Anruf m; (visit) Besuch m; **be on ~** ⟨doctor:⟩ Bereitschaftsdienst haben □ vt rufen; (Teleph) anrufen; (wake) wecken; ausrufen ⟨strike⟩; (name) nennen; **be ~ed** heißen □ vi rufen; (Teleph) anrufen. **~ back** vt zurückrufen □ vi noch einmal vorbeikommen. **~ for** vt rufen nach; (demand) verlangen;

(*fetch*) abholen. ~ **off** *vt* zurückrufen ⟨*dog*⟩; (*cancel*) absagen. ~
on *vt* bitten (**for** um); (*appeal to*)
appellieren an (+ *acc*); (*visit*) besuchen. ~ **out** *vt* rufen; aufrufen
⟨*names*⟩ □*vi* rufen. ~ **up** *vt* (*Mil*)
einberufen; (*Teleph*) anrufen
call: ~**-box** *n* Telefonzelle *f.* ~**er**
n Besucher *m*; (*Teleph*) Anrufer
m. ~**ing** *n* Berufung *f*
'call-up *n* (*Mil*) Einberufung *f*
callous /'kæləs/ *a* gefühllos
calm /kɑ:m/ *a* (-**er**, -**est**), -**ly** *adv*
ruhig □ *n* Ruhe *f* □*vt* ~ [**down**]
beruhigen □*vi* ~ **down** sich beruhigen. ~**ness** *n* Ruhe *f*; (*of sea*)
Stille *f*
calorie /'kælərɪ/ *n* Kalorie *f*
calves /kɑ:vz/ *npl see* **calf**[1] & [2]
camber /'kæmbə(r)/ *n* Wölbung *f*
came /keɪm/ *see* **come**
camel /'kæml/ *n* Kamel *nt*
camera /'kæmərə/ *n* Kamera *f.* ~
man *n* Kameramann *m*
camouflage /'kæməflɑ:ʒ/ *n* Tar-
nung *f* □*vt* tarnen
camp /kæmp/ *n* Lager *nt* □*vi* campen; (*Mil*) kampieren
campaign /kæm'peɪn/ *n* Feldzug
m; (*Comm, Pol*) Kampagne *f* □*vi*
kämpfen; (*Pol*) im Wahlkampf
arbeiten
camp: ~**-bed** *n* Feldbett *nt.* ~**er** *n*
Camper *m*; (*Auto*) Wohnmobil *nt.*
~**ing** *n* Camping *nt.* ~**site** *n*
Campingplatz *m*
campus /'kæmpəs/ *n* (*pl* **-puses**)
(*Univ*) Campus *m*
can[1] /kæn/ *n* (*for petrol*) Kanister
m; (*tin*) Dose *f*, Büchse *f*; **a** ~ **of**
beer eine Dose Bier □*vt* in Dosen
od Büchsen konservieren
can[2] /kæn, *unbetont* kən/ *v aux*
(*pres* **can**; *pt* **could**) können; **I**
cannot/can't go ich kann nicht
gehen; **he could not go** er konnte
nicht gehen; **if I could go** wenn
ich gehen könnte
Canada /'kænədə/ *n* Kanada *nt.*
~**ian** /kə'neɪdɪən/ *a* kanadisch
□*n* Kanadier(in) *m(f)*

canal /kə'næl/ *n* Kanal *m*
Canaries /kə'neərɪz/ *npl* Kana-
rische Inseln *pl*
canary /kə'neərɪ/ *n* Kanarienvogel *m*
cancel /'kænsl/ *vt/i* (*pt/pp* **cancelled**) absagen; entwerten
⟨*stamp*⟩; (*annul*) rückgängig machen; (*Comm*) stornieren; abbestellen ⟨*newspaper*⟩; **be** ~**led**
ausfallen. ~**lation** /-ə'leɪʃn/ *n* Absage *f*
cancer /'kænsə(r)/ *n*, & (*Astr*) **C** ~
Krebs *m.* ~**ous** /-rəs/ *a* krebsig
candelabra /kændə'lɑ:brə/ *n*
Armleuchter *m*
candid /'kændɪd/ *a*, -**ly** *adv* offen
candidate /'kændɪdət/ *n* Kandi-
dat(in) *m(f)*
candied /'kændɪd/ *a* kandiert
candle /'kændl/ *n* Kerze *f.* ~**stick**
n Kerzenständer *m*, Leuchter *m*
candour /'kændə(r)/ *n* Offenheit *f*
candy /'kændɪ/ *n* (*Amer*) Süßig-
keiten *pl*; [**piece of**] ~ Bonbon *m*.
~**floss** /-flɒs/ *n* Zuckerwatte *f*
cane /keɪn/ *n* Rohr *nt*; (*stick*) Stock
m □*vt* mit dem Stock züchtigen
canine /'keɪnaɪn/ *a* Hunde-.
~**tooth** *n* Eckzahn *m*
canister /'kænɪstə(r)/ *n* Blech-
dose *f*
cannabis /'kænəbɪs/ *n* Haschisch
nt
canned /kænd/ *a* Dosen-, Büch-
sen-; ~ **music** (*fam*) Musik *f* aus
der Konserve
cannibal /'kænɪbl/ *n* Kannibale
m. ~**ism** *n* Kannibalismus *m*
cannon /'kænən/ *n inv* Kanone *f.*
~**-ball** *n* Kanonenkugel *f*
cannot /'kænɒt/ *see* **can**[2]
canny /'kænɪ/ *a* schlau
canoe /kə'nu:/ *n* Paddelboot *nt*;
(*Sport*) Kanu *nt* □*vi* paddeln;
(*Sport*) Kanu fahren
canon /'kænən/ *n* Kanon *m*; (*person*) Kanonikus *m.* ~**ize** /-aɪz/ *vt*
kanonisieren
'can-opener *n* Dosenöffner *m*,
Büchsenöffner *m*

canopy /'kænəpɪ/ n Baldachin m

cant /kænt/ n Heuchelei f

can't /ka:nt/ = cannot. See can[2]

cantankerous /kæn'tæŋkərəs/ a zänkisch

canteen /kæn'ti:n/ n Kantine f; ~ of cutlery Besteckkasten m

canter /'kæntə(r)/ n Kanter m □ vi kantern

canvas /'kænvəs/ n Segeltuch nt; (Art) Leinwand f; (painting) Gemälde nt

canvass /'kænvəs/ vi um Stimmen werben

canyon /'kænjən/ n Cañon m

cap /kæp/ n Kappe f, Mütze f; (nurse's) Haube f; (top, lid) Verschluß m □ vt (pt/pp capped) (fig) übertreffen

capability /keɪpə'bɪlətɪ/ n Fähigkeit f

capable /'keɪpəbl/ a, -bly adv fähig; be ~ of doing sth fähig sein, etw zu tun

capacity /kə'pæsətɪ/ n Fassungsvermögen nt; (ability) Fähigkeit f; in my ~ as in meiner Eigenschaft als

cape[1] /keɪp/ n (cloak) Cape nt

cape[2] n (Geog) Kap nt

caper[1] /'keɪpə(r)/ vi herumspringen

caper[2] n (Culin) Kaper f

capital /'kæpɪtl/ a ⟨letter⟩ groß □ n (town) Hauptstadt f; (money) Kapital nt; (letter) Großbuchstabe m

capital|ism /'kæpɪtəlɪzm/ n Kapitalismus m. ~ist /-ɪst/ a kapitalistisch □ n Kapitalist m. ~ize /-aɪz/ vi ~ize on (fig) Kapital schlagen aus. ~ letter n Großbuchstabe m. ~ 'punishment n Todesstrafe f

capitulat|e /kə'pɪtjʊleɪt/ vi kapitulieren. ~ion /-'leɪʃn/ n Kapitulation f

capricious /kə'prɪʃəs/ a launisch

Capricorn /'kæprɪkɔ:n/ n (Astr) Steinbock m

capsize /kæp'saɪz/ vi kentern □ vt zum Kentern bringen

capsule /'kæpsjʊl/ n Kapsel f

captain /'kæptɪn/ n Kapitän m; (Mil) Hauptmann m □ vt anführen ⟨team⟩

caption /'kæpʃn/ n Überschrift f; (of illustration) Bildtext m

captivate /'kæptɪveɪt/ vt bezaubern

captive /'kæptɪv/ a hold/take ~ gefangenhalten/-nehmen □ n Gefangene(r) m/f. ~ity /-'tɪvətɪ/ n Gefangenschaft f

capture /'kæptʃə(r)/ n Gefangennahme f □ vt gefangennehmen; [ein]fangen ⟨animal⟩; (Mil) einnehmen ⟨town⟩

car /ka:(r)/ n Auto nt, Wagen m; by ~ mit dem Auto od Wagen

carafe /kə'ræf/ n Karaffe f

caramel /'kærəmel/ n Karamel m

carat /'kærət/ n Karat nt

caravan /'kærəvæn/ n Wohnwagen m; (procession) Karawane f

carbohydrate /ka:bə'haɪdreɪt/ n Kohlenhydrat nt

carbon /'ka:bən/ n Kohlenstoff m; (paper) Kohlepapier nt; (copy) Durchschlag m

carbon: ~ copy n Durchschlag m. ~ di'oxide n Kohlendioxyd nt; (in drink) Kohlensäure f. ~ paper n Kohlepapier nt

carburettor /ka:bju'retə(r)/ n Vergaser m

carcass /'ka:kəs/ n Kadaver m

card /ka:d/ n Karte f

'cardboard n Pappe f, Karton m. ~ 'box n Pappschachtel f; (large) [Papp]karton m

card-game n Kartenspiel nt

cardiac /'ka:dɪæk/ a Herz-

cardigan /'ka:dɪgən/ n Strickjacke f

cardinal /'ka:dɪnl/ a Kardinal-; ~ number Kardinalzahl f □ n (Relig) Kardinal m

card 'index n Kartei f

care /keə(r)/ n Sorgfalt f; (caution) Vorsicht f; (protection) Obhut f; (looking after) Pflege f; (worry) Sorge f; ~ of (on letter abbr c/o) bei; **take** ~ vorsichtig sein; **take into** ~ in Pflege nehmen; **take ~ of** sich kümmern um □ *vi* ~ **about** sich kümmern um; ~ **for** (*like*) mögen; (*look after*) betreuen; **I don't** ~ das ist mir gleich

career /kə'rɪə(r)/ *n* Laufbahn *f*; (*profession*) Beruf *m* □ *vi* rasen

care: ~ **free** *a* sorglos. ~ **ful** *a*, **-ly** *adv* sorgfältig; (*cautious*) vorsichtig. ~ **less** *a*, **-ly** *adv* nachlässig. ~ **lessness** *n* Nachlässigkeit *f*

caress /kə'res/ *n* Liebkosung *f* □ *vt* liebkosen

'**caretaker** *n* Hausmeister *m*

'**car ferry** *n* Autofähre *f*

cargo /'kɑ:gəʊ/ *n* (*pl* **-es**) Ladung *f*

Caribbean /kærɪ'bi:ən/ *n* **the** ~ die Karibik

caricature /'kærɪkətjʊə(r)/ *n* Karikatur *f* □ *vt* karikieren

caring /'keərɪŋ/ *a* (*parent*) liebevoll; (*profession, attitude*) sozial

carnage /'kɑ:nɪdʒ/ *n* Gemetzel *nt*

carnal /'kɑ:nl/ *a* fleischlich

carnation /kɑ:'neɪʃn/ *n* Nelke *f*

carnival /'kɑ:nɪvl/ *n* Karneval *m*

carnivorous /kɑ:'nɪvərəs/ *a* fleischfressend

carol /'kærəl/ *n* [**Christmas**] ~ Weihnachtslied *nt*

carp[1] /kɑ:p/ *n inv* Karpfen *m*

carp[2] *vi* nörgeln; ~ **at** herumnörgeln an (+ *dat*)

'**car park** *n* Parkplatz *m*; (*multistorey*) Parkhaus *nt*; (*underground*) Tiefgarage *f*

carpent|er /'kɑ:pɪntə(r)/ *n* Zimmermann *m*; (*joiner*) Tischler *m*. ~ **ry** *n* Tischlerei *f*

carpet /'kɑ:pɪt/ *n* Teppich *m* □ *vt* mit Teppich auslegen

carriage /'kærɪdʒ/ *n* Kutsche *f*; (*Rail*) Wagen *m*; (*of goods*) Beförderung *f*; (*cost*) Frachtkosten *pl*; (*bearing*) Haltung *f*. ~ **way** *n* Fahrbahn *f*

carrier /'kærɪə(r)/ *n* Träger(in) *m(f)*; (*Comm*) Spediteur *m*; ~ [-**bag**] Tragetasche *f*

carrot /'kærət/ *n* Möhre *f*, Karotte *f*

carry /'kærɪ/ *vt/i* (*pt/pp* **-ied**) tragen; **be carried away** (*fam*) hingerissen sein. ~ **off** *vt* wegtragen; gewinnen (*prize*). ~ **on** *vi* weitermachen; ~ **on at** (*fam*) herumnörgeln an (+ *dat*); ~ **on with** (*fam*) eine Affäre haben mit □ *vt* führen; (*continue*) fortführen. ~ **out** *vt* hinaus-/heraustragen; (*perform*) ausführen

'**carry-cot** *n* Babytragetasche *f*

cart /kɑ:t/ *n* Karren *m*; **put the ~ before the horse** *fig* das Pferd beim Schwanz aufzäumen □ *vt* karren; (*fam: carry*) schleppen

cartilage /'kɑ:tɪlɪdʒ/ *n* (*Anat*) Knorpel *m*

carton /'kɑ:tn/ *n* [Papp]karton *m*; (*for drink*) Tüte *f*; (*of cream, yoghurt*) Becher *m*

cartoon /kɑ:'tu:n/ *n* Karikatur *f*; (*joke*) Witzzeichnung *f*; (*strip*) Comic Strips *pl*; (*film*) Zeichentrickfilm *m*; (*Art*) Karton *m*. ~ **ist** *n* Karikaturist *m*

cartridge /'kɑ:trɪdʒ/ *n* Patrone *f*; (*for film, typewriter ribbon*) Kassette *f*; (*of record player*) Tonabnehmer *m*

carve /kɑ:v/ *vt* schnitzen; (*in stone*) hauen; (*Culin*) aufschneiden

carving /'kɑ:vɪŋ/ *n* Schnitzerei *f*. ~ **knife** *n* Tranchiermesser *nt*

'**car wash** *n* Autowäsche *f*; (*place*) Autowaschanlage *f*

case[1] /keɪs/ *n* Fall *m*; **in any** ~ auf jeden Fall; **just in** ~ für alle Fälle; **in** ~ **he comes** falls er kommt

case[2] *n* Kasten *m*; (*crate*) Kiste *f*; (*for spectacles*) Etui *nt*; (*suitcase*) Koffer *m*; (*for display*) Vitrine *f*

cash /kæʃ/ *n* Bargeld *nt*; **pay** [**in**] ~ [in] bar bezahlen; ~ **on delivery** per Nachnahme □ *vt*

einlösen ⟨cheque⟩. ~ **desk** n
Kasse f

cashier /kæˈʃɪə(r)/ n Kassierer(in)
m(f)

'cash register n Registrierkasse f

casino /kəˈsiːnəʊ/ n Kasino nt

cask /kɑːsk/ n Faß nt

casket /ˈkɑːskɪt/ n Kasten m;
(Amer: coffin) Sarg m

casserole /ˈkæsərəʊl/ n Schmor-
topf m; (stew) Eintopf m

cassette /kəˈset/ n Kassette f. ~
recorder n Kassettenrecorder m

cast /kɑːst/ n (throw) Wurf m;
(mould) Form f; (model) Abguß
m; (Theat) Besetzung f;
[**plaster**] ~ (Med) Gipsverband
m □vt (pt/pp cast) (throw) werfen; (shed) abwerfen; abgeben
⟨vote⟩; gießen ⟨metal⟩; (Theat)
besetzen ⟨role⟩. ~ **a glance** at
einen Blick werfen auf (+ acc). ~
off vi (Naut) ablegen □vt (Knitting) abketten. ~ **on** vt (Knitting)
anschlagen

castanets /kæstəˈnets/ npl Kastagnetten pl

castaway /ˈkɑːstəweɪ/ n Schiff-
brüchige(r) m/f

caste /kɑːst/ n Kaste f

cast 'iron n Gußeisen nt

cast-'iron a gußeisern

castle /ˈkɑːsl/ n Schloß nt; (forti-
fied) Burg f; (Chess) Turm m

'cast-offs npl abgelegte Kleidung f

castor /ˈkɑːstə(r)/ n (wheel)
[Lauf]rolle f

'castor sugar n Streuzucker m

castrat|e /kæˈstreɪt/ vt kastrieren.
~**ion** -eɪʃn/ n Kastration f

casual /ˈkæʒʊəl/ a, **-ly** adv ⟨chance⟩
zufällig; (offhand) lässig; (informal) zwanglos; (not permanent)
Gelegenheits-; ~ **wear** Freizeit-
bekleidung f

casualty /ˈkæʒʊəltɪ/ n [Todes]-
opfer nt; (injured person) Verletz-
te(r) m/f; ~ [**department**] Unfall-
station f

cat /kæt/ n Katze f

catalogue /ˈkætəlɒg/ n Katalog m
□vt katalogisieren

catalyst /ˈkætəlɪst/ n (Chem & fig)
Katalysator m

catalytic /kætəˈlɪtɪk/ a ~ **converter** (Auto) Katalysator m

catapult /ˈkætəpʌlt/ n Katapult m
□vt katapultieren

cataract /ˈkætərækt/ n (Med)
grauer Star m

catarrh /kəˈtɑː(r)/ n Katarrh m

catastrophe /kəˈtæstrəfɪ/ n Katastrophe f. ~**ic** /kætəˈstrɒfɪk/ a
katastrophal

catch /kætʃ/ n (of fish) Fang m;
(fastener) Verschluß m; (on door)
Klinke f; (fam: snag) Haken m
(fam) □v (pt/pp caught) □vt fangen; (be in time for) erreichen;
(travel by) fahren mit; bekommen
⟨illness⟩; ~ **a cold** sich erkälten;
~ **sight of** entdecken; ~ **s.o.
stealing** jdn beim Stehlen erwischen; ~ **one's finger in the
door** sich (dat) den Finger in der
Tür [ein]klemmen □vi (burn) anbrennen; (get stuck) klemmen. ~
on vi (fam) (understand) kapieren; (become popular) sich durchsetzen. ~ **up** vt einholen □vi
aufholen; ~ **up with** einholen
⟨s.o.⟩; nachholen ⟨work⟩

catching /ˈkætʃɪŋ/ a ansteckend

catch: ~**phrase** n, ~**word** n
Schlagwort nt

catchy /ˈkætʃɪ/ a (-ier, -iest) ein-
prägsam

catechism /ˈkætɪkɪzm/ n Katechismus m

categor|ical /kætɪˈgɒrɪkl/ a, **-ly**
adv kategorisch. ~**y** /ˈkætɪgərɪ/ n
Kategorie f

cater /ˈkeɪtə(r)/ vi ~ **for** bekösti-
gen; ⟨firm:⟩ das Essen liefern für
⟨party⟩; (fig) eingestellt sein auf
(+ acc). ~**ing** n (trade) Gast-
stättengewerbe nt

caterpillar /ˈkætəpɪlə(r)/ n
Raupe f

cathedral /kəˈθiːdrl/ n Dom m, Kathedrale f

Catholic /'kæθəlɪk/ *a* katholisch
□*n* Katholik(in) *m(f)*. **C~ism**
/kə'θɒlɪsɪzm/ *n* Katholizismus *m*

catkin /'kætkɪn/ *n (Bot)* Kätzchen
nt

cattle /'kætl/ *npl* Vieh *nt*

catty /'kætɪ/ *a* (-ier, -iest) boshaft

caught /kɔ:t/ *see* catch

cauldron /'kɔ:ldrən/ *n (großer)*
Kessel *m*

cauliflower /'kɒlɪ-/ *n* Blumen-
kohl *m*

cause /kɔ:z/ *n* Ursache *f; (reason)*
Grund *m; good ~* gute Sache *f*
□*vt* verursachen; *~ s.o. to do sth*
jdn veranlassen, etw zu tun

'causeway *n* [Insel]damm *m*

caustic /'kɔ:stɪk/ *a* ätzend; *(fig)*
beißend

cauterize /'kɔ:təraɪz/ *vt* kauterisieren

caution /'kɔ:ʃn/ *n* Vorsicht *f;*
(warning) Warnung *f* □*vt*
(Jur) verwarnen

cautious /'kɔ:ʃəs/ *a*, **-ly** *adv* vorsichtig

cavalry /'kævəlrɪ/ *n* Kavallerie *f*

cave /keɪv/ *n* Höhle *f* □*vi* **~ in**
einstürzen

cavern /'kævən/ *n* Höhle *f*

caviare /'kævɪɑ:(r)/ *n* Kaviar *m*

caving /'keɪvɪŋ/ *n* Höhlenfor-
schung *f*

cavity /'kævətɪ/ *n* Hohlraum *m;*
(in tooth) Loch *nt*

cavort /kə'vɔ:t/ *vi* tollen

cease /si:s/ *n without ~* unaufhörlich □*vt/i* aufhören. **~-**
fire *n* Waffenruhe *f.* **~less** *a*, **-ly**
adv unaufhörlich

cedar /'si:də(r)/ *n* Zeder *f*

cede /si:d/ *vt* abtreten (**to** an +
acc)

ceiling /'si:lɪŋ/ *n* [Zimmer]decke *f;*
(fig) oberste Grenze *f*

celebrat|e /'selɪbreɪt/ *vt/i* feiern.
~ed *a* berühmt (**for** wegen).
~ion /-'breɪʃn/ *n* Feier *f*

celebrity /sɪ'lebrətɪ/ *n* Berühmt-
heit *f*

celery /'selərɪ/ *n* [Stangen]selle-
rie *m & f*

celiba|cy /'selɪbəsɪ/ *n* Zölibat *nt.*
~te /-ə/ *a* **be ~te** im Zölibat leben

cell /sel/ *n* Zelle *f*

cellar /'selə(r)/ *n* Keller *m*

cellist /'tʃelɪst/ *n* Cellist(in) *m(f)*

cello /'tʃeləʊ/ *n* Cello *nt*

Celsius /'selsɪəs/ *a* Celsius

Celt /kelt/ *n* Kelte *m*/Keltin *f.* **~ic**
a keltisch

cement /sɪ'ment/ *n* Zement *m; (ad-*
hesive) Kitt *m* □*vt* zementieren;
(stick) kitten

cemetery /'semətrɪ/ *n* Friedhof *m*

censor /'sensə(r)/ *n* Zensor *m* □*vt*
zensieren. **~ship** *n* Zensur *f*

censure /'senʃə(r)/ *n* Tadel *m* □*vt*
tadeln

census /'sensəs/ *n* Volkszählung *f*

cent /sent/ *n (coin)* Cent *m*

centenary /sen'ti:nərɪ/ *n*, *(Amer)*
centennial /sen'tenɪəl/ *n* Hun-
dertjahrfeier *f*

center /'sentə(r)/ *n (Amer)* =
centre

centigrade /'sentɪ-/ *a* Celsius-;
5° ~ 5° Celsius. **~metre** *m* Zentimeter *m & nt.* **~pede** /-pi:d/ *n*
Tausendfüßler *m*

central /'sentrəl/ *a*, **-ly** *adv* zentral.
~ 'heating *n* Zentralheizung *f.*
~ize *vt* zentralisieren. **~ reser-**
'vation *n (Auto)* Mittelstreifen *m*

centre /'sentə(r)/ *n* Zentrum *nt;*
(middle) Mitte *f* □*v (pt/pp* cen-
tred) □*vt* zentrieren; **~ on** *(fig)*
sich drehen um. **~'forward** *n*
Mittelstürmer *m*

centrifugal /sentrɪ'fju:gl/ *a*
~ force Fliehkraft *f*

century /'sentʃərɪ/ *n* Jahrhundert
nt

ceramic /sɪ'ræmɪk/ *a* Keramik-.
~s *n* Keramik *f*

cereal /'sɪərɪəl/ *n* Getreide *nt;*
(breakfast food) Frühstücks-
flocken *pl*

cerebral /'serɪbrl/ *a* Gehirn-

ceremon|ial /serɪ'məʊnɪəl/ *a*, **-ly**
adv zeremoniell, feierlich □*n*

Zeremoniell *nt*. ~**ious** /-ɪəs/ *a*, -**ly** *adv* formell

ceremony /'serɪmənɪ/ *n* Zeremonie *f*, Feier *f*; *without* ~ ohne weitere Umstände

certain /'sɜːtn/ *a* sicher; (*not named*) gewiß; *for* ~ mit Bestimmtheit; **make** ~ (*check*) sich vergewissern (*that* daß); (*ensure*) dafür sorgen (*that* daß); **he is** ~ **to win** er wird ganz bestimmt siegen. ~**ly** *adv* bestimmt, sicher; ~**ly not!** auf keinen Fall! ~**ty** *n* Sicherheit *f*, Gewißheit *f*; **it's a** ~**ty** es ist sicher

certificate /sə'tɪfɪkət/ *n* Bescheinigung *f*; (*Jur*) Urkunde *f*; (*Sch*) Zeugnis *nt*

certify /'sɜːtɪfaɪ/ *vt* (*pt/pp* -**ied**) bescheinigen; (*declare insane*) für geisteskrank erklären

cessation /se'seɪʃn/ *n* Ende *nt*

cesspool /'ses-/ *n* Senkgrube *f*

cf *abbr* (*compare*) vgl

chafe /tʃeɪf/ *vt* wund reiben

chaff /tʃɑːf/ *n* Spreu *f*

chaffinch /'tʃæfɪntʃ/ *n* Buchfink *m*

chain /tʃeɪn/ *n* Kette *f* □ *vt* ketten (**to** an + *acc*). ~ **up** *vt* anketten

chain: ~ **re'action** *n* Kettenreaktion *f*. ~**-smoker** *n* Kettenraucher *m*. ~ **store** *n* Kettenladen *m*

chair /tʃeə(r)/ *n* Stuhl *m*; (*Univ*) Lehrstuhl *m* □ *vt* den Vorsitz führen bei. ~**-lift** *n* Sessellift *m*. ~**man** *n* Vorsitzende(r) *m/f*

chalet /'ʃæleɪ/ *n* Chalet *nt*

chalice /'tʃælɪs/ *n* (*Relig*) Kelch *m*

chalk /tʃɔːk/ *n* Kreide *f*. ~**y** *a* kreidig

challenge /'tʃælɪndʒ/ *n* Herausforderung *f*; (*Mil*) Anruf *m* □ *vt* herausfordern; (*Mil*) anrufen; (*fig*) anfechten ⟨*statement*⟩. ~**er** *n* Herausforderer *m*. ~**ing** *a* herausfordernd; (*demanding*) anspruchsvoll

chamber /'tʃeɪmbə(r)/ *n* Kammer *f*. ~**s** *pl* (*Jur*) [Anwalts]büro *nt*;

C~ **of Commerce** Handelskammer *f*

chamber: ~ **maid** *n* Zimmermädchen *nt*. ~ **music** *n* Kammermusik *f*. ~**-pot** *n* Nachttopf *m*

chamois[1] /'ʃæmwɑː/ *n inv* (*animal*) Gemse *f*

chamois[2] /'ʃæmɪ/ *n* ~**[-leather]** Ledertuch *nt*

champagne /ʃæm'peɪn/ *n* Champagner *m*

champion /'tʃæmpɪən/ *n* (*Sport*) Meister(in) *m(f)*; (*of cause*) Verfechter *m* □ *vt* sich einsetzen für. ~**ship** *n* (*Sport*) Meisterschaft *f*

chance /tʃɑːns/ *n* Zufall *m*; (*prospect*) Chancen *pl*; (*likelihood*) Aussicht *f*; (*opportunity*) Gelegenheit *f*; **by** ~ zufällig; **take a** ~ ein Risiko eingehen; **give s.o. a** ~ jdm eine Chance geben □ *attrib* zufällig □ *vt* ~ **it** es riskieren

chancellor /'tʃɑːnsələ(r)/ *n* Kanzler *m*; (*Univ*) Rektor *m*; C~ **of the Exchequer** Schatzkanzler *m*

chancy /'tʃɑːnsɪ/ *a* riskant

chandelier /ʃændə'lɪə(r)/ *n* Kronleuchter *m*

change /tʃeɪndʒ/ *n* Veränderung *f*; (*alteration*) Änderung *f*; (*money*) Wechselgeld *nt*; **for a** ~ zur Abwechslung □ *vt* wechseln; (*alter*) ändern; (*exchange*) umtauschen (**for** gegen); (*transform*) verwandeln; trocken legen ⟨*baby*⟩; ~ **one's clothes** sich umziehen; ~ **trains** umsteigen □ *vi* sich verändern; (*change*) sich umziehen; (~ *clothes*) umsteigen; **all** ~! alles aussteigen!

changeable /'tʃeɪndʒəbl/ *a* wechselhaft

'**changing-room** *n* Umkleideraum *m*

channel /'tʃænl/ *n* Rinne *f*; (*Radio, TV*) Kanal *m*; (*fig*) Weg *m*; **the [English]** C~ der Ärmelkanal; **the C~ Islands** die Kanalinseln □ *vt* (*pt/pp* channelled) leiten; (*fig*) lenken

chant /tʃɑːnt/ n liturgischer Gesang m □ vt singen; ⟨demonstrators:⟩ skandieren

chaos /'keɪɒs/ n Chaos nt. ~**tic** /-'ɒtɪk/ a chaotisch

chap /tʃæp/ n (fam) Kerl m

chapel /'tʃæpl/ n Kapelle f

chaperon /'ʃæpərəʊn/ n Anstandsdame f □ vt begleiten

chaplain /'tʃæplɪn/ n Geistliche(r) m

chapped /tʃæpt/ a ⟨skin⟩ aufgesprungen

chapter /'tʃæptə(r)/ n Kapitel nt

char¹ /tʃɑː(r)/ n (fam) Putzfrau f

char² vt (pt/pp charred) (burn) verkohlen

character /'kærɪktə(r)/ n Charakter m; (in novel, play) Gestalt f; (Typ) Schriftzeichen nt; out of ~ uncharakteristisch; quite a ~ (fam) ein Original

characteristic /kærɪktə'rɪstɪk/ a, -ally adv charakteristisch (of für) □ n Merkmal nt

characterize /'kærɪktəraɪz/ vt charakterisieren

charade /ʃə'rɑːd/ n Scharade f

charcoal /'tʃɑː-/ n Holzkohle f

charge /tʃɑːdʒ/ n (price) Gebühr f; (Electr) Ladung f; (attack) Angriff m; (Jur) Anklage f; free of ~ kostenlos; **be in** ~ verantwortlich sein (of für); **take** ~ die Aufsicht übernehmen (of über + acc) □ vt berechnen ⟨fee⟩; (Electr) laden; (attack) angreifen; (Jur) anklagen (with gen); ~ s.o. for sth jdm etw berechnen □ vi (attack) angreifen

chariot /'tʃærɪət/ n Wagen m

charisma /kə'rɪzmə/ n Charisma nt. ~**tic** /kærɪz'mætɪk/ a charismatisch

charitable /'tʃærɪtəbl/ a wohltätig; (kind) wohlwollend

charity /'tʃærətɪ/ n Nächstenliebe f; (organization) wohltätige Einrichtung f; **for** ~ für Wohltätigkeitszwecke; **live on** ~ von Almosen leben

charlatan /'ʃɑːlətən/ n Scharlatan m

charm /tʃɑːm/ n Reiz m; (of person) Charme f; (object) Amulett nt □ vt bezaubern. ~**ing**, -ly adv reizend; ⟨person, smile⟩ charmant

chart /tʃɑːt/ n Karte f; (table) Tabelle f

charter /'tʃɑːtə(r)/ n ~ **[flight]** Charterflug m □ vt chartern; ~**ed accountant** n Wirtschaftsprüfer(in) m(f)

charwoman /'tʃɑː-/ n Putzfrau f

chase /tʃeɪs/ n Verfolgungsjagd f □ vt jagen, verfolgen. ~ **away** or **off** vt wegjagen

chasm /'kæzm/ n Kluft f

chassis /'ʃæsɪ/ n (pl chassis /-sɪz/) Chassis nt

chaste /tʃeɪst/ a keusch

chastise /tʃæ'staɪz/ vt züchtigen

chastity /'tʃæstətɪ/ n Keuschheit f

chat /tʃæt/ n Plauderei f; **have a** ~ with plaudern mit □ vi (pt/pp chatted) plaudern. ~ **show** n Talk-Show f

chatter /'tʃætə(r)/ n Geschwätz nt □ vi schwatzen; ⟨child:⟩ plappern; ⟨teeth:⟩ klappern. ~**box** n (fam) Plappermaul nt

chatty /'tʃætɪ/ a (-ier, -iest) geschwätzig

chauffeur /'ʃəʊfə(r)/ n Chauffeur m

chauvinism /'ʃəʊvɪnɪzm/ n Chauvinismus m. ~**ist** n Chauvinist m; **male** ~**ist** (fam) Chauvi m

cheap /tʃiːp/ a & adv (-er, -est), -ly adv billig. ~**en** vt entwürdigen; ~ **en oneself** sich erniedrigen

cheat /tʃiːt/ n Betrüger(in) m(f); (at games) Mogler m □ vt betrügen □ vi (at games) mogeln (fam)

check¹ /tʃek/ a (squared) kariert □ n Karo nt

check² n Überprüfung f; (inspection) Kontrolle f; (Chess) Schach nt; (Amer: bill) Rechnung f; (Amer: cheque) Scheck m; (Amer: tick) Haken m; **keep a** ~ **on**

kontrollieren □ *vt* [über]prüfen;
(*inspect*) kontrollieren; (*restrain*) hemmen; (*stop*) aufhalten
□ *vi* [**go and**] ~ nachsehen. ~ **in**
vi sich anmelden; (*Aviat*) einchecken □ *vt* abfertigen; einchecken. ~ **out** *vi* sich abmelden.
~ **up** *vi* prüfen, kontrollieren; ~
up on überprüfen

check|ed /tʃekt/ *a* kariert. ~**ers** *n*
(*Amer*) Damespiel *nt*

check: ~**mate** *int* schachmatt!
~**out** *n* Kasse *f*. ~**room** *n*
(*Amer*) Garderobe *f*. ~**-up** *n*
(*Med*) [Kontroll]untersuchung *f*

cheek /tʃiːk/ *n* Backe *f*; (*impudence*) Frechheit *f*. ~ **y** *a*, **-ily** *adv*
frech

cheep /tʃiːp/ *vi* piepen

cheer /tʃɪə(r)/ *n* Beifallsruf *m*;
three ~**s** ein dreifaches Hoch
(**for** auf + *acc*); ~ **s!** prost! (*goodbye*) tschüs! □ *vt* zujubeln (+ *dat*)
□ *vi* jubeln. ~ **up** *vt* aufmuntern;
aufheitern □ *vi* munterer werden.
~**ful** *a*, **-ly** *adv* fröhlich. ~**fulness** *n* Fröhlichkeit *f*

cheerio /tʃɪərɪ'əʊ/ *int* (*fam*) tschüs!

'**cheerless** *a* trostlos

cheese /tʃiːz/ *n* Käse *m*. ~**cake** *n*
Käsekuchen *m*

cheetah /tʃiːtə/ *n* Gepard *m*

chef /ʃef/ *n* Koch *m*

chemical /kemɪkl/ *a*, **-ly** *adv* chemisch □ *n* Chemikalie *f*

chemist /kemɪst/ *n* (*pharmacist*)
Apotheker(in) *m(f)*; (*scientist*)
Chemiker(in) *m(f)*; ~**'s [shop]**
Drogerie *f*; (*dispensing*) Apo-
theke *f*. ~**ry** *n* Chemie *f*

cheque /tʃek/ *n* Scheck *m*.
~**book** *n* Scheckbuch *nt*. ~
card *n* Scheckkarte *f*

cherish /tʃerɪʃ/ *vt* lieben; (*fig*)
hegen

cherry /tʃerɪ/ *n* Kirsche *f* □ *attrib*
Kirsch-

cherub /tʃerəb/ *n* Engelchen *nt*

chess /tʃes/ *n* Schach *nt*

chess: ~ **board** *n* Schachbrett *nt*.
~ **man** *n* Schachfigur *f*

chest /tʃest/ *n* Brust *f*; (*box*)
Truhe *f*

chestnut /tʃesnʌt/ *n* Eßkastanie
f, Marone *f*; (*horse-*) [Roß]kasta-
nie *f*

chest of 'drawers *n* Kommode *f*

chew /tʃuː/ *vt* kauen. ~**ing-gum**
n Kaugummi *m*

chic /ʃiːk/ *a* schick

chick /tʃɪk/ *n* Küken *nt*

chicken /tʃɪkɪn/ *n* Huhn *nt* □
attrib Hühner- □ *a* (*fam*) feige □
vi ~ **out** (*fam*) kneifen. ~**pox**
n Windpocken *pl*

chicory /tʃɪkərɪ/ *n* Chicorée *f*; (*in
coffee*) Zichorie *f*

chief /tʃiːf/ *a* Haupt- □ *n* Chef *m*;
(*of tribe*) Häuptling *m*. ~**ly** *adv*
hauptsächlich

chilblain /tʃɪlbleɪn/ *n* Frost-
beule *f*

child /tʃaɪld/ *n* (*pl* ~**ren**) Kind *nt*

child: ~**birth** *n* Geburt *f*. ~**hood**
n Kindheit *f*. ~**ish** *a* kindisch.
~**less** *a* kinderlos. ~**like** *a* kind-
lich. ~**minder** *n* Tagesmutter *f*

children /tʃɪldrən/ *npl see* **child**

Chile /tʃɪlɪ/ *n* Chile *nt*

chill /tʃɪl/ *n* Kälte *f*; (*illness*) Erkältung *f* □ *vt* kühlen

chilli /tʃɪlɪ/ *n* (*pl* **-es**) Chili *m*

chilly /tʃɪlɪ/ *a* kühl; **I felt** ~ **mich**
fröstelte [es]

chime /tʃaɪm/ *vi* läuten; ⟨*clock:*⟩
schlagen

chimney /tʃɪmnɪ/ *n* Schornstein
m. ~**pot** *n* Schornsteinaufsatz
m. ~**sweep** *n* Schornsteinfeger
m

chimpanzee /tʃɪmpænziː/ *n*
Schimpanse *m*

chin /tʃɪn/ *n* Kinn *nt*

china /tʃaɪnə/ *n* Porzellan *nt*

China /tʃaɪnə/ *n* China *nt*. ~**ese** /-'niːz/ *a*
chinesisch □ *n* (*Lang*) Chinesisch
nt; **the** ~**ese** *pl* die Chinesen.
~**ese** '**lantern** *n* Lampion *m*

chink[1] /tʃɪŋk/ *n* (*slit*) Ritze *f*

chink[2] *n* Geklirr *nt* □ *vi* klirren;
⟨*coins:*⟩ klimpern

chip /tʃɪp/ n (fragment) Span m; (in china, paintwork) angeschlagene Stelle f; (Computing, Gambling) Chip m; ~s pl (Culin) Pommes frites pl; (Amer: crisps) Chips pl □ vt (pt/pp chipped) (damage) anschlagen. ~ped a angeschlagen

chiropodist /kɪˈrɒpədɪst/ n Fußpfleger(in) m(f). ~y n Fußpflege f

chirp /tʃɜːp/ vi zwitschern; ⟨cricket:⟩ zirpen. ~y a (fam) munter

chisel /ˈtʃɪzl/ n Meißel m □ vt/i (pt/pp chiselled) meißeln

chit /tʃɪt/ n Zettel m

chivalr|ous /ˈʃɪvlrəs/ a, -ly adv ritterlich. ~ry n Ritterlichkeit f

chives /tʃaɪvz/ npl Schnittlauch m

chlorine /ˈklɔːriːn/ n Chlor nt

chloroform /ˈklɔːrəfɔːm/ n Chloroform nt

chocolate /ˈtʃɒkələt/ n Schokolade f; (sweet) Praline f

choice /tʃɔɪs/ n Wahl f; (variety) Auswahl f □ a auserlesen

choir /ˈkwaɪə(r)/ n Chor m. ~boy n Chorknabe m

choke /tʃəʊk/ n (Auto) Choke m □ vt würgen; (to death) erwürgen □ vi sich verschlucken; ~ on [fast] ersticken an (+ dat)

cholera /ˈkɒlərə/ n Cholera f

cholesterol /kəˈlestərɒl/ n Cholesterin nt

choose /tʃuːz/ vt/i (pt chose, pp chosen) wählen; (select) sich (dat) aussuchen; to do/go [freiwillig] tun/gehen; as you ~ wie Sie wollen

choos[e]y /ˈtʃuːzɪ/ a (fam) wählerisch

chop /tʃɒp/ n (blow) Hieb m; (Culin) Kotelett nt □ vt (pt/pp chopped) hacken. ~ down vt abhacken; fällen ⟨tree⟩. ~ off vt abhacken

chop|per /ˈtʃɒpə(r)/ n Beil nt; (fam) Hubschrauber m. ~py a kabbelig

'chopsticks npl Eßstäbchen pl

choral /ˈkɔːrəl/ a Chor-; ~ society Gesangverein m

chord /kɔːd/ n (Mus) Akkord m

chore /tʃɔː(r)/ n lästige Pflicht f; [household] ~s Hausarbeit f

choreography /kɒrɪˈɒɡrəfɪ/ n Choreographie f

chortle /ˈtʃɔːtl/ vi [vor Lachen] glucksen

chorus /ˈkɔːrəs/ n Chor m; (of song) Refrain m

chose, chosen /tʃəʊz, ˈtʃəʊzn/ see choose

Christ /kraɪst/ n Christus m

christen /ˈkrɪsn/ vt taufen. ~ing n Taufe f

Christian /ˈkrɪstʃən/ a christlich □ n Christ(in) m(f). ~ity /-tʃiˈænətɪ/ n Christentum nt. ~ name n Vorname m

Christmas /ˈkrɪsməs/ n Weihnachten nt. ~ card n Weihnachtskarte f. ~ 'Day n erster Weihnachtstag m. ~ 'Eve n Heiligabend m. ~ tree n Weihnachtsbaum m

chrome /krəʊm/ n, **chromium** /ˈkrəʊmɪəm/ n Chrom nt

chromosome /ˈkrəʊməsəʊm/ n Chromosom nt

chronic /ˈkrɒnɪk/ a chronisch

chronicle /ˈkrɒnɪkl/ n Chronik f

chronological /krɒnəˈlɒdʒɪkl/ a, -ly adv chronologisch

chrysalis /ˈkrɪsəlɪs/ n Puppe f

chrysanthemum /krɪˈsænθəməm/ n Chrysantheme f

chubby /ˈtʃʌbɪ/ a (-ier, -iest) mollig

chuck /tʃʌk/ vt (fam) schmeißen. ~ out vt (fam) rausschmeißen

chuckle /ˈtʃʌkl/ vi in sich (acc) hineinlachen

chum /tʃʌm/ n Freund(in) m(f)

chunk /tʃʌŋk/ n Stück nt

church /tʃɜːtʃ/ n Kirche f. ~yard n Friedhof m

churlish /ˈtʃɜːlɪʃ/ a unhöflich

churn 408 claret

churn /tʃɜːn/ n Butterfaß nt; (for milk) Milchkanne f □vt ~ **out** am laufenden Band produzieren

chute /ʃuːt/ n Rutsche f; (for rubbish) Müllschlucker m

CID abbr (**Criminal Investigation Department**) Kripo f

cider /'saɪdə(r)/ n Apfelwein m

cigar /sɪ'gɑː(r)/ n Zigarre f

cigarette /sɪgə'ret/ n Zigarette f

cine-camera /'sɪnɪ-/ n Filmkamera f

cinema /'sɪnɪmə/ n Kino nt

cinnamon /'sɪnəmən/ n Zimt m

cipher /'saɪfə(r)/ n (code) Chiffre f; (numeral) Ziffer f; (fig) Null f

circle /'sɜːkl/ n Kreis m; (Theat) Rang m □vt umkreisen □vi kreisen

circuit /'sɜːkɪt/ n Runde f; (race-track) Rennbahn f; (Electr) Stromkreis m. ~**ous** /sə'kjuːɪtəs/ a ~ route Umweg m

circular /'sɜːkjʊlə(r)/ a kreisförmig □n Rundschreiben nt. ~ '**saw** n Kreissäge f. ~ '**tour** n Rundfahrt f

circulat|e /'sɜːkjʊleɪt/ vt in Umlauf setzen □vi zirkulieren. ~**ion** /-'leɪʃn/ n Kreislauf m; (of newspaper) Auflage f

circumcis|e /'sɜːkəmsaɪz/ vt beschneiden. ~**ion** /-'sɪʒn/ n Beschneidung f

circumference /sə'kʌmfərəns/ n Umfang m

circumspect /'sɜːkəmspekt/ a, -**ly** adv umsichtig

circumstance /'sɜːkəmstəns/ n Umstand m; ~**s** pl Umstände pl; (financial) Verhältnisse pl

circus /'sɜːkəs/ n Zirkus m

CIS abbr (**Commonwealth of Independent States**) GUS f

cistern /'sɪstən/ n (tank) Wasserbehälter m; (of WC) Spülkasten m

cite /saɪt/ vt zitieren

citizen /'sɪtɪzn/ n Bürger(in) m(f). ~**ship** n Staatsangehörigkeit f

citrus /'sɪtrəs/ n ~ [**fruit**] Zitrusfrucht f

city /'sɪtɪ/ n [Groß]stadt f

civic /'sɪvɪk/ a Bürger-

civil /'sɪvl/ a bürgerlich; (aviation, defence) zivil; (polite) höflich. ~ **engi'neering** n Hoch- und Tiefbau m

civilian /sɪ'vɪljən/ a Zivil-; **in ~ clothes** in Zivil □n Zivilist m

civility /sɪ'vɪlətɪ/ n Höflichkeit f

civiliz|ation /sɪvəlaɪ'zeɪʃn/ n Zivilisation f. ~**e** /'sɪvəlaɪz/ vt zivilisieren

civil: ~ '**servant** n Beamte(r) m/ Beamtin f. **C ~ 'Service** n Staatsdienst m

clad /klæd/ a gekleidet (**in** in + acc)

claim /kleɪm/ n Anspruch m; (application) Antrag m; (demand) Forderung f; (assertion) Behauptung f □vt beanspruchen; (apply for) beantragen; (demand) fordern; (assert) behaupten; (collect) abholen. ~**ant** n Antragsteller m

clairvoyant /kleə'vɔɪənt/ n Hellseher(in) m(f)

clam /klæm/ n Klaffmuschel f

clamber /'klæmbə(r)/ vi klettern

clammy /'klæmɪ/ a (-ier, -iest) feucht

clamour /'klæmə(r)/ n Geschrei nt □vi ~ **for** schreien nach

clamp /klæmp/ n Klammer f □vt [ein]spannen □vi (fam) ~ **down** durchgreifen; ~ **down on** vorgehen gegen

clan /klæn/ n Clan m

clandestine /klæn'destɪn/ a geheim

clang /klæŋ/ n Schmettern nt. ~**er** n (fam) Schnitzer m

clank /klæŋk/ vi klirren

clap /klæp/ n **give s.o. a** ~ jdm Beifall klatschen; ~ **of thunder** Donnerschlag m □vt/i (pt/pp **clapped**) Beifall klatschen (+ dat); ~ **one's hands** [in die Hände] klatschen

claret /'klærət/ n roter Bordeaux m

clarification /klærɪfɪˈkeɪʃn/ n Klärung f. **~fy** /ˈklærɪfaɪ/ vt/i (pt/pp -ied) klären

clarinet /klærɪˈnet/ n Klarinette f

clarity /ˈklærətɪ/ n Klarheit f

clash /klæʃ/ n Geklirr nt; ⟨fig⟩ Konflikt m □ vi klirren; ⟨colours:⟩ sich beißen; ⟨events:⟩ ungünstig zusammenfallen

clasp /klɑːsp/ n Verschluß m □ vt ergreifen; ⟨hold⟩ halten

class /klɑːs/ n Klasse f; **first/second ~** erster/zweiter Klasse □ vt einordnen

classic /ˈklæsɪk/ a klassisch □ n Klassiker m; **~al** a klassisch

classification /klæsɪfɪˈkeɪʃn/ n Klassifikation f. **~fy** /ˈklæsɪfaɪ/ vt (pt/pp -ied) klassifizieren

'classroom n Klassenzimmer nt

classy /ˈklɑːsɪ/ a (-ier, -iest) ⟨fam⟩ schick

clatter /ˈklætə(r)/ n Geklapper nt □ vi klappern

clause /klɔːz/ n Klausel f; ⟨Gram⟩ Satzteil m

claustrophobia /klɔːstrəˈfəʊbɪə/ n Klaustrophobie f, ⟨fam⟩ Platzangst m

claw /klɔː/ n Kralle f; ⟨of bird of prey & Techn⟩ Klaue f; ⟨of crab, lobster⟩ Schere f □ vt kratzen

clay /kleɪ/ n Lehm m; ⟨pottery⟩ Ton m

clean /kliːn/ a (-er, -est) sauber □ adv glatt □ vt saubermachen; putzen ⟨shoes, windows⟩; **~ one's teeth** sich ⟨dat⟩ die Zähne putzen; **have sth ~ed** etw reinigen lassen. **~ up** vt saubermachen

cleaner /ˈkliːnə(r)/ n Putzfrau f; ⟨substance⟩ Reinigungsmittel nt; **[dry] ~'s** chemische Reinigung f

cleanliness /ˈklenlɪnɪs/ n Sauberkeit f

cleanse /klenz/ vt reinigen. **~r** n Reinigungsmittel nt

clean-shaven a glattrasiert

cleansing cream /ˈklenz-/ n Reinigungscreme f

clear /klɪə(r)/ a (-er, -est), **-ly** adv klar; ⟨obvious⟩ eindeutig; ⟨distinct⟩ deutlich; ⟨conscience⟩ rein; ⟨without obstacles⟩ frei; **make sth ~** etw klarmachen (**to** dat) □ adv stand — zurücktreten; **keep ~ of** aus dem Wege gehen (+ dat) □ vt räumen; abräumen ⟨table⟩; ⟨acquit⟩ freisprechen; ⟨authorize⟩ genehmigen; ⟨jump over⟩ überspringen; **~ one's throat** sich räuspern □ vi ⟨fog:⟩ sich auflösen. **~ away** vt wegräumen. **~ off** vi ⟨fam⟩ abhauen. **~ out** vt ausräumen □ vi ⟨fam⟩ abhauen. **~ up** vt ⟨tidy⟩ aufräumen; ⟨solve⟩ aufklären □ vi ⟨weather:⟩ sich aufklären

clearance /ˈklɪərəns/ n Räumung f; ⟨authorization⟩ Genehmigung f; ⟨customs⟩ [Zoll]abfertigung f; ⟨Techn⟩ Spielraum m. **~ sale** n Räumungsverkauf m

clearing /ˈklɪərɪŋ/ n Lichtung f. **~way** n ⟨Auto⟩ Straße f mit Halteverbot

cleavage /ˈkliːvɪdʒ/ n Spaltung f; ⟨woman's⟩ Dekolleté nt

clef /klef/ n Notenschlüssel m

cleft /kleft/ n Spalte f

clemency /ˈklemənsɪ/ n Milde f. **~t** a mild

clench /klentʃ/ vt **~ one's fist** die Faust ballen; **~ one's teeth** die Zähne zusammenbeißen

clergy /ˈklɜːdʒɪ/ npl Geistlichkeit f. **~man** n Geistliche(r) m

cleric /ˈklerɪk/ n Geistliche(r) m. **~al** a Schreib-; ⟨Relig⟩ geistlich

clerk /klɑːk, Amer: klɜːk/ n Büroangestellte(r) m/f; ⟨Amer: shop assistant⟩ Verkäufer(in) m(f)

clever /ˈklevə(r)/ a (-er, -est), **-ly** adv klug; ⟨skilful⟩ geschickt

cliché /ˈkliːʃeɪ/ n Klischee nt

click /klɪk/ vi klicken

client /ˈklaɪənt/ n Kunde m/ Kundin f; ⟨Jur⟩ Klient(in) m(f)

clientele /kli:ɒn'tel/ n Kundschaft f

cliff /klɪf/ n Kliff nt

climat|e /'klaɪmət/ n Klima nt. ~ic /-'mætɪk/ a klimatisch

climax /'klaɪmæks/ n Höhepunkt m

climb /klaɪm/ n Aufstieg m □vt besteigen 〈mountain〉; steigen auf (+ acc) 〈ladder, tree〉 □vi klettern; 〈rise〉 steigen; 〈road:〉 ansteigen. **~ down** vi hinunter-/herunterklettern; 〈from ladder, tree〉 heruntersteigen; (fam) nachgeben.

climber /'klaɪmə(r)/ n Bergsteiger m; (plant) Kletterpflanze f

clinch /klɪntʃ/ vt perfekt machen 〈deal〉 □vi (boxing) clinchen

cling /klɪŋ/ vi (pt/pp clung) sich klammern (**to an** + acc); (stick) haften (**to an** + dat). **~ film** n Sichtfolie f mit Hafteffekt

clinic /'klɪnɪk/ n Klinik f. **~al** a, **-ly** adv klinisch

clink /klɪŋk/ n Klirren nt; (fam: prison) Knast m □vi klirren

clip¹ /klɪp/ n Klammer f; (jewellery) Klipp m □vt (pt/pp clipped) anklammern (**to an** + acc)

clip² n (extract) Ausschnitt m □vt schneiden; knipsen 〈ticket〉. **~board** n Klemmbrett nt. **~pers** npl Schere f. **~ping** n (extract) Ausschnitt m

clique /kli:k/ n Clique f

cloak /kləʊk/ n Umhang m. **~room** n Garderobe f; (toilet) Toilette f

clobber /'klɒbə(r)/ n (fam) Zeug nt □vt (fam: hit, defeat) schlagen

clock /klɒk/ n Uhr f; (fam: speedometer) Tacho m □vi. **in/out** stechen

clock: **~ tower** n Uhrenturm m. **~wise** a & adv im Uhrzeigersinn. **~work** n Uhrwerk nt; (of toy) Aufziehmechanismus m; **like ~work** (fam) wie am Schnürchen

clod /klɒd/ n Klumpen m

clog /klɒg/ n Holzschuh m □vt/i (pt/pp clogged) **~ [up]** verstopfen

cloister /'klɔɪstə(r)/ n Kreuzgang m

close¹ /kləʊs/ a (-r, -st) nah[e] (**to** dat); 〈friend〉 eng; 〈weather〉 schwül; **have a ~ shave** (fam) mit knapper Not davonkommen □adv nahe; **~ by** nicht weit weg □n (street) Sackgasse f

close² /kləʊz/ n Ende nt; **draw to a ~** sich dem Ende nähern □vt zumachen, schließen; (bring to an end) beenden; sperren 〈road〉 □vi sich schließen; 〈shop:〉 schließen, zumachen; (end) enden. **~ down** vt schließen, stillegen 〈factory〉 □vi schließen; 〈factory:〉 stillgelegt werden

closed 'shop /kləʊzd-/ n ≈ Gewerkschaftszwang m

closely /'kləʊslɪ/ adv eng, nah[e]; (with attention) genau

close season /kləʊs-/ n Schonzeit f

closet /'klɒzɪt/ n (Amer) Schrank m

close-up /'kləʊs-/ n Nahaufnahme f

closure /'kləʊʒə(r)/ n Schließung f; (of factory) Stillegung f; (of road) Sperrung f

clot /klɒt/ n [Blut]gerinnsel nt; (fam: idiot) Trottel m □vi (pt/pp clotted) 〈blood:〉 gerinnen

cloth /klɒθ/ n Tuch nt

clothe /kləʊð/ vt kleiden

clothes /kləʊðz/ npl Kleider pl. **~-brush** n Kleiderbürste f. **~-line** n Wäscheleine f

clothing /'kləʊðɪŋ/ n Kleidung f

cloud /klaʊd/ n Wolke f □vi. over sich bewölken. **~burst** n Wolkenbruch m

cloudy /'klaʊdɪ/ a (-ier, -iest) wolkig, bewölkt; 〈liquid〉 trübe

clout /klaʊt/ n (fam) Schlag m; (influence) Einfluß m □vt (fam) hauen

clove /kləʊv/ n [Gewürz]nelke f; **~ of garlic** Knoblauchzehe f

clover /'kləʊvə(r)/ n Klee m. ~leaf n Kleeblatt nt

clown /klaʊn/ n Clown m □ vi ~ [about] herumalbern

club /klʌb/ n Klub m; (weapon) Keule f; (Sport) Schläger m; ~s pl (Cards) Kreuz nt, Treff nt □ vt (pt/pp clubbed) □ vt knüppeln □ vi ~ together zusammenlegen

cluck /klʌk/ vi glucken

clue /kluː/ n Anhaltspunkt m; (in crossword) Frage f; I haven't a ~ (fam) ich habe keine Ahnung

clump /klʌmp/ n Gruppe f

clumsiness /'klʌmzɪnɪs/ n Ungeschicklichkeit f

clumsy /'klʌmzɪ/ a (-ier, -iest), -ily adv ungeschickt; (unwieldy) unförmig

clung /klʌŋ/ see cling

cluster /'klʌstə(r)/ n Gruppe f; (of flowers) Büschel nt □ vi sich scharen (round um)

clutch /klʌtʃ/ n Griff m; (Auto) Kupplung f; be in s.o.'s ~es (fam) in jds Klauen sein □ vt festhalten; (grab) ergreifen □ vi ~ at greifen nach

clutter /'klʌtə(r)/ n Kram m □ vt ~ [up] vollstopfen

c/o abbr (care of) bei

coach /kəʊtʃ/ n [Reise]bus m; (Rail) Wagen m; (horse-drawn) Kutsche f; (Sport) Trainer m □ vt Nachhilfestunden geben (+ dat); (Sport) trainieren

coagulate /kəʊ'ægjʊleɪt/ vi gerinnen

coal /kəʊl/ n Kohle f

coalition /kəʊə'lɪʃn/ n Koalition f

'coal-mine n Kohlenbergwerk nt

coarse /kɔːs/ a (-r, -st), -ly adv grob

coast /kəʊst/ n Küste f □ vi (freewheel) im Freilauf fahren; (Auto) im Leerlauf fahren. ~al a Küsten-. ~er n (mat) Untersatz m. coast: ~guard n Küstenwache f. ~line n Küste f

coat /kəʊt/ n Mantel m; (of animal) Fell nt; (of paint) Anstrich m; ~

of arms Wappen nt □ vt überziehen; (with paint) [an]streichen. ~-hanger n Kleiderbügel m. ~-hook n Kleiderhaken m

coating /'kəʊtɪŋ/ n Überzug m, Schicht f; (of paint) Anstrich m

coax /kəʊks/ vt gut zureden (+ dat)

cob /kɒb/ n (of corn) [Mais]kolben m

cobble[1] /kɒbl/ n Kopfstein m; ~s pl Kopfsteinpflaster nt

cobble[2] vt flicken. ~r m Schuster m

'cobblestones npl = cobbles

cobweb /'kɒbweb/ n Spinnengewebe nt

cocaine /kə'keɪn/ n Kokain nt

cock /kɒk/ n Hahn m; (any male bird) Männchen nt □ vt (animal:) ~ its ears die Ohren spitzen; ~ the gun den Hahn spannen. ~-and-'bull story n (fam) Lügengeschichte f

cockerel /'kɒkərəl/ n [junger] Hahn m

cock-'eyed a (fam) schief; (absurd) verrückt

cockle /'kɒkl/ n Herzmuschel f

cockney /'kɒknɪ/ n (dialect) Cockney nt; (person) Cockney m

cock: ~pit n (Aviat) Cockpit nt. ~roach /-rəʊtʃ/ n Küchenschabe f. ~tail n Cocktail m. ~-up n (sl) make a ~up Mist bauen (fam)

cocky /'kɒkɪ/ a (-ier, -iest) (fam) eingebildet

cocoa /'kəʊkəʊ/ n Kakao m

coconut /'kəʊkənʌt/ n Kokosnuß f

cocoon /kə'kuːn/ n Kokon m

cod /kɒd/ n inv Kabeljau m

COD abbr (cash on delivery) per Nachnahme

coddle /'kɒdl/ vt verhätscheln

code /kəʊd/ n Kode m; (Computing) Code m; (set of rules) Kodex m. ~d a verschlüsselt

coedu'cational /kəʊ-/ a gemischt. ~ school n Koedukationsschule f

coerc|e /kəʊˈɜːs/ vt zwingen. ~ion
/-ˈɜːʃn/ n Zwang m

coe'xist vi koexistieren. ~ence n
Koexistenz f

coffee /ˈkɒfɪ/ n Kaffee m

coffee: ~-grinder n Kaffee-
mühle f. ~-pot n Kaffeekanne f.
~-table n Couchtisch m

coffin /ˈkɒfɪn/ n Sarg m

cog /kɒg/ n (Techn) Zahn m

cogent /ˈkəʊdʒənt/ a überzeugend

cog-wheel n Zahnrad nt

cohabit /kəʊˈhæbɪt/ vi (Jur) zu-
sammenleben

coherent /kəʊˈhɪərənt/ a zusammenhängend; (comprehensible)
verständlich

coil /kɔɪl/ n Rolle f; (Electr) Spule
f; (one ring) Windung f □ vt ~ [up]
zusammenrollen

coin /kɔɪn/ n Münze f □ vt prägen

coincide /kəʊɪnˈsaɪd/ vi zusammenfallen; (agree) übereinstimmen

coinciden|ce /kəʊˈɪnsɪdəns/ n Zu-
fall m. ~tal /-ˈdentl/ a, -ly adv
zufällig

coke /kəʊk/ n Koks m

Coke (P) n (drink) Cola f

colander /ˈkʌləndə(r)/ n (Culin)
Durchschlag m

cold /kəʊld/ a (-er, -est) kalt; I am
or feel ~ mir ist kalt □ n Kälte f;
(Med) Erkältung f

cold: ~-'blooded a kaltblütig. ~-
'hearted a kaltherzig. ~ly adv
(fig) kalt, kühl. ~ness n Kälte f

coleslaw /ˈkəʊlslɔː/ n Krautsalat m

colic /ˈkɒlɪk/ n Kolik f

collaborat|e /kəˈlæbəreɪt/ vi zu-
sammenarbeiten (with mit); ~e
on sth mitarbeiten bei etw. ~ion
/-ˈreɪʃn/ n Zusammenarbeit f; Mitarbeit f; (with enemy) Kollabora-
tion f. ~or n Mitarbeiter(in)
m(f); Kollaborateur m

collaps|e /kəˈlæps/ n Zusammen-
bruch m; Einsturz m □ vi zusammenbrechen; ⟨roof, building:⟩
einstürzen. ~ible a zusammen-
klappbar

collar /ˈkɒlə(r)/ n Kragen m; (for
animal) Halsband nt. ~-bone n
Schlüsselbein nt

colleague /ˈkɒliːg/ n Kollege m/
Kollegin f

collect /kəˈlekt/ vt sammeln;
(fetch) abholen; einsammeln
(tickets); einziehen (taxes) □ vi
sich [an]sammeln □ adv call ~
(Amer) ein R-Gespräch führen.
~ed /-ɪd/ a gesammelt; (calm)
gefaßt

collection /kəˈlekʃn/ n Sammlung
f; (in church) Kollekte f; (of post)
Leerung f; (designer's) Kollek-
tion f

collective /kəˈlektɪv/ a gemeinsam; (Pol) kollektiv. ~ 'noun n
Kollektivum nt

collector /kəˈlektə(r)/ n Samm-
ler(in) m(f)

college /ˈkɒlɪdʒ/ n College nt

collide /kəˈlaɪd/ vi zusammenstoßen

colliery /ˈkɒljərɪ/ n Kohlengrube f

collision /kəˈlɪʒn/ n Zusammenstoß m

colloquial /kəˈləʊkwɪəl/ a, -ly adv
umgangssprachlich. ~ism n um-
gangssprachlicher Ausdruck m

Cologne /kəˈləʊn/ n Köln nt

colon /ˈkəʊlən/ n Doppelpunkt m;
(Anat) Dickdarm m

colonel /ˈkɜːnl/ n Oberst m

colonial /kəˈləʊnɪəl/ a Kolonial-

colon|ize /ˈkɒlənaɪz/ vt kolonisie-
ren. ~y n Kolonie f

colossal /kəˈlɒsl/ a riesig

colour /ˈkʌlə(r)/ n Farbe f;
(complexion) Gesichtsfarbe f;
(race) Hautfarbe f; ~s pl (of flag)
Fahne f. off ~ (fam) nicht ganz
auf der Höhe □ vt färben; ~ [in]
ausmalen □ vi (blush) erröten

colour: ~ bar n Rassenschranke
f. ~-blind a farbenblind. ~ed a
farbig □ n (person) Farbige(r) m/f.
~-fast a farbecht. ~ film n
Farbfilm m. ~ful a farbenfroh.

~**less** *a* farblos. ~ **photo-
[graph]** *n* Farbaufnahme *f.* ~
television *n* Farbfernsehen *nt*

colt /kəʊlt/ *n* junger Hengst *m*

column /'kɒləm/ *n* Säule *f;* (*of sol-
diers, figures*) Kolonne *f;* (*Typ*)
Spalte *f;* (*Journ*) Kolumne *f.* ~**ist**
/-nɪst/ *n* Kolumnist *m*

coma /'kəʊmə/ *n* Koma *nt*

comb /kəʊm/ *n* Kamm *m* □ *vt* kämmen;
(*search*) absuchen; ~ **one's
hair** *sich* (*dat*) [die Haare] kämmen

combat /'kɒmbæt/ *n* Kampf *m* □ *vt*
(*pt/pp* **combated**) bekämpfen

combination /kɒmbɪ'neɪʃn/ *n*
Verbindung *f;* (*for lock*) Kombi-
nation *f*

combine¹ /kəm'baɪn/ *vt* verbinden
□ *vi* sich verbinden; ⟨*people:*⟩ sich
zusammenschließen

combine² /'kɒmbaɪn/ *n* (*Comm*)
Konzern *m.* ~ **[harvester]** *n*
Mähdrescher *m*

combustion /kəm'bʌstʃn/ *n* Verbrennung *f*

come /kʌm/ *vi* (*pt* **came,** *pp* **come**)
kommen; (*reach*) reichen (**to** an
+ *acc*); **that** ~**s to £10** das macht
£10; ~ **into money** zu Geld kommen; ~ **true** wahr werden; ~ **in
two sizes** in zwei Größen erhältlich sein; **the years to** ~ die
kommenden Jahre; **how** ~?
(*fam*) wie das? ~ **about** *vi* geschehen. ~ **across** *vi* herüber-
kommen; (*fam*) klar sein; ~ **across**
stoßen auf (+ *acc*). ~ **apart** *vi*
sich auseinandernehmen lassen;
(*accidentally*) auseinandergehen.
~ **away** *vi* weggehen; ⟨*thing:*⟩
abgehen. ~ **back** *vi* zurückkommen. ~ **by** *vi* vorbeikommen □ *vt*
(*obtain*) bekommen. ~ **in** *vi* hereinkommen. ~ **off** *vi* abgehen;
(*take place*) stattfinden; (*succeed*)
klappen (*fam*). ~ **out** *vi* herauskommen; ⟨*book:*⟩ erscheinen;
⟨*stain:*⟩ herausgehen. ~ **round**
vi vorbeikommen; (*after fainting*)
[wieder] zu sich kommen; (*change*

one's mind) sich umstimmen lassen. ~ **to** *vi* [wieder] zu sich
kommen. ~ **up** *vi* heraufkommen; ⟨*plant:*⟩ aufgehen; (*reach*)
reichen (**to bis**); ~ **up with** *sich*
(*dat*) einfallen lassen

'**come-back** *n* Comeback *nt*

comedian /kə'miːdɪən/ *n* Komiker
m

'**come-down** *n* Rückschritt *m*

comedy /'kɒmədɪ/ *n* Komödie *f*

comet /'kɒmɪt/ *n* Komet *m*

come-uppance /kʌm'ʌpəns/ *n* **get
one's** ~ (*fam*) sein Fett abkrie-
gen

comfort /'kʌmfət/ *n* Bequemlichkeit *f;* (*consolation*) Trost *m*
□ *vt* trösten

comfortable /'kʌmfətəbl/ *a,* -**bly**
adv bequem

'**comfort station** *n* (*Amer*) öffentliche Toilette *f*

comfy /'kʌmfɪ/ *a* (*fam*) bequem

comic /'kɒmɪk/ *a* komisch □ *n* Komiker *m;* (*periodical*) Comic-Heft
nt. ~**al** *a,* -**ly** *adv* komisch. ~
strip *n* Comic Strips *pl*

coming /'kʌmɪŋ/ *a* kommend □ *n*
Kommen *nt;* ~**s and goings**
Kommen und Gehen *nt*

comma /'kɒmə/ *n* Komma *nt*

command /kə'mɑːnd/ *n* Befehl *m;*
(*Mil*) Kommando *nt;* (*mastery*)
Beherrschung *f* □ *vt* befehlen (+
dat); kommandieren (*army*)

commandeer /kɒmən'dɪə(r)/ *vt*
beschlagnahmen

command|er /kə'mɑːndə(r)/ *n* Be-
fehlshaber *m;* (*of unit*) Komman-
deur *m;* (*of ship*) Kommandant *m.*
~**ing** ⟨*view*⟩ beherrschend.
~**ing officer** *n* Befehlshaber *m.*
~**ment** *n* Gebot *nt*

commemorat|e /kə'meməreɪt/ *vt*
gedenken (+ *gen*). ~**ion** /-'reɪʃn/
n Gedenken *nt.* ~**ive** /-ətɪv/ *a*
Gedenk-

commence /kə'mens/ *vt/i* anfangen, beginnen. ~**ment** *n* Anfang
m, Beginn *m*

commend /kə'mend/ vt loben; (recommend) empfehlen (**to** dat).
~able /-əbl/ a lobenswert.
~ation /kɒmen'deɪʃn/ n Lob nt
commensurate /kə'menʃərət/ a
angemessen; **be ~ with** entsprechen (+ dat)
comment /'kɒment/ n Bemerkung f; **no ~!** kein Kommentar!
□ vi sich äußern (**on** zu); **~ on**
(Journ) kommentieren
commentary /'kɒməntrɪ/ n Kommentar m; **[running] ~** (Radio,
TV) Reportage f
commentator /'kɒmənteɪtə(r)/ n
Kommentator m; (Sport) Reporter m
commerce /'kɒmɜːs/ n Handel m
commercial /kə'mɜːʃl/, **-ly** adv
kommerziell □ n (Radio, TV)
Werbespot m. **~ize** vt kommerzialisieren
commiserate /kə'mɪzəreɪt/ vi sein
Mitleid ausdrücken (**with** dat)
commission /kə'mɪʃn/ n (order for
work) Auftrag m; (body of people)
Kommission f; (payment) Provision f; (Mil) [Offiziers]patent nt;
out of ~ außer Betrieb □ vt beauftragen ⟨s.o.⟩; in Auftrag geben ⟨thing⟩; (Mil) zum Offizier
ernennen
commissionaire /kəmɪʃə'neə(r)/
n Portier m
commissioner /kə'mɪʃənə(r)/ n
Kommissar m; **~ for oaths** Notar m
commit /kə'mɪt/ vt (pt/pp commit-
ted) begehen; (entrust) anvertrauen (**to** dat); (consign) einwei-
sen (**to in** + acc); **~ oneself** sich
festlegen; (involve oneself) sich
engagieren; **~ sth to memory**
sich (dat) etw einprägen. **~ment**
n Verpflichtung f; (involvement)
Engagement nt. **~ted** a enga-
giert
committee /kə'mɪtɪ/ n Ausschuß
m, Komitee nt
commodity /kə'mɒdətɪ/ n Ware f

common /'kɒmən/ a (**-er, -est**) gemeinsam; (frequent) häufig; (ordinary) gewöhnlich; (vulgar) ordinär □ n Gemeindeland nt; **have
in ~** gemeinsam haben; **House
of C~s** Unterhaus nt. **~er** n
Bürgerliche(r) m/f
common: ~ law n Gewohnheits-
recht m. **~ly** adv allgemein. **C~
'Market** n Gemeinsamer Markt
m. **~place** a häufig. **~-room** n
Aufenthaltsraum m. **~'sense** n
gesunder Menschenverstand m
commotion /kə'məʊʃn/ n Tumult
m
communal /'kɒmjʊnl/ a gemeinschaftlich
communicable /kə'mjuːnɪkəbl/ a
⟨disease⟩ übertragbar
communicate /kə'mjuːnɪkeɪt/ vt
mitteilen (**to** dat); übertragen
⟨disease⟩ □ vi sich verständigen;
(be in touch) Verbindung haben
communication /kəmjuːnɪ'keɪʃn/
n Verständigung f; (contact) Verbindung f; (of disease) Übertragung f; (message) Mitteilung f;
~s pl (technology) Nachrichten-
wesen nt. **~ cord** n Notbremse f
communicative /kə'mjuːnɪkətɪv/
a mitteilsam
Communion /kə'mjuːnɪən/ n
[Holy] ~ das [heilige] Abend-
mahl; (Roman Catholic) die [hei-
lige] Kommunion
communiqué /kə'mjuːnɪkeɪ/ n
Kommuniqué nt
Communis|m /'kɒmjʊnɪzm/ n
Kommunismus m. **~t** /-ɪst/ a
kommunistisch □ n Kommu-
nist(in) m(f)
community /kə'mjuːnətɪ/ n Gemeinschaft f; **local ~** Gemeinde
f. **~ centre** n Gemeinschafts-
zentrum nt
commute /kə'mjuːt/ vi pendeln
□ vt (Jur) umwandeln. **~r** n
Pendler(in) m(f)
compact[1] /kəm'pækt/ a kompakt
compact[2] /'kɒmpækt/ n Puder-
dose f. **~ disc** n CD f

companion /kəm'pænjən/ n Begleiter(in) m(f). **~ship** n Gesellschaft f

company /'kʌmpəni/ n Gesellschaft f; (firm) Firma f; (Mil) Kompanie f; (fam: guests) Besuch m. **~ car** n Firmenwagen m

comparable /'kɒmpərəbl/ a vergleichbar

comparative /kəm'pærətɪv/ a vergleichend; (relative) relativ □ n (Gram) Komparativ m. **~ly** adv verhältnismäßig

compare /kəm'peə(r)/ vt vergleichen (with/to mit) □ vi sich vergleichen lassen

comparison /kəm'pærɪsn/ n Vergleich m

compartment /kəm'pɑ:tmənt/ n Fach nt; (Rail) Abteil nt

compass /'kʌmpəs/ n Kompaß m. **~es** npl pair of ~es Zirkel m

compassion /kəm'pæʃn/ n Mitleid nt. **~ate** /-ʃənət/ a mitfühlend

compatible /kəm'pætəbl/ a vereinbar; (drugs) verträglich; (Techn) kompatibel; be ~ (people:) [gut] zueinander passen

compatriot /kəm'pætrɪət/ n Landsmann m /-männin f

compel /kəm'pel/ vt (pt/pp compelled) zwingen

compensat|e /'kɒmpənseɪt/ vt entschädigen □ vi ~e for (fig) ausgleichen. **~ion** /-'seɪʃn/ n Entschädigung f; (fig) Ausgleich m

compère /'kɒmpeə(r)/ n Conférencier m

compete /kəm'pi:t/ vi konkurrieren; (take part) teilnehmen (in an + dat)

competen|ce /'kɒmpɪtəns/ n Tüchtigkeit f; (ability) Fähigkeit f; (Jur) Kompetenz f. **~t** a tüchtig; fähig; (Jur) kompetent

competition /kɒmpə'tɪʃn/ n Konkurrenz f; (contest) Wettbewerb m; (in newspaper) Preisausschreiben nt

competitive /kəm'petɪtɪv/ a (Comm) konkurrenzfähig

competitor /kəm'petɪtə(r)/ n Teilnehmer m; (Comm) Konkurrent m

compile /kəm'paɪl/ vt zusammenstellen; verfassen (dictionary)

complacen|cy /kəm'pleɪsənsɪ/ n Selbstzufriedenheit f. **~t** a, **-ly** adv selbstzufrieden

complain /kəm'pleɪn/ vi klagen (about/of über + acc); (formally) sich beschweren. **~t** n Klage f; (formal) Beschwerde f; (Med) Leiden nt

complement¹ /'kɒmplɪmənt/ n Ergänzung f; full ~ volle Anzahl f

complement² /'kɒmplɪment/ vt ergänzen; ~ each other sich ergänzen. **~ary** /-'mentəri/ a sich ergänzend; be ~ary sich ergänzen

complete /kəm'pli:t/ a vollständig; (finished) fertig; (utter) völlig □ vt vervollständigen; (finish) abschließen; (fill in) ausfüllen. **~ly** adv völlig

completion /kəm'pli:ʃn/ n Vervollständigung f; (end) Abschluß m

complex /'kɒmpleks/ a komplex □ n Komplex m

complexion /kəm'plekʃn/ n Teint m; (colour) Gesichtsfarbe f; (fig) Aspekt m

complexity /kəm'pleksətɪ/ n Komplexität f

compliance /kəm'plaɪəns/ n Einverständnis nt; in ~ with gemäß (+ dat)

complicat|e /'kɒmplɪkeɪt/ vt komplizieren. **~ed** a kompliziert. **~ion** /-'keɪʃn/ n Komplikation f

complicity /kəm'plɪsətɪ/ n Mitterschaft f

compliment /'kɒmplɪmənt/ n Kompliment nt; **~s** pl Grüße pl □ vt ein Kompliment machen (+ dat). **~ary** /-'mentəri/ a schmeichelhaft; (given free) Frei-

comply /kəm'plaɪ/ vi (pt/pp -ied) ~ with nachkommen (+ dat)

component /kəm'pəʊnənt/ *a & n* ~ [part] Bestandteil *m*, Teil *m*

compose /kəm'pəʊz/ *vt* verfassen; *(Mus)* komponieren; ~ **oneself** sich fassen; **be ~d of** sich zusammensetzen aus. ~ **d** *a (calm)* gefaßt. ~ **r** *n* Komponist *m*

composition /kɒmpə'zɪʃn/ *n* Komposition *f*; *(essay)* Aufsatz *m*

compost /'kɒmpɒst/ *n* Kompost *m*

composure /kəm'pəʊʒə(r)/ *n* Fassung *f*

compound¹ /kəm'paʊnd/ *vt (make worse)* verschlimmern

compound² /'kɒmpaʊnd/ *a* zusammengesetzt; kompliziert □ *n (Chem)* Verbindung *f*; *(Gram)* Kompositum *nt*; *(enclosure)* Einfriedigung *f*. ~ '**interest** *n* Zinseszins *m*

comprehen|d /kɒmprɪ'hend/ *vt* begreifen, verstehen; *(include)* umfassen. ~ **sible** *a*, **-bly** *adv* verständlich. ~ **sion** /-'henʃn/ *n* Verständnis *nt*

comprehensive /kɒmprɪ'hensɪv/ *a & n* umfassend; ~ [school] Gesamtschule *f*. ~ **insurance** *n* *(Auto)* Vollkaskoversicherung *f*

compress¹ /'kɒmpres/ *n* Kompresse *f*

compress² /kəm'pres/ *vt* zusammenpressen; ~ **ed air** Druckluft *f*

comprise /kəm'praɪz/ *vt* umfassen, bestehen aus

compromise /'kɒmprəmaɪz/ *n* Kompromiß *m* □ *vt* kompromittieren *(person)* □ *vi* einen Kompromiß schließen

compuls|ion /kəm'pʌlʃn/ *n* Zwang *m*. ~ **ive** /-sɪv/ *a* zwanghaft; ~ **eating** Eßzwang *m*. ~ **ory** /-sərɪ/ *a* obligatorisch; ~ **ory subject** Pflichtfach *nt*

compunction /kəm'pʌŋkʃn/ *n* Gewissensbisse *pl*

comput|er /kəm'pjuːtə(r)/ *n* Computer *m*. ~ **erize** *vt* computerisieren *(data)*; auf Computer umstellen *(firm)*. ~ **ing** *n* Computertechnik *f*

comrade /'kɒmreɪd/ *n* Kamerad *m*; *(Pol)* Genosse *m*/Genossin *f*. ~ **ship** *n* Kameradschaft *f*

con¹ /kɒn/ *see* **pro**

con² /kɒn/ *(fam)* Schwindel *m* □ *vt (pt/pp* conned*) (fam)* beschwindeln

concave /'kɒŋkeɪv/ *a* konkav

conceal /kən'siːl/ *vt* verstecken; *(keep secret)* verheimlichen

concede /kən'siːd/ *vt* zugeben; *(give up)* aufgeben

conceit /kən'siːt/ *n* Einbildung *f*. ~ **ed** *a* eingebildet

conceivable /kən'siːvəbl/ *a* denkbar

conceive /kən'siːv/ *vt (Biol)* empfangen; *(fig)* sich *(dat)* ausdenken □ *vi* schwanger werden. ~ **of** *(fig)* sich *(dat)* vorstellen

concentrat|e /'kɒnsəntreɪt/ *vt* konzentrieren □ *vi* sich konzentrieren. ~ **ion** /-'treɪʃn/ *n* Konzentration *f*. ~ **ion camp** *n* Konzentrationslager *nt*

concept /'kɒnsept/ *n* Begriff *m*. ~ **ion** /kən'sepʃn/ *n* Empfängnis *f*; *(idea)* Vorstellung *f*

concern /kən'sɜːn/ *n* Angelegenheit *f*; *(worry)* Sorge *f*; *(Comm)* Unternehmen *nt* □ *vt (be about, affect)* betreffen; *(worry)* kümmern; **be ~ed about** besorgt sein um; ~ **oneself with** sich beschäftigen mit; **as far as I am ~ed** was mich angeht od betrifft. ~ **ing** *prep* bezüglich (+ *gen*)

concert /'kɒnsət/ *n* Konzert *nt*; **in** ~ im Chor. ~ **ed** /kən'sɜːtɪd/ *a* gemeinsam

concertina /kɒnsə'tiːnə/ *n* Konzertina *f*

'**concertmaster** *n* *(Amer)* Konzertmeister *m*

concerto /kən'tʃeətəʊ/ *n* Konzert *nt*

concession /kən'seʃn/ *n* Zugeständnis *nt*; *(Comm)* Konzession *f*; *(reduction)* Ermäßigung *f*. ~ **ary** *a (reduced)* ermäßigt

conciliation /kənsɪlɪ'eɪʃn/ n Schlichtung f

concise /kən'saɪs/ a, **-ly** adv kurz

conclude /kən'klu:d/ vt/i schließen

conclusion /kən'klu:ʒn/ n Schluß m; **in** ~ abschließend, zum Schluß

conclusive /kən'klu:sɪv/ a schlüssig

concoct /kən'kɒkt/ vt zusammenstellen; (fig) fabrizieren. **~ion** /-'ɒkʃn/ n Zusammenstellung f; (drink) Gebräu nt

concourse /'kɒŋkɔ:s/ n Halle f

concrete /'kɒŋkri:t/ a konkret □ n Beton m □ vt betonieren

concur /kən'kɜ:(r)/ vi (pt/pp concurred) übereinstimmen

concurrently /kən'kʌrəntlɪ/ adv gleichzeitig

concussion /kən'kʌʃn/ n Gehirnerschütterung f

condemn /kən'dem/ vt verurteilen; (declare unfit) für untauglich erklären. **~ation** /kɒndem-'neɪʃn/ n Verurteilung f

condensation /kɒnden'seɪʃn/ n Kondensation f

condense /kən'dens/ vt zusammenfassen; (Phys) kondensieren □ vi sich kondensieren. **~d milk** n Kondensmilch f

condescend /kɒndɪ'send/ vi sich herablassen (to zu). **~ing, -ly** adv herablassend

condiment /'kɒndɪmənt/ n Gewürz nt

condition /kən'dɪʃn/ n Bedingung f; (state) Zustand m; **~s** pl Verhältnisse pl: on ~ that unter der Bedingung, daß □ vt (Psych) konditionieren. **~al** a bedingt; be **~al on** abhängen von (Gram) Konditional m. **~er** n Haarkur f; (for fabrics) Weichspüler m

condolences /kən'dəʊlənsɪz/ npl Beileid nt

condom /'kɒndəm/ n Kondom nt

condominium /kɒndə'mɪnɪəm/ n (Amer) ≈ Eigentumswohnung f

condone /kən'dəʊn/ vt hinwegsehen über (+ acc)

conducive /kən'dju:sɪv/ a förderlich (to dat)

conduct[1] /'kɒndʌkt/ n Verhalten nt; (Sch) Betragen nt

conduct[2] /kən'dʌkt/ vt führen; (Phys) leiten; (Mus) dirigieren. **~or** n Dirigent m; (of bus) Schaffner m; (Phys) Leiter m. **~ress** n Schaffnerin f

cone /kəʊn/ n Kegel m; (Bot) Zapfen m; (for ice-cream) [Eis]tüte f; (Auto) Leitkegel m

confectioner /kən'fekʃənə(r)/ n Konditor m. **~y** n Süßwaren pl

confederation /kənfedə'reɪʃn/ n Bund m; (Pol) Konföderation f

confer /kən'fɜ:(r)/ v (pt/pp conferred) □ vt verleihen (on dat) □ vi sich beraten

conference /'kɒnfərəns/ n Konferenz f

confess /kən'fes/ vt/i gestehen; (Relig) beichten. **~ion** /-eʃn/ n Geständnis nt; (Relig) Beichte f. **~ional** /-eʃənəl/ n Beichtstuhl m. **~or** n Beichtvater m

confetti /kən'fetɪ/ n Konfetti nt

confide /kən'faɪd/ vt anvertrauen □ vi **~ in s.o.** sich jdm anvertrauen

confidence /'kɒnfɪdəns/ n (trust) Vertrauen nt; (self-assurance) Selbstvertrauen nt; (secret) Geheimnis nt; **in** ~ im Vertrauen. **~ trick** n Schwindel m

confident /'kɒnfɪdənt/ a, **-ly** adv zuversichtlich; (self-assured) selbstsicher

confidential /kɒnfɪ'denʃl/ a, **-ly** adv vertraulich

confine /kən'faɪn/ vt beschränken; (keep shut up) einsperren; ~ **one-self** to sich beschränken auf (+ acc); be **~d to bed** das Bett hüten müssen. **~d** a (narrow) eng. **~ment** n Haft f

confines /'kɒnfaɪnz/ npl Grenzen pl

confirm /kən'fɜːm/ vt bestätigen; (Relig) konfirmieren; (Roman Catholic) firmen. **~ation** /kɒnfə-'meɪʃn/ n Bestätigung f; Konfirmation f; Firmung f. **~ed** a **~ed bachelor** eingefleischter Junggeselle m

confiscat|e /'kɒnfɪskeɪt/ vt beschlagnahmen. **~ion** /-'keɪʃn/ n Beschlagnahme f

conflict¹ /'kɒnflɪkt/ n Konflikt m

conflict² /kən'flɪkt/ vi im Widerspruch stehen (with zu). **~ing** a widersprüchlich

conform /kən'fɔːm/ vi (person:) sich anpassen; (thing:) entsprechen (to dat). **~ist** n Konformist m

confounded /kən'faʊndɪd/ a (fam) verflixt

confront /kən'frʌnt/ vt konfrontieren. **~ation** /kɒnfrʌn'teɪʃn/ n Konfrontation f

confus|e /kən'fjuːz/ vt verwirren; (mistake for) verwechseln (with mit). **~ing** a verwirrend. **~ion** /-ʒn/ n Verwirrung f; (muddle) Durcheinander n

congeal /kən'dʒiːl/ vi fest werden; (blood:) gerinnen

congenial /kən'dʒiːnɪəl/ a angenehm

congenital /kən'dʒenɪtl/ a angeboren

congest|ed /kən'dʒestɪd/ a verstopft; (with people) überfüllt. **~ion** /-estʃn/ n Verstopfung f; Überfüllung f

congratulat|e /kən'grætjʊleɪt/ vt gratulieren (+ dat) (on zu). **~ions** /-'leɪʃnz/ npl Glückwünsche pl; **~ions!** gratuliere!

congregat|e /'kɒngrɪgeɪt/ vi sich versammeln. **~ion** /-'geɪʃn/ n (Relig) Gemeinde f

congress /'kɒngres/ n Kongreß m. **~man** n Kongreßabgeordnete(r) m

conical /'kɒnɪkl/ a kegelförmig

conifer /'kɒnɪfə(r)/ n Nadelbaum m

conjecture /kən'dʒektʃə(r)/ n Mutmaßung f ⃞ vt/i mutmaßen

conjugal /'kɒndʒʊgl/ a ehelich

conjugat|e /'kɒndʒʊgeɪt/ vt konjugieren. **~ion** /-'geɪʃn/ n Konjugation f

conjunction /kən'dʒʌŋkʃn/ n Konjunktion f; **in ~ with** zusammen mit

conjunctivitis /kəndʒʌŋktɪ'vaɪtɪs/ n Bindehautentzündung f

conjur|e /'kʌndʒə(r)/ vi zaubern ⃞ vt **~e up** heraufbeschwören. **~or** n Zauberkünstler m

conk /kɒŋk/ vi **~ out** (fam) (machine:) kaputtgehen; (person:) zusammenklappen

conker /'kɒŋkə(r)/ n (fam) [Roß]-kastanie f

'con-man n (fam) Schwindler m

connect /kə'nekt/ vt/i verbinden (to mit); (Electr) anschließen (to an + acc) ⃞ vi verbunden sein; (train:) Anschluß haben (with an + acc); **be ~ed with** zu tun haben mit; (be related to) verwandt sein mit

connection /kə'nekʃn/ n Verbindung f; (Rail, Electr) Anschluß m; **in ~ with** in Zusammenhang mit. **~s** npl Beziehungen pl

conniv|ance /kə'naɪvns/ n stillschweigende Duldung f. **~e** vi **~e at** stillschweigend dulden

connoisseur /kɒnə'sɜː(r)/ n Kenner m

connotation /kɒnə'teɪʃn/ n Assoziation f

conquer /'kɒŋkə(r)/ vt erobern; (fig) besiegen. **~or** n Eroberer m

conquest /'kɒŋkwest/ n Eroberung f

conscience /'kɒnʃəns/ n Gewissen nt

conscientious /kɒnʃɪ'enʃəs/ a, **-ly** adv gewissenhaft. **~ objector** n Kriegsdienstverweigerer m

conscious /'kɒnʃəs/ a, **-ly** adv bewußt; **[fully] ~** bei [vollem] Bewußtsein; **be/become ~ of sth**

sich ⟨dat⟩ etw ⟨gen⟩ bewußt sein; werden. ~**ness** n Bewußtsein nt

conscript[1] /'kɒnskrɪpt/ n Einberufene(r) m

conscript[2] /kən'skrɪpt/ vt einberufen. ~**ion** /-ɪpʃn/ n allgemeine Wehrpflicht f

consecrat|**e** /'kɒnsɪkreɪt/ vt weihen; einweihen ⟨church⟩. ~**ion** /-'kreɪʃn/ n Weihe f; Einweihung f

consecutive /kən'sekjʊtɪv/ a aufeinanderfolgend. ~**ly** adv fortlaufend

consensus /kən'sensəs/ n Übereinstimmung f

consent /kən'sent/ n Einwilligung f, Zustimmung f ○ vi einwilligen (to in + acc), zustimmen (to dat)

consequen|**ce** /'kɒnsɪkwəns/ n Folge f; ⟨importance⟩ Bedeutung f. ~**t** a daraus folgend. ~**tly** adv folglich

conservation /kɒnsə'veɪʃn/ n Erhaltung f, Bewahrung f. ~**ist** n Umweltschützer m

conservative /kən'sɜːvətɪv/ a konservativ; ⟨estimate⟩ vorsichtig. C~ (Pol) a konservativ □ n konservative(r) m/f

conservatory /kən'sɜːvətrɪ/ n Wintergarten m

conserve /kən'sɜːv/ vt erhalten, bewahren; sparen ⟨energy⟩

consider /kən'sɪdə(r)/ vt erwägen; ⟨think over⟩ sich ⟨dat⟩ überlegen; ⟨take into account⟩ berücksichtigen; ⟨regard as⟩ betrachten als; ~ doing sth erwägen, etw zu tun. ~**able** /-əbl/ a, -**bly** adv erheblich

consider|**ate** /kən'sɪdərət/ a, -**ly** adv rücksichtsvoll. ~**ation** /-'reɪʃn/ n Erwägung f; ⟨thoughtfulness⟩ Rücksicht f; ⟨payment⟩ Entgelt nt; **take into** ~**ation** berücksichtigen. ~**ing** prep wenn man bedenkt ⟨that, daß⟩; ~**ing the circumstances** unter den Umständen

consign /kən'saɪn/ vt übergeben (to dat). ~**ment** n Lieferung f

consist /kən'sɪst/ vi ~ **of** bestehen aus

consisten|**cy** /kən'sɪstənsɪ/ n Konsequenz f; ⟨density⟩ Konsistenz f. ~**t** a konsequent; ⟨unchanging⟩ gleichbleibend; **be** ~ **with** entsprechen (+ dat). ~**tly** adv konsequent; ⟨constantly⟩ ständig

consolation /kɒnsə'leɪʃn/ n Trost m. ~ **prize** n Trostpreis m

console /kən'səʊl/ vt trösten

consolidate /kən'sɒlɪdeɪt/ vt konsolidieren

consonant /'kɒnsənənt/ n Konsonant m

consort /'kɒnsɔːt/ n Gemahl(in) m(f)

conspicuous /kən'spɪkjʊəs/ a auffällig

conspiracy /kən'spɪrəsɪ/ n Verschwörung f

conspire /kən'spaɪə(r)/ vi sich verschwören

constable /'kʌnstəbl/ n Polizist m

constant /'kɒnstənt/ a, -**ly** adv ständig; ⟨continuous⟩ ständig

constellation /kɒnstə'leɪʃn/ n Sternbild nt

consternation /kɒnstə'neɪʃn/ n Bestürzung f

consti|**pated** /'kɒnstɪpeɪtɪd/ a verstopft. ~**ion** /-'peɪʃn/ n Verstopfung f

constituency /kən'stɪtjʊənsɪ/ n Wahlkreis m

constituent /kən'stɪtjʊənt/ n Bestandteil m; ⟨Pol⟩ Wähler(in) m(f)

constitute /'kɒnstɪtjuːt/ vt bilden. ~**ion** /-'tjuːʃn/ n ⟨Pol⟩ Verfassung f; ⟨of person⟩ Konstitution f. ~**ional** /-'tjuːʃənl/ a Verfassungs- □ n Verdauungsspaziergang m

constrain /kən'streɪn/ vt zwingen. ~**t** n Zwang m; ⟨restriction⟩ Beschränkung f; ⟨strained manner⟩ Gezwungenheit f

constrict /kən'strɪkt/ vt einengen

construct /kən'strʌkt/ vt bauen. ~**ion** /-ʌkʃn/ n Bau m; ⟨Gram⟩

Konstruktion f; (interpretation)
Deutung f; under ~ion im Bau.
~ive /-ɪv/ a konstruktiv

construe /kən'stru:/ vt deuten

consul /'kɒnsl/ n Konsul m. ~ate
/'kɒnsjʊlət/ n Konsulat nt

consult /kən'sʌlt/ vt [um Rat] fragen; konsultieren ⟨doctor⟩; nachschlagen in (+ dat) ⟨book⟩. ~ant
n Berater m; (Med) Chefarzt m.
~ation /kɒnsl'teɪʃn/ n Beratung
f; (Med) Konsultation f

consume /kən'sju:m/ vt verzeh-
ren; (use) verbrauchen. ~r n
Verbraucher m. ~r goods npl
Konsumgüter pl

consummat|e /'kɒnsəmeɪt/ vt
vollziehen. ~ion /-'meɪʃn/ n
Vollzug m

consumption /kən'sʌmpʃn/ n
Konsum m; (use) Verbrauch m

contact /'kɒntækt/ n Kontakt m;
(person) Kontaktperson f □ vt
sich in Verbindung setzen mit. ~
'lenses npl Kontaktlinsen pl

contagious /kən'teɪdʒəs/ a direkt
übertragbar

contain /kən'teɪn/ vt enthalten;
(control) beherrschen. ~er n Behälter m; (Comm) Container m

contaminat|e /kən'tæmɪneɪt/ vt
verseuchen. ~ion /-'neɪʃn/ n
Verseuchung f

contemplat|e /'kɒntəmpleɪt/ vt
betrachten; (meditate) nachdenken über (+ acc); ~e doing sth
daran denken, etw zu tun.
~ion /-'pleɪʃn/ n Betrachtung f;
Nachdenken nt

contemporary /kən'tempərəri/ a
zeitgenössisch □n Zeitgenosse m/
-genossin f

contempt /kən'tempt/ n Verachtung f; beneath ~ verab-
scheuungswürdig; ~ of court
Mißachtung f des Gerichts.
~ible /-əbl/ a verachtenswert.
~uous /-tjʊəs/ a, -ly adv verächtlich

contend /kən'tend/ vi kämpfen
(with mit) □ vt (assert) behaupten. ~er n Bewerber(in) m(f);
(Sport) Wettkämpfer(in) m(f)

content¹ /'kɒntent/ n & contents
pl Inhalt m

content² /kən'tent/ a zufrieden □ n
to one's heart's ~ nach Her-
zenslust □ vt ~ oneself sich begnügen (with mit). ~ed a, -ly
adv zufrieden

contention /kən'tenʃn/ n (assertion) Behauptung f

contentment /kən'tentmənt/ n
Zufriedenheit f

contest¹ /'kɒntest/ n Kampf m;
(competition) Wettbewerb m

contest² /kən'test/ vt (dispute) bestreiten; (Jur) anfechten; (Pol)
kandidieren in (+ dat). ~ant n
Teilnehmer m

context /'kɒntekst/ n Zusammenhang m

continent /'kɒntɪnənt/ n Kontinent m

continental /kɒntɪ'nentl/ a Kon-
tinental-. ~ breakfast n kleines
Frühstück nt. ~ quilt n Daunendecke f

contingen|cy /kən'tɪndʒənsɪ/ n
Eventualität f. ~t a be ~t upon
abhängen von □ n (Mil) Kontingent nt

continual /kən'tɪnjʊəl/ a, -ly adv
dauernd

continuation /kəntɪnjʊ'eɪʃn/ n
Fortsetzung f

continue /kən'tɪnju:/ vt fortsetzen;
~ doing or to do sth fortfahren,
etw zu tun; to be ~d Fortsetzung
folgt □ vi weitergehen; (doing sth)
weitermachen; (speaking) fortfahren; (weather:) anhalten

continuity /kɒntɪ'nju:ətɪ/ n Kontinuität f

continuous /kən'tɪnjʊəs/ a, -ly adv
anhaltend, ununterbrochen

contort /kən'tɔ:t/ vt verzerren.
~ion /-ɔ:ʃn/ n Verzerrung f

contour /'kɒntʊə(r)/ n Kontur f;
(line) Höhenlinie f

contraband /'kɒntrəbænd/ n Schmuggelware f

contracep|tion /kɒntrə'sepʃn/ n Empfängnisverhütung f. **~tive** /-tɪv/ a empfängnisverhütend □ n Empfängnisverhütungsmittel nt

contract¹ /'kɒntrækt/ n Vertrag m

contract² /kən'trækt/ vi sich zusammenziehen; sich (dat) zuziehen ⟨illness⟩. **~ion** /-ækʃn/ n Zusammenziehung f; (abbreviation) Abkürzung f; (in childbirth) Wehe f. **~or** n Unternehmer m

contradict /kɒntrə'dɪkt/ vt widersprechen (+ dat). **~ion** /-ɪkʃn/ n Widerspruch m. **~ory** a widersprüchlich

contra-flow /'kɒntrə-/ n Umleitung f [auf die entgegengesetzte Fahrbahn]

contralto /kən'træltəʊ/ n Alt m; (singer) Altistin f

contraption /kən'træpʃn/ n (fam) Apparat m

contrary¹ /'kɒntrərɪ/ a & adv entgegengesetzt; **~ to** entgegen (+ dat) □ n Gegenteil nt; **on the ~** im Gegenteil

contrary² /kən'treərɪ/ a widerspenstig

contrast¹ /'kɒntrɑːst/ n Kontrast m

contrast² /kən'trɑːst/ vt gegenüberstellen (with dat) □ vi einen Kontrast bilden (with zu). **~ing** a gegensätzlich; ⟨colour⟩ Kontrast-

contraven|e /kɒntrə'viːn/ vt verstoßen gegen. **~tion** /-'venʃn/ n Verstoß m (of gegen)

contribut|e /kən'trɪbjuːt/ vt/i beitragen; beisteuern ⟨money⟩; (donate) spenden. **~ion** /kɒntrɪ'bjuːʃn/ n Beitrag m; (donation) Spende f. **~or** n Beitragende(r) m/f

contrite /kən'traɪt/ a reuig

contrivance /kən'traɪvəns/ n Vorrichtung f

contrive /kən'traɪv/ vt verfertigen; **~ to do sth** es fertigbringen, etw zu tun

control /kən'trəʊl/ n Kontrolle f; (mastery) Beherrschung f; (Techn) Regler m; **~s** pl (of car, plane) Steuerung f; **get out of ~** außer Kontrolle geraten □ vt (pt/pp **controlled**) kontrollieren; (restrain) unter Kontrolle halten; **~ oneself** sich beherrschen

controvers|ial /kɒntrə'vɜːʃl/ a umstritten. **~y** /'kɒntrəvɜːsɪ/ n Kontroverse f

conundrum /kə'nʌndrəm/ n Rätsel nt

conurbation /kɒnɜː'beɪʃn/ n Ballungsgebiet nt

convalesce /kɒnvə'les/ vi sich erholen. **~nce** n Erholung f

convalescent /kɒnvə'lesnt/ a **be ~** noch erholungsbedürftig sein. **~ home** n Erholungsheim nt

convector /kən'vektə(r)/ n ~ [heater] Konvektor m

convene /kən'viːn/ vt einberufen □ vi sich versammeln

convenience /kən'viːnɪəns/ n Bequemlichkeit f; [public] öffentliche Toilette f; **with all modern ~s** mit allem Komfort

convenient /kən'viːnɪənt/ a, **-ly** adv günstig; **be ~ for s.o.** jdm gelegen sein od jdm passen; **if it is ~ [for you]** wenn es Ihnen paßt

convent /'kɒnvənt/ n [Nonnen]-kloster nt

convention /kən'venʃn/ n (custom) Brauch m, Sitte f; (agreement) Konvention f; (assembly) Tagung f. **~al** a, **-ly** adv konventionell

converge /kən'vɜːdʒ/ vi zusammenlaufen

conversant /kən'vɜːsənt/ a ~ **with** vertraut mit

conversation /kɒnvə'seɪʃn/ n Gespräch nt; (Sch) Konversation f

converse¹ /kən'vɜːs/ vi sich unterhalten

converse² /'kɒnvɜ:s/ n Gegenteil nt. **~ly** adv umgekehrt

conversion /kən'vɜ:ʃn/ n Umbau m; (Relig) Bekehrung f; (calculation) Umrechnung f

convert¹ /'kɒnvɜ:t/ n Bekehrte(r) m/f, Konvertit m

convert² /kən'vɜ:t/ vt bekehren ⟨person⟩; (change) umwandeln (into in + acc); umbauen ⟨building⟩; (calculate) umrechnen; (Techn) umstellen. **~ible** /-əbl/ a verwandelbar □n (Auto) Kabriolett nt

convex /'kɒnveks/ a konvex

convey /kən'veɪ/ vt befördern; vermitteln ⟨idea, message⟩. **~ance** n Beförderung f; (vehicle) Beförderungsmittel nt. **~or belt** n Förderband nt

convict¹ /'kɒnvɪkt/ n Sträfling m

convict² /kən'vɪkt/ vt verurteilen (of wegen). **~ion** /-ɪkʃn/ n Verurteilung f; (belief) Überzeugung f; **previous ~ion** Vorstrafe f

convince /kən'vɪns/ vt überzeugen. **~ing** a, **-ly** adv überzeugend

convivial /kən'vɪvɪəl/ a gesellig

convoluted /'kɒnvəlu:tɪd/ a verschlungen; (fig) verwickelt

convoy /'kɒnvɔɪ/ n Konvoi m

convulse /kən'vʌls/ vt be sich krümmen (with vor + dat). **~ion** /-ʌlʃn/ n Krampf m

coo /ku:/ vi gurren

cook /kʊk/ n Koch m/ Köchin f □vt/i kochen; **is it ~ed?** ist es gar? **~ the books** (fam) die Bilanz frisieren. **~book** n (Amer) Kochbuch nt

cooker /'kʊkə(r)/ n (Koch)herd m; (apple) Kochapfel m. **~y** n Kochen nt. **~y book** n Kochbuch f

cookie /'kʊkɪ/ n (Amer) Keks m

cool /ku:l/ a (-er, -est), **-ly** adv kühl □n Kühle f □vt kühlen □vi abkühlen. **~box** n Kühlbox f. **~ness** n Kühle f

coop /ku:p/ n [Hühner]stall m □vt **~ up** einsperren

co-operate /kəʊ'ɒpəreɪt/ vi zusammenarbeiten. **~ion** /-'reɪʃn/ n Kooperation f

co-operative /kəʊ'ɒpərətɪv/ a hilfsbereit □n Genossenschaft f

co-opt /kəʊ'ɒpt/ vt hinzuwählen

co-ordinate /kəʊ'ɔ:dɪneɪt/ vt koordinieren. **~ion** /-'neɪʃn/ n Koordination f

cop /kɒp/ n (fam) Polizist m

cope /kəʊp/ vi (fam) zurechtkommen; **~ with** fertig werden mit

copious /'kəʊpɪəs/ a reichlich

copper¹ /'kɒpə(r)/ n Kupfer nt; **~s** pl Kleingeld nt □a kupfern

copper² /'kɒpə(r)/ n (fam) Polizist m

copper 'beech n Blutbuche f

coppice /'kɒpɪs/ n, **copse** /kɒps/ n Gehölz nt

copulate /'kɒpjʊleɪt/ vi sich begatten

copy /'kɒpɪ/ n Kopie f; (book) Exemplar nt □vt (pt/pp -ied) kopieren; (imitate) nachmachen; (Sch) abschreiben. **~right** n Copyright nt. **~writer** n Texter m

coral /'kɒrəl/ n Koralle f

cord /kɔ:d/ n Schnur f; (fabric) Cordsamt m; **~s** pl Cordhose f

cordial /'kɔ:dɪəl/ a, **-ly** adv herzlich □n Fruchtsirup m

cordon /'kɔ:dn/ n Kordon m □vt **~ off** absperren

corduroy /'kɔ:dərɔɪ/ n Cordsamt m

core /kɔ:(r)/ n Kern m; (of apple, pear) Kerngehäuse nt

cork /kɔ:k/ n Kork m; (for bottle) Korken m. **~screw** n Korkenzieher m

corn¹ /kɔ:n/ n Korn nt; (Amer: maize) Mais m

corn² n (Med) Hühnerauge nt

cornea /'kɔ:nɪə/ n Hornhaut f

corned beef /kɔ:nd'bi:f/ n Corned beef nt

corner /'kɔ:nə(r)/ n Ecke f; (bend) Kurve f; (football) Eckball m □vt (fig) in die Enge treiben; (Comm) monopolisieren ⟨market⟩. **~stone** n Eckstein m

cornet /'kɔːnɪt/ n (Mus) Kornett nt; (for ice-cream) [Eis]tüte f

corn: ~ **flour** n, (Amer) ~ **starch** n Stärkemehl nt

corny /'kɔːnɪ/ a (fam) abgedroschen

coronary /'kɒrənərɪ/ a & n ~ **[thrombosis]** Koronarthrombose f

coronation /kɒrə'neɪʃn/ n Krönung f

coroner /'kɒrənə(r)/ n Beamte(r) m, der verdächtige Todesfälle untersucht

coronet /'kɒrənet/ n Adelskrone f

corporal[1] /'kɔːpərəl/ n (Mil) Stabsunteroffizier m

corporal[2] a körperlich; ~ **punishment** körperliche Züchtigung f

corporate /'kɔːpərət/ a gemeinschaftlich

corporation /kɔːpə'reɪʃn/ n Körperschaft f; (of town) Stadtverwaltung f

corps /kɔː(r)/ n (pl **corps** /kɔːz/) Korps nt

corpse /kɔːps/ n Leiche f

corpulent /'kɔːpjʊlənt/ a korpulent

corpuscle /'kɔːpʌsl/ n Blutkörperchen nt

correct /kə'rekt/ a, -ly adv richtig; (proper) korrekt □ vt verbessern; (Sch, Typ) korrigieren. ~**ion** /-ekʃn/ n Verbesserung f; (Typ) Korrektur f

correlation /kɒrə'leɪʃn/ n Wechselbeziehung f

correspond /kɒrɪ'spɒnd/ vi entsprechen (**to** dat); (two things:) sich entsprechen; (write) korrespondieren. ~**ence** n Briefwechsel m; (Comm) Korrespondenz f. ~**ent** n Korrespondent(in) m(f). ~**ing** a, -ly adv entsprechend

corridor /'kɒrɪdɔː(r)/ n Gang m; (Pol, Aviat) Korridor m

corroborate /kə'rɒbəreɪt/ vt bestätigen

corro|de /kə'rəʊd/ vt zerfressen □ vi rosten. ~**sion** /-'rəʊʒn/ n Korrosion f

corrugated /'kɒrəgeɪtɪd/ a gewellt. ~ **iron** n Wellblech nt

corrupt /kə'rʌpt/ a korrupt □ vt korrumpieren; (spoil) verderben. ~**ion** /-ʌpʃn/ n Korruption f

corset /'kɔːsɪt/ n & -s pl Korsett nt

Corsica /'kɔːsɪkə/ n Korsika nt

cortège /kɔː'teɪʒ/ n **[funeral]** ~ Leichenzug m

cosh /kɒʃ/ n Totschläger m

cosmetic /kɒz'metɪk/ a kosmetisch □ n ~s pl Kosmetika pl

cosmic /'kɒzmɪk/ a kosmisch

cosmonaut /'kɒzmənɔːt/ n Kosmonaut(in) m(f)

cosmopolitan /kɒzmə'pɒlɪtən/ a kosmopolitisch

cosmos /'kɒzmɒs/ n Kosmos m

cosset /'kɒsɪt/ vt verhätscheln

cost /kɒst/ n Kosten pl; ~**s** pl (Jur) Kosten; **at all** ~**s** um jeden Preis; **I learnt to my** ~ es ist mich teuer zu stehen gekommen □ vt (pt/pp cost) kosten; **it** ~ **me £20** es hat mich £20 gekostet □ vt (pt/pp costed) ~ **[out]** die Kosten kalkulᵘⁱᵉren für

costly /'kɒstlɪ/ a (-ier, -iest) teuer

cost: ~ **of living** n Lebenshaltungskosten pl. ~ **price** n Selbstkostenpreis m

costume /'kɒstjuːm/ n Kostüm nt; (national) Tracht f. ~ **jewellery** n Modeschmuck m

cosy /'kəʊzɪ/ a (-ier, -iest) gemütlich □ n (tea-, egg-) Wärmer m

cot /kɒt/ n Kinderbett nt; (Amer: camp-bed) Feldbett nt

cottage /'kɒtɪdʒ/ n Häuschen nt. ~ **'cheese** n Hüttenkäse m

cotton /'kɒtn/ n Baumwolle f; (thread) Nähgarn nt □ a baumwollen □ vi ~ **on** (fam) kapieren

cotton 'wool n Watte f

couch /kaʊtʃ/ n Liege f

couchette /kuːˈʃet/ n (Rail) Liegeplatz m

cough /kɒf/ n Husten m □vi husten. ~ **up** vt/i husten; (fam: pay) blechen

'cough mixture n Hustensaft m

could /kʊd, unbetont kəd/ see **can²**

council /'kaʊnsl/ n Rat m; (Admin) Stadtverwaltung f; (rural) Gemeindeverwaltung f. ~ **house** n ≈ Sozialwohnung f

councillor /'kaʊnsələ(r)/ n Stadtverordnete(r) m/f

'council tax n Gemeindesteuer f

counsel /'kaʊnsl/ n Rat m; (Jur) Anwalt m □vt (pt/pp counselled) beraten. ~**lor** n Berater(in) m(f)

count¹ /kaʊnt/ n Graf m

count² n Zählung f; keep ~ zählen □vt/i zählen. ~ **on** vt rechnen auf (+ acc)

countenance /'kaʊntənəns/ n Gesicht nt □vt dulden

counter¹ /'kaʊntə(r)/ n (in shop) Ladentisch m; (in bank) Schalter m; (in café) Theke f; (Games) Spielmarke f

counter² adv ~ **to** gegen (+ acc) □a Gegen- □vt/i kontern

counter'act vt entgegenwirken (+ dat)

'counter-attack n Gegenangriff m

counter-'espionage n Spionageabwehr f

'counterfeit /-fɪt/ a gefälscht □n Fälschung f □vt fälschen

'counterfoil n Kontrollabschnitt m

'counterpart n Gegenstück nt

counter-pro'ductive a be ~ das Gegenteil bewirken

'countersign vt gegenzeichnen

countess /'kaʊntɪs/ n Gräfin f

countless /'kaʊntlɪs/ a unzählig

countrified /'kʌntrɪfaɪd/ a ländlich

country /'kʌntrɪ/ n Land nt; (native land) Heimat f; (countryside) Landschaft f; **in the** ~ auf dem Lande. ~**man** n [fellow] ~**man** Landsmann m. ~**side** n Landschaft f

county /'kaʊntɪ/ n Grafschaft f

coup /ku:/ n (Pol) Staatsstreich m

couple /'kʌpl/ n Paar nt; **a** ~ **of** (two) zwei □vt verbinden; (Rail) koppeln

coupon /'ku:pɒn/ n Kupon m; (voucher) Gutschein m; (entry form) Schein m

courage /'kʌrɪdʒ/ n Mut m. ~**ous** /kə'reɪdʒəs/ a, **-ly** adv mutig

courgette /kʊə'ʒets/ npl Zucchini pl

courier /'kʊrɪə(r)/ n Bote m; (diplomatic) Kurier m; (for tourists) Reiseleiter(in) m(f)

course /kɔ:s/ n (Naut, Sch) Kurs m; (Culin) Gang m; (for golf) Platz m; ~ **of treatment** (Med) Kur f; **of** ~ natürlich, selbstverständlich; **in the** ~ **of** im Lauf[e] (+ gen)

court /kɔ:t/ n Hof m; (Sport) Platz m; (Jur) Gericht nt □vt werben um; herausfordern ⟨danger⟩

courteous /'kɜ:tɪəs/ a, **-ly** adv höflich

courtesy /'kɜ:təsɪ/ n Höflichkeit f

court: ~'martial n (pl ~**s -martial**) Militärgericht nt. ~ **shoes** npl Pumps pl. ~**yard** n Hof m

cousin /'kʌzn/ n Vetter m, Cousin m; (female) Kusine f

cove /kəʊv/ n kleine Bucht f

cover /'kʌvə(r)/ n Decke f; (of cushion) Bezug m; (of umbrella) Hülle f; (of typewriter) Haube f; (of book, lid) Deckel m; (of magazine) Umschlag m; (protection) Deckung f, Schutz m; **take** ~ Deckung nehmen; **under separate** ~ mit getrennter Post □vt bedecken; beziehen ⟨cushion⟩; decken ⟨costs, needs⟩; zurücklegen ⟨distance⟩; (Journ) berichten über (+ acc); (insure) versichern. ~ **up** vt zudecken; (fig) vertuschen

coverage /'kʌvərɪdʒ/ n (Journ) Berichterstattung f (of über + acc)

cover: ~ **charge** n Gedeck nt.
~**ing** n Decke f; (for floor) Belag
m. ~-**up** n Vertuschung f
covet /ˈkʌvɪt/ vt begehren
cow /kaʊ/ n Kuh f
coward /ˈkaʊəd/ n Feigling m.
~**ice** /-ɪs/ n Feigheit f. ~**ly** a feige
'**cowboy** n Cowboy m; (fam) un-
solider Handwerker m
cower /ˈkaʊə(r)/ vi sich [ängstlich]
ducken
'**cowshed** n Kuhstall m
cox /kɒks/ n, **coxswain** /ˈkɒksn/ n
Steuermann m
coy /kɔɪ/ a (-er, -est) gespielt
schüchtern
crab /kræb/ n Krabbe f. ~-**apple**
n Holzapfel m
crack /kræk/ n Riß m; (in china,
glass) Sprung m; (noise) Knall m;
(fam: joke) Witz m; (fam: attempt) Versuch m □ a (fam) erstklassig □ vt knacken ⟨nut, code⟩;
einen Sprung machen in (+ acc)
⟨china, glass⟩; (fam) reißen
⟨joke⟩; (fam) lösen ⟨problem⟩ □ vi
⟨china, glass:⟩ springen; ⟨whip:⟩
knallen. ~ **down** vi (fam) durchgreifen
cracked /krækt/ a gesprungen;
⟨rib⟩ angebrochen; (fam: crazy)
verrückt
cracker /ˈkrækə(r)/ n (biscuit)
Kräcker m; (firework) Knallkör-
per m; [Christmas] ~ Knallbon-
bon m. ~**s** a be ~**s** (fam) einen
Knacks haben
crackle /ˈkrækl/ vi knistern
cradle /ˈkreɪdl/ n Wiege f
craft[1] /krɑːft/ n inv (boat) [Was-
ser]fahrzeug nt
craft[2] n Handwerk nt; (technique)
Fertigkeit f. ~**sman** n Handwerker m
crafty /ˈkrɑːftɪ/ a (-ier, -iest), -**ily**
adv gerissen
crag /kræg/ n Felszacken m. ~**gy**
a felsig; ⟨face⟩ kantig
cram /kræm/ v (pt/pp **crammed**)
□ vt hineinstopfen (into in +

acc); vollstopfen (with mit) □ vi
(for exams) pauken
cramp /kræmp/ n Krampf m. ~**ed**
a eng
crampon /ˈkræmpən/ n Steig-
eisen nt
cranberry /ˈkrænbərɪ/ n (Culin)
Preiselbeere f
crane /kreɪn/ n Kran m; (bird)
Kranich m □ vt ~ **one's neck** den
Hals recken
crank[1] /kræŋk/ n (fam) Exzentriker m
crank[2] n (Techn) Kurbel f.
~**shaft** n Kurbelwelle f
cranky /ˈkræŋkɪ/ a exzentrisch;
(Amer: irritable) reizbar
cranny /ˈkrænɪ/ n Ritze f
crash /kræʃ/ n (noise) Krach m;
(Auto) Zusammenstoß m; (Aviat)
Absturz m □ vi krachen (into gegen); ⟨cars:⟩ zusammenstoßen;
⟨plane:⟩ abstürzen □ vt einen Unfall haben mit ⟨car⟩
crash: ~ **course** n Schnellkurs
m. ~-**helmet** n Sturzhelm m. ~-
landing n Bruchlandung f
crate /kreɪt/ n Kiste f
crater /ˈkreɪtə(r)/ n Krater m
craˈ**vat** /krəˈvæt/ n Halstuch nt
crave /kreɪv/ vi ~ **e for** sich sehnen nach. ~**ing** n Gelüst m
crawl /krɔːl/ n (Swimming) Kraul
nt; **do the** ~ kraulen; **at a** ~ im
Kriechtempo □ vi kriechen;
⟨baby:⟩ krabbeln; ~ **with** wimmeln von. ~**er lane** n (Auto)
Kriechspur f
crayon /ˈkreɪən/ n Wachsstift m;
(pencil) Buntstift m
craze /kreɪz/ n Mode f
crazy /ˈkreɪzɪ/ a (-ier, -iest) verrückt; **be** ~ **about** verrückt sein
nach
creak /kriːk/ n Knarren nt □ vi
knarren
cream /kriːm/ n Sahne f; (Cosmetic, Med, Culin) Creme f □ a
(colour) cremefarben □ vt (Culin)
cremig rühren. ~ '**cheese** n ≈

Quark *m*. ~y *a* sahnig; (*smooth*) cremig

crease /kriːs/ *n* Falte *f*; (*unwanted*) Knitterfalte *f* □*vt* falten; (*accidentally*) zerknittern □*vi* knittern. ~**-resistant** *a* knitterfrei

create|e /kriːˈeɪt/ *vt* schaffen. ~**ion** /-ˈeɪʃn/ *n* Schöpfung *f*. ~**ive** /-ɪv/ *a* schöpferisch. ~**or** *n* Schöpfer *m*

creature /ˈkriːtʃə(r)/ *n* Geschöpf *nt*

crèche /kreʃ/ *n* Kinderkrippe *f*

credentials /krɪˈdenʃlz/ *npl* Beglaubigungsschreiben *nt*

credibility /kredəˈbɪlətɪ/ *n* Glaubwürdigkeit *f*

credible /ˈkredəbl/ *a* glaubwürdig

credit /ˈkredɪt/ *n* Kredit *m*; (*honour*) Ehre *f* □*vt* glauben; ~ **s.o. with sth** (*Comm*) jdm etw gutschreiben; (*fig*) jdm etw zuschreiben. ~**able** /-əbl/ *a* lobenswert

credit: ~ **card** *n* Kreditkarte *f*. ~ **or** *n* Gläubiger *m*

creed /kriːd/ *n* Glaubensbekenntnis *nt*

creek /kriːk/ *n* enge Bucht *f*; (*Amer: stream*) Bach *m*

creep /kriːp/ *vi* (*pt/pp* crept) schleichen □*n* (*fam*) fieser Kerl *m*; **it gives me the ~s** es ist mir unheimlich. ~**er** *n* Kletterpflanze *f*. ~**y** *a* gruselig

cremat|e /krɪˈmeɪt/ *vt* einäschern. ~**ion** /-eɪʃn/ *n* Einäscherung *f*.

crematorium /kreməˈtɔːrɪəm/ *n* Krematorium *nt*

crêpe /kreɪp/ *n* Krepp *m*. ~ **paper** *n* Kreppapier *nt*

crept /krept/ *see* creep

crescent /ˈkresnt/ *n* Halbmond *m*

cress /kres/ *n* Kresse *f*

crest /krest/ *n* Kamm *m*; (*coat of arms*) Wappen *nt*

Crete /kriːt/ *n* Kreta *nt*

crevasse /krɪˈvæs/ *n* [Gletscher]-spalte *f*

crevice /ˈkrevɪs/ *n* Spalte *f*

crew /kruː/ *n* Besatzung *f*; (*gang*) Bande *f*. ~ **cut** *n* Bürstenschnitt *m*

crib[1] /krɪb/ *n* Krippe *f*

crib[2] *vt/i* (*pt/pp* cribbed) (*fam*) abschreiben

crick /krɪk/ *n* ~ **in the neck** steifes Genick *nt*

cricket[1] /ˈkrɪkɪt/ *n* (*insect*) Grille *f*

cricket[2] *n* Kricket *nt*. ~**er** *n* Kricketspieler *m*

crime /kraɪm/ *n* Verbrechen *nt*; (*rate*) Kriminalität *f*

criminal /ˈkrɪmɪnl/ *a* kriminell, verbrecherisch; ⟨*law, court*⟩ Straf- □*n* Verbrecher *m*

crimson /ˈkrɪmzn/ *a* purpurrot

cringe /krɪndʒ/ *vi* sich [ängstlich] ducken

crinkle /ˈkrɪŋkl/ *vt/i* knittern

cripple /ˈkrɪpl/ *n* Krüppel *m* □*vt* zum Krüppel machen; (*fig*) lahmlegen. ~**d** *a* verkrüppelt

crisis /ˈkraɪsɪs/ *n* (*pl* -ses /-siːz/) Krise *f*

crisp /krɪsp/ *a* (-**er**, -**est**) knusprig. ~ **bread** *n* Knäckebrot *nt*. ~**s** *npl* Chips *pl*

criss-cross /ˈkrɪs-/ *a* schräg gekreuzt

criterion /kraɪˈtɪərɪən/ *n* (*pl* -ria /-rɪə/) Kriterium *nt*

critic /ˈkrɪtɪk/ *n* Kritiker *m*. ~**al** *a* kritisch. ~**ally** *adv* kritisch; ~**ally ill** schwer krank

criticism /ˈkrɪtɪsɪzm/ *n* Kritik *f*

criticize /ˈkrɪtɪsaɪz/ *vt* kritisieren

croak /krəʊk/ *vi* krächzen; ⟨*frog:*⟩ quaken

crochet /ˈkrəʊʃeɪ/ *n* Häkelarbeit *f* □*vt/i* häkeln. ~**-hook** *n* Häkelnadel *f*

crock /krɒk/ *n* (*fam*) **old ~** (*person*) Wrack *m*; (*car*) Klapperkiste *f*

crockery /ˈkrɒkərɪ/ *n* Geschirr *nt*

crocodile /ˈkrɒkədaɪl/ *n* Krokodil *nt*

crocus /ˈkrəʊkəs/ *n* (*pl* -es) Krokus *m*

crony /ˈkrəʊnɪ/ *n* Kumpel *m*

crook /krʊk/ n (stick) Stab m; (fam: criminal) Schwindler m, Gauner m

crooked /'krʊkɪd/ a schief; (bent) krumm; (fam: dishonest) unehrlich

crop /krɒp/ n Feldfrucht f; (harvest) Ernte f; (of bird) Kropf m □v (pt/pp cropped) □vt stutzen □n ~ up (fam) zur Sprache kommen; (occur) dazwischenkommen

croquet /'krəʊkeɪ/ n Krocket nt

croquette /krəʊ'ket/ n Krokette f

cross /krɒs/ a, -ly adv (annoyed) böse (with auf + acc); talk at ~ purposes aneinander vorbeireden □n Kreuz nt; (Bot, Zool) Kreuzung f; on the ~ schräg □vt kreuzen ⟨cheque, animals⟩; überqueren ⟨road⟩; ~ oneself sich bekreuzigen; ~ one's arms die Arme verschränken; ~ one's legs die Beine übereinanderschlagen; keep one's fingers ~ed for s.o. jdm die Daumen drücken; it ~ed my mind es fiel mir ein □ vi (go across) hinübergehen/-fahren; ⟨lines:⟩ sich kreuzen. ~ out vt durchstreichen

cross: ~bar n Querlatte f; (on bicycle) Stange f. ~'country n (Sport) Crosslauf m. ~-ex'amine vt ins Kreuzverhör nehmen. ~-exami'nation n Kreuzverhör nt. ~-eyed a schielend; be ~-eyed schielen. ~fire n Kreuzfeuer nt. ~ing n (Übergang m; (sea journey) Überfahrt f. ~-'reference n Querverweis m. ~roads n [Straßen]kreuzung f. ~-'section n Querschnitt m. ~-stitch n Kreuzstich m. ~wise adv quer. ~word n ~word [puzzle] Kreuzworträtsel nt

crotchet /'krɒtʃɪt/ n Viertelnote f

crotchety /'krɒtʃɪtɪ/ a griesgrämig

crouch /kraʊtʃ/ vi kauern

crow /krəʊ/ n Krähe f; as the ~ flies Luftlinie □vi krähen. ~bar n Brechstange f

crowd /kraʊd/ n [Menschen]menge f □vi sich drängen. ~ed /'kraʊdɪd/ a (gedrängt) voll

crown /kraʊn/ n Krone f □vt krönen; überkronen ⟨tooth⟩

crucial /'kruːʃl/ a höchst wichtig; (decisive) entscheidend (to für)

crucifix /'kruːsɪfɪks/ n Kruzifix nt

cruci'fixion /kruːsɪ'fɪkʃn/ n Kreuzigung f. ~y /'kruːsɪfaɪ/ vt (pt/pp -ied) kreuzigen

crude /kruːd/ a (-r, -st) (raw) roh

cruel /'kruːəl/ a (crueller, cruellest), -ly adv grausam (to gegen). ~ty n Grausamkeit f; ~ty to animals Tierquälerei f

cruise /kruːz/ n Kreuzfahrt f □vi kreuzen; ⟨car:⟩ fahren. ~er n (Mil) Kreuzer m; (motor boat) Kajütboot nt. ~ing speed n Reisegeschwindigkeit f

crumb /krʌm/ n Krümel m

crumble /'krʌmbl/ vt/i krümeln; (collapse) einstürzen. ~ly a krümelig

crumple /'krʌmpl/ vt zerknittern □vi knittern

crunch /krʌntʃ/ n (fam) when it comes to the ~ wenn es [wirklich], drauf ankommt □vt mampfen □vi knirschen

crusade /kruː'seɪd/ n Kreuzzug m; (fig) Kampagne f. ~r n Kreuzfahrer m; (fig) Kämpfer m

crush /krʌʃ/ n (crowd) Gedränge nt □vt zerquetschen; zerknittern ⟨clothes⟩; (fig: subdue) niederschlagen

crust /krʌst/ n Kruste f

crutch /krʌtʃ/ n Krücke f

crux /krʌks/ n (fig) springender Punkt m

cry /kraɪ/ n Ruf m; (shout) Schrei m; a far ~ from (fig) weit entfernt von □vi (pt/pp cried) (weep) weinen; ⟨baby:⟩ schreien; (call) rufen

crypt /krɪpt/ n Krypta f. ~ic a rätselhaft

crystal /'krɪstl/ n Kristall m; (glass) Kristall nt. ~lize vi [sich] kristallisieren

cub /kʌb/ n (Zool) Junge(s) nt; C~ [Scout] Wölfling m

Cuba /'kju:bə/ n Kuba nt

cubby-hole /'kʌbɪ-/ n Fach nt

cub|e /kju:b/ n Würfel m. ~ic a Kubik-

cubicle /'kju:bɪkl/ n Kabine f

cuckoo /'kuku:/ n Kuckuck m. ~ clock n Kuckucksuhr f

cucumber /'kju:kʌmbə(r)/ n Gurke f

cuddl|e /'kʌdl/ vt herzen □ vi ~ e up to sich kuscheln an (+ acc). ~y a kuschelig. ~y 'toy n Plüschtier nt

cudgel /'kʌdʒl/ n Knüppel m

cue[1] /kju:/ n Stichwort nt

cue[2] n (Billiards) Queue nt

cuff /kʌf/ n Manschette f; (Amer: turn-up) [Hosen]aufschlag m; (blow) Klaps m; off the ~ (fam) aus dem Stegreif □ vt einen Klaps geben (+ dat). ~-link n Manschettenknopf m

cul-de-sac /'kʌldəsæk/ n Sackgasse f

culinary /'kʌlɪnərɪ/ a kulinarisch

cull /kʌl/ vt pflücken ⟨flowers⟩; (kill) ausmerzen

culminat|e /'kʌlmɪneɪt/ vi gipfeln (in in + dat). ~ion /-'neɪʃn/ n Gipfelpunkt m

culottes /kjʊ'lɒts/ npl Hosenrock m

culprit /'kʌlprɪt/ n Täter m

cult /kʌlt/ n Kult m

cultivate /'kʌltɪveɪt/ vt anbauen ⟨crop⟩; bebauen ⟨land⟩

cultural /'kʌltʃərəl/ a kulturell

culture /'kʌltʃə(r)/ n Kultur f. ~d a kultiviert

cumbersome /'kʌmbəsəm/ a hinderlich; (unwieldy) unhandlich

cumulative /'kju:mjʊlətɪv/ a kumulativ

cunning /'kʌnɪŋ/ a listig □ n List f

cup /kʌp/ n Tasse f; (prize) Pokal m

cupboard /'kʌbəd/ n Schrank m

Cup 'Final n Pokalendspiel nt

Cupid /'kju:pɪd/ n Amor m

curable /'kjʊərəbl/ a heilbar

curate /'kjʊərət/ n Vikar m; (Roman Catholic) Kaplan m

curator /kjʊə'reɪtə(r)/ n Kustos m

curb /kɜ:b/ vt zügeln

curdle /'kɜ:dl/ vi gerinnen

cure /kjʊə(r)/ n [Heil]mittel nt □ vt heilen; (salt) pökeln; (smoke) räuchern; gerben ⟨skin⟩

curfew /'kɜ:fju:/ n Ausgangssperre f

curio /'kjʊərɪəʊ/ n Kuriosität f

curiosity /kjʊərɪ'ɒsətɪ/ n Neugier f; (object) Kuriosität f

curious /'kjʊərɪəs/ a, -ly adv neugierig; (strange) merkwürdig, seltsam

curl /kɜ:l/ n Locke f □ vt locken □ vi sich locken. ~ up vi sich zusammenrollen

curler /'kɜ:lə(r)/ n Lockenwickler m

curly /'kɜ:lɪ/ a (-ier, -iest) lockig

currant /'kʌrənt/ n (dried) Korinthe f

currency /'kʌrənsɪ/ n Geläufigkeit f; (money) Währung f; foreign ~ Devisen pl

current /'kʌrənt/ a augenblicklich, gegenwärtig; (in general use) geläufig, gebräuchlich □ n Strömung f; (Electr) Strom m. ~ affairs or events npl Aktuelle(s) nt. ~ly adv zur Zeit

curriculum /kə'rɪkjʊləm/ n Lehrplan m. ~ vitae /-'vi:taɪ/ n Lebenslauf m

curry /'kʌrɪ/ n Curry nt & m; (meal) Currygericht nt □ vt (pt/pp -ied) ~ favour sich einschmeicheln (with bei)

curse /kɜ:s/ n Fluch m □ vt verfluchen □ vi fluchen

cursory /'kɜ:sərɪ/ a flüchtig

curt /kɜ:t/ a, -ly adv barsch

curtail /kɜ:'teɪl/ vt abkürzen

curtain /'kɜːtn/ n Vorhang m

curtsy /'kɜːtsɪ/ n Knicks m □vi (pt/pp -ied) knicksen

curve /kɜːv/ n Kurve f □vi einen Bogen machen; ~ to the right/ left nach rechts/links biegen. ~d a gebogen

cushion /'kʊʃn/ n Kissen nt □vt dämpfen; (protect) beschützen

cushy /'kʊʃɪ/ a (-ier, -iest) (fam) bequem

custard /'kʌstəd/ n Vanillesoße f

custodian /kʌ'stəʊdɪən/ n Hüter m

custody /'kʌstədɪ/ n Obhut f; (of child) Sorgerecht nt; (imprisonment) Haft f

custom /'kʌstəm/ n Brauch m; (habit) Gewohnheit f; (Comm) Kundschaft f. ~ary a üblich; (habitual) gewohnt. ~er n Kunde m / Kundin f

customs /'kʌstəmz/ npl Zoll m. ~ officer n Zollbeamte(r) m

cut /kʌt/ n Schnitt m; (Med) Schnittwunde f; (reduction) Kürzung f; (in price) Senkung f; ~ [of meat] [Fleisch]stück nt □vt/i (pt/pp cut, pres p cutting) schneiden; (mow) mähen; abheben ⟨cards⟩; (reduce) kürzen; senken ⟨price⟩; ~ one's finger sich in den Finger schneiden; s.o.'s hair jdm die Haare schneiden; ~ short abkürzen; (fig) einschränken, kürzen. ~ back vt zurückschneiden; (fig) einschränken, kürzen. ~ down vt fällen; (fig) einschränken. ~ off vt abschneiden; (disconnect) abstellen; be ~ off (Teleph) unterbrochen werden. ~ out vt ausschneiden; (delete) streichen; be ~ out for (fam) geeignet sein zu. ~ up vt zerschneiden; (slice) aufschneiden

'cut-back n Kürzung f, Einschränkung f

cute /kjuːt/ a (-r, -st) (fam) niedlich

cut 'glass n Kristall nt

cuticle /'kjuːtɪkl/ n Nagelhaut f

cutlery /'kʌtlərɪ/ n Besteck nt

cutlet /'kʌtlɪt/ n Kotelett nt

'cut-price a verbilligt

cutting /'kʌtɪŋ/ a ⟨remark⟩ bissig □n (from newspaper) Ausschnitt m; (of plant) Ableger m

CV abbr of curriculum vitae

cyclamen /'sɪkləmən/ n Alpenveilchen nt

cycle /'saɪkl/ n Zyklus m; (bicycle) [Fahr]rad nt □vi mit dem Rad fahren. ~ing n Radfahren nt. ~ist n Radfahrer(in) m(f)

cyclone /'saɪkləʊn/ n Wirbelsturm m

cylind|er /'sɪlɪndə(r)/ n Zylinder m. ~rical /-'lɪndrɪkl/ a zylindrisch

cymbals /'sɪmblz/ npl (Mus) Becken nt

cynic /'sɪnɪk/ n Zyniker m. ~al a, -ly adv zynisch. ~ism /-sɪzm/ n Zynismus m

cypress /'saɪprəs/ n Zypresse f

Cyprus /'saɪprəs/ n Zypern nt

cyst /sɪst/ n Zyste f. ~itis /-'taɪtɪs/ n Blasenentzündung f

Czech /tʃek/ a tschechisch □n Tscheche m / Tschechin f

Czechoslovak /tʃekə'sləʊvæk/ a tschechoslowakisch. ~ia /-'væk-ɪə/ n die Tschechoslowakei. ~ian /-'vækɪən/ a tschechoslowakisch

D

dab /dæb/ n Tupfer m; (of butter) Klecks m; a ~ of ein bißchen □vt (pt/pp dabbed) abtupfen; betupfen (with mit)

dabble /'dæbl/ vi ~ in sth (fig) sich nebenbei mit etw befassen

dachshund /'dækshʊnd/ n Dackel m

dad[dy] /'dæd[ɪ]/ n (fam) Vati m

daddy-'long-legs n [Kohl]schnake f; (Amer: spider) Weberknecht m

daffodil /'dæfədɪl/ n Osterglocke f, gelbe Narzisse f

daft /dɑːft/ a (-er, -est) dumm

dagger /'dægə(r)/ n Dolch m; (Typ)
Kreuz nt; **be at ~s drawn** (fam)
auf Kriegsfuß stehen

dahlia /'deɪlɪə/ n Dahlie f

daily /'deɪlɪ/ a & adv täglich □ n
(newspaper) Tageszeitung f;
(fam: cleaner) Putzfrau f

dainty /'deɪntɪ/ a (-ier, -iest) zierlich

dairy /'deərɪ/ n Molkerei f; (shop)
Milchgeschäft nt. **~ cow** n
Milchkuh f. **~ products** pl
Milchprodukte pl

dais /'deɪɪs/ n Podium nt

daisy /'deɪzɪ/ n Gänseblümchen nt

dale /deɪl/ n (liter) Tal nt

dally /'dælɪ/ vi (pt/pp -ied) trödeln

dam /dæm/ n [Stau]damm m □ vt
(pt/pp dammed) eindämmen

damage /'dæmɪdʒ/ n Schaden m
(to an + dat); **~es** pl (Jur) Scha-
denersatz m □ vt beschädigen;
(fig) beeinträchtigen. **~ing** a
schädlich

damask /'dæməsk/ n Damast m

dame /deɪm/ n (liter) Dame f;
(Amer sl) Weib nt

damn /dæm/ a, int & adv (fam)
verdammt □ n **I don't care or
give a ~** (fam) ich schere mich
einen Dreck darum □ vt verdammen. **~ation** /-'neɪʃn/ n Ver-
dammnis f □ int (fam) verdammt!

damp /dæmp/ a (-er, -est) feucht
□ n Feuchtigkeit f □ vt = **dampen**

dampen vt anfeuchten; (fig)
dämpfen. **~ness** n Feuchtigkeit f

dance /dɑːns/ n Tanz m; (function)
Tanzveranstaltung f □ vt/i tanzen. **~hall** n Tanzlokal nt.
~ music n Tanzmusik f

dancer /'dɑːnsə(r)/ n Tänzer(in)
m(f)

dandelion /'dændɪlaɪən/ n Löwen-
zahn m

dandruff /'dændrʌf/ n Schuppen
pl

Dane /deɪn/ n Däne m/Dänin f;
Great ~ [deutsche] Dogge f

danger /'deɪndʒə(r)/ n Gefahr f;
in/out of ~ in/außer Gefahr.

~ous /-rəs/ a, **-ly** adv gefährlich;
~ously ill schwer erkrankt

dangle /'dæŋgl/ vi baumeln □ vt
baumeln lassen

Danish /'deɪnɪʃ/ a dänisch. **~
'pastry** n Hefeteilchen nt, Plunderstück nt

dank /dæŋk/ a (-er, -est) naßkalt

Danube /'dænjuːb/ n Donau f

dare /deə(r)/ n Mutprobe f □ vt/i
(challenge) herausfordern (to
zu); **~ [to] do sth** [es] wagen, etw
zu tun; **I ~ say!** das mag wohl
sein! **~devil** n Draufgänger m

daring /'deərɪŋ/ a verwegen □ n
Verwegenheit f

dark /dɑːk/ a (-er, -est) dunkel; **~
blue/brown** dunkelblau/-braun;
~ horse (fig) stilles Wasser nt;
keep sth ~ (fig) etw geheimhal-
ten □ n Dunkelheit f; **after ~**
nach Einbruch der Dunkelheit;
in the ~ im Dunkeln; **keep in
the ~** (fig) im dunkeln lassen

darken /'dɑːkn/ vt verdunkeln
□ vi dunkler werden. **~ness** n
Dunkelheit f

'dark-room n Dunkelkammer f

darling /'dɑːlɪŋ/ a allerliebst □ n
Liebling m

darn /dɑːn/ vt stopfen. **~ing-
needle** n Stopfnadel f

dart /dɑːt/ n Pfeil m; (Sewing)
Abnäher m; **~s** sg (game)
[Wurf]pfeil m □ vi flitzen

dash /dæʃ/ n (Typ) Gedanken-
strich m; (in Morse) Strich m; **a ~
of milk** ein Schuß Milch; **make a
~** losstürzen (for auf + acc) □ vi
rennen □ vt schleudern. **~ off** vi
losstürzen □ vt (write quickly)
hinwerfen

'dashboard n Armaturenbrett nt

dashing /'dæʃɪŋ/ a schneidig

data /'deɪtə/ npl & sg Daten pl. **~
processing** n Datenverar-
beitung f

date¹ /deɪt/ n (fruit) Dattel f

date² n Datum nt; (fam) Verabredung f; **to ~** bis heute; **out of ~**
überholt; (expired) ungültig; **be**

up to ~ auf dem laufenden sein □ *vt/i* datieren; (*Amer, fam: go out with*) ausgehen mit (+ *acc*)

dated /'dertɪd/ *a* altmodisch

'date-line *n* Datumsgrenze *f*

dative /'dertɪv/ *a & n* (*Gram*) ~ [**case**] Dativ *m*

daub /dɔːb/ *vt* beschmieren (**with** mit); schmieren ⟨*paint*⟩

daughter /'dɔːtə(r)/ *n* Tochter *f*. **~-in-law** *n* (*pl* **s-in-law**) Schwiegertochter *f*

daunt /dɔːnt/ *vt* entmutigen; **nothing** ~**ed** unverzagt. **~less** *a* furchtlos

dawdle /'dɔːdl/ *vi* trödeln

dawn /dɔːn/ *n* Morgendämmerung *f*; **at** ~ bei Tagesanbruch □ *vi* anbrechen; **it** ~**ed on me** *(fig)* es ging mir auf

day /deɪ/ *n* Tag *m*; ~ **by** ~ Tag für Tag; ~ **after** ~ Tag um Tag; **these** ~**s** heutzutage; **in those** ~**s** zu der Zeit; **it's had its** ~ ⟨*fam*⟩ es hat ausgedient

day: ~**break** *n* at ~**break** bei Tagesanbruch *m*. **~dream** *n* Tagtraum *m* □ *vi* [mit offenen Augen] träumen. **~light** *n* Tageslicht *nt*. ~ **re'turn** *n* (*ticket*) Tagesrückfahrkarte *f*. **~time** *n* **in the** ~**time** am Tage

daze /deɪz/ *n* **in a** ~ wie benommen. ~**d** *a* benommen

dazzle /'dæzl/ *vt* blenden

deacon /'diːkn/ *n* Diakon *m*

dead /ded/ *a* tot; ⟨*flower*⟩ verwelkt; (*numb*) taub; ~ **body** Leiche *f*; **be** ~ **on time** auf die Minute pünktlich kommen; ~ **centre** genau in der Mitte □ *adv* ~ **tired** todmüde; ~ **slow** sehr langsam; **stop** ~ stehenbleiben □ *n the* ~ *pl* die Toten; **in the** ~ **of night** mitten in der Nacht

deaden /'dedn/ *vt* dämpfen ⟨*sound*⟩; betäuben ⟨*pain*⟩

dead: ~ **'end** *n* Sackgasse *f*. ~ **'heat** *n* totes Rennen *nt*. **~line** *n* [letzter] Termin *m*. **~lock** *n*

reach ~**lock** *(fig)* sich festfahren

deadly /'dedlɪ/ *a* (**-ier, -iest**) tödlich; (*fam: dreary*) sterbenslangweilig; ~ **sins** *pl* Todsünden *pl*

deaf /def/ *a* (**-er, -est**) taub; ~ **and dumb** taubstumm. **--aid** *n* Hörgerät *nt*

deafen /'defn/ *vt* betäuben; (*permanently*) taub machen. **~ening** *a* ohrenbetäubend. **~ness** *n* Taubheit *f*

deal /diːl/ *n* (*transaction*) Geschäft *nt*; **who's** ~? (*Cards*) wer gibt? **a good** *or* **great** ~ eine Menge; **get a raw** ~ *(fam)* sehr schlecht abschneiden □ *v* (*pt/pp* **dealt** /delt/) *vt* (*Cards*) geben; ~ **out** austeilen; ~ **s.o. a blow** jdm einen Schlag versetzen □ *vi* ~ **in** handeln mit; ~ **with** zu tun haben mit; (*handle*) sich befassen mit; (*cope with*) fertig werden mit; (*be about*) handeln von; **that's been dealt with** das ist schon erledigt

dealer /'diːlə(r)/ *n* Händler *m*; (*Cards*) Kartengeber *m*. **~ings** *npl* **have** ~**ings with** zu tun haben mit

de· /diː/ *n* Dekan *m*

dear /dɪə(r)/ *a* (**-er, -est**) lieb; (*expensive*) teuer; (*in letter*) liebe(r,s); (*formal*) sehr geehrte(r,s) □ *n* Liebe(r) *m/f* □ *int* **oh** ~! **oje! ~ly** *adv* ⟨*love*⟩ sehr; ⟨*pay*⟩ teuer

dearth /dɜːθ/ *n* Mangel *m* (**of** an + *dat*)

death /deθ/ *n* Tod *m*; **three** ~**s** drei Todesfälle. ~ **certificate** *n* Sterbeurkunde *f*. ~ **duty** *n* Erbschaftssteuer *f*

deathly *a* ~ **silence** Totenstille *f* □ *adv* ~ **pale** totenblaß

death: ~ **penalty** *n* Todesstrafe *f*. **~'s head** *n* Totenkopf *m*. **~-trap** *n* Todesfalle *f*

debar /dɪ'bɑː(r)/ *vt* (*pt/pp* **debarred**) ausschließen

debase /dɪ'beɪs/ *vt* erniedrigen

debatable /dɪ'bertəbl/ a strittig

debate /dɪ'bert/ n Debatte f ▢ vt/i debattieren

debauchery /dɪ'bɔːtʃərɪ/ n Ausschweifung f

debility /dɪ'bɪlətɪ/ n Entkräftung f

debit /'debɪt/ n Schuldbetrag m; ~ [side] Soll nt ▢ vt (pt/pp **debited**) (Comm) belasten; abbuchen ⟨sum⟩

debris /'debriː/ n Trümmer pl

debt /det/ n Schuld f; in ~ verschuldet. ~ or n Schuldner m

début /'derbuː/ n Debüt nt

decade /'dekeɪd/ n Jahrzehnt nt

decaden|ce /'dekədəns/ n Dekadenz f. ~t a dekadent

decaffeinated /diː'kæfɪnertɪd/ a koffeinfrei

decant /dɪ'kænt/ vt umfüllen. ~er n Karaffe f

decapitate /dɪ'kæpɪteɪt/ vt köpfen

decay /dɪ'keɪ/ n Verfall m; (rot) Verwesung f; (of tooth) Zahnfäule f ▢ vi verfallen; (rot) verwesen; (tooth:) schlecht werden

decease /dɪ'siːs/ n Ableben nt. ~d a verstorben ▢ n the ~d der/die Verstorbene

deceit /dɪ'siːt/ n Täuschung f. ~ful a, -ly adv unaufrichtig

deceive /dɪ'siːv/ vt täuschen; (be unfaithful to) betrügen

December /dɪ'sembə(r)/ n Dezember m

decency /'diːsənsɪ/ n Anstand m

decent /'diːsənt/ a, -ly adv anständig

decentralize /diː'sentrəlaɪz/ vt dezentralisieren

decept|ion /dɪ'sepʃn/ n Täuschung f; (fraud) Betrug m. ~ive /-tɪv/ a, -ly adv täuschend

decibel /'desɪbel/ n Dezibel nt

decide /dɪ'saɪd/ vt entscheiden ▢ vi sich entscheiden (on für)

decided /dɪ'saɪdɪd/ a, -ly adv entschieden

deciduous /dɪ'sɪdjʊəs/ a ~ tree Laubbaum m

decimal /'desɪml/ a Dezimal- ▢ n Dezimalzahl f. ~ 'point n Komma nt. ~ system n Dezimalsystem nt

decimate /'desɪmeɪt/ vt dezimieren

decipher /dɪ'saɪfə(r)/ vt entziffern

decision /dɪ'sɪʒn/ n Entscheidung f; (firmness) Entschlossenheit f

decisive /dɪ'saɪsɪv/ a ausschlaggebend; (firm) entschlossen

deck¹ /dek/ vt schmücken

deck² n (Naut) Deck nt; on ~ an Deck; top ~ (of bus) Oberdeck nt; ~ of cards (Amer) [Karten]spiel nt. ~-chair n Liegestuhl m

declaration /deklə'reɪʃn/ n Erklärung f

declare /dɪ'kleə(r)/ vt erklären; angeben ⟨goods⟩; anything to ~? etwas zu verzollen?

declension /dɪ'klenʃn/ n Deklination f

decline /dɪ'klaɪn/ n Rückgang m; (in health) Verfall m ▢ vt ablehnen; (Gram) deklinieren ▢ vi ablehnen; (fall) sinken; (decrease) nachlassen

decode /diː'kəʊd/ vt entschlüsseln

decompose /diːkəm'pəʊz/ vi sich zersetzen

décor /'deɪkɔː(r)/ n Ausstattung f

decorat|e /'dekəreɪt/ vt (adorn) schmücken, verzieren ⟨cake⟩; (paint) streichen; (wallpaper) tapezieren; (award medal to) einen Orden verleihen (+ dat). ~ion /-'reɪʃn/ n Verzierung f; (medal) Orden m; ~ions pl Schmuck m. ~ive /-rətɪv/ a dekorativ. ~or n painter and ~or Maler und Tapezierer m

decorous /'dekərəs/ a, -ly adv schamhaft

decorum /dɪ'kɔːrəm/ n Anstand m

decoy¹ /'diːkɔɪ/ n Lockvogel m

decoy² /dɪ'kɔɪ/ vt locken

decrease¹ /'diːkriːs/ n Verringerung f; (in number) Rückgang m; be on the ~ zurückgehen

decrease² /dɪˈkriːs/ vt verringern; herabsetzen ⟨price⟩ □ vi sich verringern; ⟨price⟩ sinken

decree /dɪˈkriː/ n Erlaß m □ vt ⟨pt/pp decreed⟩ verordnen

decrepit /dɪˈkrepɪt/ a altersschwach

dedicat|e /ˈdedɪkeɪt/ vt widmen; ⟨Relig⟩ weihen. ~ed a hingebungsvoll; ⟨person⟩ aufopfernd. ~ion /-ˈkeɪʃn/ n Hingabe f; ⟨in book⟩ Widmung f

deduce /dɪˈdjuːs/ vt folgern (from aus)

deduct /dɪˈdʌkt/ vt abziehen

deduction /dɪˈdʌkʃn/ n Abzug m; ⟨conclusion⟩ Folgerung f

deed /diːd/ n Tat f; ⟨Jur⟩ Urkunde f

deem /diːm/ vt halten für

deep /diːp/ a ⟨-er, -est⟩, -ly adv tief; go off the ~ end ⟨fam⟩ auf die Palme gehen □ adv tief

deepen /ˈdiːpn/ vt vertiefen □ vi tiefer werden; ⟨fig⟩ sich vertiefen

deep-'freeze n Gefriertruhe f; ⟨upright⟩ Gefrierschrank m

deer /dɪə(r)/ n inv Hirsch m; ⟨roe⟩ Reh nt

deface /dɪˈfeɪs/ vt beschädigen

defam|ation /defəˈmeɪʃn/ n Verleumdung f. ~ory /dɪˈfæmətərɪ/ a verleumderisch

default /dɪˈfɔːlt/ n ⟨Jur⟩ Nichtzahlung f; ⟨failure to appear⟩ Nichterscheinen nt; win by ~ ⟨Sport⟩ kampflos gewinnen □ vi nicht zahlen; nicht erscheinen

defeat /dɪˈfiːt/ n Niederlage f; ⟨defeating⟩ Besiegung f; ⟨rejection⟩ Ablehnung f □ vt besiegen; ablehnen; ⟨frustrate⟩ vereiteln

defect¹ /dɪˈfekt/ vi ⟨Pol⟩ überlaufen

defect² /ˈdiːfekt/ n Fehler m; ⟨Techn⟩ Defekt m. ~ive /dɪˈfektɪv/ a fehlerhaft; ⟨Techn⟩ defekt

defence /dɪˈfens/ n Verteidigung f. ~less a wehrlos

defend /dɪˈfend/ vt verteidigen; ⟨justify⟩ rechtfertigen. ~ant n

⟨Jur⟩ Beklagte(r) m/f; ⟨in criminal court⟩ Angeklagte(r) m/f

defensive /dɪˈfensɪv/ a defensiv □ n Defensive f

defer /dɪˈfɜː(r)/ vt ⟨pt/pp deferred⟩ ⟨postpone⟩ aufschieben; ~ to s.o. sich jdm fügen

deferen|ce /ˈdefərəns/ n Ehrerbietung f. ~tial /-ˈrenʃl/ a, -ly adv ehrerbietig

defian|ce /dɪˈfaɪəns/ n Trotz m; in ~ce of zum Trotz (+ dat). ~t a, -ly adv aufsässig

deficien|cy /dɪˈfɪʃnsɪ/ n Mangel m. ~t a mangelhaft; he is ~t in ... ihm mangelt es an ... ⟨dat⟩

deficit /ˈdefɪsɪt/ n Defizit nt

defile /dɪˈfaɪl/ vt ⟨fig⟩ schänden

define /dɪˈfaɪn/ vt bestimmen; definieren ⟨word⟩

definite /ˈdefɪnɪt/ a, -ly adv bestimmt; ⟨certain⟩ sicher

definition /defɪˈnɪʃn/ n Definition f; ⟨Phot, TV⟩ Schärfe f

definitive /dɪˈfɪnɪtɪv/ a endgültig; ⟨authoritative⟩ maßgeblich

deflat|e /dɪˈfleɪt/ vt die Luft auslassen aus. ~ion /-eɪʃn/ n ⟨Comm⟩ Deflation f

de'flect /dɪˈflekt/ vt ablenken

deform|ed /dɪˈfɔːmd/ a mißgebildet. ~ity n Mißbildung f

defraud /dɪˈfrɔːd/ vt betrügen (of um)

defray /dɪˈfreɪ/ vt bestreiten

defrost /diːˈfrɒst/ vt entfrosten; abtauen ⟨fridge⟩; auftauen ⟨food⟩

deft /deft/ a ⟨-er, -est⟩, -ly adv geschickt. ~ness n Geschicklichkeit f

defunct /dɪˈfʌŋkt/ a aufgelöst; ⟨law⟩ außer Kraft gesetzt

defuse /diːˈfjuːz/ vt entschärfen

defy /dɪˈfaɪ/ vt ⟨pt/pp -ied⟩ trotzen (+ dat); widerstehen (+ dat) ⟨attempt⟩

degenerate¹ /dɪˈdʒenəreɪt/ vi degenerieren; ~ into ⟨fig⟩ ausarten in (+ acc)

degenerate[2] /dɪˈdʒenərət/ a degeneriert

degrading /dɪˈɡreɪdɪŋ/ a entwürdigend

degree /dɪˈɡriː/ n Grad m; ⟨Univ⟩ akademischer Grad m; **20 ~s** 20 Grad

dehydrate /diːˈhaɪdreɪt/ vt Wasser entziehen (+ dat). **~d** /-ɪd/ a ausgetrocknet

de-ice /diːˈaɪs/ vt enteisen

deign /deɪn/ vi **~ to do sth** sich herablassen, etw zu tun

deity /ˈdiːɪtɪ/ n Gottheit f

dejected /dɪˈdʒektɪd/ a, **-ly** adv niedergeschlagen

delay /dɪˈleɪ/ n Verzögerung f; ⟨of train, aircraft⟩ Verspätung f; **without ~** unverzüglich □ vt aufhalten; ⟨postpone⟩ aufschieben; **be ~ed** ⟨person:⟩ aufgehalten werden; ⟨train, aircraft:⟩ Verspätung haben □ vi zögern

delegate[1] /ˈdelɪɡət/ n Delegierte(r) m/f

delegat|**e**[2] /ˈdelɪɡeɪt/ vt delegieren. **~ion** /-ˈɡeɪʃn/ n Delegation f

delete /dɪˈliːt/ vt streichen. **~ion** /-iːʃn/ n Streichung f

deliberate[1] /dɪˈlɪbərət/ a, **-ly** adv absichtlich; ⟨slow⟩ bedächtig

deliberat|**e**[2] /dɪˈlɪbəreɪt/ vt/i überlegen. **~ion** /-ˈreɪʃn/ n Überlegung f; **with ~ion** mit Bedacht

delicacy /ˈdelɪkəsɪ/ n Feinheit f; Zartheit f; ⟨food⟩ Delikatesse f

delicate /ˈdelɪkət/ a fein; ⟨fabric, health⟩ zart; ⟨situation⟩ heikel; ⟨mechanism⟩ empfindlich

delicatessen /delɪkəˈtesn/ n Delikatessengeschäft nt

delicious /dɪˈlɪʃəs/ a köstlich

delight /dɪˈlaɪt/ n Freude f □ vt entzücken □ vi **~ in** sich erfreuen an (+ dat). **~ed** a hocherfreut; **be ~ed** sich sehr freuen. **~ful** a reizend

delinquen|**cy** /dɪˈlɪŋkwənsɪ/ n Kriminalität f. **~t** a straffällig □ n Straffällige(r) m/f

deli|**rious** /dɪˈlɪrɪəs/ a **be ~rious** im Delirium sein. **~rium** /-rɪəm/ n Delirium nt

deliver /dɪˈlɪvə(r)/ vt liefern; zustellen ⟨post, newspaper⟩; halten ⟨speech⟩; überbringen ⟨message⟩; versetzen ⟨blow⟩; ⟨set free⟩ befreien; **~ a baby** ein Kind zur Welt bringen. **~ance** n Erlösung f. **~y** n Lieferung f; ⟨of post⟩ Zustellung f; ⟨Med⟩ Entbindung f; **cash on ~** per Nachnahme

delta /ˈdeltə/ n Delta nt

delude /dɪˈluːd/ vt täuschen; **~ oneself** sich (dat) Illusionen machen

deluge /ˈdeljuːdʒ/ n Flut f; ⟨heavy rain⟩ schwerer Guß □ vt überschwemmen

delusion /dɪˈluːʒn/ n Täuschung f

de luxe /dɪˈlʌks/ a Luxus-

delve /delv/ vi hineingreifen (into in + acc); ⟨fig⟩ eingehen (into auf + acc)

demand /dɪˈmɑːnd/ n Forderung f; ⟨Comm⟩ Nachfrage f; **in ~** gefragt; **on ~** auf Verlangen □ vt verlangen, fordern (of/from von). **~ing** a anspruchsvoll

demarcation /diːmɑːˈkeɪʃn/ n Abgrenzung f

demean /dɪˈmiːn/ vt **~ oneself** sich erniedrigen

demeanour /dɪˈmiːnə(r)/ n Verhalten nt

demented /dɪˈmentɪd/ a verrückt

demise /dɪˈmaɪz/ n Tod m

demister /diːˈmɪstə(r)/ n ⟨Auto⟩ Defroster m

demo /ˈdeməʊ/ n (pl **~s**) ⟨fam⟩ Demonstration f

demobilize /diːˈməʊbəlaɪz/ vt ⟨Mil⟩ entlassen

democracy /dɪˈmɒkrəsɪ/ n Demokratie f

democrat /ˈdeməkræt/ n Demokrat m. **~ic** /-ˈkrætɪk/ a, **-ally** adv demokratisch

demol|**ish** /dɪˈmɒlɪʃ/ vt abbrechen; ⟨destroy⟩ zerstören. **~lition** /deməˈlɪʃn/ n Abbruch m

demon /'diːmən/ n Dämon m

demonstrat|e /'demənstreɪt/ vt beweisen; vorführen ⟨appliance⟩ □vi (Pol) demonstrieren. **~ion** /-'streɪʃn/ n Vorführung f; (Pol) Demonstration f

demonstrative /dɪ'mɒnstrətɪv/ a (Gram) demonstrativ; **be ~** seine Gefühle zeigen

demonstrator /'demənstreɪtə(r)/ n Vorführer m; (Pol) Demonstrant m

demoralize /dɪ'mɒrəlaɪz/ vt demoralisieren

demote /dɪ'məʊt/ vt degradieren

demure /dɪ'mjʊə(r)/ a, **-ly** adv sittsam

den /den/ n Höhle f; (room) Bude f

denial /dɪ'naɪəl/ n Leugnen nt; **official ~** Dementi nt

denigrate /'denɪɡreɪt/ vt herabsetzen

denim /'denɪm/ n Jeansstoff m; **~s** pl Jeans pl

Denmark /'denmɑːk/ n Dänemark nt

denomination /dɪnɒmɪ'neɪʃn/ n (Relig) Konfession f; (money) Nennwert m

denote /dɪ'nəʊt/ vt bezeichnen

denounce /dɪ'naʊns/ vt denunzieren; (condemn) verurteilen

dens|e /dens/ a (-r, -st), **-ly** adv dicht; (fam: stupid) blöd[e]. **~ity** n Dichte f

dent /dent/ n Delle f, Beule f □vt einbeulen; **~ed** /-ɪd/ verbeult

dental /'dentl/ a Zahn-; ⟨treatment⟩ zahnärztlich. **~ floss** /flɒs/ n Zahnseide f. **~ surgeon** n Zahnarzt m

dentist /'dentɪst/ n Zahnarzt m/ -ärztin f. **~ry** n Zahnmedizin f

denture /'dentʃə(r)/ n Zahnprothese f; **~s** pl künstliches Gebiß nt

denude /dɪ'njuːd/ vt entblößen

denunciation /dɪnʌnsɪ'eɪʃn/ n Denunziation f; (condemnation) Verurteilung f

deny /dɪ'naɪ/ vt (pt/pp -ied) leugnen; (officially) dementieren; **~ s.o. sth** jdm etw verweigern

deodorant /diː'əʊdərənt/ n Deodorant nt

depart /dɪ'pɑːt/ vi abfahren; (Aviat) abfliegen; (go away) weggehen/-fahren; (deviate) abweichen (from von)

department /dɪ'pɑːtmənt/ n Abteilung f; (Pol) Ministerium nt. **~ store** n Kaufhaus nt

departure /dɪ'pɑːtʃə(r)/ n Abfahrt f; (Aviat) Abflug m; (from rule) Abweichung f; **new ~** Neuerung f

depend /dɪ'pend/ vi abhängen (on von); (rely) sich verlassen (on auf + acc); **it all ~s** das kommt darauf an. **~able** /-əbl/ a zuverlässig. **~ant** n Abhängige(r) m/f. **~ence** n Abhängigkeit f. **~ent** a abhängig (on von)

depict /dɪ'pɪkt/ vt darstellen

depilatory /dɪ'pɪlətərɪ/ n Enthaarungsmittel nt

deplete /dɪ'pliːt/ vt verringern

deplor|able /dɪ'plɔːrəbl/ a bedauerlich. **~e** vt bedauern

dep̲loy /dɪ'plɔɪ/ vt (Mil) einsetzen □vi sich aufstellen

depopulate /diː'pɒpjʊleɪt/ vt entvölkern

deport /dɪ'pɔːt/ vt deportieren, ausweisen. **~ation** /diːpɔː'teɪʃn/ n Ausweisung f

deportment /dɪ'pɔːtmənt/ n Haltung f

depose /dɪ'pəʊz/ vt absetzen

deposit /dɪ'pɒzɪt/ n Anzahlung f; (against damage) Kaution f; (on bottle) Pfand nt; (sediment) Bodensatz m; (Geol) Ablagerung f □vt (pt/pp deposited) legen; (for safety) deponieren; (Geol) ablagern. **~ account** n Sparkonto nt

depot /'depəʊ/ n Depot nt; (Amer: railway station) Bahnhof m

deprav|e /dɪˈpreɪv/ vt verderben. **~ed** a verkommen. **~ity** /-ˈprævətɪ/ n Verderbtheit f

deprecate /ˈdeprəkeɪt/ vt mißbilligen

depreciat|e /dɪˈpriːʃɪeɪt/ vi an Wert verlieren. **~ion** /-ˈeɪʃn/ n Wertminderung f; (Comm) Abschreibung f

depress /dɪˈpres/ vt deprimieren; (press down) herunterdrücken. **~ed** a deprimiert; **~ed area** Notstandsgebiet nt. **~ing** a deprimierend. **~ion** /-eʃn/ n Vertiefung f; (Med) Depression f; (Meteorol) Tief nt

deprivation /deprɪˈveɪʃn/ n Entbehrung f

deprive /dɪˈpraɪv/ vt entziehen; **~ s.o. of sth** jdm etw entziehen. **~d** a benachteiligt

depth /depθ/ n Tiefe f; **in ~** gründlich; **in the ~s of winter** im tiefsten Winter

deputation /depjʊˈteɪʃn/ n Abordnung f

deputize /ˈdepjʊtaɪz/ vi **~ for** vertreten

deputy /ˈdepjʊtɪ/ n Stellvertreter m □ attrib stellvertretend

derail /dɪˈreɪl/ vt **be ~ed** entgleisen. **~ment** n Entgleisung f

deranged /dɪˈreɪndʒd/ a geistesgestört

derelict /ˈderəlɪkt/ a verfallen; (abandoned) verlassen

deri|de /dɪˈraɪd/ vt verhöhnen. **~sion** /-ˈrɪʒn/ n Hohn m

derisive /dɪˈraɪsɪv/ a, **-ly** adv höhnisch

derisory /dɪˈraɪsərɪ/ a höhnisch; (offer) lächerlich

derivation /derɪˈveɪʃn/ n Ableitung f

derivative /dɪˈrɪvətɪv/ a abgeleitet □ n Ableitung f

derive /dɪˈraɪv/ vt/i (obtain) gewinnen (from aus); **be ~d from** (word:) hergeleitet sein aus

dermatologist /dɜːməˈtɒlədʒɪst/ n Hautarzt m /-ärztin f

derogatory /dɪˈrɒgətrɪ/ a abfällig

derrick /ˈderɪk/ n Bohrturm m

derv /dɜːv/ n Diesel[kraftstoff] m

descend /dɪˈsend/ vt/i hinunter-/heruntergehen; (vehicle, lift:) hinunter-/herunterfahren; **be ~ed from** abstammen von. **~ant** n Nachkomme m

descent /dɪˈsent/ n Abstieg m; (lineage) Abstammung f

describe /dɪˈskraɪb/ vt beschreiben

descrip|tion /dɪˈskrɪpʃn/ n Beschreibung f; (sort) Art f. **~tive** /-tɪv/ a beschreibend; (vivid) anschaulich

desecrat|e /ˈdesɪkreɪt/ vt entweihen. **~ion** /-ˈkreɪʃn/ n Entweihung f

desert[1] /ˈdezət/ n Wüste f □ a Wüsten-; **~ island** verlassene Insel f

desert[2] /dɪˈzɜːt/ vt verlassen □ vi desertieren. **~ed** a verlassen. **~er** n (Mil) Deserteur m. **~ion** /-ɜːʃn/ n Fahnenflucht f

deserts /dɪˈzɜːts/ npl **get one's ~** seinen verdienten Lohn bekommen

deserv|e /dɪˈzɜːv/ vt verdienen. **~edly** /-ɪdlɪ/ adv verdientermaßen. **~ing** a verdienstvoll; **~ing cause** guter Zweck m

design /dɪˈzaɪn/ n Entwurf m; (pattern) Muster nt; (construction) Konstruktion f; (aim) Absicht f □ vt entwerfen; (construct) konstruieren; **be ~ed for** bestimmt sein für

designat|e /ˈdezɪgneɪt/ vt bezeichnen; (appoint) ernennen. **~ion** /-ˈneɪʃn/ n Bezeichnung f

designer /dɪˈzaɪnə(r)/ n Designer m; (Techn) Konstrukteur m; (Theat) Bühnenbildner m

desirable /dɪˈzaɪərəbl/ a wünschenswert; (sexually) begehrenswert

desire /dɪˈzaɪə(r)/ n Wunsch m; (longing) Verlangen nt (for nach); (sexual) Begierde f □ vt [sich (dat)] wünschen; (sexually) begehren

desk /desk/ n Schreibtisch m; (Sch) Pult nt; (Comm) Kasse f; (in hotel) Rezeption f

desolate /'desələt/ a trostlos. **~ion** /-'leɪʃn/ n Trostlosigkeit f

despair /dɪ'speə(r)/ n Verzweiflung f; **in ~** verzweifelt □ vi verzweifeln

desperate /'despərət/ a, **-ly** adv verzweifelt; (urgent) dringend; **be ~e** (criminal:) zum Äußersten entschlossen sein; **be ~e for** dringend brauchen. **~ion** /-'reɪʃn/ n Verzweiflung f; **in ~ion** aus Verzweiflung

despicable /dɪ'spɪkəbl/ a verachtenswert

despise /dɪ'spaɪz/ vt verachten

despite /dɪ'spaɪt/ prep trotz (+ gen)

despondent /dɪ'spɒndənt/ a niedergeschlagen

despot /'despɒt/ n Despot m

dessert /dɪ'zɜːt/ n Dessert nt, Nachtisch m. **~ spoon** n Dessertlöffel m

destination /destɪ'neɪʃn/ n [Reise]ziel nt; (of goods) Bestimmungsort m

destine /'destɪn/ vt bestimmen

destiny /'destɪnɪ/ n Schicksal nt

destitute /'destɪtjuːt/ a völlig mittellos

destroy /dɪ'strɔɪ/ vt zerstören; (totally) vernichten. **~er** n (Naut) Zerstörer m

destruction /dɪ'strʌkʃn/ n Zerstörung f; Vernichtung f. **-tive** /-tɪv/ a zerstörerisch; (fig) destruktiv

detach /dɪ'tætʃ/ vt abnehmen; (tear off) abtrennen. **~able** /-əbl/ a abnehmbar. **~ed** a (fig) distanziert; **~ed house** Einzelhaus nt

detachment /dɪ'tætʃmənt/ n Distanz f; (objectivity) Abstand m; (Mil) Sonderkommando nt

detail /'diːteɪl/ n Einzelheit f, Detail nt; **in ~** ausführlich □ vt einzeln aufführen; (Mil) abkommandieren. **~ed** a ausführlich

detain /dɪ'teɪn/ vt aufhalten; (police:) in Haft behalten; (take into custody) in Haft nehmen. **~ee** /diːteɪ'niː/ n Häftling m

detect /dɪ'tekt/ vt entdecken; (perceive) wahrnehmen. **~ion** /-ekʃn/ n Entdeckung f

detective /dɪ'tektɪv/ n Detektiv m. **~ story** n Detektivroman m

detector /dɪ'tektə(r)/ n Suchgerät nt; (for metal) Metalldetektor m

detention /dɪ'tenʃn/ n Haft f; (Sch) Nachsitzen nt

deter /dɪ'tɜː(r)/ vt (pt/pp deterred) abschrecken; (prevent) abhalten

detergent /dɪ'tɜːdʒənt/ n Waschmittel nt

deteriorate /dɪ'tɪərɪəreɪt/ vi sich verschlechtern. **~ion** /-'reɪʃn/ n Verschlechterung f

determination /dɪtɜːmɪ'neɪʃn/ n Entschlossenheit f

determine /dɪ'tɜːmɪn/ vt bestimmen; **~ to** (resolve) sich entschließen zu. **~d** a entschlossen

deterrent /dɪ'terənt/ n Abschreckungsmittel nt

detest /dɪ'test/ vt verabscheuen. **~able** /-əbl/ a abscheulich

detonate /'detəneɪt/ vt zünden □ vi explodieren. **~or** n Zünder m

detour /'diːtʊə(r)/ n Umweg m; (for traffic) Umleitung f

detract /dɪ'trækt/ vi **~ from** beeinträchtigen

detriment /'detrɪmənt/ n **to the ~** zum Schaden (of gen). **~al** /-'mentl/ a schädlich (to dat)

deuce /djuːs/ n (Tennis) Einstand m

devaluation /diːvæljʊ'eɪʃn/ n Abwertung f

de'value vt abwerten (currency)

devastat|e /'devəsteɪt/ vt verwüsten. **~ed** /-ɪd/ a (fam) erschüttert. **~ing** a verheerend. **~ion** /-'steɪʃn/ n Verwüstung f

develop /dɪ'veləp/ vt entwickeln; bekommen ⟨illness⟩; erschließen ⟨area⟩ □vi sich entwickeln (into zu). **~er** n [property] ~er Bodenspekulant m

de'veloping country n Entwicklungsland nt

development /dɪ'veləpmənt/ n Entwicklung f

deviant /'di:vɪənt/ a abweichend

deviat|e /'di:vɪeɪt/ vi abweichen. **~ion** /-'eɪʃn/ n Abweichung f

device /dɪ'vaɪs/ n Gerät nt; (fig) Mittel nt; leave s.o. to his own ~s jdn sich (dat) selbst überlassen

devil /'devl/ n Teufel m. **~ish** a teuflisch

devious /'di:vɪəs/ a verschlagen; ~ route Umweg m

devise /dɪ'vaɪz/ vt sich (dat) ausdenken

devoid /dɪ'vɔɪd/ a ~ of ohne

devolution /di:və'lu:ʃn/ n Dezentralisierung f; (of power) Übertragung f

devot|e /dɪ'vəʊt/ vt widmen (to dat). **~ed** a, -ly adv ergeben; ⟨care⟩ liebevoll; be ~ed to s.o. sehr an jdm hängen. **~ee** /devə'ti:/ n Anhänger(in) m(f)

devotion /dɪ'vəʊʃn/ n Hingabe f; **~s** pl (Relig) Andacht f

devour /dɪ'vaʊə(r)/ vt verschlingen

devout /dɪ'vaʊt/ a fromm

dew /dju:/ n Tau m

dexterity /dek'sterətɪ/ n Geschicklichkeit f

diabet|es /daɪə'bi:ti:z/ n Zuckerkrankheit f. **~ic** /-'betɪk/ a zuckerkrank □n Zuckerkranke(r) m/f, Diabetiker(in) m(f)

diabolical /daɪə'bɒlɪkl/ a teuflisch

diagnose /daɪəg'nəʊz/ vt diagnostizieren

diagnosis /daɪəg'nəʊsɪs/ n (pl -oses /-si:z/) Diagnose f

diagonal /daɪ'æɡənl/ a, -ly adv diagonal □n Diagonale f

diagram /'daɪəɡræm/ n Diagramm nt

dial /'daɪəl/ n (of clock) Zifferblatt nt; (Techn) Skala f; (Teleph) Wählscheibe f □vt/i (pt/pp dialled) (Teleph) wählen; ~ direct durchwählen

dialect /'daɪəlekt/ n Dialekt m

dialling: ~ code n Vorwahlnummer f. ~ tone n Amtszeichen nt

dialogue /'daɪəlɒɡ/ n Dialog m

'dial tone n (Amer, Teleph) Amtszeichen nt

diameter /daɪ'æmɪtə(r)/ n Durchmesser m

diametrically /daɪə'metrɪkəlɪ/ adv ~ opposed genau entgegengesetzt (to dat)

diamond /'daɪəmənd/ n Diamant m; (cut) Brillant m; (shape) Raute f; ~s pl (Cards) Karo nt

diaper /'daɪəpə(r)/ n (Amer) Windel f

diaphragm /'daɪəfræm/ n (Anat) Zwerchfell nt; (Phot) Blende f

diarrhoea /daɪə'ri:ə/ n Durchfall m

diary /'daɪərɪ/ n Tagebuch nt; (for appointments) [Termin]kalender m

dice /daɪs/ n inv Würfel m □vt (Culin) in Würfel schneiden

dicey /'daɪsɪ/ a (fam) riskant

dictat|e /dɪk'teɪt/ vt/i diktieren. **~ion** /-eɪʃn/ n Diktat nt

dictator /dɪk'teɪtə(r)/ n Diktator m. **~ial** /-tə'tɔ:rɪəl/ a diktatorisch. **~ship** n Diktatur f

diction /'dɪkʃn/ n Aussprache f

dictionary /'dɪkʃənrɪ/ n Wörterbuch nt

did /dɪd/ see do

didactic /dɪ'dæktɪk/ a didaktisch

diddle /'dɪdl/ vt (fam) übers Ohr hauen

didn't /'dɪdnt/ = did not

die¹ /daɪ/ n (Techn) Prägestempel m; (metal mould) Gußform f

die² vi (pres p dying) sterben (of an + dat); (plant, animal:) eingehen; (flower:) verwelken; **be dying to do sth** (fam) darauf brennen, etw zu tun; **be dying for sth** (fam) sich nach etw sehnen. **~ down** vi nachlassen; (fire:) herunterbrennen. **~ out** vi aussterben

diesel /'diːzl/ n Diesel m. **~ engine** n Dieselmotor m

diet /'daɪət/ n Kost f; (restricted) Diät f; (for slimming) Schlankheitskur f; **be on a ~** diät leben; eine Schlankheitskur machen □vi diät leben; eine Schlankheitskur machen

dietician /daɪə'tɪʃn/ n Diätassistent(in) m(f)

differ /'dɪfə(r)/ vi sich unterscheiden; (disagree) verschiedener Meinung sein

differen|ce /'dɪfrəns/ n Unterschied m; (disagreement) Meinungsverschiedenheit f. **~t** a andere(r,s); (various) verschiedene; **be ~t** anders sein (from als)

differential /dɪfə'renʃl/ a Differential- □n Unterschied m; (Techn) Differential nt

differentiate /dɪfə'renʃɪeɪt/ vt/i unterscheiden (between zwischen + dat)

differently /'dɪfrəntlɪ/ adv anders

difficult /'dɪfɪkəlt/ a schwierig, schwer. **~y** n Schwierigkeit f

diffiden|ce /'dɪfɪdəns/ n Zaghaftigkeit f. **~ t** a zaghaft

diffuse¹ /dɪ'fjuːs/ a ausgebreitet; (wordy) langatmig

diffuse² /dɪ'fjuːz/ vt (Phys) streuen

dig /dɪg/ n (poke) Stoß m; (remark) spitze Bemerkung f; (Archaeol) Ausgrabung f; **~ s** pl (fam) möbliertes Zimmer nt □vt/i (pt/pp **dug**, pres p **digging**) graben; umgraben (garden); **~ s.o. in the ribs** jdm einen Rippenstoß ge-

ben. **~ out** vt ausgraben. **~ up** vt ausgraben; umgraben (garden); aufreißen (street)

digest¹ /'daɪdʒest/ n Kurzfassung f

digest² /dɪ'dʒest/ vt verdauen. **~ible** a verdaulich. **~ion** /-estʃn/ n Verdauung f

digger /'dɪgə(r)/ n (Techn) Bagger m

digit /'dɪdʒɪt/ n Ziffer f; (finger) Finger m; (toe) Zehe f

digital /'dɪdʒɪtl/ a Digital-; **~ clock** n Digitaluhr f

dignified /'dɪgnɪfaɪd/ a würdevoll

dignitary /'dɪgnɪtərɪ/ n Würdenträger m

dignity /'dɪgnɪtɪ/ n Würde f

digress /daɪ'gres/ vi abschweifen. **~ion** /-eʃn/ n Abschweifung f

dike /daɪk/ n Deich m; (ditch) Graben m

dilapidated /dɪ'læpɪdeɪtɪd/ a baufällig

dilate /daɪ'leɪt/ vt erweitern □vi sich erweitern

dilatory /'dɪlətərɪ/ a langsam

dilemma /dɪ'lemə/ n Dilemma nt

dilettante /dɪlɪ'tæntɪ/ n Dilettant(in) m(f)

diligen|ce /'dɪlɪdʒəns/ n Fleiß m. **~ t** a, **-ly** adv fleißig

dill /dɪl/ n Dill m

dilly-dally /'dɪlɪdælɪ/ vi (pt/pp **-ied**) (fam) trödeln

dilute /daɪ'luːt/ vt verdünnen

dim /dɪm/ a (**dimmer, dimmest**), **-ly** adv (weak) schwach; (dark) trüb[e]; (indistinct) undeutlich; (fam: stupid) dumm, (fam) doof □v (pt/pp **dimmed**) □vt dämpfen □vi schwächer werden

dime /daɪm/ n (Amer) Zehncentstück n

dimension /daɪ'menʃn/ n Dimension f; **~ s** pl Maße pl

diminish /dɪ'mɪnɪʃ/ vt verringern □vi sich verringern

diminutive /dɪ'mɪnjʊtɪv/ a winzig □n Verkleinerungsform f

dimple /'dɪmpl/ n Grübchen nt

din /dɪn/ n Krach m, Getöse nt

dine /daɪn/ *vi* speisen. **~r** *n* Speisende(r) *m/f*; (*Amer: restaurant*) Eßlokal *nt*

dinghy /'dɪŋgɪ/ *n* Dinghi *nt*; (*inflatable*) Schlauchboot *nt*

dingy /'dɪndʒɪ/ *a* (**-ier, -iest**) trübe

dining /'daɪnɪŋ/: **~-car** *n* Speisewagen *m*. **~-room** *n* Eßzimmer *nt*. **~-table** *n* Eßtisch *m*

dinner /'dɪnə(r)/ *n* Abendessen *nt*; (*at midday*) Mittagessen *nt*; (*formal*) Essen *nt*. **~-jacket** *n* Smoking *m*

dinosaur /'daɪnəsɔ:(r)/ *n* Dinosaurier *m*

dint /dɪnt/ *n* **by ~ of** durch (+ *acc*)

diocese /'daɪəsɪs/ *n* Diözese *f*

dip /dɪp/ *n* (*in ground*) Senke *f*; (*Culin*) Dip *m*; **go for a ~** kurz schwimmen gehen □*v* (*pt/pp* dipped) *vt* [ein]tauchen; **~ one's headlights** (*Auto*) [die Scheinwerfer] abblenden □*vt* sich senken

diphtheria /dɪf'θɪərɪə/ *n* Diphtherie *f*

diphthong /'dɪfθɒŋ/ *n* Diphthong *m*

diploma /dɪ'pləʊmə/ *n* Diplom *nt*

diplomacy /dɪ'pləʊməsɪ/ *n* Diplomatie *f*

diplomat /'dɪpləmæt/ *n* Diplomat *m*. **~ic** /-'mætɪk/ *a*, **-ally** *adv* diplomatisch

'dip-stick *n* (*Auto*) Ölmeßstab *m*

dire /'daɪə(r)/ *a* (**-r, -st**) bitter; ⟨*situation, consequences*⟩ furchtbar

direct /dɪ'rekt/ *a* & *adv* direkt □*vt* (*aim*) richten (*at* auf / (*fig*) an + *acc*); (*control*) leiten; (*order*) anweisen; **~ s.o.** (*show the way*) jdm den Weg sagen; **~ a film/play** bei einem Film/Theaterstück Regie führen. **~ 'current** *n* Gleichstrom *m*

direction /dɪ'rekʃn/ *n* Richtung *f*; (*control*) Leitung *f*; (*of play, film*) Regie *f*; **~s** *pl* Anweisungen *pl*; **~s for use** Gebrauchsanweisung *f*

directly /dɪ'rektlɪ/ *adv* direkt; (*at once*) sofort □*conj* (*fam*) sobald

director /dɪ'rektə(r)/ *n* (*Comm*) Direktor *m*; (*of play, film*) Regisseur *m*

directory /dɪ'rektərɪ/ *n* Verzeichnis *nt*; (*Teleph*) Telefonbuch *nt*

dirt /dɜ:t/ *n* Schmutz *m*; (*soil*) Erde *f*; **~ cheap** (*fam*) spottbillig

dirty /'dɜ:tɪ/ *a* (**-ier, -iest**) schmutzig □*vt* schmutzig machen

dis|a'bility /dɪs-/ *n* Behinderung *f*. **~abled** /dɪ'seɪbld/ *a* [körper]behindert

disad'vantage *n* Nachteil *m*; **at a ~tage** im Nachteil. **~taged** *a* benachteiligt. **~'tageous** *a* nachteilig

disaf'fected *a* unzufrieden; (*disloyal*) illoyal

disa'gree *vi* nicht übereinstimmen (**with** mit); **I ~** ich bin anderer Meinung; **we ~** wir sind verschiedener Meinung; **oysters ~ with me** Austern bekommen mir nicht

disa'greeable *a* unangenehm

disa'greement *n* Meinungsverschiedenheit *f*

disap'pear *vi* verschwinden. **~ance** *n* Verschwinden *nt*

disap'point *vt* enttäuschen. **~ment** *n* Enttäuschung *f*

disap'proval *n* Mißbilligung *f*

disap'prove *vi* dagegen sein; **~ of** mißbilligen

dis'arm *vt* entwaffnen □*vi* (*Mil*) abrüsten. **~ament** *n* Abrüstung *f*. **~ing** *a* entwaffnend

disar'ray *n* Unordnung *f*

disast|er /dɪ'za:stə(r)/ *n* Katastrophe *f*; (*accident*) Unglück *nt*. **~rous** /-rəs/ *a* katastrophal

dis'band *vt* auflösen □*vi* sich auflösen

disbe'lief *n* Unglaube *m*; **in ~** ungläubig

disc /dɪsk/ *n* Scheibe *f*; (*record*) [Schall]platte *f*; (*CD*) CD *f*

discard /dɪ'ska:d/ *vt* ablegen; (*throw away*) wegwerfen

discern /dɪˈsɜːn/ vt wahrnehmen. **~ible** a wahrnehmbar. **~ing** a anspruchsvoll

'discharge¹ n Ausstoßen nt; (Naut, Electr) Entladung f; (dismissal) Entlassung f; (Jur) Freispruch m; (Med) Ausfluß m

dis'charge² vt ausstoßen; (Naut, Electr) entladen; (dismiss) entlassen; (Jur) freisprechen ⟨accused⟩; **~ a duty** sich einer Pflicht entledigen

disciple /dɪˈsaɪpl/ n Jünger m; (fig) Schüler m

disciplinary /ˈdɪsɪplɪnərɪ/ a disziplinarisch

discipline /ˈdɪsɪplɪn/ n Disziplin f □vt Disziplin beibringen (+ dat); (punish) bestrafen

'disc jockey n Diskjockey m

dis'claim vt abstreiten. **~er** n Verzichterklärung f

dis'close vt enthüllen. **~ure** n Enthüllung f

disco /ˈdɪskəʊ/ n (fam) Disko f

dis'colour vt verfärben □vi sich verfärben

dis'comfort n Beschwerden pl; (fig) Unbehagen nt

disconcert /dɪskənˈsɜːt/ vt aus der Fassung bringen

discon'nect vt trennen; (Electr) ausschalten; (cut supply) abstellen

disconsolate /dɪsˈkɒnsələt/ a untröstlich

discon'tent n Unzufriedenheit f. **~ed** a unzufrieden

discon'tinue vt einstellen; (Comm) nicht mehr herstellen

'discord n Zwietracht f; (Mus & fig) Mißklang m. **~ant** /dɪˈskɔːdənt/ a **~ant note** Mißklang m

discothèque /ˈdɪskətek/ n Diskothek f

'discount¹ n Rabatt m

dis'count² vt außer acht lassen

dis'courage vt entmutigen; (dissuade) abraten (+ dat)

'discourse n Rede f

dis'courteous a, **-ly** adv unhöflich

discover /dɪˈskʌvə(r)/ vt entdecken. **~y** n Entdeckung f

dis'credit n Mißkredit m □vt in Mißkredit bringen

discreet /dɪˈskriːt/ a, **-ly** adv diskret

discrepancy /dɪˈskrepənsɪ/ n Diskrepanz f

discretion /dɪˈskreʃn/ n Diskretion f; (judgement) Ermessen nt

discriminate /dɪˈskrɪmɪneɪt/ vi unterscheiden (between zwischen + dat); **~e against** diskriminieren. **~ing** a anspruchsvoll. **~ion** /-ˈneɪʃn/ n Diskriminierung f; (quality) Urteilskraft f

discus /ˈdɪskəs/ n Diskus m

discuss /dɪˈskʌs/ vt besprechen; (examine critically) diskutieren. **~ion** /-ʌʃn/ n Besprechung f; Diskussion f

disdain /dɪsˈdeɪn/ n Verachtung f □vt verachten. **~ful** a verächtlich

disease /dɪˈziːz/ n Krankheit f. **~d** a krank

disem'bark vi an Land gehen

disen'chant vt ernüchtern. **~ment** n Ernüchterung f

disen'gage vt losmachen; (Techn) **~ the clutch** (Auto) auskuppeln

disen'tangle vt entwirren

dis'favour n Ungnade f; (disapproval) Mißfallen nt

dis'figure vt entstellen

dis'gorge vt ausspeien

dis'grace n Schande f; **in ~** in Ungnade □vt Schande machen (+ dat). **~ful** a schändlich

disgruntled /dɪsˈgrʌntld/ a verstimmt

disguise /dɪsˈgaɪz/ n Verkleidung f; **in ~** verkleidet □vt verkleiden; verstellen ⟨voice⟩; (conceal) verhehlen

disgust /dɪsˈgʌst/ n Ekel m; **in ~** empört □vt anekeln; (appal) empören. **~ing** a eklig; (appalling) abscheulich

dish /dɪʃ/ n Schüssel f; (shallow) Schale f; (small) Schälchen nt; (food) Gericht nt. ~ **out** vt austeilen. ~ **up** vt auftragen

'**dishcloth** n Spültuch nt

dis'**hearten** vt entmutigen. ~**ing** a entmutigend

dishevelled /dɪ'ʃevld/ a zerzaust

dis'**honest** a, -**ly** adv unehrlich. ~**y** n Unehrlichkeit f

dis'**honour** n Schande f □vt entehren; nicht honorieren (cheque). ~**able** a, -**bly** adv unehrenhaft

'**dishwasher** n Geschirrspülmaschine f

disil'**lusion** vt ernüchtern. ~**ment** n Ernüchterung f

disin'**fect** vt desinfizieren. ~**ant** n Desinfektionsmittel nt

disin'**herit** vt enterben

dis'**integrate** vi zerfallen

dis'**interested** a unvoreingenommen; (uninterested) uninteressiert

dis'**jointed** a unzusammenhängend

disk /dɪsk/ n = disc

dis'**like** n Abneigung f □vt nicht mögen

dislocate /'dɪsləkeɪt/ vt ausrenken; ~ **one's shoulder** sich (dat) den Arm auskugeln

dis'**lodge** vt entfernen

dis'**loyal** a, -**ly** adv illoyal. ~**ty** n Illoyalität f

dismal /'dɪzml/ a trüb[e]; (person) trübselig; (fam: poor) kläglich

dismantle /dɪs'mæntl/ vt auseinandernehmen; (take down) abbauen

dis'**may** n Bestürzung f. ~**ed** a bestürzt

dis'**miss** vt entlassen; (reject) zurückweisen. ~**al** n Entlassung f; Zurückweisung f

dis'**mount** vi absteigen

diso'**bedien|ce** n Ungehorsam m. ~**t** a ungehorsam

diso'**bey** vt/i nicht gehorchen (+ dat); nicht befolgen (rule)

dis'**order** n Unordnung f; (Med) Störung f. ~**ly** a unordentlich; ~**ly conduct** ungebührliches Benehmen nt

dis'**organized** a unorganisiert

dis'**orientate** vt verwirren; **be ~d** die Orientierung verloren haben

dis'**own** vt verleugnen

disparaging /dɪs'pærɪdʒɪŋ/ a, -**ly** adv abschätzig

disparity /dɪs'pærətɪ/ n Ungleichheit f

dispassionate /dɪs'pæʃənət/ a, -**ly** adv gelassen; (impartial) unparteiisch

dispatch /dɪs'pætʃ/ n (Comm) Versand m; (Mil) Nachricht f; (report) Bericht m; **with** ~ prompt □vt [ab]senden; (deal with) erledigen; (kill) töten. ~**rider** n Meldefahrer m

dispel /dɪs'pel/ vt (pt/pp dispelled) vertreiben

dispensable /dɪs'spensəbl/ a entbehrlich

dispensary /dɪs'spensərɪ/ n Apotheke f

dispense /dɪs'spens/ vt austeilen; ~ **with** verzichten auf (+ acc). ~**r** n Apotheker(in) m(f); (device) Automat m

dispers|al /dɪs'spɜ:sl/ n Zerstreuung f. ~**e** /dɪs'spɜ:s/ vt zerstreuen □vi sich zerstreuen

dispirited /dɪs'spɪrɪtɪd/ a entmutigt

dis'**place** vt verschieben; ~**d person** Vertriebene(r) m/f

display /dɪs'pleɪ/ n Ausstellung f; (Comm) Auslage f; (performance) Vorführung f □vt zeigen; ausstellen (goods)

dis'**please** vt mißfallen (+ dat)

dis'**pleasure** n Mißfallen nt

disposable /dɪs'spəʊzəbl/ a Wegwerf-; (income) verfügbar

disposal /dɪˈspəʊzl/ n Beseitigung f; **be at s.o.'s** ~ jdm zur Verfügung stehen

dispose /dɪˈspəʊz/ vi ~ **of** beseitigen; (deal with) erledigen; **be well** ~**d** wohlgesinnt sein (**to** dat)

disposition /dɪspəˈzɪʃn/ n Veranlagung f; (nature) Wesensart f

disproportionate /dɪsprəˈpɔː-ʃənət/ a, **-ly** adv unverhältnismäßig

dis'prove vt widerlegen

dispute /dɪˈspjuːt/ n Disput m; (quarrel) Streit m ◻ vt bestreiten

disqualifi'cation n Disqualifikation f

dis'qualify vt disqualifizieren; ~ **s.o. from driving** jdm den Führerschein entziehen

disquieting /dɪsˈkwaɪətɪŋ/ a beunruhigend

disre'gard n Nichtbeachtung f ◻ vt nicht beachten, ignorieren

disre'pair n **fall into** ~ verfallen

dis'reputable a verrufen

disre'pute n Verruf m

disre'spect n Respektlosigkeit f. ~ **ful** a, **-ly** adv respektlos

disrupt /dɪsˈrʌpt/ vt stören. ~**ion** /-ʌpʃn/ n Störung f. ~**ive** /-tɪv/ a störend

dissatis'faction n Unzufriedenheit f

dis'satisfied a unzufrieden

dissect /dɪˈsekt/ vt zergliedern; (Med) sezieren. ~**ion** /-ekʃn/ n Zergliederung f; (Med) Sektion f

disseminate /dɪˈsemɪneɪt/ vt verbreiten. ~**ion** /-ˈneɪʃn/ n Verbreitung f

dissent /dɪˈsent/ n Nichtübereinstimmung f ◻ vi nicht übereinstimmen

dissertation /dɪsəˈteɪʃn/ n Dissertation f

dis'service n schlechter Dienst m

dissident /ˈdɪsɪdənt/ n Dissident m

dis'similar a unähnlich (**to** dat)

dissociate /dɪˈsəʊʃɪeɪt/ vt trennen; ~ **oneself** sich distanzieren (**from** von)

dissolute /ˈdɪsəluːt/ a zügellos; ⟨life⟩ ausschweifend

dissolution /dɪsəˈluːʃn/ n Auflösung f

dissolve /dɪˈzɒlv/ vt auflösen ◻ vi sich auflösen

dissuade /dɪˈsweɪd/ vt abbringen (**from** von)

distance /ˈdɪstəns/ n Entfernung f; **long/short** ~ lange/kurze Strecke f; **in the/from a** ~ in/aus der Ferne

distant /ˈdɪstənt/ a fern; (aloof) kühl; ⟨relative⟩ entfernt

dis'taste n Abneigung f. ~ **ful** a unangenehm

distend /dɪˈstend/ vi sich [auf]blähen

distil /dɪˈstɪl/ vt (pt/pp distilled) brennen; (Chem) destillieren. ~ **lation** /-ˈleɪʃn/ n Destillation f. ~**lery** /-əri/ n Brennerei f

distinct /dɪˈstɪŋkt/ a deutlich; (different) verschieden. ~**ion** /-ɪŋkʃn/ n Unterschied m; (Sch) Auszeichnung f. ~**ive** /-tɪv/ a kennzeichnend; (unmistakable) unverwechselbar. ~**ly** adv deutlich

distinguish /dɪˈstɪŋgwɪʃ/ vt/i unterscheiden; (make out) erkennen; ~ **oneself** sich auszeichnen. ~ **ed** a angesehen; ⟨appearance⟩ distinguiert

distort /dɪˈstɔːt/ vt verzerren; (fig) verdrehen. ~**ion** /-ɔːʃn/ n Verzerrung f; (fig) Verdrehung f

distract /dɪˈstrækt/ vt ablenken. ~ **ed** /-ɪd/ a [völlig] aufgelöst. ~**ion** /-ækʃn/ n Ablenkung f; (despair) Verzweiflung f

distraught /dɪˈstrɔːt/ a [völlig] aufgelöst

distress /dɪˈstres/ n Kummer m; (pain) Schmerz m; (poverty, danger) Not f ◻ vt Kummer/Schmerz bereiten (+ dat); (sadden) bekümmern; (shock) erschüttern.

~**ing** a schmerzlich; (shocking) erschütternd. ~ **signal** n Notsignal nt

distribut|e /dɪˈstrɪbjuːt/ vt verteilen; (Comm) vertreiben. ~**ion** /-ˈbjuːʃn/ n Verteilung f; Vertrieb m. ~**or** n Verteiler m

district /ˈdɪstrɪkt/ n Gegend f; (Admin) Bezirk m. ~ **nurse** n Gemeindeschwester f

dis'trust n Mißtrauen nt □vt mißtrauen (+ dat). ~**ful** a mißtrauisch

disturb /dɪˈstɜːb/ vt stören; (perturb) beunruhigen; (touch) anrühren. ~**ance** n Unruhe f; (interruption) Störung f. ~**ed** a beunruhigt; [**mentally**] ~**ed** geistig gestört. ~**ing** a beunruhigend

dis'used a stillgelegt; (empty) leer

ditch /dɪtʃ/ n Graben m □vt (fam: abandon) fallenlassen ⟨plan⟩; wegschmeißen ⟨thing⟩

dither /ˈdɪðə(r)/ vi zaudern

ditto /ˈdɪtəʊ/ n dito; (fam)ebenfalls

divan /dɪˈvæn/ n Polsterbett nt

dive /daɪv/ n [Kopf]sprung m; (Aviat) Sturzflug m; (fam: place) Spelunke f □vi einen Kopfsprung machen; (when in water) tauchen; (Aviat) einen Sturzflug machen; (fam: rush) stürzen

diver /ˈdaɪvə(r)/ n Taucher m; (Sport) Kunstspringer m

diverg|e /daɪˈvɜːdʒ/ vi auseinandergehen. ~**gent** /-ənt/ a abweichend

diverse /daɪˈvɜːs/ a verschieden

diversif|y /daɪˈvɜːsɪfaɪ/ vt/i (pt/pp -**ied**) variieren; (Comm) diversifizieren

diversion /daɪˈvɜːʃn/ n Umleitung f; (distraction) Ablenkung f

diversity /daɪˈvɜːsəti/ n Vielfalt f

divert /daɪˈvɜːt/ vt umleiten; ablenken ⟨attention⟩; (entertain) unterhalten

divest /daɪˈvest/ vt sich entledigen (of + gen); (fig) entkleiden

divide /dɪˈvaɪd/ vt teilen; (separate) trennen; (Math) dividieren (by durch) □vi sich teilen

dividend /ˈdɪvɪdend/ n Dividende f

divine /dɪˈvaɪn/ a göttlich

diving /ˈdaɪvɪŋ/ n (Sport) Kunstspringen nt. ~**board** n Sprungbrett nt. ~**-suit** n Taucheranzug m

divinity /dɪˈvɪnəti/ n Göttlichkeit f; (subject) Theologie f

divisible /dɪˈvɪzɪbl/ a teilbar (by durch)

division /dɪˈvɪʒn/ n Teilung f; (separation) Trennung f; (Math, Mil) Division f; (Parl) Hammelsprung m; (line) Trennlinie f; (group) Abteilung f

divorce /dɪˈvɔːs/ n Scheidung f □vt sich scheiden lassen von. ~**d** a geschieden; get ~**d** sich scheiden lassen

divorcee /dɪvɔːˈsiː/ n Geschiedene(r) m/f

divulge /daɪˈvʌldʒ/ vt preisgeben

DIY abbr of do-it-yourself

dizziness /ˈdɪzɪnɪs/ n Schwindel m

dizzy /ˈdɪzɪ/ a (-ier, -iest) schwindlig; I feel ~ mir ist schwindlig

do /duː/ n (pl dos or do's) (fam) Veranstaltung f □ v □ vt/i (3 sg pres tense does; pt did; pp done) □vt/i tun, machen; (be suitable) passen; (be enough) reichen, genügen; (cook) kochen; (clean) putzen; (Sch: study) durchnehmen; (fam: cheat) beschwindeln (out of um); do without auskommen ohne; do away with abschaffen; be done (Culin) gar sein; well done gut gemacht! (Culin) gut durchgebraten; done in (fam) kaputt, fertig; done for (fam) verloren, erledigt; do the flowers die Blumen arrangieren; do the potatoes die Kartoffeln schälen; do the washing up abwaschen, spülen; do one's hair sich frisieren; do well/badly gut/schlecht abschneiden; how is he

doing? wie geht es ihm? **this won't do** das geht nicht; **are you doing anything today?** haben Sie heute etwas vor? **I could do with a spanner** ich könnte einen Schraubenschlüssel gebrauchen □v aux **do you speak German?** sprechen Sie deutsch? **yes, I do** ja; (emphatic) **no, I don't** nein; **I don't smoke** ich rauche nicht; **don't you/doesn't he?** nicht [wahr]? **so do I** ich auch; **do come in** kommen Sie doch herein; **how do you do?** guten Tag. **do in** vt (fam) um die Ecke bringen. **do up** vt (fasten) zumachen; (renovate) renovieren; (wrap) einpacken

docile /'dəʊsaɪl/ a fügsam

dock[1] /dɒk/ n (Jur) Anklagebank f

dock[2] n Dock nt □vi anlegen, docken □vt docken. **~er** n Hafenarbeiter m. **~yard** n Werft f

doctor /'dɒktə(r)/ n Arzt m/ Ärztin f; (Univ) Doktor m □vt kastrieren; (spay) sterilisieren. **~ate** /-ət/ n Doktorwürde f

doctrine /'dɒktrɪn/ n Lehre f, Doktrin f

document /'dɒkjʊmənt/ n Dokument nt. **~ary** /-'mentərɪ/ a Dokumentar- n Dokumentarbericht m; (film) Dokumentarfilm m

doddery /'dɒdərɪ/ a (fam) tatterig

dodge /dɒdʒ/ n (fam) Trick m, Kniff m □vt/i ausweichen (+ dat); **~ out of the way** zur Seite springen

dodgems /'dɒdʒəmz/ npl Autoskooter pl

dodgy /'dɒdʒɪ/ a (-ier, -iest) (fam) (awkward) knifflig; (dubious) zweifelhaft

doe /dəʊ/ n Ricke f; (rabbit) [Kaninchen]weibchen nt

does /dʌz/ see **do**

doesn't /'dʌznt/ = does not

dog /dɒg/ n Hund m □vt (pt/pp dogged) verfolgen

dog: **~-biscuit** n Hundekuchen m. **~-collar** n Hundehalsband

nt; (Relig, fam) Kragen m eines Geistlichen. **~-eared** a be **~-eared** Eselsohren haben

dogged /'dɒgɪd/ a, **-ly** adv beharrlich

dogma /'dɒgmə/ n Dogma nt. **~tic** /-'mætɪk/ a dogmatisch

dogsbody n (fam) Mädchen nt für alles

doily /'dɔɪlɪ/ n Deckchen nt

do-it-yourself /'duːɪtjə'self/ n Heimwerken nt. **~ shop** n Heimwerkerladen m

doldrums /'dɒldrəmz/ npl **be in the ~** niedergeschlagen sein; ⟨business⟩ darniederliegen

dole /dəʊl/ n (fam) Stempelgeld nt; **be on the ~** arbeitslos sein □vt **~ out** austeilen

doleful /'dəʊlfl/ a, **-ly** adv trauervoll

doll /dɒl/ n Puppe f □vt (fam) **~ oneself up** sich herausputzen

dollar /'dɒlə(r)/ n Dollar m

dollop /'dɒləp/ n (fam) Klecks m

dolphin /'dɒlfɪn/ n Delphin m

domain /də'meɪn/ n Gebiet nt

dome /dəʊm/ n Kuppel m

domestic /də'mestɪk/ a häuslich; (Pol) Innen-; (Comm) Binnen-. **~ animal** n Haustier m

domesticated /də'mestɪkeɪtɪd/ a häuslich; ⟨animal⟩ zahm

domestic: **~ flight** n Inlandflug m. **~ 'servant** n Hausangestellte(r) m/f

dominant /'dɒmɪnənt/ a vorherrschend

dominat|e /'dɒmɪneɪt/ vt beherrschen □vi dominieren; **~e over** beherrschen. **~ion** /-'neɪʃn/ n Vorherrschaft f

domineer /dɒmɪ'nɪə(r)/ vi **~ over** tyrannisieren; **~ing** a herrschsüchtig

dominion /də'mɪnjən/ n Herrschaft f

domino /'dɒmɪnəʊ/ n (pl -es) Dominostein m; **~es** sg (game) Domino nt

don[1] /dɒn/ *vt* (*pt/pp* **donned**) (*liter*) anziehen

don[2] *n* [Universitäts]dozent *m*

donat|e /dəʊ'neɪt/ *vt* spenden. **~ion** /-eɪʃn/ *n* Spende *f*

done /dʌn/ *see* **do**

donkey /'dɒŋkɪ/ *n* Esel *m*; **~'s years** (*fam*) eine Ewigkeit. **~-work** *n* Routinearbeit *f*

donor /'dəʊnə(r)/ *n* Spender(in) *m(f)*

don't /dəʊnt/ = **do not**

doodle /'du:dl/ *vi* kritzeln

doom /du:m/ *n* Schicksal *nt*; (*ruin*) Verhängnis *f*. **~ed** *vt* **be ~ed to failure** zum Scheitern verurteilt sein

door /dɔ:(r)/ *n* Tür *f*; **out of ~s** im Freien

door: **~man** *n* Portier *m*. **~mat** *n* [Fuß]abtreter *m*. **~step** *n* Türschwelle *f*; **on the ~step** vor der Tür. **~way** *n* Türöffnung *f*

dope /dəʊp/ *n* (*fam*) Drogen *pl*; (*fam: information*) Informationen *pl*; (*fam: idiot*) Trottel *m* □ *vt* betäuben; (*Sport*) dopen

dopey /'dəʊpɪ/ *a* (*fam*) benommen; (*stupid*) blöd[e]

dormant /'dɔ:mənt/ *a* ruhend

dormer /'dɔ:mə(r)/ *n* **~ [window]** Mansardenfenster *nt*

dormitory /'dɔ:mɪtərɪ/ *n* Schlafsaal *m*

dormouse /'dɔ:-/ *n* Haselmaus *f*

dosage /'dəʊsɪdʒ/ *n* Dosierung *f*

dose /dəʊs/ *n* Dosis *f*

doss /dɒs/ *vi* (*sl*) pennen. **~er** *n* Penner *m*. **~-house** *n* Penne *f*

dot /dɒt/ *n* Punkt *m*; **on the ~** pünktlich

dote /dəʊt/ *vi* **~ on** vernarrt sein in (+ *acc*)

dotted /'dɒtɪd/ *a* **~ line** punktierte Linie *f*; **be ~ with** bestreut sein mit

dotty /'dɒtɪ/ *a* (*-ier, -iest*) (*fam*) verdreht

double /'dʌbl/ *a & adv* doppelt; (*bed, chin*) Doppel-; (*flower*) gefüllt □ *n* das Doppelte; (*person*)

Doppelgänger *m*; **~s** *pl* (*Tennis*) Doppel *nt*; **at the ~** im Laufschritt □ *vt* verdoppeln; (*fold*) falten □ *vi* sich verdoppeln. **~ back** *vi* zurückgehen. **~ up** *vi* sich krümmen (**with** vor + *dat*)

double: **~-'bass** *n* Kontrabaß *m*. **~-'breasted** *a* zweireihig. **~-'cross** *vt* ein Doppelspiel treiben mit. **~-'decker** *n* Doppeldecker *m*. **~ 'Dutch** *n* Kauderwelsch *nt*. **~ 'glazing** *n* Doppelverglasung *f*. **~ 'room** *n* Doppelzimmer *nt*

doubly /'dʌblɪ/ *adv* doppelt

doubt /daʊt/ *n* Zweifel *m* □ *vt* bezweifeln. **~ful** *a*, **-ly** *adv* zweifelhaft; (*disbelieving*) skeptisch. **~less** *adv* zweifellos

dough /dəʊ/ *n* [fester] Teig *m*; (*fam: money*) Pinke *f*. **~nut** *n* Berliner [Pfannkuchen] *m*, Krapfen *m*

douse /daʊs/ *vt* übergießen; ausgießen (*flames*)

dove /dʌv/ *n* Taube *f*. **~tail** *n* (*Techn*) Schwalbenschwanz *m*

dowdy /'daʊdɪ/ *a* (*-ier, -iest*) unschick

down[1] /daʊn/ *n* (*feathers*) Daunen *pl*

down[2] *adv* unten; (*with movement*) nach unten; **go ~** untergehen; **come ~** herunterkommen; **~ there** da unten; **£50 ~** £50 Anzahlung; **~s** (*to dog*) Platz! **~ with ...!** nieder mit ...! □ *prep* **~ the road/stairs** die Straße/ Treppe hinunter; **~ the river** den Fluß abwärts; **be ~ the pub** (*fam*) in der Kneipe sein □ *vt* (*fam*) (*drink*) runterkippen; **~ tools** die Arbeit niederlegen

down: **~-and-'out** *n* Penner *m*. **~-cast** *a* niedergeschlagen. **~-fall** *n* Sturz *m*; (*ruin*) Ruin *m*. **~-grade** *vt* niedriger einstufen. **~-'hearted** *a* entmutigt. **~-'hill** *adv* bergab. **~ payment** *n* Anzahlung *f*. **~-pour** *n* Platzregen *m.* ~**right** *a* & *adv* ausgesprochen. ~**stairs** *adv* unten; ⟨*go*⟩ nach unten □*a* /'·•/ im Erdgeschoß. ~**stream** *adv* stromabwärts. ~**to·earth** *a* sachlich. ~**town** *adv* (*Amer*) im Stadtzentrum. ~**trodden** *a* unterdrückt. ~**ward** *a* nach unten; ⟨*slope*⟩ abfallend □*adv* & ~**wards** abwärts, nach unten

downy /'dauni/ *a* (-ier, -iest) flaumig

dowry /'dauri/ *n* Mitgift *f*

doze /dəuz/ *n* Nickerchen *nt* □*vi* dösen. ~ **off** *vi* einnicken

dozen /'dʌzn/ *n* Dutzend *nt*

Dr *abbr of* **doctor**

draft¹ /drɑːft/ *n* Entwurf *m*; (*Comm*) Tratte *f*; (*Amer Mil*) Einberufung *f* □*vt* entwerfen; (*Amer Mil*) einberufen

draft² *n* (*Amer*) = **draught**

drag /dræg/ *n* (*fam*) Klotz *m* am Bein; **in** ~ (*fam*) ⟨*man*⟩ als Frau gekleidet □*vt* (*pt/pp* **dragged**) schleppen; absuchen ⟨*river*⟩. ~ **on** *vi* sich in die Länge ziehen

dragon /'drægən/ *n* Drache *m*. ~**fly** *n* Libelle *f*

'**drag show** *n* Transvestitenshow *f*

drain /drein/ *n* Abfluß *m*; (*underground*) Kanal *m*; **the** ~**s** die Kanalisation □*vt* entwässern ⟨*land*⟩; ablassen ⟨*liquid*⟩; abgießen ⟨*vegetables*⟩; austrinken ⟨*glass*⟩ □*vi* ~ [**away**] ablaufen; **leave sth to** ~ etw abtropfen lassen

drain|age /'dreinidʒ/ *n* Kanalisation *f*; (*of land*) Dränage *f*. ~**ing board** *n* Abtropfbrett *nt*. ~**pipe** *n* Abflußrohr *nt*

drake /dreik/ *n* Enterich *m*

drama /'drɑːmə/ *n* Drama *nt*; (*quality*) Dramatik *f*

dramatic /drə'mætik/ *a*, **-ally** *adv* dramatisch

dramat|ist /'dræmətist/ *n* Dramatiker *m*. ~**ize** *vt* für die Bühne bearbeiten; (*fig*) dramatisieren

drank /dræŋk/ *see* **drink**

drape /dreip/ *n* (*Amer*) Vorhang *m* □*vt* drapieren

drastic /'dræstik/ *a*, **-ally** *adv* drastisch

draught /drɑːft/ *n* [Luft]zug *m*; ~**s** *sg* (*game*) Damespiel *nt*; **there is a** ~ es zieht

draught: ~ **beer** *n* Bier *nt* vom Faß. ~**sman** *n* technischer Zeichner *m*

draughty /'drɑːfti/ *a* zugig; **it's** ~ es zieht

draw /drɔː/ *n* Attraktion *f*; (*Sport*) Unentschieden *nt*; (*in lottery*) Ziehung *f* □*v* (*pt* **drew**, *pp* **drawn**) □*vt* ziehen; (*attract*) anziehen; zeichnen ⟨*picture*⟩; abheben ⟨*money*⟩; holen ⟨*water*⟩; ~ **the curtains** die Vorhänge zuziehen/ (*back*) aufziehen; ~ **lots losen** (**for** um) □*vi* ⟨*tea:*⟩ ziehen; (*Sport*) unentschieden spielen. ~**back** *vt* zurückziehen □*vi* (*recoil*) zurückweichen. ~ **in** *vt* einziehen □*vi* einfahren; ⟨*days:*⟩ kürzer werden. ~ **out** *vt* herausziehen; abheben ⟨*money*⟩ □*vi* ausfahren; ⟨*days:*⟩ länger werden. ~ **up** *vt* aufsetzen ⟨*document*⟩; herrücken ⟨*chair*⟩; ~ **oneself up** sich aufrichten □*vi* [an]halten

draw: ~**back** *n* Nachteil *m*. ~**bridge** *n* Zugbrücke *f*

drawer /drɔː(r)/ *n* Schublade *f*

drawing /'drɔːiŋ/ *n* Zeichnung *f*

drawing: ~**board** *n* Reißbrett *nt*. ~**pin** *n* Reißzwecke *f*. ~**room** *n* Wohnzimmer *nt*

drawl /drɔːl/ *n* schleppende Aussprache *f*

drawn /drɔːn/ *see* **draw**

dread /dred/ *n* Furcht *f* (**of** vor + *dat*) □*vt* fürchten

dreadful *a*, **-ly** *adv* fürchterlich

dream /driːm/ *n* Traum *m* □*attrib* Traum- □*vt/i* (*pt/pp* **dreamt**

/dremt/ *or* **dreamed**) träumen
(about/of von)

dreary /'drɪərɪ/ *a* (-ier, -iest)
trüb[e]; (*boring*) langweilig

dredge /dredʒ/ *vt/i* baggern. ~**r** *n*
[Naß]bagger *m*

dregs /dregz/ *npl* Bodensatz *m*

drench /drentʃ/ *vt* durchnässen

dress /dres/ *n* Kleid *nt*; (*clothing*)
Kleidung *f* □*vt* anziehen; (*decorate*) schmücken; (*Culin*) anmachen; (*Med*) verbinden; ~ one-
self, get ~ed sich anziehen □*vi*
sich anziehen. ~ **up** *vi* sich schön
anziehen; (*in disguise*) sich verkleiden (as als)

dress: ~ **circle** *n* (*Theat*) erster
Rang *m*. ~**er** *n* (*furniture*) An-
richte *f*; (*Amer: dressing-table*)
Frisiertisch *m*

dressing *n* (*Culin*) Soße *f*; (*Med*)
Verband *m*

dressing: ~ **'down** *n* (*fam*)
Standpauke *f*. ~**gown** *n* Mor-
genmantel *m*. ~-**room** *n* Anklei-
dezimmer *nt*; (*Theat*) [Künstler]-
garderobe *f*. ~-**table** *n* Frisiertisch *m*

dress: ~**maker** *n* Schneiderin *f*.
~**making** *n* Damenschneiderei
f. ~ **rehearsal** *n* Generalprobe *f*

dressy /'dresɪ/ *a* (-ier, -iest)
schick

drew /dru:/ *see* **draw**

dribble /'drɪbl/ *vi* sabbern; (*Sport*)
dribbeln

dried /draɪd/ *a* getrocknet; ~
fruit Dörrobst *nt*

drier /'draɪə(r)/ *n* Trockner *m*

drift /drɪft/ *n* Abtrift *f*; (*of snow*)
Schneewehe *f*; (*meaning*) Sinn *m*
□*vi* treiben; (*off course*) abtreiben; (*snow*:) Wehen bilden; (*fig*
person:) sich treiben lassen; ~
apart (*persons*:) sich ausein-
anderleben. ~**wood** *n* Treibholz
nt

drill /drɪl/ *n* Bohrer *m*; (*Mil*) Drill
m □*vt/i* bohren (**for** nach); (*Mil*)
drillen

drily /'draɪlɪ/ *adv* trocken

drink /drɪŋk/ *n* Getränk *nt*; (*alcoholic*) Drink *m*; (*alcohol*) Alkohol
m; **have a** ~ etwas trinken □*vt/i*
(*pt* **drank**, *pp* **drunk**) trinken. ~
up *vt/i* austrinken

drinkable /'drɪŋkəbl/ *a* trinkbar.
~**er** *n* Trinker *m*

'drinking-water *n* Trinkwasser
nt

drip /drɪp/ *n* Tropfen *m*; (*drop*)
Tropfen *m*; (*Med*) Tropf *m*; (*fam:
person*) Niete *f* □*vi* (*pt/pp*
dripped) tropfen. ~'**dry** *a* bügelfrei. ~**ping** *n* Schmalz *nt*

drive /draɪv/ *n* [Auto]fahrt *f*; (*entrance*) Einfahrt *f*; (*energy*) Elan
m; (*Psych*) Trieb *m*; (*Pol*) Aktion
f; (*Sport*) Treibschlag *m*; (*Techn*)
Antrieb *m* □*v* (*pt* **drove**, *pp* **driv-
en**) □*vt* treiben; fahren ⟨*car*⟩;
(*Sport: hit*) schlagen; (*Techn*)
antreiben; **s.o. mad** (*fam*) jdn
verrückt machen; **what are you
driving at?** (*fam*) worauf willst
du hinaus? □*vi* fahren. ~ **away**
vt vertreiben □*vi* abfahren. ~ **in**
vi hinein-/hereinfahren. ~ **off** *vt*
vertreiben □*vi* abfahren. ~ **on** *vi*
weiterfahren. ~ **up** *vi* vorfahren

'drive-in *a* ~ **cinema** Autokino
nt

drivel /'drɪvl/ *n* (*fam*) Quatsch *m*

driven /'drɪvn/ *see* **drive**

driver /'draɪvə(r)/ *n* Fahrer(in)
m(*f*); (*of train*) Lokführer *m*

driving /'draɪvɪŋ/ *a* ⟨*rain*⟩ peit-
schend; ⟨*force*⟩ treibend

driving: ~ **lesson** *n* Fahrstunde
f. ~ **licence** *n* Führerschein *m*.
~ **school** *n* Fahrschule *f*. ~ **test**
Fahrprüfung *f*; **take one's** ~ **test**
den Führerschein machen

drizzle /'drɪzl/ *n* Nieselregen *m*
□*vi* nieseln

drone /drəʊn/ *n* Drohne *f*; (*sound*)
Brummen *nt*

droop /dru:p/ *vi* herabhängen;
⟨*flowers*:⟩ die Köpfe hängen lassen

drop /drɒp/ *n* Tropfen *m*; (*fall*)
Fall *m*; (*in price, temperature*)

Rückgang m □v (pt/pp dropped)
□vt fallen lassen; abwerfen
⟨bomb⟩; (omit) auslassen; (give
up) aufgeben □vi fallen; (fall lower) sinken; ⟨wind:⟩ nachlassen.
~ in vi vorbeikommen. ~ off vt
absetzen ⟨person⟩ □vi abfallen;
(fall asleep) einschlafen. ~ out
vi herausfallen; (give up) aufgeben

drop-out n Aussteiger m
droppings /'drɒpɪŋz/ npl Kot m
drought /draʊt/ n Dürre f
drove /drəʊv/ see **drive**
droves /drəʊvz/ npl in ~ in
Scharen
drown /draʊn/ vi ertrinken □vt
ertränken; übertönen ⟨noise⟩; be
~ed ertrinken
drowsy /'draʊzɪ/ a schläfrig
drudgery /'drʌdʒərɪ/ n Plackerei f
drug /drʌg/ n Droge f □vt (pt/pp
drugged) betäuben
drug: ~ **addict** n Drogenab-
hängige(r) m/f. ~**gist** n (Amer)
Apotheker m. ~**store** n (Amer)
Drogerie f; (dispensing) Apotheke f
drum /drʌm/ n Trommel f; (for
oil) Tonne f □v (pt/pp drummed)
□vi trommeln □vt ~ **sth into s.o.**
(fam) jdm etw einbleuen. ~**mer**
n Trommler m; (in pop-group)
Schlagzeuger m. ~**stick** n Trom-
melschlegel m; (Culin) Keule f
drunk /drʌŋk/ see **drink** □a betrunken; **get** ~ sich betrinken □n
Betrunkene(r) m
drunk|ard /'drʌŋkəd/ n Trinker
m. ~**en** a betrunken; ~**en driving** Trunkenheit f am Steuer
dry /draɪ/ a (drier, driest)
trocken □vt/i trocknen; ~**one's
eyes** sich die Tränen abwischen. ~ **up** vi austrocknen; (fig)
versiegen □vt austrocknen; abtrocknen ⟨dishes⟩
dry: ~'**clean** vt chemisch reinigen.
~-'**cleaner's** n (shop) chemische Reinigung f. ~**ness** n
Trockenheit f

dual /'dju:əl/ a doppelt
dual: ~ '**carriageway** n ≈
Schnellstraße f. ~-'**purpose** a
zweifach verwendbar
dub /dʌb/ vt (pt/pp dubbed)
synchronisieren ⟨film⟩; kopieren ⟨tape⟩; (name) nennen
dubious /'dju:bɪəs/ a zweifelhaft;
be ~ **about** Zweifel haben über
(+ acc)
duchess /'dʌtʃɪs/ n Herzogin f
duck /dʌk/ n Ente f □vt (in water)
untertauchen; **one's head** den
Kopf einziehen □vi sich ducken.
~**ling** n Entchen nt; (Culin)
Ente f
duct /dʌkt/ n Rohr nt; (Anat)
Gang m
dud /dʌd/ a (fam) nutzlos; ⟨coin⟩
falsch; ⟨cheque⟩ ungedeckt; (forged) gefälscht □n (fam) (banknote) Blüte f; (Mil: shell) Blind-
gänger m
due /dju:/ a angemessen; **be** ~
fällig sein; ⟨baby:⟩ erwartet werden; ⟨train:⟩ planmäßig ankommen; ~ **to** (owing to) wegen (+
gen); **be** ~ **to** zurückzuführen
sein auf (+ acc); **in** ~ **course** im
Laufe der Zeit; ⟨write⟩ zu gegebe-
ner Zeit □adv ~ **west** genau westlich
duel /'dju:əl/ n Duell nt
dues /dju:z/ npl Gebühren pl
duet /dju:'et/ n Duo nt; (vocal)
Duett nt
dug /dʌg/ see **dig**
duke /dju:k/ n Herzog m
dull /dʌl/ a (-er, -est) (overcast,
not bright) trüb[e]; (not shiny)
matt; ⟨sound⟩ dumpf; (boring)
langweilig; (stupid) schwerfällig
□vt betäuben ⟨pain⟩; abstumpfen
⟨mind⟩
duly /'dju:lɪ/ adv ordnungsgemäß
dumb /dʌm/ a (-er, -est) stumm;
(fam: stupid) dumm. ~**founded**
a sprachlos
dummy /'dʌmɪ/ n (tailor's)
[Schneider]puppe f; (for baby)
Schnuller m; (Comm) Attrappe f

dump /dʌmp/ n Abfallhaufen m; (for refuse) Müllhalde f, Deponie f; (fam: town) Kaff nt; **be down in the ~s** (fam) deprimiert sein □ vt abladen; (fam: put down) hinwerfen (**on** auf + acc)

dumpling /ˈdʌmplɪŋ/ n Kloß m, Knödel m

dunce /dʌns/ n Dummkopf m

dune /djuːn/ n Düne f

dung /dʌŋ/ n Mist m

dungarees /dʌŋgəˈriːz/ npl Latzhose f

dungeon /ˈdʌndʒən/ n Verlies nt

dunk /dʌŋk/ vt eintunken

duo /ˈdjuːəʊ/ n Paar nt; (Mus) Duo nt

dupe /djuːp/ n Betrogene(r) m/f □ vt betrügen

duplicate[1] /ˈdjuːplɪkət/ a Zweit-□n Doppel nt; (document) Duplikat nt; **in ~** in doppelter Ausfertigung f

duplicat|e[2] /ˈdjuːplɪkeɪt/ vt kopieren; (do twice) zweimal machen. **~or** n Vervielfältigungsapparat m

durable /ˈdjʊərəbl/ a haltbar

duration /djʊəˈreɪʃn/ n Dauer f

duress /djʊəˈres/ n Zwang m

during /ˈdjʊərɪŋ/ prep während (+ gen)

dusk /dʌsk/ n [Abend]dämmerung f

dust /dʌst/ n Staub m □ vt abstauben; (sprinkle) bestäuben (**with** mit) □ vi Staub wischen

dust: **~bin** n Mülltonne f. **~-cart** n Müllwagen m. **~er** n Staubtuch nt. **~-jacket** n Schutzumschlag m. **~man** n Müllmann m. **~pan** n Kehrschaufel f

dusty /ˈdʌstɪ/ a (-ier, -iest) staubig

Dutch /dʌtʃ/ a u holländisch; **go ~** (fam) getrennte Kasse machen □ n (Lang) Holländisch nt; **the ~** pl die Holländer. **~man** n Holländer m

dutiable /ˈdjuːtɪəbl/ a zollpflichtig

dutiful /ˈdjuːtɪfl/ a, **-ly** adv pflichtbewußt; (obedient) gehorsam

duty /ˈdjuːtɪ/ n Pflicht f; (task) Aufgabe f; (tax) Zoll m; **on ~** Dienst haben. **~-free** a zollfrei

duvet /ˈduːveɪ/ n Steppdecke f

dwarf /dwɔːf/ n (pl -s or dwarves) Zwerg m

dwell /dwel/ vi (pt/pp dwelt) (liter) wohnen; **~ on** (fig) verweilen bei. **~ing** n Wohnung f

dwindle /ˈdwɪndl/ vi abnehmen, schwinden

dye /daɪ/ n Farbstoff m □ vt (pres p dyeing) färben

dying /ˈdaɪɪŋ/ see **die**[2]

dynamic /daɪˈnæmɪk/ a dynamisch. **~s** n Dynamik f

dynamite /ˈdaɪnəmaɪt/ n Dynamit nt

dynamo /ˈdaɪnəməʊ/ n Dynamo m

dynasty /ˈdɪnəstɪ/ n Dynastie f

dysentery /ˈdɪsəntrɪ/ n Ruhr f

dyslex|ia /dɪsˈleksɪə/ n Legasthenie f. **~ic** a legasthenisch; **be ~ic** Legastheniker sein

E

each /iːtʃ/ a & pron jede(r,s); (per) je; **~ other** einander; **£1 ~** £1 pro Person; (for thing) pro Stück

eager /ˈiːgə(r)/ a, **-ly** adv eifrig; **be ~ to do sth** etw gerne machen wollen. **~ness** n Eifer m

eagle /ˈiːgl/ n Adler m

ear[1] /ɪə(r)/ n (of corn) Ähre f

ear[2] n Ohr nt. **~ache** n Ohrenschmerzen pl. **~-drum** n Trommelfell nt

earl /ɜːl/ n Graf m

early /ˈɜːlɪ/ a & adv (-ier, -iest) früh; (reply) baldig; **be ~** früh dran sein; **~ in the morning** früh am Morgen

earmark vt **~ for** bestimmen für

earn /ɜːn/ vt verdienen

earnest /ˈɜːnɪst/ a, **-ly** adv ernsthaft □ n **in ~** im Ernst

earnings /ˈɜːnɪŋz/ npl Verdienst m

ear: ~**phones** npl Kopfhörer pl.
~**ring** n Ohrring m; (clip-on)
Ohrklips m. ~**shot** n within/out
of ~ shot in/außer Hörweite

earth /ɜːθ/ n Erde f; (of fox) Bau m;
where/what on ~? wo/was in
aller Welt? □ vt (Electr) erden

earthenware /ˈɜːθn-/ n Tonwaren
pl

earthly /ˈɜːθlɪ/ a irdisch; **be no** ~
use (fam) völlig nutzlos sein

'**earthquake** n Erdbeben nt

earthy /ˈɜːθɪ/ a erdig; (coarse) derb

earwig /ˈɪəwɪɡ/ n Ohrwurm m

ease /iːz/ n Leichtigkeit f; **at** ~!
(Mil) rührt euch! **be/feel ill at** ~
ein ungutes Gefühl haben □ vt
erleichtern; lindern (pain) □ vi
(pain:) nachlassen; (situation:)
sich entspannen

easel /ˈiːzl/ n Staffelei f

easily /ˈiːzɪlɪ/ adv leicht, mit
Leichtigkeit

east /iːst/ n Osten m; **to the** ~ **of**
östlich von □ a Ost-, ost- □ adv
nach Osten

Easter /ˈiːstə(r)/ n Ostern nt □
attrib Oster-. ~ **egg** n Osterei nt

east|**erly** /ˈiːstəlɪ/ a östlich. ~**ern**
a östlich. ~**ward[s]** /-wəd[z]/ adv
nach Osten

easy /ˈiːzɪ/ a (-ier, -iest) leicht;
take it ~ (fam) sich schonen;
take it ~! beruhige dich! **go** ~
with (fam) sparsam umgehen
mit

easy: ~ **chair** n Sessel m.
~**going** a gelassen; **too** ~**going**
lässig

eat /iːt/ vt/i (pt **ate**, pp **eaten**)
essen; (animal:) fressen. ~ **up**
vt aufessen

eat|**able** /ˈiːtəbl/ a genießbar. ~**er**
n (apple) Eßapfel m

eau-de-Cologne /əʊdəkəˈləʊn/ n
Kölnisch Wasser nt

eaves /iːvz/ npl Dachüberhang m.
~**drop** vi (pt/pp ~**dropped**)
[heimlich] lauschen; ~**drop on**
belauschen

ebb /eb/ n (tide) Ebbe f; **at a low** ~
(fig) auf einem Tiefstand □ vi zurückgehen; (fig) verebben

ebony /ˈebənɪ/ n Ebenholz nt

ebullient /ɪˈbʌlɪənt/ a überschwenglich

EC abbr (**European Community**) EG f

eccentric /ɪkˈsentrɪk/ a exzentrisch □ n Exzentriker m

ecclesiastical /ɪkliːzɪˈæstɪkl/ a
kirchlich

echo /ˈekəʊ/ n (pl -es) Echo nt,
Widerhall m □ v (pt/pp **echoed**,
pres p **echoing**) zurückwerfen;
(imitate) nachsagen □ vi widerhallen (with von)

eclipse /ɪˈklɪps/ n (Astr) Finster-
nis f □ vt (fig) in den Schatten
stellen

ecolog|**ical** /iːkəˈlɒdʒɪkl/ a ökolo-
gisch. ~**y** /iːˈkɒlədʒɪ/ n Ökologie f

economic /iːkəˈnɒmɪk/ a wirtschaftlich. ~**al** a sparsam.
~**ally** adv wirtschaftlich; (thrift-
ily) sparsam. ~**s** n Volkswirt-
schaft f

economist /ɪˈkɒnəmɪst/ n Volks-
wirt m; (Univ) Wirtschaftswis-
senschaftler m

economize /ɪˈkɒnəmaɪz/ vi sparen
(on an + dat)

economy /ɪˈkɒnəmɪ/ n Wirtschaft
f; (thrift) Sparsamkeit f

ecstasy /ˈekstəsɪ/ n Ekstase f

ecstatic /ɪkˈstætɪk/ a, ~**ally** adv
ekstatisch

ecu /ˈeɪkjuː/ n Ecu m

ecumenical /iːkjʊˈmenɪkl/ a ökumenisch

eczema /ˈeksɪmə/ n Ekzem nt

eddy /ˈedɪ/ n Wirbel m

edge /edʒ/ n Rand m; (of table,
lawn) Kante f; (of knife) Schneide
f; **on** ~ (fam) nervös; **have the**
on (fam) etwas besser sein als
□ vt einfassen. ~ **forward** vi sich
nach vorn schieben

edging /ˈedʒɪŋ/ n Einfassung f

edgy /ˈedʒɪ/ a (fam) nervös

edible /ˈedɪbl/ a eßbar

edict /'iːdɪkt/ n Erlaß m

edifice /'edɪfɪs/ n [großes] Gebäude nt

edify /'edɪfaɪ/ vt (pt/pp -ied) erbauen. ~ing a erbaulich

edit /'edɪt/ vt (pt/pp edited) redigieren; herausgeben ⟨anthology, dictionary⟩; schneiden ⟨film, tape⟩

edition /ɪ'dɪʃn/ n Ausgabe f; (impression) Auflage f

editor /'edɪtə(r)/ n Redakteur m; (of anthology, dictionary) Herausgeber m; (of newspaper) Chefredakteur m; (of film) Cutter(in) m(f)

editorial /edɪ'tɔːrɪəl/ a redaktionell, Redaktions- □n (Journ) Leitartikel m

educate /'edjʊkeɪt/ vt erziehen; be~d at X auf die X-Schule gehen. ~d a gebildet

education /edjʊ'keɪʃn/ n Erziehung f; (culture) Bildung f. ~al a pädagogisch; ⟨visit⟩ kulturell

eel /iːl/ n Aal m

eerie /'ɪərɪ/ a (-ier, -iest) unheimlich

effect /ɪ'fekt/ n Wirkung f, Effekt m; in ~ in Wirklichkeit; take ~ in Kraft treten □vt bewirken

effective /ɪ'fektɪv/ a, -ly adv wirksam, effektiv; ⟨striking⟩ wirkungsvoll, effektvoll; (actual) tatsächlich. ~ness n Wirksamkeit f

effeminate /ɪ'femɪnət/ a unmännlich

effervescent /efə'vesnt/ a sprudelnd

efficiency /ɪ'fɪʃənsɪ/ n Tüchtigkeit f; (of machine, organization) Leistungsfähigkeit f

efficient /ɪ'fɪʃnt/ a tüchtig; ⟨machine, organization⟩ leistungsfähig; ⟨method⟩ rationell. ~ly adv gut; ⟨function⟩ rationell

effigy /'efɪdʒɪ/ n Bildnis nt

effort /'efət/ n Anstrengung f; make an ~ sich (dat) Mühe geben. ~less a, -ly adv mühelos

effrontery /ɪ'frʌntərɪ/ n Unverschämtheit f

effusive /ɪ'fjuːsɪv/ a, -ly adv überschwenglich

e.g. abbr (exempli gratia) z.B.

egalitarian /ɪgælɪ'teərɪən/ a egalitär

egg¹ /eg/ vt ~ on (fam) anstacheln

egg² n Ei nt. ~-cup n Eierbecher m. ~shell n Eierschale f. ~-timer n Eieruhr f

ego /'iːgəʊ/ n Ich nt. ~centric /-'sentrɪk/ a egozentrisch. ~ism n Egoismus m. ~ist n Egoist m. ~tism n Ichbezogenheit f. ~tist n ichbezogener Mensch m

Egypt /'iːdʒɪpt/ n Ägypten nt. ~ian /ɪ'dʒɪpʃn/ a ägyptisch □n Ägypter(in) m(f)

eiderdown /'aɪdə-/ n (quilt) Daunendecke f

eight /eɪt/ a acht □n Acht f; (boat) Achter m. ~'teen a achtzehn. ~'teenth a achtzehnte(r,s)

eighth /eɪtθ/ a achte(r,s) □n Achtel nt

eightieth /'eɪtɪɪθ/ a achtzigste(r,s)

eighty /'eɪtɪ/ a achtzig

either /'aɪðə(r)/ a & pron ~ [of them] einer von [den] beiden; (both) beide; on ~ side auf beiden Seiten □adv I don't ~ ich auch nicht □conj ~ ... or entweder ... oder

eject /ɪ'dʒekt/ vt hinauswerfen

eke /iːk/ vt ~ out strecken; (increase) ergänzen; ~ out a living sich kümmerlich durchschlagen

elaborate¹ /ɪ'læbərət/ a, -ly adv kunstvoll; (fig) kompliziert

elaborate² /ɪ'læbəreɪt/ vi ausführlicher sein; ~ on näher ausführen

elapse /ɪ'læps/ vi vergehen

elastic /ɪ'læstɪk/ a elastisch □n Gummiband nt. ~ 'band n Gummiband nt

elasticity /ɪlæs'tɪsətɪ/ n Elastizität f

elated /ɪ'leɪtɪd/ a überglücklich

elbow /'elbəʊ/ n Ellbogen m

elder¹ /'eldə(r)/ n Holunder m

eld|er² /a/ ältere(r,s) □n the ~ der/die Ältere. **~erly** /a/ alt. **~est** /a/ älteste(r,s) □n the ~est der/die Älteste

elect /ɪˈlekt/ a **the president ~** der designierte Präsident □vt wählen; **~ to do sth** sich dafür entscheiden, etw zu tun. **~ion** /-ekʃn/ n Wahl f

elector /ɪˈlektə(r)/ n Wähler(in) m(f). **~al** a Wahl-; **~al roll** Wählerverzeichnis nt. **~ate** /-rət/ n Wählerschaft f

electric /ɪˈlektrɪk/ a, **-ally** adv elektrisch

electrical /ɪˈlektrɪkl/ a elektrisch; **~ engineering** Elektrotechnik f

electric: ~ 'blanket n Heizdecke f. **~ 'fire** n elektrischer Heizofen m

electrician /ɪlekˈtrɪʃn/ n Elektriker m

electricity /ɪlekˈtrɪsəti/ n Elektrizität f; (supply) Strom m

electrify /ɪˈlektrɪfaɪ/ vt (pt/pp -ied) elektrifizieren. **~ing** a (fig) elektrisierend

electrocute /ɪˈlektrəkjuːt/ vt durch einen elektrischen Schlag töten; (execute) auf dem elektrischen Stuhl hinrichten

electrode /ɪˈlektrəʊd/ n Elektrode f

electron /ɪˈlektrɒn/ n Elektron nt

electronic /ɪlekˈtrɒnɪk/ a elektronisch. **~s** n Elektronik f

elegance /ˈelɪɡəns/ n Eleganz f

elegant /ˈelɪɡənt/ a, **-ly** adv elegant

elegy /ˈelɪdʒɪ/ n Elegie f

element /ˈelɪmənt/ n Element nt. **~ary** /-ˈmentərɪ/ a elementar

elephant /ˈelɪfənt/ n Elefant m

elevate /ˈelɪveɪt/ vt heben; (fig) erheben. **~ion** /-ˈveɪʃn/ n Erhebung f

elevator /ˈelɪveɪtə(r)/ n (Amer) Aufzug m, Fahrstuhl m

eleven /ɪˈlevn/ a elf □n Elf f. **~th** a elfte(r,s); **at the ~th hour** (fam) in letzter Minute

elf /elf/ n (pl **elves**) Elfe f

elicit /ɪˈlɪsɪt/ vt herausbekommen

eligible /ˈelɪdʒəbl/ a berechtigt; **~ young man** gute Partie f

eliminate /ɪˈlɪmɪneɪt/ vt ausschalten; (excrete) ausscheiden

élite /eɪˈliːt/ n Elite f

ellipse /ɪˈlɪps/ n Ellipse f. **~tical** a elliptisch

elm /elm/ n Ulme f

elocution /eləˈkjuːʃn/ n Sprecherziehung f

elongate /ˈiːlɒŋɡeɪt/ vt verlängern

elope /ɪˈləʊp/ vi durchbrennen (fam)

eloquen|ce /ˈeləkwəns/ n Beredsamkeit f. **~t** a, **-ly** adv beredt

else /els/ adv sonst; **who ~?** wer sonst? **nothing ~** sonst nichts; **or ~** oder; (otherwise) sonst; **someone/somewhere ~** jemand/irgendwo anders; **anyone ~** jeder andere; (as question) sonst noch jemand? **anything ~** alles andere; (as question) sonst noch etwas? **~where** adv woanders

elucidate /ɪˈluːsɪdeɪt/ vt erläutern

elude /ɪˈluːd/ vt entkommen (+ dat); (avoid) ausweichen (+ dat)

elusive /ɪˈluːsɪv/ a **be ~** schwer zu fassen sein

emaciated /ɪˈmeɪsɪeɪtɪd/ a abgezehrt

emanate /ˈeməneɪt/ vi ausgehen (from von)

emancipat|ed /ɪˈmænsɪpeɪtɪd/ a emanzipiert. **~ion** /-ˈpeɪʃn/ n Emanzipation f; (of slaves) Freilassung f

embalm /ɪmˈbɑːm/ vt einbalsamieren

embankment /ɪmˈbæŋkmənt/ n Böschung f; (of railway) Bahndamm m

embargo /emˈbɑːɡəʊ/ n (pl **-es**) Embargo nt

embark /ɪmˈbɑːk/ vi sich einschiffen; **~ on** anfangen mit. **~ation** /embɑːˈkeɪʃn/ n Einschiffung f

embarrass /ɪmˈbærəs/ vt in Verlegenheit bringen. **~ed** a verlegen.

~ing *a* peinlich. **~ment** *n* Verlegenheit *f*

embassy /'embəsɪ/ *n* Botschaft *f*

embedded /ɪm'bedɪd/ *a* **be deeply ~ in** tief stecken in (+ *dat*)

embellish /ɪm'belɪʃ/ *vt* verzieren; (*fig*) ausschmücken

embers /'embəz/ *npl* Glut *f*

embezzle /ɪm'bezl/ *vt* unterschlagen. **~ment** *n* Unterschlagung *f*

embitter /ɪm'bɪtə(r)/ *vt* verbittern

emblem /'embləm/ *n* Emblem *nt*

embodiment /ɪm'bɒdɪmənt/ *n* Verkörperung *f*

embody /ɪm'bɒdɪ/ *vt* (*pt/pp* -**ied**) verkörpern; (*include*) enthalten

emboss /ɪm'bɒs/ *vt* prägen

embrace /ɪm'breɪs/ *n* Umarmung *f* □*vt* umarmen; (*fig*) umfassen □*vi* sich umarmen

embroider /ɪm'brɔɪdə(r)/ *vt* besticken; sticken ⟨*design*⟩; (*fig*) ausschmücken □*vi* sticken. **~y** *n* Stickerei *f*

embroil /ɪm'brɔɪl/ *vt* **become ~ed in sth** in etw (*acc*) verwickelt werden

embryo /'embrɪəʊ/ *n* Embryo *m*

emerald /'emərəld/ *n* Smaragd *m*

emerge /ɪ'mɜːdʒ/ *vi* auftauchen (**from** aus); (*become known*) sich herausstellen; (*come into being*) entstehen. **~gence** /-əns/ *n* Auftauchen *nt*; Entstehung *f*

emergency /ɪ'mɜːdʒənsɪ/ *n* Notfall *m*; **in an ~** im Notfall. **~ exit** *n* Notausgang *m*

emery-paper /'emərɪ-/ *n* Schmirgelpapier *nt*

emigrant /'emɪgrənt/ *n* Auswanderer *m*

emigrat|e /'emɪgreɪt/ *vi* auswandern. **~ion** /-'greɪʃn/ *n* Auswanderung *f*

eminent /'emɪnənt/ *a*, **-ly** *adv* eminent

emission /ɪ'mɪʃn/ *n* Ausstrahlung *f*; (*of pollutant*) Emission *f*

emit /ɪ'mɪt/ *vt* (*pt/pp* emitted) ausstrahlen ⟨*light, heat*⟩; ausstoßen ⟨*smoke, fumes, cry*⟩

emotion /ɪ'məʊʃn/ *n* Gefühl *nt*. **~al** *a* emotional; **become ~al** sich erregen

emotive /ɪ'məʊtɪv/ *a* emotional

empath|ize /'empəθaɪz/ *vi* **~ize with s.o.** sich in jdn einfühlen. **~y** *n* Einfühlungsvermögen *nt*

emperor /'empərə(r)/ *n* Kaiser *m*

emphasis /'emfəsɪs/ *n* Betonung *f*

emphasize /'emfəsaɪz/ *vt* betonen

emphatic /ɪm'fætɪk/ *a*, **-ally** *adv* nachdrücklich

empire /'empaɪə(r)/ *n* Reich *nt*

empirical /em'pɪrɪkl/ *a* empirisch

employ /ɪm'plɔɪ/ *vt* beschäftigen; (*appoint*) einstellen; (*fig*) anwenden. **~ ee** /emplɔɪ'iː/ *n* Beschäftigte(r) *m*/*f*; (*in contrast to employer*) Arbeitnehmer *m*. **~ er** *n* Arbeitgeber *m*. **~ ment** *n* Beschäftigung *f*; (*work*) Arbeit *f*. **~ ment agency** *n* Stellenvermittlung *f*

empower /ɪm'paʊə(r)/ *vt* ermächtigen

empress /'emprɪs/ *n* Kaiserin *f*

empties /'emptɪz/ *npl* leere Flaschen *pl*

emptiness /'emptɪnɪs/ *n* Leere *f*

empty /'emptɪ/ *a* leer □*vt* leeren; ausleeren ⟨*container*⟩ □*vi* sich leeren

emulate /'emjʊleɪt/ *vt* nacheifern (+ *dat*)

emulsion /ɪ'mʌlʃn/ *n* Emulsion *f*

enable /ɪ'neɪbl/ *vt* **~ s.o. to** es jdm möglich machen, zu

enact /ɪ'nækt/ *vt* (*Theat*) aufführen

enamel /ɪ'næml/ *n* Email *nt*; (*on teeth*) Zahnschmelz *m*; (*paint*) Lack *m* □*vt* (*pt/pp* enamelled) emaillieren

enamoured /ɪ'næməd/ *a* **be ~ of** sehr angetan sein von

enchant /ɪn'tʃɑːnt/ *vt* bezaubern. **~ing** *a* bezaubernd. **~ment** *n* Zauber *m*

encircle /ɪn'sɜːkl/ *vt* einkreisen

enclave /'enkleɪv/ *n* Enklave *f*

enclos|e /ɪn'kləʊz/ *vt* einschließen; (*in letter*) beilegen (**with** *dat*).

~ure /-ʒə(r)/ n (at zoo) Gehege nt; (in letter) Anlage f

encompass /ɪnˈkʌmpəs/ vt umfassen

encore /ˈɒŋkɔː(r)/ n Zugabe f □ int bravo!

encounter /ɪnˈkaʊntə(r)/ n Begegnung f; (battle) Zusammenstoß m □ vt begegnen (+ dat); (fig) stoßen auf (+ acc)

encourag|e /ɪnˈkʌrɪdʒ/ vt ermutigen; (promote) fördern. **~ement** n Ermutigung f. **~ing** a ermutigend

encroach /ɪnˈkrəʊtʃ/ vi **~ on** eindringen in (+ acc) ⟨land⟩; beanspruchen ⟨time⟩

encumb|er /ɪnˈkʌmbə(r)/ vt belasten (**with** mit). **~rance** n Belastung f

encyclopaed|ia /ɪnsaɪkləˈpiːdɪə/ n Enzyklopädie f, Lexikon nt. **~ic** a enzyklopädisch

end /end/ n Ende nt; (purpose) Zweck m; **in the ~** schließlich; **at the ~ of May** Ende Mai; **on ~** hochkant; **for days on ~** tagelang; **make ~s meet** (fam) [gerade] auskommen; **no ~ of** (fam) unheimlich viel(e) □ vt beenden □ vi enden; **~ up in** (fam: arrive at) landen in (+ dat)

endanger /ɪnˈdeɪndʒə(r)/ vt gefährden

endear|ing /ɪnˈdɪərɪŋ/ a liebenswert. **~ment** n term of **~ment** Kosewort nt

endeavour /ɪnˈdevə(r)/ n Bemühung f □ vi sich bemühen (**to** zu)

ending /ˈendɪŋ/ n Schluß m, Ende nt; (Gram) Endung f

endive /ˈendaɪv/ n Endivie f

endless /ˈendlɪs/ a, **-ly** adv endlos

endorse /ɪnˈdɔːs/ vt (Comm) indossieren; (confirm) bestätigen. **~ment** n (Comm) Indossament nt; (fig) Bestätigung f; (on driving licence) Strafvermerk m

endow /ɪnˈdaʊ/ vt stiften; **be ~ed with** (fig) haben. **~ment** n Stiftung f

endur|able /ɪnˈdjʊərəbl/ a erträglich. **~ance** /-rəns/ n Durchhaltevermögen nt; **beyond ~ance** unerträglich

endur|e /ɪnˈdjʊə(r)/ vt ertragen □ vi (lange) bestehen. **~ing** a dauernd

enemy /ˈenəmɪ/ n Feind m □ attrib feindlich

energetic /enəˈdʒetɪk/ a tatkräftig; **be ~** voller Energie sein

energy /ˈenədʒɪ/ n Energie f

enforce /ɪnˈfɔːs/ vt durchsetzen. **~d** a unfreiwillig

engage /ɪnˈgeɪdʒ/ vt einstellen ⟨staff⟩; (Theat) engagieren; (Auto) einlegen ⟨gear⟩ □ vi sich beteiligen (**in** an + dat); (Techn) ineinandergreifen. **~d** a besetzt; ⟨person⟩ beschäftigt; (to be married) verlobt; **get ~d** sich verloben (**to** mit). **~ment** n Verlobung f; (appointment) Verabredung f; (Mil) Gefecht nt

engaging /ɪnˈgeɪdʒɪŋ/ a einnehmend

engender /ɪnˈdʒendə(r)/ vt (fig) erzeugen

engine /ˈendʒɪn/ n Motor m; (Naut) Maschine f; (Rail) Lokomotive f; (of jet-plane) Triebwerk nt. **~-driver** n Lokomotivführer m

engineer /endʒɪˈnɪə(r)/ n Ingenieur m; (service, installation) Techniker m; (Naut) Maschinist m; (Amer) Lokomotivführer m □ vt (fig) organisieren. **~ing** n [mechanical] **~ing** Maschinenbau m

England /ˈɪŋglənd/ n England nt

English /ˈɪŋglɪʃ/ a englisch; **the ~ Channel** der Ärmelkanal □ n (Lang) Englisch nt; **in ~** auf englisch; **into ~** ins Englische; **the ~** pl die Engländer. **~man** n Engländer m. **~woman** n Engländerin f

engrav|e /ɪnˈgreɪv/ vt eingravieren. **~ing** n Stich m

engross /ɪn'grəʊs/ vt be ~ed in vertieft sein in (+ acc)

engulf /ɪn'gʌlf/ vt verschlingen

enhance /ɪn'hɑːns/ vt verschönern; (fig) steigern

enigma /ɪ'nɪgmə/ n Rätsel nt. ~tic /enɪg'mætɪk/ a rätselhaft

enjoy /ɪn'dʒɔɪ/ vt genießen; ~ oneself sich amüsieren; ~ cooking/painting gern kochen/malen; I ~ed it es hat mir gut gefallen; (food:) geschmeckt. ~able /-əbl/ a angenehm, nett. ~ment n Vergnügen nt

enlarge /ɪn'lɑːdʒ/ vt vergrößern □ vi ~ upon sich näher auslassen über (+ acc). ~ment n Vergrößerung f

enlighten /ɪn'laɪtn/ vt aufklären. ~ment n Aufklärung f

enlist /ɪn'lɪst/ vt (Mil) einziehen; ~ s.o.'s help jdn zur Hilfe heranziehen □ vi (Mil) sich melden

enliven /ɪn'laɪvn/ vt beleben

enmity /'enmətɪ/ n Feindschaft f

enormity /ɪ'nɔːmətɪ/ n Ungeheuerlichkeit f

enormous /ɪ'nɔːməs/ a, -ly adv riesig

enough /ɪ'nʌf/ a, adv & n genug; be ~ reichen; **funnily ~** komischerweise; **I've had ~!** (fam) jetzt reicht's mir aber!

enquir|e /ɪn'kwaɪə(r)/ vi sich erkundigen (**about** nach) □ vt sich erkundigen nach. ~y n Erkundigung f; (investigation) Untersuchung f

enrage /ɪn'reɪdʒ/ vt wütend machen

enrich /ɪn'rɪtʃ/ vt bereichern; (improve) anreichern

enrol /ɪn'rəʊl/ v (pt/pp -rolled) □ vt einschreiben □ vi sich einschreiben. ~ment n Einschreibung f

ensemble /ɒn'sɒmbl/ n (clothing & Mus) Ensemble nt

ensign /'ensaɪn/ n Flagge f

enslave /ɪn'sleɪv/ vt versklaven

ensue /ɪn'sjuː/ vi folgen; (result:) sich ergeben (**from** aus)

ensure /ɪn'ʃʊə(r)/ vt sicherstellen; ~ that dafür sorgen, daß

entail /ɪn'teɪl/ vt erforderlich machen; **what does it ~?** was ist damit verbunden?

entangle /ɪn'tæŋgl/ vt get ~d sich verfangen (**in** in + dat); (fig) sich verstricken (**in** in + acc)

enter /'entə(r)/ vt eintreten/ (vehicle:) einfahren in (+ acc); einreisen in (+ acc) (country); (register) eintragen; sich anmelden zu (competition) □ vi eintreten; (vehicle:) einfahren; (Theat) auftreten; (register as competitor) sich anmelden; (take part) sich beteiligen (**in** an + dat)

enterpris|e /'entəpraɪz/ n Unternehmen nt; (quality) Unternehmungsgeist m. ~ing a unternehmend

entertain /entə'teɪn/ vt unterhalten; (invite) einladen; (to meal) bewirten (guest); (fig) in Erwägung ziehen □ vi unterhalten; (have guests) Gäste haben. ~er n Unterhalter m. ~ment n Unterhaltung f

enthral /ɪn'θrɔːl/ vt (pt/pp enthralled) be ~led gefesselt sein (**by** von)

enthuse /ɪn'θjuːz/ vi ~ over schwärmen von

enthusias|m /ɪn'θjuːzɪæzm/ n Begeisterung f. ~t n Enthusiast m. ~tic /-'æstɪk/ a, -ally adv begeistert

entice /ɪn'taɪs/ vt locken. ~ment n Anreiz m

entire /ɪn'taɪə(r)/ a ganz. ~ly adv ganz, völlig. ~ty /-rətɪ/ n in its ~ty in seiner Gesamtheit

entitle /ɪn'taɪtl/ vt berechtigen; ~d ... mit dem Titel ...; be ~d to sth das Recht auf etw (acc) haben. ~ment n Berechtigung f; (claim) Anspruch m (**to** auf + acc)

entity /'entətɪ/ n Wesen nt

entomology /entə'mɒlədʒɪ/ n Entomologie f

entourage /'ɒntʊraːʒ/ n Gefolge nt

entrails /'entreɪlz/ npl Eingeweide pl

entrance¹ /ɪn'traːns/ vt bezaubern

entrance² /'entrəns/ n Eintritt m; (Theat) Auftritt m; (way in) Eingang m; (for vehicle) Einfahrt f. ~ examination n Aufnahmeprüfung f. ~ fee n Eintrittsgebühr f

entrant /'entrənt/ n Teilnehmer(in) m(f)

entreat /ɪn'triːt/ vt anflehen (for um)

entrench /ɪn'trentʃ/ vt be ~ed in verwurzelt sein in (+ dat)

entrust /ɪn'trʌst/ vt ~ s.o. with sth, ~ sth to s.o. jdm etw anvertrauen

entry /'entrɪ/ n Eintritt m; (into country) Einreise f; (on list) Eintrag m; no ~ Zutritt (Auto) Einfahrt verboten. ~ form n Anmeldeformular nt. ~ visa n Einreisevisum nt

enumerate /ɪ'njuːmərət/ vt aufzählen

enunciate /ɪ'nʌnsɪeɪt/ vt [deutlich] aussprechen; (state) vorbringen

envelop /ɪn'veləp/ vt (pt/pp enveloped) einhüllen

envelope /'envələʊp/ n [Brief]umschlag m

enviable /'envɪəbl/ a beneidenswert

envious /'envɪəs/ a, -ly adv neidisch (of auf + acc)

environment /ɪn'vaɪərənmənt/ n Umwelt f

environmental /ɪnvaɪərən'mentl/ a Umwelt-. ~ist n Umweltschützer m. ~ly adv ~ly friendly umweltfreundlich

envisage /ɪn'vɪzɪdʒ/ vt sich (dat) vorstellen

envoy /'envɔɪ/ n Gesandte(r) m

envy /'envɪ/ n Neid m □vt (pt/pp -ied) ~ s.o. sth jdn um etw beneiden

enzyme /'enzaɪm/ n Enzym nt

epic /'epɪk/ a episch □n Epos nt

epidemic /epɪ'demɪk/ n Epidemie f

epilep|sy /'epɪlepsɪ/ n Epilepsie f. ~tic /-'leptɪk/ a epileptisch □n Epileptiker(in) m(f)

epilogue /'epɪlɒg/ n Epilog m

episode /'epɪsəʊd/ n Episode f; (instalment) Folge f

epistle /ɪ'pɪsl/ n (liter) Brief m

epitaph /'epɪtaːf/ n Epitaph m

epithet /'epɪθet/ n Beiname m

epitom|e /ɪ'pɪtəmɪ/ n Inbegriff m. ~ize vt verkörpern

epoch /'iːpɒk/ n Epoche f. ~-making a epochemachend

equal /'iːkwl/ a gleich (to dat); be ~ to a task einer Aufgabe gewachsen sein □n Gleichgestellte(r) m(f) □vt (pt/pp equalled) gleichen (+ dat); (fig) gleichkommen (+ dat). ~ity /ɪ'kwɒlətɪ/ n Gleichheit f

equalize /'iːkwəlaɪz/ vt/i ausgleichen. ~r n (Sport) Ausgleich[streffer] m

equally /'iːkwəlɪ/ adv gleich; (divide) gleichmäßig; (just as) genauso

equanimity /ekwə'nɪmətɪ/ n Gleichmut f

equat|e /ɪ'kweɪt/ vt gleichsetzen (with mit). ~ion /-eɪʒn/ n (Math) Gleichung f

equator /ɪ'kweɪtə(r)/ n Äquator m. ~ial /ekwə'tɔːrɪəl/ a Äquator-

equestrian /ɪ'kwestrɪən/ a Reit-

equilibrium /iːkwɪ'lɪbrɪəm/ n Gleichgewicht nt

equinox /'iːkwɪnɒks/ n Tagundnachtgleiche f

equip /ɪ'kwɪp/ vt (pt/pp equipped) ausrüsten; (furnish) ausstatten. ~ment n Ausrüstung f; Ausstattung f

equitable /'ekwɪtəbl/ a gerecht

equity /'ekwətɪ/ n Gerechtigkeit f

equivalent /ɪ'kwɪvələnt/ a gleichwertig; (corresponding) entsprechend □n Äquivalent nt; (value)

Gegenwert *m*; *(counterpart)* Gegenstück *nt*

equivocal /ɪˈkwɪvəkl/ *a* zweideutig

era /ˈɪərə/ *n* Ära *f*, Zeitalter *nt*

eradicate /ɪˈrædɪkeɪt/ *vt* ausrotten

erase /ɪˈreɪz/ *vt* ausradieren; *(from tape)* löschen; *(fig)* auslöschen. ~ **r** *n* Radiergummi *m*

erect /ɪˈrekt/ *a* aufrecht □ *vt* errichten. ~**ion** /-ekʃn/ *n* Errichtung *f*; *(building)* Bau *m*; *(Biol)* Erektion *f*

ermine /ˈɜːmɪn/ *n* Hermelin *m*

ero|de /ɪˈrəʊd/ *vt* ⟨water:⟩ auswaschen; ⟨acid:⟩ angreifen. ~ **sion** /-əʊʒn/ *n* Erosion *f*

erotic /ɪˈrɒtɪk/ *a* erotisch. ~**ism** /-tɪsɪzm/ *n* Erotik *f*

err /ɜː(r)/ *vi* sich irren; *(sin)* sündigen

errand /ˈerənd/ *n* Botengang *m*

erratic /ɪˈrætɪk/ *a* unregelmäßig; ⟨person:⟩ unberechenbar

erroneous /ɪˈrəʊnɪəs/ *a* falsch; ⟨belief, assumption:⟩ irrig. ~**ly** *adv* fälschlich; irrigerweise

error /ˈerə(r)/ *n* Irrtum *m*; *(mistake)* Fehler *m*; **in** ~ irrtümlicherweise

erudit|e /ˈeruːdaɪt/ *a* gelehrt. ~**ion** /-ˈdɪʃn/ *n* Gelehrsamkeit *f*

erupt /ɪˈrʌpt/ *vi* ausbrechen. ~**ion** /-ʌpʃn/ *n* Ausbruch *m*

escalat|e /ˈeskəleɪt/ *vt/i* eskalieren. ~**ion** /-ˈleɪʃn/ *n* Eskalation *f*. ~**or** *n* Rolltreppe *f*

escapade /ˈeskəpeɪd/ *n* Eskapade *f*

escape /ɪˈskeɪp/ *n* Flucht *f*; *(from prison)* Ausbruch *m*; **have a narrow** ~ gerade noch davonkommen □ *vi* flüchten; ⟨prisoner:⟩ ausbrechen; entkommen (**from** aus; **from s.o.** jdm); ⟨gas:⟩ entweichen □ *vt* ~ **notice** unbemerkt bleiben; **the name** ~ **s me** der Name entfällt mir

escapism /ɪˈskeɪpɪzm/ *n* Flucht *f* vor der Wirklichkeit, Eskapismus *m*

escort[1] /ˈeskɔːt/ *n* *(of person)* Begleiter *m*; *(Mil)* Eskorte *f*; **under** ~ unter Bewachung

escort[2] /ɪˈskɔːt/ *vt* begleiten; *(Mil)* eskortieren

Eskimo /ˈeskɪməʊ/ *n* Eskimo *m*

esoteric /esəˈterɪk/ *a* esoterisch

especial /ɪˈspeʃl/ *a* besondere(r,s). ~**ly** *adv* besonders

espionage /ˈespɪənɑːʒ/ *n* Spionage *f*

essay /ˈeseɪ/ *n* Aufsatz *m*

essence /ˈesns/ *n* Wesen *nt*; *(Chem, Culin)* Essenz *f*; **in** ~ im wesentlichen

essential /ɪˈsenʃl/ *a* wesentlich; *(indispensable)* unentbehrlich □ **the** ~**s** das Wesentliche; *(items)* das Nötigste. ~**ly** *adv* im wesentlichen

establish /ɪˈstæblɪʃ/ *vt* gründen; *(form)* bilden; *(prove)* beweisen. ~**ment** *n* *(firm)* Unternehmen *nt*

estate /ɪˈsteɪt/ *n* Gut *nt*; *(possessions)* Besitz *m*; *(after death)* Nachlaß *m*; *(housing)* [Wohn]siedlung *f*. ~ **agent** *n* Immobilienmakler *m*. ~ **car** *n* Kombi[wagen] *m*

esteem /ɪˈstiːm/ *n* Achtung *f* □ *vt* hochschätzen

estimate[1] /ˈestɪmət/ *n* Schätzung *f*; *(Comm)* [Kosten]voranschlag *m*; **at a rough** ~ grob geschätzt

estimate[2] /ˈestɪmeɪt/ *vt* schätzen. ~**ion** /-ˈmeɪʃn/ *n* Einschätzung *f*; *(esteem)* Achtung *f*; **in my** ~**ion** meiner Meinung nach

estuary /ˈestʊərɪ/ *n* Mündung *f*

etc. /et'setərə/ *abbr* (**et cetera**) und so weiter, usw.

etching /ˈetʃɪŋ/ *n* Radierung *f*

eternal /ɪˈtɜːnl/ *a* ewig. ~**ly** *adv* ewig

eternity /ɪˈtɜːnətɪ/ *n* Ewigkeit *f*

ether /ˈiːθə(r)/ *n* Äther *m*

ethic /ˈeθɪk/ *n* Ethik *f*. ~**al** *a* ethisch; *(morally correct)* moralisch einwandfrei. ~**s** *n* Ethik *f*

Ethiopia /iːθɪˈəʊpɪə/ *n* Äthiopien *nt*

ethnic /'eθnɪk/ a ethnisch

etiquette /'etɪket/ n Etikette f

etymology /etɪ'mɒlədʒɪ/ n Etymologie f

eucalyptus /juːkə'lɪptəs/ n Eukalyptus m

eulogy /'juːlədʒɪ/ n Lobrede f

euphemism /'juːfəmɪzm/ n Euphemismus m. ~tic /-'mɪstɪk/ a, -ally adv verhüllend

euphoria /juː'fɔːrɪə/ n Euphorie f

Euro-: /'juərəu-/ pref ~cheque n Euroscheck m. ~passport n Europaß m

Europe /'juərəp/ n Europa nt

European /juərə'pɪən/ a europäisch; ~ Community Europäische Gemeinschaft f □ n Europäer(in) m(f)

evacuat|e /ɪ'vækjuət/ vt evakuieren; räumen ⟨building, area⟩. ~ion /-'eɪʃn/ n Evakuierung f; Räumung f

evade /ɪ'veɪd/ vt sich entziehen (+ dat); hinterziehen ⟨taxes⟩; ~ the issue ausweichen

evaluate /ɪ'væljuət/ vt einschätzen

evangel|ical /iːvæn'dʒelɪkl/ a evangelisch. ~ist /ɪ'vændʒəlɪst/ n Evangelist m

evaporat|e /ɪ'væpəreɪt/ vi verdunsten; ~ed milk Kondensmilch f, Dosenmilch f. ~ion /-'reɪʃn/ n Verdampfung f

evasion /ɪ'veɪʒn/ n Ausweichen nt; ~ of taxes Steuerhinterziehung f

evasive /ɪ'veɪsɪv/ a, -ly adv ausweichend; be ~ ausweichen

eve /iːv/ n ⟨liter⟩ Vorabend m

even /'iːvn/ a ⟨level⟩ eben; ⟨same, equal⟩ gleich; ⟨regular⟩ gleichmäßig; ⟨number⟩ gerade; get ~ with ⟨fam⟩ es jdm heimzahlen □ adv sogar, selbst; ~ so trotzdem; not ~ nicht einmal □ vt ~ the score ausgleichen. ~ up vt ausgleichen □ vi sich ausgleichen

evening /'iːvnɪŋ/ n Abend m; this ~ heute abend; in the ~ abends,

am Abend. ~ class n Abendkurs m

evenly /'iːvnlɪ/ adv gleichmäßig

event /ɪ'vent/ n Ereignis nt; ⟨function⟩ Veranstaltung f; ⟨Sport⟩ Wettbewerb m; in the ~ of im Falle (+ gen); in the ~ wie es sich ergab. ~ful a ereignisreich

eventual /ɪ'ventjʊəl/ a his ~ success der Erfolg, der ihm schließlich zuteil wurde. ~ity /-'ælətɪ/ n Eventualität f, Fall m. ~ly adv schließlich

ever /'evə(r)/ adv je[mals]; not ~ nie; for ~ für immer; hardly ~ fast nie; ~ since seitdem; ~ so ⟨fam⟩ sehr, furchtbar ⟨fam⟩

'evergreen n immergrüner Strauch m/ ⟨tree⟩ Baum m

ever'lasting a ewig

every /'evrɪ/ a jede(r,s); ~ one jede(r,s) einzelne; ~ other day jeden zweiten Tag

every: ~body pron jeder[mann]; alle pl. ~day a alltäglich. ~one pron jeder[mann]; alle pl. ~thing pron alles. ~where adv überall

evict /ɪ'vɪkt/ vt [aus der Wohnung] hinausweisen. ~ion /-ɪkʃn/ n Ausweisung f

eviden|ce /'evɪdəns/ n Beweise pl; ⟨Jur⟩ Beweismaterial nt; ⟨testimony⟩ Aussage f; give ~ce aussagen. ~t a, -ly adv offensichtlich

evil /'iːvl/ a böse □ n Böse nt

evocative /ɪ'vɒkətɪv/ a be ~ of heraufbeschwören

evoke /ɪ'vəʊk/ vt heraufbeschwören

evolution /iːvə'luːʃn/ n Evolution f

evolve /ɪ'vɒlv/ vt entwickeln □ vi sich entwickeln

ewe /juː/ n Schaf nt

exacerbate /ek'sæsəbeɪt/ vt verschlimmern; verschärfen ⟨situation⟩

exact /ɪg'zækt/ a, -ly adv genau; not ~ly nicht gerade. □ vt erzwingen. ~ing a anspruchsvoll.

~**itude** /-ɪtjuːd/ n, ~**ness** n Genauigkeit f

exaggerat|e /ɪgˈzædʒəreɪt/ vt/i übertreiben. ~**ion** /-ˈreɪʃn/ n Übertreibung f

exalt /ɪgˈzɔːlt/ vt erheben; (praise) preisen

exam /ɪgˈzæm/ n (fam) Prüfung f

examination /ɪgzæmɪˈneɪʃn/ n Untersuchung f; (Sch) Prüfung f

examine /ɪgˈzæmɪn/ vt untersuchen; (Sch) prüfen; (Jur) verhören. ~**r** n (Sch) Prüfer m

example /ɪgˈzɑːmpl/ n Beispiel nt (of für); for ~ zum Beispiel; make an ~ of ein Exempel statuieren an (+ dat)

exasperat|e /ɪgˈzæspəreɪt/ vt zur Verzweiflung treiben. ~**ion** /-ˈreɪʃn/ n Verzweiflung f

excavat|e /ˈekskəveɪt/ vt ausschachten; (Archaeol) ausgraben. ~**ion** /-ˈveɪʃn/ n Ausgrabung f

exceed /ɪkˈsiːd/ vt übersteigen. ~**ingly** adv äußerst

excel /ɪkˈsel/ v (pt/pp **excelled**) vi sich auszeichnen □ vt ~ **oneself** sich selbst übertreffen

excellen|ce /ˈeksələns/ n Vorzüglichkeit f. E~**cy** n (title) Exzellenz f. ~**t**, **-ly** adv ausgezeichnet, vorzüglich

except /ɪkˈsept/ prep außer (+ dat); ~ **for** abgesehen von □ vt ausnehmen. ~**ing** prep außer (+ dat)

exception /ɪkˈsepʃn/ n Ausnahme f; **take** ~ **to** Anstoß nehmen an (+ dat). ~**al**, **-ly** adv außergewöhnlich

excerpt /ˈeksɜːpt/ n Auszug m

excess /ɪkˈses/ n Übermaß nt (of an + dat); (surplus) Überschuß m; ~**es** pl Exzesse pl; in ~ of über (+ dat)

excess 'fare /ˈekses-/ n Nachlösegebühr f

excessive /ɪkˈsesɪv/ a, **-ly** adv übermäßig

exchange /ɪksˈtʃeɪndʒ/ n Austausch m; (Teleph) Fernsprechamt nt; (Comm) [Geld]wechsel m; [stock] ~ Börse f; in ~ dafür □ vt austauschen (for gegen); tauschen ⟨places, greetings, money⟩. ~ **rate** n Wechselkurs m

exchequer /ɪksˈtʃekə(r)/ n (Pol) Staatskasse f

excise[1] /ˈeksaɪz/ n ~ **duty** Verbrauchssteuer f

excise[2] /ekˈsaɪz/ vt herausschneiden

excitable /ɪkˈsaɪtəbl/ a [leicht] erregbar

excit|e /ɪkˈsaɪt/ vt aufregen; (cause) erregen. ~**ed** a, **-ly** adv aufgeregt; **get** ~**ed** sich aufregen. ~**ement** n Aufregung f; Erregung f. ~**ing** a aufregend; ⟨story⟩ spannend

exclaim /ɪkˈskleɪm/ vt/i ausrufen

exclamation /ekskləˈmeɪʃn/ n Ausruf m. ~ **mark** n, (Amer) ~ **point** n Ausrufezeichen nt

exclu|de /ɪkˈskluːd/ vt ausschließen. ~**ding** pron ausschließlich (+ gen). ~**sion** /-ʒn/ n Ausschluß m

exclusive /ɪkˈskluːsɪv/ a, **-ly** adv ausschließlich; (select) exklusiv; ~ **of** ausschließlich (+ gen)

excommunicate /ekskəˈmjuːnɪkeɪt/ vt exkommunizieren

excrement /ˈekskrɪmənt/ n Kot m.

excrete /ɪkˈskriːt/ vt ausscheiden

excruciating /ɪkˈskruːʃɪeɪtɪŋ/ a gräßlich

excursion /ɪkˈskɜːʃn/ n Ausflug m

excusable /ɪkˈskjuːzəbl/ a entschuldbar

excuse[1] /ɪkˈskjuːs/ n Entschuldigung f; (pretext) Ausrede f

excuse[2] /ɪkˈskjuːz/ vt entschuldigen; ~ **from** freistellen von; ~ **me!** Entschuldigung!

ex-di'rectory a **be** ~ nicht im Telefonbuch stehen

execute /ˈeksɪkjuːt/ vt ausführen; (put to death) hinrichten

execution /eksɪˈkjuːʃn/ n (see execute) Ausführung f; Hinrichtung f. ~ er n Scharfrichter m

executive /ɪgˈzekjʊtɪv/ a leitend □ n leitende(r) Angestellte(r) m/f; (Pol) Exekutive f

executor /ɪgˈzekjʊtə(r)/ n (Jur) Testamentsvollstrecker m

exemplary /ɪgˈzemplərɪ/ a beispielhaft; (as a warning) exemplarisch

exemplify /ɪgˈzemplɪfaɪ/ vt (pt/pp -ied) veranschaulichen

exempt /ɪgˈzempt/ a befreit □vt befreien (from von). ~ion /-empʃn/ n Befreiung f

exercise /ˈeksəsaɪz/ n Übung f; physical ~ körperliche Bewegung f; take ~ sich bewegen □vt (use) ausüben; bewegen (horse); spazierenführen (dog) □vi sich bewegen. ~ book n [Schul]heft nt

exert /ɪgˈzɜːt/ vt ausüben; ~ oneself sich anstrengen. ~ion /-ɜːʃn/ n Anstrengung f

exhale /eksˈheɪl/ vt/i ausatmen

exhaust /ɪgˈzɔːst/ n (Auto) Auspuff m; (pipe) Auspuffrohr nt; (fumes) Abgase pl □vt erschöpfen. ~ed a erschöpft. ~ing a anstrengend. ~ion /-ɔːstʃn/ n Erschöpfung f. ~ive /-ɪv/ a (fig) erschöpfend

exhibit /ɪgˈzɪbɪt/ n Ausstellungsstück nt; (Jur) Beweisstück n □vt ausstellen; (fig) zeigen

exhibition /eksɪˈbɪʃn/ n Ausstellung f; (Univ) Stipendium nt. ~ist n Exhibitionist(in) m(f)

exhibitor /ɪgˈzɪbɪtə(r)/ n Aussteller m

exhilarat|ed /ɪgˈzɪləreɪtɪd/ a beschwingt. ~ing a berauschend. ~ion /-ʃn/ n Hochgefühl nt

exhort /ɪgˈzɔːt/ vt ermahnen

exhume /ɪgˈzjuːm/ vt exhumieren

exile /ˈeksaɪl/ n Exil nt; (person) im Exil Lebende(r) m/f □vt ins Exil schicken

exist /ɪgˈzɪst/ vi bestehen, existieren. ~ence /-əns/ n Existenz f; be in ~ence existieren

exit /ˈeksɪt/ n Ausgang m; (Auto) Ausfahrt f; (Theat) Abgang m □vi (Theat) abgehen. ~ visa n Ausreisevisum nt

exonerate /ɪgˈzɒnəreɪt/ vt entlasten

exorbitant /ɪgˈzɔːbɪtənt/ a übermäßig hoch

exorcize /ˈeksɔːsaɪz/ vt austreiben

exotic /ɪgˈzɒtɪk/ a exotisch

expand /ɪkˈspænd/ vt ausdehnen; (explain better) weiter ausführen □vi sich ausdehnen; (Comm) expandieren; ~ on (fig) weiter ausführen

expans|e /ɪkˈspæns/ n Weite f. ~ion /-ænʃn/ n Ausdehnung f; (Techn, Pol, Comm) Expansion f. ~ive /-ɪv/ a mitteilsam

expatriate /eksˈpætrɪət/ n be an ~ im Ausland leben

expect /ɪkˈspekt/ vt erwarten; (suppose) annehmen; I ~ so wahrscheinlich; we ~ to arrive on Monday wir rechnen damit, daß wir am Montag ankommen

expectan|cy /ɪkˈspektənsɪ/ n Erwartung f. ~t a, -ly adv erwartungsvoll; ~t mother werdende Mutter f

expectation /ekspekˈteɪʃn/ n Erwartung f; ~ of life Lebenserwartung f

expedient /ɪkˈspiːdɪənt/ a zweckdienlich

expedite /ˈekspɪdaɪt/ vt beschleunigen

expedition /ekspɪˈdɪʃn/ n Expedition f. ~ary a (Mil) Expeditions-

expel /ɪkˈspel/ vt (pt/pp expelled) ausweisen (from aus); (from school) von der Schule verweisen

expend /ɪkˈspend/ vt aufwenden. ~able /-əbl/ a entbehrlich

expenditure /ɪkˈspendɪtʃə(r)/ n Ausgaben pl

expense /ɪk'spens/ n Kosten pl; **business** ~ s pl Spesen pl; **at my** ~ auf meine Kosten; **at the** ~ **of** (fig) auf Kosten (+ gen)

expensive /ɪk'spensɪv/ a, **-ly** adv teuer

experience /ɪk'spɪərɪəns/ n Erfahrung f; (event) Erlebnis nt □vt erleben. ~ **d** a erfahren

experiment /ɪk'sperɪmənt/ n Versuch m, Experiment nt □/-ment/ vi experimentieren. ~ **al** /-'mentl/ a experimentell

expert /'ekspɜːt/ a, **-ly** adv fachmännisch □n Fachmann m, Experte m

expertise /ekspɜː'tiːz/ n Sachkenntnis f; (skill) Geschick nt

expire /ɪk'spaɪə(r)/ vi ablaufen

expiry /ɪk'spaɪərɪ/ n Ablauf m. ~ **date** n Verfallsdatum nt

explain /ɪk'spleɪn/ vt erklären

explana|tion /eksplə'neɪʃn/ n Erklärung f. ~ **tory** /ɪk'splænətərɪ/ a erklärend

expletive /ɪk'spliːtɪv/ n Kraftausdruck m

explicit /ɪk'splɪsɪt/ a, **-ly** adv deutlich

explode /ɪk'spləʊd/ vi explodieren □vt zur Explosion bringen

exploit[1] /'eksplɔɪt/ n [Helden]tat f

exploit[2] /ɪk'splɔɪt/ vt ausbeuten. ~ **ation** /eksplɔɪ'teɪʃn/ n Ausbeutung f

explora|tion /eksplə'reɪʃn/ n Erforschung f. ~ **tory** /ɪk'splɒrətərɪ/ a Probe-

explore /ɪk'splɔː(r)/ vt erforschen. ~ **r** n Forschungsreisende(r) m

explosi|on /ɪk'spləʊʒn/ n Explosion f. ~ **ive** /-sɪv/ a explosiv □n Sprengstoff m

exponent /ɪk'spəʊnənt/ n Vertreter m

export[1] /'ekspɔːt/ n Export m, Ausfuhr f

export[2] /ɪk'spɔːt/ vt exportieren, ausführen. ~ **er** n Exporteur m

expos|e /ɪk'spəʊz/ vt freilegen; (to danger) aussetzen (**to** dat); (reveal) aufdecken; (Phot) belichten. ~ **ure** /-ʒə(r)/ n Aussetzung f; (Med) Unterkühlung f; (Phot) Belichtung f; **24** ~ **ures** 24 Aufnahmen

expound /ɪk'spaʊnd/ vt erläutern

express /ɪk'spres/ a ausdrücklich; ⟨purpose⟩ fest □adv ⟨send⟩ per Eilpost □n (train) Schnellzug m □vt ausdrücken; ~ **oneself** sich ausdrücken. ~ **ion** /-ʃn/ n Ausdruck m. ~ **ive** /-ɪv/ a ausdrucksvoll. ~ **ly** adv ausdrücklich

expulsion /ɪk'spʌlʃn/ n Ausweisung f; (Sch) Verweisung f von der Schule

expurgate /'ekspəgeɪt/ vt zensieren

exquisite /ek'skwɪzɪt/ a erlesen

ex-'serviceman n Veteran m

extempore /ɪk'stempərɪ/ adv ⟨speak⟩ aus dem Stegreif

extend /ɪk'stend/ vt verlängern; (stretch out) ausstrecken; (enlarge) vergrößern □vi sich ausdehnen; ⟨table:⟩ sich ausziehen lassen

extension /ɪk'stenʃn/ n Verlängerung f; (to house) Anbau m; (Teleph) Nebenanschluß m; ~ **7** Apparat 7

extensive /ɪk'stensɪv/ a weit; (fig) umfassend. ~ **ly** adv viel

extent /ɪk'stent/ n Ausdehnung f; (scope) Ausmaß nt, Umfang m; **to a certain** ~ in gewissem Maße

extenuating /ɪk'stenjʊeɪtɪŋ/ a mildernd

exterior /ɪk'stɪərɪə(r)/ a äußere(r,s) □n **the** ~ das Äußere

exterminat|e /ɪk'stɜːmɪneɪt/ vt ausrotten. ~ **ion** /-'neɪʃn/ n Ausrottung f

external /ɪk'stɜːnl/ a äußere(r,s); **for** ~ **use only** (Med) nur äußerlich. ~ **ly** adv äußerlich

extinct /ɪk'stɪŋkt/ a ausgestorben; ⟨volcano⟩ erloschen. ~ **ion** /-ɪŋkʃn/ n Aussterben nt

extinguish /ɪkˈstɪŋgwɪʃ/ *vt* löschen. **~er** *n* Feuerlöscher *m*

extol /ɪkˈstəʊl/ *vt* (*pt/pp* extolled) preisen

extort /ɪkˈstɔːt/ *vt* erpressen. **~ion** /-ɔːʃn/ *n* Erpressung *f*

extortionate /ɪkˈstɔːʃənət/ *a* übermäßig hoch

extra /ˈekstrə/ *a* zusätzlich □ *adv* extra; (*especially*) besonders; **~ strong** extrastark □ *n* (*Theat*) Statist(in) *m(f)*; **~s** *pl* Nebenkosten *pl*; (*Auto*) Extras *pl*

extract[1] /ˈekstrækt/ *n* Auszug *m*; (*Culin*) Extrakt *m*

extract[2] /ɪkˈstrækt/ *vt* herausziehen; ziehen (*tooth*); (*fig*) erzwingen. **~or** [**fan**] *n* Entlüfter *m*

extradit|e /ˈekstrədaɪt/ *vt* (*Jur*) ausliefern. **~ion** /-ˈdɪʃn/ *n* (*Jur*) Auslieferung *f*

extra'marital *a* außerehelich

extraordinary /ɪkˈstrɔːdɪnərɪ/ *a*, **-ily** *adv* außerordentlich; (*strange*) seltsam

extravagan|ce /ɪkˈstrævəgəns/ *n* Verschwendung *f*; an **~ce** ein Luxus *m*. **~t** *a* verschwenderisch; (*exaggerated*) extravagant

extrem|e /ɪkˈstriːm/ *a* äußerste(r,s); (*fig*) extrem □ *n* Extrem *nt*; **in the ~e** im höchsten Grade. **~ely** *adv* äußerst. **~ist** *n* Extremist *m*

extremity /ɪkˈstremətɪ/ *n* (*distress*) Not *f*; **the ~ies** *pl* die Extremitäten *pl*

extricate /ˈekstrɪkeɪt/ *vt* befreien

extrovert /ˈekstrəvɜːt/ *n* extravertierter Mensch *m*

exuberant /ɪgˈzjuːbərənt/ *a* überglücklich

exude /ɪgˈzjuːd/ *vt* absondern; (*fig*) ausstrahlen

exult /ɪgˈzʌlt/ *vi* frohlocken

eye /aɪ/ *n* Auge *nt*; (*of needle*) Öhr *nt*; (*for hook*) Öse *f*; **keep an ~ on** aufpassen auf (+ *acc*); **see ~ to ~** einer Meinung sein □ *vt* (*pt/pp* eyed, *pres p* ey[e]ing) ansehen

eye: **~ball** *n* Augapfel *m*. **~brow** *n* Augenbraue *f*. **~lash** *n* Wimper *f*. **~let** /-lɪt/ *n* Öse *f*. **~lid** *n* Augenlid *nt*. **~-shadow** *n* Lidschatten *m*. **~sight** *n* Sehkraft *f*. **~sore** *n* (*fam*) Schandfleck *m*. **~-tooth** *n* Eckzahn *m*. **~-witness** *n* Augenzeuge *m*

F

fable /ˈfeɪbl/ *n* Fabel *f*

fabric /ˈfæbrɪk/ *n* Stoff *m*; (*fig*) Gefüge *nt*

fabrication /fæbrɪˈkeɪʃn/ *n* Erfindung *f*

fabulous /ˈfæbjʊləs/ *a* (*fam*) phantastisch

façade /fəˈsɑːd/ *n* Fassade *f*

face /feɪs/ *n* Gesicht *nt*; (*grimace*) Grimasse *f*; (*surface*) Fläche *f*; (*of clock*) Zifferblatt *nt*; **pull ~s** Gesichter schneiden; **in the ~ of** angesichts (+ *gen*); **on the ~ of it** allem Anschein nach □ *vt/i* gegenüberstehen (+ *dat*); (*house:*) nach Norden liegen; **~ me!** sieh mich an! **~ the fact that** sich damit abfinden, daß; **~ up to** s.o. jdm die Stirn bieten

face: **~-flannel** *n* Waschlappen *m*. **~less** *a* anonym. **~-lift** *n* Gesichtsstraffung *f*

facet /ˈfæsɪt/ *n* Facette *f*; (*fig*) Aspekt *m*

facetious /fəˈsiːʃəs/ *a*, **-ly** *adv* spöttisch

'face value *n* Nennwert *m*

facial /ˈfeɪʃl/ *a* Gesichts-

facile /ˈfæsaɪl/ *a* oberflächlich

facilitate /fəˈsɪlɪteɪt/ *vt* erleichtern

facility /fəˈsɪlətɪ/ *n* Leichtigkeit *f*; (*skill*) Gewandtheit *f*; **~ies** *pl* Einrichtungen *pl*

facing /ˈfeɪsɪŋ/ *n* Besatz *m*

facsimile /fækˈsɪməlɪ/ *n* Faksimile *nt*

fact /fækt/ *n* Tatsache *f*; **in ~** tatsächlich; (*actually*) eigentlich

faction /ˈfækʃn/ *n* Gruppe *f*

factor /'fæktə(r)/ n Faktor m

factory /'fæktərɪ/ n Fabrik f

factual /'fæktʃʊəl/ a, **-ly** adv sachlich

faculty /'fækltɪ/ n Fähigkeit f; ⟨Univ⟩ Fakultät f

fad /fæd/ n Fimmel m

fade /feɪd/ vi verblassen; ⟨material:⟩ verbleichen; ⟨sound:⟩ abklingen; ⟨flower:⟩ verwelken. **~ in/out** vt ⟨Radio, TV⟩ ein-/ausblenden

fag /fæg/ n ⟨chore⟩ Plage f; ⟨fam: cigarette⟩ Zigarette f; ⟨Amer sl:⟩ Homosexuelle(r) m

fagged /fægd/ a **~ out** ⟨fam⟩ völlig erledigt

Fahrenheit /'færənhaɪt/ a Fahrenheit

fail /feɪl/ n **without ~** unbedingt □ vi ⟨attempt:⟩ scheitern; ⟨grow weak⟩ nachlassen; ⟨break down⟩ versagen; ⟨in exam⟩ durchfallen; **~ to do sth** etw nicht tun; **he ~ed to break the record** es gelang ihm nicht, den Rekord zu brechen □ vt nicht bestehen ⟨exam⟩; durchfallen lassen ⟨candidate⟩; ⟨disappoint⟩ enttäuschen; **words ~ me** ich weiß nicht, was ich sagen soll

failing /'feɪlɪŋ/ n Fehler m □ prep **~ that** andernfalls

failure /'feɪljə(r)/ n Mißerfolg m; ⟨breakdown⟩ Versagen nt; ⟨person⟩ Versager m

faint /feɪnt/ a ⟨-er, -est⟩, **-ly** adv schwach; **I feel ~** mir ist schwach □ n Ohnmacht f □ vi ohnmächtig werden

faint: **~-'hearted** a zaghaft. **~ness** n Schwäche f

fair[1] /feə(r)/ n Jahrmarkt m; ⟨Comm⟩ Messe f

fair[2] a ⟨-er, -est⟩ ⟨hair⟩ blond; ⟨skin⟩ hell; ⟨weather⟩ heiter; ⟨just⟩ gerecht, fair; ⟨quite good⟩ ziemlich gut; ⟨Sch⟩ genügend; **a ~ amount** ziemlich viel □ adv **play ~** fair sein. **~ly** adv gerecht; ⟨rather⟩ ziemlich. **~ness** n

Blondheit f; Helle f; Gerechtigkeit f; ⟨Sport⟩ Fairneß f

fairy /'feərɪ/ n Elfe f; **good/wicked ~** gute/böse Fee f. **~ story**, **~-tale** n Märchen nt

faith /feɪθ/ n Glaube m; ⟨trust⟩ Vertrauen nt (in zu); **in good ~** in gutem Glauben

faithful /'feɪθfl/ a, **-ly** adv treu; ⟨exact⟩ genau; **Yours ~ly** Hochachtungsvoll. **~ness** n Treue f; Genauigkeit f

'faith-healer n Gesundbeter(in) m(f)

fake /feɪk/ a falsch □ n Fälschung f; ⟨person⟩ Schwindler m □ vt fälschen; ⟨pretend⟩ vortäuschen

falcon /'fɔːlkən/ n Falke m

fall /fɔːl/ n Fall m; ⟨heavy⟩ Sturz m; ⟨in prices⟩ Fallen nt; ⟨Amer: autumn⟩ Herbst m; **have a ~** fallen □ vi ⟨pt fell, pp fallen⟩ fallen; ⟨heavily⟩ stürzen; ⟨night:⟩ anbrechen; **~ in love** sich verlieben; **~ back on** zurückgreifen auf (+ acc); **~ for s.o.** ⟨fam⟩ sich in jdn verlieben; **~ for sth** ⟨fam⟩ auf etw ⟨acc⟩ hereinfallen. **~ about** vi ⟨with laughter⟩ sich vor Lachen⟩ kringeln. **~ down** vi umfallen; ⟨thing:⟩ herunterfallen; ⟨building:⟩ einstürzen. **~ in** vi hineinfallen; ⟨collapse⟩ einfallen; ⟨Mil⟩ antreten; **~ in with** sich anschließen (+ dat). **~ off** vi herunterfallen; ⟨diminish⟩ abnehmen. **~ out** vi herausfallen; ⟨hair:⟩ ausfallen; ⟨quarrel⟩ sich überwerfen. **~ over** vi hinfallen. **~ through** vi durchfallen; ⟨plan:⟩ ins Wasser fallen

fallacy /'fæləsɪ/ n Irrtum m

fallible /'fæləbl/ a fehlbar

'fall-out n [radioaktiver] Niederschlag m

fallow /'fæləʊ/ a **lie ~** brachliegen

false /fɔːls/ a falsch; ⟨artificial⟩ künstlich; **~ start** ⟨Sport⟩ Fehlstart m. **~hood** n Unwahrheit f. **~ly** adv falsch. **~ness** n Falschheit f

false 'teeth *npl* [künstliches] Gebiß *nt*

falsify /'fɔːlsɪfaɪ/ *vt* (*pt/pp* **-ied**) fälschen; (*misrepresent*) verfälschen

falter /'fɔːltə(r)/ *vi* zögern; (*stumble*) straucheln

fame /feɪm/ *n* Ruhm *m*. **~d** *a* berühmt

familiar /fə'mɪljə(r)/ *a* vertraut; (*known*) bekannt; **too ~** familiär. **~ity** /-lɪ'ærətɪ/ *n* Vertrautheit *f*. **~ize** *vt* vertraut machen (**with** mit)

family /'fæməlɪ/ *n* Familie *f*

family: **~ al'lowance** *n* Kindergeld *nt*. **~ 'doctor** *n* Hausarzt *m*. **~ 'life** *n* Familienleben *nt*. **~ 'planning** *n* Familienplanung *f*. **~ 'tree** *n* Stammbaum *m*

famine /'fæmɪn/ *n* Hungersnot *f*

famished /'fæmɪʃt/ *a* sehr hungrig

famous /'feɪməs/ *a* berühmt

fan[1] /fæn/ *n* Fächer *m*; (*Techn*) Ventilator *m* □*v* (*pt/pp* **fanned**) □*vt* fächeln; **~ oneself** sich fächeln □*vi* **~ out** sich fächerförmig ausbreiten

fan[2] *n* (*admirer*) Fan *m*

fanatic /fə'nætɪk/ *n* Fanatiker *m*. **~al** *a*, **-ly** *adv* fanatisch. **~ism** /-sɪzm/ *n* Fanatismus *m*

'fan belt *n* Keilriemen *m*

fanciful /'fænsɪfl/ *a* phantastisch; (*imaginative*) phantasiereich

fancy /'fænsɪ/ *n* Phantasie *f*; **have a ~ to** Lust haben, zu; **I have taken a real ~ to** ihm er hat es mir angetan □*a* ausgefallen; **~ cakes and biscuits** Feingebäck *nt* □*vt* (*believe*) meinen; (*imagine*) sich [*dat*] einbilden; (*fam: want*) Lust haben auf (+ *acc*); **~ that!** stell dir vor! (*really*) tatsächlich! **~ 'dress** *n* Kostüm *nt*

fanfare /'fænfeə(r)/ *n* Fanfare *f*

fang /fæŋ/ *n* Fangzahn *m*; (*of snake*) Giftzahn *m*

fan: **~ heater** *n* Heizlüfter *m*. **~light** *n* Oberlicht *nt*

fantas|ize /'fæntəsaɪz/ *vi* phantasieren. **~tic** /-'tæstɪk/ *a* phantastisch. **~y** *n* Phantasie *f*; (*Mus*) Fantasie *f*

far /fɑː(r)/ *adv* weit; (*much*) viel; **by ~** am besten; **~ away** weit weg; **as ~ as I know** soviel ich weiß; **as ~ as the church** bis zur Kirche □*a* **at the ~ end** am anderen Ende; **the F~ East** der Ferne Osten

farce /fɑːs/ *n* Farce *f*. **~ical** *a* lächerlich

fare /feə(r)/ *n* Fahrpreis *m*; (*money*) Fahrgeld *nt*; (*food*) Kost *f*; **air ~** Flugpreis *m*. **~-dodger** /-dɒdʒə(r)/ *n* Schwarzfahrer *m*

farewell /feə'wel/ *int* (*liter*) lebe wohl! □*n* Lebewohl *nt*; **~ dinner** Abschiedsessen *nt*

far-'fetched *a* weit hergeholt; **be ~** an den Haaren herbeigezogen sein

farm /fɑːm/ *n* Bauernhof *m* □*vi* Landwirtschaft betreiben □*vt* bewirtschaften (*land*). **~er** *n* Landwirt *m*

farm: **~house** *n* Bauernhaus *nt*. **~ing** *n* Landwirtschaft *f*. **~yard** *n* Hof *m*

far: **~-'reaching** *a* weitreichend. **~-'sighted** *a* (*fig*) weitsichtig; (*Amer: long-sighted*) weitsichtig

fart /fɑːt/ *n* (*vulg*) Furz *m* □*vi* (*vulg*) furzen

farther /'fɑːðə(r)/ *adv* weiter; **~ off** weiter entfernt □*a* **at the ~ end** am anderen Ende

fascinate /'fæsɪneɪt/ *vt* faszinieren. **~ing** *a* faszinierend. **~ion** /-'neɪʃn/ *n* Faszination *f*

fascism /'fæʃɪzm/ *n* Faschismus *m*. **~t** *n* Faschist *m* □*a* faschistisch

fashion /'fæʃn/ *n* Mode *f*; (*manner*) Art *f* □*vt* machen; (*mould*) formen. **~able** /-əbl/ *a*, **-bly** *adv* modisch; **be ~able** Mode sein

fast[1] /fɑːst/ *a* & *adv* (**-er**, **-est**) schnell; (*firm*) fest; ⟨*colour*⟩

waschecht; be ~ ⟨clock:⟩ vorgehen; be ~ asleep fest schlafen

fast² n Fasten nt □ vi fasten

'fastback n (Auto) Fließheck nt

fasten /'fɑːsn/ vt zumachen; ⟨fix⟩ befestigen (**to** an + dat); ~ **one's seatbelt** sich anschnallen. ~**er** n, ~**ing** n Verschluß m

fastidious /fə'stɪdɪəs/ a wählerisch; ⟨particular⟩ penibel

fat /fæt/ a (**fatter, fattest**) dick; ⟨meat⟩ fett □ n Fett nt

fatal /'feɪtl/ a tödlich; ⟨error⟩ verhängnisvoll. ~**ism** /-təlɪzm/ n Fatalismus m. ~**ist** /-təlɪst/ n Fatalist m. ~**ity** /fə'tælətɪ/ n Todesopfer nt. ~**ly** adv tödlich

fate /feɪt/ n Schicksal nt. ~**ful** a verhängnisvoll

'fat-head n (fam) Dummkopf m

father /'fɑːðə(r)/ n Vater m; **F~ Christmas** der Weihnachtsmann □ vt zeugen

father: ~**hood** n Vaterschaft f. ~**in-law** n (pl ~**s-in-law**) Schwiegervater m. ~**ly** a väterlich

fathom /'fæðəm/ n (Naut) Faden m □ vt verstehen; ~ **out** ergründen

fatigue /fə'tiːg/ n Ermüdung f □ vt ermüden

fatten /'fætn/ vt mästen ⟨animal⟩. ~**ing** a cream is ~**ing** Sahne macht dick

fatty /'fætɪ/ a fett; ⟨foods⟩ fetthaltig

fatuous /'fætjʊəs/ a, -**ly** adv albern

faucet /'fɔːsɪt/ n (Amer) Wasserhahn m

fault /fɔːlt/ n Fehler m; (Techn) Defekt m; (Geol) Verwerfung f; **at ~** im Unrecht; **find ~ with** etwas auszusetzen haben an (+ dat); **it's your ~** du bist schuld □ vt etwas auszusetzen haben an (+ dat). ~**less** a, -**ly** adv fehlerfrei

faulty /'fɔːltɪ/ a fehlerhaft

fauna /'fɔːnə/ n Fauna f

favour /'feɪvə(r)/ n Gunst f; **I am in ~** ich bin dafür; **do s.o. a ~** jdm einen Gefallen tun □ vt begünstigen; (prefer) bevorzugen. ~**able** /-əbl/ a, -**bly** adv günstig; ⟨reply⟩ positiv

favourit|e /'feɪvərɪt/ a Lieblings- □ n Liebling m; (Sport) Favorit(in) m(f). ~**ism** n Bevorzugung f

fawn¹ /fɔːn/ a rehbraun □ n Hirschkalb nt

fawn² vi sich einschmeicheln (**on** bei)

fax /fæks/ vt faxen (s.o. jdm). ~ **machine** n Faxgerät nt

fear /fɪə(r)/ n Furcht f, Angst f (**of** vor + dat); **no ~!** (fam) keine Angst! □ vt/i fürchten

fear|ful /'fɪəfl/ a besorgt; (awful) furchtbar. ~**less** a, -**ly** adv furchtlos. ~**some** /-səm/ a furchterregend

feasib|ility /fiːzə'bɪlətɪ/ n Durchführbarkeit f. ~**ible** a durchführbar; (possible) möglich

feast /fiːst/ n Festmahl nt; (Relig) Fest nt □ vi ~ [**on**] schmausen

feat /fiːt/ n Leistung f

feather /'feðə(r)/ n Feder f

feature /'fiːtʃə(r)/ n Gesichtszug m; (quality) Merkmal nt; (Journ) Feature nt □ vt darstellen; ⟨film:⟩ in der Hauptrolle zeigen. ~ **film** n Hauptfilm m

February /'febrʊərɪ/ n Februar m

feckless /'feklɪs/ a verantwortungslos

fed /fed/ see **feed** □ a **be ~ up** (fam) die Nase voll haben (**with** von)

federal /'fedərəl/ a Bundes-

federation /fedə'reɪʃn/ n Föderation f

fee /fiː/ n Gebühr f; (professional) Honorar nt

feeble /'fiːbl/ a (-**r**, -**st**), -**bly** adv schwach

feed /fiːd/ n Futter nt; (for baby) Essen nt □ v (pt/pp **fed**) □ vt füttern; (support) ernähren; (into

machine) eingeben; speisen ⟨*computer*⟩ □*vi* sich ernähren (**on** von)
'feedback *n* Feedback *nt*

feel /fiːl/ *v* (*pt/pp* **felt**) □*vt* fühlen; (*experience*) empfinden; (*think*) meinen □*vi* sich fühlen; ~ **soft/ hard** sich weich/hart anfühlen; **I** ~ **hot/ill** mir ist heiß/schlecht; **I don't** ~ **like it** ich habe keine Lust dazu. ~**er** *n* Fühler *m*. ~**ing** *n* Gefühl *nt*; **no hard** ~**ings** nichts für ungut

feet /fiːt/ *see* **foot**

feign /feɪn/ *vt* vortäuschen

feint /feɪnt/ *n* Finte *f*

feline /'fiːlaɪn/ *a* Katzen-; (*catlike*) katzenartig

fell[1] /fel/ *vt* fällen

fell[2] *see* **fall**

fellow /'feləʊ/ *n* (*of society*) Mitglied *nt*; (*fam: man*) Kerl *m*

fellow: ~'**countryman** *n* Landsmann *m*. ~ **men** *pl* Mitmenschen *pl*. ~**ship** *n* Kameradschaft *f*; (*group*) Gesellschaft *f*

felony /'feləni/ *n* Verbrechen *nt*

felt[1] /felt/ *see* **feel**

felt[2] *n* Filz *m*. ~ **[-tipped] 'pen** *n* Filzstift *m*

female /'fiːmeɪl/ *a* weiblich □*nt* Weibchen *nt*; (*pej: woman*) Weib *nt*

feminine /'feminin/ *a* weiblich □*n* (*Gram*) Femininum *nt*. ~**inity** /-'nɪnəti/ *n* Weiblichkeit *f*. ~**ist** *a* feministisch □*n* Feminist(in) *m(f)*

fence /fens/ *n* Zaun *m*; (*fam: person*) Hehler *m* □*vi* (*Sport*) fechten □*vt* ~ **e in** einzäunen. ~**er** *n* Fechter *m*. ~**ing** *n* Zaun *m*; (*Sport*) Fechten *nt*

fend /fend/ *vi* ~ **for oneself** sich allein durchschlagen. ~ **off** *vt* abwehren

fender /'fendə(r)/ *n* Kaminvorsetzer *m*; (*Naut*) Fender *m*; (*Amer: wing*) Kotflügel *m*

fennel /'fenl/ *n* Fenchel *m*

ferment[1] /'fɜːment/ *n* Erregung *f*

ferment[2] /fə'ment/ *vi* gären □*vt* gären lassen. ~**ation** /fɜːmen-'teɪʃn/ *n* Gärung *f*

ferocious /fə'rəʊʃəs/ *a* wild. ~**ity** /-'rɒsəti/ *n* Wildheit *f*

ferret /'ferɪt/ *n* Frettchen *nt*

ferry /'feri/ *n* Fähre *f* □*vt* ~ **[across]** übersetzen

fertile /'fɜːtaɪl/ *a* fruchtbar. ~**ity** /fə'tɪləti/ *n* Fruchtbarkeit *f*

fertilize /'fɜːtəlaɪz/ *vt* befruchten; düngen ⟨*land*⟩. ~**r** *n* Dünger *m*

fervent /'fɜːvənt/ *a* leidenschaftlich

fervour /'fɜːvə(r)/ *n* Leidenschaft *f*

fester /'festə(r)/ *vi* eitern

festival /'festɪvl/ *n* Fest *nt*; (*Mus, Theat*) Festspiele *pl*

festive /'festɪv/ *a* festlich; ~**e season** Festzeit *f*. ~**ities** /fe'stɪv-ətɪz/ *npl* Feierlichkeiten *pl*

festoon /fe'stuːn/ *vt* behängen (**with** mit)

fetch /fetʃ/ *vt* holen; (*collect*) abholen; (*be sold for*) einbringen

fetching /'fetʃɪŋ/ *a* anziehend

fête /feɪt/ *n* Fest *nt* □*vt* feiern

fetish /'fetɪʃ/ *n* Fetisch *m*

fetter /'fetə(r)/ *vt* fesseln

fettle /'fetl/ *n* **in fine** ~ **in bester Form**

feud /fjuːd/ *n* Fehde *f*

feudal /'fjuːdl/ *a* Feudal-

fever /'fiːvə(r)/ *n* Fieber *nt*. ~**ish** *a* fiebrig; (*fig*) fieberhaft

few /fjuː/ *a* (**-er, -est**) wenige; **every** ~ **days** alle paar Tage □*n* **a** ~ ein paar; **quite a** ~ ziemlich viele

fiancé /fɪ'ɒnseɪ/ *n* Verlobte(r) *m*.
fiancée *n* Verlobte *f*

fiasco /fɪ'æskəʊ/ *n* Fiasko *nt*

fib /fɪb/ *n* kleine Lüge; **tell a** ~ schwindeln

fibre /'faɪbə(r)/ *n* Faser *f*

fickle /'fɪkl/ *a* unbeständig

fiction /'fɪkʃn/ *n* Erfindung *f*; **[works of]** ~ Erzählungsliteratur *f*. ~**al** *a* erfunden

fictitious /fɪk'tɪʃəs/ a [frei] erfunden

fiddle /'fɪdl/ n (fam) Geige f; (cheating) Schwindel m □vi herumspielen (with mit) □vt (fam) frisieren ⟨accounts⟩; (arrange) arrangieren

fiddly /'fɪdlɪ/ a knifflig

fidelity /fɪ'delətɪ/ n Treue f

fidget /'fɪdʒɪt/ vi zappeln. ~y a zappelig

field /fiːld/ n Feld nt; (meadow) Wiese f; (subject) Gebiet nt

field: ~ **events** npl Sprung- und Wurfdisziplinen pl. ~**glasses** npl Feldstecher m. F ~ **'Marshal** n Feldmarschall m. ~**work** n Feldforschung f

fiend /fiːnd/ n Teufel m. ~**ish** a teuflisch

fierce /fɪəs/ a (-r, -st), **-ly** adv wild; (fig) heftig. ~**ness** n Wildheit f; (fig) Heftigkeit f

fiery /'faɪərɪ/ a (-ier, -iest) feurig

fifteen /fɪf'tiːn/ a u fünfzehn □n Fünfzehn f. ~**th** a fünfzehnte(r,s)

fifth /fɪfθ/ a fünfte(r,s)

fiftieth /'fɪftɪɪθ/ a fünfzigste(r,s)

fifty /'fɪftɪ/ a u fünfzig

fig /fɪg/ n Feige f

fight /faɪt/ n Kampf m; (brawl) Schlägerei f; (between children, dogs) Rauferei f □v (pt/pp **fought**) □vt bekämpfen □vi kämpfen; (brawl) sich schlagen; ⟨children, dogs:⟩ sich raufen. ~**er** n Kämpfer m; (Aviat) Jagdflugzeug nt. ~**ing** n Kampf m

figment /'fɪgmənt/ n ~ **of the imagination** Hirngespinst nt

figurative /'fɪgjərətɪv/ a, **-ly** adv bildlich, übertragen

figure /'fɪgə(r)/ n (digit) Ziffer f; (number) Zahl f; (sum) Summe f; (carving, sculpture, woman's) Figur f; (form) Gestalt f; (illustration) Abbildung f; ~ **of speech**

Redefigur f; **good at** ~ **s** gut im Rechnen □vi (appear) erscheinen □vt (Amer: think) glauben. ~ **out** vt ausrechnen

figure: ~**head** n Galionsfigur f; (fig) Repräsentationsfigur f. ~ **skating** n Eiskunstlauf m

filament /'fɪləmənt/ n Faden m; (Electr) Glühfaden m

filch /fɪltʃ/ vt (fam) klauen

file¹ /faɪl/ n Akte f; (for documents) [Akten]ordner m □vt ablegen ⟨documents⟩; (Jur) einreichen

file² n (line) Reihe f; **in single** ~ im Gänsemarsch

file³ n (Techn) Feile f □vt feilen

filigree /'fɪlɪgriː/ n Filigran nt

filings /'faɪlɪŋz/ npl Feilspäne pl

fill /fɪl/ n **eat one's** ~ sich satt essen □vt füllen; plombieren ⟨tooth⟩ □vi sich füllen. ~ **in** vt auffüllen; ausfüllen ⟨form⟩. ~ **out** vt ausfüllen ⟨form⟩. ~ **up** vi sich füllen □vt vollfüllen; (Auto) volltanken; ausfüllen ⟨form⟩

fillet /'fɪlɪt/ n Filet nt □vt (pt/pp **filleted**) entgräten

filling /'fɪlɪŋ/ n Füllung f; (of tooth) Plombe f. ~ **station** n Tankstelle f

filly /'fɪlɪ/ n junge Stute f

film /fɪlm/ n Film m; (Culin) [cling] ~ Klarsichtfolie f □vt/i filmen; verfilmen ⟨book⟩. ~ **star** n Filmstar m

filter /'fɪltə(r)/ n Filter m □vt filtern. ~ **through** vi durchsickern. ~ **tip** n Filter m; (cigarette) Filterzigarette f

filth /fɪlθ/ n Dreck m. ~**y** a (-ier, -iest) dreckig

fin /fɪn/ n Flosse f

final /'faɪnl/ a letzte(r,s); (conclusive) endgültig; ~ **result** Endresultat nt □n (Sport) Finale nt, Endspiel nt; ~**s** pl (Univ) Abschlußprüfung f

finale /fɪ'nɑːlɪ/ n Finale nt

final|ist /'faɪnəlɪst/ n Finalist(in) m(f). **~ity** /-'nælətɪ/ n Endgültig-keit f

final|ize /'faɪnəlaɪz/ vt endgültig festlegen. **~ly** adv schließlich

finance /faɪˈnæns/ n Finanz f □vt finanzieren

financial /faɪˈnænʃl/ a, **-ly** adv finanziell

finch /fɪntʃ/ n Fink m

find /faɪnd/ n Fund m □vt (pt/pp found) finden; (establish) feststellen; **go and ~** holen; **try to ~** suchen; **~ guilty** (Jur) schuldig sprechen. **~ out** vt herausfinden; (learn) erfahren □vi (enquire) sich erkundigen

findings /'faɪndɪŋz/ npl Ergebnisse pl

fine¹ /faɪn/ n Geldstrafe f □vt zu einer Geldstrafe verurteilen

fine² a (-r, -st), **-ly** adv fein; (weather) schön; **he's ~** es geht ihm gut □adv gut; **cut it ~** (fam) sich (dat) wenig Zeit lassen. **~ arts** npl schöne Künste pl

finery /'faɪnərɪ/ n Putz m, Staat m

finesse /fɪˈnes/ n Gewandtheit f

finger /'fɪŋgə(r)/ n Finger m □vt anfassen

finger|mark n Fingerabdruck m. **~nail** n Fingernagel m. **~print** n Fingerabdruck m. **~tip** n Fingerspitze f; **have sth at one's ~tips** etw im kleinen Finger haben

finicky /'fɪnɪkɪ/ a knifflig; (choosy) wählerisch

finish /'fɪnɪʃ/ n Schluß m; Finish nt; (line) Ziel nt; (of product) Ausführung f □vt beenden; (use up) aufbrauchen; **~ one's drink** austrinken; **~ reading** zu Ende lesen □vi fertig werden; (performance:) zu Ende sein; (runner:) durchs Ziel gehen

finite /'faɪnaɪt/ a begrenzt

Finland /'fɪnlənd/ n Finnland nt

Finn /fɪn/ n Finne m/ Finnin f. **~ish** a finnisch

fiord /fjɔːd/ n Fjord m

fir /fɜː(r)/ n Tanne f

fire /faɪə(r)/ n Feuer nt; (forest, house) Brand m; **be on ~** brennen; **catch ~** Feuer fangen; **set ~ to** anzünden; (arsonist:) in Brand stecken; **under ~** unter Beschuß □vt brennen (pottery); abfeuern (shot); schießen mit (gun); (fam: dismiss) feuern □vi schießen (**at** auf + acc); (engine:) anspringen

fire: ~ alarm n Feueralarm m; (apparatus) Feuermelder m. **~arm** n Schußwaffe f. **~brigade** n Feuerwehr f. **~engine** n Löschfahrzeug nt. **~escape** n Feuertreppe f. **~extinguisher** n Feuerlöscher m. **~man** n Feuerwehrmann m. **~place** n Kamin m. **~side** n by or at the **~side** am Kamin. **~station** n Feuerwache f. **~wood** n Brennholz nt. **~work** n Feuerwerkskörper m; **~works** pl (display) Feuerwerk nt

'firing squad n Erschießungskommando nt

firm¹ /fɜːm/ n Firma f

firm² a (-er, -est), **-ly** adv fest; (resolute) entschlossen; (strict) streng

first /fɜːst/ a & n erste(r,s); **at ~** zuerst; **who's ~?** wer ist der erste? **at ~ sight** auf den ersten Blick; **for the ~ time** zum ersten Mal; **from the ~** von Anfang an. □adv zuerst; (firstly) erstens

first: ~ aid n Erste Hilfe. **~-'aid kit** n Verbandkasten m. **~-class** a erstklassig; (Rail) erster Klasse □/-'-/ adv (travel) erster Klasse. **~ e'dition** n Erstausgabe f. **'floor** n erster Stock; (Amer: ground floor) Erdgeschoß nt. **~ly** adv erstens. **~ name** n Vorname m. **~-rate** a erstklassig

fish /fɪʃ/ n Fisch m □vt/i fischen; (with rod) angeln. **~ out** vt herausfischen

fish: ~ **bone** n Gräte f. ~ **erman** n
Fischer m. ~ **farm** n Fischzucht
f. ~ '**finger** n Fischstäbchen nt

fishing /'fɪʃɪŋ/ n Fischerei f. ~
boat n Fischerboot nt. ~ **-rod** n
Angel[rute] f

fish: ~ **monger** /-mʌŋgə(r)/ n
Fischhändler m. ~ **-slice** n Fisch-
heber m. ~ **y** a Fisch-; (fam: suspicious) verdächtig

fission /'fɪʃn/ n (Phys) Spaltung f

fist /fɪst/ n Faust f

fit[1] /fɪt/ n (attack) Anfall m

fit[2] a (fitter, fittest) (suitable)
geeignet; (healthy) gesund;
(Sport) fit; ~ **to eat** eßbar; **keep**
~ **sich fit halten; see** ~ **es für**
angebracht halten (to zu)

fit[3] n (of clothes) Sitz m; **be a good**
~ **gut passen** □ v (pt/pp fitted)
□ vi (be the right size) passen □ vt
anbringen (to an + dat); (install)
einbauen; <clothes:> passen (+
dat); ~ **with** versehen mit. ~ **in**
vi hineinpassen; (adapt) sich einfügen (**with** in + acc) □ vt (accommodate) unterbringen

fit|**ful** /'fɪtfl/ a, **-ly** adv <sleep>
unruhig. ~ **ment** n Einrich-
tungsgegenstand m; (attachment) Zusatzgerät nt. ~ **ness** n
Eignung f; [physical] ~ **ness** Gesundheit f; (Sport) Fitneß f. ~ **ted**
a eingebaut; <garment> tailliert

fitted: ~ **'carpet** n Teppichboden
m. ~ **'cupboard** n Einbau-
schrank m. ~ **'kitchen** n Ein-
bauküche f. ~ **'sheet** n Spannla-
ken nt

fitter /'fɪtə(r)/ n Monteur m

fitting /'fɪtɪŋ/ a passend □ n (of
clothes) Anprobe f; (of shoes)
Weite f; (Techn) Zubehörteil nt;
~ **s** pl Zubehör nt. ~ **room** n
Anprobekabine f

five /faɪv/ a fünf □ n Fünf f. ~ **r** n
Fünfpfundschein m

fix /fɪks/ n (sl: drugs) Fix m; **be in**
a ~ (fam) in der Klemme sitzen
□ vt befestigen (**to** an + dat);

(arrange) festlegen; (repair) reparieren; (Phot) fixieren; ~ **a meal**
(Amer) Essen machen

fixation /fɪk'seɪʃn/ n Fixierung f

fixed /'fɪkst/ a fest

fixture /'fɪkstʃə(r)/ n (Sport) Veranstaltung f; ~ **s and fittings** zu
einer Wohnung gehörende Einrichtungen pl

fizz /fɪz/ vi sprudeln

fizzle /'fɪzl/ vi ~ **out** verpuffen

fizzy /'fɪzɪ/ a sprudelnd. ~ **drink**
n Brauselimonade] f

flabbergasted /'flæbəgɑːstɪd/ a
be ~ platt sein (fam)

flabby /'flæbɪ/ a schlaff

flag[1] /flæg/ n Fahne f; (Naut)
Flagge f □ vt (pt/pp flagged) ~
down anhalten <taxi>

flag[2] vi (pt/pp flagged) ermüden

flagon /'flægən/ n Krug m

'flag-pole n Fahnenstange f

flagrant /'fleɪgrənt/ a flagrant

'flagstone n [Pflaster]platte f

flair /fleə(r)/ n Begabung f

flake /fleɪk/ n Flocke f □ vi ~ [off]
abblättern

flaky /'fleɪkɪ/ a blättrig. ~ **pastry**
n Blätterteig m

flamboyant /flæm'bɔɪənt/ a extravagant

flame /fleɪm/ n Flamme f

flammable /'flæməbl/ a feuergefährlich

flan /flæn/ n [**fruit**] ~ Obsttorte f

flank /flæŋk/ n Flanke f □ vt flan-
kieren

flannel /'flænl/ n Flanell m; (for
washing) Waschlappen m

flannelette /flænə'let/ n (Tex) Biber m

flap /flæp/ n Klappe f; **in a** ~
(fam) aufgeregt □ v (pt/pp flap-
ped) vi flattern; (fam) sich aufregen □ vt ~ **its wings** mit den
Flügeln schlagen

flare /fleə(r)/ n Leuchtsignal nt.
□ vi ~ **up** auflodern; (fam: get
angry) aufbrausen. ~ **d** a <gar-
ment> ausgestellt

flash /flæʃ/ n Blitz m; **in a** ~ (fam) im Nu □ vi blitzen; (repeatedly) blinken; ~ **past** vorbeirasen □ vt aufleuchten lassen; ~ **one's headlights** die Lichthupe betätigen

flash: ~**back** n Rückblende f. ~**bulb** n (Phot) Blitzbirne f. ~**er** n (Auto) Blinker m. ~**light** n (Phot) Blitzlicht nt; (Amer: torch) Taschenlampe f. ~**y** a auffällig

flask /flɑ:sk/ n Flasche f; (Chem) Kolben m; (vacuum~) Thermosflasche (P) f

flat /flæt/ a (flatter, flattest) flach; (surface) eben; (refusal) glatt; (beer) schal; (battery) verbraucht; (Auto) leer; (tyre) platt; (Mus) A ~ As nt; B ~ B nt □ n Wohnung f; (Mus) · Erniedrigungszeichen nt; (fam: puncture) Reifenpanne f

flat: ~**feet** npl Plattfüße pl. ~**fish** n Plattfisch m. ~**ly** adv (refuse) glatt. ~ **rate** n Einheitspreis m

flatten /ˈflætn/ vt platt drücken

flatter /ˈflætə(r)/ vt schmeicheln (+ dat). ~**y** n Schmeichelei f

flat 'tyre n Reifenpanne f

flatulence /ˈflætjʊləns/ n Blähungen pl

flaunt /flɔ:nt/ vt prunken mit

flautist /ˈflɔ:tɪst/ n Flötist(in) m(f)

flavour /ˈfleɪvə(r)/ n Geschmack m □ vt abschmecken. ~**ing** n Aroma nt

flaw /flɔ:/ n Fehler m. ~**less** a tadellos; (complexion) makellos

flax /flæks/ n Flachs m. ~**en** a flachsblond

flea /fli:/ n Floh m. ~ **market** n Flohmarkt m

fleck /flek/ n Tupfen m.

fled /fled/ see flee

flee /fli:/ v (pt/pp fled) □ vi fliehen (from vor + dat) □ vt flüchten aus

fleece /fli:s/ n Vlies nt □ vt (fam) schröpfen. ~**y** a flauschig

fleet /fli:t/ n Flotte f; (of cars) Wagenpark m

fleeting /ˈfli:tɪŋ/ a flüchtig

Flemish /ˈflemɪʃ/ a flämisch

flesh /fleʃ/ n Fleisch nt; **in the** ~ (fam) in Person. ~**y** a fleischig

flew /flu:/ see fly²

flex¹ /fleks/ vt anspannen (muscle)

flex² n (Electr) Schnur f

flex|ibility /fleksəˈbɪlətɪ/ n Biegsamkeit f; (fig) Flexibilität f. ~**le** a biegsam; (fig) flexibel

flexitime /ˈfleksɪ-/ n Gleitzeit f

flick /flɪk/ vt schnippen. ~ **through** vi schnell durchblättern

flicker /ˈflɪkə(r)/ vi flackern

flier /ˈflaɪə(r)/ n = flyer

flight¹ /flaɪt/ n (fleeing) Flucht f; **take** ~ die Flucht ergreifen

flight² n (flying) Flug m; ~ **of stairs** Treppe f

flight: ~ **path** n Flugschneise f. ~ **recorder** n Flugschreiber m

flighty /ˈflaɪtɪ/ a (-ier, -iest) flatterhaft

flimsy /ˈflɪmzɪ/ a (-ier, -iest) dünn; (excuse) fadenscheinig

flinch /flɪntʃ/ vi zurückzucken

fling /flɪŋ/ n **have a** ~ (fam) sich austoben □ vt (pt/pp **flung**) schleudern

flint /flɪnt/ n Feuerstein m

flip /flɪp/ vt/i schnippen; ~ **through** durchblättern

flippant /ˈflɪpənt/ a, -**ly** adv leichtfertig

flipper /ˈflɪpə(r)/ n Flosse f

flirt /flɜ:t/ n kokette Frau f □ vi flirten

flirtation /flɜ:ˈteɪʃn/ n Flirt m. ~**ious** /-ʃəs/ a kokett

flit /flɪt/ vi (pt/pp **flitted**) flattern

float /fləʊt/ n Schwimmer m; (in procession) Festwagen m; (money) Wechselgeld nt □ vi (thing:) schwimmen; (person:) sich treiben lassen; (in air) schweben; (Comm) floaten

flock /flɒk/ n Herde f; (of birds) Schwarm m □vi strömen

flog /flɒg/ vt (pt/pp **flogged**) auspeitschen; (fam: sell) verkloppen

flood /flʌd/ n Überschwemmung f; (fig) Flut f; **be in** ~ ⟨river:⟩ Hochwasser führen □vi überschwemmen □vi ⟨river:⟩ über die Ufer treten

floodlight n Flutlicht nt □vt (pt/pp **floodlit**) anstrahlen

floor /flɔː(r)/ n Fußboden m; (storey) Stock m □vt (baffle) verblüffen

floor: ~**board** n Dielenbrett nt. ~**cloth** n Scheuertuch nt. ~**polish** n Bohnerwachs nt. ~**show** n Kabarettvorstellung f

flop /flɒp/ n (fam: failure) Reinfall m; (Theat) Durchfall m □vi (pt/pp **flopped**) (fam) (fail) durchfallen; ~ **down** sich plumpsen lassen

floppy /ˈflɒpɪ/ a schlapp. ~ **'disc** n Diskette f

flora /ˈflɔːrə/ n Flora f

floral /ˈflɔːrəl/ a Blumen-

florid /ˈflɒrɪd/ a ⟨complexion⟩ gerötet; ⟨style⟩ blumig

florist /ˈflɒrɪst/ n Blumenhändler(in) m(f)

flounce /flaʊns/ n Volant m □vi ~ **out** hinausstolzieren

flounder[1] /ˈflaʊndə(r)/ vi zappeln

flounder[2] n (fish) Flunder f

flour /ˈflaʊə(r)/ n Mehl nt

flourish /ˈflʌrɪʃ/ n große Geste f; (scroll) Schnörkel m □vi gedeihen; (fig) blühen □vt schwenken

floury /ˈflaʊərɪ/ a mehlig

flout /flaʊt/ vt mißachten

flow /fləʊ/ n Fluß m; (of traffic, blood) Strom m □vi fließen

flower /ˈflaʊə(r)/ n Blume f □vi blühen

flower: ~**bed** n Blumenbeet nt. ~**ed** a geblümt. ~**pot** n Blumentopf m. ~**y** a blumig

flown /fləʊn/ see **fly**[2]

flu /fluː/ n (fam) Grippe f

fluctuat|e /ˈflʌktjʊeɪt/ vi schwanken. ~**ion** /-ˈeɪʃn/ n Schwankung f

fluent /ˈfluːənt/ a, **-ly** adv fließend

fluff /flʌf/ n Fusseln pl; (down) Flaum m. ~**y** a (**-ier, -iest**) flauschig

fluid /ˈfluːɪd/ a flüssig; (fig) veränderlich □n Flüssigkeit f

fluke /fluːk/ n (glücklicher) Zufall m

flung /flʌŋ/ see **fling**

flunk /flʌŋk/ vt/i (Amer, fam) durchfallen (in + dat)

fluorescent /flʊəˈresnt/ a fluoreszierend; ~ **lighting** Neonbeleuchtung f

fluoride /ˈflʊəraɪd/ n Fluor nt

flurry /ˈflʌrɪ/ n (snow) Gestöber nt; (fig) Aufregung f

flush /flʌʃ/ n (blush) Erröten nt □vi rot werden □vt spülen □a in einer Ebene (**with** mit); (fam: affluent) gut bei Kasse

flustered /ˈflʌstəd/ a nervös

flute /fluːt/ n Flöte f

flutter /ˈflʌtə(r)/ n Flattern nt □vi flattern

flux /flʌks/ n **in a state of** ~ im Fluß

fly[1] /flaɪ/ n (pl **flies**) Fliege f

fly[2] v (pt **flew**, pp **flown**) □vi fliegen; ⟨flag:⟩ wehen; (rush) sausen □vt fliegen; führen ⟨flag⟩

fly[3] n & **flies** pl (on trousers) Hosenschlitz m

flyer /ˈflaɪə(r)/ n Flieger(in) m(f); (Amer: leaflet) Flugblatt nt

flying: ~ **'buttress** n Strebebogen m. ~ **'saucer** n fliegende Untertasse f. ~ **'visit** n Stippvisite f

fly: ~**leaf** n Vorsatzblatt nt. ~**over** n Überführung f

foal /fəʊl/ n Fohlen nt

foam /fəʊm/ n Schaum m; (synthetic) Schaumstoff m □vi schäumen. ~ **'rubber** n Schaumgummi m

fob /fɒb/ vt (pt/pp **fobbed**) ~ **sth off** etw andrehen (on s.o. jdm); ~ **s.o. off** jdn abspeisen (**with** mit)

focal /ˈfəʊkl/ a Brenn-

focus /ˈfəʊkəs/ n Brennpunkt m; **in** ~ scharf eingestellt □ v (pt/pp **focused** or **focussed**) □ vt einstellen (**on** auf + acc); (fig) konzentrieren (**on** auf + acc) □ vi (fig) sich konzentrieren (**on** auf + acc)

fodder /ˈfɒdə(r)/ n Futter nt

foe /fəʊ/ n Feind m

foetus /ˈfiːtəs/ n (pl -tuses) Fötus m

fog /fɒg/ n Nebel m

foggy /ˈfɒgɪ/ a (**foggier, foggiest**) neblig

'fog-horn n Nebelhorn nt

fogy /ˈfəʊgɪ/ n **old** ~ alter Knacker m

foible /ˈfɔɪbl/ n Eigenart f

foil[1] /fɔɪl/ n Folie f; (Culin) Alufolie f

foil[2] vt (thwart) vereiteln

foil[3] n (Fencing) Florett nt

foist /fɔɪst/ vt andrehen (**on** s.o. jdm)

fold[1] /fəʊld/ n (for sheep) Pferch m

fold[2] n Falte f; (in paper) Kniff m □ vt falten; ~ **one's arms** die Arme verschränken □ vi sich falten lassen; (fail) eingehen. ~ **up** vt zusammenfalten; zusammenklappen ⟨chair⟩ □ vi sich zusammenklappen/-klappen lassen; (fam) ⟨business:⟩ eingehen

folder /ˈfəʊldə(r)/ n Mappe f. ~**ing** a Klapp-

foliage /ˈfəʊlɪdʒ/ n Blätter pl; (of tree) Laub nt

folk /fəʊk/ npl Leute pl

folk: ~**-dance** n Volkstanz m. ~**lore** n Folklore f. ~**-song** n Volkslied nt

follow /ˈfɒləʊ/ vt/i folgen (+ dat); (pursue) verfolgen; (in vehicle) nachfahren (+ dat); ~ **suit** (fig) dasselbe tun. ~ **up** vt nachgehen (+ dat)

follower /ˈfɒləʊə(r)/ n Anhänger(in) m(f). ~**ing** a folgend □ n

Folgende(s) nt; (supporters) Anhängerschaft f □prep im Anschluß an (+ acc)

folly /ˈfɒlɪ/ n Torheit f

fond /fɒnd/ a (-**er**, -**est**), -**ly** adv liebevoll; **be** ~ **of** gern haben; gern essen ⟨food⟩

fondle /ˈfɒndl/ vt liebkosen

fondness /ˈfɒndnɪs/ n Liebe f (**for** zu)

font /fɒnt/ n Taufstein m

food /fuːd/ n Essen nt; (for animals) Futter nt; (groceries) Lebensmittel pl

food: ~ **mixer** n Küchenmaschine f. ~ **poisoning** n Lebensmittelvergiftung f. ~ **processor** n Küchenmaschine f. ~ **value** n Nährwert m

fool[1] /fuːl/ n (Culin) Fruchtcreme f

fool[2] n Narr m; **you are a** ~ du bist dumm; **make a** ~ **of oneself** sich lächerlich machen □vt hereinlegen □vi ~ **around** herumalbern

'fool|hardy a tollkühn. ~**ish** a, -**ly** adv dumm. ~**ishness** n Dummheit f. ~**proof** a narrensicher

foot /fʊt/ n (pl **feet**) Fuß m; (measure) Fuß m (30,48 cm); (of bed) Fußende nt; **on** ~ zu Fuß; **on one's feet** auf den Beinen; **put one's** ~ **in it** (fam) ins Fettnäpfchen treten

foot: ~**-and-'mouth disease** n Maul- und Klauenseuche f. ~**ball** n Fußball m. ~**baller** n Fußballspieler m. ~**ball pools** npl Fußballtoto nt. ~**-brake** n Fußbremse f. ~**-bridge** n Fußgängerbrücke f. ~**hills** npl Vorgebirge nt. ~**hold** n Halt m. ~**ing** n Halt m; (fig) Basis f. ~**lights** npl Rampenlicht nt. ~**man** n Lakai m. ~**note** n Fußnote f. ~**path** n Fußweg m. ~**print** n Fußabdruck m. ~**step** n Schritt m; **follow in s.o.'s** ~**steps** (fig) in jds Fußstapfen treten. **~stool** n Fußbank f. **~ wear** n Schuhwerk nt

for /fə(r), betont fɔː(r)/ prep für (+ acc); ⟨send, long⟩ nach; ⟨ask, fight⟩ um; what ~? wozu? ~ **supper** zum Abendessen; ~ **nothing** umsonst; ~ **all that** trotz allem; ~ **this reason** aus diesem Grund; ~ **a month** einen Monat; **I have lived here** ~ **ten years** ich wohne seit zehn Jahren hier □conj denn

forage /ˈfɒrɪdʒ/ n Futter nt □vi ~ **for** suchen nach

forbade /fəˈbæd/ see **forbid**

forbear|ance /fɔːˈbeərəns/n Nachsicht f. **~ing** a nachsichtig

forbid /fəˈbɪd/ vt (pt **forbade**, pp **forbidden**) verbieten (s.o. jdm). **~ding** a bedrohlich; (stern) streng

force /fɔːs/ n Kraft f; (of blow) Wucht f; (violence) Gewalt f; **in** ~ gültig; (in large numbers) in großer Zahl; **come into** ~ in Kraft treten; **the** ~ **s** pl die Streitkräfte pl □vt zwingen; (break open) aufbrechen; ~ **sth on s.o.** jdm etw aufdrängen

forced /fɔːst/ a gezwungen; ~ **landing** Notlandung f

force: ~-**feed** vt (pt/pp **-fed**) zwangsernähren. ~**ful** a, **-ly** adv energisch

forceps /ˈfɔːseps/ n inv Zange f

forcibl|e /ˈfɔːsəbl/ a gewaltsam. ~**y** adv mit Gewalt

ford /fɔːd/ n Furt f □vt durchwaten; (in vehicle) durchfahren

fore /fɔː(r)/ a vordere(r,s) □n **to the** ~ im Vordergrund

fore: ~**arm** n Unterarm m. ~**boding** /-ˈbəʊdɪŋ/n Vorahnung f. ~**cast** n Voraussage f; (for weather) Vorhersage f □vt (pt/pp ~**cast**) voraussagen, vorhersagen. ~**court** n Vorhof m. ~**fathers** npl Vorfahren pl. ~**finger** n Zeigefinger m. ~**front** n **be in the** ~**front** führend sein. ~**gone** a **be a** ~**gone**

conclusion von vornherein feststehen. ~**ground** n Vordergrund m. ~**head** /ˈfɒrɪd/ n Stirn f. ~**hand** n Vorhand f

foreign /ˈfɒrən/ a ausländisch; (country) fremd; **he is** ~ **er ist** Ausländer. ~ **currency** n Devisen pl. ~ **er** n Ausländer(in) m(f). ~ **language** n Fremdsprache f

Foreign: ~ **Office** n ≈ Außenministerium m. ~ **'Secretary** n ≈ Außenminister m

fore: ~**leg** n Vorderbein nt. ~**man** n Vorarbeiter m. ~**most** a führend □adv **first and** ~**most** zuallererst. ~**name** n Vorname m

forensic /fəˈrensɪk/ a ~ **medicine** Gerichtsmedizin f

'forerunner n Vorläufer m

fore'see vt (pt **-saw**, pp **-seen**) voraussehen, vorhersehen. ~**able** /-əbl/ a **in the** ~**able future** in absehbarer Zeit

'foresight n Weitblick m

forest /ˈfɒrɪst/ n Wald m. ~**er** n Förster m

fore'stall vt zuvorkommen (+ dat)

forestry /ˈfɒrɪstrɪ/ n Forstwirtschaft f

'foretaste n Vorgeschmack m

fore'tell vt (pt/pp **-told**) vorhersagen

forever /fəˈrevə(r)/ adv für immer

fore'warn vt vorher warnen

'foreword n Vorwort nt

forfeit /ˈfɔːfɪt/ n (in game) Pfand nt □vt verwirken

forgave /fəˈgeɪv/ see **forgive**

forge[1] /fɔːdʒ/ vt ~ **ahead** (fig) Fortschritte machen

forge[2] n Schmiede f □vt schmieden; (counterfeit) fälschen. ~**r** n Fälscher m. ~**ry** n Fälschung f

forget /fəˈget/ vt/i (pt **-got**, pp **-gotten**) vergessen; verlernen ⟨language, skill⟩. ~**ful** a vergeßlich. ~**fulness** n Vergeßlichkeit f. ~-**me-not** n Vergißmeinnicht nt

forgive /fə'gɪv/ vt (pt **-gave**, pp **-given**) ~ s.o. for sth jdm etw vergeben od verzeihen. **~ness** f Vergebung f, Verzeihung f

forgo /fɔ:'gəʊ/ vt (pt **-went**, pp **-gone**) verzichten auf (+ acc)

forgot(ten) /fə'gɒt(n)/ see forget

fork /fɔ:k/ n Gabel f; (in road) Gabelung f □ vi ⟨road:⟩ sich gabeln; ~ **right** rechts abzweigen. ~ **out** vt ⟨right (fam) blechen

fork-lift 'truck n Gabelstapler m

forlorn /fə'lɔ:n/ a verlassen; ⟨hope⟩ schwach

form /fɔ:m/ n Form f; (document) Formular nt; (bench) Bank f; (Sch) Klasse f □ vt formen (into zu); (create) bilden □ vi sich bilden; (idea:) Gestalt annehmen

formal /'fɔ:ml/ a, **-ly** adv formell, förmlich. **~ity** /-'mælətɪ/ n Förmlichkeit f; (requirement) Formalität f

format /'fɔ:mæt/ n Format nt

formation /fɔ:'meɪʃn/ n Formation f

formative /'fɔ:mətɪv/ a ~ **years** Entwicklungsjahre pl

former /'fɔ:mə(r)/ a ehemalig; the ~ der/die/das erstere. **~ly** adv früher

formidable /'fɔ:mɪdəbl/ a gewaltig

formula /'fɔ:mjʊlə/ n (pl **-ae** /-li:/ or **-s**) Formel f

formulate /'fɔ:mjʊleɪt/ vt formulieren

forsake /fə'seɪk/ vt (pt **-sook** /-sʊk/, pp **-saken**) verlassen

fort /fɔ:t/ n (Mil) Fort nt

forte /'fɔ:teɪ/ n Stärke f

forth /fɔ:θ/ adv back and ~ hin und her; **and so ~** und so weiter

forth: **~coming** a bevorstehend; (fam: communicative) mitteilsam. **~right** a direkt. **~'with** adv umgehend

fortieth /'fɔ:tɪɪθ/ a vierzigste(r,s)

fortification /fɔ:tɪfɪ'keɪʃn/ n Befestigung f

fortify /'fɔ:tɪfaɪ/ vt (pt/pp **-ied**) befestigen; (fig) stärken

fortitude /'fɔ:tɪtju:d/ n Standhaftigkeit f

fortnight /'fɔ:t-/ n vierzehn Tage pl. **~ly** a vierzehntäglich □ adv alle vierzehn Tage

fortress /'fɔ:trɪs/ n Festung f

fortuitous /fɔ:'tju:ɪtəs/ a, **-ly** adv zufällig

fortunate /'fɔ:tʃʊnət/ a glücklich; **be ~** Glück haben. **~ly** adv glücklicherweise

fortune /'fɔ:tʃu:n/ n Glück nt; (money) Vermögen nt. **~-teller** n Wahrsagerin f

forty /'fɔ:tɪ/ a vierzig; **have ~ winks** (fam) ein Nickerchen machen □ n Vierzig f

forum /'fɔ:rəm/ n Forum nt

forward /'fɔ:wəd/ adv vorwärts; (to the front) nach vorn □ a Vorwärts-; (presumptuous) anmaßend □ n (Sport) Stürmer m □ vt nachsenden (letter). **~s** adv vorwärts

fossil /'fɒsl/ n Fossil nt. **~ized** a versteinert

foster /'fɒstə(r)/ vt fördern; in Pflege nehmen (child). **~-child** n Pflegekind nt. **~-mother** n Pflegemutter f

fought /fɔ:t/ see fight

foul /faʊl/ a (**-er**, **-est**) widerlich; (language) unflätig; ~ **play** (Jur) Mord m □ n (Sport) Foul nt □ vt verschmutzen; (obstruct) blockieren; (Sport) foulen. **~-smelling** a übelriechend

found[1] /faʊnd/ see find

found[2] vt gründen

foundation /faʊn'deɪʃn/ n (basis) Grundlage f; (charitable) Stiftung f; **~s** pl Fundament nt. **~-stone** n Grundstein m

founder[1] /'faʊndə(r)/ n Gründer(in) m(f)

founder[2] vi ⟨ship:⟩ sinken; (fig) scheitern

foundry /'faʊndrɪ/ n Gießerei f

fountain /'faʊntɪn/ n Brunnen m. **~-pen** n Füllfederhalter m

four /fɔ:(r)/ a vier □ n Vier f

four: ~-'**poster** /n Himmelbett nt. ~ **some** /'fɔːsəm/ n in a ~ some zu viert. ~ **teen** /a vierzehn □ n Vierzehn f. ~ '**teenth** /a vierzehnte(r,s)

fourth /fɔːθ/ a vierte(r,s)

fowl /faʊl/ n Geflügel nt

fox /fɒks/ n Fuchs m □ vt (puzzle) verblüffen

foyer /'fɔɪeɪ/ n Foyer nt; (in hotel) Empfangshalle f

fraction /'frækʃn/ n Bruchteil m; (Math) Bruch m

fracture /'fræktʃə(r)/ n Bruch m □ vt/i brechen

fragile /'frædʒaɪl/ a zerbrechlich

fragment /'frægmənt/ n Bruchstück nt, Fragment nt. ~**ary** /a bruchstückhaft

fragran|ce /'freɪgrəns/ n Duft m. ~**t** a duftend

frail /freɪl/ a (-er, -est) gebrechlich

frame /freɪm/ n Rahmen m; (of spectacles) Gestell nt; (Anat) Körperbau m; ~ **of mind** Gemütsverfassung f □ vt einrahmen; (sl) ein Verbrechen anhängen (+ dat). ~ **work** n Gerüst nt; (fig) Gerippe nt

franc /fræŋk/ n (French, Belgian) Franc m; (Swiss) Franken m

France /frɑːns/ n Frankreich nt

franchise /'fræntʃaɪz/ n (Pol) Wahlrecht nt; (Comm) Franchise nt

frank[1] /fræŋk/ vt frankieren

frank[2] a, ~**ly** adv offen

frankfurter /'fræŋkfɜːtə(r)/ n Frankfurter f

frantic /'fræntɪk/ a, ~**ally** adv verzweifelt; **be** ~ außer sich (dat) sein (**with** vor)

fraternal /frə'tɜːnl/ a brüderlich

fraud /frɔːd/ n Betrug m; (person) Betrüger(in) m(f). ~**ulent** /-jʊlənt/ a betrügerisch

fraught /frɔːt/ a ~ **with danger** gefahrvoll

fray[1] /freɪ/ n Kampf m

fray[2] vi ausfransen

freak /friːk/ n & attrib a (person) Mißgeburt f; (phenomenon) Ausnahmeerscheinung f □ a anormal. ~**ish** a anormal

freckle /'frekl/ n Sommersprosse f. ~**d** a sommersprossig

free /friː/ a (**freer, freest**) frei; (ticket, copy, time) Frei-; (lavish) freigebig; ~ **[of charge]** kostenlos; **set** ~ (rescue) befreien; **you are** ~ **to ...** es steht Ihnen frei, zu ... □ vt (pt/pp **freed**) freilassen; (rescue) befreien; (disentangle) freibekommen

free: ~**dom** n Freiheit f. ~ **hand** adv aus freier Hand. ~ **hold** n [freier] Grundbesitz m. ~ '**kick** n Freistoß m. ~ **lance** a & adv freiberuflich. ~**ly** adv frei; (voluntarily) freiwillig; (generously) großzügig. **F**~**mason** n Freimaurer m. **F**~**masonry** n Freimaurerei f. ~**range** a ~-**range eggs** Landeier pl. ~ **sample** n Gratisprobe f. ~-**style** n Freistil m. ~**way** n (Amer) Autobahn f. ~-**wheel** vi im Freilauf fahren

freez|e /friːz/ vt (pt froze, pp frozen) einfrieren; stoppen ⟨wages⟩ □ vi gefrieren; **it's** ~**ing** es friert

freezer /'friːzə(r)/ n Gefriertruhe f; (upright) Gefrierschrank m. ~**ing** a eiskalt □ n **below** ~**ing** unter Null

freight /freɪt/ n Fracht f. ~**er** n Frachter m. ~ **train** n (Amer) Güterzug m

French /frentʃ/ a französisch □ n (Lang) Französisch nt; **the** ~ pl die Franzosen

French: ~ '**beans** npl grüne Bohnen pl. ~ '**bread** n Stangenbrot nt. ~ '**fries** npl Pommes frites pl. ~-**man** n Franzose m. ~'**window** n Terrassentür f. ~-**woman** n Französin f

frenzied /'frenzɪd/ a rasend

frenzy /'frenzɪ/ n Raserei f

frequency /'friːkwənsɪ/ n Häufigkeit f; (Phys) Frequenz f

frequent[1] /'fri:kwənt/ a, **-ly** adv häufig

frequent[2] /fri'kwent/ vt regelmäßig besuchen

fresco /'freskəʊ/ n Fresko nt

fresh /freʃ/ a (-er, -est), **-ly** adv frisch; ⟨new⟩ neu; ⟨Amer: cheeky⟩ frech

freshen /'freʃn/ vi ⟨wind:⟩ auffrischen. **~ up** vt auffrischen □ vi sich frisch machen

freshness /'freʃnɪs/ n Frische f

'freshwater a Süßwasser-

fret /fret/ vi (pt/pp **fretted**) sich grämen. **~ful** a weinerlich

'fretsaw n Laubsäge f

friar /'fraɪə(r)/ n Mönch m

friction /'frɪkʃn/ n Reibung f; ⟨fig⟩ Reibereien pl

Friday /'fraɪdeɪ/ n Freitag m

fridge /frɪdʒ/ n Kühlschrank m

fried /fraɪd/ see **fry**[2] □ a gebraten; **~ egg** Spiegelei nt

friend /frend/ n Freund(in) m(f). **~liness** n Freundlichkeit f. **~ly** a (-ier, -iest) freundlich; **~ly with** befreundet mit. **~ship** n Freundschaft f

frieze /fri:z/ n Fries m

fright /fraɪt/ n Schreck m

frighten /'fraɪtn/ vt angst machen (+ dat); ⟨startle⟩ erschrecken; **be ~ed** Angst haben (of vor + dat). **~ing** a angsterregend

frightful /'fraɪtfl/ a, **-ly** adv schrecklich

frigid /'frɪdʒɪd/ a frostig; ⟨Psych⟩ frigide. **~ity** /-'dʒɪdətɪ/ n Frostigkeit f; Frigidität f

frill /frɪl/ n Rüsche f; ⟨paper⟩ Manschette f. **~y** a rüschenbesetzt

fringe /frɪndʒ/ n Fransen pl; ⟨of hair⟩ Pony m; ⟨fig: edge⟩ Rand m. **~ benefits** npl zusätzliche Leistungen pl

frisk /frɪsk/ vi herumspringen □ vt ⟨search⟩ durchsuchen; ⟨fam⟩ filzen

frisky /'frɪskɪ/ a (-ier, -iest) lebhaft

fritter /'frɪtə(r)/ vt **~ [away]** verplempern ⟨fam⟩

frivol|ity /frɪ'vɒlətɪ/ n Frivolität f. **~ous** /'frɪvələs/ a, **-ly** adv frivol, leichtfertig

frizzy /'frɪzɪ/ a kraus

fro /frəʊ/ see **to**

frock /frɒk/ n Kleid nt

frog /frɒg/ n Frosch m. **~man** n Froschmann m. **~-spawn** n Froschlaich m

frolic /'frɒlɪk/ vi (pt/pp **frolicked**) herumtollen

from /frɒm/ prep von (+ dat); ⟨out of⟩ aus (+ dat); ⟨according to⟩ nach (+ dat); **~ Monday** ab Montag; **~ that day** seit dem Tag

front /frʌnt/ n Vorderseite f; ⟨fig⟩ Fassade f; ⟨of garment⟩ Vorderteil nt; ⟨sea⟩ Strandpromenade f; ⟨Mil, Pol, Meteorol⟩ Front f; **in ~ of** vor; **in** or **at the ~** vorne; **to the ~** nach vorne □ a vordere(r,s); ⟨page, row⟩ erste(r,s); ⟨tooth, wheel⟩ Vorder-

frontal /'frʌntl/ a Frontal-

front: **~ 'door** n Haustür f. **~ 'garden** n Vorgarten m

frontier /'frʌntɪə(r)/ n Grenze f

front-wheel 'drive n Vorderradantrieb m

frost /frɒst/ n Frost m; ⟨hoar-⟩ Raureif m; **ten degrees of ~** zehn Grad Kälte. **~bite** n Erfrierung f. **~bitten** a erfroren

frost|ed /'frɒstɪd/ a **~ed glass** Mattglas nt. **~ing** n ⟨Amer Culin⟩ Zuckerguß m. **~y** a, **-ly** adv frostig

froth /frɒθ/ n Schaum m □ vi schäumen. **~y** a schaumig

frown /fraʊn/ n Stirnrunzeln nt □ vi die Stirn runzeln; **~ on** mißbilligen

froze /frəʊz/ see **freeze**

frozen /'frəʊzn/ see **freeze** □ a gefroren; ⟨Culin⟩ tiefgekühlt; **I'm ~** ⟨fam⟩ mir ist eiskalt. **~ food** n Tiefkühlkost f

frugal /'fru:gl/ a, **-ly** adv sparsam; ⟨meal⟩ frugal

fruit /fruːt/ n Frucht f; (collectively) Obst nt. ~ **cake** n englischer [Tee]kuchen m

fruiterer /ˈfruːtərə(r)/ n Obsthändler m. ~**ful** a fruchtbar

fruition /fruːˈɪʃn/ n come to ~ sich verwirklichen

fruit: ~ **juice** n Obstsaft m. ~**less** a, -**ly** adv fruchtlos. ~ **machine** n Spielautomat m. ~ **'salad** n Obstsalat m

fruity /ˈfruːtɪ/ a fruchtig

frumpy /ˈfrʌmpɪ/ a unmodisch

frustrat|**e** /frʌˈstreɪt/ vt vereiteln; (Psych) frustrieren. ~**ing** a frustrierend. ~**ion** /-eɪʃn/ n Frustration f

fry¹ /fraɪ/ n inv small ~ (fig) kleine Fische pl

fry² vt/i (pt/pp **fried**) [in der Pfanne] braten. ~**ing-pan** n Bratpfanne f

fuck /fʌk/ vt/i (vulg) ficken. ~**ing** a (vulg) Scheiß-

fuddy-duddy /ˈfʌdɪdʌdɪ/ n (fam) verknöcherter Kerl m

fudge /fʌdʒ/ n weiche Karamellen pl

fuel /ˈfjuːəl/ n Brennstoff m; (for car) Kraftstoff m; (for aircraft) Treibstoff m

fugitive /ˈfjuːdʒɪtɪv/ n Flüchtling m

fugue /fjuːg/ n (Mus) Fuge f

fulfil /fʊlˈfɪl/ vt (pt/pp -**filled**) erfüllen. ~**ment** n Erfüllung f

full /fʊl/ a & adv (-**er**, -**est**) voll; (detailed) ausführlich; (skirt) weit; ~ **of** voll von (+ dat), voller (+ gen); **at** ~ **speed** in voller Fahrt □ n in ~ vollständig

full: ~ **'moon** n Vollmond m. ~**-scale** a (model) in Originalgröße; (rescue, alert) großangelegt. ~ **'stop** n Punkt m. ~**-time** a ganztägig □ adv ganztags

fully /ˈfʊlɪ/ adv völlig; (in detail) ausführlich

fulsome /ˈfʊlsəm/ a übertrieben

fumble /ˈfʌmbl/ vi herumfummeln (with an + dat)

fume /fjuːm/ vi vor Wut schäumen

fumes /fjuːmz/ npl Dämpfe pl; (from car) Abgase pl

fumigate /ˈfjuːmɪgeɪt/ vt ausräuchern

fun /fʌn/ n Spaß m; **for** ~ aus od zum Spaß; **make** ~ **of** sich lustig machen über (+ acc); **have** ~! viel Spaß!

function /ˈfʌŋkʃn/ n Funktion f; (event) Veranstaltung f □ vi funktionieren; (serve) dienen (as als). ~**al** a zweckmäßig

fund /fʌnd/ n Fonds m; (fig) Vorrat m; ~**s** pl Geldmittel pl □ vt finanzieren

fundamental /fʌndəˈmentl/ a grundlegend; (essential) wesentlich

funeral /ˈfjuːnərl/ n Beerdigung f; (cremation) Feuerbestattung f

funeral: ~ **directors** pl, (Amer) ~ **home** n Bestattungsinstitut nt. ~ **march** n Trauermarsch m. ~ **parlour** n (Amer) Bestattungsinstitut nt. ~ **service** n Trauergottesdienst m

'funfair n Jahrmarkt m, Kirmes f

fungus /ˈfʌŋgəs/ n (pl -**gi** /-gaɪ/) Pilz m

funicular /fjuːˈnɪkjʊlə(r)/ n Seilbahn f

funnel /ˈfʌnl/ n Trichter m; (on ship, train) Schornstein m

funnily /ˈfʌnɪlɪ/ adv komisch; ~ **enough** komischerweise

funny /ˈfʌnɪ/ a (-**ier**, -**iest**) komisch. ~**-bone** n (fam) Musikantenknochen m

fur /fɜː(r)/ n Fell nt; (for clothing) Pelz m; (in kettle) Kesselstein m. ~ **'coat** n Pelzmantel m

furious /ˈfjʊərɪəs/ a, -**ly** adv wütend (with auf + acc)

furnace /ˈfɜːnɪs/ n (Techn) Ofen m

furnish /ˈfɜːnɪʃ/ vt einrichten; (supply) liefern. ~**ed** a ~**ed room** möbliertes Zimmer nt. ~**ings** npl Einrichtungsgegenstände pl

furniture /ˈfɜːnɪtʃə(r)/ n Möbel pl

furred /fɜːd/ a ‹tongue› belegt

furrow /ˈfarəʊ/ n Furche f

furry /ˈfɜːrɪ/ a ‹animal› Pelz-; ‹toy› Plüsch-

further /ˈfɜːðə(r)/ a weitere(r,s); at the ~ end am anderen Ende; until ~ notice bis auf weiteres □adv weiter; ~ off weiter entfernt □vt fördern

further: ~ edu'cation n Weiterbildung f. ~'more adv überdies

furthest /ˈfɜːðɪst/ a am weitesten entfernt □adv am weitesten

furtive /ˈfɜːtɪv/ a, -ly adv verstohlen

fury /ˈfjʊərɪ/ n Wut f

fuse¹ /fjuːz/ n ‹of bomb› Zünder m; ‹cord› Zündschnur f

fuse² n ‹Electr› Sicherung f □vt/i verschmelzen; the lights have ~d die Sicherung [für das Licht] ist durchgebrannt. ~-box n Sicherungskasten m

fuselage /ˈfjuːzəlɑːʒ/ n ‹Aviat› Rumpf m

fusion /ˈfjuːʒn/ n Verschmelzung f, Fusion f

fuss /fʌs/ n Getue nt; make a ~ of verwöhnen; ‹caress› liebkosen □vi Umstände machen

fussy /ˈfasɪ/ a (-ier, -iest) wählerisch; ‹particular› penibel

fusty /ˈfastɪ/ a moderig

futile /ˈfjuːtaɪl/ a zwecklos. ~ity /-ˈtɪlɪtɪ/ n Zwecklosigkeit f

future /ˈfjuːtʃə(r)/ a zukünftig □n Zukunft f; ‹Gram› [erstes] Futur nt; ~ perfect zweites Futur nt; in ~ in Zukunft

futuristic /fjuːtʃəˈrɪstɪk/ a futuristisch

fuzz /faz/ n the ~ ‹sl› die Bullen pl

fuzzy /ˈfazɪ/ a (-ier, -iest) ‹hair› kraus; ‹blurred› verschwommen

G

gab /gæb/ n ‹fam› have the gift of the ~ gut reden können

gabble /ˈgæbl/ vi schnell reden

gable /ˈgeɪbl/ n Giebel m

gad /gæd/ vi (pt/pp gadded) ~ about dauernd ausgehen

gadget /ˈgædʒɪt/ n [kleines] Gerät nt

Gaelic /ˈgeɪlɪk/ n Gälisch nt

gaffe /gæf/ n Fauxpas m

gag /gæg/ n Knebel m; ‹joke› Witz m; ‹Theat› Gag m □vt (pt/pp gagged) knebeln

gaiety /ˈgeɪətɪ/ n Fröhlichkeit f

gaily /ˈgeɪlɪ/ adv fröhlich

gain /geɪn/ n Gewinn m; ‹increase› Zunahme f □vt gewinnen; ‹obtain› erlangen; ~ weight zunehmen □vi ‹clock:› vorgehen. ~ful a ~ful employment Erwerbstätigkeit f

gait /geɪt/ n Gang m

gala /ˈgɑːlə/ n Fest nt; swimming ~ Schwimmfest nt □attrib Gala-

galaxy /ˈgæləksɪ/ n Galaxie f; the G~ die Milchstraße

gale /geɪl/ n Sturm m

gall /gɔːl/ n Galle f; ‹impudence› Frechheit f

gallant /ˈgælənt/ a, -ly adv tapfer; ‹chivalrous› galant. ~ry n Tapferkeit f

'gall-bladder n Gallenblase f

gallery /ˈgælərɪ/ n Galerie f

galley /ˈgælɪ/ n ‹ship's kitchen› Kombüse f; ~ [proof] [Druck]fahne f

gallivant /ˈgælɪvænt/ vi ‹fam› ausgehen

gallon /ˈgælən/ n Gallone f (= 4,5 l; Amer = 3,7 l)

gallop /ˈgæləp/ n Galopp m □vi galoppieren

gallows /ˈgæləʊz/ n Galgen m

'gallstone n Gallenstein m

galore /gəˈlɔː(r)/ adv in Hülle und Fülle

galvanize /ˈgælvənaɪz/ vt galvanisieren

gambit /ˈgæmbɪt/ n Eröffnungsmanöver nt

gamble /ˈgæmbl/ n ‹risk› Risiko nt □vi [um Geld] spielen; ~ on ‹rely›

sich verlassen auf (+ acc). ~r n
Spieler(in) m(f)

game /geɪm/ n Spiel nt; (animals,
birds) Wild nt; ~s (Sch) Sport m
□a (brave) tapfer; (willing) bereit
(for zu). ~**keeper** n Wildhüter m

gammon /ˈgæmən/ n [geräucher-
ter] Schinken m

gamut /ˈgæmət/ n Skala f

gander /ˈgændə(r)/ n Gänserich m

gang /gæŋ/ n Bande f; (of work-
men) Kolonne f □vi ~ **up** sich
zusammenrotten (on gegen)

gangling /ˈgæŋglɪŋ/ a schlaksig

gangrene /ˈgæŋgriːn/ n Wund-
brand m

gangster /ˈgæŋstə(r)/ n Gangster
m

gangway /ˈgæŋweɪ/ n Gang m;
(Naut, Aviat) Gangway f

gaol /dʒeɪl/ n Gefängnis nt □vt ins
Gefängnis sperren. ~**er** n Ge-
fängniswärter m

gap /gæp/ n Lücke f; (interval)
Pause f; (difference) Unterschied
m

gap|e /geɪp/ vi gaffen; ~e at an-
starren. ~**ing** a klaffend

garage /ˈgærɑːʒ/ n Garage f; (for
repairs) Werkstatt f; (for petrol)
Tankstelle f

garb /gɑːb/ n Kleidung f

garbage /ˈgɑːbɪdʒ/ n Müll m. ~
can n (Amer) Mülleimer m

garbled /ˈgɑːbld/ a verworren

garden /ˈgɑːdn/ n Garten m;
[**public**] ~**s** pl [öffentliche] Anlagen pl □vi im Garten arbeiten.
~**er** n Gärtner(in) m(f). ~**ing** n
Gartenarbeit f

gargle /ˈgɑːgl/ n (liquid) Gurgel-
wasser nt □vi gurgeln

gargoyle /ˈgɑːgɔɪl/ n Wasser-
speier m

garish /ˈgeərɪʃ/ a grell

garland /ˈgɑːlənd/ n Girlande f

garlic /ˈgɑːlɪk/ n Knoblauch m

garment /ˈgɑːmənt/ n Kleidungsstück nt

garnet /ˈgɑːnɪt/ n Granat m

garnish /ˈgɑːnɪʃ/ n Garnierung f
□vt garnieren

garret /ˈgærɪt/ n Dachstube f

garrison /ˈgærɪsn/ n Garnison f

garrulous /ˈgærʊləs/ a geschwätzig

garter /ˈgɑːtə(r)/ n Strumpfband
nt; (Amer: suspender) Strumpf-
halter m

gas /gæs/ n Gas nt; (Amer fam:
petrol) Benzin nt □v (pt/pp
gassed) □vt vergasen □vi (fam)
schwatzen. ~**cooker** n Gasherd
m. ~**fire** n Gasofen m

gash /gæʃ/ n Schnitt m; (wound)
klaffende Wunde f □vt ~ **one's
arm** sich (dat) den Arm aufschlitzen

gasket /ˈgæskɪt/ n (Techn) Dichtung f

gas: ~ **mask** n Gasmaske f.
~**-meter** n Gaszähler m

gasoline /ˈgæsəliːn/ n (Amer) Benzin nt

gasp /gɑːsp/ vi keuchen; (in surprise) hörbar die Luft einziehen

gas station n (Amer) Tankstelle f

gastric /ˈgæstrɪk/ a Magen-.
~**flu** n Darmgrippe f. ~ **ulcer** n
Magengeschwür nt

gastronomy /gæˈstrɒnəmɪ/ n
Gastronomie f

gate /geɪt/ n Tor nt; (to field) Gatter nt; (barrier) Schranke f; (at
airport) Flugsteig m

gâteau /ˈgætəʊ/ n Torte f

gate: ~**crasher** n ungeladener
Gast m. ~**way** n Tor nt

gather /ˈgæðə(r)/ vt sammeln;
(pick) pflücken; (conclude) folgern (from aus); (Sewing) kräuseln; ~ **speed** schneller werden
□vi sich versammeln; ⟨storm:⟩
sich zusammenballen. ~**ing** n
family ~**ing** Familientreffen nt

gaudy /ˈgɔːdɪ/ a (-ier, -iest) knallig

gauge /geɪdʒ/ n Stärke f; (Rail)
Spurweite f; (device) Meßinstru-
ment nt □vt messen; (estimate)
schätzen

gaunt /gɔ:nt/ a hager

gauntlet /'gɔ:ntlɪt/ n run the ~ Spießruten laufen

gauze /gɔ:z/ n Gaze f

gave /geɪv/ see give

gawky /'gɔ:kɪ/ a (-ier, -iest) schlaksig

gawp /gɔ:p/ vi (fam) glotzen; ~ at anglotzen

gay /geɪ/ a (-er, -est) fröhlich; (fam) homosexuell, (fam) schwul

gaze /geɪz/ n [langer] Blick m □vi sehen; ~ at ansehen

gazelle /gə'zel/ n Gazelle f

GB abbr of Great Britain

gear /gɪə(r)/ n Ausrüstung f; (Techn) Getriebe nt; (Auto) Gang m; in ~ mit eingelegtem Gang; change ~ schalten □vt anpassen (to dat)

gear: ~**box** n (Auto) Getriebe nt. ~-**lever** n, (Amer) ~-**shift** n Schalthebel m

geese /gi:s/ see goose

geezer /'gi:zə(r)/n (sl) Typ m

gel /dʒel/ n Gel nt

gelatine /'dʒelətɪn/ n Gelatine f

gelignite /'dʒelɪgnaɪt/ n Gelatinedynamit nt

gem /dʒem/ n Juwel nt

Gemini /'dʒemɪnaɪ/ n (Astr) Zwillinge pl

gender /'dʒendə(r)/ n (Gram) Geschlecht nt

gene /dʒi:n/ n Gen nt

genealogy /dʒi:nɪ'ælədʒɪ/ n Genealogie f

general /'dʒenrəl/ a allgemein □n General m; in ~ im allgemeinen. ~ **e'lection** n allgemeine Wahlen pl

generaliz|ation /dʒenrəlar'zeɪʃn/ n Verallgemeinerung f. ~**e** /'dʒenrəlaɪz/ vi verallgemeinern

generally /'dʒenrəlɪ/ adv im allgemeinen

general prac'titioner n praktischer Arzt m

generate /'dʒenəreɪt/ vt erzeugen

generation /dʒenə'reɪʃn/ n Generation f

generator /'dʒenəreɪtə(r)/n Generator m

generic /dʒɪ'nerɪk/ a ~ **term** Oberbegriff m

generosity /dʒenə'rɒsɪtɪ/ n Großzügigkeit f

generous /'dʒenərəs/ a, -ly adv großzügig

genetic /dʒɪ'netɪk/ a genetisch. ~ **engineering** n Gentechnologie f. ~**s** n Genetik f

Geneva /dʒɪ'ni:və/ n Genf nt

genial /'dʒi:nɪəl/ a, -ly adv freundlich

genitals /'dʒenɪtlz/ pl [äußere] Geschlechtsteile pl

genitive /'dʒenɪtɪv/ a & n ~ [**case**] Genitiv m

genius /'dʒi:nɪəs/ n (pl -**uses**) Genie nt; (quality) Genialität f

genocide /'dʒenəsaɪd/ n Völkermord m

genre /'ʒɑ̃rə/ n Gattung f, Genre f

gent /dʒent/ n (fam) Herr m; the ~**s** sg die Herrentoilette f

genteel /dʒen'ti:l/ a vornehm

gentle /'dʒentl/ a (-r, -st) sanft

gentleman /'dʒentlmən/n Herr m; (well-mannered) Gentleman m

gent|leness /'dʒentlnɪs/ n Sanftheit f. ~**ly** adv sanft

genuine /'dʒenjʊɪn/ a echt; (sincere) aufrichtig. ~**ly** adv (honestly) ehrlich

genus /'dʒi:nəs/ n (Biol) Gattung f

geographical /dʒɪə'græfɪkl/ a, -ly adv geographisch. ~**y** /dʒɪ'ɒgrəfɪ/ n Geographie f, Erdkunde f

geological /dʒɪə'lɒdʒɪkl/ a, -ly adv geologisch

geolog|ist /dʒɪ'ɒlədʒɪst/ n Geologe m/-gin f. ~**y** n Geologie f

geometr|ic(al) /dʒɪə'metrɪk(l)/ a geometrisch. ~**y** /dʒɪ'ɒmətrɪ/ n Geometrie f

geranium /dʒə'reɪnɪəm/ n Geranie f

geriatric /dʒerɪˈætrɪk/ a geriatrisch □n geriatrischer Patient m. ~s n Geriatrie f

germ /dʒɜːm/ n Keim m; ~s pl (fam) Bazillen pl

German /ˈdʒɜːmən/ a deutsch □n (person) Deutsche(r) m/f; (Lang) Deutsch nt; in ~ auf deutsch; into ~ ins Deutsche

Germanic /dʒəˈmænɪk/ a germanisch

German: ~ 'measles n Röteln pl. ~ 'shepherd [dog] n [deutscher] Schäferhund m

Germany /ˈdʒɜːmənɪ/ n Deutschland nt

germinate /ˈdʒɜːmɪneɪt/ vi keimen

gesticulate /dʒeˈstɪkjʊleɪt/ vi gestikulieren

gesture /ˈdʒestʃə(r)/ n Geste f

get /get/ v (pt/pp got, pp Amer also gotten, pres p getting) □vt bekommen, (fam) kriegen; (procure) besorgen; (buy) kaufen; (fetch) holen; (take) bringen; (on telephone) erreichen; (fam: understand) kapieren; machen (meal); ~ s.o. to do sth jdn dazu bringen, etw zu tun □vi (become) werden; ~ to kommen zu/nach (town); (reach) erreichen; ~ dressed sich anziehen; ~ married heiraten. ~ at vt herankommen an (+ acc); what are you ~ting at? worauf willst du hinaus? ~ away vi (leave) wegkommen; (escape) entkommen. ~ back vi zurückkommen □vt (recover) zurückbekommen; ~ one's own back sich revanchieren. ~ by vi vorbeikommen; (manage) sein Auskommen haben. ~ down vi heruntersteigen; ~ down to sich [heran]machen an (+ acc) □vt (depress) deprimieren. ~ in vi einsteigen □vt (fetch) hereinholen. ~ off vi (dismount) absteigen; (from bus) aussteigen; (leave) wegkommen □vt (Jur) freigesprochen werden □vt (remove)

abbekommen. ~ on vi (mount) aufsteigen; (to bus) einsteigen; (be on good terms) gut auskommen (with mit); (make progress) Fortschritte machen; how are you ~ting on? wie geht's? ~ out vi herauskommen; (of car) aussteigen; (avoid doing) sich drücken um □vt herausholen; herauskommen (cork, stain). ~ over vi hinübersteigen □vt (fig) hinwegkommen über (+ acc). ~ round vi herumkommen; (avoid) umgehen; I never ~ round to it ich komme nie dazu □vt herumkriegen. ~ through vi durchkommen. ~ up vi aufstehen

get: ~away n Flucht f. ~-up n Aufmachung f

geyser /ˈgiːzə(r)/ n Durchlauferhitzer m; (Geol) Geysir m

ghastly /ˈgɑːstlɪ/ a (-ier, -iest) gräßlich; (pale) blaß

gherkin /ˈgɜːkɪn/ n Essiggurke f

ghetto /ˈgetəʊ/ n Getto nt

ghost /ɡəʊst/ n Geist m, Gespenst nt. ~ly a geisterhaft

ghoulish /ˈguːlɪʃ/ a makaber

giant /ˈdʒaɪənt/ n Riese m □a riesig

gibberish /ˈdʒɪbərɪʃ/ n Kauderwelsch nt

gibe /dʒaɪb/ n spöttische Bemerkung f □vi spotten (at über + acc)

giblets /ˈdʒɪblɪts/ npl Geflügelklein nt

giddiness /ˈgɪdɪnɪs/ n Schwindel m

giddy /ˈgɪdɪ/ a (-ier, -iest) schwindlig; I feel ~ mir ist schwindlig

gift /gɪft/ n Geschenk nt; (to charity) Gabe f; (talent) Begabung f. ~ed /-ɪd/ a begabt. ~-wrap vt als Geschenk einpacken

gig /gɪg/ n (fam, Mus) Gig m

gigantic /dʒaɪˈgæntɪk/ a riesig, riesengroß

giggle /ˈgɪgl/ n Kichern nt □vi kichern

gild /gɪld/ vt vergolden

gills /gɪlz/ npl Kiemen pl

gilt /gɪlt/ a vergoldet □n Vergoldung f. **~-edged** a (Comm) mündelsicher

gimmick /'gɪmɪk/ n Trick m

gin /dʒɪn/ n Gin m

ginger /'dʒɪndʒə(r)/ a rotblond; ⟨cat⟩ rot □n Ingwer m. **~ bread** n Pfefferkuchen m

gingerly /'dʒɪndʒəlɪ/ adv vorsichtig

gipsy /'dʒɪpsɪ/ n = **gypsy**

giraffe /dʒɪ'rɑːf/ n Giraffe f

girder /'gɜːdə(r)/ n (Techn) Träger m

girdle /'gɜːdl/ n Bindegürtel m; (corset) Hüfthalter m

girl /gɜːl/ n Mädchen nt; (young woman) junge Frau f. **~ friend** n Freundin f. **~ ish**, **-ly** adv mädchenhaft

giro /'dʒaɪərəʊ/ n Giro nt; (cheque) Postscheck m

girth /gɜːθ/ n Umfang m; (for horse) Bauchgurt m

gist /dʒɪst/ n the **~** das Wesentliche

give /gɪv/ n Elastizität f □v (pt gave, pp given) (a) geben/(as present) schenken (to dat); (donate) spenden; (lecture) halten; ⟨one's name⟩ angeben □vi geben; (yield) nachgeben. **~ away** vt verschenken; (betray) verraten; (distribute) verteilen; **~ away the bride** ≈ Brautführer sein. **~ back** vt zurückgeben. **~ in** vt einreichen □vi (yield) nachgeben. **~ off** vt abgeben. **~ up** vt/i aufgeben; **~ oneself up** sich stellen. **~ way** vi nachgeben; (Auto) die Vorfahrt beachten

given /'gɪvn/ see **give** □a **~ name** Vorname m

glacier /'glæsɪə(r)/ n Gletscher m

glad /glæd/ a froh (**of** + acc). **~den** /'glædn/ vt erfreuen

glade /gleɪd/ n Lichtung f

gladly /'glædlɪ/ adv gern[e]

glamorous /'glæmərəs/ a glanzvoll; ⟨film star⟩ glamourös

glamour /'glæmə(r)/ n [betörender] Glanz m

glance /glɑːns/ n [flüchtiger] Blick m □vi **~ at** einen Blick werfen auf (+ acc). **~ up** n aufblicken

gland /glænd/ n Drüse f

glandular /'glændjʊlə(r)/ a Drüsen-

glare /gleə(r)/ n grelles Licht nt; (look) ärgerlicher Blick m □vi **~ at** böse ansehen

glaring /'gleərɪŋ/ a grell; ⟨mistake⟩ kraß

glass /glɑːs/ n Glas nt; (mirror) Spiegel m; **~es** pl (spectacles) Brille f. **~y** a glasig

glaze /gleɪz/ n Glasur f □vt verglasen; (Culin, Pottery) glasieren

glazier /'gleɪzɪə(r)/ n Glaser m

gleam /gliːm/ n Schein m □vi glänzen

glean /gliːn/ vi Ähren lesen □vt (learn) erfahren

glee /gliː/ n Frohlocken nt. **~ful** a, **-ly** adv frohlockend

glen /glen/ n [enges] Tal nt

glib /glɪb/ a, **-ly** adv (pej) gewandt

glide /glaɪd/ vi gleiten; (through the air) schweben. **~er** n Segelflugzeug nt. **~ing** n Segelfliegen nt

glimmer /'glɪmə(r)/ n Glimmen nt □vi glimmen

glimpse /glɪmps/ n **catch a ~ of** flüchtig sehen □vt flüchtig sehen

glint /glɪnt/ n Blitzen nt □vi blitzen

glisten /'glɪsn/ vi glitzern

glitter /'glɪtə(r)/ vi glitzern

gloat /gləʊt/ vi schadenfroh sein; **~ over** sich weiden an (+ dat)

global /'gləʊbl/ a, **-ly** adv global

globe /gləʊb/ n Kugel f; (map) Globus m

gloom /gluːm/ n Düsterkeit f; (fig) Pessimismus m

gloomy /'glu:mɪ/ a ⟨-ier, -iest⟩, **-ily** adv düster; ⟨fig⟩ pessimistisch

glorify /'glɔ:rɪfaɪ/ vt ⟨pt/pp -ied⟩ verherrlichen; **a ~ied waitress** eine bessere Kellnerin f

glorious /'glɔ:rɪəs/ a herrlich; ⟨deed, hero⟩ glorreich

glory /'glɔ:rɪ/ n Ruhm m; ⟨splendour⟩ Pracht f □vi ~ **in** genießen

gloss /glɒs/ n Glanz m □a Glanz- □vi ~ **over** beschönigen

glossary /'glɒsərɪ/ n Glossar nt

glossy /'glɒsɪ/ a ⟨-ier, -iest⟩ glänzend

glove /glʌv/ n Handschuh m. ~ **compartment** n ⟨Auto⟩ Handschuhfach nt

glow /gləʊ/ n Glut f; ⟨of candle⟩ Schein m □vi glühen; ⟨candle:⟩ scheinen. ~**ing** a glühend; ⟨account⟩ begeistert

'glow-worm n Glühwürmchen nt

glucose /'glu:kəʊs/ n Traubenzucker m, Glukose f

glue /glu:/ n Klebstoff m □vt ⟨pres p **gluing**⟩ kleben (**to** an + acc)

glum /glʌm/ a ⟨glummer, glummest⟩, **-ly** adv niedergeschlagen

glut /glʌt/ n Überfluß m ⟨of + dat⟩; ~ **of fruit** Obstschwemme f

glutton /'glʌtən/ n Vielfraß m. ~**ous** /-əs/ a gefräßig. ~**y** n Gefräßigkeit f

gnarled /nɑ:ld/ a knorrig; ⟨hands⟩ knotig

gnash /næʃ/ vt ~ **one's teeth** mit den Zähnen knirschen

gnat /næt/ n Mücke f

gnaw /nɔ:/ vt/i nagen ⟨at an + dat⟩

gnome /nəʊm/ n Gnom m

go /gəʊ/ n ⟨pl **goes**⟩ Energie f; ⟨attempt⟩ Versuch m; **on the go** auf Trab; **at one go** auf einmal; **it's your go** du bist dran; **make a go of it** Erfolg haben □vi ⟨pt **went**, pp **gone**⟩ gehen; ⟨in vehicle⟩ fahren; ⟨leave⟩ weggehen; ⟨on journey⟩ abfahren; ⟨time:⟩ vergehen; ⟨vanish⟩ verschwinden;

versagen; ⟨become⟩ werden; ⟨belong⟩ kommen; **go swimming/shopping** schwimmen/einkaufen gehen; **where are you going?** wo gehst du hin? **it's all gone** es ist nichts mehr übrig; **I am not going to** ich werde es nicht tun; **'to go'** ⟨Amer⟩ 'zum Mitnehmen'. **go away** vi weggehen/-fahren. **go back** vi zurückgehen/-fahren. **go by** vi vorbeigehen/-fahren; ⟨time:⟩ vergehen. **go down** vi hinuntergehen/-fahren; ⟨sun, ship:⟩ untergehen; ⟨prices:⟩ fallen; ⟨temperature, swelling:⟩ zurückgehen. **go for** vt holen; ⟨fam: attack⟩ losgehen auf (+ acc). **go in** vi hineingehen/-fahren; **go in for** teilnehmen an (+ dat) ⟨competition⟩; ⟨take up⟩ sich verlegen auf (+ acc). **go off** vi weggehen/-fahren; ⟨alarm:⟩ klingeln; ⟨gun, bomb:⟩ losgehen; ⟨go bad⟩ schlecht werden; **go off well** gut verlaufen. **go on** vi weitergehen/-fahren; ⟨continue⟩ weitermachen; ⟨talking⟩ fortfahren; ⟨happen⟩ vorgehen; **go on at** ⟨fam⟩ herumnörgeln an (+ dat.). **go out** vi ausgehen; ⟨leave⟩ hinausgehen/-fahren. **go over** vi hinübergehen/-fahren □vt ⟨check⟩ durchgehen. **go round** vi herumgehen/-fahren; ⟨visit⟩ vorbeigehen; ⟨turn⟩ sich drehen; ⟨be enough⟩ reichen. **go through** vi durchgehen/-fahren □vt ⟨suffer⟩ durchmachen; ⟨check⟩ durchgehen. **go under** vi untergehen; ⟨fail⟩ scheitern. **go up** vi hinaufgehen/-fahren; ⟨lift:⟩ hochfahren; ⟨prices:⟩ steigen. **go without** vt verzichten auf (+ acc) □vi darauf verzichten

goad /gəʊd/ vt anstacheln ⟨into zu⟩; ⟨taunt⟩ reizen

'go-ahead a fortschrittlich; ⟨enterprising⟩ unternehmend □n ⟨fig⟩ grünes Licht nt

goal /gəʊl/ n Ziel nt; (Sport) Tor nt.
~-**keeper** n Torwart m. ~-**post** n
Torpfosten m

goat /gəʊt/ n Ziege f

gobble /'gɒbl/ vt hinunterschlingen

'**go-between** n Vermittler(in)
m(f)

goblet /'gɒblɪt/ n Pokal m; (glass)
Kelchglas nt

goblin /'gɒblɪn/ n Kobold m

God, god /gɒd/ n Gott m

god: ~-**child** n Patenkind nt. ~-
daughter n Patentochter f.
~**dess** n Göttin f. ~-**father** n
Pate m. G~-**forsaken** a gottver-
lassen. ~-**mother** n Patin f.
~**parents** npl Paten pl. ~-**send** n
Segen m. ~-**son** n Patensohn m

goggle /'gɒgl/ vi (fam) ~ at glotzen. ~**s** npl Schutzbrille f

going /'gəʊɪŋ/ a (price, rate) gängig; (concern) gutgehend □n it is
hard ~ es ist schwierig; while
the ~ is good solange es noch
geht. ~**s-'on** npl [seltsame] Vor-
gänge pl

gold /gəʊld/ n Gold nt □ a golden

golden /'gəʊldn/ a golden. ~-
'**handshake** n hohe Abfindungs-
summe f. ~'**wedding** n goldene
Hochzeit f

gold: ~-**fish** n inv Goldfisch m. ~-
mine n Goldgrube f. ~-**plated** a
vergoldet. ~-**smith** n Gold-
schmied m

golf /gɒlf/ n Golf nt

golf: ~-**club** n Golfklub m; (implement) Golfschläger m. ~-**course**
n Golfplatz m. ~-**er** n Golf-
spieler(in) m(f)

gondola /'gɒndələ/ n Gondel f.
~-**lier** /-'lɪə(r)/ n Gondoliere m

gone /gɒn/ see **go**

gong /gɒŋ/ n Gong m

good /gʊd/ a (better, best) gut;
(well-behaved) brav, artig; ~ at
gut in (+ dat); a ~ **deal** ziemlich
viel; as ~ as so gut wie; (almost)
fast; ~ **morning/evening** guten
Morgen/Abend; ~ **afternoon**

guten Tag; ~ **night** gute Nacht
□n the ~ das Gute; for ~ für immer; do ~ Gutes tun; do s.o. ~
jdm guttun; it's no ~ es ist nutzlos; (hopeless) da ist nichts zu
machen; be up to no ~ nichts
Gutes im Schilde führen

goodbye /gʊd'baɪ/ int auf Wiedersehen; (Teleph, Radio) auf
Wiederhören

good: ~-**for-nothing** a nichts-
nutzig □n Taugenichts m. G~-
'**Friday** n Karfreitag m. ~-'**looking** a gutaussehend. ~-'**natured**
a gutmütig

goodness /'gʊdnɪs/ n Güte f; **my**
~! du meine Güte! **thank** ~! Gott
sei Dank!

goods /gʊdz/ npl Waren pl. ~-
train n Güterzug m

good'will n Wohlwollen nt;
(Comm) Goodwill m

goody /'gʊdɪ/ n (fam) Gute(r) m/f.
~-**goody** n Musterkind nt

gooey /'guːɪ/ a (fam) klebrig

goof /guːf/ vi (fam) einen Schnitzer machen

goose /guːs/ n (pl **geese**) Gans f

gooseberry /'gʊzbərɪ/ n Stachel-
beere f

goose /guːs/: ~-**flesh** n, ~-
pimples npl Gänsehaut f

gore[1] /gɔː(r)/ n Blut nt

gore[2] vt mit den Hörnern aufspießen

gorge /gɔːdʒ/ n (Geog) Schlucht f
□vt ~ **oneself** sich vollessen

gorgeous /'gɔːdʒəs/ a prachtvoll;
(fam) herrlich

gorilla /gə'rɪlə/ n Gorilla m

gormless /'gɔːmlɪs/ a (fam) doof

gorse /gɔːs/ n inv Stechginster m

gory /'gɔːrɪ/ a (-ier, -iest) blutig;
(story) blutrünstig

gosh /gɒʃ/ int (fam) Mensch!

go-'slow n Bummelstreik m

gospel /'gɒspl/ n Evangelium nt

gossip /'gɒsɪp/ n Klatsch m; (person) Klatschbase f □vi klatschen.
~-**y** a geschwätzig

got /gɒt/ *see* get; **have ~ haben**; **have ~ to müssen**; **have ~ to do sth** etw tun müssen

Gothic /'gɒθɪk/ *a* gotisch

gotten /'gɒtn/ *see* get

gouge /gaʊdʒ/ *vt ~* **out** aushöhlen

goulash /'guːlæʃ/ *n* Gulasch *nt*

gourmet /'gʊəmeɪ/ *n* Feinschmecker *m*

gout /gaʊt/ *n* Gicht *f*

govern /'gʌvn/ *vt/i* regieren; *(determine)* bestimmen. **~ess** *n* Gouvernante *f*

government /'gʌvnmənt/ *n* Regierung *f*. **~al** /-'mentl/ *a* Regierungs-

governor /'gʌvənə(r)/ *n* Gouverneur *m*; *(on board)* Vorstandsmitglied *nt*; *(of prison)* Direktor *m*; *(fam: boss)* Chef *m*

gown /gaʊn/ *n* [elegantes] Kleid *nt*; *(Univ, Jur)* Talar *m*

GP *abbr of* general practitioner

grab /græb/ *vt (pt/pp* grabbed*)* ergreifen; *~* **[hold of]** packen

grace /greɪs/ *n* Anmut *f*; *(before meal)* Tischgebet *nt*; *(Relig)* Gnade *f*; **with good ~** mit Anstand; **say ~** [vor dem Essen] beten; **three days' ~** drei Tage Frist. **~ful**, **~fully** *a*, *-ly adv* anmutig

gracious /'greɪʃəs/ *a* gnädig; *(elegant)* vornehm

grade /greɪd/ *n* Stufe *f*; *(Comm)* Güteklasse *f*; *(Sch)* Note *f*; *(Amer, Sch: class)* Klasse *f*; *(Amer)* = **gradient** □*vt* einstufen; *(Comm)* sortieren. **~ crossing** *n (Amer)* Bahnübergang *m*

gradient /'greɪdɪənt/ *n* Steigung *f*; *(downward)* Gefälle *nt*

gradual /'grædʒʊəl/ *a*, *-ly adv* allmählich

graduate¹ /'grædʒʊət/ *n* Akademiker(in) *m(f)*

graduate² /'grædʒʊeɪt/ *vi (Univ)* sein Examen machen. **~d** *a* abgestuft; *(container)* mit Maßeinteilung

graffiti /grə'fiːtiː/ *npl* Graffiti *pl*

graft /grɑːft/ *n (Bot)* Pfropfreis *nt*; *(Med)* Transplantat *nt*; *(fam: hard work)* Plackerei *f* □*vt (Bot)* aufpfropfen; *(Med)* übertragen

grain /greɪn/ *n (sand, salt, rice)* Korn *nt*; *(cereals)* Getreide *nt*; *(in wood)* Maserung *f*; **against the ~** *(fig)* gegen den Strich

gram /græm/ *n* Gramm *nt*

grammar /'græmə(r)/ *n* Grammatik *f*. **~ school** *n* ≈ Gymnasium *nt*

grammatical /grə'mætɪkl/ *a*, *-ly adv* grammatisch

granary /'grænərɪ/ *n* Getreidespeicher *m*

grand /grænd/ *a* (-er, -est) großartig

grandad /'grændæd/ *n (fam)* Opa *m*

'grandchild *n* Enkelkind *nt*

'granddaughter *n* Enkelin *f*

grandeur /'grændʒə(r)/ *n* Pracht *f*

'grandfather *n* Großvater *m*. **~ clock** *n* Standuhr *f*

grandiose /'grændɪəʊs/ *a* grandios

grand: **~mother** *n* Großmutter *f*. **~parents** *npl* Großeltern *pl*. **~pi'ano** *n* Flügel *m*. **~son** *n* Enkel *m*. **~stand** *n* Tribüne *f*

granite /'grænɪt/ *n* Granit *m*

granny /'grænɪ/ *n (fam)* Oma *f*

grant /grɑːnt/ *n* Subvention *f*; *(Univ)* Studienbeihilfe *f* □*vt* gewähren; *(admit)* zugeben; **take sth for ~ed** etw als selbstverständlich hinnehmen

granular /'grænjʊlə(r)/ *a* körnig

granulated /'grænjʊleɪtɪd/ *a* **~ sugar** Kristallzucker *m*

granule /'grænjuːl/ *n* Körnchen *nt*

grape /greɪp/ *n* [Wein]traube *f*; **bunch of ~s** [ganze] Weintraube *f*

grapefruit /'greɪp-/ *n inv* Grapefruit *f*, Pampelmuse *f*

graph /grɑːf/ *n* Kurvendiagramm *nt*

graphic /'græfɪk/ *a*, **-ally** *adv* grafisch; (*vivid*) anschaulich. **~s** *n* (*design*) grafische Gestaltung *nt*

'graph paper *n* Millimeterpapier *nt*

grapple /'græpl/ *vi* ringen

grasp /grɑːsp/ *n* Griff *m* □ *vt* ergreifen; (*understand*) begreifen. **~ing** *a* habgierig

grass /grɑːs/ *n* Gras *nt*; (*lawn*) Rasen *m*; **at the ~ roots** an der Basis. **~ hopper** *n* Heuschrecke *f*. **~ land** *n* Weideland *nt*

grassy /'grɑːsɪ/ *a* grasig

grate[1] /greɪt/ *n* Feuerrost *m*; (*hearth*) Kamin *m*

grate[2] *vt* (*Culin*) reiben; **~ one's teeth** mit den Zähnen knirschen

grateful /'greɪtfl/ *a*, **-ly** *adv* dankbar (**to** *dat*)

grater /'greɪtə(r)/ *n* (*Culin*) Reibe *f*

gratify /'grætɪfaɪ/ *vt* (*pt/pp* **-ied**) befriedigen. **~ing** *a* erfreulich

grating /'greɪtɪŋ/ *n* Gitter *nt*

gratis /'grɑːtɪs/ *adv* gratis

gratitude /'grætɪtjuːd/ *n* Dankbarkeit *f*

gratuitous /grə'tjuːɪtəs/ *a* (*uncalled for*) überflüssig

gratuity /grə'tjuːətɪ/ *n* (*tip*) Trinkgeld *nt*

grave[1] /greɪv/ *a* (**-r, -st**), **-ly** *adv* ernst; **~ly ill** schwer krank

grave[2] *n* Grab *nt*. **~-digger** *n* Totengräber *m*

gravel /'grævl/ *n* Kies *m*

grave: **~ stone** *n* Grabstein *m*. **~ yard** *n* Friedhof *m*

gravitate /'grævɪteɪt/ *vi* gravitieren

gravity /'grævətɪ/ *n* Ernst *m*; (*force*) Schwerkraft *f*

gravy /'greɪvɪ/ *n* [Braten]soße *f*

gray /greɪ/ *a* (*Amer*) = **grey**

graze[1] /greɪz/ *vi* ⟨*animal*⟩ weiden

graze[2] *n* Schürfwunde *f* □ *vt* ⟨*car*⟩ streifen; ⟨*knee*⟩ aufschürfen

grease /griːs/ *n* Fett *nt*; (*lubricant*) Schmierfett *nt* □ *vt* einfetten; (*lubricate*) schmieren. **~-proof 'paper** *n* Pergamentpapier *nt*

greasy /'griːsɪ/ *a* (**-ier, -iest**) fettig

great /greɪt/ *a* (**-er, -est**) groß; (*fam: marvellous*) großartig

great: **~'aunt** *n* Großtante *f*. **G~ 'Britain** *n* Großbritannien *nt*. **~ 'grandchildren** *npl* Urenkel *pl*. **~'grandfather** *n* Urgroßvater *m*. **~'grandmother** *n* Urgroßmutter *f*

greatly /'greɪtlɪ/ *adv* sehr. **~ness** *n* Größe *f*

great-'uncle *n* Großonkel *m*

Greece /griːs/ *n* Griechenland *nt*

greed /griːd/ *n* [Hab]gier *f*

greedy /'griːdɪ/ *a* (**-ier, -iest**), **-ily** *adv* gierig; **don't be ~** sei nicht so unbescheiden

Greek /griːk/ *a* griechisch □ *n* Grieche *m*/Griechin *f*; (*Lang*) Griechisch *nt*

green /griːn/ *a* (**-er, -est**) grün; (*fig*) unerfahren □ *n* Grün *nt*; (*grass*) Wiese *f*; **~s** *pl* Kohl *m*; **the G~s** *pl* (*Pol*) die Grünen *pl*

greenery /'griːnərɪ/ *n* Grün *nt*

'greenfly *n* Blattlaus *f*

greengage /'griːngeɪdʒ/ *n* Reneklode *f*

green: **~grocer** *n* Obst- und Gemüsehändler *m*. **~house** *n* Gewächshaus *nt*. **~house effect** *n* Treibhauseffekt *m*

Greenland /'griːnlənd/ *n* Grönland *nt*

greet /griːt/ *vt* grüßen; (*welcome*) begrüßen. **~ing** *n* Gruß *m*; (*welcome*) Begrüßung *f*. **~ings card** *n* Glückwunschkarte *f*

gregarious /grɪ'geərɪəs/ *a* gesellig

grenade /grɪ'neɪd/ *n* Granate *f*

grew /gruː/ *see* **grow**

grey /greɪ/ *a* (**-er, -est**) grau □ *n* Grau *nt* □ *vi* grau werden. **~ hound** *n* Windhund *m*

grid /grɪd/ *n* Gitter *nt*; (*on map*) Gitternetz *nt*; (*Electr*) Überlandleitungsnetz *nt*

grief /griːf/ *n* Trauer *f*; **come to ~** scheitern

grievance /'griːvəns/ *n* Beschwerde *f*

grieve /griːv/ vt betrüben □ vi
trauern (for um)

grievous /ˈgriːvəs/ a, **-ly** adv
schwer

grill /grɪl/ n Gitter nt; (Culin) Grill
m; **mixed ~** Gemischtes nt
vom Grill □ vt/i grillen; (interrogate) [streng] verhören

grille /grɪl/ n Gitter nt

grim /grɪm/ a (**grimmer, grim-
mest**), **-ly** adv ernst; (determination) verbissen

grimace /grɪˈmeɪs/ n Grimasse f
□ vi Grimassen schneiden

grime /graɪm/ n Schmutz m

grimy /ˈgraɪmɪ/ a (**-ier, -iest**)
schmutzig

grin /grɪn/ n Grinsen nt □ vi (pt/pp
grinned) grinsen

grind /graɪnd/ n (fam: hard work)
Plackerei f □ vt (pt/pp **ground**)
mahlen; (smooth, sharpen)
schleifen; (Amer: mince) durchdrehen; **~ one's teeth** mit den
Zähnen knirschen

grip /grɪp/ n Griff m; (bag) Reise-
tasche f □ vt (pt/pp **gripped**) ergreifen; (hold) festhalten; fesseln
(interest)

gripe /graɪp/ vi (sl: grumble)
meckern

gripping /ˈgrɪpɪŋ/ a fesselnd

grisly /ˈgrɪzlɪ/ a (**-ier, -iest**)
grausig

gristle /ˈgrɪsl/ n Knorpel m

grit /grɪt/ n [grober] Sand m; (for
roads) Streugut nt; (courage) Mut
m □ vt (pt/pp **gritted**) streuen
(road); **~ one's teeth** die Zähne
zusammenbeißen

grizzle /ˈgrɪzl/ vi quengeln

groan /grəʊn/ n Stöhnen nt □ vi
stöhnen

grocer /ˈgrəʊsə(r)/ n Lebensmittel-
händler m; **~'s [shop]** Lebens-
mittelgeschäft nt; **~ies** npl Lebensmittel pl

groggy /ˈgrɒgɪ/ a schwach; (unsteady) wackelig [auf den Beinen]

groin /grɔɪn/ n (Anat) Leiste f

groom /gruːm/ n Bräutigam m;
(for horse) Pferdepfleger(in) m(f)
□ vt striegeln (horse)

groove /gruːv/ n Rille f

grope /grəʊp/ vi tasten (for nach)

gross /grəʊs/ a (**-er, -est**) fett;
(coarse) derb; (glaring) grob;
(Comm) brutto; (of coffee) Satz
m □ vi (ship:) auflaufen □ vt aus
dem Verkehr ziehen (aircraft);
(Amer, Electr) erden

ground /graʊnd/ a (very) sehr
Brutto- □ n inv Gros nt. **~ly** adv
(very) sehr

grotesque /grəʊˈtesk/ a, **-ly** adv
grotesk

grotto /ˈgrɒtəʊ/ n (pl **-es**) Grotte f

grotty /ˈgrɒtɪ/ a (fam) mies

ground¹ /graʊnd/ see **grind**

ground² n Boden m; (terrain) Gelände nt; (reason) Grund m;
(Amer, Electr) Erde f; **~s** pl
(park) Anlagen pl; (of coffee) Satz
m □ vt (ship:) auflaufen □ vt aus
dem Verkehr ziehen (aircraft);
(Amer, Electr) erden

ground: ~ floor n Erdgeschoß
nt. **~ing** n Grundlage f. **~less**
a grundlos. **~'meat** n Hackfleisch
nt. **~sheet** n Bodenplane f.
~work n Vorarbeiten pl

group /gruːp/ n Gruppe f □ vt gruppieren □ vi sich gruppieren

grouse¹ /graʊs/ n inv schottisches
Moorschneehuhn nt

grouse² /graʊs/ vi (fam) meckern

grovel /ˈgrɒvl/ vi (pt/pp **grov-
elled**) kriechen. **~ling** a krie-
cherisch

grow /grəʊ/ v (pt **grew**, pp **grown**)
□ vi wachsen; (become) werden;
(increase) zunehmen □ vt anbauen; **~ one's hair** sich (dat)
die Haare wachsen lassen. **~ up**
vi aufwachsen; (town:) entstehen

growl /graʊl/ n Knurren nt □ vi
knurren

grown /grəʊn/ see **grow**. **~-up** a
erwachsen □ n Erwachsene(r) m/f

growth /grəʊθ/ n Wachstum nt;
(increase) Zunahme f; (Med) Gewächs nt

grub /grʌb/ n (larva) Made f;
(fam: food) Essen nt

grubby /'grʌbɪ/ a (-ier, -iest) schmuddelig

grudge /grʌdʒ/ n Groll m; **bear s.o. a ~e** einen Groll gegen jdn hegen □vt **~ e s.o. sth** jdm etw mißgönnen. **~ing** a, **-ly** adv widerwillig

gruelling /'gru:əlɪŋ/ a strapaziös

gruesome /'gru:səm/ a grausig

gruff /grʌf/ a, **-ly** adv barsch

grumble /'grʌmbl/ vi schimpfen (**at** mit)

grumpy /'grʌmpɪ/ a (-ier, -iest) griesgrämig

grunt /grʌnt/ n Grunzen nt □vi grunzen

guarantee /gærən'ti:/ n Garantie f; (document) Garantieschein m □vt garantieren; garantieren für (quality, success); **be ~eed** (product:) Garantie haben. **~or** n Bürge m

guard /gɑ:d/ n Wache f; (security) Wächter m; (on train) ≈ Zugführer m; (Techn) Schutz m; **be on ~** Wache stehen; **on one's ~** auf der Hut □vt bewachen; (protect) schützen □vi ~ **against** sich hüten vor (+ dat). **~-dog** n Wachhund m

guarded /gɑ:dɪd/ a vorsichtig

guardian /'gɑ:dɪən/ n Vormund m

guerrilla /gə'rɪlə/ n Guerillakämpfer m. **~ warfare** n Partisanenkrieg m

guess /ges/ n Vermutung f □vt erraten □vi raten; (Amer: believe) glauben. **~work** n Vermutung f

guest /gest/ n Gast m. **~-house** n Pension f

guffaw /gʌ'fɔ:/ n derbes Lachen nt □vi derb lachen

guidance /'gaɪdəns/ n Führung f, Leitung f; (advice) Beratung f

guide /gaɪd/ n Führer(in) m(f); (book) Führer m; **[Girl] G ~** Pfadfinderin f □vt führen, leiten. **~book** n Führer m

guided /'gaɪdɪd/ a ~ **missile** Fernlenkgeschoß nt; ~ **tour** Führung f

guide: **~-dog** n Blindenhund m. **~ lines** npl Richtlinien pl

guild /gɪld/ n Gilde f, Zunft f

guile /gaɪl/ n Arglist f

guillotine /'gɪlətiːn/ n Guillotine f; (for paper) Papierschneidemaschine f

guilt /gɪlt/ n Schuld f. **~ily** adv schuldbewußt

guilty /'gɪltɪ/ a (-ier, -iest) a schuldig (**of** gen); (look) schuldbewußt; (conscience) schlecht

guinea-pig /'gɪnɪ-/ n Meerschweinchen nt; (person) Versuchskaninchen nt

guise /gaɪz/ n **in the ~ of** in Gestalt (+ gen)

guitar /gɪ'tɑ:(r)/ n Gitarre f. **~ist** n Gitarrist(in) m(f)

gulf /gʌlf/ n (Geog) Golf m; (fig) Kluft f

gull /gʌl/ n Möwe f

gullet /'gʌlɪt/ n Speiseröhre f; (throat) Kehle f

gullible /'gʌlɪbl/ a leichtgläubig

gully /'gʌlɪ/ n Schlucht f; (drain) Rinne f

gulp /gʌlp/ n Schluck m □vi schlucken □vt ~ **down** hinunterschlucken

gum¹ /gʌm/ n & **-s** pl (Anat) Zahnfleisch nt

gum² n Gummi[harz] nt; (glue) Klebstoff m; (chewing-gum) Kaugummi m □vt (pt/pp **gummed**) kleben (**to** an + acc). **~boot** n Gummistiefel m

gummed /gʌmd/ see **gum²** □a (label) gummiert

gumption /'gʌmpʃn/ n (fam) Grips m

gun /gʌn/ n Schußwaffe f; (pistol) Pistole f; (rifle) Gewehr nt; (cannon) Geschütz nt □vt (pt/pp **gunned**) ~ **down** niederschießen

gun: **~fire** n Geschützfeuer nt. **~man** n bewaffneter Bandit m

gunner /'gʌnə(r)/ n Artillerist m

gun: **~powder** n Schießpulver nt. **~shot** n Schuß m

gurgle /'gɜːgl/ vi gluckern; (of baby) glucksen

gush /gʌʃ/ vi strömen; (enthuse) schwärmen (over von). ~ out vi herausströmen

gusset /'gʌsɪt/ n Zwickel m

gust /gʌst/ n (of wind) Windstoß m; (Naut) Bö f

gusto /'gʌstəʊ/ n with ~ mit Schwung

gusty /'gʌstɪ/ a böig

gut /gʌt/ n Darm m. ~s pl Eingeweide pl; (fam: courage) Schneid m □vt (pt/pp gutted) (Culin) ausnehmen; ~ted by fire ausgebrannt

gutter /'gʌtə(r)/ n Rinnstein m; (fig) Gosse f; (on roof) Dachrinne f

guttural /'gʌtərəl/ a guttural

guy /gaɪ/ n (fam) Kerl m

guzzle /'gʌzl/ vt/i schlingen; (drink) schlürfen

gym /dʒɪm/ n (fam) Turnhalle f; (gymnastics) Turnen nt

gymnasium /dʒɪm'neɪzɪəm/ n Turnhalle f

gymnast /'dʒɪmnæst/ n Turner(in) m(f). ~ics /-'næstɪks/ n Turnen nt

gym: ~ shoes pl Turnschuhe pl. ~-slip n (Sch) Trägerkleid nt

gynaecologist /gaɪnɪ'kɒlədʒɪst/ n Frauenarzt m, -ärztin f. ~y n Gynäkologie f

gypsy /'dʒɪpsɪ/ n Zigeuner(in) m(f)

gyrate /dʒaɪə'reɪt/ vi sich drehen

H

haberdashery /'hæbədæʃərɪ/ n Kurzwaren pl; (Amer) Herrenmoden pl

habit /'hæbɪt/ n Gewohnheit f; (Relig: costume) Ordenstracht f; **be in the ~** die Angewohnheit haben (of zu)

habitable /'hæbɪtəbl/ a bewohnbar

habitat /'hæbɪtæt/ n Habitat nt

habitation /hæbɪ'teɪʃn/ n **unfit for human ~** für Wohnzwecke ungeeignet

habitual /hə'bɪtjʊəl/ a gewohnt; (inveterate) gewohnheitsmäßig. ~ly adv gewohnheitsmäßig; (constantly) ständig

hack[1] /hæk/ n (writer) Schreiberling m; (hired horse) Mietpferd nt

hack[2] vt hacken; ~ **to pieces** zerhacken

hackneyed /'hæknɪd/ a abgedroschen

'hacksaw n Metallsäge f

had /hæd/ see **have**

haddock /'hædək/ n inv Schellfisch m

haemorrhage /'hemərɪdʒ/ n Blutung f

haemorrhoids /'hemərɔɪdz/ npl Hämorrhoiden pl

hag /hæg/ n **old** ~ alte Hexe f

haggard /'hægəd/ a abgehärmt

haggle /'hægl/ vi feilschen (over um)

hail[1] /heɪl/ vt begrüßen; herbeirufen (taxi) □vi ~ **from** kommen aus

hail[2] n Hagel m □vi hageln. ~**stone** n Hagelkorn nt

hair /heə(r)/ n Haar nt; **wash one's** ~ sich (dat) die Haare waschen

hair: ~**brush** n Haarbürste f. ~**cut** n Haarschnitt m; **have a ~ cut** sich (dat) die Haare schneiden lassen. ~**do** n (fam) Frisur f. ~**dresser** n Friseur m/Friseuse f. ~**drier** n Haartrockner m; (hand-held) Fön (P) m. ~**grip** n [Haar]klemme f. ~**pin** n Haarnadel f. ~**pin 'bend** n Haarnadelkurve f. ~**raising** a haarsträubend. ~**style** n Frisur f

hairy /'heərɪ/ a (-ier, -iest) behaart; (excessively) haarig; (fam: frightening) brenzlig

hake /heɪk/ n inv Seehecht m

hale /heɪl/ a ~ **and hearty** gesund und munter

half /hɑ:f/ n (pl **halves**) Hälfte f;
cut in ~ halbieren; **one and a**
~ eineinhalb, anderthalb; **a** ~
dozen ein halbes Dutzend; ~
an hour eine halbe Stunde □a &
adv halb; ~ **past** two halb drei;
[at] ~ **price** zum halben Preis

half-: ~-**board** n Halbpension f.
~-**caste** n Mischling m.
~-**hearted** a lustlos. ~-'**hourly**
a & adv halbstündlich. ~-'**mast**
n at ~-**mast** auf halbmast. ~-
measure n Halbheit f. ~-**term**
n schulfreie Tage nach dem halben Trimester. ~-'**timbered** a
Fachwerk-. ~-'**time** n (Sport)
Halbzeit f. ~-'**way** a the ~-**way**
mark/stage die Hälfte □adv auf
halbem Weg; **get** ~-**way** den halben Weg zurücklegen; (fig) bis
zur Hälfte kommen. ~-**wit** n
Idiot m

halibut /ˈhælɪbət/ n inv Heilbutt m
hall /hɔ:l/ n Halle f; (room) Saal m;
(Sch) Aula f; (entrance) Flur m;
(mansion) Gutshaus nt; ~ **of re-**
sidence (Univ) Studentenheim nt
hallmark n [Feingehalts]stem-
pel m; (fig) Kennzeichen nt (of
für) □vt stempeln
hallo /həˈləʊ/ int [guten] Tag!
(fam) hallo!
Hallowe'en /hæləʊˈi:n/ n der Tag
vor Allerheiligen
hallucination /həlu:sɪˈneɪʃn/ n
Halluzination f
halo /ˈheɪləʊ/ n (pl -es) Heiligen-
schein m; (Astr) Hof m
halt /hɔ:lt/ n Halt m; **come to a** ~
stehenbleiben; (traffic:) zum
Stillstand kommen □vi haltmachen; ~! halt! ~**ing** a, adv -ly
zögernd
halve /hɑ:v/ vt halbieren; (reduce)
um die Hälfte reduzieren
ham /hæm/ n Schinken m
hamburger /ˈhæmbɜ:gə(r)/ n
Hamburger m
hamlet /ˈhæmlɪt/ n Weiler m
hammer /ˈhæmə(r)/ n Hammer m
□vt/i hämmern (**at** an + acc)

hammock /ˈhæmək/ n Hänge-
matte f
hamper[1] /ˈhæmpə(r)/ n Picknick-
korb m; [gift] ~ Geschenkkorb m
hamper[2] vt behindern
hamster /ˈhæmstə(r)/ n Hamster
m

hand /hænd/ n Hand f; (of clock)
Zeiger m; (writing) Handschrift f;
(worker) Arbeiter(in) m(f);
(Cards) Blatt nt; **all** ~**s** (Naut)
alle Mann; **at** ~ in der Nähe; **on**
the one/other ~ einer-/anderer-
seits; **out of** ~ außer Kontrolle;
(summarily) kurzerhand; **in** ~
unter Kontrolle; (available) verfügbar; **give s.o. a** ~ jdm behilflich sein □vt reichen (**to** dat). ~
in vt abgeben. ~ **out** vt austeilen. ~ **over** vt überreichen

hand-: ~**bag** n Handtasche f.
~**book** n Handbuch nt. ~**brake**
n Handbremse f. ~**cuffs** npl
Handschellen pl. ~**ful** n Hand-
voll f; **be [quite] a** ~**ful** (fam)
nicht leicht zu haben sein
handicap /ˈhændɪkæp/ n Behinderung f; (Sport & fig) Handikap
nt. ~**ped** a **mentally/physic-**
ally ~**ped** geistig/körperlich
behindert
handi|craft /ˈhændɪkrɑ:ft/ n Ba-
steln nt; (Sch) Werken nt.
~**work** n Werk nt
handkerchief /ˈhæŋkətʃɪf/ n (pl
~**s** & -**chieves**) Taschentuch nt
handle /ˈhændl/ n Griff m; (of
door) Klinke f; (of cup) Henkel m;
(of broom) Stiel m; **fly off the** ~
(fam) aus der Haut fahren □vt
handhaben; (treat) umgehen mit;
(touch) anfassen. ~**bars** npl
Lenkstange f

hand-: ~**luggage** n Handgepäck
nt. ~**made** a handgemacht.
~**out** n Prospekt m; (money)
Unterstützung f. ~**rail** n Handlauf m. ~**shake** n Händedruck m
handsome /ˈhænsəm/ a gutaussehend; (generous) großzügig;
(large) beträchtlich

hand: ~**stand** n Handstand m.
~**writing** n Handschrift f. ~-
'written a handgeschrieben

handy /'hændɪ/ a (-ier, -iest)
handlich; ⟨person⟩ geschickt;
have/ keep ~ griffbereit haben/
halten. ~**man** n [home] ~**man**
Heimwerker m

hang /hæŋ/ vt/i (pt/pp hung) hängen; ~ **wallpaper** tapezieren □ vt
(pt/pp hanged) hängen ⟨crim-
inal⟩; ~ **oneself** sich erhängen
□ n get the ~ **of it** (fam) den Dreh
herauskriegen. ~ **about** vi sich
herumdrücken. ~ **on** vi sich festhalten (**to an** + dat); (fam: wait)
warten. ~ **out** vi heraushängen;
(fam: live) wohnen □ vt draußen
aufhängen ⟨washing⟩. ~ **up** vt/i
aufhängen

hangar /'hæŋə(r)/ n Flugzeug-
halle f

hanger /'hæŋə(r)/ n [Kleider]-
bügel m

hang: ~-**glider** n Drachenflieger
m. ~-**gliding** n Drachenfliegen
nt. ~**man** n Henker m. ~-**over** n
(fam) Kater m (fam).
~-**up** n (fam) Komplex m

hanker /'hæŋkə(r)/ vi ~ **after**
sth sich (dat) etw wünschen

hanky /'hæŋkɪ/ n (fam) Taschentuch nt

hanky-panky /hæŋkɪ'pæŋkɪ/ n
(fam) Mauscheleien pl

haphazard /hæp'hæzəd/ a, -ly
adv planlos

happen /'hæpn/ vi geschehen,
passieren; **as it** ~**s** zufällig-
erweise; **I** ~**ed to be there** ich war
zufällig da; **what has** ~**ed to**
him? was ist mit ihm los? ⟨become
of⟩ was ist aus ihm geworden?
~**ing** n Ereignis nt

happily /'hæpɪlɪ/ adv glücklich;
(fortunately) glücklicherweise.
~**ness** n Glück nt

happy /'hæpɪ/ a (-ier, -iest) glücklich. ~-**go-'lucky** a sorglos

harass /'hærəs/ vt schikanieren.
~**ed** a abgehetzt. ~**ment** n
Schikane f; (sexual) Belästigung f

harbour /'hɑːbə(r)/ n Hafen m □ vt
Unterschlupf gewähren (+ dat);
hegen ⟨grudge⟩

hard /hɑːd/ a (-er, -est) hart; (difficult) schwer; ~ **of hearing**
schwerhörig □ adv hart; ⟨work⟩
schwer; ⟨pull⟩ kräftig; ⟨rain,
snow⟩ stark; **think** ~! denk mal
nach! **be** ~ **up** (fam) knapp bei
Kasse sein; **be** ~ **done by** (fam)
ungerecht behandelt werden

hard: ~**back** n gebundene Ausgabe f. ~**board** n Hartfaserplatte
f. ~-**boiled** a hartgekocht

harden /'hɑːdn/ vi hart werden

hard-'hearted a hartherzig

hard|**ly** /'hɑːdlɪ/ adv kaum; ~**ly**
ever kaum [jemals]. ~**ness** n
Härte f. ~**ship** n Not f

hard: ~'**shoulder** n (Auto)
Randstreifen m. ~**ware** n Haus-
haltswaren pl; (Computing)
Hardware f. ~-'**wearing** a strapazierfähig. ~-'**working** a
fleißig

hardy /'hɑːdɪ/ a (-ier, -iest) abge-
härtet; ⟨plant⟩ winterhart

hare /heə(r)/ n Hase m. ~-**lip** n
Hasenscharte f

hark /hɑːk/ vi ~! hört! ~ **back** vi
~ **back to** (fig) zurückkommen
auf (+ acc)

harm /hɑːm/ n Schaden m; **out of**
~**'s way** in Sicherheit; **it won't**
do any ~ es kann nichts schaden
□ vt ~ **s.o.** jdm etwas antun. ~**ful**
a schädlich. ~**less** a harmlos

harmonica /hɑː'mɒnɪkə/ n Mundharmonika f

harmonious /hɑː'məʊnɪəs/ a, -ly
adv harmonisch

harmonize /'hɑːmənaɪz/ vi (fig)
harmonieren. ~**y** n Harmonie f

harness /'hɑːnɪs/ n Geschirr nt;
(of parachute) Gurtwerk nt □ vt
anschirren ⟨horse⟩; (use) nutzbar machen

harp /hɑːp/ *n* Harfe *f* □ *vi* ~ **on** [**about**] (*fam*) herumreiten auf (+ *dat*). ~**ist** *n* Harfenist(in) *m(f)*

harpoon /hɑːˈpuːn/ *n* Harpune *f*

harpsichord /ˈhɑːpsɪkɔːd/ *n* Cembalo *nt*

harrow /ˈhærəʊ/ *n* Egge *f*. ~**ing** *a* grauenhaft

harsh /hɑːʃ/ *a* (-**er**, -**est**), -**ly** *adv* hart; ⟨*voice*⟩ rauh; ⟨*light*⟩ grell. ~**ness** *n* Härte *f*; Rauheit *f*

harvest /ˈhɑːvɪst/ *n* Ernte *f* □ *vt* ernten

has /hæz/ *see* **have**

hash /hæʃ/ *n* (*Culin*) Haschee *nt*; **make a ~ of** (*fam*) verpfuschen

hashish /ˈhæʃɪʃ/ *n* Haschisch *nt*

hassle /ˈhæsl/ *n* (*fam*) Ärger *m* □ *vt* schikanieren

hassock /ˈhæsək/ *n* Kniekissen *nt*

haste /heɪst/ *n* Eile *f*; **make ~** sich beeilen

hasten /ˈheɪsn/ *vi* sich beeilen (**to** zu); (*go quickly*) eilen □ *vt* beschleunigen

hasty /ˈheɪstɪ/ *a* (-**ier**, -**iest**), -**ily** *adv* hastig; ⟨*decision*⟩ voreilig

hat /hæt/ *n* Hut *m*; (*knitted*) Mütze *f*

hatch[1] /hætʃ/ *n* (*for food*) Durchreiche *f*; (*Naut*) Luke *f*

hatch[2] *vi* ~ [**out**] ausschlüpfen □ *vt* ausbrüten

'hatchback *n* (*Auto*) Modell *nt* mit Hecktür

hatchet /ˈhætʃɪt/ *n* Beil *nt*

hate /heɪt/ *n* Haß *m* □ *vt* hassen. ~**ful** *a* abscheulich

hatred /ˈheɪtrɪd/ *n* Haß *m*

haughty /ˈhɔːtɪ/ *a* (-**ier**, -**iest**), -**ily** *adv* hochmütig

haul /hɔːl/ *n* (*fish*) Fang *m*; (*loot*) Beute *f* □ *vt/i* ziehen (**on an** + *dat*). ~**age** /-ɪdʒ/ *n* Transport *m*. ~**ier** /-ɪə(r)/ *n* Spediteur *m*

haunt /hɔːnt/ *n* Lieblingsaufenthalt *m* □ *vt* umgehen in (+ *dat*); **this house is** ~**ed** in diesem Haus spukt es

have /hæv/ *vt* (*3 sg pres tense* **has**; *pt/pp* **had**) haben; bekommen ⟨*baby*⟩; holen ⟨*doctor*⟩; ~ **a meal/drink** etwas essen/trinken; ~ **lunch** zu Mittag essen; ~ **a walk** spazierengehen; ~ **a dream** träumen; ~ **a rest** sich ausruhen; ~ **a swim** schwimmen; ~ **sth done** etw machen lassen; ~ **sth made** sich (*dat*) etw machen lassen; ~ **to do sth** etw tun müssen; ~ **it out** with zur Rede stellen; **so I** ~ **!** tatsächlich! **he has [got] two houses** er hat zwei Häuser; **you have got the money, haven't you?** du hast das Geld, nicht [wahr]? □ *v aux* haben; (*with verbs of motion & some others*) sein; **I** ~ **seen him** ich habe ihn gesehen; **he has never been there** er ist nie da gewesen. ~ **on** *vt* (*be wearing*) anhaben; (*dupe*) anführen

haven /ˈheɪvn/ *n* (*fig*) Zuflucht *f*

haversack /ˈhævə-/ *n* Rucksack *m*

havoc /ˈhævək/ *n* Verwüstung *f*; **play** ~ **with** (*fig*) völlig durcheinanderbringen

haw /hɔː/ *see* **hum**

hawk[1] /hɔːk/ *n* Falke *m*

hawk[2] *vt* hausieren mit. ~**er** *n* Hausierer *m*

hawthorn /ˈhɔː-/ *n* Hagedorn *m*

hay /heɪ/ *n* Heu *nt*. ~ **fever** *n* Heuschnupfen *m*. ~**stack** *n* Heuschober *m*

'haywire *a* (*fam*) **go** ~ verrückt spielen; ⟨*plans*⟩ über den Haufen geworfen werden

hazard /ˈhæzəd/ *n* Gefahr *f*; (*risk*) Risiko *nt* □ *vt* riskieren. ~**ous** /-əs/ *a* gefährlich; (*risky*) riskant. ~ [**warning**] **lights** *npl* (*Auto*) Warnblinkanlage *f*

haze /heɪz/ *n* Dunst *m*

hazel /ˈheɪzl/ *n* Haselbusch *m*. ~-**nut** *n* Haselnuß *f*

hazy /ˈheɪzɪ/ *a* (-**ier**, -**iest**) dunstig; (*fig*) unklar

he /hiː/ *pron* er

head /hed/ n Kopf m; (chief) Oberhaupt nt; (of firm) Chef(in) m(f); (of school) Schulleiter(in) m(f); (on beer) Schaumkrone f; (of bed) Kopfende nt; **20 ~ of cattle** 20 Stück Vieh; **~ first** kopfüber □vt anführen; (Sport) köpfen ⟨ball⟩ □vi **~ for** zusteuern auf (+ acc). **~ache** n Kopfschmerzen pl. **~dress** n Kopfschmuck m

head|er /'hedə(r)/ n Kopfball m; (dive) Kopfsprung m. **~ing** n Überschrift f

head: **~lamp** n (Auto) Scheinwerfer m. **~land** n Landspitze f. **~light** n (Auto) Scheinwerfer m. **~line** n Schlagzeile f. **~long** adv kopfüber. **~'master** n Schulleiter m. **~'mistress** n Schulleiterin f. **~-on** a & adv frontal. **~phones** npl Kopfhörer m. **~quarters** npl Hauptquartier nt; (Pol) Zentrale f. **~rest** n Kopfstütze f. **~room** n lichte Höhe f. **~scarf** n Kopftuch nt. **~strong** a eigenwillig. **~'waiter** n Oberkellner m. **~way** n **make ~way** Fortschritte machen. **~wind** n Gegenwind m. **~word** n Stichwort nt

heady /'hedɪ/ a berauschend

heal /hi:l/ vt/i heilen

health /helθ/ n Gesundheit f

health: **~ farm** n Schönheitsfarm f. **~ foods** npl Reformkost f. **~-food shop** n Reformhaus nt. **~ insurance** n Krankenversicherung f

healthy /'helθɪ/ a (-ier, -iest), **-ily** adv gesund

heap /hi:p/ n Haufen m; **~s** (fam) jede Menge □vt **~ [up]** häufen; **~ed teaspoon** n gehäufter Teelöffel

hear /hɪə(r)/ vt/i (pt/pp **heard**) hören; **~,~!** hört, hört! **he would not ~ of it** er ließ es nicht zu

hearing /'hɪərɪŋ/ n Gehör nt; (Jur) Verhandlung f. **~-aid** n Hörgerät nt

hearsay n **from ~** vom Hörensagen

hearse /hɜ:s/ n Leichenwagen m

heart /hɑ:t/ n Herz nt; (courage) Mut m; **~s** pl (Cards) Herz nt; **by ~** auswendig

heart: **~ache** n Kummer m. **~attack** n Herzanfall m. **~beat** n Herzschlag m. **~break** n Leid nt. **~breaking** a herzzerreißend. **~broken** a untröstlich. **~burn** n Sodbrennen nt. **~en** vt ermutigen. **~felt** a herzlich(st)

hearth /hɑ:θ/ n Herd m; (fireplace) Kamin m. **~-rug** n Kaminvorleger m

heart|ily /'hɑ:tɪlɪ/ adv herzlich; (eat) viel. **~less** a, **-ly** adv herzlos. **~y** a herzlich; ⟨meal⟩ groß; ⟨person⟩ burschikos

heat /hi:t/ n Hitze f; (Sport) Vorlauf m □vt heiß machen; heizen ⟨room⟩. **~ed** a geheizt; ⟨swimming pool⟩ beheizt; ⟨discussion⟩ hitzig. **~er** n Heizgerät nt; (Auto) Heizanlage f

heath /hi:θ/ n Heide f

heathen /'hi:ðn/ a heidnisch □n Heide m/Heidin f

heather /'heðə(r)/ n Heidekraut nt

heating /'hi:tɪŋ/ n Heizung f

heat: **~stroke** n Hitzschlag m. **~wave** n Hitzewelle f

heave /hi:v/ vt/i ziehen; (lift) heben; (fam: throw) schmeißen; **~ a sigh** einen Seufzer ausstoßen

heaven /'hevn/ n Himmel m. **~ly** a himmlisch

heavy /'hevɪ/ a (-ier, -iest), **-ily** adv schwer; ⟨traffic, rain⟩ stark; ⟨sleep⟩ tief. **~weight** n Schwergewicht nt

Hebrew /'hi:bru:/ a hebräisch

heckle /'hekl/ vt [durch Zwischenrufe] unterbrechen. **~r** n Zwischenrufer m

hectic /'hektɪk/ a hektisch

hedge /hedʒ/ n Hecke f □vi (fig) ausweichen. **~hog** n Igel m

heed /hi:d/ *n* **pay ~ to** Beachtung schenken (+ *dat*) □ *vt* beachten.
~ less *a* ungeachtet (**of** *gen*)

heel /hi:l/ *n* Ferse *f*; (*of shoe*) Absatz *m*; **down at ~** heruntergekommen; **take to one's ~s** (*fam*) Fersengeld geben

heel *vi* **~ over** (*Naut*) sich auf die Seite legen

hefty /'hefti/ *a* (**-ier, -iest**) kräftig; (*heavy*) schwer

heifer /'hefə(r)/ *n* Färse *f*

height /hait/ *n* Höhe *f*; (*of person*) Größe *f*. **~ en** *vt* (*fig*) steigern

heir /eə(r)/ *n* Erbe *m*. **~ ess** *n* Erbin *f*. **~ loom** *n* Erbstück *nt*

held /held/ *see* **hold**²

helicopter /'helikɒptə(r)/ *n* Hubschrauber *m*

hell /hel/ *n* Hölle *f*; **go to ~!** (*sl*) geh zum Teufel! □ *int* verdammt!

hello /hə'ləu/ *int* [guten] Tag! (*fam*) hallo!

helm /helm/ *n* [Steuer]ruder *nt*; **at the ~** (*fig*) am Ruder

helmet /'helmit/ *n* Helm *m*

help /help/ *n* Hilfe *f*; (*employees*) Hilfskräfte *pl*; **that's no ~** das nützt nichts □ *vt/i* helfen (s.o. jdm); **~ oneself to sth** sich (*dat*) etw nehmen; **~ yourself** (*at table*) greif zu; **I could not ~ laughing** ich mußte lachen; **it cannot be ~ ed** es läßt sich nicht ändern; **I can't ~ it** ich kann nichts dafür

help|er /'helpə(r)/ *n* Helfer(in) *m(f)*. **~ ful** *a*, **-ly** *adv* hilfsbereit; (*advice*) nützlich. **~ ing** *n* Portion *f*. **~ less** *a*, **-ly** *adv* hilflos

helter-skelter /heltə'skeltə(r)/ *adv* holterdiepolter □ *n* Rutschbahn *f*

hem /hem/ *n* Saum *m* □ *vt* (*pt/pp* **hemmed**) säumen; **~ in** umzingeln

hemisphere /'hemi-/ *n* Hemisphäre *f*

'hem-line *n* Rocklänge *f*

hemp /hemp/ *n* Hanf *m*

hen /hen/ *n* Henne *f*; (*any female bird*) Weibchen *nt*

hence /hens/ *adv* daher; **five years ~** in fünf Jahren. **~ 'forth** *adv* von nun an

henchman /'hent∫mən/ *n* (*pej*) Gefolgsmann *m*

'henpecked *a* **~ husband** Pantoffelheld *m*

her /hɜ:(r)/ *a* ihr □ *pron* (*acc*) sie; (*dat*) ihr; **I know ~** ich kenne sie; **give ~ the money** gib ihr das Geld

herald /'herəld/ *vt* verkünden. **~ ry** *n* Wappenkunde *f*

herb /hɜ:b/ *n* Kraut *nt*

herbaceous /hɜ:'bei∫əs/ *a* krautartig; **~ border** Staudenrabatte *f*

herd /hɜ:d/ *n* Herde *f* □ *vt* (*tend*) hüten; (*drive*) treiben. **~ together** *vi* sich zusammendrängen □ *vt* zusammentreiben

here /hiə(r)/ *adv* hier; (*to this place*) hierher; **in ~** hier drinnen; **come/bring ~** herkommen/herbringen. **~ 'after** *adv* im folgenden. **~ 'by** *adv* hiermit

heredit|ary /hə'reditəri/ *a* erblich. **~ y** *n* Vererbung *f*

here|sy /'herəsi/ *n* Ketzerei *f*. **~ tic** *n* Ketzer(in) *m(f)*

here'with *adv* (*Comm*) beiliegend

heritage /'heritidʒ/ *n* Erbe *nt*

hermetic /hɜ:'metik/ *a*, **-ally** *adv* hermetisch

hermit /'hɜ:mit/ *n* Einsiedler *m*

hernia /'hɜ:niə/ *n* Bruch *m*, Hernie *f*

hero /'hiərəu/ *n* (*pl* **-es**) Held *m*

heroic /hi'rəuik/ *a*, **-ally** *adv* heldenhaft

heroin /'herəuin/ *n* Heroin *nt*

hero|ine /'herəuin/ *n* Heldin *f*. **~ ism** *n* Heldentum *nt*

heron /'herən/ *n* Reiher *m*

herring /'heriŋ/ *n* Hering *m*; **red ~** (*fam*) falsche Spur *f*. **~ bone** *n* (*pattern*) Fischgrätenmuster *nt*

hers /hɜ:z/ *poss pron* ihre(r), ihrs; **a friend of ~** ein Freund von ihr; **that is ~** das gehört ihr

her'self *pron* selbst; *(refl)* sich; by ~ allein

hesitant /'hezɪtənt/ *a*, **-ly** *adv* zögernd

hesitat|e /'hezɪteɪt/ *vi* zögern. **~ion** /-'teɪʃn/ *n* Zögern *nt*; **without ~ion** ohne zu zögern

het /het/ *a* **~ up** *(fam)* aufgeregt

hetero'sexual /hetərəʊ-/ *a* heterosexuell

hew /hjuː/ *vt* *(pt* hewed, *pp* hewed *or* hewn*)* hauen

hexagonal /hek'sægənl/ *a* sechseckig

heyday /'heɪ-/ *n* Glanzzeit *f*

hi /haɪ/ *int* he! *(hallo)* Tag!

hiatus /haɪ'eɪtəs/ *n* *(pl* **-tuses***)* Lücke *f*

hibernat|e /'haɪbəneɪt/ *vi* Winterschlaf halten. **~ion** /-'neɪʃn/ *n* Winterschlaf *m*

hiccup /'hɪkʌp/ *n* Hick *m*; *(fam: hitch)* Panne *f*; **have the ~s** den Schluckauf haben □ *vi* hick machen

hid /hɪd/, **hidden** *see* **hide²**

hide¹ /haɪd/ *n* *(Comm)* Haut *f*; *(leather)* Leder *nt*

hide² *vt* *(pt* hid, *pp* hidden*)* verstecken; *(keep secret)* verheimlichen □ *vi* sich verstecken. **~-and-'seek** *n* play **~-and-seek** Verstecke spielen

hideous /'hɪdɪəs/ *a*, **-ly** *adv* häßlich; *(horrible)* gräßlich

'hide-out *n* Versteck *nt*

hiding¹ /'haɪdɪŋ/ *n* *(fam)* **give s.o. a ~** jdn verdreschen

hiding² *n* **go into ~** untertauchen

hierarchy /'haɪərɑːkɪ/ *n* Hierarchie *f*

hieroglyphics /haɪərə'glɪfɪks/ *npl* Hieroglyphen *pl*

higgledy-piggledy /hɪgldɪ'pɪgldɪ/ *adv* kunterbunt durcheinander

high /haɪ/ *a* (**-er, -est**) hoch; *attrib* hohe(r,s); *(meat)* angegangen; *(wind)* stark; *(on drugs)* high; **it's ~ time** es ist höchste Zeit □ *adv* hoch; **~ and low** überall

□ *n* Hoch *nt*; *(temperature)* Höchsttemperatur *f*

high: **~brow** *a* intellektuell. **~ chair** *n* Kinderhochstuhl *m*. **~-'handed** *a* selbstherrlich. **~-'heeled** *a* hochhackig. **~ jump** *n* Hochsprung *m*

highlight *n* *(fig)* Höhepunkt *m*; **~s** *pl* *(in hair)* helle Strähnen *pl* □ *vt* *(emphasize)* hervorheben

highly /'haɪlɪ/ *adv* hoch; **speak ~ of** loben; **think ~ of** sehr schätzen. **~-'strung** *a* nervös

Highness /'haɪnɪs/ *n* Hoheit *f*

high: **~-rise** *a* **~-rise flats** *pl* Wohnturm *m*. **~ season** *n* Hochsaison *f*. **~ street** *n* Hauptstraße *f*. **~ 'tide** *n* Hochwasser *nt*. **~way** *n* **public ~way** öffentliche Straße *f*

hijack /'haɪdʒæk/ *vt* entführen. **~er** *n* Entführer *m*

hike /haɪk/ *n* Wanderung *f* □ *vi* wandern. **~r** *n* Wanderer *m*

hilarious /hɪ'leərɪəs/ *a* sehr komisch

hill /hɪl/ *n* Berg *m*; *(mound)* Hügel *m*; *(slope)* Hang *m*

hill: **~billy** *n* *(Amer)* Hinterwäldler *m*. **~side** *n* Hang *m*. **~y** *a* hügelig

hilt /hɪlt/ *n* Griff *m*; **to the ~** *(fam)* voll und ganz

him /hɪm/ *pron* *(acc)* ihn; *(dat)* ihm; **I know ~** ich kenne ihn; **give ~ the money** gib ihm das Geld. **~'self** *pron* selbst; *(refl)* sich; **by ~** self allein

hind /haɪnd/ *a* Hinter-

hind|er /'hɪndə/r/ *vt* hindern. **~rance** /-rəns/ *n* Hindernis *nt*

hindsight /'haɪnd-/ *n* **with ~** rückblickend

Hindu /'hɪnduː/ *n* Hindu *m* □ *a* Hindu-. **~ism** *n* Hinduismus *m*

hinge /hɪndʒ/ *n* Scharnier *nt*; *(on door)* Angel *f* □ *vi* **~ on** *(fig)* ankommen auf *(+ acc)*

hint /hɪnt/ *n* Wink *m*, Andeutung *f*; *(advice)* Hinweis *m*; *(trace)* Spur *f* □ *vi* **~ at** anspielen auf *(+ acc)*

hip /hɪp/ n Hüfte f

hippie /'hɪpɪ/ n Hippie m

hip 'pocket n Gesäßtasche f

hippopotamus /hɪpə'pɒtəməs/ n (pl -muses or -mi /-maɪ/) Nilpferd nt

hire /'haɪə(r)/ vt mieten ⟨car⟩; leihen ⟨suit⟩; einstellen ⟨person⟩; ~ [out] vermieten; verleihen □n Mieten nt; Leihen nt. ~-car n Leihwagen m

his /hɪz/ a sein □ poss pron seine(r), seins; **a friend of** ~ ein Freund von ihm; **that is** ~ das gehört ihm

hiss /hɪs/ n Zischen nt □vt/i zischen

historian /hɪ'stɔːrɪən/ n Historiker(in) m(f)

historic /hɪ'stɒrɪk/ a historisch. ~**al** a, -**ly** adv geschichtlich, historisch

history /'hɪstərɪ/ n Geschichte f

hit /hɪt/ n ⟨blow⟩ Schlag m; ⟨fam: success⟩ Erfolg m; **direct** ~ Volltreffer m □vt/i ⟨pt/pp hit, pres p hitting⟩ schlagen; ⟨knock against, collide with, affect⟩ treffen; ~ **the target** das Ziel treffen; ~ **on** ⟨fig⟩ kommen auf (+ acc); ~ **it off** gut auskommen ⟨with mit⟩; ~ **one's head on sth** sich ⟨dat⟩ den Kopf an etw ⟨dat⟩ stoßen

hitch /hɪtʃ/ n Problem nt; **technical** ~ Panne f □vt festmachen ⟨to an + dat⟩; ~ **up** hochziehen; ~ **a lift** per Anhalter fahren, ⟨fam⟩ trampen. ~-**hike** vi per Anhalter fahren, ⟨fam⟩ trampen. ~-**hiker** n Anhalter(in) m(f)

hither /'hɪðə(r)/ adv hierher; ~ **and thither** hin und her. ~'**to** adv bisher

hive /haɪv/ n Bienenstock m. ~ **off** vt ⟨Comm⟩ abspalten

hoard /hɔːd/ n Hort m □vt horten, hamstern

hoarding /'hɔːdɪŋ/ n Bauzaun m; ⟨with advertisements⟩ Reklamewand f

hoar-frost /'hɔː-/ n Rauhreif m

hoarse /hɔːs/ a (-r, -st), -**ly** adv heiser. ~**ness** n Heiserkeit f

hoax /həʊks/ n übler Scherz m; ⟨false alarm⟩ blinder Alarm m

hob /hɒb/ n Kochmulde f

hobble /'hɒbl/ vi humpeln

hobby /'hɒbɪ/ n Hobby nt. ~-**horse** n ⟨fig⟩ Lieblingsthema nt

hobnailed /'hɒb-/ a ~ **boots** pl genagelte Schuhe pl

hock /hɒk/ n [weißer] Rheinwein m

hockey /'hɒkɪ/ n Hockey nt

hoe /həʊ/ n Hacke f □ vt ⟨pres p hoeing⟩ hacken

hog /hɒg/ n [Mast]schwein nt □vt ⟨pt/pp hogged⟩ ⟨fam⟩ mit Beschlag belegen

hoist /hɔɪst/ n Lastenaufzug m □vt hochziehen; hissen ⟨flag⟩

hold[1] n ⟨Naut, Aviat⟩ Laderaum m

hold[2] /həʊld/ n Halt m; ⟨Sport⟩ Griff m; ⟨fig: influence⟩ Einfluß m; **get** ~ **of** fassen; ⟨fam: contact⟩ erreichen □v ⟨pt/pp held⟩ □vt halten; ⟨container:⟩ fassen; ⟨believe⟩ meinen; ⟨possess⟩ haben; anhalten ⟨breath⟩; ~ **one's tongue** den Mund halten □vi ⟨rope:⟩ halten; ⟨weather:⟩ sich halten; **not** ~ **with** ⟨fam⟩ nicht einverstanden sein mit. ~ **back** vt zurückhalten □vi zögern. ~ **on** vi ⟨wait⟩ warten; ⟨on telephone⟩ am Apparat bleiben; ~ **on to** ⟨keep⟩ behalten; ⟨cling to⟩ sich festhalten an (+ dat). ~ **out** vt hinhalten □vi ⟨resist⟩ aushalten. ~ **up** vt hochhalten; ⟨delay⟩ aufhalten; ⟨rob⟩ überfallen

'hold|**all** n Reisetasche f. ~-**er** n Inhaber(in) m(f); ⟨container⟩ Halter m. ~-**up** n Verzögerung f; ⟨attack⟩ Überfall m

hole /həʊl/ n Loch nt

holiday /'hɒlədeɪ/ n Urlaub m; ⟨Sch⟩ Ferien pl; ⟨public⟩ Feiertag m; ⟨day off⟩ freier Tag m; **go on** ~

in Urlaub fahren. **~-maker** n
Urlauber(in) m(f)

holiness /'həʊlɪnɪs/ n Heiligkeit f

Holland /'hɒlənd/ n Holland nt

hollow /'hɒləʊ/ a hohl; ⟨promise⟩
leer □ n Vertiefung f; (in ground)
Mulde f. **~ out** vt aushöhlen

holly /'hɒlɪ/ n Stechpalme f

'hollyhock n Stockrose f

hologram /'hɒləgræm/ n Holo-
gramm nt

holster /'həʊlstə(r)/ n Pistolen-
tasche f

holy /'həʊlɪ/ a (-ier, -iest) heilig.
H~ Ghost or Spirit n Heiliger
Geist m. **~ water** n Weihwasser
nt. **H~ Week** n Karwoche f

homage /'hɒmɪdʒ/ n Huldigung f;
pay ~ to huldigen (+ dat)

home /həʊm/ n Zuhause nt;
(house) Haus nt; (institution)
Heim nt; (native land) Heimat f
□ adv at ~ zu Hause; **come/go**
nach Hause kommen/gehen

home: **~ ad'dress** n Heimatan-
schrift f. **~ com'puter** n Heim-
computer m. **~ game** n Heim-
spiel nt. **~ help** n Haushaltshilfe
f. **~ land** n Heimatland m. **~ less**
a obdachlos

homely /'həʊmlɪ/ a (-ier, -iest) a
gemütlich; (Amer: ugly) unscheinbar

home: **~'made** a selbstgemacht.
H~ Office n Innenministerium
nt. **H~ 'Secretary** Innenmini-
ster m. **~ sick** a be ~ sick Heimweh haben (for nach). **~ sickness** n Heimweh nt. **~ 'town** n
Heimatstadt f. **~ work** n (Sch)
Hausaufgaben pl

homicide /'hɒmɪsaɪd/ n Totschlag
m; (murder) Mord m

homoeopath|ic /həʊmɪə'pæθɪk/ a
homöopathisch. **~ y** /-'ɒpəθɪ/ n
Homöopathie f

homogeneous /hɒmə'dʒiːnɪəs/ a
homogen

homo'sexual a homosexuell □ n
Homosexuelle(r) m/f

---

honest /'ɒnɪst/ a, **-ly** adv ehrlich.
~ y n Ehrlichkeit f

honey /'hʌnɪ/ n Honig m; (fam:
darling) Schatz m

honey: ~comb n Honigwabe f.
~moon n Flitterwochen pl;
(journey) Hochzeitsreise f.
~suckle n Geißblatt nt

honk /hɒŋk/ vi hupen

honorary /'ɒnərərɪ/ a ehrenamt-
lich; ⟨member, doctorate⟩ Ehren-

honour /'ɒnə(r)/ n Ehre f □ vt
ehren; honorieren ⟨cheque⟩. **~ -
able** /-əbl/ a, **-bly** adv ehrenhaft

hood /hʊd/ n Kapuze f; (of pram)
[Klapp]verdeck nt; (over cooker)
Abzugshaube f; (Auto, Amer)
Kühlerhaube f

hoodlum /'huːdləm/ n Rowdy m

'hoodwink vt (fam) reinlegen

hoof /huːf/ n (pl ~ s or hooves)
Huf m

hook /hʊk/ n Haken m; by ~ or by
crook mit allen Mitteln □ vt
festhaken (to an + acc)

hook|ed /hʊkt/ a **~ ed nose** Ha-
kennase f; **~ ed on** (fam) abhängig von; (keen on) besessen von.
~ er n (Amer, sl) Nutte f

hookey /'hʊkɪ/ n **play ~** (Amer,
fam) schwänzen

hooligan /'huːlɪgən/ n Rowdy m.
~ ism n Rowdytum nt

hoop /huːp/ n Reifen m

hooray /hʊ'reɪ/ int & n = hurrah

hoot /huːt/ n Ruf m; **~ s of laughter** schallendes Gelächter nt □ vi
⟨owl:⟩ rufen; ⟨car:⟩ hupen; ⟨jeer⟩
johlen. **~ er** n (of factory) Sirene
f; (Auto) Hupe f

hoover /'huːvə(r)/ n H~ (P) Staubsauger m □ vt/i [staub]saugen

hop¹ /hɒp/ n, **~ s** pl Hopfen m

hop² n Hüpfer m; **catch s.o. on
the ~** (fam) jdm ungelegen kommen □ vi (pt/pp hopped) hüpfen;
~ it! (fam) hau ab! **~ in** vi (fam)
einsteigen. **~ out** vi (fam) aussteigen

hope /həʊp/ n Hoffnung f; (prospect) Aussicht f (of auf + acc)

□ *vt/i* hoffen (**for** auf + *acc*) I ~ **so** hoffentlich

hope|ful /ˈhəʊpfl/ *a* hoffnungsvoll; **be ~ful that** hoffen, daß. ~**fully** *adv* hoffnungsvoll; (*it is hoped*) hoffentlich. ~**less** *a*, ~**ly** *adv* hoffnungslos; (*useless*) nutzlos; (*incompetent*) untauglich

horde /hɔːd/ *n* Horde *f*

horizon /həˈraɪzn/ *n* Horizont *m*; **on the ~** am Horizont

horizontal /hɒrɪˈzɒntl/ *a*, ~**ly** *adv* horizontal. ~ **'bar** *n* Reck *nt*

horn /hɔːn/ *n* Horn *nt*; (*Auto*) Hupe *f*

hornet /ˈhɔːnɪt/ *n* Hornisse *f*

horny /ˈhɔːnɪ/ *a* schwielig

horoscope /ˈhɒrəskəʊp/ *n* Horoskop *nt*

horrible /ˈhɒrɪbl/ *a*, ~**bly** *adv* schrecklich

horrid /ˈhɒrɪd/ *a* gräßlich

horrific /həˈrɪfɪk/ *a* entsetzlich

horrify /ˈhɒrɪfaɪ/ *vt* (*pt/pp* -**ied**) entsetzen

horror /ˈhɒrə(r)/ *n* Entsetzen *nt*. ~ **film** *n* Horrorfilm *m*

hors-d'œuvre /ɔːˈdɜːvr/ *n* Vorspeise *f*

horse /hɔːs/ *n* Pferd *nt*

horse: ~**back** *n* **on ~back** zu Pferde. ~**chestnut** *n* [Roß]kastanie *f*. ~**man** *n* Reiter *m*. ~**play** *n* Toben *nt*. ~**power** *n* Pferdestärke *f*. ~**racing** *n* Pferderennen *nt*. ~**radish** *n* Meerrettich *m*. ~**shoe** *n* Hufeisen *nt*

horti'cultural *a* Garten-. **'horticulture** *n* Gartenbau *m*

hose /həʊz/ *n* (*pipe*) Schlauch *m* □ *vt* ~ **down** abspritzen

hosiery /ˈhəʊzərɪ/ *n* Strumpfwaren *pl*

hospice /ˈhɒspɪs/ *n* Heim *nt*; (*for the terminally ill*) Sterbeklinik *f*

hospitable /hɒˈspɪtəbl/ *a*, -**bly** *adv* gastfreundlich

hospital /ˈhɒspɪtl/ *n* Krankenhaus *nt*

hospitality /hɒspɪˈtælətɪ/ *n* Gastfreundschaft *f*

host¹ /həʊst/ *n* **a ~ of** eine Menge von

host² *n* Gastgeber *m*

host³ *n* (*Relig*) Hostie *f*

hostage /ˈhɒstɪdʒ/ *n* Geisel *f*

hostel /ˈhɒstl/ *n* [Wohn]heim *nt*

hostess /ˈhəʊstɪs/ *n* Gastgeberin *f*

hostile /ˈhɒstaɪl/ *a* feindlich; (*unfriendly*) feindselig

hostilit|y /hɒˈstɪlətɪ/ *n* Feindschaft *f*; ~ **ies** *pl* Feindseligkeiten *pl*

hot /hɒt/ *a* (**hotter, hottest**) heiß; ⟨*meal*⟩ warm; (*spicy*) scharf; **I am** or **feel ~** mir ist heiß

'hotbed *n* (*fig*) Brutstätte *f*

hotchpotch /ˈhɒtʃpɒtʃ/ *n* Mischmasch *m*

hotel /həʊˈtel/ *n* Hotel *nt*. ~**ier** /-ɪə(r)/ *n* Hotelier *m*

hot: ~**head** *n* Hitzkopf *m*. ~**'headed** *a* hitzköpfig. ~**house** *n* Treibhaus *nt*. ~**ly** *adv* (*fig*) heiß, heftig. ~**plate** *n* Tellerwärmer *m*; (*of cooker*) Kochplatte *f*. ~**tap** *n* Warmwasserhahn *m*. ~**tempered** *a* jähzornig. ~**'water bottle** *n* Wärmflasche *f*

hound /haʊnd/ *n* Jagdhund *m* □ *vt* (*fig*) verfolgen

hour /ˈaʊə(r)/ *n* Stunde *f*. ~**ly** *a* & *adv* stündlich. ~**ly pay** or **rate** Stundenlohn *m*

house¹ /haʊs/ *n* Haus *nt*; **at my ~** bei mir

house² /haʊz/ *vt* unterbringen

house: /haʊs/. ~**boat** *n* Hausboot *nt*. ~**breaking** *n* Einbruch *m*. ~**hold** *n* Haushalt *m*. ~**holder** *n* Hausinhaber(in) *m(f)*. ~**keeper** *n* Haushälterin *f*. ~**keeping** *n* Hauswirtschaft *f*; (*money*) Haushaltsgeld *nt*. ~**plant** *n* Zimmerpflanze *f*. ~**trained** *a* stubenrein. ~**warming** *n* **have a ~ warming party** Einstand feiern. ~**wife** *n* Hausfrau *f*. ~**work** *n* Hausarbeit *f*

housing /'haʊzɪŋ/ n Wohnungen pl; (Techn) Gehäuse nt. ~ **estate** n Wohnsiedlung f

hovel /'hɒvl/ n elende Hütte f

hover /'hɒvə(r)/ vi schweben; (be undecided) schwanken; (linger) herumstehen. ~**craft** n Luftkissenfahrzeug nt

how /haʊ/ adv wie; ~ **do you do?** guten Tag! ~ **many** wie viele; ~ **much** wieviel; and ~! und ob!

how'ever adv (in question) wie; (nevertheless) jedoch, aber; ~ **small** wie klein es auch sein mag

howl /haʊl/ n Heulen nt □ vi heulen; (baby:) brüllen. ~**er** n (fam) Schnitzer m

hub /hʌb/ n Nabe f; (fig) Mittelpunkt m

hubbub /'hʌbʌb/ n Stimmengewirr nt

'hub-cap n Radkappe f

huddle /'hʌdl/ vi ~ **together** sich zusammendrängen

hue[1] /hju:/ n Farbe f

hue[2] n ~ **and cry** Aufruhr m

huff /hʌf/ n **in a** ~ beleidigt

hug /hʌg/ n Umarmung f □ vt (pt/pp **hugged**) umarmen

huge /hju:dʒ/ a, **-ly** adv riesig

hulking /'hʌlkɪŋ/ a (fam) ungeschlacht

hull /hʌl/ n (Naut) Rumpf m

hullo /hə'ləʊ/ int = **hallo**

hum /hʌm/ n Summen nt; Brummen nt □ vt/i (pt/pp **hummed**) summen; (motor:) brummen; ~ **and haw** nicht mit der Sprache herauswollen

human /'hju:mən/ a menschlich □ n Mensch m. ~ **being** n Mensch m

humane /hju:'meɪn/ a, **-ly** adv human

humanitarian /hju:mænɪ'teərɪən/ a humanitär

humanit|y /hju:'mænətɪ/ n Menschheit f; ~**ies** pl (Univ) Geisteswissenschaften pl

humble /'hʌmbl/ a (-r, -st), **-bly** adv demütig □ vt demütigen

humdrum a eintönig

humid /'hju:mɪd/ a feucht. ~**ity** /-'mɪdətɪ/ n Feuchtigkeit f

humiliat|e /hju:'mɪlɪeɪt/ vt demütigen. ~**ion** /-'eɪʃn/ n Demütigung f

humility /hju:'mɪlətɪ/ n Demut f

'humming-bird n Kolibri m

humorous /'hju:mərəs/ a, **-ly** adv humorvoll; (story) humoristisch

humour /'hju:mə(r)/ n Humor m; (mood) Laune f; **have a sense of** ~ Humor haben □ vt ~ **s.o.** jdm seinen Willen lassen

hump /hʌmp/ n Buckel m; (of camel) Höcker m □ vt schleppen

hunch[1] /hʌntʃ/ n (idea) Ahnung f

'hunch|back n Bucklige(r) m/f. ~**ed** a ~ **ed up** gebeugt

hundred /'hʌndrəd/ a **one/a** ~ [ein]hundert □ n Hundert nt; (written figure) Hundert f. ~**th** a hundertste(r,s) □ n Hundertstel nt. ~**weight** n ≈ Zentner m

hung /hʌŋ/ see **hang**

Hungarian /hʌŋ'geərɪən/ a ungarisch □ n Ungar(in) m(f)

Hungary /'hʌŋgərɪ/ n Ungarn nt

hunger /'hʌŋgə(r)/ n Hunger m. ~**strike** n Hungerstreik m

hungry /'hʌŋgrɪ/ a (-ier, -iest), **-ily** adv hungrig; **be** ~ Hunger haben

hunk /hʌŋk/ n [großes] Stück nt

hunt /hʌnt/ n Jagd f; (for criminal) Fahndung f □ vt/i jagen; fahnden nach (criminal); ~ **for** suchen. ~**er** n Jäger m; (horse) Jagdpferd nt. ~**ing** n Jagd f

hurdle /'hɜ:dl/ n (Sport & fig) Hürde f. ~**r** n Hürdenläufer(in) m(f)

hurl /hɜ:l/ vt schleudern

hurrah /hʊ'rɑ:/, **hurray** /hʊ'reɪ/ int Hurra! □ n Hurra nt

hurricane /'hʌrɪkən/ n Orkan m

hurried /'hʌrɪd/ a, **-ly** adv eilig; (superficial) flüchtig

hurry /'hʌrɪ/ n Eile f; **be in a** ~ es eilig haben □ vi (pt/pp **-ied**) sich beeilen; (go quickly) eilen. ~ **up** vi sich beeilen □ vt antreiben

hurt /hɜːt/ n Schmerz m □ vt/i (pt/pp **hurt**) weh tun (+ dat); (injure) verletzen; (offend) kränken. ~**ful** a verletzend

hurtle /ˈhɜːtl/ vi ~ **along** rasen

husband /ˈhʌzbənd/ n [Ehe]mann m

hush /hʌʃ/ n Stille f □ vt ~ **up** vertuschen. ~**ed** a gedämpft. ~-**hush** a (fam) streng geheim

husk /hʌsk/ n Spelze f

husky /ˈhʌskɪ/ a (-ier, -iest) heiser; (burly) stämmig

hustle /ˈhʌsl/ vt drängen □ n Gedränge nt; ~ **and bustle** geschäftiges Treiben f

hut /hʌt/ n Hütte f

hutch /hʌtʃ/ n [Kaninchen]stall m

hybrid /ˈhaɪbrɪd/ a hybrid □ n Hybride f

hydrangea /haɪˈdreɪndʒə/ n Hortensie f

hydrant /ˈhaɪdrənt/ n [fire] ~ Hydrant m

hydraulic /haɪˈdrɔːlɪk/ a, ~**ally** adv hydraulisch

hydrochloric /haɪdrəˈklɔːrɪk/ a ~ **acid** Salzsäure f

hydroe'lectric /haɪdrəʊ-/ a hydroelektrisch. ~ **power station** n Wasserkraftwerk nt

hydrofoil /ˈhaɪdrə-/ n Tragflügelboot nt

hydrogen /ˈhaɪdrədʒən/ n Wasserstoff m

hyena /haɪˈiːnə/ n Hyäne f

hygiene /ˈhaɪdʒiːn/ n Hygiene f. ~**ic** /haɪˈdʒiːnɪk/ a, ~**ally** adv hygienisch

hymn /hɪm/ n Kirchenlied nt. ~**book** n Gesangbuch nt

hyphen /ˈhaɪfn/ n Bindestrich m. ~**ate** vt mit Bindestrich schreiben

hypno|sis /hɪpˈnəʊsɪs/ n Hypnose f. ~**tic** /-ˈnɒtɪk/ a hypnotisch

hypno|tism /ˈhɪpnətɪzm/ n Hypnotik f. ~**tist** /-tɪst/ n Hypnotiseur m. ~**tize** vt hypnotisieren

hypochondriac /haɪpəˈkɒndrɪæk/ a hypochondrisch □ n Hypochonder m

hypocrisy /hɪˈpɒkrəsɪ/ n Heuchelei f

hypocrit|e /ˈhɪpəkrɪt/ n Heuchler(in) m(f). ~**ical** /-ˈkrɪtɪkl/ a, -ly adv heuchlerisch

hypodermic /haɪpəˈdɜːmɪk/ a & n ~ [syringe] Injektionsspritze f

hypothe|sis /haɪˈpɒθəsɪs/ n Hypothese f. ~**tical** /-əˈθetɪkl/ a, -ly adv hypothetisch

hyster|ia /hɪˈstɪərɪə/ n Hysterie f. ~**ical** /-ˈsterɪkl/ a, -ly adv hysterisch. ~**ics** /hɪˈsterɪks/ npl hysterischer Anfall m

I

I /aɪ/ pron ich

ice /aɪs/ n Eis nt □ vt mit Zuckerguß überziehen ⟨cake⟩

ice: ~ **age** n Eiszeit f. ~-**axe** n Eispickel m. ~**berg** /-bɜːg/ n Eisberg m. ~**box** n (Amer) Kühlschrank m. ~-**'cream** n [Speise]eis nt. ~-**'cream parlour** n Eisdiele f. ~-**cube** n Eiswürfel m

Iceland /ˈaɪslənd/ n Island f

ice: ~-**'lolly** n Eis nt am Stiel. ~**rink** n Eisbahn f

icicle /ˈaɪsɪkl/ n Eiszapfen m

icing /ˈaɪsɪŋ/ n Zuckerguß m. ~ **sugar** n Puderzucker m

icon /ˈaɪkɒn/ n Ikone f

icy /ˈaɪsɪ/ a (-ier, -iest), -ily adv eisig; ⟨road⟩ vereist

idea /aɪˈdɪə/ n Idee f; (conception) Vorstellung f; **I have no** ~! ich habe keine Ahnung!

ideal /aɪˈdɪəl/ a ideal □ n Ideal nt. ~**ism** n Idealismus m. ~**ist** n Idealist(in) m(f). ~**istic** a idealistisch. ~**ize** vt idealisieren. ~**ly** adv ideal; (in ideal circumstances) idealerweise

identical /aɪˈdentɪkl/ a identisch; ⟨twins⟩ eineiig

identi|fication /aɪdentɪfɪ'keɪʃn/ n
Identifizierung f; (proof of identity) Ausweispapiere pl. ~**fy**
/ar'dentɪfaɪ/ vt (pt/pp -ied) identifizieren

identity /aɪ'dentətɪ/ n Identität f.
~ **card** n [Personal]ausweis m

ideolog|ical /aɪdɪə'lɒdʒɪkl/ a
ideologisch. ~**y** /aɪdɪ'ɒlədʒɪ/ n
Ideologie f

idiom /'ɪdɪəm/ n [feste] Redewendung f. ~**atic** /-'mætɪk/ a, -**ally**
adv idiomatisch

idiosyncrasy /ɪdɪə'sɪŋkrəsɪ/ n Eigenart f

idiot /'ɪdɪət/ n Idiot m. ~**ic** /-'ɒtɪk/ a
idiotisch

idle /'aɪdl/ a (-r, -st), -**ly** adv untätig; (lazy) faul; (empty) leer; (machine) nicht in Betrieb ○ vi faulenzen; (engine:) leer laufen.
~**ness** n Untätigkeit f; Faulheit f

idol /'aɪdl/ n Idol nt. ~**ize** /'aɪd-
əlaɪz/ vt vergöttern

idyllic /ɪ'dɪlɪk/ a idyllisch

i.e. abbr (id est) d.h.

if /ɪf/ conj wenn; (whether) ob; **as if**
als ob

ignite /ɪg'naɪt/ vt entzünden ○ vi
sich entzünden

ignition /ɪg'nɪʃn/ n (Auto) Zündung f. ~ **key** n Zündschlüssel m

ignoramus /ɪgnə'reɪməs/ n Igno-
rant m

ignoran|ce /'ɪgnərəns/ n Unwis-
senheit f. ~**t** a unwissend;
(rude) ungehobelt

ignore /ɪg'nɔː(r)/ vt ignorieren

ilk /ɪlk/ n (fam) of that~ von der
Sorte

ill /ɪl/ a krank; (bad) schlecht; **feel
~ at ease** sich unbehaglich füh-
len □adv schlecht □n Schlech-
te(s) nt; (evil) Übel nt. ~**advised**
a unklug. ~**bred** a schlecht erzogen

illegal /ɪ'liːgl/ a, -**ly** adv illegal

illegible /ɪ'ledʒəbl/ a, -**bly** adv
unleserlich

illegitima|cy /ɪlɪ'dʒɪtɪməsɪ/ n Un-
ehelichkeit f. ~**te** /-mət/ a unehelich; (claim) unberechtigt

illicit /ɪ'lɪsɪt/ a, -**ly** adv illegal

illitera|cy /ɪ'lɪtərəsɪ/ n Analphabe-
tentum nt. ~**te** /-rət/ a **be ~te**
nicht lesen und schreiben können □n Analphabet(in) m(f)

illness /'ɪlnɪs/ n Krankheit f

illogical /ɪ'lɒdʒɪkl/ a, -**ly** adv unlogisch

ill-treat /ɪl'triːt/ vt mißhandeln.
~ **ment** n Mißhandlung f

illuminat|e /ɪ'luːmɪnent/ vt be-
leuchten. ~**ing** a aufschlußreich. ~**ion** /-'neɪʃn/ n Beleuchtung f

illusion /ɪ'luːʒn/ n Illusion f; **be
under the ~** that sich (dat) einbilden, daß

illusory /ɪ'luːsərɪ/ a illusorisch

illustrat|e /'ɪləstreɪt/ vt illustrie-
ren. ~**ion** /-'streɪʃn/ n Illustration f

illustrious /ɪ'lʌstrɪəs/ a berühmt

image /'ɪmɪdʒ/ n Bild nt; (statue)
Standbild nt; (figure) Figur f;
(exact likeness) Ebenbild nt;
(public) ~ Image nt

imagin|able /ɪ'mædʒɪnəbl/ a vor-
stellbar. ~**ary** /-ərɪ/ a eingebildet

imaginat|ion /ɪmædʒɪ'neɪʃn/ n
Phantasie f; (fancy) Einbildung f.
~**ive** /ɪ'mædʒɪnətɪv/ a, -**ly** adv
phantasievoll; (full of ideas) ein-
fallsreich

imagine /ɪ'mædʒɪn/ vt sich (dat)
vorstellen; (wrongly) sich (dat)
einbilden

im'balance n Unausgeglichen-
heit f

imbecile /'ɪmbəsiːl/ n Schwach-
sinnige(r) m/f; (pej) Idiot m

imbibe /ɪm'baɪb/ vt trinken; (fig)
aufnehmen

imbue /ɪm'bjuː/ vt **be ~d with**
erfüllt sein von

imitat|e /'ɪmɪteɪt/ vt nachahmen,
imitieren. ~**ion** /-'teɪʃn/ n Nachahmung f, Imitation f

immaculate /ɪˈmækjʊlət/ a, **-ly** adv tadellos; (Relig) unbefleckt

imma'terial a (unimportant) unwichtig, unwesentlich

imma'ture a unreif

immediate /ɪˈmiːdɪət/ a sofortig; (nearest) nächste(r,s). **~ly** adv sofort; **~ly next to** unmittelbar neben □ conj sobald

immemorial /ɪməˈmɔːrɪəl/ a from time ~ seit Urzeiten

immense /ɪˈmens/ a, **-ly** adv riesig; (fam) enorm; (extreme) äußerst

immers|e /ɪˈmɜːs/ vt untertauchen; **be ~ed in** (fig) vertieft sein in (+ acc). **~ion** /-ʃn/ n Untertauchen nt. **~ion heater** n Heißwasserbereiter m

immigrant /ˈɪmɪɡrənt/ n Einwanderer m

immigrat|e /ˈɪmɪɡreɪt/ vi einwandern. **~ion** /-ˈɡreɪʃn/ n Einwanderung f

imminent /ˈɪmɪnənt/ a be ~ unmittelbar bevorstehen

immobil|e /ɪˈməʊbaɪl/ a unbeweglich. **~ize** /-bəlaɪz/ vt (fig) lähmen; (Med) ruhigstellen

immoderate /ɪˈmɒdərət/ a übermäßig

immodest /ɪˈmɒdɪst/ a unbescheiden

immoral /ɪˈmɒrəl/ a, **-ly** adv unmoralisch. **~ity** /ɪməˈrælətɪ/ n Unmoral f

immortal /ɪˈmɔːtl/ a unsterblich. **~ity** /-ˈtælɪtɪ/ n Unsterblichkeit f. **~ize** vt verewigen

immovable /ɪˈmuːvəbl/ a unbeweglich; (fig) fest

immune /ɪˈmjuːn/ a immun (to/from gegen). **~ system** n Abwehrsystem nt

immunity /ɪˈmjuːnətɪ/ n Immunität f

immunize /ˈɪmjʊnaɪz/ vt immunisieren

imp /ɪmp/ n Kobold m

impact /ˈɪmpækt/ n Aufprall m; (collision) Zusammenprall m; (of

bomb) Einschlag m; (fig) Auswirkung f

impair /ɪmˈpeə(r)/ vt beeinträchtigen

impale /ɪmˈpeɪl/ vt aufspießen

impart /ɪmˈpɑːt/ vt übermitteln (to dat); vermitteln ⟨knowledge⟩

im'partial a unparteiisch. **~'ality** n Unparteilichkeit f

im'passable a unpassierbar

impasse /æmˈpɑːs/ n (fig) Sackgasse f

impassioned /ɪmˈpæʃnd/ a leidenschaftlich

im'passive a, **-ly** adv unbeweglich

im'patien|ce n Ungeduld f. **~t** a, **-ly** adv ungeduldig

impeach /ɪmˈpiːtʃ/ vt anklagen

impeccable /ɪmˈpekəbl/ a, **-bly** adv tadellos

impede /ɪmˈpiːd/ vt behindern

impediment /ɪmˈpedɪmənt/ n Hindernis nt; (in speech) Sprachfehler m

impel /ɪmˈpel/ vt (pt/pp **impelled**) treiben; **feel ~led** sich genötigt fühlen (to zu)

impending /ɪmˈpendɪŋ/ a bevorstehend

impenetrable /ɪmˈpenɪtrəbl/ a undurchdringlich

imperative /ɪmˈperətɪv/ a be ~ dringend notwendig sein □ n (Gram) Imperativ m, Befehlsform f

imper'ceptible a nicht wahrnehmbar

im'perfect a unvollkommen; (faulty) fehlerhaft □ n (Gram) Imperfekt nt. **~ion** /-ˈfekʃn/ n Unvollkommenheit f; (fault) Fehler m

imperial /ɪmˈpɪərɪəl/ a kaiserlich. **~ism** n Imperialismus m

imperil /ɪmˈperɪl/ vt (pt/pp imperilled) gefährden

imperious /ɪmˈpɪərɪəs/ a, **-ly** adv herrisch

im'personal a unpersönlich

impersonat|e /ɪmˈpɜːsəneɪt/ vt sich ausgeben als; (*Theat*) nachahmen, imitieren. **~or** n Imitator m

impertinen|ce /ɪmˈpɜːtɪnəns/ n Frechheit f. **~t** a frech

imperturbable /ɪmpəˈtɜːbəbl/ a unerschütterlich

impervious /ɪmˈpɜːvɪəs/ a **~ to** (*fig*) unempfänglich für

impetuous /ɪmˈpetjʊəs/ a, **-ly** adv ungestüm

impetus /ˈɪmpɪtəs/ n Schwung m

impish /ˈɪmpɪʃ/ a schelmisch

implacable /ɪmˈplækəbl/ a unerbittlich

im'plant¹ vt einpflanzen

'implant² n Implantat nt

implement¹ /ˈɪmplɪmənt/ n Gerät nt

implement² /ˈɪmplɪment/ vt ausführen

implicat|e /ˈɪmplɪkeɪt/ vt verwickeln. **~ion** /-ˈkeɪʃn/ n Verwicklung f; **~ions** pl Auswirkungen pl; **by ~ion** implizit

implicit /ɪmˈplɪsɪt/ a, **-ly** adv unausgesprochen; (*absolute*) unbedingt

implore /ɪmˈplɔː(r)/ vt anflehen

imply /ɪmˈplaɪ/ vt (pt/pp **-ied**) andeuten; **what are you ~ing?** was wollen Sie damit sagen?

impo'lite a, **-ly** adv unhöflich

import¹ /ˈɪmpɔːt/ n Import m, Einfuhr f; (*importance*) Wichtigkeit f; (*meaning*) Bedeutung f

import² /ɪmˈpɔːt/ vt importieren, einführen

importan|ce /ɪmˈpɔːtns/ n Wichtigkeit f. **~t** a wichtig

importer /ɪmˈpɔːtə(r)/ n Importeur m

impos|e /ɪmˈpəʊz/ vt auferlegen (on *dat*) □vi sich aufdrängen (on *dat*). **~ing** a eindrucksvoll. **~ition** /ɪmpəˈzɪʃn/ n **be an ~ition** eine Zumutung sein

impossi'bility n Unmöglichkeit f

im'possible a, **-bly** adv unmöglich

impostor /ɪmˈpɒstə(r)/ n Betrüger(in) m(f)

impoten|ce /ˈɪmpətəns/ n Machtlosigkeit f; (*Med*) Impotenz f. **~t** a machtlos; (*Med*) impotent

impound /ɪmˈpaʊnd/ vt beschlagnahmen

impoverished /ɪmˈpɒvərɪʃt/ a verarmt

im'practicable a undurchführbar

im'practical a unpraktisch

impre'cise a ungenau

impregnable /ɪmˈpregnəbl/ a uneinnehmbar

impregnate /ˈɪmpregneɪt/ vt tränken; (*Biol*) befruchten

im'press vt beeindrucken; **~ sth [up]on s.o.** jdm etw einprägen

impression /ɪmˈpreʃn/ n Eindruck m; (*imitation*) Nachahmung f; (*imprint*) Abdruck m; (*edition*) Auflage f. **~ism** n Impressionismus m

impressive /ɪmˈpresɪv/ a eindrucksvoll

'imprint¹ n Abdruck m

im'print² vt prägen; (*fig*) einprägen (on *dat*)

im'prison vt gefangenhalten; (*put in prison*) ins Gefängnis sperren

im'probable a unwahrscheinlich

impromptu /ɪmˈprɒmptjuː/ a improvisiert □adv aus dem Stegreif

im'proper a, **-ly** adv inkorrekt; (*indecent*) unanständig

impro'priety n Unkorrektheit f

improve /ɪmˈpruːv/ vt verbessern; verschönern (*appearance*) □vi sich bessern; **~ [up]on** übertreffen. **~ment** /-mənt/ n Verbesserung f; (*in health*) Besserung f

improvise /ˈɪmprəvaɪz/ vt/i improvisieren

im'prudent a unklug

impuden|ce /ˈɪmpjʊdəns/ n Frechheit f. **~t** a, **-ly** adv frech

impuls|e /ˈɪmpʌls/ n Impuls m; **on [an] ~e** impulsiv. **~ive** /-ˈpʌlsɪv/ a, **-ly** adv impulsiv

impunity /ɪmˈpjuːnətɪ/ n with ~ ungestraft

im'pur|e a unrein. ~**ity** n Unreinheit f; ~**ities** pl Verunreinigungen pl

impute /ɪmˈpjuːt/ vt zuschreiben (to dat)

in /ɪn/ prep in (+ dat/into) + acc); **sit in the garden** im Garten sitzen; **go in the garden** in den Garten gehen; **in May** im Mai; **in the summer/winter** im Sommer/Winter; **in 1992** [im Jahre] 1992; **in this heat** bei dieser Hitze; **in the rain/sun** im Regen/in der Sonne; **in the evening** am Abend; **in the sky** am Himmel; **in the world** auf der Welt; **in the street** auf der Straße; **deaf in one ear** auf einem Ohr taub; **in the army** beim Militär; **in English/German** auf englisch/deutsch; **in ink/pencil** mit Tinte/Bleistift; **in a soft/loud voice** mit leiser/lauter Stimme; **in doing this, he ...** indem er das tut/tat, ... er ▢ adv (at home) zu Hause; (indoors) drinnen; **he's not in yet** er ist noch nicht da; **all in** alles inbegriffen; (fam: exhausted) kaputt; **day in, day out** tagaus, tagein; **keep in with s.o.** sich mit jdm gut stellen; **have it in for s.o.** (fam) es auf jdn abgesehen haben; **let oneself in for sth** sich auf etw (acc) einlassen; **send/go in** hineinschicken/-gehen; **come/bring in** hereinkommen/-bringen ▢ a (fam: in fashion) in ▢ **the ins and outs** alle Einzelheiten pl

ina'bility n Unfähigkeit f

inac'cessible a unzugänglich

in'accura|cy n Ungenauigkeit f. ~**te** a, **-ly** adv ungenau

in'act|ive a untätig. ~**tivity** n Untätigkeit f

in'adequate a, **-ly** adv unzulänglich; **feel** ~ sich der Situation nicht gewachsen fühlen

inad'missable a unzulässig

inadvertently /ɪnədˈvɜːtəntlɪ/ adv versehentlich

inad'visable a nicht ratsam

inane /ɪˈneɪn/ a, **-ly** adv albern

in'animate a unbelebt

in'applicable a nicht zutreffend

inap'propriate a unangebracht

inar'ticulate a undeutlich; **be** ~ sich nicht gut ausdrücken können

inat'tentive a unaufmerksam

in'audible a, **-bly** adv unhörbar

inaugural /ɪˈnɔːgjʊrl/ a Antrittsinaugurate /ɪˈnɔːgjʊreɪt/ vt [feierlich] in sein Amt einführen. ~**ion** /-ˈreɪʃn/ n Amtseinführung f

inau'spicious a ungünstig

inborn /ˈɪnbɔːn/ a angeboren

inbred /ɪnˈbred/ a angeboren

incalculable /ɪnˈkælkjʊləbl/ a nicht berechenbar; (fig) unabsehbar

in'capable a unfähig; **be** ~ **of doing sth** nicht fähig sein, etw zu tun

incapacitate /ɪnkəˈpæsɪteɪt/ vt unfähig machen

incarcerate /ɪnˈkɑːsəreɪt/ vt einkerkern

incarnat|e /ɪnˈkɑːnət/ a **the devil** ~ der leibhaftige Satan. ~**ion** /-ˈneɪʃn/ n Inkarnation f

incendiary /ɪnˈsendɪərɪ/ a & n ~ [**bomb**] Brandbombe f

incense[1] /ˈɪnsens/ n Weihrauch m

incense[2] /ɪnˈsens/ vt wütend machen

incentive /ɪnˈsentɪv/ n Anreiz m

inception /ɪnˈsepʃn/ n Beginn m

incessant /ɪnˈsesnt/ a, **-ly** adv unaufhörlich

incest /ˈɪnsest/ n Inzest m, Blutschande f

inch /ɪntʃ/ n Zoll m ▢ vi ~ **forward** sich ganz langsam vorwärtsschieben

incidence /ˈɪnsɪdəns/ n Vorkommen nt. ~**t** n Zwischenfall m

incidental /ɪnsɪˈdentl/ a nebensächlich; ⟨remark⟩ beiläufig; ⟨expenses⟩ Neben-. **~ly** adv übrigens

incinerat|e /ɪnˈsɪnəreɪt/ vt verbrennen. **~or** n Verbrennungsofen m

incipient /ɪnˈsɪpɪənt/ a angehend

incision /ɪnˈsɪʒn/ n Einschnitt m

incisive /ɪnˈsaɪsɪv/ a scharfsinnig

incisor /ɪnˈsaɪzə(r)/ n Schneidezahn m

incite /ɪnˈsaɪt/ vt aufhetzen. **~ment** n Aufhetzung f

inci'vility n Unhöflichkeit f

in'clement a rauh

inclination /ɪnklɪˈneɪʃn/ n Neigung f

incline¹ /ɪnˈklaɪn/ vt neigen; **be ~d to do sth** dazu neigen, etw zu tun □ vi sich neigen

incline² /ˈɪnklaɪn/ n Neigung f

inclu|de /ɪnˈkluːd/ vt einschließen; ⟨contain⟩ enthalten; ⟨incorporate⟩ aufnehmen (in + acc). **~ding** a einschließlich (+ gen). **~sion** /-ˈuːʒn/ n Aufnahme f

inclusive /ɪnˈkluːsɪv/ a Inklusiv-; **~ of** einschließlich (+ gen) □ adv inklusive

incognito /ɪnkɒgˈniːtəʊ/ adv inkognito

inco'herent a, **-ly** adv zusammenhanglos; ⟨incomprehensible⟩ unverständlich

income /ˈɪnkəm/ n Einkommen nt. **~ tax** n Einkommensteuer f

'incoming a ankommend; ⟨mail, call⟩ eingehend. **~ tide** n steigende Flut f

in'comparable a unvergleichlich

incom'patible a unvereinbar; **be ~ ⟨people:⟩** nicht zueinander passen

in'competen|ce n Unfähigkeit f. **~t** a unfähig

incom'plete a unvollständig

incompre'hensible a unverständlich

incon'ceivable a undenkbar

incon'clusive a nicht schlüssig

incongruous /ɪnˈkɒŋgrʊəs/ a unpassend

inconse'quential /ɪnkɒnsɪˈkwen-ʃl/ a unbedeutend

incon'siderate a rücksichtslos

incon'sistent a, **-ly** adv widersprüchlich; ⟨illogical⟩ inkonsequent; **be ~** nicht übereinstimmen

inconsolable /ɪnkənˈsəʊləbl/ a untröstlich

incon'spicuous a unauffällig

inconti'nen|ce /ɪnˈkɒntɪnəns/ n Inkontinenz f. **~t** a inkontinent

incon'venien|ce n Unannehmlichkeit f; ⟨drawback⟩ Nachteil m; **put s.o. to ~ce** jdm Umstände machen. **~t** a, **-ly** adv ungünstig; **be ~t for s.o.** jdm nicht passen

incorporate /ɪnˈkɔːpəreɪt/ vt aufnehmen; ⟨contain⟩ enthalten

incor'rect a, **-ly** adv inkorrekt

incorrigible /ɪnˈkɒrɪdʒəbl/ a unverbesserlich

incorruptible /ɪnkəˈrʌptəbl/ a unbestechlich

increase¹ /ˈɪnkriːs/ n Zunahme f; ⟨rise⟩ Erhöhung f; **be on the ~** zunehmen

increas|e² /ɪnˈkriːs/ vt vergrößern; ⟨raise⟩ erhöhen □ vi zunehmen; ⟨rise⟩ sich erhöhen. **~ing** a, **-ly** adv zunehmend

in'credible a, **-bly** adv unglaublich

incredulous /ɪnˈkredjʊləs/ a ungläubig

increment /ˈɪnkrɪmənt/ n Gehaltszulage f

incriminate /ɪnˈkrɪmɪneɪt/ vt ⟨Jur⟩ belasten

incubat|e /ˈɪnkjʊbeɪt/ vt ausbrüten. **~ion** /-ˈbeɪʃn/ n Ausbrüten nt. **~ion period** n ⟨Med⟩ Inkubationszeit f. **~or** n ⟨for baby⟩ Brutkasten m

inculcate /ˈɪnkʌlkeɪt/ vt einprägen (in dat)

incumbent /ɪnˈkʌmbənt/ a **be ~ on s.o.** jds Pflicht sein

incur /ɪn'kɜ:(r)/ vt (pt/pp incurred) sich (dat) zuziehen; machen ⟨debts⟩

in'curable a, -bly adv unheilbar

incursion /ɪn'kɜ:ʃn/ n Einfall m

indebted /ɪn'detɪd/ a verpflichtet (to dat)

in'decent a, -ly adv unanständig

inde'cision n Unentschlossenheit f

inde'cisive a ergebnislos; ⟨person⟩ unentschlossen

indeed /ɪn'di:d/ adv in der Tat, tatsächlich; **yes** ~ ! allerdings! ~ **I am/do** oh doch! **very much** ~ sehr; **thank you very much** ~ vielen herzlichen Dank

indefatigable /ɪndɪ'fætɪgəbl/ a unermüdlich

in'definite a unbestimmt. ~**ly** adv unbegrenzt; ⟨postpone⟩ auf unbestimmte Zeit

indelible /ɪn'delɪbl/ a, -bly adv nicht zu entfernen; (fig) unauslöschlich

indemnify /ɪn'demnɪfaɪ/ vt (pt/pp -ied) versichern, (compensate) entschädigen. ~**ty** n Versicherung f; Entschädigung f

indent /ɪn'dent/ vt (Typ) einrücken. ~**ation** /-'teɪʃn/ n Einrückung f; (notch) Kerbe f

inde'pendence n Unabhängigkeit f; (self-reliance) Selbständigkeit f. ~ t a, -ly adv unabhängig; selbständig

indescribable /ɪndɪ'skraɪbəbl/ a, -bly adv unbeschreiblich

indestructible /ɪndɪ'strʌktəbl/ a unzerstörbar

indeterminate /ɪndɪ'tɜ:mɪnət/ a unbestimmt

index /'ɪndeks/ n Register nt

index: ~ **card** n Karteikarte f. ~ **finger** n Zeigefinger m. ~-**linked** a ⟨pension⟩ dynamisch

India /'ɪndɪə/ n Indien nt. ~**n** a indisch; (American) indianisch □n Inder(in) m(f); (American) Indianer(in) m(f)

Indian: ~ **'ink** n Tusche f. ~ **'summer** n Nachsommer m

indicate /'ɪndɪkeɪt/ vt zeigen; (point at) zeigen auf (+ acc); (hint) andeuten; (register) anzeigen □vi (Auto) blinken. ~**ion** /-'keɪʃn/ n Anzeichen nt

indicative /ɪn'dɪkətɪv/ a **be** ~ **of** schließen lassen auf (+ acc) □n (Gram) Indikativ m

indicator /'ɪndɪkeɪtə(r)/ n (Auto) Blinker m

indict /ɪn'daɪt/ vt anklagen. ~**ment** n Anklage f

in'difference n Gleichgültigkeit f. ~ t a, -ly adv gleichgültig; (not good) mittelmäßig

indigenous /ɪn'dɪdʒɪnəs/ a einheimisch

indi'gestible a unverdaulich; (difficult to digest) schwerverdaulich. ~**ion** n Magenverstimmung f

indignant /ɪn'dɪgnənt/ a, -ly adv entrüstet, empört. ~**tion** /-'neɪʃn/ n Entrüstung f, Empörung f

in'dignity n Demütigung f

indi'rect a, -ly adv indirekt

indi'screet a indiskret

indis'cretion n Indiskretion f

indiscriminate /ɪndɪ'skrɪmɪnət/ a, -ly adv wahllos

indi'spensable a unentbehrlich

indisposed /ɪndɪ'spəʊzd/ a indisponiert

indisputable /ɪndɪ'spju:təbl/ a, -bly adv unbestreitbar

indi'stinct a, -ly adv undeutlich

indistinguishable /ɪndɪ'stɪŋgwɪʃəbl/ a **be** ~ nicht zu unterscheiden sein; (not visible) nicht erkennbar sein

individual /ɪndɪ'vɪdjʊəl/ a, -ly adv individuell; (single) einzeln □n Individuum nt. ~**ity** /-'ælətɪ/ n Individualität f

indi'visible a unteilbar

indoctrinate /ɪn'dɒktrɪneɪt/ vt indoktrinieren

indolen|ce /'ɪndələns/ *n* Faulheit *f.* ~**t** *a* faul

indomitable /ɪn'dɒmɪtəbl/ *a* unbeugsam

indoor /'ɪndɔ:(r)/ *a* Innen-; ⟨*clothes*⟩ Haus-; ⟨*plant*⟩ Zimmer-; ⟨*Sport*⟩ Hallen-. ~**s** /-'dɔ:z/ *adv* im Haus, drinnen; **go** ~**s** ins Haus gehen

induce /ɪn'dju:s/ *vt* dazu bewegen (**to** zu); ⟨*produce*⟩ herbeiführen. ~**ment** *n* (*incentive*) Anreiz *m*

indulge /ɪn'dʌldʒ/ *vt* frönen (+ *dat*); verwöhnen ⟨*child*⟩□□ ti ~ **in** frönen (+ *dat*). ~**nce** /-əns/ *n* Nachgiebigkeit *f;* (*leniency*) Nachsicht *f.* ~**nt** *a* [zu] nachgiebig; nachsichtig

industrial /ɪn'dʌstrɪəl/ *a* Industrie-; **take** ~ **action** streiken. ~**ist** *n* Industrielle(r) *m.* ~**ized** *a* industrialisiert

industr|ious /ɪn'dʌstrɪəs/ *a, -ly adv* fleißig. ~**y** /'ɪndəstrɪ/ *n* Industrie *f;* (*zeal*) Fleiß *m*

inebriated /ɪ'ni:brɪeɪtɪd/ *a* betrunken

in'edible *a* nicht eßbar

inef'fective *a, -ly adv* unwirksam; ⟨*person*⟩ untauglich

inef'fectual /ɪnɪ'fektʃʊəl/ *a* unwirksam; ⟨*person*⟩ untauglich

inef'ficient *a* unfähig; ⟨*organization*⟩ nicht leistungsfähig; ⟨*method*⟩ nicht rationell

in'eligible *a* nicht berechtigt

inept /ɪ'nept/ *a* ungeschickt

ine'quality *n* Ungleichheit *f*

inert /ɪ'nɜ:t/ *a* unbeweglich; (*Phys*) träge. ~**ia** /ɪ'nɜ:ʃə/ *n* Trägheit *f*

inescapable /ɪnɪ'skeɪpəbl/ *a* unvermeidlich

inestimable /ɪn'estɪməbl/ *a* unschätzbar

inevitab|le /ɪn'evɪtəbl/ *a* unvermeidlich. ~**ly** *adv* zwangsläufig

ine'xact *a* ungenau

inex'cusable *a* unverzeihlich

inexhaustible /ɪnɪg'zɔ:stəbl/ *a* unerschöpflich

inexorable /ɪn'eksərəbl/ *a* unerbittlich

inex'pensive *a, -ly adv* preiswert

inex'perience *n* Unerfahrenheit *f.* ~**d** *a* unerfahren

inexplicable /ɪnɪk'splɪkəbl/ *a* unerklärlich

in'fallible *a* unfehlbar

infam|ous /'ɪnfəməs/ *a* niederträchtig; (*notorious*) berüchtigt. ~**y** *n* Niedertracht *f*

infan|cy /'ɪnfənsɪ/ *n* frühe Kindheit *f;* (*fig*) Anfangsstadium *nt.* ~**t** *n* Kleinkind *nt.* ~**tile** *a* kindisch

infantry /'ɪnfəntrɪ/ *n* Infanterie *f*

infatuated /ɪn'fætʃʊeɪtɪd/ *a* vernarrt (**with in** + *acc*)

infect /ɪn'fekt/ *vt* anstecken, infizieren; **become** ~**ed** ⟨*wound*:⟩ sich infizieren. ~**ion** /-'fekʃn/ *n* Infektion *f.* ~**ious** /-'fekʃəs/ *a* ansteckend

infer /ɪn'fɜ:(r)/ *vt* (*pt/pp* **inferred**) folgern (**from** aus); (*imply*) andeuten. ~**ence** /'ɪnfərəns/ *n* Folgerung *f*

inferior /ɪn'fɪərɪə(r)/ *a* minderwertig; (*in rank*) untergeordnet □*n* Untergebene(r) *m/f*

inferiority /ɪnfɪərɪ'ɒrətɪ/ *n* Minderwertigkeit *f.* ~ **complex** *n* Minderwertigkeitskomplex *m*

infern|al /ɪn'fɜ:nl/ *a* höllisch. ~**o** *n* flammendes Inferno *nt*

in'fertile *a* unfruchtbar. ~**'tility** *n* Unfruchtbarkeit *f*

infest /ɪn'fest/ *vt* befallen; **be** ~**ed with** befallen sein von; ⟨*place*⟩ verseucht sein mit

infi'delity *n* Untreue *f*

infighting /'ɪnfaɪtɪŋ/ *n* (*fig*) interne Machtkämpfe *pl*

infiltrate /'ɪnfɪltreɪt/ *vt* infiltrieren; (*Pol*) unterwandern

infinite /'ɪnfɪnət/ *a, -ly adv* unendlich

infinitesimal /ɪnfɪnɪ'tesɪml/ *a* unendlich klein

infinitive /ɪn'fɪnətɪv/ *n* (*Gram*) Infinitiv *m*

infinity /ɪn'fɪnəti/ n Unendlichkeit f

infirm /ɪn'fɜːm/ a gebrechlich. ~**ary** n Krankenhaus nt. ~**ity** n Gebrechlichkeit f

inflame /ɪn'fleɪm/ vt entzünden; **become** ~**d** sich entzünden. ~**d** a entzündet

in'flammable a feuergefährlich

inflammation /ɪnflə'meɪʃn/ n Entzündung f

inflammatory /ɪn'flæmətri/ a aufrührerisch

inflatable /ɪn'fleɪtəbl/ a aufblasbar

inflat|e /ɪn'fleɪt/ vt aufblasen; (with pump) aufpumpen. ~**ion** /-eɪʃn/ n Inflation f. ~**ionary** /-eɪʃənəri/ a inflationär

in'flexible a starr; ⟨person⟩ unbeugsam

inflexion /ɪn'flekʃn/ n Tonfall m; (Gram) Flexion f

inflict /ɪn'flɪkt/ vt zufügen (on dat); versetzen ⟨blow⟩ (on dat)

influen|ce /'ɪnfluəns/ n Einfluß m □ vt beeinflussen. ~**tial** /-'enʃl/ a einflußreich

influenza /ɪnflu'enzə/ n Grippe f

influx /'ɪnflʌks/ n Zustrom m

inform /ɪn'fɔːm/ vt benachrichtigen; (officially) informieren; ~ **s.o. of sth** jdm etw mitteilen; **keep s.o.** ~**ed** jdn auf dem laufenden halten □ vi ~ **against** denunzieren

in'for|mal a, -**ly** adv zwanglos; (unofficial) inoffiziell. ~'**mality** n Zwanglosigkeit f

informant /ɪn'fɔːmənt/ n Gewährsmann m

information /ɪnfə'meɪʃn/ n Auskunft f; **a piece of** ~**ion** eine Auskunft. ~**ive** /ɪn'fɔːmətɪv/ a aufschlußreich; (instructive) lehrreich

informer /ɪn'fɔːmə(r)/ n Spitzel m; (Pol) Denunziant m

infra-red /ɪnfrə-/ a infrarot

in'frequent a, -**ly** adv selten

infringe /ɪn'frɪndʒ/ vt/i ~ [**on**] verstoßen gegen. ~**ment** n Verstoß m

infuriat|e /ɪn'fjʊərɪeɪt/ vt wütend machen. ~**ing** a ärgerlich; **he is** ~**ing** er kann einen zur Raserei bringen

infusion /ɪn'fjuːʒn/ n Aufguß m

ingenious /ɪn'dʒiːnɪəs/ a erfinderisch; ⟨thing⟩ raffiniert

ingenuity /ɪndʒɪ'njuːəti/ n Geschicklichkeit f

ingenuous /ɪn'dʒenjʊəs/ a unschuldig

ingot /'ɪŋgət/ n Barren m

ingrained /ɪn'greɪnd/ a eingefleischt; **be** ~ ⟨dirt:⟩ tief sitzen

ingratiate /ɪn'greɪʃɪeɪt/ vt ~ **oneself** sich einschmeicheln (**with** bei)

in'gratitude n Undankbarkeit f

ingredient /ɪn'griːdɪənt/ n (Culin) Zutat f

ingrowing /'ɪngrəʊɪŋ/ a ⟨nail⟩ eingewachsen

inhabit /ɪn'hæbɪt/ vt bewohnen. ~**ant** n Einwohner(in) m(f)

inhale /ɪn'heɪl/ vt/i einatmen; (Med & when smoking) inhalieren

inherent /ɪn'hɪərənt/ a natürlich

inherit /ɪn'herɪt/ vt erben. ~**ance** /-əns/ n Erbschaft f, Erbe nt

inhibit /ɪn'hɪbɪt/ vt hemmen. ~**ed** a gehemmt. ~**ion** /-'bɪʃn/ n Hemmung f

inho'spitable a ungastlich

in'human a unmenschlich

inimitable /ɪ'nɪmɪtəbl/ a unnachahmlich

iniquitous /ɪ'nɪkwɪtəs/ a schändlich; (unjust) ungerecht

initial /ɪ'nɪʃl/ a anfänglich, Anfangs- □ n Anfangsbuchstabe m; **my** ~**s** meine Initialen □ vt (pt/pp **initialled**) abzeichnen; (Pol) paraphieren. ~**ly** adv anfangs, am Anfang

initiat|e /ɪ'nɪʃɪeɪt/ vt einführen. ~**ion** /-'eɪʃn/ n Einführung f

initiative /ɪ'nɪʃətɪv/ n Initiative f

inject /ɪn'dʒekt/ vt einspritzen, injizieren. ~**ion** /-ekʃn/ n Spritze f, Injektion f

injunction /ɪn'dʒʌŋkʃn/ n gerichtliche Verfügung f

injur|e /'ɪndʒə(r)/ vt verletzen. ~**y** n Verletzung f

injustice n Ungerechtigkeit f; **do s.o. an** ~ jdm unrecht tun

ink /ɪŋk/ n Tinte f

inkling /'ɪŋklɪŋ/ n Ahnung f

inlaid /ɪn'leɪd/ a eingelegt

inland /'ɪnlənd/ a Binnen- □ adv landeinwärts. **I~ Revenue** n ≈ Finanzamt nt

in-laws /'ɪnlɔːz/ npl (fam) Schwiegereltern pl

inlay /'ɪnleɪ/ n Einlegearbeit f

inlet /'ɪnlet/ n schmale Bucht f; (Techn) Zuleitung f

inmate /'ɪnmeɪt/ n Insasse m

inn /ɪn/ n Gasthaus nt

innards /'ɪnədz/ npl (fam) Eingeweide pl

innate /ɪ'neɪt/ a angeboren

inner /'ɪnə(r)/ a innere(r,s). ~**most** a innerste(r,s)

'innkeeper n Gastwirt m

innocen|ce /'ɪnəsns/ n Unschuld f. ~**t** a unschuldig. ~**tly** adv in aller Unschuld

innocuous /ɪ'nɒkjʊəs/ a harmlos

innovat|e /'ɪnəveɪt/ vi neu einführen. ~**ion** /-'veɪʃn/ n Neuerung f. ~**or** n Neuerer m

innuendo /ɪnjuː'endəʊ/ n (pl -es) [versteckte] Anspielung f

innumerable /ɪ'njuːmərəbl/ a unzählig

inoculat|e /ɪ'nɒkjʊlet/ vt impfen. ~**ion** /-'leɪʃn/ n Impfung f

inoffensive a harmlos

in'operable a nicht operierbar

in'opportune a unpassend

inordinate /ɪ'nɔːdɪnət/ a, -ly adv übermäßig

inor'ganic a anorganisch

'in-patient n [stationär behandelter] Krankenhauspatient m

input /'ɪnpʊt/ n Input m & nt

inquest /'ɪnkwest/ n gerichtliche Untersuchung f

inquir|e /ɪn'kwaɪə(r)/ vi sich erkundigen (**about** nach); ~ **e into** untersuchen □ vt sich erkundigen nach. ~**y** n Erkundigung f; (investigation) Untersuchung f

inquisitive /ɪn'kwɪzətɪv/ a, -ly adv neugierig

inroad /'ɪnrəʊd/ n Einfall m; **make** ~**s into sth** etw angreifen

in'sane a geisteskrank; (fig) wahnsinnig

in'sanitary a unhygienisch

in'sanity n Geisteskrankheit f

insatiable /ɪn'seɪʃəbl/ a unersättlich

inscri|be /ɪn'skraɪb/ vt eingravieren. ~**ption** /-'skrɪpʃn/ n Inschrift f

inscrutable /ɪn'skruːtəbl/ a unergründlich; (expression) undurchdringlich

insect /'ɪnsekt/ n Insekt nt. ~**icide** /-'sektɪsaɪd/ n Insektenvertilgungsmittel nt

inse'cur|e a nicht sicher; (fig) unsicher. ~**ity** n Unsicherheit f

insemination /ɪnsemɪ'neɪʃn/ n Besamung f; (Med) Befruchtung f

in'sensible a (unconscious) bewußtlos

in'sensitive a gefühllos; ~ **to** unempfindlich gegen

in'separable a untrennbar; (people) unzertrennlich

insert¹ /'ɪnsɜːt/ n Einsatz m

insert² /ɪn'sɜːt/ vt einfügen, einsetzen; einstecken ⟨key⟩; einwerfen ⟨coin⟩. ~**ion** /-ɜːʃn/ n (insert) Einsatz m; (in text) Einfügung f

inside /ɪn'saɪd/ n Innenseite f; (of house) Innere(s) nt □ attrib Innen- □ adv innen; (indoors) drinnen; **go** ~ hineingehen; **come** ~ hereinkommen; ~ **out** links [herum]; **know sth** ~ **out** etw in- und auswendig kennen □ prep ~ [**of**] in (+ dat/(into) + acc)

insidious /ɪn'sɪdɪəs/ a, -ly adv heimtückisch

insight /'ɪnsaɪt/ n Einblick m
(**into** in + acc); (understanding)
Einsicht f

insignia /ɪn'sɪgnɪə/ npl Insignien
pl

insig'nificant a unbedeutend

insin'cere a unaufrichtig

insinuat|e /ɪn'sɪnjʊeɪt/ vt andeu-
ten. ~**ion** /-'eɪʃn/ n Andeutung f

insipid /ɪn'sɪpɪd/ a fade

insist /ɪn'sɪst/ vi darauf bestehen;
~ **on** bestehen auf (+ dat)□ vt ~
that darauf bestehen, daß.
~**ence** n Bestehen nt. ~**ent** a,
-ly adv beharrlich; **be** ~**ent** darauf bestehen

'insole n Einlegesohle f

insolen|ce /'ɪnsələns/ n Unver-
schämtheit f. ~**t** a, **-ly** adv unverschämt

in'soluble a unlöslich; (fig) un-
lösbar

in'solvent a zahlungsunfähig

insomnia /ɪn'sɒmnɪə/ n Schlaflo-
sigkeit f

inspect /ɪn'spekt/ vt inspizieren;
(test) prüfen; kontrollieren
⟨ticket⟩. ~**ion** /-ekʃn/ n Inspektion f. ~**or** n Inspektor m; (of
tickets) Kontrolleur m

inspiration /ɪnspə'reɪʃn/ n Inspiration f

inspire /ɪn'spaɪə(r)/ vt inspirieren;
~ **sth in** s.o. jdm etw einflößen

insta'bility n Unbeständigkeit f;
(of person) Labilität f

install /ɪn'stɔːl/ vt installieren; [in
ein Amt] einführen ⟨person⟩.
~**ation** /-stə'leɪʃn/ n Installation f; Amtseinführung f

instalment /ɪn'stɔːlmənt/ n
(Comm) Rate f; (of serial) Fortsetzung f; (Radio, TV) Folge f

instance /'ɪnstəns/ n Fall m;
(example) Beispiel nt; **in the first**
~ zunächst; **for** ~ zum Beispiel

instant /'ɪnstənt/ a sofortig;
(Culin) Instant- □ n Augenblick
m, Moment m. ~**aneous** /-'teɪ-
nɪəs/ a unverzüglich, unmittel-

bar; **death was** ~**aneous** der
Tod trat sofort ein

instant 'coffee n Pulverkaffee m

instantly /'ɪnstəntlɪ/ adv sofort

instead /ɪn'sted/ adv statt dessen;
~ **of** statt (+ gen); anstelle von;
~ **of me** an meiner Stelle; ~ **of
going** anstatt zu gehen

'instep n Spann m, Rist m

instigat|e /'ɪnstɪgeɪt/ vt anstiften;
einleiten ⟨proceedings⟩. ~**ion**
/-'geɪʃn/ n Anstiftung f; **at his**
~**ion** auf seine Veranlassung.
~**or** n Anstifter(in) m(f)

instil /ɪn'stɪl/ vt (pt/pp **instilled**)
einprägen (**into** s.o. jdm)

instinct /'ɪnstɪŋkt/ n Instinkt m.
~**ive** /ɪn'stɪŋktɪv/ a, **-ly** adv instinktiv

institut|e /'ɪnstɪtjuːt/ n Institut nt
□ vt einführen; einleiten
⟨search⟩. ~**ion** /-'tjuːʃn/ n Institution f; (home) Anstalt f

instruct /ɪn'strʌkt/ vt unterrichten; (order) anweisen. ~**ion**
/-ʌkʃn/ n Unterricht m; Anweisung f; ~**ions** pl for use Gebrauchsanweisung f. ~**ive** /-ɪv/ a
lehrreich. ~**or** n Lehrer(in)
m(f); (Mil) Ausbilder(in) m(f)

instrument /'ɪnstrʊmənt/ n Instrument nt. ~**al** /-'mentl/ a In-
strumental-; **be** ~**al** in eine ent-
scheidende Rolle spielen bei

insu'bordinat|e a ungehorsam.
~**nation** /-'neɪʃn/ n Ungehorsam
m; (Mil) Insubordination f

in'sufferable a unerträglich

insuf'ficient a, **-ly** adv nicht genügend

insular /'ɪnsjʊlə(r)/ a (fig) engstirnig

insulat|e /'ɪnsjʊleɪt/ vt isolieren.
~**ing tape** n Isolierband nt.
~**ion** /-'leɪʃn/ n Isolierung f

insulin /'ɪnsjʊlɪn/ n Insulin nt

insult[1] /'ɪnsʌlt/ n Beleidigung f

insult[2] /ɪn'sʌlt/ vt beleidigen

insuperable /ɪn'suːpərəbl/ a un-
überwindlich

insur|ance /ɪn'ʃʊərəns/ n Versicherung f. ~e vt versichern
insurrection /ɪnsə'rekʃn/ n Aufstand m
intact /ɪn'tækt/ a unbeschädigt; (complete) vollständig
'intake n Aufnahme f
in'tangible /a nicht greifbar
integral /'ɪntɪgrl/ a wesentlich
integrat|e /'ɪntɪgreɪt/ vt integrieren □vi sich integrieren. ~ion /-'greɪʃn/ n Integration f
integrity /ɪn'tegrətɪ/ n Integrität f
intellect /'ɪntəlekt/ n Intellekt m. ~ual /-'lektjʊəl/ a intellektuell
intelligen|ce /ɪn'telɪdʒəns/ n Intelligenz f; (Mil) Nachrichtendienst m; (information) Meldungen pl. ~t a, -ly adv intelligent
intelligentsia /ɪntelɪ'dʒentsɪə/ n Intelligenz f
intelligible /ɪn'telɪdʒəbl/ a verständlich
intend /ɪn'tend/ vt beabsichtigen; be ~ed for bestimmt sein für
intense /ɪn'tens/ a intensiv; (pain) stark. ~ly adv äußerst; (study) intensiv
intensi|fication /ɪntensɪfɪ'keɪʃn/ n Intensivierung f. ~fy /-'tensɪfaɪ/ v (pt/pp -ied) □vt intensivieren □vi zunehmen
intensity /ɪn'tensətɪ/ n Intensität f
intensive /ɪn'tensɪv/ a, -ly adv intensiv; be in ~ care auf der Intensivstation sein
intent /ɪn'tent/ a, -ly adv aufmerksam; ~ on (absorbed in) vertieft in (+ acc); be ~ on doing sth fest entschlossen sein, etw zu tun □n Absicht f; to all ~s and purposes im Grunde
intention /ɪn'tenʃn/ n Absicht f. ~al a, -ly adv absichtlich
inter /ɪn'tɜ:(r)/ vt (pt/pp interred) bestatten
inter'action n Wechselwirkung f
intercede /ɪntə'si:d/ vi Fürsprache einlegen (on behalf of für)
intercept /ɪntə'sept/ vt abfangen

'interchange[1] n Austausch m; (Auto) Autobahnkreuz nt
inter'change[2] vt austauschen. ~able a austauschbar
intercom /'ɪntəkɒm/ n [Gegen]sprechanlage f
'intercourse n Verkehr m; (sexual) Geschlechtsverkehr m
interest /'ɪntrəst/ n Interesse nt; (Comm) Zinsen pl; have an ~ (Comm) beteiligt sein (in an + dat) □vt interessieren; be ~ed sich interessieren (in für). ~ing a interessant. ~ rate n Zinssatz m
interfere /ɪntə'fɪə(r)/ vi sich einmischen. ~nce /-əns/ n Einmischung f; (Radio, TV) Störung f
interim /'ɪntərɪm/ a Zwischen-; (temporary) vorläufig □n in the ~ in der Zwischenzeit
interior /ɪn'tɪərɪə(r)/ a innere(r,s), Innen- □n Innere(s) nt
interject /ɪntə'dʒekt/ vt einwerfen. ~ion /-ekʃn/ n Interjektion f; (remark) Einwurf m
inter'lock vi ineinandergreifen
interloper /'ɪntələʊpə(r)/ n Eindringling m
interlude /'ɪntəlu:d/ n Pause f; (performance) Zwischenspiel nt
inter'marry vi untereinander heiraten; (different groups:) Mischen schließen
intermediary /ɪntə'mi:dɪərɪ/ n Vermittler(in) m(f)
intermediate /ɪntə'mi:dɪət/ a Zwischen-
interminable /ɪn'tɜ:mɪnəbl/ a endlos [lang]
intermission /ɪntə'mɪʃn/ n Pause f
intermittent /ɪntə'mɪtənt/ a in Abständen auftretend
intern /ɪn'tɜ:n/ vt internieren
internal /ɪn'tɜ:nl/ a innere(r,s); (matter, dispute) intern. ~ly adv innerlich; (deal with) intern
inter'national a, -ly adv international □n Länderspiel nt; (player) Nationalspieler(in) m(f)

internist /ɪnˈtɜːnɪst/ n (Amer) Internist m

internment /ɪnˈtɜːnmənt/ n Internierung f

'interplay n Wechselspiel nt

interpolate /ɪnˈtɜːpəleɪt/ vt einwerfen

interpret /ɪnˈtɜːprɪt/ vt interpretieren; auslegen ⟨text⟩; deuten ⟨dream⟩; (translate) dolmetschen □vi dolmetschen. **~ation** /-ˈteɪʃn/ n Interpretation f. **~er** n Dolmetscher(in) m(f)

inter'related a verwandt; ⟨facts⟩ zusammenhängend

interrogate /ɪnˈterəgeɪt/ vt verhören. **~ion** /-ˈgeɪʃn/ n Verhör nt

interrogative /ɪntəˈrɒgətɪv/ a & n **~ [pronoun]** Interrogativpronomen nt

interrupt /ɪntəˈrʌpt/ vt/i unterbrechen; **don't ~ !** red nicht dazwischen! **~ion** /-ʌpʃn/ n Unterbrechung f

intersect /ɪntəˈsekt/ vi sich kreuzen; (Geom) sich schneiden. **~ion** /-ekʃn/ n Kreuzung f

interspersed /ɪntəˈspɜːst/ a ~ **with** durchsetzt mit

inter'twine vi sich ineinanderschlingen

interval /ˈɪntəvl/ n Abstand m; (Theat) Pause f; (Mus) Intervall nt; **at hourly ~s** alle Stunde; **bright ~s** pl Aufheiterungen pl

intervene /ɪntəˈviːn/ vi eingreifen; (occur) dazwischenkommen. **~tion** /-ˈvenʃn/ n Eingreifen nt; (Mil, Pol) Intervention f

interview /ˈɪntəvjuː/ n (Journ) Interview nt; (for job) Vorstellungsgespräch nt; **go for an ~** sich vorstellen □vt interviewen; ein Vorstellungsgespräch führen mit. **~er** n Interviewer(in) m(f)

intestine /ɪnˈtestɪn/ n Darm m

intimacy /ˈɪntɪməsɪ/ n Vertrautheit f; (sexual) Intimität f

intimate¹ /ˈɪntɪmət/ a, **-ly** adv vertraut; ⟨friend⟩ eng; (sexually) intim

intimate² /ˈɪntɪmeɪt/ vt zu verstehen geben; (imply) andeuten

intimidate /ɪnˈtɪmɪdeɪt/ vt einschüchtern. **~ion** /-ˈdeɪʃn/ n Einschüchterung f

into /ˈɪntə, vor einem Vokal ɪntʊ/ prep in (+ acc); **go ~ the house** ins Haus [hinein]gehen; **be ~** (fam) sich auskennen mit; **7 ~ 21** 21 [geteilt] durch 7

in'tolerable a unerträglich

in'tolerance n Intoleranz f. **~t** a intolerant

intonation /ɪntəˈneɪʃn/ n Tonfall m

intoxicated /ɪnˈtɒksɪkeɪtɪd/ a betrunken; (fig) berauscht. **~ion** /-ˈkeɪʃn/ n Rausch m

intractable /ɪnˈtræktəbl/ a widerspenstig; ⟨problem⟩ hartnäckig

intransigent /ɪnˈtrænsɪdʒənt/ a unnachgiebig

in'transitive a, **-ly** adv intransitiv

intravenous /ɪntrəˈviːnəs/ a, **-ly** adv intravenös

intrepid /ɪnˈtrepɪd/ a kühn, unerschrocken

intricate /ˈɪntrɪkət/ a kompliziert

intrigue /ɪnˈtriːg/ n Intrige f □vt faszinieren □vi intriguieren. **~ing** a faszinierend

intrinsic /ɪnˈtrɪnsɪk/ a ~ **value** Eigenwert m

introduce /ɪntrəˈdjuːs/ vt vorstellen; (bring in, insert) einführen

introduction /ɪntrəˈdʌkʃn/ n Einführung f; (to person) Vorstellung f; (to book) Einleitung f. **~ory** /-tərɪ/ a einleitend

introspective /ɪntrəˈspektɪv/ a in sich (acc) gerichtet

introvert /ˈɪntrəvɜːt/ n introvertierter Mensch m

intrude /ɪnˈtruːd/ vi stören. **~er** n Eindringling m. **~sion** /-uːʒn/ n Störung f

intuition /ɪntjuːˈɪʃn/ n Intuition f. **~ive** /-ˈtjuːɪtɪv/ a, **-ly** adv intuitiv

inundate /ˈɪnəndeɪt/ vt überschwemmen

invade /ɪn'veɪd/ vt einfallen in (+ acc). ~ r n Angreifer m

invalid¹ /'ɪnvəlɪd/ n Kranke(r) m/f

invalid² /ɪn'vælɪd/ a ungültig. ~ate vt ungültig machen

in'valuable a unschätzbar; ⟨person⟩ unersetzlich

in'variab|le a unveränderlich. ~ly adv immer

invasion /ɪn'veɪʒn/ n Invasion f

invective /ɪn'vektɪv/ n Beschimpfungen pl

invent /ɪn'vent/ vt erfinden. ~ion /-enʃn/ n Erfindung f. ~ive /-tɪv/ a erfinderisch. ~or n Erfinder m

inventory /'ɪnvəntrɪ/ n Bestandsliste f; **make an** ~ ein Inventar aufstellen

inverse /ɪn'vɜːs/ a, -ly adv umgekehrt □ n Gegenteil nt

invert /ɪn'vɜːt/ vt umkehren. ~ed **commas** npl Anführungszeichen pl

invest /ɪn'vest/ vt investieren, anlegen; ~ **in** (fam: buy) sich (dat) zulegen

investigat|e /ɪn'vestɪgeɪt/ vt untersuchen. ~ion /-'geɪʃn/ n Untersuchung f

invest|ment /ɪn'vestmənt/ n Anlage f; **be a good** ~**ment** ⟨fig⟩ sich bezahlt machen. ~or n Kapitalanleger m

inveterate /ɪn'vetərət/ a Gewohnheits-; ⟨liar⟩ unverbesserlich

invidious /ɪn'vɪdɪəs/ a unerfreulich; ⟨unfair⟩ ungerecht

invigilate /ɪn'vɪdʒɪleɪt/ vi (Sch) Aufsicht führen

invigorate /ɪn'vɪgəreɪt/ vt beleben

invincible /ɪn'vɪnsəbl/ a unbesiegbar

inviolable /ɪn'vaɪələbl/ a unantastbar

in'visible a unsichtbar. ~ **mending** n Kunststopfen nt

invitation /ɪnvɪ'teɪʃn/ n Einladung f

invit|e /ɪn'vaɪt/ vt einladen. ~**ing** a einladend

invoice /'ɪnvɔɪs/ n Rechnung f □ vt ~ **s.o.** jdm eine Rechnung schicken

invoke /ɪn'vəʊk/ vt anrufen

in'voluntary a, -ily adv unwillkürlich

involve /ɪn'vɒlv/ vt beteiligen; ⟨affect⟩ betreffen; ⟨implicate⟩ verwickeln; ⟨entail⟩ mit sich bringen; ⟨mean⟩ bedeuten; **be** ~**d in** beteiligt sein an (+ dat); ⟨implicated⟩ verwickelt sein in (+ acc); **get** ~**d with s.o.** sich mit jdm einlassen. ~**d** a kompliziert

in'vulnerable a unverwundbar; ⟨position⟩ unangreifbar

inward /'ɪnwəd/ a innere(r,s). ~**ly** adv innerlich. ~**s** adv nach innen

iodine /'aɪədiːn/ n Jod nt

iota /aɪ'əʊtə/ n Jota nt; (fam) Funke m

IOU abbr (**I owe you**) Schuldschein m

Iran /ɪ'rɑːn/ n der Iran

Iraq /ɪ'rɑːk/ n der Irak

irascible /ɪ'ræsəbl/ a aufbrausend

irate /aɪ'reɪt/ a wütend

Ireland /'aɪələnd/ n Irland nt

iris /'aɪərɪs/ n (Anat) Regenbogenhaut f, Iris f; (Bot) Schwertlilie f

Irish /'aɪərɪʃ/ a irisch □ n the ~ pl die Iren. ~**man** n Ire m. ~**woman** n Irin f

irk /ɜːk/ vt ärgern. ~**some** /-səm/ a lästig

iron /'aɪən/ a Eisen-; ⟨fig⟩ eisern □ n Eisen nt; ⟨appliance⟩ Bügeleisen nt □ vt/i bügeln. ~ **out** vt ausbügeln

ironic[al] /aɪ'rɒnɪk[l]/ a ironisch

ironing /'aɪənɪŋ/ n Bügeln nt; ⟨articles⟩ Bügelwäsche f; **do the** ~ bügeln. ~**-board** n Bügelbrett nt

ironmonger /'-mʌŋgə(r)/ n ~**'s [shop]** Haushaltswarengeschäft nt

irony /'aɪərənɪ/ n Ironie f

irradiate /ɪ'reɪdɪeɪt/ vt bestrahlen

irrational /ɪ'ræʃənl/ a irrational

irreconcilable /ɪ'rekənsaɪləbl/ a unversöhnlich

irrefutable /ɪrɪˈfjuːtəbl/ a unwiderlegbar

irregular /ɪˈregjʊlə(r)/ a, **-ly** adv unregelmäßig; (against rules) regelwidrig. **~ity** /-ˈlærətɪ/ n Unregelmäßigkeit f; Regelwidrigkeit f

irrelevant /ɪˈreləvənt/ a irrelevant

irreparable /ɪˈrepərəbl/ a unersetzlich; be ~ nicht wiedergutzumachen sein

irreplaceable /ɪrɪˈpleɪsəbl/ a unersetzlich

irrepressible /ɪrɪˈpresəbl/ a unverwüstlich; be ~ ⟨person:⟩ nicht unterzukriegen sein

irresistible /ɪrɪˈzɪstəbl/ a unwiderstehlich

irresolute /ɪˈrezəluːt/ a unentschlossen

irrespective /ɪrɪˈspektɪv/ a ~ of ungeachtet (+ gen)

irresponsible /ɪrɪˈspɒnsəbl/ a, **-bly** adv unverantwortlich; ⟨person⟩ verantwortungslos

irreverent /ɪˈrevərənt/ a, **-ly** adv respektlos

irreversible /ɪrɪˈvɜːsəbl/ a unwiderruflich; (Med) irreversibel

irrevocable /ɪˈrevəkəbl/ a, **-bly** adv unwiderruflich

irrigat|e /ˈɪrɪgeɪt/ vt bewässern. **~ion** /-ˈgeɪʃn/ n Bewässerung f

irritability /ɪrɪtəˈbɪlətɪ/ n Gereiztheit f

irritable /ˈɪrɪtəbl/ a reizbar

irritant /ˈɪrɪtnt/ n Reizstoff m

irritat|e /ˈɪrɪteɪt/ vt irritieren; (Med) reizen. **~ion** /-ˈteɪʃn/ n Ärger m; (Med) Reizung f

is /ɪz/ see **be**

Islam /ˈɪzlɑːm/ n der Islam. **~ic** /-ˈlæmɪk/ a islamisch

island /ˈaɪlənd/ n Insel f. **~er** n Inselbewohner(in) m(f)

isle /aɪl/ n Insel f

isolat|e /ˈaɪsəleɪt/ vt isolieren. **~ed** a (remote) abgelegen; (single) einzeln. **~ion** /-ˈleɪʃn/ n Isoliertheit f; (Med) Isolierung f

Israel /ˈɪzreɪl/ n Israel nt. **~i** /ɪzˈreɪlɪ/ a israelisch □n Israeli m/f

issue /ˈɪʃuː/ n Frage f; (outcome) Ergebnis nt; (of magazine, stamps) Ausgabe f; (offspring) Nachkommen pl; **what is at ~?** worum geht es? **take ~ with s.o.** jdm widersprechen □ vt ausgeben; ausstellen ⟨passport⟩; erteilen ⟨order⟩; herausgeben ⟨book⟩; **be ~ d with sth** etw erhalten □ vi **~ from** herausströmen aus

isthmus /ˈɪsməs/ n (pl **-muses**) Landenge f

it /ɪt/ pron es; (m) er; (f) sie; (as direct object) es; (m) ihn; (f) sie; (as indirect object) ihm; (f) ihr; **it is raining** es regnet; **it's me** ich bin's; **who is it?** wer ist da? **of/from it** davon; **with it** damit; **out of it** daraus

Italian /ɪˈtæljən/ a italienisch □ n Italiener(in) m(f); (Lang) Italienisch nt

italic /ɪˈtælɪk/ a kursiv. **~s** npl Kursivschrift f; **in ~s** kursiv

Italy /ˈɪtəlɪ/ n Italien nt

itch /ɪtʃ/ n Juckreiz m; **I have an ~** es juckt mich □ vi jucken; **I'm ~ing** (fam) es juckt mich (to zu). **~y** a be ~ jucken

item /ˈaɪtəm/ n Gegenstand m; (Comm) Artikel m; (on agenda) Punkt m; (on invoice) Posten m; (act) Nummer f; ~ **[of news]** Nachricht f. **~ize** vt einzeln aufführen; spezifizieren ⟨bill⟩

itinerant /aɪˈtɪnərənt/ a Wander-

itinerary /aɪˈtɪnərərɪ/ n [Reise]route f

its /ɪts/ poss pron sein; (f) ihr

it's = it is, it has

itself /ɪtˈself/ pron selbst; (refl) sich; **by ~** von selbst; (alone) allein

ivory /ˈaɪvərɪ/ n Elfenbein nt □ attrib Elfenbein-

ivy /ˈaɪvɪ/ n Efeu m

J

jab /dʒæb/ n Stoß m; (fam: injection) Spritze f □ vt (pt/pp jabbed) stoßen

jabber /'dʒæbə(r)/ vi plappern

jack /dʒæk/ n (Auto) Wagenheber m; (Cards) Bube m □ vt ~ up (Auto) aufbocken

jackdaw /'dʒækdɔː/ n Dohle f

jacket /'dʒækɪt/ n Jacke f; (of book) Schutzumschlag m. ~ po-**tato** n in der Schale gebackene Kartoffel f

'jackpot n hit the ~ das Große Los ziehen

jade /dʒeɪd/ n Jade m

jaded /'dʒeɪdɪd/ a abgespannt

jagged /'dʒægɪd/ a zackig

jail /dʒeɪl/ = **gaol**

jalopy /dʒə'lɒpɪ/ n (fam) Klapperkiste f

jam¹ /dʒæm/ n Marmelade f

jam² n Gedränge nt; (fam: difficulty) Klemme f □ v (pt/pp jammed) □ vt klemmen (in in + acc); stören ⟨broadcast⟩ □ vi klemmen

Jamaica /dʒə'meɪkə/ n Jamaika nt

jangle /'dʒæŋgl/ vi klimpern □ vt klimpern mit

janitor /'dʒænɪtə(r)/ n Hausmeister m

January /'dʒænjʊərɪ/ n Januar m

Japan /dʒə'pæn/ n Japan nt. ~**ese** /dʒæpə'niːz/ a japanisch □ n Japaner(in) m(f); (Lang) Japanisch nt

jar¹ /dʒɑː(r)/ n Glas nt; (earthenware) Topf m

jar² v (pt/pp jarred) vi stören □ vt erschüttern

jargon /'dʒɑːgən/ n Jargon m

jaundice /'dʒɔːndɪs/ n Gelbsucht f. ~**d** a (fig) zynisch

jaunt /dʒɔːnt/ n Ausflug m

jaunty /'dʒɔːntɪ/ a (-ier, -iest), -ily adv keck

javelin /'dʒævlɪn/ n Speer m

jaw /dʒɔː/ n Kiefer m; ~s pl Rachen m □ vi (fam) quatschen

jay /dʒeɪ/ n Eichelhäher m. ~-**walker** n achtloser Fußgänger m

jazz /dʒæz/ n Jazz m. ~**y** a knallig

jealous /'dʒeləs/ a, -ly adv eifersüchtig (of auf + acc). ~**y** n Eifersucht f

jeans /dʒiːnz/ npl Jeans pl

jeer /dʒɪə(r)/ n Johlen nt □ vi johlen; ~ **at** verhöhnen

jell /dʒel/ vi gelieren

jelly /'dʒelɪ/ n Gelee nt; (dessert) Götterspeise f. ~**fish** n Qualle f

jemmy /'dʒemɪ/ n Brecheisen nt

jeopardize /'dʒepədaɪz/ vt gefährden. ~**dy** /-dɪ/ n in ~ gefährdet

jerk /dʒɜːk/ n Ruck m □ vt stoßen; (pull) reißen □ vi rucken; ⟨limb, muscle:⟩ zucken. ~**ily** adv ruckweise. ~**y** a ruckartig

jersey /'dʒɜːzɪ/ n Pullover m; (Sport) Trikot nt; (fabric) Jersey m

jest /dʒest/ n Scherz m; **in** ~ im Spaß □ vi scherzen

jet¹ /dʒet/ n (Miner) Jett m

jet² n (of water) [Wasser]strahl m; (nozzle) Düse f; (plane) Düsenflugzeug nt

jet: ~-**black** a pechschwarz. ~-**lag** n Jet-lag m. ~-**pro'pelled** a mit Düsenantrieb

jettison /'dʒetɪsn/ vt über Bord werfen

jetty /'dʒetɪ/ n Landesteg m; (breakwater) Buhne f

Jew /dʒuː/ n Jude m /Jüdin f

jewel /'dʒuːəl/ n Edelstein m; (fig) Juwel nt. ~**ler** n Juwelier m; ~**ler's [shop]** Juweliergeschäft nt. ~**lery** n Schmuck m

Jewess /'dʒuːɪs/ n Jüdin f. ~**ish** a jüdisch

jib /dʒɪb/ vi (pt/pp jibbed) (fig) sich sträuben (at gegen)

jiffy /'dʒɪfɪ/ n (fam) **in a** ~ in einem Augenblick

jigsaw /'dʒɪgsɔː/ n ~ **[puzzle]** Puzzlespiel nt

jilt /dʒɪlt/ vt sitzenlassen

jingle /'dʒɪŋgl/ n (rhyme) Verschen nt □vi klimpern □vt klimpern mit

jinx /dʒɪŋks/ n (fam) it's got a ~ on it es ist verhext

jitter|s /'dʒɪtəz/ npl (fam) have the ~s nervös sein. ~y a (fam) nervös

job /dʒɒb/ n Aufgabe f; (post) Stelle f, (fam) Job m; be a ~ (fam) nicht leicht sein; it's a good ~ that es ist [nur] gut, daß. ~centre n Arbeitsvermittlungsstelle f. ~less a arbeitslos

jockey /'dʒɒkɪ/ n Jockei m

jocular /'dʒɒkjʊlə(r)/ a, -ly adv spaßhaft

jog /dʒɒg/ n Stoß m; at a ~ im Dauerlauf □v (pt/pp jogged) □vt anstoßen; ~ s.o.'s memory jds Gedächtnis nachhelfen □vi (Sport) joggen. ~ging n Jogging nt

john /dʒɒn/ n (Amer, fam) Klo nt

join /dʒɔɪn/ n Nahtstelle f □vt verbinden (to mit); sich anschließen (+ dat) ⟨person⟩; (become member of) beitreten (+ dat); eintreten in (+ acc) ⟨firm⟩ □vi ⟨roads:⟩ sich treffen. ~ in vi mitmachen. ~ up vi (Mil) Soldat werden □vt zusammenfügen

joiner /'dʒɔɪnə(r)/ n Tischler m

joint /dʒɔɪnt/ a, -ly adv gemeinsam □n Gelenk nt; (in wood, brickwork) Fuge f; (Culin) Braten m; (fam: bar) Lokal nt

joist /dʒɔɪst/ n Dielenbalken m

jok|e /dʒəʊk/ n Scherz m; (funny story) Witz m; (trick) Streich m □vi scherzen. ~er n Witzbold m; (Cards) Joker m. ~ing n ~ing apart Spaß beiseite. ~ingly adv im Spaß

jollity /'dʒɒlətɪ/ n Lustigkeit f

jolly /'dʒɒlɪ/ a (-ier, -iest) lustig □adv (fam) sehr

jolt /dʒəʊlt/ n Ruck m □vt einen Ruck versetzen (+ dat) □vi holpern

Jordan /'dʒɔːdn/ n Jordanien nt

jostle /'dʒɒsl/ vt anrempeln □vi drängeln

jot /dʒɒt/ n Jota nt □vt (pt/pp jotted) ~ [down] sich (dat) notieren. ~ter n Notizblock m

journal /'dʒɜːnl/ n Zeitschrift f; (diary) Tagebuch nt. ~ese /-ə'liːz/ n Zeitungsjargon m. ~ism m Journalismus m. ~ist n Journalist(in) m(f)

journey /'dʒɜːnɪ/ n Reise f

jovial /'dʒəʊvɪəl/ a lustig

joy /dʒɔɪ/ n Freude f. ~ful a, ~adv freudig, froh. ~ride n (fam) Spritztour f [im gestohlenen Auto]

jubil|**ant** /'dʒuːbɪlənt/ a überglücklich. ~ation /-'leɪʃn/ n Jubel m

jubilee /'dʒuːbɪliː/ n Jubiläum nt

Judaism /'dʒuːdeɪɪzm/ n Judentum nt

judder /'dʒʌdə(r)/ vi rucken

judge /dʒʌdʒ/ n Richter m; (of competition) Preisrichter m □vt beurteilen; (estimate) [ein]schätzen □vi urteilen (by nach). ~ment n Beurteilung f; (Jur) Urteil nt; (fig) Urteilsvermögen nt

judic|**ial** /dʒuː'dɪʃl/ a gerichtlich. ~iary /-ʃərɪ/ n Richterstand m. ~ious /-ʃəs/ a klug

judo /'dʒuːdəʊ/ n Judo nt

jug /dʒʌg/ n Kanne f; (small) Kännchen nt; (for water, wine) Krug m

juggernaut /'dʒʌgənɔːt/ n (fam) Riesenlaster m

juggle /'dʒʌgl/ vi jonglieren. ~r n Jongleur m

juice /dʒuːs/ n Saft m. ~ extractor n Entsafter m

juicy /'dʒuːsɪ/ a (-ier, -iest) saftig; (fam) ⟨story⟩ pikant

juke-box /'dʒuːk-/ n Musikbox f

July /dʒʊ'laɪ/ n Juli m

jumble /'dʒʌmbl/ n Durcheinander nt □vt ~ [up] durcheinanderbringen. ~ sale n [Wohltätigkeits]basar m

jumbo /ˈdʒʌmbəʊ/ n ~ **[jet]** Jumbo[-Jet] m

jump /dʒʌmp/ n Sprung m; (in prices) Anstieg m; (in horse racing) Hindernis nt □ vi springen; (start) zusammenzucken; **make s.o.** ~ jdn erschrecken; ~ **at** (fig) sofort zugreifen bei (offer); ~ **to conclusions** voreilige Schlüsse ziehen □ vt überspringen; ~ **the gun** (fig) vorschnell handeln. ~ **up** vi aufspringen

jumper /ˈdʒʌmpə(r)/ n Pullover m, Pulli m

jumpy /ˈdʒʌmpɪ/ a nervös

junction /ˈdʒʌŋkʃn/ n Kreuzung f; (Rail) Knotenpunkt m

juncture /ˈdʒʌŋktʃə(r)/ n at this ~ zu diesem Zeitpunkt

June /dʒuːn/ n Juni m

jungle /ˈdʒʌŋgl/ n Dschungel m

junior /ˈdʒuːnɪə(r)/ a jünger; (in rank) untergeordnet; (Sport) Junioren- □ n Junior m. ~ **school** n Grundschule f

juniper /ˈdʒuːnɪpə(r)/ n Wacholder m

junk /dʒʌŋk/ n Gerümpel m, Trödel m

junkie /ˈdʒʌŋkɪ/ n (sl) Fixer m

junk-shop n Trödelladen m

juris|diction /dʒʊərɪsˈdɪkʃn/ n Gerichtsbarkeit f. ~**'prudence** n Rechtswissenschaft f

juror /ˈdʒʊərə(r)/ n Geschworene(r) m/f

jury /ˈdʒʊərɪ/ n **the** ~ die Geschworenen pl; (for competition) die Jury

just /dʒʌst/ a gerecht □ adv gerade; (only) nur; (simply) einfach; (exactly) genau; ~ **as tall** ebenso groß; ~ **listen!** hör doch mal! I'm ~ **going** ich gehe schon; ~ **put it down** stell es nur hin

justice /ˈdʒʌstɪs/ n Gerechtigkeit f; **do** ~ **to** gerecht werden (+ dat); **J**~ **of the Peace** ≈ Friedensrichter m

justifiab|le /ˈdʒʌstɪfaɪəbl/ a berechtigt. ~**ly** adv berechtigterweise

justi|fication /dʒʌstɪfɪˈkeɪʃn/ n Rechtfertigung f. ~**fy** /ˈdʒʌstɪfaɪ/ vt (pt/pp -**ied**) rechtfertigen

justly /ˈdʒʌstlɪ/ adv zu Recht

jut /dʒʌt/ vi (pt/pp **jutted**) ~ **out** vorstehen

juvenile /ˈdʒuːvənaɪl/ a jugendlich; (childish) kindisch □ n Jugendliche(r) m/f. ~ **delinquency** n Jugendkriminalität f

juxtapose /dʒʌkstəˈpəʊz/ vt nebeneinanderstellen

K

kangaroo /kæŋgəˈruː/ n Känguruh nt

karate /kəˈrɑːtɪ/ n Karate nt

kebab /kɪˈbæb/ n (Culin) Spießchen nt

keel /kiːl/ n Kiel m □ vi ~ **over** umkippen; (Naut) kentern

keen /kiːn/ a (-**r**, -**est**) (sharp) scharf; (intense) groß; (eager) eifrig, begeistert; ~ **on** (fam) erpicht auf (+ acc); ~ **on s.o.** von jdm sehr angetan; **be** ~ **to do sth** etw gerne machen wollen. ~**ly** adv tief. ~**ness** n Eifer m, Begeisterung f

keep /kiːp/ n (maintenance) Unterhalt m; (of castle) Bergfried m; **for** ~ **s** für immer □ v (pt/pp **kept**) □ vt behalten; (store) aufbewahren; (not throw away) aufheben; (support) unterhalten; (detain) aufhalten; freihalten (seat); halten (promise, animals); führen, haben (shop); einhalten (law, rules); ~ **sth hot** etw warm halten; ~ **s.o. from doing sth** jdn davon abhalten, etw zu tun; ~ **s.o. waiting** jdn warten lassen; ~ **sth to oneself** etw nicht weitersagen; **where do you** ~ **the sugar?** wo hast du den Zucker? □ vi (remain) bleiben; (food:) sich halten;

~ **left/right** sich links/rechts halten; ~ **doing sth** etw dauernd machen; ~ **on doing sth** etw weitermachen; ~ **in** with sich gut stellen mit. ~ **up** vi Schritt halten □vt (continue) weitermachen

keeper /'ki:pə(r)/ n Wärter(in) m(f). ~**ing** n Obhut f; **be in** ~**ing** with passen zu. ~**sake** n Andenken nt

keg /keg/ n kleines Faß nt

kennel /'kenl/ n Hundehütte f; ~**s** pl (boarding) Hundepension f; (breeding) Zwinger m

Kenya /'kenjə/ n Kenia nt

kept /kept/ see **keep**

kerb /kɜːb/ n Bordstein m

kernel /'kɜːnl/ n Kern m

kerosene /'kerəsiːn/ n (Amer) Petroleum nt

ketchup /'ketʃʌp/ n Ketchup m

kettle /'ketl/ n [Wasser]kessel m; **put the** ~ **on** Wasser aufsetzen; **a pretty** ~ **of fish** (fam) eine schöne Bescherung f

key /kiː/ n Schlüssel m; (Mus) Tonart f; (of piano, typewriter) Taste f □vt ~ **in** vt eintasten

key: ~**board** n Tastatur f; (Mus) Klaviatur f. ~**boarder** n Taster(in) m(f). ~**hole** n Schlüsselloch nt. ~**ring** n Schlüsselring m

khaki /'kɑːkɪ/ a khakifarben □n Khaki nt

kick /kɪk/ n [Fuß]tritt m; **for** ~**s** (fam) zum Spaß □vt/i treten; **the bucket** (fam) abkratzen □vi (animal:) ausschlagen. ~**off** n (Sport) Anstoß m

kid /kɪd/ n Kitz nt; (fam: child) Kind nt □vt (pt/pp **kidded**) (fam) ~ **s.o.** jdm etwas vormachen. ~ **gloves** npl Glacéhandschuhe pl

kidnap /'kɪdnæp/ vt (pt/pp -**napped**) entführen. ~**per** n Entführer m. ~**ping** n Entführung f

kidney /'kɪdnɪ/ n Niere f. ~ **machine** n künstliche Niere f

kill /kɪl/ vt töten; (fam) totschlagen ⟨time⟩; ~ **two birds with one stone** zwei Fliegen mit einer Klappe schlagen. ~**er** n Mörder(in) m(f). ~**ing** n Tötung f; (murder) Mord m

killjoy n Spielverderber m

kiln /kɪln/ n Brennofen m

kilo /'kiːləʊ/ n Kilo nt

kilo: ~**gram** n Kilogramm nt. ~**hertz** /-hɜːts/ n Kilohertz nt. ~**metre** n Kilometer m. ~**watt** n Kilowatt nt

kilt /kɪlt/ n Schottenrock m

kin /kɪn/ n Verwandtschaft f; **next of** ~ nächster Verwandter m/nächste Verwandte f

kind¹ /kaɪnd/ n Art f; (brand, type) Sorte f; **what** ~ **of car?** was für ein Auto? ~ **of** (fam) irgendwie

kind² a (-er, -est) nett; ~ **to animals** gut zu Tieren; ~ **regards** herzliche Grüße

kindergarten /'kɪndəgɑːtn/ n Vorschule f

kindle /'kɪndl/ vt anzünden

kind|ly /'kaɪndlɪ/ a (-ier, -iest) nett □adv netterweise; (if you please) gefälligst. ~**ness** n Güte f; (favour) Gefallen m

kindred /'kɪndrɪd/ a ~ **spirit** Gleichgesinnte(r) m/f

kinetic /kɪ'netɪk/ a kinetisch

king /kɪŋ/ n König m; (Draughts) Dame f. ~**dom** n Königreich nt; (fig & Relig) Reich nt

king: ~**fisher** n Eisvogel m. ~**sized** a extragroß

kink /kɪŋk/ n Knick m. ~**y** a (fam) pervers

kiosk /'kiːɒsk/ n Kiosk m

kip /kɪp/ n **have a** ~ (fam) pennen □vi (pt/pp **kipped**) (fam) pennen

kipper /'kɪpə(r)/ n Räucherhering m

kiss /kɪs/ n Kuß m □vt/i küssen

kit /kɪt/ n Ausrüstung f; (tools) Werkzeug nt; (construction ~) Bausatz m □vt (pt/pp **kitted**) ~ **out** ausrüsten. ~**bag** n Seesack m

kitchen /'kɪtʃɪn/ n Küche f □ attrib
Küchen-. ~**ette** /kɪtʃɪˈnet/ n
Kochnische f

kitchen: ~'**garden** n Gemüse-
garten m. ~'**sink** n Spülbecken
nt

kite /kaɪt/ n Drachen m

kith /kɪθ/ n **with** ~ **and kin** mit
der ganzen Verwandtschaft

kitten /'kɪtn/ n Kätzchen nt

kitty /'kɪtɪ/ n (money) [gemein-
same] Kasse f

kleptomaniac /kleptə'meɪnɪæk/
n Kleptomane m/-manin f

knack /næk/ n Trick m, Dreh m

knapsack /'næp-/ n Tornister m

knead /ni:d/ vt kneten

knee /ni:/ n Knie nt. ~**cap** n
Kniescheibe f

kneel /ni:l/ vi (pt/pp knelt) knien;
~ [**down**] sich [nieder]knien

knelt /nelt/ see kneel

knew /nju:/ see know

knickers /'nɪkəz/ npl Schlüpfer m

knick-knacks /'nɪknæks/ npl
Nippsachen pl

knife /naɪf/ n (pl knives) Messer
nt □ vt einen Messerstich versetzen (+ dat); (to death) erstechen

knight /naɪt/ n Ritter m; (Chess)
Springer m □ vt adeln

knit /nɪt/ vt/i (pt/pp knitted)
stricken; ~ **one, purl one** eine
rechts, eine links; ~ **one's brow**
die Stirn runzeln. ~**ting** n
Stricken nt; (work) Strickzeug
nt. ~**ting-needle** n Stricknadel
f. ~**wear** n Strickwaren pl

knives /naɪvz/ npl see knife

knob /nɒb/ n Knopf m; (on door)
Knauf m; (small lump) Beule f;
(small piece) Stückchen nt. ~**bly**
a knorrig; (bony) knochig

knock /nɒk/ n Klopfen nt; (blow)
Schlag m; **there was a** ~ **at the
door** es klopfte □ vt anstoßen; (at
door) klopfen an (+ acc); (fam:
criticize) heruntermachen; ~ **a
hole in sth** ein Loch in etw (acc)
schlagen; ~ **one's head** sich
(dat) den Kopf stoßen (**on an** +

dat) □ vi klopfen. ~ **about** vt
schlagen □ vi (fam) herumkommen. ~ **down** vt herunterwerfen; (with fist) niederschlagen;
(in car) anfahren; (demolish) abreißen; (fam: reduce) herabsetzen. ~ **off** vt herunterwerfen;
(fam: steal) klauen; (fam: complete quickly) hinhauen □ vi (fam:
cease work) Feierabend machen.
~ **out** vt ausschlagen; (make
unconscious) bewußtlos schlagen; (Boxing) k.o. schlagen. ~
over vt umwerfen; (in car) anfahren

knock: ~-**down** a ~-**down**
prices Schleuderpreise pl. ~-**er** n
Türklopfer m. ~-**kneed** /-'ni:d/ a
X-beinig. ~-**out** n (Boxing) K.o.
m

knot /nɒt/ n Knoten m □ vt (pt/pp
knotted) knoten

knotty /'nɒtɪ/ a (-ier, -iest) (fam)
verwickelt

know /nəʊ/ vt/i (pt knew, pp
known) wissen; kennen (person); können (language); **get to**
~ kennenlernen □ n **in the** ~
(fam) im Bild

know: ~-**all** n (fam) Alleswisser
m. ~-**how** n (fam) [Sach]kennt-
nis f. ~-**ing** a wissend. ~**ingly**
adv wissend; (intentionally)
wissentlich

knowledge /'nɒlɪdʒ/ n Kenntnis f
(of von/gen); (general) Wissen nt;
(specialized) Kenntnis pl.
~**able** /-əbl/ a **be** ~**able** viel
wissen

known /nəʊn/ see know □ a bekannt

knuckle /'nʌkl/ n [Finger]knö-
chel m; (Culin) Hachse f □ vi ~
under sich fügen; ~ **down** sich
dahinterklemmen

kosher /'kəʊʃə(r)/ a koscher

kowtow /kaʊ'taʊ/ vi Kotau machen (**to** vor + dat)

kudos /'kju:dɒs/ n (fam) Prestige
nt

L

lab /læb/ *n (fam)* Labor *nt*

label /'leɪbl/ *n* Etikett *nt* □ *vt (pt/pp* **labelled**) etikettieren

laboratory /lə'bɒrətrɪ/ *n* Labor *nt*

laborious /lə'bɔːrɪəs/ *a, -ly adv* mühsam

labour /'leɪbə(r)/ *n* Arbeit *f; (workers)* Arbeitskräfte *pl; (Med)* Wehen *pl;* **L~** *(Pol)* die Labourpartei □ *attrib* Labour- □ *vi* arbeiten □ *vt (fig)* sich lange auslassen über (+ *acc.).* **~er** *n* Arbeiter *m*

'labour-saving *a* arbeitssparend

laburnum /lə'bɜːnəm/ *n* Goldregen *m*

labyrinth /'læbərɪnθ/ *n* Labyrinth *nt*

lace /leɪs/ *n* Spitze *f; (of shoe)* Schnürsenkel *m* □ *vt* schnüren; **~d with** Rum mit einem Schuß Rum

lacerate /'læsəreɪt/ *vt* zerreißen

lack /læk/ *n* Mangel *m (of an* + *dat)* □ *vt* **I ~ the time** mir fehlt die Zeit □ *vi* **be ~ing** fehlen

lackadaisical /lækə'deɪzɪk/ *a* lustlos

laconic /lə'kɒnɪk/ *a, -ally adv* lakonisch

lacquer /'lækə(r)/ *n* Lack *m; (for hair)* [Haar]spray *m*

lad /læd/ *n* Junge *m*

ladder /'lædə(r)/ *n* Leiter *f; (in fabric)* Laufmasche *f*

laden /'leɪdn/ *a* beladen

ladle /'leɪdl/ *n* [Schöpf]kelle *f* □ *vt* schöpfen

lady /'leɪdɪ/ *n* Dame *f; (title)* Lady *f*

lady: **~bird** *n, (Amer)* **~bug** *n* Marienkäfer *m.* **~like** *a* damenhaft

lag¹ /læg/ *vi (pt/pp* **lagged**) *(~ behind)* zurückbleiben; *(fig)* nachhinken

lag² *vt (pt/pp* **lagged**) umwickeln ⟨pipes⟩

lager /'lɑːgə(r)/ *n* Lagerbier *nt*

lagoon /lə'guːn/ *n* Lagune *f*

laid /leɪd/ *see* lay³

lain /leɪn/ *see* lie²

lair /leə(r)/ *n* Lager *nt*

laity /'leɪətɪ/ *n* Laienstand *m*

lake /leɪk/ *n* See *m*

lamb /læm/ *n* Lamm *nt*

lame /leɪm/ *a (-r, -st)* lahm

lament /lə'ment/ *n* Klage *f; (song)* Klagelied *nt* □ *vt* beklagen □ *vi* klagen. **~able** /'læməntəbl/ *a* beklagenswert

laminated /'læmɪnertɪd/ *a* laminiert

lamp /læmp/ *n* Lampe *f; (in street)* Laterne *f.* **~post** *n* Laternenpfahl *m.* **~shade** *n* Lampenschirm *m*

lance /lɑːns/ *n* Lanze *f* □ *vt (Med)* aufschneiden. **~-corporal** *n* Gefreite(r) *m*

land /lænd/ *n* Land *nt;* **plot of ~** Grundstück *nt* □ *vt/i* landen; **~ s.o. with sth** *(fam)* jdm etw aufhalsen

landing /'lændɪŋ/ *n* Landung *f; (top of stairs)* Treppenflur *m.* **~-stage** *n* Landesteg *m*

land: **~lady** *n* Wirtin *f.* **~-locked** *a* **~-locked country** Binnenstaat *m.* **~lord** *n* Wirt *m; (of land)* Grundbesitzer *m; (of building)* Hausbesitzer *m.* **~mark** *n* Erkennungszeichen *nt; (fig)* Meilenstein *m.* **~owner** *n* Grundbesitzer *m.* **~scape** /-skeɪp/ *n* Landschaft *f.* **~slide** *n* Erdrutsch *m*

lane /leɪn/ *n* kleine Landstraße *f; (Auto)* Spur *f; (Sport)* Bahn *f;* **'get in ~'** *(Auto)* 'bitte einordnen'

language /'læŋgwɪdʒ/ *n* Sprache *f; (speech, style)* Ausdrucksweise *f.* **~ laboratory** *n* Sprachlabor *nt*

languid /'læŋgwɪd/ *a, -ly adv* träge

languish /'læŋgwɪʃ/ *vi* schmachten

lank /læŋk/ *a ⟨hair⟩* strähnig

lanky /'læŋkɪ/ *a (-ier, -iest)* schlaksig

lantern /'læntən/ n Laterne f
lap¹ /læp/ n Schoß m
lap² n (Sport) Runde f; (of journey)
Etappe f □vi (pt/pp lapped) plätschern (against gegen)
lap³ vt (pt/pp lapped) ~ up aufschlecken
lapel /lə'pel/ n Revers nt
lapse /læps/ n Fehler m; (moral)
Fehltritt m; (of time) Zeitspanne f
□vi (expire) erlöschen; ~ into verfallen in (+ acc)
larceny /'lɑ:sənɪ/ n Diebstahl m
lard /lɑ:d/ n [Schweine]schmalz nt
larder /'lɑ:də(r)/ n Speisekammer f
large /lɑ:dʒ/ a (-r, -st) & adv groß;
by and ~ im großen und ganzen;
at ~ auf freiem Fuß; (in general)
im allgemeinen. ~ly adv großenteils
lark¹ /lɑ:k/ n (bird) Lerche f
lark² n (joke) Jux m □vi ~ about
herumalbern
larva /'lɑ:və/ n (pl -vae /-vi:/)
Larve f
laryngitis /lærɪn'dʒaɪtɪs/ n Kehlkopfentzündung f
larynx /'lærɪŋks/ n Kehlkopf m
lascivious /lə'sɪvɪəs/ a lüstern
laser /'leɪzə(r)/ n Laser m
lash /læʃ/ n Peitschenhieb m; (eyelash) Wimper f □vt peitschen;
(tie) festbinden (to an + acc). ~
out vi um sich schlagen; (spend)
viel Geld ausgeben (on für)
lashings /'læʃɪŋz/ npl ~ of (fam)
eine Riesenmenge von
lass /læs/ n Mädchen nt
lasso /lə'su:/ n Lasso nt
last¹ /lɑ:st/ n (for shoe) Leisten m
last² a & n letzte(r,s); ~ night
heute od gestern nacht; (evening)
gestern abend; at ~ endlich; the
~ time das letztemal; for the ~
time zum letztenmal; the ~ but
one der/die/das vorletzte; that's
the ~ straw (fam) das schlägt
dem Faß den Boden aus □adv
zuletzt; (last time) das letztemal;
do sth ~ etw zuletzt od als letztes
machen; he/she went ~ er/sie

ging als letzter/letzte □vi dauern;
(weather:) sich halten; (relationship:) halten. ~ing a dauerhaft. ~ly adv schließlich, zum
Schluß
latch /lætʃ/ n [einfache] Klinke f;
on the ~ nicht verschlossen
late /leɪt/ a & adv (-r, -st) (delayed) verspätet; (deceased)
verstorben; the ~st news die
neuesten Nachrichten; **stay up**
~ bis spät aufbleiben; of ~ in
letzter Zeit; **arrive** ~ zu spät
ankommen; **I am** ~ ich komme
zu spät od habe mich verspätet;
the train is ~ der Zug hat Verspätung. ~comer n Zuspätkommende(r) m/f. ~ly adv in letzter
Zeit. ~ness n Zuspätkommen nt;
(delay) Verspätung f
latent /'leɪtnt/ a latent
later /'leɪtə(r)/ a & adv später; ~
on nachher
lateral /'lætərəl/ a seitlich
lathe /leɪð/ n Drehbank f
lather /'lɑ:ðə(r)/ n [Seifen]schaum
m □vt einseifen □vi schäumen
Latin /'lætɪn/ a lateinisch □n Latein nt. ~ **America** n Lateinamerika nt
latitude /'lætɪtju:d/ n (Geog) Breite f; (fig) Freiheit f
latter /'lætə(r)/ a & n the ~ der/
die/das letztere. ~ly adv in letzter Zeit
lattice /'lætɪs/ n Gitter nt
Latvia /'lætvɪə/ n Lettland nt
laudable /'lɔ:dəbl/ a lobenswert
laugh /lɑ:f/ n Lachen nt; with a ~
lachend □vi lachen (at/about
über + acc); at s.o. (mock) jdn
auslachen. ~able /-əbl/ a lachhaft, lächerlich. ~ing-stock n
Gegenstand m des Spottes
laughter /'lɑ:ftə(r)/ n Gelächter nt
launch¹ /lɔ:ntʃ/ n (boat) Barkasse f
launch² n Stapellauf m; (of rocket) Abschuß m; (of product) Lancierung f □vt vom Stapel lassen

⟨ship⟩; zu Wasser lassen ⟨life-
boat⟩; ⟨rocket⟩; star-
ten ⟨attack⟩; (Comm) lancieren
⟨product⟩

launder /'lɔːndə(r)/ vt waschen.
~**ette** /-'dret/ n Münzwäscherei f

laundry /'lɔːndrɪ/ n Wäscherei f;
(clothes) Wäsche f

laurel /'lɒrl/ n Lorbeer m

lava /'lɑːvə/ n Lava f

lavatory /'lævətrɪ/ n Toilette f

lavender /'lævəndə(r)/ n Lavendel m

lavish /'lævɪʃ/ a, **-ly** adv großzügig; (wasteful) verschwende-
risch; **on a ~ scale** mit viel Aufwand □vt ~ **sth on s.o.** jdn mit
etw überschütten

law /lɔː/ n Gesetz nt; (system)
Recht nt; **study ~** Jura studie-
ren; ~ **and order** Recht und
Ordnung

law: ~**-abiding** a gesetzestreu.
~**court** n Gerichtshof m. ~**ful** a
rechtmäßig. ~**less** a gesetzlos

lawn /lɔːn/ n Rasen m. ~**mower**
n Rasenmäher m

'law suit n Prozeß m

lawyer /'lɔːjə(r)/ n Rechtsanwalt
m /-anwältin f

lax /læks/ a lax, locker

laxative /'læksətɪv/ n Abführmit-
tel nt

laxity /'læksətɪ/ n Laxheit f

lay¹ /leɪ/ a Laien-

lay² see **lie**²

lay³ vt (pt/pp **laid**) legen; decken
⟨table⟩; ~ **a trap** eine Falle stellen. ~ **down** vt hinlegen; festlegen ⟨rules, conditions⟩. ~ **off** vt
entlassen ⟨workers⟩ □vi (fam:
stop) aufhören. ~ **out** vt hinlegen; aufbahren ⟨corpse⟩; anlegen
⟨garden⟩; (Typ) gestalten

lay: ~**about** n Faulenzer m. ~
by n Parkbucht f; (on motorway)
Rastplatz m

layer /'leɪə(r)/ n Schicht f

layette /leɪ'et/ n Babyausstat-
tung f

lay: ~**man** n Laie m. ~**out** n
Anordnung f; (design) Gestaltung f; (Typ) Layout nt. ~ **'preacher** n Laienprediger m

laze /leɪz/ vi ~ **[about]** faulenzen

laziness /'leɪzɪnɪs/ n Faulheit f

lazy /'leɪzɪ/ a (-ier, -iest) faul.
~**bones** n Faulenzer m

lb /paʊnd/ abbr (**pound**) Pfd.

lead¹ /led/ n Blei nt; (of pencil)
[Bleistift]mine f

lead² /liːd/ n Führung f; (leash)
Leine f; (flex) Schnur f; (clue)
Hinweis m, Spur f; (Theat)
Hauptrolle f; (distance ahead)
Vorsprung m; **be in the ~** in
Führung liegen □vt/i (pt/pp **led**)
führen; leiten ⟨team⟩; (induce)
bringen; ⟨at cards⟩ ausspielen; ~
the way vorangehen. ~ **up to**
sth (fig) etw (dat) vorangehen.
~ **away** vt wegführen

leaded /'ledɪd/ a verbleit

leader /'liːdə(r)/ n Führer m; (of
expedition, group) Leiter(in
m(f); (of orchestra) Konzertmeister m; (in newspaper) Leitartikel
m. ~**ship** n Führung f; Leitung f

leading /'liːdɪŋ/ a führend; ~
lady Hauptdarstellerin f; ~
question n Suggestivfrage f

leaf /liːf/ n (pl **leaves**) Blatt nt; (of
table) Ausziehplatte f □vi ~
through sth etw durchblättern.
~**let** n Merkblatt nt; (advertising) Reklameblatt nt; (political) Flugblatt nt

league /liːg/ n Liga f; **be in ~ with**
unter einer Decke stecken mit

leak /liːk/ n (hole) undichte Stelle
f; (Naut) Leck nt; (of gas) Gasaus-
fluß m □vi undicht sein; ⟨ship⟩
leck sein, lecken; ⟨liquid:⟩ auslaufen; ⟨gas:⟩ ausströmen □vt
auslaufen lassen; ~ **sth to s.o.**
(fig) jdm etw zuspielen. ~**y** a
undicht; (Naut) leck

lean¹ /liːn/ a (-er, -est) mager

lean² v (pt/pp **leaned** or **leant**
/lent/) □vt lehnen (**against/on an**

+ acc) □ vi ⟨pers:⟩ sich lehnen
(against/on an + acc); (not be
straight) sich neigen; be ~ing
against lehnen an (+ dat); ~ on
s.o. (depend) bei jdm festen Halt
finden. ~ **back** vi sich zurücklehnen. ~ **forward** vi sich vorbeugen. ~ **out** vi sich hinausleh-
nen. ~ **over** vi sich vorbeugen

leaning /'li:nɪŋ/ a schief □ n Neigung f

leap /li:p/ n Sprung m □ vi (pt/pp
leapt /lept/ or leaped) springen;
he leapt at it (fam) er griff sofort
zu. ~-**frog** n Bockspringen nt. ~
year n Schaltjahr nt

learn /lɜ:n/ vt/i (pt/pp learnt or
learned) lernen; (hear) erfahren;
~ **to swim** schwimmen lernen

learn|ed /'lɜ:nɪd/ a gelehrt. ~**er** n
Anfänger m; ~**er** [driver] Fahr-
schüler(in) m(f). ~**ing** n Gelehr-
samkeit f

lease /li:s/ n Pacht f; (contract)
Mietvertrag m; (Comm) Pachtvertrag m □ vt pachten; ~ [out]
verpachten

leash /li:ʃ/ n Leine f

least /li:st/ a geringste(r,s); have
~ **time** am wenigsten Zeit haben
□ n the ~ das wenigste; at ~
wenigstens, mindestens; **not in
the** ~ nicht im geringsten □ adv
am wenigsten

leather /'leðə(r)/ n Leder nt. ~**y** a
ledern; (tough) zäh

leave /li:v/ n Erlaubnis f; (holiday) Urlaub m; **on** ~ auf Urlaub;
take one's ~ sich verabschieden
□ v (pt/pp left) □ vt lassen; (go out
of, abandon) verlassen; (forget)
liegenlassen; (bequeath) vermach-
en (to dat); ~ **it to me!** überlassen Sie es mir! **there is
nothing left** es ist nichts
mehr übrig □ vi [weg]gehen/-fah-
ren; ⟨train, bus:⟩ abfahren. ~
behind vt zurücklassen; (forget)
liegenlassen. ~ **out** vt liegenlassen; (leave outside) draußen
lassen; (omit) auslassen

leaves /li:vz/ see leaf

Lebanon /'lebənən/ n Libanon m

lecherous /'letʃərəs/ a lüstern

lectern /'lektɜ:n/ n [Lese]pult nt

lecture /'lektʃə(r)/ n Vortrag m;
(Univ) Vorlesung f; (reproof)
Strafpredigt f □ vi einen Vortrag/
eine Vorlesung halten (on über
+ acc) □ vt ~ **s.o.** jdm eine Strafpredigt halten. ~**r** n Vortragen-
de(r) m/f; (Univ) Dozent(in) m(f)

led /led/ see lead²

ledge /ledʒ/ n Leiste f; (shelf, of
window) Sims m; (in rock) Vorsprung m

ledger /'ledʒə(r)/ n Hauptbuch nt

lee /li:/ n (Naut) Lee f

leech /li:tʃ/ n Blutegel m

leek /li:k/ n Stange f Porree; ~**s**
pl Porree m

leer /lɪə(r)/ n anzügliches Grinsen
nt □ vi anzüglich grinsen

lee|ward /'li:wad/ adv nach Lee.
~**way** n (fig) Spielraum m

left¹ /left/ see leave

left² a linke(r,s) □ adv links; ⟨go⟩
nach links □ n linke Seite f; **on
the** ~ links; **from/to the** ~ von/
nach links; **the** ~ (Pol) die Linke.
left: ~-**handed** a linkshändig.
~-**luggage** [**office**] n Gepäck-
aufbewahrung f. ~-**overs** npl
Reste pl. ~-**wing** a (Pol) lin-
ke(r,s)

leg /leg/ n Bein nt; (Culin) Keule f;
(of journey) Etappe f

legacy /'legəsɪ/ n Vermächtnis nt,
Erbschaft f

legal /'li:gl/ a, -**ly** adv gesetzlich;
⟨matters⟩ rechtlich; ⟨depart-
ment, position⟩ Rechts-; **be** ~
[gesetzlich] erlaubt sein; **take** ~
action gerichtlich vorgehen

legality /lɪ'gælətɪ/ n Legalität f

legalize /'li:gəlaɪz/ vt legalisieren

legend /'ledʒənd/ n Legende f.
~**ary** a legendär

legible /'ledʒəbl/ a, -**bly** adv leserlich

legion /'li:dʒn/ n Legion f

legislate /'ledʒisleit/ vi Gesetze
erlassen. **~ion** /-'leiʃn/ n Gesetz-
gebung f; (laws) Gesetze pl
legislat|**ive** /'ledʒislətiv/ a gesetz-
gebend. **~ure** /-lətʃə(r)/ n Legislative f
legitimate /lɪ'dʒɪtɪmət/ a rechtmäßig; (justifiable) berechtigt;
⟨child⟩ ehelich
leisure /'leʒə(r)/ n Freizeit f; **at
your ~** wenn Sie Zeit haben.
~ly a gemächlich
lemon /'lemən/ n Zitrone f. **~ade**
/-'neid/ n Zitronenlimonade f
lend /lend/ vt (pt/pp lent) leihen;
~ s.o. sth jdm etw leihen; **~ a
hand** (fam) helfen. **~ing library** n Leihbücherei f
length /leŋθ/ n Länge f; (piece)
Stück nt; (of wallpaper) Bahn f;
(of time) Dauer f; **at ~** ausführlich; (at last) endlich
lengthen /'leŋθən/ vt etw länger machen □vi länger werden. **~ways**
adv der Länge nach, längs
lengthy /'leŋθɪ/ a (-ier, -iest) lang-
wierig
lenien|**ce** /'li:nɪəns/ n Nachsicht f.
~t a, **-ly** adv nachsichtig
lens /lenz/ n Linse f; (Phot) Objektiv nt; (of spectacles) Glas nt
lent /lent/ see **lend**
Lent n Fastenzeit f
lentil /'lentl/ n (Bot) Linse f
Leo /'li:əʊ/ n (Astr) Löwe m
leopard /'lepəd/ n Leopard m
leotard /'li:ətɑːd/ n Trikot nt
leper /'lepə(r)/ n Leprakranke(r)
m|f; (Bible & fig) Aussätzige(r)
m|f
leprosy /'leprəsɪ/ n Lepra f
lesbian /'lezbɪən/ a lesbisch □n
Lesbierin f
lesion /'li:ʒn/ n Verletzung f
less /les/ a, adv, & prep weniger;
~ and ~ immer weniger; **not
any the ~** um nichts weniger
lessen /'lesn/ vt verringern □vi
nachlassen; ⟨value:⟩ abnehmen
lesser /'lesə(r)/ a geringere(r,s)

lesson /'lesn/ n Stunde f; (in text-
book) Lektion f; (Relig) Lesung f;
teach s.o. a ~ (fig) jdm eine
Lehre erteilen
lest /lest/ conj (liter) damit ...
nicht
let /let/ vt (pt/pp **let**, pres p **let-
ting**) lassen; (rent) vermieten; **~
alone** (not to mention) geschweige denn; **'to ~'** 'zu vermieten'; **~
us go** gehen wir; **~ me know**
sagen Sie mir Bescheid; **~ him**
do it laß ihn das machen; **just ~
him!** soll er doch! **~ sleep/
win** jdn schlafen/gewinnen lassen; **~ oneself in for sth** (fam)
sich (dat) etw einbrocken. **~
down** vt hinunter-/herunterlas-
sen; (lengthen) länger machen;
s.o. down (fam) jdn im Stich
lassen; (disappoint) jdn enttäuschen. **~ in** vt hereinlassen. **~
off** vt abfeuern ⟨gun⟩; hochgehen
lassen ⟨firework, bomb⟩; (emit)
ausstoßen; (excuse from) befreien
von; (not punish) frei ausgehen
lassen. **~ out** vt hinaus-/heraus-
lassen; (make larger) auslassen.
~ through vt durchlassen. **~
up** vi (fam) nachlassen
'let-down n Enttäuschung f,
(fam) Reinfall m
lethal /'li:θl/ a tödlich
letharg|**ic** /lɪ'θɑːdʒɪk/ a lethar-
gisch. **~y** /'leθədʒɪ/ n Lethargie f
letter /'letə(r)/ n Brief m; (of alphabet) Buchstabe m; **by ~** brieflich.
~-box n Briefkasten m. **~-head**
n Briefkopf m. **~ing** n Beschrif-
tung f
lettuce /'letɪs/ n [Kopf]salat m
'let-up n (fam) Nachlassen nt
leukaemia /lu:'ki:mɪə/ n Leukämie f
level /'levl/ a eben; (horizontal)
waagerecht; (in height) auf glei-
cher Höhe; ⟨spoonful⟩ gestrichen; **draw ~ with** gleichziehen
mit; **one's ~ best** sein möglichstes □n Höhe f; (fig) Ebene f;
Niveau nt; (stage) Stufe f; **on the**

~ *(fam)* ehrlich □ *vt (pt/pp* level-led) einebnen; *(aim)* richten ⟨at auf + *acc*⟩

level: ~ '**crossing** *n* Bahnübergang *m*. ~-'**headed** *a* vernünftig

lever /'li:və(r)/ *n* Hebel *m* □ *vt* ~ **up** mit einem Hebel anheben. ~**age** /-rɪdʒ/ *n* Hebelkraft *f*

levity /'levəti/ *n* Heiterkeit *f*; *(frivolity)* Leichtfertigkeit *f*

levy /'levɪ/ *vt (pt/pp* levied) erheben ⟨*tax*⟩

lewd /lju:d/ *a* (-er, -est) anstößig

liability /laɪə'bɪlətɪ/ *n* Haftung *f*; ~**ies** *pl* Verbindlichkeiten *pl*

liable /'laɪəbl/ *a* haftbar; be ~ to do sth etw leicht tun können

liaise /lɪ'eɪz/ *vi (fam)* Verbindungsperson sein

liaison /lɪ'eɪzɒn/ *n* Verbindung *f*; *(affair)* Verhältnis *nt*

liar /'laɪə(r)/ *n* Lügner(in) *m(f)*

libel /'laɪbl/ *n* Verleumdung *f* □ *vt (pt/pp* libelled) verleumden. ~**lous** *a* verleumderisch

liberal /'lɪbərl/ *a*, **-ly** *adv* tolerant; *(generous)* großzügig. **L**~ *a (Pol)* liberal □ *n* Liberale(r) *m/f*

liberate /'lɪbəreɪt/ *vt* befreien. ~**ed** *a* ⟨*woman*⟩ emanzipiert. ~**ion** /-'reɪʃn/ *n* Befreiung *f*. ~ **or** *n* Befreier *m*

liberty /'lɪbətɪ/ *n* Freiheit *f*; take the ~ of doing sth sich *(dat)* erlauben, etw zu tun; take liberties sich *(dat)* Freiheiten erlauben

Libra /'li:brə/ *n (Astr)* Waage *f*

librarian /laɪ'breərɪən/ *n* Bibliothekar(in) *m(f)*

library /'laɪbrərɪ/ *n* Bibliothek *f*

Libya /'lɪbɪə/ *n* Libyen *nt*

lice /laɪs/ *see* **louse**

licence /'laɪsns/ *n* Genehmigung *f*; *(Comm)* Lizenz *f*; *(for TV)* ≈ Fernsehgebühr *f*; *(for driving)* Führerschein *m*; *(for alcohol)* Schankkonzession *f*; *(freedom)* Freiheit *f*

license /'laɪsns/ *vt* eine Genehmigung/*(Comm)* Lizenz erteilen (+

dat); be ~**d** ⟨*car:*⟩ zugelassen sein; *(restaurant:)* Schankkonzession haben. ~-**plate** *n* Nummernschild *nt*

licentious /laɪ'senʃəs/ *a* lasterhaft

lichen /'laɪkən/ *n (Bot)* Flechte *f*

lick /lɪk/ *n* Lecken *nt*; a ~ of paint ein bißchen Farbe □ *vt* lecken; *(fam: defeat)* schlagen

lid /lɪd/ *n* Deckel *m*; *(of eye)* Lid *nt*

lie[1] /laɪ/ *n* Lüge *f*; tell a ~ lügen □ *vi (pt/pp* lied, pres p lying) lügen; ~ to belügen

lie[2] *vi (pt* lay, *pp* lain, pres p lying) liegen; here ~s ... hier ruht ... ~ **down** *vi* sich hinlegen

Liège /lɪ'eɪʒ/ *n* Lüttich *nt*

lie-in *n* have a ~ [sich] ausschlafen

lieu /lju:/ *n* in ~ of statt (+ *gen)*

lieutenant /lef'tenənt/ *n* Oberleutnant *m*

life /laɪf/ *n (pl* lives) Leben *nt*; *(biography)* Biographie *f*; lose one's ~ ums Leben kommen

life: ~-**belt** *n* Rettungsring *m*. ~-**boat** *n* Rettungsboot *nt*. ~-**buoy** *n* Rettungsring *m*. ~-**guard** *n* Lebensretter *m*. ~-**jacket** *n* Schwimmweste *f*. ~-**less** *a* leblos. ~-**like** *a* naturgetreu. ~-**line** *n* Rettungsleine *f*. ~-**long** *a* lebenslang. ~-**preserver** *n (Amer)* Rettungsring *m*. ~-**size(d)** *a* ... in Lebensgröße. ~-**time** *n* Leben *nt*; in s.o.'s ~-**time** zu jds Lebzeiten; the chance of a ~-**time** eine einmalige Gelegenheit

lift /lɪft/ *n* Aufzug *m*, Lift *m*; give s.o. a ~ jdn mitnehmen; get a ~ mitgenommen werden □ *vt* heben; aufheben ⟨*restrictions*⟩ □ *vi* ⟨*fog:*⟩ sich lichten. ~ **up** *vt* hochheben

'lift-off *n* Abheben *nt*

ligament /'lɪgəmənt/ *n (Anat)* Band *nt*

light[1] /laɪt/ *a* (-er, -est) *(not dark)* hell; ~ **blue** hellblau □ *n* Licht *nt*; *(lamp)* Lampe *f*; in the ~ of *(fig)* angesichts (+ *gen*); **have you [got] a ~ ?** haben Sie Feuer? □ *vt* (*pt*/*pp* **lit** or **lighted**) anzünden ⟨*fire*, *cigarette*⟩; anmachen ⟨*lamp*⟩; (*illuminate*) beleuchten. **~ up** *vi* ⟨*face*:⟩ sich erhellen

light² *a* (-er, -est) (*not heavy*) leicht; **~ sentence** milde Strafe *f* □ *adv* **travel ~** mit wenig Gepäck reisen

'light-bulb *n* Glühbirne *f*

lighten¹ /'laɪtn/ *vt* heller machen □ *vi* heller werden

lighten² *vt* leichter machen ⟨*load*⟩

lighter /'laɪtə(r)/ *n* Feuerzeug *nt*

light: **~-'headed** *a* benommen. **~-'hearted** *a* unbekümmert. **~house** *n* Leuchtturm *m*. **~ing** *n* Beleuchtung *f*. **~ly** *adv* leicht; (*casually*) leichthin; **get off ~ly** glimpflich davonkommen

lightning /'laɪtnɪŋ/ *n* Blitz *m*. **~-conductor** *n* Blitzableiter *m*

'lightweight *a* leicht □ *n* (*Boxing*) Leichtgewicht *nt*

like¹ /laɪk/ *a* ähnlich; (*same*) gleich □ *prep* wie; (*similar to*) ähnlich (+ *dat*); **~ this** so; **a man ~ that** so ein Mann; **what's he ~?** wie ist er denn? □ *conj* (*fam*: *as*) wie; (*Amer*: *as if*) als ob

like² *vt* mögen; **I should/would ~ ich** möchte; **I ~ the car** das Auto gefällt mir; **I ~ chocolate** ich esse gern Schokolade; **~ dancing/singing** gern tanzen/singen; **I ~ that!** (*fam*) das ist doch die Höhe! □ *n* ~**s and dislikes** *pl* Vorlieben und Abneigungen *pl*

like|able /'laɪkəbl/ *a* sympathisch. **~lihood** /-lɪhʊd/ *n* Wahrscheinlichkeit *f*. **~ly** *a* (-ier, -iest) & *adv* wahrscheinlich; **not ~ly!** (*fam*) auf gar keinen Fall!

'like-minded *a* gleichgesinnt

liken /'laɪkən/ *vt* vergleichen (**to** mit)

like|ness /'laɪknɪs/ *n* Ähnlichkeit *f*. **~wise** *adv* ebenso

liking /'laɪkɪŋ/ *n* Vorliebe *f*; **is it to your ~?** gefällt es Ihnen?

lilac /'laɪlək/ *n* Flieder *m* □ *a* fliederfarben

lily /'lɪlɪ/ *n* Lilie *f*. **~ of the valley** *n* Maiglöckchen *nt*

limb /lɪm/ *n* Glied *nt*

limber /'lɪmbə(r)/ *vi* **~ up** Lockerungsübungen machen

lime¹ /laɪm/ *n* (*fruit*) Limone *f*; (*tree*) Linde *f*

lime² /laɪm/ *n* Kalk *m*. **~light** *n* **be in the ~light** im Rampenlicht stehen. **~stone** *n* Kalkstein *m*

limit /'lɪmɪt/ *n* Grenze *f*; (*limitation*) Beschränkung *f*; **that's the ~!** (*fam*) das ist doch die Höhe! □ *vt* beschränken (**to** auf + *acc*). **~ation** /-'teɪʃn/ *n* Beschränkung *f*. **~ed** *a* beschränkt; **~ed company** Gesellschaft *f* mit beschränkter Haftung

limousine /'lɪməzi:n/ *n* Limousine *f*

limp¹ /lɪmp/ *n* Hinken *nt*; **have a ~** hinken □ *vi* hinken

limp² *a* (-er, -est), **-ly** *adv* schlaff

limpet /'lɪmpɪt/ *n* **like a ~** (*fig*) wie eine Klette

limpid /'lɪmpɪd/ *a* klar

linctus /'lɪŋktəs/ *n* [**cough**] **~** Hustensirup *m*

line¹ /laɪn/ *n* Linie *f*; (*length of rope*, *cord*) Leine *f*; (*Teleph*) Leitung *f*; (*of writing*) Zeile *f*; (*row*) Reihe *f*; (*wrinkle*) Falte *f*; (*of business*) Branche *f*; (*Amer*: *queue*) Schlange *f*; **in ~ with** gemäß (+ *dat*) □ *vt* säumen ⟨*street*,⟩. **~ up** *vi* sich aufstellen □ *vt* aufstellen

line² *vt* füttern ⟨*garment*⟩; (*Techn*) auskleiden

lineage /'lɪnɪɪdʒ/ *n* Herkunft *f*

linear /'lɪnɪə(r)/ *a* linear

lined¹ /laɪnd/ *a* (*wrinkled*) faltig; ⟨*paper*⟩ liniert

lined² *a* ⟨*garment*⟩ gefüttert

linen /'lɪnɪn/ *n* Leinen *nt*; (*articles*) Wäsche *f*

liner /'laɪnə(r)/ *n* Passagierschiff *nt*

'linesman n (Sport) Linienrichter m

linger /'lɪŋgə(r)/ vi [zurück]bleiben

lingerie /'læʒərɪ/ n Damenunterwäsche f

linguist /'lɪŋgwɪst/ n Sprachkundige(r) m/f

linguistic /lɪŋ'gwɪstɪk/ a, **-ally** adv sprachlich. ~s n Linguistik f

lining /'laɪnɪŋ/ n (of garment) Futter nt; (Techn) Auskleidung f

link /lɪŋk/ n (of chain) Glied nt; (fig) Verbindung f □ vt verbinden; ~ **arms** sich unterhaken

links /lɪŋks/ n or npl Golfplatz m

lino /'laɪnəʊ/ n, **linoleum** /lɪ'nəʊlɪəm/ n Linoleum nt

lint /lɪnt/ n Verbandstoff m

lion /'laɪən/ n Löwe m; ~'s **share** (fig) Löwenanteil m. ~**ess** n Löwin f

lip /lɪp/ n Lippe f; (edge) Rand m; (of jug) Schnabel m

lip: ~**-reading** n Lippenlesen nt. ~**-service** n pay **-service** ein Lippenbekenntnis ablegen (to zu). ~**stick** n Lippenstift m

liquefy /'lɪkwɪfaɪ/ vt (pt/pp **-ied**) verflüssigen □ vi sich verflüssigen

liqueur /lɪ'kjʊə(r)/ n Likör m

liquid /'lɪkwɪd/ n Flüssigkeit f □ a flüssig

liquidat|e /'lɪkwɪdeɪt/ vt liquidieren. ~**ion** /-'deɪʃn/ n Liquidation f

liquidize /'lɪkwɪdaɪz/ vt (im Mixer) pürieren. ~**r** n (Culin) Mixer m

liquor /'lɪkə(r)/ n Alkohol m; (juice) Flüssigkeit f

liquorice /'lɪkərɪs/ n Lakritze f

'liquor store n (Amer) Spirituosengeschäft nt

lisp /lɪsp/ n Lispeln nt □ vt/i lispeln

list¹ /lɪst/ n Liste f □ vt aufführen

list vi (ship:) Schlagseite haben

listen /'lɪsn/ vi zuhören (to dat); ~ **to the radio** Radio hören. ~**er** n

Zuhörer(in) m(f); (Radio) Hörer(in) m(f)

listless /'lɪstlɪs/ a, **-ly** adv lustlos

lit /lɪt/ see **light¹**

litany /'lɪtənɪ/ n Litanei f

literacy /'lɪtərəsɪ/ n Lese- und Schreibfertigkeit f

literal /'lɪtərəl/ a wörtlich. ~**ly** adv buchstäblich

literary /'lɪtərərɪ/ a literarisch

literate /'lɪtərət/ a be ~ lesen und schreiben können

literature /'lɪtrətʃə(r)/ n Literatur f; (fam) Informationsmaterial nt

lithe /laɪð/ a geschmeidig

Lithuania /lɪθjʊ'eɪnɪə/ n Litauen f

litigation /lɪtɪ'geɪʃn/ n Rechtsstreit m

litre /'liːtə(r)/ n Liter m & nt

litter /'lɪtə(r)/ n Abfall m; (Zool) Wurf m □ vt be ~**ed** with übersät sein mit. ~**-bin** n Abfalleimer m

little /'lɪtl/ a klein; (not much) wenig □ adv & n wenig; a ~ ein bißchen/wenig; ~ **by** ~ nach und nach

liturgy /'lɪtədʒɪ/ n Liturgie f

live¹ /laɪv/ a lebendig; ⟨ammunition⟩ scharf; ~ **broadcast** Live-Sendung f; be ~ (Electr) unter Strom stehen □ adv ⟨Radio, TV⟩ live

live² /lɪv/ vi leben; (reside) wohnen; ~ **up to** gerecht werden (+ dat). ~ **on** vt leben von; (eat) sich ernähren von □ vi weiterleben

livelihood /'laɪvlɪhʊd/ n Lebensunterhalt m. ~**ness** n Lebendigkeit f

lively /'laɪvlɪ/ a (-ier, -iest) lebhaft, lebendig

liven /'laɪvn/ v ~ **up** vt beleben □ vi lebhaft werden

liver /'lɪvə(r)/ n Leber f

lives /laɪvz/ see **life**

livestock /'laɪv-/ n Vieh nt

livid /'lɪvɪd/ a (fam) wütend

living /'lɪvɪŋ/ a lebend □ n **earn** one's ~ seinen Lebensunterhalt verdienen; **the ~** *pl* die Lebenden. **~-room** *n* Wohnzimmer *nt*

lizard /'lɪzəd/ *n* Eidechse *f*

load /ləʊd/ *n* Last *f*; (*quantity*) Ladung *f*; (*Electr*) Belastung *f*; **~ s of** (*fam*) jede Menge □*vt* laden (*goods, gun*); beladen (*vehicle*); **~ a camera** einen Film in eine Kamera einlegen. **~ed** *a* beladen; (*fam: rich*) steinreich; **~ed question** Fangfrage *f*

loaf[1] /ləʊf/ *n* (*pl* **loaves**) Brot *nt*

loaf[2] *vi* faulenzen

loan /ləʊn/ *n* Leihgabe *f*; (*money*) Darlehen *nt*; **on ~** geliehen □*vt* leihen (**to** *dat*)

loath /ləʊθ/ *a* **be ~ to do sth** etw ungern tun

loathe /ləʊð/ *vt* verabscheuen. **~ing** *n* Abscheu *m*. **~some** *a* abscheulich

loaves /ləʊvz/ *see* loaf

lobby /'lɒbɪ/ *n* Foyer *nt*; (*anteroom*) Vorraum *m*; (*Pol*) Lobby *f*

lobe /ləʊb/ *n* (*of ear*) Ohrläppchen *nt*

lobster /'lɒbstə(r)/ *n* Hummer *m*

local /'ləʊkl/ *a* hiesig; (*time, traffic*) Orts-; **under ~ anaesthetic** unter örtlicher Betäubung; **I'm not ~** ich bin nicht von hier □*n* Hiesige(r) *m*/*f*; (*fam: public house*) Stammkneipe *f*. **~ au'thority** *n* Kommunalbehörde *f*. **~ call** *n* (*Teleph*) Ortsgespräch *nt*

locality /ləʊ'kælətɪ/ *n* Gegend *f*

localized /'ləʊkəlaɪzd/ *a* lokalisiert

locally /'ləʊkəlɪ/ *adv* am Ort

locate /ləʊ'keɪt/ *vt* ausfindig machen; **be ~ed** sich befinden. **~ion** /-'keɪʃn/ *n* Lage *f*; **filmed on ~ion** als Außenaufnahme gedreht

lock[1] /lɒk/ *n* (*hair*) Strähne *f*

lock[2] *n* (*on door*) Schloß *nt*; (*on canal*) Schleuse *f* □*vt* abschließen □*vi* sich abschließen lassen. **~ in** *vt* einschließen. **~ out** *vt* aussperren. **~ up** *vt* abschließen; einsperren ⟨*person*⟩ □*vi* zuschließen

locker /'lɒkə(r)/ *n* Schließfach *nt*; (*Mil*) Spind *m*; (*in hospital*) kleiner Schrank *m*

locket /'lɒkɪt/ *n* Medaillon *nt*

lock: **~-out** *n* Aussperrung *f*. **~ smith** *n* Schlosser *m*

locomotion /ləʊkə'məʊʃn/ *n* Fortbewegung *f*

locomotive /ləʊkə'məʊtɪv/ *n* Lokomotive *f*

locum /'ləʊkəm/ *n* Vertreter(in) *m*(*f*)

locust /'ləʊkəst/ *n* Heuschrecke *f*

lodge /lɒdʒ/ *n* (*porter's*) Pförtnerhaus *nt*; (*masonic*) Loge *f* □*vt* (*submit*) einreichen; (*deposit*) deponieren □*vi* zur Untermiete wohnen (**with** bei); (*become fixed*) steckenbleiben. **~r** *n* Untermieter(in) *m*(*f*)

lodging /'lɒdʒɪŋ/ *n* Unterkunft *f*. **~s** *npl* möbliertes Zimmer *nt*

loft /lɒft/ *n* Dachboden *m*

lofty /'lɒftɪ/ *a* (**-ier, -iest**) hoch; (*haughty*) hochmütig

log /lɒg/ *n* Baumstamm *m*; (*for fire*) [Holz]scheit *nt*; **sleep like a ~** (*fam*) wie ein Murmeltier schlafen

logarithm /'lɒgərɪðm/ *n* Logarithmus *m*

'log-book *n* (*Naut*) Logbuch *nt*

loggerheads /'lɒgə-/ *npl* **be at ~** (*fam*) sich in den Haaren liegen

logic /'lɒdʒɪk/ *n* Logik *f*. **~al** *a*, **-ly** *adv* logisch

logistics /lə'dʒɪstɪks/ *npl* Logistik *f*

logo /'ləʊgəʊ/ *n* Symbol *nt*, Logo *nt*

loin /lɔɪn/ *n* (*Culin*) Lende *f*

loiter /'lɔɪtə(r)/ *vi* herumlungern

loll /lɒl/ *vi* sich lümmeln

lolli|pop /'lɒlɪpɒp/ *n* Lutscher *m*. **~y** *n* Lutscher *m*; (*fam: money*) Moneten *pl*

London /'lʌndən/ *n* London *nt* □*attrib* Londoner. **~er** *n* Londoner(in) *m*(*f*)

lone /ləʊn/ *a* einzeln. **~liness** *n* Einsamkeit *f*

lonely /ˈləʊnlɪ/ *a* (-ier, -iest) einsam

lone|r /ˈləʊnə(r)/ *n* Einzelgänger *m*. **~some** *a* einsam

long[1] /lɒŋ/ *a* (-er /ˈlɒŋgə(r)/, -est /ˈlɒŋgɪst/) lang; ⟨*journey*⟩ lang; **~ time** lange; **a ~ way** weit; **in the ~ run** letzten Endes □*adv* lange; **all day ~** den ganzen Tag; **not ~ ago** vor kurzem; **before ~** bald; **no ~er** nicht mehr; **as** *or* **so ~ as** solange; **so ~!** (*fam*) tschüs! **will you be ~?** dauert es noch lange [bei dir]? **it won't take ~** es dauert nicht lange

long[2] *vi* **~ for** sich sehnen nach

long-'distance *a* Fern-; (*Sport*) Langstrecken-

longevity /lɒnˈdʒevətɪ/ *n* Langlebigkeit *f*

'longhand *n* Langschrift *f*

longing /ˈlɒŋɪŋ/ *a*, **-ly** *adv* sehnsüchtig □*n* Sehnsucht *f*

longitude /ˈlɒŋgɪtjuːd/ *n* (*Geog*) Länge *f*

long|~ jump *n* Weitsprung *m*. **~-life 'milk** *n* H-Milch *f*. **~-lived** /-lɪvd/ *a* langlebig. **~-range** *a* (*Mil, Aviat*) Langstrecken-; ⟨*forecast*⟩ langfristig. **~-sighted** *a* weitsichtig. **~-sleeved** *a* langärmelig. **~-suffering** *a* langmütig. **~-term** *a* langfristig. **~ wave** *n* Langwelle *f*. **~-winded** /-ˈwɪndɪd/ *a* langatmig

loo /luː/ *n* (*fam*) Klo *nt*

look /lʊk/ *n* Blick *m*; (*appearance*) Aussehen *nt*; [**good**] **~s** *pl* [gutes] Aussehen *nt*; **have a ~ at** sich (*dat*) ansehen; **go and have a ~** sieh mal nach □*vi* sehen; (*search*) nachsehen; (*seem*) aussehen; **don't ~** sieh nicht hin; **~ here!** hören Sie mal! **~ at** ansehen; **~ for** suchen; **~ forward to** sich freuen auf (+ *acc*); **~ in on**

vorbeischauen bei; **~ into** (*examine*) nachgehen (+ *dat*); **~ like** aussehen wie; **~ on to** ⟨*room:*⟩ gehen auf (+ *acc*). **~ after** *vt* betreuen. **~ down** *vi* hinuntersehen; **~ down on s.o.** (*fig*) auf jdn herabsehen. **~ out** *vi* hinausheraussehen; (*take care*) aufpassen; **~ out for** Ausschau halten nach; **~ out!** Vorsicht! **~ round** *vi* sich umsehen. **~ up** *vi* aufblicken; **~ up to s.o.** (*fig*) zu jdm aufsehen □*vt* nachschlagen ⟨*word*⟩

'look-out *n* Wache *f*; (*prospect*) Aussicht *f*; **be on the ~ for** Ausschau halten nach

loom[1] /luːm/ *n* Webstuhl *m*

loom[2] *vi* auftauchen; (*fig*) sich abzeichnen

loony /ˈluːnɪ/ *a* (*fam*) verrückt

loop /luːp/ *n* Schlinge *f*; (*in road*) Schleife *f*; (*on garment*) Aufhänger *m* □*vt* schlingen. **~hole** *n* Hintertürchen *nt*; (*in the law*) Lücke *f*

loose /luːs/ *a* (-r, -st), **-ly** *adv* lose; (*not tight enough*) locker; (*inexact*) frei; **be at a ~ end** nichts zu tun haben; **set ~** freilassen; **run ~** frei herumlaufen. **~ 'change** *n* Kleingeld *nt*. **~ 'chippings** *npl* Rollsplit *m*

loosen /ˈluːsn/ *vt* lockern □*vi* sich lockern

loot /luːt/ *n* Beute *f* □*vt/i* plündern. **~er** *n* Plünderer *m*

lop /lɒp/ *vt* (*pt/pp* lopped) stutzen. **~ off** *vt* abhacken

lop'sided *a* schief

loquacious /ləˈkweɪʃəs/ *a* redselig

lord /lɔːd/ *n* Herr *m*; (*title*) Lord *m*; **House of L~s** ≈ Oberhaus *nt*; **the L~'s Prayer** das Vaterunser; **good L~!** du liebe Zeit!

lore /lɔː(r)/ *n* Überlieferung *f*

lorry /ˈlɒrɪ/ *n* Last[kraft]wagen *m*

lose /luːz/ *v* (*pt/pp* lost) □*vt* verlieren; (*miss*) verpassen □*vi* verlieren; ⟨*clock:*⟩ nachgehen; **get lost**

verlorengehen; ~r n Verlierer m

loss /lɒs/ n Verlust m; **be at a** ~ nicht mehr weiter wissen; **be at a** ~ **for words** nicht wissen, was man sagen soll

lost /lɒst/ see **lose**. ~ '**property office** n Fundbüro nt

lot¹ /lɒt/ n Los nt; (at auction) Posten m; **draw** ~**s** losen (for um)

lot² n the ~ alle; (everything) alles; **a** ~ [**of**] viel; (many) viele; ~**s of** (fam) eine Menge; **it has changed a** ~ es hat sich sehr verändert

lotion /'ləʊʃn/ n Lotion f

lottery /'lɒtərɪ/ n Lotterie f. ~ **ticket** n Los nt

loud /laʊd/ a (-er, -est), **-ly** adv laut; (colours) grell □adv [out] ~ laut. ~ '**hailer** n Megaphon nt. ~**speaker** n Lautsprecher m

lounge /laʊndʒ/ n Wohnzimmer nt; (in hotel) Aufenthaltsraum m. □vi sich lümmeln. ~ **suit** n Straßenanzug m

louse /laʊs/ n (pl **lice**) Laus f

lousy /'laʊzɪ/ a (-ier, -iest) (fam) lausig

lout /laʊt/ n Flegel m, Lümmel m. ~**ish** a flegelhaft

lovable /'lʌvəbl/ a liebenswert

love /lʌv/ n Liebe f; (Tennis) null; **in** ~ verliebt □vt lieben; (like) ~ **doing sth** etw sehr gerne machen; **I** ~ **chocolate** ich esse sehr gerne Schokolade. ~**affair** n Liebesverhältnis nt. ~ **letter** n Liebesbrief m

lovely /'lʌvlɪ/ a (-ier, -iest) schön; **we had a** ~ **time** es war sehr schön

lover /'lʌvə(r)/ n Liebhaber m

love: ~ **song** n Liebeslied nt. ~ **story** n Liebesgeschichte f

loving /'lʌvɪŋ/ a, **-ly** adv liebevoll

low /ləʊ/ a (-er, -est) niedrig; (cloud, note) tief; (voice) leise; (depressed) niedergeschlagen □adv niedrig; (fly, sing) tief;

(speak) leise; **feel** ~ deprimiert sein □n (Meteorol) Tief nt; (fig) Tiefstand m

low: ~**brow** a geistig anspruchslos. ~**cut** a (dress) tief ausgeschnitten

lower /'ləʊə(r)/ a & adv see **low** □vt niedriger machen; (let down) herunterlassen; (reduce) senken; ~ **oneself** sich herabwürdigen

low: ~**fat** a fettarm. ~**grade** a minderwertig. ~**lands** /-ləndz/ npl Tiefland nt. ~ '**tide** n Ebbe f

loyal /'lɔɪəl/ a, **-ly** adv treu. ~**ty** n Treue f

lozenge /'lɒzɪndʒ/ n Pastille f

Ltd abbr (Limited) GmbH

lubricant /'lu:brɪkənt/ n Schmiermittel nt

lubricat|e /'lu:brɪkeɪt/ vt schmieren. ~**ion** /-'keɪʃn/ n Schmierung f

lucid /'lu:sɪd/ a klar. ~**ity** /-'sɪdətɪ/ n Klarheit f

luck /lʌk/ n Glück nt; **bad** ~ Pech nt; **good** ~! viel Glück! ~**ily** adv glücklicherweise, zum Glück

lucky /'lʌkɪ/ a (-ier, -iest) glücklich; (day, number) Glücks-; **be** ~ Glück haben; (thing:) Glück bringen. ~ '**charm** n Amulett nt

lucrative /'lu:krətɪv/ a einträglich

ludicrous /'lu:dɪkrəs/ a lächerlich

lug /lʌg/ vt (pt/pp **lugged**) (fam) schleppen

luggage /'lʌgɪdʒ/ n Gepäck nt

luggage: ~**rack** n Gepäckablage f. ~ **trolley** n Kofferkuli m. ~**van** n Gepäckwagen m

lugubrious /lu:'gu:brɪəs/ a traurig

lukewarm /'lu:k-/ a lauwarm

lull /lʌl/ n Pause f □vt ~ **to sleep** einschläfern

lullaby /'lʌləbaɪ/ n Wiegenlied nt

lumbago /lʌm'beɪgəʊ/ n Hexenschuß m

lumber /'lʌmbə(r)/ n Gerümpel nt; (Amer: timber) Bauholz nt □vt ~ **s.o. with sth** jdm etw aufhalsen. ~**jack** n (Amer) Holzfäller m

luminous /'lu:mɪnəs/ a leuchtend; be ~ leuchten

lump¹ /lʌmp/ n Klumpen m; (of sugar) Stück nt; (swelling) Beule f; (in breast) Knoten m; (tumour) Geschwulst f; **a ~ in one's throat** (fam) ein Kloß im Hals □ vt ~ **together** zusammentun

lump² vt ~ **it** (fam) sich damit abfinden

lump: ~ **sugar** n Würfelzucker m. ~ '**sum** n Pauschalsumme f

lumpy /'lʌmpi/ a (-ier, -iest) klumpig

lunacy /'lu:nəsi/ n Wahnsinn m

lunar /'lu:nə(r)/ a Mond-

lunatic /'lu:nətɪk/ n Wahnsinnige(r) m|f

lunch /lʌntʃ/ n Mittagessen nt □ vi zu Mittag essen

luncheon /'lʌntʃn/ n Mittagessen nt. ~ **meat** n Frühstücksfleisch nt. ~ **voucher** n Essensbon m

lunch: ~-**hour** n Mittagspause f. ~-**time** n Mittagszeit f

lung /lʌŋ/ n Lungenflügel m; ~**s** pl Lunge f. ~ **cancer** n Lungenkrebs m

lunge /lʌndʒ/ vi sich stürzen (at auf + acc)

lurch¹ /lɜ:tʃ/ n **leave in the ~** (fam) im Stich lassen

lurch² vi schleudern; ⟨person:⟩ torkeln

lure /lʊə(r)/ n Lockung f; (bait) Köder m □ vt locken

lurid /'lʊərɪd/ a grell; (sensational) reißerisch

lurk /lɜ:k/ vi lauern

luscious /'lʌʃəs/ a lecker, köstlich

lush /lʌʃ/ a üppig

lust /lʌst/ n Begierde f □ vi ~ **after** gieren nach. ~**ful** a lüstern

lustre /'lʌstə(r)/ n Glanz m

lusty /'lʌsti/ a (-ier, -iest) kräftig

lute /luːt/ n Laute f

luxuriant /lʌg'ʒʊərɪənt/ a üppig

luxurious /lʌg'ʒʊərɪəs/ a, -ly adv luxuriös

luxury /'lʌkʃərɪ/ n Luxus m □ attrib Luxus-

lying /'laɪɪŋ/ see lie¹, lie²

lymph gland /'lɪmf-/ n Lymphdrüse f

lynch /lɪntʃ/ vt lynchen

lynx /lɪŋks/ n Luchs m

lyric /'lɪrɪk/ a lyrisch. ~**al** a lyrisch; (fam: enthusiastic) schwärmerisch. ~ **poetry** n Lyrik f. ~**s** npl [Lied]text m

M

mac /mæk/ n (fam) Regenmantel m

macabre /mə'kɑ:br/ a makaber

macaroni /mækə'rəʊnɪ/ n Makkaroni pl

macaroon /mækə'ru:n/ n Makrone f

mace¹ /meɪs/ n Amtsstab m

mace² n (spice) Muskatblüte f

machinations /mækɪ'neɪʃnz/ pl Machenschaften pl

machine /mə'ʃi:n/ n Maschine f □ vt (sew) mit der Maschine nähen; (Techn) maschinell bearbeiten. ~-**gun** n Maschinengewehr nt

machinery /mə'ʃi:nərɪ/ n Maschinerie f

machine **tool** n Werkzeugmaschine f

machinist /mə'ʃi:nɪst/ n Maschinist m; (on sewing machine) Maschinennäherin f

mackerel /'mækrl/ n inv Makrele f

mackintosh /'mækɪntɒʃ/ n Regenmantel m

mad /mæd/ a (madder, maddest) verrückt; (dog) tollwütig; (fam: angry) böse (at auf + acc)

madam /'mædəm/ n gnädige Frau f

madden /'mædn/ vt (make angry) wütend machen

made /meɪd/ see make; ~ **to measure** maßgeschneidert

Madeira cake /mə'dɪərə-/ n Sandkuchen m

madly /'mædlɪ/ adv (fam) wahnsinnig. **~man** n Irre(r) m. **~ness** n Wahnsinn m

madonna /mə'dɒnə/ n Madonna f

magazine /mægə'ziːn/ n Zeitschrift f; (Mil, Phot) Magazin nt

maggot /'mægət/ n Made f. **~y** a madig

Magi /'meɪdʒaɪ/ npl the ~ die Heiligen Drei Könige

magic /'mædʒɪk/ n Zauber m; (tricks) Zauberkunst f □a magisch; (word, wand, flute) Zauber-. **~al** a zauberhaft

magician /mə'dʒɪʃn/ n Zauberer m; (entertainer) Zauberkünstler m

magistrate /'mædʒɪstreɪt/ n ≈ Friedensrichter m

magnanim|ity /mægnə'nɪmətɪ/ n Großmut f. **~ous** /-'nænɪməs/ a großmütig

magnesia /mæg'niːʃə/ n Magnesia f

magnet /'mægnɪt/ n Magnet m. **~ic** /-'netɪk/ a magnetisch. **~ism** n Magnetismus m. **~ize** vt magnetisieren

magnification /mægnɪfɪ'keɪʃn/ n Vergrößerung f

magnificen|ce /mæg'nɪfɪsəns/ n Großartigkeit f. **~t** a, **-ly** adv großartig

magnify /'mægnɪfaɪ/ vt (pt/pp -ied) vergrößern; (exaggerate) übertreiben. **~ing glass** n Vergrößerungsglas nt

magnitude /'mægnɪtjuːd/ n Größe f; (importance) Bedeutung f

magpie /'mægpaɪ/ n Elster f

mahogany /mə'hɒgənɪ/ n Mahagoni nt

maid /meɪd/ n Dienstmädchen nt; (liter: girl) Maid f; old ~ (pej) alte Jungfer f

maiden /'meɪdn/ n (liter) Maid f □a (speech, voyage) Jungfern-. **'~aunt** n unverheiratete Tante f. **~ name** n Mädchenname m

mail¹ /meɪl/ n Kettenpanzer m

mail² n Post f □vt mit der Post schicken; (send off) abschicken

mail: **~bag** n Postsack m. **~box** n (Amer) Briefkasten m. **~ing list** n Postversandliste f. **~man** n (Amer) Briefträger m. **~order firm** n Versandhaus nt

maim /meɪm/ vt verstümmeln

main¹ /meɪn/ n (water, gas, electricity) Hauptleitung f

main² a Haupt- □n in the ~ im großen und ganzen

main: **~land** /-lənd/ n Festland nt. **~ly** adv hauptsächlich. **~stay** n (fig) Stütze f. **~ street** n Hauptstraße f

maintain /meɪn'teɪn/ vt aufrechterhalten; (keep in repair) instand halten; (support) unterhalten; (claim) behaupten

maintenance /'meɪntənəns/ n Aufrechterhaltung f; (care) Instandhaltung f; (allowance) Unterhalt m

maisonette /meɪzə'net/ n Wohnung f [auf zwei Etagen]

maize /meɪz/ n Mais m

majestic /mə'dʒestɪk/ a, **-ally** adv majestätisch

majesty /'mædʒəstɪ/ n Majestät f

major /'meɪdʒə(r)/ a größer □n (Mil) Major m; (Mus) Dur nt □vi (Amer) ~ in als Hauptfach studieren

Majorca /mə'jɔːkə/ n Mallorca nt

majority /mə'dʒɒrətɪ/ n Mehrheit f; in the ~ in der Mehrzahl

major road n Hauptverkehrsstraße f

make /meɪk/ n (brand) Marke f □v (pt/pp made) □vt machen; (force) zwingen; (earn) verdienen; halten (speech); treffen (decision); erreichen (destination) □vi ~ as if to Miene machen zu. **~ do** vi zurechtkommen (with mit). **~ for** vi zusteuern auf (+ acc). **~ off** vi sich davonmachen (with mit). **~ out** vt (distinguish) ausmachen; (write out) ausstellen; (assert) behaupten.

~ **over** vt überschreiben (to auf + acc). ~ **up** vt (constitute) bilden; (invent) erfinden; (apply cosmetics to) schminken; ~ **up one's mind** sich entschließen □vi sich versöhnen; ~ **up for sth** etw wiedergutmachen; ~ **up for lost time** verlorene Zeit aufholen

'**make-believe** n Phantasie f

'**maker** /'meɪkə(r)/ n Hersteller m

'**make**: ~**shift** a behelfsmäßig □n Notbehelf m. ~**-up** n Make-up nt

'**making** /'meɪkɪŋ/ n **have the ~s of das** Zeug haben zu

maladjusted /mælə'dʒʌstɪd/ a verhaltensgestört

malaise /mə'leɪz/ n (fig) Unbehagen nt

male /meɪl/ a männlich □n Mann m; (animal) Männchen nt. ~ '**nurse** n Krankenpfleger m. ~ '**voice 'choir** n Männerchor m

malevolen|ce /mə'levələns/ n Bosheit f. ~**t** a boshaft

malfunction /mæl'fʌŋkʃn/ n technische Störung f; (Med) Funktionsstörung f □vi nicht richtig funktionieren

malice /'mælɪs/ n Bosheit f; **bear s.o.** ~ einen Groll gegen jdn hegen

malicious /mə'lɪʃəs/ a, **-ly** adv böswillig

malign /mə'laɪn/ vt verleumden

malignan|cy /mə'lɪgnənsɪ/ n Bösartigkeit f. ~**t** a bösartig

malinger /mə'lɪŋgə(r)/ vi simulieren, sich krank stellen. ~**er** n Simulant m

malleable /'mælɪəbl/ a formbar

mallet /'mælɪt/ n Holzhammer m

malnu'trition /mæl-/ n Unterernährung f

mal'practice n Berufsvergehen nt

malt /mɔːlt/ n Malz nt

mal'treat /mæl-/ vt mißhandeln. ~**ment** n Mißhandlung f

mammal /'mæml/ n Säugetier nt

mammoth /'mæməθ/ a riesig □n Mammut nt

man /mæn/ n (pl **men**) Mann m; (mankind) der Mensch; (chess) Figur f; (draughts) Stein m □vt (pt/pp **manned**) bemannen ⟨ship⟩; bedienen ⟨pump⟩; besetzen ⟨counter⟩

manacle /'mænəkl/ vt fesseln (to an + acc); (cope with) fertig werden mit; ~ **to do sth** es schaffen, etw zu tun □vi zurechtkommen; ~ **on** auskommen mit. ~**able** /-əbl/ a ⟨tool⟩ handlich; ⟨person⟩ fügsam. ~**ment** /-mənt/ n the ~**ment die Geschäftsleitung f

manager /'mænɪdʒə(r)/ n Geschäftsführer m; (of bank) Direktor m; (of estate) Verwalter m; (Sport) [Chef]trainer m. ~**ess** n Geschäftsführerin f. ~**ial** /-dʒɪərɪəl/ a. ~**ial staff** Führungskräfte pl

managing /'mænɪdʒɪŋ/ a ~ **director** Generaldirektor m

mandarin /'mændərɪn/ n [**orange**] Mandarine f

mandat|e /'mændeɪt/ n Mandat nt. ~**ory** /-dətrɪ/ a obligatorisch

mane /meɪn/ n Mähne f

manful /'mænfl/ a, **-ly** adv mannhaft

manger /'meɪndʒə(r)/ n Krippe f

mangle[1] /'mæŋgl/ n Wringmaschine f; (for smoothing) Mangel f

mangle[2] vt (damage) verstümmeln

mango /'mæŋgəʊ/ n (pl **-es**) Mango f

mangy /'meɪndʒɪ/ a ⟨dog⟩ räudig

man: ~'**handle** vt grob behandeln ⟨person⟩. ~'**hole** n Kanalschacht m. ~**hole cover** n Kanaldeckel m. ~'**hood** n Mannesalter nt; (quality) Männlichkeit f. ~'**-hour** n Arbeitsstunde f. ~'**-hunt** n Fahndung f

man|ia /'meɪnɪə/ n Manie f. ~**iac** /-ɪæk/ n Wahnsinnige(r) m/f

manicur|e /'mænɪkjʊə(r)/ n Mani-
küre f □vt maniküren. ~ist n
Maniküre f

manifest /'mænɪfest/ a, -ly adv
offensichtlich □vt ~ itself sich
manifestieren

manifesto /mænɪ'festəʊ/ n Manifest nt

manifold /'mænɪfəʊld/ a mannigfaltig

manipulat|e /mə'nɪpjʊleɪt/ vt
handhaben; (pej) manipulieren.
~ion /-'leɪʃn/ n Manipulation f

man'kind n Die Menschheit

manly /'mænlɪ/ a männlich

'man-made a künstlich. ~ fibre
n Kunstfaser f

manner /'mænə(r)/ n Weise f;
(kind, behaviour) Art f; in this
~ auf diese Weise; [good/bad]
~ s [gute/schlechte] Manieren pl.
~ism n Angewohnheit f

mannish /'mænɪʃ/ a männlich

manœuvrable /mə'nu:vrəbl/ a
manövrierfähig

manœuvre /mə'nu:və(r)/ n Manöver nt □vt/i manövrieren

manor /'mænə(r)/ n Gutshof m;
(house) Gutshaus nt

man: ~power n Arbeitskräfte pl.
~servant n (pl menservants)
Diener m

mansion /'mænʃn/ n Villa f

'manslaughter n Totschlag m

mantelpiece /'mæntl-/ n Kamin-
sims m & nt

manual /'mænjʊəl/ a Hand- □n
Handbuch nt

manufacture /mænjʊ'fæktʃə(r)/
vt herstellen □n Herstellung f.
~r n Hersteller m

manure /mə'njʊə(r)/ n Mist m

manuscript /'mænjʊskrɪpt/ n
Manuskript nt

many /'menɪ/ a viele; ~ a time oft
□n a good/great ~ sehr viele

map /mæp/ n Landkarte f; (of
town) Stadtplan m □vt (pt/pp
mapped) ~ out (fig) ausarbeiten

maple /'meɪpl/ n Ahorn m

mar /ma:(r)/ vt (pt/pp marred)
verderben

marathon /'mærəθən/ n Marathon m

marauding /mə'rɔ:dɪŋ/ a plün-
dernd

marble /'ma:bl/ n Marmor m; (for
game) Murmel f

March /ma:tʃ/ n März m

march n Marsch m □vi marschieren □vt marschieren lassen; ~
s.o. off jdn abführen

mare /'meə(r)/ n Stute f

margarine /ma:dʒə'ri:n/ n Margarine f

margin /'ma:dʒɪn/ n Rand m; (lee-
way) Spielraum m; (Comm) Spanne f. ~al a, -ly adv geringfügig

marigold /'mærɪgəʊld/ n Ringel-
blume f

marijuana /mærɪ'hwa:nə/ n Marihuana nt

marina /mə'ri:nə/ n Jachthafen m

marinade /mærɪ'neɪd/ n Marinade f □vt marinieren

marine /mə'ri:n/ a Meeres- □n
Marine f; (sailor) Marineinfante-
rist m

marionette /mærɪə'net/ n Marionette f

marital /'mærɪtl/ a ehelich. ~
status n Familienstand m

maritime /'mærɪtaɪm/ a See-

marjoram /'ma:dʒərəm/ n Majoran m

mark¹ /ma:k/ n (currency) Mark f

mark² n Fleck m; (sign) Zeichen
nt; (trace) Spur f; (target) Ziel nt;
(Sch) Note f □vt markieren;
(spoil) beschädigen; (characterize) kennzeichnen; (Sch) korrigieren; (Sport) decken; ~ time
(Mil) auf der Stelle treten; (fig)
abwarten; ~ my words das
[eine] will ich dir sagen. ~ out vt
markieren

marked /ma:kt/ a, ~ly /-kɪdlɪ/
adv deutlich; (pronounced) ausgeprägt

marker /'ma:kə(r)/ n Marke f; (of
exam) Korrektor(in) m(f)

market /'mɑːkɪt/ n Markt m ⊡ vt vertreiben; (*launch*) auf den Markt bringen. ~**ing** n Marketing nt. ~ **re'search** n Marktforschung f

marking /'mɑːkɪŋ/ n Markierung f; (*on animal*) Zeichnung f

marksman /'mɑːksmən/ n Scharfschütze m

marmalade /'mɑːməleɪd/ n Orangenmarmelade f

marmot /'mɑːmət/ n Murmeltier nt

maroon /mə'ruːn/ a dunkelrot

marooned /mə'ruːnd/ a (*fig*) von der Außenwelt abgeschnitten

marquee /mɑː'kiː/ n Festzelt nt; (*Amer: awning*) Markise f

marquetry /'mɑːkɪtrɪ/ n Einlegearbeit f

marquis /'mɑːkwɪs/ n Marquis m

marriage /'mærɪdʒ/ n Ehe f; (*wedding*) Hochzeit f. ~**able** /-əbl/ a heiratsfähig

married /'mærɪd/ see **marry** ⊡ a verheiratet. ~ **life** n Eheleben nt

marrow /'mærəʊ/ n (*Anat*) Mark nt; (*vegetable*) Kürbis m

marr|y /'mærɪ/ vt/i (pt/pp **married**) heiraten; (*unite*) trauen; get ~ **ied** heiraten

marsh /mɑːʃ/ n Sumpf m

marshal /'mɑːʃl/ n Marschall m; (*steward*) Ordner m ⊡ vt (pt/pp **marshalled**) (*Mil*) formieren; (*fig*) ordnen

marshy /'mɑːʃɪ/ a sumpfig

marsupial /mɑː'sjuːpɪəl/ n Beuteltier nt

martial /'mɑːʃl/ a kriegerisch. ~ **'law** n Kriegsrecht nt

martyr /'mɑːtə(r)/ n Märtyrer(in) m(f) ⊡ vt zum Märtyrer machen. ~**dom** /-dəm/ n Martyrium nt

marvel /'mɑːvl/ n Wunder nt ⊡ vi (pt/pp **marvelled**) staunen (**at** über + acc). ~**lous** /-vələs/ a, -**ly** adv wunderbar

Marxis|m /'mɑːksɪzm/ n Marxismus m. ~**t** a marxistisch ⊡ n Marxist(in) m(f)

marzipan /'mɑːzɪpæn/ n Marzipan nt

mascara /mæ'skɑːrə/ n Wimperntusche f

mascot /'mæskət/ n Maskottchen nt

masculin|e /'mæskjʊlm/ a männlich ⊡ n (*Gram*) Maskulinum nt. ~**ity** /-'lɪnətɪ/ n Männlichkeit f

mash /mæʃ/ n (*fam, Culin*) Kartoffelpüree nt ⊡ vt stampfen. ~**ed potatoes** npl Kartoffelpüree nt

mask /mɑːsk/ n Maske f ⊡ vt maskieren

masochis|m /'mæsəkɪzm/ n Masochismus m. ~**t** /-ɪst/ n Masochist m

mason /'meɪsn/ n Steinmetz m

Mason n Freimaurer m. ~**ic** /mə-'sɒnɪk/ a freimaurerisch

masonry /'meɪsnrɪ/ n Mauerwerk nt

masquerade /mæskə'reɪd/ n (*fig*) Maskerade f ⊡ vi ~ **as** (*pose*) sich ausgeben als

mass[1] /mæs/ n (*Relig*) Messe f

mass[2] n Masse f ⊡ vi sich sammeln; (*Mil*) sich massieren

massacre /'mæsəkə(r)/ n Massaker nt ⊡ vt niedermetzeln

massage /'mæsɑːʒ/ n Massage f ⊡ vt massieren

masseu|r /mæ'sɜː(r)/ n Masseur m. ~**se** /-'sɜːz/ n Masseuse f

massive /'mæsɪv/ a massiv; (*huge*) riesig

mass: ~ **media** npl Massenmedien pl. ~-**'pro'duce** vt in Massenproduktion herstellen. ~-**pro'duction** n Massenproduktion f

mast /mɑːst/ n Mast m

master /'mɑːstə(r)/ n Herr m; (*teacher*) Lehrer m; (*craftsman, artist*) Meister m; (*of ship*) Kapitän m ⊡ vt meistern; beherrschen (*language*)

master: ~-**key** n Hauptschlüssel m. ~-**ly** a meisterhaft. ~-**mind** n führender Kopf m □ vt der führende Kopf sein von. **~piece** n Meisterwerk nt. **~y** n (of subject) Beherrschung f

masturbat|e /'mæstəbeɪt/ vi masturbieren. **~ion** n /-'beɪʃn/ n Masturbation f

mat /mæt/ n Matte f; (on table) Untersatz m

match[1] /mætʃ/ n Wettkampf m; (in ball games) Spiel nt; (Tennis) Match nt; (marriage) Heirat f; **be a good ~** (colours:) gut zusammenpassen; **be no ~ for** s.o. jdm nicht gewachsen sein □ vt (equal) gleichkommen (+ dat); (be like) passen zu; (find sth similar) etwas Passendes finden zu □ vi zusammenpassen

match[2] n Streichholz nt. **~box** n Streichholzschachtel f

matching /'mætʃɪŋ/ a (zusammen)passend

mate[1] /meɪt/ n Kumpel m; (assistant) Gehilfe m; (Naut) Maat m; (Zool) Männchen nt; (female) Weibchen nt □ vi sich paaren □ vt paaren

mate[2] n (Chess) Matt nt

material /mə'tɪərɪəl/ n Material nt; (fabric) Stoff m; raw **~s** Rohstoffe pl □ a materiell

material|ism /mə'tɪərɪəlɪzm/ n Materialismus m. **~istic** /-'lɪstɪk/ a materialistisch. **~ize** /-laɪz/ vi sich verwirklichen

maternal /mə'tɜːnl/ a mütterlich

maternity /mə'tɜːnətɪ/ n Mutterschaft f. **~ clothes** npl Umstandskleidung f. **~ ward** n Entbindungsstation f

matey /'meɪtɪ/ a (fam) freundlich

mathematic|al /mæθə'mætɪkl/ a, **-ly** adv mathematisch. **~ian** /-mə'tɪʃn/ n Mathematiker(in) m(f)

mathematics /mæθə'mætɪks/ n Mathematik f

maths /mæθs/ n (fam) Mathe f

matinée /'mætɪneɪ/ n (Theat) Nachmittagsvorstellung f

matriculat|e /mə'trɪkjʊleɪt/ vi sich immatrikulieren. **~ion** /-'leɪʃn/ n Immatrikulation f

matrimon|ial /mætrɪ'məʊnɪəl/ a Ehe-. **~y** /'mætrɪmənɪ/ n Ehe f

matrix /'meɪtrɪks/ n (pl **matrices** /-siːz/) n (Techn: mould) Matrize f

matron /'meɪtrən/ n (of hospital) Oberin f; (of school) Hausmutter f. **~ly** a matronenhaft

matt /mæt/ a matt

matted /'mætɪd/ a verfilzt

matter /'mætə(r)/ n (affair) Sache f; (pus) Eiter m; (Phys: substance) Materie f; **money ~s** Geldangelegenheiten pl; **as a ~ of fact** eigentlich; **what is the ~?** was ist los? □ vi wichtig sein; **~ to** s.o. jdm etwas ausmachen; **it doesn't ~** es macht nichts. **~-of-fact** a sachlich

matting /'mætɪŋ/ n Matten pl

mattress /'mætrɪs/ n Matratze f

matur|e /mə'tjʊə(r)/ a reif; (Comm) fällig □ vi reifen; (person:) reif werden; (Comm) fällig werden □ vt reifen lassen. **~ity** n Reife f; (Comm) Fälligkeit f

maul /mɔːl/ vt übel zurichten

Maundy /'mɔːndɪ/ n **~ Thursday** Gründonnerstag m

mauve /məʊv/ a lila

mawkish /'mɔːkɪʃ/ a rührselig

maxim /'mæksɪm/ n Maxime f

maximum /'mæksɪməm/ a maximal □ n (pl -ima) Maximum nt. **~ speed** /meɪ/ v aux (nur Präsens) (be allowed to) dürfen; (be possible) können; **may I come in?** darf ich reinkommen? **may he succeed** möge es ihm gelingen; **I may as well stay** am besten bleibe ich hier; **it may be true** es könnte wahr sein

May n Mai m

maybe /'meɪbɪ/ adv vielleicht

'May Day n der Erste Mai

mayonnaise /meɪə'neɪz/ n Mayonnaise f

mayor /'meə(r)/ n Bürgermeister m. **~ess** n Bürgermeisterin f; (wife of mayor) Frau Bürgermeister f

maze /meɪz/ n Irrgarten m; (fig) Labyrinth n

me /miː/ pron (acc) mich; (dat) mir; he knows ~ er kennt mich; give ~ the money gib mir das Geld; it's ~ (fam) ich bin es

meadow /'medəʊ/ n Wiese f

meagre /'miːgə(r)/ a dürftig

meal[1] /miːl/ n Mahlzeit f; (food) Essen nt

meal[2] n (grain) Schrot m

mealy-mouthed /miːlɪ'maʊðd/ a heuchlerisch

mean[1] /miːn/ a (-er, -est) geizig; (unkind) gemein; (poor) schäbig

mean[2] a mittlere(r,s) (in (average) Durchschnitt m; the golden ~ die goldene Mitte

mean[3] vt (pt/pp meant) heißen; (signify) bedeuten; (intend) beabsichtigen; I ~ it das ist mein Ernst; ~ well es gut meinen; be meant for (present:) bestimmt sein für; (remark:) gerichtet sein an (+ acc)

meander /mɪ'ændə(r)/ vi sich schlängeln; (person:) schlendern

meaning /'miːnɪŋ/ n Bedeutung f. ~ful a bedeutungsvoll. ~less a bedeutungslos

means /miːnz/ n Möglichkeit f, Mittel nt; ~ of transport Verkehrsmittel nt; by ~ of durch; by all ~! aber natürlich! by no ~ keineswegs □ npl (resources) [Geld]mittel pl. ~ test n Bedürftigkeitsnachweis m

meant /ment/ see **mean**[3]

'meantime n in the ~ in der Zwischenzeit □ adv inzwischen

'meanwhile adv inzwischen

measles /'miːzlz/ n Masern pl

measly /'miːzlɪ/ a (fam) mickerig

measurable /'meʒərəbl/ a meßbar

measure /'meʒə(r)/ n Maß nt; (action) Maßnahme f □ vt/i messen; ~ up to (fig) herankommen an

(+ acc). ~d a gemessen. ~ment /-mənt/ n Maß nt

meat /miːt/ n Fleisch nt. ~ball n (Culin) Klops m. ~ loaf n falscher Hase m

mechanic /mɪ'kænɪk/ n Mechaniker m. ~ical a, ~ly adv mechanisch. ~ical engineering Maschinenbau m. ~ics n Mechanik f □ n pl Mechanismus m

mechanism /'mekənɪzm/ n Mechanismus m. ~ize vt mechanisieren

medal /medl/ n Orden m; (Sport) Medaille f

medallion /mɪ'dælɪən/ n Medaillon nt

medallist /'medəlɪst/ n Medaillengewinner(in) m(f)

meddle /medl/ vi sich einmischen (in in + acc); (tinker) herumhantieren (with an + acc)

media /'miːdɪə/ see **medium** □ n pl the ~ die Medien pl

median /'miːdɪən/ a ~ strip (Amer) Mittelstreifen m

mediate /'miːdɪeɪt/ vi vermitteln. ~or n Vermittler(in) m(f)

medical /'medɪkl/ a medizinisch; (treatment) ärztlich □ n ärztliche Untersuchung f. ~ insurance n Krankenversicherung f. ~ student n Medizinstudent m

medicated /'medɪkeɪtɪd/ a medizinisch. ~ion /-'keɪʃn/ n (drugs) Medikamente pl

medicinal /mɪ'dɪsɪnl/ a medizinisch; (plant) heilkräftig

medicine /'medsən/ n Medizin f; (preparation) Medikament nt

medieval /medɪ'iːvl/ a mittelalterlich

mediocre /miːdɪ'əʊkə(r)/ a mittelmäßig. ~ity /-'ɒkrətɪ/ n Mittelmäßigkeit f

meditate /'medɪteɪt/ vi nachdenken (on über + acc); (Relig) meditieren. ~ion /-'teɪʃn/ n Meditation f

Mediterranean /medɪtə'reɪnɪən/ n Mittelmeer nt □ a Mittelmeer-

medium /ˈmiːdɪəm/ a mittlere(r,s); ⟨steak⟩ medium; of ~ size von mittlerer Größe □n (pl media) Medium nt; (means) Mittel nt □(pl -s) (person) Medium nt

medium: ~-sized a mittelgroß. ~ **wave** n Mittelwelle f

medley /ˈmedlɪ/ n Gemisch nt; (Mus) Potpourri nt

meek /miːk/ a (-er, -est), -ly adv sanftmütig; (unprotesting) widerspruchslos

meet /miːt/ v (pt/pp met) □vt treffen; (by chance) begegnen (+ dat); (at station) abholen; (make the acquaintance of) kennenlernen; stoßen auf (+ acc) ⟨problem⟩; bezahlen ⟨bill⟩; erfüllen ⟨requirements⟩ □vi sich treffen; (for the first time) sich kennenlernen; ~ with stoßen auf (+ acc) ⟨problem⟩; sich treffen mit ⟨person⟩ □n Jagdtreffen nt

meeting /ˈmiːtɪŋ/ n Treffen nt; (by chance) Begegnung f; (discussion) Besprechung f; (of committee) Sitzung f; (large) Versammlung f

megalomania /meɡələˈmeɪnɪə/ n Größenwahnsinn m

megaphone /ˈmeɡəfəʊn/ n Megaphon nt

melancholy /ˈmelənkəlɪ/ a melancholisch □n Melancholie f

mellow /ˈmeləʊ/ a (-er, -est) ⟨fruit⟩ ausgereift; ⟨sound, person⟩ sanft □vi reifer werden

melodic /mɪˈlɒdɪk/ a melodisch

melodious /mɪˈləʊdɪəs/ a melodiös

melodrama /ˈmelə-/ n Melodrama nt. ~tic /-drəˈmætɪk/ a, -ally adv melodramatisch

melody /ˈmelədɪ/ n Melodie f

melon /ˈmelən/ n Melone f

melt /melt/ vt/i schmelzen. ~ **down** vt einschmelzen. ~ing-**pot** n (fig) Schmelztiegel m

member /ˈmembə(r)/ n Mitglied nt; (of family) Angehörige(r) m/f;

M~ of Parliament Abgeordnete(r) m/f. ~**ship** n Mitgliedschaft f; (members) Mitgliederzahl f

membrane /ˈmembreɪn/ n Membran f

memento /mɪˈmentəʊ/ n Andenken nt

memo /ˈmeməʊ/ n Mitteilung f

memoirs /ˈmemwɑːz/ n pl Memoiren pl

memorable /ˈmemərəbl/ a denkwürdig

memorandum /meməˈrændəm/ n Mitteilung f

memorial /mɪˈmɔːrɪəl/ n Denkmal nt. ~ **service** n Gedenkfeier f

memorize /ˈmeməraɪz/ vt sich (dat) einprägen

memory /ˈmemərɪ/ n Gedächtnis nt; (thing remembered) Erinnerung f; (of computer) Speicher m; **from** ~ auswendig; **in** ~ **of** zur Erinnerung an (+ acc)

men /men/ see **man**

menace /ˈmenɪs/ n Drohung f; (nuisance) Plage f □vt bedrohen. ~ **ing** a, -ly adv drohend

mend /mend/ vt reparieren; (patch) flicken; ausbessern ⟨clothes⟩ □n **on the** ~ auf dem Weg der Besserung

menfolk n pl Männer pl

menial /ˈmiːnɪəl/ a niedrig

meningitis /menɪnˈdʒaɪtɪs/ n Hirnhautentzündung f, Meningitis f

menopause /ˈmenə-/ n Wechseljahre pl

menstruate /ˈmenstruet/ vi menstruieren. ~**ion** /-ˈeɪʃn/ n Menstruation f

mental /ˈmentl/ a, -ly adv geistig; (fam: mad) verrückt. ~ a**rith-metic** n Kopfrechnen nt. ~ **ill-ness** n Geisteskrankheit f

mentality /menˈtælətɪ/ n Mentalität f

mention /ˈmenʃn/ n Erwähnung f □vt erwähnen; **don't** ~ **it** keine Ursache; bitte

menu /ˈmenjuː/ n Speisekarte f

mercantile /'mɜːkəntaɪl/ a Handels-

mercenary /'mɜːsɪnərɪ/ a geldgierig ◻ n Söldner m

merchandise /'mɜːtʃəndaɪz/ n Ware f

merchant /'mɜːtʃənt/ n Kaufmann m; (dealer) Händler m. ~ **'navy** n Handelsmarine f

merci|ful /'mɜːsɪfl/ a barmherzig. ~**fully** adv (fam) glücklicherweise. ~**less** a, -ly adv erbarmungslos

mercury /'mɜːkjʊrɪ/ n Quecksilber nt

mercy /'mɜːsɪ/ n Barmherzigkeit f, Gnade f; be at s.o.'s ~ jdm ausgeliefert sein

mere /mɪə(r)/ a, -ly adv bloß

merest /'mɪərɪst/ a kleinste(r,s)

merge /mɜːdʒ/ vi zusammenlaufen; (Comm) fusionieren ◻ vt (Comm) zusammenschließen

merger /'mɜːdʒə(r)/ n Fusion f

meridian /mə'rɪdɪən/ n Meridian m

meringue /mə'ræŋ/ n Baiser nt

merit /'merɪt/ n Verdienst nt; (advantage) Vorzug m; (worth) Wert m ◻ vt verdienen

mermaid /'mɜːmeɪd/ n Meerjungfrau f

merri|ly /'merɪlɪ/ adv fröhlich. ~**ment** /-mənt/ n Fröhlichkeit f; (laughter) Gelächter nt

merry /'merɪ/ a (-ier, -iest) fröhlich; ~ **Christmas!** fröhliche Weihnachten!

merry: ~**-go-round** n Karussell nt. ~**-making** n Feiern nt

mesh /meʃ/ n Masche f; (size) Maschenweite f; (fig: network) Netz nt

mesmerize /'mezməraɪz/ vt hypnotisieren. ~**d** a (fig) [wie] gebannt

mess /mes/ n Durcheinander nt; (trouble) Schwierigkeiten pl; (something spilt) Bescherung f (fam); (Mil) Messe f. make a ~ of (botch) verpfuschen ◻ vt ~ up

in Unordnung bringen; (botch) verpfuschen ◻ vi ~ **about** herumalbern; (tinker) herumspielen (with mit)

message /'mesɪdʒ/ n Nachricht f; **give s.o. a** ~ jdm etwas ausrichten

messenger /'mesɪndʒə(r)/ n Bote m

Messiah /mɪ'saɪə/ n Messias m

Messrs /'mesəz/ n pl see Mr; (on letter) ~ Smith Firma Smith

messy /'mesɪ/ a (-ier, -iest) schmutzig; (untidy) unordentlich

met /met/ see meet

metabolism /mɪ'tæbəlɪzm/ n Stoffwechsel m

metal /'metl/ n Metall nt ◻ a Metall-. ~**lic** /mɪ'tælɪk/ a metallisch. ~**lurgy** /mɪ'tælədʒɪ/ n Metallurgie f

metamorphosis /metə'mɔːfəsɪs/ n (pl -phoses /-siːz/) Metamorphose f

metaphor /'metəfə(r)/ n Metapher f. ~**ical** /-'fɒrɪkl/ a, -ly adv metaphorisch

meteor /'miːtɪə(r)/ n Meteor m. ~**ic** /-'ɒrɪk/ a kometenhaft

meteorological /miːtɪərə'lɒdʒɪkl/ a Wetter-

meteorolog|ist /miːtɪə'rɒlədʒɪst/ n Meteorologe m/ -gin f. ~**y** n Meteorologie f

meter[1] /'miːtə(r)/ n Zähler m

meter[2] n (Amer) = metre

method /'meθəd/ n Methode f; (Culin) Zubereitung f

methodical /mɪ'θɒdɪkl/ a, -ly adv systematisch, methodisch

Methodist /'meθədɪst/ n Methodist(in) m(f)

meths /meθs/ n (fam) Brennspiritus m

methylated /'meθɪleɪtɪd/ a ~ **spirit[s]** Brennspiritus m

meticulous /mɪ'tɪkjʊləs/ a, -ly adv sehr genau

metre /'miːtə(r)/ n Meter m & n; (rhythm) Versmaß nt

metric /'metrɪk/ a metrisch

metropolis /mɪˈtrɒpəlɪs/ n Metropole f

metropolitan /metrəˈpɒlɪtən/ a hauptstädtisch; (international) weltstädtisch

mettle /ˈmetl/ n Mut m

mew /mjuː/ n Miau nt □ vi miauen

Mexican /ˈmeksɪkən/ a mexikanisch □n Mexikaner(in) m(f).
'Mexico n Mexiko nt

miaow /mɪaʊ/ n Miau nt □ vi miauen

mice /maɪs/ see mouse

microbe /ˈmaɪkrəʊb/ n Mikrobe f

micro /ˈmaɪkrəʊ/: ~chip n Mikrochip nt. ~computer n Mikrocomputer m. ~film n Mikrofilm m. ~phone n Mikrophon nt. ~processor n Mikroprozessor m. ~scope /-skəʊp/ n Mikroskop nt. ~scopic /-ˈskɒpɪk/ a mikroskopisch. ~wave n Mikrowelle f. ~wave [oven] n Mikrowellenherd m

mid /mɪd/ a ~ May Mitte Mai; in ~ air in der Luft

midday /mɪdˈdeɪ/ n Mittag m

middle /ˈmɪdl/ a mittlere(r, s); the M ~ Ages das Mittelalter; the ~ class[es] der Mittelstand; the M ~ East der Nahe Osten □n Mitte f; in the ~ of the night mitten in der Nacht

middle: ~aged a mittleren Alters. ~class a bürgerlich. ~man n (Comm) Zwischenhändler m

middling /ˈmɪdlɪŋ/ a mittelmäßig

midge /mɪdʒ/ n [kleine] Mücke f

midget /ˈmɪdʒɪt/ n Liliputaner(in) m(f)

Midlands /ˈmɪdləndz/ npl the ~ Mittelengland n

'midnight n Mitternacht f

midriff /ˈmɪdrɪf/ n (fam) Taille f

midst /mɪdst/ n in the ~ of mitten in (+ dat); in our ~ unter uns

mid: ~summer n Hochsommer m; (solstice) Sommersonnenwende f. ~way adv auf halbem Wege. ~wife n Hebamme f.

~wifery /-wɪfrɪ/ n Geburtshilfe f. ~'winter n Mitte f des Winters

might[1] /maɪt/ v aux I — vielleicht; it — be true es könnte wahr sein; I — as well stay am besten bleibe ich hier; he asked if he — go er fragte, ob er gehen dürfte; you — have drowned du hättest ertrinken können

might[2] n Macht f

mighty /ˈmaɪtɪ/ a (-ier, -iest) mächtig

migraine /ˈmiːɡreɪn/ n Migräne f

migrant /ˈmaɪɡrənt/ a Wandern; □n (bird) Zugvogel m

migrate /maɪˈɡreɪt/ vi abwandern; ⟨birds:⟩ ziehen. ~ion /-ˈɡreɪʃn/ n Wanderung f; (of birds) Zug m

mike /maɪk/ n (fam) Mikrophon nt

mild /maɪld/ a (-er, -est) mild

mildew /ˈmɪldjuː/ n Schimmel m; (Bot) Mehltau m

mild|**ly** /ˈmaɪldlɪ/ adv leicht; to put it ~ly gelinde gesagt. ~ness n Milde f

mile /maɪl/ n Meile f (= 1,6 km); ~s too big (fam) viel zu groß

mile|**age** /-ɪdʒ/ n Meilenzahl f; (of car) Meilenstand m. ~stone /-stəʊn/ n Meilenstein m

militant /ˈmɪlɪtənt/ a militant

military /ˈmɪlɪtrɪ/ a militärisch. ~ service n Wehrdienst m

militate /ˈmɪlɪteɪt/ vi ~ against sprechen gegen

militia /mɪˈlɪʃə/ n Miliz f

milk /mɪlk/ n Milch f □ vt melken

milk: ~man n Milchmann m. ~ shake n Milchmixgetränk nt

milky /ˈmɪlkɪ/ a (-ier, -iest) milchig. M~ Way n (Astr) Milchstraße f

mill /mɪl/ n Mühle f; (factory) Fabrik f □ vt/i mahlen; (Techn) fräsen. ~ about, ~ around vi umherlaufen

millenium /mɪˈleniəm/ n Jahrtausend nt

miller /ˈmɪlə(r)/ n Müller m

millet /'mɪlɪt/ n Hirse f

milli|gram /'mɪlɪ-/ n Milligramm nt. **~metre** n Millimeter m & nt

milliner /'mɪlɪnə(r)/ n Modistin f; (man) Hutmacher m. **~y** n Damenhüte pl

million /'mɪljən/ n Million f; a ~ pounds eine Million Pfund. **~aire** /-'neə(r)/ n Millionär(in) m(f)

'millstone n Mühlstein m

mime /maɪm/ n Pantomime f □ vt pantomimisch darstellen

mimic /'mɪmɪk/ n Imitator m □ vt (pt/pp **mimicked**) nachahmen. **~ry** n Nachahmung f

mimosa /mɪ'məʊzə/ n Mimose f

mince /mɪns/ n Hackfleisch nt □ vt (Culin) durchdrehen; **not ~ words** kein Blatt vor den Mund nehmen

mince: **~meat** n Masse f aus Korinthen, Zitronat usw; **make ~meat of** (fig) vernichtend schlagen. **~'pie** n mit 'mince-meat' gefülltes Pastetchen

mincer /'mɪnsə(r)/ n Fleischwolf m

mind /maɪnd/ n Geist m; (sanity) Verstand m; **to my ~** meiner Meinung nach; **give s.o. a piece of one's ~** jdm gehörig die Meinung sagen; **make up one's ~** sich entschließen; **be out of one's ~** nicht bei Verstand sein; **have sth in ~** etw im Sinn haben; **bear sth in ~** an etw (acc) denken; **have a good ~ to** große Lust haben, zu; **I have changed my ~** ich habe es mir anders überlegt □ vt aufpassen auf (+ acc); **I don't ~ the noise** der Lärm stört mich nicht; **~ the step!** Achtung Stufe! □ vi (care) sich kümmern (about um); **I don't ~** mir macht es nichts aus; **never ~!** macht nichts! **do you ~ if?** haben Sie etwas dagegen, wenn? **~ out** vi aufpassen

mind|ful a ~**ful of** eingedenk (+ gen). **~less** a geistlos

mine¹ /maɪn/ poss pron meine(r), meins; **a friend of ~** ein Freund von mir; **that is ~** das gehört mir

mine² n Bergwerk nt; (explosive) Mine f □ vt abbauen; (Mil) verminen. **~ detector** n Minensuchgerät nt. **~field** n Minenfeld nt

miner /'maɪnə(r)/ n Bergarbeiter m

mineral /'mɪnərəl/ n Mineral nt. **~ogy** /-'rælədʒɪ/ n Mineralogie f. **~ water** n Mineralwasser nt

minesweeper /'maɪn-/ n Minenräumboot nt

mingle /'mɪŋgl/ vi ~ **with** sich mischen unter (+ acc)

miniature /'mɪnɪtʃə(r)/ a Klein- □ n Miniatur f

mini|bus /'mɪnɪ-/ n Kleinbus m. **~cab** n Taxi nt

minim /'mɪnɪm/ n (Mus) halbe Note f

minim|al /'mɪnɪməl/ a minimal. **~ize** vt auf ein Minimum reduzieren. **~um** n (pl **-ima**) Minimum nt □ a Mindest-

mining /'maɪnɪŋ/ n Bergbau m

miniskirt /'mɪnɪ-/ n Minirock m

minister /'mɪnɪstə(r)/ n Minister m; (Relig) Pastor m. **~erial** /-'stɪərɪəl/ a ministeriell

ministry /'mɪnɪstrɪ/ n (Pol) Ministerium nt; **the ~** (Relig) das geistliche Amt

mink /mɪŋk/ n Nerz m

minor /'maɪnə(r)/ a kleiner; (less important) unbedeutend □ n Minderjährige(r) m/f; (Mus) Moll nt

minority /maɪ'nɒrətɪ/ n Minderheit f; (age) Minderjährigkeit f

minor road n Nebenstraße f

mint¹ /mɪnt/ n Münzstätte f □ a ⟨stamp⟩ postfrisch; **in ~ condition** wie neu □ vt prägen

mint² n (herb) Minze f; (sweet) Pfefferminzbonbon m & nt

minuet /mɪnjʊ'et/ n Menuett nt

minus /'maɪnəs/ prep minus, weniger; (fam: without) ohne □ n ~ [**sign**] Minuszeichen nt

minute¹ /'mɪnɪt/ n Minute f; in a ~ (shortly) gleich; ~ s pl (of meeting) Protokoll nt

minute² /maɪ'njuːt/ a winzig; (precise) genau

mirac|le /'mɪrəkl/ n Wunder nt. ~ulous /-'rækjʊləs/ a wunderbar

mirage /'mɪrɑːʒ/ n Fata Morgana f

mire /'maɪə(r)/ n Morast m

mirror /'mɪrə(r)/ n Spiegel m □vt widerspiegeln

mirth /mɜːθ/ n Heiterkeit f

misad'venture /mɪs-/ n Mißgeschick nt

misanthropist /mɪ'zænθrəpɪst/ n Menschenfeind m

misappre'hension n Mißverständnis nt; be under a ~ sich irren

misbe'hav|e vi sich schlecht benehmen. ~iour n schlechtes Benehmen nt

mis'calcul|ate vt falsch berechnen □vi sich verrechnen. ~lation n Fehlkalkulation f

'miscarriage n Fehlgeburt f; ~ of justice Justizirrtum m. mis'carry vi eine Fehlgeburt haben

miscellaneous /mɪsə'leɪnɪəs/ a vermischt

mischief /'mɪstʃɪf/ n Unfug m; (harm) Schaden m

mischievous /'mɪstʃɪvəs/ a, -ly adv schelmisch; (malicious) boshaft

miscon'ception n falsche Vorstellung f

mis'conduct n unkorrektes Verhalten nt; (adultery) Ehebruch m

miscon'strue vt mißdeuten

mis'deed n Missetat f

misde'meanour n Missetat f

miser /'maɪzə(r)/ n Geizhals m

miserable /'mɪzrəbl/ a, -bly adv unglücklich; (wretched) elend

miserly /'maɪzəlɪ/ adv geizig

misery /'mɪzərɪ/ n Elend nt; (fam: person) Miesepeter m

mis'fire vi fehlzünden; (go wrong) fehlschlagen

'misfit n Außenseiter(in) m(f)

mis'fortune n Unglück nt

mis'givings npl Bedenken pl

mis'guided a töricht

mishap /'mɪshæp/ n Mißgeschick nt

misin'form vt falsch unterrichten

misin'terpret vt mißdeuten

mis'judge vt falsch beurteilen; (estimate wrongly) falsch einschätzen

mis'lay vt (pt/pp -laid) verlegen

mis'lead vt (pt/pp -led) irreführen. ~ing a irreführend

mis'manage vt schlecht verwalten. ~ment n Mißwirtschaft f

misnomer /mɪs'nəʊmə(r)/ n Fehlbezeichnung f

'misprint n Druckfehler m

mis'quote vt falsch zitieren

misrepre'sent vt falsch darstellen

miss /mɪs/ n Fehltreffer m □vt verpassen; (fail to hit or find) verfehlen; (fail to attend) versäumen; (fail to notice) übersehen; (feel the loss of) vermissen □vi (fail to hit) nicht treffen. ~ out vt auslassen

Miss n (pl -es) Fräulein nt

misshapen /mɪs'ʃeɪpən/ a mißgestaltet

missile /'mɪsaɪl/ n [Wurf]geschoß nt; (Mil) Rakete f

missing /'mɪsɪŋ/ a fehlend; (lost) verschwunden; (Mil) vermißt; be ~ fehlen

mission /'mɪʃn/ n Auftrag m; (Mil) Einsatz m; (Relig) Mission f

missionary /'mɪʃənrɪ/ n Missionar(in) m(f)

mis'spell vt (pt/pp -spelt or -spelled) falsch schreiben

mist /mɪst/ n Dunst m; (fog) Nebel m; (on window) Beschlag m □vi ~ up beschlagen

mistake /mɪ'steɪk/ n Fehler m; by ~ aus Versehen □vt (pt mistook, pp mistaken) mißverstehen; ~ for verwechseln mit

mistaken /mɪˈsteɪkən/ *a* falsch; be ~ sich irren; ~ **identity** Verwechslung *f*. ~**ly** *adv* irrtümlicherweise

mistletoe /ˈmɪsltəʊ/ *n* Mistel *f*

mistress /ˈmɪstrɪs/ *n* Herrin *f*; (*teacher*) Lehrerin *f*; (*lover*) Geliebte *f*

mis'trust *n* Mißtrauen □ *vt* mißtrauen (+ *dat*)

misty /ˈmɪstɪ/ *a* (-ier, -iest) dunstig; (*foggy*) neblig; (*fig*) unklar

misunder'stand *vt* (*pt/pp*-stood) mißverstehen. ~**ing** *n* Mißverständnis *nt*

misuse¹ /mɪsˈjuːz/ *vt* mißbrauchen

misuse² /mɪsˈjuːs/ *n* Mißbrauch *m*

mite /maɪt/ *n* (*Zool*) Milbe *f*; **little** ~ (*child*) kleines Ding *nt*

mitigat|e /ˈmɪtɪgeɪt/ *vt* mildern. ~**ing** *a* mildernd

mitten /ˈmɪtn/ *n* Fausthandschuh *m*

mix /mɪks/ *n* Mischung *f* □ *vt* mischen □ *vi* sich mischen; ~ **with** (*associate with*) verkehren mit. ~ **up** *vt* mischen; (*muddle*) durcheinanderbringen; (*mistake for*) verwechseln (**with** mit)

mixed /mɪkst/ *a* gemischt; be ~ **up** durcheinander sein

mixer /ˈmɪksə(r)/ *n* Mischmaschine *f*; (*Culin*) Küchenmaschine *f*

mixture /ˈmɪkstʃə(r)/ *n* Mischung *f*; (*medicine*) Mixtur *f*; (*Culin*) Teig *m*

'mix-up *n* Durcheinander *nt*; (*confusion*) Verwirrung *f*; (*mistake*) Verwechslung *f*

moan /məʊn/ *n* Stöhnen *nt* □ *vi* stöhnen; (*complain*) jammern

moat /məʊt/ *n* Burggraben *m*

mob /mɒb/ *n* Horde *f*; (*rabble*) Pöbel *m*; (*fam: gang*) Bande *f* □ *vt* (*pt/pp* mobbed) herfallen über (+ *acc*); belagern (*celebrity*)

mobile /ˈməʊbaɪl/ *a* beweglich □ *n* Mobile *nt*. ~ **'home** *n* Wohnwagen *m*

mobility /məˈbɪlətɪ/ *n* Beweglichkeit *f*

mobiliz|ation /məʊbɪlaɪˈzeɪʃn/ *n* Mobilisierung *f*. ~**ize** /ˈməʊbɪlaɪz/ *vt* mobilisieren

mocha /ˈmɒkə/ *n* Mokka *m*

mock /mɒk/ *a* Schein- □ *vt* verspotten □ *vi* spotten. ~**ery** *n* Spott *m*

'mock-up *n* Modell *nt*

modal /ˈməʊdl/ *a* ~ **auxiliary** Modalverb *nt*

mode /məʊd/ *n* [Art und] Weise *f*; (*fashion*) Mode *f*

model /ˈmɒdl/ *n* Modell *nt*; (*example*) Vorbild *nt*; [**fashion**] ~ Mannequin *nt* □ *a* Modell-; (*exemplary*) Muster- □ *v* (*pt/pp* modelled) □ *vt* formen, modellieren; vorführen (*clothes*) □ *vi* Mannequin sein; (*for artist*) Modell stehen

moderate¹ /ˈmɒdəreɪt/ *vt* mäßigen □ *vi* sich mäßigen

moderate² /ˈmɒdərət/ *a* mäßig; (*opinion*) gemäßigt □ *n* (*Pol*) Gemäßigte(r) *m/f*. ~**ly** *adv* mäßig; (*fairly*) einigermaßen

moderation /mɒdəˈreɪʃn/ *n* Mäßigung *f*; **in** ~ mit Maß[en]

modern /ˈmɒdn/ *a* modern. ~**ize** *vt* modernisieren. ~ **languages** *npl* neuere Sprachen *pl*

modest /ˈmɒdɪst/ *a* bescheiden; (*decorous*) schamhaft. ~**y** *n* Bescheidenheit *f*

modicum /ˈmɒdɪkəm/ *n* a ~ **of** ein bißchen

modif|ication /mɒdɪfɪˈkeɪʃn/ *n* Abänderung *f*. ~**y** /ˈmɒdɪfaɪ/ *vt* (*pt/pp* -fied) abändern

modulate /ˈmɒdjʊleɪt/ *vt/i* modulieren

moist /mɔɪst/ *a* (-er, -est) feucht

moisten /ˈmɔɪsn/ *vt* befeuchten

moistur|e /ˈmɔɪstʃə(r)/ *n* Feuchtigkeit *f*. ~**izer** *n* Feuchtigkeitscreme *f*

molar /ˈməʊlə(r)/ *n* Backenzahn *m*

molasses /məˈlæsɪz/ *n* (*Amer*) Sirup *m*

mole¹ /məʊl/ *n* Leberfleck *m*

mole² n (Zool) Maulwurf m

mole³ n (breakwater) Mole f

molecule /'mɒlɪkjuːl/ n Molekül nt

'molehill n Maulwurfshaufen m

molest /mə'lest/ vt belästigen

mollify /'mɒlɪfaɪ/ vt (pt/pp -ied) besänftigen

mollusc /'mɒləsk/ n Weichtier nt

mollycoddle /'mɒlɪkɒdl/ vt verzärteln

molten /'məʊltən/ a geschmolzen

mom /mɒm/ n (Amer fam) Mutti f

moment /'məʊmənt/ n Moment m, Augenblick m; **at the ~** im Augenblick, augenblicklich. **~ary** a vorübergehend

momentous /mə'mentəs/ a bedeutsam

momentum /mə'mentəm/ n Schwung m

monarch /'mɒnək/ n Monarch(in) m(f). **~y** n Monarchie f

monast|ery /'mɒnəstrɪ/ n Kloster nt. **~ic** /mə'næstɪk/ a Kloster-

Monday /'mʌndeɪ/ n Montag m

money /'mʌnɪ/ n Geld nt

money: ~-box n Sparbüchse f. **~-lender** n Geldverleiher m. **~ order** n Zahlungsanweisung f

mongrel /'mʌŋgrəl/ n Promenadenmischung f

monitor /'mɒnɪtə(r)/ n (Techn) Monitor m ⃝ vt überwachen ⟨progress⟩; abhören ⟨broadcast⟩

monk /mʌŋk/ n Mönch m

monkey /'mʌŋkɪ/ n Affe m. **~-nut** n Erdnuß f. **~-wrench** n (Techn) Engländer m

mono /'mɒnəʊ/ n Mono nt

monocle /'mɒnəkl/ n Monokel nt

monogram /'mɒnəgræm/ n Monogramm nt

monologue /'mɒnəlɒg/ n Monolog m

monopol|ize /mə'nɒpəlaɪz/ vt monopolisieren. **~y** n Monopol nt

monosyll|abic /mɒnəsɪ'læbɪk/ a einsilbig. **~able** /'mɒnəsɪləbl/ n einsilbiges Wort nt

monotone /'mɒnətəʊn/ n **in a ~** mit monotoner Stimme

monoton|ous /mə'nɒtənəs/ a, **-ly** adv eintönig, monoton; ⟨tedious⟩ langweilig. **~y** n Eintönigkeit f, Monotonie f

monsoon /mɒn'suːn/ n Monsun m

monster /'mɒnstə(r)/ n Ungeheuer nt; ⟨cruel person⟩ Unmensch m

monstrosity /mɒn'strɒsətɪ/ n Monstrosität f

monstrous /'mɒnstrəs/ a ungeheuer; ⟨outrageous⟩ ungeheuerlich

montage /mɒn'tɑːʒ/ n Montage f

month /mʌnθ/ n Monat m. **~ly** a & adv monatlich ⃝ n (periodical) Monatszeitschrift f

monument /'mɒnjʊmənt/ n Denkmal nt. **~al** /-'mentl/ a ⟨fig⟩ monumental

moo /muː/ n Muh nt ⃝ vi (pt/pp mooed) muhen

mooch /muːtʃ/ vi **~ about** ⟨fam⟩ herumschleichen

mood /muːd/ n Laune f; **be in a good/bad ~** gute/schlechte Laune haben

moody /'muːdɪ/ a (-ier, -iest) launisch

moon /muːn/ n Mond m; **over the ~** ⟨fam⟩ überglücklich

moon: ~light n Mondschein m. **~lighting** n ⟨fam⟩ ≈ Schwarzarbeit f. **~lit** a mondhell

moor¹ /mʊə(r)/ n Moor nt

moor² vt (Naut) festmachen ⃝ vi anlegen. **~ings** npl ⟨chains⟩ Verankerung f; ⟨place⟩ Anlegestelle f

moose /muːs/ n Elch m

moot /muːt/ a **it's a ~ point** darüber läßt sich streiten ⃝ vt aufwerfen ⟨question⟩

mop /mɒp/ n Mop m; **~ of hair** Wuschelkopf m ⃝ vt (pt/pp mopped) wischen. **~ up** vt aufwischen

mope /məʊp/ vi Trübsal blasen

moped /'məʊped/ n Moped nt

moral /'mɒrəl/ a, -ly adv moralisch, sittlich; (virtuous) tugendhaft □n Moral f; ~s pl Moral f

morale /mə'rɑːl/ n Moral f

morality /mə'ræləti/ n Sittlichkeit f

moralize /'mɒrəlaɪz/ vi moralisieren

morbid /'mɔːbɪd/ a krankhaft; (gloomy) trübe

more /mɔː(r)/ a, adv & n mehr; (in addition) noch; a few ~ noch ein paar; any ~ noch etwas; once ~ noch einmal; ~ or less mehr oder weniger; some ~ tea? noch etwas Tee? ~ interesting interessanter; ~ [and ~] quickly [immer] schneller; the ~ ... the ~ je mehr ... desto; ~ and ~ quickly immer schneller; no ~, thank you, nichts mehr danke; no ~ bread kein Brot mehr; no ~ apples keine Äpfel mehr

moreover /mɔːˈrəʊvə(r)/ adv außerdem

morgue /mɔːg/ n Leichenschauhaus nt

moribund /'mɒrɪbʌnd/ a sterbend

morning /'mɔːnɪŋ/ n Morgen m; in the ~ morgens, am Morgen; (tomorrow) morgen früh

Morocco /mə'rɒkəʊ/ n Marokko nt

moron /'mɔːrɒn/ n (fam) Idiot m

morose /mə'rəʊs/ a, -ly adv mürrisch

morphine /'mɔːfiːn/ n Morphium nt

Morse /mɔːs/ n ~ [code] Morsealphabet nt

morsel /'mɔːsl/ n (food) Happen m

mortal /'mɔːtl/ a sterblich; (fatal) tödlich □n Sterbliche(r) m/f. ~ity /-'tæləti/ n Sterblichkeit f. ~ly adv tödlich

mortar /'mɔːtə(r)/ n Mörtel m

mortgage /'mɔːgɪdʒ/ n Hypothek f □vt hypothekarisch belasten

mortify /'mɔːtɪfaɪ/ vt (pt/pp -ied) demütigen

mortuary /'mɔːtjʊərɪ/ n Leichenhalle f; (public) Leichenschauhaus nt; (Amer: undertaker's) Bestattungsinstitut nt

mosaic /məʊ'zeɪɪk/ n Mosaik nt

Moscow /'mɒskəʊ/ n Moskau nt

Moselle /məʊ'zel/ n Mosel f; (wine) Moselwein m

mosque /mɒsk/ n Moschee f

mosquito /mɒs'kiːtəʊ/ n (pl -es) [Stech]mücke f, Schnake f; (tropical) Moskito m

moss /mɒs/ n Moos nt. ~y a moosig

most /məʊst/ a der/die/das meiste; (majority) die meisten; for the ~ part zum größten Teil □adv am meisten; (very) höchst; the ~ interesting day der interessanteste Tag; ~ unlikely höchst unwahrscheinlich □n das meiste; ~ of them die meisten [von ihnen]; at [the] ~ höchstens; ~ of the time die meiste Zeit. ~ly adv meist

MOT n ≈ TÜV m

motel /məʊ'tel/ n Motel nt

moth /mɒθ/ n Nachtfalter m; [clothes-] ~ Motte f

moth: ~ball n Mottenkugel f. ~-eaten a mottenzerfressen

mother /'mʌðə(r)/ n Mutter f; M~'s Day Muttertag m □vt bemuttern

mother: ~hood n Mutterschaft f. ~-in-law n (pl ~s-in-law) Schwiegermutter f. ~land n Mutterland nt. ~ly a mütterlich. ~-of-pearl n Perlmutter f. ~-to-be n werdende Mutter f. ~ tongue n Muttersprache f

mothproof /'mɒθ-/ a mottenfest

motif /məʊ'tiːf/ n Motiv nt

motion /'məʊʃn/ n Bewegung f; (proposal) Antrag m □vt/i ~ [to] s.o. jdm ein Zeichen geben (to zu). ~less a, -ly adv bewegungslos

motivate /'məʊtɪveɪt/ vt motivieren. ~ion /-'veɪʃn/ n Motivation f

motive /'məʊtɪv/ n Motiv nt

motley /'mɒtlɪ/ a bunt

motor /'məʊtə(r)/ n Motor m; (car) Auto nt □ a Motor-; (Anat) motorisch □ vi [mit dem Auto] fahren

Motorail /'məʊtəreɪl/ n Autozug m

motor: ~ **bike** n (fam) Motorrad nt. ~ **boat** n Motorboot nt. ~**cade** /-keɪd/ n (Amer) Autokolonne f. ~ **car** n Auto nt, Wagen m. ~ **cycle** n Motorrad nt. ~**cyclist** n Motorradfahrer m. ~**ing** n Autofahren nt. ~**ist** n Autofahrer(in) m(f.) ~**ize** vt motorisieren. ~ **vehicle** n Kraftfahrzeug nt. ~**way** n Autobahn f

mottled /'mɒtld/ a gesprenkelt

motto /'mɒtəʊ/ n (pl -es) Motto nt

mould¹ /məʊld/ n (fungus) Schimmel m

mould² n Form f □ vt formen (**into** zu). ~**ing** n (Archit) Fries m

mouldy /'məʊldɪ/ a schimmelig; (fam: worthless) schäbig

moult /məʊlt/ vi (bird:) sich mausern; (animal:) sich haaren

mound /maʊnd/ n Hügel m; (of stones) Haufen m

mount¹ /maʊnt/ n Berg m

mount² n (animal) Reittier nt; (of jewel) Fassung f; (of photo, picture) Passepartout nt □ vt (get on) steigen auf (+ acc); (on pedestal) montieren auf (+ acc); besteigen (horse); fassen (jewel); aufziehen (photo, picture) □ vi aufsteigen; (tension:) steigen. ~ **up** vi sich häufen; (add up) sich anhäufen

mountain /'maʊntɪn/ n Berg m

mountaineer /maʊntɪ'nɪə(r)/ n Bergsteiger(in) m(f). ~**ing** n Bergsteigen nt

mountainous /'maʊntɪnəs/ a bergig, gebirgig

mourn /mɔːn/ vt betrauern □ vi trauern (**for** um). ~**er** n Trauernde(r) m/f. ~**ful** a, -**ly** adv trauervoll. ~**ing** n Trauer f

mouse /maʊs/ n (pl mice) Maus f. ~**trap** n Mausefalle f

mousse /muːs/ n Schaum m; (Culin) Mousse f

moustache /mə'stɑːʃ/ n Schnurrbart m

mousy /'maʊsɪ/ a graubraun; (person) farblos

mouth¹ /maʊð/ vt ~ **sth** etw lautlos mit den Lippen sagen

mouth² /maʊθ/ n Mund m; (of animal) Maul nt; (of river) Mündung f

mouth: ~**ful** n Mundvoll m; (bite) Bissen m. ~**organ** n Mundharmonika f. ~**piece** n Mundstück nt; (fig: person) Sprachrohr n. ~**wash** n Mundwasser nt

movable /'muːvəbl/ a beweglich

move /muːv/ n Bewegung f; (fig) Schritt m; (moving house) Umzug m; (in board-game) Zug m; **on the** ~ unterwegs; **get a** ~ **on** (fam) sich beeilen □ vt bewegen; (emotionally) rühren; (move along) rücken; (in board-game) ziehen; (take away) wegnehmen; wegfahren (car); (rearrange) umstellen; (transfer) versetzen (person); verlegen (office); (propose) beantragen; ~ **house** umziehen □ vi sich bewegen; (move house) umziehen; **don't** ~! stillhalten! (stop) stillstehen! ~ **along** vt/i weiterrücken. ~ **away** vt/i wegrücken; (move house) wegziehen. ~ **forward** vt/i vorrücken; (vehicle:) vorwärts fahren. ~ **in** vi einziehen. ~ **off** vi (vehicle:) losfahren. ~ **out** vi ausziehen. ~ **over** vt/i [zur Seite] rücken. ~ **up** vi aufrücken

movement /'muːvmənt/ n Bewegung f; (Mus) Satz m; (of clock) Uhrwerk nt

movie /'muːvɪ/ n (Amer) Film m; **go to the** ~**s** ins Kino gehen

moving /'muːvɪŋ/ a beweglich; (touching) rührend

mow /məʊ/ vt (pt **mowed**, pp **mown** or **mowed**) mähen. ~ **down** vt (destroy) niedermähen

mower /'məʊə(r)/ n Rasenmäher m

MP abbr see **Member of Parliament**

Mr /'mɪstə(r)/ *n* (*pl* **Messrs**) Herr *m*

Mrs /'mɪsɪz/ *n* Frau *f*

Ms /mɪz/ *n* Frau *f*

much /mʌtʃ/ *a, adv & n* viel; **as ~ as** soviel wie; **very ~ loved/ interested** sehr geliebt/ interessiert

muck /mʌk/ *n* Mist *m*; (*fam: filth*) Dreck *m*. **~ about** *vi* herumalbern; (*tinker*) herumspielen (**with** mit). **~ in** *vi* (*fam*) mitmachen. **~ out** *vt* ausmisten. **~ up** *vt* (*fam*) vermasseln; (*make dirty*) schmutzig machen

mucky /'mʌkɪ/ *a* (**-ier, -iest**) dreckig

mucus /'mjuːkəs/ *n* Schleim *m*

mud /mʌd/ *n* Schlamm *m*

muddle /'mʌdl/ *n* Durcheinander *nt*; (*confusion*) Verwirrung *f* □ *vt* **~ [up]** durcheinanderbringen

muddy /'mʌdɪ/ *a* (**-ier, -iest**) schlammig; (*shoes*) schmutzig

mudguard *n* Kotflügel *m*; (*on bicycle*) Schutzblech *nt*

muesli /'muːzlɪ/ *n* Müsli *nt*

muff /mʌf/ *n* Muff *m*

muffle /'mʌfl/ *vt* dämpfen ⟨*sound*⟩; **~ [up]** (*for warmth*) einhüllen (**in** in + *acc*)

muffler /'mʌflə(r)/ *n* Schal *m*; (*Amer, Auto*) Auspufftopf *m*

mufti /'mʌftɪ/ *n* **in ~** in Zivil

mug[1] /mʌg/ *n* Becher *m*; (*for beer*) Bierkrug *m*; (*fam: face*) Visage *f*; (*fam: simpleton*) Trottel *m*

mug[2] *vt* (*pt/pp* **mugged**) überfallen. **~ger** *n* Straßenräuber *m*. **~ging** *n* Straßenraub *m*

muggy /'mʌgɪ/ *a* (**-ier, -iest**) schwül

mule[1] /mjuːl/ *n* Maultier *nt*

mule[2] *n* (*slipper*) Pantoffel *m*

mull /mʌl/ *vt* **~ over** nachdenken über (+ *acc*)

mulled /mʌld/ *a* **~ wine** Glühwein *m*

multi /'mʌltɪ/: **~-coloured** *a* vielfarbig, bunt. **~lingual** /-'lɪŋgwəl/

a mehrsprachig. **~'national** *a* multinational

multiple /'mʌltɪpl/ *a* vielfach; (*with pl*) mehrere □ *n* Vielfache(s) *nt*

multiplication /mʌltɪplɪ'keɪʃn/ *n* Multiplikation *f*

multiply /'mʌltɪplaɪ/ *v* (*pt/pp* **-ied**) □ *vt* multiplizieren (**by** mit) □ *vi* sich vermehren

multistorey *a* **~ car park** Parkhaus *nt*

mum[1] /mʌm/ *a* **keep ~** (*fam*) den Mund halten

mum[2] *n* (*fam*) Mutti *f*

mumble /'mʌmbl/ *vt/i* murmeln

mummy[1] *n* (*fam*) Mutti *f*

mummy[2] /'mʌmɪ/ *n* (*Archaeol*) Mumie *f*

mumps /mʌmps/ *n* Mumps *m*

munch /mʌntʃ/ *vt/i* mampfen

mundane /mʌn'deɪn/ *a* banal; (*worldly*) weltlich

municipal /mjuː'nɪsɪpl/ *a* städtisch

munitions /mjuː'nɪʃnz/ *npl* Kriegsmaterial *nt*

mural /'mjʊərəl/ *n* Wandgemälde *nt*

murder /'mɜːdə(r)/ *n* Mord *m* □ *vt* ermorden; (*fam: ruin*) verhunzen. **~er** *n* Mörder *m*. **~ess** *n* Mörderin *f*. **~ous** /-rəs/ *a* mörderisch

murky /'mɜːkɪ/ *a* (**-ier, -iest**) düster

murmur /'mɜːmə(r)/ *n* Murmeln *nt* □ *vt/i* murmeln

muscle /'mʌsl/ *n* Muskel *m*

muscular /'mʌskjʊlə(r)/ *a* Muskel-; (*strong*) muskulös

muse /mjuːz/ *vi* nachsinnen (**on** über + *acc*)

museum /mjuː'zɪəm/ *n* Museum *nt*

mush /mʌʃ/ *n* Brei *m*

mushroom /'mʌʃrʊm/ *n* [eßbarer] Pilz *m*, *esp* Champignon *m* □ *vi* (*fig*) wie Pilze aus dem Boden schießen

mushy /'mʌʃɪ/ *a* breiig

music /'mju:zɪk/ n Musik f; (written) Noten pl; set to ~ vertonen

musical /'mju:zɪkl/ a musikalisch □n Musical nt. ~ **box** n Spieldose f. ~ **instrument** n Musikinstrument nt

'music-hall n Varieté nt

musician /mju:'zɪʃn/ n Musiker(in) m(f)

'music-stand n Notenständer m

Muslim /'muzlɪm/ a mohammedanisch □n Mohammedaner(in) m(f)

muslin /'mʌzlɪn/ n Musselin m

mussel /'mʌsl/ n [Mies]muschel f

must /mʌst/ v aux (nur Präsens) müssen; (with negative) dürfen □n a ~ (fam) ein Muß nt

mustard /'mʌstəd/ n Senf m

muster /'mʌstə(r)/ vt versammeln; aufbringen ⟨strength⟩ □vi sich versammeln

musty /'mʌstɪ/ a (-ier, -iest) muffig

mutation /mju:'teɪʃn/ n Veränderung f; (Biol) Mutation f

mute /mju:t/ a stumm

muted /'mju:tɪd/ a gedämpft

mutilat|e /'mju:tɪleɪt/ vt verstümmeln. ~**ion** /-'leɪʃn/ n Verstümmelung f

mutin|ous /'mju:tɪnəs/ a meuterisch. ~**y** n Meuterei f □vi (pt/pp -ied) meutern

mutter /'mʌtə(r)/ n Murmeln n □vt/i murmeln

mutton /'mʌtn/ n Hammelfleisch nt

mutual /'mju:tjʊəl/ a gegenseitig; (fam: common) gemeinsam. ~**ly** adv gegenseitig

muzzle /'mʌzl/ n (of animal) Schnauze f; (of firearm) Mündung f; (for dog) Maulkorb m □vt einen Maulkorb anlegen (+ dat)

my /maɪ/ a mein

myopic /maɪ'ɒpɪk/ a kurzsichtig

myself /maɪ'self/ pron selbst; (refl) mich; **by** ~ allein; I

thought to ~ ich habe mir gedacht

mysterious /mɪ'stɪərɪəs/ a, -**ly** adv geheimnisvoll; (puzzling) mysteriös, rätselhaft

mystery /'mɪstərɪ/ n Geheimnis nt; (puzzle) Rätsel nt; ~ **[story]** Krimi m

mystic[al] /'mɪstɪk[l]/ a mystisch. ~**cism** /-sɪzm/ n Mystik f

mystification /mɪstɪfɪ'keɪʃn/ n Verwunderung f

mystified /'mɪstɪfaɪd/ a be ~ vor einem Rätsel stehen

mystique /mɪ'sti:k/ n geheimnisvoller Zauber m

myth /mɪθ/ n Mythos m; (fam: untruth) Märchen nt. ~**ical** a mythisch; (fig) erfunden

mythology /mɪ'θɒlədʒɪ/ n Mythologie f

N

nab /næb/ vt (pt/pp nabbed) (fam) erwischen

nag[1] /næg/ n (horse) Gaul m

nag[2] /næg/ vt/i (pt/pp nagged) herumnörgeln (s.o. an jdm). ~**ging** a ⟨pain⟩ nagend □n Nörgelei f

nail /neɪl/ n (Anat, Techn) Nagel m; on the ~ (fam) sofort □vt nageln (to an + acc). ~ **down** vt festnageln; (close) zunageln

nail: ~**brush** n Nagelbürste f. ~**file** n Nagelfeile f. ~ **polish** n Nagellack m. ~ **scissors** npl Nagelschere f. ~ **varnish** n Nagellack m

naïve /naɪ'i:v/ a, -**ly** adv naiv. ~**ety** /-ətɪ/ n Naivität f

naked /'neɪkɪd/ a nackt; ⟨flame⟩ offen; **with the** ~ **eye** mit bloßem Auge. ~**ness** n Nacktheit f

name /neɪm/ n Name m; (reputation) Ruf m; by ~ dem Namen nach; by the ~ of namens; call s.o. ~**s** (fam) jdn beschimpfen □vt nennen; (give a name to) einen Namen geben (+ *dat*); *(announce publicly)* den Namen bekanntgeben von. **~less** *a* namenlos. **~ly** *adv* nämlich.

name: **~plate** *n* Namensschild *nt*. **~sake** *n* Namensvetter *m/* Namensschwester *f*

nanny /'nænɪ/ *n* Kindermädchen *nt*. **~-goat** *n* Ziege *f*

nap /næp/ *n* Nickerchen *nt*; **have a ~** ein Nickerchen machen □ *vi* catch s.o. **~ping** jdn überrumpeln

nape /neɪp/ *n* **[of the neck]** Nacken *m*

napkin /'næpkɪn/ *n* Serviette *f*; *(for baby)* Windel *f*

nappy /'næpɪ/ *n* Windel *f*

narcotic /nɑː'kɒtɪk/ *a* betäubend □ *n* Narkotikum *nt*; *(drug)* Rauschgift *nt*

narrat|e /nə'reɪt/ *vt* erzählen. **~ion** -ɪʃn/ *n* Erzählung *f*

narrative /'nærətɪv/ *a* erzählend □ *n* Erzählung *f*

narrator /nə'reɪtə(r)/ *n* Erzähler(in) *m(f)*

narrow /'nærəʊ/ *a* (-er, -est) schmal; *(restricted)* eng; *(margin, majority)* knapp; *(fig)* beschränkt; **have a ~ escape**, eine Notlage; **~ly escape** mit knapper Not davonkommen □ *vi* sich verengen. **~-'minded** *a* engstirnig

nasal /'neɪzl/ *a* nasal; *(Med & Anat)* Nasen-

nastily /'nɑːstɪlɪ/ *adv* boshaft

nasturtium /nə'stɜːʃəm/ *n* Kapuzinerkresse *f*

nasty /'nɑːstɪ/ *a* (-ier, -iest) übel; *(unpleasant)* unangenehm; *(unkind)* boshaft; *(serious)* schlimm; **turn ~** gemein werden

nation /neɪʃn/ *n* Nation *f*; *(people)* Volk *nt*

national /'næʃənl/ *a* national; *(newspaper)* überregional; *(campaign)* landesweit □ *n* Staatsbürger(in) *m(f)*

national: **~ 'anthem** *n* Nationalhymne *f*. **N~ 'Health Service** *n*

staatlicher Gesundheitsdienst *m*. **N~ In'surance** *n* Sozialversicherung *f*

nationalism /'næʃənəlɪzm/ *n* Nationalismus *m*

nationality /næʃə'nælətɪ/ *n* Staatsangehörigkeit *f*

national|ization /næʃənəlaɪ'zeɪʃn/ *n* Verstaatlichung *f*. **~ize** /'næʃənəlaɪz/ *vt* verstaatlichen. **~ly** /'næʃənəlɪ/ *adv* landesweit

'nation-wide *a* landesweit

native /'neɪtɪv/ *a* einheimisch; *(innate)* angeboren □ *n* Eingeborene(r) *m/f*; *(local inhabitant)* Einheimische(r) *m/f*; **a ~ of Vienna** ein gebürtiger Wiener

native: **~ 'land** *n* Heimatland *nt*. **~ 'language** *n* Muttersprache *f*

Nativity /nə'tɪvətɪ/ *n* **the ~** Christi Geburt *f*. **~ play** *n* Krippenspiel *nt*

natter /'nætə(r)/ *n* **have a ~** *(fam)* einen Schwatz halten □ *vi* *(fam)* schwatzen

natural /'nætʃrəl/ *a*, **-ly** *adv* natürlich; **~-[coloured]** naturfarben

natural: **~ 'gas** *n* Erdgas *nt*. **~ 'history** *n* Naturkunde *f*

naturalist /'nætʃrəlɪst/ *n* Naturforscher *m*

natural|ization /nætʃrəlaɪ'zeɪʃn/ *n* Einbürgerung *f*. **~ize** /'nætʃrəlaɪz/ *vt* einbürgern

nature /'neɪtʃə(r)/ *n* Natur *f*; *(kind)* Art *f*; **by ~** von Natur aus. **~ reserve** *n* Naturschutzgebiet *nt*

naturism /'neɪtʃərɪzm/ *n* Freikörperkultur *f*

naught /nɔːt/ *n* = **nought**

naughty /'nɔːtɪ/ *a* (-ier, -iest), **-ily** *adv* unartig; *(slightly indecent)* gewagt

nausea /'nɔːzɪə/ *n* Übelkeit *f*

nause|ate /'nɔːzɪeɪt/ *vt* anekeln. **~ating** *a* ekelhaft. **~ous** /-ɪəs/ *a* **I feel ~ous** mir ist übel

nautical /'nɔːtɪkl/ *a* nautisch. **~ mile** *n* Seemeile *f*

naval /'neɪvl/ *a* Marine-

nave /neɪv/ *n* Kirchenschiff *nt*

navel /'neɪvl/ n Nabel m

navigable /'nævɪgəbl/ a schiffbar

navigat|e /'nævɪgeɪt/ vi navigieren □vt befahren *<river>*. **~ion** /-'geɪʃn/ n Navigation f. **~or** n Navigator m

navvy /'nævɪ/ n Straßenarbeiter m

navy /'neɪvɪ/ n [Kriegs]marine f □a ~ **[blue]** marineblau

near /nɪə(r)/ a (-er, -est) nah[e]; **the ~est bank** die nächste Bank □adv nahe; **~ by** weit weg; **~ at hand** in der Nähe; **draw ~** sich nähern □prep nahe an (+ dat/acc); in der Nähe von; **~ to tears** den Tränen nahe; **go ~ [to] sth** nahe an etw (acc) herangehen □vt sich nähern (+ dat)

near: **~by** a nahegelegen. **~ly** adv fast, beinahe; **not ~ly** bei weitem nicht. **~ness** n Nähe f. **~ side** n Beifahrerseite f. **~-sighted** a (Amer) kurzsichtig

neat /niːt/ a (-er, -est), **-ly** adv adrett; (tidy) ordentlich; (clever) geschickt; (undiluted) pur. **~ness** n Ordentlichkeit f

necessarily /'nesəserəlɪ/ adv notwendigerweise; **not ~** nicht unbedingt

necessary /'nesəsərɪ/ a nötig, notwendig

necessit|ate /nɪ'sesɪteɪt/ vt notwendig machen. **~y** n Notwendigkeit f; **she works from ~y** sie arbeitet, weil sie es nötig hat

neck /nek/ n Hals m; **~ and ~** Kopf an Kopf

necklace /'neklɪs/ n Halskette f

neck: **~line** n Halsausschnitt m. **~tie** n Schlips m

nectar /'nektə(r)/ n Nektar m

neé /neɪ/ a **~ Brett** geborene Brett

need /niːd/ n Bedürfnis nt; (misfortune) Not f; **be in ~** Not leiden; **be in ~ of** brauchen; **in case of ~** notfalls; **if ~ be** wenn nötig; **there is a ~** for es besteht ein Bedarf an (+ dat); **there is no ~ for that** das ist nicht nötig; **there**

is no ~ for you to go du brauchst nicht zu gehen □vt brauchen; **you ~ not go** du brauchst nicht zu gehen; **~ I come?** muß ich kommen? **I ~ to know** ich muß es wissen; **it ~s to be done** es muß gemacht werden (annoy) ärgern

needle /'niːdl/ n Nadel f □vt (annoy) ärgern

needless /'niːdlɪs/ a, **-ly** adv unnötig; **~ to say** selbstverständlich, natürlich

'needlework n Nadelarbeit f

needy /'niːdɪ/ a (-ier, -iest) bedürftig

negation /nɪ'geɪʃn/ n Verneinung f

negative /'negətɪv/ a negativ □n Verneinung f; (photo) Negativ nt

neglect /nɪ'glekt/ n Vernachlässigung f; **state of ~** verwahrloster Zustand m □vt vernachlässigen; (omit) versäumen (to zu). **~ed** a verwahrlost. **~ful** a nachlässig; **be ~ful of** vernachlässigen

negligen|ce /'neglɪdʒəns/ n Nachlässigkeit f; (Jur) Fahrlässigkeit f. **~t a**, **-ly** adv nachlässig; (Jur) fahrlässig

negligible /'neglɪdʒəbl/ a unbedeutend

negotiable /nɪ'gəʊʃəbl/ a (road) befahrbar; (Comm) unverbindlich; **not ~** nicht übertragbar

negotiat|e /nɪ'gəʊʃɪeɪt/ vt aushandeln; (Auto) nehmen (bend) □vi verhandeln. **~ion** /-'eɪʃn/ n Verhandlung f. **~or** n Unterhändler(in) m(f)

Negro /'niːgrəʊ/ a Neger- □n (pl -es) Neger m

neigh /neɪ/ vi wiehern

neighbour /'neɪbə(r)/ n Nachbar(in) m(f). **~hood** n Nachbarschaft f; **in the ~hood of** in der Nähe von; (fig) um ... herum. **~ing** a Nachbar-. **~ly** a [gut]nachbarlich

neither /'naɪðə(r)/ a & pron keine(r, s) [von beiden] □adv

~... **nor** weder ... noch □*conj* auch nicht

neon /'niːɒn/ *n* Neon *nt*. **~ light** *n* Neonlicht *nt*

nephew /'nevjuː/ *n* Neffe *m*

nepotism /'nepətɪzm/ *n* Vetternwirtschaft *f*

nerve /nɜːv/ *n* Nerv *m*; (*fam: courage*) Mut *m*; (*fam: impudence*) Frechheit *f*; **lose one's ~** den Mut verlieren. **~-racking** *a* nervenaufreibend

nervous /'nɜːvəs/ *a*, **-ly** *adv* (*afraid*) ängstlich; (*highly-strung*) nervös; (*Anat, Med*) Nerven-; **be ~** Angst haben. **~ 'breakdown** *n* Nervenzusammenbruch *m*. **~ness** Ängstlichkeit *f*; (*Med*) Nervosität *f*

nervy /'nɜːvɪ/ *a* (**-ier, -iest**) nervös; (*Amer: impudent*) frech

nest /nest/ *n* Nest *nt* □*vi* nisten. **~-egg** *n* Notgroschen *m*

nestle /'nesl/ *vi* sich schmiegen (**against an** + *acc*)

net[1] /net/ *n* Netz *nt*; (*curtain*) Store *m* □*vt* (*pt/pp* netted) (*catch*) [mit dem Netz] fangen

net[2] *a* netto; ⟨*salary, weight*⟩ Netto- □*vt* (*pt/pp* netted) netto einnehmen; (*yield*) einbringen

netball *n* ≈ Korbball *m*

Netherlands /'neðələndz/ *npl* **the ~** die Niederlande *pl*

netting /'netɪŋ/ *n* [wire] **~** Maschendraht *m*

nettle /'netl/ *n* Nessel *f*

network *n* Netz *nt*

neuralgia /njʊəˈrældʒə/ *n* Neuralgie *f*

neurolog|ist /njʊəˈrɒlədʒɪst/ *n* Neurologe *m*/-gin *f*. **~y** *n* Neurologie *f*

neur|osis /njʊəˈrəʊsɪs/ *n* (*pl* -oses /-siːz/) Neurose *f*. **~otic** /-ˈrɒtɪk/ *a* neurotisch

neuter /'njuːtə(r)/ *a* (*Gram*) sächlich □*n* (*Gram*) Neutrum *nt* □*vt* kastrieren; (*spay*) sterilisieren

neutral /'njuːtrl/ *a* neutral □*n* **in ~** (*Auto*) im Leerlauf. **~ity**

/-'trælɪtɪ/ *n* Neutralität *f*. **~ize** *vt* neutralisieren

never /'nevə(r)/ *adv* nie, niemals; (*fam: not*) nicht; **~ mind** macht nichts; **well I ~!** ja so was! **~-ending** *a* endlos

nevertheless /nevəðə'les/ *adv* dennoch, trotzdem

new /njuː/ *a* (**-er, -est**) neu

new: ~-born *a* neugeboren. **~-comer** *n* Neuankömmling *m*. **~-fangled** /-'fæŋgld/ *a* (*pej*) neumodisch. **~-laid** *a* frisch gelegt

newly *adv* frisch. **~-weds** *npl* jungverheiratetes Paar *nt*

new: ~'moon *n* Neumond *m*. **~ness** *n* Neuheit *f*

news /njuːz/ *n* Nachricht *f*; (*Radio, TV*) Nachrichten *pl*; **piece of ~** Neuigkeit *f*

news: ~agent *n* Zeitungshändler *m*. **~ bulletin** *n* Nachrichtensendung *f*. **~caster** *n* Nachrichtensprecher(in) *m*(*f*). **~flash** *n* Kurzmeldung *f*. **~letter** *n* Mitteilungsblatt *nt*. **~paper** *n* Zeitung *f*; (*material*) Zeitungspapier *nt*. **~reader** *n* Nachrichtensprecher(in) *m*(*f*)

newt /njuːt/ *n* Molch *m*

New: ~ Year's 'Day *n* Neujahr *nt*. **~ Year's 'Eve** *n* Silvester *nt*. **~ Zealand** /'ziːlənd/ *n* Neuseeland *nt*

next /nekst/ *a* & *n* nächste(r, s); **who's ~?** wer kommt als nächster dran? **the ~ best** das nächstbeste; **~ door** nebenan; **my ~ of kin** mein nächster Verwandter; **~ to nothing** fast gar nichts; **the week after ~** übernächste Woche □*adv* als nächstes; **~ to** neben

NHS *abbr see* **National Health Service**

nib /nɪb/ *n* Feder *f*

nibble /'nɪbl/ *vt*/*i* knabbern (**at** an + *dat*)

nice /naɪs/ *a* (**-r, -st**) nett; ⟨*day, weather*⟩ schön; ⟨*food*⟩ gut; ⟨*distinction*⟩ fein. **~ly** *adv* nett;

(*well*) gut. ~**ties** /'naɪsətɪz/ *npl* Feinheiten *pl*

niche /niːʃ/ *n* Nische *f*; (*fig*) Platz *m*

nick /nɪk/ *n* Kerbe *f*; (*fam: prison*) Knast *m*; (*fam: police station*) Revier *nt*; **in the ~ of time** (*fam*) gerade noch rechtzeitig; **in good ~** (*fam*) in gutem Zustand □*vt* einkerben; (*steal*) klauen; (*fam: arrest*) schnappen

nickel /'nɪkl/ *n* Nickel *nt*; (*Amer*) Fünfcentstück *nt*

'nickname *n* Spitzname *m*

nicotine /'nɪkətiːn/ *n* Nikotin *nt*

niece /niːs/ *n* Nichte *f*

Nigeria /naɪ'dʒɪərɪə/ *n* Nigeria *nt*. ~**n** *a* nigerianisch □*n* Nigerianer(in) *m(f)*

niggardly /'nɪgədlɪ/ *a* knauserig

niggling /'nɪglɪŋ/ *a* gering; (*petty*) kleinlich; (*pain*) quälend

night /naɪt/ *n* Nacht *f*; (*evening*) Abend *m*; **at ~** nachts; **Monday ~** Montag nacht/abend

night: ~**cap** *n* Schlafmütze *f*; (*drink*) Schlaftrunk *m*. ~**club** *n* Nachtklub *m*. ~**dress** *n* Nachthemd *nt*. ~**fall** *n* **at ~fall** bei Einbruch der Dunkelheit. ~**gown** *n*, (*fam*) ~**ie** /'naɪtɪ/ *n* Nachthemd *nt*

nightingale /'naɪtɪŋgeɪl/ *n* Nachtigall *f*

night: ~**-life** *n* Nachtleben *nt*. ~**ly** *a* nächtlich □*adv* jede Nacht. ~**mare** *n* Alptraum *m*. ~**shade** *n* (*Bot*) **deadly ~shade** Tollkirsche *f*. ~**time** *n* **at ~-time** bei Nacht. ~'**watchman** *n* Nachtwächter *m*

nil /nɪl/ *n* null

nimble /'nɪmbl/ *a* (-**r**, -**st**), -**bly** *adv* flink

nine /naɪn/ *a* neun □*n* Neun *f*. ~'**teen** *a* neunzehn. ~'**teenth** *a* neunzehnte(r, s)

ninetieth /'naɪntɪɪθ/ *a* neunzigste(r, s)

ninety /'naɪntɪ/ *a* neunzig

ninth /naɪnθ/ *a* neunte(r, s)

nip /nɪp/ *n* Kniff *m*; (*bite*) Biß *m* □*vt* kneifen; (*bite*) beißen; ~ **in the bud** (*fig*) im Keim ersticken □*vi* (*fam: run*) laufen

nipple /'nɪpl/ *n* Brustwarze *f*; (*Amer: on bottle*) Sauger *m*

nippy /'nɪpɪ/ *a* (-**ier**, -**iest**) (*cold*) frisch; (*quick*) flink

nitrate /'naɪtreɪt/ *n* Nitrat *nt*

nitrogen /'naɪtrədʒən/ *n* Stickstoff *m*

nitwit /'nɪtwɪt/ *n* (*fam*) Dummkopf *m*

no /nəʊ/ *adv* nein □ *n* (*pl* **noes**) Nein *nt* □*a* kein(e); (*pl*) keine; **in no time** [sehr] schnell; **no parking/smoking** Parken/Rauchen verboten; **no one** = **nobody**

nobility /nəʊ'bɪlətɪ/ *n* Adel *m*

noble /'nəʊbl/ *a* (-**r**, -**st**) edel; (*aristocratic*) adlig. ~**man** *n* Adlige(r) *m*

nobody /'nəʊbədɪ/ *pron* niemand, keiner; **he knows ~** er kennt niemanden *od* keinen □ *n* **a ~** ein Niemand *m*

nocturnal /nɒk'tɜːnl/ *a* nächtlich; ⟨*animal, bird*⟩ Nacht-

nod /nɒd/ *n* Nicken *nt* □ *v* (*pt/pp* **nodded**) □ *vi* nicken □ *vt* ~ **one's head** mit dem Kopf nicken. ~ **off** *vi* einnicken

nodule /'nɒdjuːl/ *n* Knötchen *nt*

noise /nɔɪz/ *n* Geräusch *nt*; (*loud*) Lärm *m*. ~**less** *a*, -**ly** *adv* geräuschlos

noisy /'nɔɪzɪ/ *a* (-**ier**, -**iest**), -**ily** *adv* laut; (*eater*) geräuschvoll

nomad /'nəʊmæd/ *n* Nomade *m*. ~**ic** /-'mædɪk/ *a* nomadisch; ⟨*life, tribe*⟩ Nomaden-

nominal /'nɒmɪnl/ *a*, -**ly** *adv* nominell

nominat|e /'nɒmɪneɪt/ *vt* nominieren, aufstellen; (*appoint*) ernennen. ~**ion** /-'neɪʃn/ *n* Nominierung *f*; Ernennung *f*

nominative /'nɒmɪnətɪv/ *a & n* (*Gram*) ~ **[case]** Nominativ *m*

nonchalent /'nɒnʃələnt/ a, -ly adv nonchalant; ⟨gesture⟩ lässig

non-com'missioned /nɒn-/ a ~ officer Unteroffizier m

non-com'mittal a unverbindlich; be ~ sich nicht festlegen

nondescript /'nɒndɪskrɪpt/ a unbestimmbar; ⟨person⟩ unscheinbar

none /nʌn/ pron keine(r)/keins; ~ of us keiner von uns; ~ of it/ this nichts davon □ adv ~ too nicht gerade; ~ too soon [um] keine Minute zu früh; ~ the wiser um nichts klüger; ~ the less dennoch

nonentity /nɒ'nentətɪ/ n Null f

non-ex'istent a nichtvorhanden; be ~ nicht vorhanden sein

non-'fiction n Sachliteratur f

non-'iron a bügelfrei

nonplussed /nɒn'plʌst/ a verblüfft

nonsens|e /'nɒnsəns/ n Unsinn m. ~ical /-'sensɪkl/ a unsinnig

non-'smoker n Nichtraucher m; ⟨compartment⟩ Nichtraucherabteil nt

non-'stop adv ununterbrochen; ⟨fly⟩ nonstop; ~ 'flight Nonstopflug m

non-'swimmer n Nichtschwimmer m

non-'violent a gewaltlos

noodles /'nu:dlz/ npl Bandnudeln pl

nook /nʊk/ n Eckchen nt, Winkel m

noon /nu:n/ n Mittag m; at ~ um 12 Uhr mittags

noose /nu:s/ n Schlinge f

nor /nɔ:(r)/ adv noch □ conj auch nicht

Nordic /'nɔ:dɪk/ a nordisch

norm /nɔ:m/ n Norm f

normal /'nɔ:ml/ a normal. ~ity /-'mælətɪ/ n Normalität f. ~ly adv normal; (usually) normalerweise

north /nɔ:θ/ n Norden m; to the ~ of nördlich von □ a Nord-, nord- □ adv nach Norden

north: N~ America n Nordamerika nt. ~-east a Nordost- □ n Nordosten m

norther|ly /'nɔ:ðəlɪ/ a nördlich. ~n a nördlich. N~n Ireland n Nordirland n

north: N~ 'Pole n Nordpol m. N~ 'Sea n Nordsee f. ~ward[s] /-wəd[z]/ adv nach Norden. ~-west a Nordwest- □ n Nordwesten m

Nor|way /'nɔ:weɪ/ n Norwegen nt. ~wegian /-'wi:dʒn/ a norwegisch □ n Norweger(in) m(f)

nose /nəʊz/ n Nase f □ vi ~ about herumschnüffeln

nose: ~bleed n Nasenbluten nt. ~dive n (Aviat) Sturzflug m

nostalgia /nɒ'stældʒɪə/ n Nostalgie f. ~ic a nostalgisch

nostril /'nɒstrəl/ n Nasenloch nt; (of horse) Nüster f

nosy /'nəʊzɪ/ a (-ier, -iest) (fam) neugierig

not /nɒt/ adv nicht; ~ a kein(e); if ~ wenn nicht; ~ at all gar nicht; ~ a bit kein bißchen; ~ even nicht mal; ~ yet noch nicht; he is ~ a German er ist kein Deutscher

notab|le /'nəʊtəbl/ a bedeutend; (remarkable) bemerkenswert. ~ly adv insbesondere

notary /'nəʊtərɪ/ n ~ 'public ≈ Notar m

notation /nəʊ'teɪʃn/ n Notation f; (Mus) Notenschrift f

notch /nɒtʃ/ n Kerbe f. ~ up vt (score) erzielen

note /nəʊt/ n (written comment) Notiz f, Anmerkung f; (short letter) Briefchen nt, Zettel m; (bank~) Banknote f, Schein m; (Mus) Note f; (sound) Ton m; (on piano) Taste f; eighth/quarter ~ (Amer) Achtel-/Viertelnote f; half/whole ~ (Amer) halbe/ganze Note f; of ~ von Bedeutung; make a ~ of notieren □ vt beachten; (notice) bemerken (that daß). ~ down vt notieren

'notebook n Notizbuch nt

noted /'nəʊtɪd/ a bekannt (for für)

note: ~**paper** n Briefpapier nt. ~**worthy** a beachtenswert

nothing /'nʌθɪŋ/ n, pron & adv nichts; for ~ umsonst; ~ **but** nichts als; ~ **much** nicht viel; ~ **interesting** nichts Interessantes; **it's** ~ **to do with you** das geht dich nichts an

notice /'nəʊtɪs/ n (on board) Anschlag m, Bekanntmachung f; (announcement) Anzeige f; (review) Kritik f; (termination of lease, employment) Kündigung f; **[advance]** ~ Bescheid m; **give [in one's]** ~ kündigen; **give s.o.** ~ jdm kündigen; **take no** ~ **of** keine Notiz nehmen von; **take no** ~! ignoriere es! ~**able** /-əbl/ a, -**bly** adv merklich. ~**-board** n Anschlagbrett nt

noti|fication /nəʊtɪfɪ'keɪʃn/ n Benachrichtigung f. ~**fy** /'nəʊtɪfaɪ/ vt (pt/pp -ied) benachrichtigen

notion /'nəʊʃn/ n Idee f; ~**s** pl (Amer: haberdashery) Kurzwaren pl

notorious /nəʊ'tɔːrɪəs/ a berüchtigt

notwith'standing prep trotz (+ gen) □adv trotzdem, dennoch

nought /nɔːt/ n Null f

noun /naʊn/ n Substantiv nt

nourish /'nʌrɪʃ/ vt nähren. ~**ing** a nahrhaft. ~**ment** n Nahrung f

novel /'nɒvl/ a neu[artig] □n Roman m. ~**ist** n Romanschriftsteller(in) m(f). ~**ty** n Neuheit f; ~**ties** pl kleine Geschenkartikel pl

November /nəʊ'vembə(r)/ n November m

novice /'nɒvɪs/ n Neuling m; (Relig) Novize m/Novizin f

now /naʊ/ adv & conj jetzt; ~ **[that]** jetzt, wo; **just** ~ gerade, eben; **right** ~ sofort; ~ **and again** hin und wieder; **now now!** na, na!

'nowadays adv heutzutage

nowhere /'nəʊ-/ adv nirgendwo, nirgends

noxious /'nɒkʃəs/ a schädlich

nozzle /'nɒzl/ n Düse f

nuance /'njuːɑ̃s/ n Nuance f

nuclear /'njuːklɪə(r)/ a Kern-. ~**de'terrent** n nukleares Abschreckungsmittel nt

nucleus /'njuːklɪəs/ n (pl -**lei** /-lɪaɪ/) Kern m

nude /njuːd/ a nackt □n (Art) Akt m; **in the** ~ nackt

nudge /nʌdʒ/ n Stups m □vt stupsen

nud|ist /'njuːdɪst/ n Nudist m. ~**ity** n Nacktheit f

nugget /'nʌgɪt/ n [Gold]klumpen m

nuisance /'njuːsns/ n Ärgernis nt; (pest) Plage f; **be a** ~ ärgerlich sein; (person:) lästig sein; **what a** ~! wie ärgerlich!

null /nʌl/ a ~ **and void** null und nichtig. ~**ify** /'nʌlɪfaɪ/ vt (pt/pp -ied) für nichtig erklären

numb /nʌm/ a gefühllos, taub; ~ **with cold** taub vor Kälte □vt betäuben

number /'nʌmbə(r)/ n Nummer f; (amount) Anzahl f; (Math) Zahl f □vt numerieren; (include) zählen (among zu). ~**-plate** n Nummernschild nt

numeral /'njuːmərəl/ n Ziffer f

numerate /'njuːmərət/ a be ~ rechnen können

numerical /njuː'merɪkl/ a, -**ly** adv numerisch; **in** ~ **order** zahlenmäßig geordnet

numerous /'njuːmərəs/ a zahlreich

nun /nʌn/ n Nonne f

nuptial /'nʌpʃl/ a Hochzeits-. ~**s** npl (Amer) Hochzeit f

nurse /nɜːs/ n [Kranken]schwester f; (male) Krankenpfleger m; **children's** ~ Kindermädchen nt □vt pflegen. ~**maid** n Kindermädchen nt

nursery /ˈnɜːsərɪ/ n Kinderzimmer nt; (Hort) Gärtnerei f; **[day]** ~ Kindertagesstätte f. ~ **rhyme** n Kinderreim m. ~ **school** n Kindergarten m

nursing /ˈnɜːsɪŋ/ n Krankenpflege f. ~ **home** n Pflegeheim nt

nurture /ˈnɜːtʃə(r)/ vt nähren; (fig) hegen

nut /nʌt/ n Nuß f; (Techn) [Schrauben]mutter f; (fam: head) Birne f (fam); **be** ~ **s** (fam) spinnen (fam). ~**crackers** npl Nußknacker m. ~**meg** n Muskat m

nutrient /ˈnjuːtrɪənt/ n Nährstoff m

nutrit|ion /njuːˈtrɪʃn/ n Ernährung f. ~**ious** /-ʃəs/ a nahrhaft

'nutshell n Nußschale f; **in a** ~ (fig) kurz gesagt

nuzzle /ˈnʌzl/ vt beschnüffeln

nylon /ˈnaɪlɒn/ n Nylon nt; ~**s** pl Nylonstrümpfe pl

nymph /nɪmf/ n Nymphe f

O

O /əʊ/ n (Teleph) null

oaf /əʊf/ n (pl oafs) Trottel m

oak /əʊk/ n Eiche f; □ attrib Eichen-

OAP abbr (old-age pensioner) Rentner(in) f(m)

oar /ɔː(r)/ n Ruder nt. ~**sman** n Ruderer m

oasis /əʊˈeɪsɪs/ n (pl oases /-siːz/) Oase f

oath /əʊθ/ n Eid m; (swear-word) Fluch m

oatmeal /ˈəʊt-/ n Hafermehl nt

oats /əʊts/ npl Hafer m; (Culin) **[rolled]** ~ Haferflocken pl

obedien|ce /əˈbiːdɪəns/ n Gehorsam m. ~**t** a, **-ly** adv gehorsam

obese /əʊˈbiːs/ a fettleibig. ~**ity** n Fettleibigkeit f

obey /əˈbeɪ/ vt/i gehorchen (+ dat); befolgen (instructions, rules)

obituary /əˈbɪtjʊərɪ/ n Nachruf m; (notice) Todesanzeige f

object¹ /ˈɒbdʒɪkt/ n Gegenstand m; (aim) Zweck m; (intention) Absicht f; (Gram) Objekt nt; **money is no** ~ Geld spielt keine Rolle

object² /əbˈdʒekt/ vi Einspruch erheben (**to** gegen); (be against) etwas dagegen haben

objection /əbˈdʒekʃn/ n Einwand m; **have no** ~ nichts dagegen haben. ~**able** /-əbl/ a anstößig; (person) unangenehm

objectiv|e /əbˈdʒektɪv/ a, **-ly** adv objektiv □n Ziel nt. ~**ity** /-ˈtɪvətɪ/ n Objektivität f

objector /əbˈdʒektə(r)/ n Gegner m

obligation /ɒblɪˈgeɪʃn/ n Pflicht f; **be under an** ~ verpflichtet sein; **without** ~ unverbindlich

obligatory /əˈblɪgətrɪ/ a obligatorisch; **be** ~ Vorschrift sein

oblig|e /əˈblaɪdʒ/ vt verpflichten; (compel) zwingen; (do a small service) einen Gefallen tun (+ dat); **much** ~**ed!** vielen Dank! ~**ing** a entgegenkommend

oblique /əˈbliːk/ a schräg; (angle) schief; (fig) indirekt. ~ **stroke** n Schrägstrich m

obliterate /əˈblɪtəreɪt/ vt auslöschen

oblivion /əˈblɪvɪən/ n Vergessenheit f

oblivious /əˈblɪvɪəs/ a **be** ~ sich (dat) nicht bewußt sein (**of** or to gen)

oblong /ˈɒblɒŋ/ a rechteckig □n Rechteck nt

obnoxious /əbˈnɒkʃəs/ a widerlich

oboe /ˈəʊbəʊ/ n Oboe f

obscen|e /əbˈsiːn/ a obszön; (atrocious) abscheulich. ~**ity** /-ˈsenətɪ/ n Obszönität f; Abscheulichkeit f

obscur|e /əbˈskjʊə(r)/ a dunkel; (unknown) unbekannt □vt verdecken; (confuse) verwischen. ~**ity** n Dunkelheit f; Unbekanntheit f

obsequious /əbˈsiːkwɪəs/ a unterwürfig

observa|nce /əbˈzɜːvns/ n (of custom) Einhaltung f. ~nt a aufmerksam. ~tion /ɒbzəˈveɪʃn/ n Beobachtung f; (remark) Bemerkung f

observatory /əbˈzɜːvətrɪ/ n Sternwarte f; (weather) Wetterwarte f

observe /əbˈzɜːv/ vt beobachten; (say, notice) bemerken; (keep, celebrate) feiern; (obey) einhalten. ~r n Beobachter m

obsess /əbˈses/ vt be ~ed by besessen sein von. ~ion /-eʃn/ n Besessenheit f; (persistent idea) fixe Idee f. ~ive /-ɪv/ a, -ly adv zwanghaft

obsolete /ˈɒbsəliːt/ a veraltet

obstacle /ˈɒbstəkl/ n Hindernis nt

obstetrician /ɒbstəˈtrɪʃn/ n Geburtshelfer m. **obstetrics** /-ˈste-trɪks/ n Geburtshilfe f

obstina|cy /ˈɒbstɪnəsɪ/ n Starrsinn m. ~te /-nət/ a, -ly adv starrsinnig; (refusal) hartnäckig

obstreperous /əbˈstrepərəs/ a widerspenstig

obstruct /əbˈstrʌkt/ vt blockieren; (hinder) behindern. ~ion /-ʌkʃn/ n Blockierung f; Behinderung f; (obstacle) Hindernis nt. ~ive /-ɪv/ a be ~ive Schwierigkeiten bereiten

obtain /əbˈteɪn/ vt erhalten, bekommen □ vi gelten. ~able /-əbl/ a erhältlich

obtrusive /əbˈtruːsɪv/ a aufdringlich; (thing) auffällig

obtuse /əbˈtjuːs/ a (Geom) stumpf; (stupid) begriffsstutzig

obviate /ˈɒbvɪeɪt/ vt beseitigen

obvious /ˈɒbvɪəs/ a, -ly adv offensichtlich, offenbar

occasion /əˈkeɪʒn/ n Gelegenheit f; (time) Mal nt; (event) Ereignis nt; (cause) Anlaß m, Grund m; on ~ gelegentlich, hin und wieder; on the ~ of anläßlich (+ gen) □ vt veranlassen

occasiona|l /əˈkeɪʒənl/ a gelegentlich; he has the ~ glass of wine er trinkt gelegentlich ein

Glas Wein. ~ly adv gelegentlich, hin und wieder

occult /ɒˈkʌlt/ a okkult

occupant /ˈɒkjupənt/ n Bewohner(in) m(f); (of vehicle) Insasse m

occupation /ɒkjuˈpeɪʃn/ n Beschäftigung f; (job) Beruf m; (Mil) Besetzung f; (period) Besatzung f. ~al a Berufs-. ~al therapy n Beschäftigungstherapie f

occupier /ˈɒkjupaɪə(r)/ n Bewohner(in) m(f)

occupy /ˈɒkjupaɪ/ vt (pt/pp occupied) besetzen (seat, Mil country); einnehmen (space); in Anspruch nehmen (time); (live in) bewohnen; (fig) bekleiden (office); (keep busy) beschäftigen; ~ oneself sich beschäftigen

occur /əˈkɜː(r)/ vi (pt/pp occurred) geschehen; (exist) vorkommen, auftreten; it ~red to me that es fiel mir ein, daß. **occurrence** /əˈkʌrəns/ n Auftreten nt; (event) Ereignis nt

ocean /ˈəʊʃn/ n Ozean m

o'clock /əˈklɒk/ adv [at] 7 ~ [um] 7 Uhr

octagonal /ɒkˈtægənl/ a achteckig

octave /ˈɒktɪv/ n (Mus) Oktave f

October /ɒkˈtəʊbə(r)/ n Oktober m

octopus /ˈɒktəpəs/ n (pl -puses) Tintenfisch m

odd /ɒd/ a (-er, -est) seltsam, merkwürdig; (number) ungerade; (not of set) einzeln; forty ~ über vierzig; ~ jobs Gelegenheitsarbeiten pl; the ~ one out die Ausnahme; at ~ moments zwischendurch; have the ~ glass of wine gelegentlich ein Glas Wein trinken

odd|ity /ˈɒdɪtɪ/ n Kuriosität f. ~ly adv merkwürdig; ~ly enough merkwürdigerweise. ~ment n (of fabric) Rest m

odds /ɒdz/ npl (chances) Chancen pl; at ~ uneinig; ~ and ends Kleinkram m; it makes no ~ es spielt keine Rolle

ode /əʊd/ n Ode f

odious /ˈəʊdɪəs/ a widerlich, abscheulich

odour /ˈəʊdə(r)/ n Geruch m. **~less** a geruchlos

oesophagus /iːˈsɒfəgəs/ n Speiseröhre f

of /ɒv, unbetont əv/ prep von (+ dat); (made of) aus (+ dat); **the two of us** wir zwei; **a child of three** ein dreijähriges Kind; **the fourth of January** der vierte Januar; **a pound of butter** ein Pfund Butter; **a cup of tea/coffee** eine Tasse Tee/Kaffee; **a bottle of wine** eine Flasche Wein; **half of it** die Hälfte davon; **the whole of the room** das ganze Zimmer

off /ɒf/ prep von (+ dat); **£10 ~ the price** £10 Nachlaß; **the coast vor der Küste; get ~ the ladder/bus** von der Leiter/aus dem Bus steigen; **take/leave the lid ~ the saucepan** den Topf abdecken/nicht zudecken □ adv weg; ⟨button, lid, handle⟩ ab; ⟨light⟩ aus; ⟨brake⟩ los; ⟨machine⟩ abgeschaltet; ⟨tap⟩ zu; (on appliance) 'off' 'aus'; **2 kilometres ~** 2 Kilometer entfernt; **a long way ~** weit weg; (time) noch lange hin; **~ and on** hin und wieder; **with his hat/coat ~** ohne Hut/Mantel; **with the light/lid ~** ohne Licht/Deckel; **20% ~** 20% Nachlaß; **be ~** (leave) [weg]gehen; (Sport) starten; ⟨food:⟩ schlecht/(all gone) alle sein; **be better/worse ~** besser/schlechter dran sein; **be well ~** gut dran sein; (financially) wohlhabend sein; **have a day ~** einen freien Tag haben; **go/drive ~** weggehen/-fahren; **turn/take sth ~** etw abdrehen/nehmen

offal /ˈɒfl/ n (Culin) Innereien pl

offence /əˈfens/ n (illegal act) Vergehen nt; **give/take ~** Anstoß erregen/nehmen (at an + dat)

offend /əˈfend/ vt beleidigen. **~er** n (Jur) Straftäter m

offensive /əˈfensɪv/ a anstößig; (Mil, Sport) offensiv □ n Offensive f

offer /ˈɒfə(r)/ n Angebot nt; **on special ~** im Sonderangebot □ vt anbieten (to s.o. jdm); leisten ⟨resistance⟩; **~ s.o. sth** jdm etw anbieten; **~ to do sth** sich anbieten, etw zu tun. **~ing** n Gabe f

off'hand a brüsk; (casual) lässig □ adv so ohne weiteres

office /ˈɒfɪs/ n Büro nt; (post) Amt nt; **in ~** im Amt; **~ hours** pl Dienststunden pl

officer /ˈɒfɪsə(r)/ n Offizier m; (official) Beamte(r) m/ Beamtin f; (police) Polizeibeamte(r) m/-beamtin f

official /əˈfɪʃl/ a offiziell, amtlich □ n Beamte(r) m/ Beamtin f; (Sport) Funktionär m. **~ly** adv offiziell

officiate /əˈfɪʃɪeɪt/ vi amtieren

officious /əˈfɪʃəs/ a, **-ly** adv übereifrig

offing n **in the ~** in Aussicht

off-licence n Wein- und Spirituosenhandlung f

off-load vt ausladen

off-putting a (fam) abstoßend

off'set vt (pt/pp -set, pres p -setting) ausgleichen

offshoot n Schößling m; (fig) Zweig m

offshore a offshore-. **~ rig** n Bohrinsel f

off'side a (Sport) abseits

offspring n Nachwuchs m

off'stage adv hinter den Kulissen

off-white a fast weiß

often /ˈɒfn/ adv oft; **every so ~** von Zeit zu Zeit

ogle /ˈəʊgl/ vt beäugeln

ogre /ˈəʊgə(r)/ n Menschenfresser m

oh /əʊ/ int oh! ach! **oh dear!** o weh!

oil /ɔɪl/ n Öl nt; (petroleum) Erdöl nt □ vt ölen

oil: ~**cloth** n Wachstuch nt. ~**field** n Ölfeld nt. ~**painting** n Ölgemälde nt. ~**refinery** n [Erd]ölraffinerie f. ~**skins** npl Ölzeug nt. ~**slick** n Ölteppich m. ~**tanker** n Öltanker m. ~**well** n Ölquelle f

oily /ˈɔɪlɪ/ a (-ier, -iest) ölig

ointment /ˈɔɪntmənt/ n Salbe f

OK /əʊˈkeɪ/ a & int (fam) in Ordnung; okay □adv (well) gut □vt (auch okay) (pt/pp okayed) genehmigen

old: ~**'age** n Alter nt. ~**age 'pensioner** n Rentner(in) m(f). ~ **boy** n ehemaliger Schüler. ~**'fashioned** a altmodisch. ~**'girl** n ehemalige Schülerin f. ~**'maid** n alte Jungfer f

olive /ˈɒlɪv/ n Olive f; (colour) Oliv nt □a olivgrün. ~ **branch** n Ölzweig m; (fig) Friedensangebot nt. ~**'oil** n Olivenöl nt

Olympic /əˈlɪmpɪk/ a olympisch □n the ~**s** die Olympischen Spiele pl

omelette /ˈɒmlɪt/ n Omelett nt

omen /ˈəʊmən/ n Omen nt

ominous /ˈɒmɪnəs/ a bedrohlich

omission /əˈmɪʃn/ n Auslassung f; (failure to do) Unterlassung f

omit /əˈmɪt/ vt (pt/pp omitted) auslassen; ~ **to do sth** es unterlassen, etw zu tun

omnipotent /ɒmˈnɪpətənt/ a allmächtig

on /ɒn/ prep auf (+ dat/(on to) + acc); (on vertical surface) an (+ dat/(on to) + acc); (about) über (+ acc); **on Monday** [am] Montag; **on Mondays** montags; **on the first of May** am ersten Mai; **on arriving** als ich ankam; **on one's finger** am Finger; **on the right/left** rechts/links; **on the Rhine/Thames** am Rhein/an der Themse; **on the radio/television** im Radio/Fernsehen; **on the bus/train** im Bus/Zug; **go on the**

bus/train mit dem Bus/Zug fahren; **get on the bus/train** in den Bus/Zug einsteigen; **on me** (with me) bei mir; **it's on me** (fam) das spendiere ich □adv (further on) weiter; (switched on) an; ⟨brake⟩ angezogen; ⟨machine⟩ angeschaltet; (on appliance) 'on' 'ein'; **with/without his hat/coat on** mit/ohne Hut/Mantel; **with/without the lid on** mit/ohne Deckel; **be on** ⟨film:⟩ laufen; ⟨event:⟩ stattfinden; **be on at** (fam) bedrängen (zu to); **it's not on** (fam) das geht nicht; **on and on** immer weiter; **on and off** hin und wieder; **and so on** und so weiter; **later on** später; **move/drive on** weitergehen/-fahren; **stick/sew on** ankleben/-nähen

once /wʌns/ adv einmal; (formerly) früher; **at** ~ sofort; (at the same time) gleichzeitig; ~ **and for all** ein für allemal □conj wenn; (with past tense) als. ~**over** n (fam) **give s.o./sth the** ~**over** sich (dat) jdn/etw kurz ansehen

'oncoming a ~ **traffic** Gegenverkehr m

one /wʌn/ a ein(e); (only) einzig; **not** ~ kein(e); ~ **day/evening** eines Tages/Abends □n Eins f □pron eine(r)/eins; (impersonal) man; **which** ~ welche(r,s); **another** einander; ~ **by** ~ einzeln; ~ **never knows** man kann nie wissen

one: ~**'eyed** a einäugig. ~**'parent 'family** n Einelternfamilie f. ~**'self** pron selbst; (refl) sich; **by** ~**self** allein. ~**sided** a einseitig. ~**way** a ⟨street⟩ Einbahn-; ⟨ticket⟩ einfach

onion /ˈʌnjən/ n Zwiebel f

'onlooker n Zuschauer(in) m(f)

only /ˈəʊnlɪ/ a einzige(r,s); **an** ~ **child** ein Einzelkind nt □adv & conj nur; ~ **just** gerade erst; (barely) gerade noch '**onset** n Beginn m; (of winter) Einsetzen nt

onslaught /'ɒnslɔ:t/ n heftiger Angriff m

onus /'əʊnəs/ n the ~ is on me es liegt an mir (to zu)

onward[s] /'ɒnwəd[z]/ adv vorwärts; from then ~ von der Zeit an

ooze /u:z/ vi sickern

opal /'əʊpl/ n Opal m

opaque /əʊ'peɪk/ a undurchsichtig

open /'əʊpən/ a, -ly adv offen; be ~ ⟨shop:⟩ geöffnet sein; in the ~ air im Freien □n in the ~ im Freien □vt öffnen, aufmachen; (start, set up) eröffnen □vi sich öffnen; ⟨flower:⟩ aufgehen; ⟨shop:⟩ öffnen, aufmachen; (be started) eröffnet werden. ~ up vt öffnen, aufmachen; (fig) eröffnen □vi sich öffnen; (fig) sich eröffnen

open: ~-**air** '**swimming pool** n Freibad nt. ~ **day** n Tag m der offenen Tür

opener /'əʊpənə(r)/ n Öffner m

opening /'əʊpənɪŋ/ n Öffnung f; (beginning) Eröffnung f; (job) Einstiegsmöglichkeit f. ~ **hours** npl Öffnungszeiten f

open: ~-'**minded** a aufgeschlossen. ~-**plan** a ~-**plan office** Großraumbüro nt. ~ '**sandwich** n belegtes Brot nt

opera /'ɒpərə/ n Oper f

operable /'ɒpərəbl/ a operierbar

opera: ~-**glasses** npl Opernglas nt. ~-**house** n Opernhaus nt. ~-**singer** n Opernsänger(in) m(f)

operate /'ɒpəreɪt/ vt bedienen ⟨machine, lift⟩; betätigen ⟨lever, brake⟩; (fig: run) betreiben □vi (Techn) funktionieren; (be in action) in Betrieb sein; (Mil & fig) operieren; ~ [**on**] (Med) operieren

operatic /ɒpə'rætɪk/ a Opern-

operation /ɒpə'reɪʃn/ n (see operate) Bedienung f; Betätigung f;

Operation f; in ~ (Techn) in Betrieb; **come into** ~ (fig) in Kraft treten; **have an** ~ (Med) operiert werden. ~**al** a be ~**al** in Betrieb sein; ⟨law:⟩ in Kraft sein

operative /'ɒpərətɪv/ a wirksam

operator /'ɒpəreɪtə(r)/ n (user) Bedienungsperson f; (Teleph) Vermittlung f

operetta /ɒpə'retə/ n Operette f

opinion /ə'pɪnjən/ n Meinung f; in my ~ meiner Meinung nach. ~**ated** a rechthaberisch

opium /'əʊpɪəm/ n Opium nt

opponent /ə'pəʊnənt/ n Gegner(in) m(f)

opportune /'ɒpətju:n/ a günstig. ~**ist** /-'tju:nɪst/ a opportunistisch □n Opportunist m

opportunity /ɒpə'tju:nətɪ/ n Gelegenheit f

oppos|**e** /ə'pəʊz/ vt Widerstand leisten (+ dat); (argue against) sprechen gegen; be ~**ed to sth** gegen etw sein; **as** ~**ed to** im Gegensatz zu. ~**ing** a gegnerisch; (opposite) entgegengesetzt

opposite /'ɒpəzɪt/ a entgegengesetzt; ⟨house, side⟩ gegenüberliegend; ~ **number** (fig) Gegenstück nt; the ~ **sex** das andere Geschlecht □n Gegenteil nt □adv gegenüber □prep gegenüber (+ dat)

opposition /ɒpə'zɪʃn/ n Widerstand m; (Pol) Opposition f

oppress /ə'pres/ vt unterdrücken. ~**ion** /-eʃn/ n Unterdrückung f. ~**ive** /-ɪv/ a tyrannisch; ⟨heat⟩ drückend. ~**or** n Unterdrücker m

opt /ɒpt/ vi ~ **for** sich entscheiden für; ~ **out** ausscheiden (**of** aus)

optical /'ɒptɪkl/ a optisch; ~ illusion optische Täuschung f

optician /ɒp'tɪʃn/ n Optiker m

optics /'ɒptɪks/ n Optik f

optim|**ism** /'ɒptɪmɪzm/ n Optimismus m. ~**t** /-mɪst/ n Optimist m. ~**tic** /-'mɪstɪk/ a, -**ally** adv optimistisch

optimum /'ɒptɪməm/ a optimal□n (pl -ima) Optimum nt

option /'ɒpʃn/ n Wahl f; (Comm) Option f. **~al** a auf Wunsch erhältlich; ⟨subject⟩ wahlfrei; **~al extras** pl Extras pl

opulence /'ɒpjʊləns/ n Prunk m; (wealth) Reichtum m. **~t** a prunkvoll; (wealthy) sehr reich

or /ɔ:(r)/ conj oder; (after negative) noch; **or [else]** sonst; **in a year or two** in ein bis zwei Jahren

oracle /'ɒrəkl/ n Orakel nt

oral /'ɔ:rəl/ a, **-ly** adv mündlich; (Med) oral □n (fam) Mündliche(s) nt

orange /'ɒrɪndʒ/ n Apfelsine f, Orange f; (colour) Orange nt □a orangefarben. **~ade** /-'dʒeɪd/ n Orangeade f

oration /ə'reɪʃn/ n Rede f

orator /'ɒrətə(r)/ n Redner m

oratorio /ɒrə'tɔ:rɪəʊ/ n Oratorium nt

oratory /'ɒrətərɪ/ n Redekunst f

orbit /'ɔ:bɪt/ n Umlaufbahn f □vt umkreisen. **~al** a **~al road** Ringstraße f

orchard /'ɔ:tʃəd/ n Obstgarten m

orches|tra /'ɔ:kɪstrə/ n Orchester nt. **~tral** /-'kestrəl/ a Orchester-. **~trate** vt orchestrieren

orchid /'ɔ:kɪd/ n Orchidee f

ordain /ɔ:'deɪn/ vt bestimmen; (Relig) ordinieren

ordeal /ɔ:'di:l/ n (fig) Qual f

order /'ɔ:də(r)/ n Ordnung f; (sequence) Reihenfolge f; (condition) Zustand m; (command) Befehl m; (in restaurant) Bestellung f; (Comm) Auftrag m; (Relig, medal) Orden m; **out of ~** ⟨machine⟩ außer Betrieb; **in ~ that** damit; **in ~ to help** um zu helfen; **take holy ~s** Geistlicher werden □vt (put in ~) ordnen; (command) befehlen (+ dat); (Comm, in restaurant) bestellen; (prescribe) verordnen

orderly /'ɔ:dəlɪ/ a ordentlich; (not unruly) friedlich □n (Mil, Med) Sanitäter m

ordinary /'ɔ:dɪnərɪ/ a gewöhnlich, normal; ⟨meeting⟩ ordentlich

ordination /ɔ:dɪ'neɪʃn/ n (Relig) Ordination f

ore /ɔ:(r)/ n Erz nt

organ /'ɔ:gən/ n (Biol & fig) Organ nt; (Mus) Orgel f

organic /ɔ:'gænɪk/ a, **-ally** adv organisch; (without chemicals) biodynamisch; ⟨crop⟩ biologisch angebaut; ⟨food⟩ Bio-; **~ally grown** biologisch angebaut. **~ farm** n Biohof m. **~ farming** n biologischer Anbau m

organism /'ɔ:gənɪzm/ n Organismus m

organist /'ɔ:gənɪst/ n Organist m

organization /ɔ:gənaɪ'zeɪʃn/ n Organisation f

organize /'ɔ:gənaɪz/ vt organisieren; veranstalten ⟨event⟩. **~r** n Organisator m; Veranstalter m

orgasm /'ɔ:gæzm/ n Orgasmus m

orgy /'ɔ:dʒɪ/ n Orgie f

Orient /'ɔ:rɪənt/ n Orient m. **o~al** /-'entl/ a orientalisch; **~al carpet** Orientteppich m □n Orientale m/ Orientalin f

orient|ate /'ɔ:rɪəntert/ vt **~ate oneself** sich orientieren. **~ation** /-'teɪʃn/ n Orientierung f

orifice /'ɒrɪfɪs/ n Öffnung f

origin /'ɒrɪdʒɪn/ n Ursprung m; (of person, goods) Herkunft f

original /ə'rɪdʒənl/ a ursprünglich; (not copied) original; (new) originell □n Original nt. **~ity** /-'nælətɪ/ n Originalität f. **~ly** adv ursprünglich

originate /ə'rɪdʒɪnert/ vi entstehen □vt hervorbringen. **~or** n Urheber m

ornament /'ɔ:nəmənt/ n Ziergegenstand m; (decoration) Verzierung f. **~al** /-'mentl/ a dekorativ. **~ation** /-'teɪʃn/ n Verzierung f

ornate /ɔ:'neɪt/ a reich verziert

ornithology /ɔːnɪˈθɒlədʒɪ/ n
Vogelkunde f

orphan /ˈɔːfn/ n Waisenkind nt,
Waise f □ vt zur Waise machen;
~ed verwaist. ~age /-ɪdʒ/ n Waisenhaus nt

orthodox /ˈɔːθədɒks/ a orthodox

orthography /ɔːˈθɒɡrəfɪ/ n Rechtschreibung f

orthopaedic /ɔːθəˈpiːdɪk/ a orthopädisch

oscillate /ˈɒsɪleɪt/ vi schwingen

ostensible /ɒˈstensəbl/ a, **-bly** adv
angeblich

ostentat|ion /ɒstenˈteɪʃn/ n Protzerei f (fam). ~ious /-ʃəs/ a protzig (fam)

osteopath /ˈɒstɪəpæθ/ n Osteopath
m

ostracize /ˈɒstrəsaɪz/ vt ächten

ostrich /ˈɒstrɪtʃ/ n Strauß m

other /ˈʌðə(r)/ a, pron & n andere(r,s); the ~ [one] der/die/
das andere; the ~ two die zwei
anderen; two ~s zwei andere; no
(more) noch zwei; no ~s sonst
keine; any ~ questions? sonst
noch Fragen? every ~ day jeden
zweiten Tag; the ~ day neulich;
the ~ evening neulich abends;
someone/something or ~ irgend jemand/etwas; someone or
~ than him außer ihm; somehow/somewhere or ~ irgend-
wie/irgendwo

otherwise adv sonst; (differently)
anders

otter /ˈɒtə(r)/ n Otter m

ouch /aʊtʃ/ int autsch

ought /ɔːt/ v aux I/we ~ to stay
ich sollte/wir sollten eigentlich
bleiben; he ~ not to have done
it er hätte es nicht machen sollen; that ~ to be enough das
sollte eigentlich genügen

ounce /aʊns/ n Unze f (28,35 g)

our /ˈaʊə(r)/ a unser

ours /ˈaʊəz/ poss pron unsere(r,s);
a friend of ~ ein Freund von
uns; that is ~ das gehört uns

ourselves /aʊəˈselvz/ pron selbst;
(refl) uns; **by** ~ allein

oust /aʊst/ vt entfernen

out /aʊt/ adv (not at home) weg;
(outside) draußen; (not alight)
aus; (unconscious) bewußtlos; be
~ ⟨sun:⟩ scheinen; ⟨flower:⟩ blühen; ⟨workers:⟩ streiken; ⟨calculation:⟩ nicht stimmen; (Sport)
aus sein; (fig: not feasible) nicht
in Frage kommen; ~ and about
unterwegs; have it ~ with s.o.
(fam) jdn zur Rede stellen; get ~!
(fam) raus! ~ with it! (fam)
heraus damit! go/send ~ hinausgehen/-schicken; come/bring ~
herauskommen/-bringen □ prep
~ of aus (+ dat); go ~ of the
door zur Tür hinausgehen; be ~
of bed/ the room nicht im Bett/
im Zimmer sein; ~ of breath/
danger außer Atem/Gefahr; ~ of
work arbeitslos; nine ~ of ten
neun von zehn; be ~ of sugar/
bread keinen Zucker/kein Brot
mehr haben □ prep aus (+ dat);
go ~ the door zur Tür hinausgehen

out'bid vt (pt/pp -bid, pres p -bidding) überbieten

'outboard a ~ motor Außenbordmotor m

'outbreak n Ausbruch m

'outbuilding n Nebengebäude nt

'outburst n Ausbruch m

'outcast n Ausgestoßene(r) m/f

'outcome n Ergebnis nt

'outcry n Aufschrei m [der Entrüstung]

out'dated a überholt

out'do vt (pt -did, pp -done) übertreffen, übertrumpfen

'outdoor a ⟨life, sports⟩ im Freien; ~ shoes pl Straßenschuhe pl;
~ swimming pool Freibad nt

out'doors adv draußen; go ~
nach draußen gehen

'outer a äußere(r,s)

'outfit n Ausstattung f; (clothes)
Ensemble nt; (fam: organization)

Betrieb m; (fam) Laden m. ~ter
n men's ~ter's Herrenbeklei-
dungsgeschäft nt

'outgoing a ausscheidend; ⟨mail⟩
ausgehend; (sociable) kontakt-
freudig. ~s npl Ausgaben pl

out'grow vt (pt-grew, pp-grown)
herauswachsen aus

'outhouse n Nebengebäude nt

outing /'aʊtɪŋ/ n Ausflug m

outlandish /aʊt'lændɪʃ/ a ungewöhnlich

'outlaw n Geächtete(r) m/f □ vt
ächten

'outlay n Auslagen pl

'outlet n Abzug m; (for water)
Abfluß m; (fig) Ventil nt; (Comm)
Absatzmöglichkeit f

'outline n Umriß m; (summary)
kurze Darstellung f □ vt umrei-
ßen

out'live vt überleben

'outlook n Aussicht f; (future prospect) Aussichten pl; (attitude)
Einstellung f

'outlying a entlegen; ~ areas pl
Außengebiete pl

out'moded a überholt

out'number vt zahlenmäßig
überlegen sein (+ dat)

'out-patient n ambulanter Patient m; ~s' department Ambu-
lanz f

'outpost n Vorposten m

'output n Leistung f, Produktion f

'outrage n Greueltat f; (fig) Skandal m; (indignation) Empörung f
□ vt empören. ~ous /-'reɪdʒəs/ a
empörend

'outright¹ a völlig, total; ⟨refu-
sal⟩ glatt

out'right² adv ganz; (at once) sofort; (frankly) offen

'outset n Anfang m; from the ~
von Anfang an

'outside¹ a äußere(r,s); ~ wall
Außenwand f □ n Außenseite f;
from the ~ von außen; at the ~
höchstens

out'side² adv außen; (out of
doors) draußen; go ~ nach draußen gehen □ prep außerhalb (+
gen); (in front of) vor (+ dat/acc)

'outsider n Außenseiter m

'outsize a übergroß

'outskirts npl Rand m

out'spoken a offen; be ~ kein
Blatt vor den Mund nehmen

out'standing a hervorragend;
(conspicuous) bemerkenswert;
(not settled) unerledigt; (Comm)
ausstehend

out'stretched a ausgestreckt

out'strip vt (pt/pp -stripped) davonlaufen (+ dat); (fig) übertreffen

out'vote vt überstimmen

'outward /-wəd/ a äußerlich; ~
journey Hinreise f □ adv nach
außen; be ~ bound ⟨ship:⟩ auslaufen. ~ly adv nach außen hin,
äußerlich. ~s adv nach außen

out'weigh vt überwiegen

out'wit vt (pt/pp -witted) überlisten

oval /'əʊvl/ a oval □ n Oval nt

ovary /'əʊvərɪ/ n (Anat) Eierstock
m

ovation /əʊ'veɪʃn/ n Ovation f

oven /'ʌvn/ n Backofen m.
~-ready a bratfertig

over /'əʊvə(r)/ prep über (+ acc/
dat); ~ dinner beim Essen; ~
the weekend übers Wochen-
ende; ~ the phone am Telefon;
~ the page auf der nächsten
Seite; all ~ Germany in ganz
Deutschland; ⟨travel⟩ durch ganz
Deutschland; all ~ the place
(fam) überall □ adv (remaining)
übrig; (ended) zu Ende. ~ again
noch einmal; ~ and ~ immer
wieder; ~ here/there hier/da
drüben; all ~ (everywhere) überall; it's all ~ es ist vorbei; I ache
all ~ mir tut alles weh; go/
drive ~ hinübergehen/-fahren;
come/bring ~ herüberkom-
men/-bringen; turn ~ herum-
drehen

overall¹ /'əʊvərɔ:l/ n Kittel m;
~ s pl Overall m

overall² /'əʊvərɔ:l/ a gesamt;
(general) allgemein □adv insgesamt

over'awe vt (fig) überwältigen

over'balance vi das Gleichgewicht verlieren

over'bearing a herrisch

over'board adv (Naut) über Bord

over'cast a bedeckt

over'charge v ~ s.o. jdm zu viel
berechnen □vi zu viel verlangen

overcoat n Mantel m

over'come vt (pt -came, pp
-come) überwinden; be ~ by
überwältigt werden von

over'crowded a überfüllt

over'do vt (pt -did, pp -done)
übertreiben; (cook too long) zu
lange kochen; ~ it (fam: do too
much) sich übernehmen

overdose n Überdosis f

overdraft n (Konto)überziehung
f; have an ~ sein Konto überzo-
gen haben

over'draw vt (pt -drew, pp
-drawn) (Comm) überziehen

over'due a überfällig

over'estimate vt überschätzen

overflow¹ n Überschuß m; (outlet) Überlauf m

over'flow² vi überlaufen

over'grown a (garden) überwachsen

overhang¹ n Überhang m

over'hang² vt/i (pt/pp -hung)
überhängen (über + acc)

overhaul¹ n Überholung f

over'haul² vt (Techn) überholen

overhead¹ adv oben

over'head² a Ober-; (ceiling)
Decken-. ~ s npl allgemeine Unkosten pl

over'hear vt (pt/pp -heard) mit
anhören (conversation); I over-
heard him saying it ich hörte
zufällig, wie er das sagte

over'heat vi zu heiß werden □vt
zu stark erhitzen

over'joyed a überglücklich

'overland a & adv /---/ auf dem
Landweg; ~ route Landroute f

over'lap v (pt/pp -lapped) □vi
sich überschneiden □vt überlap-
pen

over'leaf adv umseitig

over'load vt überladen; (Electr)
überlasten

'overlook¹ n (Amer) Aussichtspunkt m

over'look² vt überblicken; (fail to
see, ignore) übersehen

overly /'əʊvlɪ/ adv übermäßig

over'night¹ adv über Nacht; stay
~ übernachten

'overnight² a Nacht-; ~ stay
Übernachtung f

overpass n Überführung f

over'pay vt (pt/pp -paid) überbe-
zahlen

over'populated a übervölkert

over'power vt überwältigen.
~ing a überwältigend

over'priced a zu teuer

overpro'duce vt überproduzie-
ren

over'rate vt überschätzen. ~d a
überbewertet

over'reach vt ~ oneself sich
übernehmen

overre'act vi überreagieren.
~ion n Überreaktion f

over'ride vt (pt -rode, pp -rid-
den) sich hinwegsetzen über (+
acc). ~ing a Haupt-

over'rule vt ablehnen; we were
~ d wir wurden überstimmt

over'run vt (pt -ran, pp -run, pres
p -running) überrennen; überschreiten (time); be ~ with überlaufen sein von

over'seas¹ adv in Übersee; go ~
nach Übersee gehen

'overseas² a Übersee-

over'see vt (pt -saw, pp -seen)
beaufsichtigen

'overseer /-si:ə(r)/ n Aufseher m

over'shadow vt überschatten

over'shoot vt (pt/pp -shot) hin-
ausschießen über (+ acc)

'oversight n Versehen nt

over'sleep vi (pt/pp **-slept**) [sich] verschlafen

over'step vt (pt/pp **-stepped**) überschreiten

over'strain vt überanstrengen

overt /'əʊvɜ:t/ a offen

over'take vt/i (pt **-took**, pp **-taken**) überholen. **~ing** n Überholen nt; **no ~ing** Überholverbot nt

over'tax vt zu hoch besteuern; (fig) überfordern

'overthrow[1] n (Pol) Sturz m

over'throw[2] vt (pt **-threw**, pp **-thrown**) (Pol) stürzen

'overtime n Überstunden pl □adv **work ~** Überstunden machen

over'tired a übermüdet

'overtone n (fig) Unterton m

overture /'əʊvətjʊə(r)/ n (Mus) Ouvertüre f; **~s** pl (fig) Annäherungsversuche pl

over'turn vt umstoßen □vi umkippen

over'weight a übergewichtig; **be ~** Übergewicht haben

overwhelm /-'welm/ vt überwältigen. **~ing** a überwältigend

over'work n Überarbeitung f □vt überfordern □vi sich überarbeiten

over'wrought a überreizt

ovulation /ɒvjʊ'leɪʃn/ n Eisprung m

owe /əʊ/ vt schulden / (fig) verdanken ([to] s.o. jdm); **~e s.o. sth** jdm etw schuldig sein; **be ~ing** (money:) ausstehen. **'~ing to** prep wegen (+ gen)

owl /aʊl/ n Eule f

own[1] /əʊn/ a & pron eigen; **it's my ~** es gehört mir; **a car of my ~** mein eigenes Auto; **on one's ~** allein; **hold one's ~** sich behaupten; **get one's ~ back** (fam) sich revanchieren

own[2] vt besitzen; (confess) zugeben; **I don't ~** it es gehört mir nicht. **~ up** vi es zugeben

owner /'əʊnə(r)/ n Eigentümer(in) m(f), Besitzer(in) m(f); (of shop)

Inhaber(in) m(f). **~ship** n Besitz m

ox /ɒks/ n (pl **oxen**) Ochse m

oxide /'ɒksaɪd/ n Oxyd nt

oxygen /'ɒksɪdʒən/ n Sauerstoff m

oyster /'ɔɪstə(r)/ n Auster f

ozone /'əʊzəʊn/ n Ozon nt. **~-'friendly** a ≈ ohne FCKW. **~ layer** n Ozonschicht f

P

pace /peɪs/ n Schritt m; (speed) Tempo nt; **keep ~ with** Schritt halten mit □vi **~ up and down** auf und ab gehen. **~-maker** n (Sport & Med) Schrittmacher m

Pacific /pə'sɪfɪk/ a & n **the ~ [Ocean]** der Pazifik

pacifier /'pæsɪfaɪə(r)/ n (Amer) Schnuller m

pacifist /'pæsɪfɪst/ n Pazifist m

pacify /'pæsɪfaɪ/ vt (pt/pp **-ied**) beruhigen

pack /pæk/ n Packung f; (Mil) Tornister m; (of cards) [Karten]spiel nt; (gang) Bande f; (of wolves) Meute f; (of hounds) Meute f; **a ~ of lies** ein Haufen Lügen □vt/i packen; einpacken (article); **be ~ed** (crowded) [gedrängt] voll sein; **send s.o. ~ing** (fam) jdn wegschicken. **~ up** vt einpacken □vi (fam) (machine:) kaputtgehen; (person:) einpacken (fam)

package /'pækɪdʒ/ n Paket nt □vt verpacken. **~ holiday** n Pauschalreise f

packed 'lunch n Lunchpaket nt

packet /'pækɪt/ n Päckchen nt; **cost a ~** (fam) einen Haufen Geld kosten

packing /'pækɪŋ/ n Verpackung f

pact /pækt/ n Pakt m

pad[1] /pæd/ n Polster nt; (for writing) [Schreib]block m; (fam: home) Wohnung f □vt (pt/pp **padded**) polstern

pad[2] vi (pt/pp **padded**) tappen

padding /'pædɪŋ/ n Polsterung f; (in written work) Füllwerk nt

paddle[1] /'pædl/ n Paddel nt □vt (row) paddeln

paddle[2] vi waten

paddock /'pædək/ n Koppel f

padlock /'pædlɒk/ n Vorhängeschloß nt □vt mit einem Vorhängeschloß verschließen

paediatrician /pi:dɪə'trɪʃn/ n Kinderarzt m /-ärztin f

pagan /'peɪgən/ a heidnisch □n Heide m/Heidin f

page[1] /peɪdʒ/ n Seite f

page[2] n (boy) Page m □vt ausrufen (person)

pageant /'pædʒənt/ n Festzug m. **~ry** n Prunk m

paid /peɪd/ see **pay** □a bezahlt; **put ~ to** (fam) zunichte machen

pail /peɪl/ n Eimer m

pain /peɪn/ n Schmerz m; **be in ~** Schmerzen haben; **take ~s** sich (dat) Mühe geben; **~ in the neck** (fam) Nervensäge f □vt (fig) schmerzen

pain: **~ful** a schmerzhaft; (fig) schmerzlich. **~killer** n schmerzstillendes Mittel nt. **~less** a, **-ly** adv schmerzlos

painstaking /'peɪnzteɪkɪŋ/ a sorgfältig

paint /peɪnt/ n Farbe f □vt/i streichen; (artist:) malen. **~brush** n Pinsel m. **~er** n Maler m; (decorator) Anstreicher m. **~ing** n Malerei f; (picture) Gemälde nt

pair /peə(r)/ n Paar nt; **~ of trousers** Hose f; **~ of scissors** Schere f □vt paaren □vi **~ off** Paare bilden

pajamas /pə'dʒɑ:məz/ n pl (Amer) Schlafanzug m

Pakistan /pɑ:kɪ'stɑ:n/ n Pakistan nt. **~i** a pakistanisch □n Pakistaner(in) m(f)

pal /pæl/ n Freund(in) m(f)

palace /'pælɪs/ n Palast m

palatable /'pælətəbl/ a schmackhaft

palate /'pælət/ n Gaumen m

palatial /pə'leɪʃl/ a palastartig

palaver /pə'lɑ:və(r)/ n (fam: fuss) Theater nt (fam)

pale[1] /peɪl/ n (stake) Pfahl m; **beyond the ~** (fam) unmöglich

pale[2] a (-r, -st) blaß □vi blaß werden. **~ness** n Blässe f

Palestin|e /'pælɪstaɪn/ n Palästina nt. **~ian** /pælə'stɪnɪən/ a palästinensisch □n Palästinenser(in) m(f)

palette /'pælɪt/ n Palette f

pall /pɔ:l/ n Sargtuch nt; (fig) Decke f □vi an Reiz verlieren

pallid /'pælɪd/ a bleich. **~ness** n Blässe f

palm /pɑ:m/ n Handfläche f; (tree, symbol) Palme f □vt **~ sth off on s.o.** jdm etw andrehen. **P~ 'Sunday** n Palmsonntag m

palpable /'pælpəbl/ a tastbar; (perceptible) spürbar

palpitat|e /'pælpɪteɪt/ vi klopfen. **~ions** /-'teɪʃnz/ npl Herzklopfen nt

paltry /'pɔ:ltrɪ/ a (-ier, -iest) armselig

pamper /'pæmpə(r)/ vt verwöhnen

pamphlet /'pæmflɪt/ n Broschüre f

pan /pæn/ n Pfanne f; (saucepan) Topf m; (of scales) Schale f □vt (pt/pp panned) (fam) verreißen

panacea /pænə'si:ə/ n Allheilmittel nt

panache /pə'næʃ/ n Schwung m

pancake n Pfannkuchen m

pancreas /'pæŋkrɪəs/ n Bauchspeicheldrüse f

panda /'pændə/ n Panda m. **~ car** n Streifenwagen m

pandemonium /pændɪ'məʊnɪəm/ n Höllenlärm m

pander /'pændə(r)/ vi **~ to s.o.** jdm zu sehr nachgeben

pane /peɪn/ n [Glas]scheibe f

panel /'pænl/ n Tafel f, Platte f; **~ of experts** Expertenrunde f;

~ of judges Jury f. ~ling n Täfelung f

pang /pæŋ/ n ~s of hunger Hungergefühl nt; ~s of conscience Gewissensbisse pl

panic /'pænɪk/ n Panik f (pt/pp **panicked**) in Panik geraten. ~-stricken a von Panik ergriffen

panoram|a /pænə'rɑːmə/ n Panorama nt. ~ic /-'ræmɪk/ a Panorama-

pansy /'pænzɪ/ n Stiefmütterchen nt

pant /pænt/ vi keuchen; ⟨dog:⟩ hecheln

pantechnicon /pæn'teknɪkən/ n Möbelwagen m

panther /'pænθə(r)/ n Panther m

panties /'pæntɪz/ npl [Damen]slip m

pantomime /'pæntəmaɪm/ n [zu Weihnachten aufgeführte] Märchenvorstellung f

pantry /'pæntrɪ/ n Speisekammer f

pants /pænts/ npl Unterhose f; ⟨woman's⟩ Schlüpfer m; ⟨trousers⟩ Hose f

'**pantyhose** n (Amer) Strumpfhose f

papal /'peɪpl/ a päpstlich

paper /'peɪpə(r)/ n Papier nt; ⟨wall~⟩ Tapete f; ⟨newspaper⟩ Zeitung f; ⟨exam~⟩ Testbogen m; ⟨exam⟩ Klausur f; ⟨treatise⟩ Referat nt; ~s pl ⟨documents⟩ Unterlagen pl; ⟨for identification⟩ [Ausweis]papiere pl; on ~ schriftlich □vt tapezieren

paper: ~back n Taschenbuch nt. ~-clip n Büroklammer f. ~-knife n Brieföffner m. ~-weight n Briefbeschwerer m. ~work n Schreibarbeit f

par /pɑː(r)/ n (Golf) Par nt; on a ~ gleichwertig (with dat); feel below ~ sich nicht ganz auf der Höhe fühlen

parable /'pærəbl/ n Gleichnis nt

parachut|e /'pærəʃuːt/ n Fallschirm m □vi [mit dem Fallschirm] abspringen. ~ist n Fallschirmspringer m

parade /pə'reɪd/ n Parade f; ⟨procession⟩ Festzug m □vi marschieren □vt ⟨show off⟩ zur Schau stellen

paradise /'pærədaɪs/ n Paradies nt

paradox /'pærədɒks/ n Paradox nt. ~ical /-'dɒksɪkl/ paradox

paraffin /'pærəfɪn/ n Paraffin nt

paragon /'pærəgən/ n ~ of virtue Ausbund m der Tugend

paragraph /'pærəgrɑːf/ n Absatz m

parallel /'pærəlel/ a & adv parallel □n (Geog) Breitenkreis m; ⟨fig⟩ Parallele f

paralyse /'pærəlaɪz/ vt lähmen; ⟨fig⟩ lahmlegen

paralysis /pə'ræləsɪs/ n (pl -ses /-siːz/) Lähmung f

paramount /'pærəmaʊnt/ a überragend; be ~ vorgehen

paranoid /'pærənɔɪd/ a ⟨krankhaft⟩ mißtrauisch

parapet /'pærəpɪt/ n Brüstung f

paraphernalia /pærəfə'neɪlɪə/ n Kram m

paraphrase /'pærəfreɪz/ n Umschreibung f □vt umschreiben

paraplegic /pærə'pliːdʒɪk/ a querschnittsgelähmt □n Querschnittsgelähmte(r) m/f

parasite /'pærəsaɪt/ n Parasit m, Schmarotzer m

parasol /'pærəsɒl/ n Sonnenschirm m

paratrooper /'pærətruːpə(r)/ n Fallschirmjäger m

parcel /'pɑːsl/ n Paket nt

parch /pɑːtʃ/ vt austrocknen; be ~ed ⟨person:⟩ einen furchtbaren Durst haben

parchment /'pɑːtʃmənt/ n Pergament nt

pardon /'pɑːdn/ n Verzeihung f; ⟨Jur⟩ Begnadigung f; ~? ⟨fam⟩ bitte? I beg your ~ wie bitte?

(sorry) Verzeihung! □vt verzeihen; (Jur) begnadigen

pare /peə(r)/ vt (peel) schälen

parent /'peərənt/ n Elternteil m;
~s pl Eltern pl. ~al /pə'rentl/ a
elterlich

parenthesis /pə'renθəsɪs/ n (pl
-ses /-si:z/) Klammer f

parish /'pærɪʃ/ n Gemeinde f.
~ioner /pə'rɪʃənə(r)/ n Ge-
meindemitglied nt

parity /'pærətɪ/ n Gleichheit f

park /pɑːk/ n Park m □vt/i parken

parking /'pɑːkɪŋ/ n Parken nt; 'no
~' 'Parken verboten'. ~-lot n
(Amer) Parkplatz m. ~-meter n
Parkuhr f. ~ space n Parkplatz
m

parliament /'pɑːləmənt/ n Parlament nt. ~ary /-'mentərɪ/ a parla-
mentarisch

parlour /'pɑːlə(r)/ n Wohnzimmer
nt

parochial /pə'rəʊkɪəl/ a Ge-
meinde-; (fig) beschränkt

parody /'pærədɪ/ n Parodie f □vt
(pt/pp -ied) parodieren

parole /pə'rəʊl/ n on ~ auf Be-
währung

paroxysm /'pærəksɪzm/ n Anfall
m

parquet /'pɑːkeɪ/ n ~ floor Parkett nt

parrot /'pærət/ n Papagei m

parry /'pærɪ/ vt (pt/pp -ied) abwehren ⟨blow⟩; (Fencing) parieren

parsimonious /pɑːsɪ'məʊnɪəs/ a
geizig

parsley /'pɑːslɪ/ n Petersilie f

parsnip /'pɑːsnɪp/ n Pastinake f

parson /'pɑːsn/ n Pfarrer m

part /pɑːt/ n Teil m; (Techn) Teil
nt; (area) Gegend f; (Theat) Rolle
f; (Mus) Part m; spare ~ Ersatzteil nt; for my ~ meinerseits; on
the ~ of von Seiten (+ gen); take
s.o.'s ~ für jdn Partei ergreifen;
take ~ in teilnehmen an (+ dat)

□adv teils □vt trennen; scheiteln
⟨hair⟩ □vi ⟨people:⟩ sich trennen;
~ with sich trennen von

partake /pɑː'teɪk/ vi (pt -took, pp
-taken) teilnehmen; ~ of ⟨eat⟩ zu
sich nehmen

part-ex'change n take in ~ in
Zahlung nehmen

partial /'pɑːʃl/ a Teil-; be ~ to
mögen. ~ity /pɑːʃɪ'ælətɪ/ n Voreingenommenheit f; (liking) Vorliebe f. ~ly adv teilweise

participant /pɑː'tɪsɪpənt/ n Teil-
nehmer(in) m(f). ~ate /-peɪt/ vi
teilnehmen (in an + dat).
~ation /-'peɪʃn/ n Teilnahme f

participle /'pɑːtɪsɪpl/ n Partizip
nt; present/past ~ erstes/zwei-
tes Partizip nt

particle /'pɑːtɪkl/ n Körnchen nt;
(Phys) Partikel nt; (Gram) Partikel f

particular /pə'tɪkjʊlə(r)/ a beson-
dere(r,s); (precise) genau; (fastidious) penibel; in ~ besonders.
~ly adv besonders. ~s npl
nähere Angaben pl

parting /'pɑːtɪŋ/ n Abschied m; (in
hair) Scheitel m □attrib Ab-
schieds-

partition /pɑː'tɪʃn/ n Trennwand
f; (Pol) Teilung f □vt teilen. ~ off
vt abtrennen

partly /'pɑːtlɪ/ adv teilweise

partner /'pɑːtnə(r)/ n Partner(in)
m(f); (Comm) Teilhaber m.
~ship n Partnerschaft f;
(Comm) Teilhaberschaft f

partridge /'pɑːtrɪdʒ/ n Rebhuhn
nt

part-time a & adv Teilzeit-; be or
work ~ Teilzeitarbeit machen

party /'pɑːtɪ/ n Party f, Fest nt;
(group) Gruppe f; (Pol, Jur) Partei f; be ~ to sich beteiligen an (+
dat)

'party line[1] n (Teleph) Gemein-
schaftsanschluß m

party 'line[2] n (Pol) Parteilinie f

pass /pɑ:s/ n Ausweis m; (Geog, Sport) Paß m; (Sch) ≈ ausreichend; **get a** ~ bestehen □ vt vorbeigehen/-fahren an (+ dat); (overtake) überholen; (hand) reichen; (Sport) abgeben, abspielen; (approve) annehmen; (exceed) übersteigen; bestehen (exam); machen (remark); fällen (judgement); (Jur) verhängen (sentence); ~ **water** Wasser lassen; ~ **the time** sich (dat) die Zeit vertreiben; ~ **sth off as sth** etw als etw ausgeben; ~ **one's hand over sth** mit der Hand über etw (acc) fahren □ vi vorbeigehen/-fahren; (get by) vorbeikommen; (overtake) überholen; (time:) vergehen; (in exam) bestehen; **let sth** ~ (fig) etw übergehen; **[I]** ~! [ich] passe! ~ **away** vi sterben. ~ **down** vt herunterreichen; (fig) weitergeben. ~ **out** vi ohnmächtig werden. ~ **round** vt herumreichen. ~ **up** vt heraufreichen. (fam: miss) vorübergehen lassen

passable /'pɑ:səbl/ a (road) befahrbar; (satisfactory) passabel

passage /'pæsɪdʒ/ n Durchgang m; (corridor) Gang m; (voyage) Überfahrt f; (in book) Passage f

passenger /'pæsɪndʒə(r)/ n Fahrgast m; (Naut, Aviat) Passagier m; (in car) Mitfahrer m. ~ **seat** n Beifahrersitz m

passer-by /pɑ:sə'baɪ/ n (pl -s-by) Passant|in m(f)

'passing place n Ausweichstelle f

passion /'pæʃn/ n Leidenschaft f. ~**ate** /-ət/ a, ~**ly** adv leidenschaftlich

passive /'pæsɪv/ a passiv □ n Passiv nt

Passover /'pɑ:səʊvə(r)/ n Passah nt

pass: ~**port** n [Reise]paß m. ~**word** n Kennwort nt; (Mil) Losung f

past /pɑ:st/ a vergangene(r,s); (former) ehemalig; **in the** ~ **few days** in den letzten paar Tagen;

that's all ~ das ist jetzt vorbei □ n Vergangenheit f □ prep an (+ dat) ... vorbei; (after) nach; **at ten** ~ **two** um zehn nach zwei □ adv vorbei; **go/come** ~ vorbeigehen/-kommen

pasta /'pæstə/ n Nudeln pl

paste /peɪst/ n Brei m; (dough) Teig m; (fish-, meat-) Paste f; (adhesive) Kleister m; (jewellery) Straß m □ vt kleistern

pastel /'pæstl/ n Pastellfarbe f; (crayon) Pastellstift m; (drawing) Pastell n □ attrib Pastell-

pasteurize /'pɑ:stʃəraɪz/ vt pasteurisieren

pastille /'pæstɪl/ n Pastille f

pastime /'pɑ:staɪm/ n Zeitvertreib m

pastoral /'pɑ:stərəl/ a ländlich; (care) seelsorgerisch

pastry /'peɪstrɪ/ n Teig m; **cakes and** ~**ies** Kuchen und Gebäck

pasture /'pɑ:stʃə(r)/ n Weide f

pasty¹ /'pæstɪ/ n Pastete f

pasty² /'peɪstɪ/ a blaß, (fam) käsig

pat /pæt/ n Klaps m; (of butter) Stückchen nt □ adv **have sth off** ~ etw aus dem Effeff können □ vt (pt/pp patted) tätscheln; ~ **s.o. on the back** jdm auf die Schulter klopfen

patch /pætʃ/ n Flicken m; (spot) Fleck m; **not a** ~ **on** (fam) gar nicht zu vergleichen mit □ vt flicken. ~ **up** vt [zusammen]-flicken; beilegen (quarrel)

patchy /'pætʃɪ/ a ungleichmäßig

pâté /'pæteɪ/ n Pastete f

patent /'peɪtnt/ a, ~**ly** adv offensichtlich □ n Patent nt □ vt patentieren. ~ **leather** n Lackleder nt

paternal /pə'tɜ:nl/ a väterlich. ~**ity** n Vaterschaft f

path /pɑ:θ/ n (pl ~s /pɑ:ðz/) [Fuß]-weg m, Pfad m; (orbit, track) Bahn f; (fig) Weg m

pathetic /pə'θetɪk/ a mitleiderregend; (attempt) erbärmlich

patholog|ical /ˌpæθəˈlɒdʒɪkl/ a pathologisch. ~**ist**/pəˈθɒlədʒɪst/n Pathologe m

pathos /ˈpeɪθɒs/ n Rührseligkeit f

patience /ˈpeɪʃns/ n Geduld f; (game) Patience f

patient /ˈpeɪʃnt/ a, -ly adv geduldig □n Patient(in) m(f)

patio /ˈpætɪəʊ/ n Terrasse f

patriot /ˈpætrɪət/ n Patriot(in) m(f). ~**ic** /-ˈɒtɪk/ a patriotisch. ~**ism** n Patriotismus m

patrol /pəˈtrəʊl/ n Patrouille f □ vt/i patrouillieren [in (+ dat)]; (police:) auf Streife gehen/fahren [in (+ dat)]. ~ **car** n Streifenwagen m

patron /ˈpeɪtrən/ n Gönner m; (of charity) Schirmherr m; (of the arts) Mäzen m; (customer) Kunde m/Kundin f; (Theat) Besucher m. ~ **age** /ˈpætrənɪdʒ/ n Schirmherrschaft f

patroniz|e /ˈpætrənaɪz/ vt (fig) herablassend behandeln. ~**ing** a, -ly adv gönnerhaft

patter¹ /ˈpætə(r)/ n Getrippel nt; (of rain) Plätschern nt □ vi trippeln; plätschern

patter² n (speech) Gerede nt

pattern /ˈpætn/ n Muster nt

paunch /pɔːntʃ/ n [Schmer]bauch m

pauper /ˈpɔːpə(r)/ n Arme(r) m/f

pause /pɔːz/ n Pause f □ vi innehalten

pave /peɪv/ vt pflastern; ~ the way den Weg bereiten (for dat). ~**ment** n Bürgersteig m

pavilion /pəˈvɪljən/ n Pavillon m; (Sport) Klubhaus nt

paw /pɔː/ n Pfote f; (of large animal) Pranke f, Tatze f

pawn¹ /pɔːn/ n (Chess) Bauer m; (fig) Schachfigur f

pawn² vt verpfänden □n in ~ verpfändet. ~**broker** n Pfandleiher m. ~**shop** n Pfandhaus nt

pay /peɪ/ n Lohn m; (salary) Gehalt nt; be in the ~ of bezahlt werden von □v (pt/pp paid) □vt

bezahlen; zahlen (money); ~ s.o. a visit jdm einen Besuch abstatten; ~ s.o. a compliment jdm ein Kompliment machen □vi zahlen; (be profitable) sich bezahlt machen; (fig) sich lohnen; ~ for sth etw bezahlen. ~ back vt zurückzahlen. ~ in vt einzahlen. ~ off vt abzahlen (debt) □vi (fig) sich auszahlen. ~ up vi zahlen

payable /ˈpeɪəbl/ a zahlbar; make ~ to ausstellen auf (+ acc)

payee /peɪˈiː/ n [Zahlungs]empfänger m

payment /ˈpeɪmənt/ n Bezahlung f; (amount) Zahlung f

pay: ~ packet n Lohntüte f; ~ **phone** n Münzfernsprecher m

pea /piː/ n Erbse f

peace /piːs/ n Frieden m; for my ~ of mind zu meiner eigenen Beruhigung

peace|able /ˈpiːsəbl/ a friedlich. ~**ful** a, -ly adv friedlich. ~**maker** n Friedensstifter m

peach /piːtʃ/ n Pfirsich m

peacock /ˈpiːkɒk/ n Pfau m

peak /piːk/ n Gipfel m; (fig) Höhepunkt m. ~**ed** '**cap** n Schirmmütze f. ~ **hours** npl Hauptbelastungszeit f; (for traffic) Hauptverkehrszeit f

peaky /ˈpiːkɪ/ a kränklich

peal /piːl/ n (of bells) Glockengeläut nt; ~s of laughter schallendes Gelächter nt

peanut /ˈpiːnʌt/ n Erdnuß f; for ~s (fam) für einen Apfel und ein Ei

pear /peə(r)/ n Birne f

pearl /pɜːl/ n Perle f

peasant /ˈpeznt/ n Bauer m

peat /piːt/ n Torf m

pebble /ˈpebl/ n Kieselstein m

peck /pek/ n Schnabelhieb m; (kiss) flüchtiger Kuß m □vt/i picken(nip) hacken (at nach). ~**ing order** n Hackordnung f

peckish /ˈpekɪʃ/ a be ~ (fam) Hunger haben

peculiar /prˈkjuːlɪə(r)/ a eigenartig, seltsam; ~ to eigentümlich

(+ *dat*). ~ity /-'ærətɪ/ *n* Eigenart *f*

pedal /'pedl/ *n* Pedal *nt* □ *vt* fahren ⟨*bicycle*⟩ □ *vi* treten. ~ **bin** *n* Treteimer *m*

pedantic /pr'dæntɪk/ *a*, **-ally** *adv* pedantisch

peddle /'pedl/ *vt* handeln mit

pedestal /'pedɪstl/ *n* Sockel *m*

pedestrian /pr'destrɪən/ *n* Fußgänger(in) *m(f)* □ *a* ⟨*fig*⟩ prosaisch. ~ **'crossing** *n* Fußgängerüberweg *m*. ~ **precinct** *n* Fußgängerzone *f*

pedicure /'pedɪkjʊə(r)/ *n* Pediküre *f*

pedigree /'pedɪgri:/ *n* Stammbaum *m* □ *attrib* ⟨*animal*⟩ Rasse-

pedlar /'pedlə(r)/ *n* Hausierer *m*

pee /pi:/ *vi* ⟨*pt/pp* peed⟩ ⟨*fam*⟩ pinkeln

peek /pi:k/ *vi* ⟨*fam*⟩ gucken

peel /pi:l/ *n* Schale *f* □ *vt* schälen □ *vi* ⟨*skin:*⟩ sich schälen; ⟨*paint:*⟩ abblättern. ~ings *npl* Schalen *pl*

peep /pi:p/ *n* kurzer Blick *m* □ *vi* gucken. ~-**hole** *n* Guckloch *nt*. P~ing 'Tom *n* ⟨*fam*⟩ Spanner *m*

peer[1] /pɪə(r)/ *vi* ~ **at** forschend ansehen

peer[2] *n* Peer *m*; his ~s *pl* seinesgleichen

peeved /pi:vd/ *a* ⟨*fam*⟩ ärgerlich. ~**ish** *a* reizbar

peg /peg/ *n* ⟨*hook*⟩ Haken *m*; ⟨*for tent*⟩ Pflock *m*, Hering *m*; ⟨*for clothes*⟩ [Wäsche]klammer *f*; off the ~ ⟨*fam*⟩ von der Stange □ *vt* ⟨*pt/pp* pegged⟩ anpflocken; anklammern ⟨*washing*⟩

pejorative /pr'dʒɒrətɪv/ *a*, **-ly** *adv* abwertend

pelican /'pelɪkən/ *n* Pelikan *m*

pellet /'pelɪt/ *n* Kügelchen *nt*

pelt[1] /pelt/ *n* ⟨*skin*⟩ Pelz *m*, Fell *nt*

pelt[2] *vt* bewerfen □ *vi* ⟨*fam:* run fast⟩ rasen; ~ **[down]** ⟨*rain:*⟩ [hernieder]prasseln

pelvis /'pelvɪs/ *n* ⟨*Anat*⟩ Becken *nt*

pen[1] /pen/ *n* ⟨*for animals*⟩ Hürde *f*

pen[2] *n* Federhalter *m*; ⟨*ball-point*⟩ Kugelschreiber *m*

penal /'pi:nl/ *a* Straf-. ~**ize** *vt* bestrafen; ⟨*fig*⟩ benachteiligen

penalty /'penltɪ/ *n* Strafe *f*; ⟨*fine*⟩ Geldstrafe *f*; ⟨*Sport*⟩ Strafstoß *m*; ⟨*Football*⟩ Elfmeter *m*

penance /'penəns/ *n* Buße *f*

pence /pens/ *see* **penny**

pencil /'pensl/ *n* Bleistift *m* □ *vt* ⟨*pt/pp* pencilled⟩ mit Bleistift schreiben. ~-**sharpener** *n* Bleistiftspitzer *m*

pendant /'pendənt/ *n* Anhänger *m*

pending /'pendɪŋ/ *a* unerledigt □ *prep* bis zu

pendulum /'pendjʊləm/ *n* Pendel *nt*

penetrat|e /'penɪtreɪt/ *vt* durchdringen; ~**e [into]** eindringen in (+ *acc*). ~**ing** *a* durchdringend. ~**ion** /-'treɪʃn/ *n* Durchdringen *nt*

'penfriend *n* Brieffreund(in) *m(f)*

penguin /'peŋgwɪn/ *n* Pinguin *m*

penicillin /penɪ'sɪlɪn/ *n* Penizillin *nt*

peninsula /pə'nɪnsʊlə/ *n* Halbinsel *f*

penis /'pi:nɪs/ *n* Penis *m*

peniten|ce /'penɪtəns/ *n* Reue *f*. ~**t** *a* reuig □ *n* Büßer *m*

penitentiary /penɪ'tenʃərɪ/ *n* ⟨*Amer*⟩ Gefängnis *nt*

pen|:-knife *n* Taschenmesser *nt*. ~**-name** *n* Pseudonym *nt*

pennant /'penənt/ *n* Wimpel *m*

penniless /'penɪlɪs/ *a* mittellos

penny /'penɪ/ *n* ⟨*pl* pence *or* single coins* pennies⟩ Penny *m*; ⟨*Amer*⟩ Centstück *nt*; spend a ~ ⟨*fam*⟩ mal verschwinden; the ~'s dropped ⟨*fam*⟩ der Groschen ist gefallen

pension /'penʃn/ *n* Rente *f*; ⟨*of civil servant*⟩ Pension *f*. ~**er** *n* Rentner(in) *m(f)*; Pensionär(in) *m(f)*

pensive /'pensɪv/ *a* nachdenklich

Pentecost /'pentɪkɒst/ n Pfingsten nt

pent-up /'pentʌp/ a angestaut

penultimate /pe'nʌltɪmət/ a vorletzte(r,s)

penury /'penjʊrɪ/ n Armut f

peony /'pɪənɪ/ n Pfingstrose f

people /'piːpl/ npl Leute pl, Menschen pl; (citizens) Bevölkerung f; the ~ das Volk; **English** ~ die Engländer; ~ **say** man sagt; **for four** ~ für vier Personen □vt bevölkern

pep /pep/ n (fam) Schwung m

pepper /'pepə(r)/ n Pfeffer m; (vegetable) Paprika m □vt (Culin) pfeffern

pepper: ~**corn** n Pfefferkorn nt. ~**mint** n Pfefferminz nt (bot) Pfefferminze f. ~**pot** n Pfefferstreuer m

per /pɜː(r)/ prep pro; ~ **cent** Prozent nt

perceive /pə'siːv/ vt wahrnehmen

percentage /pə'sentɪdʒ/ n Prozentsatz m; (part) Teil m

perceptible /pə'septəbl/ a wahrnehmbar

percept|ion /pə'sepʃn/ n Wahrnehmung f. ~**ive** /-tɪv/ a feinsinnig

perch[1] /pɜːtʃ/ n Stange f □vi ⟨bird:⟩ sich niederlassen

perch[2] n inv ⟨fish⟩ Barsch m

percolat|e /'pɜːkəleɪt/ vi durchsickern. ~**or** n Kaffeemaschine f

percussion /pə'kʌʃn/ n Schlagzeug nt. ~ **instrument** n Schlaginstrument nt

peremptory /pə'remptərɪ/ a herrisch

perennial /pə'renɪəl/ a ⟨problem⟩ immer wiederkehrend □n (Bot) mehrjährige Pflanze f

perfect[1] /'pɜːfɪkt/ a perfekt, vollkommen; (fam: utter) völlig □n (Gram) Perfekt nt

perfect[2] /pə'fekt/ vt vervollkommnen. ~**ion** /-ekʃn/ n Vollkommenheit f; **to** ~**ion** perfekt

perfectly /'pɜːfɪktlɪ/ adv perfekt; (completely) vollkommen, völlig

perforate /'pɜːfəreɪt/ vt perforieren; (make a hole in) durchlöchern. ~**d** a perforiert

perform /pə'fɔːm/ vt ausführen; erfüllen ⟨duty⟩; (Theat) aufführen ⟨play⟩; spielen ⟨role⟩ □vi (Theat) auftreten; (Techn) laufen. ~**ance** n Aufführung f; (at theatre, cinema) Vorstellung f; (Techn) Leistung f. ~**er** n Künstler(in) m(f)

perfume /'pɜːfjuːm/ n Parfüm nt; (smell) Duft m

perfunctory /pə'fʌŋktərɪ/ a flüchtig

perhaps /pə'hæps/ adv vielleicht

peril /'perəl/ n Gefahr f. ~**ous** /-əs/ a gefährlich

perimeter /pə'rɪmɪtə(r)/ n [äußere] Grenze f; (Geom) Umfang m

period /'pɪərɪəd/ n Periode f; (Sch) Stunde f; (full stop) Punkt m □attrib ⟨costume⟩ zeitgenössisch; ⟨furniture⟩ antik. ~**ic** /-'ɒdɪk/ a, **-ally** adv periodisch. ~**ical** /-'ɒdɪkl/ n Zeitschrift f

peripher|al /pə'rɪfərl/ a nebensächlich. ~**y** n Peripherie f

periscope /'perɪskəʊp/ n Periskop nt

perish /'perɪʃ/ vi ⟨rubber:⟩ verrotten; ⟨food:⟩ verderben; (die) ums Leben kommen. ~**able** /-əbl/ a leicht verderblich. ~**ing** a ⟨fam: cold⟩ eiskalt

perjur|e /'pɜːdʒə(r)/ vt ~ **e oneself** einen Meineid leisten. ~**y** n Meineid m

perk[1] /pɜːk/ n (fam) [Sonder]vergünstigung f

perk[2] vi ~ **up** munter werden

perky /'pɜːkɪ/ a munter

perm /pɜːm/ n Dauerwelle f □vt ~ **s.o.'s hair** jdm eine Dauerwelle machen

permanent /'pɜːmənənt/ a ständig; ⟨job, address⟩ fest. ~**ly** adv ständig; ⟨work, live⟩ dauernd, permanent; ⟨employed⟩ fest

permeable /'pɜ:mɪəbl/ a durchlässig

permeate /'pɜ:mɪeɪt/ vt durchdringen

permissible /pə'mɪsəbl/ a erlaubt

permission /pə'mɪʃn/ n Erlaubnis f

permissive /pə'mɪsɪv/ a ⟨society⟩ permissiv

permit[1] /pə'mɪt/ vt (pt/pp -mitted) erlauben (s.o. jdm); ~ me! gestatten Sie!

permit[2] /'pɜ:mɪt/ n Genehmigung f

pernicious /pə'nɪʃəs/ a schädlich; (Med) perniziös

perpendicular /pɜ:pən'dɪkjʊlə(r)/ a senkrecht □ n Senkrechte f

perpetrat|e /'pɜ:pɪtreɪt/ vt begehen. **~or** n Täter m

perpetual /pə'petjʊəl/ a, **-ly** adv ständig, dauernd

perpetuate /pə'petjʊeɪt/ vt bewahren; verewigen ⟨error⟩

perplex /pə'pleks/ vt verblüffen. **~ed** a verblüfft. **~ity** n Verblüffung f

persecut|e /'pɜ:sɪkju:t/ vt verfolgen. **~ion** /-'kju:ʃn/ n Verfolgung f

perseverance /pɜ:sɪ'vɪərəns/ n Ausdauer f

persever|e /pɜ:sɪ'vɪə(r)/ vi beharrlich weitermachen. **~ing** a ausdauernd

Persia /'pɜ:ʃə/ n Persien nt

Persian /'pɜ:ʃn/ a persisch; ⟨cat, carpet⟩ Perser-

persist /pə'sɪst/ vi beharrlich weitermachen; (continue) anhalten; ⟨view:⟩ weiter bestehen; ~ in doing sth dabei bleiben, etw zu tun. **~ence** n Beharrlichkeit f. **~ent** a, **-ly** adv beharrlich; (continuous) anhaltend

person /'pɜ:sn/ n Person f; in ~ persönlich

personal /'pɜ:sənl/ a, **-ly** adv persönlich. **~ 'hygiene** n Körperpflege f

personality /pɜ:sə'næləti/ n Persönlichkeit f

personify /pə'sɒnɪfaɪ/ vt (pt/pp -ied) personifizieren, verkörpern

personnel /pɜ:sə'nel/ n Personal nt

perspective /pə'spektɪv/ n Perspektive f

perspicacious /pɜ:spɪ'keɪʃəs/ a scharfsichtig

persp|iration /pɜ:spɪ'reɪʃn/ n Schweiß m. **~ire** /-'spaɪə(r)/ vi schwitzen

persua|de /pə'sweɪd/ vt überreden; (convince) überzeugen. **~sion** /-eɪʒn/ n Überredung f; (powers of ~sion) Überredungskunst f; (belief) Glaubensrichtung f

persuasive /pə'sweɪsɪv/ a, **-ly** adv beredsam; (convincing) überzeugend

pert /pɜ:t/ a, **-ly** adv keß

pertain /pə'teɪn/ vi ~ to betreffen; (belong) gehören zu

pertinent /'pɜ:tɪnənt/ a relevant (to für)

perturb /pə'tɜ:b/ vt beunruhigen

peruse /pə'ru:z/ vt lesen

perva|de /pə'veɪd/ vt durchdringen. **~sive** /-sɪv/ a durchdringend

pervers|e /pə'vɜ:s/ a eigensinnig. **~ion** /-ʃn/ n Perversion f

pervert[1] /pə'vɜ:t/ vt verdrehen; verführen ⟨person⟩

pervert[2] /'pɜ:vɜ:t/ n Perverse(r) m

perverted /pə'vɜ:tɪd/ a abartig

pessimis|m /'pesɪmɪzm/ n Pessimismus m. **~t** /-mɪst/ n Pessimist m. **~tic** /-'mɪstɪk/ a, **-ally** adv pessimistisch

pest /pest/ n Schädling m; (fam: person) Nervensäge f

pester /'pestə(r)/ vt belästigen; ~ s.o. for sth jdm wegen etw in den Ohren liegen

pesticide /'pestɪsaɪd/ n Schädlingsbekämpfungsmittel nt

pet /pet/ n Haustier nt; (favourite) Liebling m □vt (pt/pp **petted**) liebkosen

petal /ˈpetl/ n Blütenblatt nt

peter /ˈpiːtə(r)/ vi ~ **out** allmählich aufhören; ⟨stream:⟩ versickern

petite /pəˈtiːt/ a klein und zierlich

petition /pəˈtɪʃn/ n Bittschrift f □vt eine Bittschrift richten an (+ acc)

pet 'name n Kosename m

petrify /ˈpetrɪfaɪ/ vt/i (pt/pp -ied) versteinern; ~**ied** (frightened) vor Angst wie versteinert

petrol /ˈpetrl/ n Benzin nt

petroleum /pɪˈtrəʊliəm/ n Petroleum nt

petrol: ~-**pump** n Zapfsäule f. ~ **station** n Tankstelle f. ~ **tank** n Benzintank m

pet shop n Tierhandlung f

petticoat /ˈpetɪkəʊt/ n Unterrock m

petty /ˈpetɪ/ a (-ier, -iest) kleinlich. ~ **'cash** n Portokasse f

petulant /ˈpetjʊlənt/ a gekränkt

pew /pjuː/ n [Kirchen]bank f

pewter /ˈpjuːtə(r)/ n Zinn nt

phantom /ˈfæntəm/ n Gespenst nt

pharmaceutical /fɑːməˈsjuːtɪkl/ a pharmazeutisch

pharmacist /ˈfɑːməsɪst/ n Apotheker(in) m(f). ~**y** n Pharmazie f; (shop) Apotheke f

phase /feɪz/ n Phase f □vt ~ **in/out** allmählich einführen/abbauen

Ph.D. (abbr of Doctor of Philosophy) Dr. phil.

pheasant /ˈfeznt/ n Fasan m

phenomenal /fɪˈnɒmɪnl/ a phänomenal. ~**on** n (pl -na) Phänomen nt

phial /ˈfaɪəl/ n Fläschchen nt

philanderer /fɪˈlændərə(r)/ n Verführer m

philanthropic /fɪlənˈθrɒpɪk/ a menschenfreundlich. ~**ist** /fɪˈlænθrəpɪst/ n Philanthrop m

philately /fɪˈlætəlɪ/ n Philatelie f, Briefmarkenkunde f

philharmonic /fɪlɑːˈmɒnɪk/ n (orchestra) Philharmoniker pl

Philippines /ˈfɪlɪpiːnz/ npl Philippinen pl

philistine /ˈfɪlɪstaɪn/ n Banause m

philosopher /fɪˈlɒsəfə(r)/ n Philosoph m. ~**ical** /fɪləˈsɒfɪkl/ a, -**ly** adv philosophisch. ~**y** n Philosophie f

phlegm /flem/ n (Med) Schleim m

phlegmatic /flegˈmætɪk/ a phlegmatisch

phobia /ˈfəʊbɪə/ n Phobie f

phone /fəʊn/ n Telefon nt; **be on the** ~ Telefon haben; (be phoning) telefonieren □vt anrufen □vi telefonieren. ~ **back** vt/i zurückrufen. ~ **book** n Telefonbuch nt. ~ **box** n Telefonzelle f. ~ **card** n Telefonkarte f. ~-**in** n (Radio) Hörersendung f. ~ **number** n Telefonnummer f

phonetic /fəˈnetɪk/ a phonetisch. ~**s** n Phonetik f

phoney /ˈfəʊnɪ/ a (-ier, -iest) falsch; (forged) gefälscht

phosphorus /ˈfɒsfərəs/ n Phosphor m

photo /ˈfəʊtəʊ/ n Foto nt, Aufnahme f. ~**copier** n Fotokopiergerät nt. ~**copy** n Fotokopie f □vt fotokopieren

photogenic /fəʊtəʊˈdʒenɪk/ a fotogen

photograph /ˈfəʊtəgrɑːf/ n Fotografie f, Aufnahme f □vt fotografieren

photographer /fəˈtɒgrəfə(r)/ n Fotograf(in) m(f). ~**ic** /fəʊtəˈgræfɪk/ a, -**ally** adv fotografisch. ~**y** n Fotografie f

phrase /freɪz/ n Redensart f □vt formulieren. ~-**book** n Sprachführer m

physical /ˈfɪzɪkl/ a, -**ly** adv körperlich; ⟨geography, law⟩ physikalisch. ~ edu'cation n Turnen nt

physician /fɪˈzɪʃn/ n Arzt m/Ärztin f

physicist /ˈfɪzɪsɪst/ n Physiker(in) m(f). ~**s** n Physik f

physiology /fɪzɪ'ɒlədʒɪ/ n Physiologie f

physio|therap|ist /fɪzɪəʊ-/ n Physiotherapeut(in) m(f). **~y** n Physiotherapie f

physique /fɪ'ziːk/ n Körperbau m

pianist /'pɪənɪst/ n Klavierspieler(in) m(f); ⟨professional⟩ Pianist(in) m(f)

piano /pɪ'ænəʊ/ n Klavier nt

pick¹ /pɪk/ n Spitzhacke f

pick² n Auslese f; **take one's ~** sich (dat) aussuchen □vt/i ⟨pluck⟩ pflücken; ⟨select⟩ wählen, sich (dat) aussuchen; **~ and choose** wählerisch sein; **~ one's nose** in der Nase bohren; **~ a quarrel** einen Streit anfangen; **~ a hole in sth** ein Loch in etw (acc) machen; **~ holes in** ⟨fam⟩ kritisieren; **~ at one's food** beim Essen herumstochern. **~ on** vt wählen; ⟨fam: find fault with⟩ herumhacken auf (+ dat). **~ up** vt in die Hand nehmen; ⟨off the ground⟩ aufheben; hochnehmen ⟨baby⟩; ⟨learn⟩ lernen; ⟨acquire⟩ erwerben; ⟨buy⟩ kaufen; ⟨Teleph⟩ abnehmen ⟨receiver⟩; auffangen ⟨signal⟩; ⟨collect⟩ abholen; aufnehmen ⟨passengers⟩; ⟨police:⟩ aufgreifen ⟨criminal⟩; sich holen ⟨illness⟩; ⟨fam⟩ aufgabeln ⟨girl⟩; **~ oneself up** aufstehen □vi ⟨improve⟩ sich bessern

'pickaxe n Spitzhacke f

picket /'pɪkɪt/ n Streikposten m □vt Streikposten aufstellen vor (+ dat). **~ line** n Streikpostenkette f

pickle /'pɪkl/ n ⟨Amer: gherkin⟩ Essiggurke f; **~s** pl [Mixed] Pickles pl □vt einlegen

pick: ~pocket n Taschendieb m. **~-up** n ⟨truck⟩ Lieferwagen m; ⟨on record-player⟩ Tonabnehmer m

picnic /'pɪknɪk/ n Picknick nt □vi ⟨pt/pp **-nicked**⟩ picknicken

pictorial /pɪk'tɔːrɪəl/ a bildlich

picture /'pɪktʃə(r)/ n Bild nt; ⟨film⟩ Film m; **as pretty as a ~** bildhübsch; **put s.o. in the ~** ⟨fig⟩ jdn ins Bild setzen □vt ⟨imagine⟩ sich (dat) vorstellen

picturesque /pɪktʃə'resk/ a malerisch

pie /paɪ/ n Pastete f; ⟨fruit⟩ Kuchen m

piece /piːs/ n Stück nt; ⟨of set⟩ Teil nt; ⟨in game⟩ Stein m; ⟨Journ⟩ Artikel m; **a ~ of bread/paper** ein Stück Brot/Papier; **a ~ of news/advice** eine Nachricht/ein Rat; **take to ~s** auseinandernehmen □vt **~ together** zusammensetzen; ⟨fig⟩ zusammenstückeln. **~meal** adv stückweise. **~work** n Akkordarbeit f

pier /pɪə(r)/ n Pier m; ⟨pillar⟩ Pfeiler m

pierc|e /pɪəs/ vt durchstechen; **~e a hole in sth** ein Loch in etw (acc) stechen. **~ing** a durchdringend

piety /'paɪətɪ/ n Frömmigkeit f

piffle /'pɪfl/ n ⟨fam⟩ Quatsch m

pig /pɪg/ n Schwein nt

pigeon /'pɪdʒɪn/ n Taube f. **~-hole** n Fach nt

piggy /'pɪgɪ/ n ⟨fam⟩ Schweinchen nt. **~back** n **give s.o. a ~back** jdn huckepack tragen. **~ bank** n Sparschwein nt

pig'headed a ⟨fam⟩ starrköpfig

pigment /'pɪgmənt/ n Pigment nt. **~ation** /-men'teɪʃn/ n Pigmentierung f

pig: ~skin n Schweinsleder nt. **~sty** n Schweinestall m. **~tail** n ⟨fam⟩ Zopf m

pike /paɪk/ n inv ⟨fish⟩ Hecht m

pilchard /'pɪltʃəd/ n Sardine f

pile¹ /paɪl/ n ⟨of fabric⟩ Flor m

pile² n Haufen m □vt **~ sth on to sth** etw auf etw (acc) häufen. **~ up** vt häufen □vi sich häufen

piles /paɪlz/ npl ⟨fam⟩ Hämorrhoiden pl

'pile-up n Massenkarambolage f

pilfer /'pɪlfə(r)/ vt/i stehlen

pilgrim /'pɪlgrɪm/ n Pilger(in) m(f). **~age** /-ɪdʒ/ n Pilgerfahrt f, Wallfahrt f

pill /pɪl/ n Pille f

pillage /'pɪlɪdʒ/ vt plündern

pillar /'pɪlə(r)/ n Säule f. **~-box** n Briefkasten m

pillion /'pɪljən/ n Sozius[sitz] m

pillory /'pɪlərɪ/ n Pranger m □vt (pt/pp **-ied**) anprangern

pillow /'pɪləʊ/ n Kopfkissen nt. **~case** n Kopfkissenbezug m

pilot /'paɪlət/ n Pilot m; (Naut) Lotse m □vt fliegen (plane); lotsen (ship). **~-light** n Zündflamme f

pimp /pɪmp/ n Zuhälter m

pimple /'pɪmpl/ n Pickel m

pin /pɪn/ n Stecknadel f; (Techn) Bolzen m, Stift m; (Med) Nagel m; **I have ~ s and needles in my leg** (fam) mein Bein ist eingeschlafen □vt (pt/pp **pinned**) anstecken (**to/on** an + acc); (sewing) stecken; (hold down) festhalten; **~ sth on s.o.** (fam) jdm etw anhängen. **~ up** vt hochstecken; (on wall) anheften, anschlagen

pinafore /'pɪnəfɔ:(r)/ n Schürze f. **~ dress** n Kleiderrock m

pincers /'pɪnsəz/ npl Kneifzange f; (Zool) Scheren fpl

pinch /pɪntʃ/ n Kniff m; (of salt) Prise f; **at a ~** (fam) zur Not □vt kneifen, zwicken; (fam: steal) klauen; **~ one's finger** sich (dat) den Finger klemmen □vi (shoe) drücken

'pincushion n Nadelkissen nt

pine[1] /paɪn/ n (tree) Kiefer f

pine[2] vi **~** for sich sehnen nach; **~ away** sich verzehren

pineapple /'paɪn-/ n Ananas f

ping /pɪŋ/ n Klingeln nt

'ping-pong n Tischtennis nt

pink /pɪŋk/ a rosa

pinnacle /'pɪnəkl/ n Gipfel m; (on roof) Turmspitze f

pin: ~point vt genau festlegen. **~stripe** n Nadelstreifen m

pint /paɪnt/ n Pint nt (0,57 l, Amer: 0,47 l)

'pin-up n Pin-up-Girl nt

pioneer /paɪə'nɪə(r)/ n Pionier m □vt bahnbrechende Arbeit leisten für

pious /'paɪəs/ a, **-ly** adv fromm

pip[1] /pɪp/ n (seed) Kern m

pip[2] n (sound) Tonsignal nt

pipe /paɪp/ n Pfeife f; (for water, gas) Rohr nt □vt in Rohren leiten; (Culin) spritzen. **~ down** vi (fam) den Mund halten

pipe: ~dream n Luftschloß nt. **~line** n Pipeline f; **in the ~ line** (fam) in Vorbereitung

piper /'paɪpə(r)/ n Pfeifer m

piping /'paɪpɪŋ/ a **~ hot** kochend heiß

piquant /'pi:kənt/ a pikant

pique /pi:k/ n **in a fit of ~** beleidigt

pirate /'paɪərət/ n Pirat m

Pisces /'paɪsi:z/ n (Astr) Fische pl

piss /pɪs/ vi (sl) pissen

pistol /'pɪstl/ n Pistole f

piston /'pɪstən/ n (Techn) Kolben m

pit /pɪt/ n Grube f; (for orchestra) Orchestergraben m □vt (pt/pp **pitted**) (fig) messen (**against** mit)

pitch[1] /pɪtʃ/ n (steepness) Schräge f; (of voice) Stimmlage f; (of sound) [Ton]höhe f; (Sport) Feld nt; (of street-trader) Standplatz m; (fig: degree) Grad m □vt werfen; aufschlagen (tent) □vi fallen

pitch[2] n (tar) Pech nt. **~-'black** a pechschwarz. **~-'dark** a stockdunkel

pitcher /'pɪtʃə(r)/ n Krug m

piteous /'pɪtɪəs/ a erbärmlich

pitfall n (fig) Falle f

pith /pɪθ/ n (Bot) Mark nt; (of orange) weiße Haut f; (fig) Wesentliche(s) nt

pithy /'pɪθɪ/ a (-ier, -iest) (fig) prägnant

piti|**ful** /'pɪtɪfl/ a bedauernswert. **~less** a mitleidslos

pittance /'pɪtns/ n Hungerlohn m

pity /'pɪtɪ/ n Mitleid nt, Erbarmen nt; [what a] ~! [wie] schade! take ~ on sich erbarmen über (+ acc) □ vt bemitleiden

pivot /'pɪvət/ n Drehzapfen m; (fig) Angelpunkt m □ vi sich drehen (on um)

pixie /'pɪksɪ/ n Kobold m

pizza /'piːtsə/ n Pizza f

placard /'plækɑːd/ n Plakat nt

placate /plə'keɪt/ vt beschwichtigen

place /pleɪs/ n Platz m; (spot) Stelle f; (town, village) Ort m; (fam: house) Haus nt; out of ~ fehl am Platze; take ~ stattfinden; all over the ~ überall □ vt setzen; (upright) stellen; (flat) legen; (remember) unterbringen (fam); ~ an order eine Bestellung aufgeben; be ~d (in race) sich plazieren. ~-mat n Set nt

placid /'plæsɪd/ a gelassen

plagiar|ism /'pleɪdʒərɪzm/ n Plagiat nt. ~ize vt plagiieren

plague /pleɪg/ n Pest f □ vt plagen

plaice /pleɪs/ n inv Scholle f

plain /pleɪn/ a (-er, -est) klar; (simple) einfach; (not pretty) nicht hübsch; (not patterned) einfarbig; ⟨chocolate⟩ zartbitter; in ~ clothes in Zivil □ adv (simply) einfach □ n Ebene f; (Knitting) linke Masche f. ~ly adv klar, deutlich; (simply) einfach; (obviously) offensichtlich

plaintiff /'pleɪntɪf/ n (Jur) Kläger(in) m(f)

plaintive /'pleɪntɪv/ a, -ly adv klagend

plait /plæt/ n Zopf m □ vt flechten

plan /plæn/ n Plan m □ vt (pt/pp planned) planen; (intend) vorhaben

plane[1] /pleɪn/ n (tree) Platane f

plane[2] n Flugzeug nt; (Geom & fig) Ebene f

plane[3] n (Techn) Hobel m □ vt hobeln

planet /'plænɪt/ n Planet m

plank /plæŋk/ n Brett nt; (thick) Planke f

planning /'plænɪŋ/ n Planung f. ~ permission n Baugenehmigung f

plant /plɑːnt/ n Pflanze f; (Techn) Anlage f; (factory) Werk nt □ vt pflanzen; (place in position) setzen; ~ oneself in front of s.o. sich vor jdn hinstellen. ~ation /plæn'teɪʃn/ n Plantage f

plaque /plɑːk/ n [Gedenk]tafel f; (on teeth) Zahnbelag m

plasma /'plæzmə/ n Plasma nt

plaster /'plɑːstə(r)/ n Verputz m; (sticking ~) Pflaster nt; ~ [of Paris] Gips m □ vt verputzen ⟨wall⟩; (cover) bedecken mit. ~ed a (sl) besoffen. ~er n Gipser m

plastic /'plæstɪk/ n Kunststoff m, Plastik nt □ a Kunststoff-, Plastik-; (malleable) formbar, plastisch

Plasticine (P) /'plæstɪsiːn/ n Knetmasse f

plastic surgery n plastische Chirurgie f

plate /pleɪt/ n Teller m; (flat sheet) Platte f; (with name, number) Schild nt; (gold and silverware) vergoldete/versilberte Ware f; (in book) Tafel f □ vt (with gold) vergolden; (with silver) versilbern

plateau /'plætəʊ/ n (pl -x /-əʊz/) Hochebene f

platform /'plætfɔːm/ n Plattform f; (stage) Podium nt; (Rail) Bahnsteig m; ~ 5 Gleis 5

platinum /'plætɪnəm/ n Platin nt

platitude /'plætɪtjuːd/ n Platitüde f

platonic /plə'tɒnɪk/ a platonisch

platoon /plə'tuːn/ n (Mil) Zug m

platter /'plætə(r)/ n Platte f

plausible /'plɔːzəbl/ a plausibel

play /pleɪ/ n Spiel nt; (Theater)-stück nt; (Radio) Hörspiel nt; (TV) Fernsehspiel nt; ~ on words Wortspiel nt □ vt/i spielen;

ausspielen ⟨card⟩; ~ **safe** sicher-gehen. ~ **down** vt herunterspie-len. ~ **up** vi (fam) Mätzchen machen

play: ~**boy** n Playboy m. ~**er** n Spieler(in) m(f). ~**ful** a, -**ly** adv verspielt. ~**ground** n Spielplatz m; (Sch) Schulhof m. ~**group** n Kindergarten m

playing: ~**card** n Spielkarte f. ~**field** n Sportplatz m

play: ~**mate** n Spielkamerad m. ~**pen** n Laufstall m, Laufgitter nt. ~**thing** n Spielzeug nt. ~**wright** /-raɪt/ n Dramatiker m

plc abbr (public limited com-pany) ≈ GmbH

plea /pliː/ n Bitte f; **make a ~ for** bitten um

plead /pliːd/ vt vorschützen; (Jur) vertreten ⟨case⟩ □vi flehen (for um); ~ **guilty** sich schuldig be-kennen; ~ **with s.o.** jdn anflehen

pleasant /ˈpleznt/ a angenehm; ⟨person⟩ nett. ~**ly** adv ange-nehm; ⟨say, smile⟩ freundlich

pleas|e /pliːz/ adv bitte □vt gefal-len (+ dat); ~**e s.o.** jdm eine Freude machen; ~**e oneself** tun, was man will. ~**ed** a erfreut; **be** ~**ed with/about** sth sich über etw (acc) freuen. ~**ing** a erfreu-lich

pleasurable /ˈpleʒərəbl/ a ange-nehm

pleasure /ˈpleʒə(r)/ n Vergnü-gen nt; (Joy) Freude f; **with** ~ gern[e]

pleat /pliːt/ n Falte f □vt fälteln. ~**ed 'skirt** n Faltenrock m

plebiscite /ˈplebɪsɪt/ n Volksab-stimmung f

pledge /pledʒ/ n Pfand nt; (pro-mise) Versprechen nt □vt ver-pfänden; versprechen

plentiful /ˈplentɪfl/ a reichlich; **be** ~ reichlich vorhanden sein

plenty /ˈplentɪ/ n eine Menge; (enough) reichlich; ~ **of money/ people** viel Geld/viele Leute

pleurisy /ˈplʊərəsɪ/ n Rippen-fellentzündung f

pliable /ˈplaɪəbl/ a biegsam

pliers /ˈplaɪəz/ npl [Flach]zange f

plight /plaɪt/ n [Not]lage f

plimsolls /ˈplɪmsəlz/ npl Turn-schuhe pl

plinth /plɪnθ/ n Sockel m

plod /plɒd/ vi (pt/pp **plodded**) trotten; (work hard) sich abmü-hen

plonk /plɒŋk/ n (fam) billiger Wein m

plot /plɒt/ n Komplott nt; (of novel) Handlung f. ~ **of land** Stück nt Land □vt einzeichnen □vi ein Komplott schmieden

plough /plaʊ/ n Pflug m □vt/i pflügen. ~ **back** vt (Comm) wieder investieren

ploy /plɔɪ/ n (fam) Trick m

pluck /plʌk/ n Mut m □vt zupfen; rupfen ⟨bird⟩; pflücken ⟨flower⟩; ~ **up courage** Mut fassen

plucky /ˈplʌkɪ/ a (-ier, -iest) tap-fer, mutig

plug /plʌg/ n Stöpsel m; (wood) Zapfen m; (cotton wool) Bausch m; (Electr) Stecker m; (Auto) Zündkerze f; (fam: advertise-ment) Schleichwerbung f □vt zustopfen; (fam: advertise) Schleichwerbung machen für. ~ **in** vt (Electr) einstecken

plum /plʌm/ n Pflaume f

plumage /ˈpluːmɪdʒ/ n Gefieder nt

plumb /plʌm/ n Lot m □adv lot-recht □vt loten. ~ **in** vt installie-ren

plumb|er /ˈplʌmə(r)/ n Klempner m. ~**ing** n Wasserleitungen pl

'plumb-line n [Blei]lot nt

plume /pluːm/ n Feder f

plummet /ˈplʌmɪt/ vi herunter-stürzen

plump /plʌmp/ a (-er, -est) mollig, rundlich □vt ~ **for** wählen

plunder /ˈplʌndə(r)/ n Beute f □vt plündern

plunge /plʌndʒ/ n Sprung m; **take the** ~ (fam) den Schritt wagen □vt/i tauchen

plu·perfect /plu:-/ n Plusquamperfekt nt

plural /'plʊərl/ a pluralisch □n Mehrzahl f, Plural m

plus /plʌs/ prep plus (+ dat) □a Plus-□ n Pluszeichen nt; (advantage) Plus nt

plush[y] /plʌʃ[ɪ]/ a luxuriös

ply /plaɪ/ vt (pt/pp plied) ausüben ⟨trade⟩; ~ s.o. with drink jdm ein Glas nach dem anderen eingießen. ~-wood n Sperrholz nt

p.m. adv (abbr of post meridiem) nachmittags

pneumatic /njuː'mætɪk/ a pneumatisch. ~-drill n Preßlufthammer m

pneumonia /njuː'məʊnɪə/ f Lungenentzündung f

poach /pəʊtʃ/ vt (Culin) pochieren; (steal) wildern. ~er n Wilddieb m

pocket /'pɒkɪt/ n Tasche f; ~ of resistance Widerstandsnest nt; be out of ~ [an einem Geschäft] verlieren □vt einstecken. ~-book n Notizbuch nt; (wallet) Brieftasche f. ~-money n Taschengeld nt

pock-marked /'pɒk-/ a pockennarbig

pod /pɒd/ n Hülse f

podgy /'pɒdʒɪ/ a (-ier, -iest) dick

poem /'pəʊɪm/ n Gedicht nt

poet /'pəʊɪt/ n Dichter(in) m(f). ~ic /-'etɪk/ a dichterisch

poetry /'pəʊɪtrɪ/ n Dichtung f

poignant /'pɔɪnjənt/ a ergreifend

point /pɔɪnt/ n Punkt m; (sharp end) Spitze f; (meaning) Sinn m; (purpose) Zweck m; (Electr) Steckdose f; ~s pl (Rail) Weiche f; ~ of view Standpunkt m; good/bad ~s gute/schlechte Seiten; what is the ~? wozu? the ~ is es geht darum; I don't see the ~ das sehe ich nicht ein; up to a ~ bis zu einem gewissen Grade; be on the ~ of doing sth im Begriff sein, etw zu tun □vt richten (at auf + acc); ausfugen ⟨brickwork⟩

□vi deuten (at/to auf + acc); (with finger) mit dem Finger zeigen. ~ out vt zeigen auf (+ acc); ~ sth out to s.o. jdn auf etw (acc) hinweisen

point-'blank a aus nächster Entfernung; (fig) rundweg

point|ed /'pɔɪntɪd/ a spitz; ⟨question⟩ gezielt. ~er n (hint) Hinweis m. ~less a zwecklos, sinnlos

poise /pɔɪz/ n Haltung f. ~d a (confident) selbstsicher; ~d to bereit zu

poison /'pɔɪzn/ n Gift nt □vt vergiften. ~ous a giftig

poke /pəʊk/ n Stoß m □vt stoßen; schüren ⟨fire⟩; (put) stecken; ~ fun at sich lustig machen über (+ acc)

poker[1] /'pəʊkə(r)/ n Schüreisen nt

poker[2] n (Cards) Poker nt

poky /'pəʊkɪ/ a (-ier, -iest) eng

Poland /'pəʊlənd/ n Polen nt

polar /'pəʊlə(r)/ a Polar-. ~ bear n Eisbär m. ~ize vt polarisieren

Pole /pəʊl/ n Pole m/Polin f

pole[1] n Stange f

pole[2] n (Geog, Electr) Pol m

polecat n Iltis m

'pole-star n Polarstern m

'pole-vault n Stabhochsprung m

police /pə'liːs/ npl Polizei f □vt polizeilich kontrollieren

police: ~man n Polizist m. ~ state n Polizeistaat m. ~ station n Polizeiwache f. ~woman n Polizistin f

policy[1] /'pɒlɪsɪ/ n Politik f

policy[2] n (insurance) Police f

polio /'pəʊlɪəʊ/ n Kinderlähmung f

Polish /'pəʊlɪʃ/ a polnisch

polish /'pɒlɪʃ/ n (shine) Glanz m; (for shoes) [Schuh]creme f; (for floor) Bohnerwachs nt; (for furniture) Politur f; (for silver) Putzmittel nt; (for nails) Lack m; (fig) Schliff m □vt polieren; bohnern ⟨floor⟩; ~ off vt (fam) verputzen ⟨food⟩; erledigen ⟨task⟩

polisher /ˈpɒlɪʃə(r)/ n (machine) Poliermaschine f; (for floor) Bohnermaschine f

polite /pəˈlaɪt/ a, **-ly** adv höflich. **~ness** n Höflichkeit f

politic /ˈpɒlɪtɪk/ a ratsam

politic|al /pəˈlɪtɪkl/ a, **-ly** adv politisch. **~ian** /pɒlɪˈtɪʃn/ n Politiker(in) m(f)

politics /ˈpɒlɪtɪks/ n Politik f

polka /ˈpɒlkə/ n Polka f

poll /pəʊl/ n Abstimmung f; (election) Wahl f; **[opinion] ~** [Meinungs]umfrage f; **go to the ~s** wählen ▢ vt erhalten ⟨votes⟩

pollen /ˈpɒlən/ n Blütenstaub m, Pollen m

polling /ˈpəʊlɪŋ/: **~-booth** n Wahlkabine f. **~-station** n Wahllokal nt

'poll tax n Kopfsteuer f

pollutant /pəˈluːtənt/ n Schadstoff m

pollut|e /pəˈluːt/ vt verschmutzen. **~ion** /-ˈuːʃn/ n Verschmutzung f

polo /ˈpəʊləʊ/ n Polo nt. **~-neck** n Rollkragen m. **~ shirt** n Polohemd nt

polyester /pɒlɪˈestə(r)/ n Polyester m

polystyrene (P) /pɒlɪˈstaɪriːn/ n Polystyrol m; (for packing) Styropor (P) nt

polytechnic /pɒlɪˈteknɪk/ n ≈ technische Hochschule f

polythene /ˈpɒlɪθiːn/ n Polyäthylen nt. **~ bag** n Plastiktüte f

polyun'saturated a mehrfachungesättigt

pomegranate /ˈpɒmɪgrænɪt/ n Granatapfel m

pomp /pɒmp/ n Pomp m

pompon /ˈpɒmpɒn/ n Pompon m

pompous /ˈpɒmpəs/ a, **-ly** adv großspurig

pond /pɒnd/ n Teich m

ponder /ˈpɒndə(r)/ vi nachdenken

ponderous /ˈpɒndərəs/ a schwerfällig

pong /pɒŋ/ n (fam) Mief m

pony /ˈpəʊnɪ/ n Pony nt. **~-tail** n Pferdeschwanz m. **~-trekking** n Ponyreiten nt

poodle /ˈpuːdl/ n Pudel m

pool¹ /puːl/ n [Schwimm]becken nt; (pond) Teich m; (of blood) Lache f

pool² n (common fund) [gemeinsame] Kasse f; **~s** pl (Fußball)toto nt ▢ vt zusammenlegen

poor /pʊə(r)/ a (-er, -est) arm; (not good) schlecht; **in ~ health** nicht gesund ▢ npl **the ~** die Armen. **~-ly** a **be ~ly** krank sein ▢ adv ärmlich; (badly) schlecht

pop¹ /pɒp/ n Knall m; (drink) Brause f ▢ v (pt/pp popped) ▢ vt (fam: put) stecken (in in + acc) ▢ vi knallen; (burst) platzen. **~ in** vi (fam) reinschauen. **~ out** vi (fam) kurz rausgehen

pop² n (fam) Popmusik f, Pop m ▢ attrib Pop-

popcorn n Puffmais m

pope /pəʊp/ n Papst m

poplar /ˈpɒplə(r)/ n Pappel f

poppy /ˈpɒpɪ/ n Mohn m

popular /ˈpɒpjʊlə(r)/ a beliebt, populär; ⟨belief⟩ volkstümlich. **~ity** /-ˈlærətɪ/ n Beliebtheit f, Popularität f

populat|e /ˈpɒpjʊleɪt/ vt bevölkern. **~ion** /-ˈleɪʃn/ n Bevölkerung f

porcelain /ˈpɔːsəlɪn/ n Porzellan nt

porch /pɔːtʃ/ n Vorbau m; (Amer) Veranda f

porcupine /ˈpɔːkjʊpaɪn/ n Stachelschwein nt

pore¹ /pɔː(r)/ n Pore f

pore² vi **~ over** studieren

pork /pɔːk/ n Schweinefleisch nt

porn /pɔːn/ n (fam) Porno m

pornograph|ic /pɔːnəˈgræfɪk/ a pornographisch. **~y** /-ˈnɒgrəfɪ/ n Pornographie f

porous /ˈpɔːrəs/ a porös

porpoise /ˈpɔːpəs/ n Tümmler m

porridge /ˈpɒrɪdʒ/ n Haferbrei m

port¹ /pɔːt/ n Hafen m; (town) Hafenstadt f

port² n (Naut) Backbord nt

port³ n (wine) Portwein m

portable /'po:təbl/ a tragbar

porter /'po:tə(r)/ n Portier m; (for luggage) Gepäckträger m

portfolio /po:t'fəʊliəʊ/ n Mappe f; (Comm) Portefeuille nt

'porthole n Bullauge nt

portion /'po:ʃn/ n Portion f; (part, share) Teil m

portly /'po:tlɪ/ a (-ier, -iest) beleibt

portrait /'po:trɪt/ n Porträt nt

portray /po:'treɪ/ vt darstellen. ~**al** n Darstellung f

Portug|al /'po:tjʊgl/ n Portugal nt. ~**uese** /-'gi:z/ a portugiesisch □ n Portugiese m/-giesin f

pose /pəʊz/ n Pose f □ vt aufwerfen ⟨problem⟩; stellen ⟨question⟩ □ vi posieren; (for painter) Modell stehen; ~ **as** sich ausgeben als

posh /pɒʃ/ a (fam) feudal

position /pə'zɪʃn/ n Platz m; (posture) Haltung f; (job) Stelle f; (situation) Lage f, Situation f; (status) Stellung f □ vt plazieren; ~ **oneself** sich stellen

positive /'pɒzətɪv/ a, **-ly** adv positiv; (definite) eindeutig; (real) ausgesprochen □ n Positiv nt

possess /pə'zes/ vt besitzen. ~**ion** /pə'zeʃn/ n Besitz m; ~**ions** pl Sachen pl

possess|ive /pə'zesɪv/ a Possessiv-; **be** ~**ive** zu sehr an jdm hängen. ~**or** n Besitzer m

possibility /pɒsə'bɪlətɪ/ n Möglichkeit f

possib|le /'pɒsəbl/ a möglich. ~**ly** adv möglicherweise; **not** ~**ly** unmöglich

post¹ /pəʊst/ n (pole) Pfosten m □ vt anschlagen ⟨notice⟩

post² n (place of duty) Posten m; (job) Stelle f □ vt postieren; (transfer) versetzen

post³ n (mail) Post f; **by** ~ mit der Post □ vt aufgeben ⟨letter⟩; (send by ~) mit der Post schicken;

keep s.o. ~ **ed** jdn auf dem laufenden halten

postage /'pəʊstɪdʒ/ n Porto nt. ~ **stamp** f Briefmarke f

postal /'pəʊstl/ a Post-. ~ **order** f ≈ Geldanweisung f

post: ~**box** n Briefkasten m. ~**card** n Postkarte f. (picture) Ansichtskarte f. ~**code** n Postleitzahl f. ~'**date** vt vordatieren

poster /'pəʊstə(r)/ n Plakat nt

posterior /pɒ'stɪərɪə(r)/ a hintere(r,s) □ n (fam) Hintern m

posterity /pɒ'sterətɪ/ n Nachwelt f

posthumous /'pɒstjʊməs/ a, **-ly** adv postum

post: ~**man** n Briefträger m. ~**mark** n Poststempel m

post-mortem /-'mɔ:təm/ n Obduktion f

'post office n Post f

postpone /pəʊst'pəʊn/ vt aufschieben; ~ **until** verschieben auf (+ acc). ~**ment** n Verschiebung f

postscript /'pəʊstskrɪpt/ n Nachschrift f

posture /'pɒstʃə(r)/ n Haltung f

post-'war a Nachkriegs-

posy /'pəʊzɪ/ n Sträußchen nt

pot /pɒt/ n Topf m; (for tea, coffee) Kanne f; ~ **s of money** (fam) eine Menge Geld; **go to** ~ (fam) herunterkommen

potassium /pə'tæsɪəm/ n Kalium nt

potato /pə'teɪtəʊ/ n (pl **-es**) Kartoffel f

poten|cy /'pəʊtənsɪ/ n Stärke f. ~**t** a stark

potential /pə'tenʃl/ a, **-ly** adv potentiell □ n Potential nt

pot: ~**hole** n Höhle f; (in road) Schlagloch nt. ~**holer** n Höhlenforscher m. ~**shot** n **take a** ~**shot** at schießen auf (+ acc)

potted /'pɒtɪd/ a eingemacht; (shortened) gekürzt. ~'**plant** n Topfpflanze f

potter¹ /'pɒtə(r)/ vi ~ **[about]** herumwerkeln

potter² n Töpfer(in) m(f). **~y** n Töpferei f; ⟨articles⟩ Töpferwaren pl

potty /'pɒtɪ/ a (-ier, -iest) ⟨fam⟩ verrückt □ n Töpfchen nt

pouch /pautʃ/ n Beutel m

pouffe /pu:f/ n Sitzkissen nt

poultry /'pəʊltrɪ/ n Geflügel nt

pounce /pauns/ vi zuschlagen; **~ on** sich stürzen auf (+ acc)

pound¹ /paund/ n ⟨money & 0,454 kg⟩ Pfund nt

pound² vt hämmern □ vi ⟨heart:⟩ hämmern; ⟨run heavily⟩ stampfen

pour /pɔ:(r)/ vt gießen; einschenken ⟨drink⟩ □ vi strömen; ⟨with rain⟩ gießen. **~ out** vi ausströmen □ vt ausschütten; einschenken ⟨drink⟩

pout /paut/ vi einen Schmollmund machen

poverty /'pɒvətɪ/ n Armut f

powder /'paudə(r)/ n Pulver nt; ⟨cosmetic⟩ Puder m □ vt pudern. **~y** a pulverig

power /'pauə(r)/ n Macht f; ⟨strength⟩ Kraft f; ⟨Electr⟩ Strom m; ⟨nuclear⟩ Energie f; ⟨Math⟩ Potenz f. **~ cut** n Stromsperre f. **~ed** a betrieben (by mit); **~ed by electricity** mit Elektroantrieb. **~ful** a mächtig; ⟨strong⟩ stark. **~less** a machtlos. **~station** n Kraftwerk nt

practicable /'præktɪkəbl/ a durchführbar, praktikabel

practical /'præktɪkl/ a, **-ly** adv praktisch. **~ 'joke** n Streich m

practice /'præktɪs/ n Praxis f; ⟨custom⟩ Brauch m; ⟨habit⟩ Gewohnheit f; ⟨exercise⟩ Übung f; ⟨Sport⟩ Training nt; **in ~** ⟨in reality⟩ in der Praxis; **out of ~** außer Übung; **put into ~** ausführen

practise /'præktɪs/ vt üben; ⟨carry out⟩ praktizieren; ausüben ⟨profession⟩ □ vi üben; ⟨doctor:⟩ praktizieren. **~d** a geübt

pragmatic /præg'mætɪk/ a, **~ally** adv pragmatisch

praise /preɪz/ n Lob nt □ vt loben. **~worthy** a lobenswert

pram /præm/ n Kinderwagen m

prance /prɑ:ns/ vi herumhüpfen; ⟨horse:⟩ tänzeln

prank /præŋk/ n Streich m

prattle /'prætl/ vi plappern

prawn /prɔ:n/ n Garnele f, Krabbe f. **~ 'cocktail** n Krabbencocktail m

pray /preɪ/ vi beten. **~er** /preə(r)/ n Gebet nt; **~ers** pl ⟨service⟩ Andacht f

preach /pri:tʃ/ vt/i predigen. **~er** n Prediger m

preamble /pri:'æmbl/ n Einleitung f

pre-ar'range /pri:-/ vt im voraus arrangieren

precarious /prɪ'keərɪəs/ a, **-ly** adv unsicher

precaution /prɪ'kɔ:ʃn/ n Vorsichtsmaßnahme f; **as a ~** zur Vorsicht. **~ary** a Vorsichts-

precede /prɪ'si:d/ vt vorangehen (+ dat)

preceden|ce /'presɪdəns/ n Vorrang m. **~t** n Präzedenzfall m

preceding /prɪ'si:dɪŋ/ a vorhergehend

precinct /'pri:sɪŋkt/ n Bereich m; ⟨traffic-free⟩ Fußgängerzone f; ⟨Amer: district⟩ Bezirk m

precious /'preʃəs/ a kostbar; ⟨style⟩ preziös □ adv ⟨fam⟩ **~ little** recht wenig

precipice /'presɪpɪs/ n Steilabfall m

precipitate¹ /prɪ'sɪpɪtət/ a voreilig

precipitat|e² /prɪ'sɪpɪteɪt/ vt schleudern; ⟨fig: accelerate⟩ beschleunigen. **~ion** /-'teɪʃn/ n ⟨Meteorol⟩ Niederschlag m

précis /'preɪsi:/ n (pl précis /-si:z/) Zusammenfassung f

precis|e /prɪ'saɪs/ a, **-ly** adv genau. **~ion** /-'sɪʒn/ n Genauigkeit f

preclude /prɪ'klu:d/ vt ausschließen

precocious /prɪˈkəʊʃəs/ a frühreif

pre|con'ceived /priː-/ a vorgefaßt. ~**con'ception** n vorgefaßte Meinung f

precursor /priːˈkɜːsə(r)/ n Vorläufer m

predator /ˈpredətə(r)/ n Raubtier nt

predecessor /ˈpriːdisesə(r)/ n Vorgänger(in) m(f)

predicament /prɪˈdɪkəmənt/ n Zwangslage f

predicat|e /ˈpredɪkət/ n (Gram) Prädikat nt. ~**ive** /prɪˈdɪkətɪv/ a, -**ly** adv prädikativ

predict /prɪˈdɪkt/ vt voraussagen. ~**able** /-əbl/ a voraussehbar; ⟨person⟩ berechenbar. ~**ion** /-ˈdɪkʃn/ n Voraussage f

pre'domin|ant /priː-/ a vorherrschend. ~**antly** adv hauptsächlich, überwiegend. ~**ate** vi vorherrschen

pre-'eminent /priː-/ a hervorragend

pre-empt /priːˈempt/ vt zuvorkommen (+ dat)

preen /priːn/ vt putzen; ~ **oneself** (fig) selbstgefällig tun

pre|fab /ˈpriːfæb/ n (fam) [einfaches] Fertighaus nt. ~**'fabricated** a vorgefertigt

preface /ˈprefɪs/ n Vorwort nt

prefect /ˈpriːfekt/ n Präfekt m

prefer /prɪˈfɜː(r)/ vt (pt/pp -ferred) vorziehen; I ~ to **walk** ich gehe lieber zu Fuß; I ~ **wine** ich trinke lieber Wein

prefera|ble /ˈprefərəbl/ a be ~**ble** vorzuziehen sein (to dat). ~**bly** adv vorzugsweise

preferen|ce /ˈprefərəns/ n Vorzug m. ~**tial** /-ˈrenʃl/ a bevorzugt

prefix /ˈpriːfɪks/ n Vorsilbe f

pregnan|cy /ˈpregnənsɪ/ n Schwangerschaft f. ~**t** a schwanger; ⟨animal⟩ trächtig

prehi'storic /priː-/ a prähistorisch

prejudice /ˈpredʒʊdɪs/ n Vorurteil nt; (bias) Voreingenommenheit f □ vt einnehmen (**against** gegen). ~**d** a voreingenommen

preliminary /prɪˈlɪmɪnərɪ/ a Vor-

prelude /ˈpreljuːd/ n Vorspiel nt

pre-'marital /priː-/ a vorehelich

premature /ˈpremətjʊə(r)/ a vorzeitig; ⟨birth⟩ Früh-. ~**ly** adv zu früh

pre'meditated /priː-/ a vorsätzlich

premier /ˈpremɪə(r)/ a führend □ n (Pol) Premier[minister] m

première /ˈpremɪeə(r)/ n Premiere f

premises /ˈpremɪsɪz/ npl Räumlichkeiten pl; **on the** ~ im Haus

premiss /ˈpremɪs/ n Prämisse f

premium /ˈpriːmɪəm/ n Prämie f; **be at a** ~ hoch im Kurs stehen

premonition /premə'nɪʃn/ n Vorahnung f

preoccupied /prɪˈɒkjʊpaɪd/ a (in Gedanken) beschäftigt

prep /prep/ n (Sch) Hausaufgaben pl

pre-'packed /priː-/ a abgepackt

preparation /prepəˈreɪʃn/ n Vorbereitung f; (substance) Präparat nt

preparatory /prɪˈpærətrɪ/ a Vor-
□ adv ~ **to** vor (+ dat)

prepare /prɪˈpeə(r)/ vt vorbereiten; anrichten ⟨meal⟩ □ vi sich vorbereiten (**for** auf + acc); ~**d** to **be** bereit zu

pre'pay /priː-/ vt (pt/pp -**paid**) im voraus bezahlen

preposition /prepəˈzɪʃn/ n Präposition f

prepossessing /priːpəˈzesɪŋ/ a ansprechend

preposterous /prɪˈpɒstərəs/ a absurd

prerequisite /priːˈrekwɪzɪt/ n Voraussetzung f

prerogative /prɪˈrɒgətɪv/ n Vorrecht nt

Presbyterian /prezbɪ'tɪərɪən/ *a* presbyterianisch □*n* Presbyterianer(in) *m(f)*

prescribe /prɪ'skraɪb/ *vt* vorschreiben; ⟨Med⟩ verschreiben

prescription /prɪ'skrɪpʃn/ *n* ⟨Med⟩ Rezept *nt*

presence /'prezns/ *n* Anwesenheit *f*, Gegenwart *f*; ~ **of mind** Geistesgegenwart *f*

present[1] /'preznt/ *a* gegenwärtig; **be** ~ anwesend sein; ⟨occur⟩ vorkommen □*n* Gegenwart *f*; ⟨Gram⟩ Präsens *nt*; **at** ~ zur Zeit; **for the** ~ vorläufig

present[2] *n* ⟨gift⟩ Geschenk *nt*

present[3] /prɪ'zent/ *vt* überreichen; ⟨show⟩ zeigen; vorlegen ⟨cheque⟩; ⟨introduce⟩ vorstellen; ~ **s.o. with sth** jdm etw überreichen. **~able** /-əbl/ *a* **be** ~**able** sich zeigen lassen können

presentation /prezn'teɪʃn/ *n* Überreichung *f*. ~ **ceremony** *n* Verleihungszeremonie *f*

presently /'prezntlɪ/ *adv* nachher; ⟨Amer: now⟩ zur Zeit

preservation /prezə'veɪʃn/ *n* Erhaltung *f*

preservative /prɪ'zɜːvətɪv/ *n* Konservierungsmittel *nt*

preserve /prɪ'zɜːv/ *vt* erhalten; ⟨Culin⟩ konservieren; ⟨bottle⟩ einmachen □*n* ⟨Hunting & fig⟩ Revier *nt*; ⟨jam⟩ Konfitüre *f*

preside /prɪ'zaɪd/ *vi* den Vorsitz haben ⟨over bei⟩

presidency /'prezɪdənsɪ/ *n* Präsidentschaft *f*

president /'prezɪdnt/ *n* Präsident *m*; ⟨Amer: chairman⟩ Vorsitzende(r) *m/f*. ~**ial** /-'denʃl/ *a* Präsidenten- ⟨election⟩ Präsidentschafts-

press /pres/ *n* Presse *f* □*vt/i* drücken; drücken auf (+ *acc*) ⟨button⟩; pressen ⟨flower⟩; ⟨iron⟩ bügeln; ⟨urge⟩ bedrängen; ~ **for** drängen auf (+ *acc*); **be** ~**ed for time** in Zeitdruck sein. ~ **on** *vi*

weitergehen/-fahren; ⟨fig⟩ weitermachen

press: ~ **cutting** *n* Zeitungsausschnitt *m*. ~**ing** *a* dringend. ~**stud** *n* Druckknopf *m*. ~**up** *n* Liegestütz *m*

pressure /'preʃə(r)/ *n* Druck *m* □ *vt* = **pressurize**. ~**cooker** *n* Schnellkochtopf *m*. ~ **group** *n* Interessengruppe *f*

pressurize /'preʃəraɪz/ *vt* Druck ausüben auf (+ *acc*). ~**d** *a* Druck-

prestige /pre'stiːʒ/ *n* Prestige *nt*. ~**ious** /-'stɪdʒəs/ *a* Prestige-

presumably /prɪ'zjuːməblɪ/ *adv* vermutlich

presume /prɪ'zjuːm/ *vt* vermuten; ~ **to do sth** sich (*dat*) anmaßen, etw zu tun □ *vi* ~ **on** ausnutzen

presumption /prɪ'zʌmpʃn/ *n* Vermutung *f*; ⟨boldness⟩ Anmaßung *f*. ~**uous** /-'zʌmptjuəs/ *a*, **-ly** *adv* anmaßend

presup'pose /priː-/ *vt* voraussetzen

pretence /prɪ'tens/ *n* Verstellung *f*; ⟨pretext⟩ Vorwand *m*; **it's all** ~ das ist alles gespielt

pretend /prɪ'tend/ *vt* ⟨claim⟩ vorgeben; ~ **that** so tun, als ob; ~ **to** be sich ausgeben als

pretentious /prɪ'tenʃəs/ *a* protzig

pretext /'priːtekst/ *n* Vorwand *m*

pretty /'prɪtɪ/ *a* (**-ier, -iest**), **-ily** *adv* hübsch □*adv* ⟨fam: fairly⟩ ziemlich

pretzel /'pretsl/ *n* Brezel *f*

prevail /prɪ'veɪl/ *vi* siegen; ⟨custom:⟩ vorherrschen; ~ **on s.o. to do sth** jdn dazu bringen, etw zu tun

prevalen|ce /'prevələns/ *n* Häufigkeit *f*. ~**t** *a* vorherrschend

prevent /prɪ'vent/ *vt* verhindern, verhüten; ~ **s.o.** ⟨**from**⟩ **doing sth** jdn daran hindern, etw zu tun. ~**able** /-əbl/ *a* vermeidbar. ~**ion** /-enʃn/ *n* Verhinderung *f*, Verhütung *f*. ~**ive** /-ɪv/ *a* vorbeugend

preview /'priːvjuː/ *n* Voraufführung *f*

previous /'priːvɪəs/ *a* vorhergehend; ~ **to** vor (+ *dat.*). ~ **ly** *adv* vorher, früher

pre-'war /priː-/ *a* Vorkriegs-

prey /preɪ/ *n* Beute *f*; **bird of** ~ Raubvogel *m* □*vi* ~ **on** Jagd machen auf (+ *acc*); ~ **on s.o.'s mind** jdm schwer auf der Seele liegen

price /praɪs/ *n* Preis *m* □*vt* (*Comm*) auszeichnen. ~**less** *a* unschätzbar; (*fig*) unbezahlbar

prick /prɪk/ *n* Stich *m* □*vt/i* stechen; ~ **up one's ears** die Ohren spitzen

prickle /'prɪkl/ *n* Stachel *m*; (*thorn*) Dorn *m*. ~**y** *a* stachelig; ⟨*sensation*⟩ stechend

pride /praɪd/ *n* Stolz *m*; (*arrogance*) Hochmut *m*; (*of lions*) Rudel *nt* □*vt* ~ **oneself on** stolz sein auf (+ *acc*)

priest /priːst/ *n* Priester *m*

prig /prɪg/ *n* Tugendbold *m*

prim /prɪm/ *a* (**primmer, primmest**) prüde

primarily /'praɪmərɪlɪ/ *adv* hauptsächlich, in erster Linie

primary /'praɪmərɪ/ *a* Haupt-. ~ **school** *n* Grundschule *f*

prime[1] /praɪm/ *a* Haupt-; (*first-rate*) erstklassig □*n* **be in one's** ~ in den besten Jahren sein

prime[2] *vt* scharf machen ⟨*bomb*⟩; grundieren ⟨*surface*⟩; (*fig*) instruieren

Prime Minister /praɪ'mɪnɪstə(r)/ *n* Premierminister(in) *m(f)*

primeval /praɪ'miːvl/ *a* Ur-

primitive /'prɪmɪtɪv/ *a* primitiv

primrose /'prɪmrəʊz/ *n* gelbe Schlüsselblume *f*

prince /prɪns/ *n* Prinz *m*

princess /prɪn'ses/ *n* Prinzessin *f*

principal /'prɪnsəpl/ *a* Haupt- □*n* (*Sch*) Rektor(in) *m(f)*

principality /prɪnsɪ'pælətɪ/ *n* Fürstentum *nt*

principally /'prɪnsəplɪ/ *adv* hauptsächlich

principle /'prɪnsəpl/ *n* Prinzip *nt*, Grundsatz *m*; **in/on** ~ im/aus Prinzip

print /prɪnt/ *n* Druck *m*; (*Phot*) Abzug *m*; **in** ~ gedruckt; (*available*) erhältlich; **out of** ~ vergriffen □*vt* drucken; (*write in capitals*) in Druckschrift schreiben; (*Computing*) ausdrucken; (*Phot*) abziehen. ~**ed matter** *n* Drucksache *f*

printer /'prɪntə(r)/ *n* Drucker *m*. ~**ing** *n* Druck *m*

'printout *n* (*Computing*) Ausdruck *m*

prior /'praɪə(r)/ *a* frühere(r,s); ~ **to** vor (+ *dat*)

priority /praɪ'ɒrətɪ/ *n* Priorität *f*, Vorrang *m*; (*matter*) vordringliche Sache *f*

prise /praɪz/ *vt* ~ **open/up** aufstemmen/hochstemmen

prism /'prɪzm/ *n* Prisma *nt*

prison /'prɪzn/ *n* Gefängnis *nt*. ~**er** *n* Gefangene(r) *m/f*

pristine /'prɪstiːn/ *a* tadellos

privacy /'prɪvəsɪ/ *n* Privatsphäre *f*; **have no** ~ nie für sich sein

private /'praɪvət/ *a*, **-ly** *adv* privat; (*confidential*) vertraulich; ⟨*car, secretary, school*⟩ Privat- □*n* (*Mil*) [einfacher] Soldat *m*; **in** ~ privat; (*confidentially*) vertraulich

privation /praɪ'veɪʃn/ *n* Entbehrung *f*

privatize /'praɪvətaɪz/ *vt* privatisieren

privilege /'prɪvəlɪdʒ/ *n* Privileg *nt*. ~**d** *a* privilegiert

privy /'prɪvɪ/ *a* **be** ~ **to** wissen

prize /praɪz/ *n* Preis *m* □*vt* schätzen. ~**-giving** *n* Preisverteilung *f*. ~**-winner** *n* Preisgewinner(in) *m(f)*

pro /prəʊ/ *n* (*fam*) Profi *m*; **the** ~**s and cons** das Für und Wider

probability /prɒbə'bɪlətɪ/ *n* Wahrscheinlichkeit *f*

probable /'prɒbəbl/ *a,* -bly *adv*
wahrscheinlich

probation /prə'beɪʃn/ *n* (*Jur*) Be-
währung *f.* ~**ary** *a* Probe-;
~**ary period** Probezeit *f*

probe /prəʊb/ *n* Sonde *f;* (*fig: in-*
vestigation) Untersuchung *f* □
vt/i ~ [**into**] untersuchen

problem /'prɒbləm/ *n* Problem *nt;*
(*Math*) Textaufgabe *f.* ~**atic**
/-'mætɪk/ *a* problematisch

procedure /prə'siːdʒə(r)/ *n* Verfahren *nt*

proceed /prə'siːd/ *vi* gehen; (*in*
vehicle) fahren; (*continue*) weiter-
gehen/-fahren; (*speaking*) fortfahren; (*act*) verfahren □ *vt* ~ **to**
do sth anfangen, etw zu tun

proceedings /prə'siːdɪŋz/ *npl* Verfahren *nt;* (*Jur*) Prozeß *m*

proceeds /'prəʊsiːdz/ *npl* Erlös *m*

process /'prəʊses/ *n* Prozeß *m;*
(*procedure*) Verfahren *nt;* **in the**
~ **dabei** □ *vt* verarbeiten; (*Admin*)
bearbeiten; (*Phot*) entwickeln

procession /prə'seʃn/ *n* Umzug *m,*
Prozession *f*

proclaim /prə'kleɪm/ *vt* ausrufen

proclamation /prɒklə'meɪʃn/ *n*
Proklamation *f*

procure /prə'kjʊə(r)/ *vt* beschaffen

prod /prɒd/ *n* Stoß *m* □ *vt* stoßen;
(*fig*) einen Stoß geben (+ *dat*)

prodigal /'prɒdɪgl/ *a* verschwenderisch

prodigious /prə'dɪdʒəs/ *a* gewaltig

prodigy /'prɒdɪdʒɪ/ *n* [**infant**] ~
Wunderkind *nt*

produce[1] /'prɒdjuːs/ *n* landwirt-
schaftliche Erzeugnisse *pl*

produce[2] /prə'djuːs/ *vt* erzeugen,
produzieren; (*manufacture*) herstellen; (*bring out*) hervorholen;
(*cause*) hervorrufen; inszenieren
(*play*); (*Radio, TV*) redigieren.
~**r** *n* Erzeuger *m,* Produzent *m;*
Hersteller *m;* (*Theat*) Regisseur
m; (*Radio, TV*) Redakteur(in)
m(f)

product /'prɒdʌkt/ *n* Erzeugnis
nt, Produkt *nt.* ~**ion** /prə'dʌkʃn/

n Produktion *f;* (*Theat*) Inszenie-
rung *f*

productive /prə'dʌktɪv/ *a* produktiv; (*land, talks*) fruchtbar.
~**ity** /-'tɪvətɪ/ *n* Produktivität *f*

profane /prə'feɪn/ *a* weltlich;
(*blasphemous*) [gottes]lästerlich.
~**ity** /-'fænətɪ/ *n* (*oath*) Fluch *m*

profess /prə'fes/ *vt* behaupten; be-
kennen (*faith*)

profession /prə'feʃn/ *n* Beruf *m.*
~**al** *a,* -ly *adv* beruflich; (*not*
amateur) Berufs-; (*expert*) fachmännisch; (*Sport*) professionell
□ *n* Fachmann *m;* (*Sport*) Profi *m*

professor /prə'fesə(r)/ *n* Professor
m

proficien|cy /prə'fɪʃnsɪ/ *n* Können
nt. ~**t** *a* **be** ~**t** in beherrschen

profile /'prəʊfaɪl/ *n* Profil *nt;* (*char-*
acter study) Porträt *nt*

profit /'prɒfɪt/ *n* Gewinn *m,* Profit
m □ *vi* ~ **from** profitieren von.
~**able** /-əbl/ *a,* -bly *adv* gewinn-
bringend; (*fig*) nutzbringend

profound /prə'faʊnd/ *a,* -ly *adv* tief

profuse /prə'fjuːs/ *a,* -ly *adv* üppig; (*fig*) überschwenglich. ~**ion**
/-'juːʒn/ *n* **in** ~ **ion** in großer Fülle

progeny /'prɒdʒənɪ/ *n* Nachkom-
menschaft *f*

program /'prəʊgræm/ *n* Programm *nt* □ *vt* (*pt/pp* **program-**
med) programmieren

programme /'prəʊgræm/ *n* Programm *nt;* (*Radio, TV*) Sendung
f. ~**r** *n* (*Computing*) Program-
mierer(in) *m(f)*

progress[1] /'prəʊgres/ *n* Vorankommen *nt;* (*fig*) Fortschritt *m;*
in ~ im Gange; **make** ~ (*fig*)
Fortschritte machen

progress[2] /prə'gres/ *vi* vorankommen; (*fig*) fortschreiten. ~**ion**
/-ʃn/ *n* Folge *f;* (*development*)
Entwicklung *f*

progressive /prə'gresɪv/ *a* fortschrittlich; (*disease*) fortschrei-
tend. ~**ly** *adv* zunehmend

prohibit /prə'hɪbɪt/ vt verbieten (s.o. jdm). ~**ive** /-ɪv/ a unerschwinglich

project¹ /'prɒdʒekt/ n Projekt nt; (Sch) Arbeit f

project² /prə'dʒekt/ vt projizieren ⟨film⟩; ⟨plan⟩ planen □vi ⟨jut out⟩ vorstehen

projectile /prə'dʒektaɪl/ n Geschoß nt

projector /prə'dʒektə(r)/ n Projektor m

proletariat /prəʊlɪ'teərɪət/ n Proletariat nt

prolific /prə'lɪfɪk/ a fruchtbar; (fig) produktiv

prologue /'prəʊlɒg/ n Prolog m

prolong /prə'lɒŋ/ vt verlängern

promenade /prɒmə'nɑːd/ n Promenade f □ vi spazierengehen

prominent /'prɒmɪnənt/ a vorstehend; (important) prominent; (conspicuous) auffällig; ⟨place⟩ gut sichtbar

promiscu|ity /prɒmɪ'skjuːəti/ n Promiskuität f. ~**ous** /prə'mɪskjʊəs/ a be ~**ous** häufig den Partner wechseln

promis|e /'prɒmɪs/ n Versprechen nt □ vt/i versprechen (s.o. jdm); **the P~ed Land** das Gelobte Land. ~**ing** a vielversprechend

promote /prə'məʊt/ vt befördern; (advance) fördern; (publicize) Reklame machen für; **be** ~**ed** (Sport) aufsteigen. ~**ion** /-əʊʃn/ n Beförderung f; (Sport) Aufstieg m; (Comm) Reklame f

prompt /prɒmpt/ a prompt, unverzüglich; (punctual) pünktlich □ adv pünktlich □ vt/i veranlassen (**to** zu); (Theat) soufflieren (+ dat). ~**er** n Souffleur m/ Souffleuse f. ~**ly** adv prompt

prone /prəʊn/ a **be/lie** ~ auf dem Bauch liegen; **be** ~ **to** neigen zu; **be** ~ **to do sth** dazu neigen, etw zu tun

prong /prɒŋ/ n Zinke f

pronoun /'prəʊnaʊn/ n Fürwort nt, Pronomen nt

pronounce /prə'naʊns/ vt aussprechen; (declare) erklären. ~**d** a ausgeprägt; (noticeable) deutlich. ~**ment** n Erklärung f

pronunciation /prənʌnsɪ'eɪʃn/ n Aussprache f

proof /pruːf/ n Beweis m; (Typ) Korrekturbogen m □ a ~ **against** water/theft wasserfest/diebessicher. ~**reader** n Korrektor m

prop¹ /prɒp/ n Stütze f □ vt (pt/pp propped) ~ **open** offenhalten; ~ **against** (lean) lehnen an (+ acc). ~ **up** vt stützen

prop² n (Theat, fam) Requisit nt

propaganda /prɒpə'gændə/ n Propaganda f

propagate /'prɒpəgeɪt/ vt vermehren; (fig) verbreiten, propagieren

propel /prə'pel/ vt (pt/pp propelled) [an]treiben. ~**ler** n Propeller m. ~**ling 'pencil** n Drehbleistift m

propensity /prə'pensəti/ n Neigung f (**for** zu)

proper /'prɒpə(r)/ a, -**ly** adv richtig; (decent) anständig. ~ '**name**, ~ '**noun** n Eigenname m

property /'prɒpəti/ n Eigentum nt; (quality) Eigenschaft f; (Theat) Requisit nt; ⟨land⟩ [Grund]besitz m; (house) Haus nt. ~ **market** n Immobilienmarkt m

prophecy /'prɒfəsi/ n Prophezeiung f

prophesy /'prɒfəsaɪ/ vt (pt/pp -ied) prophezeien

prophet /'prɒfɪt/ n Prophet m. ~**ic** /prə'fetɪk/ a prophetisch

proportion /prə'pɔːʃn/ n Verhältnis nt; (share) Teil m; ~**s** pl Proportionen; (dimensions) Maße. ~**al** a, -**ly** adv proportional

proposal /prə'pəʊzl/ n Vorschlag m; (of marriage) [Heirats]antrag m

propose /prə'pəʊz/ vt vorschlagen; (intend) vorhaben; einbringen

⟨*motion*⟩; ausbringen ⟨*toast*⟩ □ *vi* einen Heiratsantrag machen

proposition /propə'zıʃn/ *n* Vorschlag *m*

propound /prə'paund/ *vt* darlegen

proprietor /prə'praıətə(r)/ *n* Inhaber(in) *m(f)*

propriety /prə'praıətı/ *n* Korrektheit *f*; (*decorum*) Anstand *m*

propulsion /prə'pʌlʃn/ *n* Antrieb *m*

prosaic /prə'zeıık/ *a* prosaisch

prose /prəuz/ *n* Prosa *f*

prosecut|e /'prosıkju:t/ *vt* strafrechtlich verfolgen. **~ion** /-'kju:ʃn/ *n* strafrechtliche Verfolgung *f*; the ~ion die Anklage. **~or** *n* [Public] P~or Staatsanwalt *m*

prospect¹ /'prospekt/ *n* Aussicht *f*

prospect² /prə'spekt/ *vi* suchen (for nach)

prospect|ive /prə'spektıv/ *a* (*future*) zukünftig. **~or** *n* Prospektor *m*

prospectus /prə'spektəs/ *n* Prospekt *m*

prosper /'prospə(r)/ *vi* gedeihen, florieren; ⟨*person*⟩ Erfolg haben. **~ity** /-'sperətı/ *n* Wohlstand *m*

prosperous /'prospərəs/ *a* wohlhabend

prostitut|e /'prostıtju:t/ *n* Prostituierte *f*. **~ion** /-'tju:ʃn/ *n* Prostitution *f*

prostrate /'prostreıt/ *a* ausgestreckt; **~ with grief** (*fig*) vor Kummer gebrochen

protagonist /prəu'tægənıst/ *n* Kämpfer *m*; (*fig*) Protagonist *m*

protect /prə'tekt/ *vt* schützen (from vor + *dat*); beschützen ⟨*person*⟩. **~ion** /-ekʃn/ *n* Schutz *m*. **~ive** /-ıv/ *a* Schutz-; (*fig*) beschützend. **~or** *n* Beschützer *m*

protégé /'protıʒeı/ *n* Schützling *m*, Protegé *m*

protein /'prəuti:n/ *n* Eiweiß *nt*

protest¹ /'prəutest/ *n* Protest *m*

protest² /prə'test/ *vi* protestieren

Protestant /'protıstənt/ *a* protestantisch, evangelisch □ *n* Protestant(in) *m(f)*, Evangelische(r) *m/f*

protester /prə'testə(r)/ *n* Protestierende(r) *m/f*

protocol /'prəutəkɒl/ *n* Protokoll *nt*

prototype /'prəutə-/ *n* Prototyp *m*

protract /prə'trækt/ *vt* verlängern. **~or** *n* Winkelmesser *m*

protrude /prə'tru:d/ *vi* [her]vorstehen

proud /praud/ *a*, **-ly** *adv* stolz (of auf + *acc*)

prove /pru:v/ *vt* beweisen □ *vi* **~ to be** sich erweisen als

proverb /'provз:b/ *n* Sprichwort *nt*. **~ial** /prə'vз:bıəl/ *a* sprichwörtlich

provide /prə'vaıd/ *vt* zur Verfügung stellen; gewähren ⟨*shade*⟩; **~ s.o. with sth** jdn mit etw versorgen *od* versehen □ *vi* **~ for** sorgen für

provided /prə'vaıdıd/ *conj* **~** [that] vorausgesetzt [daß]

providen|ce /'provıdəns/ *n* Vorsehung *f*. **~tial** /-'denʃl/ *a* **be ~tial** ein Glück sein

providing /prə'vaıdıŋ/ *conj* = **provided**

provinc|e /'provıns/ *n* Provinz *f*; (*fig*) Bereich *m*. **~ial** /prə'vınʃl/ *a* provinziell

provision /prə'vıʒn/ *n* Versorgung *f* (of mit); **~s** *pl* Lebensmittel *pl*. **~al**, **-ly** *adv* vorläufig

proviso /prə'vaızəu/ *n* Vorbehalt *m*

provocat|ion /provə'keıʃn/ *n* Provokation *f*. **~ive** /prə'vɒkətıv/ *a*, **-ly** *adv* provozierend; (*sexually*) aufreizend

provoke /prə'vəuk/ *vt* provozieren; (*cause*) hervorrufen

prow /prau/ *n* Bug *m*

prowess /'prauıs/ *n* Kraft *f*

prowl /praul/ *vi* herumschleichen □ *n* **be on the ~** herumschleichen

proximity /prok'sımətı/ *n* Nähe *f*

proxy /'prɒksɪ/ n Stellvertreter(in) m(f); (power) Vollmacht f
prude /pruːd/ n be a ~ prüde sein
pruden|ce /'pruːdns/ n Umsicht f. ~t a, -ly adv umsichtig; (wise) klug
prudish /'pruːdɪʃ/ a prüde
prune[1] /pruːn/ n Backpflaume f
prune[2] vt beschneiden
pry /praɪ/ vi (pt/pp pried) neugierig sein

psalm /sɑːm/ n Psalm m
pseudonym /'sjuːdənɪm/ n Pseudonym nt
psychiatric /saɪkɪˈætrɪk/ a psychiatrisch
psychiatr|ist /saɪˈkaɪətrɪst/ n Psychiater(in) m(f). ~y n Psychiatrie f
psychic /'saɪkɪk/ a übersinnlich; I'm not ~ ich kann nicht hellsehen
psycho|'**analyse** /saɪkəʊ-/ vt psychoanalysieren. ~a'nalysis n Psychoanalyse f. ~'analyst Psychoanalytiker(in) m(f)
psychological /saɪkə'lɒdʒɪkl/ a, -ly adv psychologisch; ⟨illness⟩ psychisch
psycholog|ist /saɪˈkɒlədʒɪst/ n Psychologe m/ -login f. ~y n Psychologie f
psychopath /'saɪkəpæθ/ n Psychopath(in) m(f)
P.T.O. abbr (please turn over) b.w.
pub /pʌb/ n (fam) Kneipe f
puberty /'pjuːbətɪ/ n Pubertät f
public /'pʌblɪk/ a, -ly adv öffentlich; make ~ publik machen □ n the ~ die Öffentlichkeit; in ~ in aller Öffentlichkeit
publican /'pʌblɪkən/ n [Gast]wirt m
publication /pʌblɪ'keɪʃn/ n Veröffentlichung f
public: ~ con'venience n öffentliche Toilette f. ~'holiday n gesetzlicher Feiertag m. ~'house n [Gast]wirtschaft f

publicity /pʌb'lɪsətɪ/ n Publicity f; (advertising) Reklame f
publicize /'pʌblɪsaɪz/ vt Reklame machen für
public: ~'library n öffentliche Bücherei f. ~'school n Privatschule f; (Amer) staatliche Schule f. ~'spirited a be ~spirited Gemeinsinn haben. ~ 'transport n öffentliche Verkehrsmittel pl
publish /'pʌblɪʃ/ vt veröffentlichen. ~er n Verleger(in) m(f); (firm) Verlag m. ~ing n Verlagswesen nt
pucker /'pʌkə(r)/ vt kräuseln
pudding /'pʊdɪŋ/ n Pudding m; (course) Nachtisch m
puddle /'pʌdl/ n Pfütze f
puerile /'pjʊəraɪl/ a kindisch
puff /pʌf/ n (of wind) Hauch m; (of smoke) Wölkchen nt; (for powder) Quaste f □ vt blasen, pusten; ~ out ausstoßen. □ vi keuchen; ~ at paffen an (+ dat) ⟨pipe⟩. ~ed a (out of breath) aus der Puste. ~ **pastry** n Blätterteig m
puffy /'pʌfɪ/ a geschwollen
pugnacious /pʌg'neɪʃəs/ a, -ly adv aggressiv
pull /pʊl/ n Zug m; (jerk) Ruck m; (fam: influence) Einfluß m □ vt ziehen; ziehen an (+ dat) ⟨rope⟩; ~ a muscle sich (dat) einen Muskel zerren; ~ oneself together sich zusammennehmen; ~ one's weight tüchtig mitarbeiten; ~ s.o.'s leg (fam) jdn auf den Arm nehmen. ~ **down** vt herunterziehen; (demolish) abreißen. ~ **in** vt hereinziehen □ vi (Auto) einscheren. ~ **off** vt abziehen; (fam) schaffen. ~ **out** vt herausziehen □ vi (Auto) ausscheren. ~ **through** vt durchziehen □ vi (recover) durchkommen. ~ **up** vt heraufziehen; ausziehen ⟨plant⟩; (reprimand) zurechtweisen □ vi (Auto) anhalten
pulley /'pʊlɪ/ n (Techn) Rolle f

pullover /'pʊləʊvə(r)/ n Pullover m

pulp /pʌlp/ n Brei m; (of fruit) [Frucht]fleisch nt

pulpit /'pʊlpɪt/ n Kanzel f

pulsate /pʌl'seɪt/ vi pulsieren

pulse /pʌls/ n Puls m

pulses /'pʌlsɪz/ npl Hülsenfrüchte pl

pulverize /'pʌlvəraɪz/ vt pulverisieren

pumice /'pʌmɪs/ n Bimsstein m

pummel /'pʌml/ vt (pt/pp pummelled) mit den Fäusten bearbeiten

pump /pʌmp/ n Pumpe f □ vt pumpen; (fam) aushorchen. ~ up vt hochpumpen; (inflate) aufpumpen

pumpkin /'pʌmpkɪn/ n Kürbis m

pun /pʌn/ n Wortspiel nt

punch¹ /pʌntʃ/ n Faustschlag m; (device) Locher m □ vt boxen; lochen ⟨ticket⟩; stanzen ⟨hole⟩

punch² n (drink) Bowle f

punch: ~ **line** n Pointe f. ~**-up** n Schlägerei f

punctual /'pʌŋktjʊəl/ a, **-ly** adv pünktlich. ~**ity** /-'ælətɪ/ n Pünktlichkeit f

punctuate /'pʌŋktjʊeɪt/ vt mit Satzzeichen versehen. ~**ion** /-'eɪʃn/ n Interpunktion f. ~**ion mark** n Satzzeichen nt

puncture /'pʌŋktʃə(r)/ n Loch nt; (tyre) Reifenpanne f □ vt durchstechen

pundit /'pʌndɪt/ n Experte m

pungent /'pʌndʒənt/ a scharf

punish /'pʌnɪʃ/ vt bestrafen. ~**able** /-əbl/ a strafbar. ~**ment** n Strafe f

punitive /'pjuːnɪtɪv/ a Straf-

punnet /'pʌnɪt/ n Körbchen nt

punt /pʌnt/ n (boat) Stechkahn m

punter /'pʌntə(r)/ n (gambler) Wetter m; (client) Kunde m

puny /'pjuːnɪ/ a (-ier, -iest) mickerig

pup /pʌp/ n = puppy

pupil /'pjuːpl/ n Schüler(in) m(f); (of eye) Pupille f

puppet /'pʌpɪt/ n Puppe f; (fig) Marionette f

puppy /'pʌpɪ/ n junger Hund m

purchase /'pɜːtʃəs/ n Kauf m; (leverage) Hebelkraft f □ vt kaufen. ~**r** n Käufer m

pure /pjʊə(r)/ a (-r, -st), **-ly** adv rein

purée /'pjʊəreɪ/ n Püree nt, Brei m

purgatory /'pɜːgətrɪ/ n (Relig) Fegefeuer nt; (fig) Hölle f

purge /pɜːdʒ/ n (Pol) Säuberungsaktion f □ vt reinigen; (Pol) säubern

puri|fication /pjʊərɪfɪ'keɪʃn/ n Reinigung f. ~**fy** /'pjʊərɪfaɪ/ vt (pt/pp -ied) reinigen

puritanical /pjʊərɪ'tænɪkl/ a puritanisch

purity /'pjʊərɪtɪ/ n Reinheit f

purl /pɜːl/ n (Knitting) linke Masche f □ vt/i links stricken

purple /'pɜːpl/ a [dunkel]lila

purport /pə'pɔːt/ vt vorgeben

purpose /'pɜːpəs/ n Zweck m; (intention) Absicht f; (determination) Entschlossenheit f; **on** ~ absichtlich; **to no** ~ unnützerweise. ~**ful** a, **-ly** adv entschlossen. ~**ly** adv absichtlich

purr /pɜː(r)/ vi schnurren

purse /pɜːs/ n Portemonnaie nt; (Amer: handbag) Handtasche f □ vt schürzen ⟨lips⟩

pursue /pə'sjuː/ vt verfolgen; (fig) nachgehen (+ dat). ~**r** /-ə(r)/ n Verfolger m

pursuit /pə'sjuːt/ n Verfolgung f; Jagd f; (pastime) Beschäftigung f; **in** ~ hinterher

pus /pʌs/ n Eiter m

push /pʊʃ/ n Stoß m, (fam) Schubs m; **get the** ~ (fam) hinausfliegen □ vt/i schieben; (press) drücken; (roughly) stoßen; **be** ~**ed for time** (fam) unter Zeitdruck stehen. ~ **off** vt hinunterstoßen □ vi (fam: leave) abhauen. ~ **on**

vi (*continue*) weitergehen/-fahren; (*with activity*) weitermachen. ~ **up** *vt* hochschieben; hochtreiben (*price*)

push: ~-**button** *n* Druckknopf *m.* ~-**chair** *n* [Kinder]sportwagen *m.* ~-**over** *n* (*fam*) Kinderspiel *nt.* ~-**up** *n* (*Amer*) Liegestütz *m*

pushy /'pʊʃɪ/ *a* (*fam*) aufdringlich

puss /pʊs/ *n*, **pussy** /'pʊsɪ/ *n* Mieze *f*

put /pʊt/ *vt* (*pt/pp* put, *pres p* putting) (*place*) setzen; (*upright*) stellen; (*flat*) legen; (*express*) ausdrücken; (*say*) sagen; (*estimate*) schätzen (at auf + *acc*); ~ **aside** *or* by beiseite legen; ~ **one's foot down** (*fam*) energisch werden; (*Auto*) Gas geben □ *vi* ~ **to sea** auslaufen □ **stay** ~ dableiben. ~ **away** *vt* wegräumen. ~ **back** *vt* wieder hineinsetzen/-stellen/-legen; zurückstellen (*clock*). ~ **down** *vt* hinsetzen/-stellen/-legen; (*suppress*) niederschlagen; (*kill*) töten; (*write*) niederschreiben; (*attribute*) zuschreiben (to *dat*). ~ **forward** *vt* vorbringen; vorstellen (*clock*). ~ **in** *vt* hineinsetzen/-stellen/-legen; (*insert*) einstecken; (*submit*) einreichen □ *vi* ~ **in for** beantragen. ~ **off** *vt* ausmachen (*light*); (*postpone*) verschieben; ~ **s.o. off** jdn abbestellen; (*disconcert*) jdn aus der Fassung bringen; ~ **s.o. off sth** jdm etw verleiden. ~ **on** *vt* anziehen (*clothes, brake*); sich (*dat*) aufsetzen (*hat*); (*Culin*) aufsetzen; anmachen (*light*); aufführen (*play*); annehmen (*accent*); ~ **on weight** zunehmen. ~ **out** *vt* hinaussetzen/-stellen/-legen; ausmachen (*fire, light*); ausstrecken (*hand*); (*disconcert*) aus der Fassung bringen; ~ **s.o./oneself out** jdm/sich Umstände machen. ~ **through** *vt* durchstecken; (*Teleph*) verbinden (to

mit). ~ **up** *vt* errichten (*building*); aufschlagen (*tent*); aufspannen (*umbrella*); anschlagen (*notice*); erhöhen (*price*); unterbringen (*guest*); ~ **s.o. up to sth** jdn zu etw anstiften □ *vi* (*at hotel*) absteigen (in + *dat*); ~ **up with sth** sich (*dat*) etw bieten lassen

putrefy /'pju:trɪfaɪ/ *vi* (*pt/pp* -ied) verwesen

putrid /'pju:trɪd/ faulig

putty /'pʌtɪ/ *n* Kitt *m*

put-up /'pʊtʌp/ *a* **a** ~ **job** ein abgekartetes Spiel *nt*

puzzle /'pʌzl/ *n* Rätsel *nt*; (*jigsaw*) Puzzlespiel *nt* □ *vt* **it** ~ **es me** es ist mir rätselhaft □ *vi* ~ **e over** sich (*dat*) den Kopf zerbrechen über (+ *acc*). ~ **ing** *a* rätselhaft

pyjamas /pə'dʒɑ:məz/ *npl* Schlafanzug *m*

pylon /'paɪlən/ *n* Mast *m*

pyramid /'pɪrəmɪd/ *n* Pyramide *f*

python /'paɪθn/ *n* Pythonschlange *f*

Q

quack[1] /kwæk/ *n* Quaken *nt* □ *vi* quaken

quack[2] *n* (*doctor*) Quacksalber *m*

quad /kwɒd/ *n*; (*fam: court*) Hof *m*; ~ **s** *pl* = **quadruplets**

quadrangle /'kwɒdræŋgl/ *n* Viereck *nt*; (*court*) Hof *m*

quadruped /'kwɒdruped/ *n* Vierfüßer *m*

quadruple /'kwɒdrʊpl/ *a* vierfach □ *vt* vervierfachen □ *vi* sich vervierfachen. ~ **ts** /-plɪts/ *npl* Vierlinge *pl*

quagmire /'kwɒgmaɪə(r)/ *n* Sumpf *m*

quaint /kweɪnt/ *a* (-er, -est) malerisch; (*odd*) putzig

quake /kweɪk/ *n* (*fam*) Erdbeben *nt* □ *vi* beben; (*with fear*) zittern

Quaker /'kweɪkə(r)/ *n* Quäker(in) *m(f)*

qualification /kwɒlɪfɪˈkeɪʃn/ n Qualifikation f; (reservation) Einschränkung f. ~**ied** /-faɪd/ a qualifiziert; (trained) ausgebildet; (limited) bedingt

qualify /ˈkwɒlɪfaɪ/ v (pt/pp -ied) □vt qualifizieren; (entitle) berechtigen; (limit) einschränken □vi sich qualifizieren

quality /ˈkwɒlətɪ/ n Qualität f; (characteristic) Eigenschaft f

qualm /kwɑːm/ n Bedenken pl

quandary /ˈkwɒndərɪ/ n Dilemma nt

quantity /ˈkwɒntətɪ/ n Quantität f, Menge f; **in ~** in großen Mengen

quarantine /ˈkwɒrəntiːn/ n Quarantäne f

quarrel /ˈkwɒrl/ n Streit m □vi (pt/pp **quarrelled**) sich streiten. ~**some** a streitsüchtig

quarry¹ /ˈkwɒrɪ/ n (prey) Beute f

quarry² n Steinbruch m

quart /kwɔːt/ n Quart nt

quarter /ˈkwɔːtə(r)/ n Viertel nt; (of year) Vierteljahr nt; (Amer) 25-Cent-Stück nt; ~**s** pl Quartier pl; **at [a] ~ to six** um Viertel vor sechs; **from all ~s** aus allen Richtungen □vt vierteln; (Mil) einquartieren (on bei). ~'**final** n Viertelfinale nt

quarterly /ˈkwɔːtəlɪ/ a & adv vierteljährlich

quartet /kwɔːˈtet/ n Quartett nt

quartz /kwɔːts/ n Quarz m. ~ **watch** n Quarzuhr f

quash /kwɒʃ/ vt aufheben; niederschlagen (rebellion)

quaver /ˈkweɪvə(r)/ n (Mus) Achtelnote f □vi zittern

quay /kiː/ n Kai m

queasy /ˈkwiːzɪ/ a **I feel ~** mir ist übel

queen /kwiːn/ n Königin f; (Cards, Chess) Dame f

queer /kwɪə(r)/ a (-er, -est) eigenartig; (dubious) zweifelhaft; (ill) unwohl; (fam: homosexual) schwul □n (fam) Schwule(r) m

quell /kwel/ vt unterdrücken

quench /kwentʃ/ vt löschen

query /ˈkwɪərɪ/ n Frage f; (question mark) Fragezeichen nt □vt (pt/pp -ied) in Frage stellen; reklamieren (bill)

quest /kwest/ n Suche f (for nach)

question /ˈkwestʃn/ n Frage f; (for discussion) Thema nt; **out of the ~** ausgeschlossen; **without ~** ohne Frage; **the person in ~** die fragliche Person □vt in Frage stellen; ~ (police:) jdn verhören. ~**able** /-əbl/ a zweifelhaft. ~ **mark** n Fragezeichen nt

questionnaire /kwestʃəˈneə(r)/ n Fragebogen m

queue /kjuː/ n Schlange f □vi ~ **[up]** Schlange stehen, sich anstellen (for nach)

quibble /ˈkwɪbl/ vi Haarspalterei treiben

quick /kwɪk/ a (-er, -est), -**ly** adv schnell; **be ~!** mach schnell! **have a ~ meal** schnell etwas essen □adv schnell □n **cut to the ~** (fig) bis ins Mark getroffen. ~**en** vt beschleunigen □vi sich beschleunigen

quick: ~**sand** n Treibsand m. ~-**tempered** a aufbrausend

quid /kwɪd/ n inv (fam) Pfund nt

quiet /ˈkwaɪət/ a (-er, -est), -**ly** adv still; (calm) ruhig; (soft) leise; **keep ~ about** (fam) nichts sagen von □n Stille f; Ruhe f; **on the ~** heimlich

quiet|en /ˈkwaɪətn/ vt beruhigen □vi ~**en down** ruhig werden. ~**ness** n (see quiet) Stille f; Ruhe f

quill /kwɪl/ n Feder f; (spine) Stachel m

quilt /kwɪlt/ n Steppdecke f. ~**ed** a Stepp-

quince /kwɪns/ n Quitte f

quins /kwɪnz/ npl (fam) = **quintuplets**

quintet /kwɪnˈtet/ n Quintett nt

quintuplets /ˈkwɪntjʊplɪts/ npl Fünflinge pl

quip /kwɪp/ n Scherz m □ vi (pt/pp **quipped**) scherzen

quirk /kwɜːk/ n Eigenart f

quit /kwɪt/ v (pt/pp **quitted** or **quit**) vt verlassen; (give up) aufgeben; ~ **doing sth** aufhören, etw zu tun □ vi gehen; **give s.o. notice to** ~ jdm die Wohnung kündigen

quite /kwaɪt/ adv ganz; (really) wirklich; ~ [**so**]! genau! ~ **a few** ziemlich viele

quits /kwɪts/ a quitt

quiver /ˈkwɪvə(r)/ vi zittern

quiz /kwɪz/ n Quiz nt □ vt (pt/pp **quizzed**) ausfragen. ~**zical** a, **-ly** adv fragend

quorum /ˈkwɔːrəm/ n **have a** ~ beschlußfähig sein

quota /ˈkwəʊtə/ n Anteil m; (Comm) Kontingent nt

quotation /kwəʊˈteɪʃn/ n Zitat nt; (price) Kostenvoranschlag m; (of shares) Notierung f. ~ **marks** npl Anführungszeichen pl

quote /kwəʊt/ n (fam) = **quotation**; **in** ~**s** in Anführungszeichen □ vt/i zitieren

R

rabbi /ˈræbaɪ/ n Rabbiner m; (title) Rabbi m

rabbit /ˈræbɪt/ n Kaninchen nt

rabble /ˈræbl/ n **the** ~ der Pöbel

rabid /ˈræbɪd/ a fanatisch; (animal) tollwütig

rabies /ˈreɪbiːz/ n Tollwut f

race[1] /reɪs/ n Rasse f

race[2] /reɪs/ n Rennen nt; (fig) Wettlauf m □ vi [am Rennen] teilnehmen; (athlete, horse:) laufen; (fam: rush) rasen □ vt um die Wette laufen mit; an einem Rennen teilnehmen lassen (horse)

race: ~**course** n Rennbahn f. ~**horse** n Rennpferd nt. ~**track** n Rennbahn f

racial /ˈreɪʃl/ a, **-ly** adv rassisch; (discrimination, minority) Rassen-

racing /ˈreɪsɪŋ/ n Rennsport m; (horse-) Pferderennen nt. ~ **car** n Rennwagen m. ~ **driver** n Rennfahrer m

racism /ˈreɪsɪzm/ n Rassismus m. ~**t** /-ɪst/ a rassistisch □ n Rassist m

rack[1] /ræk/ n Ständer m; (for plates) Gestell nt □ vt ~ **one's brains** sich (dat) den Kopf zerbrechen

rack[2] n **go to** ~ **and ruin** verfallen; (fig) heruntarkommen

racket[1] /ˈrækɪt/ n (Sport) Schläger m

racket[2] n (din) Krach m; (swindle) Schwindelgeschäft nt

racy /ˈreɪsɪ/ a (**-ier, -iest**) schwungvoll; (risqué) gewagt

radar /ˈreɪdɑː(r)/ n Radar m

radian|ce /ˈreɪdɪəns/ n Strahlen nt. ~**t** a, **-ly** adv strahlend

radiate /ˈreɪdɪeɪt/ vt ausstrahlen □ vi (heat:) ausgestrahlt werden; (roads:) strahlenförmig ausgehen. ~**ion** /-ˈeɪʃn/ n Strahlung f

radiator /ˈreɪdɪeɪtə(r)/ n Heizkörper m; (Auto) Kühler m

radical /ˈrædɪkl/ a, **-ly** adv radikal □ n Radikale(r) m/f

radio /ˈreɪdɪəʊ/ n Radio nt; by ~ über Funk □ vt funken (message)

radio|active a radioaktiv. ~**activity** n Radioaktivität f

radiography /reɪdɪˈɒɡrəfɪ/ n Röntgenographie f

'radio ham n Hobbyfunker m

radio'therapy n Strahlenbehandlung f

radish /ˈrædɪʃ/ n Radieschen nt

radius /ˈreɪdɪəs/ n (pl **-dii** /-dɪaɪ/) Radius m, Halbmesser m

raffle /ˈræfl/ n Tombola f □ vt verlosen

raft /rɑːft/ n Floß nt

rafter /ˈrɑːftə(r)/ n Dachsparren m

rag[1] /ræg/ n Lumpen m; (pej: newspaper) Käseblatt nt; in ~s in Lumpen

rag[2] vt (pt/pp ragged) (fam) aufziehen

rage /reɪdʒ/ n Wut f; **all the** ~ (fam) der letzte Schrei ●vi rasen; ⟨storm:⟩ toben

ragged /'rægɪd/ a zerlumpt; ⟨edge⟩ ausgefranst

raid /reɪd/ n Überfall m; (Mil) Angriff m; (police) Razzia f ●vt überfallen; (Mil) angreifen; ⟨police:⟩ eine Razzia durchführen in (+ dat); (break in) eindringen in (+ acc). ~**er** n Eindringling m; (of bank) Bankräuber m

rail /reɪl/ n Schiene f; (pole) Stange f; (hand ~) Handlauf m; (Naut) Reling f; **by** ~ mit der Bahn

railings /'reɪlɪŋz/ npl Geländer nt

'railroad n (Amer) = **railway**

'railway n [Eisen]bahn f. ~**man** n Eisenbahner m. ~ **station** n Bahnhof m

rain /reɪn/ n Regen m ●vi regnen

rain: ~**bow** n Regenbogen m. ~**check** n (Amer) **take a** ~**check on** aufschieben. ~**coat** n Regenmantel m. ~**fall** n Niederschlag m

rainy /'reɪnɪ/ a (-ier, -iest) regnerisch

raise /reɪz/ n (Amer) Lohnerhöhung f ●vt erheben; (upright) aufrichten; (make higher) erhöhen; (lift) [hoch]heben; lüften ⟨hat⟩; [auf]ziehen ⟨children, animals⟩; aufwerfen ⟨question⟩; aufbringen ⟨money⟩

raisin /'reɪzn/ n Rosine f

rake /reɪk/ n Harke f, Rechen m ●vt harken, rechen. ~ **up** vt zusammenharken. (fam) wieder aufrühren

'rake-off n (fam) Prozente pl

rally /'rælɪ/ n Versammlung f; (Auto) Rallye f; (Tennis) Ballwechsel m ●vt sammeln ●vi sich sammeln; ⟨recover strength⟩ sich erholen

ram /ræm/ n Schafbock m; (Astr) Widder m ●vt (pt/pp rammed)

rambl|e /'ræmbl/ n Wanderung f ●vi wandern; (in speech) irrereden. ~**er** n Wanderer m; (rose) Kletterrose f. ~**ing** a weitschweifig; ⟨club⟩ Wander-

ramp /ræmp/ n Rampe f; (Aviat) Gangway f

rampage[1] /'ræmpeɪdʒ/ n be/go **on the** ~ randalieren

rampage[2] /ræm'peɪdʒ/ vi randalieren

rampant /'ræmpənt/ a weit verbreitet; (in heraldry) aufgerichtet

rampart /'ræmpɑːt/ n Wall m

ramshackle /'ræmʃækl/ a baufällig

ran /ræn/ see **run**

ranch /rɑːntʃ/ n Ranch f

rancid /'rænsɪd/ a ranzig

rancour /'ræŋkə(r)/ n Groll m

random /'rændəm/ a willkürlich; **a** ~ **sample** eine Stichprobe ●n **at** ~ aufs Geratewohl; ⟨choose⟩ willkürlich

randy /'rændɪ/ a (-ier, -iest) (fam) geil

rang /ræŋ/ see **ring**[2]

range /reɪndʒ/ n Serie f, Reihe f; (Comm) Auswahl f, Angebot nt (of an + dat); (of mountains) Kette f; (Mus) Umfang m; (distance) Reichweite f; (for shooting) Schießplatz m; (stove) Kohlenherd m; **at a** ~ **of** auf eine Entfernung von ●vi reichen; ~ **from … to** gehen von … bis. ~**r** n Aufseher m

rank[1] /ræŋk/ n (row) Reihe f; (Mil) Rang m; (social position) Stand m; **the** ~ **and file** die breite Masse; **the** ~**s** pl die gemeinen Soldaten ●vt/i einstufen; ~ **among** zählen zu

rank[2] a (bad) übel; ⟨plants⟩ üppig; (fig) kraß

ransack /'rænsæk/ vt durchwühlen; (pillage) plündern

ransom /ˈrænsəm/ n Lösegeld nt;
hold s.o. to ~ Lösegeld für jdn
fordern

rant /rænt/ vi rasen

rap /ræp/ n Klopfen nt; (blow)
Schlag m □v (pt/pp **rapped**) □vt
klopfen auf (+ acc) □vi ~ **at/on**
klopfen an/auf (+ acc)

rape¹ /reɪp/ n (Bot) Raps m

rape² /reɪp/ n Vergewaltigung f □vt ver-
gewaltigen

rapid /ˈræpɪd/ a, **-ly** adv schnell.
~ity /rəˈpɪdətɪ/ n Schnelligkeit f

rapids /ˈræpɪdz/ npl Stromschnel-
len pl

rapist /ˈreɪpɪst/ n Vergewaltiger m

rapport /ræˈpɔː(r)/ n (innerer)
Kontakt m

rapt /ræpt/ a, **-ly** adv gespannt;
(look) andächtig; **~ in** versunken in (+ acc)

raptur|e /ˈræptʃə(r)/ n Entzücken
nt. **~ous** /-rəs/ a, **-ly** adv begeistert

rare¹ /reə(r)/ a (-r, -st), **-ly** adv
selten

rare² /reə(r)/ a (Culin) englisch gebraten

rarefied /ˈreərɪfaɪd/ a dünn

rarity /ˈreərətɪ/ n Seltenheit f

rascal /ˈrɑːskl/ n Schlingel m

rash¹ /ræʃ/ n (Med) Ausschlag m

rash² (-er, -est), **-ly** adv voreilig

rasher /ˈræʃə(r)/ n Speckscheibe f

rasp /rɑːsp/ n Raspel f

raspberry /ˈrɑːzbərɪ/ n Himbeere f

rat /ræt/ n Ratte f; (fam: person)
Schuft m; **smell a ~** (fam) Lunte
riechen

rate /reɪt/ n Rate f; (speed) Tempo
nt; (of payment) Satz m; (of exchange) Kurs m; **~s** pl (taxes) ≈
Grundsteuer f; **at any ~** auf
jeden Fall; **at this ~** auf diese
Weise □vt einschätzen; **~ among**
zählen zu □vi **~ as** gelten als

rather /ˈrɑːðə(r)/ adv lieber; (fairly) ziemlich; **~!** und ob!

ratification /rætɪfɪˈkeɪʃn/ n Rati-
fizierung f. **~fy** /ˈrætɪfaɪ/ vt
(pt/pp **-ied**) ratifizieren

rating /ˈreɪtɪŋ/ n Einschätzung f;
(class) Klasse f; (sailor) [einfa-
cher] Matrose m; **~s** pl (Radio,
TV) ≈ Einschaltquote f

ratio /ˈreɪʃɪəʊ/ n Verhältnis nt

ration /ˈræʃn/ n Ration f □vt ratio-
nieren

rational /ˈræʃənl/ a, **-ly** adv rational. **~ize** /-aɪz/ vt rationalisieren

'rat race n (fam) Konkurrenzkampf m

rattle /ˈrætl/ n Rasseln nt; (of
china, glass) Klirren nt; (of win-
dows) Klappern nt; (toy) Klapper
f □vi rasseln; klirren; klappern
□vt rasseln mit; (shake) schütteln. **~ off** vt herunterrasseln

'rattlesnake n Klapperschlange f

raucous /ˈrɔːkəs/ a rauh

ravage /ˈrævɪdʒ/ vt verwüsten,
verheeren

rave /reɪv/ vi toben; **~ about**
schwärmen von

raven /ˈreɪvn/ n Rabe m

ravenous /ˈrævənəs/ a heißhung-
rig

ravine /rəˈviːn/ n Schlucht f

raving /ˈreɪvɪŋ/ a **~ mad** (fam)
total verrückt

ravishing /ˈrævɪʃɪŋ/ a hinreißend

raw /rɔː/ a (-er, -est) roh; (not
processed) Roh-; (skin) wund;
(weather) naßkalt; (inexperienced) unerfahren; **get a ~ deal**
(fam) schlecht wegkommen. **~
materials** npl Rohstoffe pl

ray /reɪ/ n Strahl m; **~ of hope**
Hoffnungsschimmer m

raze /reɪz/ vt **~ to the ground**
dem Erdboden gleichmachen

razor /ˈreɪzə(r)/ n Rasierapparat
m. **~ blade** n Rasierklinge f

re /riː/ prep betreffs (+ gen)

reach /riːtʃ/ n Reichweite f; (of
river) Strecke f; **within/out of ~**
in/außer Reichweite; **within
easy ~** leicht erreichbar □vt erreichen; (arrive at) ankommen in
(+ dat); (**~ as far as**) reichen bis
zu; kommen zu (decision, conclusion); (pass) reichen □vi reichen

(to bis zu); ~ **for** greifen nach; I **can't** ~ ich komme nicht daran

re'act /rɪ-/ *vi* reagieren

re'action /rɪ-/ *n* Reaktion *f*. ~**ary** *a* reaktionär

reactor /rɪˈæktə(r)/ *n* Reaktor *m*

read /riːd/ *vt/i* (*pt/pp* **read** /red/) lesen; (*aloud*) vorlesen (**to** *dat*); (*Univ*) studieren; ableseπ ⟨*meter*⟩. ~ **out** *vt* vorlesen

readable /ˈriːdəbl/ *a* lesbar

reader /ˈriːdə(r)/ *n* Leser(in) *m*(*f*); (*book*) Lesebuch *nt*

readily /ˈredɪlɪ/ *adv* bereitwillig; (*easily*) leicht. ~**ness** *n* Bereitschaft *f*; **in** ~**ness** bereit

reading /ˈriːdɪŋ/ *n* Lesen *nt*; (*Pol, Relig*) Lesung *f*

rea'djust /riː-/ *vt* neu einstellen □ *vi* sich umstellen (**to** *auf* + *acc*)

ready /ˈredɪ/ *a* (**-ier, -iest**) fertig; (*willing*) bereit; (*quick*) schnell; **get** ~ sich fertigmachen; (*prepare to*) sich bereitmachen

ready: ~**-made** *a* fertig. ~ **'money** *n* Bargeld *nt*. ~**-to- 'wear** *a* Konfektions-

real /rɪəl/ *a* wirklich; (*genuine*) echt; (*actual*) eigentlich □ *adv* (*Amer, fam*) echt. ~ **estate** *n* Immobilien *pl*

realis|m /ˈrɪəlɪzm/ *n* Realismus *m*. ~**t** /-lɪst/ *n* Realist *m*. ~**tic** /-ˈlɪstɪk/ *a*, ~**ally** *adv* realistisch

reality /rɪˈælətɪ/ *n* Wirklichkeit *f*, Realität *f*

realization /rɪəlaɪˈzeɪʃn/ *n* Erkenntnis *f*

realize /ˈrɪəlaɪz/ *vt* einsehen; (*become aware*) gewahr werden; verwirklichen ⟨*hopes, plans*⟩; (*Comm*) realisieren; einbringen ⟨*price*⟩; **I didn't** ~ das wußte ich nicht

really /ˈrɪəlɪ/ *adv* wirklich; (*actually*) eigentlich

realm /relm/ *n* Reich *nt*

realtor /ˈrɪəltə(r)/ *n* (*Amer*) Immobilienmakler *m*

reap /riːp/ *vt* ernten

reap'pear /riː-/ *vi* wiederkommen

rear¹ /rɪə(r)/ *a* Hinter-; (*Auto*) Heck-. □ *n* **the** ~ der hintere Teil; **at the** ~ von hinten

rear² *vt* aufziehen □ *vi* ~ **[up]** ⟨*horse:*⟩ sich aufbäumen

'rear-light *n* Rücklicht *nt*

re'arm /riː-/ *vi* wieder aufrüsten

re'arrange /riː-/ *vt* umstellen

rear-view 'mirror *n* (*Auto*) Rückspiegel *m*

reason /ˈriːzn/ *n* Grund *m*; (*good sense*) Vernunft *f*; (*ability to think*) Verstand *m*; **within** ~ in vernünftigen Grenzen □ *vi* argumentieren; ~ **with** vernünftig reden mit. ~**able** /-əbl/ *a* vernünftig; (*not expensive*) preiswert. ~**ably** /-əblɪ/ *adv* (*fairly*) ziemlich

reas'sur|ance /riː-/ *n* Beruhigung *f*; Versicherung *f*. ~**e** *vt* beruhigen; ~ **s.o. of sth** jdm etw (*gen*) versichern

rebate /ˈriːbeɪt/ *n* Rückzahlung *f*; (*discount*) Nachlaß *m*

rebel¹ /ˈrebl/ *n* Rebell *m*

rebel² /rɪˈbel/ *vi* (*pt/pp* rebelled) rebellieren. ~**lion** /-ɪən/ *n* Rebellion *f*. ~**lious** /-ɪəs/ *a* rebellisch

re'bound¹ /rɪ-/ *vi* abprallen

rebound² /riː-/ *n* Rückprall *m*

rebuff /rɪˈbʌf/ *n* Abweisung *f* □ *vt* abweisen; eine Abfuhr erteilen (*s.o.* jdm)

re'build /riː-/ *vt* (*pt/pp* -**built**) wieder aufbauen; (*fig*) wiederaufbauen

rebuke /rɪˈbjuːk/ *n* Tadel *m* □ *vt* tadeln

rebuttal /rɪˈbʌtl/ *n* Widerlegung *f*

re'call /rɪ-/ *n* Erinnerung *f*; **beyond** ~ unwiderruflich □ *vt* zurückrufen; abberufen ⟨*diplomat*⟩; vorzeitig einberufen ⟨*parliament*⟩; (*remember*) sich erinnern an (+ *acc*)

recant /rɪ-/ *vi/i* widerrufen

recap /ˈriːkæp/ *vt/i* (*fam*) = **recapitulate**

recapitulate /riːkəˈpɪtjʊleɪt/ *vt/i* zusammenfassen; rekapitulieren

re'capture /riː-/ vt wieder gefangennehmen ⟨person⟩; wieder einfangen ⟨animal⟩

reced|e /rɪˈsiːd/ vi zurückgehen. ~**ing** a ⟨forehead, chin⟩ fliehend; ~**ing hair** Stirnglatze f

receipt /rɪˈsiːt/ n Quittung f; (receiving) Empfang m; ~**s** pl (Comm) Einnahmen pl

receive /rɪˈsiːv/ vt erhalten, bekommen; empfangen ⟨guests⟩. ~**r** n (Teleph) Hörer m; (Radio, TV) Empfänger m; (of stolen goods) Hehler m

recent /ˈriːsnt/ a kürzlich erfolgte(r,s). ~**ly** adv in letzter Zeit; (the other day) kürzlich, vor kurzem

receptacle /rɪˈseptəkl/ n Behälter m

reception /rɪˈsepʃn/ n Empfang m; ~ [**desk**] (in hotel) Rezeption f. ~**ist** n Empfangsdame f

receptive /rɪˈseptɪv/ a aufnahmefähig; ~ **to** empfänglich für

recess /rɪˈses/ n Nische f; (holiday) Ferien pl; (Amer, Sch) Pause f

recession /rɪˈseʃn/ n Rezession f

re'charge /riː-/ vt [wieder] aufladen

recipe /ˈresəpɪ/ n Rezept nt

recipient /rɪˈsɪpɪənt/ n Empfänger m

recipro|cal /rɪˈsɪprəkl/ a gegenseitig. ~**cate** /-keɪt/ vt erwidern

recital /rɪˈsaɪtl/ n (of poetry, songs) Vortrag m; (on piano) Konzert nt

recite /rɪˈsaɪt/ vt aufsagen; (before audience) vortragen; (list) aufzählen

reckless /ˈreklɪs/ a, -**ly** adv leichtsinnig; (careless) rücksichtslos. ~**ness** n Leichtsinn m; Rücksichtslosigkeit f

reckon /ˈrekən/ vt rechnen; (consider) glauben □ vi ~ **on/with** rechnen mit

re'claim /riː-/ vt zurückfordern; zurückgewinnen ⟨land⟩

reclin|e /rɪˈklaɪn/ vi liegen. ~**ing seat** n Liegesitz m

recluse /rɪˈkluːs/ n Einsiedler(in) m(f)

recognition /rekəgˈnɪʃn/ n Erkennen nt; (acknowledgement) Anerkennung f; **in** ~ **als** Anerkennung (of gen); **beyond** ~ nicht wiederzuerkennen sein

recognize /ˈrekəgnaɪz/ vt erkennen; (know again) wiedererkennen; (acknowledge) anerkennen

re'coil /rɪ-/ vi zurückschnellen; (in fear) zurückschrecken

recollect /rekəˈlekt/ vt sich erinnern an (+ acc). ~**ion** /-ekʃn/ n Erinnerung f

recommend /rekəˈmend/ vt empfehlen. ~**ation** /-deɪʃn/ n Empfehlung f

recompense /ˈrekəmpens/ n Entschädigung f □ vt entschädigen

recon|cile /ˈrekənsaɪl/ vt versöhnen; ~**cile oneself to** sich abfinden mit. ~**ciliation** /-sɪlɪˈeɪʃn/ n Versöhnung f

recon'dition /riː-/ vt generalüberholen. ~**ed engine** n Austauschmotor m

reconnaissance /rɪˈkɒnɪsns/ n (Mil) Aufklärung f

reconnoitre /rekəˈnɔɪtə(r)/ vi (pres p -**tring**) auf Erkundung ausgehen

recon'sider /riː-/ vt sich (dat) noch einmal überlegen

recon'struct /riː-/ vt wieder aufbauen; rekonstruieren ⟨crime⟩. ~**ion** n Wiederaufbau m; Rekonstruktion f

record¹ /rɪˈkɔːd/ vt aufzeichnen; (register) registrieren; (on tape) aufnehmen

record² /ˈrekɔːd/ n Aufzeichnung f; (Jur) Protokoll nt; (Mus) [Schall]platte f; (Sport) Rekord m; ~**s** pl Unterlagen pl; **keep a** ~ **of** sich (dat) notieren; **off the** ~ inoffiziell; **have a [criminal]** ~ vorbestraft sein

recorder /rɪˈkɔːdə(r)/ n (Mus) Blockflöte f

recording /rɪˈkɔːdɪŋ/ n Aufzeichnung f, Aufnahme f

'record-player n Plattenspieler m

recount /rɪˈkaʊnt/ vt erzählen

re-'count¹ /riː-/ vt nachzählen

're-count² /riː-/ n (Pol) Nachzählung f

recoup /rɪˈkuːp/ vt wiedereinbringen; ausgleichen ⟨losses⟩

recourse /rɪˈkɔːs/ n have ∼ to Zuflucht nehmen zu

re-'cover /riː-/ vt neu beziehen

recover /rɪˈkʌvə(r)/ vt zurückbekommen; bergen ⟨wreck⟩ □vi sich erholen. ∼y n Wiedererlangung f; Bergung f; (of health) Erholung f

recreation /rekrɪˈeɪʃn/ n Erholung f; (hobby) Hobby nt. ∼al a Freizeit-; be ∼al erholsam sein

recrimination /rɪkrɪmɪˈneɪʃn/ n Gegenbeschuldigung f

recruit /rɪˈkruːt/ n (Mil) Rekrut m; new ∼ (member) neues Mitglied nt; (worker) neuer Mitarbeiter □vt rekrutieren; anwerben ⟨staff⟩. ∼ment n Rekrutierung f; Anwerbung f

rectangle /ˈrektæŋgl/ n Rechteck nt. ∼ular /-ˈtæŋgjʊlə(r)/ a rechteckig

rectify /ˈrektɪfaɪ/ vt (pt/pp -ied) berichtigen

rector /ˈrektə(r)/ n Pfarrer m; (Univ) Rektor m. ∼y n Pfarrhaus nt

recuperate /rɪˈkjuːpəreɪt/ vi sich erholen. ∼ion /-ˈreɪʃn/ n Erholung f

recur /rɪˈkɜː(r)/ vi (pt/pp recurred) sich wiederholen; ⟨illness:⟩ wiederkehren

recurrence /rɪˈkʌrəns/ n Wiederkehr f. ∼t a wiederkehrend

recycle /riːˈsaɪkl/ vt wiederverwerten. ∼d paper n Umweltschutzpapier nt

red /red/ a (redder, reddest) rot □n Rot nt. ∼'currant n rote Johannisbeere f

redden /ˈredn/ vt röten □vi rot werden. ∼ish a rötlich

re'decorate /riː-/ vt renovieren; (paint) neu streichen; (wallpaper) neu tapezieren

redeem /rɪˈdiːm/ vt einlösen; (Relig) erlösen

redemption /rɪˈdempʃn/ n Erlösung f

rede'ploy /riː-/ vt an anderer Stelle einsetzen

red: ∼-'haired a rothaarig. ∼-'handed a catch s.o. ∼-handed jdn auf frischer Tat ertappen. ∼ 'herring n falsche Spur f. ∼-hot a glühend heiß. R∼ 'Indian n Indianer(in) m(f)

redi'rect /riː-/ vt nachsenden ⟨letter⟩; umleiten ⟨traffic⟩

re'do /riː-/ vt (pt -did, pp -done) noch einmal machen

re'double /riː-/ vt verdoppeln

redress /rɪˈdres/ n Entschädigung f □vt wiedergutmachen; wiederherstellen ⟨balance⟩

red 'tape n (fam) Bürokratie f

reduce /rɪˈdjuːs/ vt verringern, vermindern; (in size) verkleinern; ermäßigen ⟨costs⟩; herabsetzen ⟨price, goods⟩; (Culin) einkochen lassen. ∼tion /-ˈdʌkʃn/ n Verringerung f; (in price) Ermäßigung f; (in size) Verkleinerung f

redundancy /rɪˈdʌndənsɪ/ n Beschäftigungslosigkeit f; (payment) Abfindung f. ∼t a überflüssig; make ∼t entlassen; be made ∼t beschäftigungslos werden

reed /riːd/ n [Schilf]rohr nt; ∼s pl Schilf nt

reef /riːf/ n Riff nt

reek /riːk/ vi riechen (of nach)

reel /riːl/ n Rolle f, Spule f □vi (stagger) taumeln □vt ~ **off** (fig) herunterrasseln

refectory /rɪˈfektərɪ/ n Refektorium nt; (Univ) Mensa f

refer /rɪˈfɜː(r)/ v (pt/pp **referred**) □vt verweisen (**to an** + acc); übergeben, weiterleiten (matter) (**to an** + acc) □vi ~ **to** sich beziehen auf (+ acc); (mention) erwähnen; (concern) betreffen; (consult) sich wenden an (+ acc); nachschlagen in (+ dat) (book); **are you ~ring to me?** meinen Sie mich?

referee /refəˈriː/ n Schiedsrichter m; (Boxing) Ringrichter m; (for job) Referenz f □vt/i (pt/pp **refereed**) Schiedsrichter/Ringrichter sein (bei)

reference /ˈrefərəns/ n Erwähnung f; (in book) Verweis m; (for job) Referenz f; (Comm) ‘**your ~**’ ‘Ihr Zeichen’; **with ~ to** sich auf (+ acc) beziehen; (in letter) unter Bezugnahme auf (+ acc); **make [a] ~ to** erwähnen. **~ book** n Nachschlagewerk nt. **~ number** n Aktenzeichen nt

referendum /refəˈrendəm/ n Volksabstimmung f

re'fill[1] /riː-/ vt nachfüllen
'refill[2] /riː-/ n (for pen) Ersatzmine f

refine /rɪˈfaɪn/ vt raffinieren. **~d** a fein, vornehm. **~ment** n Vornehmheit f; (Techn) Verfeinerung f. **~ry** /-ərɪ/ n Raffinerie f

reflect /rɪˈflekt/ vt reflektieren; (mirror-) [wider]spiegeln; **be ~ed in** sich spiegeln in (+ dat) □vi nachdenken (**on** über + acc); **~ badly upon s.o.** (fig) jdn in ein schlechtes Licht stellen. **~ion** /-ekʃn/ n Reflexion f; (image) Spiegelbild nt; **on ~ion** nach nochmaliger Überlegung. **~ive** /-ɪv/ a, **-ly** adv nachdenklich. **~or** n Rückstrahler m

reflex /ˈriːfleks/ a Reflex m □attrib Reflex-

reflexive /rɪˈfleksɪv/ a reflexiv

reform /rɪˈfɔːm/ n Reform f □vt reformieren □vi sich bessern. **R~ation** /refəˈmeɪʃn/ n (Relig) Reformation f. **~er** n Reformer m; (Relig) Reformator m

refract /rɪˈfrækt/ vt (Phys) brechen

refrain[1] /rɪˈfreɪn/ n Refrain m
refrain[2] vi ~ **from doing sth** etw nicht tun

refresh /rɪˈfreʃ/ vt erfrischen. **~ing** a erfrischend. **~ments** npl Erfrischungen pl

refrigerate /rɪˈfrɪdʒəreɪt/ vt kühlen. **~or** n Kühlschrank m

re'fuel /riː-/ v (pt/pp **-fuelled**) vt/i auftanken

refuge /ˈrefjuːdʒ/ n Zuflucht f; **take ~** in Zuflucht nehmen in (+ dat)

refugee /refjʊˈdʒiː/ n Flüchtling m

re'fund[1] /riː-/ **get a ~** sein Geld zurückbekommen
re'fund[2] /rɪ-/ vt zurückerstatten

refurbish /riːˈfɜːbɪʃ/ vt renovieren

refusal /rɪˈfjuːzl/ n (see **refuse**[1]) Ablehnung f, Weigerung f

refuse[1] /rɪˈfjuːz/ vt ablehnen; (not grant) verweigern; **~ to do** sth sich weigern, etw zu tun □vi ablehnen; sich weigern

refuse[2] /ˈrefjuːs/ n Müll m, Abfall m. **~ collection** n Müllabfuhr f

regain /rɪˈgeɪn/ vt wiedergewinnen

regal /ˈriːgl/ a, **-ly** adv königlich

regalia /rɪˈgeɪlɪə/ npl Insignien pl

regard /rɪˈgɑːd/ n (heed) Rücksicht f; (respect) Achtung f; **~s** pl Grüße pl; **with ~ to** in bezug auf (+ acc) □vt ansehen, betrachten (**as** als); **as ~s** in bezug auf (+ acc). **~ing** prep bezüglich (+ gen). **~less** adv ohne Rücksicht (**of** auf + acc)

regatta /rɪˈgætə/ n Regatta f

regenerate /rɪˈdʒenəreɪt/ vt regenerieren □vi sich regenerieren

regime /reɪˈʒiːm/ n Regime nt

regiment /'redʒɪmənt/ n Regiment nt. **~al** /-'mentl/ a Regiments-. **~ation** /-'teɪʃn/ n Reglementierung f

region /'riːdʒən/ n Region f; **in the ~ of** (fig) ungefähr. **~al** a, **-ly** adv regional

register /'redʒɪstə(r)/ n Register nt; (Sch) Anwesenheitsliste f □ vt registrieren; (report) anmelden; einschreiben ⟨letter⟩; aufgeben ⟨luggage⟩ □ vi (report) sich anmelden; **it didn't ~** (fig) ich habe es nicht registriert

registrar /redʒɪ'strɑː(r)/ n Standesbeamte(r) m

registration /redʒɪ'streɪʃn/ n Registrierung f; Anmeldung f; **~ number** n Autonummer f

registry office /'redʒɪstrɪ-/ n Standesamt nt

regret /rɪ'gret/ n Bedauern nt □ vt (pt/pp regretted) bedauern. **~fully** adv mit Bedauern

regrettab|le /rɪ'gretəbl/ a bedauerlich. **~ly** adv bedauerlicherweise

regular /'regjʊlə(r)/ a, **-ly** adv regelmäßig; (usual) üblich; (Mil) Berufs- □ n Berufssoldat m; (in pub) Stammgast m; (in shop) Stammkunde m. **~ity** /-'lærətɪ/ n Regelmäßigkeit f

regulat|e /'regjʊleɪt/ vt regulieren. **~ion** /-'leɪʃn/ n (rule) Vorschrift f

rehabilitat|e /riːhə'bɪlɪteɪt/ vt rehabilitieren. **~ion** /-'teɪʃn/ n Rehabilitation f

rehears|al /rɪ'hɜːsl/ n (Theat) Probe f. **~e** vt proben

reign /reɪn/ n Herrschaft f □ vi herrschen, regieren

reimburse /riːɪm'bɜːs/ vt **~ s.o. for sth** jdm etw zurückerstatten

rein /reɪn/ n Zügel m

reincarnation /riːɪnkɑː'neɪʃn/ f Reinkarnation f, Wiedergeburt f

reindeer /'reɪndɪə(r)/ n inv Rentier nt

reinforce /riːɪn'fɔːs/ vt verstärken. **~d 'concrete** n Stahlbeton

m. **~ment** n Verstärkung f; **send ~ments** Verstärkung schicken

reinstate /riːɪn'steɪt/ vt wiedereinstellen; (to office) wiedereinsetzen

reiterate /riː'ɪtəreɪt/ vt wiederholen

reject /rɪ'dʒekt/ vt ablehnen. **~ion** /-ekʃn/ n Ablehnung f

rejects /'riːdʒekts/ npl (Comm) Ausschußware f

rejoice /rɪ'dʒɔɪs/ vi (liter) sich freuen. **~ing** n Freude f

re'join /riː-/ vt sich wieder anschließen (+ dat); wieder beitreten (+ dat) ⟨club, party⟩; (answer) erwidern

rejuvenate /rɪ'dʒuːvəneɪt/ vt verjüngen

relapse /rɪ'læps/ n Rückfall m □ vi einen Rückfall erleiden

relate /rɪ'leɪt/ vt (tell) erzählen; (connect) verbinden □ vi zusammenhängen (**to** mit). **~d** a verwandt (**to** mit)

relation /rɪ'leɪʃn/ n Beziehung f; (person) Verwandte(r) m/f. **~ship** n Beziehung f; (link) Verbindung f; (blood tie) Verwandtschaft f; (affair) Verhältnis m

relative /'relətɪv/ n Verwandte(r) m/f □ a relativ; (Gram) Relativ-. **~ly** adv relativ, verhältnismäßig

relax /rɪ'læks/ vt lockern, entspannen □ vi sich lockern, sich entspannen. **~ation** /-'seɪʃn/ n Entspannung f. **~ing** a entspannend

relay[1] /rɪ'leɪ/ vt (pt/pp -laid) weitergeben; (Radio, TV) übertragen

relay[2] /'riːleɪ/ n (Electr) Relais nt; **work in ~s** sich bei der Arbeit ablösen. **~ [race]** n Staffel f

release /rɪ'liːs/ n Freilassung f, Entlassung f; (Techn) Auslöser m □ vt freilassen; (let go of) loslassen; (Techn) auslösen; veröffentlichen ⟨information⟩

relegate /ˈreligeit/ vt verbannen; **be ~d** (Sport) absteigen

relent /rɪˈlent/ vi nachgeben. **~less** a, **~ly** adv erbarmungslos; (unceasing) unaufhörlich

relevan|ce /ˈrelevans/ n Relevanz f. **~t** a relevant (to für)

reliab|ility /rɪlaɪəˈbɪlətɪ/ n Zuverlässigkeit f. **~le** /-ˈlaɪəbl/ a, **-ly** adv zuverlässig

relian|ce /rɪˈlaɪəns/ n Abhängigkeit f (on von). **~t** a angewiesen (on auf + acc)

relic /ˈrelɪk/ n Überbleibsel nt; (Relig) Reliquie f

relief /rɪˈliːf/ n Erleichterung f; (assistance) Hilfe f; (distraction) Abwechslung f; (replacement) Ablösung f; (Art) Relief nt; **in ~** im Relief. **~ map** n Reliefkarte f. **~ train** n Entlastungszug m

relieve /rɪˈliːv/ vt erleichtern; (take over from) ablösen; **~ of** entlasten von

religion /rɪˈlɪdʒən/ n Religion f

religious /rɪˈlɪdʒəs/ a religiös. **~ly** adv (conscientiously) gewissenhaft

relinquish /rɪˈlɪŋkwɪʃ/ vt loslassen; (give up) aufgeben

relish /ˈrelɪʃ/ n Genuß m; (Culin) Würze f ◻ vt genießen

relo'cate /riː-/ vt verlegen

reluctan|ce /rɪˈlʌktəns/ n Widerstreben nt. **~t** a widerstrebend; **be ~t** zögern (to zu). **~tly** adv ungern, widerstrebend

rely /rɪˈlaɪ/ vi (pt/pp -ied) **~ on** sich verlassen auf (+ acc); (be dependent on) angewiesen sein auf (+ acc)

remain /rɪˈmeɪn/ vi bleiben; (be left) übrigbleiben. **~der** n Rest m. **~ing** a restlich. **~s** npl Reste pl; [mortal] **~s** [sterbliche] Überreste pl

remand /rɪˈmɑːnd/ n **on ~** in Untersuchungshaft ◻ vt **~ in custody** in Untersuchungshaft schicken

remark /rɪˈmɑːk/ n Bemerkung f ◻ vt bemerken. **~able** /-əbl/ a, **-bly** adv bemerkenswert

re'marry /riː-/ vi wieder heiraten

remedial /rɪˈmiːdɪəl/ a Hilfs-; (Med) Heil-

remedy /ˈremədɪ/ n [Heil]mittel nt (for gegen); (fig) Abhilfe f ◻ vt (pt/pp -ied) abhelfen (+ dat); beheben (fault)

remember /rɪˈmembə(r)/ vt sich erinnern an (+ acc); **~ er to do sth** daran denken, etw zu tun; **~ er me to him** grüßen Sie ihn von mir ◻ vi sich erinnern. **~rance** n Erinnerung f

remind /rɪˈmaɪnd/ vt erinnern (of an + acc). **~er** n Andenken nt; (letter, warning) Mahnung f

reminisce /remɪˈnɪs/ vi sich seinen Erinnerungen hingeben. **~nces** /-ənsɪz/ npl Erinnerungen pl. **~nt** a **be ~nt of** erinnern an (+ acc)

remiss /rɪˈmɪs/ a nachlässig

remission /rɪˈmɪʃn/ n Nachlaß m; (of sentence) [Straf]erlaß m; (Med) Remission f

remit /rɪˈmɪt/ vt (pt/pp remitted) überweisen (money). **~tance** n Überweisung f

remnant /ˈremnənt/ n Rest m

remonstrate /ˈremənstreɪt/ vi protestieren; **~ with s.o.** jdm Vorhaltungen machen

remorse /rɪˈmɔːs/ n Reue f. **~ful** a, **-ly** adv reumütig. **~less** a, **-ly** adv unerbittlich

remote /rɪˈməʊt/ a fern; (isolated) abgelegen; (slight) gering. **~ con'trol** n Fernsteuerung f; (for TV) Fernbedienung f. **~-con'trolled** a ferngesteuert; fernbedient

remotely /rɪˈməʊtlɪ/ adv entfernt; **not ~** nicht im entferntesten

re'movable /rɪ-/ a abnehmbar

removal /rɪˈmuːvl/ n Entfernung f; (from house) Umzug m. **~ van** n Möbelwagen m

remove /rɪˈmuːv/ vt entfernen; (take off) abnehmen; (take out) herausnehmen

remunerat|e /rɪˈmjuːnəreɪt/ vt bezahlen. ~**ion** /-ˈreɪʃn/ n Bezahlung f. ~**ive** /-ətɪv/ a einträglich

render /ˈrendə(r)/ vt machen; erweisen ⟨service⟩; ⟨translate⟩ wiedergeben; (Mus) vortragen

renegade /ˈrenɪgeɪd/ n Abtrünnige(r) m/f

renew /rɪˈnjuː/ vt erneuern; verlängern ⟨contract⟩. ~**al** n Erneuerung f; Verlängerung f

renounce /rɪˈnaʊns/ vt verzichten auf (+ acc); (Relig) abschwören (+ dat)

renovat|e /ˈrenəveɪt/ vt renovieren. ~**ion** /-ˈveɪʃn/ n Renovierung f

renown /rɪˈnaʊn/ n Ruf m. ~**ed** a berühmt

rent /rent/ n Miete f □ vt mieten; (hire) leihen; ~ [out] vermieten; verleihen. ~**al** n Mietgebühr f; Leihgebühr f

renunciation /rɪnʌnsɪˈeɪʃn/ n Verzicht m

re'open /riː-/ vt/i wieder aufmachen

re'organize /riː-/ vt reorganisieren

rep /rep/ n (fam) Vertreter m

repair /rɪˈpeə(r)/ n Reparatur f; in good/bad ~ in gutem/schlechtem Zustand □ vt reparieren

repartee /repɑːˈtiː/ n piece of ~ schlagfertige Antwort f

repatriat|e /riːˈpætrɪeɪt/ vt repatriieren. ~**ion** /-ˈeɪʃn/ n Repatriierung f

re'pay /riː-/ vt (pt/pp -**paid**) zurückzahlen; ~ **s.o. for sth** jdm etw zurückzahlen. ~**ment** n Rückzahlung f

repeal /rɪˈpiːl/ n Aufhebung f □ vt aufheben

repeat /rɪˈpiːt/ n Wiederholung f □ vt/i wiederholen; ~ **after me**

sprechen Sie mir nach. ~**ed** a, -**ly** adv wiederholt

repel /rɪˈpel/ vt (pt/pp repelled) abwehren; (fig) abstoßen. ~**lent** a abstoßend

repent /rɪˈpent/ vi Reue zeigen. ~**ance** n Reue f. ~**ant** a reuig

repercussions /riːpəˈkʌʃnz/ npl Auswirkungen pl

repertoire /ˈrepətwɑː(r)/ n Repertoire nt

repertory /ˈrepətrɪ/ n Repertoire nt

repetit|ion /repɪˈtɪʃn/ n Wiederholung f. ~**ive** /rɪˈpetɪtɪv/ a eintönig

re'place /rɪ-/ vt zurücktun; (take the place of) ersetzen; (exchange) austauschen, auswechseln. ~**ment** n Ersatz m. ~**ment part** n Ersatzteil nt

'replay /riː-/ n (Sport) Wiederholungsspiel nt; [action] ~ Wiederholung f

replenish /rɪˈplenɪʃ/ vt auffüllen ⟨stocks⟩; (refill) nachfüllen

replete /rɪˈpliːt/ a gesättigt

replica /ˈreplɪkə/ n Nachbildung f

reply /rɪˈplaɪ/ n Antwort f (to auf + acc) □ vt/i (pt/pp replied) antworten

report /rɪˈpɔːt/ n Bericht m; (Sch) Zeugnis nt; (rumour) Gerücht nt; (of gun) Knall m □ vt berichten; (notify) melden; ~ **s.o. to the police** jdn anzeigen □ vi berichten (on über + acc); (present oneself) sich melden (to bei). ~**er** n Reporter(in) m(f)

repose /rɪˈpəʊz/ n Ruhe f

repos'sess /riː-/ vt wieder in Besitz nehmen

reprehensible /reprɪˈhensəbl/ a tadelnswert

represent /reprɪˈzent/ vt darstellen; (act for) vertreten, repräsentieren. ~**ation** /-ˈteɪʃn/ n Darstellung f; **make** ~**ations to** vorstellig werden bei

representative /reprɪˈzentətɪv/ a repräsentativ (of für) □ n Bevollmächtigte(r) m/f; (Comm) Vertreter(in) m(f); (Amer, Pol) Abgeordnete(r) m/f

repress /rɪˈpres/ vt unterdrücken. ~ion /-ʃn/ n Unterdrückung f. ~ive /-ɪv/ a repressiv

reprieve /rɪˈpriːv/ n Begnadigung f; (postponement) Strafaufschub m; (fig) Gnadenfrist f □ vt begnadigen

reprimand /ˈreprɪmɑːnd/ n Tadel m □ vt tadeln

'reprint[1] /riː-/ n Nachdruck m

re'print[2] /riː-/ vt neu auflegen

reprisal /rɪˈpraɪzl/ n Vergeltungsmaßnahme f

reproach /rɪˈprəʊtʃ/ n Vorwurf m □ vt Vorwürfe pl machen (+ dat). ~ful a, -ly adv vorwurfsvoll

repro'duce /riː-/ vt wiedergeben, reproduzieren □ vi sich fortpflanzen. ~tion /-ˈdʌkʃn/ n Reproduktion f; (Biol) Fortpflanzung f. ~tion furniture n Stilmöbel pl. ~tive /-ˈdʌktɪv/ a Fortpflanzungs-

reprove /rɪˈpruːv/ vt tadeln

reptile /ˈreptaɪl/ n Reptil n

republic /rɪˈpʌblɪk/ n Republik f. ~an a republikanisch □ n Republikaner(in) m(f)

repudiate /rɪˈpjuːdɪeɪt/ vt zurückweisen

repugnan|ce /rɪˈpʌɡnəns/ n Widerwille m. ~t a widerlich

repuls|e /rɪˈpʌls/ vt zurückschlagen; (fig) abweisen. ~ion /-ʌlʃn/ n Widerwille m. ~ive /-ɪv/ a abstoßend, widerlich

reputable /ˈrepjʊtəbl/ a ⟨firm⟩ von gutem Ruf; ⟨respectable⟩ anständig

reputation /repjʊˈteɪʃn/ n Ruf m

repute /rɪˈpjuːt/ n Ruf m. ~d /-ɪd/ a, -ly adv angeblich

request /rɪˈkwest/ n Bitte f □ vt bitten. ~ stop n Bedarfshaltestelle f

require /rɪˈkwaɪə(r)/ vt (need) brauchen; (demand) erfordern; **be ~d to do sth** etw tun müssen. ~ment n Bedürfnis nt; (condition) Erfordernis nt

requisite /ˈrekwɪzɪt/ a erforderlich □ n toilet/travel ~s pl Toiletten-/Reiseartikel pl

requisition /rekwɪˈzɪʃn/ n ~ [order] Anforderung f □ vt anfordern

re'sale /riː-/ n Weiterverkauf m

rescind /rɪˈsɪnd/ vt aufheben

rescue /ˈreskjuː/ n Rettung f □ vt retten. ~r n Retter m

research /rɪˈsɜːtʃ/ n Forschung f □ vt erforschen; (Journ) recherchieren □ vi ~ into erforschen. ~er n Forscher m; (Journ) Rechercheur m

resem|blance /rɪˈzembləns/ n Ähnlichkeit f. ~ble /-bl/ vt ähneln (+ dat)

resent /rɪˈzent/ vt übelnehmen; einen Groll hegen gegen ⟨person⟩. ~ful a, -ly adv verbittert. ~ment n Groll m

reservation /rezəˈveɪʃn/ n Reservierung f; (doubt) Vorbehalt m; (enclosure) Reservat nt

reserve /rɪˈzɜːv/ n Reserve f; (for animals) Reservat nt; (Sport) Reservespieler(in) m(f) □ vt reservieren; ⟨client:⟩ reservieren lassen; (keep) aufheben; sich (dat) vorbehalten ⟨right⟩. ~d a reserviert

reservoir /ˈrezəvwɑː(r)/ n Reservoir n

re'shape /riː-/ vt umformen

re'shuffle /riː-/ n (Pol) Umbildung f □ vt (Pol) umbilden

reside /rɪˈzaɪd/ vi wohnen

residence /ˈrezɪdəns/ n Wohnsitz m; (official) Residenz f; (stay) Aufenthalt m. ~ permit n Aufenthaltsgenehmigung f

resident /ˈrezɪdənt/ a ansässig (in in + dat); ⟨housekeeper, nurse⟩ im Haus wohnend □ n Bewohner(in) *m(f)*; *(of street)* Anwohner *m.* ~**ial** /-'denʃl/ *a* Wohn-

residue /'rezɪdjuː/ *n* Rest *m*; *(Chem)* Rückstand *m*

resign /rɪ'zaɪn/ *vt* ~ oneself to sich abfinden mit □*vi* kündigen; *(from public office)* zurücktreten. ~**ation** /rezɪg'neɪʃn/ *n* Resignation *f*; *(from job)* Kündigung *f*; Rücktritt *m.* ~**ed** *a*, -**ly** *adv* resigniert

resilient /rɪ'zɪlɪənt/ *a* federnd; *(fig)* widerstandsfähig

resin /'rezɪn/ *n* Harz *nt*

resist /rɪ'zɪst/ *vt/i* sich widersetzen (+ *dat*); *(fig)* widerstehen (+ *dat*). ~**ance** *n* Widerstand *m*. ~**ant** *a* widerstandsfähig

resolut|**e** /'rezəluːt/ *a*, -**ly** *adv* entschlossen. ~**ion** /-'luːʃn/ *n* Entschlossenheit *f*; *(intention)* Vorsatz *m*; *(Pol)* Resolution *f*

resolve /rɪ'zɒlv/ *n* Entschlossenheit *f*; *(decision)* Beschluß *m* □*vt* beschließen; *(solve)* lösen. ~**d** *a* entschlossen

resonan|**ce** /'rezənəns/ *n* Resonanz *f.* ~**t** *a* klangvoll

resort /rɪ'zɔːt/ *n* *(place)* Urlaubsort *m*; **as a last** ~ wenn alles andere fehlschlägt □*vi* ~ **to** (*fig*) greifen zu

resound /rɪ'zaʊnd/ *vi* widerhallen. ~**ing** *a* widerhallend; *(loud)* laut; *(notable)* groß

resource /rɪ'sɔːs/ *n* ~*s pl* Ressourcen *pl.* ~**ful** *a* findig. ~**fulness** *n* Findigkeit *f*

respect /rɪ'spekt/ *n* Respekt *m*, Achtung *f* **(for** vor + *dat)*; *(aspect)* Hinsicht *f*; **with** ~ **to** in bezug auf (+ *acc)* □*vt* respektieren, achten

respectability /rɪspektə'bɪlətɪ/ *n* (*see* **respectable**) Ehrbarkeit *f*; Anständigkeit *f*

respect|**able** /rɪ'spektəbl/ *a*, -**bly** *adv* ehrbar; *(decent)* anständig; *(considerable)* ansehnlich. ~**ful** *a*, -**ly** *adv* respektvoll

respective /rɪ'spektɪv/ *a* jeweilig. ~**ly** *adv* beziehungsweise

respiration /respə'reɪʃn/ *n* Atmung *f*

respite /'respaɪt/ *n* [Ruhe]pause *f*; *(delay)* Aufschub *m*

resplendent /rɪ'splendənt/ *a* glänzend

respond /rɪ'spɒnd/ *vi* antworten; *(react)* reagieren **(to** auf + *acc)*; *⟨patient:⟩* ansprechen **(to** auf + *acc)*

response /rɪ'spɒns/ *n* Antwort *f*; Reaktion *f*

responsibility /rɪspɒnsɪ'bɪlətɪ/ *n* Verantwortung *f*; *(duty)* Verpflichtung *f*

responsib|**le** /rɪ'spɒnsəbl/ *a* verantwortlich; *(trustworthy)* verantwortungsvoll. ~**ly** *adv* verantwortungsbewußt

responsive /rɪ'spɒnsɪv/ *a* **be** ~ reagieren

rest[1] /rest/ *n* Ruhe *f*; *(holiday)* Erholung *f*; *(interval & Mus)* Pause *f*; **have a** ~ eine Pause machen; *(rest)* sich ausruhen □*vt* ausruhen; *(lean)* lehnen **(on** an/ auf + *acc)* □*vi* ruhen; *(have a rest)* sich ausruhen

rest[2] *n* **the** ~ der Rest; *(people)* die Übrigen *pl* □*vi* **it** ~**s with you** es ist an Ihnen *(to* zu)

restaurant /'restərɒnt/ *n* Restaurant *nt*, Gaststätte *f.* ~ **car** *n* Speisewagen *m*

restful /'restfl/ *a* erholsam

restitution /restɪ'tjuːʃn/ *n* Entschädigung *f*; *(return)* Rückgabe *f*

restive /'restɪv/ *a* unruhig

restless /'restlɪs/ *a*, -**ly** *adv* unruhig

restoration /restə'reɪʃn/ *n* (*of building*) Restaurierung *f*

restore /rɪ'stɔː(r)/ *vt* wiederherstellen; restaurieren *(building)*; *(give back)* zurückgeben

restrain /rɪ'streɪn/ *vt* zurückhalten; ~ **oneself** sich beherrschen. ~**ed** *a* zurückhaltend. ~**t** *n* Zurückhaltung *f*

restrict /rɪ'strɪkt/ *vt* einschränken; ~ **to** beschränken auf (+ *acc*). ~**ion** /-ɪkʃn/ *n* Einschränkung *f*; Beschränkung *f*. ~**ive** /-ɪv/ *a* einschränkend

'**rest room** *n* (*Amer*) Toilette *f*

result /rɪ'zʌlt/ *n* Ergebnis *nt*, Resultat *nt*; (*consequence*) Folge *f*; **as a** ~ als Folge (**of** *gen*) □ *vi* sich ergeben (**from** aus); ~ **in** enden in (+ *dat*); (*lead to*) führen zu

resume /rɪ'zju:m/ *vt* wiederaufnehmen; wieder einnehmen ⟨*seat*⟩ □ *vi* wieder beginnen

résumé /'rezʊmeɪ/ *n* Zusammenfassung *f*

resumption /rɪ'zʌmpʃn/ *n* Wiederaufnahme *f*

resurgence /rɪ'sɜ:dʒəns/ *n* Wiederaufleben *nt*

resurrect /rezə'rekt/ *vt* (*fig*) wiederbeleben. ~**ion** /-ekʃn/ *n* **the R**~**ion** (*Relig*) die Auferstehung

resuscitat|e /rɪ'sʌsɪteɪt/ *vt* wiederbeleben. ~**ion** /-'teɪʃn/ *n* Wiederbelebung *f*

retail /'ri:teɪl/ *n* Einzelhandel *m* □ *a* Einzelhandels- □ *adv* im Einzelhandel □ *vt* im Einzelhandel verkaufen □ *vi* ~ **at** im Einzelhandel kosten. ~**er** *n* Einzelhändler *m*. ~ **price** *n* Ladenpreis *m*

retain /rɪ'teɪn/ *vt* behalten

retaliat|e /rɪ'tælɪeɪt/ *vi* zurückschlagen. ~**ion** /-'eɪʃn/ *n* Vergeltung *f*; **in** ~**ion** als Vergeltung

retarded /rɪ'tɑ:dɪd/ *a* zurückgeblieben

retentive /rɪ'tentɪv/ *a* ⟨*memory*⟩ gut

retic|ence /'retɪsns/ *n* Zurückhaltung *f*. ~**t** *a* zurückhaltend

retina /'retɪnə/ *n* Netzhaut *f*

retinue /'retɪnju:/ *n* Gefolge *nt*

retire /rɪ'taɪə(r)/ *vi* in den Ruhestand treten; (*withdraw*) sich zurückziehen. ~**d** *a* im Ruhestand. ~**ment** *n* Ruhestand *m*; **since**

my ~**ment** seit ich nicht mehr arbeite

retiring /rɪ'taɪərɪŋ/ *a* zurückhaltend

retort /rɪ'tɔ:t/ *n* scharfe Erwiderung *f*; (*Chem*) Retorte *f* □ *vt* scharf erwidern

re'touch /ri:-/ *vt* (*Phot*) retuschieren

re'trace /rɪ-/ *vt* zurückverfolgen; ~ **one's steps** denselben Weg zurückgehen

retract /rɪ'trækt/ *vt* einziehen; zurücknehmen ⟨*remark*⟩ □ *vi* widerrufen

re'train /ri:-/ *vt* umschulen □ *vi* umgeschult werden

retreat /rɪ'tri:t/ *n* Rückzug *m*; (*place*) Zufluchtsort *m* □ *vi* sich zurückziehen

re'trial /ri:-/ *n* Wiederaufnahmeverfahren *nt*

retribution /retrɪ'bju:ʃn/ *n* Vergeltung *f*

retrieve /rɪ'tri:v/ *vt* zurückholen; (*from wreckage*) bergen; (*Computing*) wiederauffinden; ⟨*dog:*⟩ apportieren

retrograde /'retrəgreɪd/ *a* rückschrittlich

retrospect /'retrəspekt/ *n* **in** ~ rückblickend. ~**ive** /-ɪv/ *a*, **-ly** *adv* rückwirkend; (*looking back*) rückblickend

return /rɪ'tɜ:n/ *n* Rückkehr *f*; (*giving back*) Rückgabe *f*; (*Comm*) Ertrag *m*; (*ticket*) Rückfahrkarte *f*; (*Aviat*) Rückflugschein *m*; **by** ~ [**of post**] postwendend; **in** ~ dafür; **in** ~ **for** für; **many happy** ~**s!** herzlichen Glückwunsch zum Geburtstag! □ *vi* zurückgehen/-fahren; (*come back*) zurückkommen □ *vt* zurückgeben; (*put back*) zurückstellen/ -legen; (*send back*) zurückschicken; (*elect*) wählen

return: ~ **flight** *n* Rückflug *m*. ~ **match** *n* Rückspiel *nt*. ~ **ticket** *n* Rückfahrkarte *f*; (*Aviat*) Rückflugschein *m*

reunion /riːˈjuːnɪən/ n Wiedervereinigung f; (social gathering) Treffen nt

reunite /riːjuːˈnaɪt/ vt wiedervereinigen □vi sich wiedervereinigen

re'usable /riː-/ a wiederverwendbar. **~e** vt wiederverwenden

rev /rev/ n (Auto, fam) Umdrehung f □vt/i ~ [up] den Motor auf Touren bringen

reveal /rɪˈviːl/ vt jdn Vorschein bringen; (fig) enthüllen. **~ing** a (fig) aufschlußreich

revel /ˈrevl/ vi (pt/pp revelled) ~ in sth etw genießen

revelation /revəˈleɪʃn/ n Offenbarung f, Enthüllung f

revelry /ˈrevlrɪ/ n Lustbarkeit f

revenge /rɪˈvendʒ/ n Rache f; (fig & Sport) Revanche f □vt rächen

revenue /ˈrevənjuː/ n [Staats]einnahmen pl

reverberate /rɪˈvɜːbəreɪt/ vi nachhallen

revere /rɪˈvɪə(r)/ vt verehren. **~nce** /ˈrevərəns/ n Ehrfurcht f

Reverend /ˈrevərənd/ a the ~ X Pfarrer X; (Catholic) Hochwürden X

reverent /ˈrevərənt/ a, **-ly** adv ehrfürchtig

reverie /ˈrevərɪ/ n Träumerei f

revers /rɪˈvɪə/ n (pl revers /-z/) Revers nt

reversal /rɪˈvɜːsl/ n Umkehrung f

reverse /rɪˈvɜːs/ a umgekehrt □n Gegenteil nt; (back) Rückseite f; (Auto) Rückwärtsgang m □vt umkehren; (Auto) zurücksetzen; ~ **the charges** (Teleph) ein R-Gespräch führen □vi zurücksetzen

revert /rɪˈvɜːt/ vi ~ **to** zurückfallen an (+ acc); zurückkommen auf (+ acc) (topic)

review /rɪˈvjuː/ n Rückblick m (of auf + acc); (re-examination) Überprüfung f; (Mil) Truppenschau f; (of book, play) Kritik f, Rezension f □vt zurückblicken

auf (+ acc); überprüfen (situation); (Mil) besichtigen; kritisieren, rezensieren (book, play). **~er** n Kritiker m, Rezensent m

revile /rɪˈvaɪl/ vt verunglimpfen

revis|e /rɪˈvaɪz/ vt revidieren; (for exam) wiederholen. **~ion** /-ˈvɪʒn/ n Revision f; Wiederholung f

revival /rɪˈvaɪvl/ n Wiederbelebung f

revive /rɪˈvaɪv/ vt wiederbeleben; (fig) wieder aufleben lassen □vi wieder aufleben

revoke /rɪˈvəʊk/ vt aufheben; widerrufen (command, decision)

revolt /rɪˈvəʊlt/ n Aufstand m □vi rebellieren □vt anwidern. **~ing** a widerlich, eklig

revolution /revəˈluːʃn/ n Revolution f; (Auto) Umdrehung f. **~ary** /-ərɪ/ a revolutionär. **~ize** vt revolutionieren

revolve /rɪˈvɒlv/ vi sich drehen; ~ **around** kreisen um

revolv|er /rɪˈvɒlvə(r)/ n Revolver m. **~ing** a Dreh-

revue /rɪˈvjuː/ n Revue f; (satirical) Kabarett nt

revulsion /rɪˈvʌlʃn/ n Abscheu m

reward /rɪˈwɔːd/ n Belohnung f □vt belohnen. **~ing** a lohnend

re'write /riː-/ vt (pt rewrote, pp rewritten) noch einmal [neu] schreiben; (alter) umschreiben

rhapsody /ˈræpsədɪ/ n Rhapsodie f

rhetoric /ˈretərɪk/ n Rhetorik f. **~al** /rɪˈtɒrɪkl/ a rhetorisch

rheuma|tic /ruːˈmætɪk/ a rheumatisch. **~tism** /ˈruːmətɪzm/ n Rheumatismus m, Rheuma nt

Rhine /raɪn/ n Rhein m

rhinoceros /raɪˈnɒsərəs/ n Nashorn nt, Rhinozeros nt

rhubarb /ˈruːbɑːb/ n Rhabarber m

rhyme /raɪm/ n Reim m □vt reimen □vi sich reimen

rhythm /ˈrɪðm/ n Rhythmus m. **~ic[al]** a, **-ally** adv rhythmisch

rib /rɪb/ n Rippe f □vt (pt/pp ribbed) (fam) aufziehen (fam)

ribald /ˈrɪbld/ a derb

ribbon /'rɪbən/ n Band nt; (for typewriter) Farbband nt; **in ~s** in Fetzen

rice /raɪs/ n Reis m

rich /rɪtʃ/ a (-er, -est), -ly adv reich; ⟨food⟩ gehaltvoll; (heavy) schwer □n **the ~** pl die Reichen; **~es** pl Reichtum m

rickets /'rɪkɪts/ n Rachitis f

rickety /'rɪkətɪ/ a wackelig

ricochet /'rɪkəʃeɪ/ vi abprallen

rid /rɪd/ vt (pt/pp **rid**, pres p **ridding**) befreien (**of** von); **get ~ of** loswerden

riddance /'rɪdns/ n **good ~!** auf Nimmerwiedersehen!

ridden /'rɪdn/ see **ride**

riddle /'rɪdl/ n Rätsel nt

riddled /'rɪdld/ a **~ with** durchlöchert mit

ride /raɪd/ n Ritt m; (in vehicle) Fahrt f; **take s.o. for a ~** (fam) jdn reinlegen □v (pt **rode**, pp **ridden**) vt reiten ⟨horse⟩; fahren mit ⟨bicycle⟩ □vi reiten; (in vehicle) fahren. **~r** n Reiter(in) m(f); (on bicycle) Fahrer(in) m(f); (in document) Zusatzklausel f

ridge /rɪdʒ/ n Erhebung f; (on roof) First m; (of mountain) Grat m, Kamm m; (of high pressure) Hochdruckkeil m

ridicule /'rɪdɪkjuːl/ n Spott m □vt verspotten, spotten über (+ acc)

ridiculous /rɪ'dɪkjʊləs/ a, -ly adv lächerlich

riding /'raɪdɪŋ/ n Reiten nt □attrib Reit-

rife /raɪf/ a **be ~** weit verbreitet sein

riff-raff /'rɪfræf/ n Gesindel nt

rifle /'raɪfl/ n Gewehr nt □vt plündern; **~ through** durchwühlen

rift /rɪft/ n Spalt m; (fig) Riß m

rig[1] /rɪg/ n Ölbohrturm m; (at sea) Bohrinsel f □vt (pt/pp **rigged**) **~ out** ausrüsten; **~ up** aufbauen

rig[2] vt (pt/pp **rigged**) manipulieren

right /raɪt/ a richtig; (not left) rechte(r,s); **be ~** ⟨person:⟩ recht

haben; ⟨clock:⟩ richtig gehen; **put ~** wieder in Ordnung bringen; (fig) richtigstellen; **that's ~!** das stimmt! □adv richtig; (directly) direkt; (completely) ganz; (not left) rechts; ⟨go⟩ nach rechts; **~ away** sofort □n Recht nt; (not left) rechte Seite f; **on the ~** rechts; **from/to the ~** von/nach rechts; **be in the ~** recht haben; **by ~s** eigentlich; **the R~** (Pol) die Rechte. **~ angle** n rechter Winkel m

righteous /'raɪtʃəs/ a rechtschaffen

rightful /'raɪtfl/ a, -ly adv rechtmäßig

right: ~-'handed a rechtshändig. **~-hand 'man** n (fig) rechte Hand f

rightly /'raɪtlɪ/ adv mit Recht

right: ~ of way n Durchgangsrecht nt; (path) öffentlicher Fußweg m; (Auto) Vorfahrt f. **~-'wing** a (Pol) rechte(r,s)

rigid /'rɪdʒɪd/ a starr; (strict) streng. **~ity** /-'dʒɪdətɪ/ n Starrheit f; Strenge f

rigmarole /'rɪgmərəʊl/ n Geschwätz nt; (procedure) Prozedur f

rigorous /'rɪgərəs/ a, -ly adv streng

rigour /'rɪgə(r)/ n Strenge f

rile /raɪl/ vt (fam) ärgern

rim /rɪm/ n Rand m; (of wheel) Felge f

rind /raɪnd/ n (on fruit) Schale f; (on cheese) Rinde f; (on bacon) Schwarte f

ring[1] /rɪŋ/ n Ring m; (for circus) Manege f; **stand in a ~** im Kreis stehen □vt umringen; **~ in red** rot einkreisen

ring[2] n Klingeln nt; **give s.o. a ~** (Teleph) jdn anrufen □v (pt **rang**, pp **rung**) vt läuten; **[up]** (Teleph) anrufen □vi läuten, klingeln. **~ back** vt/i (Teleph) zurückrufen. **~ off** vi (Teleph) auflegen

ring: ~**leader** *n* Rädelsführer *m.*
~ **road** *n* Umgehungsstraße *f*

rink /rɪŋk/ *n* Eisbahn *f*

rinse /rɪns/ *n* Spülung *f*; ⟨*hair colour*⟩ Tönung *f* □*vt* spülen; tönen ⟨*hair*⟩. ~ **off** *vt* abspülen

riot /ˈraɪət/ *n* Aufruhr *m*; ~**s** *pl* Unruhen *pl*; ~ **of colours** bunte Farbenpracht *f*; **run** ~ randalieren □*vi* randalieren. ~ **er** *n* Randalierer *m.* ~ **ous** /-/əs/ *a* aufrührerisch; ⟨*boisterous*⟩ wild

rip /rɪp/ *n* Riß *m* □*vt/i* ⟨*pt/pp* **ripped**⟩ zerreißen; ~ **open** aufreißen. ~ **off** *vt* ⟨*fam*⟩ neppen

ripe /raɪp/ *a* (**-r, -st**) reif

ripen /ˈraɪpn/ *vi* reifen □*vt* reifen lassen

ripeness /ˈraɪpnɪs/ *n* Reife *f*

rip-off /ˈrɪp-/ *n* Nepp *m*

ripple /ˈrɪpl/ *n* kleine Welle *f* □*vt* kräuseln □*vi* sich kräuseln

rise /raɪz/ *n* Anstieg *m*; ⟨*fig*⟩ Aufstieg *m*; ⟨*increase*⟩ Zunahme *f*; ⟨*in wages*⟩ Lohnerhöhung *f*; ⟨*in salary*⟩ Gehaltserhöhung *f*; **give** ~ **to** Anlaß geben zu □*vi* ⟨*pt* **rose,** *pp* **risen**⟩ steigen; ⟨*ground:*⟩ ansteigen; ⟨*sun, dough:*⟩ aufgehen; ⟨*river:*⟩ entspringen; ⟨*get up*⟩ aufstehen; ⟨*fig*⟩ aufsteigen ⟨*to* zu⟩; ⟨*rebel*⟩ sich erheben; ⟨*court:*⟩ sich vertagen. ~ **r** *n* **early** ~ **r** Frühaufsteher *m*

rising /ˈraɪzɪŋ/ *a* steigend; ⟨*sun*⟩ aufgehend; **the** ~ **generation** die heranwachsende Generation □*n* ⟨*revolt*⟩ Aufstand *m*

risk /rɪsk/ *n* Risiko *nt*; **at one's own** ~ auf eigene Gefahr □*vt* riskieren

risky /ˈrɪskɪ/ *a* (**-ier, -iest**) riskant

risqué /ˈrɪskeɪ/ *a* gewagt

rissole /ˈrɪsəʊl/ *n* Frikadelle *f*

rite /raɪt/ *n* Ritus *m*; **last** ~ **s** Letzte Ölung *f*

ritual /ˈrɪtjʊəl/ *a* rituell □*n* Ritual *nt*

rival /ˈraɪvl/ *a* rivalisierend □*n* Rivale *m*/Rivalin *f*; ~ **s** *pl* ⟨*Comm*⟩ Konkurrenten *pl* □*vt* ⟨*pt/pp* **rivalled**⟩ gleichkommen (+ *dat*); ⟨*compete with*⟩ rivalisieren mit. ~ **ry** *n* Rivalität *f*; ⟨*Comm*⟩ Konkurrenzkampf *m*

river /ˈrɪvə(r)/ *n* Fluß *m.* ~ **bed** *n* Flußbett *nt*

rivet /ˈrɪvɪt/ *n* Niete *f* □*vt* [ver]nieten; ~ **ed by** ⟨*fig*⟩ gefesselt von

road /rəʊd/ *n* Straße *f*; ⟨*fig*⟩ Weg *m*

road: ~ **block** *n* Straßensperre *f.* ~ **hog** *n* ⟨*fam*⟩ Straßenschreck *m.* ~ **map** *n* Straßenkarte *f.* ~ **safety** *n* Verkehrssicherheit *f.* ~ **sense** *n* Verkehrssinn *m.* ~ **side** *n* Straßenrand *m.* ~ **way** *n* Fahrbahn *f.* ~ **works** *npl* Straßenarbeiten *pl.* ~ **worthy** *a* verkehrssicher

roam /rəʊm/ *vi* wandern

roar /rɔː(r)/ *n* Gebrüll *nt*; ~ **s of laughter** schallendes Gelächter □*vi* brüllen; ⟨*with laughter*⟩ schallend lachen. ~ **ing** *a* ⟨*fire*⟩ prasselnd; **do a** ~ **ing trade** ⟨*fam*⟩ ein Bombengeschäft machen

roast /rəʊst/ *a* gebraten, Brat-; ~ **beef/pork** Rinder-/Schweinebraten *m* □*n* Braten *m* □*vt/i* braten; rösten ⟨*coffee, chestnuts*⟩

rob /rɒb/ *vt* ⟨*pt/pp* **robbed**⟩ berauben ⟨*of* gen⟩; ausrauben ⟨*bank*⟩. ~ **ber** *n* Räuber *m.* ~ **bery** *n* Raub *m*

robe /rəʊb/ *n* Robe *f*; ⟨*Amer: bathrobe*⟩ Bademantel *m*

robin /ˈrɒbɪn/ *n* Rotkehlchen *nt*

robot /ˈrəʊbɒt/ *n* Roboter *m*

robust /rəʊˈbʌst/ *a* robust

rock[1] /rɒk/ *n* Fels *m*; **stick of** ~ Zuckerstange *f*; **on the** ~ **s** ⟨*ship*⟩ aufgelaufen; ⟨*marriage*⟩ kaputt; ⟨*drink*⟩ mit Eis

rock[2] *vt/i* schaukeln

rock[3] *n* ⟨*Mus*⟩ Rock *m*

rock-'bottom *n* Tiefpunkt *m*

rockery /ˈrɒkərɪ/ *n* Steingarten *m*

rocket /ˈrɒkɪt/ *n* Rakete *f* □*vi* in die Höhe schießen

rocking: **~-chair** n Schaukel-
stuhl m. **~-horse** n Schaukel-
pferd nt

rocky /'rɒkɪ/ a (-ier, -iest) felsig;
(unsteady) wackelig

rod /rɒd/ n Stab m; (stick) Rute f;
(for fishing) Angel[rute] f

rode /rəʊd/ see **ride**

rodent /'rəʊdnt/ n Nagetier nt

roe¹ /rəʊ/ n Rogen m; (soft) Milch f

roe² n (pl roe or roes) **~-**[deer]
Reh nt

rogue /rəʊg/ n Gauner m

role /rəʊl/ n Rolle f

roll /rəʊl/ n Rolle f; (bread) Brötchen nt; (list) Liste f; (of drum)
Wirbel m ● vi rollen; be **~ing in
money** (fam) Geld wie Heu haben ● vt rollen; walzen (lawn);
ausrollen (pastry). **~ over** vi
sich auf die andere Seite rollen.
~ up vt aufrollen; hochkrempeln
(sleeves) ● vi (fam) auftauchen

'roll-call n Namensaufruf m;
(Mil) Appell m

roller /'rəʊlə(r)/ n Rolle f; (lawn,
road) Walze f; (hair) Lockenwickler m. **~ blind** n Rollo m. **~-
coaster** n Berg-und-Talbahn f.
~-skate n Rollschuh m

'rolling-pin n Teigrolle f

Roman /'rəʊmən/ a römisch ● n
Römer(in) m(f)

romance /rə'mæns/ n Romantik f;
(love-affair) Romanze f; (book)
Liebesgeschichte f

Romania /rəʊ'meɪnɪə/ n Rumänien nt. **~ n** a rumänisch ● n Ru-
mäne m/-nin f

romantic /rə'mæntɪk/ a, **-ally**
adv romantisch. **~ism** /-tɪsɪzm/ n
Romantik f

Rome /rəʊm/ n Rom nt

romp /rɒmp/ n Tollen nt ● vi [her-
um]tollen. **~ers** npl Strampel-
höschen nt

roof /ruːf/ n Dach nt; (of mouth)
Gaumen m ● vt **~ over** überda-
chen. **~-rack** n Dachgepäckträ-
ger m. **~-top** n Dach nt

rook /rʊk/ n Saatkrähe f; (Chess)
Turm m ● vt (fam: swindle)
schröpfen

room /ruːm/ n Zimmer nt; (for
functions) Saal m; (space) Platz
m. **~y** a geräumig

roost /ruːst/ n Hühnerstange f ● vi
schlafen

root¹ /ruːt/ n Wurzel f; **take ~**
anwachsen ● vi Wurzeln schla-
gen. **~ out** vt (fig) ausrotten

root² vi **~ about** wühlen; **~ for**
s.o. (Amer, fam) für jdn sein

rope /rəʊp/ n Seil nt; **know the ~s**
(fam) sich auskennen. **~ in** vt
(fam) einspannen

rope-ladder n Strickleiter f

rosary /'rəʊzərɪ/ n Rosenkranz m

rose¹ /rəʊz/ n Rose f; (of watering-
can) Brause f

rose² see **rise**

rosemary /'rəʊzmərɪ/ n Rosmarin
m

rosette /rəʊ'zet/ n Rosette f

roster /'rɒstə(r)/ n Dienstplan m

rostrum /'rɒstrəm/ n Podest nt,
Podium nt

rosy /'rəʊzɪ/ a (-ier, -iest) rosig

rot /rɒt/ n Fäulnis f; (fam: nonsense) Quatsch m ● vi (pt/pp rot-
ted) [ver]faulen

rota /'rəʊtə/ n Dienstplan m

rotary /'rəʊtərɪ/ a Dreh-; (Techn)
Rotations-

rotate /rəʊ'teɪt/ vt drehen; im
Wechsel anbauen (crops) ● vi
sich drehen; (Techn) rotieren.
~ion /-eɪʃn/ n Drehung f; (of
crops) Fruchtfolge f; **in ~ion** im
Wechsel

rote /rəʊt/ n **by ~** auswendig

rotten /'rɒtn/ a faul; (fam) mies;
(person) fies

rotund /rəʊ'tʌnd/ a rundlich

rough /rʌf/ a (-er, -est) rauh; (uneven) uneben; (coarse, not gentle)
grob; (brutal) roh; (turbulent)
stürmisch; (approximate) ungefähr ● adv **sleep ~** im Freien
übernachten; **play ~** holzen

□n do sth in ~ etw ins unreine schreiben □vt ~ it primitiv leben. ~ out vt im Groben entwerfen

roughage /'rʌfɪdʒ/ n Ballaststoffe pl

rough 'draft n grober Entwurf m

rough|ly /'rʌflɪ/ adv (approx) rauh; grob; roh; ungefähr. ~ness n Rauheit f

'rough paper n Konzeptpapier nt

round /raʊnd/ a (-er, -est) rund □n Runde f; (slice) Scheibe f; do one's ~s seine Runde machen □prep um (+ acc); ~ the clock rund um die Uhr □adv all ~ ringsherum; ~ and ~ im Kreis; ask s.o. ~ jdn einladen; turn/look ~ sich umdrehen/umsehen □vt biegen um ⟨corner⟩ □vi ~ on s.o. jdn anfahren. ~ off vt abrunden. ~ up vt aufrunden; zusammentreiben ⟨animals⟩; festnehmen ⟨criminals⟩

roundabout /'raʊndəbaʊt/ a ~ route Umweg m □n Karussell nt; (for traffic) Kreisverkehr m

round: ~-'shouldered a mit einem runden Rücken. ~ 'trip n Rundreise f

rous|e /raʊz/ vt wecken; (fig) erregen. ~ing a mitreißend

route /ru:t/ n Route f; (of bus) Linie f

routine /ru:'ti:n/ a, -ly adv routinemäßig □n Routine f; (Theat) Nummer f

roux /ru:/ n Mehlschwitze f

rove /rəʊv/ vi wandern

row¹ /rəʊ/ n (line) Reihe f; in a ~ (one after the other) nacheinander

row² /rəʊ/ vt/i rudern

row³ /raʊ/ n (fam) Krach m □vi (fam) sich streiten

rowan /'rəʊən/ n Eberesche f

rowdy /'raʊdɪ/ a (-ier, -iest) laut

rowing boat /'rəʊɪŋ-/ n Ruderboot nt

royal /'rɔɪəl/ a, -ly adv königlich

royal|ty /'rɔɪəltɪ/ n Königtum nt; (persons) Mitglieder pl der königlichen Familie; ~ies pl (payments) Tantiemen pl

rub /rʌb/ n give sth a ~ etw reiben/(polish) polieren □vt (pt/pp rubbed) reiben; (polish) polieren; don't ~ it in (fam) reib es mir nicht unter die Nase. ~ off vt abreiben □vi abgehen; ~ off on abfärben auf (+ acc). ~ out vt ausradieren

rubber /'rʌbə(r)/ n Gummi m; (eraser) Radiergummi m. ~ band n Gummiband nt. ~-y a gummiartig

rubbish /'rʌbɪʃ/ n Abfall m, Müll m; (fam: nonsense) Quatsch m; (fam: junk) Plunder m, Kram m □vt (fam) schlechtmachen. ~ bin n Mülleimer m, Abfalleimer m. ~ dump n Abfallhaufen m; (official) Müllhalde f

rubble /'rʌbl/ n Trümmer pl, Schutt m

ruby /'ru:bɪ/ n Rubin m

rucksack /'rʌksæk/ n Rucksack m

rudder /'rʌdə(r)/ n [Steuer]ruder nt

ruddy /'rʌdɪ/ a (-ier, -iest) rötlich; (sl) verdammt

rude /ru:d/ a (-r, -st), -ly adv unhöflich; (improper) unanständig. ~ness n Unhöflichkeit f

rudiment /'ru:dɪmənt/ n ~s pl Anfangsgründe pl. ~ary /-'mentərɪ/ a elementar; (Biol) rudimentär

rueful /'ru:fl/ a, -ly adv reumütig

ruffian /'rʌfɪən/ n Rüpel m

ruffle /'rʌfl/ n Rüsche f □vt zerzausen

rug /rʌg/ n Vorleger m, [kleiner] Teppich m; (blanket) Decke f

rugged /'rʌgɪd/ a ⟨coastline⟩ zerklüftet

ruin /'ru:ɪn/ n Ruine f; (fig) Ruin m □vt ruinieren. ~ous /-əs/ a ruinös

rule /ruːl/ n Regel f; (control) Herrschaft f; (government) Regierung f; (for measuring) Lineal nt; **as a ~** in der Regel □ vt regieren, herrschen über (+ acc); (fig) beherrschen; (decide) entscheiden; ziehen ⟨line⟩ □ vi regieren, herrschen. **~ out** vt ausschließen

ruled /ruːld/ a ⟨paper⟩ liniert

ruler /ˈruːlə(r)/ n Herrscher(in) m(f); (measure) Lineal nt

ruling /ˈruːlɪŋ/ a herrschend; ⟨factor⟩ entscheidend; (Pol) regierend □ n Entscheidung f

rum /rʌm/ n Rum m

rumble /ˈrʌmbl/ n Grollen nt □ vi grollen; ⟨stomach:⟩ knurren

ruminant /ˈruːmɪnənt/ n Wiederkäuer m

rummage /ˈrʌmɪdʒ/ vi wühlen; **~ through** durchwühlen

rummy /ˈrʌmɪ/ n Rommé f

rumour /ˈruːmə(r)/ n Gerücht n □ vt **is is ~ed that** es geht das Gerücht, daß

rump /rʌmp/ n Hinterteil nt. **~ steak** n Rumpsteak nt

rumpus /ˈrʌmpəs/ n (fam) Spektakel m

run /rʌn/ n Lauf m; (journey) Fahrt f; (series) Serie f, Reihe f; (Theat) Laufzeit f; (Skiing) Abfahrt f; (enclosure) Auslauf m; (Amer: ladder) Laufmasche f; **at a ~** im Laufschritt; **of bad luck** Pechsträhne f; **be on the ~** flüchtig sein; **have the ~ of sth** etw zu seiner freien Verfügung haben; **in the long ~** auf lange Sicht □ v (pt **ran**, pp **run**, pres p **running**) □ vi laufen; (flow) fließen; ⟨eyes:⟩ tränen; ⟨bus:⟩ verkehren, fahren; ⟨butter, ink:⟩ zerfließen; ⟨colours:⟩ [ab]färben; (in election) kandidieren; **~ across s.o./sth** auf jdn/ etw stoßen □ vt laufen lassen; einlaufen lassen ⟨bath⟩; (manage) führen, leiten; (drive) fahren; (risk) eingehen; (Journ) bringen ⟨article⟩; **~ one's hand over sth** mit der Hand über etw

(acc) fahren. **~ away** vi weglaufen. **~ down** vi hinunter-/herunterlaufen; ⟨clockwork:⟩ ablaufen; ⟨stocks:⟩ sich verringern □ vt (run over) überfahren; (reduce) verringern; (fam: criticize) heruntermachen. **~ in** vi hineinlaufen; hereinlaufen. **~ off** vi weglaufen □ vt abziehen ⟨copies⟩. **~ out** vi hinaus-/herauslaufen; ⟨supplies, money:⟩ ausgehen; **I've ~ out of sugar** ich habe keinen Zucker mehr. **~ over** vi hinüber-/herüberlaufen; ⟨overflow⟩ überlaufen □ vt überfahren. **~ through** vi durchlaufen. **~ up** vi hinauf-/herauflaufen; ⟨towards⟩ hinlaufen □ vt machen ⟨debts⟩; auflaufen lassen ⟨bill⟩; (sew) schnell nähen

runaway n Ausreißer m

run-down a ⟨area⟩ verkommen

rung[1] /rʌŋ/ n (of ladder) Sprosse f

rung[2] see **ring**[2]

runner /ˈrʌnə(r)/ n Läufer m; (Bot) Ausläufer m; (on sledge) Kufe f. **~ bean** n Stangenbohne f. **~-up** n Zweite(r) m/f

running /ˈrʌnɪŋ/ a laufend; ⟨water⟩ fließend; **four times ~** viermal nacheinander □ n Laufen nt; (management) Führung f, Leitung f; **be/not be in the ~** eine/keine Chance haben. **~ 'commentary** n fortlaufender Kommentar m

runny /ˈrʌnɪ/ a flüssig

run-of-the-'mill a gewöhnlich. **~-up** n (Sport) Anlauf m; (to election) Zeit f vor der Wahl. **~way** n Start- und Landebahn f, Piste f

rupture /ˈrʌptʃə(r)/ n Bruch m □ vt/i brechen; **~ oneself** sich (dat) einen Bruch heben

rural /ˈrʊərəl/ a ländlich

ruse /ruːz/ n List f

rush[1] /rʌʃ/ n (Bot) Binse f

rush[2] n Hetze f; **in a ~** in Eile □ vi sich hetzen; (run) rasen; ⟨water:⟩ rauschen □ vt hetzen, drängen;

~ **s.o. to hospital** jdn schnellstens ins Krankenhaus bringen. **~-hour** n Hauptverkehrszeit f, Stoßzeit f

rusk /rʌsk/ n Zwieback m

Russia /'rʌʃə/ n Rußland nt. **~n** a russisch □n Russe m/Russin f; (Lang) Russisch nt

rust /rʌst/ n Rost m □vi rosten

rustic /'rʌstɪk/ a bäuerlich; (furniture) rustikal

rustle /'rʌsl/ vi rascheln □vt rascheln mit; (Amer) stehlen (cattle). ~ **up** vt (fam) improvisieren

'rustproof a rostfrei

rusty /'rʌstɪ/ a (-ier, -iest) rostig

rut /rʌt/ n Furche f; **be in a** ~ (fam) aus dem alten Trott nicht herauskommen

ruthless /'ruːθlɪs/ a, -ly adv rücksichtslos. **~ness** n Rücksichtslosigkeit f

rye /raɪ/ n Roggen m

S

sabbath /'sæbəθ/ n Sabbat m

sabbatical /sə'bætɪkl/ n (Univ) Forschungsurlaub m

sabotage /'sæbətɑːʒ/ n Sabotage f □vt sabotieren. **~eur** /-'tɜː(r)/ n Saboteur m

sachet /'sæʃeɪ/ n Beutel m; (scented) Kissen nt

sack[1] /sæk/ vt (plunder) plündern

sack[2] n Sack m; **get the** ~ (fam) rausgeschmissen werden □vt (fam) rausschmeißen. **~ing** n Sackleinen nt; (fam: dismissal) Rausschmiß m

sacrament /'sækrəmənt/ n Sakrament nt

sacred /'seɪkrɪd/ a heilig

sacrifice /'sækrɪfaɪs/ n Opfer nt □vt opfern

sacrilege /'sækrɪlɪdʒ/ n Sakrileg nt

sad /sæd/ a (sadder, saddest) traurig; ⟨loss, death⟩ schmerzlich. **~den** vt traurig machen

saddle /'sædl/ n Sattel m □vt satteln; ~ **s.o. with sth** (fam) jdm etw aufhalsen

sadis|m /'seɪdɪzm/ n Sadismus m. **~t** /-dɪst/ n Sadist m. **~tic** /sə-'dɪstɪk/ a, **-ally** adv sadistisch

sad|ly /'sædlɪ/ adv traurig; (unfortunately) leider. **~ness** n Traurigkeit f

safe /seɪf/ a (-r, -st) sicher; ⟨journey⟩ gut; (not dangerous) ungefährlich; **~ and sound** gesund und wohlbehalten □n Safe m. **~guard** n Schutz m □vt schützen. **~ly** adv sicher; ⟨arrive⟩ gut

safety /'seɪftɪ/ n Sicherheit f. **~-belt** n Sicherheitsgurt m. **~-pin** n Sicherheitsnadel f. **~-valve** n [Sicherheits]ventil nt

sag /sæg/ vi (pt/pp sagged) durchhängen

saga /'sɑːgə/ n Saga f; (fig) Geschichte f

sage[1] /seɪdʒ/ n (herb) Salbei m

sage[2] n Weise(r) m □n Weise(r) m

Sagittarius /sædʒɪ'teərɪəs/ n (Astr) Schütze m

said /sed/ see **say**

sail /seɪl/ n Segel nt; (trip) Segelfahrt f □vi segeln; (on liner) fahren; (leave) abfahren (nach for) □vt segeln mit

'sailboard n Surfbrett nt. **~ing** n Windsurfen nt

sailing /'seɪlɪŋ/ n Segelsport m. **~-boat** n Segelboot nt. **~-ship** n Segelschiff nt

sailor /'seɪlə(r)/ n Seemann m; (in navy) Matrose m

saint /seɪnt/ n Heilige(r) m/f. **~ly** a heilig

sake /seɪk/ n **for the** ~ **of** . . . um . . . (gen) willen; **for my/your** ~ um meinet-/deinetwillen

salad /'sæləd/ n Salat m. **~-cream** n ≈ Mayonnaise f. **~-dressing** n Salatsoße f

salary /'sælərɪ/ n Gehalt nt

sale /seɪl/ n Verkauf m; (event) Basar m; (at reduced prices) Schlußverkauf m; **for** ~ zu verkaufen

sales|man n Verkäufer m. ~**woman** n Verkäuferin f

salient /'seɪlɪənt/ a wichtigste(r,s)

saliva /sə'laɪvə/ n Speichel m

sallow /'sæləʊ/ a (-er, -est) bleich

salmon /'sæmən/ n Lachs m. ~-**pink** a lachsrosa

saloon /sə'luːn/ n Salon m; (Auto) Limousine f; (Amer: bar) Wirtschaft f

salt /sɔːlt/ n Salz m □a salzig; ⟨water, meat⟩ Salz- □vt salzen; (cure) pökeln; streuen ⟨road⟩. ~-**cellar** n Salzfaß nt. ~ '**water** n Salzwasser nt. ~**y** a salzig

salutary /'sæljʊtərɪ/ a heilsam

salute /sə'luːt/ n (Mil) Gruß m □vt/i (Mil) grüßen

salvage /'sælvɪdʒ/ n (Naut) Bergung f □vt bergen

salvation /sæl'veɪʃn/ n Rettung f; (Relig) Heil nt. **S~ Army** n Heilsarmee f

salvo /'sælvəʊ/ n Salve f

same /seɪm/ a & pron the ~ der/die/das gleiche; (pl) die gleichen; (identical) der-/die-/dasselbe; (pl) dieselben □adv the ~ gleich; **all the** ~ trotzdem; **the** ~ **to you** gleichfalls

sample /'sɑːmpl/ n Probe f; (Comm) Muster nt □vt probieren, kosten

sanatorium /sænə'tɔːrɪəm/ n Sanatorium nt

sanctify /'sæŋktɪfaɪ/ vt (pt/pp -fied) heiligen

sanctimonious /sæŋktɪ'məʊnɪəs/ a, -**ly** adv frömmlerisch

sanction /'sæŋkʃn/ n Sanktion f □vt sanktionieren

sanctity /'sæŋktətɪ/ n Heiligkeit f

sanctuary /'sæŋktjʊərɪ/ n (Relig) Heiligtum nt; (refuge) Zuflucht f; (for wildlife) Tierschutzgebiet nt

sand /sænd/ n Sand m □vt ~ [**down**] [ab]schmirgeln

sandal /'sændl/ n Sandale f

sand: ~**bank** n Sandbank f. ~**paper** n Sandpapier nt □vt [ab]schmirgeln. ~**pit** n Sandkasten m

sandwich /'sænwɪdʒ/ n ≈ belegtes Brot nt; Sandwich m □vt ~**ed between** eingeklemmt zwischen

sandy /'sændɪ/ a (-ier, -iest) sandig; ⟨beach, soil⟩ Sand-; ⟨hair⟩ rotblond

sane /seɪn/ a (-r, -st) geistig normal; (sensible) vernünftig

sang /sæŋ/ see **sing**

sanitary /'sænɪtərɪ/ a hygienisch; ⟨system⟩ sanitär. ~ **napkin** n (Amer), ~ **towel** n [Damen]binde f

sanitation /sænɪ'teɪʃn/ n Kanalisation und Abfallbeseitigung pl

sanity /'sænətɪ/ n [gesunder] Verstand m

sank /sæŋk/ see **sink**

sap /sæp/ n (Bot) Saft m □vt (pt/pp sapped) schwächen

sapphire /'sæfaɪə(r)/ n Saphir m

sarcas|m /'sɑːkæzm/ n Sarkasmus m. ~**tic** /-'kæstɪk/ a, -**ally** adv sarkastisch

sardine /sɑː'diːn/ n Sardine f

Sardinia /sɑː'dɪnɪə/ n Sardinien nt

sardonic /sɑː'dɒnɪk/ a, -**ally** adv höhnisch; ⟨smile⟩ sardonisch

sash /sæʃ/ n Schärpe f

sat /sæt/ see **sit**

satanic /sə'tænɪk/ a satanisch

satchel /'sætʃl/ n Ranzen m

satellite /'sætəlaɪt/ n Satellit m. ~ **dish** n Satellitenschüssel f. ~ **television** n Satellitenfernsehen nt

satin /'sætɪn/ n Satin m

satire /'sætaɪə(r)/ n Satire f

satirical /sə'tɪrɪkl/ a, -**ly** adv satirisch

satir|ist /'sætərɪst/ n Satiriker(in) m(f). ~**ize** vt satirisch darstellen; ⟨book:⟩ eine Satire sein auf (+ acc)

satisfaction /sætɪsˈfækʃn/ n Befriedigung f; **to my ~** zu meiner Zufriedenheit

satisfactory /sætɪsˈfæktərɪ/ a, **-ily** adv zufriedenstellend

satisf|y /ˈsætɪsfaɪ/ vt (pt/pp **-fied**) befriedigen; zufriedenstellen (customer); (convince) überzeugen; **be ~ied** zufrieden sein. **~ying** a befriedigend; (meal) sättigend

saturat|e /ˈsætʃəreɪt/ vt durchtränken; (Chem & fig) sättigen. **~ed** a durchnäßt; (fat) gesättigt

Saturday /ˈsætədeɪ/ n Samstag m, Sonnabend m

sauce /sɔːs/ n Soße f; (cheek) Frechheit f. **~pan** n Kochtopf m

saucer /ˈsɔːsə(r)/ n Untertasse f

saucy /ˈsɔːsɪ/ a (-ier, -iest) frech

Saudi Arabia /saʊdɪəˈreɪbɪə/ n Saudi-Arabien nt

sauna /ˈsɔːnə/ n Sauna f

saunter /ˈsɔːntə(r)/ vi schlendern

sausage /ˈsɒsɪdʒ/ n Wurst f

savage /ˈsævɪdʒ/ a wild; (fierce) scharf; (brutal) brutal □ n Wilde(r) m/f □ vt anfallen. **~ry** n Brutalität f

save /seɪv/ n (Sport) Abwehr f □ vt retten (**from** + dat); (keep) aufheben; (not waste) sparen; (collect) sammeln; (avoid) ersparen; (Sport) verhindern (goal) □ vi ~ [**up**] sparen □ prep außer (+ dat), mit Ausnahme (+ gen)

saver /ˈseɪvə(r)/ n Sparer m

saving /ˈseɪvɪŋ/ n (see save) Rettung f; Sparen nt; Ersparnis f; **~s** pl (money) Ersparnisse pl. **~s account** n Sparkonto nt. **~s bank** n Sparkasse f

saviour /ˈseɪvjə(r)/ n Retter m

savour /ˈseɪvə(r)/ n Geschmack m □ vt auskosten. **~y** a herzhaft, würzig; (fig) angenehm

saw¹ /sɔː/ see **see¹**

saw² n Säge f □ vt (pt **sawed**, pp **sawn** or **sawed**) sägen. **~dust** n Sägemehl nt

saxophone /ˈsæksəfəʊn/ n Saxo-

phon nt

say /seɪ/ n Mitspracherecht nt; **have one's ~** seine Meinung sagen □ vt/i (pt/pp **said**) sagen; sprechen (prayer); **that is to ~** das heißt; **that goes without ~ing** das versteht sich von selbst; **when all is said and done** letzten Endes; **I ~!** (attracting attention) hallo! **~ing** n Redensart f

scab /skæb/ n Schorf m; (pej) Streikbrecher m

scaffold /ˈskæfəld/ n Schafott nt. **~ing** n Gerüst nt

scald /skɔːld/ vt verbrühen

scale¹ /skeɪl/ n (of fish) Schuppe f

scale² n Skala f; (Mus) Tonleiter f; (ratio) Maßstab m; **on a grand ~** in großem Stil □ vt (climb) erklettern. **~ down** vt verkleinern

scales /skeɪlz/ npl (for weighing) Waage f

scalp /skælp/ n Kopfhaut f □ vt skalpieren

scalpel /ˈskælpl/ n Skalpell nt

scam /skæm/ n (fam) Schwindel m

scamper /ˈskæmpə(r)/ vi huschen

scan /skæn/ n (Med) Szintigramm nt □ v (pt/pp **scanned**) □ vt absuchen; (quickly) flüchtig ansehen; (Med) szintigraphisch untersuchen □ vi (poetry:) das richtige Versmaß haben

scandal /ˈskændl/ n Skandal m; (gossip) Skandalgeschichten pl. **~ize** /-dəlaɪz/ vt schockieren. **~ous** /-əs/ a skandalös

Scandinavia /skændɪˈneɪvɪə/ n Skandinavien nt. **~n** a skandinavisch □ n Skandinavier(in) m(f)

scant /skænt/ a wenig

scanty /ˈskæntɪ/ a (-ier, -iest), **-ily** adv spärlich; (clothing) knapp

scapegoat /ˈskeɪp-/ n Sündenbock m

scar /skɑː(r)/ n Narbe f □ vt (pt/pp **scarred**) eine Narbe hinterlassen auf (+ dat)

scarce /skeəs/ a (-r, -st) knapp; **make oneself ~e** (fam) sich aus

dem Staub machen. **~ely** *adv*
kaum. **~ity** *n* Knappheit *f*
scare /skeə(r)/ *n* Schreck *m*;
(*panic*) [allgemeine] Panik *f*;
(*bomb* **~**) Bombendrohung *f* □ *vt*
Angst machen (+ *dat*); **be ~d**
Angst haben (**of** vor + *dat*)
'scarecrow *n* Vogelscheuche *f*
scarf /skɑːf/ *n* (*pl* **scarves**) Schal
m; (*square*) Tuch *nt*
scarlet /'skɑːlət/ *a* scharlachrot.
~ 'fever *n* Scharlach *m*
scary /'skeərɪ/ *a* unheimlich
scathing /'skeɪðɪŋ/ *a* bissig
scatter /'skætə(r)/ *vt* verstreuen;
(*disperse*) zerstreuen □ *vi* sich
zerstreuen. **~-brained** *a* (*fam*)
schusselig. **~ed** *a* verstreut;
⟨*showers*⟩ vereinzelt
scatty /'skætɪ/ *a* (**-ier, -iest**) (*fam*)
verrückt
scavenge /'skævɪndʒ/ *vi* [im Ab-
fall] Nahrung suchen; ⟨*animal*⟩
Aas fressen. **~r** *n* Aasfresser *m*
scenario /sɪ'nɑːrɪəʊ/ *n* Szenario *nt*
scene /siːn/ *n* Szene *f*; (*sight*) Anblick *m*; (*place of event*) Schauplatz *m*; **behind the ~s** hinter
den Kulissen; **~ of the crime**
Tatort *m*
scenery /'siːnərɪ/ *n* Landschaft *f*;
(*Theat*) Szenerie *f*
scenic /'siːnɪk/ *a* landschaftlich
schön; (*Theat*) Bühnen-
scent /sent/ *n* Duft *m*; (*trail*)
Fährte *f*; (*perfume*) Parfüm *nt*.
~ed *a* parfümiert
sceptic|al /'skeptɪkl/ *a*, **-ly** *adv*
skeptisch. **~ism** /-tɪsɪzm/ *n* Skep-
sis *f*
schedule /'ʃedjuːl/ *n* Programm
nt; (*of work*) Zeitplan *m*; (*timetable*) Fahrplan *m*; **behind ~** im
Rückstand; **according to ~** planmäßig □ *vt* planen. **~d flight** *n*
Linienflug *m*
scheme /skiːm/ *n* Programm *nt*;
(*plan*) Plan *m*; (*plot*) Komplott *nt*
□ *vi* Ränke schmieden

schizophren|ia /skɪtsə'friːnɪə/ *n*
Schizophrenie *f*. **~ic** /-'frenɪk/ *a*
schizophren
scholar /'skɒlə(r)/ *n* Gelehrte(r)
m/f. **~ly** *a* gelehrt. **~ship** *n* Ge-
lehrtheit *f*; (*grant*) Stipendium *nt*
school /skuːl/ *n* Schule *f*; (*Univ*)
Fakultät *f* □ *vt* schulen; dressieren ⟨*animal*⟩
school: ~boy *n* Schüler *m*. **~girl**
n Schülerin *f*. **~ing** *n* Schulbil-
dung *f*. **~master** *n* Lehrer *m*.
~mistress *n* Lehrerin *f*. **~-
teacher** *n* Lehrer(in) *m(f)*
sciatica /saɪ'ætɪkə/ *n* Ischias *m*
scien|ce /'saɪəns/ *n* Wissenschaft *f*.
~tific /-'tɪfɪk/ *a* wissenschaft-
lich. **~tist** *n* Wissenschaftler *m*
scintillating /'sɪntɪleɪtɪŋ/ *a* sprü-
hend
scissors /'sɪzəz/ *npl* Schere *f*; **a
pair of ~** eine Schere
scoff[1] /skɒf/ *vi* **~ at** spotten über
(+ *acc*)
scoff[2] *vt* (*fam*) verschlingen
scold /skəʊld/ *vt* ausschimpfen
scoop /skuːp/ *n* Schaufel *f*; (*Culin*)
Portionierer *m*; (*Journ*) Exklu-
sivmeldung *f* □ *vt* **~ out** aushöhlen; (*remove*) auslöffeln; **~ up**
schaufeln; schöpfen ⟨*liquid*⟩
scoot /skuːt/ *vi* (*fam*) rasen. **~er**
n Roller *m*
scope /skəʊp/ *n* Bereich *m*; (*opportunity*) Möglichkeiten *pl*
scorch /skɔːtʃ/ *vt* versengen.
~ing *a* glühend heiß
score /skɔː(r)/ *n* [Spiel]stand *m*;
(*individual*) Punktzahl *f*; (*Mus*)
Partitur *f*; (*Cinema*) Filmmusik *f*;
a ~ [of] (*twenty*) zwanzig; **keep
[the] ~** zählen; (*written*) aufschreiben; **on that ~** was das
betrifft □ *vt* erzielen; schießen
⟨*goal*⟩; (*cut*) einritzen □ *vi* Punkte
erzielen; (*Sport*) ein Tor schießen; (*keep score*) Punkte zählen.
~r *n* Punktezähler *m*; (*of goals*)
Torschütze *m*

scorn /skɔːn/ n Verachtung f □ vt verachten. **~ful** a, **-ly** adv verächtlich

Scorpio /'skɔːpɪəʊ/ n (Astr) Skorpion m

scorpion /'skɔːpɪən/ n Skorpion m

Scot /skɒt/ n Schotte m/Schottin f

Scotch /skɒtʃ/ a schottisch □ n (whisky) Scotch m

scotch vt unterbinden

scot-'free a **get off ~** straffrei ausgehen

Scot|land /'skɒtlənd/ n Schottland nt. **~s, ~tish** a schottisch

scoundrel /'skaʊndrl/ n Schurke m

scour¹ /'skaʊə(r)/ vt (search) absuchen

scour² vt (clean) scheuern

scourge /skɜːdʒ/ n Geißel f

scout /skaʊt/ n (Mil) Kundschafter m □ vi **~ for** Ausschau halten nach

Scout n [Boy] ~ Pfadfinder m

scowl /skaʊl/ n böser Gesichtsausdruck m □ vi ein böses Gesicht machen

scraggy /'skrægɪ/ a (**-ier, -iest**) (pej) dürr, hager

scram /skræm/ vi (fam) abhauen

scramble /'skræmbl/ n Gerangel nt □ vi klettern; **~ for** sich drängen nach □ vt (Teleph) verschlüsseln. **~d 'egg[s]** n[pl] Rührei nt

scrap¹ /skræp/ n (fam: fight) Rauferei f □ vi sich raufen

scrap² /skræp/ n (metal) Schrott m; **~s** pl Reste; **not a ~** kein bißchen □ vt (pt/pp scrapped) aufgeben

'scrap-book n Sammelalbum nt

scrape /skreɪp/ vt schaben; (clean) abkratzen; (damage) [ver]-schrammen. **~ through** vi gerade noch durchkommen. **~ together** vt zusammenkriegen

scraper /'skreɪpə(r)/ n Kratzer m

'scrap iron n Alteisen nt

scrappy /'skræpɪ/ a lückenhaft

'scrap-yard n Schrottplatz m

scratch /skrætʃ/ n Kratzer m; **start from ~** von vorne anfangen; **not be up to ~** zu wünschen übriglassen □ vt/i kratzen; (damage) zerkratzen

scrawl /skrɔːl/ n Gekrakel nt □ vt/i krakeln

scrawny /'skrɔːnɪ/ a (**-ier, -iest**) (pej) dürr, hager

scream /skriːm/ n Schrei m □ vt/i schreien

screech /skriːtʃ/ n Kreischen nt □ vt/i kreischen

screen /skriːn/ n Schirm m; (Cinema) Leinwand f; (TV) Bildschirm m □ vt schützen; (conceal) verdecken; vorführen ⟨film⟩; (examine) überprüfen (Med) untersuchen. **~ing** n (Med) Reihenuntersuchung f. **~ play** n Drehbuch nt

screw /skruː/ n Schraube f □ vt schrauben. **~ up** vt festschrauben; (crumple) zusammenknüllen; zusammenkneifen ⟨eyes⟩; (sl: bungle) vermasseln; **~ up one's courage** seinen Mut zusammennehmen

'screwdriver n Schraubenzieher m

screwy /'skruːɪ/ a (**-ier, -iest**) (fam) verrückt

scribble /'skrɪbl/ n Gekritzel nt □ vt/i kritzeln

script /skrɪpt/ n Schrift f; (of speech, play) Text m; (Radio, TV) Skript nt; (of film) Drehbuch nt

Scripture /'skrɪptʃə(r)/ n (Sch) Religion f; **the ~s** pl die Heilige Schrift f

scroll /skrəʊl/ n Schriftrolle f; (decoration) Volute f

scrounge /skraʊndʒ/ vt/i schnorren. **~r** n Schnorrer m

scrub¹ /skrʌb/ n (land) Buschland nt, Gestrüpp nt

scrub² /skrʌb/ vt/i (pt/pp scrubbed) schrubben; (fam: cancel) absagen; fallenlassen ⟨plan⟩

scruff /skrʌf/ n **by the ~ of the neck** beim Genick

scruffy /'skrʌfɪ/ a (-ier, -iest) vergammelt

scrum /skrʌm/ n Gedränge nt

scruple /'skru:pl/ n Skrupel m

scrupulous /'skru:pjʊləs/ a, **-ly** adv gewissenhaft

scrutin|ize /'skru:tɪnaɪz/ vt (genau) ansehen. **~y** n (look) prüfender Blick m

scuff /skʌf/ vt abstoßen

scuffle /'skʌfl/ n Handgemenge nt

scullery /'skʌlərɪ/ n Spülküche f

sculpt|or /'skʌlptə(r)/ n Bildhauer(in) m(f). **~ure** /-tʃə(r)/ n Bildhauerei f; (piece of work) Skulptur f, Plastik f

scum /skʌm/ n Schmutzschicht f; (people) Abschaum m

scurrilous /'skʌrɪləs/ a niederträchtig

scurry /'skʌrɪ/ vi (pt/pp -ied) huschen

scuttle[1] /'skʌtl/ n Kohleneimer m

scuttle[2] vt versenken ⟨ship⟩

scuttle[3] vi schnell krabbeln

scythe /saɪð/ n Sense f

sea /si:/ n Meer nt, See f; **at** ~ auf See; **by** ~ mit dem Schiff. **~board** n Küste f. **~food** n Meeresfrüchte pl. **~gull** n Möwe f

seal[1] /si:l/ n (Zool) Seehund m

seal[2] n Siegel nt; (Techn) Dichtung f ⸱ vt versiegeln; (Techn) abdichten; (fig) besiegeln. ~ **off** vt abriegeln

'sea-level n Meeresspiegel m

seam /si:m/ n Naht f; (of coal) Flöz nt

'seaman n Seemann m; (sailor) Matrose m

seamless /si:mlɪs/ a nahtlos

seance /'seɪɑ:ns/ n spiritistische Sitzung f

'sea|plane n Wasserflugzeug nt. **~port** n Seehafen m

search /sɜ:tʃ/ n Suche f; (official) Durchsuchung f ⸱ vt durchsuchen; absuchen ⟨area⟩ ⸱ vi suchen (**for** nach). **~ing** a prüfend, forschend

search: **~light** n [Such]scheinwerfer m. **~party** n Suchmannschaft f

sea: **~sick** a seekrank. **~side** n at/to the **~side** am/ans Meer

season /'si:zn/ n Jahreszeit f; (social, tourist, sporting) Saison f ⸱ vt (flavour) würzen. **~able** /-əbl/ a der Jahreszeit gemäß. **~al** a Saison-. **~ing** n Gewürze pl

'season ticket n Dauerkarte f

seat /si:t/ n Sitz m; (place) Sitzplatz m; (bottom) Hintern m; **take a** ~ Platz nehmen ⸱ vt setzen; (have seats for) Sitzplätze bieten (+ dat); **remain** ~**ed** sitzen bleiben. **~-belt** n Sicherheitsgurt m; **fasten one's** ~**-belt** sich anschnallen

sea: **~weed** n [See]tang m. **~worthy** a seetüchtig

secateurs /sekə'tɜːz/ npl Gartenschere f

seclu|de /sɪ'klu:d/ vt absondern. **~ded** a abgelegen. **~sion** /-ʒn/ n Zurückgezogenheit f

second[1] /sɪ'kɒnd/ vt (transfer) [vorübergehend] versetzen

second[2] /'sekənd/ a zweite(r,s); **on** ~ **thoughts** ⸱ n Sekunde f; (Sport) Sekundant m; ~**s** pl (goods) Waren zweiter Wahl; **the** ~ der/die/das zweite ⸱ adv (in race) an zweiter Stelle ⸱ vt unterstützen ⟨proposal⟩

secondary /'sekəndrɪ/ a zweitrangig; (Phys) Sekundär-. ~ **school** n höhere Schule f

second: **~best** a zweitbeste(r,s). ~ **'class** adv ⟨travel, send⟩ zweiter Klasse. **~-class** a zweitklassig

'second hand n (on clock) Sekundenzeiger m

second-'hand a gebraucht ⸱ adv aus zweiter Hand

secondly /'sekəndlɪ/ adv zweitens

second-'rate a zweitklassig

secrecy /'si:krəsɪ/ n Heimlichkeit f

secret /'si:krɪt/ a geheim; ⟨agent, police⟩ Geheim-; ⟨drinker, lover⟩ heimlich □ n Geheimnis nt

secretarial /sekrə'teərɪəl/ a Sekretärinnen-; ⟨work, staff⟩ Sekretariats-

secretary /'sekrətərɪ/ n Sekretär(in) m(f)

secret|e /sɪ'kri:t/ vt absondern. **~ion** /-i:ʃn/ n Absonderung f

secretive /'si:krətɪv/ a geheimniskrämerisch. **~ness** n Heimlichtuerei f

secretly /'si:krɪtlɪ/ adv heimlich

sect /sekt/ n Sekte f

section /'sekʃn/ n Teil m; ⟨of text⟩ Abschnitt m; ⟨of firm⟩ Abteilung f; ⟨of organization⟩ Sektion f

sector /'sektə(r)/ n Sektor m

secular /'sekjʊlə(r)/ a weltlich

secure /sɪ'kjʊə(r)/ a, **-ly** adv sicher; ⟨firm⟩ fest; ⟨emotionally⟩ geborgen □ vt sichern; ⟨fasten⟩ festmachen; ⟨obtain⟩ sich ⟨dat⟩ sichern

securit|y /sɪ'kjʊərətɪ/ n Sicherheit f; ⟨emotional⟩ Geborgenheit f; **~ies** pl Wertpapiere pl; ⟨Fin⟩ Effekten pl

sedan /sɪ'dæn/ n ⟨Amer⟩ Limousine f

sedate¹ /sɪ'deɪt/ a, **-ly** adv gesetzt

sedate² vt sedieren

sedation /sɪ'deɪʃn/ n Sedierung f; **be under ~** sediert sein

sedative /'sedətɪv/ a beruhigend □ n Beruhigungsmittel nt

sedentary /'sedntərɪ/ a sitzend

sediment /'sedɪmənt/ n [Boden]satz m

seduce /sɪ'dju:s/ vt verführen

seduct|ion /sɪ'dʌkʃn/ n Verführung f. **~ive** /-tɪv/ a, **-ly** adv verführerisch

see¹ /si:/ v ⟨pt saw, pp seen⟩ □ vt sehen; ⟨understand⟩ einsehen; ⟨imagine⟩ sich ⟨dat⟩ vorstellen; ⟨escort⟩ begleiten; **go and ~** nachsehen; ⟨visit⟩ besuchen; **~ you later!** bis nachher! **~ing that** da/⟨in view of⟩ da; ⟨check⟩ nachsehen; **~ about** sich kümmern um. **~ off** vt verabschieden; ⟨chase

away⟩ vertreiben. **~ through** vi durchsehen □ vt ⟨fig⟩ **~ through** s.o. jdn durchschauen

see² n ⟨Relig⟩ Bistum nt

seed /si:d/ n Samen m; ⟨of grape⟩ Kern m; ⟨fig⟩ Saat f; ⟨Tennis⟩ gesetzter Spieler m; **go to ~** Samen bilden; ⟨fig⟩ herunterkommen. **~ed** a ⟨Tennis⟩ gesetzt. **~ling** n Sämling m

seedy /'si:dɪ/ a ⟨-ier, -iest⟩ schäbig; ⟨area⟩ heruntergekommen

seek /si:k/ vt ⟨pt/pp sought⟩ suchen

seem /si:m/ vi scheinen. **~ingly** adv scheinbar

seemly /'si:mlɪ/ a schicklich

seen /si:n/ see **see¹**

seep /si:p/ vi sickern

see-saw /'si:sɔ:/ n Wippe f

seethe /si:ð/ vi **~ with anger** vor Wut schäumen

'see-through a durchsichtig

segment /'segmənt/ n Teil m; ⟨of worm⟩ Segment m; ⟨of orange⟩ Spalte f

segregat|e /'segrɪgeɪt/ vt trennen. **~ion** /-'geɪʃn/ n Trennung f

seize /si:z/ vt ergreifen; ⟨Jur⟩ beschlagnahmen; **~ s.o. by the arm** jdn am Arm packen. **~ up** vi ⟨Techn⟩ sich festfressen

seizure /'si:ʒə(r)/ n ⟨Jur⟩ Beschlagnahme f; ⟨Med⟩ Anfall m

seldom /'seldəm/ adv selten

select /sɪ'lekt/ a ausgewählt; ⟨exclusive⟩ exklusiv □ vt auswählen; aufstellen ⟨team⟩. **~ion** /-ekʃn/ n Auswahl f. **~ive** /-ɪv/ a, **-ly** adv selektiv; ⟨choosy⟩ wählerisch

self /self/ n ⟨pl **selves**⟩ Ich nt

self: **~-ad'dressed** a adressiert. **~-ad'hesive** a selbstklebend. **~-as'surance** n Selbstsicherheit f. **~-as'sured** a selbstsicher. **~-'catering** n Selbstversorgung f. **~-'centred** a egozentrisch. **~-'confidence** n Selbstbewußtsein nt, Selbstvertrauen nt. ~-'**confident** a selbstbewußt. ~-'**conscious** a befangen. ~-con'tained a ⟨flat⟩ abgeschlossen. ~-con'trol n Selbstbeherrschung f. ~-de'fence n Selbstverteidigung f; ⟨Jur⟩ Notwehr f. ~-de'nial n Selbstverleugnung f. ~-determi'nation n Selbstbestimmung f. ~-em'ployed selbständig. ~-e'steem n Selbstachtung f. ~-'evident a offensichtlich. ~-'governing a selbstverwaltet. ~-'help n Selbsthilfe f. ~-in-'dulgent a maßlos. ~-'interest n Eigennutz m

self|ish /'selfɪʃ/ a, -ly adv egoistisch, selbstsüchtig. ~less a, -ly adv selbstlos

self: ~-'pity n Selbstmitleid nt. ~-'portrait n Selbstporträt nt. ~-pos'sessed a selbstbeherrscht. ~-preser'vation n Selbsterhaltung f. ~-re'spect n Selbstachtung f. ~-'righteous a selbstgerecht. ~-'sacrifice n Selbstaufopferung f. ~-'satisfied a selbstgefällig. ~-'service n Selbstbedienung f □attrib Selbstbedienungs-. ~-'sufficient a selbständig. ~-'willed a eigenwillig

sell /sel/ v (pt/pp sold) □vt verkaufen; be sold out ausverkauft sein □vi sich verkaufen. ~ off vt verkaufen

seller /'selə(r)/ n Verkäufer m

Sellotape (P) /'seləʊ-/ n ≈ Tesafilm (P) m

'sell-out n be a ~ ausverkauft sein; ⟨fam: betrayal⟩ Verrat sein

selves /selvz/ see self

semblance /'sembləns/ n Anschein m

semen /'siːmən/ n ⟨Anat⟩ Samen m

semester /sɪ'mestə(r)/ n ⟨Amer⟩ Semester nt

semi|breve /'semɪbriːv/ n ⟨Mus⟩ ganze Note f. ~circle n Halbkreis m. ~'circular a halbkreisförmig. ~'colon n Semikolon nt.

~-de'tached a & n ~-detached [house] Doppelhaushälfte f. ~'final n Halbfinale nt

seminar /'semɪnɑː(r)/ n Seminar nt. ~y /-nərɪ/ n Priesterseminar nt

'semitone n ⟨Mus⟩ Halbton m

semolina /semə'liːnə/ n Grieß m

senat|e /'senət/ n Senat m. ~or n Senator m

send /send/ vt/i (pt/pp sent) schicken; ~ one's regards grüßen lassen; ~ for somebody lassen ⟨person⟩; sich ⟨dat⟩ schicken lassen ⟨thing⟩. ~er n Absender m. ~-off n Verabschiedung f

senile /'siːnaɪl/ a senil. ~ity /sɪ-'nɪlətɪ/ n Senilität f

senior /'siːnɪə(r)/ a älter; ⟨in rank⟩ höher □n Ältere(r) m/f; ⟨in rank⟩ Vorgesetzte(r) m/f. ~ 'citizen n Senior(in) m(f)

seniority /siːnɪ'ɒrətɪ/ n höheres Alter nt; ⟨in rank⟩ höherer Rang m

sensation /sen'seɪʃn/ n Sensation f; ⟨feeling⟩ Gefühl nt. ~al a, -ly adv sensationell

sense /sens/ n Sinn m; ⟨feeling⟩ Gefühl nt; ⟨common-⟩ Verstand m; in a ~ in gewisser Hinsicht; make ~ Sinn ergeben □vt spüren. ~less a, -ly adv sinnlos; ⟨unconscious⟩ bewußtlos

sensible /'sensəbl/ a, -bly adv vernünftig; ⟨suitable⟩ zweckmäßig

sensitiv|e /'sensɪtɪv/ a, -ly adv empfindlich; ⟨understanding⟩ einfühlsam. ~ity /-'tɪvətɪ/ Empfindlichkeit f

sensory /'sensərɪ/ a Sinnes-

sensual /'sensjʊəl/ a sinnlich. ~ity /-'ælətɪ/ n Sinnlichkeit f

sensuous /'sensjʊəs/ a sinnlich

sent /sent/ see send

sentence /'sentəns/ n Satz m; ⟨Jur⟩ Urteil nt; ⟨punishment⟩ Strafe f □vt verurteilen

sentiment /'sentɪmənt/ n Gefühl nt; ⟨opinion⟩ Meinung f; ⟨sentimentality⟩ Sentimentalität f.

~**-al** /'mentl/ *a* sentimental.
~**ality** /-'tæləti/ *n* Sentimentalität *f*

sentry /'sentri/ *n* Wache *f*

separable /'sepərəbl/ *a* trennbar

separate[1] /'sepərət/ *a*, **-ly** *adv* getrennt, separat

separate[2] /'sepəreɪt/ *vt* trennen □*vi* sich trennen. ~**ion** /-'reɪʃn/ *n* Trennung *f*

September /sep'tembə(r)/ *n* September *m*

septic /'septɪk/ *a* vereitert; **go** ~ vereitern

sequel /'si:kwəl/ *n* Folge *f*; (*fig*) Nachspiel *nt*

sequence /'si:kwəns/ *n* Reihenfolge *f*

sequin /'si:kwɪn/ *n* Paillette *f*

serenade /serə'neɪd/ *n* Ständchen *nt* □*vt* ~ **s.o.** jdm ein Ständchen bringen

seren|e /sɪ'ri:n/ *a*, **-ly** *adv* gelassen. ~**ity** /-'renəti/ *n* Gelassenheit *f*

sergeant /'sɑ:dʒənt/ *n* (*Mil*) Feldwebel *m*; (*in police*) Polizeimeister *m*

serial /'sɪərɪəl/ *n* Fortsetzungsgeschichte *f*; (*Radio, TV*) Serie *f*. ~**ize** *vt* in Fortsetzungen veröffentlichen (*Radio, TV*) senden

series /'sɪəri:z/ *n* Serie *f*

serious /'sɪərɪəs/ *a*, **-ly** *adv* ernst; ⟨*illness, error*⟩ schwer. ~**ness** *n* Ernst *m*

sermon /'sɜ:mən/ *n* Predigt *f*

serpent /'sɜ:pənt/ *n* Schlange *f*

serrated /se'reɪtɪd/ *a* gezackt

serum /'sɪərəm/ *n* Serum *nt*

servant /'sɜ:vənt/ *n* Diener(in) *m(f)*

serve /sɜ:v/ *n* (*Tennis*) Aufschlag *m* □*vt* dienen (+ *dat*); bedienen ⟨*customer, guest*⟩; servieren ⟨*food*⟩; (*Jur*) zustellen (**on s.o.** jdm); verbüßen ⟨*sentence*⟩; ~ **its purpose** seinen Zweck erfüllen; **it** ~**s you right!** das geschieht

dir recht! ~ **s two** für zwei Personen □*vi* dienen; (*Tennis*) aufschlagen

service /'sɜ:vɪs/ *n* Dienst *m*; (*Relig*) Gottesdienst *m*; (*in shop, restaurant*) Bedienung *f*; (*transport*) Verbindung *f*; (*maintenance*) Wartung *f*; (*set of crockery*) Service *nt*; (*Tennis*) Aufschlag *m*; ~**s** *pl* Dienstleistungen *pl*; (*on motorway*) Tankstelle und Raststätte *f*; **in the** ~**s** beim Militär; **be of** ~ nützlich sein; **out of/in** ~ ⟨*machine:*⟩ außer/ in Betrieb □*vt* (*Techn*) warten. ~**able** /-əbl/ *a* nützlich; ⟨*durable*⟩ haltbar

service: ~ **area** *n* Tankstelle und Raststätte *f*. ~ **charge** *n* Bedienungszuschlag *m*. ~ **man** *n* Soldat *m*. ~ **station** *n* Tankstelle *f*

serviette /sɜ:vɪ'et/ *n* Serviette *f*

servile /'sɜ:vaɪl/ *a* unterwürfig

session /'seʃn/ *n* Sitzung *f*; (*Univ*) Studienjahr *nt*

set /set/ *n* Satz *m*; (*of crockery*) Service *nt*; (*of cutlery*) Garnitur *f*; (*TV, Radio*) Apparat *m*; (*Math*) Menge *f*; (*Theat*) Bühnenbild *nt*; (*Cinema*) Szenenaufbau *m*; (*of people*) Kreis *m*; **shampoo and** ~ Waschen und Legen □*a* ⟨*ready*⟩ fertig, bereit; ⟨*rigid*⟩ fest; ⟨*book*⟩ vorgeschrieben; **be** ~ **on doing sth** entschlossen sein, etw zu tun; **be** ~ **in one's ways** in seinen Gewohnheiten festgefahren sein □*v* (*pt/pp* **set**, *pres p* **setting**) □*vt* setzen; (*adjust*) einstellen; stellen ⟨*task, alarm clock*⟩; festsetzen, festlegen ⟨*date, limit*⟩; aufgeben ⟨*homework*⟩; zusammenstellen ⟨*questions*⟩; [ein]fassen ⟨*gem*⟩; einrichten ⟨*bone*⟩; legen ⟨*hair*⟩; decken ⟨*table*⟩ □*vi* ⟨*sun:*⟩ untergehen; (*become hard*) fest werden; ~ **about sth** sich an etw ⟨*acc*⟩ machen; ~ **about doing sth** sich daranmachen, etw zu tun. ~ **back** *vt* zurücksetzen; (*hold up*) aufhalten; (*fam: cost*) kosten.

~ **off** vi losgehen; (in vehicle)
losfahren □vt auslösen (alarm);
explodieren lassen ⟨bomb⟩. ~
out vi losgehen; (in vehicle) losfahren; ~**out to do sth** sich vornehmen, etw zu tun □vt auslegen; ⟨state⟩ darlegen. ~ **up** vt
aufbauen; ⟨fig⟩ gründen

set 'meal n Menü nt

settee /se'ti:/ n Sofa nt, Couch f

setting /'setɪŋ/ n Rahmen m; (surroundings) Umgebung f; (of
sun) Untergang m; (of jewel) Fassung f

settle /'setl/ vt (decide) entscheiden; (agree) regeln; (fix) festsetzen; (calm) beruhigen; (pay) bezahlen □vi sich niederlassen;
⟨snow, dust⟩ liegenbleiben;
(subside) sich senken; ⟨sedi-
ment:⟩ sich absetzen. ~ **down** vi
sich beruhigen; (permanently)
seßhaft werden. ~ **up** vi abrech-
nen

settlement /'setlmənt/ n (see
settle) Entscheidung f; Regelung
f; Bezahlung f; ⟨Jur⟩ Vergleich m;
(colony) Siedlung f

settler /'setlə(r)/ n Siedler m

'set-to n (fam) Streit m

'set-up n System nt

seven /'sevn/ a sieben. ~**teen** a
siebzehn. ~**teenth** a siebzehn-
te(r,s)

seventh /'sevnθ/ a siebte(r,s)

seventieth /'sevntɪɪθ/ a siebzig-
ste(r,s)

seventy /'sevntɪ/ a siebzig

sever /'sevə(r)/ vt durchtrennen;
abbrechen ⟨relations⟩

several /'sevrl/ a & pron mehrere,
einige

severe|e /sɪ'vɪə(r)/ a (-r, -st), **-ly** adv
streng; ⟨pain⟩ stark; ⟨illness⟩
schwer. ~**ity** /-'verətɪ/ n Strenge
f; Schwere f

sew /səʊ/ vt/i (pt sewed, pp sewn
or sewed) nähen. ~ **up** vt zu-
nähen

sewage /'su:ɪdʒ/ n Abwasser nt

sewer /'su:ə(r)/ n Abwasserkanal
m

sewing /'səʊɪŋ/ n Nähen nt; (work)
Näharbeit f. ~ **machine** n Näh-
maschine f

sewn /səʊn/ see sew

sex /seks/ n Geschlecht nt;
(sexuality, intercourse) Sex m.
~**ist** a sexistisch. ~ **offender** n
Triebverbrecher m

sexual /'seksjʊəl/ a, **-ly** adv sexuell. ~ '**intercourse** n Geschlechtsverkehr m

sexuality /seksjʊ'ælətɪ/ n Sexuali-
tät f

sexy /'seksɪ/ a (-ier, -iest) sexy

shabby /'ʃæbɪ/ a (-ier, -iest), **-ily**
adv schäbig

shack /ʃæk/ n Hütte f

shackles /'ʃæklz/ npl Fesseln pl

shade /ʃeɪd/ n Schatten m; (of
colour) [Farb]ton m; (of lamp)
[Lampen]schirm m; (Amer: win-
dow-blind) Jalousie f □vt beschatten; (draw lines on) schat-
tieren

shadow /'ʃædəʊ/ n Schatten m □vt
(follow) beschatten. ~**y** a schat-
tenhaft

shady /'ʃeɪdɪ/ a (-ier, -iest) schattig; (fam: disreputable) zwie-
lichtig

shaft /ʃɑ:ft/ n Schaft m; (Techn)
Welle f; (of light) Strahl m; (of lift)
Schacht m; ~**s** pl (of cart) Gabel-
deichsel f

shaggy /'ʃægɪ/ a (-ier, -iest) zottig

shake /ʃeɪk/ n Schütteln nt □v (pt
shook, pp **shaken**) □vt schütteln; (cause to tremble, shock) erschüttern; ~ **hands with s.o.**
jdm die Hand geben □vi wackeln;
(tremble) zittern. ~ **off** vt ab-
schütteln

shaky /'ʃeɪkɪ/ a (-ier, -iest) wackelig; ⟨hand, voice⟩ zittrig

shall /ʃæl/ v aux I ~ **go** ich werde
gehen; **we** ~ **see** wir werden
sehen; **what** ~ **I do?** was soll ich
machen? **I'll come too,** ~ **I?** ich

komme mit, ja? **thou shalt not
kill** (*liter*) du sollst nicht töten

shallow /ˈʃæləʊ/ *a* (**-er, -est**)
seicht; (*dish*) flach; (*fig*) oberflächlich

sham /ʃæm/ *a* unecht □ *n* Heuchelei *f*; (*person*) Heuchler(in) *m(f)*
□ *vt* (*pt/pp* **shammed**) vortäuschen

shambles /ˈʃæmblz/ *n* Durcheinander *nt*

shame /ʃeɪm/ *n* Scham *f*; (*disgrace*) Schande *f*; **be a ~** schade
sein; **what a ~!** wie schade! **~-
faced** *a* betreten

shame|ful /ˈʃeɪmfl/ *a*, **-ly** *adv*
schändlich. **~less** *a*, **-ly** *adv*
schamlos

shampoo /ʃæmˈpuː/ *n* Shampoo *nt*
□ *vt* schamponieren

shandy /ˈʃændɪ/ *n* Radler *m*

shan't /ʃɑːnt/ = **shall not**

shape /ʃeɪp/ *n* Form *f*; (*figure*)
Gestalt *f*; **take ~** Gestalt annehmen □ *vt* formen (**into** zu) □ *vi* **~
up** sich entwickeln. **~less** *a*
formlos; (*clothing*) unförmig

shapely /ˈʃeɪplɪ/ *a* (**-ier, -iest**)
wohlgeformt

share /ʃeə(r)/ *n* [An]teil *m*; (*Comm*)
Aktie *f* □ *vt/i* teilen. **~holder** *n*
Aktionär(in) *m(f)*

shark /ʃɑːk/ *n* Hai[fisch] *m*

sharp /ʃɑːp/ *a* (**-er, -est**), **-ly** *adv*
scharf; (*pointed*) spitz; (*severe*)
heftig; (*sudden*) steil; (*alert*) clever; (*unscrupulous*) gerissen
□ *adv* scharf; (*Mus*) zu hoch; **at
six o'clock ~** Punkt sechs Uhr;
look ~! beeil dich! □ *n* (*Mus*)
Kreuz *nt*. **~en** *vt* schärfen; [an]spitzen ⟨*pencil*⟩

shatter /ˈʃætə(r)/ *vt* zertrümmern;
(*fig*) zerstören; **be ~ed** ⟨*person*:⟩
erschüttert sein □ *vi* zersplittern

shave /ʃeɪv/ *n* Rasur *f*; **have a ~**
sich rasieren □ *vt* rasieren □ *vi*
sich rasieren. **~r** *n* Rasierapparat *m*

shaving /ˈʃeɪvɪŋ/ *n* Rasieren *nt*.

~-brush *n* Rasierpinsel *m*

shawl /ʃɔːl/ *n* Schultertuch *nt*

she /ʃiː/ *pron* sie

sheaf /ʃiːf/ *n* (*pl* **sheaves**) Garbe *f*;
(*of papers*) Bündel *nt*

shear /ʃɪə(r)/ *vt* (*pt* **sheared**, *pp*
shorn *or* **sheared**) scheren

shears /ʃɪəz/ *npl* [große] Schere *f*

sheath /ʃiːθ/ *n* (*pl* **~s** /ʃiːðz/)
Scheide *f*

sheaves /ʃiːvz/ *see* **sheaf**

shed[1] /ʃed/ *n* Schuppen *m*; (*for
cattle*) Stall *m*

shed[2] *vt* (*pt/pp* **shed**, *pres p* **shedding**) verlieren; vergießen
⟨*blood, tears*⟩; **~ light on** Licht
bringen in (+ *acc*)

sheen /ʃiːn/ *n* Glanz *m*

sheep /ʃiːp/ *n inv* Schaf *nt*. **~-dog**
n Hütehund *m*

sheepish /ˈʃiːpɪʃ/ *a*, **-ly** *adv* verlegen

'**sheepskin** *n* Schaffell *nt*

sheer /ʃɪə(r)/ *a* rein; (*steep*) steil;
(*transparent*) hauchdünn □ *adv*
steil

sheet /ʃiːt/ *n* Laken *nt*, Bettuch *nt*;
(*of paper*) Blatt *nt*; (*of glass,
metal*) Platte *f*

sheikh /ʃeɪk/ *n* Scheich *m*

shelf /ʃelf/ *n* (*pl* **shelves**) Brett *nt*,
Bord *nt*; (*set of shelves*) Regal *nt*

shell /ʃel/ *n* Schale *f*; (*of snail*)
Haus *nt*; (*of tortoise*) Panzer *m*;
(*on beach*) Muschel *f*; (*of unfinished building*) Rohbau *m*; (*Mil*)
Granate *f* □ *vt* pellen; enthülsen
⟨*peas*⟩; (*Mil*) [mit Granaten] beschießen. **~ out** *vi* (*fam*) blechen

'**shellfish** *n inv* Schalentiere *pl*;
(*Culin*) Meeresfrüchte *pl*

shelter /ˈʃeltə(r)/ *n* Schutz *m*; (*air-
raid* **~**) Luftschutzraum *m* □ *vt*
schützen (**from** vor + *dat*) □ *vi*
sich unterstellen. **~ed** *a* geschützt; ⟨*life*⟩ behütet

shelve /ʃelv/ *vt* auf Eis legen;
(*abandon*) aufgeben □ *vi* ⟨*slope:*⟩
abfallen

shelves /ʃelvz/ *see* **shelf**

shelving /'ʃelvɪŋ/ n (shelves)
Regale pl
shepherd /'ʃepəd/ n Schäfer m;
(Relig) Hirte m ⊔vt führen. ~ess
n Schäferin f. ~'s pie n Auflauf
m aus mit Kartoffelbrei bedeck-
tem Hackfleisch
sherry /'ʃerɪ/ n Sherry m
shield /ʃiːld/ n Schild m; (for eyes)
Schirm m; (Techn & fig) Schutz m
⊔vt schützen (from vor +dat)
shift /ʃɪft/ n Verschiebung f; (at
work) Schicht f; make ~ sich
(dat) behelfen (with mit) ⊔vt
rücken; (take away) wegnehmen;
(rearrange) umstellen; schieben
(blame: on to auf + acc) ⊔vi sich
verschieben; (fam: move quickly)
rasen
'shift work n Schichtarbeit f
shifty /'ʃɪftɪ/ a (-ier, -iest) (pej)
verschlagen
shilly-shally /'ʃɪlɪʃælɪ/ vi fackeln
(fam)
shimmer /'ʃɪmə(r)/ n Schimmer m
⊔vi schimmern
shin /ʃɪn/ n Schienbein n
shine /ʃaɪn/ n Glanz m ⊔v (pt/pp
shone) ⊔vi leuchten; (reflect
light) glänzen; (sun:) scheinen
⊔vt ~ a light on beleuchten
shingle /'ʃɪŋgl/ n (pebbles) Kiesel
pl
shingles /'ʃɪŋglz/ n (Med) Gürtel-
rose f
shiny /'ʃaɪnɪ/ a (-ier, -iest) glänzend
ship /ʃɪp/ n Schiff nt ⊔vt (pt/pp
shipped) verschiffen
ship: ~building n Schiffbau m
~ment n Sendung f. ~per n
Spediteur m. ~ping n Versand
m; (traffic) Schiffahrt f. ~shape
a & adv in Ordnung. ~wreck n
Schiffbruch m. ~wrecked a
schiffbrüchig. ~yard n Werft f
shirk /ʃɜːk/ vt sich drücken vor
(+ dat). ~er n Drückeberger m
shirt /ʃɜːt/ n [Ober]hemd nt; (for
woman) Hemdbluse f

shit /ʃɪt/ n (vulg) Scheiße f ⊔vi
(pt/pp shit) (vulg) scheißen
shiver /'ʃɪvə(r)/ n Schauder m ⊔vi
zittern
shoal /ʃəʊl/ n (of fish) Schwarm m
shock /ʃɒk/ n Schock m; (Electr)
Schlag m; (impact) Erschütterung f ⊔vt einen Schock versetzen (+ dat); (scandalize)
schockieren. ~ing a schockie-
rend; (fam: dreadful) fürchterlich
shod /ʃɒd/ see shoe
shoddy /'ʃɒdɪ/ a (-ier, -iest) minderwertig
shoe /ʃuː/ n Schuh m; (of horse)
Hufeisen nt ⊔vt (pt/pp shod, pres
p shoeing) beschlagen (horse)
shoe: ~horn n Schuhanzieher m.
~lace n Schnürsenkel m.
~maker n Schuhmacher m.
~string n on a ~string (fam)
mit ganz wenig Geld
shone /ʃɒn/ see shine
shoo /ʃuː/ vt scheuchen ⊔int sch!
shook /ʃʊk/ see shake
shoot /ʃuːt/ n (Bot) Trieb m;
(hunt) Jagd f ⊔v (pt/pp shot) ⊔vt
schießen; (kill) erschießen; drehen (film) ⊔vi schießen. ~
down vt abschießen. ~ out vi
(rush) herausschießen. ~ up vi
(grow) in die Höhe schießen; (prices:) schnellen
'shooting-range n Schießstand
m
shop /ʃɒp/ n Laden m, Geschäft nt;
(workshop) Werkstatt f; talk ~
(fam) fachsimpeln ⊔vi (pt/pp
shopped, pres p shopping) einkaufen; go ~ping einkaufen gehen
shop: ~ assistant n Verkäu-
fer(in) m(f). ~keeper n Laden-
besitzer(in) m(f). ~lifter n La-
dendieb m. ~lifting n Laden-
diebstahl m
shopping /'ʃɒpɪŋ/ n Einkaufen nt;
(articles) Einkäufe pl; do the ~

einkaufen. ~ **bag** n Einkaufstasche f. ~ **centre** n Einkaufszentrum nt. ~ **trolley** n Einkaufswagen m

shop: ~**steward** n [gewerkschaftlicher] Vertrauensmann m. ~'**window** n Schaufenster nt

shore /ʃɔː(r)/ n Strand m; (of lake) Ufer nt

shorn /ʃɔːn/ see shear

short /ʃɔːt/ a (-er, -est) kurz; ⟨person⟩ klein; (curt) schroff; a ~ **time ago** vor kurzem; be ~ **of** ... zuwenig ... haben; be in ~ **supply** knapp sein ▢ adv kurz; (abruptly) plötzlich; (curtly) kurz angebunden; in ~ kurzum; ~ **of** (except) außer; go ~ Mangel leiden; **stop** ~ **of doing sth** davor zurückschrecken, etw zu tun

shortage /ʃɔːtɪdʒ/ n Mangel m (of an + dat); (scarcity) Knappheit f

short: ~**bread** n Mürbekekse pl. ~**'circuit** n Kurzschluß m. ~**coming** n Fehler m. ~**'cut** n Abkürzung f

shorten /ʃɔːtn/ vt [ab]kürzen; kürzer machen ⟨garment⟩

short: ~**hand** n Kurzschrift f, Stenographie f. ~'**handed** a be ~**handed** zuwenig Personal haben. ~**hand typist** n Stenotypistin f. ~ **list** n engere Auswahl f. ~**lived** a kurzlebig

short|ly /ʃɔːtlɪ/ adv in Kürze; ~**ly before/after** kurz vorher/danach. ~**ness** n Kürze f; (of person) Kleinheit f

shorts /ʃɔːts/ npl kurze Hose f, Shorts pl

short: ~**sighted** a kurzsichtig. ~**sleeved** a kurzärmelig. ~**staffed** a be ~**staffed** zuwenig Personal haben. ~**'story** n Kurzgeschichte f. ~**tempered** a aufbrausend. ~**term** a kurzfristig. ~ **wave** n Kurzwelle f

shot /ʃɒt/ see shoot ▢ n Schuß m; (pellets) Schrot m; (person) Schütze m; (Phot) Aufnahme f;

(injection) Spritze f; (fam: attempt) Versuch m; **like a** ~ (fam) sofort. ~**gun** n Schrotflinte f. ~**putting** n (Sport) Kugelstoßen nt

should /ʃʊd/ v aux **you** ~ **go** du solltest gehen; **I** ~ **have seen him** ich hätte ihn sehen sollen; **I** ~ **like** ich möchte; **this** ~ **be enough** das müßte eigentlich reichen; **if he** ~ **be there** falls er da sein sollte

shoulder /ʃəʊldə(r)/ n Schulter f ▢ vt schultern; (fig) auf sich (acc) nehmen. ~**blade** n Schulterblatt nt. ~**strap** n Trägriemen m; (on garment) Träger m

shout /ʃaʊt/ n Schrei m ▢ vt/i schreien. ~ **down** vt niederschreien

shouting /ʃaʊtɪŋ/ n Geschrei nt

shove /ʃʌv/ n Stoß m; (fam) Schubs m ▢ vt stoßen; (fam) schubsen; (fam: put) tun ▢ vi drängeln. ~ **off** vi (fam) abhauen

shovel /ʃʌvl/ n Schaufel f ▢ vt (pt/pp shovelled) schaufeln

show /ʃəʊ/ n (display) Pracht f; (exhibition) Ausstellung f, Schau f; (performance) Vorstellung f; (Theat, TV) Show f; **on** ~ ausgestellt ▢ v (pt showed, pp shown) ▢ vt zeigen; (put on display) ausstellen; vorführen ⟨film⟩ ▢ vi sichtbar sein; ⟨film:⟩ gezeigt werden. ~ **in** vt hereinführen. ~ **off** vi (fam) angeben ▢ vt vorführen; (flaunt) angeben mit. ~ **up** vi [deutlich] zu sehen sein; (fam: arrive) auftauchen ▢ vt deutlich zeigen; (fam: embarrass) blamieren

'**show-down** n Entscheidungskampf m

shower /ʃaʊə(r)/ n Dusche f; (of rain) Schauer m; **have a** ~ duschen ▢ vt ~ **with** überschütten mit ▢ vi duschen. ~**proof** a regendicht. ~**y** a regnerisch

'**show-jumping** n Springreiten nt

shown /ʃəʊn/ see show

show: ~**-off** n Angeber(in) m(f).
~**-piece** n Paradestück nt.
~**room** n Ausstellungsraum m

showy /'ʃəʊɪ/ a protzig

shrank /ʃræŋk/ see shrink

shred /ʃred/ n Fetzen m; ⟨fig⟩
Spur f □vt (pt/pp **shredded**)
zerkleinern; ⟨Culin⟩ schnitzeln.
~**der** n Reißwolf m; ⟨Culin⟩
Schnitzelwerk nt

shrewd /ʃruːd/ a (-er, -est), -ly
adv klug. ~**ness** n Klugheit f

shriek /ʃriːk/ n Schrei m □vt/i
schreien

shrift /ʃrɪft/ n give s.o. short ~
jdn kurz abfertigen

shrill /ʃrɪl/ a, -y adv schrill

shrimp /ʃrɪmp/ n Garnele f,
Krabbe f

shrine /ʃraɪn/ n Heiligtum nt

shrink /ʃrɪŋk/ vi (pt **shrank**, pp
shrunk) schrumpfen; ⟨gar-
ment:⟩ einlaufen; ⟨draw back⟩ zurückschrecken (**from** vor + dat)

shrivel /'ʃrɪvl/ vi (pt/pp **shrivel-
led**) verschrumpeln

shroud /ʃraʊd/ n Leichentuch nt;
⟨fig⟩ Schleier m

Shrove /ʃrəʊv/ n ~ '**Tuesday** Fast-
nachtsdienstag m

shrub /ʃrʌb/ n Strauch m

shrug /ʃrʌg/ n Achselzucken nt
□vt/i (pt/pp **shrugged**) ~ [**one's
shoulders**] mit den Achseln zucken

shrunk /ʃrʌŋk/ see **shrink**. ~**en**
a geschrumpft

shudder /'ʃʌdə(r)/ n Schauder m
□vi schaudern; ⟨tremble⟩ zittern

shuffle /'ʃʌfl/ vi schlurfen □vt mischen ⟨cards⟩

shun /ʃʌn/ vt (pt/pp **shunned**)
meiden

shunt /ʃʌnt/ vt rangieren

shush /ʃʊʃ/ int sch!

shut /ʃʌt/ v (pt/pp **shut**, pres p
shutting) □vt zumachen, schließen; ~ **one's finger in the door**
sich ⟨dat⟩ den Finger in der Tür
einklemmen □vi sich schließen;
⟨shop:⟩ schließen, zumachen. ~
down vt schließen; stillegen

⟨factory⟩ □vi schließen; ⟨fact-
ory:⟩ stillgelegt werden. ~ **up** vt
abschließen; ⟨lock in⟩ einsperren
□vi ⟨fam⟩ den Mund halten

'**shut-down** n Stillegung f

shutter /'ʃʌtə(r)/ n [Fenster]laden
m; ⟨Phot⟩ Verschluß m

shuttle /'ʃʌtl/ n ⟨Tex⟩ Schiffchen
nt □vi pendeln

shuttle: ~**cock** n Federball m. ~
service n Pendelverkehr m

shy /ʃaɪ/ a (-er, -est), -ly adv
schüchtern; ⟨timid⟩ scheu □vi
(pt/pp **shied**) ⟨horse:⟩ scheuen.
~**ness** n Schüchternheit f

Siamese /saɪə'miːz/ a siamesisch

siblings /'sɪblɪŋz/ npl Geschwister pl

Sicily /'sɪsɪlɪ/ n Sizilien nt

sick /sɪk/ a krank; ⟨humour⟩
makaber; **be** ~ ⟨vomit⟩ sich übergeben; **be** ~ **of sth** ⟨fam⟩ etw satt
haben; **I feel** ~ mir ist schlecht

sicken /'sɪkn/ vt anwidern □vi **be**
~ **ing for something** krank werden

sickle /'sɪkl/ n Sichel f

sick|ly /'sɪklɪ/ a (-ier, -iest) kränk-
lich. ~**ness** n Krankheit f; ⟨vom-
iting⟩ Erbrechen nt

'**sick-room** n Krankenzimmer nt

side /saɪd/ n Seite f; **on the** ~ ⟨as
sideline⟩ nebenbei; ~ **by** ~ nebeneinander; ⟨fig⟩ Seite an Seite;
take ~**s** Partei ergreifen (**with**
für); **to be on the safe** ~ vor-
sichtshalber □attrib Seiten- □vi
~ **with** Partei ergreifen für

side: ~**board** n Anrichte f.
~**burns** npl Koteletten pl. ~-
effect n Nebenwirkung f.
~**lights** npl Standlicht nt.
~**line** n Nebenbeschäftigung f.
~**-show** n Nebenattraktion f. ~-
step vt ausweichen (+ dat). ~-
track vt ablenken. ~**walk** n
⟨Amer⟩ Bürgersteig m. ~**ways**
adv seitwärts

siding /'saɪdɪŋ/ n Abstellgleis nt

sidle /'saɪdl/ vi sich heranschlei-
chen (**up to** an + acc)

siege /siːdʒ/ n Belagerung f; (by police) Umstellung f

sieve /sɪv/ n Sieb nt □ vt sieben

sift /sɪft/ vt sieben; (fig) durchsehen

sigh /saɪ/ n Seufzer m □ vi seufzen

sight /saɪt/ n Sicht f; (faculty) Sehvermögen nt; (spectacle) Anblick m; (on gun) Visier nt; ~s pl Sehenswürdigkeiten pl; **at first ~** auf den ersten Blick; **within/out of ~** in/außer Sicht; **lose ~ of** aus dem Auge verlieren; **know by ~** vom Sehen kennen; **have bad ~** schlechte Augen haben □ vt sichten

'sightseeing n go ~ die Sehenswürdigkeiten besichtigen

sign /saɪn/ n Zeichen nt; (notice) Schild nt □ vt/i unterschreiben; (author, artist:) signieren. ~ **on** vi (as unemployed) sich arbeitslos melden; (Mil) sich verpflichten

signal /'sɪgnl/ n Signal nt □ vt/i (pt/pp **signalled**) signalisieren; ~ **to s.o.** jdm ein Signal geben (to zu). ~-**box** n Stellwerk nt

signature /'sɪgnətʃə(r)/ n Unterschrift f; (of artist) Signatur f. ~-**tune** n Kennmelodie f

signet-ring /'sɪgnɪt-/ n Siegelring m

significan|ce /sɪg'nɪfɪkəns/ n Bedeutung f. ~ **t** a, -**ly** adv bedeutungsvoll; (important) bedeutend

signify /'sɪgnɪfaɪ/ vt (pt/pp -**ied**) bedeuten

signpost /'saɪn-/ n Wegweiser m

silence /'saɪləns/ n Stille f; (of person) Schweigen nt □ vt zum Schweigen bringen. ~ **r** n (on gun) Schalldämpfer m; (Auto) Auspufftopf m

silent /'saɪlənt/ a, -**ly** adv still; (without speaking) schweigend; **remain ~** schweigen. ~ **film** n Stummfilm m

silhouette /sɪluː'et/ n Silhouette f; (picture) Schattenriß m □ vt **be ~d** sich als Silhouette abheben

silicon /'sɪlɪkən/ n Silizium nt

silk /sɪlk/ n Seide f □ attrib Seiden-. ~-**worm** n Seidenraupe f

silky /'sɪlkɪ/ a (-**ier**, -**iest**) seidig

sill /sɪl/ n Sims m & nt

silly /'sɪlɪ/ a (-**ier**, -**iest**) dumm, albern

silo /'saɪləʊ/ n Silo m

silt /sɪlt/ n Schlick m

silver /'sɪlvə(r)/ a silbern; (coin, paper) Silber- □ n Silber nt

silver: ~-**plated** a versilbert. ~**ware** n Silber nt. ~ **wedding** n Silberhochzeit f

similar /'sɪmɪlə(r)/ a, -**ly** adv ähnlich. ~**ity** /-'lærətɪ/ n Ähnlichkeit f

simile /'sɪmɪlɪ/ n Vergleich m

simmer /'sɪmə(r)/ vi/t leise kochen, ziehen □ vt ziehen lassen

simple /'sɪmpl/ a (-**r**, -**st**) einfach; (person) einfältig. ~-'**minded** a einfältig. ~-**ton** /'sɪmpltən/ n Einfaltspinsel m

simplicity /sɪm'plɪsətɪ/ n Einfachheit f

simplif|ication /sɪmplɪfɪ'keɪʃn/ n Vereinfachung f. ~-**fy** /'sɪmplɪfaɪ/ vt (pt/pp -**ied**) vereinfachen

simply /'sɪmplɪ/ adv einfach

simulate /'sɪmjʊleɪt/ vt vortäuschen; (Techn) simulieren. ~**ion** /-'leɪʃn/ n Vortäuschung f; Simulation f

simultaneous /sɪml'teɪnɪəs/ a, -**ly** adv gleichzeitig; (interpreting) Simultan-

sin /sɪn/ n Sünde f □ vi (pt/pp **sinned**) sündigen

since /sɪns/ prep seit (+ dat) □ adv seitdem □ conj seit; (because) da

sincere /sɪn'sɪə(r)/ a aufrichtig; (heartfelt) herzlich. ~-**ly** adv aufrichtig; **Yours ~ly** Mit freundlichen Grüßen

sincerity /sɪn'serətɪ/ n Aufrichtigkeit f

sinew /'sɪnjuː/ n Sehne f

sinful /'sɪnfl/ a sündhaft

sing /sɪŋ/ vt/i (pt **sang**, pp **sung**) singen

singe /sɪndʒ/ vt (pres p **singeing**) versengen

singer /'sɪŋə(r)/ n Sänger(in) m(f)

single /'sɪŋgl/ a einzeln; (one only) einzig; (unmarried) ledig; ⟨ticket⟩ einfach; ⟨room, bed⟩ Einzel- □ n ⟨ticket⟩ einfache Fahrkarte f; ⟨record⟩ Single f; ~s pl (Tennis) Einzel nt □ vt ~ **out** auswählen

single: ~-breasted a einreihig. **~-handed** a & adv allein. **~-minded** a zielstrebig. **~ 'parent** n Alleinerziehende(r) m/f

singlet /'sɪŋglɪt/ n Unterhemd nt

singly /'sɪŋglɪ/ adv einzeln

singular /'sɪŋgjʊlə(r)/ a eigenartig; (Gram) im Singular □ n Singular m. **~ly** adv außerordentlich

sinister /'sɪnɪstə(r)/ a finster

sink /sɪŋk/ n Spülbecken nt □ v (pt **sank**, pp **sunk**) □ vi sinken □ vt versenken ⟨ship⟩; senken ⟨shaft⟩. **~ in** vi einsinken; (fam: be understood) kapiert werden

'sink unit n Spüle f

sinner /'sɪnə(r)/ n Sünder(in) m(f)

sinus /'saɪnəs/ n Nebenhöhle f

sip /sɪp/ n Schlückchen nt □ vt (pt/pp **sipped**) in kleinen Schlucken trinken

siphon /'saɪfn/ n ⟨bottle⟩ Siphon m. **~ off** vt mit einem Saugheber ablassen

sir /sɜ:(r)/ n mein Herr; **S~** ⟨title⟩ Sir; **Dear S~s** Sehr geehrte Herren

siren /'saɪrən/ n Sirene f

sissy /'sɪsɪ/ n Waschlappen m

sister /'sɪstə(r)/ n Schwester f; (nurse) Oberschwester f. **~-in-law** n (pl **~s-in-law**) Schwägerin f. **~ly** a schwesterlich

sit /sɪt/ v (pt/pp **sat**, pres p **sitting**) □ vi sitzen; (sit down) sich setzen; ⟨committee:⟩ tagen □ vt setzen; machen ⟨exam⟩. **~ back** vi sich zurücklehnen. **~ down** vi sich setzen. **~ up** vi (aufrecht) sitzen; (rise) sich aufsetzen; (not slouch) gerade sitzen; (stay up) aufbleiben

site /saɪt/ n Gelände nt; (for camping) Platz m; (Archaeol) Stätte f □ vt legen

sitting /'sɪtɪŋ/ n Sitzung f; (for meals) Schub m

situate /'sɪtjʊeɪt/ vt legen; be **~ed** liegen. **~ion** /-'eɪʃn/ n Lage f; (circumstances) Situation f; (job) Stelle f

six /sɪks/ a sechs. **~teen** a sechzehn. **~teenth** a sechzehnte(r,s)

sixth /sɪksθ/ a sechste(r,s)

sixtieth /'sɪkstɪɪθ/ a sechzigste(r,s)

sixty /'sɪkstɪ/ a sechzig

size /saɪz/ n Größe f □ vt ~ **up** (fam) taxieren

sizeable /'saɪzəbl/ a ziemlich groß

sizzle /'sɪzl/ vi brutzeln

skate[1] /skeɪt/ n inv (fish) Rochen m

skate[2] n Schlittschuh m; (roller-) Rollschuh m □ vi Schlittschuh/ Rollschuh laufen. **~r** n Eisläufer(in) m(f); Rollschuhläufer(in) m(f)

skating /'skeɪtɪŋ/ n Eislaufen nt. **~-rink** n Eisbahn f

skeleton /'skelɪtn/ n Skelett nt. **~ 'key** n Dietrich m. **~ 'staff** n Minimalbesetzung f

sketch /sketʃ/ n Skizze f; (Theat) Sketch m □ vt skizzieren

sketchy /'sketʃɪ/ a (-ier, -iest), **-ily** adv skizzenhaft

skew /skju:/ n on the **~** schräg

skewer /'skjʊə(r)/ n [Brat]spieß m

ski /ski:/ n Ski m □ vi (pt/pp **skied**, pres p **skiing**) Ski fahren or laufen

skid /skɪd/ n Schleudern nt □ vi (pt/pp **skidded**) schleudern

skier /'ski:ə(r)/ n Skiläufer(in) m(f)

skiing /'ski:ɪŋ/ n Skilaufen nt

skilful /'skɪlfl/ a, **-ly** adv geschickt

skill /skɪl/ n Geschick nt. **~ed** a geschickt; (trained) ausgebildet

skim /skɪm/ vt (pt/pp **skimmed**) entrahmen ⟨milk⟩. **~ off** vt abschöpfen. **~ through** vt überfliegen

skimp /skɪmp/ vt sparen an (+ dat)

skimpy /'skɪmpɪ/ a (-ier, -iest) knapp

skin /skɪn/ n Haut f; (on fruit) Schale f □ vt (pt/pp skinned) häuten; schälen ⟨fruit⟩

skin: ~**-deep** a oberflächlich. ~**-diving** n Sporttauchen nt

skinflint /'skɪnflɪnt/ n Geizhals m

skinny /'skɪnɪ/ a (-ier, -iest) dünn

skip[1] /skɪp/ n Container m

skip[2] /skɪp/ n Hüpfer m □ v (pt/pp skipped) vi hüpfen; (with rope) seilspringen □ vt überspringen

skipper /'skɪpə(r)/ n Kapitän m

'skipping-rope n Sprungseil nt

skirmish /'skɜːmɪʃ/ n Gefecht m

skirt /skɜːt/ n Rock m □ vt herumgehen um

skit /skɪt/ n parodistischer Sketch m

skittle /'skɪtl/ n Kegel m

skive /skaɪv/ vi (fam) blaumachen

skulk /skʌlk/ vi lauern

skull /skʌl/ n Schädel m

skunk /skʌŋk/ n Stinktier nt

sky /skaɪ/ n Himmel m. ~**light** n Dachluke f. ~**scraper** n Wolkenkratzer m

slab /slæb/ n Platte f; (slice) Scheibe f; (of chocolate) Tafel f

slack /slæk/ a (-er, -est) schlaff, locker; ⟨person⟩ nachlässig; (Comm) flau □ vi bummeln

slacken /'slækn/ vi sich lockern; (diminish) nachlassen; ⟨speed:⟩ sich verringern □ vt lockern; (diminish) verringern

slacks /slæks/ npl Hose f

slag /slæg/ n Schlacke f

slain /sleɪn/ see slay

slake /sleɪk/ vt löschen

slam /slæm/ v (pt/pp slammed) □ vt zuschlagen; (put) knallen (fam); (criticize) verreißen □ vi zuschlagen

slander /'slɑːndə(r)/ n Verleumdung f □ vt verleumden. ~**ous** /-rəs/ a verleumderisch

slang /slæŋ/ n Slang m. ~**y** a salopp

slant /slɑːnt/ n Schräge f; **on the** ~ schräg □ vt abschrägen; (fig) färben ⟨report⟩ □ vi sich neigen

slap /slæp/ n Schlag m □ vt (pt/pp slapped) schlagen; (put) knallen (fam) □ adv direkt

slap: ~**-dash** a (fam) schludrig. ~**-up** a (fam) toll

slash /slæʃ/ n Schlitz m □ vt aufschlitzen; [drastisch] reduzieren ⟨prices⟩

slat /slæt/ n Latte f

slate /sleɪt/ n Schiefer m □ vt (fam) heruntermachen; verreißen ⟨performance⟩

slaughter /'slɔːtə(r)/ n Schlachten nt; (massacre) Gemetzel nt □ vt schlachten; abschlachten. ~**house** n Schlachthaus nt

Slav /slɑːv/ a slawisch □ n Slawe m/Slawin f

slave /sleɪv/ n Sklave m/Sklavin f □ vi ~ [away] schuften. ~**driver** n Leuteschinder m

slav|ery /'sleɪvərɪ/ n Sklaverei f. ~**ish** a, ~**ly** adv sklavisch

Slavonic /slə'vɒnɪk/ a slawisch

slay /sleɪ/ vt (pt slew, pp slain) ermorden

sleazy /'sliːzɪ/ a (-ier, -iest) schäbig

sledge /sledʒ/ n Schlitten m. ~**-hammer** n Vorschlaghammer m

sleek /sliːk/ a (-er, -est) seidig; (well-fed) wohlgenährt

sleep /sliːp/ n Schlaf m; **go to** ~ einschlafen; **put to** ~ einschläfern □ v (pt/pp slept) □ vi schlafen □ vt (accommodate) Unterkunft bieten für. ~**er** n Schläfer(in) m(f); (Rail) Schlafwagen m; (on track) Schwelle f

sleeping: ~**-bag** n Schlafsack m. ~**-car** n Schlafwagen m. ~**-pill** n Schlaftablette f

sleep: ~**less** a schlaflos. ~**walking** n Schlafwandeln nt

sleepy /'sli:pɪ/ a (-ier, -iest), **-ily** adv schläfrig

sleet /sli:t/ n Schneeregen m □ vi it is ~ing es gibt Schneeregen

sleeve /sli:v/ n Ärmel m; (for record) Hülle f. **~less** a ärmellos

sleigh /sleɪ/ n [Pferde]schlitten m

sleight /slaɪt/ n ~ of hand Taschenspielerei f

slender /'slendə(r)/ a schlank; (fig) gering

slept /slept/ see **sleep**

sleuth /slu:θ/ n Detektiv m

slew¹ /slu:/ vi schwenken

slew² see **slay**

slice /slaɪs/ n Scheibe f □ vt in Scheiben schneiden; **~d bread** Schnittbrot nt

slick /slɪk/ a clever □ n (of oil) Ölteppich m

slid|e /slaɪd/ n Rutschbahn f; (for hair) Spange f; (Phot) Dia nt □ vi (pt/pp **slid**) rutschen □ vt schieben. **~ing** a gleitend; (door, seat) Schiebe-

slight /slaɪt/ a (-er, -est), **-ly** adv leicht; (importance) gering; (acquaintance) flüchtig; (slender) schlank; **not in the ~est** nicht im geringsten; **~ly better** ein bißchen besser □ vt kränken, beleidigen □ n Beleidigung f

slim /slɪm/ a (slimmer, slimmest) schlank; (volume) schmal; (fig) gering □ vi eine Schlankheitskur machen

slim|e /slaɪm/ n Schleim m. **~y** a schleimig

sling /slɪŋ/ n (Med) Schlinge f □ vt (pt/pp **slung**) (fam) schmeißen

slip /slɪp/ n (mistake) Fehler m, (fam) Patzer m; (petticoat) Unterrock m; (for pillow) Bezug m; (paper) Zettel m; **give s.o. the ~** (fam) jdm entwischen; **~ of the tongue** Versprecher m □ v (pt/pp **slipped**) □ vi rutschen; (fall) ausrutschen; (go quickly) schlüpfen; (decline) nachlassen □ vt schieben; **~ s.o.'s mind** jdm entfallen. **~ away** vi sich fortschleichen;

(time:) verfliegen. **~ up** vi (fam) einen Schnitzer machen

slipped 'disc n (Med) Bandscheibenvorfall m

slipper /'slɪpə(r)/ n Hausschuh m

slippery /'slɪpərɪ/ a glitschig; (surface) glatt

slipshod /'slɪpʃɒd/ a schludrig

'slip-up n (fam) Schnitzer m

slit /slɪt/ n Schlitz m □ vt (pt/pp **slit**) aufschlitzen

slither /'slɪðə(r)/ vi rutschen

sliver /'slɪvə(r)/ n Splitter m

slobber /'slɒbə(r)/ vi sabbern

slog /slɒg/ n [hard] ~ Schinderei f □ v (pt/pp **slogged**) □ vi schuften □ vt schlagen

slogan /'sləʊgən/ n Schlagwort nt; (advertising) Werbespruch m

slop /slɒp/ v (pt/pp **slopped**) □ vt verschütten □ vi ~ over überschwappen. **~s** npl Schmutzwasser nt

slop|e /sləʊp/ n Hang m; (inclination) Neigung f □ vi sich neigen. **~ing** a schräg

sloppy /'slɒpɪ/ a (-ier, -iest) schludrig; (sentimental) sentimental

slosh /slɒʃ/ vi (fam) platschen; (water:) schwappen □ vt (fam: hit) schlagen

slot /slɒt/ n Schlitz m; (TV) Sendezeit f □ v (pt/pp **slotted**) □ vt einfügen □ vi sich einfügen (**in** in + acc)

sloth /sləʊθ/ n Trägheit f

'slot-machine n Münzautomat m; (for gambling) Spielautomat m

slouch /slaʊtʃ/ vi sich schlecht halten

slovenly /'slʌvnlɪ/ a schlampig

slow /sləʊ/ a (-er, -est), **-ly** adv langsam; **be ~** (clock:) nachgehen; **in ~ motion** in Zeitlupe □ adv langsam □ vt verlangsamen □ vi ~ **down**, ~ **up** langsamer werden

slow: **~coach** n (fam) Trödler m. **~ness** n Langsamkeit f

sludge /slʌdʒ/ n Schlamm m

slug /slʌg/ n Nacktschnecke f

sluggish /ˈslʌgɪʃ/ a, **-ly** adv träge

sluice /sluːs/ n Schleuse f

slum /slʌm/ n (house) Elendsquartier nt; **~s** pl Elendsviertel nt

slumber /ˈslʌmbə(r)/ n Schlummer m □vi schlummern

slump /slʌmp/ n Sturz m □vi fallen; (crumple) zusammensacken; ⟨prices:⟩ stürzen; ⟨sales:⟩ zurückgehen

slung /slʌŋ/ see sling

slur /slɜː(r)/ n (discredit) Schande f □vt (pt/pp **slurred**) undeutlich sprechen

slurp /slɜːp/ vt/i schlürfen

slush /slʌʃ/ n [Schnee]matsch m; (fig) Kitsch m. **~ fund** n Fonds m für Bestechungsgelder

slushy /ˈslʌʃɪ/ a matschig; (sentimental) kitschig

slut /slʌt/ n Schlampe f (fam)

sly /slaɪ/ a (-er, -est), **-ly** adv verschlagen □ on the **~** heimlich

smack[1] /smæk/ n Schlag m, Klaps m □vt schlagen; **~ one's lips** mit den Lippen schmatzen □adv (fam) direkt

smack[2] vi **~ of** (fig) riechen nach

small /smɔːl/ a (-er, -est) klein; **in the ~ hours** in den frühen Morgenstunden □adv **chop up ~** kleinhacken □n **~ of the back** Kreuz nt

small: **~ ads** npl Kleinanzeigen pl. **~ 'change** n Kleingeld nt. **~-holding** n landwirtschaftlicher Kleinbetrieb m. **~pox** n Pocken pl. **~ talk** n leichte Konversation f

smarmy /ˈsmɑːmɪ/ a (-ier, -iest) (fam) ölig

smart /smɑːt/ a (-er, -est), **-ly** adv schick; (clever) schlau, clever; (brisk) flott; (Amer fam: cheeky) frech □vi brennen

smarten /ˈsmɑːtn/ vt **~ oneself up** mehr auf sein Äußeres achten

smash /smæʃ/ n Krach m; (collision) Zusammenstoß m; (Tennis) Schmetterball m □vt zerschlagen; (strike) schlagen; (Tennis) schmettern □vi zerschmettern; (crash) krachen (into gegen). **~ing** a (fam) toll

smattering /ˈsmætərɪŋ/ n **a ~ of German** ein paar Brocken Deutsch

smear /smɪə(r)/ n verschmierter Fleck m; (Med) Abstrich m; (fig) Verleumdung f □vt schmieren; (coat) beschmieren (with mit); (fig) verleumden □vi schmieren

smell /smel/ n Geruch m; (sense) Geruchssinn m □n (pt/pp **smelt** or **smelled**) □vt riechen; (sniff) riechen an (+ dat) □vi riechen (of nach)

smelly /ˈsmelɪ/ a (-ier, -iest) übelriechend

smelt[1] /smelt/ see smell

smelt[2] vt schmelzen

smile /smaɪl/ n Lächeln nt □vi lächeln; **~ at** anlächeln

smirk /smɜːk/ vi feixen

smith /smɪθ/ n Schmied m

smithereens /smɪðəˈriːnz/ npl **smash to ~** in tausend Stücke schlagen

smitten /ˈsmɪtn/ a **~ with** sehr angetan von

smock /smɒk/ n Kittel m

smog /smɒg/ n Smog m

smoke /sməʊk/ n Rauch m □vt/i rauchen; (Culin) räuchern. **~less** a rauchfrei; ⟨fuel⟩ rauchlos

smoker /ˈsməʊkə(r)/ n Raucher m; (Rail) Raucherabteil nt

'smoke-screen n [künstliche] Nebelwand f

smoking /ˈsməʊkɪŋ/ n Rauchen nt; **'no ~'** 'Rauchen verboten'

smoky /ˈsməʊkɪ/ a (-ier, -iest) verraucht; ⟨taste⟩ rauchig

smooth /smuːð/ a (-er, -est), **-ly** adv glatt □vt glätten. **~ out** vt glattstreichen

smother /'smʌðə(r)/ *vt* ersticken; *(cover)* bedecken; *(suppress)* unterdrücken

smoulder /'smǝuldǝ(r)/ *vi* schwelen

smudge /smʌdʒ/ *n* Fleck *m* □*vt* verwischen □*vi* schmieren

smug /smʌg/ *a* (smugger, smuggest), **-ly** *adv* selbstgefällig

smuggl|e /'smʌgl/ *vt* schmuggeln. **~er** *n* Schmuggler *m*. **~ing** *n* Schmuggel *m*

smut /smʌt/ *n* Rußflocke *f*; *(mark)* Rußfleck *m*; *(fig)* Schmutz *m*

smutty /'smʌti/ *a* (-ier, -iest) schmutzig

snack /snæk/ *n* Imbiss *m*. **~-bar** *n* Imbißstube *f*

snag /snæg/ *n* Schwierigkeit *f*, *(fam)* Haken *m*

snail /sneɪl/ *n* Schnecke *f*; **at a ~'s pace** im Schneckentempo

snake /sneɪk/ *n* Schlange *f*

snap /snæp/ *n* Knacken *nt*; *(photo)* Schnappschuß *m* □*attrib* ⟨decision⟩ plötzlich □*v* *(pt/pp* snapped) □*vi* [entzwei]brechen; **~ at** *(bite)* schnappen nach; *(speak sharply)* [scharf] anfahren □*vt* zerbrechen; *(say)* fauchen; *(Phot)* knipsen. **~ up** *vt* wegschnappen

snappy /'snæpi/ *a* (-ier, -iest) bissig; *(smart)* flott; **make it ~!** ein bißchen schnell!

'**snapshot** *n* Schnappschuß *m*

snare /sneǝ(r)/ *n* Schlinge *f*

snarl /snɑːl/ *vi* [mit gefletschten Zähnen] knurren

snatch /snætʃ/ *n* *(fragment)* Fetzen *pl*; *(theft)* Raub *m*; **make a ~ at** greifen nach □*vt* schnappen; *(steal)* klauen; entführen ⟨*child*⟩; **~ sth from s.o.** jdm etw entreißen

sneak /sniːk/ *n* *(fam)* Petze *f* □*vi* schleichen; *(fam: tell tales)* petzen □*vt* *(take)* mitgehen lassen □*vi* — **in/out** sich hinein-/hinausschleichen

sneakers /'sniːkǝz/ *npl* *(Amer)* Turnschuhe *pl*

sneaking /'sniːkɪŋ/ *a* heimlich; ⟨*suspicion*⟩ leise

sneaky /'sniːkɪ/ *a* hinterhältig

sneer /snɪǝ(r)/ *vi* höhnisch lächeln; *(mock)* spotten

sneeze /sniːz/ *n* Niesen *nt* □*vi* niesen

snide /snaɪd/ *a* *(fam)* abfällig

sniff /snɪf/ *vi* schnüffeln □*vt* schnüffeln an (+ *dat)*; schnüffeln ⟨*glue*⟩

snigger /'snɪgǝ(r)/ *vi* [boshaft] kichern

snip /snɪp/ *n* Schnitt *m*; *(fam: bargain)* günstiger Kauf *m* □*vt/i* **~ [at]** schnippeln an (+ *dat)*

snipe /snaɪp/ *vi* — **at** aus dem Hinterhalt schießen auf (+ *acc)*; *(fig)* anschießen. **~r** *n* Heckenschütze *m*

snippet /'snɪpɪt/ *n* Schnipsel *m*; *(of information)* Bruchstück *nt*

snivel /'snɪvl/ *vi* *(pt/pp* snivelled) flennen

snob /snɒb/ *n* Snob *m*. **~bery** *n* Snobismus *m*. **~bish** *a* snobistisch

snoop /snuːp/ *vi* *(fam)* schnüffeln

snooty /'snuːti/ *a* *(fam)* hochnäsig

snooze /snuːz/ *n* Nickerchen *nt* □*vi* dösen

snore /snɔː(r)/ *vi* schnarchen

snorkel /'snɔːkl/ *n* Schnorchel *m*

snort /snɔːt/ *vi* schnauben

snout /snaʊt/ *n* Schnauze *f*

snow /snǝu/ *n* Schnee *m* □*vi* schneien; **~ed under with** *(fig)* überhäuft mit

snow: **~ball** *n* Schneeball *m* □*vi* lawinenartig anwachsen. **~drift** *n* Schneewehe *f*. **~drop** *n* Schneeglöckchen *nt*. **~fall** *n* Schneefall *m*. **~flake** *n* Schneeflocke *f*. **~ flurry** *n* Schneegestöber *m*. **~man** *n* Schneemann *m*. **~plough** *n* Schneepflug *m*. **~storm** *n* Schneesturm *m*

snub /snʌb/ *n* Abfuhr *f* □*vt* *(pt/pp* snubbed) brüskieren

'**snub-nosed** a stupsnasig
snuff¹ /snʌf/ n Schnupftabak m
snuff² vt ~ [out] löschen
snuffle /'snʌfl/ vi schnüffeln
snug /snʌg/ a (**snugger**, **snuggest**) behaglich, gemütlich
snuggle /'snʌgl/ vi sich kuscheln (**up to** an + acc)
so /səʊ/ adv so; **not so fast** nicht so schnell; **so am I** ich auch; **so does** he er auch; **so I see** das sehe ich; **that is so** das stimmt; **so much the better** um so besser; **so it is** tatsächlich; **if so** wenn ja; **so as to** um zu; **so long!** (fam) tschüs! □pron **I hope so** hoffentlich; **I think so** ich glaube schon; **I told you so** ich hab's dir gleich gesagt; **because I say so** weil ich es sage; **I'm afraid so** leider ja; **so saying/doing, he/she** . . . indem er/sie das sagte/tat, . . .; **an hour or so** eine Stunde oder so; **very much so** durchaus □conj (therefore) also; **so that** damit; **so there!** fertig! **so what!** na und! **so you see** wie du siehst; **so where have you been?** wo warst du denn?
soak /səʊk/ vt naß machen; (steep) einweichen; (fam: fleece) schröpfen □vi weichen; (liquid:) sickern. ~ **up** vt aufsaugen
soaking /'səʊkɪŋ/ a & adv ~ [**wet**] patschnaß (fam)
soap /səʊp/ n Seife f. ~ **opera** n Seifenoper f. ~ **powder** n Seifenpulver nt
soapy /'səʊpɪ/ a (-**ier**, -**iest**) seifig
soar /sɔ:(r)/ vi aufsteigen; (prices:) in die Höhe schnellen
sob /sɒb/ n Schluchzer m □vi (pt/pp **sobbed**) schluchzen
sober /'səʊbə(r)/ a, -**ly** adv nüchtern; (serious) ernst; (colour) gedeckt. ~ **up** vi nüchtern werden
'**so-called** a sogenannt
soccer /'sɒkə(r)/ n (fam) Fußball m
sociable /'səʊʃəbl/ a gesellig
social /'səʊʃl/ a gesellschaftlich; (Admin, Pol, Zool) sozial

socialis|m /'səʊʃəlɪzm/ n Sozialismus m. ~**t** /-ɪst/ a sozialistisch □n Sozialist m
socialize /'səʊʃəlaɪz/ vi (gesellschaftlich) verkehren
socially /'səʊʃəlɪ/ adv gesellschaftlich; **know** ~ privat kennen
social: ~ se'**curity** n Sozialhilfe f. ~ **work** n Sozialarbeit f. ~ **worker** n Sozialarbeiter(in) m(f)
society /sə'saɪətɪ/ n Gesellschaft f; (club) Verein m
sociolog|ist /səʊsɪ'ɒlədʒɪst/ n Soziologe m. ~**y** n Soziologie f
sock¹ /sɒk/ n Socke f; (kneelength) Kniestrumpf m
sock² n (fam) Schlag m □vt (fam) hauen
socket /'sɒkɪt/ n (of eye) Augenhöhle f; (of joint) Gelenkpfanne f; (wall plug) Steckdose f; (for bulb) Fassung f
soda /'səʊdə/ n Soda nt; (Amer) Limonade f. ~ **water** n Sodawasser nt
sodden /'sɒdn/ a durchnäßt
sodium /'səʊdɪəm/ n Natrium nt
sofa /'səʊfə/ n Sofa nt. ~ **bed** n Schlafcouch f
soft /sɒft/ a (-**er**, -**est**), -**ly** adv weich; (quiet) leise; (gentle) sanft; (fam: silly) dumm; **have a** ~ **spot for s.o.** jdn mögen. ~ **drink** n alkoholfreies Getränk nt
soften /'sɒfn/ vt weich machen; (fig) mildern □vi weich werden
soft: ~ **toy** n Stofftier nt. ~ **ware** n Software f
soggy /'sɒgɪ/ a (-**ier**, -**iest**) aufgeweicht
soil¹ /sɔɪl/ n Erde f, Boden m
soil² vt verschmutzen
solace /'sɒlɪs/ n Trost m
solar /'səʊlə(r)/ a Sonnen-
sold /səʊld/ see **sell**
solder /'səʊldə(r)/ n Lötmetall nt □vt löten
soldier /'səʊldʒə(r)/ n Soldat m □vi ~ **on** [unbeirrbar] weitermachen
sole¹ /səʊl/ n Sohle f

sole² n (*fish*) Seezunge f

sole³ a einzig. ~**ly** adv einzig und allein

solemn /ˈsɒləm/ a, **-ly** adv feierlich; (*serious*) ernst. ~**ity** /sɪˈlemnətɪ/ n Feierlichkeit f; Ernst m

solicit /səˈlɪsɪt/ vt bitten um □vi (*prostitute:*) sich an Männer heranmachen

solicitor /səˈlɪsɪtə(r)/ n Rechtsanwalt m/-anwältin f

solicitous /səˈlɪsɪtəs/ a besorgt

solid /ˈsɒlɪd/ a fest; (*sturdy*) stabil; (*not hollow, of same substance*) massiv; (*unanimous*) einstimmig; (*complete*) ganz □n (Geom) Körper m; ~**s** pl (*food*) feste Nahrung f

solidarity /sɒlɪˈdærətɪ/ n Solidarität f

solidify /səˈlɪdɪfaɪ/ vi (pt/pp **-ied**) fest werden

soliloquy /səˈlɪləkwɪ/ n Selbstgespräch nt

solitary /ˈsɒlɪtərɪ/ a einsam; (*sole*) einzig. ~ **confinement** n Einzelhaft f

solitude /ˈsɒlɪtjuːd/ n Einsamkeit f

solo /ˈsəʊləʊ/ n Solo nt □ a Solo-; (*flight*) Allein-□adv solo. ~ **ist** n Solist(in) m(f)

solstice /ˈsɒlstɪs/ n Sonnenwende f

soluble /ˈsɒljʊbl/ a löslich; (*solvable*) lösbar

solution /səˈluːʃn/ n Lösung f

solvable /ˈsɒlvəbl/ a lösbar

solve /sɒlv/ vt lösen

solvent /ˈsɒlvənt/ a zahlungsfähig; (Chem) lösend □n Lösungsmittel nt

sombre /ˈsɒmbə(r)/ a dunkel; (*mood*) düster

some /sʌm/ a & pron etwas; (*a little*) ein bißchen; (*with pl noun*) einige; (*a few*) ein paar; (*certain*) manche(r,s); (*one or the other*) [irgend]ein; ~ **day** eines Tages; I want ~ ich möchte etwas; (*pl*) welche; will you have ~ ich möchten Sie Wein? I need ~ **money/books** ich brauche

Geld/Bücher; do ~ **shopping** einkaufen

some: ~**body** /-bədɪ/ pron & n jemand; (*emphatic*) irgend jemand. ~**how** adv irgendwie. ~**one** pron & n = somebody

somersault /ˈsʌməsɔːlt/ n Purzelbaum m (*fam*); (Sport) Salto m; **turn a** ~ einen Purzelbaum schlagen; einen Salto springen

'something pron & adv etwas; (*emphatic*) irgend etwas; ~ **different** etwas anderes; ~ **like** so etwas wie; **see** ~ **of s.o.** jdn mal sehen

some: ~**time** adv irgendwann □a ehemalig. ~**times** adv manchmal. ~**what** adv ziemlich. ~**where** adv irgendwo; ⟨go⟩ irgendwohin

son /sʌn/ n Sohn m

sonata /səˈnɑːtə/ n Sonate f

song /sɒŋ/ n Lied nt. ~ **bird** n Singvogel m

sonic /ˈsɒnɪk/ a Schall-. ~ '**boom** n Überschallknall m

'son-in-law n (pl ~**s-in-law**) Schwiegersohn m

soon /suːn/ adv (**-er, -est**) bald; (*quickly*) schnell; **too** ~ zu früh; **as** ~ **as** sobald; **as** ~ **as possible** so bald wie möglich; ~**er or later** früher oder später; **no** ~**er had I arrived than** … kaum war ich angekommen, da …; **I would** ~**er stay** ich würde lieber bleiben

soot /sʊt/ n Ruß m

soothe /suːð/ vt beruhigen; lindern ⟨*pain*⟩. ~**ing** a, **-ly** adv beruhigend; lindernd

sooty /ˈsʊtɪ/ a rußig

sop /sɒp/ n Beschwichtigungsmittel nt

sophisticated /səˈfɪstɪkeɪtɪd/ a weltgewandt; (*complex*) hochentwickelt

soporific /sɒpəˈrɪfɪk/ a einschläfernd

sopping /ˈsɒpɪŋ/ a & adv ~[**wet**] durchnäßt

soppy /'sɒpɪ/ a (-ier, -iest) (fam) rührselig

soprano /sə'prɑːnəʊ/ n Sopran m; (woman) Sopranistin f

sordid /'sɔːdɪd/ a schmutzig

sore /sɔː(r)/ a (-r, -st) wund; (painful) schmerzhaft; **have a ~ throat** Halsschmerzen haben □ n wunde Stelle f. **~ly** adv sehr

sorrow /'sɒrəʊ/ n Kummer m, Leid nt. **~ful** a traurig

sorry /'sɒrɪ/ a (-ier, -iest) (sad) traurig; (wretched) erbärmlich; **I am ~** es tut mir leid; **she is** or **feels ~ for him** er tut ihr leid; **I am ~ to say** leider; **~!** Entschuldigung!

sort /sɔːt/ n Art f; (brand) Sorte f; **he's a good ~** (fam) er ist in Ordnung; **be out of ~s** (fam) nicht auf der Höhe sein □ vt sortieren. **~ out** vt sortieren; (fig) klären

sought /sɔːt/ see **seek**

soul /səʊl/ n Seele f. **~ful** a gefühlvoll

sound¹ /saʊnd/ a (-er, -est) gesund; (sensible) vernünftig; (secure) solide; (thorough) gehörig □ adv **be ~ asleep** fest schlafen

sound² vt (Naut) loten. **~ out** vt (fig) aushorchen

sound³ n (strait) Meerenge f

sound⁴ n Laut m; (noise) Geräusch nt; (Phys) Schall m; (Radio, TV) Ton m; (of bells, music) Klang m; **I don't like the ~ of it** (fam) das hört sich nicht gut an □ vi [er]tönen; (seem) sich anhören □ vt (pronounce) aussprechen; schlagen ⟨alarm⟩; (Med) abhorchen ⟨chest⟩. **~ barrier** n Schallmauer f. **~less** a, **-ly** adv lautlos

soundly /'saʊndlɪ/ adv solide; (sleep) fest; (defeat) vernichtend

'soundproof a schalldicht

soup /suːp/ n Suppe f. **~ed-up a** (fam) (engine) frisiert

soup: ~-plate n Suppenteller m. **~-spoon** n Suppenlöffel m

sour /'saʊə(r)/ a (-er, -est) sauer; (bad-tempered) griesgrämig, verdrießlich

source /sɔːs/ n Quelle f

south /saʊθ/ n Süden m; **to the ~ of** südlich von □ a Süd-, süd- □ adv nach Süden

south: S~ 'Africa n Südafrika nt. **S~ A'merica** n Südamerika nt. **~-'east** n Südosten m

southerly /'sʌðəlɪ/ a südlich

southern /'sʌðən/ a südlich

South 'Pole n Südpol m

'southward[s] /-wəd[z]/ adv nach Süden

souvenir /suːvə'nɪə(r)/ n Andenken nt, Souvenir nt

sovereign /'sɒvrɪn/ a souverän □ n Souverän m. **~ty** n Souveränität f

Soviet /'səʊvɪət/ a sowjetisch; **~ Union** Sowjetunion f

sow¹ /saʊ/ n Sau f

sow² /səʊ/ vt (pt sowed, pp sown or sowed) säen

soya /'sɔɪə/ n **~ bean** Sojabohne f

spa /spɑː/ n Heilbad nt

space /speɪs/ n Raum m; (gap) Platz m; (Astr) Weltraum m; **leave/clear a ~** Platz lassen/schaffen □ vt **~ [out]** [in Abständen] verteilen

space: ~craft n Raumfahrzeug nt. **~ship** n Raumschiff nt

spacious /'speɪʃəs/ a geräumig

spade /speɪd/ n Spaten m; (for child) Schaufel f; **~s** pl (Cards) Pik nt; **call a ~ a ~** das Kind beim rechten Namen nennen. **~work** n Vorarbeit f

Spain /speɪn/ n Spanien nt

span¹ /spæn/ n Spanne f; (of arch) Spannweite f □ vt (pt/pp **spanned**) überspannen; umspannen ⟨time⟩

span² see **spick**

Spaniard /'spænjəd/ n Spanier(in) m(f). **~ish** a spanisch □ n (Lang) Spanisch nt; **the ~ish** pl die Spanier

spank /spæŋk/ vt verhauen

spanner /'spænə(r)/ n Schraubenschlüssel m

spar /spɑ:(r)/ vi (pt/pp **sparred**)
(Sport) sparren; (argue) sich zanken

spare /speə(r)/ a (surplus) übrig;
(additional) zusätzlich; ⟨seat,
time⟩ frei; ⟨room⟩ Gäste-; ⟨bed,
cup⟩ Extra- □ n (part) Ersatzteil
nt □ vt ersparen; (not hurt) verschonen; (do without) entbehren;
(afford to give) erübrigen; **to** ~
(surplus) übrig. ~ 'wheel n Re-
serverad nt

sparing /'speərɪŋ/ a, **-ly** adv sparsam

spark /spɑ:k/ n Funke m □ vt ~ **off**
zünden; (fig) auslösen. ~ **off**-
plug n (Auto) Zündkerze f

sparkl|**e** /'spɑ:kl/ n Funkeln nt □ vi
funkeln. ~**ing** a funkelnd;
⟨wine⟩ Schaum-

sparrow /'spærəʊ/ n Spatz m

sparse /spɑ:s/ a spärlich. ~**ly** adv
spärlich; ⟨populated⟩ dünn

Spartan /'spɑ:tn/ a spartanisch

spasm /'spæzm/ n Anfall m;
(cramp) Krampf m. ~**odic**
/-'mɒdɪk/ a, **-ally** adv sporadisch;
(Med) krampfartig

spastic /'spæstɪk/ a spastisch [ge-
lähmt] □ n Spastiker(in) m(f)

spat /spæt/ see spit²

spate /speɪt/ n Flut f; (series) Serie
f; **be in full** ~ Hochwasser führen

spatial /'speɪʃl/ a räumlich

spatter /'spætə(r)/ vt spritzen; ~
with bespritzen mit

spatula /'spætjʊlə/ n Spachtel m;
(Med) Spatel m

spawn /spɔ:n/ n Laich m □ vi lai-
chen □ vt (fig) hervorbringen

spay /speɪ/ vt sterilisieren

speak /spi:k/ v (pt **spoke**, pp
spoken) □ vi sprechen (**to** mit); ~
ing! (Teleph) am Apparat! □ vt
sprechen; sagen ⟨truth⟩. ~ **up**
vi lauter sprechen; ~ **up for**
oneself seine Meinung äußern

speaker /'spi:kə(r)/ n Sprecher(in)
m(f); (in public) Redner(in) m(f);
(loudspeaker) Lautsprecher m

spear /spɪə(r)/ n Speer m □ vt aufspießen. ~**head** vt (fig) anführen

spec /spek/ n **on** ~ (fam) auf gut
Glück

special /'speʃl/ a besondere(r,s),
speziell. ~**ist** n Spezialist m;
(Med) Facharzt m/-ärztin f. ~**ity**
/-ʃɪ'ælətɪ/ n Spezialität f

special|**ize** /'speʃəlaɪz/ vi sich spe-
zialisieren (**in** auf + acc). ~**ly**
adv speziell; (particularly) besonders

species /'spi:ʃi:z/ n Art f

specific /spə'sɪfɪk/ a bestimmt;
(precise) genau; (Phys) spezifisch. ~**ally** adv ausdrücklich

specification /spesɪfɪ'keɪʃn/ n &
~ **s** pl (einzel) Angaben pl

specify /'spesɪfaɪ/ vt (pt/pp -**ied**)
(genau) angeben

specimen /'spesɪmən/ n Exemplar
nt; (sample) Probe f; (of
urine) Urinprobe f

speck /spek/ n Fleck m; (particle)
Teilchen nt

speckled /'spekld/ a gesprenkelt

specs /speks/ npl (fam) Brille f

spectacle /'spektəkl/ n (show)
Schauspiel nt; (sight) Anblick m.
~**s** npl Brille f

spectacular /spek'tækjʊlə(r)/ a
spektakulär

spectator /spek'teɪtə(r)/ n Zu-
schauer(in) m(f)

spectre /'spektə(r)/ n Gespenst nt;
(fig) Schreckgespenst nt

spectrum /'spektrəm/ n (pl -**tra**)
Spektrum nt

speculat|**e** /'spekjʊleɪt/ vi speku-
lieren. ~**ion** /-'leɪʃn/ n Spekula-
tion f. ~**or** n Spekulant m

sped /sped/ see speed

speech /spi:tʃ/ n Sprache f; (address) Rede f. ~**less** a sprachlos

speed /spi:d/ n Geschwindigkeit f;
(rapidity) Schnelligkeit f; (gear)

Gang *m*; at ~ mit hoher Geschwindigkeit □*vi* (*pt/pp* speeded) schnell fahren □*vt* (*pt/pp* speeded) (*go too fast*) zu schnell fahren. ~ up (*pt/pp* speeded up) □*vt* beschleunigen □*vi* schneller werden; (*vehicle*): schneller fahren

speed: ~boat *n* Rennboot *nt*. ~ing *n* Geschwindigkeitsüberschreitung *f*. ~ limit *n* Geschwindigkeitsbeschränkung *f*

speedometer /spiːˈdɒmɪtə(r)/ *n* Tachometer *m*

speedy /ˈspiːdɪ/ *a* (-ier, -iest), -ily *adv* schnell

spell[1] /spel/ *n* Weile *f*; (*of weather*) Periode *f*

spell[2] *v* (*pt/pp* spelled *or* spelt) □*vt* schreiben; (*aloud*) buchstabieren; (*fig: mean*) bedeuten □*vi* richtig schreiben; (*aloud*) buchstabieren. ~ out *vt* buchstabieren; (*fig*) genau erklären

spell[3] *n* Zauber *m*; (*words*) Zauberspruch *m*. ~bound *a* wie verzaubert

spelling /ˈspelɪŋ/ *n* Schreibweise *f*; (*orthography*) Rechtschreibung *f*

spelt /spelt/ *see* spell[2]

spend /spend/ *vt/i* (*pt/pp* spent) ausgeben; verbringen (*time*)

spent /spent/ *see* spend

sperm /spɜːm/ *n* Samen *m*

spew /spjuː/ *vt* speien

spher|**e** /sfɪə(r)/ *n* Kugel *f*; (*fig*) Sphäre *f*. ~ical /ˈsferɪk/ *a* kugelförmig

spice /spaɪs/ *n* Gewürz *nt*; (*fig*) Würze *f*

spick /spɪk/ *a* ~ and span blitzsauber

spicy /ˈspaɪsɪ/ *a* würzig, pikant

spider /ˈspaɪdə(r)/ *n* Spinne *f*

spik|**e** /spaɪk/ *n* Spitze *f*; (*Bot, Zool*) Stachel *m*; (*on shoe*) Spike *m*. ~y *a* stachelig

spill /spɪl/ *v* (*pt/pp* spilt *or* spilled) □*vt* verschütten; vergießen (*blood*) □*vi* überlaufen

spin /spɪn/ *v* (*pt/pp* spun, *pres p* spinning) □*vt* drehen; spinnen (*wool*); schleudern (*washing*) □*vi* sich drehen. ~ out *vt* in die Länge ziehen

spinach /ˈspɪnɪdʒ/ *n* Spinat *m*

spinal /ˈspaɪnl/ *a* Rückgrat-. ~ 'cord *n* Rückenmark *nt*

spindl|**e** /ˈspɪndl/ *n* Spindel *f*. ~y *a* spindeldürr

spin-'drier *n* Wäscheschleuder *f*

spine /spaɪn/ *n* Rückgrat *nt*; (*of book*) [Buch]rücken *m*; (*Bot, Zool*) Stachel *m*. ~less *a* (*fig*) rückgratlos

spinning /ˈspɪnɪŋ/ *n* Spinnen *nt*. ~-wheel *n* Spinnrad *nt*

'spin-off *n* Nebenprodukt *nt*

spinster /ˈspɪnstə(r)/ *n* ledige Frau *f*

spiral /ˈspaɪrl/ *a* spiralig □*n* Spirale *f* □*vi* (*pt/pp* spiralled) sich hochwinden; (*smoke*): in einer Spirale aufsteigen. ~ 'staircase *n* Wendeltreppe *f*

spire /ˈspaɪə(r)/ *n* Turmspitze *f*

spirit /ˈspɪrɪt/ *n* Geist *m*; (*courage*) Mut *m*; ~s *pl* (*alcohol*) Spirituosen *pl*; in high ~s in gehobener Stimmung; in low ~s niedergedrückt. ~ away *vt* verschwinden lassen

spirited /ˈspɪrɪtɪd/ *a* lebhaft; (*courageous*) beherzt

spirit: ~-level *n* Wasserwaage *f*. ~ stove *n* Spirituskocher *m*

spiritual /ˈspɪrɪtjʊəl/ *a* geistig; (*Relig*) geistlich. ~ism *n* -[-ɪzm/ *n* Spiritismus *m*. ~ist *n* -[-ɪst/ *a* spiritistisch □*n* Spiritist *m*

spit[1] /spɪt/ *n* (*for roasting*) [Brat]spieß *m*

spit[2] *n* Spucke *f* □*vt/i* (*pt/pp* spat, *pres p* spitting) spucken; (*cat*): fauchen; (*fat*): spritzen; it's ~ting with rain es tröpfelt; be the ~ting image of s.o. jdm wie aus dem Gesicht geschnitten sein

spite /spaɪt/ *n* Boshaftigkeit *f*; in ~ of trotz (+ *gen*) □*vt* ärgern. ~ful *a*, -ly *adv* gehässig

spittle /'spɪtl/ n Spucke f

splash /splæʃ/ n Platschen nt; (fam: drop) Schuß m; ~ of colour Farbfleck m □vt spritzen; ~ s.o. with sth jdn mit etw bespritzen □vi spritzen. ~ about vi planschen

spleen /spli:n/ n Milz f

splendid /'splendɪd/ a herrlich, großartig

splendour /'splendə(r)/ n Pracht f

splint /splɪnt/ n (Med) Schiene f

splinter /'splɪntə(r)/ n Splitter m □vi zersplittern

split /splɪt/ n Spaltung f; (Pol) Bruch m; (tear) Riß m □v (pt/pp **split**, pres p **splitting**) □vt spalten; (share) teilen; (tear) zerreißen; ~ one's sides sich kaputtlachen □vi sich spalten; (tear) zerreißen; ~ on s.o. (sl) jdn verpfeifen. ~ **up** vt aufteilen □vi (couple:) sich trennen

splutter /'splʌtə(r)/ vi prusten

spoil /spɔɪl/ n ~s pl Beute f □v (pt/pp **spoilt** or **spoiled**) □vt verderben; verwöhnen (person) □vi verderben. ~**sport** n Spielverderber m

spoke[1] /spəʊk/ n Speiche f

spoke[2], **spoken** /'spəʊkn/ see speak

'spokesman n Sprecher m

sponge /spʌndʒ/ n Schwamm m □vt abwaschen □vi ~ **on** schmarotzen bei. ~**bag** n Waschbeutel m. ~**cake** n Biskuitkuchen m

sponger /'spʌndʒə(r)/ n Schmarotzer m. ~**y** a schwammig

sponsor /'spɒnsə(r)/ n Sponsor m; (god-parent) Pate m/Patin f; (for membership) Bürge m □vt sponsern; bürgen für

spontaneous /spɒn'teɪnɪəs/ a, -ly adv spontan

spoof /spu:f/ n (fam) Parodie f

spooky /'spu:kɪ/ a (-ier, -iest) (fam) gespenstisch

spool /spu:l/ n Spule f

spoon /spu:n/ n Löffel m □vt löffeln. ~-**feed** vt (pt/pp -**fed**) (fig)

alles vorkauen (+ dat). ~**ful** n Löffel m

sporadic /spə'rædɪk/ a, -ally adv sporadisch

sport /spɔ:t/ n Sport m; (amusement) Spaß m □vt (stolz) tragen. ~**ing** a sportlich; a ~**ing** chance eine faire Chance

sports: ~ **car** n Sportwagen m. ~ **coat** n, ~ **jacket** n Sakko m. ~**man** n Sportler m. ~**woman** n Sportlerin f

sporty /'spɔ:tɪ/ a (-ier, -iest) sportlich

spot /spɒt/ n Fleck m; (place) Stelle f; (dot) Punkt m; (drop) Tropfen m; (pimple) Pickel m; ~**s** pl (rash) Ausschlag m; a ~ **of** (fam) ein bißchen; on the ~ auf der Stelle; be in a tight ~ (fam) in der Klemme sitzen □vt (pt/pp **spotted**) entdecken

spot: ~ '**check** n Stichprobe f. ~**less** a makellos; (fam: very clean) blitzsauber. ~**light** n Scheinwerfer m; (fig) Rampenlicht nt

spotted /'spɒtɪd/ a gepunktet

spotty /'spɒtɪ/ a (-ier, -iest) fleckig; (pimply) pickelig

spouse /spaʊz/ n Gatte m/Gattin f

spout /spaʊt/ n Schnabel m, Tülle f □vi schießen (from aus)

sprain /spreɪn/ n Verstauchung f □vt verstauchen

sprang /spræŋ/ see **spring**

sprat /spræt/ n Sprotte f

sprawl /sprɔ:l/ vi sich ausstrecken; (fall) der Länge nach hinfallen

spray[1] /spreɪ/ n (of flowers) Strauß m

spray[2] n Sprühnebel m; (from sea) Gischt m; (device) Spritze f; (container) Sprühdose f; (preparation) Spray m □vt spritzen; (with aerosol) sprühen

spread /spred/ n Verbreitung f; (paste) Aufstrich m; (fam: feast) Festessen nt □v (pt/pp **spread**) □vt ausbreiten; streichen (butter, *jam*⟩; bestreichen ⟨*bread, sur-face*⟩; streuen ⟨*sand, manure*⟩; verbreiten ⟨*news, disease*⟩; verteilen ⟨*payments*⟩ □*vi* sich ausbreiten. ~ **out** *vt* ausbreiten; (*space out*) verteilen □*vi* sich verteilen

spree /spriː/ *n* (*fam*) go on a ~ shopping ~ groß einkaufen gehen

sprig /sprɪg/ *n* Zweig *m*

sprightly /ˈspraɪtlɪ/ *a* (-ier, -iest) rüstig

spring[1] /sprɪŋ/ *n* Frühling *m* □ *attrib* Frühlings-

spring[2] *n* (*jump*) Sprung *m*; (*water*) Quelle *f*; (*device*) Feder *f*; (*elasticity*) Elastizität *f* □*v* (*pt* sprang, *pp* sprung) □*vi* springen; (*arise*) entspringen (from *dat*) □*vt* ~ sth on s.o. jdn mit etw überfallen

spring: ~**board** *n* Sprungbrett *nt*. ~ -ˈcleaning *n* Frühjahrsputz *m*. ~**time** *n* Frühling *m*

sprinkle /ˈsprɪŋkl/ *vt* sprengen; (*scatter*) streuen; bestreuen ⟨*surface*⟩. ~**er** *n* Sprinkler *m*; (*Hort*) Sprenger *m*. ~**ing** *n* dünne Schicht *f*

sprint /sprɪnt/ *n* Sprint *m* □*vi* rennen; (*Sport*) sprinten. ~**er** *n* Kurzstreckenläufer(in) *m*(*f*)

sprout /spraʊt/ *n* Trieb *m*; [**Brussels**] ~**s** *pl* Rosenkohl *m* □*vi* sprießen

spruce /spruːs/ *a* gepflegt □*n* Fichte *f*

sprung /sprʌŋ/ *see* spring[2] □*a* gefedert

spry /spraɪ/ *a* (-er, -est) rüstig

spud /spʌd/ *n* (*fam*) Kartoffel *f*

spun /spʌn/ *see* spin

spur /spɜː(r)/ *n* Sporn *m*; (*stimulus*) Ansporn *m*; (*road*) Nebenstraße *f*; **on the** ~ **of the moment** ganz spontan □*vt* (*pt/pp* spurred) ~ [**on**] (*fig*) anspornen

spurious /ˈspjʊərɪəs/ *a*, **-ly** *adv* falsch

spurn /spɜːn/ *vt* verschmähen

spurt /spɜːt/ *n* Strahl *m*; (*Sport*) Spurt *m*; **put on a** ~ spurten □*vi* spritzen

spy /spaɪ/ *n* Spion(in) *m*(*f*) □*vi* spionieren □*vt* (*fam: see*) sehen. ~ **on** *vt* nachspionieren (s.o. jdm). ~ **out** *vt* auskundschaften

spying /ˈspaɪɪŋ/ *n* Spionage *f*

squabble /ˈskwɒbl/ *n* Zank *m* □*vi* sich zanken

squad /skwɒd/ *n* Gruppe *f*; (*Sport*) Mannschaft *f*

squadron /ˈskwɒdrən/ *n* (*Mil*) Geschwader *nt*

squalid /ˈskwɒlɪd/ *a*, **-ly** *adv* schmutzig

squall /skwɔːl/ *n* Bö *f* □*vi* brüllen

squalor /ˈskwɒlə(r)/ *n* Schmutz *m*

squander /ˈskwɒndə(r)/ *vt* vergeuden

square /skweə(r)/ *a* quadratisch; ⟨*metre, mile*⟩ Quadrat-; ⟨*meal*⟩ anständig; **all** ~ (*fam*) quitt □*n* Quadrat *nt*; (*area*) Platz *m*; (on *chessboard*) Feld *nt* □*vt* (*settle*) klären; (*Math*) quadrieren □*vi* (*agree*) übereinstimmen

squash /skwɒʃ/ *n* Gedränge *nt*; (*drink*) Fruchtsaftgetränk *nt*; (*Sport*) Squash *nt* □*vt* zerquetschen; (*suppress*) niederschlagen. ~**y** *a* weich

squat /skwɒt/ *a* gedrungen □*n* (*fam*) besetztes Haus *nt* □*vi* (*pt/pp* squatted) hocken; ~ **in a house** ein Haus besetzen. ~**ter** *n* Hausbesetzer *m*

squawk /skwɔːk/ *vi* krächzen

squeak /skwiːk/ *n* Quieken *nt*; (*of hinge, brakes*) Quietschen *nt* □*vi* quieken; quietschen

squeal /skwiːl/ *n* Schrei *m*; (*screech*) Kreischen *nt* □*vi* schreien; kreischen

squeamish /ˈskwiːmɪʃ/ *a* empfindlich

squeeze /skwiːz/ *n* Druck *m*; (*crush*) Gedränge *nt* □*vt* drücken; (*to get juice*) ausdrücken; (*force*

zwängen; (*fam: extort*) heraus-
pressen (**from** aus) □ *vi* ~ **in/out**
sich hinein-/hinauszwängen

squelch /skweltʃ/ *vi* quatschen

squid /skwɪd/ *n* Tintenfisch *m*

squiggle /ˈskwɪgl/ *n* Schnörkel *m*

squint /skwɪnt/ *n* Schielen *nt* □ *vi*
schielen

squire /ˈskwaɪə(r)/ *n* Gutsherr *m*

squirm /skwɜ:m/ *vi* sich winden

squirrel /ˈskwɪrl/ *n* Eichhörnchen *nt*

squirt /skwɜ:t/ *n* Spritzer *m* □ *vt/i*
spritzen

St *abbr* (**Saint**) St.; (**Street**) Str.

stab /stæb/ *n* Stich *m*; (*fam: attempt*) Versuch *m* □ *vt* (*pt/pp*
stabbed) stechen; (*to death*) erstechen

stability /stəˈbɪlətɪ/ *n* Stabilität *f*

stabilize /ˈsteɪbɪlaɪz/ *vt* stabilisieren □ *vi* sich stabilisieren

stable[1] /ˈsteɪbl/ *a* (**-r, -st**) stabil

stable[2] *n* Stall *m*; (*establishment*)
Reitstall *m*

stack /stæk/ *n* Stapel *m*; (*of chimney*) Schornstein *m*; (*fam: large
quantity*) Haufen *m* □ *vt* stapeln

stadium /ˈsteɪdɪəm/ *n* Stadion *nt*

staff /stɑ:f/ *n* (*stick & Mil*) Stab *m*
□ (*& pl*) (*employees*) Personal *nt*;
(*Sch*) Lehrkräfte *pl* □ *vt* mit Personal besetzen. **~room** *n* (*Sch*)
Lehrerzimmer *nt*

stag /stæg/ *n* Hirsch *m*

stage /steɪdʒ/ *n* Bühne *f*; (*in journey*) Etappe *f*; (*in process*) Stadium *nt*; **by** *or* **in** ~**s** in Etappen
□ *vt* aufführen; (*arrange*) veranstalten

stage: ~ **door** *n* Bühneneingang
m. ~ **fright** *n* Lampenfieber *nt*

stagger /ˈstægə(r)/ *vi* taumeln □ *vt*
staffeln ⟨*holidays*⟩; versetzt anordnen ⟨*seats*⟩; **I was ~ed** ich hatte
mir die Sprache verschlagen.
~ing *a* unglaublich

stagnant /ˈstægnənt/ *a* stehend;
(*fig*) stagnierend

stagnat|e /stægˈneɪt/ *vi* (*fig*) sta-
gnieren. **~ion** /-ˈneɪʃn/ *n* Stagna-
tion *f*

staid /steɪd/ *a* gesetzt

stain /steɪn/ *n* Fleck *m*; (*for wood*)
Beize *f* □ *vt* färben; beizen ⟨*wood*⟩;
(*fig*) beflecken; **~ed glass** farbi-
ges Glas *nt*. **~less** *a* fleckenlos;
⟨*steel*⟩ rostfrei. ~ **remover** *n*
Fleckentferner *m*

stair /steə(r)/ *n* Stufe *f*; **~s** *pl*
Treppe *f*. **~case** *n* Treppe *f*

stake /steɪk/ *n* Pfahl *m*; (*wager*)
Einsatz *m*; (*Comm*) Anteil *m*; **be
at** ~ auf dem Spiel stehen □ *vt* [an
einem Pfahl] anbinden; (*wager*)
setzen; ~ **a claim to sth** Anspruch auf etw (*acc*) erheben

stale /steɪl/ *a* (**-r, -st**) alt; ⟨*air*⟩
verbraucht. **~mate** *n* Patt *nt*

stalk[1] /stɔ:k/ *n* Stiel *m*, Stengel *m*

stalk[2] *vt* pirschen auf (+ *acc*) □ *vi*
stolzieren

stall /stɔ:l/ *n* Stand *m*; ~**s** *pl*
(*Theat*) Parkett *nt* □ *vi* ⟨*engine:*⟩
stehenbleiben; (*fig*) ausweichen
□ *vt* abwürgen ⟨*engine*⟩

stallion /ˈstæljən/ *n* Hengst *m*

stalwart /ˈstɔ:lwət/ *a* treu □ *n*
treuer Anhänger *m*

stamina /ˈstæmɪnə/ *n* Ausdauer *f*

stammer /ˈstæmə(r)/ *n* Stottern *nt*
□ *vt/i* stottern

stamp /stæmp/ *n* Stempel *m*;
(*postage* ~) [Brief]marke *f* □ *vt*
stempeln; (*impress*) prägen;
(*put postage on*) frankieren;
~ **one's feet** mit den Füßen
stampfen □ *vi* stampfen. ~ **out** *vt*
[aus]stanzen; (*fig*) ausmerzen

stampede /stæmˈpi:d/ *n* wilde
Flucht *f*; (*fam*) Ansturm *m* □ *vi* in
Panik fliehen

stance /stɑ:ns/ *n* Haltung *f*

stand /stænd/ *n* Stand *m*; (*rack*)
Ständer *m*; (*pedestal*) Sockel *m*;
(*Sport*) Tribüne *f* □ *v* (*pt/pp* **stood**) □ *vi*
stehen; (*rise*) aufstehen; (*be can-
didate*) kandidieren; (*stay valid*)
gültig bleiben; ~ **still** stillstehen;

~ **firm** (*fig*) festbleiben; ~ **to-gether** zusammenhalten; ~ **to lose / gain** gewinnen / verlieren können; ~ **to reason** logisch sein; ~ **in for** vertreten; ~ **for** (*mean*) bedeuten; **I won't ~ for that** das lasse ich mir nicht bieten □*vt* stellen; (*withstand*) standhalten (+ *dat*); (*endure*) ertragen; vertragen ⟨*climate*⟩; (*put up with*) aushalten; been ⟨*chance*⟩; ~ **one's ground** nicht nachgeben; ~ **the test of time** sich bewähren; **I can't ~ her** (*fam*) ich kann sie nicht ausstehen. ~ **by** vi danebenstehen; (*be ready*) sich bereithalten □*vt* **by s.o.** (*fig*) zu jdm stehen. ~ **down** vi (*retire*) zurücktreten. ~ **out** vi hervorstehen; (*fig*) herausragen. ~ **up** vi aufstehen; ~ **up for** eintreten für; ~ **up to** sich wehren gegen

standard /'stændəd/ *a* Normal-; **be ~ practice** allgemein üblich sein □*n* Maßstab *m*; (*Techn*) Norm *f*; (*level*) Niveau *nt*; (*flag*) Standarte *f*; ~**s** *pl* (*morals*) Prinzipien *pl*; ~ **of living** Lebensstandard *m*. ~**ize** *vt* standardisieren; (*Techn*) normen

'**standard lamp** *n* Stehlampe *f*

'**stand-in** *n* Ersatz *m*

standing /'stændɪŋ/ *a* (*erect*) stehend; (*permanent*) ständig □*n* Rang *m*; (*duration*) Dauer *f*. ~ '**order** *n* Dauerauftrag *m*. ~**room** *n* Stehplätze *pl*

stand: ~-**offish** /stænd'ɒfɪʃ/ *a* distanziert. ~**point** *n* Standpunkt *m*. ~**still** *n* Stillstand *m*; **come to a ~still** zum Stillstand kommen

stank /stæŋk/ *see* **stink**

staple[1] /'steɪpl/ *a* Grund-. □*n* (*product*) Haupterzeugnis *nt*

staple[2] *n* Heftklammer *f* □*vt* heften. ~**r** *n* Heftmaschine *f*

star /stɑː(r)/ *n* Stern *m*; (*asterisk*) Sternchen *nt*; (*Theat, Sport*) Star

m □*vi* (*pt/pp* **starred**) die Hauptrolle spielen

starboard /'stɑːbəd/ *n* Steuerbord *nt*

starch /stɑːtʃ/ *n* Stärke *f* □*vt* stärken. ~**y** *a* stärkehaltig; (*fig*) steif

stare /steə(r)/ *n* Starren *nt* □*vi* starren; ~ **at** anstarren

'**starfish** *n* Seestern *m*

stark /stɑːk/ *a* (-**er**, -**est**) scharf; (*contrast*) krass □*adv* ~ **naked** splitternackt

starling /'stɑːlɪŋ/ *n* Star *m*

'**starlit** *a* sternhell

starry /'stɑːrɪ/ *a* sternklar

start /stɑːt/ *n* Anfang *m*, Beginn *m*; (*departure*) Aufbruch *m*; (*Sport*) Start *m*; **from the ~** von Anfang an; **for a ~** erstens □*vi* anfangen, beginnen; (*set out*) aufbrechen; (*engine*:) anspringen; (*Auto, Sport*) starten; (*jump*) aufschrecken; **to ~ with** zuerst □*vt* anfangen, beginnen; (*cause*) verursachen; (*found*) gründen; starten ⟨*car, race*⟩; in Umlauf setzen ⟨*rumour*⟩. ~**er** *n* (*Culin*) Vorspeise *f*; (*Auto, Sport*) Starter *m*. ~**ing-point** *n* Ausgangspunkt *m*

startle /'stɑːtl/ *vt* erschrecken

starvation /stɑː'veɪʃn/ *n* Verhungern *nt*

starve /stɑːv/ *vi* hungern; (*to death*) verhungern □*vt* verhungern lassen

stash /stæʃ/ *vt* (*fam*) **[away]** beiseite schaffen

state /steɪt/ *n* Zustand *m*; (*grand style*) Prunk *m*; (*Pol*) Staat *m*; ~ **of play** Spielstand *m*; **be in a ~** ⟨*person*:⟩ aufgeregt sein; **lie in ~** feierlich aufgebahrt sein □*attrib* Staats-, staatlich □*vt* erklären; (*specify*) angeben. ~-**aided** *a* staatlich gefördert. ~**less** *a* staatenlos

stately /'steɪtlɪ/ *a* (-**ier**, -**iest**) stattlich. ~ '**home** *n* Schloß *nt*

statement /'steɪtmənt/ *n* Erklärung *f*; (*Jur*) Aussage *f*; (*Banking*) Auszug *m*

'statesman n Staatsmann m

static /'stætk/ a statisch; **remain ~** unverändert bleiben

station /'steɪʃn/ n Bahnhof m; (police) Wache f; (radio) Sender m; (space, weather) Station f; (Mil) Posten m; (status) Rang m □vt stationieren; (post) postieren. **~ary** /-ərɪ/ a stehend; **be ~ary** stehen

stationer /'steɪʃənə(r)/ n **~'s [shop]** Schreibwarengeschäft nt. **~y** n Briefpapier nt; (writing-materials) Schreibwaren pl

'station-wagon n (Amer) Kombi[wagen] m

statistic /stə'tɪstɪk/ n statistische Tatsache f. **~al** a, **-ly** adv statistisch. **~s** n & pl Statistik f

statue /'stætju:/ n Statue f

stature /'stætʃə(r)/ n Statur f; (fig) Format m

status /'steɪtəs/ n Status m, Rang m. **~ symbol** n Statussymbol nt

statut|e /'stætju:t/ n Statut nt. **~ory** a gesetzlich

staunch /stɔ:ntʃ/ a (-er, -est), **-ly** adv treu

stave /steɪv/ vt **~ off** abwenden

stay /steɪ/ n Aufenthalt m □vi bleiben; (reside) wohnen; **~ the night** übernachten; **~ put** dableiben □vt **~ the course** durchhalten. **~ away** vi wegbleiben. **~ behind** vi zurückbleiben. **~ in** vi zu Hause bleiben; (Sch) nachsitzen. **~ up** vi oben bleiben; (upright) stehen bleiben; (on wall) hängen bleiben; ⟨person:⟩ aufbleiben

stead /sted/ n in his **~** an seiner Stelle; **stand s.o. in good ~** jdm zustatten kommen. **~fast**, a, **-ly** adv standhaft

steadily /'stedɪlɪ/ adv fest; (continually) stetig

steady /'stedɪ/ a (-ier, -iest) fest, (not wobbly) stabil; ⟨hand⟩ ruhig; (regular) regelmäßig; (dependable) zuverlässig

steak /steɪk/ n Steak nt

steal /sti:l/ vt/i (pt **stole**, pp **stolen**) stehlen (from dat). **~ in/out** vi sich hinein-/hinausstehlen

stealth /stelθ/ n Heimlichkeit f; **by ~** heimlich. **~y** a heimlich

steam /sti:m/ n Dampf m; **under one's own ~** (fam) aus eigener Kraft □vt (Culin) dämpfen, dünsten □vi dampfen. **~ up** vi beschlagen

'steam-engine n Dampfmaschine f; (Rail) Dampflokomotive f

steamer /'sti:mə(r)/ n Dampfer m

'steamroller n Dampfwalze f

steamy /'sti:mɪ/ a dampfig

steel /sti:l/ n Stahl m □vt **~** oneself allen Mut zusammennehmen

steep¹ /sti:p/ vt (soak) einweichen

steep² a, **-ly** adv steil; (fam: exorbitant) gesalzen

steeple /'sti:pl/ n Kirchturm m. **~chase** n Hindernisrennen nt

steer /stɪə(r)/ vt/i steuern; **~ clear of s.o./sth** jdm/etw aus dem Weg gehen. **~ing** n (Auto) Steuerung f. **~ing-wheel** n Lenkrad nt

stem¹ /stem/ n Stiel m; (of word) Stamm m □vi (pt/pp **stemmed**) **~ from** zurückzuführen sein auf (+ acc)

stem² vt (pt/pp **stemmed**) eindämmen; stillen ⟨bleeding⟩

stench /stentʃ/ n Gestank m

stencil /'stensl/ n Schablone f; (for typing) Matrize f

step /step/ n Schritt m; (stair) Stufe f; **~s** pl (ladder) Trittleiter f; **in ~** im Schritt; **~ by ~** Schritt für Schritt; **take ~s** (fig) Schritte unternehmen □vi (pt/pp **stepped**) treten. **~ in** (fig) eingreifen; **~ into s.o.'s shoes** an jds Stelle treten. **~ out of line** aus der Reihe tanzen. **~ up** vt hinaufsteigen □vt (increase) erhöhen, steigern; verstärken ⟨efforts⟩

step-: ~brother n Stiefbruder m. **~child** n Stiefkind nt. **~daughter** n Stieftochter f. **~father** n

Stiefvater m. ~**-ladder** n Trittleiter f. ~**mother** n Stiefmutter f

'**stepping-stone** n Trittstein m; (fig) Sprungbrett nt

step: ~**-sister** n Stiefschwester f. ~**son** n Stiefsohn m

stereo /'steriəʊ/ n Stereo nt; (equipment) Stereoanlage f; **in** ~ stereo. ~**phonic** /-'fɒnɪk/ a stereophon

stereotype /'steriətaɪp/ n stereotype Figur f. ~**d** a stereotyp

steril|e /'steraɪl/ a steril. ~**ity** /stə'rɪlətɪ/ n Sterilität f

steriliz|ation /sterəlaɪ'zeɪʃn/ n Sterilisation f. ~**e** vt sterilisieren

sterling /'stɜːlɪŋ/ a Sterling-; (fig) gediegen □ n Sterling m

stern[1] /stɜːn/ a (-er, -est), **-ly** adv streng

stern[2] n (of boat) Heck nt

stew /stjuː/ n Eintopf m; **in a** ~ (fam) aufgeregt □ vt/i schmoren; ~**ed fruit** Kompott nt

steward /'stjuːəd/ n Ordner m; (on ship, aircraft) Steward m. ~**ess** n Stewardeß f

stick[1] /stɪk/ n Stock m; (of chalk) Stück nt; (of rhubarb) Stange f; (Sport) Schläger m

stick[2] v (pt/pp **stuck**) □ vt stecken; (stab) stechen; (glue) kleben; (fam: put) tun; (fam: endure) aushalten □ vi stecken; (adhere) kleben, haften (**to an** + dat); (jam) klemmen; ~ **to sth** (fig) bei etw bleiben; ~ **at it** (fam) dranbleiben; ~ **at nothing** (fam) vor nichts zurückschrecken; ~ **up for** (fam) eintreten für; **be stuck** nicht weiterkönnen; (vehicle:) festsitzen, festgefahren sein; (drawer:) klemmen; **be stuck with sth** (fam) etw am Hals haben. ~ **out** vi abstehen; (project) vorstehen □ vt (fam) hinausstrecken; herausstrecken (tongue)

sticker /'stɪkə(r)/ n Aufkleber m

'**sticking plaster** n Heftpflaster nt

stickler /'stɪklə(r)/ n **be a** ~ **for** es sehr genau nehmen mit

sticky /'stɪkɪ/ a (-ier, -iest) klebrig; (adhesive) Klebe-

stiff /stɪf/ a (-er, -est), **-ly** adv steif; (brush) hart; (dough) fest; (difficult) schwierig; (penalty) schwer; **be bored** ~ (fam) sich zu Tode langweilen. ~**en** vt steif machen □ vi steif werden. ~**ness** n Steifheit f

stifl|e /'staɪfl/ vt ersticken; (fig) unterdrücken. ~**ing** a **be** ~**ing** zum Ersticken sein

stigma /'stɪgmə/ n Stigma nt

stile /staɪl/ n Zauntritt m

stiletto /stɪ'letəʊ/ n Stilett nt; (heel) Bleistiftabsatz m

still[1] /stɪl/ n Destillierapparat m

still[2] a still; (drink) ohne Kohlensäure; **keep** ~ stillhalten; **stand** ~ stillstehen □ n Stille f □ adv noch; (emphatic) immer noch; (nevertheless) trotzdem; ~ **not** immer noch nicht

'**stillborn** a totgeboren

still 'life n Stilleben nt

stilted /'stɪltɪd/ a gestelzt, geschraubt

stilts /stɪlts/ npl Stelzen pl

stimulant /'stɪmjʊlənt/ n Anregungsmittel nt

stimulat|e /'stɪmjʊleɪt/ vt anregen. ~**ion** /-'leɪʃn/ n Anregung f

stimulus /'stɪmjʊləs/ n (pl **-li** /-laɪ/) Reiz m

sting /stɪŋ/ n Stich m; (from nettle, jellyfish) Brennen nt; (organ) Stachel m □ v (pt/pp **stung**) □ vt stechen □ vi brennen; (insect:) stechen. ~**ing nettle** n Brennessel f

stingy /'stɪndʒɪ/ a (-ier, -iest) geizig, (fam) knauserig

stink /stɪŋk/ n Gestank m □ vi (pt **stank**, pp **stunk**) stinken (**of** nach)

stint /stɪnt/ n Pensum nt □ vi ~ **on** sparen an (+ dat)

stipulat|e /'strpjulert/ vt vorschreiben. **~ion** /-'leɪʃn/ n Bedingung f

stir /stɜː(r)/ n (commotion) Aufregung f □ v (pt/pp **stirred**) vt rühren □ vi sich rühren

stirrup /'strɪrəp/ n Steigbügel m

stitch /stɪtʃ/ n Stich m; (Knitting) Masche f; (pain) Seitenstechen nt; **be in ~es** (fam) sich kaputtlachen □ vt nähen

stoat /stəʊt/ n Hermelin nt

stock /stɒk/ n Vorrat m (**of** an + dat); (in shop) [Waren]bestand m; (livestock) Vieh nt; (lineage) Abstammung f; (Finance) Wertpapiere pl; (Culin) Brühe f; (plant) Levkoje f; **in/out of ~** vorrätig/nicht vorrätig; **take ~** (fig) Bilanz ziehen □ a Standard- □ vt (shop:) führen; auffüllen (shelves). **~ up** vi sich eindecken (**with** mit)

stock: ~broker n Börsenmakler m. **~ cube** n Brühwürfel m. **S~ Exchange** n Börse f

stocking /'stɒkɪŋ/ n Strumpf m

stockist /'stɒkɪst/ n Händler m

stock: ~market n Börse f. **~pile** vt horten; anhäufen (weapons). **~-still** a bewegungslos. **~-taking** n (Comm) Inventur f

stocky /'stɒkɪ/ a (-ier, -iest) untersetzt

stodgy /'stɒdʒɪ/ a pappig [und schwer verdaulich]

stoical /'stəʊɪkl/ a, **-ly** adv stoisch

stoke /stəʊk/ vt heizen

stole¹ /stəʊl/ n Stola f

stole², stolen /stəʊln/ see **steal**

stolid /'stɒlɪd/ a, **-ly** adv stur

stomach /'stʌmək/ n Magen m □ vt vertragen. **~ache** n Magenschmerzen pl

stone /stəʊn/ n Stein m; (weight) 6,35 kg □ a steinern; (wall, Age) Stein- □ vt mit Steinen bewerfen; entsteinen (fruit). **~-cold** a eiskalt. **~-deaf** a (fam) stocktaub

stony /'stəʊnɪ/ a steinig

stood /stʊd/ see **stand**

stool /stuːl/ n Hocker m

stoop /stuːp/ n **walk with a ~** gebeugt gehen □ vi sich bücken; (fig) sich erniedrigen

stop /stɒp/ n Halt m; (break) Pause f; (for bus) Haltestelle f; (for train) Station f; (Gram) Punkt m; (on organ) Register nt; **come to a ~** stehenbleiben; **put a ~ to** etw unterbinden □ v (pt/pp **stopped**) □ vt anhalten, stoppen; (switch off) abstellen; (plug, block) zustopfen; (prevent) verhindern; **~ s.o. doing sth** jdn daran hindern, etw zu tun; **~ doing sth** aufhören, etw zu tun; **~ that!** hör auf damit! laß das sein! □ vi anhalten; (cease) aufhören; (clock:) stehenbleiben; (fam: stay) bleiben (**with** bei) □ int halt! stopp!

stop: ~gap n Notlösung f. **~over** n Zwischenaufenthalt m; (Aviat) Zwischenlandung f

stoppage /'stɒpɪdʒ/ n Unterbrechung f; (strike) Streik m; (deduction) Abzug m

stopper /'stɒpə(r)/ n Stöpsel m

stop: ~press n letzte Meldungen pl. **~watch** n Stoppuhr f

storage /'stɔːrɪdʒ/ n Aufbewahrung f; (in warehouse) Lagerung f; (Computing) Speicherung f

store /stɔː(r)/ n (stock) Vorrat m; (shop) Laden m; (department ~) Kaufhaus nt; (depot) Lager nt; **in ~ auf Lager; put in ~** lagern; **set great ~ by** großen Wert legen auf (+ acc); **be in ~ for s.o.** (fig) jdm bevorstehen □ vt aufbewahren; (in warehouse) lagern; (Computing) speichern. **~-room** n Lagerraum m

storey /'stɔːrɪ/ n Stockwerk nt

stork /stɔːk/ n Storch m

storm /stɔːm/ n Sturm m; (with thunder) Gewitter nt □ vt/i stürmen. **~y** a stürmisch

story /'stɔːrɪ/ n Geschichte f; (in newspaper) Artikel m; (fam: lie) Märchen nt

stout /staʊt/ a (-er, -est) beleibt; (strong) fest

stove /stəʊv/ n Ofen m; (for cooking) Herd m

stow /stəʊ/ vt verstauen. ~away n blinder Passagier m

straddle /ˈstrædl/ vt rittlings sitzen auf (+ dat); (standing) mit gespreizten Beinen über (+ dat)

straggl|e /ˈstrægl/ vi hinterherhinken. ~er n Nachzügler m. ~y a strähnig

straight /streɪt/ a (-er, -est) gerade; (direct) direkt; (clear) klar; (hair) glatt; (drink) pur; be ~ (tidy) in Ordnung sein □ adv gerade; (directly) direkt, geradewegs; (clearly) klar; ~ away sofort; ~ on or ahead geradeaus; ~ out (fig) geradeheraus; go ~ (fam) ein ehrliches Leben führen; put sth ~ etw in Ordnung bringen; sit/stand up ~ gerade sitzen/-stehen

straighten /ˈstreɪtn/ vt gerademachen; (put straight) geraderichten □ vi gerade werden; ~ [up] (person:) sich aufrichten. ~ out vt geradebiegen

straight'forward a offen; (simple) einfach

strain[1] /streɪn/ n Rasse f; (Bot) Sorte f; (of virus) Art f

strain[2] n Belastung f; ~s pl (of music) Klänge pl □ vt belasten; (overexert) überanstrengen; (injure) zerren (muscle); (Culin) durchseihen; abgießen (vegetables) □ vi sich anstrengen. ~ed a (relations) gespannt. ~er n Sieb nt

strait /streɪt/ n Meerenge f; in dire ~s in großen Nöten. ~-jacket n Zwangsjacke f. ~-'laced a puritanisch

strand[1] /strænd/ n (of thread) Faden m; (of beads) Kette f; (of hair) Strähne f

strand[2] vt be ~ed festsitzen

strange /streɪndʒ/ a (-r, -st) fremd; (odd) seltsam, merkwürdig. ~r n Fremde(r) m/f

strangely /ˈstreɪndʒlɪ/ adv seltsam, merkwürdig; ~ enough seltsamerweise

strangle /ˈstræŋgl/ vt erwürgen; (fig) unterdrücken

strangulation /stræŋgjʊˈleɪʃn/ n Erwürgen nt

strap /stræp/ n Riemen m; (for safety) Gurt m; (to grasp in vehicle) Halteriemen m; (of watch) Armband nt; (shoulder-) Träger m □ vt (pt/pp strapped) schnallen; ~ in or down festschnallen

strapping /ˈstræpɪŋ/ a stramm

strata /ˈstrɑːtə/ npl see stratum

stratagem /ˈstrætədʒəm/ n Kriegslist f

strategic /strəˈtiːdʒɪk/ a, -ally adv strategisch

strategy /ˈstrætədʒɪ/ n Strategie f

stratum /ˈstrɑːtəm/ n (pl strata) Schicht f

straw /strɔː/ n Stroh nt; (single piece, drinking) Strohhalm m; that's the last ~ jetzt reicht's aber

strawberry /ˈstrɔːbərɪ/ n Erdbeere f

stray /streɪ/ a streunend □ n streunendes Tier nt □ vi sich verirren; (deviate) abweichen

streak /striːk/ n Streifen m; (in hair) Strähne f; (fig: trait) Zug m □ vi flitzen. ~y a streifig; (bacon) durchwachsen

stream /striːm/ n Bach m; (flow) Strom m; (current) Strömung f; (Sch) Parallelzug m □ vi strömen; ~ in/out hinaus-/herausströmen

streamer /ˈstriːmə(r)/ n Luftschlange f; (flag) Wimpel m

streamline vt (fig) rationalisieren. ~d a stromlinienförmig

street /striːt/ n Straße f. ~-car n (Amer) Straßenbahn f. ~ lamp n Straßenlaterne f

strength /streŋθ/ n Stärke f;
(power) Kraft f; **on the ~ of** auf
Grund (+ gen). **~en** vt stärken;
(reinforce) verstärken

strenuous /'strenjʊəs/ a anstrengend

stress /stres/ n (emphasis) Betonung f; (strain) Belastung f;
(mental) Streß m □vt betonen;
(put a strain on) belasten. **~ful** a
stressig (fam)

stretch /stretʃ/ n (of road) Strecke
f; (elasticity) Elastizität f; **at a ~**
ohne Unterbrechung; **a long ~**
eine lange Zeit; **have a ~** sich
strecken □vt strecken; (widen)
dehnen; (spread) ausbreiten; fordern ⟨person⟩; **~ one's legs** sich
(dat) die Beine vertreten □vi sich
erstrecken; (become wider) sich
dehnen; ⟨person:⟩ sich strecken.
~er n Tragbahre f

strew /struː/ vt (pp strewn or
strewed) streuen

stricken /'strɪkn/ a betroffen; **~
with** heimgesucht von

strict /strɪkt/ a (-er, -est), **-ly** adv
streng; **~ly speaking** streng-
genommen

stride /straɪd/ n [großer] Schritt
m; **make great ~s** (fig) große
Fortschritte machen; **take sth in
one's ~** mit etw gut fertig werden □vi (pt strode, pp stridden)
[mit großen Schritten] gehen

strident /'straɪdnt/ a, **-ly** adv
schrill; ⟨colour⟩ grell

strife /straɪf/ n Streit m

strike /straɪk/ n Streik m; (Mil)
Angriff m; **be on ~** streiken □v
(pt/pp struck) □vt schlagen;
(knock against, collide with) treffen; prägen ⟨coin⟩; anzünden
⟨match⟩; stoßen auf (+ acc) ⟨oil,
gold⟩; abbrechen ⟨camp⟩; (delete)
streichen; (impress) beeindrucken; (occur to) einfallen (+
dat); (Mil) angreifen; **~ s.o. a
blow** jdm einen Schlag versetzen
□vi treffen; ⟨lightning:⟩ einschlagen; ⟨clock:⟩ schlagen; (attack)

zuschlagen; ⟨workers:⟩ streiken;
~ lucky Glück haben. **~-break-
er** n Streikbrecher m

striker /'straɪkə(r)/ n Streiken-
de(r) m/f

striking /'straɪkɪŋ/ a auffallend

string /strɪŋ/ n Schnur f; (thin)
Bindfaden m; (of musical instrument, racket) Saite f; (of bow)
Sehne f; (of pearls) Kette f; **the
~s** (Mus) die Streicher pl; **pull
~s** (fam) seine Beziehungen
spielen lassen, Fäden ziehen □vt
(pt/pp strung) (thread) aufziehen ⟨beads⟩. **~ed** a (Mus)
Saiten-; (played with a bow)
Streich-

stringent /'strɪndʒnt/ a streng

strip /strɪp/ n Streifen m □v (pt/pp
stripped) □vt ablösen; ausziehen
⟨clothes⟩; abziehen ⟨bed⟩; abbeizen ⟨wood, furniture⟩; auseinandernehmen ⟨machine⟩; (deprive) berauben (of gen); **~ sth
off** sth etw von etw entfernen
□vi (undress) sich ausziehen. **~
club** n Stripteaselokal nt

stripe /straɪp/ n Streifen m. **~d** a
gestreift

'striplight n Neonröhre f

stripper /'strɪpə(r)/ n Stripperin f;
(male) Stripper m

strip-'tease n Striptease m

strive /straɪv/ vi (pt strove, pp
striven) sich bemühen (to zu); **~
for** streben nach

strode /strəʊd/ see **stride**

stroke¹ /strəʊk/ n Schlag m; (of
pen) Strich m; (Swimming) Zug
m; (style) Stil m; (Med) Schlag-
anfall m; **~ of luck** Glücksfall m;
put s.o. off his ~ jdn aus dem
Konzept bringen

stroke² □vt streicheln

stroll /strəʊl/ n Spaziergang m,
(fam) Bummel m □vi spazieren,
(fam) bummeln. **~er** n (Amer:
push-chair) [Kinder]sportwagen
m

strong /strɒŋ/ a (-er /-gə(r)/, -est
/-gɪst/), **-ly** adv stark; (powerful,

healthy) kräftig; (_severe_) streng; (_sturdy_) stabil; (_convincing_) gut

strong: ~**-box** n Geldkassette f. ~**hold** n Festung f; (_fig_) Hochburg f. ~**-minded** a willensstark. ~**-room** n Tresorraum m

stroppy /'strɒpɪ/ a widerspenstig

strove /strəʊv/ see **strive**

struck /strʌk/ see **strike**

structural /'strʌktʃərl/ a, **-ly** adv baulich

structure /'strʌktʃə(r)/ n Struktur f; (_building_) Bau m

struggle /'strʌgl/ n Kampf m; **with a** ~ mit Mühe □ vi kämpfen; ~ **for breath** nach Atem ringen; ~ **to do sth** sich abmühen, etw zu tun; ~ **to one's feet** mühsam aufstehen

strum /strʌm/ v (_pt/pp_ **strummed**) □ vt klimpern auf (+ _dat_) □ vi klimpern

strung /strʌŋ/ see **string**

strut¹ /strʌt/ n Strebe f

strut² vi (_pt/pp_ **strutted**) stolzieren

stub /stʌb/ n Stummel m; (_counterfoil_) Abschnitt m □ vt (_pt/pp_ **stubbed**) ~ **one's toe** sich (_dat_) den Zeh stoßen (_on an + dat_). ~ **out** vt ausdrücken (_cigarette_)

stubble /'stʌbl/ n Stoppeln _pl_. ~**ly** a stoppelig

stubborn /'stʌbən/ a, **-ly** adv starrsinnig; (_refusal_) hartnäckig

stubby /'stʌbɪ/ a (**-ier, -iest**) kurz und dick

stucco /'stʌkəʊ/ n Stuck m

stuck /stʌk/ see **stick²**. ~**-'up** a (_fam_) hochnäsig

stud¹ /stʌd/ n Nagel m; (_on clothes_) Niete f; (_for collar_) Kragenknopf m; (_for ear_) Ohrstecker m

stud² n (_of horses_) Gestüt nt

student /'stju:dnt/ n Student(in) m(f); (_Sch_) Schüler(in) m(f). ~ **nurse** n Lernschwester f

studied /'stʌdɪd/ a gewollt

studio /'stju:dɪəʊ/ n Studio nt; (_for artist_) Atelier nt

studious /'stju:dɪəs/ a lerneifrig; (_earnest_) ernsthaft

study /'stʌdɪ/ n Studie f; (_room_) Studierzimmer nt; (_investigation_) Untersuchung f; ~**ies** _pl_ Studium nt □ v (_pt/pp_ **studied**) □ vt studieren; (_examine_) untersuchen □ vi lernen; (_at university_) studieren

stuff /stʌf/ n Stoff m; (_fam: things_) Zeug nt □ vt vollstopfen; (_with padding, Culin_) füllen; ausstopfen (_animal_); ~ **sth into sth** etw in etw (_acc_) [hinein]stopfen. ~**ing** n Füllung f

stuffy /'stʌfɪ/ a (**-ier, -iest**) stickig; (_old-fashioned_) spießig

stumble /'stʌmbl/ vi stolpern; ~**e across** zufällig stoßen auf (+ _acc_). ~**ing-block** n Hindernis nt

stump /stʌmp/ n Stumpf m □ ~ **up** vt/i (_fam_) blechen. ~**ed** a (_fam_) überfragt

stun /stʌn/ vt (_pt/pp_ **stunned**) betäuben; ~**ned by** (_fig_) wie betäubt von

stung /stʌŋ/ see **sting**

stunk /stʌŋk/ see **stink**

stunning /'stʌnɪŋ/ a (_fam_) toll

stunt¹ /stʌnt/ n (_fam_) Kunststück nt

stunt² vt hemmen. ~**ed** a verkümmert

stupendous /stju:'pendəs/ a, **-ly** adv enorm

stupid /'stju:pɪd/ a dumm. ~**ity** /-'pɪdətɪ/ n Dummheit f. ~**ly** adv dumm; ~**ly** [**enough**] dummerweise

stupour /'stju:pə(r)/ n Benommenheit f

sturdy /'stɜ:dɪ/ a (**-ier, -iest**) stämmig; (_furniture_) stabil; (_shoes_) fest

stutter /'stʌtə(r)/ n Stottern nt □ vt/i stottern

sty¹ /staɪ/ n (_pl_ **sties**) Schweinestall m

sty², **stye** n (_pl_ **styes**) (_Med_) Gerstenkorn nt

style /staɪl/ n Stil m; (fashion) Mode f; (sort) Art f; (hair ~) Frisur f; **in ~** in großem Stil

stylish /'staɪlɪʃ/ a, **-ly** adv stilvoll

stylist /'staɪlɪst/ n Friseur m/ Friseuse f. **~ic** /-'lɪstɪk/ a, **-ally** adv stilistisch

stylized /'staɪlaɪzd/ a stilisiert

stylus /'staɪləs/ n (on record-player) Nadel f

suave /swɑːv/ a (pej) gewandt

sub'conscious /sʌb-/ a, **-ly** adv unterbewußt □ n Unterbewußtsein nt

subcon'tract vt [vertraglich] weitervergeben (to an + acc)

'subdivide vt unterteilen. **~sion** n Unterteilung f

subdue /səb'djuː/ vt unterwerfen; (make quieter) beruhigen. **~d** a gedämpft; (person) still

subject¹ /'sʌbdʒɪkt/ a **be ~ to** sth etw (dat) unterworfen sein □ n Staatsbürger(in) m(f); (of ruler) Untertan m; (theme) Thema nt; (of investigation) Gegenstand m; (Sch) Fach nt; (Gram) Subjekt nt

subject² /səb'dʒekt/ vt unterwerfen (to dat); (expose) aussetzen (to dat)

subjective /səb'dʒektɪv/ a, **-ly** adv subjektiv

subjugate /'sʌbdʒʊgeɪt/ vt unterjochen

subjunctive /səb'dʒʌŋktɪv/ n Konjunktiv m

sub'let vt (pt/pp **-let**) untervermieten

sublime /sə'blaɪm/ a, **-ly** adv erhaben

subliminal /sʌ'blɪmɪnl/ a unterschwellig

sub-ma'chine-gun n Maschinenpistole f

subma'rine n Unterseeboot nt

submerge /səb'mɜːdʒ/ vt untertauchen; **be ~d** unter Wasser stehen □ vi tauchen

submiss|ion /səb'mɪʃn/ n Unterwerfung f. **~ive** /-sɪv/ a gehorsam; (pej) unterwürfig

submit /səb'mɪt/ v (pt/pp **-mitted**, pres p **-mitting**) □ vt vorlegen (to dat); (hand in) einreichen □ vi sich unterwerfen (to dat)

subordinate¹ /sə'bɔːdɪnət/ a untergeordnet □ n Untergebene(r) m/f

subordinate² /sə'bɔːdɪneɪt/ vt unterordnen (to dat)

subscribe /səb'skraɪb/ vi spenden; **~ to** (fig) sich anschließen (+ dat); abonnieren ⟨newspaper⟩. **~r** n Spender m; Abonnent m

subscription /səb'skrɪpʃn/ n (to club) [Mitglieds]beitrag m; (to newspaper) Abonnement nt; **by ~** mit Spenden

subsequent /'sʌbsɪkwənt/ a, **-ly** adv folgend; (later) später

subservient /səb'sɜːvɪənt/ a, **-ly** adv untergeordnet; (servile) unterwürfig

subside /səb'saɪd/ vi sinken; ⟨ground:⟩ sich senken; ⟨storm:⟩ nachlassen

subsidiary /səb'sɪdɪərɪ/ a untergeordnet □ n Tochtergesellschaft f

subsid|ize /'sʌbsɪdaɪz/ vt subventionieren. **~y** n Subvention f

subsist /səb'sɪst/ vi leben (on von). **~ence** n Existenz f

substance /'sʌbstəns/ n Substanz f

sub'standard a unzulänglich; ⟨goods⟩ minderwertig

substantial /səb'stænʃl/ a solide; ⟨meal⟩ reichhaltig; (considerable) beträchtlich. **~ly** adv solide; (essentially) im wesentlichen

substantiate /səb'stænʃɪeɪt/ vt erhärten

substitut|e /'sʌbstɪtjuːt/ n Ersatz m; (Sport) Ersatzspieler(in) m(f) □ vt **~e A for B** B durch A ersetzen □ vi **~e for s.o.** jdn vertreten. **~ion** /-'tjuːʃn/ n Ersetzung f

subterfuge /'sʌbtəfjuːdʒ/ n List f

subterranean /sʌbtə'reɪnɪən/ a unterirdisch

'subtitle n Untertitel m

subtle /'sʌtl/ a (-r, -st), -tly adv fein; (fig) subtil

subtract /səb'trækt/ vt abziehen, subtrahieren. ~ion /-ækʃn/ n Subtraktion f

suburb /'sʌbɜ:b/ n Vorort m; in the ~s am Stadtrand. ~an /sə-'bɜ:bən/ a Vorort-; (pej) spießig. ~ia /sə'bɜ:brə/ n die Vororte pl

subversive /səb'vɜ:sɪv/ a subversiv

'**subway** n Unterführung f; (Amer: railway) U-Bahn f

succeed /sək'si:d/ vi Erfolg haben; (plan:) gelingen; (follow) nachfolgen (+dat); I ~ed es ist mir gelungen; he ~ed in escaping es gelang ihm zu entkommen □vt folgen (+dat). ~ing a folgend

success /sək'ses/ n Erfolg m. ~ful a, -ly adv erfolgreich

succession /sək'seʃn/ n Folge f; (series) Serie f; (to title, office) Nachfolge f; (to throne) Thronfolge f; in ~ hintereinander

successive /sək'sesɪv/ a aufeinanderfolgend. ~ly adv hintereinander

successor /sək'sesə(r)/ n Nachfolger(in) m(f)

succinct /sək'sɪŋkt/ a, -ly adv prägnant

succulent /'sʌkjʊlənt/ a saftig

succumb /sə'kʌm/ vi erliegen (to dat)

such /sʌtʃ/ a solche(r,s); ~ a book ein solches od solch ein Buch; ~ a thing so etwas; ~ a long time so lange; there is no ~ thing das gibt es gar nicht; there is no ~ person eine solche Person gibt es nicht □pron as ~ als solche(r,s); (strictly speaking) an sich; ~ as wie [zum Beispiel]; and ~ und dergleichen. ~like pron (fam) dergleichen

suck /sʌk/ vt/i saugen; lutschen (sweet). ~ up vt aufsaugen □vi ~ up to s.o. (fam) sich bei jdm einschmeicheln

sucker /'sʌkə(r)/ n (Bot) Ausläufer m; (fam: person) Dumme(r) m/f

suckle /'sʌkl/ vt säugen

suction /'sʌkʃn/ n Saugwirkung f

sudden /'sʌdn/ a, -ly adv plötzlich; (abrupt) jäh □n all of a ~ auf einmal

sue /su:/ vt (pres p suing) verklagen (for auf +acc) □vi klagen

suede /sweɪd/ n Wildleder nt

suet /'su:ɪt/ n [Nieren]talg m

suffer /'sʌfə(r)/ vi leiden (from an + dat) □vt erleiden; (tolerate) dulden. ~ance /-əns/ n on ~ance bloß geduldet. ~ing n Leiden nt

suffice /sə'faɪs/ vi genügen

sufficient /sə'fɪʃnt/ a, -ly adv genug, genügend; be ~ genügen

suffix /'sʌfɪks/ n Nachsilbe f

suffocate /'sʌfəkeɪt/ vt/i ersticken. ~ion /-'keɪʃn/ n Ersticken nt

sugar /'ʃʊɡə(r)/ n Zucker m □vt zuckern; (fig) versüßen. ~basin, ~bowl n Zuckerschale f. ~y a süß; (fig) süßlich

suggest /sə'dʒest/ vt vorschlagen; (indicate, insinuate) andeuten. ~ion /-estʃən/ n Vorschlag m; Andeutung f; (trace) Spur f. ~ive /-ɪv/ a, -ly adv anzüglich; be ~ive of schließen lassen auf (+acc)

suicidal /su:ɪ'saɪdl/ a selbstmörderisch

suicide /'su:ɪsaɪd/ n Selbstmord m; (person) Selbstmörder(in) m(f); commit ~ Selbstmord begehen

suit /su:t/ n Anzug m; (woman's) Kostüm nt; (Cards) Farbe f; (Jur) Prozeß m; follow ~ (fig) das Gleiche tun □vt (adapt) anpassen (to dat); (be convenient for) passen (+dat); (go with) passen zu; (clothing:) stehen (s.o. jdm); be ~ed for geeignet sein für; ~ yourself! wie du willst!

suit|able /'su:təbl/ a geeignet; (convenient) passend; (appropriate) angemessen; (for weather, activity) zweckmäßig. ~ably adv angemessen; zweckmäßig

'**suitcase** n Koffer m

suite /swi:t/ n Suite f; (of furniture) Garnitur f

sulk /sʌlk/ vi schmollen. ~y a schmollend

sullen /'sʌlən/ a, -ly adv mürrisch

sulphur /'sʌlfə(r)/ n Schwefel m. ~ic /-'fju:rɪk/ a ~ic acid Schwefelsäure f

sultana /sʌl'tɑ:nə/ n Sultanine f

sultry /'sʌltrɪ/ a (-ier, -iest) ⟨weather⟩ schwül

sum /sʌm/ n Summe f; (Sch) Rechenaufgabe f □ vt/i (pt/pp summed) ~ up zusammenfassen; ⟨assess⟩ einschätzen

summarize /'sʌmərazz/ vt zusammenfassen. ~y n Zusammenfassung f □ a, -ily adv summarisch; ⟨dismissal⟩ fristlos

summer /'sʌmə(r)/ n Sommer m. ~house n [Garten]laube f. ~time n Sommer m

summery /'sʌmərɪ/ a sommerlich

summit /'sʌmɪt/ n Gipfel m. ~ conference n Gipfelkonferenz f

summon /'sʌmən/ vt rufen; holen ⟨help⟩; (Jur) vorladen. ~ up vt aufbringen

summons /'sʌmənz/ n (Jur) Vorladung f □ vt vorladen

sump /sʌmp/ n (Auto) Ölwanne f

sumptuous /'sʌmptjʊəs/ a, -ly adv prunkvoll; ⟨meal⟩ üppig

sun /sʌn/ n Sonne f □ vt (pt/pp sunned) ~ oneself sich sonnen

sun: ~bathe vi sich sonnen. ~bed n Sonnenbank f. ~burn n Sonnenbrand m

sundae /'sʌndeɪ/ n Eisbecher m

Sunday /'sʌndeɪ/ n Sonntag m

sundial /'sʌndaɪəl/ n Sonnenuhr f

sundry /'sʌndrɪ/ a verschiedene pl; all and ~ alle pl

sunflower n Sonnenblume f

sung /sʌŋ/ see sing

'sun-glasses npl Sonnenbrille f

sunk /sʌŋk/ see sink

sunken /'sʌŋkn/ a gesunken; ⟨eyes⟩ eingefallen

sunny /'sʌnɪ/ a (-ier, -iest) sonnig

sun: ~rise n Sonnenaufgang m. ~-roof n (Auto) Schiebedach nt.

~set n Sonnenuntergang m. ~shade n Sonnenschirm m. ~shine n Sonnenschein m. ~stroke n Sonnenstich m. ~tan n [Sonnen]bräune f. ~tanned a braun[gebrannt]. ~tan oil n Sonnenöl nt

super /'su:pə(r)/ a (fam) prima, toll

superb /su'pɜ:b/ a erstklassig

supercilious /su:pə'sɪlɪəs/ a überlegen

superficial /su:pə'fɪʃl/ a, -ly adv oberflächlich

superfluous /su'pɜ:flʊəs/ a überflüssig

super'human a übermenschlich

superintendent /su:pərɪn'ten-dənt/ n (of police) Kommissar m

superior /su:'pɪərɪə(r)/ a überlegen; (in rank) höher □ n Vorgesetzte(r) m/f. ~ity /-'ɒrətɪ/ n Überlegenheit f

superlative /su:'pɜ:lətɪv/ a untrefflich □ n Superlativ m

'superman n Übermensch m

'supermarket n Supermarkt m

super'natural a übernatürlich

'superpower n Supermacht f

super'sonic a Überschall-

superstition /su:pə'stɪʃn/ n Aberglaube m. ~ous /-'stɪʃəs/ a, -ly adv abergläubisch

supervise /'su:pəvaɪz/ vt beaufsichtigen; überwachen ⟨work⟩. ~ion /-'vɪʒn/ n Aufsicht f; Überwachung f. ~or n Aufseher(in) m(f)

supper /'sʌpə(r)/ n Abendessen nt

supple /'sʌpl/ a geschmeidig

supplement /'sʌplɪmənt/ n Ergänzung f; (addition) Zusatz m; (to fare) Zuschlag m; (book) Ergänzungsband m; (to newspaper) Beilage f □ vt ergänzen. ~ary /-'men-tərɪ/ a zusätzlich

supplier /sə'plaɪə(r)/ n Lieferant m

supply /sə'plaɪ/ n Vorrat m; supplies pl (Mil) Nachschub m □ vt (pt/pp -ied) liefern; ~ s.o. with sth jdn mit etw versorgen

support /sə'pɔːt/ *n* Stütze *f*; (*fig*) Unterstützung *f* □ *vt* stützen; (*bear weight of*) tragen; (*keep* *alive*) ernähren; (*give money to*) unterstützen; (*speak in favour of*) befürworten; (*Sport*) Fan sein von. ~**er** *n* Anhänger(in) *m(f)*; (*Sport*) Fan *m*. ~**ive** /-ɪv/ *a* be ~**ive [to s.o.]** [jdm] eine große Stütze sein

suppose /sə'pəʊz/ *vt* annehmen; (*presume*) vermuten; (*imagine*) sich (*dat*) vorstellen; be ~**d to** do sth etw tun sollen; not be ~**d to** (*fam*) nicht dürfen; I ~ so vermutlich. ~**dly** /-ɪdlɪ/ *adv* angeblich

supposition /sʌpə'zɪʃn/ *n* Vermutung *f*

suppository /sʌ'pɒzɪtrɪ/ *n* Zäpfchen *nt*

suppress /sə'pres/ *vt* unterdrücken. ~**ion** /-eʃn/ *n* Unterdrückung *f*

supremacy /su:'preməsɪ/ *n* Vorherrschaft *f*

supreme /su:'pri:m/ *a* höchste(r,s); (*court*) oberste(r,s)

surcharge /'sɜːtʃɑːdʒ/ *n* Zuschlag *m*

sure /ʃʊə(r)/ *a* (-**r**, -**st**) sicher; **make** ~ sich vergewissern (**of** *gen*); (*check*) nachprüfen; **be** ~ **to** do it sieh zu, daß du es tust □ *adv* (*Amer, fam*) klar; ~ **enough** tatsächlich. ~**ly** *adv* sicher; (*for* *emphasis*) doch; (*Amer: gladly*) gern

surety /'ʃʊərətɪ/ *n* Bürgschaft *f*; **stand** ~ **for** bürgen für

surf /sɜːf/ *n* Brandung *f*

surface /'sɜːfɪs/ *n* Oberfläche *f* □ *vi* (*emerge*) auftauchen. ~ **mail** *n* **by** ~ **mail** auf dem Land-/Seeweg

'surfboard *n* Surfbrett *nt*

surfeit /'sɜːfɪt/ *n* Übermaß *nt*

surfing /'sɜːfɪŋ/ *n* Surfen *nt*

surge /sɜːdʒ/ *n* (*of sea*) Branden *nt*; (*fig*) Welle *f* □ *vi* branden; ~ **forward** nach vorn drängen

surgeon /'sɜːdʒən/ *n* Chirurg(in) *m(f)*

surgery /'sɜːdʒərɪ/ *n* Chirurgie *f*; (*place*) Praxis *f*; (*room*) Sprechzimmer *nt*; (*hours*) Sprechstunde *f*; **have** ~ operiert werden

surgical /'sɜːdʒɪkl/ *a*, **-ly** *adv* chirurgisch

surly /'sɜːlɪ/ *a* (-**ier**, -**iest**) mürrisch

surmise /sə'maɪz/ *vt* mutmaßen

surmount /sə'maʊnt/ *vt* überwinden

surname /'sɜːneɪm/ *n* Nachname *m*

surpass /sə'pɑːs/ *vt* übertreffen

surplus /'sɜːpləs/ *a* überschüssig; **be** ~ **to requirements** nicht benötigt werden □ *n* Überschuß *m* (**of** an + *dat*)

surprise /sə'praɪz/ *n* Überraschung *f* □ *vt* überraschen; **be** ~**ed** sich wundern (**at** über + *acc*). ~**ing** *a*, **-ly** *adv* überraschend

surrender /sə'rendə(r)/ *n* Kapitulation *f* □ *vi* sich ergeben; (*Mil*) kapitulieren □ *vt* aufgeben

surreptitious /sʌrəp'tɪʃəs/ *a*, **-ly** *adv* heimlich, verstohlen

surrogate /'sʌrəgət/ *n* Ersatz *m*. ~ **'mother** *n* Leihmutter *f*

surround /sə'raʊnd/ *vt* umgeben; (*encircle*) umzingeln; ~**ed by** umgeben von. ~**ing** *a* umliegend. ~**ings** *npl* Umgebung *f*

surveillance /sə'veɪləns/ *n* Überwachung *f*; **be under** ~ überwacht werden

survey[1] /'sɜːveɪ/ *n* Überblick *m*; (*poll*) Umfrage *f*; (*investigation*) Untersuchung *f*; (*of land*) Vermessung *f*; (*of house*) Gutachten *nt*

survey[2] /sə'veɪ/ *vt* betrachten; vermessen ⟨*land*⟩; begutachten ⟨*building*⟩. ~**or** *n* Landvermesser *m*; Gutachter *m*

survival /sə'vaɪvl/ *n* Überleben *nt*; (*of tradition*) Fortbestand *m*

surviv|e /sə'vaɪv/ vt überleben □vi überleben; (tradition:) erhalten bleiben. **~or** n Überlebende(r) m/f; **be a ~or** (fam) nicht unterzukriegen sein

susceptible /sə'septəbl/ a empfänglich; (Med) anfällig (**to** für)

suspect¹ /sə'spekt/ vt verdächtigen; (assume) vermuten; **he ~s nothing** er ahnt nichts

suspect² /'sʌspekt/ a verdächtig □n Verdächtige(r) m/f

suspend /sə'spend/ vt aufhängen; (stop) [vorläufig] einstellen; (from duty) vorläufig beurlauben. **~er belt** n Strumpfbandgürtel m. **~ers** npl Strumpfbänder pl; (Amer: braces) Hosenträger pl

suspense /sə'spens/ n Spannung f

suspension /sə'spenʃn/ n (Auto) Federung f. **~ bridge** n Hängebrücke f

suspici|on /sə'spɪʃn/ n Verdacht m; (mistrust) Mißtrauen nt; (trace) Spur f. **~ous** /-ɪʃəs/ a, **-ly** adv mißtrauisch; (arousing suspicion) verdächtig

sustain /sə'steɪn/ vt tragen; (fig) aufrechterhalten; erhalten (life); erleiden (injury)

sustenance /'sʌstɪnəns/ n Nahrung f

swab /swɒb/ n (Med) Tupfer m; (specimen) Abstrich m

swagger /'swægə(r)/ vi stolzieren

swallow¹ /'swɒləʊ/ vt/i schlucken. **~ up** vt verschlucken; verschlingen (resources)

swallow² n (bird) Schwalbe f

swam /swæm/ see **swim**

swamp /swɒmp/ n Sumpf m □vt überschwemmen. **~y** a sumpfig

swan /swɒn/ n Schwan m

swank /swæŋk/ vi (fam) angeben

swap /swɒp/ n (fam) Tausch m □vt/i (pt/pp swapped) (fam) tauschen (for gegen)

swarm /swɔːm/ n Schwarm m □vi schwärmen; **be ~ing with** wimmeln von

swarthy /'swɔːðɪ/ a (-ier, -iest) dunkel

swastika /'swɒstɪkə/ n Hakenkreuz nt

swat /swɒt/ vt (pt/pp swatted) totschlagen

sway /sweɪ/ n (fig) Herrschaft f □vi schwanken; (gently:) sich wiegen □vt wiegen; (influence) beeinflussen

swear /sweə(r)/ v (pt swore, pp sworn) □vt schwören □vi schwören (**by** auf + acc); (curse) fluchen. **~-word** n Kraftausdruck m

sweat /swet/ n Schweiß m □vi schwitzen

sweater /'swetə(r)/ n Pullover m

sweaty /'swetɪ/ a verschwitzt

swede /swiːd/ n Kohlrübe f

Swede n Schwede m /-din f. **~en** n Schweden nt. **~ish** a schwedisch

sweep /swiːp/ n Schornsteinfeger m; (curve) Bogen m; (movement) ausholende Bewegung f; **make a clean ~** (fig) gründlich aufräumen □v (pt/pp swept) □vt fegen, kehren □vi (go swiftly) rauschen; (wind:) fegen. **~ up** vt zusammenfegen/-kehren

sweeping /'swiːpɪŋ/ a ausholend; (statement) pauschal; (changes) weitreichend

sweet /swiːt/ a (-er, -est) süß; **have a ~ tooth** gern Süßes mögen □n Bonbon m & nt; (dessert) Nachtisch m. **~ corn** n [Zucker]mais m

sweeten /'swiːtn/ vt süßen. **~er** n Süßstoff m; (fam: bribe) Schmiergeld nt

sweet: ~heart n Schatz m. **~-shop** n Süßwarenladen m. **~ness** n Süße f. **~'pea** n Wicke f

swell /swel/ n Dünung f □v (pt swelled, pp swollen or swelled) □vi [an]schwellen; (sails:) sich blähen; (wood:) aufquellen □vt anschwellen lassen; (in-

crease) vergrößern. ~**ing** n Schwellung f

swelter /'swelta(r)/ vi schwitzen

swept /swept/ see **sweep**

swerve /swɜ:v/ vi einen Bogen machen

swift /swift/ a (-er, -est), -ly adv schnell

swig /swig/ n (fam) Schluck m, Zug m □vt (pt/pp swigged) (fam) [herunter]kippen

swill /swil/ n (for pigs) Schweinefutter nt □vt ~ [out] [aus]spülen

swim /swim/ n have a ~ schwimmen □vi (pt swam, pp swum) schwimmen; my head is ~ming mir dreht sich der Kopf. ~mer n Schwimmer(in) m(f)

swimming /'swimiŋ/ n Schwimmen nt. ~-**baths** npl Schwimmbad nt. ~-**pool** n Schwimmbecken nt; (private) Swimmingpool m

'**swim-suit** n Badeanzug m

swindle /'swindl/ n Schwindel m, Betrug m □vt betrügen. ~**r** n Schwindler m

swine /swain/ n Schwein nt

swing /swiŋ/ n Schwung m; (shift) Schwenk m; (seat) Schaukel f; in full ~ in vollem Gange □v (pt/pp swung) □vi schwingen; (on swing) schaukeln; (sway) schwanken; (dangle) baumeln; (turn) schwenken □vt schwingen; (influence) beeinflussen. ~-'**door** n Schwingtür f

swingeing /'swindʒiŋ/ a hart; (fig) drastisch

swipe /swaip/ n (fam) Schlag m □vt (fam) knallen; (steal) klauen

swirl /swɜ:l/ n Wirbel m □vt/i wirbeln

swish /swiʃ/ a (fam) schick □vi zischen

Swiss /swis/ a Schweizer, schweizerisch □n Schweizer(in) m(f); the ~ pl die Schweizer. ~ '**roll** n Biskuitrolle f

switch /switʃ/ n Schalter m; (change) Wechsel m; (Amer, Rail)

Weiche f □vt wechseln; (exchange) tauschen □vi wechseln; ~ **to** umstellen auf (+ acc.). ~ **off** vt ausschalten; abschalten (engine). ~ **on** vt einschalten, anschalten

switch: ~**back** n Achterbahn f. ~**board** n [Telefon]zentrale f

Switzerland /'switsələnd/ n die Schweiz

swivel /'swivl/ v (pt/pp swivelled) □vt drehen □vi sich drehen

swollen /'swəulən/ see **swell** □a geschwollen. ~-'**headed** a eingebildet

swoop /swu:p/ n Sturzflug m; (by police) Razzia f □vi ~ **down** herabstoßen

sword /sɔ:d/ n Schwert nt

swore /swɔ:(r)/ see **swear**

sworn /swɔ:n/ see **swear**

swot /swɒt/ n (fam) Streber m □vt/i (pt/pp swotted) (fam) büffeln

swum /swʌm/ see **swim**

swung /swʌŋ/ see **swing**

syllable /'siləbl/ n Silbe f

syllabus /'siləbəs/ n Lehrplan m; (for exam) Studienplan m

symbol /'simbl/ n Symbol nt (of für). ~**ic** /-'bɒlik/ a, -**ally** adv symbolisch. ~**ism** /-izm/ n Symbolik f. ~**ize** vt symbolisieren

symmetr|ical /si'metrikl/ a, -**ly** adv symmetrisch. ~**y** /'simətri/ n Symmetrie f

sympathetic /simpə'θetik/ a, -**ally** adv mitfühlend; (likeable) sympathisch

sympathize /'simpəθaiz/ vi mitfühlen. ~**r** n (Pol) Sympathisant m

sympathy /'simpəθi/ n Mitgefühl nt; (condolences) Beileid nt

symphony /'simfəni/ n Sinfonie f

symptom /'simptəm/ n Symptom nt. ~**atic** /-'mætik/ a symptomatisch (of für)

synagogue /'sinəgɒg/ n Synagoge f

synchronize /'sɪŋkrənaɪz/ *vt* synchronisieren

syndicate /'sɪndɪkət/ *n* Syndikat *nt*

syndrome /'sɪndrəʊm/ *n* Syndrom *nt*

synonym /'sɪnənɪm/ *n* Synonym *nt*. **~ous** /-'nɒnɪməs/ *a*, **-ly** *adv* synonym

synopsis /sɪ'nɒpsɪs/ *n* (*pl* **-opses** /-siːz/) Zusammenfassung *f*; (*of opera, ballet*) Inhaltsangabe *f*

syntax /'sɪntæks/ *n* Syntax *f*

synthesis /'sɪnθəsɪs/ *n* (*pl* **-ses** /-siːz/) Synthese *f*

synthetic /sɪn'θetɪk/ *a* synthetisch □ *n* Kunststoff *m*

Syria /'sɪrɪə/ *n* Syrien *nt*

syringe /sɪ'rɪndʒ/ *n* Spritze *f* □ *vt* spritzen; ausspritzen ⟨*ears*⟩

syrup /'sɪrəp/ *n* Sirup *m*

system /'sɪstəm/ *n* System *nt*. **~atic** /-'mætɪk/ *a*, **-ally** *adv* systematisch

T

tab /tæb/ *n* (*projecting*) Zunge *f*; (*with name*) Namensschild *nt*; (*loop*) Aufhänger *m*; **keep ~s on** (*fam*) [genau] beobachten; **pick up the ~** (*fam*) bezahlen

tabby /'tæbɪ/ *n* getigerte Katze *f*

table /'teɪbl/ *n* Tisch *m*; (*list*) Tabelle *f*; **at [the]** ~ bei Tisch □ *vt* einbringen. **~-cloth** *n* Tischdecke *f*, Tischtuch *nt*. **~ spoon** *n* Servierlöffel *m*

tablet /'tæblɪt/ *n* Tablette *f*; (*of soap*) Stück *nt*; (*slab*) Tafel *f*

'table tennis *n* Tischtennis *nt*

tabloid /'tæblɔɪd/ *n* kleinformatige Zeitung *f*; (*pej*) Boulevardzeitung *f*

taboo /tə'buː/ *a* tabu □ *n* Tabu *nt*

tacit /'tæsɪt/ *a*, **-ly** *adv* stillschweigend

taciturn /'tæsɪtɜːn/ *a* wortkarg

tack /tæk/ *n* (*nail*) Stift *m*; (*stitch*) Heftstich *m*; (*Naut & fig*) Kurs *m* □ *vt* festnageln; (*sew*) heften □ *vi* (*Naut*) kreuzen

tackle /'tækl/ *n* Ausrüstung *f* □ *vt* angehen

tacky /'tækɪ/ *a* klebrig

tact /tækt/ *n* Takt *m*, Taktgefühl *nt*. **~ful** *a*, **-ly** *adv* taktvoll

tactic|al /'tæktɪkl/ *a*, **-ly** *adv* taktisch. **~s** *npl* Taktik *f*

tactless /'tæktlɪs/ *a*, **-ly** *adv* taktlos. **~ness** *n* Taktlosigkeit *f*

tadpole /'tædpəʊl/ *n* Kaulquappe *f*

tag¹ /tæg/ *n* (*label*) Schild *nt* □ *vt* (*pt/pp* **tagged**) **~ along** mitkommen

tag² *n* (*game*) Fangen *nt*

tail /teɪl/ *n* Schwanz *m*; **~s** *pl* (*tailcoat*) Frack *m*; **heads or ~s?** Kopf oder Zahl? □ *vt* (*fam: follow*) beschatten □ *vi* **~ off** zurückgehen

tail: **~-back** *n* Rückstau *m*. **~-coat** *n* Frack *m*. **~-end** *n* Ende *nt*. **~-light** *n* Rücklicht *nt*

tailor /'teɪlə(r)/ *n* Schneider *m*. **~-made** *a* maßgeschneidert

'tail wind *n* Rückenwind *m*

taint /teɪnt/ *vt* verderben

take /teɪk/ *v* (*pt* **took**, *pp* **taken**) □ *vt* nehmen; (*with one*) mitnehmen; (*take to a place*) bringen; (*steal*) stehlen; (*win*) gewinnen; (*capture*) einnehmen; (*require*) brauchen; (*last*) dauern; (*teach*) geben; machen ⟨*exam, subject, holiday, photograph*⟩; messen ⟨*pulse, temperature*⟩; **~ s.o. home** jdn nach Hause bringen; **~ sth to the cleaner's** etw in die Reinigung bringen; **~ s.o. prisoner** jdn gefangennehmen; **be ~ n ill** krank werden; **~ sth calmly** etw gelassen aufnehmen □ *vi* ⟨*plant:*⟩ angehen; **~ after** s.o. jdm nachschlagen; (*in looks*) jdm ähnlich sehen; **~ to** ⟨*like*⟩ mögen; (*as a habit*) sich ⟨*dat*⟩ angewöhnen. **~ away** *vt* wegbringen; (*remove*) wegnehmen; (*subtract*) abziehen; **'to ~ away'**

'zum Mitnehmen'. ~ **back** vt zurücknehmen; (*return*) zurückbringen. ~ **down** vt herunternehmen; (*remove*) abnehmen; (*write down*) aufschreiben. ~ **in** vt hineinbringen; (*bring indoors*) hereinholen; (*to one's home*) aufnehmen; (*understand*) begreifen; (*deceive*) hereinlegen; (*make smaller*) enger machen. ~ **off** vt abnehmen; (*coat*), sich (*dat*) ausziehen (*clothes*); (*deduct*) abziehen; (*mimic*) nachmachen; ~ **time off** sich (*dat*) frei nehmen; ~ **oneself off** [fort]gehen □vi (*Aviat*) starten. ~ **on** vt annehmen; (*undertake*) übernehmen; (*engage*) einstellen; (*as opponent*) antreten gegen. ~ **out** vt hinausbringen; (*for pleasure*) ausgehen mit; ausführen (*dog*); (*remove*) herausnehmen; (*withdraw money*); (*from library*) ausleihen; ~ **out a subscription to** sth etw abonnieren; ~ **it out on** s.o. (*fam*) seinen Ärger an jdm auslassen. ~ **over** vt hinüberbringen; übernehmen (*firm, control*) □vi ~ **over from** s.o. jdn ablösen. ~ **up** vt hinaufbringen; annehmen (*offer*); ergreifen (*profession*); sich (*dat*) zulegen (*hobby*); in Anspruch nehmen (*time*); einnehmen (*space*); aufreißen (*floorboards*); ~ **sth up with** s.o. mit jdm über etw (*acc*) sprechen □vi ~ **up with** s.o. sich mit jdm einlassen

take: ~**-away** n Essen nt zum Mitnehmen; (*restaurant*) Restaurant nt mit Straßenverkauf. ~**-off** n (*Aviat*) Start m, Abflug m. ~**-over** n Übernahme f

takings /ˈteɪkɪŋz/ npl Einnahmen pl

talcum /ˈtælkəm/ n ~ [**powder**] Körperpuder m

tale /teɪl/ n Geschichte f

talent /ˈtælənt/ n Talent nt. ~**ed** a talentiert

talk /tɔːk/ n Gespräch nt; (*lecture*) Vortrag m; **make small** ~ Konversation machen □vi reden, sprechen (**to/with** mit) □vt reden; ~ s.o. **into** sth jdn zu etw überreden. ~ **over** vt besprechen

talkative /ˈtɔːkətɪv/ a gesprächig

'talking-to n Standpauke f

tall /tɔːl/ a (**-er, -est**) groß; (*building, tree*) hoch; **that's a** ~ **order** das ist ziemlich viel verlangt. ~**boy** n hohe Kommode f. ~ **'story** n übertriebene Geschichte f

tally /ˈtælɪ/ n **keep a** ~ **of** Buch führen über (+ acc) □vi übereinstimmen

talon /ˈtælən/ n Klaue f

tambourine /tæmbəˈriːn/ n Tamburin nt

tame /teɪm/ a (**-r, -st**), **-ly** adv zahm; (*dull*) lahm (*fam*) □vt zähmen. ~**r** n Dompteur m

tamper /ˈtæmpə(r)/ vi ~ **with** sich (*dat*) zu schaffen machen an (+ dat)

tampon /ˈtæmpɒn/ n Tampon m

tan /tæn/ a gelbbraun □n Gelbbraun nt; (*from sun*) Bräune f □v (pt/pp **tanned**) □vt gerben (*hide*) □vi braun werden

tang /tæŋ/ n herber Geschmack m; (*smell*) herber Geruch m

tangent /ˈtændʒənt/ n Tangente f; **go off at a** ~ (*fam*) vom Thema abschweifen

tangible /ˈtændʒɪbl/ a greifbar

tangle /ˈtæŋgl/ n Gewirr nt; (*in hair*) Verfilzung f □vt ~ [**up**] verheddern □vi sich verheddern

tango /ˈtæŋgəʊ/ n Tango m

tank /tæŋk/ n Tank m; (*Mil*) Panzer m

tankard /ˈtæŋkəd/ n Krug m

tanker /ˈtæŋkə(r)/ n Tanker m; (*lorry*) Tank[last]wagen m

tantaliz|e /ˈtæntəlaɪz/ vt quälen. ~**ing** a verlockend

tantamount /ˈtæntəmaʊnt/ a **be** ~ **to** gleichbedeutend sein mit

tantrum /'tæntrəm/ n Wutanfall m

tap /tæp/ n Hahn m; (knock) Klopfen nt; **on** ~ zur Verfügung ○ (pt/pp **tapped**) □vt klopfen an (+ acc); anzapfen ⟨barrel, tree⟩; erschließen ⟨resources⟩; abhören ⟨telephone⟩ □vi klopfen. **~dance** n Step[tanz] m □vi Step tanzen, steppen

tape /teip/ n Band nt; (adhesive) Klebstreifen m; (for recording) Tonband nt □vt mit Klebstreifen zukleben; (record) auf Band aufnehmen

'tape-measure n Bandmaß nt

taper /'teipə(r)/ n dünne Wachskerze f □vi sich verjüngen

'tape recorder n Tonbandgerät nt

tapestry /'tæpistri/ n Gobelinstickerei f

'tapeworm n Bandwurm m

'tap water n Leitungswasser nt

tar /ta:(r)/ n Teer m □vt (pt/pp **tarred**) teeren

tardy /'ta:di/ a (-ier, -iest) langsam; (late) spät

target /'ta:git/ n Ziel nt; (board) [Ziel]scheibe f

tariff /'tærif/ n Tarif m; (duty) Zoll m

tarnish /'ta:niʃ/ vi anlaufen

tarpaulin /ta:'pɔ:lin/ n Plane f

tarragon /'tærəgən/ n Estragon m

tart¹ /ta:t/ a (-er, -est) sauer; (fig) scharf

tart² n ≈ Obstkuchen m; (individual) Törtchen nt; (sl: prostitute) Nutte f □vt ~ **oneself up** (fam) sich auftakeln

tartan /'ta:tn/ n Schottenmuster nt; (cloth) Schottenstoff □attrib schottisch kariert

tartar /'ta:tə(r)/ n (on teeth) Zahnstein m

tartar 'sauce /ta:tə-/ n ≈ Remouladensoße f

task /ta:sk/ n Aufgabe f; **take s.o. to** ~ jdm Vorhaltungen machen. ~ **force** n Sonderkommando nt

tassel /'tæsl/ n Quaste f

taste /teist/ n Geschmack m; (sample) Kostprobe f □vt kosten, probieren; schmecken ⟨flavour⟩ □vi schmecken (**of** nach). ~**ful** a, **-ly** adv geschmackvoll. ~**less** a, **-ly** adv geschmacklos

tasty /'teisti/ a (-ier, -iest) lecker, schmackhaft

tat /tæt/ see **tit²**

tatter|ed /'tætəd/ a zerlumpt; ⟨pages⟩ zerfleddert. ~**s** npl **in** ~**s** in Fetzen

tattoo¹ /tə'tu:/ n Tätowierung f □vt tätowieren

tattoo² n (Mil) Zapfenstreich m

tatty /'tæti/ a (-ier, -iest) schäbig; ⟨book⟩ zerfleddert

taught /tɔ:t/ see **teach**

taunt /tɔ:nt/ n höhnische Bemerkung f □vt verhöhnen

Taurus /'tɔ:rəs/ n (Astr) Stier m

taut /tɔ:t/ a straff

tavern /'tævən/ n (liter) Schenke f

tawdry /'tɔ:dri/ a (-ier, -iest) billig und geschmacklos

tawny /'tɔ:ni/ a gelbbraun

tax /tæks/ n Steuer f □vt besteuern; (fig) strapazieren; ~ **with** beschuldigen (+ gen). ~**able** /-əbl/ a steuerpflichtig. ~**ation** /-'seiʃn/ n Besteuerung f. ~**-free** a steuerfrei

taxi /'tæksi/ n Taxi nt □vi (pt/pp **taxied**, pres p **taxiing**) ⟨aircraft:⟩ rollen. ~ **driver** n Taxifahrer m. ~ **rank** n Taxistand m

taxpayer n Steuerzahler m

tea /ti:/ n Tee m. ~**-bag** n Teebeutel m. ~**-break** n Teepause f

teach /ti:tʃ/ vt/i (pt/pp **taught**) unterrichten; ~ **s.o. sth** jdm etw beibringen. ~**er** n Lehrer(in) m(f)

tea: ~**cloth** n (for drying) Geschirrtuch nt. ~**cup** n Teetasse f

teak /ti:k/ n Teakholz nt

team /ti:m/ n Mannschaft f; (fig) Team nt; (of animals) Gespann nt □vi ~ **up** sich zusammentun

'team-work n Teamarbeit f

'teapot n Teekanne f

tear[1] /teə(r)/ n Riß m ▢ v (pt tore, pp torn) ▢ vt reißen; (damage) zerreißen; ~ **open** aufreißen; ~ **oneself away** sich losreißen ▢ vi [zer]reißen; (run) rasen. ~ **up** vt zerreißen

tear[2] /tɪə(r)/ n Träne f. ~**ful** a weinend. ~**fully** adv unter Tränen. ~**gas** n Tränengas nt

tease /tiːz/ vt necken

tea: ~**set** n Teeservice nt. ~ **shop** n Café nt. ~**spoon** n Teelöffel m. ~**strainer** n Teesieb nt

teat /tiːt/ n Zitze f; (on bottle) Sauger m

'tea-towel n Geschirrtuch nt

technical /'teknɪkl/ a technisch; (specialized) fachlich. ~**ity** /-'kælətɪ/ n technisches Detail nt; (Jur) Formfehler m. ~**ly** adv technisch; (strictly) streng genommen. ~ **term** n Fachausdruck m

technician /tek'nɪʃn/ n Techniker m

technique /tek'niːk/ n Technik f

technological /teknə'lɒdʒɪkl/ a, -**ly** adv technologisch

technology /tek'nɒlədʒɪ/ n Technologie f

teddy /'tedɪ/ n ~ [**bear**] Teddybär m

tedious /'tiːdɪəs/ a langweilig

tedium /'tiːdɪəm/ n Langeweile f

teem /tiːm/ vi (rain) in Strömen gießen; **be** ~**ing with** (full of) wimmeln von

teenage /'tiːneɪdʒ/ a Teenager-; ~ **boy/girl** Junge m/Mädchen nt im Teenageralter. ~**r** n Teenager m

teens /tiːnz/ npl **the** ~ die Teenagerjahre pl

teeny /'tiːnɪ/ a (-ier, -iest) winzig

teeter /'tiːtə(r)/ vi schwanken

teeth /tiːθ/ see **tooth**

teethe /tiːð/ vi zahnen. ~**ing troubles** npl (fig) Anfangsschwierigkeiten pl

teetotal /tiː'təʊtl/ a abstinent. ~**ler** n Abstinenzler m

telecommunications /telɪkə-mjuːnɪ'keɪʃnz/ npl Fernmeldewesen nt

telegram /'telɪɡræm/ n Telegramm nt

telegraph /'telɪɡrɑːf/ n Telegraf m. ~**ic** /-'ɡræfɪk/ a telegrafisch. ~ **pole** n Telegrafenmast m

telepathy /tɪ'lepəθɪ/ n Telepathie f; **by** ~ telepathisch

telephone /'telɪfəʊn/ n Telefon nt; **be on the** ~ Telefon haben; (be telephoning) telefonieren ▢ vt anrufen ▢ vi telefonieren

telephone: ~ **book** n Telefonbuch nt. ~ **booth** n, ~ **box** n Telefonzelle f. ~ **directory** n Telefonbuch nt. ~ **number** n Telefonnummer f

telephonist /tɪ'lefənɪst/ n Telefonist(in) m(f)

tele'photo /telɪ-/ a ~ **lens** Teleobjektiv nt

teleprinter /'telɪ-/ n Fernschreiber m

telescop|e /'telɪskəʊp/ n Teleskop nt, Fernrohr nt. ~**ic** /-'skɒpɪk/ a teleskopisch; (collapsible) ausziehbar

televise /'telɪvaɪz/ vt im Fernsehen übertragen

television /'telɪvɪʒn/ n Fernsehen nt; **watch** ~ fernsehen. ~ **set** n Fernsehapparat m, Fernseher m

telex /'teleks/ n Telex nt ▢ vt telexen

tell /tel/ vt/i (pt/pp told) sagen (s.o. jdm); (relate) erzählen; (know) wissen; (distinguish) erkennen; ~ **the time** die Uhr lesen; **time will** ~ das wird man erst sehen; **his age is beginning to** ~ sein Alter macht sich bemerkbar; **don't** ~ **me** sag es mir nicht; **you mustn't** ~ du darfst nichts sagen. ~ **off** vt ausschimpfen

teller /'telə(r)/ n (cashier) Kassierer(in) m(f)

telly /'telɪ/ n (fam) = **television**

temerity /tɪ'merətɪ/ n Kühnheit f

temp /temp/ n (fam) Aushilfs-
sekretärin f

temper /'tempə(r)/ n (disposition)
Naturell nt; (mood) Laune f; (anger) Wut f; **lose one's ~** wütend
werden □ vt (fig) mäßigen

temperament /'tempramant/ n
Temperament nt. **~al** /-'mentl/ a
temperamentvoll; (moody) launisch

temperance /'temparans/ n Mäßigung f; (abstinence) Abstinenz f

temperate /'temparat/ a gemäßigt

temperature /'tempratʃə(r)/ n
Temperatur f; **have or run a ~**
Fieber haben

tempest /'tempist/ n Sturm m.
~uous /-'pestjʊəs/ a stürmisch

template /'templit/ n Schablone f

temple[1] /'templ/ n Tempel m

temple[2] n (Anat) Schläfe f

tempo /'tempəʊ/ n Tempo m

temporary /'temprəri/ a, -ly adv
vorübergehend; (measure, building) provisorisch

tempt /tempt/ vt verleiten; (Relig)
versuchen; herausfordern (fate);
(entice) [ver]locken; **be ~ed** versucht sein (to zu); **I am ~ed by it**
es lockt mich. **~ation** /-'teɪʃn/ n
Versuchung f. **~ing** a verlockend

ten /ten/ a zehn

tenable /'tenəbl/ a (fig) haltbar

tenacious /tɪ'neɪʃəs/ a, -ly adv
hartnäckig. **~ty** /-'næsəti/ n Hartnäckigkeit f

tenant /'tenənt/ n Mieter(in) m(f);
(Comm) Pächter(in) m(f)

tend[1] /tend/ vt (look after) sich
kümmern um

tend[2] vi **~ to do sth** dazu neigen,
etw zu tun

tendency /'tendənsɪ/ n Tendenz f;
(inclination) Neigung f

tender[1] /'tendə(r)/ n (Comm) Angebot nt; **legal ~** gesetzliches
Zahlungsmittel nt □ vt anbieten;
einreichen (resignation)

tender[2] a zart; (loving) zärtlich;
(painful) empfindlich. **~ly** adv

zärtlich. **~ness** n Zartheit f;
Zärtlichkeit f

tendon /'tendən/ n Sehne f

tenement /'tenəmənt/ n Mietshaus nt

tenet /'tenɪt/ n Grundsatz m

tenner /'tenə(r)/ n (fam) Zehnpfundschein m

tennis /'tenɪs/ n Tennis nt.
~-court n Tennisplatz m

tenor /'tenə(r)/ n Tenor m

tense[1] /tens/ n (Gram) Zeit f

tense[2] a (-r, -st) gespannt □ vt
anspannen (muscle)

tension /'tenʃn/ n Spannung f

tent /tent/ n Zelt nt

tentacle /'tentəkl/ n Fangarm m

tentative /'tentətɪv/ a, -ly adv vorläufig; (hesitant) zaghaft

tenterhooks /'tentəhʊks/ npl **be
on ~** wie auf glühenden Kohlen
sitzen

tenth /tenθ/ a zehnte(r,s) □ n Zehntel
nt

tenuous /'tenjʊəs/ a (fig) schwach

tepid /'tepɪd/ a lauwarm

term /tɜːm/ n Zeitraum m; (Sch) ≈
Halbjahr nt; (Univ) ≈ Semester
nt; (expression) Ausdruck m; **~s**
pl (conditions) Bedingungen pl;
~ of office Amtszeit f; **in the
short/long ~** kurz-/langfristig;
be on good/bad ~s gut/nicht gut
miteinander auskommen; **come
to ~s with** sich abfinden mit

terminal /'tɜːmɪnl/ a End-; (Med)
unheilbar □ n (Aviat) Terminal
m; (of bus) Endstation f; (on battery) Pol m; (Computing) Terminal nt

terminate /'tɜːmɪneɪt/ vt beenden; lösen (contract); unterbrechen (pregnancy) □ vi enden.
~ion /-'neɪʃn/ n Beendigung f;
(Med) Schwangerschaftsabbruch m

terminology /tɜːmɪ'nɒlədʒɪ/ n
Terminologie f

terminus /'tɜːmɪnəs/ n (pl **-ni**
/-naɪ/) Endstation f

terrace /ˈterəs/ n Terrasse f; (houses) Häuserreihe f; the ~s (Sport) die [Steh]ränge pl. ~d house n Reihenhaus nt

terrain /teˈreɪn/ n Gelände nt

terrible /ˈterəbl/ a, -bly adv schrecklich

terrier /ˈterɪə(r)/ n Terrier m

terrific /təˈrɪfɪk/ a (fam) (excellent) sagenhaft; (huge) riesig

terri|fy /ˈterɪfaɪ/ vt (pt/pp -ied) angst machen (+ dat); be ~fied Angst haben. ~fying a furchterregend

territorial /terɪˈtɔːrɪəl/ a Territorial-

territory /ˈterɪtərɪ/ n Gebiet nt

terror /ˈterə(r)/ n (panische] Angst f; (Pol) Terror m. ~ism /-ɪzm/ n Terrorismus m. ~ist /-ɪst/ n Terrorist m. ~ize vt terrorisieren

terse /tɜːs/ a, -ly adv kurz, knapp

test /test/ n Test m; (Sch) Klassenarbeit f; **put to the** ~ auf die Probe stellen □ vt prüfen; (examine) untersuchen (for auf + acc)

testament /ˈtestəmənt/ n Testament nt; **Old/New T~** Altes/ Neues Testament nt

testicle /ˈtestɪkl/ n Hoden m

testi|fy /ˈtestɪfaɪ/ v (pt/pp -ied) □ vt beweisen; ~ that bezeugen, daß □ vi aussagen. ~to bezeugen

testimonial /testɪˈməʊnɪəl/ n Zeugnis nt

testimony /ˈtestɪmənɪ/ n Aussage f

'test-tube n Reagenzglas nt. ~ **baby** n (fam) Retortenbaby nt

testy /ˈtestɪ/ a gereizt

tetanus /ˈtetənəs/ n Tetanus m

tetchy /ˈtetʃɪ/ a gereizt

tether /ˈteðə(r)/ n **be at the end of one's** ~ am Ende seiner Kraft sein □ vt anbinden

text /tekst/ n Text m. ~**book** n Lehrbuch nt

textile /ˈtekstaɪl/ a Textil- □ n ~**s** pl Textilien pl

texture /ˈtekstʃə(r)/ n Beschaffenheit f; (Tex) Struktur f

Thai /taɪ/ a thailändisch. ~**land** n Thailand nt

Thames /temz/ n Themse f

than /ðən, betont ðæn/ conj als; **older** ~ **me** älter als ich

thank /θæŋk/ vt danken (+ dat); ~ **you [very much]** danke [schön]. ~**ful** a, -ly adv dankbar. ~**less** a undankbar

thanks /θæŋks/ npl Dank m; ~! (fam) danke! ~ **to** dank (+ dat or gen)

that /ðæt/ a & pron (pl those) der/die/das; (pl) die; ~ **one** der/die/das; **I'll take** ~ ich nehme den/die/das; **I don't like those** die mag ich nicht; ~ **is** das heißt; **is** ~ **you?** bist du es? **who is** ~? wer ist da? **with/after** ~ damit/ danach; **like** ~ so; **a man like** ~ so ein Mann; ~ **is why** deshalb; ~ **'s it!** genau! **all** ~ **I know** alles was ich weiß; **the day** ~ **I saw him** an dem Tag, als ich ihn sah □ adv so; ~ **good/hot** so gut/heiß □ conj daß

thatch /θætʃ/ n Strohdach nt. ~**ed** a strohgedeckt

thaw /θɔː/ n Tauwetter nt □ vt/i auftauen; **it's** ~**ing** es taut

the /ðə, vor einem Vokal ðiː/ def art der/die/das; (pl) die; **play** ~ **piano/violin** Klavier/Geige spielen □ adv ~ **more** ~ **better** je mehr, desto besser; **all** ~ **better** um so besser

theatre /ˈθɪətə(r)/ n Theater nt; (Med) Operationssaal m

theatrical /θɪˈætrɪkl/ a Theater-; (showy) theatralisch

theft /θeft/ n Diebstahl m

their /ðeə(r)/ a ihr

theirs /ðeəz/ poss pron ihre(r), ihrs; **a friend of** ~ ein Freund von ihnen; **those are** ~ die gehören ihnen

them /ðem/ pron (acc) sie; (dat) ihnen; **I know** ~ ich kenne sie; **give** ~ **the money** gib ihnen das Geld

theme /θiːm/ n Thema nt

them'selves *pron* selbst; (*refl*) sich; **by** ~ allein

then /ðen/ *adv* dann; (*at that time in past*) damals; **by** ~ bis dahin; **since** ~ seitdem; **before** ~ vorher; **from** ~ **on** von da an; **now and** ~ dann und wann; **there and** ~ auf der Stelle □ *a* damalig

theolog|ian /θɪəˈləʊdʒɪən/ *n* Theologe *m*. ~**y** /-ˈɒlədʒɪ/ *n* Theologie *f*

theorem /ˈθɪərəm/ *n* Lehrsatz *m*

theoretical /θɪəˈretɪk/ *a*, **-ly** *adv* theoretisch

theory /ˈθɪərɪ/ *n* Theorie *f*; **in** ~ theoretisch

therapeutic /θerəˈpjuːtɪk/ *a* therapeutisch

therap|ist /ˈθerəpɪst/ *n* Therapeut(in) *m(f)*. ~**y** *n* Therapie *f*

there /ðeə(r)/ *adv* da; (*with movement*) dahin, dorthin; **down/up** ~ da unten/oben; ~ **is/are** da ist/sind; (*in existence*) es gibt; ~ **he/she is** da ist er/sie; **send/take** ~ hinschicken/-bringen □ *int* **there, there!** nun, nun!

there: ~**abouts** *adv* da [in der Nähe]; **or** ~**abouts** (*roughly*) ungefähr. ~'**after** *adv* danach. ~**by** *adv* dadurch. ~**fore** /-fɔː(r)/ *adv* deshalb, also

thermal /ˈθɜːml/ *a* Thermal-; ~ **'underwear** *n* Thermowäsche *f*

thermometer /θəˈmɒmɪtə(r)/ *n* Thermometer *nt*

Thermos (P) /ˈθɜːməs/ *n* ~ **[flask]** Thermosflasche (P) *f*

thermostat /ˈθɜːməstæt/ *n* Thermostat *m*

these /ðiːz/ *see* **this**

thesis /ˈθiːsɪs/ *n* (*pl* **-ses** /-siːz/) Dissertation *f*; (*proposition*) These *f*

they /ðeɪ/ *pron* sie; ~ **say** (*generalizing*) man sagt

thick /θɪk/ *a* (**-er, -est**), **-ly** *adv* dick; (*dense*) dicht; (*liquid*) dickflüssig; (*fam: stupid*) dumm □ *adv* dick □ *n* **in the** ~ **of** mitten in (+ *dat*). ~**en** *vt* dicker machen; eindicken (*sauce*) □ *vi*

dicker werden; (*fog:*) dichter werden; (*plot:*) kompliziert werden. ~**ness** *n* Dicke *f*; Dichte *f*; Dickflüssigkeit *f*

thick: ~**set** *a* untersetzt. ~'**skinned** *a* (*fam*) dickfellig

thief /θiːf/ *n* (*pl* **thieves**) Dieb(in) *m(f)*

thieving /ˈθiːvɪŋ/ *a* diebisch □ *n* Stehlen *nt*

thigh /θaɪ/ *n* Oberschenkel *m*

thimble /ˈθɪmbl/ *n* Fingerhut *m*

thin /θɪn/ *a* (**thinner, thinnest**), **-ly** *adv* dünn □ *adv* dünn □ *v* (*pt/pp* **thinned**) □ *vt* verdünnen (*liquid*) □ *vi* sich lichten. ~ **out** *vt* ausdünnen

thing /θɪŋ/ *n* Ding *nt*; (*subject, affair*) Sache *f*; ~**s** *pl* (*belongings*) Sachen *pl*; **for one** ~ erstens; **the right** ~ das Richtige; **just the** ~! genau das Richtige! **how are** ~**s?** wie geht's? **the latest** ~ (*fam*) der letzte Schrei; **the best** ~ **would be am besten wäre es

think /θɪŋk/ *vt/i* (*pt/pp* **thought**) denken (**about/of** an + *acc*); (*believe*) meinen; (*consider*) nachdenken; (*regard as*) halten für; ~ **so** ich glaube schon; **what do you** ~? was meinen Sie? **what do you** ~ **of it?** was halten Sie davon? ~ **better of it** es sich (*dat*) anders überlegen. ~ **over** *vt* sich (*dat*) überlegen. ~ **up** *vt* sich (*dat*) ausdenken

third /θɜːd/ *a* dritte(r,s) □ *n* Drittel *nt*. ~**ly** *adv* drittens. ~**-rate** *a* drittrangig

thirst /θɜːst/ *n* Durst *m*. ~**y** *a*, **-ily** *adv* durstig; **be** ~**y** Durst haben

thirteen /θɜːˈtiːn/ *a* dreizehn. ~**th** *a* dreizehnte(r,s)

thirtieth /ˈθɜːtɪɪθ/ *a* dreißigste(r,s)

thirty /ˈθɜːtɪ/ *a* dreißig

this /ðɪs/ *a* (*pl* **these**) diese(r,s); (*pl*) diese; ~ **one** diese(r,s) da; **I'll take** ~ ich nehme diesen/ diese/ dieses; ~ **evening/morning** heute abend/morgen; **these**

days heutzutage □ *pron* (*pl* these)
das, dies[es]; (*pl*) die, diese; ~
and that dies und das; ~ **or that**
dieses oder das das; **like** ~ so; ~ **is
Peter** das ist Peter; (*Teleph*) hier
[spricht] Peter; **who is** ~ wer ist da?
(*Teleph, Amer*) wer ist am
Apparat?

thistle /ˈθɪsl/ *n* Distel *f*

thorn /θɔːn/ *n* Dorn *m*. ~**y** *a*
dornig

thorough /ˈθʌrə/ *a* gründlich

thorough: ~**bred** *n* reinrassiges
Tier *nt*; (*horse*) Rassepferd *nt*.
~**fare** *n* Durchfahrtsstraße *f*;
'**no** ~ **fare**' 'keine Durchfahrt'

thorough|**ly** /ˈθʌrəlɪ/ *adv* gründ-
lich; (*completely*) völlig; (*extremely*) äußerst. ~**ness** *n* Gründ-
lichkeit *f*

those /ðəʊz/ *see* that

though /ðəʊ/ *conj* obgleich, ob-
wohl; **as** ~ als ob □ *adv* (*fam*)
doch

thought /θɔːt/ *see* think □ *n* Gedanke *m*; (*thinking*) Denken *nt*.
~**ful** *a*, **-ly** *adv* nachdenklich;
(*considerate*) rücksichtsvoll.
~**less** *a*, **-ly** *adv* gedankenlos

thousand /ˈθaʊznd/ *a* one/a
~ [ein]tausend □ *n* Tausend *nt*;
~**s of** Tausende von. ~**th** *a* tau-
sendste(r,s) □ *n* Tausend-
stel *nt*

thrash /θræʃ/ *vt* verprügeln; (*defeat*) [vernichtend] schlagen. ~
about *vi* sich herumwerfen;
⟨*fish:*⟩ zappeln. ~ **out** *vt* ausdis-
kutieren

thread /θred/ *n* Faden *m*; (*of
screw*) Gewinde *nt* □ *vt* einfädeln;
auffädeln ⟨*beads*⟩. ~ **one's way
through** sich schlängeln durch.
~**bare** *a* fadenscheinig

threat /θret/ *n* Drohung *f*; (*danger*) Bedrohung *f*

threaten /ˈθretn/ *vt* drohen (+
dat); (*with weapon*) bedrohen; ~
to do sth drohen, etw zu tun; ~
s.o. with sth jdm etw androhen

□ *vi* drohen. ~**ing** *a*, **-ly** *adv* drohend; (*ominous*) bedrohlich

three /θriː/ *a* drei. ~**fold** *a* & *adv*
dreifach. ~**some** /-səm/ *n* Trio *nt*

thresh /θreʃ/ *vt* dreschen

threshold /ˈθreʃəʊld/ *n* Schwelle *f*

threw /θruː/ *see* throw

thrift /θrɪft/ *n* Sparsamkeit *f*. ~**y**
a sparsam

thrill /θrɪl/ *n* Erregung *f*; (*fam*)
Nervenkitzel *m* □ *vt* (*excite*) erregen; **be ~ed with** sich sehr freu-
en über (+ *acc*). ~**er** *n* Thriller
m. ~**ing** *a* erregend

thrive /θraɪv/ *vi* (*pt* thrived *or*
throve, *pp* thrived *or* thriven
/ˈθrɪvn/) gedeihen (**on** bei); ⟨*business:*⟩ florieren

throat /θrəʊt/ *n* Hals *m*; **sore** ~
Halsschmerzen *pl*; **cut s.o.'s** ~
jdm die Kehle durchschneiden

throb /θrɒb/ *n* Pochen *nt* □ *vi*
(*pt/pp* throbbed) pochen; (*vibrate*) vibrieren

throes /θrəʊz/ *npl* **in the** ~ **of**
(*fig*) mitten in (+ *dat*)

thrombosis /θrɒmˈbəʊsɪs/ *n*
Thrombose *f*

throne /θrəʊn/ *n* Thron *m*

throng /θrɒŋ/ *n* Menge *f*

throttle /ˈθrɒtl/ *vt* erdrosseln

through /θruː/ *prep* durch (+
acc); (*during*) während (+ *gen*);
(*Amer: up to & including*) bis
einschließlich □ *adv* durch; **all** ~
die ganze Zeit; ~ **and** ~ durch
und durch; **wet** ~ durch und
durch naß; **read sth** ~ etw
durchlesen; **let/walk** ~ durch-
lassen/-gehen □ *a* ⟨*train*⟩ durch-
gehend; **be** ~ (*finished*) fertig
sein; (*Teleph*) durch sein

throughout /θruːˈaʊt/ *prep* ~ **the
country** im ganzen Land; ~ **the
night** die Nacht durch □ *adv*
ganz; (*time*) die ganze Zeit

throve /θrəʊv/ *see* thrive

throw /θrəʊ/ *n* Wurf *m* □ *vt* (*pt*
threw, *pp* thrown) werfen;
schütten ⟨*liquid*⟩; betätigen
⟨*switch*⟩; abwerfen ⟨*rider*⟩; (*fam:*

disconcert) aus der Fassung bringen; (fam) geben ⟨party⟩; ~ **sth to** s.o. jdm etw zuwerfen; ~ **sth at** s.o. etw nach jdm werfen; (pelt with) jdn mit etw bewerfen). ~ **away** vt wegwerfen. ~ **out** vt hinauswerfen; (~ away) wegwerfen; verwerfen ⟨plan⟩. ~ **up** vt hochwerfen □vi (fam) sich übergeben

'**throw-away** a Wegwerf-

thrush /θrʌʃ/ n Drossel f

thrust /θrʌst/ n Stoß m; (Phys) Schub m □vt (pt/pp thrust) stoßen; (insert) stecken; ~ [up]on aufbürden (s.o. jdm)

thud /θʌd/ n dumpfer Schlag m

thug /θʌg/ n Schläger m

thumb /θʌm/ n Daumen m; **rule of** ~ Faustregel f; **under** s.o.'s ~ unter jds Fuchtel □vt ~ **a lift** (fam) per Anhalter fahren. ~**-index** n Daumenregister nt. ~**tack** n (Amer) Reißzwecke f

thump /θʌmp/ n dumpfer Schlag m □vt schlagen □vi hämmern (**on** an/auf + acc); ⟨heart:⟩ pochen

thunder /ˈθʌndə(r)/ n Donner m □vi donnern. ~**clap** n Donnerschlag m. ~**storm** n Gewitter nt. ~**y** a gewittrig

Thursday /ˈθɜːzdeɪ/ n Donnerstag m

thus /ðʌs/ adv so

thwart /θwɔːt/ vt vereiteln; ~ s.o. jdm einen Strich durch die Rechnung machen

thyme /taɪm/ n Thymian m

thyroid /ˈθaɪrɔɪd/ n Schilddrüse f

tiara /tɪˈɑːrə/ n Diadem nt

tick[1] /tɪk/ n on ~ (fam) auf Pump

tick[2] n (sound) Ticken nt; (mark) Häkchen nt; (fam: instant) Sekunde f □vi ticken □vt abhaken. ~ **off** vt abhaken; (fam) rüffeln. ~ **over** vi ⟨engine:⟩ im Leerlauf laufen

ticket /ˈtɪkɪt/ n Karte f; (for bus, train) Fahrschein m; (Aviat) Flugschein m; (for lottery) Los nt; (for article deposited) Schein m; (label) Schild nt; (for library) Lesekarte f; (fine) Strafzettel m. ~**-collector** n Fahrkartenkontrolleur m. ~**-office** n Fahrkartenschalter m; (for entry) Kasse f

tick[le] /ˈtɪkl/ n Kitzeln nt □vt/i kitzeln. ~**lish** /ˈtɪklɪʃ/ a kitzlig

tidal /ˈtaɪdl/ a ⟨river, harbour⟩ Tide-. ~ **wave** n Flutwelle f

tiddly-winks /ˈtɪdlɪwɪŋks/ n Flohspiel nt

tide /taɪd/ n Gezeiten pl; (of events) Strom m; **the** ~ **is in/out** es ist Flut/Ebbe □vt ~ **s.o. over** jdm über die Runden helfen

tidiness /ˈtaɪdɪnɪs/ n Ordentlichkeit f

tidy /ˈtaɪdɪ/ a (-ier, -iest), -ily adv ordentlich □vt ~ [up] aufräumen; ~ **oneself up** sich zurechtmachen

tie /taɪ/ n Krawatte f, Schlips m; (cord) Schnur f; (fig: bond) Band nt; (restriction) Bindung f; (Sport) Unentschieden nt; (in competition) Punktgleichheit f □v (pres p tying) □vt binden; machen ⟨knot⟩ □vi (Sport) unentschieden spielen; (have equal scores, votes) punktgleich sein; ~ **in with** passen zu. ~ **up** vt festbinden; verschnüren ⟨parcel⟩; fesseln ⟨person⟩; **be** ~**d up** (busy) beschäftigt sein

tier /tɪə(r)/ n Stufe f; (of cake) Etage f; (in stadium) Rang m

tiff /tɪf/ n Streit m, (fam) Krach m

tiger /ˈtaɪgə(r)/ n Tiger m

tight /taɪt/ a (-er, -est), -ly adv fest; (taut) straff; ⟨clothes⟩ eng; ⟨control⟩ streng; (fam: drunk) blau; **in a** ~ **corner** (fam) in der Klemme □adv fest

tighten /ˈtaɪtn/ vt festerziehen; straffen ⟨rope⟩; anziehen ⟨screw⟩; verschärfen ⟨control⟩ □vi sich spannen

tight: ~**-fisted** a knauserig. ~**rope** n Hochseil nt

tights /taɪts/ npl Strumpfhose f

tile /taɪl/ *n* Fliese *f*; (*on wall*) Kachel *f*; (*on roof*) [Dach]ziegel *m* □ *vt* mit Fliesen auslegen; kacheln ⟨*wall*⟩; decken ⟨*roof*⟩

till[1] /tɪl/ *prep & conj* = **until**

till[2] *n* Kasse *f*

tiller /'tɪlə(r)/ *n* Ruderpinne *f*

tilt /tɪlt/ *n* Neigung *f*; **at full ~** mit voller Wucht □ *vt* neigen; [zur Seite] neigen ⟨*head*⟩ □ *vi* sich neigen

timber /'tɪmbə(r)/ *n* [Nutz]holz *nt*

time /taɪm/ *n* Zeit *f*; (*occasion*) Mal *nt*; (*rhythm*) Takt *m*; **~s** (*Math*) mal; **at any ~** jederzeit; **this ~** dieses Mal, diesmal; **at ~s** manchmal; **~ and again** immer wieder; **two at a ~** zwei auf einmal; **on ~** pünktlich; **in ~** rechtzeitig; (*eventually*) mit der Zeit; **in no ~** im Handumdrehen; **in a year's ~** in einem Jahr; **behind ~** verspätet; **behind the ~s** rückständig; **for the ~ being** vorläufig; **what is the ~?** wie spät ist es? wieviel Uhr ist es? **by the ~ we arrive** bis wir ankommen; **did you have a nice ~?** hast du dich gut amüsiert? **have a good ~!** viel Vergnügen! □ *vt* stoppen ⟨*race*⟩; **be well ~d** gut abgepaßt sein

time: **~ bomb** *n* Zeitbombe *f*. **~-lag** *n* Zeitdifferenz *f*. **~less** *a* zeitlos. **~ly** *a* rechtzeitig. **~-switch** *n* Zeitschalter *m*. **~-table** *n* Fahrplan *m*; (*Sch*) Stundenplan *m*

timid /'tɪmɪd/ *a*, **-ly** *adv* scheu; (*hesitant*) zaghaft

timing /'taɪmɪŋ/ *n* Wahl *f* des richtigen Zeitpunkts; (*Sport, Techn*) Timing *nt*

tin /tɪn/ *n* Zinn *nt*; (*container*) Dose *f* □ *vt* (*pt/pp* **tinned**) in Dosen *od* Büchsen konservieren. **~ foil** *n* Stanniol *nt*; (*Culin*) Alufolie *f*

tinge /tɪndʒ/ *n* Hauch *m* □ *vt* **~d with** mit einer Spur von

tingle /'tɪŋgl/ *vi* kribbeln

tinker /'tɪŋkə(r)/ *vi* herumbasteln (**with an** + *dat*)

tinkle /'tɪŋkl/ *n* Klingeln *nt* □ *vi* klingeln

tinned /tɪnd/ *a* Dosen-, Büchsen-

'tin opener *n* Dosen-/Büchsenöffner *m*

'tinpot *a* (*pej*) ⟨*firm*⟩ schäbig

tinsel /'tɪnsl/ *n* Lametta *nt*

tint /tɪnt/ *n* Farbton *m* □ *vt* tönen

tiny /'taɪnɪ/ *a* (**-ier, -iest**) winzig

tip[1] /tɪp/ *n* Spitze *f*

tip[2] /tɪp/ *n* (*money*) Trinkgeld *nt*; (*advice*) Rat *m*, (*fam*) Tip *m*; (*for rubbish*) Müllhalde *f* □ *v* (*pt/pp* **tipped**) □ *vt* (*tilt*) kippen; (*reward*) Trinkgeld geben (**s.o. jdm**) □ *vi* kippen. **~ off** *vt* **~ s.o. off** jdm einen Hinweis geben. **~ out** *vt* auskippen. **~ over** *vt/i* umkippen

'tip-off *n* Hinweis *m*

tipped /tɪpt/ *a* Filter-

tipsy /'tɪpsɪ/ *a* (*fam*) beschwipst

tiptoe /'tɪptəʊ/ *n* **on ~** auf Zehenspitzen

tiptop /tɪp'tɒp/ *a* (*fam*) erstklassig

tire /taɪə(r)/ *vt/i* ermüden. **~d** *a* müde; **be ~d of sth** etw satt haben; **~d out** [völlig] erschöpft. **~less** *a*, **-ly** *adv* unermüdlich. **~some** /-səm/ *a* lästig

tiring /'taɪrɪŋ/ *a* ermüdend

tissue /'tɪʃuː/ *n* Gewebe *nt*; (*handkerchief*) Papiertaschentuch *nt*. **~-paper** *n* Seidenpapier *nt*

tit[1] /tɪt/ *n* (*bird*) Meise *f*

tit[2] *n* **~ for tat** wie du mir, so ich dir

'titbit *n* Leckerbissen *m*

titillate /'tɪtɪleɪt/ *vt* erregen

title /'taɪtl/ *n* Titel *m*. **~-role** *n* Titelrolle *f*

tittle-tattle /'tɪtltætl/ *n* Klatsch *m*

titular /'tɪtjʊlə(r)/ *a* nominell

to /tuː, *unbetont* tə/ *prep* zu (+ *dat*); (*with place, direction*) nach; (*to cinema, theatre*) in (+ *acc*); (*to wedding, party*) auf (+ *acc*); ⟨*address, send, fasten*⟩ an (+ *acc*); (*per*) pro; (*up to, until*) bis;

to the station zum Bahnhof;
to Germany/Switzerland nach
Deutschland/ in die Schweiz; **to
the toilet/one's room** auf die
Toilette/sein Zimmer; **to the of-
fice/an exhibition** ins Büro/ in
eine Ausstellung; **to university**
auf die Universität; **twenty/
quarter to eight** zwanzig/Vier-
tel vor acht; **5 to 6 pounds** 5 bis 6
Pfund; **to the end** bis zum
Schluß; **to this day** bis heute; **to
the best of my knowledge** nach
meinem besten Wissen; **give/say
sth to s.o.** jdm etw geben/sagen;
go/come to s.o. zu jdm gehen/
kommen; **I've never been to
Berlin** ich war noch nie in Berlin; **there's nothing to it** es ist
nichts dabei □ *verbal construc-
tions* **to go** gehen; **to stay** bleiben; **learn to swim** schwimmen
lernen; **want to/have to go** gehen wollen/müssen; **be easy/
difficult to forget** leicht/schwer
zu vergessen sein; **too ill/tired
to go** zu krank/müde, um zu gehen; **he did it to annoy me** er tat
es, um mich zu ärgern; **you have
to** du mußt; **I don't want to** ich
will nicht; **I'd love to** gern; **I
forgot to** ich habe es vergessen;
he wants to be a teacher er will
Lehrer werden; **live to be 90** 90
werden; **he was the last to arrive** er kam als letzter; **to be
honest** ehrlich gesagt □ *adv* **pull
to** anlehnen; **to and fro** hin und
her

toad /təʊd/ *n* Kröte *f.* **~stool** *n*
Giftpilz *m*

toast /təʊst/ *n* Toast *m* □ *vt* toasten
⟨*bread*⟩; (*drink a ~ to*) trinken
auf (+ *acc*). **~er** *n* Toaster *m*

tobacco /təˈbækəʊ/ *n* Tabak *m*.
~nist's [shop] *n* Tabakladen *m*

toboggan /təˈbɒgən/ *n* Schlitten *m*
□ *vi* Schlitten fahren

today /təˈdeɪ/ *n* & *adv* heute; **~
week** heute in einer Woche; **~'s
paper** die heutige Zeitung

toddler /ˈtɒdlə(r)/ *n* Kleinkind *nt*

to-do /təˈduː/ *n* (*fam*) Getue *nt*,
Theater *nt*

toe /təʊ/ *n* Zeh *m*; (*of footwear*)
Spitze *f* □ *vt* **~ the line** spuren.
~nail *n* Zehennagel *m*

toffee /ˈtɒfɪ/ *n* Karamelbonbon *m*
& *nt*

together /təˈgeðə(r)/ *adv* zusammen; (*at the same time*) gleichzeitig

toil /tɔɪl/ *n* [harte] Arbeit *f* □ *vi*
schwer arbeiten

toilet /ˈtɔɪlɪt/ *n* Toilette *f.* **~ bag** *n*
Kulturbeutel *m.* **~ paper** *n* Toi-
lettenpapier *nt*

toiletries /ˈtɔɪlɪtrɪz/ *npl* Toilet-
tenartikel *pl*

toilet: ~ roll *n* Rolle *f* Toiletten-
papier. **~ water** *n* Toilettenwas-
ser *nt*

token /ˈtəʊkən/ *n* Zeichen *nt*; (*counter*) Marke *f*; (*voucher*) Gutschein
m □ *attrib* symbolisch

told /təʊld/ *see* **tell** □ **all ~** insgesamt

tolerable /ˈtɒlərəbl/ *a*, **-bly** *adv* erträglich; (*not bad*) leidlich

toleran|ce /ˈtɒlərəns/ *n* Toleranz *f.*
~t *a*, **-ly** *adv* tolerant

tolerate /ˈtɒləreɪt/ *vt* dulden, tole-
rieren; (*bear*) ertragen

toll[1] /təʊl/ *n* Gebühr *f*; (*for road*)
Maut *f* (*Aust*); **death ~** Zahl *f* der
Todesopfer; **take a heavy ~** ei-
nen hohen Tribut fordern

toll[2] *vi* läuten

tom /tɒm/ *n* (*cat*) Kater *m*

tomato /təˈmɑːtəʊ/ *n* (*pl* **-es**) Tomate *f.* **~ purée** *n* Tomatenmark *nt*

tomb /tuːm/ *n* Grabmal *nt*

tomboy *n* Wildfang *m*

tombstone *n* Grabstein *m*

tom-cat *n* Kater *m*

tome /təʊm/ *n* dicker Band *m*

tomfoolery /tɒmˈfuːlərɪ/ *n* Blödsinn *m*

tomorrow /təˈmɒrəʊ/ *n* & *adv* morgen; **~ morning** morgen früh;

the day after ~ übermorgen; see you ~! bis morgen!

ton /tʌn/ n Tonne f; ~s of (fam) jede Menge

tone /təʊn/ n Ton m; (colour) Farbton m □ vt ~ **down** dämpfen; (fig) mäßigen. ~ **up** vt kräftigen; straffen ⟨muscles⟩

tongs /tɒŋz/ npl Zange f

tongue /tʌŋ/ n Zunge f; ~ in cheek (fam) nicht ernst. ~**twister** n Zungenbrecher m

tonic /'tɒnɪk/ n Tonikum nt; (for hair) Haarwasser nt; (fig) Wohltat f; ~ [**water**] Tonic nt

tonight /tə'naɪt/ n & adv heute nacht; (evening) heute abend

tonne /tʌn/ n Tonne f

tonsil /'tɒnsl/ n (Anat) Mandel f. ~**litis** /-sə'laɪtɪs/ n Mandelentzündung f

too /tuː/ adv zu; (also) auch; ~ much/little zuviel/zuwenig

took /tʊk/ see **take**

tool /tuːl/ n Werkzeug nt; (for gardening) Gerät nt

toot /tuːt/ n Hupsignal nt □ vi tuten; (Auto) hupen

tooth /tuːθ/ n (pl teeth) Zahn m

tooth: ~**ache** n Zahnschmerzen pl. ~**brush** n Zahnbürste f. ~**less** a zahnlos. ~**paste** n Zahnpasta f. ~**pick** n Zahnstocher m

top[1] /tɒp/ n (toy) Kreisel m

top[2] /tɒp/ n oberer Teil m; (apex) Spitze f; (summit) Gipfel m; (Sch) Erste(r) m/f; (top part or half) Oberteil nt; (head) Kopfende nt; (of road) oberes Ende nt; (upper surface) Oberfläche f; (lid) Deckel m; (of bottle) Verschluß m; (garment) Top nt; at the/on ~ oben; on ~ of oben auf (+ dat/ acc); on ~ of that (besides) obendrein; from ~ to bottom von oben bis unten □ a oberste(r,s); (highest) höchste(r,s); (best) beste(r,s) □ vt (pt/pp topped) an erster Stelle stehen auf (+ dat)

⟨list⟩; (exceed) übersteigen; (remove the ~ of) die Spitze abschneiden. ~ **up** vt nachfüllen, auffüllen

top: ~'**hat** n Zylinder[hut] m. ~**heavy** a kopflastig

topic /'tɒpɪk/ n Thema nt. ~**al** a aktuell

top: ~**less** a & adv oben ohne. ~**most** a oberste(r,s)

topple /'tɒpl/ vt/i umstürzen. ~ **off** vi stürzen

top'secret a streng geheim

topsy-turvy /tɒpsɪ'tɜːvɪ/ adv völlig durcheinander

torch /tɔːtʃ/ n Taschenlampe f; (flaming) Fackel f

tore /tɔː(r)/ see **tear**[1]

torment[1] /'tɔːment/ n Qual f

torment[2] /tɔː'ment/ vt quälen

torn /tɔːn/ see **tear**[1] □ a zerrissen

tornado /tɔː'neɪdəʊ/ n (pl -es) Wirbelsturm m

torpedo /tɔː'piːdəʊ/ n (pl -es) Torpedo m □ vt torpedieren

torrent /'tɒrənt/ n reißender Strom m. ~**ial** /tə'renʃl/ a ⟨rain⟩ wolkenbruchartig

torso /'tɔːsəʊ/ n Rumpf m; (Art) Torso m

tortoise /'tɔːtəs/ n Schildkröte f. ~**shell** n Schildpatt nt

tortuous /'tɔːtjʊəs/ a verschlungen; (fig) umständlich

torture /'tɔːtʃə(r)/ n Folter f; (fig) Qual f □ vt foltern; (fig) quälen

toss /tɒs/ vt werfen; (into the air) hochwerfen; (shake) schütteln; (unseat) abwerfen; mischen ⟨salad⟩; wenden ⟨pancake⟩; ~ **a** coin mit einer Münze losen □ vi ~ **and turn** (in bed) sich [schlaflos] im Bett wälzen. ~ **up** vi [mit einer Münze] losen

tot[1] /tɒt/ n kleines Kind nt; (fam: of liquor) Gläschen nt

tot[2] /tɒt/ v (pt/pp totted) ~ **up** (fam) zusammenzählen

total /'təʊtl/ a gesamt; (complete) völlig, total □ n Gesamtzahl f; (sum) Gesamtsumme f □ vt *(pt/pp* **totalled)** zusammenzählen; *(amount to)* sich belaufen auf (+ *acc)*

totalitarian /təʊtælɪ'teəriən/ *a* totalitär

totally /'təʊtəlɪ/ *adv* völlig, total

totter /'tɒtə(r)/ *vi* taumeln; *(rock)* schwanken. **~ y** *a* wackelig

touch /tʌtʃ/ *n* Berührung *f*; *(sense)* Tastsinn *m*; *(Mus)* Anschlag *m*; *(contact)* Kontakt *m*; *(trace)* Spur *f*; *(fig)* Anflug *m*; **get/be in ~** sich in Verbindung setzen/in Verbindung stehen **(with** mit) □ *vt* berühren; *(get hold of)* anfassen; *(lightly)* tippen auf/an (+ *acc)*; *(brush against)* streifen [gegen]; *(reach)* erreichen; *(equal)* herankommen an (+ *acc)*; *(fig: move)* rühren; anrühren *(food, subject)*; **don't ~ that!** faß das nicht an! □ *vi* sich berühren; **~ on** *(fig)* berühren. **~ down** *vi (Aviat)* landen. **~ up** *vt* ausbessern

touch|ing /'tʌtʃɪŋ/ *a* rührend. **~ y** *a* empfindlich; *(subject)* heikel

tough /tʌf/ *a* (-er, -est) zäh; *(severe, harsh)* hart; *(difficult)* schwierig; *(durable)* strapazierfähig

toughen /'tʌfn/ *vt* härten; **~ up** abhärten

tour /tʊə(r)/ *n* Reise *f*, Tour *f*; *(of building, town)* Besichtigung *f*; *(Theat, Sport)* Tournee *f*; *(of duty)* Dienstzeit *f* □ *vt* fahren durch; besichtigen *(building)* □ *vi* herumreisen

touris|m /'tʊərɪzm/ *n* Tourismus *m*, Fremdenverkehr *m*. **~ t** /-rɪst/ *n* Tourist(in) *m(f)* □ *attrib* Touristen-. **~ t office** *n* Fremdenverkehrsbüro *nt*

tournament /'tʊənəmənt/ *n* Turnier *nt*

'tour operator *n* Reiseveranstalter *m*

tousle /'taʊzl/ *vt* zerzausen

tout /taʊt/ *n* Anreißer *m*; *(ticket ~)* Kartenschwarzhändler *m* □ *vi* **~ for customers** Kunden werben

tow /təʊ/ *n* **give s.o./a car a ~** jdn/ein Auto abschleppen; **'on ~'** 'wird geschleppt'; **in ~** *(fam)* im Schlepptau □ *vt* schleppen; ziehen *(trailer)*. **~ away** *vt* abschleppen

toward[s] /tə'wɔːd(z)/ *prep* zu (+ *dat)*; *(with time)* gegen (+ *acc)*; *(with respect to)* gegenüber (+ *dat)*

towel /'taʊəl/ *n* Handtuch *nt*. **~ling** *n (Tex)* Frottee *nt*

tower /'taʊə(r)/ *n* Turm *m* □ *vi* **above** überragen. **~ block** *n* Hochhaus *nt*. **~ing** *a* hochragend

town /taʊn/ *n* Stadt *f*. **~ 'hall** *n* Rathaus *nt*

tow: ~path *n* Treidelpfad *m*. **~rope** *n* Abschleppseil *nt*

toxic /'tɒksɪk/ *a* giftig. **~ 'waste** *n* Giftmüll *m*

toxin /'tɒksɪn/ *n* Gift *nt*

toy /tɔɪ/ *n* Spielzeug *nt* □ *vi* **~ with** spielen mit; stochern in (+ *dat)* *(food)*. **~shop** *n* Spielwarengeschäft *nt*

trac|e /treɪs/ *n* Spur *f* □ *vt* folgen (+ *dat)*; *(find)* finden; *(draw)* zeichnen; *(with tracing-paper)* durchpausen. **~ing-paper** *n* Pauspapier *nt*

track /træk/ *n* Spur *f*; *(path)* [unbefestigter] Weg *m*; *(Sport)* Bahn *f*; *(Rail)* Gleis *nt*; **keep ~ of** im Auge behalten □ *vt* verfolgen. **~ down** *vt* aufspüren; *(find)* finden

'tracksuit *n* Trainingsanzug *m*

tract[1] /trækt/ *n (land)* Gebiet *nt*

tract[2] *n (pamphlet)* [Flugschrift *f*

tractor /'træktə(r)/ *n* Traktor *m*

trade /treɪd/ *n* Handel *m*; *(line of business)* Gewerbe *nt*; *(business)* Geschäft *nt*; *(craft)* Handwerk *nt*; **by ~** von Beruf □ *vt* tauschen; **~ in** *(give in part exchange)* in Zahlung geben □ *vi* handeln **(in** mit)

'trade mark *n* Warenzeichen *nt*

trader /'treɪdə(r)/ n Händler m
trade: ~ **union** n Gewerkschaft
f. ~ **unionist** n Gewerk-
schaftler(in) m(f)

trading /'treɪdɪŋ/ n Handel m. ~
estate n Gewerbegebiet o. ~
stamp n Rabattmarke f

tradition /trə'dɪʃn/ n Tradition f.
~ **al** a, **-ly** adv traditionell

traffic /'træfɪk/ n Verkehr m;
(trading) Handel m ●vi handeln
(in mit)

traffic: ~ **circle** n (Amer) Kreisverkehr m. ~ **jam** n [Verkehrs]-
stau m. ~ **lights** npl [Verkehrs]-
ampel f. ~ **warden** n ≈ Hilfspo-
lizist m; (woman) Politesse f

tragedy /'trædʒədɪ/ n Tragödie f

tragic /'trædʒɪk/ a, **-ally** adv tra-
gisch

trail /treɪl/ n Spur f; (path) Weg m,
Pfad m ●vi schleifen; (plant)
sich ranken; (be behind) zurückbleiben; (Sport) zurückliegen ●vt
verfolgen, folgen (+ dat); (drag)
schleifen

trailer /'treɪlə(r)/ n (Auto) Anhänger m; (Amer: caravan) Wohnwagen m; (film) Vorschau f

train /treɪn/ n Zug m; (of dress)
Schleppe f; ~ **of thought** Gedan-
kengang m ●vt ausbilden; (Sport)
trainieren; (aim) richten auf (+
acc); erziehen (child); abrichten/
(to do tricks) dressieren (animal); ziehen (plant) ●vi eine
Ausbildung machen; (Sport) trainieren. ~**ed** a ausgebildet

trainee /treɪ'niː/ n Auszubil-
dende(r) m/f; (Techn) Prakti-
kant(in) m(f)

train|er /'treɪnə(r)/ n (Sport) Trai-
ner m; (in circus) Dompteur m;
~**ers** pl Trainingsschuhe pl.
~**ing** n Ausbildung f; (Sport)
Training nt; (of animals) Dres-
sur f

traipse /treɪps/ vi (fam) latschen

trait /treɪt/ n Eigenschaft f

traitor /'treɪtə(r)/ n Verräter m

tram /træm/ n Straßenbahn f.
~**-lines** npl Straßenbahnschie-
nen pl

tramp /træmp/ n Landstreicher
m; (hike) Wanderung f ●vi stapfen; (walk) marschieren

trample /'træmpl/ vt/i trampeln
(on auf + acc)

trampoline /'træmpəliːn/ n Tram-
polin nt

trance /trɑːns/ n Trance f

tranquil /'træŋkwɪl/ a ruhig.
~**lity** /-'kwɪlətɪ/ n Ruhe f

tranquillizer /'træŋkwɪlaɪzə(r)/
n Beruhigungsmittel nt

transact /træn'zækt/ vt abschließen. ~**ion** /-ækʃn/ n Transaktion f

transcend /træn'send/ vt übersteigen

transcript /'trænskrɪpt/ n Ab-
schrift f; (of official proceedings)
Protokoll nt. ~**ion** /-'skrɪpʃn/ n
Abschrift f

transept /'trænsept/ n Querschiff
nt

transfer[1] /'trænsfɜː(r)/ n (see
transfer[2]) Übertragung f; Verle-
gung f; Versetzung f; Überweisung f; (Sport) Transfer m; (design) Abziehbild nt

transfer[2] /træns'fɜː(r)/ v (pt/pp
transferred) ●vt übertragen;
verlegen (firm, prisoners); versetzen (employee); überweisen
(money); (Sport) transferieren
●vi [über]wechseln; (when travelling) umsteigen. ~**able** /-əbl/ a
übertragbar

transform /træns'fɔːm/ vt verwandeln. ~**ation** /-fə'meɪʃn/ n
Verwandlung f. ~**er** n Transfor-
mator m

transfusion /træns'fjuːʒn/ n
Transfusion f

transient /'trænzɪənt/ a kurzlebig; (life) kurz

transistor /træn'zɪstə(r)/ n Transistor m

transit /'trænsɪt/ n Transit m; (of goods) Transport m; **in** ~ ⟨goods⟩ auf dem Transport

transition /træn'sɪʒn/ n Übergang m. ~**al** a Übergangs-

transitive /'trænsɪtɪv/ a, **-ly** adv transitiv

transitory /'trænsɪtərɪ/ a vergänglich; ⟨life⟩ kurz

translat|e /træns'leɪt/ vt übersetzen. ~**ion** /-'leɪʃn/ n Übersetzung f. ~**or** n Übersetzer(in) m(f)

translucent /trænz'lu:snt/ a durchscheinend

transmission /trænz'mɪʃn/ n Übertragung f

transmit /trænz'mɪt/ vt (pt/pp transmitted) übertragen. ~**ter** n Sender m

transparen|cy /træns'pærənsɪ/ n (Phot) Dia nt. ~**t** a durchsichtig

transpire /træn'spaɪə(r)/ vi sich herausstellen; (fam: happen) passieren

transplant¹ /'trænspla:nt/ n Verpflanzung f; Transplantation f

transplant² /træns'pla:nt/ vt umpflanzen; (Med) verpflanzen

transport¹ /'trænspɔ:t/ n Transport m

transport² /træn'spɔ:t/ vt transportieren. ~**ation** /-'teɪʃn/ n Transport m

transpose /træns'pəʊz/ vt umstellen

transvestite /trænz'vestaɪt/ n Transvestit m

trap /træp/ n Falle f; (fam: mouth) Klappe f; **pony and** ~ Einspänner m □ vt (pt/pp trapped) [mit einer Falle] fangen; (jam) einklemmen; **be** ~**ped** festsitzen; (shut in) eingeschlossen sein; (cut off) abgeschnitten sein. ~'**door** n Falltür f

trapeze /trə'pi:z/ n Trapez nt

trash /træʃ/ n Schund m; (rubbish) Abfall m; (nonsense) Quatsch m. ~**can** n (Amer) Mülleimer m. ~**y** a Schund-

trauma /'trɔ:mə/ n Trauma nt. ~**tic** /-'mætɪk/ a traumatisch

travel /'trævl/ n Reisen nt □ v (pt/pp travelled) □ vi reisen; (go in vehicle) fahren; ⟨light, sound⟩ sich fortpflanzen; (Techn) sich bewegen □ vt bereisen; fahren ⟨distance⟩. ~ **agency** n Reisebüro nt. ~ **agent** n Reisebürokaufmann m

traveller /'trævələ(r)/ n Reisende(r) m/f; (Comm) Vertreter m; ~**s** pl (gypsies) Zigeuner pl. ~'**s cheque** n Reisescheck m

trawler /'trɔ:lə(r)/ n Fischdampfer m

tray /treɪ/ n Tablett nt; (for baking) [Back]blech nt; (for documents) Ablagekorb m

treacher|ous /'tretʃərəs/ a treulos; (dangerous, deceptive) tückisch. ~**y** n Verrat m

treacle /'tri:kl/ n Sirup m

tread /tred/ n Schritt m; (step) Stufe f; (of tyre) Profil nt □ v (pt trod, pp trodden) □ vi (walk) gehen; ~ **on/in** treten auf/in (+ acc) □ vt treten

treason /'tri:zn/ n Verrat m

treasure /'treʒə(r)/ n Schatz m □ vt in Ehren halten. ~**r** n Kassenwart m

treasury /'treʒərɪ/ n Schatzkammer f; **the T** ~ das Finanzministerium

treat /tri:t/ n [besonderes] Vergnügen nt; **give s.o. a** ~ jdm etwas Besonderes bieten □ vt behandeln; ~ **s.o. to sth** jdm etw spendieren

treatise /'tri:tɪz/ n Abhandlung f

treatment /'tri:tmənt/ n Behandlung f

treaty /'tri:tɪ/ n Vertrag m

treble /'trebl/ a dreifach; ~ **the amount** dreimal soviel □ n (Mus) Diskant m; (voice) Sopran m □ vt verdreifachen □ vi sich verdreifachen. ~ **clef** n Violinschlüssel m

tree /tri:/ n Baum m

trek /trek/ n Marsch m □ vi (pt/pp
trekked) latschen

trellis /'trelɪs/ n Gitter nt

tremble /'trembl/ vi zittern

tremendous /trɪ'mendəs/ a, -ly
adv gewaltig; (fam: excellent)
großartig

tremor /'tremə(r)/ n Zittern nt;
[earth] ~ Beben nt

trench /trentʃ/ n Graben m; (Mil)
Schützengraben m

trend /trend/ n Tendenz f;
(fashion) Trend m. ~y a (-ier,
-iest) (fam) modisch

trepidation /trepɪ'deɪʃn/ n Be-
klommenheit f

trespass /'trespəs/ vi ~ on unerlaubt betreten. ~er n Unbe-
fugte(r) m/f

trial /'traɪəl/ n (Jur) [Gerichts]ver-
fahren nt, Prozeß m; (test) Probe
f; (ordeal) Prüfung f; be on ~ auf
Probe sein; (Jur) angeklagt sein
(for wegen); by ~ and error
durch Probieren

triang|le /'traɪæŋgl/ n Dreieck nt;
(Mus) Triangel m. ~ular
/-'æŋgjʊlə(r)/ a dreieckig

tribe /traɪb/ n Stamm m

tribulation /trɪbjʊ'leɪʃn/ n Kummer m

tribunal /traɪ'bjuːnl/ n Schieds-
gericht nt

tributary /'trɪbjʊtəri/ n Neben-
fluß m

tribute /'trɪbjuːt/ n Tribut m; pay
~ Tribut zollen (to dat)

trice /traɪs/ n in a ~ im Nu

trick /trɪk/ n Trick m; (joke)
Streich m; (Cards) Stich m; (feat
of skill) Kunststück nt; that
should do the ~ (fam) damit
dürfte es klappen □ vt täuschen,
(fam) hereinlegen

trickle /'trɪkl/ vi rinnen

trick|ster /'trɪkstə(r)/ n Schwind-
ler m. ~y a (-ier, -iest) a schwierig

tricycle /'traɪsɪkl/ n Dreirad nt

tried /traɪd/ see try

trifl|e /'traɪfl/ n Kleinigkeit f; (Cu-
lin) Trifle nt. ~ing a unbedeu-
tend

trigger /'trɪgə(r)/ n Abzug m; (fig)
Auslöser m □ vt ~ [off] auslösen

trigonometry /trɪgə'nɒmɪtri/ n
Trigonometrie f

trim /trɪm/ a (trimmer, trim-
mest) gepflegt □ n (cut) Nach-
schneiden nt; (decoration) Verzierung f; (condition) Zustand m □ vt
schneiden; (decorate) besetzen;
(Naut) trimmen. ~ming n Besatz m; ~mings pl (accessories)
Zubehör nt; (decorations) Verzie-
rungen pl; with all the ~mings
mit allem Drum und Dran

Trinity /'trɪnəti/ n the [Holy] ~
die [Heilige] Dreieinigkeit f

trinket /'trɪŋkɪt/ n Schmuck-
gegenstand m

trio /'triːəʊ/ n Trio nt

trip /trɪp/ n Reise f; (excursion)
Ausflug m □ v (pt/pp tripped) □ vt
~ s.o. up jdm ein Bein stellen □ vi
stolpern (on/over über + acc)

tripe /traɪp/ n Kaldaunen pl; (nonsense) Quatsch m

triple /'trɪpl/ a dreifach □ vt verdreifachen □ vi sich verdreifachen

triplets /'trɪplɪts/ npl Drillinge pl

triplicate /'trɪplɪkət/ n in ~ in
dreifacher Ausfertigung

tripod /'traɪpɒd/ n Stativ nt

tripper /'trɪpə(r)/ n Ausflügler m

trite /traɪt/ a banal

triumph /'traɪʌmf/ n Triumph m
□ vi triumphieren (over über +
acc). ~ant /-'ʌmfnt/ a, -ly adv
triumphierend

trivial /'trɪvɪəl/ a belanglos. ~ity
/-'ælɪti/ n Belanglosigkeit f

trod, trodden /trɒd, 'trɒdn/ see
tread

trolley /'trɒli/ n (for serving food)
Servierwagen m; (for shopping)
Einkaufswagen m; (for luggage)
Kofferkuli m; (Amer: tram)
Straßenbahn f. ~ bus n O-Bus m

trombone /trɒm'bəʊn/ n Posaune f

troop /truːp/ n Schar f; ~**s** pl Truppen pl □vi ~ **in/out** hinein-/hinausströmen

trophy /'trəʊfɪ/ n Trophäe f; (in competition) ≈ Pokal m

tropic /'trɒpɪk/ n Wendekreis m; ~**s** pl Tropen pl. ~**al** a tropisch; ⟨fruit⟩ Süd-

trot /trɒt/ n Trab m □vi (pt/pp trotted) traben

trouble /'trʌbl/ n Ärger m; (difficulties) Schwierigkeiten pl; (inconvenience) Mühe f; (conflict) Unruhe f; (Med) Beschwerden pl; (Techn) Probleme pl; **get into ~** Ärger bekommen; **take ~** sich (dat) Mühe geben □vt (disturb) stören; (worry) beunruhigen □vi sich bemühen. ~-**maker** n Unruhestifter m. ~**some** /-səm/ a schwierig; ⟨flies, cough⟩ lästig

trough /trɒf/ n Trog m

trounce /traʊns/ vt vernichtend schlagen; (thrash) verprügeln

troupe /truːp/ n Truppe f

trousers /'traʊzəz/ npl Hose f

trousseau /'truːsəʊ/ n Aussteuer f

trout /traʊt/ n inv Forelle f

trowel /'traʊəl/ n Kelle f; (for gardening) Pflanzkelle f

truant /'truːənt/ n **play ~** die Schule schwänzen

truce /truːs/ n Waffenstillstand m

truck /trʌk/ n Last[kraft]wagen m; (Rail) Güterwagen m

truculent /'trʌkjʊlənt/ a aufsässig

trudge /trʌdʒ/ n [mühseliger] Marsch m □vi latschen

true /truː/ a (-r, -st) wahr; (loyal) treu; (genuine) echt; **come ~** in Erfüllung gehen; **is that ~?** stimmt das?

truism /'truːɪzm/ n Binsenwahrheit f

truly /'truːlɪ/ adv wirklich; (faithfully) treu; **Yours ~** Hochachtungsvoll

trump /trʌmp/ n (Cards) Trumpf m □vt übertrumpfen. ~ **up** vt (fam) erfinden

trumpet /'trʌmpɪt/ n Trompete f. ~**er** n Trompeter m

truncheon /'trʌntʃn/ n Schlagstock m

trundle /'trʌndl/ vt/i rollen

trunk /trʌŋk/ n [Baum]stamm m; (body) Rumpf m; (of elephant) Rüssel m; (for travelling) [Über-see]koffer m; (for storage) Truhe f; (Amer: of car) Kofferraum m; ~**s** pl Badehose f

truss /trʌs/ n (Med) Bruchband nt

trust /trʌst/ n Vertrauen nt; (group of companies) Trust m; (organization) Treuhandgesellschaft f; (charitable) Stiftung f □vt trauen (+ dat), vertrauen (+ dat); (hope) hoffen □vi vertrauen (in/to auf + acc)

trustee /trʌsˈtiː/ n Treuhänder m

trust|**ful** /'trʌstfl/ a, **-ly** adv vertrauensvoll. ~**ing** a vertrauensvoll. ~**worthy** a vertrauenswürdig

truth /truːθ/ n (pl **-s** /truːðz/) Wahrheit f. ~**ful** a, **-ly** adv ehrlich

try /traɪ/ n Versuch m □v (pt/pp tried) □vt versuchen; (sample, taste) probieren; (be a strain on) anstrengen; (Jur) vor Gericht stellen; verhandeln ⟨case⟩ □vi versuchen; (make an effort) sich bemühen. ~ **on** vt anprobieren; aufprobieren ⟨hat⟩. ~ **out** vt ausprobieren

trying /'traɪɪŋ/ a schwierig

T-shirt /'tiː-/ n T-Shirt nt

tub /tʌb/ n Kübel m; (carton) Becher m; (bath) Wanne f

tuba /'tjuːbə/ n (Mus) Tuba f

tubby /'tʌbɪ/ a (-ier, -iest) rundlich

tube /tjuːb/ n Röhre f; (pipe) Rohr nt; (flexible) Schlauch m; (of toothpaste) Tube f; (Rail, fam) U-Bahn f

tuber /'tjuːbə(r)/ n Knolle f

tuberculosis /tjuːbɜːkjʊˈləʊsɪs/ n Tuberkulose f

tubing /'tju:bɪŋ/ n Schlauch m

tubular /'tju:bjʊlə(r)/ a röhrenförmig

tuck /tʌk/ n (decorative) Biese f □ vt (put) stecken. **~ in** vt hineinstecken; **s.o. in** jdn zudecken □ vi (fam: eat) zulangen. **~ up** vt hochkrempeln ⟨sleeves⟩; (in bed) zudecken

Tuesday /'tju:zdeɪ/ n Dienstag m

tuft /tʌft/ n Büschel nt

tug /tʌg/ n Ruck m; (Naut) Schleppdampfer m □ v (pt/pp **tugged**) □ vt ziehen □ vi zerren (at an + dat). **~ of war** n Tauziehen nt

tuition /tju:'ɪʃn/ n Unterricht m

tulip /'tju:lɪp/ n Tulpe f

tumble /'tʌmbl/ n Sturz m □ vi fallen; **~ to sth** (fam) etw kapieren. **~down** a verfallen. **~drier** n Wäschetrockner m

tumbler /'tʌmblə(r)/ n Glas nt

tummy /'tʌmɪ/ n (fam) Magen m; (abdomen) Bauch m

tumour /'tju:mə(r)/ n Geschwulst f, Tumor m

tumult /'tju:mʌlt/ n Tumult m. **~uous** /-'mʌltjʊəs/ a stürmisch

tuna /'tju:nə/ n Thunfisch m

tune /tju:n/ n Melodie f; **out of ~** ⟨instrument⟩ verstimmt; **to the ~ of** (fam) in Höhe von □ vt stimmen; (Techn) einstellen. **in** vt einstellen □ vi **~ to a station** einen Sender einstellen. **~ up** vi (Mus) stimmen

tuneful /'tju:nfl/ a melodisch

tunic /'tju:nɪk/ n (Mil) Uniformjacke f; (Sch) Trägerkleid nt

Tunisia /tju:'nɪzɪə/ n Tunesien nt

tunnel /'tʌnl/ n Tunnel m □ vi (pt/pp **tunnelled**) einen Tunnel graben

turban /'tɜ:bən/ n Turban m

turbine /'tɜ:baɪn/ n Turbine f

turbot /'tɜ:bət/ n Steinbutt m

turbulen|ce /'tɜ:bjʊləns/ n Turbulenz f. **~t** a stürmisch

tureen /tjʊə'ri:n/ n Terrine f

turf /tɜ:f/ n Rasen m; (segment) Rasenstück nt. **~ out** vt (fam) rausschmeißen

'turf accountant n Buchmacher m

Turk /tɜ:k/ n Türke m/Türkin f

turkey /'tɜ:kɪ/ n Pute f, Truthahn m

Turk|ey n die Türkei. **~ish** a türkisch

turmoil /'tɜ:mɔɪl/ n Aufruhr m; (confusion) Durcheinander nt

turn /tɜ:n/ n (rotation) Drehung f; (in road) Kurve f; (change of direction) Wende f; (short walk) Runde f; (Theat) Nummer f; (fam: attack) Anfall m; **do s.o. a good ~** jdm einen guten Dienst erweisen; **take ~s** sich abwechseln; **in ~** der Reihe nach; **out of ~** außer der Reihe; **it's your ~** du bist an der Reihe □ vt drehen; (~ over) wenden; (reverse) umdrehen; (Techn) drechseln ⟨wood⟩; **~ the page** umblättern; **~ the corner** um die Ecke biegen □ vi sich drehen; (~ round) sich umdrehen; ⟨car:⟩ wenden; ⟨leaves:⟩ sich färben; ⟨weather:⟩ umschlagen; (become) werden; **right/left** nach rechts/links abbiegen; **~ to s.o.** sich an jdn wenden □ vt **have ~ed against s.o.** gegen jdn sein. **~ away** vt abweisen □ vi sich abwenden. **~ down** vt herunterdrehen ⟨collar⟩; herunterdrehen ⟨heat, gas⟩; leiser stellen ⟨sound⟩; (reject) ablehnen; abweisen ⟨person⟩. **~ in** vt einschlagen ⟨edges⟩ □ vi ⟨car:⟩ einbiegen; (fam: go to bed) ins Bett gehen. **~ off** vt zudrehen ⟨tap⟩; ausschalten ⟨light, radio⟩; abstellen ⟨water, gas, engine, machine⟩ □ vi abbiegen. **~ on** vt aufdrehen ⟨tap⟩; einschalten ⟨light, radio⟩; anstellen ⟨water, gas, engine, machine⟩. **~ out** vt (*expel*) vertreiben, (*fam*) hinauswerfen; ausschalten ⟨*light*⟩; abdrehen ⟨*gas*⟩; (*produce*) produzieren; (*empty*) ausleeren; [gründlich] aufräumen ⟨*room, cupboard*⟩ □ *vi* (*go out*) hinausgehen; (*transpire*) sich herausstellen; ~ **out well/badly** gut/schlecht gehen. ~ **over** *vt* umdrehen □ *vi* sich umdrehen. ~ **up** *vt* hochschlagen ⟨*collar*⟩; aufdrehen ⟨*heat, gas*⟩; lauter stellen ⟨*sound, radio*⟩ □ *vi* auftauchen

turning /'tɜːnɪŋ/ *n* Abzweigung *f.* **~-point** *n* Wendepunkt *m*

turnip /'tɜːnɪp/ *n* weiße Rübe *f*

turn-: ~out *n* (*of people*) Teilnahme *f*, Beteiligung *f*; (*of goods*) Produktion *f*. ~ **over** *n* (*Comm*) Umsatz *m*; (*of staff*) Personalwechsel *m*. ~**pike** *n* (*Amer*) gebührenpflichtige Autobahn *f*. ~ **stile** *n* Drehkreuz *nt*. ~**table** *n* Drehscheibe *f*; (*on record-player*) Plattenteller *m*. ~**-up** *n* [Hosen]aufschlag *m*

turpentine /'tɜːpəntaɪn/ *n* Terpentin *nt*

turquoise /'tɜːkwɔɪz/ *a* türkis[farben] □ *n* (*gem*) Türkis *m*

turret /'tarɪt/ *n* Türmchen *nt*

turtle /'tɜːtl/ *n* Seeschildkröte *f*

tusk /tʌsk/ *n* Stoßzahn *m*

tussle /'tʌsl/ *n* Balgerei *f*; (*fig*) Streit *m* □ *vi* sich balgen

tutor /'tjuːtə(r)/ *n* [Privat]lehrer *m*

tuxedo /tʌk'siːdəʊ/ *n* (*Amer*) Smoking *m*

TV *abbr of* television

twaddle /'twɒdl/ *n* Geschwätz *nt*

twang /twæŋ/ *n* (*in voice*) Näseln *nt* □ *vt* zupfen

tweed /twiːd/ *n* Tweed *m*

tweezers /'twiːzəz/ *npl* Pinzette *f*

twelfth /twelfθ/ *a* zwölfte(r,s)

twelve /twelv/ *a* zwölf

twentieth /'twentɪɪθ/ *a* zwanzigste(r,s)

twenty /'twentɪ/ *a* zwanzig

twerp /twɜːp/ *n* (*fam*) Trottel *m*

twice /twaɪs/ *adv* zweimal

twiddle /'twɪdl/ *vt* drehen an (+ *dat*)

twig[1] /twɪg/ *n* Zweig *m*

twig[2] /twɪg/ *vt/i* (*pt/pp* **twigged**) (*fam*) kapieren

twilight /'twaɪ-/ *n* Dämmerlicht *nt*

twin /twɪn/ *n* Zwilling *m* □ *attrib* Zwillings-. ~ **beds** *npl* zwei Einzelbetten *pl*

twine /twaɪn/ *n* Bindfaden *m* □ *vi* sich winden; ⟨*plant*:⟩ sich ranken

twinge /twɪndʒ/ *n* Stechen *nt*; ~ **of conscience** Gewissensbisse *pl*

twinkle /'twɪŋkl/ *n* Funkeln *nt* □ *vi* funkeln

twin 'town *n* Partnerstadt *f*

twirl /twɜːl/ *vt/i* herumwirbeln

twist /twɪst/ *n* Drehung *f*; (*curve*) Kurve *f*; (*unexpected occurrence*) überraschende Wendung *f* □ *vt* drehen; (*distort*) verdrehen; (*fam: swindle*) beschummeln; ~ **one's ankle** sich (*dat*) den Knöchel verrenken □ *vi* sich drehen; ⟨*road*:⟩ sich winden. ~**er** *n* (*fam*) Schwindler *m*

twit /twɪt/ *n* (*fam*) Trottel *m*

twitch /twɪtʃ/ *n* Zucken *nt* □ *vi* zucken

twitter /'twɪtə(r)/ *n* Zwitschern *nt* □ *vi* zwitschern

two /tuː/ *a* zwei

two-: ~faced *a* falsch. ~**piece** *a* zweiteilig. ~**some** /-səm/ *n* Paar *nt*. ~**way** *a* ~**way traffic** Gegenverkehr *m*

tycoon /tar'kuːn/ *n* Magnat *m*

tying /'taɪɪŋ/ *see* **tie**

type /taɪp/ *n* Art *f*, Sorte *f*; (*person*) Typ *m*; (*printing*) Type *f* □ *vt* mit der Maschine schreiben, (*fam*) tippen □ *vi* maschineschreiben, (*fam*) tippen. ~ **writer** *n* Schreibmaschine *f*. ~ **written** *a* maschinegeschrieben

typhoid /'taɪfɔɪd/ *n* Typhus *m*

typical /'tɪpɪkl/ *a*, **-ly** *adv* typisch (*of* für)

typify /'tɪpɪfaɪ/ *vt* (*pt/pp* **-ied**) typisch sein für

typing /'taɪpɪŋ/ n Maschinenschreiben nt. ~ **paper** n Schreibmaschinenpapier nt

typist /'taɪpɪst/ n Schreibkraft f

typography /taɪ'pɒgrəfi/ n Typographie f

tyrannical /tɪ'rænɪkl/ a tyrannisch

tyranny /'tɪrəni/ n Tyrannei f

tyrant /'taɪrənt/ n Tyrann m

tyre /'taɪə(r)/ n Reifen m

U

ubiquitous /ju:'bɪkwɪtəs/ a allgegenwärtig; **be** ~ überall zu finden sein

udder /'ʌdə(r)/ n Euter nt

ugl|iness /'ʌglɪnɪs/ n Häßlichkeit f. ~**y** a (-ier, -iest) häßlich; (nasty) übel

UK abbr see United Kingdom

ulcer /'ʌlsə(r)/ n Geschwür nt

ulterior /ʌl'tɪərɪə(r)/ a ~ **motive** Hintergedanke m

ultimate /'ʌltɪmət/ a letzte(r,s); (final) endgültig; (fundamental) grundlegend, eigentlich. ~**ly** adv schließlich

ultimatum /ʌltɪ'meɪtəm/ n Ultimatum nt

ultrasound /'ʌltrə-/ n (Med) Ultraschall m

ultra'violet a ultraviolett

umbilical /ʌm'bɪlɪkl/ a ~ **cord** Nabelschnur f

umbrella /ʌm'brelə/ n (Regen)schirm m

umpire /'ʌmpaɪə(r)/ n Schiedsrichter m ○ vt/i Schiedsrichter sein (bei)

umpteen /ʌmp'ti:n/ a (fam) zig. ~**th** a (fam) zigste(r,s); for the ~**th time** zum zigsten Mal

un'able /ʌn-/ a **be** ~ **to do sth** etw nicht tun können

una'bridged a ungekürzt

unac'companied a ohne Begleitung; ⟨luggage⟩ unbegleitet

unac'countabl|e a unerklärlich. ~ **ly** adv unerklärlicherweise

unac'customed a ungewohnt; **be** ~ **to sth** etw nicht gewohnt sein

una'dulterated a unverfälscht, rein; (utter) völlig

un'aided a ohne fremde Hilfe

unalloyed /ʌnə'lɔɪd/ a (fig) ungetrübt

unanimity /ju:nə'nɪmətɪ/ n Einstimmigkeit f

unanimous /ju:'nænɪməs/ a, -ly adv einmütig; ⟨vote, decision⟩ einstimmig

un'armed a unbewaffnet; ~ **combat** Kampf m ohne Waffen

unas'suming a bescheiden

unat'tached a nicht befestigt; ⟨person⟩ ungebunden

unat'tended a unbeaufsichtigt

un'authorized a unbefugt

una'voidable a unvermeidlich

una'ware a **be** ~ **of sth** sich (dat) etw (gen) nicht bewußt sein. ~**s** /-əz/ adv **catch s.o.** ~**s** jdn überraschen

un'balanced a unausgewogen; (mentally) unausgeglichen

un'bearable a, -bly adv unerträglich

unbeat|able /ʌn'bi:təbl/ a unschlagbar. ~**en** a ungeschlagen; ⟨record⟩ ungebrochen

unbeknown /ʌnbɪ'nəʊn/ a (fam) ~ **to me** ohne mein Wissen

unbe'lievable a unglaublich

un'bend vi (pt/pp -bent) (relax) aus sich herausgehen

un'biased a unvoreingenommen

un'block vt frei machen

un'bolt vt aufriegeln

un'breakable a unzerbrechlich

un'bridled /ʌn'braɪdld/ a ungezügelt

un'burden vt ~ **oneself** (fig) sich aussprechen

un'button vt aufknöpfen

uncalled-for /ʌn'kɔ:ldfɔ:(r)/ a unangebracht

un'canny a unheimlich

un'ceasing a unaufhörlich

unceremonious *a*, **-ly** *adv* formlos; *(abrupt)* brüsk

un'certain *a* *(doubtful)* ungewiß; ⟨*origins*⟩ unbestimmt; **be ~** nicht sicher sein; **in no ~ terms** ganz eindeutig. **~ty** *n* Ungewißheit *f*

un'changed *a* unverändert

un'charitable *a* lieblos

uncle /'ʌŋkl/ *n* Onkel *m*

un'comfortable *a*, **-bly** *adv* unbequem; **feel ~** *(fig)* sich nicht wohl fühlen

un'common *a* ungewöhnlich

un'compromising *a* kompromißlos

uncon'ditional *a*, **-ly** *adv* bedingungslos

un'conscious *a* bewußtlos; *(unintended)* unbewußt; **be ~ of sth** sich *(dat)* etw *(gen)* nicht bewußt sein. **~ly** *adv* unbewußt

uncon'ventional *a* unkonventionell

unco'operative *a* nicht hilfsbereit

un'cork *vt* entkorken

uncouth /ʌn'kuːθ/ *a* ungehobelt

un'cover *vt* aufdecken

unctuous /'ʌŋktjʊəs/ *a*, **-ly** *adv* salbungsvoll

unde'cided *a* unentschlossen; *(not settled)* nicht entschieden

undeniable /ʌndɪ'naɪəbl/ *a*, **-bly** *adv* unbestreitbar

under /'ʌndə(r)/ *prep* unter (+ *dat/acc*); **~ it** darunter; **~ there** da drunter; **~ repair** in Reparatur; **~ construction** im Bau; **~ age** minderjährig; **~ way** unterwegs; *(fig)* im Gange □ *adv* darunter

'**undercarriage** *n* *(Aviat)* Fahrwerk *nt*, Fahrgestell *nt*

'**underclothes** *npl* Unterwäsche *f*

under'cover *a* geheim

'**undercurrent** *n* Unterströmung *f*; *(fig)* Unterton *m*

under'cut *vt* *(pt/pp* **-cut**) *(Comm)* unterbieten

'**underdog** *n* Unterlegene(r) *m*

under'done *a* nicht gar; *(rare)* nicht durchgebraten

under'estimate *vt* unterschätzen

under'fed *a* unterernährt

under'foot *adv* am Boden; **trample ~** zertrampeln

under'go *vt* *(pt* **-went**, *pp* **-gone**) durchmachen; sich unterziehen (+ *dat*) ⟨*operation*, *treatment*⟩; **~ repairs** repariert werden

under'graduate *n* Student(in) *m(f)*

under'ground[1] *adv* unter der Erde; ⟨*mining*⟩ unter Tage

'**underground**[2] *a* unterirdisch; *(secret)* Untergrund- □ *n* *(railway)* U-Bahn *f*. **~ car park** *n* Tiefgarage *f*

'**undergrowth** *n* Unterholz *nt*

'**underhand** *a* hinterhältig

'**underlay** *n* Unterlage *f*

under'lie *vt* *(pt* **-lay**, *pp* **-lain**, *pres p* **-lying**) *(fig)* zugrundeliegen (+ *dat*)

under'line *vt* unterstreichen

underling /'ʌndəlɪŋ/ *n* *(pej)* Untergebene(r) *m/f*

under'lying *a* *(fig)* eigentlich

under'mine *vt* *(fig)* unterminieren, untergraben

underneath /ʌndə'niːθ/ *prep* unter (+ *dat/acc*); **~ it** darunter □ *adv* darunter

'**underpants** *npl* Unterhose *f*

'**underpass** *n* Unterführung *f*

under'privileged *a* unterprivilegiert

under'rate *vt* unterschätzen

'**underseal** *n* *(Auto)* Unterbodenschutz *m*

'**undershirt** *n* *(Amer)* Unterhemd *nt*

under'staffed /-'stɑːft/ *a* unterbesetzt

under'stand *vt/i* *(pt/pp* **-stood**) verstehen; **I ~ that ...** *(have heard)* ich habe gehört, daß ... **~able** /-əbl/ *a* verständlich. **~ably** /-əblɪ/ *adv* verständlicherweise

under'standing a verständnisvoll □n Verständnis nt; (agreement) Vereinbarung f; **reach an ~ sich** verständigen; **on the ~ that** unter der Voraussetzung, daß

'understatement n Untertreibung f

'understudy n (Theat) Ersatzspieler(in) m(f)

under'take vt (pt -took, pp -taken) unternehmen; ~ **to do sth** sich verpflichten, etw zu tun

'undertaker n Leichenbestatter m; [firm of] ~s Bestattungsinstitut nt

under'taking n Unternehmen nt; (promise) Versprechen nt

'undertone n (fig) Unterton m; **in an ~** mit gedämpfter Stimme

under'value vt unterbewerten

'underwater[1] a Unterwasser-

under'water[2] adv unter Wasser

'underwear n Unterwäsche f

'underweight a untergewichtig; **be ~** Untergewicht haben

'underworld n Unterwelt f

'underwriter n Versicherer m

unde'sirable a unerwünscht

undies /'ʌndɪz/ npl (fam) [Damen]unterwäsche f

un'dignified a würdelos

un'do vt (pt -did, pp -done) aufmachen; (fig) ungeschehen machen; (ruin) zunichte machen

un'done a offen; (not accomplished) unerledigt

un'doubted a unzweifelhaft. ~ly adv zweifellos

un'dress vt ausziehen; **get ~ed** sich ausziehen □vi sich ausziehen

un'due a übermäßig

undulating /'ʌndjʊleɪtɪŋ/ a Wellen-; (country) wellig

un'duly adv übermäßig

un'dying a ewig

un'earth vt ausgraben; (fig) zutage bringen. ~ly a unheimlich; **at an ~ly hour** (fam) in aller Herrgottsfrühe

un'eas|e n Unbehagen nt. ~y a unbehaglich; **I feel ~y** mir ist unbehaglich zumute

un'eatable a ungenießbar

uneco'nomic a, **-ally** adv unwirtschaftlich

uneco'nomical a verschwenderisch

unem'ployed a arbeitslos □npl **the ~** die Arbeitslosen

unem'ployment n Arbeitslosigkeit f. ~ **benefit** n Arbeitslosenunterstützung f

un'ending a endlos

un'equal a unterschiedlich; (struggle) ungleich; **be ~ to a task** einer Aufgabe nicht gewachsen sein. ~ly adv ungleichmäßig

une'quivocal /ʌnɪ'kwɪvəkl/ a, **-ly** adv eindeutig

un'erring /ʌn'ɜːrɪŋ/ a unfehlbar

un'ethical a unmoralisch; **be ~** gegen das Berufsethos verstoßen

un'even a uneben; (unequal) ungleich; (not regular) ungleichmäßig; (number) ungerade. ~ly adv ungleichmäßig

unex'pected a, **-ly** adv unerwartet

un'failing a nie versagend

un'fair a, **-ly** adv ungerecht, unfair. ~**ness** n Ungerechtigkeit f

un'faithful a untreu

unfa'miliar a ungewohnt; (unknown) unbekannt

un'fasten vt aufmachen; (detach) losmachen

un'favourable a ungünstig

un'feeling a gefühllos

un'finished a unvollendet; (business) unerledigt

un'fit a ungeeignet; (incompetent) unfähig; (Sport) nicht fit; ~ **for work** arbeitsunfähig

un'flinching /ʌn'flɪntʃɪŋ/ a unerschrocken

un'fold vt auseinanderfalten, entfalten; (spread out) ausbreiten □vi sich entfalten

unfore'seen a unvorhergesehen

unforgettable /ʌnfə'getəbl/ a unvergeßlich

unforgivable /ʌnfə'gɪvəbl/ a unverzeihlich

un'fortunate a unglücklich; (*unfavourable*) ungünstig; (*regrettable*) bedauerlich; be ~ ⟨person:⟩ Pech haben. **~ly** adv leider

un'founded a unbegründet

unfurl /ʌn'fɜ:l/ vt entrollen □vi sich entrollen

un'furnished a unmöbliert

ungainly /ʌn'geɪnlɪ/ a unbeholfen

ungodly /ʌn'gɒdlɪ/ a gottlos; at an ~ hour (*fam*) in aller Herrgottsfrühe

un'grateful a, **-ly** adv undankbar

un'happi|**ly** adv unglücklich; (*unfortunately*) leider. **~ness** n Kummer m

un'happy a unglücklich; (*not content*) unzufrieden

un'harmed a unverletzt

un'healthy a ungesund

un'hook vt vom Haken nehmen; aufhaken ⟨*dress*⟩

un'hurt a unverletzt

unhy'gienic a unhygienisch

unicorn /'ju:nɪkɔ:n/ n Einhorn nt

unification /ju:nɪfɪ'keɪʃn/ n Einigung f

uniform /'ju:nɪfɔ:m/ a, **-ly** adv einheitlich □n Uniform f

unify /'ju:nɪfaɪ/ vt (pt/pp **-ied**) einigen

uni'lateral /ju:nɪ-/ a, **-ly** adv einseitig

uni'maginable a unvorstellbar

unim'portant a unwichtig

unin'habited a unbewohnt

unin'tentional a, **-ly** adv unabsichtlich

union /'ju:nɪən/ n Vereinigung f; (*Pol*) Union f; (*trade* ~) Gewerkschaft f. **~ist** n (*Pol*) Unionist m

unique /ju:'ni:k/ a einzigartig. **~ly** adv einmalig

unison /'ju:nɪsn/ n in ~ einstimmig

unit /'ju:nɪt/ n Einheit f; (*Math*) Einer m; (*of furniture*) Teil nt, Element nt

unite /ju:'naɪt/ vt vereinigen □vi sich vereinigen

united /ju:'naɪtɪd/ a einig. **U~ 'Kingdom** n Vereinigtes Königreich nt. **U~ 'Nations** n Vereinte Nationen pl. **U~ 'States [of America]** n Vereinigte Staaten pl [von Amerika]

unity /'ju:nɪtɪ/ n Einheit f; (*harmony*) Einigkeit f

universal /ju:nɪ'vɜ:sl/ a, **-ly** adv allgemein

universe /'ju:nɪvɜ:s/ n [Welt]all nt, Universum nt

university /ju:nɪ'vɜ:sətɪ/ n Universität f □attrib Universitäts-

un'just a, **-ly** adv ungerecht

unkempt /ʌn'kempt/ a ungepflegt

un'kind a, **-ly** adv unfreundlich; (*harsh*) häßlich. **~ness** n Unfreundlichkeit f; Häßlichkeit f

un'known a unbekannt

un'lawful a, **-ly** adv gesetzwidrig

un'leaded /ʌn'ledɪd/ a bleifrei

un'leash vt (*fig*) entfesseln

unless /ən'les/ conj wenn … nicht; ~ I am mistaken wenn ich mich nicht irre

un'like a nicht ähnlich, unähnlich; (*not the same*) ungleich □prep im Gegensatz zu (+ *dat*)

un'likely a unwahrscheinlich

un'limited a unbegrenzt

un'load vt entladen; ausladen ⟨*luggage*⟩

un'lock vt aufschließen

un'lucky a unglücklich; ⟨*day, number*⟩ Unglücks-; be ~ Pech haben; ⟨*thing*:⟩ Unglück bringen

un'manned a unbemannt

un'married a unverheiratet. **~ 'mother** n ledige Mutter f

un'mask vt (*fig*) entlarven

unmistakable /ʌnmɪ'steɪkəbl/ a, **-bly** adv unverkennbar

un'mitigated a vollkommen

un'natural a, **-ly** adv unnatürlich; (*not normal*) nicht normal

un'necessary a, **-ily** adv unnötig
un'noticed a unbemerkt
unob'tainable a nicht erhältlich
unob'trusive a, **-ly** adv un-
aufdringlich; ⟨thing⟩ unauffällig
unof'ficial a, **-ly** adv inoffiziell
un'pack vt/i auspacken
un'paid a unbezahlt
un'palatable a ungenießbar
un'paralleled a beispiellos
un'pick vt auftrennen
un'pleasant a, **-ly** adv unangenehm. **~ness** n (bad feeling)
Ärger m
un'plug vt ⟨pt/pp **-plugged**⟩ den
Stecker herausziehen von
un'popular a unbeliebt
un'precedented a beispiellos
unpre'dictable a unberechenbar
unpre'meditated a nicht vorsätzlich
unpre'pared a nicht vorbereitet
unprepos'sessing a wenig attraktiv
unpre'tentious a bescheiden
un'principled a skrupellos
unpro'fessional a be ~ gegen
das Berufsethos verstoßen;
⟨Sport⟩ unsportlich sein
un'profitable a unrentabel
un'qualified a unqualifiziert;
⟨fig: absolute⟩ uneingeschränkt
un'questionable a unbezweifel-
bar; ⟨right⟩ unbestreitbar
unravel /ʌn'rævl/ vt ⟨pt/pp
-ravelled⟩ entwirren; ⟨Knitting⟩
aufziehen
un'real a unwirklich
un'reasonable a unvernünftig;
be ~ zuviel verlangen
unre'lated a unzusammenhängend; be ~ nicht verwandt sein;
⟨events:⟩ nicht miteinander zusammenhängen
unre'liable a unzuverlässig
unrequited /ʌnrɪ'kwaɪtɪd/ a
unerwidert
unre'servedly /ʌnrɪ'zɜːvɪdlɪ/ adv
uneingeschränkt; ⟨frankly⟩ offen
un'rest n Unruhen pl
un'rivalled a unübertroffen

un'roll vt aufrollen □vi sich aufrollen
unruly /ʌn'ruːlɪ/ a ungebärdig
un'safe a nicht sicher
un'said a ungesagt
un'salted a ungesalzen
unsatis'factory a unbefriedigend
un'savoury a unangenehm; ⟨fig⟩
unerfreulich
unscathed /ʌn'skeɪðd/ a unver-
sehrt
un'screw vt abschrauben
un'scrupulous a skrupellos
un'seemly a unschicklich
un'selfish a selbstlos
un'settled a ungeklärt; ⟨weather⟩
unbeständig; ⟨bill⟩ unbezahlt
unshakeable /ʌn'ʃeɪkəbl/ a unerschütterlich
unshaven /ʌn'ʃervn/ a unrasiert
unsightly /ʌn'saɪtlɪ/ a unansehnlich
un'skilled a ungelernt; ⟨work⟩
unqualifiziert
un'sociable a ungesellig
unso'phisticated a einfach
un'sound a krank, nicht gesund;
⟨building⟩ nicht sicher; ⟨advice⟩
unzuverlässig; ⟨reasoning⟩ nicht
stichhaltig; of ~ mind unzurechnungsfähig
unspeakable /ʌn'spiːkəbl/ a unbeschreiblich
un'stable a nicht stabil; ⟨men-
tally⟩ labil
un'steady a, **-ily** adv unsicher;
⟨wobbly⟩ wackelig
un'stuck a come ~ sich lösen;
⟨fam: fail⟩ scheitern
unsuc'cessful a, **-ly** adv erfolg-
los; be ~ keinen Erfolg haben
un'suitable a ungeeignet; ⟨in-
appropriate⟩ unpassend; ⟨for
weather, activity⟩ unzweckmäßig
unsu'specting a ahnungslos
un'sweetened a ungesüßt
unthinkable /ʌn'θɪŋkəbl/ a unvorstellbar
un'tidiness n Unordentlichkeit f
un'tidy a, **-ily** adv unordentlich

un'tie vt aufbinden; losbinden ⟨person, boat, horse⟩

until /ən'tɪl/ prep bis (+ acc); not ~ erst; ~ the evening bis zum Abend; ~ his arrival bis zu seiner Ankunft □conj bis; not ~ erst wenn; (in past) erst als

untimely /ʌn'taɪmlɪ/ a ungelegen; (premature) vorzeitig

un'tiring a unermüdlich

un'told a unermeßlich

unto'ward a ungünstig; (unseemly) ungehörig; **if nothing ~ happens** wenn nichts dazwischenkommt

un'true a unwahr; **that's ~** das ist nicht wahr

unused¹ /ʌn'juːzd/ a unbenutzt; (not utilized) ungenutzt

unused² /ʌn'juːst/ a **be ~ to sth** etw nicht gewohnt sein

un'usual a, **-ly** adv ungewöhnlich

un'veil vt enthüllen

un'versed a nicht bewandert (in in + dat)

un'wanted a unerwünscht

un'warranted a ungerechtfertigt

un'welcome a unwillkommen

un'well a **be** or **feel ~** sich nicht wohl fühlen

unwieldy /ʌn'wiːldɪ/ a sperrig

un'willing a, **-ly** adv widerwillig; **be ~ to do sth** etw nicht tun wollen

un'wind v (pt/pp **unwound**) □vt abwickeln □vi sich abwickeln; (fam: relax) sich entspannen

un'wise a, **-ly** adv unklug

unwitting /ʌn'wɪtɪŋ/ a, **-ly** adv unwissentlich

un'worthy a unwürdig

un'wrap vt (pt/pp **-wrapped**) auswickeln; auspacken ⟨present⟩

un'written a ungeschrieben

up /ʌp/ adv nach oben; (with movement) nach oben; (not in bed) auf; ⟨collar⟩ hochgeklappt; ⟨road⟩ aufgerissen; ⟨price⟩ gestiegen; ⟨curtains⟩ aufgehängt; ⟨shelves⟩ angebracht; ⟨notice⟩ angeschlagen;

⟨tent⟩ aufgebaut; ⟨building⟩ gebaut; **be up for sale** zu verkaufen sein; **up there** da oben; **up to** (as far as) bis; **time's up** die Zeit ist um; **what's up?** (fam) was ist los? **what's he up to?** (fam) was hat er vor? **I don't feel up to it** ich fühle mich dem nicht gewachsen; **be one up on s.o.** (fam) jdm etwas vorausohaben; **go up** hinaufgehen; **come up** heraufkommen □**prep be up on sth** [oben] auf etw (dat) sein; **up the mountain** oben am Berg; (movement) den Berg hinauf; **be up the tree** oben im Baum sein; **up the road** die Straße entlang; **up the river** stromaufwärts; **go up the stairs** die Treppe hinaufgehen; **be up the pub** (fam) in der Kneipe sein

'upbringing n Erziehung f

up'date vt auf den neuesten Stand bringen

up'grade vt aufstufen

upheaval /ʌp'hiːvl/ n Unruhe f; (Pol) Umbruch m

up'hill a (fig) mühsam □adv bergauf

up'hold vt (pt/pp **upheld**) unterstützen; bestätigen ⟨verdict⟩

upholster /ʌp'həʊlstə(r)/ vt polstern. ~**er** n Polsterer m. ~**y** n Polsterung f

'upkeep n Unterhalt m

up-'market a anspruchsvoll

upon /ə'pɒn/ prep auf (+ dat/acc)

upper /'ʌpə(r)/ a obere(r,s); ⟨deck, jaw, lip⟩ Ober-; **have the ~ hand** die Oberhand haben □ n (of shoe) Obermaterial nt

upper: ~ **circle** n zweiter Rang m. ~ **class** n Oberschicht f. ~**most** a oberste(r,s)

'upright a aufrecht □ n Pfosten m

'uprising n Aufstand m

'uproar n Aufruhr m

up'root vt entwurzeln

upset¹ vt (pt/pp **upset**, pres p **upsetting**) umstoßen; (spill) verschütten; durcheinanderbringen ⟨plan⟩ (distress) erschüttern;

⟨food:⟩ nicht bekommen (+ dat); get ~ about sth sich über etw (acc) aufregen; be very ~ sehr bestürzt sein

'upset² n Aufregung f; have a stomach ~ einen verdorbenen Magen haben

'upshot n Ergebnis nt

upside 'down adv verkehrt herum; turn ~ umdrehen

up'stairs¹ adv oben; ⟨go⟩ nach oben

up'stairs² a im Obergeschoß

'upstart n Emporkömmling m

up'stream adv stromaufwärts

'upsurge n Zunahme f

'uptake n slow on the ~ schwer von Begriff; be quick on the ~ schnell begreifen

'uptight a nervös

'upturn n Aufschwung m

upward /'ʌpwəd/ a nach oben; ⟨movement⟩ Aufwärts-; ~ slope Steigung f □ ~ [s] aufwärts, nach oben

uranium /jʊ'reɪnɪəm/ n Uran nt

urban /'ɜːbən/ a städtisch

urbane /ɜː'beɪn/ a weltmännisch

urge /ɜːdʒ/ n Trieb m, Drang m □ vt drängen; ~ on antreiben

urgen|cy /'ɜːdʒənsɪ/ n Dringlichkeit f. ~t a, ~ly adv dringend

urinate /'jʊərɪneɪt/ vi urinieren

urine /'jʊərɪn/ n Urin m, Harn m

urn /ɜːn/ n Urne f; (for tea) Teemaschine f

us /ʌs/ pron uns; it's us wir sind es

US[A] abbr USA pl

usable /'juːzəbl/ a brauchbar

usage /'juːzɪdʒ/ n Brauch m; (of word) [Sprach]gebrauch m

use¹ /juːs/ n (see use²) Benutzung f; Verwendung f; Gebrauch m; be of ~ nützlich sein; be of no ~ nichts nützen; make ~ of Gebrauch machen von; (exploit) ausnutzen; it is no ~ es hat keinen Zweck; what's the ~? wozu?

use² /juːz/ vt benutzen ⟨implement, room, lift⟩; verwenden ⟨ingredient, method, book, money⟩; gebrauchen ⟨words, force, brains⟩; ~ [up] aufbrauchen

used¹ /juːzd/ a benutzt; ⟨car⟩ gebraucht

used² /juːst/ pt be ~ to sth an etw (acc) gewöhnt sein; get ~ to sich gewöhnen an (+ acc); he ~ to say er hat immer gesagt; he ~ to live here er hat früher hier gewohnt

useful /'juːsfl/ a nützlich. ~ness n Nützlichkeit f

useless /'juːslɪs/ a nutzlos; (not usable) unbrauchbar; (pointless) zwecklos

user /'juːzə(r)/ n Benutzer(in) m(f). ~-'friendly a benutzerfreundlich

usher /'ʌʃə(r)/ n Platzanweiser m; (in court) Gerichtsdiener m □ vt ~ in hineinführen

usherette /ʌʃə'ret/ n Platzanweiserin f

USSR abbr UdSSR f

usual /'juːʒʊəl/ a üblich. ~ly adv gewöhnlich

usurp /juː'zɜːp/ vt sich (dat) widerrechtlich aneignen

utensil /juː'tensl/ n Gerät nt

uterus /'juːtərəs/ n Gebärmutter f

utilitarian /juːtɪlɪ'teərɪən/ a zweckmäßig

utility /juː'tɪlətɪ/ a Gebrauchs- □ n Nutzen m. ~ room n ≈ Waschküche f

utiliz|ation /juːtɪlaɪ'zeɪʃn/ n Nutzung f. ~e /'juːtɪlaɪz/ vt nutzen

utmost /'ʌtməʊst/ a äußerste(r,s), größte(r,s) □ n do one's ~ sein möglichstes tun

utter¹ /'ʌtə(r)/ a, ~ly adv völlig

utter² vt von sich geben ⟨sigh, sound⟩; sagen ⟨word⟩. ~ance n Äußerung f

U-turn /'juː-/ n ⟨fig⟩ Kehrtwendung f; 'no ~s' ⟨Auto⟩ 'Wenden verboten'

V

vacan|cy /'veɪkənsɪ/ n ⟨job⟩ freie Stelle f; ⟨room⟩ freies Zimmer nt; **'no ~cies** 'belegt'. **~t** a frei; ⟨look⟩ [gedanken]leer

vacate /və'keɪt/ vt räumen

vacation /və'keɪʃn/ n ⟨Univ & Amer⟩ Ferien pl

vaccinat|e /'væksɪneɪt/ vt impfen. **~ion** /-'neɪʃn/ n Impfung f

vaccine /'væksi:n/ n Impfstoff m

vacuum /'vækjʊəm/ n Vakuum nt, luftleerer Raum m □ vt saugen. **~ cleaner** n Staubsauger m. **~ flask** n Thermosflasche (P) f. **~-packed** a vakuumverpackt

vagaries /'veɪgərɪz/ npl Launen pl

vagina /və'dʒaɪnə/ n ⟨Anat⟩ Scheide f

vagrant /'veɪgrənt/ n Landstreicher m

vague /veɪg/ a (-r, -st), **-ly** adv vage; ⟨outline⟩ verschwommen

vain /veɪn/ a (-er, -est) eitel; ⟨hope, attempt⟩ vergeblich; **in ~** vergeblich. **~ly** adv vergeblich

vale /veɪl/ n ⟨liter⟩ Tal nt

valet /'væleɪ/ n Kammerdiener m

valiant /'væliənt/ a, **-ly** adv tapfer

valid /'vælɪd/ a gültig; ⟨claim⟩ berechtigt; ⟨argument⟩ stichhaltig; ⟨reason⟩ triftig. **~ate** vt ⟨confirm⟩ bestätigen. **~ity** /və'lɪdətɪ/ n Gültigkeit f

valley /'vælɪ/ n Tal nt

valour /'vælə(r)/ n Tapferkeit f

valuable /'væljʊəbl/ a wertvoll. **~s** npl Wertsachen pl

valuation /vælju'eɪʃn/ n Schätzung f

value /'vælju:/ n Wert m; ⟨usefulness⟩ Nutzen m □ vt schätzen. **~ 'added tax** n Mehrwertsteuer f

valve /vælv/ n Ventil nt; ⟨Anat⟩ Klappe f; ⟨Electr⟩ Röhre f

vampire /'væmpaɪə(r)/ n Vampir m

van /væn/ n Lieferwagen m

vandal /'vændl/ n Rowdy m. **~ism** /-ɪzm/ n mutwillige Zerstörung f. **~ize** vt demolieren

vanilla /və'nɪlə/ n Vanille f

vanish /'vænɪʃ/ vi verschwinden

vanity /'vænɪtɪ/ n Eitelkeit f. **~ bag** n Kosmetiktäschchen nt

vantage-point /'vɑ:ntɪdʒ-/ n Aussichtspunkt m

vapour /'veɪpə(r)/ n Dampf m

variable /'veərɪəbl/ a unbeständig; ⟨Math⟩ variabel; ⟨adjustable⟩ regulierbar

variance /'veərɪəns/ n **be at ~** nicht übereinstimmen

variant /'veərɪənt/ n Variante f

variation /veərɪ'eɪʃn/ n Variation f; ⟨difference⟩ Unterschied m

varicose /'værɪkəʊs/ a **~ veins** pl Krampfadern pl

varied /'veərɪd/ a vielseitig; ⟨diet⟩ abwechslungsreich

variety /və'raɪətɪ/ n Abwechslung f; ⟨quantity⟩ Vielfalt f; ⟨Comm⟩ Auswahl f; ⟨type⟩ Art f; ⟨Bot⟩ Abart f; ⟨Theat⟩ Varieté nt

various /'veərɪəs/ a verschiedene. **~ly** adv unterschiedlich

varnish /'vɑ:nɪʃ/ n Lack m □ vt lackieren

vary /'veərɪ/ v (pt/pp -ied) sich ändern; ⟨be different⟩ verschieden sein □ vt [ver]ändern; ⟨add variety to⟩ abwechslungsreicher gestalten. **~ing** a wechselnd; ⟨different⟩ unterschiedlich

vase /vɑ:z/ n Vase f

vast /vɑ:st/ a riesig; ⟨expanse⟩ weit. **~ly** adv gewaltig

vat /væt/ n Bottich m

VAT /vi:eɪ'ti:, væt/ abbr ⟨value added tax⟩ Mehrwertsteuer f, MwSt.

vault¹ /vɔ:lt/ n ⟨roof⟩ Gewölbe nt; ⟨in bank⟩ Tresor m; ⟨tomb⟩ Gruft f

vault² n Sprung m □ vt/i **~ [over]** springen über

VDU abbr ⟨visual display unit⟩ Bildschirmgerät nt

veal /vi:l/ n Kalbfleisch nt □ attrib Kalbs-

veer /vɪə(r)/ vi sich drehen; (Naut) abdrehen; (Auto) ausscheren
vegetable /ˈvedʒtəbl/ n Gemüse nt; ~ s pl Gemüse nt □attrib Gemüse-; (oil, fat) Pflanzen-
vegetarian /vedʒɪˈteərɪən/ a vegetarisch □ n Vegetarier(in) m(f)
vegetat|**e** /ˈvedʒɪteɪt/ vi dahinvegetieren. ~**ion** /-ˈteɪʃn/ n Vegetation f
vehemen|**ce** /ˈviːəməns/ n Heftigkeit f. ~**t** a, -**ly** adv heftig
vehicle /ˈviːɪkl/ n Fahrzeug nt; (fig: medium) Mittel nt
veil /veɪl/ n Schleier m □vt verschleiern
vein /veɪn/ n Ader f; (mood) Stimmung f; (manner) Art f; ~ **s and arteries** Venen und Arterien. ~**ed** a geädert
Velcro (P) /ˈvelkrəʊ/ n ~ **fastening** Klettverschluß m
velocity /vɪˈlɒsətɪ/ n Geschwindigkeit f
velvet /ˈvelvɪt/ n Samt m. ~**y** a samtig
vending-machine /ˈvendɪŋ-/ n [Verkaufs]automat m
vendor /ˈvendə(r)/ n Verkäufer(in) m(f)
veneer /vəˈnɪə(r)/ n Furnier nt; (fig) Tünche f. ~**ed** a furniert
venerable /ˈvenərəbl/ a ehrwürdig
venereal /vɪˈnɪərɪəl/ a ~ **disease** Geschlechtskrankheit f
Venetian /vɪˈniːʃn/ a venezianisch. v~ **blind** n Jalousie f
vengeance /ˈvendʒəns/ n Rache f; **with a** ~ (fam) gewaltig
Venice /ˈvenɪs/ n Venedig nt
venison /ˈvenɪsn/ n (Culin) Wild nt
venom /ˈvenəm/ n Gift nt; (fig) Haß m. ~**ous** /-əs/ a giftig
vent[1] /vent/ n Öffnung f; (fig) Ventil nt; **give** ~ **to** Luft machen (+ dat) □vt Luft machen (+ dat)
vent[2] n (in jacket) Schlitz m

ventilat|**e** /ˈventɪleɪt/ vt belüften. ~**ion** /-ˈleɪʃn/ n Belüftung f; (installation) Lüftung f. ~**or** n Lüftungsvorrichtung f; (Med) Beatmungsgerät nt
ventriloquist /venˈtrɪləkwɪst/ n Bauchredner m
venture /ˈventʃə(r)/ n Unternehmung f □vt wagen □vi sich wagen
venue /ˈvenjuː/ n Treffpunkt m; (for event) Veranstaltungsort m
veranda /vəˈrændə/ n Veranda f
verb /vɜːb/ n Verb nt. ~**al** a, -**ly** adv mündlich; (Gram) verbal
verbatim /vɜːˈbeɪtɪm/ a & adv [wort]wörtlich
verbose /vɜːˈbəʊs/ a weitschweifig
verdict /ˈvɜːdɪkt/ n Urteil nt
verge /vɜːdʒ/ n Rand m; **be on the** ~ **of doing sth** im Begriff sein, etw zu tun □vi ~ **on** (fig) grenzen an (+ acc)
verger /ˈvɜːdʒə(r)/ n Küster m
verify /ˈverɪfaɪ/ vt (pt/pp -**ied**) überprüfen; (confirm) bestätigen
vermin /ˈvɜːmɪn/ n Ungeziefer nt
vermouth /ˈvɜːməθ/ n Wermut m
vernacular /vəˈnækjʊlə(r)/ n Landessprache f
versatil|**e** /ˈvɜːsətaɪl/ a vielseitig. ~**ity** /-ˈtɪlətɪ/ n Vielseitigkeit f
verse /vɜːs/ n Strophe f; (of Bible) Vers m; (poetry) Lyrik f
version /ˈvɜːʃn/ n Version f; (translation) Übersetzung f; (model) Modell nt
versus /ˈvɜːsəs/ prep gegen (+ acc)
vertebra /ˈvɜːtɪbrə/ n (pl -**brae** /-briː/) (Anat) Wirbel m
vertical /ˈvɜːtɪkl/ a, -**ly** adv senkrecht □ n Senkrechte f
vertigo /ˈvɜːtɪgəʊ/ n (Med) Schwindel m
verve /vɜːv/ n Schwung m
very /ˈverɪ/ adv sehr; ~ **much** sehr; (quantity) sehr viel; ~ **little** sehr wenig; ~ **probably** höchstwahrscheinlich; **at the** ~ **most** allerhöchstens □ a (mere) bloß; **the** ~ **first** der/die/das allererste; **the** ~ **thing** genau

das Richtige; **at the ~ end/beginning** ganz am Ende/Anfang; **only a ~ little** nur ein ganz kleines bißchen

vessel /ˈvesl/ n Schiff nt; (receptacle & Anat) Gefäß nt

vest /vest/ n [Unter]hemd nt; (Amer: waistcoat) Weste □ vt ~ **sth in s.o.** jdm etw verleihen; **have a ~ed interest in sth** ein persönliches Interesse an etw (dat) haben

vestige /ˈvestɪdʒ/ n Spur f

vestment /ˈvestmənt/ n (Relig) Gewand nt

vestry /ˈvestrɪ/ n Sakristei f

vet /vet/ n Tierarzt m /-ärztin f □ vt (pt/pp vetted) überprüfen

veteran /ˈvetərən/ n Veteran m. ~ **car** n Oldtimer m

veterinary /ˈvetərɪnərɪ/ a tierärztlich. ~ **surgeon** n Tierarzt m /-ärztin

veto /ˈviːtəʊ/ n (pl -es) Veto nt □ vt sein Veto einlegen gegen

vex /veks/ vt ärgern. ~**ation** /-ˈseɪʃn/ n Ärger m. ~**ed** a verärgert; ~**ed question** vieldiskutierte Frage f

VHF abbr (very high frequency) UKW

via /ˈvaɪə/ prep über (+ acc)

viable /ˈvaɪəbl/ a lebensfähig; (fig) realisierbar; ⟨firm⟩ rentabel

viaduct /ˈvaɪədʌkt/ n Viadukt m

vibrant /ˈvaɪbrənt/ a (fig) lebhaft

vibrat|e /vaɪˈbreɪt/ vi vibrieren. ~**ion** /-ˈbreɪʃn/ n Vibrieren nt

vicar /ˈvɪkə(r)/ n Pfarrer m. ~**age** /-rɪdʒ/ n Pfarrhaus nt

vicarious /vɪˈkeərɪəs/ a nachempfunden

vice[1] /vaɪs/ n Laster nt

vice[2] n (Techn) Schraubstock m

vice ˈchairman n stellvertretender Vorsitzender m

vice ˈpresident n Vizepräsident m

vice versa /vaɪsɪˈvɜːsə/ adv umgekehrt

vicinity /vɪˈsɪnətɪ/ n Umgebung f; **in the ~ of** in der Nähe von

vicious /ˈvɪʃəs/ a, ~**ly** adv boshaft; ⟨animal⟩ bösartig. ~ **ˈcircle** n Teufelskreis m

victim /ˈvɪktɪm/ n Opfer nt. ~**ize** vt schikanieren

victor /ˈvɪktə(r)/ n Sieger m

victor|ious /vɪkˈtɔːrɪəs/ a siegreich. ~**y** /ˈvɪktərɪ/ n Sieg m

video /ˈvɪdɪəʊ/ n Video nt; (recorder) Videorecorder m □ attrib Video- □ vt [auf Videoband] aufnehmen

video: ~ **casˈsette** n Videokassette f. ~ **game** n Videospiel nt. ~ **ˈnasty** n Horrorvideo nt. ~ **recorder** n Videorecorder m

vie /vaɪ/ vi (pres p vying) wetteifern

Vienna /vɪˈenə/ n Wien nt. ~**ese** /vɪəˈniːz/ a Wiener

view /vjuː/ n Sicht f; (scene) Aussicht f, Blick m; (picture, opinion) Ansicht f; **in my ~** meiner Ansicht nach; **in ~ of** angesichts (+ gen); **keep/have sth in ~** etw im Auge behalten/haben; **be on ~** besichtigt werden können □ vt sich (dat) ansehen; besichtigen ⟨house⟩; (consider) betrachten □ vi (TV) fernsehen. ~**er** n (TV) Zuschauer(in) m(f); (Phot) Diabetrachter m

view: ~**finder** n (Phot) Sucher m. ~**point** n Standpunkt m

vigil /ˈvɪdʒɪl/ n Wache f

vigilan|ce /ˈvɪdʒɪləns/ n Wachsamkeit f. ~**t** a, ~**ly** adv wachsam

vigorous /ˈvɪɡərəs/ a, ~**ly** adv kräftig; (fig) heftig

vigour /ˈvɪɡə(r)/ n Kraft f; (fig) Heftigkeit f

vile /vaɪl/ a abscheulich

villa /ˈvɪlə/ n (for holidays) Ferienhaus nt

village /ˈvɪlɪdʒ/ n Dorf nt. ~**r** n Dorfbewohner(in) m(f)

villain /ˈvɪlən/ n Schurke m; (in story) Bösewicht m

vim /vɪm/ n (fam) Schwung m

vindicat|e /'vɪndɪkeɪt/ vt rechtfertigen. **~ion** /-'keɪʃn/ n Rechtfertigung f

vindictive /vɪn'dɪktɪv/ a nachtragend

vine /vaɪn/ n Weinrebe f

vinegar /'vɪnɪgə(r)/ n Essig m

vineyard /'vɪnjɑːd/ n Weinberg m

vintage /'vɪntɪdʒ/ a erlesen □n (year) Jahrgang m. **~ 'car** n Oldtimer m

viola /vɪ'əʊlə/ n (Mus) Bratsche f

violat|e /'vaɪəleɪt/ vt verletzen; (break) brechen; (disturb) stören; (defile) schänden. **~ion** /-'leɪʃn/ n Verletzung f; Schändung f

violen|ce /'vaɪələns/ n Gewalt f; (fig) Heftigkeit f. **~t** a gewalttätig; (fig) heftig. **~tly** adv brutal; (fig) heftig

violet /'vaɪələt/ a violett □n (flower) Veilchen nt

violin /vaɪə'lɪn/ n Geige f, Violine f. **~ist** n Geiger(in) m(f)

VIP abbr (very important person) Prominente(r) m/f

viper /'vaɪpə(r)/ n Kreuzotter f; (fig) Schlange f

virgin /'vɜːdʒɪn/ a unberührt □n Jungfrau f. **~ity** /-'dʒɪnətɪ/ n Unschuld f

Virgo /'vɜːgəʊ/ n (Astr) Jungfrau f

viril|e /'vɪraɪl/ a männlich. **~ity** /-'rɪlətɪ/ n Männlichkeit f

virtual /'vɜːtjʊəl/ a a - ... praktisch ein ... **~ly** adv praktisch

virtue /'vɜːtjuː/ n Tugend f; (advantage) Vorteil m; **by** or **in ~ of** auf Grund (+ gen)

virtuoso /vɜːtʊ'əʊzəʊ/ n (pl -si /-ziː/) Virtuose m

virtuous /'vɜːtjʊəs/ a tugendhaft

virulent /'vɪrʊlənt/ a bösartig; (poison) stark; (fig) scharf

virus /'vaɪərəs/ n Virus nt

visa /'viːzə/ n Visum nt

vis-à-vis /viːzaː'viː/ adv & prep gegenüber (+ dat)

viscous /'vɪskəs/ a dickflüssig

visibility /vɪzə'bɪlətɪ/ n Sichtbarkeit f; (Meteorol) Sichtweite f

visible /'vɪzəbl/ a, **-bly** adv sichtbar

vision /'vɪʒn/ n Vision f; (sight) Sehkraft f; (foresight) Weitblick m

visit /'vɪzɪt/ vt/i n Besuch m □vt besuchen; besichtigen (town, building). **~ing hours** npl Besuchszeiten pl. **~or** n Besucher(in) m(f); (in hotel) Gast m; **have ~ors** Besuch haben

visor /'vaɪzə(r)/ n Schirm m; (on helmet) Visier nt; (Auto) [Sonnen]-blende f

vista /'vɪstə/ n Aussicht f

visual /'vɪzjʊəl/ a, **-ly** adv visuell; **~ly handicapped** sehbehindert. **~ aids** npl Anschauungsmaterial nt. **~ dis'play unit** n Bildschirmgerät nt

visualize /'vɪzjʊəlaɪz/ vt sich (dat) vorstellen

vital /'vaɪtl/ a unbedingt notwendig; (essential to life) lebenswichtig. **~ity** /vaɪ'tælətɪ/ n Vitalität f. **~ly** /'vaɪtəlɪ/ adv äußerst

vitamin /'vɪtəmɪn/ n Vitamin nt

vitreous /'vɪtrɪəs/ a glasartig; (enamel) Glas-

vivacious /vɪ'veɪʃəs/ a, **-ly** adv lebhaft. **~ty** /-'væsətɪ/ n Lebhaftigkeit f

vivid /'vɪvɪd/ a, **-ly** adv lebhaft; (description) lebendig

vixen /'vɪksn/ n Füchsin f

vocabulary /və'kæbjʊlərɪ/ n Wortschatz m; (list) Vokabelverzeichnis nt; **learn ~** Vokabeln lernen

vocal /'vəʊkl/ a, **-ly** adv stimmlich; (vociferous) lautstark. **~ cords** npl Stimmbänder pl

vocalist /'vəʊkəlɪst/ n Sänger(in) m(f)

vocation /və'keɪʃn/ n Berufung f. **~al** a Berufs-

vociferous /və'sɪfərəs/ a lautstark

vodka /'vɒdkə/ n Wodka m

vogue /vəʊg/ n Mode f; **in ~** in Mode

voice /vɔɪs/ n Stimme f □vt zum Ausdruck bringen

void /vɔɪd/ a leer; (not valid) ungültig; ~ of ohne □ n Leere f

volatile /'vɒlətaɪl/ a flüchtig; ⟨person⟩ sprunghaft

volcanic /vɒl'kænɪk/ a vulkanisch

volcano /vɒl'keɪnəʊ/ n Vulkan m

volition /və'lɪʃn/ n of one's own ~ aus eigenem Willen

volley /'vɒlɪ/ n (of gunfire) Salve f; (Tennis) Volley m

volt /vəʊlt/ n Volt nt. ~age /-ɪdʒ/ n (Electr) Spannung f

voluble /'vɒljʊbl/ a, -bly adv redselig; ⟨protest⟩ wortreich

volume /'vɒljuːm/ n (book) Band m; (Geom) Rauminhalt m; (amount) Ausmaß nt; (Radio, TV) Lautstärke f. ~ control n Lautstärkeregler m

voluntary /'vɒləntərɪ/ a, -ily adv freiwillig

volunteer /vɒlən'tɪə(r)/ n Freiwillige(r) m/f □vt anbieten; geben ⟨information⟩ □vi sich freiwillig melden

voluptuous /və'lʌptjʊəs/ a sinnlich

vomit /'vɒmɪt/ n Erbrochene(s) nt □vt erbrechen □vi sich übergeben

voracious /və'reɪʃəs/ a gefräßig; ⟨appetite⟩ unbändig

vote /vəʊt/ n Stimme f; (ballot) Abstimmung f; (right) Wahlrecht nt; take a ~e on abstimmen über (+ acc) □vi abstimmen; (in election) wählen □vt ~e s.o. president zum Präsidenten wählen. ~er n Wähler(in) m(f)

vouch /vaʊtʃ/ vi ~ for sich verbürgen für. ~er n Gutschein m

vow /vaʊ/ n Gelöbnis nt; (Relig) Gelübde nt □vt geloben

vowel /'vaʊəl/ n Vokal m

voyage /'vɔɪɪdʒ/ n Seereise f; (in space) Reise f, Flug m

vulgar /'vʌlgə(r)/ a vulgär, ordinär. ~ity /-'gærətɪ/ n Vulgarität f

vulnerable /'vʌlnərəbl/ a verwundbar

vulture /'vʌltʃə(r)/ n Geier m

vying /'vaɪɪŋ/ see vie

W

wad /wɒd/ n Bausch m; (bundle) Bündel nt. ~ding n Wattierung f

waddle /'wɒdl/ vi watscheln

wade /weɪd/ vi waten; ~ through (fam) sich durchackern durch ⟨book⟩

wafer /'weɪfə(r)/ n Waffel f; (Relig) Hostie f

waffle¹ /'wɒfl/ vi (fam) schwafeln

waffle² n (Culin) Waffel f

waft /wɒft/ vt/i wehen

wag /wæg/ v (pt/pp wagged) □vt wedeln mit; ~ one's finger at s.o. jdm mit dem Finger drohen □vi wedeln

wage¹ /weɪdʒ/ vt führen

wage² n, & ~s pl Lohn m. ~ packet n Lohntüte f

wager /'weɪdʒə(r)/ n Wette f

waggle /'wægl/ vt wackeln mit □vi wackeln

wagon /'wægən/ n Wagen m; (Rail) Waggon m

wail /weɪl/ n [klagender] Schrei m □vi heulen; (lament) klagen

waist /weɪst/ n Taille f. ~coat /'weɪskəʊt/ n Weste f. ~line n Taille f

wait /weɪt/ n Wartezeit f; lie in ~ for auflauern (+ dat) □vi warten (for auf + acc); (at table) servieren; ~ on bedienen □vt ~ one's turn warten, bis man an der Reihe ist

waiter /'weɪtə(r)/ n Kellner m; ~! Herr Ober!

waiting: ~-list n Warteliste f. ~-room n Warteraum m; (doctor's) Wartezimmer nt

waitress /'weɪtrɪs/ n Kellnerin f

waive /weɪv/ vt verzichten auf (+ acc)

wake¹ /weɪk/ n Totenwache f □v (pt woke, pp woken) ~ [up] □vt [auf]wecken □vi aufwachen

wake² n (Naut) Kielwasser nt; **in the** ~ **of** im Gefolge (+ gen)

waken /ˈweɪkn/ vt [auf]wecken □vi aufwachen

Wales /weɪlz/ n Wales nt

walk /wɔːk/ n Spaziergang m; (gait) Gang m; (path) Weg m; **go for a** ~ spazierengehen □vi gehen; (not ride) laufen, zu Fuß gehen; (ramble) wandern; **learn to** ~ laufen lernen □vt ausführen (dog). ~ **out** vi hinausgehen; ⟨workers⟩: in den Streik treten; ~ **out on** s.o. jdn verlassen

walker /ˈwɔːkə(r)/ n Spaziergänger(in) m(f); (rambler) Wanderer m/Wanderin f

walking /ˈwɔːkɪŋ/ n Gehen nt; (rambling) Wandern nt. ~-**stick** n Spazierstock m

walk: ~-**out** n Streik m. ~-**over** n (fig) leichter Sieg m.

wall /wɔːl/ n Wand f; (external) Mauer f; **go to the** ~ (fam) eingehen; **drive** s.o. **up the** ~ (fam) jdn auf die Palme bringen □vt ~ **up** zumauern

wallet /ˈwɒlɪt/ n Brieftasche f

wallflower n Goldlack m

wallop /ˈwɒləp/ n (fam) Schlag m □vt (pt/pp **walloped**) (fam) schlagen

wallow /ˈwɒləʊ/ vi sich wälzen; (fig) schwelgen

wallpaper n Tapete f □vt tapezieren

walnut /ˈwɔːlnʌt/ n Walnuß f

waltz /wɔːlts/ n Walzer m □vi Walzer tanzen; **come** ~**ing up** (fam) angetanzt kommen

wan /wɒn/ a bleich

wand /wɒnd/ n Zauberstab m

wander /ˈwɒndə(r)/ vi umherwandern, (fam) bummeln; (fig: digress) abschweifen. ~ **about** vi umherwandern. ~**lust** n Fernweh nt

wane /weɪn/ n **be on the** ~ schwinden; ⟨moon:⟩ abnehmen □vi schwinden; abnehmen

wangle /ˈwæŋgl/ vt (fam) organisieren

want /wɒnt/ n Mangel m (of an + dat); (hardship) Not f; (desire) Bedürfnis nt □vt wollen; (need) brauchen; ~ **[to have] sth** etw haben wollen; ~ **to do sth** etw tun wollen; **we** ~ **to stay wir** wollen bleiben; **I** ~ **you to go** ich will, daß du gehst; **it** ~**s painting** es müßte gestrichen werden; **you** ~ **to learn to swim** du solltest schwimmen lernen □vi **he doesn't** ~ **for anything** ihm fehlt es an nichts. ~**ed** a gesucht. ~**ing** a **be** ~**ing** fehlen; **he is** ~**ing in** ihm fehlt es an + dat

wanton /ˈwɒntən/ a, -**ly** adv mutwillig

war /wɔː(r)/ n Krieg m; **be at** ~ sich im Krieg befinden

ward /wɔːd/ n [Kranken]saal m; (unit) Station f; (of town) Wahlbezirk m; (child) Mündel nt □vt ~ **off** abwehren

warden /ˈwɔːdn/ n Heimleiter(in) m(f); (of youth hostel) Herbergsvater m; (supervisor) Aufseher(in) m(f)

warder /ˈwɔːdə(r)/ n Wärter(in) m(f)

wardrobe /ˈwɔːdrəʊb/ n Kleiderschrank m; (clothes) Garderobe f

warehouse /ˈweəz/ n Lager nt; (building) Lagerhaus nt

wares /weəz/ npl Waren pl

war: ~**fare** n Krieg m. ~**head** n Sprengkopf m. ~**like** a kriegerisch

warm /wɔːm/ a (-**er**, -**est**), -**ly** adv warm; ⟨welcome⟩ herzlich; **I am** ~ mir ist warm □vt wärmen. ~ **up** vt aufwärmen □vi warm werden; (Sport) sich aufwärmen. ~-**hearted** a warmherzig

warmth /wɔːmθ/ n Wärme f

warn /wɔːn/ vt warnen (of vor + dat). ~**ing** n Warnung f; (advance notice) Vorwarnung f; (caution) Verwarnung f

warp /wɔːp/ *vt* verbiegen □*vi* sich verziehen

'war-path *n* on the ~ auf dem Kriegspfad

warrant /'wɒrənt/ *n* (*for arrest*) Haftbefehl *m*; (*for search*) Durchsuchungsbefehl *m* □*vt* (*justify*) rechtfertigen; (*guarantee*) garantieren

warranty /'wɒrənti/ *n* Garantie *f*

warrior /'wɒriə(r)/ *n* Krieger *m*

warship *n* Kriegsschiff *nt*

wart /wɔːt/ *n* Warze *f*

wartime *n* Kriegszeit *f*

wary /'weəri/ *a* (-ier, -iest), -ily *adv* vorsichtig; (*suspicious*) mißtrauisch

was /wɒz/ *see* **be**

wash /wɒʃ/ *n* Wäsche *f*; (*Naut*) Wellen *pl*; **have a ~** sich waschen □*vt* waschen; spülen (*dishes*); aufwischen (*floor*); (*flow over*) bespülen; **~ one's hands** sich (*dat*) die Hände waschen □*vi* sich waschen; (*fabric:*) sich waschen lassen. **~ out** *vt* auswaschen; ausspülen (*mouth*). **~ up** *vt* abwaschen, spülen □*vi* (*Amer*) sich waschen

washable /'wɒʃəbl/ *a* waschbar

wash: **~-basin** *n* Waschbecken *nt*. **~cloth** *n* (*Amer*) Waschlappen *m*

washed 'out *a* (*faded*) verwaschen; (*tired*) abgespannt

washer /'wɒʃə(r)/ *n* (*Techn*) Dichtungsring *m*; (*machine*) Waschmaschine *f*

washing /'wɒʃɪŋ/ *n* Wäsche *f*. **~-machine** *n* Waschmaschine *f*. **~-powder** *n* Waschpulver *nt*. **~-up** *n* Abwasch *m*; **do the ~-up** abwaschen, spülen. **~-'up liquid** *n* Spülmittel *nt*

wash: **~-out** *n* Pleite *f*; (*person*) Niete *f*. **~-room** *n* Waschraum *m*

wasp /wɒsp/ *n* Wespe *f*

wastage /'weɪstɪdʒ/ *n* Schwund *m*

waste /weɪst/ *n* Verschwendung *f*; (*rubbish*) Abfall *m*; **~s** *pl* Öde *f*; **~ of time** Zeitverschwendung *f*

□*a* (*product*) Abfall-; **lay ~** verwüsten □*vt* verschwenden □*vi* ~ **away** immer mehr abmagern

waste: **~-di'sposal unit** *n* Müllzerkleinerer *m*. **~-ful** *a* verschwenderisch. **~-land** *n* Ödland *nt*. **~ 'paper** *n* Altpapier *nt*. **~-'paper basket** *n* Papierkorb *m*

watch /wɒtʃ/ *n* Wache *f*; (*time-piece*) [Armband]uhr *f*; **be on the ~** aufpassen □*vt* beobachten; (*film, match*); sich (*dat*) ansehen (*film, match*); (*be careful of, look after*) achten auf (+ *acc*); **~ television** fernsehen □*vi* zusehen. **~ out** *vi* Ausschau halten (**for** nach); (*be careful*) aufpassen

watch: **~-dog** *n* Wachhund *m*. **~-ful** *a*, **-ly** *adv* wachsam. **~-maker** *n* Uhrmacher *m*. **~-man** *n* Wachmann *m*. **~-strap** *n* Uhrarmband *nt*. **~-tower** *n* Wachturm *m*. **~-word** *n* Parole *f*

water /'wɔːtə(r)/ *n* Wasser *nt*; **~s** *pl* Gewässer *nt* □*vt* gießen (*garden, plant*); (*dilute*) verdünnen; (*give drink to*) tränken □*vi* (*eyes:*) tränen; **my mouth was ~ing** mir lief das Wasser im Munde zusammen. **~ down** *vt* verwässern

water: **~-colour** *n* Wasserfarbe *f*; (*painting*) Aquarell *nt*. **~-cress** *n* Brunnenkresse *f*. **~-fall** *n* Wasserfall *m*

'watering-can *n* Gießkanne *f*

water: **~-lily** *n* Seerose *f*. **~-logged** *a* **be ~-logged** (*ground:*) unter Wasser stehen. **~-main** *n* Hauptwasserleitung *f*. **~-mark** *n* Wasserzeichen *nt*. **~-polo** *n* Wasserball *m*. **~-power** *n* Wasserkraft *f*. **~-proof** *a* wasserdicht. **~-shed** *n* Wasserscheide *f*; (*fig*) Wendepunkt *m*. **~-skiing** *n* Wasserskilaufen *nt*. **~-tight** *a* wasserdicht. **~-way** *n* Wasserstraße *f*

watery /'wɔːtəri/ *a* wäßrig

watt /wɒt/ *n* Watt *nt*

wave /weɪv/ n Welle f; (gesture) Handbewegung f; (as greeting) Winken nt □ vt winken mit; (brandish) schwingen; (threateningly) drohen mit; wellen ⟨hair⟩; ~ one's hand winken (to dat); ⟨flag:⟩ wehen. □ **length** n Wellenlänge f

waver /'weɪvə(r)/ vi schwanken

wavy /'weɪvɪ/ a wellig

wax[1] /wæks/ vi ⟨moon:⟩ zunehmen; (fig: become) werden

wax[2] n Wachs nt; (in ear) Schmalz nt □ vt wachsen. ~**works** n Wachsfigurenkabinett nt

way /weɪ/ n Weg m; (direction) Richtung f; (respect) Hinsicht f; (manner) Art f; (method) Art und Weise f; ~ of life Gewohnheiten pl; in the ~ im Weg; on the ~ auf dem Weg (to nach/zu); (under way) unterwegs; **a little/long ~ off** weit weg; **this** ~ hierher; (like this) so; **which** ~ in welche Richtung; (how) wie; **by the** ~ übrigens; **in some** ~s in gewisser Hinsicht; **either** ~ so oder so; **in this** ~ auf diese Weise; **in a** ~ in gewisser Weise; **in a bad** ~ ⟨person⟩ in schlechter Verfassung; **lead the** ~ vorausgehen; **make** ~ Platz machen (for dat); **'give** ~' ⟨Auto⟩ 'Vorfahrt beachten'; **go out of one's** ~ (fig) sich (dat) besondere Mühe geben (to zu); **get one's [own]** ~ seinen Willen durchsetzen □ adv weit; ~ **behind** weit zurück. ~ **'in** n Eingang m

way'lay vt (pt/pp -**laid**) überfallen; (fam: intercept) abfangen

way 'out n Ausgang m; (fig) Ausweg m

way-'out a (fam) verrückt

wayward /'weɪwəd/ a eigenwillig

WC abbr WC nt

we /wiː/ pron wir

weak /wiːk/ a (-er, -est), -ly adv schwach; ⟨liquid⟩ dünn. ~**en** vt

schwächen □ vi schwächer werden. ~**ling** n Schwächling m. ~**ness** n Schwäche f

wealth /welθ/ n Reichtum m; (fig) Fülle f (of an + dat). ~**y** a (-ier, -iest) reich

wean /wiːn/ vt entwöhnen

weapon /'wepən/ n Waffe f

wear /weə(r)/ n (clothing) Kleidung f; ~ **and tear** Abnutzung f, Verschleiß m □ v (pt wore, pp worn) □ vt tragen; (damage) abnutzen; ~ **a hole in sth** etw durchwetzen; **what shall I ~?** was soll ich anziehen? □ vi sich abnutzen; (last) halten. ~ **off** vi abgehen; ⟨effect:⟩ nachlassen. ~ **out** vt abnutzen; (exhaust) erschöpfen □ vi sich abnutzen

wearable /'weərəbl/ a tragbar

weary /'wɪərɪ/ a (-ier, -iest), -ily adv müde □ v (pt/pp **wearied**) □ vt ermüden □ vi ~ **of sth** etw (gen) überdrüssig werden

weasel /'wiːzl/ n Wiesel nt

weather /'weðə(r)/ n Wetter nt; **in this** ~ bei diesem Wetter; **under the** ~ (fam) nicht ganz auf dem Posten □ vt abwettern ⟨storm⟩; (fig) überstehen

weather: ~**beaten** a verwittert; wettergegerbt ⟨face⟩. ~**cock** n Wetterhahn m. ~ **forecast** n Wettervorhersage f. ~**vane** n Wetterfahne f

weave[1] /wiːv/ vi (pt/pp weaved) sich schlängeln (through durch)

weave[2] n (Tex) Bindung f □ vt (pt wove, pp woven) weben; (plait) flechten; (fig) einflechten (in in + acc). ~ **r** n Weber m

web /web/ n Netz nt. ~ **bed feet** npl Schwimmfüße pl

wed /wed/ vt/i (pt/pp **wedded**) heiraten. ~**ding** n Hochzeit f; (ceremony) Trauung f

wedding: ~ **day** n Hochzeitstag m. ~ **dress** n Hochzeitskleid nt. ~-**ring** n Ehering m, Trauring m

wedge /wedʒ/ n Keil m; (of cheese) [keilförmiges] Stück nt □vt festklemmen

wedlock /'wedlɒk/ n (liter) Ehe f; **in/out of ~** ehelich/unehelich

Wednesday /'wenzdeɪ/ n Mittwoch m

wee /wiː/ a (fam) klein □vi Pipi machen

weed /wiːd/ n & ~s pl Unkraut nt □vt/i jäten. **~ out** vt (fig) aussieben

'weed-killer n Unkrautvertilgungsmittel nt

weedy /'wiːdɪ/ a (fam) spillerig

week /wiːk/ n Woche f. **~day** n Wochentag m. **~end** n Wochenende nt

weekly /'wiːklɪ/ a & adv wöchentlich □n Wochenzeitschrift f

weep /wiːp/ vi (pt/pp wept) weinen. **~ing 'willow** n Trauerweide f

weigh /weɪ/ vt/i wiegen; **~ anchor** den Anker lichten. **~ down** vt (fig) niederdrücken. **~ up** vt (fig) abwägen

weight /weɪt/ n Gewicht nt; **put on/lose ~** zunehmen/abnehmen. **~ing** n (allowance) Zulage f

weight: ~lessness n Schwerelosigkeit f. **~-lifting** n Gewichtheben nt

weighty /'weɪtɪ/ a (-ier, -iest) schwer; (important) gewichtig

weir /wɪə(r)/ n Wehr nt

weird /wɪəd/ a (-er, -est) unheimlich; (bizarre) bizarr

welcome /'welkəm/ a willkommen; **you're ~!** nichts zu danken! **you're ~ to have it** das können Sie gerne haben □n Willkommen nt □vt begrüßen

weld /weld/ vt schweißen. **~er** n Schweißer m

welfare /'welfeə(r)/ n Wohl nt; (Admin) Fürsorge f. **W~ State** n Wohlfahrtsstaat m

well¹ /wel/ n Brunnen m; (oil ~) Quelle f; (of staircase) Treppenhaus nt

well² adv (better, best) gut; **as ~** auch; **as ~ as** (in addition) sowohl … als auch; **~ done!** gut gemacht! □a gesund; **he is not ~** es geht ihm nicht gut; **get ~ soon!** gute Besserung! □int nun, na

well: ~-behaved a artig. **~-being** n Wohl nt. **~-bred** a wohlerzogen. **~-heeled** a (fam) gut betucht

wellingtons /'welɪŋtənz/ npl Gummistiefel pl

well: ~-known a bekannt. **~-meaning** a wohlmeinend. **~-meant** a gutgemeint. **~-off** a wohlhabend; **be ~-off** gut dran sein. **~-read** a belesen. **~-to-do** a wohlhabend

Welsh /welʃ/ a walisisch □n (Lang) Walisisch nt; **the ~** pl die Waliser. **~man** n Waliser m. **~ rabbit** n überbackenes Käsebrot nt

went /went/ see go

wept /wept/ see weep

were /wɜː(r)/ see be

west /west/ n Westen m; **to the ~ of** westlich von □a West-, west- □adv nach Westen; **go ~** (fam) flötengehen. **~erly** a westlich. **~ern** a westlich □n Western m

West: ~ 'Germany n Westdeutschland nt. **~ 'Indian** a westindisch □n Westinder(in) m(f). **~ 'Indies** /-'ɪndɪz/ npl Westindische Inseln pl

westward[s] /-wəd[z]/ adv nach Westen

wet /wet/ a (wetter, wettest) naß; (fam: person) weichlich, lasch; **'~ paint'** 'frisch gestrichen' □vt (pt/pp wet or wetted) naß machen. **~ 'blanket** n Spaßverderber m

whack /wæk/ n (fam) Schlag m □vt (fam) schlagen. **~ed** a (fam) kaputt

whale /weɪl/ n Wal m; **have a ~ of
a time** (fam) sich toll amüsieren
wharf /wɔːf/ n Kai m
what /wɒt/ pron & int was; **~ for?**
wozu? **~ is it like?** wie ist es? **~
is your name?** wie ist Ihr Name?
~ is the weather like? wie ist
das Wetter? **~'s he talking
about?** wovon redet er? □a
welche(r,s); **~ kind of a** was für
ein(e); **at ~ time?** um wieviel
Uhr?
what'ever a [egal] welche(r,s)
□pron was … auch; **~ is it?** was
ist das bloß? **~ he does** was er
auch tut; **~ happens** was auch
geschieht; **nothing ~** überhaupt
nichts
whatso'ever pron & a ≈ **whatever**
wheat /wiːt/ n Weizen m
wheedle /ˈwiːdl/ vt gut zureden (+
dat); **~ sth out of s.o.** jdm etw
ablocken
wheel /wiːl/ n Rad nt; (pottery)
Töpferscheibe f; (steering ~)
Lenkrad nt; **at the ~** am Steuer
□vt (push) schieben □vi kehrt-
machen; (circle) kreisen
wheel: ~barrow n Schubkarre f.
~chair n Rollstuhl m.
~clamp n Parkkralle f
wheeze /wiːz/ vi keuchen
when /wen/ adv wann; **the day ~**
der Tag, an dem □conj wenn; (in
the past) als; (although) wo …
doch; **~ swimming/reading**
beim Schwimmen/Lesen
whence /wens/ adv (liter) woher
when'ever conj & adv [immer]
wenn; (at whatever time) wann
immer; **~ did it happen?** wann
ist das bloß passiert?
where /weə(r)/ adv & conj wo; **~
[to]** wohin; **~ [from]** woher
whereabouts¹ /weərəˈbaʊts/ adv
wo
'whereabouts² n Verbleib m; (of
person) Aufenthaltsort m
where'as conj während; (in contrast) wohingegen

where'by adv wodurch
whereu'pon adv worauf[hin]
wher'ever conj & adv wo immer;
(to whatever place) wohin immer;
(from whatever place) woher immer; (everywhere) überall wo; **~
is he?** wo ist er bloß? **~ possible** wenn irgend möglich
whet /wet/ vt (pt/pp whetted) wetzen; anregen (appetite)
whether /ˈweðə(r)/ conj ob
which /wɪtʃ/ a & pron welche(r,s);
~ one welche(r,s) □rel pron der/
die/das, (pl) die; (after clause)
was; **after ~** wonach; **on ~** worauf
which'ever a & pron [egal]
welche(r, s); **~ it is** was es auch
ist
whiff /wɪf/ n Hauch m
while /waɪl/ n Weile f; **a long ~**
lange; **be worth ~** sich lohnen;
it's worth my ~ es lohnt sich für
mich □conj während; (as long as)
solange; (although) obgleich □vt
~ away sich (dat) vertreiben
whilst /waɪlst/ conj während
whim /wɪm/ n Laune f
whimper /ˈwɪmpə(r)/ vi wimmern; (dog): winseln
whimsical /ˈwɪmzɪkl/ a skurril
whine /waɪn/ n Winseln nt □vi
winseln
whip /wɪp/ n Peitsche f; (Pol)
Einpeitscher m □vt (pt/pp whipped) peitschen; (Culin) schlagen
(snatch) reißen; (fam: steal)
klauen. **~ up** vt (incite) anheizen;
(fam) schnell hinzaubern
(meal). **~ped 'cream** n Schlag-
sahne f
whirl /wɜːl/ n Wirbel m; **I am in a
~** mir schwirrt der Kopf □vt/i
wirbeln. **~pool** n Strudel m.
~wind n Wirbelwind m
whirr /wɜː(r)/ vi surren
whisk /wɪsk/ n (Culin) Schnee-
besen m □vt (Culin) schlagen. **~
away** vt wegreißen

whisker /'wɪskə(r)/ n Schnurr-
haar nt; ~s pl (on man's cheek)
Backenbart m

whisky /'wɪskɪ/ n Whisky m

whisper /'wɪspə(r)/ n Flüstern nt;
(rumour) Gerücht nt; **in a** ~ im
Flüsterton □vt/i flüstern

whistle /'wɪsl/ n Pfiff m; (instrument) Pfeife f □vt/i pfeifen

white /waɪt/ a (-r, -st) weiß □n
Weiß nt; (of egg) Eiweiß nt; (person) Weiße(r) m/f

white: ~ **'coffee** n Kaffee m mit
Milch. ~-'**collar worker** n An-
gestellte(r) m. ~ **'lie** n Notlüge f

whiten /'waɪtn/ vt weiß machen
□vi weiß werden

whiteness /'waɪtnɪs/ n Weiß nt

'**whitewash** n Tünche f; (fig)
Schönfärberei f □vt tünchen

Whitsun /'wɪtsn/ n Pfingsten nt

whittle /'wɪtl/ vt ~ **down** reduzieren; kürzen ⟨list⟩

whiz[z] /wɪz/ vi (pt/pp **whizzed**)
zischen. ~-**kid** n (fam) Senk-
rechtstarter m

who /huː/ pron wer; (acc) wen;
(dat) wem □rel pron der/die/das,
(pl) die

who'ever pron wer [immer]; ~ **he**
is wer er auch ist; ~ **is it?** wer ist
das bloß?

whole /həʊl/ a ganz; ⟨truth⟩ voll
□n Ganze(s) nt; **as a** ~ als Gan-
zes; **on the** ~ im großen und
ganzen; **the** ~ **lot** alle; (everything) alles; **the** ~ **of Germany** ganz Deutschland; **the** ~
time die ganze Zeit

whole: ~-**food** n Vollwertkost f.
~-'**hearted** a rückhaltlos.
~**meal** a Vollkorn-

'**wholesale** a Großhandels- □adv
en gros; (fig) in Bausch und Bogen. ~**r** n Großhändler m

wholesome /'həʊlsəm/ a gesund

wholly /'həʊlɪ/ adv völlig

whom /huːm/ pron wen; **to** ~
wem □rel pron den/die/das, (pl)

die; (dat) dem/der/dem, (pl) denen

whooping cough /'huːpɪŋ-/ n
Keuchhusten m

whopping /'wɒpɪŋ/ a (fam) Rie-
sen-

whore /hɔː(r)/ n Hure f

whose /huːz/ pron wessen; ~ **is**
that? wem gehört das? □rel pron
dessen/deren/dessen, (pl) deren

why /waɪ/ adv warum; (for what
purpose) wozu; **that's** ~ darum
□int na

wick /wɪk/ n Docht m

wicked /'wɪkɪd/ a böse; (mischievous) frech, boshaft

wicker /'wɪkə(r)/ n Korbgeflecht
nt □attrib Korb-

wide /waɪd/ a (-r, -st) weit; (broad)
breit; (fig) groß; **be** ~ (far from
target) danebengehen □adv weit;
(off target) daneben; ~ **awake**
hellwach; **far and** ~ weit und
breit. ~**ly** adv (known, ac-
cepted) weithin; ⟨differ⟩ stark

widen /'waɪdn/ vt verbreitern;
(fig) erweitern □vi sich verbreitern

'**widespread** a weitverbreitet

widow /'wɪdəʊ/ n Witwe f. ~**ed** a
verwitwet. ~**er** n Witwer m

width /wɪdθ/ n Weite f; (breadth)
Breite f

wield /wiːld/ vt schwingen; ausüben ⟨power⟩

wife /waɪf/ n (pl **wives**) [Ehe]frau f

wig /wɪg/ n Perücke f

wiggle /'wɪgl/ vi wackeln □vt
wackeln mit

wild /waɪld/ a (-er, -est), -**ly** adv
wild; ⟨animal⟩ wildlebend;
⟨flower⟩ wildwachsend; (furious) wütend; **be** ~ **about** (keen
on) wild sein auf (+ acc) □adv
wild; **run** ~ frei herumlaufen □n
in the ~ wild; **the** ~**s** pl die
Wildnis f

'**wildcat strike** n wilder Streik m

wilderness /'wɪldənɪs/ n Wildnis f; (desert) Wüste f

wild: ~-'**goose chase** n aussichtslose Suche f. ~**life** n Tierwelt f

wilful /'wɪlfl/ a, -**ly** adv mutwillig; (self-willed) eigenwillig

will[1] /wɪl/ v aux wollen; (forming future tense) werden; **he ~ arrive tomorrow** er wird morgen kommen; ~ **you go?** gehst du? **you ~ be back soon, won't you?** du kommst doch bald wieder, nicht? **he ~ be there, won't he?** er wird doch da sein? **she ~ be there by now** sie wird jetzt schon da sein: ~ **you be quiet!** willst du wohl ruhig sein! ~ **you have some wine?** möchten Sie Wein? **the engine won't start** der Motor will nicht anspringen

will[2] n Wille m; (document) Testament nt

willing /'wɪlɪŋ/ a willig; (eager) bereitwillig; **be ~** bereit sein. ~**ly** adv bereitwillig; (gladly) gern. ~**ness** n Bereitwilligkeit f

willow /'wɪləʊ/ n Weide f

'**will-power** n Willenskraft f

willy-'nilly adv wohl oder übel

wilt /wɪlt/ vi welk werden, welken

wily /'waɪlɪ/ a (-ier, -iest) listig

wimp /wɪmp/ n Schwächling m

win /wɪn/ n Sieg m; **have a ~** gewinnen □v (pt/pp **won**; pres p **winning**) □vt gewinnen; bekommen (scholarship) □vi gewinnen; (in battle) siegen. ~ **over** vt auf seine Seite bringen

wince /wɪns/ vi zusammenzucken

winch /wɪntʃ/ n Winde f □vt ~ **up** hochwinden

wind[1] /wɪnd/ n Wind m; (breath) Atem m; (fam: flatulence) Blähungen pl; **have the ~ up** (fam) Angst haben □vt ~ **s.o.** jdm den Atem nehmen

wind[2] /waɪnd/ v (pt/pp **wound**) □vt (wrap) wickeln; (move by turning) kurbeln; aufziehen (clock) □vi (road:) sich winden. ~ **up** vt

aufziehen (clock); schließen (proceedings)

wind /wɪnd/ : ~**fall** n unerwarteter Glücksfall m; ~**falls** pl (fruit) Fallobst nt. ~ **instrument** n Blasinstrument nt. ~**mill** n Windmühle f

window /'wɪndəʊ/ n Fenster nt; (of shop) Schaufenster nt

window: ~-**box** n Blumenkasten m. ~-**cleaner** n Fensterputzer m. ~-**dresser** n Schaufensterdekorateur(in) m(f). ~-**dressing** n Schaufensterdekoration f; (fig) Schönfärberei f. ~-**pane** n Fensterscheibe f. ~-**shopping** n Schaufensterbummel m. ~-**sill** n Fensterbrett nt

'**windpipe** n Luftröhre f

'**windscreen** n, (Amer) '**windshield** n Windschutzscheibe f. ~ **washer** n Scheibenwaschanlage f. ~-**wiper** n Scheibenwischer m

wind: ~-**surfing** n Windsurfen nt. ~-**swept** a windgepeitscht; (person) zersaust

windy /'wɪndɪ/ a (-ier, -iest) windig; **be ~** (fam) Angst haben

wine /waɪn/ n Wein m

wine: ~-**bar** n Weinstube f. ~-**glass** n Weinglas nt. ~-**list** n Weinkarte f

winery /'waɪnərɪ/ n (Amer) Weingut nt

'**wine-tasting** n Weinprobe f

wing /wɪŋ/ n Flügel m; (Auto) Kotflügel m; ~**s** pl (Theat) Kulissen pl

wink /wɪŋk/ n Zwinkern nt; **not sleep a ~** kein Auge zutun □vi zwinkern; (light:) blinken

winner /'wɪnə(r)/ n Gewinner(in) m(f); (Sport) Sieger(in) m(f)

winning /'wɪnɪŋ/ a siegreich; (smile) gewinnend. ~-**post** n Zielpfosten m. ~**s** npl Gewinn m

winter /'wɪntə(r)/ n Winter m. ~**ry** a winterlich

wipe /waɪp/ n give sth a ~ etw abwischen □vt abwischen; aufwischen ⟨floor⟩; (dry) abtrocknen. ~ **off** vt abwischen; (erase) auslöschen. ~ **out** vt (cancel) löschen; (destroy) ausrotten. ~ **up** vt aufwischen; abtrocknen ⟨dishes⟩

wire /waɪə(r)/ n Draht m. ~**-haired** a rauhhaarig

wireless /waɪəlɪs/ n Radio nt

wire 'netting n Maschendraht m

wiring /waɪərɪŋ/ n [elektrische] Leitungen pl

wiry /waɪərɪ/ a (-ier, -iest) drahtig

wisdom /wɪzdəm/ n Weisheit f; (prudence) Klugheit f. ~ **tooth** n Weisheitszahn m

wise /waɪz/ a (-r, -st), -ly adv weise; (prudent) klug

wish /wɪʃ/ n Wunsch m □vt wünschen; ~ s.o. well jdm alles Gute wünschen; I ~ you could stay ich wünschte, du könntest hierbleiben □vi sich (dat) etwas wünschen. ~**ful** a ~ful thinking Wunschdenken nt

wishy-washy /wɪʃɪwɒʃɪ/ a labberig; ⟨colour⟩ verwaschen; ⟨person⟩ lasch

wisp /wɪsp/ n Büschel nt; (of hair) Strähne f; (of smoke) Fahne f

wisteria /wɪsˈtɪərɪə/ n Glyzinie f

wistful /wɪstfl/ a, -ly adv wehmütig

wit /wɪt/ n Geist m, Witz m; (intelligence) Verstand m; (person) geistreicher Mensch m; be at one's ~s' end sich (dat) keinen Rat mehr wissen; scared out of one's ~s zu Tode erschrocken

witch /wɪtʃ/ n Hexe f. ~**craft** n Hexerei f. ~**hunt** n Hexenjagd f

with /wɪð/ prep mit (+ dat); ~ fear/cold vor Angst/Kälte; ~ it damit; I'm going ~ you ich gehe mit; take it ~ you nimm es mit; I haven't got it ~ me ich habe es nicht bei mir; I'm not ~ you (fam) ich komme nicht mit

with'draw v (pt -drew, pp -drawn) □vt zurückziehen; abheben ⟨money⟩ □vi sich zurückziehen; (of money) Abhebung f; (from drugs) Entzug m. ~**al** n Zurückziehen nt; (of money) Abhebung f; (from drugs) Entzug m. ~**al symptoms** npl Entzugserscheinungen pl

with'drawn see withdraw □a ⟨person⟩ verschlossen

wither /wɪðə(r)/ vi [ver]welken

with'hold vt (pt/pp -held) vorenthalten (from s.o. jdm)

with'in prep innerhalb (+ gen); ~ the law im Rahmen des Gesetzes □adv innen

with'out prep ohne (+ acc); ~ my noticing it ohne daß ich es merkte

with'stand vt (pt/pp -stood) standhalten (+ dat)

witness /wɪtnɪs/ n Zeuge m/ Zeugin f; (evidence) Zeugnis nt □vt Zeuge/Zeugin sein (+ gen); bestätigen ⟨signature⟩. ~**-box** n, (Amer) ~**-stand** n Zeugenstand m

witticism /wɪtɪsɪzm/ n geistreicher Ausspruch m

wittingly /wɪtɪŋlɪ/ adv wissentlich

witty /wɪtɪ/ a (-ier, -iest) witzig, geistreich

wives /waɪvz/ see wife

wizard /wɪzəd/ n Zauberer m. ~**ry** n Zauberei f

wizened /wɪznd/ a verhutzelt

wobb|le /wɒbl/ vi wackeln. ~**ly** a wackelig

woe /wəʊ/ n (liter) Jammer m; ~ **is me!** wehe mir!

woke, woken /wəʊk, ˈwəʊkn/ see wake[1]

wolf /wʊlf/ n (pl wolves /wʊlvz/) Wolf m □vt ~ **[down]** hinunterschlingen

woman /wʊmən/ n (pl women) Frau f. ~**izer** n Schürzenjäger m. ~**ly** a fraulich

womb /wuːm/ n Gebärmutter f

women /ˈwɪmɪn/ npl see **woman**; **W~'s Libber** /ˈlɪbə(r)/ n Frauenrechtlerin f. **W~'s Liberation** n Frauenbewegung f

won /wʌn/ see **win**

wonder /ˈwʌndə(r)/ n Wunder nt; (surprise) Staunen nt □vt/i sich fragen; (be surprised) sich wundern; I ~ da frage ich mich; I ~ whether she is ill ob sie wohl krank ist? ~**ful** a, -**ly** adv wunderbar

won't /wəʊnt/ = will not

woo /wuː/ vt (liter) werben um; (fig) umwerben

wood /wʊd/ n Holz nt; (forest) Wald m; **touch** ~! unberufen!

wood: ~**cut** n Holzschnitt m. ~**ed** /-ɪd/ a bewaldet. ~**en** a Holz-; (fig) hölzern. ~**pecker** n Specht m. ~**wind** n Holzbläser pl. ~**work** n (wooden parts) Holzteile pl; (craft) Tischlerei f. ~**worm** n Holzwurm m. ~**y** a holzig

wool /wʊl/ n Wolle f □ attrib Woll-. ~**len** a wollen. ~**lens** npl Wollsachen pl

woolly /ˈwʊlɪ/ a (-ier, -iest) wollig; (fig) unklar

word /wɜːd/ n Wort nt; (news) Nachricht f; **by** ~ **of mouth** mündlich; **have a** ~ **with** sprechen mit; **have** ~**s** einen Wortwechsel haben. ~**ing** n Wortlaut m. ~ **processor** n Textverarbeitungssystem nt

wore /wɔː(r)/ see **wear**

work /wɜːk/ n Arbeit f; (Art, Literature) Werk nt; ~**s** pl (factory, mechanism) Werk nt; **at** ~ bei der Arbeit; **out of** ~ arbeitslos □ vi arbeiten; (machine, system:) funktionieren; (have effect) wirken; (study) lernen; **it won't** ~ (fig) es klappt nicht □ vt arbeiten lassen; bedienen (machine); betätigen (lever); ~ **one's way through sth** sich durch etw hindurcharbeiten. ~ **off** vt abarbeiten. ~ **out** vt ausrechnen; (solve)

lösen □ vi gutgehen, (fam) klappen. ~ **up** vt aufbauen; sich (dat) holen (appetite); **get** ~**ed up** sich aufregen

workable /ˈwɜːkəbl/ a (feasible) durchführbar

workaholic /wɜːkəˈhɒlɪk/ n arbeitswütiger Mensch m

worker /ˈwɜːkə(r)/ n Arbeiter(in) m(f)

working /ˈwɜːkɪŋ/ a berufstätig; (day, clothes) Arbeits-; **be in** ~ **order** funktionieren. ~ **class** n Arbeiterklasse f. ~**-class** a Arbeiter-; **be** ~**-class** zur Arbeiterklasse gehören

work: ~**man** n Arbeiter m. (craftsman) Handwerker m. ~**manship** n Arbeit f. ~**-out** n [Fitneß]training nt. ~**shop** n Werkstatt f

world /wɜːld/ n Welt f; **in the** ~ auf der Welt; **a** ~ **of difference** ein himmelweiter Unterschied; **think the** ~ **of s.o.** große Stücke auf jdn halten. ~**ly** a weltlich; (person) weltlich gesinnt. ~**-wide** a & adv /-'-/ weltweit

worm /wɜːm/ n Wurm m □ vi ~ **one's way into s.o.'s confidence** sich in jds Vertrauen einschleichen. ~**-eaten** a wurmstichig

worn /wɔːn/ see **wear** □ a abgetragen. ~**-out** a abgetragen; (carpet) abgenutzt; (person) erschöpft

worried /ˈwʌrɪd/ a besorgt

worry /ˈwʌrɪ/ n Sorge f □ v (pt/pp **worried**) □ vt beunruhigen, Sorgen machen (+ dat); (bother) stören □ vi sich beunruhigen, sich (dat) Sorgen machen. ~**ing** a beunruhigend

worse /wɜːs/ a & adv schlechter; (more serious) schlimmer □ n Schlechtere(s) nt; Schlimmere(s) nt

worsen /ˈwɜːsn/ vt verschlechtern □ vi sich verschlechtern

worship /'wɜ:ʃɪp/ n Anbetung f; (service) Gottesdienst m; Your/ His W~ Euer/Seine Ehren □v (pt/pp -shipped) □vt anbeten □vi am Gottesdienst teilnehmen

worst /wɜːst/ a schlechteste(r,s) (most serious) schlimmste(r,s) □adv am schlechtesten; am schlimmsten □n the ~ das Schlimmste; get the ~ of it den kürzeren ziehen

worsted /'wʊstɪd/ n Kammgarn m

worth /wɜːθ/ a Wert m; £10's ~ of petrol Benzin für £10 □a be ~ £5 £5 wert sein; be ~ it (fig) sich lohnen. **~less** a wertlos. **~while** a lohnend

worthy /'wɜːðɪ/ a würdig

would /wʊd/ v aux I ~ do it ich würde es tun, ich täte es; ~ you go? würdest du gehen? he said he ~n't er sagte, er würde es nicht tun; what ~ you like? was möchten Sie?

wound[1] /wuːnd/ n Wunde f □vt verwunden

wound[2] /waʊnd/ see **wind**[2]

wove, woven /wəʊv, 'wəʊvn/ see **weave**[2]

wrangle /'ræŋgl/ n Streit m □vi sich streiten

wrap /ræp/ n Umhang m □vt (pt/pp wrapped) **~[up]** wickeln; einpacken (present) □vi ~ **up** warmly sich warm einpacken; be **~ped up in** (fig) aufgehen in (+ dat). **~per** n Hülle f. **~ping** n Verpackung f. **~ping paper** n Einwickelpapier nt

wrath /rɒθ/ n Zorn m

wreak /riːk/ vt ~ havoc Verwüstungen anrichten

wreath /riːθ/ n (pl ~s /-ðz/) Kranz m

wreck /rek/ n Wrack nt □vt zerstören; zunichte machen (plans); zerrütten (marriage). **~age** /-ɪdʒ/ n Wrackteile pl; (fig) Trümmer pl

wren /ren/ n Zaunkönig m

wrench /rentʃ/ n Ruck m; (tool) Schraubenschlüssel m; be a ~ (fig) weh tun □vt reißen; ~ **sth from s.o.** jdm etw entreißen

wrest /rest/ vt entwinden (from s.o. jdm)

wrestle /'resl/ vi ringen. **~er** n Ringer m. **~ing** n Ringen nt

wretch /retʃ/ n Kreatur f. **~ed** /-ɪd/ a elend; (very bad) erbärmlich

wriggle /'rɪgl/ n Zappeln nt □vi zappeln; (move forward) sich schlängeln; ~ **out of sth** (fam) sich etw (dat) drücken

wring /rɪŋ/ vt (pt/pp wrung) wringen; (~ out) auswringen; umdrehen (neck); ringen (hands); be **~ing wet** tropfnaß sein

wrinkle /'rɪŋkl/ n Falte f; (on skin) Runzel f □vt kräuseln □vi sich kräuseln, sich falten. **~d** a runzlig

wrist /rɪst/ n Handgelenk nt. **~-watch** n Armbanduhr f

writ /rɪt/ n (Jur) Verfügung f

write /raɪt/ vt/i (pt wrote, pp written, pres p writing) schreiben. ~ **down** vt aufschreiben. ~ **off** vt abschreiben; zu Schrott fahren (car)

'write-off n ≈ Totalschaden m

writer /'raɪtə(r)/ n Schreiber(in) m(f); (author) Schriftsteller(in) m(f)

'write-up n Bericht m; (review) Kritik f

writhe /raɪð/ vi sich winden

writing /'raɪtɪŋ/ n Schreiben nt; (handwriting) Schrift f; **in** ~ schriftlich. **~paper** n Schreibpapier nt

written /'rɪtn/ see **write**

wrong /rɒŋ/ a, -ly adv falsch; (morally) unrecht; (not just) ungerecht; be ~ nicht stimmen; (person:) unrecht haben; **what's** ~? was ist los? □adv falsch; **go** ~ (person:) etwas falsch machen; (machine:) kaputtgehen; (plan:)

schiefgehen □*n* Unrecht *nt* □*vt* Unrecht tun (+ *dat*). ~**ful** *a* ungerechtfertigt. ~**fully** *adv* ⟨*accuse*⟩ zu Unrecht

wrote /rəʊt/ *see* write

wrought '**iron** /rɔːt-/ *n* Schmiedeeisen *nt* □*attrib* schmiedeeisern

wrung /rʌŋ/ *see* wring

wry /raɪ/ *a* (-er, -est) ironisch; ⟨*humour*⟩ trocken

X

xerox (P) /'zɪərɒks/ *vt* fotokopieren

Xmas /'krɪsməs, 'eksməs/ *n* ⟨*fam*⟩ Weihnachten *nt*

X-ray *n* ⟨*picture*⟩ Röntgenaufnahme *f*; ~**s** *pl* Röntgenstrahlen *pl*; **have an** ~ geröntgt werden □*vt* röntgen; durchleuchten ⟨*luggage*⟩

Y

yacht /jɒt/ *n* Jacht *f*; ⟨*for racing*⟩ Segelboot *nt*. ~**ing** *n* Segeln *nt*

yank /jæŋk/ *vt* ⟨*fam*⟩ reißen

Yank *n* ⟨*fam*⟩ Amerikaner(in) *m(f)*, ⟨*fam*⟩ Ami *m*

yap /jæp/ *vi* (*pt/pp* **yapped**) ⟨*dog*⟩ kläffen

yard[1] /jɑːd/ *n* Hof *m*; ⟨*for storage*⟩ Lager *nt*

yard[2] *n* Yard *nt* (= 0,91 m). ~**stick** *n* ⟨*fig*⟩ Maßstab *m*

yarn /jɑːn/ *n* Garn *nt*; ⟨*fam: tale*⟩ Geschichte *f*

yawn /jɔːn/ *n* Gähnen *nt* □*vi* gähnen. ~**ing** *a* gähnend

year /jɪə(r)/ *n* Jahr *nt*; ⟨*of wine*⟩ Jahrgang *m*; **for** ~**s** jahrelang. ~**book** *n* Jahrbuch *nt*. ~**ly** *a* & *adv* jährlich

yearn /jɜːn/ *vi* sich sehnen (**for** nach). ~**ing** *n* Sehnsucht *f*

yeast /jiːst/ *n* Hefe *f*

yell /jel/ *n* Schrei *m* □*vi* schreien

yellow /'jeləʊ/ *a* gelb □*n* Gelb *nt*. ~**ish** *a* gelblich

yelp /jelp/ *vi* jaulen

yen /jen/ *n* Wunsch *m* (**for** nach)

yes /jes/ *adv* ja; ⟨*contradicting*⟩ doch □*n* Ja *nt*

yesterday /'jestədeɪ/ *n* & *adv* gestern; ~'**s paper** die gestrige Zeitung; **the day before** ~ vorgestern

yet /jet/ *adv* noch; ⟨*in question*⟩ schon; ⟨*nevertheless*⟩ doch; **as** ~ bisher; **not** ~ noch nicht; **the best** ~ das bisher beste □*conj* doch

yew /juː/ *n* Eibe *f*

Yiddish /'jɪdɪʃ/ *n* Jiddisch *nt*

yield /jiːld/ *n* Ertrag *m* □*vt* bringen; abwerfen ⟨*profit*⟩ □*vi* nachgeben; ⟨*Amer, Auto*⟩ die Vorfahrt beachten

yodel /'jəʊdl/ *vi* (*pt/pp* **yodelled**) jodeln

yoga /'jəʊɡə/ *n* Yoga *m*

yoghurt /'jɒɡət/ *n* Joghurt *m*

yoke /jəʊk/ *n* Joch *nt*; ⟨*of garment*⟩ Passe *f*

yokel /'jəʊkl/ *n* Bauerntölpel *m*

yolk /jəʊk/ *n* Dotter *m*, Eigelb *nt*

yonder /'jɒndə(r)/ *adv* ⟨*liter*⟩ dort drüben

you /juː/ *pron* du; ⟨*acc*⟩ dich; ⟨*dat*⟩ dir; ⟨*pl*⟩ ihr; ⟨*acc, dat*⟩ euch; ⟨*formal*⟩ ⟨*nom* & *acc, sg* & *pl*⟩ Sie; ⟨*dat, sg* & *pl*⟩ Ihnen; ⟨*one*⟩ man; ⟨*acc*⟩ einen; ⟨*dat*⟩ einem; **all of** ~ ihr/Sie alle; **I know** ~ ich kenne dich/euch/Sie; **I'll give** ~ **the money** ich gebe dir/euch/Ihnen das Geld; **it does** ~ **good** es tut gut; **it's bad for** ~ es ist ungesund

young /jʌŋ/ *a* (-er, -ga(r)/, -est /-ɡɪst/) jung □*npl* ⟨*animals*⟩ Junge *pl*; **the** ~ die Jugend *f*. ~**ster** *n* Jugendliche(r) *m/f*; ⟨*child*⟩ Kleine(r) *m/f*

your /jɔː(r)/ *a* dein; ⟨*pl*⟩ euer; ⟨*formal*⟩ Ihr

yours /jɔːz/ *poss pron* deine(r), deins; (*pl*) eure(r), euers; (*formal, sg & pl*) Ihre(r), Ihr[e]s; a friend of ~ ein Freund von dir/Ihnen/euch; **that is** ~ das gehört dir/Ihnen/euch

your'self *pron* (*pl* **-selves**) selbst; (*refl*) dich; (*dat*) dir; (*pl*) euch; (*formal*) sich; **by** ~ allein

youth /juːθ/ *n* (*pl* **youths** /-ðz/) Jugend *f*; (*boy*) Jugendliche(r) *m*. ~**ful** *a* jugendlich. ~ **hostel** *n* Jugendherberge *f*

Yugoslav /'juːgəslɑːv/ *a* jugoslawisch. ~**ia** /-'slɑːvɪə/ *n* Jugoslawien *nt*

Z

zany /'zeɪnɪ/ *a* (**-ier, -iest**) närrisch, verrückt

zeal /ziːl/ *n* Eifer *m*

zealous /'zeləs/ *a*, **-ly** *adv* eifrig

zebra /'zebrə/ *n* Zebra *nt*. ~- 'crossing *n* Zebrastreifen *m*

zenith /'zenɪθ/ *n* Zenit *m*; (*fig*) Gipfel *m*

zero /'zɪərəʊ/ *n* Null *f*

zest /zest/ *n* Begeisterung *f*

zigzag /'zɪgzæg/ *n* Zickzack *m* □ *vi* (*pt/pp* **-zagged**) im Zickzack laufen/(*in vehicle*) fahren

zinc /zɪŋk/ *n* Zink *nt*

zip /zɪp/ *n* ~ [**fastener**] Reißverschluß *m* □ *vt* ~ [**up**] den Reißverschluß zuziehen an (+ *dat*)

'Zip code *n* (*Amer*) Postleitzahl *f*

zipper /'zɪpə(r)/ *n* Reißverschluß *m*

zither /'zɪðə(r)/ *n* Zither *f*

zodiac /'zəʊdɪæk/ *n* Tierkreis *m*

zombie /'zɒmbɪ/ *n* (*fam*) **like a** ~ ganz benommen

zone /zəʊn/ *n* Zone *f*

zoo /zuː/ *n* Zoo *m*

zoological /zəʊə'lɒdʒɪkl/ *a* zoologisch

zoolog|**ist** /zəʊ'ɒlədʒɪst/ *n* Zoologe *m* /-gin *f*. ~**y** Zoologie *f*

zoom /zuːm/ *vi* sausen. ~ **lens** *n* Zoomobjektiv *nt*

Englische unregelmäßige Verben

Ein Sternchen (*) weist darauf hin, daß die korrekte Form von der jeweiligen Bedeutung abhängt.

Infinitive *Infinitiv*	Past Tense *Präteritum*	Past Participle *2. Partizip*
arise	arose	arisen
awake	awoke	awoken
be	was *sg*, were *pl*	been
bear	bore	borne
beat	beat	beaten
become	became	become
begin	began	begun
behold	beheld	beheld
bend	bent	bent
beseech	beseeched, besought	beseeched, besought
bet	bet, betted	bet, betted
bid	*bade, bid	*bidden, bid
bind	bound	bound
bite	bit	bitten
bleed	bled	bled
blow	blew	blown
break	broke	broken
breed	bred	bred
bring	brought	brought
build	built	built
burn	burnt, burned	burnt, burned
burst	burst	burst
bust	busted, bust	busted, bust
buy	bought	bought
cast	cast	cast
catch	caught	caught
choose	chose	chosen
cling	clung	clung
come	came	come
cost	*cost, costed	*cost, costed

Infinitive *Infinitiv*	Past Tense *Präteritum*	Past Participle *2. Partizip*
creep	crept	crept
cut	cut	cut
deal	dealt	dealt
dig	dug	dug
do	did	done
draw	drew	drawn
dream	dreamt, dreamed	dreamt, dreamed
drink	drank	drunk
drive	drove	driven
dwell	dwelt	dwelt
eat	ate	eaten
fall	fell	fallen
feed	fed	fed
feel	felt	felt
fight	fought	fought
find	found	found
flee	fled	fled
fling	flung	flung
fly	flew	flown
forbid	forbade	forbidden
forget	forgot	forgotten
forgive	forgave	forgiven
forsake	forsook	forsaken
freeze	froze	frozen
get	got	got, (*Amer also*) gotten
give	gave	given
go	went	gone
grind	ground	ground
grow	grew	grown
hang	*hung, hanged	*hung, hanged
have	had	had
hear	heard	heard
hew	hewed	hewed, hewn
hide	hid	hidden
hit	hit	hit
hold	held	held
hurt	hurt	hurt
keep	kept	kept

Infinitive *Infinitiv*	Past Tense *Präteritum*	Past Participle *2. Partizip*
kneel	knelt	knelt
know	knew	known
lay	laid	laid
lead	led	led
lean	leaned, lent	leaned, lent
leap	leapt, leaped	leapt, leaped
learn	learnt, learned	learnt, learned
leave	left	left
lend	lent	lent
let	let	let
lie[2]	lay	lain
light	lit, lighted	lit, lighted
lose	lost	lost
make	made	made
mean	meant	meant
meet	met	met
mow	mowed	mown, mowed
overhang	overhung	overhung
pay	paid	paid
put	put	put
quit	quitted, quit	quitted, quit
read /riːd/	read /red/	read /red/
rid	rid	rid
ride	rode	ridden
ring[2]	rang	rung
rise	rose	risen
run	ran	run
saw	sawed	sawn, sawed
say	said	said
see	saw	seen
seek	sought	sought
sell	sold	sold
send	sent	sent
set	set	set
sew	sewed	sewn, sewed
shake	shook	shaken
shear	sheared	shorn, sheared
shed	shed	shed
shine	shone	shone

Infinitive *Infinitiv*	Past Tense *Präteritum*	Past Participle *2. Partizip*
shit	shit	shit
shoe	shod	shod
shoot	shot	shot
show	showed	shown
shrink	shrank	shrunk
shut	shut	shut
sing	sang	sung
sink	sank	sunk
sit	sat	sat
slay	slew	slain
sleep	slept	slept
slide	slid	slid
sling	slung	slung
slit	slit	slit
smell	smelt, smelled	smelt, smelled
sow	sowed	sown, sowed
speak	spoke	spoken
speed	*sped, speeded	*sped, speeded
spell	spelled, spelt	spelled, spelt
spend	spent	spent
spill	spilt, spilled	spilt, spilled
spin	spun	spun
spit	spat	spat
split	split	split
spoil	spoilt, spoiled	spoilt, spoiled
spread	spread	spread
spring	sprang	sprung
stand	stood	stood
steal	stole	stolen
stick	stuck	stuck
sting	stung	stung
stink	stank	stunk
strew	strewed	strewn, strewed
stride	strode	stridden
strike	struck	struck
string	strung	strung
strive	strove	striven
swear	swore	sworn
sweep	swept	swept

Infinitive *Infinitiv*	Past Tense *Präteritum*	Past Participle *2. Partizip*
swell	swelled	swollen, swelled
swim	swam	swum
swing	swung	swung
take	took	taken
teach	taught	taught
tear	tore	torn
tell	told	told
think	thought	thought
thrive	thrived, throve	thrived, thriven
throw	threw	thrown
thrust	thrust	thrust
tread	trod	trodden
understand	understood	understood
undo	undid	undone
wake	woke	woken
wear	wore	worn
weave[2]	wove	woven
weep	wept	wept
wet	wet, wetted	wet, wetted
win	won	won
wind[2] /waɪnd/	wound /waʊnd/	wound /waʊnd/
wring	wrung	wrung
write	wrote	written

Phonetic symbols used for German words

a	Hand	hant	ŋ	lang	laŋ	
a:	Bahn	ba:n	o	moral	mo'ra:l	
ɐ	Ober	'o:bɐ	o:	Boot	bo:t	
ɐ̯	Uhr	u:ɐ̯	ǫ	Foyer	fo̯a'je:	
ã	Conférencier	kõferã'sje:	õ	Konkurs	kõ'kurs	
ã:	Abonnement	abonə'mã:	õ:	Ballon	ba'lõ:	
aɪ̯	weit	vaɪ̯t	ɔ	Post	pɔst	
aʊ̯	Haut	haʊ̯t	ø	Ökonom	øko'no:m	
b	Ball	bal	ø:	Öl	ø:l	
ç	ich	ɪç	œ	göttlich	'gœtlɪç	
d	dann	dan	ɔʏ̯	heute	'hɔʏ̯tə	
dʒ	Gin	dʒɪn	p	Pakt	pakt	
e	Metall	me'tal	r	Rast	rast	
e:	Beet	be:t	s	Hast	hast	
ɛ	mästen	'mɛstən	ʃ	Schal	ʃa:l	
ɛ:	wählen	'vɛ:lən	t	Tal	ta:l	
ɛ̃:	Cousin	ku'zɛ̃:	ts	Zahl	tsa:l	
ə	Nase	'na:zə	tʃ	Couch	kaʊ̯tʃ	
f	Faß	fas	u	kulant	ku'lant	
g	Gast	gast	u:	Hut	hu:t	
h	haben	'ha:bən	u̯	aktuell	ak'tu̯ɛl	
i	Rivale	ri'va:lə	ʊ	Pult	pʊlt	
i:	viel	fi:l	v	was	vas	
i̯	Aktion	ak'tsi̯o:n	x	Bach	bax	
ɪ	Birke	'bɪrkə	y	Physik	fy'zi:k	
j	ja	ja:	y:	Rübe	'ry:bə	
k	kalt	kalt	y̯	Nuance	'ny̯ã:sə	
l	Last	last	ʏ	Fülle	'fʏlə	
m	Mast	mast	z	Nase	'na:zə	
n	Naht	na:t	ʒ	Regime	re'ʒi:m	

ʔ   Glottal stop, e.g. Koordination /koʔɔrdina'tsi̯o:n/.

:   Length sign after a vowel, e.g. Chrom /kro:m/.

'   Stress mark before stressed syllable, e.g. Balkon /bal'kõ:/.

Die für das Englische verwendeten Zeichen der Lautschrift

ɑː	barn	bɑːn	l	lot	lɒt
ɑ̃	nuance	'njuːɑ̃s	m	mat	mæt
æ	fat	fæt	n	not	nɒt
æ̃	lingerie	'læ̃ʒərɪ	ŋ	sing	sɪŋ
aɪ	fine	faɪn	ɒ	got	gɒt
aʊ	now	naʊ	ɔː	paw	pɔː
b	bat	bæt	ɔɪ	boil	bɔɪl
d	dog	dɒg	p	pet	pet
dʒ	jam	dʒæm	r	rat	ræt
e	met	met	s	sip	sɪp
eɪ	fate	feɪt	ʃ	ship	ʃɪp
eə	fairy	'feərɪ	t	tip	tɪp
əʊ	goat	gəʊt	tʃ	chin	tʃɪn
ə	ago	ə'gəʊ	θ	thin	θɪn
ɜː	fur	fɜː(r)	ð	the	ðə
f	fat	fæt	uː	boot	buːt
g	good	gʊd	ʊ	book	bʊk
h	hat	hæt	ʊə	tourism	'tʊərɪzm
ɪ	bit, happy	bɪt, 'hæpɪ	ʌ	dug	dʌg
ɪə	near	nɪə(r)	v	van	væn
iː	meet	miːt	w	win	wɪn
j	yet	jet	z	zip	zɪp
k	kit	kɪt	ʒ	vision	'vɪʒn

:   bezeichnet Länge des vorhergehenden Vokals, z. B. boot [buːt].

ˈ   Betonung, steht unmittelbar vor einer betonten Silbe, z. B. ago [ə'gəʊ].

(r)   Ein „r" in runden Klammern wird nur gesprochen, wenn im Textzusammenhang ein Vokal unmittelbar folgt, z. B. fire /faɪə(r); fire at /faɪər æt/.

Guide to German pronunciation

Consonants are pronounced as in English with the following exceptions:

b	as	p	*at the end of a word or*
d	as	t	*syllable*
g	as	k	

ch	as in Scottish lo<u>ch</u> *after a, o, u, au*
	like an exaggerated h as in <u>h</u>uge
	after i, e, ä, ö, ü, eu, ei

-chs	as	x	(as in bo<u>x</u>)
-ig	as	-ich /ɪç/	*when a suffix*
j	as	y	(as in <u>y</u>es)
ps			the p is pronounced
pn			
qu	as	k+v	
s	as	z	(as in <u>z</u>ero) *at the begin-ning of a word*
	as	s	(as in bu<u>s</u>) *at the end of a word or syllable, be-fore a consonant, or when doubled*
sch	as	sh	
sp	as	shp	*at the beginning of a*
st	as	sht	*word*
v	as	f	(as in <u>f</u>or)
	as	v	(as in <u>v</u>ery) *within a word*

| w | as | v (as in <u>v</u>ery) |
| z | as | ts |

Vowels are approximately as follows:

a	short	as	u	(as in b<u>u</u>t)
	long	as	a	(as in c<u>a</u>r)
e	short	as	e	(as in p<u>e</u>n)
	long	as	a	(as in p<u>a</u>per)
i	short	as	i	(as in b<u>i</u>t)
	long	as	ee	(as in qu<u>ee</u>n)
o	short	as	o	(as in h<u>o</u>t)
	long	as	o	(as in p<u>o</u>pe)
u	short	as	oo	(as in f<u>oo</u>t)
	long	as	oo	(as in b<u>oo</u>t)

Vowels are always short before a double consonant, and long when followed by an h or when double

| ie | is pronounced ee | | | (as in k<u>ee</u>p) |

Diphthongs

au		as	ow	(as in h<u>ow</u>)
ei		as	y	(as in m<u>y</u>)
ai				
eu		as	oy	(as in b<u>oy</u>)
äu				

German irregular verbs

1st, 2nd and 3rd person present are given after the infinitive, and past subjunctive after the past indicative, where there is a change of vowel or any other irregularity.

Compound verbs are only given if they do not take the same forms as the corresponding simple verb, e.g. *befehlen*, or if there is no corresponding simple verb, e.g. *bewegen*.

An asterisk (*) indicates a verb which is also conjugated regularly.

Infinitive *Infinitiv*	Past Tense *Präteritum*	Past Participle *2. Partizip*
abwägen	wog (wöge) ab	abgewogen
ausbedingen	bedang (bedänge) aus	ausbedungen
*backen (du bäckst, er bäckt)	buk (büke)	gebacken
befehlen (du befiehlst, er befiehlt)	befahl (beföhle, befähle)	befohlen
beginnen	begann (begänne)	begonnen
beißen (du/er beißt)	biß (bisse)	gebissen
bergen (du birgst, er birgt)	barg (bärge)	geborgen
bersten (du/er birst)	barst (bärste)	geborsten
bewegen²	bewog (bewöge)	bewogen
biegen	bog (böge)	gebogen
bieten	bot (böte)	geboten
binden	band (bände)	gebunden
bitten	bat (bäte)	gebeten
blasen (du/er bläst)	blies	geblasen
bleiben	blieb	geblieben
*bleichen	blich	geblichen
braten (du brätst, er brät)	briet	gebraten
brechen (du brichst, er bricht)	brach (bräche)	gebrochen
brennen	brannte (brennte)	gebrannt
bringen	brachte (brächte)	gebracht
denken	dachte (dächte)	gedacht

Infinitive *Infinitiv*	Past Tense *Präteritum*	Past Participle *2. Partizip*
dreschen (du drischst, er drischt)	drosch (drösche)	gedroschen
dringen	drang (dränge)	gedrungen
dürfen (ich/er darf, du darfst)	durfte (dürfte)	gedurft
empfehlen (du empfiehlst, er empfiehlt)	empfahl (empföhle)	empfohlen
erlöschen (du erlischst, er erlischt)	erlosch (erlösche)	erloschen
*erschallen	erscholl (erschölle)	erschollen
*erschrecken (du erschrickst, er erschrickt)	erschrak (erschräke)	erschrocken
erwägen	erwog (erwöge)	erwogen
essen (du/er ißt)	aß (äße)	gegessen
fahren (du fährst, er fährt)	fuhr (führe)	gefahren
fallen (du fällst, er fällt)	fiel	gefallen
fangen (du fängst, er fängt)	fing	gefangen
fechten (du fichtst, er ficht)	focht (föchte)	gefochten
finden	fand (fände)	gefunden
flechten (du flichtst, er flicht)	flocht (flöchte)	geflochten
fliegen	flog (flöge)	geflogen
fliehen	floh (flöhe)	geflohen
fließen (du/er fließt)	floß (flösse)	geflossen
fressen (du/er frißt)	fraß (fräße)	gefressen
frieren	fror (fröre)	gefroren
*gären	gor (göre)	gegoren
gebären (du gebierst, sie gebiert)	gebar (gebäre)	geboren
geben (du gibst, er gibt)	gab (gäbe)	gegeben
gedeihen	gedieh	gediehen
gehen	ging	gegangen
gelingen	gelang (gelänge)	gelungen
gelten (du giltst, er gilt)	galt (gölte, gälte)	gegolten
genesen (du/er genest)	genas (genäse)	genesen
genießen (du/er genießt)	genoß (genösse)	genossen
geschehen (es geschieht)	geschah (geschähe)	geschehen
gewinnen	gewann (gewönne, gewänne)	gewonnen

Infinitive *Infinitiv*	Past Tense *Präteritum*	Past Participle *2. Partizip*
gießen (du/er gießt)	goß (gösse)	gegossen
gleichen	glich	geglichen
gleiten	glitt	geglitten
glimmen	glomm (glömme)	geglommen
graben (du gräbst, er gräbt)	grub (grübe)	gegraben
greifen	griff	gegriffen
haben (du hast, er hat)	hatte (hätte)	gehabt
halten (du hältst, er hält)	hielt	gehalten
hängen[2]	hing	gehangen
hauen	haute	gehauen
heben	hob (höbe)	gehoben
heißen (du/er heißt)	hieß	geheißen
helfen (du hilfst, er hilft)	half (hülfe)	geholfen
kennen	kannte (kennte)	gekannt
klingen	klang (klänge)	geklungen
kneifen	kniff	gekniffen
kommen	kam (käme)	gekommen
können (ich/er kann, du kannst)	konnte (könnte)	gekonnt
kriechen	kroch (kröche)	gekrochen
laden (du lädst, er lädt)	lud (lüde)	geladen
lassen (du/er läßt)	ließ	gelassen
laufen (du läufst, er läuft)	lief	gelaufen
leiden	litt	gelitten
leihen	lieh	geliehen
lesen (du/er liest)	las (läse)	gelesen
liegen	lag (läge)	gelegen
lügen	log (löge)	gelogen
mahlen	mahlte	gemahlen
meiden	mied	gemieden
melken	molk (mölke)	gemolken
messen (du/er mißt)	maß (mäße)	gemessen
mißlingen	mißlang (mißlänge)	mißlungen
mögen (ich/er mag, du magst)	mochte (möchte)	gemocht
müssen (ich/er muß, du mußt)	mußte (müßte)	gemußt
nehmen (du nimmst, er nimmt)	nahm (nähme)	genommen
nennen	nannte (nennte)	genannt

Infinitive *Infinitiv*	Past Tense *Präteritum*	Past Participle *2. Partizip*
pfeifen	pfiff	gepfiffen
preisen (du/er preist)	pries	gepriesen
quellen (du quillst, er quillt)	quoll (quölle)	gequollen
raten (du rätst, er rät)	riet	geraten
reiben	rieb	gerieben
reißen (du/er reißt)	riß	gerissen
reiten	ritt	geritten
rennen	rannte (rennte)	gerannt
riechen	roch (röche)	gerochen
ringen	rang (ränge)	gerungen
rinnen	rann (ränne)	geronnen
rufen	rief	gerufen
*salzen (du/er salzt)	salzte	gesalzen
saufen (du säufst, er säuft)	soff (söffe)	gesoffen
*saugen	sog (söge)	gesogen
schaffen[1]	schuf (schüfe)	geschaffen
scheiden	schied	geschieden
scheinen	schien	geschienen
scheißen (du/er scheißt)	schiß	geschissen
schelten (du schiltst, er schilt)	schalt (schölte)	gescholten
scheren[1]	schor (schöre)	geschoren
schieben	schob (schöbe)	geschoben
schießen (du/er schießt)	schoß (schösse)	geschossen
schinden	schindete	geschunden
schlafen (du schläfst, er schläft)	schlief	geschlafen
schlagen (du schlägst, er schlägt)	schlug (schlüge)	geschlagen
schleichen	schlich	geschlichen
schleifen[2]	schliff	geschliffen
schließen (du/er schließt)	schloß (schlösse)	geschlossen
schlingen	schlang (schlänge)	geschlungen
schmeißen (du/er schmeißt)	schmiß (schmisse)	geschmissen
schmelzen (du/er schmilzt)	schmolz (schmölze)	geschmolzen
schneiden	schnitt	geschnitten
*schrecken (du schrickst, er schrickt)	schrak (schräke)	geschreckt